Archaeology, Anthropology and Cult

The Sanctuary at Gilat, Israel

Archaeology, Anthropology and Cult

The Sanctuary at Gilat, Israel

edited by

Thomas E. Levy

Routledge
Taylor & Francis Group

LONDON AND NEW YORK

First published 2006 by Equinox Publishing Ltd.

This edition published 2016 by Routledge
2 Park Square, Milton Park, Abingdon, Oxfordshire OX14 4RN
711 Third Avenue, New York, NY 10017

First issued in paperback 2016

Routledge is an imprint of the Taylor & Francis Group, an informa business

Library of Congress Cataloguing-in-Publication Data
A catalogue record for this book is available from the Library of Congress

ISBN 13: 978-1-138-66385-5 (pbk)
ISBN 13: 978-1-904768-58-6 (hbk)

Typeset by Forthcoming Publications Ltd

For my dearest wife Alina,

Who has taught me the true meaning of love
and how to tend our garden through all the seasons

With all my love always

Contents

Preface
Thomas E. Levy   ix

I. THEORY

1. **Archaeology, Anthropology and Cult:
   Exploring Religion in Formative Middle Range Societies**
   Thomas E. Levy   3

2. **Cults, Shrines, and the Emergence of Regional Ritual Centers:
   The View from New Guinea**
   Donald Tuzin   34

3. **Tribal Pilgrimages to Saints' Tombs in South Sinai**
   Emanuel Marx   54

4. **The Rise of a New Negev Cult Center Today:
   Baba Sali's Sanctuary in Netivot, Israel**
   Yoram Bilu   75

II. ARCHAEOLOGICAL FOUNDATIONS

5. **The Sanctuary Sequence: Excavations at Gilat: 1975–77, 1989, 1990–92**
   Thomas E. Levy, David Alon†, Yorke M. Rowan,
   and Morag Kersel   95

III. BIOLOGICAL DATA FROM GILAT

6. **Farming? Feasting? Herding? Large Mammals from the Chalcolithic of Gilat**
   Caroline Grigson   215

7. **Marine and Riverine Shells at Gilat**
   Daniella E. Bar-Yosef Mayer   320

8. **Death and the Sanctuary: The Human Remains from Gilat**
   Patricia Smith, Tania Zagerson, Pamela Sabari, Jonathan Golden,
   Thomas E. Levy, and Leslie Dawson   327

IV. THE EMERGENCE OF GILAT AS A REGIONAL CULT CENTER: PRODUCTION AND EXCHANGE

9. **The Technology of the Gilat Pottery Assemblage: A Reassessment**
    Yuval Goren   369

10. **Gilat's Ceramics: Cognitive Dimensions of Pottery Production**
    Catherine Commenge
    with a contribution by T.E. Levy and E. Kansa   394

11. **The Chipped Stone Assemblage at Gilat**
    Yorke M. Rowan   507

12. **Gilat's Ground Stone Assemblage: Stone Fenestrated Stands, Bowls, Palettes and Related Artifacts**
    Yorke M. Rowan, Thomas E. Levy, David Alon†, and Yuval Goren   575

13. **The Worked Bone from the Chalcolithic Site of Gilat: Interim Report**
    Caroline Grigson   685

V. PROCESSES OF INTEGRATION: THE EMERGENCE OF A PAN-REGIONAL RITUAL CENTER

14. **The Intensification of Production at Gilat: Textile Production**
    Thomas E. Levy, Wendy Conner, Yorke Rowan, and David Alon†   705

15. **Gilat's Figurines: Exploring the Social and Symbolic Dimensions of Representation**
    Catherine Commenge, Thomas E. Levy, David Alon†, and Eric Kansa   739

16. **Conclusion: The Evolution of a Levantine Prehistoric Regional Cult Center**
    Thomas E. Levy   831

VI. APPENDICES

Appendix 1. Organic Residue Analysis of Selected Vessels from Gilat: Gilat Torpedo Jars
    Margie Burton and Thomas E. Levy   849

Appendix 2. Radiocarbon Dating of Gilat
    Thomas E. Levy and Margie Burton   863

Index   867

Preface

Thomas E. Levy

This book provides an in-depth study of the role of religion in the evolution of societies. It melds anthropological theory and archaeological data to present one of the most comprehensive archaeological studies of the role of ritual as a vital force for promoting and consolidating social change. It is based on seven seasons of archaeological excavation at the Chalcolithic site of Gilat, a low mound, located in the fields of Moshav Gilat, a semi-communal farming settlement in Israel's northern Negev desert. The Chalcolithic period represents the first time that well-documented chiefdom organizations can be recognized in the archaeological record of the Holy Land when institutionalized social hierarchies, craft specialization, horticulture, temple life and other fundamental social changes occurred in this part of the ancient Near East. As one of the few Chalcolithic (ca. 4500–3600 BC) sanctuary sites in the southern Levant, Gilat provides a wonderful opportunity to explore the role of religion and ideology as a social force for influencing social relations and social evolution through one of the formative periods in the prehistory of the eastern Mediterranean. The collection of studies presented in this book aim at examining the material evidence for the ideological subsystem of Chalcolithic culture by careful analyses of relatively large sets of archaeological data through the lens of anthropological models. The book includes chapters by noted cultural anthropologists who have studied the role of religion in shaping contemporary small scale societies and Middle Eastern ethnic groups. These works provide rich models that are incorporated in the book's main focus—prehistoric and early historic religion.

The book includes hundreds of artifact drawings, photographs, maps, and data tables. By presenting the data in its entirety, it is hoped that future researchers can test their ideas with the original data. This comprehensive compendium of reference material from the late fifth - early forth millennium site of Gilat will make this an important reference for studies of formative religion throughout the Middle East and other regions.

If researchers are to genuinely construct an archaeology of cult, ritual, cognition, and religion, it is essential that they utilize complete datasets and meet the challenge of dealing with the 'ugly' facts of the archaeological record—the tens of thousands of ceramic sherds, lithics, bones, and other artifacts retrieved in modern excavations. In studying the archaeology of cult and religion, the potential for speculation is great as seen in many studies of prehistoric 'mother goddesses' and similar subjects by researchers who take an impressionistic approach to the study of ideology and religion. This study demonstrates that by studying the entire assemblages of ritual paraphernalia and associated artifacts found in the archaeological record, it is possible to move beyond personal impression and focus on the actual ritual patterns embedded in material culture datasets. In light of these and other issues, this book represents a commitment to the greater goal of promoting more systematization in the study of the archaeology of ritual and religion. *Archaeology, Anthropology and Cult—The Sanctuary at Gilat, Israel* provides a new approach to how anthropologists and archaeologists study the role of religion in social evolution and will be of interest to ancient historians, anthropologists, archaeologists, biblical scholars, students and professionals.

I first began working at Gilat in 1977 as a graduate student volunteer. That was David Alon's third season of excavation at the site, which had already gained a great deal of attention because of the wonderful Chalcolithic statuettes found several years earlier. Alon worked for the Israel Department of Antiquities (now the Israel Antiquities Authority) and this was the beginning of a long period of joint field work together. By 1987 we conducted our first joint season of excavation at Gilat under the auspices of the Nelson Glueck School of Biblical Archaeology of the Hebrew Union College-Jewish Institute of Religion, Jerusalem (NGSBA, HUC-JIR). From 1990 to 1992, thanks to the generosity of the C. Paul Johnson Family Charitable Foundation (Chicago), and especially Paul Johnson, the first large-scale HUC-JIR excavations took place at Gilat. I am especially grateful to Paul for his support of the Gilat expedition and many other projects I carried out in Israel and Jordan. There are many people to thank who have helped us along the way: Avraham Biran, Alfred Gottschalk, Paul Steinberg, Hanni Hirsh, Shaul Feinberg, Rahamim Goren, Nili Cohen, and David Ilan of the HUC-JIR. The late Amir Drori, and Ayala Sussman of the Israel Antiquities Authority kindly allowed us to published drawings of artifacts from Alon's 1975–77 excavations. Other people from the 'old; Department of Antiquities of Israel (now IAA) that I would like to thank include: Sako Ben Arieh (collections), Baruch Brandl (collections), Michal Ben Gal (illustrator), the late Moshe Hoffman (pottery restoration), Sila Sagiv and Clara Amit (photography), Teddy Mazzola (illustrator), Benny Peleg (volunteer) and the late Michael Fiest and Israel Watkin (surveyors) for all their help with Gilat. Other individuals who worked in the field and laboratory during the 1990–92 expeditions include Ibrahim al-Assam, Yorke Rowan, Morag Kersel, Jim Anderson, John Nicholson, Jonathan Golden, Alison Jones-Nassar, Yoav Arbel and numerous students and volunteers who participated in the excavations. Moshav Gilat very kindly allowed us to excavate in their fields and use the old school as our base camp. Along with the Johnson family, Steve Fossett, Neil and Karen Moss, and other friends generously supported the project. I would also like to express thanks to all the contributor/ specialists to this book who have helped in the critical analysis of the wealth of data we recovered at Gilat. A special thanks to Daniel Ladiray of the Centre National de la Recherche Scientifique (CNRS), Jerusalem, for his wonderful drawings that fill so much of this book. Thanks too many of my colleagues at UCSD for intellectual exchanges concerning religion, anthropology and archaeology while this work was in progress. Some of these individuals include Guillermo Algaze, Don Tuzin, Bob Adams, and Mel Spiro in the Department of Anthropology; and Bill Propp, Richard Elliott Friedman, David Noel Freedman, and David Goodblatt in the Judaic Studies Program.

A number of people helped with the actual production of this book. My student Adolfo Muniz kindly spent many hours bringing the Gilat work into the digital age. I appreciate Janet Joyce, my publisher at Equinox, for taking on such a large book project like this, her staff members Valerie Hall and Heidi Robbins, and Duncan Burns of typesetting this volume. Finally, I would like to sincerely thank my wife Alina and my sons Ben and Gil for accompanying me in the field, camping out in the broken down Gilat school for months on end, and giving me an unending source of love and support through the years.

I.
THEORY

1 Archaeology, Anthropology and Cult: Exploring Religion in Formative Middle Range Societies

Thomas E. Levy

Introduction

Ceremonies are the bond that holds the multitudes together, and if the bond be removed, the multitudes fall into confusion. Confucius (551–479 BC)

The discovery of one of the earliest pan-regional ritual centers in the fields of Gilat in Israel's northern Negev desert provides a rare opportunity to explore the role of religion as a critical social evolutionary force that directed, maintained and radically changed various cultural institutions at a time when Middle Eastern societies were crossing the threshold from egalitarian to hierarchical social organizations (Fig. 1.1). The role of religion in social evolution was one of the primary concerns of the nineteenth- and early twentieth-century. anthropologists and discoveries such as those at Gilat awaken the need to reexamine the power of religion for promoting social evolution. Today, anthropological archaeology is probably the singular academic discipline that consistently investigates social evolution as a principal social phenomenon. While there is no need to justify such an investigation, it is worth quoting Bruce Trigger's (Trigger 1998) remarks which highlight what cultural evolutionary studies can provide for the world community today:

> An evolutionary approach should consider the consequences of alternative courses of action in the hope that human beings may choose the course that best assures their collective survival and well-being. In that way, growing complexity may result in true progress, which involves producing the greatest possible good for the greatest number, without inflicting injustice on anyone. The belief that this is possible must not be lost sight of amidst the seductive temptations of a relativism that, despite its valid points, can all too easily descend into amorality and defeatism and end up being used to justify greed and social irresponsibility. Progress is not inherent in sociocultural evolution, but something that individuals must plan and be prepared to fight for if it is to become a reality.

Given the relevance of social evolutionary studies for today's world, we cannot forget the contributions of some of the early cultural evolutionists such as Karl Marx, Charles Darwin, Lewis Henry Morgan, Edward Tylor, Herbert Spencer, Sir James Frazer, and W. Robertson Smith— especially with regard to the study of religion and social evolution. In the Gilat study presented here, in terms of melding hard archaeological data with anthropological and sociological theory, the functionalist works of Emile Durkheim (Durkheim 1933, 1995 [orig. 1912]) and other social evolutionary theorists provide the most useful way of conceptualizing the relationship between religion and society. Durkheim viewed religion as powerfully strengthening a society's social structure as well as serving as a force for controlling change based on the sacred authority of the social group's values and rules. In this way, religion emerges out of social solidarity but also works to strengthen it. Many of the more recent archaeological studies of religion and social evolution (Bauer and Stanish 2001; Conrad and Demarest 1984; Renfrew 1985a) have relied on different aspects of Durkheim's model of religion. The contributors to this book draw directly or indirectly on some of these Durkheimian concepts as well as some of the early social evolutionary works on religion and society. The early social evolutionists were especially interested in the rise of monotheism and the history of ancient Near Eastern religions. Their control of Northwest Semitic and other languages as well as early ethnographic accounts of the 'manners and customs' of nineteenth- and early twentieth-century Middle Eastern societies make many of these works extremely valuable for our investigation of the rise of pan-regional religious institutions in this part of the world. Many of the most recent anthropological theories of religion (e.g. Boyer 1994; Boyer 2001; Geertz 1973; Mithen 1996) are too far removed from the material world to be testable in the archaeological record. Thus, from a materialist and a contextual perspective, the Gilat project is rooted in a functionalist perspective which views all elements of a culture as functional; that is, these cultural sub-systems work together to satisfy culturally defined needs of the people in that society or the society as a whole (Binford 1968; Clarke 1968).

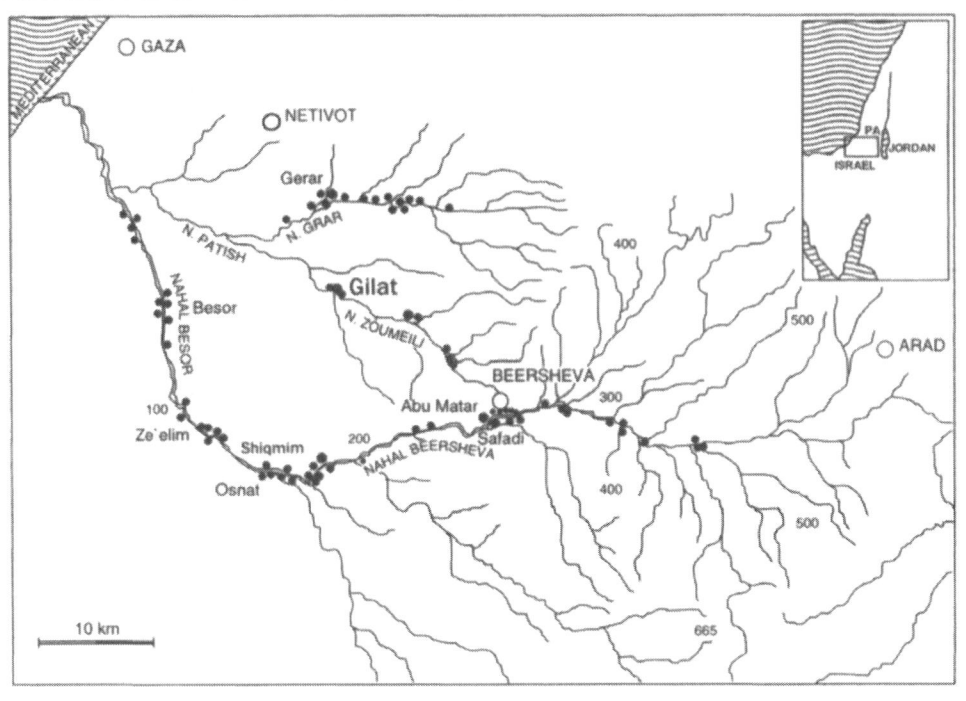

Figure 1.1. Northern Negev study area.

Religion and ideology are powerful forces that can direct, influence, maintain and radically change human societies. As Karl Marx observed long ago, 'Religion is the sign of the oppressed creature, the sentiment of a heartless world, and the soul of soulless conditions. It is the opium of the people'

(Marx 1844 [1970]). Marx was a man who rejected religious belief, but fully understood the power of religion for fundamentally structuring society. At the dawn of the twenty-first century, in a western world that is dominated by technological and material wonders, the power of religion and belief as motivational and organizational forces in human society is seen every day with the confrontations between secular and religious groups, democracy and religious fundamentalism, and the universal problem of traditional culture and society coping with modernity. Religious belief, doctrine and practice lay at the core of human culture. Does this mean that a study of religion will provide all the answers for understanding social change through time? Not necessarily. However, because Gilat is so rich in prehistoric ritual paraphernalia, the focus is on religion to help explain cultural evolution during the formative late fifth–fourth millennium BCE in the southern Levant. If religion and ritual were a key factor in the emergence of Gilat as a hierarchical social center, was this true for most other parts of the southern Levant? To answer this question, it is best to recall K.V. Flannery and Joyce Marcus's (Flannery 1983; Flannery and Marcus 1983) discussion of divergent evolution and the emergence of two complex societies (the Zapotec and Mixtec) in southern Mexico. There it was shown that two neighboring complex societies evolved along similar trajectories for a period of time from a common ancestral tradition, but took divergent evolutionary pathways to become diverse cultures. Similar divergent evolutionary processes may have occurred in the northern Negev, where some 16 km to the south of Gilat, one of the earliest Levantine chiefdom level societies evolved in the Beersheva valley along a divergent pathway (Levy 1998). Copper production and the control of copper distribution networks seem to have fueled the Beersheva chiefdom and enabled it to evolve along its own trajectory. Gilat, and its satellite sites along the Nahal Patish (Alon 1961), contains no evidence of Chalcolithic metal production activities. Thus, Gilat seems to have used religion, ritual and pilgrimage as key factors in promoting its own growth into a regional polity. This is a clear example of Flannery and Marcus's divergent cultural evolution.

As will be shown in this study, the geographic centrality of the Gilat sanctuary in the Chalcolithic settlement pattern of Israel's northern Negev desert makes religion and ritual key variables for understanding Gilat's social evolutionary role during the Chalcolithic period. Depending on the character and material culture found at a site, any one of the cultural sub-systems outlined above could be used as an analytical lens to examine cultural change. For example, archaeological sites rich in metallurgical remains or some other technological assemblage might serve as case studies for examining the role of craft production in social change (Costin 1991; Levy *et al.* 2002). Alternatively, a site with extensive evidence for agro-technology (rich faunal and paleobotanical assemblages, storage facilities, agricultural installations, etc.) would be examined using various models of subsistence to reconstruct change through time. Thus, while this study focuses primarily on the Gilat ritual center, it does seek to elicit a general investigation of the role of religion and ideology on social change in 'middle range' societies.

Social Typologies and Middle Range Societies

By 'middle range' societies, we mean those intermediate societies that are neither states nor egalitarian. Whether we call these 'chiefdoms' or intermediate societies (Earle 1991b) is a 'red herring' in academic discourse today (Rousseau 2001). With regard to Palestine and other regions around the world, Norman Yoffee (Yoffee 1998) has usefully warned about the dangers of assuming teleological trends in social evolution when scholars wed themselves to social evolutionary typologies. Kent Flannery (Flannery 1999), on the other hand, has pointed out some of the innate difficulties in recognizing chiefdoms in the archaeological record and in particular, those that may have been present in the prehistoric Near East. From the simple typological perspective, we would argue that the use of cultural typologies by anthropologists and archaeologists is essential if they are interested in identifying cross-cultural trends related to processes of culture change and adaptation.

The critical point in conceptualizing middle range or intermediate societies is the profound change they represent in the social evolutionary history of humankind. In the Levant, which is home to over 1.4 million years of human and social evolution—one of the longest human evolutionary sequences outside of Africa—the rise of institutionalized social inequality sometime during the post-Natufian Epi-Paleolithic period (c. 10,000 BP) represents a revolutionary social transformation. The fundamental question is why did people give up their social autonomy when for more than 1.39 myr they lived in relatively autonomous hunter and forager groups? The cultural evolutionary term that best characterizes these middle range or intermediate societies that mark the emergence of institutionalized social inequality is 'chiefdom'. As Carneiro (Carneiro 1981) and Earle (Earle 1987) points out, chiefdoms are polities that centrally organize a regional population in the thousands. With the rise of chiefdoms, deep-seated changes occur in the economic, subsistence, ideological, social organization and technological sub-systems of a culture. The rise of Levantine Chalcolithic chiefdoms has been documented not only in the Beersheva valley (Levy 1987) but in a number of sub-regions due in great part to recent fieldwork in areas such as Nahal Qanah in Samaria (Gopher and Tsuk 1996, Gopher et al. 1990), Peqi'in in the Galilee (Gal, Smithline and Shalem 1997), and Tuleilat Ghassul in the lower Jordan valley (Bourke 2002; Seaton 2000) and an array of studies concerning Chalcolithic craft specialization (Levy and Shalev 1989; Shalev 1994; Shalev et al. in press, Shalev and Northover 1993) Thus, the question now is not whether chiefdoms existed during the Chalcolithic, but rather, how did they emerge, maintain themselves, evolve and collapse. This study, which focuses on one of the few Chalcolithic regional ritual sites will try to answer this question by focusing on the ideological sub-system of a Chalcolithic culture that appeared in the northern Negev shortly after the end of the once vibrant Neolithic communities of the late sixth–early fifth millennium.

Early Cultural Evolutionary Perspectives on Religion. Surprisingly, Lewis Henry Morgan (1818–1881), one of the social evolutionary founders of the comparative method, hardly dealt with the evolution of religion. As M. Harris points out (Harris 2001), Morgan shied away from studying religion because he viewed religion as 'irrational'. In this sense, Morgan was dissimilar to the other nineteenth-century social evolutionists who were deeply interested in religion.

E.B. Tylor (1832–1917) is credited with stimulating interest in anthropology as a science especially when he took up being head of the University at Oxford in 1883. As Robert Carneiro (Carneiro 1973) observed, 'Tylor showed himself to be a good deal more of a cultural historian than an evolutionist. His concern was largely with tracing the history of myths, riddles, customs, games, rituals, artifacts, and the like, rather than with lying bare the general processes or stages in the evolution of culture as a whole.' There is little doubt that Tylor's concern in building a credible museum contributed to his interest in culture history. However, he was interested in evolutionary process and this is reflected in his largest contribution—the study of animism as reflected in his 1871 book *Primitive Culture: Researches into the Early History of Mankind and the Development of Civilization.* Tylor (1871) defined religion as 'a belief in spiritual beings'. As a religious worldview, animism views human life in all moving things. In band-level societies, people would see no distinction between the animate and the inanimate. Nature is alive in everything and represents soul. According to Bates (Bates 1996), Tylor viewed animism as a belief in a personified supernatural force and suggested that this was the first stage in the evolution of religion, which then passed through a belief in many gods, culminating with monotheism. Most recent scholars have question Tylor's theory that band-level societies could not discriminate whether things were animate or inanimate. The fallacy of Tylor's logic is his assumption that 'primitive' societies were also 'primitive' in ritual symbols and systems. This is inherent in his book Primitive Culture (Tylor 1871) where he develops three stages of socioreligious evolution: animism > polytheism > monotheism. Animism relates to the role of the soul used to describe the belief that animate and inanimate objects, as well as human beings, can have a soul (or life force and personality) and is still used as a general descriptive term for 'tribal' religions (Bowie 2000). Modern researchers have demonstrated the complexity of rituals, symbols and myths amongst the band-level groups that go beyond Tylor's model of animism.

Using the comparative method, Sir James Frazer (1914) produced perhaps the most comprehensive study of religion at the end of the nineteenth and early twentieth century. This 12 volume magnum opus was abridged and published as *The Golden Bough* which is still in print. Frazer's work mostly substantiates Tylor's view that modern religions evolved naturally from 'primitive' predecessors.

Frazer (Frazer 1960) wrote

> By religion, then, I understand a propitiation or conciliation of powers superior to man which are believed to direct and control the course of nature and of human life. Thus defined, religion consists of two elements, a theoretical and a practical, namely, a belief in powers higher than man and an attempt to propitiate or please them. Of the two, belief clearly comes first, since we must believe in the existence of a divine being before we can attempt to please him. But unless, the belief leads to a corresponding practice, it is not a religion but merely a theology.

According to Harris (Harris 2001), Frazer's most influential contribution was the distinction he made between religion and magic—a distinction that Tylor had ignored. Accordingly, for Frazer, magic is viewed 'as an early expression of science based on a false notion of the regularity of cause and effect processes. Religion is a higher achievement (than magic), substituting uncertainty and prayerful conciliation for misguided notions of causality. Science develops next, returning mankind to the principles of cause and effect, but on a basis of true correlations' (*ibid.*). In this sense, M. Eleade's study of alchemy—an activity imbued with magic—is indeed a precursor to science. Perhaps Frazer's biggest contribution was making a wealth of primitive customs intelligible to European thinkers of his time (Britannica 2002). Frazer's prolific writing had great influence on scholars of his time. However, his work is not based on original fieldwork. Instead he relied on personal contacts with colonial administrators and the clergy who traveled to the 'primitive'. However, the study of religion was central to Frazer's research as reflected in works such as *Totemism and Exogamy* (Frazer 1968) and *Folk-lore in the Old Testament; studies in comparative religion, legend and law* (Frazer 1927). The nineteenth- and early twentieth-century anthropologists continuously debated over social evolution and core issues such as the structure of the earliest human societies and the prehistory of religion. As David Gellner (Gellner 1999) points out, some of the questions these scholars asked included:

> Was the earliest form of religion magic? Was it the worship of forces of nature? Was it belief in spirits as apprehended in dreams and visions, a form of religion labeled 'animism'? Or was it totemism, the worship by each constituent clan of the society of its own special totem (sacred object)? There was great fascination with 'primitive' society and its religion among the reading public of the nineteenth century. For some, the difference and strangeness of exotic practices confirmed them in the rightness of their own ways. For others the historic continuity, which all believed in, between the 'primitive' and the 'modern', was a way of debunking and undermining religion as such.

Time and again, scholars return to these fundamental questions that are linked to cultural evolution and germane to the Gilat study presented here. However, social fads such as the current 'new age' interest in shamanism influence the scholarly use of nineteenth-century terms in appropriate ways. For example, it would be inappropriate to use the concept of shaman for non-hunting and gathering societies in the systematic study of religion and anthropological archaeology. As shown in the in-depth cross cultural studies of M. Winkelman (Winkelman 2000b, 1990) based on an auto-correlation multiple-regression analysis of ethnographic records, shamans are found in hunting and gathering societies who have a nomadic lifestyle and are found throughout the world—except in the Circum-Mediterranean and Insular Pacific regions. To apply this model to Mediterranean pastoral and/or agricultural societies would be unsuitable. This problem is taken up again in the concluding chapter of this book (Chapter 16). The history of anthropological approaches to the study of religion has received extensive scholarship (Aguilar 2000; Aigbe 1993; Anderson 1992; Baal, Beek and Scherer 1975; Bell 1992; Blanton 1966; Bowen 1998; Burris 1997; Coleman 2001; Feeley-harnik 1992; Fishbane 1993; Glazier 1997; Greenstein 1994; Gruber 1998; Hicks 2002; Krzyzaniak 1999; Lambek 2002; Remy 1991; Stewart 1998; Thorbjornsrud 2001; Wax 1991; Winkelman 2000a). In what follows, a distinct archaeology of religion is proposed which utilizes many of the contributions of anthropologists and other researchers of religion. In this way, the more recent literature and research on the anthropology of religion is addressed.

The Archaeology of Cult and Chalcolithic Palestine

If the anthropology of religion has been shown to be a complex area of inquiry, the archaeology of religion presents the researchers with an even more daunting challenge. This is mostly because the material remains of ancient cult activities are often few in numbers and open to different inter-pretation and debate. Hodder's (Hodder 1999) suggestion that the analysis of actual archaeological fieldwork is *both* subjective *and* objective rings true. However, by carefully outlining the assump-tions that underlie the observation and description of archaeological data (whether in the field or laboratory); it is possible to reach an objective interpretation that other observers can duplicate. This should be the goal of archaeological inquiries into ancient religion and cult. With regard to these issues, fundamental questions arise such as how much material is needed to identify a cult center or locus? When is a building a domestic structure or public building? When does a structure pass the threshold of the 'profane' into the 'sacred'? What kind of reasoning is needed to identify a locale as a locus of ritual activity? In this study, we continue to follow in the footsteps of Colin Renfrew's (Renfrew 1985a) deductive approach to the archaeology of cult applied on the island of Melos where a series of hypotheses related to ritual acts were carefully outlined and tested. Renfrew (1985:11–26) provides a general framework for examining a wealth of archaeological data found at the Late Bronze Age sanctuary at Phylakopi that we built on in our preliminary study of cult activities at Gilat (Alon and Levy 1989). It is worth reviewing this framework as the new excava-tions at Gilat (1990–1992) provide a much larger contextual basis and sample size to examine formative ritual practices in the Chalcolithic and the rise of the first pan-regional cult centers in the southern Levant.

In Palestine, Chalcolithic and Early Bronze Age religion and cult have been examined mostly in a non-systematic manner where assumptions are not clarified and quantification of data are minimal at best (Amiran 1981; Ben-Tor and Netzer 1973; Dunayevsky and Kempinski 1973; Epstein 1973, 1975, 1978, 1982, 1988, 1998; Kempinski 1972, 1987; Seton-Williams 1949; Ussishkin 1980). Since the late 1980s, a growing number of researchers have made strides to quantify and take a more explanatory perspective in studying Chalcolithic ritual (Kerner 2001; Seaton 2000). In approaching the Iron Age and early historic periods, archaeological studies of ritual and religion have made important advances to engage anthropological models, quantification and systemization of analysis. Scholars working on these issues for the Iron Age include Dever (1987), Holladay (1987), Stager (1987), and Zevit (2001) who have all argued for a 'functionalist' approach for examining the historical and archaeological record of Palestine, especially with regard to early Israelite religion. Other studies that have built on these functionalist foundations include Alpert

Nakhai (Nakhai 2001), Bloch-Smith (Bloch-Smith and Nakahi 1999; Bloch-Smith 1992), and Halpern (1998). For Middle and Late Bronze Age Cyprus, Knapp (1988) has utilized a 'structuralist' view to show how elites and other special interest groups use ideology to establish, challenge or change a specific sociopolitical order. As will be shown in this study, we have attempted to merge a wide range of these anthropological approaches to examine the formative Chalcolithic religion embedded in the archaeological record at Gilat. Some of the main issues related to formative Chalcolithic religion examined in this study and outlined in Renfrew's (1985:25–26) 'Steps in the Analysis of Prehistoric Religion' are outlined below. Like so much of Renfrew's work, this list of archaeological correlates is remarkable for its depth in tackling the links between hard archaeological data and interpretive models. Here we build on Renfrew's earlier framework for an archaeology of cult and ritual practice by addressing how the material record of societies reflects ritual practice, ideology, and the function of ritual and religion in cultural systems.

Ritual Practice: Key Questions to be Investigated

Many researchers concerned with the anthropology of religion may inappropriately use the term 'cult' as synonymous with 'ritual'. For example, in Renfrew's (1985:14ff) work entitled *The Archaeology of Cult*, he uses the terms 'cult' and 'ritual' interchangeably. According to the Webster's dictionary, cult refers to:

> a) a system of religious worship or ritual, b) a quasi-religious group, often living in a colony, with a charismatic leader who indoctrinates members with unorthodox or extremist views, practices, or beliefs, or c) devoted attachment to, or extravagant admiration for, a person, principle, or lifestyle, especially when regarded as a fad/the cult of nudism, etc.

Based on this definition, it may be perfectly appropriate to use cult and ritual interchangeably. However, since the publication of Catherine Bell's books entitled *Ritual Theory, Ritual Practice* (Bell 1992) and *Ritual: Perspectives and Dimensions* (Bell 1997), it is clear that the notion of 'ritual' should be separate from 'cult' if we are to fully investigate the role of religion in societies and social evolution. As Bell (1992:16) points out, ritual is a definitive component of the different t processes that constitute the core of religion, society and culture. 'Ritualization is fundamentally a way of doing things to trigger the perception that these practices are distinct and the associations that they engender are special' (*ibid*. 220). Bell presents a *tour de force* analysis of ritual in all its anthropological, religious studies and sociological iterations. After surveying the vast literature on ritual, she establishes the significance of a 'performance approach' to the study of ritual that was initiated by Clifford Geertz (Geertz 1973) who uses ritual as a lens which 'enables one to understand the way in which people regard their religion as "encapsulated" in specific performances that can be performed for visitors and themselves.' Thus, the term 'cult' has lost its usefulness as an anthropological construct because the media and cultural studies appropriated the term to refer to those social movements that exist on the edges of normative religion and social institutions. Ritual (as defined by Bell and others) is a more useful concept for studying religion in archaeological contexts, because it is linked to the notion of performance which has a direct material correlates that can be observed in the material record. More will be said of performance theory below in relation to the archaeological record. What then are the central questions concerning ancient ritual that can be asked of the archaeological record?

Ritual Practice at Gilat. The following questions concerning to ritual practice are investigated in the various chapters of this volume. Following each question, the chapters which discuss these issues are given in parentheses.

a) Given what is known about other late prehistoric sanctuaries in the southern Levant as well as ethnographic examples, is it possible to demonstrate the presence of a regional ritual center at Gilat? (Chapters 1, 4, 5)

b) What was the nature of cult paraphernalia used at Gilat? (Chapters 5, 10, 12, 14, 15)

c) Can local cults be distinguished from pan-regional cult practices at Gilat? (Chapters 2, 5, 3, 4, 15)

d) What was the range of offerings that were brought to Gilat and is it possible to interpret 'why' they were brought to the site? (Chapters 5, 6, 9, 10, 12, 15)

e) Is there evidence for a hierarchy of ritual practices at Gilat and how can this be demonstrated? (Chapters 14, 15)

f) What is the relation between ritual practice in the Gilat settlement and Chalcolithic cemeteries? (Chapter 8)

g) Is it possible to identify the frequency of ritual acts and/or quantify their occurrence at the site? (Chapters 6, 8, 10, 14, 15)

h) Is there evidence of animal and/or human sacrifice? (Chapters 5, 6, 8)

i) Can 'behavioral chains' (cf. Schiffer 1987) related to the flow and practice of ritual acts be identified in the archaeological record? (Chapters 6, 8, 10, 15)

j) Can the use of fire and/or water be identified as important elements of the ritual act? (Chapters 5, 6, 14, 15)

k) What is the range of cult images present in the archaeological record at Gilat? (Chapters 5, 12, 15)

l) Were cult images used as votive offerings at the site? (Chapter 12, 15)

m) Are their depictions of ritual scenes in the material culture at Gilat? (Chapter 5)

n) What religious and ideological symbolism can be inferred from the assemblage of cult related artifacts? (Chapter 15)

Ideology and Belief Underlying Cult and Ritual Practices at Gilat. To achieve an understanding of south Levantine ideology and belief systems, the following questions are asked of the Gilat data:

a) Were there anthropomorphic and/or zoomorphic deities at Gilat and how do they relate to the late fifth–fourth millennium Near Eastern world? (Chapters 1, 6, 15)

b) Are there composite deities (part human, part animal) in the archaeological record at Gilat? (Chapter 15)

c) Was there a 'pantheon' of deities at the site? (Chapters 1, 15)

d) Can the gender role differences be detected in the cult(s) at Gilat? (Chapter 15)

e) How were people vs. animals involved in cult themes at the site? (Chapters 6, 8, 15)

f) What contextual evidence accompanies the use of symbolic artifacts at Gilat? (Chapters 10, 12, 15)

g) Is it possible to reconstruct prehistoric mythology based on the distribution of cult objects and their symbolism at the site? (Chapter 15)

h) What is the role (if any) of astronomy in the ritual acts at the site? (Chapters 5, 16)

i) Can a range of separate cults be identified at the site (i.e. funerary, ancestor, fertility, etc.)? (Chapter 15)

j) What ideological meaning can be gleaned from the anthropomorphic, zoomorphic and other figurative works found at Gilat? (Chapter 15)

The Role of Ritual and Religion in Chalcolithic Society. To clarify the relationship between ritual and religion within the local community at Gilat and the network of relations between Gilat as a ritual center and other Levantine regions, the following questions are addressed in this book:

a)   Is it possible to identify the scale of investment in cult activities at Gilat? (Chapters 6, 8, 10, 15)

b)   How do scalar difference in ritual acts at Gilat compare with other extensively excavated Chalcolithic sites in Israel/Palestine and Jordan? (Chapters 6, 8, 9, 12, 15)

c)   What is the nature of religious organization at Gilat and does it extend beyond the individual settlement? (Chapters 14, 15)

d)   Can the organization of cult be linked to more general dimensions of social organization? (Chapters 13, 14)

e)   What was the role of ritual leaders in the society? (Chapters 1, 16)

f)   Is there evidence for syncretism between ritual acts carried out at Gilat and other regions in the southern Levant? (Chapters 5, 15, 16)

The Archaeological Recognition of Ritual Acts: Ritual as the Communication of Culture

Recent anthropological definitions of ritual have generally moved away from strict functionalist approaches to ones based on 'performance theory' (Austin 1975; Tambiah 1985). Performance theories, as highlighted by Robbins (Robbins 2001), are based on 'linguistic observation that certain utterances, ones that scholars classify as speech acts, do not primarily describe the world or inform people about it, but rather do something within it'. Rappaport (1999:78) uses the example of a ritual dance done by the Maring of Papua New Guinea who, by performing a special dance (*kaiko* ritual), establishes a pledge to ally himself with the host of the ritual. Similarly, a pledge to 'tell the truth, the whole truth, and nothing but the truth' in a court of law in western society, binds the speaker to a specific behavior and relationship (to tell the 'truth'). For archaeologists, performance theory is appealing because these behaviors in space and time often leave material residues that provide a window on ancient ritual acts. This does not mean that there are no problems with the application of performance theory in anthropology.

Unlike archaeology, research trends in cultural anthropology have changed over the past two decades from 'quantitative' to 'interpretive' or 'humanistic' approaches (D'andrade 1995). This is not the place to criticize this trend. However, for archaeologists who deal with masses of material culture from the observable world, functionalist views of ritual are still extremely useful. Even performance theory, when grounded in material correlates of human behavior, can be utilized within a functionalist perspective. For example, in his earlier writings, Rappaport (Rappaport 1971) defined ritual as 'both human and animal, religious and secular—as conventional acts of display through which one or more participants transmit information concerning their physiological, psychological or sociological states either to themselves or to one or more of their participants.' Accordingly, ritual behavior is especially recognized in cultural life through its formality, its repetitive elements and the fact that it is done either publicly in the form of a gathering of people or privately in the presence of the deity (Renfrew 1985a). While it is generally assumed that ritual is linked to religious activities, it should be remembered that there are also social rituals that permeate life such as greetings, acts related to trade, exchange and other domains.

In dealing with Chalcolithic ritual in this study, it is suggested that religious and social rituals are inextricably tied together. More recently, Rappaport (Rappaport 1999) defined ritual as 'the performance of more or less invariant sequences of formal acts and utterances not entirely encoded by the performers'. This is a rather open-ended definition of ritual. As Robbin's (Robbins 2001) points out, most of Rappaport's (1999) *magnum opus, Ritual and Religion in the Making of Humanity*, consists of the 'unpacking of this definition in order to show how ritual so defined creates and/or entails all of the key features of religion and many of those of social life more generally'. However, *Ritual and Religion in the Making of Humanity* falls short of the book's goal of presenting an objective, rigorous, deductive approach to the anthropological study of religion. For Rappaport (*ibid*: 3) his study is a 'treatise on ritual: first on ritual's internal logic, next on the products (like sanctity) that its logic entails, and on the nature of their truth, and finally, on the place of ritual and its products in humanity's evolution'. In Rappaport's earlier works (cf. Rappaport 1969, 1970, 1971, 1979), he was a master of analyzing and providing a framework for understanding the role of ritual an its 'products in humanity's evolution'. As Robbins (2001: 591) correctly points out, Rappaport's new work leaves deductive analysis behind and really represents Rappaport's own 'worldview' draped in a wide range of the author's own assumptions about the nature of religion. For example, to understand the meaning of symbols, Rappaport (1999:11) explains at great length the psychology of 'the lie' and 'deceit' and how these are useful concepts for understanding symbolic behavior. This is a prime example of a researcher's own worldview (in this case Rappaport's apparent cynical view of language) that results in a coloring of his analysis of data. Rappaport's (1969,1970, 1971) earlier works concerning the role of ritual in society were based on the freshness of his experience with the ethnographic world of a small-scale society in Papua New Guinea and his engagement with hard ethnographic facts that he scrupulously collected. Thus, for the study of prehistoric religion based on large assemblages of archaeological data, the methods best suited to the identification and analyses of ritual are based on the quantitative and contextual analyses of artifacts interpreted as 'cultic' that can be studied in relation to functional theories of religion as described here.

Ritual Acts and Archaeological Correlates

The most definitive archaeological study of prehistoric religion is Colin Renfrew's 'Towards a Framework for the Archaeology of Cult Practice' (Renfrew 1985b). The Gilat study presented here of the emergence of one of the first pan-regional ritual centers in the southern Levant draws very heavily on Renfrew's framework. Simply put, Renfrew has laid the foundation for studying prehistoric temple/sanctuary religion (at the Phylakopi Late Bronze Age sanctuary in the Aegean) and now, with the wealth of ritual data recovered at Gilat, we can help build the framework for an archaeological study of ritual process and social change.

Renfrew published his framework for the archaeological study of cult around the same time that Tambiah's (1985) *Culture, Thought, and Social Action: An Anthropological Perspective* appeared, and helped make performance theory a popular 'mini-paradigm' in cultural anthropology. For Renfrew (1985:18), the essence of religious ritual is 'the performance of expressive actions of worship and propitiation of the human celebrant towards the transcendent being' yet he seems to have been unaware of the growing appreciation of 'performance' in the analysis of ritual by cultural anthropologists at that time (cf. Ahern 1979; Finnegan 1969; La Fontaine 1977). However, Renfrew relied on Melford Spiro's seminal definition of religion that foreshadows the establishment of the performance theory mini-paradigm. For Spiro (1966), religion can be defined as 'culturally patterned interactions with culturally postulated superhuman beings'. Herein lies the link between the performance of ritual acts, the religious sub-system of a culture and material correlates for these behaviors. The range of ritual acts that may leave a material 'signature' includes a) attention focusing, b) the presence of 'liminal' zones (cf. Turner 1995 [1969]), c) presence of deity and associated symbolic focus, and d) participation and offering. In 1987, we conducted our first joint excavation at Gilat with the aim of clarifying the stratigraphy of the site and laying the groundwork for future large-scale excavations that took place from 1990 to 1992 (see Chapter 5, this volume). The short 1987 season enabled us to present a preliminary study of the archaeology of cult at Gilat in the *Journal of Mediterranean Archaeology* (Alon and Levy 1989). The following discussion builds on that publication and lists the various chapters where these correlates are identified and examined. Based on the dimensions of ritual behavior discussed here, the following material correlates have been suggested by Renfrew (1985) and modified for the Gilat study:

1) Ritual activities may occur in association with natural environmental features in a landscape (i.e. a hilltop, a spring, a mountain top, a grove of trees—Chapters 1, 5, 16).

2) A special building may be established for ritual acts (Chapter 5).

3) Ritual may involve 'conspicuous public display' in areas such as public courtyards, or 'hidden exclusive mysteries' where only select individuals may view ritual in secret rooms, grottos, etc; both of these dimensions of cult have an architectural signature (Chapters 5, 14, 15).

4) Ritual acts of worship may be reflected in iconography or imagery (Chapters 12, 15).

5) To induce religious experience, different devices may be used such as dance, music, drugs and alcohol. Iconography, musical instruments and residue studies can help identify this (Chapter 12).

6) The locus of ritual acts and cult paraphernalia used at a site may utilize attention-focusing devices identifiable in the architecture and mobile equipment in the facility (Chapters 5, 10, 15).

7) The presence of deities may be indicated by cult images at the site (Chapter 15).

8) The locus of ritual acts may have special installations for these activities such as altars, special benches, favisa, pools, basins, special hearths, and libation pits (Chapter 5).

9) Ritual acts may include animal and/or human sacrifice (Chapters 5, 6, 8).

10) Evidence for feasting rituals may be represented by special patterns of food and drink remains (cf. Dietler and Hayden 2001) that may represent offerings (Chapters 6, 10, 16).

11) Evidence of votive offerings may be present, some of which were intentionally broken (Chapters 12, 15).

12) Portable equipment may have been used for ritual acts (i.e. incense burners, special lamps, etc.—Chapters 10, 12).

13) Sacred areas may be identified at the site if symbolic artifacts are found, contextually, in large numbers (redundancy—Chapters 5, 10, 11, 12).

14) The symbols found at the site will often link deities worshipped with iconographic representation (Chapter 15).

15) Symbolism may be reflected in funerary architecture, the placement of the dead and grave offerings (Chapter 8).

16) Concepts of ritual cleanliness and pollution may be reflected in the animal remains at the site, the disposal of rubbish, and the general maintenance of the perceived sacred area (cf. Pearson 2000).

17) Ritual equipment should reflect a significant investment of wealth (i.e. in terms of procurement, 'value', manufacture, etc.—Chapters 12, 14, 15).

18) Architecture used for ritual should demonstrate a significant investment of wealth and resources (Chapter 5).

Test Expectations for Ritual Activities at Gilat

To analyze the wealth of ritual artifacts found at Gilat and described in this volume, we have attempted to establish a consistent theoretical framework for studying ritual behavior in the archaeological record at the site. A framework for analyzing ritual is done by suggesting seven general classes of data along with contextual evidence, provenance studies, and cross-cultural ethnographic parallels in concert with Renfrew's criteria outlined above. Generalized test expectations are made for identifying ritual activities at Gilat.

Worship and Space. While it is difficult to 'prove' that a natural environmental feature such as a mountain top was the locus of ritual activity, the human-built environment offers greater possibilities. The architectural plan of a suspected sanctuary or ritual site should show similarities with contemporary temples or sanctuary architecture from the research area. In the Negev desert example described in this book, following the 1990–1992 excavations, it is now possible to trace the evolution of ritual space at the site through six of the seven occupation phases at the site (Strata II A–IV; e.g. Chapter 5). If similarities can be established, this would help locate special buildings, facilities and open spaces used for ritual activities at the site. Based on a study of the architectural elements of the site with mobile artifacts, it should be possible to locate where hidden vs. more public ritual activities took place. These distinctions should help clarify the organization of ritual practices and the site and their ramifications for socioeconomic activities.

Ritual Practices. Within the context of the site, the material correlates for ritual acts should focus on the loci of specific cult activities within the proposed sacred area; e.g. courtyards, rooms, platforms, altars, benches, standing stone features, special hearths and storage facilities. In addition, evidence for the cartage and possible consumption of offerings such as food, drink and exotic substances should be identifiable in the suspected ritual areas.

Religious Experience. Evidence for religious or ritual experience by the ancient population may be reflected on depictions of dance or processions on artifacts and architecture, musical instruments, paleobotanical and chemical residues (of drugs, incense, alcoholic beverages, and precious commodities such as olive oil) and receptacles that may have been used to transport special substances to the ritual center. While objects specifically reflecting dance and music have not been recognized at Gilat, a large assemblage of portable ceramic and stone fenestrated stands (Chapters 10 and 12) have been found. Special ceramic vessels for the transport of rare olive oil have been isolated at Gilat (Chapter 10). These objects are examined in this study in conjunction with ethno-historical data from the Negev Bedouin and ancient textual data (from the Hebrew Bible, Mesopotamian and other sources) that may shed light on the use of these objects to facilitate religious experiences.

Attention-Focusing Devices. The lay-out of buildings, large platforms, altars, benches and other architectural features can help in inducing and enhancing religious and ritual experiences by helping to focusing the attention of the participants. In addition, portable equipment such as statuettes and figurines would have played a significant role (cf. Chapter 15). The contextual evidence of these portable objects within the sacred space at a site should provide evidence of attention-focusing activities.

Cult Images. Figurines (not toys), statuettes, statues and other forms of figurative 'art' can convey information concerning omnipotent powers and the numinous; these artifacts should contain symbols that highlight the ideology, beliefs, and concerns of the people who made these objects. In non-industrial societies these concerns might focus on fertility, the nature of deities, success in hunting and herding, agriculture, husbandry and fecundity. One way of identifying these concerns and possibly the deities worshipped is to compare the symbolic content of statuettes and figurative art with the socioeconomic dimensions of the prehistoric or pre-industrial society under study. Peltenberg (Peltenburg *et al.* 1988) suggests it is possible to identify a cult image as opposed to a votive on the basis that the former should have a special, 'less-touched', status (implying worship) than the former, which may have been manipulated more often. Thus, paint and/or delicate manufacture and features may be better preserved on a cult image than on a votive.

The study of cult images can be linked to what Merlin Donald (1991) in his book *Origins of the Modern Mind* refers to as the concept of 'external symbolic storage'—that is devices outside the human body evolved specifically or unconsciously to contain and communicate information. In terms of human cognition, this represents a fundamental advance in human evolution. By tracking the evolution of 'external symbolic storage', Donald presents a model of how symbols are used and evolve in the course of human evolution In a conference devoted to this concept and published in *Cognition and Material Culture: The Archaeology of Symbolic Storage* (Renfrew and Scarre 1998), the notion of 'external symbolic storage' is fully explored by archaeologists and anthropologists in relation to material culture. In discussing the evolution of human cognition, Donald (1991) outlines three general cognitive phases and transitions:

a) Episodic culture, which is characteristic of primate cognition (First transition)
b) Mimetic culture, characteristic of *Homo erectus* (Second transition)
c) Linguistic or mythic culture, characteristic of early *Homo sapiens* (Third transition)

Briefly, Donald suggests that mythic culture emerged during the Upper Paleolithic with the origins of visuographic representation, and extended well into Neolithic societies that foreshadow the urban world. Renfrew (1998), although appreciative of Donald's cognitive framework, criticises the fact that while Donald notes the importance of the Upper Paleolithic visuographic achievements, and highlights the role of writing systems in Mesopotamia as external symbolic storage, he neglects how middle range societies utilized this concept in their cultural evolution. Renfrew (ibid: 4), in his inimitable way, embellishes Donald's cognitive framework by linking external symbolic storage specifically with middle range societies:

a) Episodic culture, characteristic of primate cognition (First transition)
b) Mimetic culture, characteristic of Homo erectus (Second transition)
c) Linguistic or mythic culture, characteristic of early *Homo sapiens* (Third transition)
d) External symbolic storage employing symbolic material culture, characteristic of early agrarian societies with permanent settlements, monuments and valuables (Fourth transition)
e) Theoretic culture using sophisticated information retrieval systems for external symbolic storage, usually in the form of writing, frequently in urban societies.

As the Chalcolithic period in the Levant is characterized by the rise of middle range societies (Levy 1998), the cognitive dynamics underlying the evolution of external symbolic storage are significant when viewed against the background of other fundamental changes at this time including the rise in human population, transformations in agro-technology, pyro-technology (metallurgy and ceramics), and the general fabric of Levantine societies at this time. In Chapter 15, Commenge and others explore the symbolic dimensions of the Gilat figurative art in great detail.

Repetition.
> Alone, alone, all, all alone,
> Alone on a wide wide sea!
> And never a saint took pity on
> My soul in agony.
>   —Samuel Taylor Coleridge (1778)
>   *The Rime of the Ancient Mariner*

One cult object does not make a ritual site. It is the repetition of material remains linked to a range of ritual activities that provides the kind of evidence that archaeologists need to separate the sacred from everyday domestic activities and to be certain of identifying an ancient sanctuary in the archaeological record. In addition, the contextual patterns of ritual objects and the distribution of special function artifacts in large quantities and in specific loci (e.g. courtyards, small room, basins, hearths, and other features) may point to the practice of ritual acts such as the burning of incense, worship, adoration, pilgrimage, and the preparation of special substances.

Ceremonial Centers, Exchange and Ethnohistory. A ceremonial 'service center' for ritual activities should contain evidence for widespread contacts with a hinterland. In chiefdom societies, when there is a lack of economic control, as would be evidenced by land ownership or centralized storage, ritual and religion can be parlayed into power and prestige. As Tim Earle (1991a) points out, in these cases, populations, such as those in Mesoamerica or the Mississippi valley, seem to have been drawn into 'sociopolitical systems in part through manipulated "smoke and mirrors", an ideology of religiously sanctioned centrality symbolized by the ceremonial constructions and exchanges in foreign objects of sacred significance'. The archaeological evidence for exchange in ritual-related objects should reflect gifts or offerings brought to the site that highlight a concern with religion; e.g. statuettes, figurines, votives, non-local foodstuffs and 'special objects'. Provenance studies, residue analyses, and the quantification of artifacts interpreted as 'cultic' and found in the ritual center should help in detecting the direction of exchange, how the hinterland connected the regional ritual network, the extent of flow of cult objects to the site and the overall sphere of influence of the ceremonial center. Finally, a ritual center should also have functioned as a center of pilgrimage. Local and cross-cultural ethnographic and historical data concerning why a pilgrimage system may have emerged, how it functioned, and its role in the wider society can be of paramount importance for helping to understand the archaeology of ritual. In the Negev case study described in this book, a range of carefully selected studies by cultural anthropologists working in the Negev desert (Israel—Yoram Bilu, Chapter 4), Bedouin from the Sinai peninsula (Egypt—Emanuel Marx, Chapter 3) and small-scale swidden agriculturalists from Papua New Guinea (Donald Tuzin, Chapter 2) are presented and used to help provide processual models of ritual and society that are germane to the analyses of middle range societies represented at Gilat.

Ancient ethnohistorical documents can provide another source of important data for interpreting the archaeological record related to ritual. For the study of formative ritual centers, such as the Negev Chalcolithic example presented here, the earliest *local* ethnohistoric document is the Hebrew Bible. While the Hebrew Bible was codified sometime around the seventh and sixth centuries BCE (cf. Friedman 1987), millennia removed from the Chalcolithic period (c. 4500–3600 BCE), it does represent some of the earliest insights into pre-industrial societies that lived, worshipped and interacted with the local southern Levantine environment. Another important source of ethnohistoric data, but from further to the north in Syro-Mesopotamia are Ugaritic texts which scholars such as Liverani (1993, 1999) have used to build detailed socioeconomic reconstructions of the northern Levant. Important socioeconomic and subsistence data are embedded in the Hebrew Bible that has been extrapolated to understand the religious traditions reflected in the Iron Age archaeological record (cf. Zevit 2001). From an Annales perspective, the long-term processes (*la longue duree*) of south Levantine geo-history and environment both enabled and constrained social change in similar ways throughout the pre-industrial past. Thus, much can be learned from the Hebrew Bible, the ethnographies of the 'Holy Land', and the early historical texts found both in the Levant and neighboring regions about how people used ideology and religious belief to interact with their environment. While paleoenvironmental changes did occur from the Chalcolithic though the Iron Age period in the Levant (Goldberg and Rosen 1987), the fluctuations were not enormous and only several hundreds of millimeters of average annual rainfall (Fig. 1.2). Thus, any historical evidence of how the religious traditions of ancient agriculturalists and pastoralists interact with their environment can provide compelling models for late prehistory.

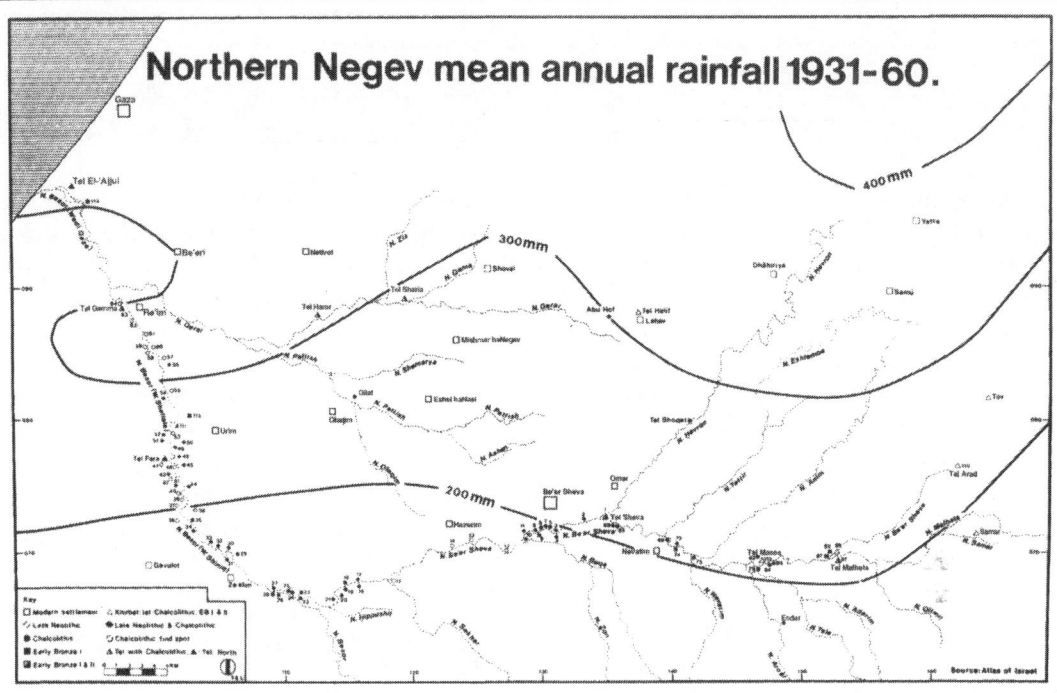

Figure 1.2. Mean Annual Rainfall, N. Negev.

The Role of Ethnography for Studying Late Prehistoric Levantine Religion

Perhaps the earliest systematic use of ethnographic data for the analysis of ancient Levantine religions is the structural approach by W. Robertson Smith 1998 (Orig. 1889), 1903 (Orig. 1885), 1956 (Orig. 1889) in various works published in the late nineteenth century. Robertson Smith falls into the category of nineteenth-century cultural evolutionists who made one of the first in-depth studies of a restricted body of ethnographic data concerning one group—Semites. As Harris (2001) notes, Robertson Smith was closer to modern structural-functionalist standards than anything produced up to that time through his detailed studies of feasting, ritual communion and sacrifice. The analysis linked these ancient Semitic religious rituals to social adaptation and social solidarity. In many respects, this work foreshadows Durkheim's *The Elementary Forms of Religious Life* which explains ritual (especially Australian totemic systems) in functionalist terms. According to Turner (1991), 'it is often difficult to distinguish between the Durkheimian conception of religion as social cement and the Marxist metaphor of religion as a social opium.' Yet, as will be shown from the Gilat data, the functional role of ritual and religion in promoting social solidarity cannot be ignored.

One of the criticisms of Robertson Smith is that his analysis was based upon insubstantial and unreliable data (Hamilton 2001). That said, there is much to be gained through his research. Robertson Smith was a Scottish Biblicist and Arabist whose command of ancient and modern Semitic languages still gives his work great authority (Propp 1999). In approaching the religion of the ancient Semites in the southern Levant, he argued against using Mesopotamian religion as the starting point for the analysis (Robertson Smith 1998 [1889]) primarily because the bulk of the Mesopotamian data available then (and now for that matter) relates to highly urban cultures. Instead, Robertson Smith argued:

> the right point of departure for a general study of Semitic religion must be sought in regions where, though our knowledge begins at a later date, it refers to a simpler state of society, and where

accordingly the religious phenomena revealed to us are of an origin less doubtful and a character less complicated. In many respects the religion of heathen Arabia, though we have few details concerning it that are not of post-Christian date, exhibits an extremely primitive character, corresponding to the primitive and unchanging character of nomadic life. And with what may be gathered from this source we must compare, above all, the invaluable notices, preserved in the Old Testament, of the religion of the small Palestinian states before their conquest by the great empires of the east.

If we filter out the nineteenth-century judgmental tone of Robertson Smith's writing, it is possible to appreciate the importance of ethnographic data from small-scale societies of the southern Levant and Arabian Peninsula for establishing closer links to local ethnohistorical documents (e.g., the Hebrew Bible). This relates to the notion of 'correspondence theory' between symbolic representations of the social world and patterns of conduct discussed below with regard to the analysis of regional cults. Scholars would have to wait almost 25 years before the first intensive, systematic, ethnographic surveys were made in the region by scholars such as Alois Musil (1868–1944) (1907, 1908, 1927a, 1927b). As Ernest Gellner (1995) points out,

> As an Old Testament scholar, he [Alois Musil] explored the toponymy of the Bible. For instance, he became convinced that the real Mount Sinai was somewhere east of Aqaba, a volcanic hill unrelated to the mountain now so named. This seems to make sense: people fleeing from Egypt were hardly likely to ascend an arid and high mountain located on the way back to Egypt. A site east of the Gulf of Aqaba is far more plausible. At about the same time as Malinowski was absorbing the philosophical ideas of Ernst Mach, which then helped him to transform anthropology from a speculative-historical-genetic discipline into a synchronic-social one, Alois Musil was similarly switching from a concern with the Arabian desert as the locale of the Old Testament to an interest in its current inhabitants: at the center of his interest were the roots of monotheism in social experience rather than in revelation. It was really the same movement of thought: the social role, not historic origin, provides the real explanation.

Seen in this perspective the early twentieth-century ethnographers provide important structural and functional links between ritual acts and social solidarity amongst pre-industrial Levantine peasant (Canaan 1979 [Orig. 1927]) and nomadic societies. These sources of data provide a rich harvest for archaeologists' interest in linking the late prehistoric archaeology of ritual with the dynamics of culture change.

While the Levant has undergone accelerated culture change and these small-scale societies are rapidly losing their traditions, as shown in the ethnographic by Abu Rab'ia (1994, 2001; Bar-Zvi, Abu-Rab'ia and Kressel 1998), Bar-Zvi (1977), Ben-David (1981), Lancaster (1997), Marx (1967, 1977b, 1977c) and others, there are still rich insights to be gained concerning the relationship between environment, social organization and ritual amongst these contemporary Negev and Sinai peoples. In this volume, Emanuel Marx (Chapter 3) presents a detailed summary of his research concerning communal and individual pilgrimage amongst some of the Sinai Bedouin and its relation to saints' tombs and pilgrimage practices. In terms of culture process, the insights gleaned by Marx highlight the role of religious ritual as a force of social consolidation and provide an important model for understanding late prehistoric pilgrimage in the nearby Negev desert.

Cultural anthropologists Donald Tuzin (Chapter 2) and Yoram Bilu (Chapter 4) present two different regional ethnographic studies that have important processual implications on the role of ritual in structuring and transforming social institutions and change. Tuzin's (1976, 1980) original research amongst the Ilahita Arapesh of Papua New Guinea represents one of the last cases of ethnographic research in that region before the widespread adoption of Christianity. Consequently, Tuzin's observations offer a unique record of a traditional tribal-scale society's interaction with population pressure, cognition and ritual that led to the emergence of one of the first regional cult centers in that part of Papua New Guinea. In search of a similar processual issue—how to explain the rise of a contemporary regional cult center—Yoram Bilu explores this problem in the modern

Israeli town of Netivot in the northern Negev desert, approximately 7 km northeast of Gilat. Bilu's long-term interest in modern Jewish saints in Moroccan-Israeli society provides a unique opportunity to study the rise (Ben-Ari and Bilu; Bilu 1988; Bilu and Ben-Ari 1992) of a cult center in the immediate vicinity of Gilat. While the scale of modern Israeli Sephardic society and late prehistoric Chalcolithic societies is in no way equivalent, the processual underpinnings of Bilu's investigation of how a regional cult center emerged in this Negev desert town provide an important local contextual source for hypothesis-building about possible similar processes in the same area, and about a traditional ethnic group (mostly Sephardic Jews) who reinterpret ancient (Biblical) textual precepts concerning pilgrimage. Bilu's work also provides general anthropological models of ritual.

Pilgrimage and Sacred Space in Anthropological Perspective

Our preliminary studies of Gilat have shown that the site was a center for a range of cult activities, amongst which pilgrimage played an important role (Alon and Levy 1987, 1989, 1990, 1996a and b; Levy 1992; Levy (ed.) 1997; Levy and Alon 1991, 1993a, 1993b, 1995; Yellin, Levy and Rowan 1996). In this section, we describe the social significance of pilgrimage in anthropological perspective with special attention to the Levant. Pilgrimage can best be defined as a journey made by a pilgrim to a shrine or holy place' (Neufeldt and Guralnik 1991). In this context, a pilgrim is a person who travels to a shrine or holy place as a religious act (*ibid.*). From an anthropological perspective, pilgrimage should be examined in relation to the use of what is perceived to be 'sacred space'. There is a rich literature on the anthropology and geography of pilgrimage that can only be touched on here (cf. Bilu 1988; Eade and Sallnow 1991; Eickelman and Piscatori 1990; Morinis 1992; Sallnow 1981; Singh and Singh 1987; Sopher 1967; Weingrod 1990; Werbner 1977b, 1989) and there are a growing number of archaeological studies on this subject (Coleman and Elsner 1994; Hammond and Bobo 1994; Harbison 1994; Petersen 1994; Ray; Silverman 1994; Stopford 1994). The Gilat study presented here goes beyond many of the earlier studies concerning the archaeology of pilgrimage, especially with regard to the Middle East, by presenting one of the largest assemblages of artifacts that can be linked to trade and pilgrimage for the late prehistoric periods. For example, Yuval Goren's (Chapter 9, this volume) petrographic analysis of torpedo jars and other ceramic vessels provides important data concerning the provenance of these objects and the range and direction of exchange to the Gilat ritual center. Amongst other topics, Commenge *et al.*'s (Chapter 10, this volume) detailed analysis of the entire ceramic assemblage demonstrates not only the on-site contextual meanings of ceramics linked to ritual, but their possible role in pilgrimage. Finally, components of the special ground stone assemblage (cf. Rowan *et al.*, Chapter 12, this volume) such as violin figurines, palettes and figurative objects are shown by Commenge *et al.* (Chapter 15, this volume) to have played an important role not only in ritual at Gilat, but also in the direction and organization of pilgrimage networks during the Chalcolithic period.

In studying the anthropology of pilgrimage, some of the more significant contributions have tried to present models that are cross-culturally valid. The main question is whether this should be the ultimate goal of an archaeological study rooted in one cultural-historic part of the world (here the Middle East). For example, M. Eliade (1971) deals with the universal notion of sacred space and suggests that all sacred spaces are conceptualized as being centers of the universe, locales where the godly and human can meet and interact. Eliade proposes that sacred spaces are equivalent to 'the cosmic navel' and are linked by three domains: the underworld (hell), the earth and heaven. However, as Seth D. Kunin (1998) points out, the main problem with Eliade's approach relates to his linkage between myth, culture and time—'He overemphasizes the cyclical understanding of myth and time, seeing many aspects of the sacred and sacred space as attempts to mirror this cycle, with myth, ritual, and sacred space seeking to return time to its sacred mythological beginnings.

This concept shapes many aspects of his analysis of sacred spaces.' Simply put, as not all cultures perceive sacred space in the same manner, it behooves the archaeologist/anthropologist to explore the unique historical and archaeological context in its own terms.

Although a religious studies scholar, Harold Turner (1979) made an enduring study of sacred space from a cross-cultural perspective where he suggests two basic categories: *domus dei* and *domus ecclesiae*. While these two distinctions are useful, they are too general and 'church-centric'. According to Kunin (1998) Turner's analysis is embedded in 'theological ethnocentricity' where the *domus ecclesiae* is consistently given preference in his work.

Victor Turner (1969, 1986; Turner and Turner 1978) was perhaps the single most influential anthropologist to have opened up the study of pilgrimage. Turner emphasized what he felt were the cross-culturally valid concepts of limnality (discussed above) and *communitas*, which, he believed, were present in all pilgrimages regardless of cultural venue. For Turner, *communitas* meant 'commonness of feeling' by the social group involved in rituals such as pilgrimage. With regard to ritual centers, Turner says, 'At major pilgrim centers, the quality and degree of the emotional impact of the devotions (with are often continuously performed, night and day), derive from the union of the separate but similar emotional dispositions of the pilgrims converging from all parts of a huge socio-geographical catchment area' (Turner and Turner 1978). The concept of *communitas*, as used by Turner for rituals such as pilgrimage, can be likened to Durkheim's (1995 [Orig. 1912]) view of religion as functioning to promote the sentiments underlying social solidarity. Indeed, *communitas* may be the singular factor that crosscuts the role of pilgrimage in all societies regardless of time or place. In our study of late prehistoric pilgrimage, we assume that *communitas* was one of the primary forces that underlay the performance of rituals that brought people from distance of up to 150 km on pilgrimage to Gilat.

Ritual Centers

To understand the centrality of ritual in promoting social change it is important to under what a religious center is and how it articulates with its hinterlands. Anthropologists and geographers provide a number of important concepts and tools concerning these issues that will help us flesh out these relationships. Over the past 30 years, it has been recognized that one of the structural characteristics that distinguishes chiefdom societies (and ultimately state level organizations) from less complex social systems is that they geographically transcend the local autonomy characteristic of the autonomous camp and village settlement patterns characteristic of band level and segmentary societies. As Carneiro (1981) points out, 'a chiefdom is an autonomous political unit comprising a number of villages or communities under the permanent control of a paramount chief' and 'chiefdoms have capital villages or towns that tend to be significantly larger than any other settlement in the political unit' (1981:54). The centers that coordinated these economic, social and ritual activities did not necessarily carry out all of these functions. Some may have specialized in trade redistribution of goods (Renfrew 1982); others may have focused on social integration (Earle 1978), and still others on ritual (Earle 1987; Yoffee 2001). The functional variability of chiefly centers foreshadows developments in urban society and does not necessarily relate to the absolute size of settlement.

For urban settlements, Richard Fox (1977) suggests that a city is a location where specific functions take place, and if those functions take place, that locale is a city, irrespective of size. For Fox, what is needed for a locale to be classed as a 'city' is for a number of centralized activities to occur that fall into three distinct categories corresponding to political, ritual and economic domains. Accordingly, he constructs an idealized typology of cities that emphasize each of these aspects: what he calls the regal-ritual city, the administrative city, and the mercantile city. While the Gilat study focuses on middle range societies, this urban anthropological construct provides a functional model that can used to conceptualize the range of 'services' that can characterize middle range societies. Thus, while a Chalcolithic chiefly center such as Shiqmim functioned primarily to coordinate social and economic activities, Gilat was a 'ritual/religious center'. According to David Sopher (1967) 'sacred places become religious centers as simple ethnic religious systems evolve into more complex ones. The religious centers, which become the primary foci of sanctity, may supplant the diffuse sacred places of the preceding simple religions, or they may merely supplement them.' In this context, we may define 'ritual/religious center' as playing an ideological role in the middle range settlement system. This evolves from the prestige and status the elite in a settlement system obtain from being linked to the organization of ritual. These 'ritual/religious centers' primarily function as ceremonial centers and the importance of this role may not be commensurate with their economic position or political power. Ritual cannot be measured quantitatively. Middle range society 'ritual/religious centers' are places that provide housing to the ritual leaders and their retinue, and sanctuary for the surrounding hinterland linked to the ritual system. Ritual/religious centers are able to obtain regional resources because their ceremonial nature is seen as necessary for the well being of the larger social system embedded in the ritual network. Examples of these are found at Chaco Canyon in New Mexico (Yoffee 2001), the nineteenth-century Nuuchalnulth Ahousaht of Clayoquot Sound along the Northwest Coast (Hayden 1995), the Early and Middle Formative periods in the Oaxaca Valley of Mexico (Blanton *et al*. 1999; Marcus and Flannery 1996), and many other regions.

Geography and Ritual: The Northern Negev, Paleoecology and Ethnohistory

Geographic Considerations. If time and space are archaeology's most precious commodities, the works of David E. Sopher (Singh and Singh 1987; Sopher 1967, 1968, 1997) concerning the geography of religion and pilgrimage represent a small treasure-trove. Born in 1923 in Shanghai, China, and of Sephardic Bagdadian Jewish background, he received all of his degrees in geography at U.C. Berkeley where he was a doctoral student of Carl O. Sauer (1889–1975). Although a specialist of South Asian cultural geography, religion and pilgrimage, he had a deep appreciation of the Hebrew Bible and it's the links between ritual and ecology. Consequently, we draw on Sopher's (1967) geographical treatment of religion here, especially with regard to the southern Levant. Religious sub-systems of culture are characterized by a number of spatial features whose identification can help archaeologists (such as those engaged in the Gilat study) move from the static archaeological record to the dynamics (cf. Binford 1982, 1983) of cultural systems. Some of the features of religious systems that are explored in this book include: a) spatial distribution in time (social–temporal context) and space (geographic context); b) an organizational network; and c) processes used by the religious sub-system to grow territorially (and in number), and d) elements which promote stability and steady states. While the environmental context in which cultural and religious systems evolved is central to understanding these phenomena, we are clearly aware of the dangers of environmental determinism (Erickson 1999; Frenkel 1992; Wright 1993). However, the further one moves in space or back in time from places and periods where industrialized technology 'rules the roost'—the more important local ecology becomes to people and their natural environment. It is in this spirit that cultural geography is used at the end of this study (Chapter 16).

Local geographical Setting. Gilat is situated in the northern Negev desert of Israel—a region characterized by a semi-arid environment (Ben-Dor *et al*. 2002; Evenari, Shanan and Tadmor 1982), consists of three geomorphologic zones: the Gaza or Negev coastal plain, the foothill zone, and the northern Negev upland zone (Israel. Ma*hle*ket ha-medidot 1970; Nir 1978). A detailed discussion of the modern environmental setting of the northern Negev can be found in Levy and Goldberg (1987).

There are two distinct trends in the distribution of average annual rainfall across the northern Negev (one east-west, the other north-south) that have played a critical role in cultural ecology of both pastoral nomads and agriculturalists in the region. Over very short distances (less than 100 km), major environmental zones change from semi-arid to arid desert zones. The highest average annual rainfall values (c. 400 mm) are found along the Negev coastal plain at the city of Gaza. Rainfall quantities drop markedly as one moves c. 45 km southeast to the city of Beersheva where the average annual values are c. 200 mm. A further 40 km east of Beersheva, the rainfall values drop to c. 140 mm at the modern town of Arad (Meteorological Service 1967). Similarly, there is a north-south rainfall gradient with high semi-arid average annual rainfall values at the city of Kiriyat Gat (c. 425 mm) to c. 200mm at Beersheva 40 km to the south, and c. 120 mm at Kibbutz Revavim 20 km south of Beersheva. Inter-annual variability in rainfall is also a key factor in determining the stability of agro-pastoral systems. Water is the key to animal, plant and human survival in the desert and the availability of average annual rainfall plays a key role in the distribution of vegetation, animals and humans in this landscape. Thus, the question arises, just how different was the northern Negev climate during the Late Neolithic and Chalcolithic periods? Paleoenvironmental data from paleolimnological studies of the Dead Sea (Hall 1996; Neev and Emery 1967; Neev and Hall 1977), sediment analyses of the Nile delta and Eastern Mediterranean basin (Butzer 1997, 2002; Stanley 2002, 2001), geomorphology in the Negev and Levant (Goldberg and Rosen 1987; Rosen 1995; Wilkinson 1996, 1999, 2000), fossil land snails from the Negev (Goodfriend 1990, 1991, 1992; Goodfriend and Magaritz 1988), and fossil pollen (Horowitz 1974, 1979, 1989) from the Levant, all point to an increase of c. 100–150 mm of average annual rainfall during the Late Neolithic/Chalcolithic periods. Thus, given the available paleoenvironmental data, it can be assumed that the same general semi-arid environmental parameters would have operated for late prehistoric agriculturalists and pastoralists in the northern Negev as today. However, given more humid conditions, it can be assumed that there was less inter-annual variability in mean annual rainfall.

Gilat's location (Figs. 1.1 and 1.2) at the boundary of two of these zones (the Negev coastal plain and inland foothill zone) played a key role in its development. The rainfall patterns outlined above coincide with the three major geomorphologic zones mentioned earlier. Briefly, the Negev coastal plain extends from 0 m amsl along the Mediterranean littoral to an altitude of c. 80–140m amsl to the east. The Negev coastal plain is characterized by an extensive, relatively flat, plain consisting primarily of loessial soils that provide the best year-round grazing lands in the Negev desert as a whole (Dan *et al.* 1976; Danin, Orshan and Zohary 1975). A wide range of plants suitable for grazing is found here (Danin 1983). Most of the Negev coastal plain has been cultivated for hundreds of years making it almost impossible to reconstruct the natural vegetation. The presence of large quantities of sand in the soil matrix here contributes to more dense vegetation dominated by *Artemisia monosperma* and other psammophytes. To the west, the inland foothill zone of the Northern extends from c. 140 m amsl in the west to c. 550 m amsl in the east. This region is dominated by Eocene chalk hills and lowland trough-shape valleys filled with loessial soils (Nir 1978; Picard and Solomonica 1936) that were re-deposited during the late Pleistocene and early Holocene periods (Goldberg and Rosen 1987). The geomorphologic history (Levy 1998; Levy and Alon 1987) of the natural terraces along these valleys show that during the Chalcolithic period they provided rich agricultural soils for the Beersheva valley farmers who used hoe-based cultivation methods to grow mostly barley, some wheat and some legumes. These two areas represent an 'ecotone'—a transition zone between two structurally different environments. Gilat's ecotonal setting along the 'fault-line' of the rich annual grazing lands along the Negev coastal plain and the more arid, inland foothill zone was an important factor in promoting its prominence as a regional ritual center. As Sahlins (1968) points out:

the chiefdom economy usually develops...toward more diversification...the independent political group is set across the ecological grain, incorporating the range of landscapes normally encountered in the general area... Spread over a hundred square miles, a chiefdom is likely to encompass greater environmental variety than is included in the few square miles of village domain. Moreover, a chiefdom has the means to organize, or at least tolerate, localized adaptations to the medley of its environmental opportunities.

As will be shown in this study, Gilat's unique ecotonal setting created a range of quite different environmental factors that contributed to its role in the late fifth–early fourth millennium social evolution in the Levant. For example, adaptation to the northern Negev's trough-shaped valleys was shown to be a critical factor in promoting agro-technological change and the rise of the Beersheva valley Chalcolithic chiefdom (Levy 1992a). At Gilat, one way of achieving greater social integration on the regional scale was to develop the site into one of the southern Levant's earliest regional cult centers. The nature of 'regional cults' is discussed in the next section.

Regional Cults

Anthropologist Richard Werbner (Werbner 1977b), perhaps more than any other scholar, has promoted the analysis of cult by situating it as a regional phenomenon. According to Werbner (1977a):

> Regional cults are found in many parts of the world. They are cults of the middle range—more far reaching than any parochial cult of the little community, yet less inclusive in belief and membership than a world religion in the most universal form. The central places are shrines in towns and villages, by crossroads or even in the wild, apart from human habitation, where great populations from various communities or their representatives, come to supplicate, sacrifice, or simply make pilgrimage. They are cults which have topography of their own, conceptually defined by the people themselves and marked apart from other features of cultural landscapes by ritual activities.

The work by Werbner and his contributors takes up the challenge raised by Max Gluckman (1940, 1942) to analyze social change in fields of relations that cross political, economic and/or ethnic boundaries. However, they do this by considering the impact of social change due to modernization, the influence of major world religions and contemporary nationalism. From the perspective of social evolution, the phenomenon of regional cults intersects with the emergence of middle range, rank or chiefdom level societies. As discussed earlier, one of the primary characteristics that distinguishes chiefdoms from family-level band and tribal level societies is the emergence of regional polities (Johnson and Earle 1987) is that they evolve out of formerly fragmented local groups into multi-community societies. As will be shown in the Gilat study, the rise of regional cults helped provide the 'social glue' that linked widespread settlements into a *communitas* web that provided solutions to persistent problems related to risk management (environmental problems), warfare, the control of technology, and trade (see conclusion, Chapter 16, this volume). The anthropological analysis of regional cults by Werbner's (1977b) group moves beyond some of the assumptions of regional analysis used by historical geographers, such as Smith (1976), who assume the existence of network hierarchies in regions. The presence of ritual, settlement or any kind of spatial hierarchy must be demonstrated and not assumed. As Werbner (1977a) points out, in regional cults flows of goods, services information and people move across major political and ethnic boundaries.

The Gilat study uses many of the findings of Regional Cults to:

   a) identify ritual activities that may not coincide with the spatial boundaries and hierarchies of regional and sub-regional Levantine cultures;
   b) define how the regional cult web changed through time during the late fifth–fourth millennium BCE;

c) examine how regional and local cults interact at Gilat through time;

d) define, if possible, boundedness and associated political divisions of regional cults in the southern Levant;

e) test whether the Gilat ritual center was 'extra-territorial' (i.e. an area beyond the territorial jurisdiction of any contemporary cultural group such as the Beersheva Chalcolithic chiefdom, etc.);

f) test whether Robertson Smith's (1998 [1889]) 'correspondence theory' (i.e. a correspondence between symbolic representations of the social world and patterns of conduct) exists in the archaeological record at Gilat (cf. Marx 1977a and Chapter 3 in support of this theory and Eickelman 1977; Eickelman and Piscatori 1990 against);

g) identify whether 'elitist' and/or 'egalitarian' regional cults are represented at Gilat. Elitist cults are characterized by processes which bring an elite and its public into dialectical inclusive domains...the religious center is the political one under the elite's own control. [An egalitarian regional cult]...is characteristically free of any political elite with special ritual roles in the cult'. (Werbner 1977a);

h) how does one or more cults establish a hierarchy with centralized control of regional cult services over the landscape?

Our Gilat study uses these and the works by Tuzin, Marx and Bilu presented in the following chapters to flesh out the character, function and evolution of regional cults during the formative Chalcolithic period in the southern Levant.

Concluding Remarks

Archaeology is the only source of deep-time data to examine the links between formative social evolution and changes in the history of religion. The analytical tools needed for making such an investigation must rely on social models of religion and society developed by anthropologists, sociologists and religious studies scholars. The study of ritual, with its associated material signature, provides the most important lens for documenting and analyzing these fundamental changes in human belief systems. In the study of the Gilat ritual center presented here, ritual practice (such as pilgrimage), local ethnohistoric data (from the Hebrew Bible and other ancient Near Eastern texts), ethnography, and the geography of religion are used to explore these changes. To test the theoretical models of religion (Chapters 1–4) and its role in culture change, an interdisciplinary approach is used to analyze the thousands of artifacts found at this ritual center in Israel's Negev desert. A range of biological data is examined including archaeozoological remains (Chapter 6), marine and riverine molluscs (Chapter 7) and human remains (Chapter 8). What is missing in the analysis of ecofacts is a detailed study of the plant remains from the site. A limited analysis of organic residues plant and liquid remains found in select pottery vessels is presented (Chapter 10). However, earlier studies from nearby sites provide a basic understanding of the role of plants in northern Negev Chalcolithic communities' (cf. Kislev 1987). Regional exchange studies of key archaeological materials (ceramics, lithics, ground stone, and bone tools) provide crucial data sets for testing models concerning the nature of ritual at Gilat, domestic activities, pilgrimage, and the evolution of regional cult systems in the southern Levant (Chapters 9–13). The socioeconomic factors that influenced the emergence of Gilat as a regional center are explored in terms of textile and other forms of manufacture (Chapter 14). Finally, some of the cognitive dimensions underlying late fifth–early fourth millennium ritual and belief are gleaned from structural analyses of the rich assemblage of figurative artifacts from the site (Chapter 15). Taken together, it is hoped that the excavations and analyses of Gilat will contribute to the growing interest in cognitive archaeology with special regard to the emergence of religious systems that transcend the local community.

Acknowledgments

TEL would like to sincerely thank Guillermo Algaze, Joel Robbins, Donald Tuzin, and Richard Werbner for their careful reading of this chapter and their critical comments. The author accepts full responsibility for any factual or conceptual errors.

References

Abu Rabi'a, A. (1994) *The Negev Bedouin and Livestock Rearing: Social, Economic and Political Aspects.* Oxford: Berg.
— (2001) *A Bedouin Century: Education and Development among the Negev Tribes in the 20th Century.* New York and Oxford: Berghahn Books.
Aguilar, M. I. (2000) History, religion, and the perils of anthropology: a response to T.O. Beidelman. *Anthropos* V95:314–15.
Ahern, E.M. (1979) The problem of efficacy: strong and weak illocutionary acts. *Man* 14:1–17.
Aigbe, S.A. (1993) *Theory of Social Involvement: A Case Study in the Anthropology of Religion, State, and Society.* Lanham: University Press of America.
Alon, D. (1961) Early settlements along the Nahal Garar and Nahal Patish. *M'befnim.*
Alon, D., and T.E. Levy (1987) Notes & News: Gilat, 1987. *Israel Exploration Journal* 37:283–84.
— (1989) The archaeology of cult and Chalcolithic sanctuary at Gilat. *Journal of Mediterranean Archeology* 2:163–221.
— (1990) The Gilat sanctuary: its centrality and influence in the southern Levant during the late 5th–early 4th millennium B.C.E. (Hebrew). *Eretz Israel* 21:23–36.
— (1996a) The demographic problem and the climatic question during the Chalcolithic Period in the Northern Negev based on the Gilat and Shiqmim sites. *Eretz Israel (Hebrew)* 25, 41:41–45.
— (1996b) Violin shape figurines and cult at Chalcolithic Gilat. *Ariel (Hebrew)* 166:6 pages.
Amiran, R. (1981) Some observations on Chalcolithic and Early Bronze Age sanctuaries and religion. In *Temples and High Places in Biblical Times*, edited by A. Bivan. Jerusalem: Hebrew Union College, pp. 47–53
Anderson, G.A. (1992) The savage in Judaism: an anthropology of Israelite religion and ancient Judaism— Eilbergschwartz, H. *Journal of Religion* V72:465–67.
Austin, J.L. (1975) *How To Do Things with Words* (2nd edition). Cambridge: Harvard University Press.
Baal, J. van, W.E.A. van Beek and J.H. Scherer (1975) *Explorations in the Anthropology of Religion: Essays in Honour of Jan van Baal.* The Hague: Martinus Nijhoff.
Bar-Zvi, S. (1977) *Bedouin Tell About Beersheba (Hebrew). Tuviaho Archives No. 13: 1-33.* Beersheva: Ben Gurion University of the Negev.
Bar-Zvi, S., A. Abu-Rab'ia, and G. Kressel (1998) *The Charm of Graves: Mourning Rituals and Tomb Worshipping Among the Negev Bedouin (Hebrew).* Tel Aviv: Israel Ministry of Defense.
Bates, D.G. (1996) *Cultural Anthropology.* Boston: Allyn and Bacon.
Bauer, B.S., and C. Stanish (2001) *Ritual and Pilgrimage in the Ancient Andes: The Islands of the Sun and the Moon* (1st edition). Austin: University of Texas Press.
Bell, C. (1992) *Ritual Theory, Ritual Practice.* New York and Oxford: Oxford University Press.
— (1997) *Ritual: Perspectives and Dimensions.* New York and Oxford: Oxford University Press.
Ben-Ari, E., and Y. Bilu. Saints' sanctuaries in Israeli development towns: on a mechanism of urban transformation. *Urban Anthropology* 16:243–72.
Ben-David, J. (1981) *Ja'baliya - A Bedouin Tribe in the Shadow of the Monastery (in Hebrew).* Jerusalem: Cana.
Ben-Dor, E., K. Patkin, A. Banin and A. Karnieli (2002) Mapping of several soil properties using DAIS-7915 hyperspectral scanner data - a case study over clayey soils in Israel. *International Journal of Remote Sensing* V23:1043–62.

Ben-Tor, A., and E. Netzer (1973) The principal architectural remains of the Early Bronze Age at Ai. *Eretz Israel* 11:1–7.

Bilu, Y. (1988) Inner limits of communitas: a covert dimension of pilgrimage experience. *Ethos* 16:302–25.

Bilu, Y., and E. Ben-Ari (1992) Making of modern saints: manufactured charisma and the Abu-Hatseiras of Israel. *American Ethnologist* 19:672–87.

Binford, L.R. (1968) Archaeological Perspectives. In *New Perspectives in Archaeology*, edited by S.R. Binford and L.R. Binford. Chicago: Aldine Publishing Company, pp. 5–32.

— (1982) The archaeology of place. *Journal of Anthropological Archaeology* 1:5–31.

— (1983 *In Pursuit of the Past: Decoding the Archaeological Record*. New York: Thames and Hudson.

Blanton, M. (ed.) (1966) *Anthropological Approaches to the Study of Religion. A.S.A. Monographs*. London: Tavistock Publications.

Blanton, R.E., G. M. Geinman, S.A. Kowalewski and L.M. Nicholas (1999) *The Monte Alban State*. Cambridge: Cambridge University Press.

Bloch-Smith, E. (1992) *Judahite Burial Practices and Beliefs about the Dead*. Sheffield: Sheffield Academic Press.

Bloch-Smith, E., and B. Nakahi Alpert (1999) A landscape comes to life: The Iron Age I. *Near Eastern Archaeology* 62:62–127.

Bourke, S. (2002) in *Egypt and the Levant*, edited by E.C.M. Van Den Brink and T.E. Levy.

Bowen, J.R. (1998) *Religions in Practice: An Approach to the Anthropology of Religion*. Boston: Allyn and Bacon.

Bowie, F. (2000) *The Anthropology of Religion*. Oxford: Blackwell Publisher.

Boyer, P. (1994) *The Naturalness of Religious Ideas - A Cognitive Theory of Religion*. Berkeley: University of California Press.

— (2001) *Religion Explained: The Evolutionary Origins of Religious Thought*. New York: Basic Books.

Britannica, E. (2002) On-line Britannica.

Burris, J.P. (1997) Religion and anthropology at nineteenth-century international expositions: from the Great Exhibition to the World's Parliament of Religions, 1851–1893.

Butzer, K.W. (1997) Sociopolitical Discontinuity in the Near East C. 2200 B.C.E.: scenarios from Palestine and Egypt. In *Third Millennium BC Climate Change and Old World Collapse.*, vol. 49, edited by H.N. Dalfes, G. Kukla and H. Weiss. Berlin: NATO ASI Series (Springer), pp. 245–96.

— (2002) Geoarchaeological implications of recent research in the Nile Delta. In *Egypt and the Levant: Interrelations from the 4th through the Early 3rd Millennium B.C.E., New Approaches to Anthropological Archaeology*. Edited by E.C.M. Van Den Brink and T.E. Levy. London: Leicester University Press.

Canaan, T. (1979) [Orig. 1927] *Mohammedan Saints and Sanctuaries in Palestine. Luzac's oriental religions series*, vol. V. Jerusalem: Ariel Publishing.

Carneiro, R.L. (1973) Classical evolution. In *Main Currents in Cultural Anthropology*, edited by R. Naroll and F. Naroll. Englewood Cliffs, NJ: Prentice–Hall.

— (1981) The Chiefdom: Precursor of the State. In *The Transition to Statehood in the New World*, edited by G.D. Jones and R.R. Kautz. Cambridge: Cambridge University Press, pp. 37–79.

Clarke, D.L. (1968) *Analytical Archaeology*. London: Metheun.

Coleman, S. (2001) Ritual and belief: readings in the anthropology of religion., (1999) (English) by D. Hicks. *Journal of the Royal Anthropological Institute* V7:579.

Coleman, S., and J. Elsner (1994) The pilgrim's progress: art, architecture and ritual movement at Sinai. *World Archaeology* 26:73–89.

Conrad, G.W., and A.A. Demarest (1984) *Religion and Empire: The Dynamics of Aztec and Inca Expansionism*. Cambridge: Cambridge University Press.

Costin, C.L. (1991) Craft specialization: issues in defining, documenting, and explaining the organization of production. *Archaeological Method and Theory* 3:1–56.

Dan, J., D.H. Ya'alon, H. Koyumdijsky and Z. Raz (1976) *The Soils of Israel (with map 1:500,000): Pamphlet No. 159*. Bet Dagan: The Volcani Center.

D'andrade, R. (1995) Objectivity and militancy: A Debate. 1. Moral Models in Anthropology. *Current Anthropology* 36:399–408.

Danin, A. (1983) *Desert Vegetation of Israel and Sinai*. Jerusalem: Cana.

Danin, A., G. Orshan and M. Zohary (1975) The Vegetation of the Northern Negev and the Judean Desert of Israel. *Israel Journal of Botany* 24:118–72.

Dever, W.G. (1987) The contribution of archaeology to the study of Canaanite and Early Israelite religion. In *Ancient Israelite Religion: Essays in Honor of Frank Moore Cross*, edited by P. Miller, P. Hanson and S. McBride. Philadelphia: Fortress Press, pp. 209–47.

Dietler, M., and B. Hayden (eds) (2001) *Feasts: Archaeological and Ethnographic Perspectives on Food, Politics, and Power*. Washington and London: Smithsonian Institution Press.

Donald, M. (1991) *Origins of the Modern Mind: Three Stages in the Evolution of Culture and Cognition*. Cambridge (MA): Harvard University Press.

Dunayevsky, I., and A. Kempinski (1973) The Megiddo temples. *Zeitschrift des Deutschen Palastina-Vereins* 89:161ff.

Durkheim, E. (1933) *The Division of Labor in Society*. Glencoe: Free Press.

— (1995) [orig. 1912] *The Elementary Forms of Religious Life (Translated and with an Introduction by Karen E. Fields)*. New York: The Free Press.

Eade, J., and M. Sallnow (1991) *Contesting the Sacred: The Anthropology of Christian Pilgrimage*. London: Routledge.

Earle, T. (1991a) The evolution of chiefdoms. In *Chiefdoms: Power, Economy, and Ideology*, edited by T. Earle. Cambridge: Cambridge University Press, pp. 1–15.

— (1991b) Preface. In *Chiefdoms: Power, Economy, and Ideology*, edited by T. Earle. Cambridge: Cambridge University Press, pp. xi–xii.

Earle, T.K. (1978) *Economic and Social Organization of a Complex Chiefdom: The Halelea District Kaua'i, Hawaii. Anthropological Papers 63*. Michigan: University of Michigan, Museum of Anthropology.

— (1987) Chiefdoms in archaeological and ethnohistorical perspective. *Annual Review of Anthropology* 16:279–308.

Eickelman, D.F. (1977) Ideological Change and Regional Cults, Maraboutism and Ties of 'Closeness' in Western Morocco. In *Regional Cults*, edited by R. P. Werbner. London: Academic Press, pp. 3–28.

Eickelman, D.F., and J. Piscatori (1990) *Muslim Travellers: Pilgrimage, Migration, and the Religious Imagination. Comparative studies on Muslim Societies 9*. Berkeley: University of California Press.

Eliade, M. (1971) *The Myth of theEternal Return, or Cosmos and History*. Princeton: Princeton University Press.

Epstein, C. (1973) The sacred area at Megiddo in Stratum XIX. *Eretz Israel* 11:54–57.

— (1975) Basalt pillar figures from the Golan. *Israel Exploration Journal* 25:193–201.

— (1978) Aspects of Symbolism in Chalcolithic Palestine. In *Archaeology in the Levant*, edited by P.R.S. Mooney and P.J. Parr. Warminster: Avis and Phillips.

— (1982) Cult symbols in Chalcolithic Palestine. *Bolletino del Centro di Studi Preistorici* 19:63–82.

— (1988) Basalt pillar figures from the Golan and the Huleh region. *Israel Exploration Journal* 38:205–23.

— (1998) *The Chalcolithic Culture of the Golan*. Jerusalem: Israel Antiquities Authority.

Erickson, C.L. (1999) Neo-environmental determinism and agrarian 'collapse' in Andean prehistory. *Antiquity* V73:634–42.

Evenari, M., L. Shanan and N. Tadmor (1982) *The Negev: The Challenge of a Desert* (2nd edition). Cambridge: Harvard University Press.

Feeleyharnik, G. (1992) The savage in Judaism: an anthropology of Israelite religion and ancient Judaism - Eilbergschwartz, H. *American Anthropologist* V94:719–20.

Finnegan, R. (1969) How to do things with words: performative utterances among the Limba of Sierra Leone. *Man* 4:537–52.

Fishbane, M. (1993) The savage in Judaism: anthropology of Israelite religion and ancient Judaism—Eilbergschwartz, H. *History of Religions* V32:306–08.

Flannery, K.V. (1983) Theoretical Framework. In *The Cloud People: Divergent Evolution of the Zapotec and Mixtec Civilizations*, edited by K.V. Flannery and J. Marcus. New York: Academic Press, pp. 1–9.

— (1999) Chiefdoms in the Early Near East: why it's so hard to identify them. In *The Iranian World: Essays on Iranian Art and Archaeology*, edited by A. Alizadeh, Y. Majidzadeh and S.M. Shahmirzadi. Tehran: Iran University Press, pp. 44–58.

Flannery, K.V., and J. Marcus (eds) (1983) *The Cloud People: Divergent Evolution of the Zapotec and Mixtec Civilizations*. New York: Academic Press.

Fox, R. (1977) *Urban Anthropology*.

Frazer, J.G. (1927) *Folk-lore in the Old Testament: Studies in Comparative Religion, Legend and Law* (abridged edition). New York: Macmillan.

— (1960) *The Golden Bough: A Study in Magic and Religion*, Vol. 1 (abridged edition). New York: Macmillan.

— (1968) *Totemism and Exogamy: A Treatise on Certain Early Forms of Superstition and Society* ([1st] reprint edition). London: Dawsons.

Frenkel, S. (1992) Geography, empire, and environmental determinism. *Geographical Review* V82:143–53.

Friedman, R.E. (1987) *Who Wrote the Bible?* New York: Summit.

Gal, Z., H. Smithline and D. Shalem (1997a) A Chalcolithic burial cave in Peqi'in, Upper Galilee. *Israel Exploration Journal* 47:145–54.

Geertz, C. (1973) *The Interpretation of Cultures*. New York: Basic Books.

Gellner, D.N. (1999) Anthropological Approaches. In *Approaches to the Study of Religion*, edited by P. Connolly. London: Cassell.

Gellner, E. (1995) *Anthropology and Politics: Revolutions in the Sacred Grove*. Oxford and Cambridge, USA: Blackwell.

Glazier, S.D. (1997) *Anthropology of Religion: A Handbook*. Westport: Greenwood Press.

Gluckman, M. (1940) Analysis of a social situation in modern Zululand. *Bantu Studies* 14:1–30, 147–74.

— (1942) Some processes of social change, illustrated with Zululand data. *African Studies* 1:243–60.

Goldberg, P., and A.M. Rosen (1987) Early Holocene paleoenvironments of Israel. In *Shiqmim I*, edited by T.E. Levy. Oxford: BAR International Series 356, pp. 22-33.

Goodfriend, G.A. (1990) Rainfall in the Negev Desert during the Middle Holocene, based on C-13 of organic matter in land snail shells. *Quaternary Research* V34:186–97.

— (1991) Holocene trends in O-18 in land snail shells from the Negev Desert and their implications for changes in rainfall source areas. *Quaternary Research* V35:417–26.

— (1992) The use of land snail shells in paleoenvironmental reconstruction. *Quaternary Science Reviews* V11:665–85.

Goodfriend, G.A., and M. Magaritz (1988) Paleosols and Late Pleistocene rainfall fluctuations in the Negev Desert. *Nature* 332:144–46.

Gopher, A., and T. Tsuk (eds) (1996) *The Nahal Qanah Cave: Earliest Gold in the Southern Levant*. Tel Aviv: Monograph Series of the Institute of Archaeology, Tel Aviv University.

Gopher, A., T. Tsuk, S. Shalev and R. Gophna (1990) Earliest gold artifacts in the Levant. *Current Anthropology* 31:436–43.

Greenstein, E.L. (1994) The savage in Judaism: an anthropology of Israelite religion and ancient Judaism-Eilbergschwartz, H. *Judaism* V43:101–09.

Gruber, M. (1998) Anthropology of religion: a handbook, by S.D. Glazier. *Journal for the Scientific Study of Religion* V37:376–78.

Hall, J.K. (1996) Digital topography and bathymetry of the area of the Dead Sea depression. *Tectonophysics* V266:177–85.

Halpern, B. (1998) Research design in archaeology: the interdisciplinary perspective. *Near Eastern Archaeology* 61:53–65.

Hamilton, M. (2001) *The Sociology of Religion*. London and New York: Routledge.

Hammond, N., and M.R. Bobo (1994) Pilgrimage's Last Mile: Late Maya Monumnet Veneration at La Milpa, Belize. *World Archaeology* 26:19–34.

Harbison, P. (1994) Early Irish pilgrim archaeology in the Dingle Peninsula. *World Archaeology* 26:90–103.

Harris, M. (2001) *The Rise of Anthropological Theory: A History of Culture, Updated Edition*. Walnut Creek: AltaMira Press.

Hayden, B. (1995) Pathways to power: principles for creating socioeconomic inequalities. In *Foundations of Social Inequality*, edited by T. D. Price and G. M. Feinman. New York and London: Plenum Press, pp. 15–86.

Hicks, D. (2002) *Ritual and belief: readings in the anthropology of religion*, 2nd edition. Boston: McGraw Hill.

Hodder, I. (1999) *The Archaeological Process - An Introduction*. Oxford: Blackwell.

Holladay, J.S. (1987) Religion in Israel and Judah under the monarchy: an explicitly archaeological approach. In *Ancient Israelite Religion: Essays in Honor of Frank Moore Cross*, edited by P. Miller, P. Hanson and S. McBride. Philadelphia: Fortress Press, pp. 249–99.

Horowitz, A. (1974) Preliminary palynological indications as to the climate of Israel during the last 6,000 years. *Paleorient* 2:407–14.

— (1979) *The Quaternary of Israel*. New York: Academic Press.

— (1989) Continuous pollen diagrams for the last 3.5 My from Israel: vegetation, climate and correlation with the oxygen isotope record. *Palaeogeography Palaeoclimatology Palaeoecology* V72:63+.

Israel. Ma*hle*ket ha-medidot (1970) *Atlas of Israel; cartography, physical geography, human and economic geography, history* (2nd edition). Jerusalem: Survey of Israel Ministry of Labour.

Israel Meteorological Service (1967) Climatological standard normals of rainfall, 1931–1960. *Series A (Meteorological Notes)* 21.

Johnson, A.W., and T. Earle (1987) *The Evolution of Human Societies: From Foraging Group to Agrarian State*. Stanford: Stanford University Press.

Kempinski, A. (1972) The Sin Temple at Khafaje and the En-Gedi Temple. *Israel Exploration Journal* 22:10–15.

— (1987) The Temples during the Chalcolithic and Early Bronze Age. In *The Architecture of Ancient Israel: From the Prehistoric to the Persian Nomads*, edited by E. Nezor, A. Kempinski and R. Reich. Jerusalem: Israel Exploration Society, pp. 49–53.

Kerner, S. (2001) *Das Chalkolithikum in der sudlichne Levante: Die Entwicklung handwerklicher Spezialisierung und ihre Beziehung zu gesellschaftlicher Komplexitat*. Orient-Archaologie Band 8. Rahden/Westf: Deutsches Archaeologisches Institut Orient-Abteilung, Verlag Marie Leidorf GmbH.

Kislev, M. (1987) Chalcolithic plant husbandry and ancient vegetation at Shiqmim. In *Shiqmim I*, edited by T.E. Levy. Oxford: BAR International Series 356, pp. 251–79.

Knapp, A.B. (1988) Ideology, archaeology, and polity. *Man* 23:133–63.

Krzyzaniak, B. (1999) Anthropology of religion. A handbook., (1997) (English translation by S.D. Glazier). *Anthropos* V94:270–71.

Kunin, S.D. (1998) *God's Place in the World: Sacred Space and Sacred Place in Judaism*. London: Cassell.

La Fontaine, J. (1977) The power of rights. *Man* 12:421–37.

Lambek, M. (2002) *A Reader in the Anthropology of Religion*. Blackwell Anthologies in Social and Cultural Anthropology 2. Malden: Blackwell.

Lancaster, W. (1997) *The Rwala Bedouin Today* (2nd edition). Prospect Heights: Waveland Press.

Levy, T.E. (1992) The Gilat Sanctuary, Northern Negev Desert, Israel. *National Geographic Research and Exploration* 8:372–74.

Levy, T.E. (ed.) (1987) *Shiqmim I: Studies Concerning Chalcolithic Societies in the Northern Negev Desert, Israel (1982–1984)*. Oxford: BAR International Series 356.

— (1992a) Transhumance, subsistence, and social evolution in the Northern Negev Desert. In *Pastoralsim in the Levant: Archaeological Material in Anthropological Perspective*, edited by A. Khaznov and O. B. Yosef. Madison, Wisconsin: Prehistory Press.

— (1997) Gilat. In *The Oxford Encyclopedia of Archaeology in the Near East*, edited by E. Meyers. Oxford: Oxford University Press, pp. 404–405.

— (1998) Cult, metallurgy and rank societies: Chalcolithic Period (c. 4500–3500 BCE). In *The Archaeology of Society in the Holy Land*, edited by T.E. Levy. London: Leicester University Press, pp. 226–44.

Levy, T.E., R.B. Adams, A. Hauptmann, M. Prange, S. Schmitt-Strecker and M. Najjar (2002) Early Bronze Age metallurgy: a newly discovered copper manufactory in southern Jordan. *Antiquity* 76:425–37.

Levy, T.E., and D. Alon (1987) Settlement patterns along the Nahal Beersheva-Lower Nahal Besor: models of subsistence in the northern Negev. In *Shiqmim I: Studies Concerning Chalcoithic Societies in the Northern Negev Desert, Israel (1982–1984)*, edited by T.E. Levy. Oxford: BAR International Series, pp. 45–138.

— (1991) Gilat-1990. *Hadashot Arkheologiyot (Hebrew)*:83–84.

— (1993a) Gilat. In *The New Encyclopedia of Archaeological Excavations in the Holy Land*, edited by E. Stern. Jerusalem: Israel Exploration Society, pp. 514–17.

— (1993b) Gilat-1991. *Excavations and Surveys in Israel* 12:91–93.

— (1995) Gilat 1992. *Excavations and Surveys in Israel* 14:111–12.

Levy, T.E., and P. Goldberg (1987) The environmental setting of the northern Negev. In *Shiqmim I*, vol. 356, edited by T.E. Levy. Oxford: BAR International Series, pp. 1–21.

Levy, T.E., and S. Shalev (1989) Prehistoric metalworking in the southern Levant: archaeometallurgy and social perspectives. *World Archaeology* 20:353–72.

Liverani, M. (1993) *Akkad: The First World Empire: Structure, Ideology, Traditions*. Padova: Sargon.

— (1999) New developments in the study of the history of the Israel of the Bible: Examining the redactional post-canonical stratum through Near Eastern archaeological and philological parallels. *Biblica* V80:488–505.

Marcus, J., and K.V. Flannery (1996) *Zapotec Civilization: How Urban Society Evolved in Mexico's Oaxaca Valley*. London: Thames and Hudson.

Marx, E. (1967) *Bedouin of the Negev*. Manchester: Manchester University Press.

— (1977a) Bedouin pilgrimage to holy tombs in southern Sinai. *Notes on the Bedouins VIII*:14–22.

— (1977b) Communal and individual pilgrimage: the region of saint's tombs in south Sinai. In *Regional Cults, Association of Social Anthropologists Monograph 16*, edited by R. P. Werbner. London, New York, San Francisco: Academic Press, pp. 29–51.

— (1977c) The tribe as a unit of subsistence: nomadic pastoralism in the Middle East. *American Anthropologist* 79:343–63.

Marx, K. (1970) [1844] *Kritik des Hegelschen Staatsrechts. English. Critique of Hegel's 'Philosophy of right'*. Translated from the German by Annette Jolin and Joseph O'Malley.Edited with an introduction and notes by Joseph O'Malley. Cambridge studies in the history and theory of politics. Cambridge: Cambridge University Press.

Mithen, S. (1996) *The Prehistory of the Mind: A Search for the Origins of Art, Religion and Science*. London: Phoenix.

Morinis, A. (ed.) (1992) *The Anthropology of Pilgrimage*. Westport: Greenwood Press.

Musil, A. (1907) *Arabia Petraea. I. Moab; II. Edom: Topograhischere Reisebericht*. Wien: Alfred Holder.

— (1908) *Arabia Petraea III: Ethnologischer Reisebericht*. Wein: Hoflen.

— (1927a) *Arabia Deserta: A Topographical Itinerary*. New York: American Geographical Society.

— (1927b) *Manners and Customs of the Rwala Bedouin*. New York: American Geographical Society.

Nakhai, B.A. (2001) *Archaeology and the religions of Canaan and Israel*. Boston, Mass.: American Schools of Oriental Research.

Neev, D., and K. O. Emery (1967) The Dead Sea. *Bulletin Geological Survey of Israel* 41:1–147.

Neev, D., and J.K. Hall (1977) Climatic fluctuations during the Holocene as reflected by the Dead Sea Levels.

Neufeldt, V., and D. B. Guralnik (eds) (1991) *Webster's New World Dictionary of American English*. New York: Prentice Hall.

Nir, D. (1978) *Geomorphological Map of Israel*. Jerusalem: Survey of Israel.

Pearson, M. Parker (2000) *The Archaeology of Death and Burial*. College Station: Texas A&M University Press.

Peltenburg, E.J., D. Bolger, E. Goring and C. Elliott (1988) Kissonerga-Mosphilia 1987: Ritual Deposit, Unit 1015. *Report of the Department of Antiquities Cyprus*:43–52.

Petersen, A. (1994) The archaeology of Syrian and Iraqi Hajj routes. *World Archaeology* 26:47–56.

Picard, L., and P. Solomonica (1936) On the Geology of the Gaza-Beersheva District. *Journal of the Palestine Oriental Society* 16:180–223.

Propp, W.H.C. (1999) *Exodus 1–18: A New Translation with Introduction and Commentary*. New York: Doubleday.

Rappaport, R.A. (1969) *Pigs for the Ancestors: Ritual in the Ecology of a New Guinea People*. New Haven: Yale University Press.

— (1970) Sanctity and adaption. *Oecology Issue* 10:46–71.

— (1971) Ritual, sanctity and cybernetics. *American Anthropologist* 73:59–76.

— (1979) *Ecology, Meaning, and Religion*. Richmond: North Atlantic Books.

— (1999) *Ritual and Religion in the Making of Humanity*. Cambridge: Cambridge University Press.

Ray, H.P. (1994) Kanheri: the archaeology of an early Buddhist pilgrimage centre in western India. *World Archaeology* 26:35–46.

Remy, J. (1991) [Socio-Anthropology of the Religious, Vol. 1, Popular Religion at the Risk of Modernism, Vol 2, the Enchanted Circle of Belief - French - Lapointe,R]. *Anthropos* V86:277–78.

Renfrew, C. (1982) Socio-economic change in ranked societies. In *Ranking, Resource and Exchange*, edited by C. Renfrew and S. Shennan. Cambridge: Cambridge University Press, pp. 1–8.

— (ed.) (1985a) *The Archaeology of Cult: The Sanctuary of Phylakopi*. London: The British School of Archaeology at Athens, Thames and Hudson.

— (1985b) Towards a framework for the archaeology of cult practice. In *The Archaeology of Cult: The Sanctuary of Phylakopi*, edited by C. Renfrew. London: The British School of Archaeology at Athens, Thames and Hudson, pp. 11–26.

— (1998) Mind and matter: cognitive archaeology and external symbolic storage. In *Cognition and Material Culture: The Archaeology of Symbolic Storage*, edited by C. Renfrew and C. Scarre. Cambrige: McDonald Institute Monographs, pp. 1–6.

Renfrew, C., and C. Scarre (eds) (1998) *Cognition and Material Culture: The Archaeology of Symbolic Storage*. Cambridge: McDonald Institute Monographs.

Robbins, J. (2001) Ritual communication and linguistic ideology. *Current Anthropology* 42:591–613.

Robertson Smith, W. (1998) [1889] Lectures on the religion of the Semites. In *The Myth and Ritual Theory*, edited by R.A. Segal. Oxford: Blackwell, pp. 17–34.

— (1903) [Orig. 1885] *Kinship and Marriage in Early Arabia*. London: Charles and Black.

— (1956) [Orig. 1889] *The Religion of the Semites*. New York: Meridian Books, World Publishing.

Rosen, A.M. (1995) The social response to environmental change in Early Bronze Age Canaan. *Journal of Anthropological Archaeology* 14:26–44.

Rousseau, J. (2001) Hereditary stratification in middle-range societies. *Journal of the Royal Anthropological Institute* 7:117–31.

Sahlins, M. (1968) *Tribesmen*. New Jersey: Prentice–Hall.

Sallnow, M. J. (1981) Communitas reconsidered: the sociology of Andean pilgrimage. *Man* 16:163–82.

Schiffer, M. B. (1987) *Formation Processes of the Archaeological Record*. Albuquerque: University of New Mexico Press.

Seaton, P. (2000) Aspects of New Research at the Chalcolithic Sanctuary Precinct at Teleilat Ghassul. In *Proceedings of the First International Congress on the Archaeology of the Ancient Near East, Rome, May 18th–23rd, 1998*, edited by P. Matthiae, A. Enea, L. Peyronel, and F. Pinnock. Rome, pp. 1503–14.

Seton-Williams, M.V. (1949) Palestinian Temples. *Iraq* 11:77–89.

Shalev, S. (1994) Change in metal production from the Chalcolithic period to the Early Bronze Age in Israel and Jordan. *Antiquity* 68:630–37.

Shalev, S., Y. Goren, T.E. Levy and P.J. Northover (in press) A Chalcolithic mace head from the Negev: technological aspects and cultural implications. *Archaeometry* 34:63–71.

Shalev, S., and J.P. Northover (1993) Metallurgy of the Nahal Mishmar hoard reconsidered. *Archaeometry* 35:35–47.

Silverman, H. (1994) The archaeological identification of an ancient Peruvian pilgrimage center. *Wolrd Archaeology* 26:1–18.

Singh, R.L., and R.P.B. Singh (eds) (1987) *Trends in the Geography of Pilgrimages: Homage to David E. Sopher*. Varanasi: The National Geographical Society of India.

Smith, C.A. (1976) *Regional Analysis*. New York: Academic Press.

Sopher, D.E. (1967) *Geography of Religions*. Englewood Cliffs: Prentice–Hall.

— (1968) Pilgrim circulation in Gujarat. *Geographical Review* 58:392–425.

— (ed.) (1997) *The goal of Indian pilgrimage: geographical considerations*. Vol. 34. *Sacred Places, Sacred Spaces: The Geography of Pilgrimages*. Baton Rouge: Geoscience Publications, Louisiana State University.

Spiro, M.E. (1966) Religion: problems of definition and explanation. In *Anthropological Approaches to the Study of Religion*, A.S.A. Monographs 3, edited by M. Banton. London: Tavistock, pp. 85–126.

Stager, L. (1987) Archaeology, ecology, and social history: background themes to the Song of Deborah. *Supplements to Vetus Testamentum* 40:221–34.

Stanley, D.J.S. (2002) Configuration of the Egypt-to-Canaan Coastal Margin and North Sinai byway in the Bronze Age. In *Egypt and the Levant: Interrelations from the 4th through the Early 3rd Millennium B.C.E.*, edited by E.C.M. van den Brink and T.E. Levy. London: Leicester University Press.

Stanley, J.D. (2001) Dating modern deltas: progress, problems, and prognostics. *Annual Review of Earth and Planetary Sciences* V29:257–94.

Stewart, C. 1998. Anthropology of religion: A handbook., (1997) (English) by S.D. Glazier. *American Ethnologist* V25:511–13.

Stopford, J. (1994) Some approaches to the archaeology of Christian pilgrimage. *World Archaeology* 26:57–72.

Tambiah, S.J. (1985) *Culture, Thought, and Social Action: An Anthropological Perspective*. Cambridge: Cambridge University Press.

Thorbjornsrud, B. (2001) Academic nomadism: The relationship between social anthropology and history of religion. *Numen-International Review for the History of Religions* V48:204–23.

Trigger, B.G. (1998) *Sociocultural Evolution: Calculation and Contingency*. Oxford: Blackwell.

Turner, H.W. (1979) *From Temple to Meeting House: The Phenomenology and Theology of Places of Worship*. The Hague; New York: Mouton.

Turner, V. 1991. *Religion and Social Theory* (2nd Edition). London: Sage.

— (1995) [1969]. *The Ritual Process: Structure and Anti-Structure*. New York: Aldine De Gruyter.

Turner, V.W. (1969) *The Ritual Process: Structure and Anti-Structure. The Lewis Henry Morgan lectures 1966*. Chicago: Aldine Pub. Co.

— (1986) *The Anthropology of Performance* (1st edition). New York: PAJ Publications.

Turner, V.W., and E.L.B. Turner (1978) *Image and Pilgrimage in Christian Culture: Anthropological Perspectives*. Lectures on the history of religions 11. Oxford: Blackwell.

Tuzin, D.F. (1976) *The Ilahita Arapesh: Dimensions of Unity*. Berkeley: University of California Press.

— (1980) *The Voice of the Tambaran: Truth and Illusion in Ilahita Arapesh Region*. Berkeley: University of California Press.

Tylor, E.B. (1871) *Primitive Culture: Researches into the Development of Mythology, Philosophy, Religion, Art, and Custom*. London: J. Murray.

Ussishkin, D. (1980) The Ghassulian Shrine at En-Gedi. *Tel Aviv*:1–44.

Wax, M.L. (1991) The savage in Judaism: an anthropology of Israelite religion and ancient Judaism-Eilbergschwartz, H. *Journal for the Scientific Study of Religion* V30:328–29.

Weingrod, A. (1990) Saints and shrines, politics, and culture: a Morocco-Israel comparison. In *Muslim Travellers: Pilgrimage, Migration, and the Religious Imagination*, edited by D. F. Eickelman and J. Piscatori. Berkeley: University of California Press, pp. 217–35.

Werbner, R.P. (1977a) Introduction. In *Regional Cults*. Association of Social Anthropologists Monograph 16, edited by R. P. Werbner. London, New York, San Francisco: Academic Press, pp. IX–XXXVII.

— (ed.) (1977b) *Regional Cults*. Association of Social Anthropologists Monograph 16. London: Academic Press.

— (1989) *Ritual Passage, Sacred Journey: The Process and Organization of Religious Movement.* Washington, D.C. and Manchester: Smithsonian Institution Press and Manchester University Press.

Wilkinson, T.J. (1996) Late quaternary chronology and palaeoclimates of the Eastern Mediterranean, by O. BarYosef, R.S. Kra. *Journal of Field Archaeology* V23:527–30.

— (1999) Holocene valley fills of southern Turkey and Northwestern Syria: recent geoarchaeological contributions. *Quaternary Science Reviews* 18:555–71.

— (2000) Regional approaches to Mesopotamian archaeology: the contribution of archaeological surveys. *Journal of Anthropological Research* 8:219–67.

Winkelman, M. (2000a) Across the boundaries of belief: contemporary issues in the anthropology of religion., (1999) (English) by M. Klass, M.K. Weisgrau. *American Anthropologist* V102:380–82.

— (2000b) *Shamanism: The Neural Ecology of Consciousness and Healing*. Westport, London: Bergin and Garvey.

Winkelman, M.J. (1990) Shamans and other magico-religious healers: a cross-cultural study of their origins, nature, and social transformations. *Ethos* V18:308–52.

Wright, H.E. (1993) Environmental determinism in Near Eastern prehistory. *Current Anthropology* V34:458–69.

Yellin, J., T.E. Levy and Y.M. Rowan (1996) New evidence on prehistoric trade routes: the obsidian evidence from Gilat, Israel. *Journal of Field Archaeology* V23: 361.

Yoffee, N. (1998) Conclusion: a mass in celebration of the conference. In *The Archaeology of Society in the Holy Land*, edited by T.E. Levy. London: Leicester University Press, pp. 542–48.

— (2001) The Chaco Rituality' revisted. In *Chaco Society and Polity: Papers from the 1999 Conference*, New Mexico Archeological Council Special Publication 4, edited by L.S. Cordell, W.J. Judge and J. Piper. Albuquerque: New Mexico Archeological Council.

Zevit, Z. (2001) *The Religions of Ancient Israel: A Synthesis of Parallactic Approaches*. London and New York: Continuum.

2 Cults, Shrines, and the Emergence of Regional Ritual Centers:

The View from New Guinea

Donald Tuzin

Introduction

For students of social and cultural evolution, the main challenge is to understand the whys and wherefores of what Karl Popper calls *emergent novelty*, that is, 'a characteristic of higher systemic levels that cannot be predicted from knowledge of lower systemic levels' (Flannery 1986:513). But if, as Popper implies, the emergent movement is not mechanistic, it is also true that nothing comes from nothing. Accordingly, the relationship between lower and higher systemic levels must be conceived to involve a *process*. In human systems this process is typically very complex, involving diverse elements, agencies, and sub-processes, the particular combination of which is highly contingent and therefore inherently improbable; hence our inability to predict the emergence of novelty.

If prediction is impossible, practically speaking, the *retro*diction of achieved novelties is somewhat less so. Anthropologists interested in sociocultural evolution have devoted considerable energy to explaining how certain forms and patterns came about, and in devising general models for the processes involved. Archaeology is perhaps especially reliant on models, insofar as the material record of particular sites is often too sparse to support meaningful evolutionary inferences; models or extrapolations from other sites can be extremely useful in such circumstances. Cultural anthropology is potentially an important contributor to archaeological methodology, in that it deals with the living intentions, contradictions, and ideologies which suffuse the evolutionary process, but which are usually absent from the material record (cf. Roscoe 2000). All the more so when the subject is the evolution of religious systems.

This chapter examines some of the material, institutional, and cultural conditions underlying the emergence of shrine centers in certain regions of New Guinea. Whatever obvious differences in content may exist between shrine phenomena there and in the ancient Near East, my working assumption is that both instances of emergent novelty involved population and settlement dynamics; preexistent exchange relations between local groups; a growing sense of regional identity and coherence; an increasingly uneven distribution of ritual knowledge and privilege across social groups and categories; a movement to hierarchy from more egalitarian preconditions; and other factors adding up to parallel processes of evolution not nearly so dissimilar as these two cases are in space and time.

Dimensions of Cult in New Guinea

New Guinea abounds with shrines. Practically wherever there is human settlement, one finds sites that are believed to be endowed with mystical power. These may be caves or built structures containing assorted bones, war and hunting trophies, or other potent relics of the ancestors or their deeds; they may be skull racks lodged in the depths of spirit-house sanctuaries, from which the dead eyelessly peer upon, and in their own fashion take part in, the affairs of the living. Very often, such shrines are the mystic headquarters of a local cult, typically predicated on graded male secrecy and initiation, and on the emphatic exclusion of females and uninitiated youths. Other sites, often associated with natural anomalies such as boulders, mountains, large trees, waterfalls, or pools, are home to demonic, non-ancestral spirits that supposedly affect humans in various ways; such spirits are usually amoral and capricious, but in some cases they do respond to human petition.

Corresponding with the atomized societal landscape of this country, shrines are nearly always local in character. An ossuary cave, for example, might belong to a local clan or to the hamlet down the hill; other clans or other hamlets would have shrines of their own. The shrines would be functionally equivalent to one another, just as the clans or settlements are, and to the outsider there would be little to choose between one bone-littered cave and another. Similarly restricted ranges characterize the other shrine forms, as well: because such sites are expressive of ritual identity, their clientele, so to speak, normally does not exceed the narrow bounds of the social group whose identity they enshrine.

A contradiction arises. On the one hand, local groups are typically unaware of the existence or specific significance of each other's shrines, the more so when the customs of these groups differ substantially. On the other hand, ancestral and spirit shrines are so common as to be virtually ubiquitous across thousands of communities and hundreds of cultures and languages. A visitor from a distant part of the country may not know the precise details of a particular shrine, but he would instantly recognize the general idea. If local groups are so isolated from one another, how does one account for this widespread recurrence of a few basic shrine forms and concepts?

Surely, part of the answer must be that these phenomena are manifestations of a universal heritage perhaps going back fifty thousand years: an enduring psychology which, even in more institutionally developed religions, flows as an undercurrent of belief in magic, spirits, and the sentiency of dead persons. The existence of shrines, therefore, cannot be entirely explained by local circumstances, but must be seen partly to reflect the primordial tendency. Shrine *centers* or complexes, on the other hand, are amenable to comparative study, insofar as they occur in correlation with specifiable historical, geographical, and sociocultural conditions.

Regional shrine centers do occur in Papua New Guinea, though they are exceedingly rare; indeed, there may be only two sites that would qualify as genuine shrine centers, in the sense that they serve as a ritual focus and, to that extent, a common cultural overlay, for a relatively large number of socially autonomous groups. One of these is in the Southern Highlands Province, where the sacred site of Kelote has been described (Goldman 1983:118) as 'an historical vatican of the Huli.'

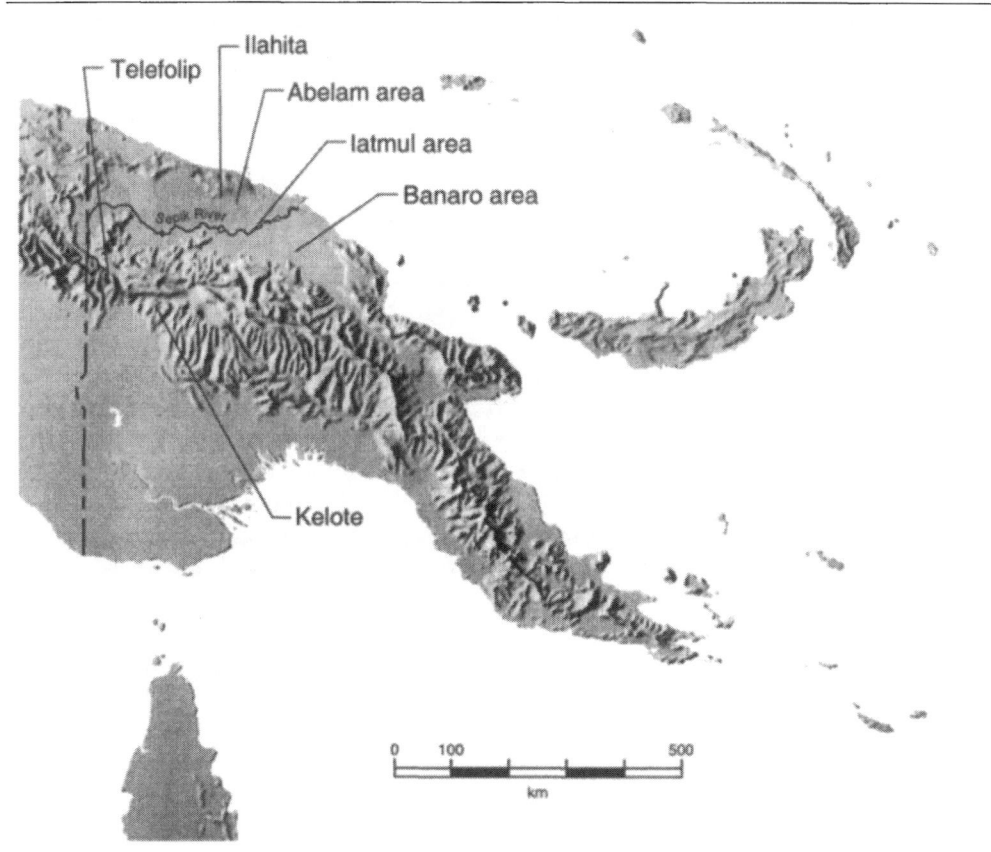

Figure 2.1. Papua New Guinea, indicating sites and areas referred to in the text.

Kelote featured a large cave, in which it was supposed that the creational spirit, Kebali, resided (Goldman 1979). This cave was the center of a network of lesser caves in the region, interlinked by mythical 'tracks,' all of which were sites of pig sacrifices conducted to promote the fertility of the people and the land. In addition to two ritually significant long houses, Kelote contained a large conical structure in which pig sacrifices to various deities occurred, and after which smaller ritual structures throughout the region were patterned. Also prominent at the shrine was a large tree—important because 'all the rivers of the Huli are felt to converge at this place, enter through this tree and pass up to the sky where [they come] down as rain' (Goldman 1979:16). All in all, Kelote was exalted as 'the middle land' and 'the root of the land' (Biersack 1995:16) The shrine 'was envisioned as an absolute, cosmic center,' a metaphorical tree, an *axis mundi*, with four roots radiating out to the Duna, Dugube, Huli, Enga and other distinct peoples, enshrining a range of some 6,500 square kilometers (*ibid.*).

The Shrine Center of Telefolip (Mountain Ok)

The other shrine center is the famous Telefolip spirit house, located in a village of the same name, among the Telefolmin. The Telefolmin are one of a dozen or more 'Min' peoples of the Mountain Ok region, a rugged, highlands area in the far west, at the headwaters of the Sepik and Strickland rivers (Map Fig. 2.1); some Min groups live across the international frontier in Irian Jaya, the Indonesian half of the continental island of New Guinea. In this steep, forested terrain, the population density is not high: as of 1983, approximately 10,000 Min speakers inhabited an area of roughly 15,000 square kilometers (Barth 1987:2); settlements are dispersed and range in size from a few score to a couple of hundred inhabitants. Subsistence is based on shifting horticulture, with an emphasis on taro, along with considerable reliance on hunting and foraging, and on the keeping of domestic pigs (*ibid.*).

Plate 2.1. The Telefolip spirit house (photograph courtesy of Dan Jorgensen).

The Telefolip is recognized as the paramount ritual center for all Min peoples by virtue of its primordial, mythic significance (Craig and Hyndman 1990; Brumbaugh 1990; Jorgensen 1990). It is the shrine of Afek, the Old Woman of the Mountain Ok. The daughter of a cassowary—a large flightless bird native to New Guinea, the off-lying islands, and northern Australia—Afek was the Primal Mother of the Min. Among her many culture- and existence-bestowing accomplishments, Afek built the Telefolip; established the secret men's cult; created the sexes; defined the gendered, magically consequential division between fertility ('Taro') and hunting ('Arrow'); allocated resources so that groups would complement one another; and ordained that humans would die. The Telefolip not only houses (and displays to senior cult initiates) the bones of Afek and Umoim, the brother whom she killed, it is also the entrance to the Land of the Dead. For the spiritual good and prosperity of all Min peoples, it is important that the Telefolip stay in good repair; only once in memory has it been destroyed when it was burned during an enemy raid.

The Telefolip stands at the head of a hierarchy of temples distributed around the entire Mountain-Ok region: lower-level cult initiations are held locally, higher-level activities occur at centers of increasingly general importance, culminating in the Telefolip. It should not be supposed, however, that the Telefolip authorities effectively organize or enforce a religious orthodoxy on the different Min groups, or that their temple is a pan-regional ceremonial or pilgrimage center. Rather, as Barth (1987) has shown, the Telefolip is a large, tolerant umbrella, overarching a religious landscape of considerable local variation in doctrine, symbolism, and ceremonial practices. Barriers of language, ethnicity, warfare, and geography deter homogeneity; so, too, does a process analogous to 'genetic drift' in biological evolution.

Like all New Guinea traditions, that of the Mountain Ok is unwritten--and, therefore, precarious. The sacred knowledge of Afek is localized, shrouded in secrecy, transmitted at infrequent initiation events, and carried in the greyest of heads. No single person or local group possesses all, or even a large proportion of, the sacred knowledge. Accordingly, groups live in 'constant fear' that vital knowledge could be lost (Barth 1987:27). Such losses are not uncommon, given the smallness of local groups and the life expectancy of old men, and when this happens the survivors' only recourse is to appeal to neighboring groups for whatever knowledge they are willing to impart. Hence the advantage of distributing sacred knowledge among different groups; hence, also, the element of 'family resemblance' which pervades the total body of cult knowledge, despite the pronounced variations, inconsistencies, and transformations at more superficial levels of comparison.

The other implication is that, by spending nearly its entire life confined within the memories and imaginations of cult elders, local sacred knowledge tends to drift stochastically within the wider parameters of Mountain-Ok cultural cognition (Barth 1987). Through this individual processing of information, innovation and thematic re-workings continually move in and out of the total corpus of knowledge. This is not a conscious or willful distortion--though in some political circumstances it could be—so much as the natural operation of individual psychology on the long-stored memories. But however much this process may generate regional variation in ritual ideation and practice, its presence imposes significant limits on the practical importance of the Telefolip as a shrine center. As Brumbaugh (1990:73) observes,

> The Telefolip origin version [of the Afek story] transfers [the model of common ancestry] from the Telefol speakers to the Min as a whole. This version invites the Min to consider themselves as one large family dispersed around the original homeplace of Telefolip, and finds in their dispersal the suggestion of a unified plan of organization, one most evident in the way Afek allocated resources to create an overall circulation of trade.
>
> This is a surprisingly ambitious ideology because it is not backed up by any economic or political control from the centre. There was no centralized ritual authority either; Afek's promise to hear all the Min people, and her sanction of intergroup variations, do not make the experts of Telefolip high priests with exclusive access to spiritual powers or competence to dictate orthodoxy. The Telefolip origin account seems ready to underwrite more centralization than anybody had yet discovered a use for; however, it may represent the direction in which ideology was moving.

In summary, the Telefolip and its charter myth of Afek are interesting for the symbolic unity they confer on the congeries of Min peoples. Like most societies in New Guinea, the Min are fiercely egalitarian in ideology, and it is therefore worthy of note that they readily concede the ritual supremacy of the Telefolip. Generally speaking, it is a common conceit of origin stories to claim application to peoples other than the immediate stakeholders—we will see another, extravagant example of this near the end of the chapter—but in New Guinea, at least, it is rare for those others to submit to being cosmogonically defined by someone else. That the Min do so is a tribute to their sense of shared history and substance, as opposed to all non-Min, who fall outside of Afek's mythic family. In the absence of political or economic infrastructure, the ideology surrounding Afek and the Telefolip may be, as Brumbaugh says, surprisingly ambitious; but it is also surprisingly restrained, as cosmogonic myths go, in embracing only groups which, by virtue of similarities in language, history, and custom, recognize themselves as related. It is this element of shared ethnic heritage, I suggest, that underwrites and confers stability on a shrine center whose purpose is otherwise difficult to fathom; conversely, without the Telefolip and the maternal image of Afek, this ethnic heritage would probably soon atrophy, because it lacks any secular rationale.

Surprising or not, the shrine system in the Mountain Ok is *fait accompli*, and, taken by itself, something of an ethnographic curiosity. The Telefolip's status as a shrine center might well have come about by an unreconstructable historical accident. Although the system's workings are observable, it is impossible to know with certainty how it arose or how it would have evolved, had it been left undisturbed by the outside world. Cross-cultural comparison offers another way, however, to clarify the conditions under which such shrine systems may develop in a New Guinea context. The case to consider is the Tambaran of the East Sepik Province: a cult complex having regionalistic features, but without a permanent shrine center of the Telefolip type, although at least one location does have the potential to become such a center. In addition, the East Sepik example holds comparative interest by possessing elements of a regional infrastructure such as are mysteriously lacking among the Mountain Ok.

Regions and Centers: The Tambaran of the East Sepik

The East Sepik region of northeastern New Guinea lies tucked between the island's great central cordillera and its rugged northern coast (Fig. 2.1). Across a varied terrain, the area's principal features are the widely meandering Sepik river, which receives major tributaries from the Highlands to the south; a large adjacency of swamps and fens, which, from the north bank of the river, soon gives way to a gently rising, grassy plain; and the coastal Prince Alexander and Torricelli mountain ranges, which, while inferior in scale and loftiness to the great mountain systems to the south, are imposing enough to restrict easy commerce between the beach and the transmontane interior. Along the coastline, these ranges plunge fairly steeply into the Bismarck Sea; but on the hinterland side they descend into a foothill region, which in turn softens into the upper reaches of the Sepik plain-- an area dissected into a hilly jumble by streams descending from the coastal ranges southwards to the great river. Between the coastal mountains and the Sepik river, then, the flow of peoples and ideas is impeded—to the extent it is impeded at all—only by social and cultural, not physical, obstacles. Such conditions not only permit, in the New Guinea context they *encourage*, the development of sociocultural forms distinctive of the region.

The East Sepik is one of the most populous provinces of Papua New Guinea. In the flatter areas of the Maprik district, local population densities are second only to those in parts of the Central Highlands, rising, under fairly traditional conditions, to just over 150 persons per square kilometer (Lea 1964:38). The many cultural groups are broadly divisible into speakers of the Sepik-Ramu phylum of languages and speakers of Torricelli-phylum languages.[1] Among the former, the ethnographically better known groups are the riverine Iatmul, Manambu, Chambri, Banaro, Bun, and Mundugumor, and their hinterland cousins, the Kwoma, Sawos, Abelam, Kwanga, and Boiken; the Torricelli taxon prominently includes the large Arapesh family of languages (Mountain Arapesh; Southern Arapesh, including Ilahita, Balif, and Supari dialects; and Bumbita Arapesh), along with the languages of numerous smaller, culturally distinct groups living in or near the coastal mountains: Urat, Wom, Urim, Kombio, and their linguistic congeners living along the mountains on the West Sepik side of the provincial border.

Subsistence regimes vary in this area according to environmental circumstances. Groups living on the Sepik river and its associated waterways depend on fish, both as a direct food source and as an item to be exchanged for sago with bush peoples through trade relationships or at barter markets held every three days at special sites near the bush villages (Gewertz 1983:18). Groups in the upper plains and foothills rejoice in yams (*Dioscorea* spp.) as their main staple food and object of prestige competition (Tuzin 1972), with taro, sago, bananas, and other garden products, along with modest amounts of meat from domestic and feral pigs, forest marsupials, and cassowaries. Among mountain dwellers, taro surpasses yams in dietary importance, and there is a greater reliance on plant and animal products of the forest.

Despite these differences in subsistence regimes, the groups of the East Sepik display certain common features, many of which were first noticed and catalogued by Margaret Mead (1938). To begin with, settlements are hamlet based; and in the larger communities of the river and the upper plain, hamlets are organized into nucleated villages. Some villages are quite large by New Guinea standards, numbering in excess of a thousand persons. Social structure is based on totemic patriclans, and there is a pronounced tendency for these clans to be classified and internally divided according to a principle of dual organization. This principle variously operates in one or more of the areas of marriage regulation, cosmological prerogative, ritualized competition, and reciprocal initiations and feasts.

Ritual life belongs to the Tambaran, a form of secret men's ritual organization that occurs locally but is broadly similar in philosophy and practice virtually wherever in the Sepik it is found. The Tambaran is a 'regional' ritual form in the sense that its cognate versions recur within, and are distinctive of, the region, not in the stronger sense that the Tambaran is *organized* at the regional level. Although the Tambaran is therefore not so fully regionalized as are the cults centered on Telefolip and Kelote, it does offer clues as to the conditions out of which such centers may have developed. To delineate these conditions, we must look more closely at the Tambaran, my view of which is taken largely from observations in Ilahita, an Arapesh-speaking village situated in the hilly, dissected plains area some twenty-five kilometers west-southwest of Maprik, the district seat.[2] While the view from Ilahita cannot take in the sweep of minor variations on ritual themes in the East Sepik, it does disclose certain structural and ideological features of the larger regional system. Furthermore, for reasons of potential relevance to this volume, Ilahita appears to have been—and possibly still is—an incipient shrine center and pilgrimage destination.

Consider, first, the village's size and local importance. At the time of my 1969–70 census, Ilahita numbered 1,490 persons,[3] making it possibly the largest village in (what was then) the Australian mandated territory of New Guinea. Ilahita is located atop a spiderlike array of ridges rising some 100–150 meters above the small streams that wind through the area. The village's residential structure consists of six named, localized wards, each semi-autonomous in terms of ritual identity and clan organization. The wards are in turn composed of named hamlets—86 in all—which typically consist of a circle of dwellings and yam houses belonging to segments of one or two patriclans; these precincts are psychological havens of a sort, and the territorial behaviors of pigs, dogs, roosters, and toddlers confirm that they regard the hamlet as 'home.' Weather permitting, most domestic activity occurs outside, in the portion of the clearing directly in front of the house.

At the time of my 1969–70 census, Ilahita boasted 478 dwelling houses, 349 yam houses, thirty-two bachelors' houses, and 100 derelict houses no longer in use but not yet fallen or torn down. With the exception of a few, non-occupied stilted houses that were failed imitations of coastal designs, all structures were A-framed ground houses thatched with sago-palm fronds and with a sheltered portico at the front.

Various lines of evidence indicate that traditionally, before the advent of Western medicine and reduced infant mortality, Ilahita's exceptional size was a result not so much of internal growth, as of the accretion of refugee groups from fighting toward the south and southeast during the last half of the 19th century. Those hostilities were the effect of Middle Sepik groups--locally, the Abelam—moving north in a disorderly, predatory expansion into areas previously occupied by Arapesh speakers (Tuzin 1976). The movement was fuelled by endemic warfare among Abelam groups, in addition to which land-use patterns created chronic, contestable resource shortages by converting arable garden land into increasing areas of impregnable sword grass. With their larger political units and more bellicose manner, the Abelam made short work of the small groups of Arapesh they encountered—variously killing, absorbing, or displacing them, along with weaker Abelam enemies.

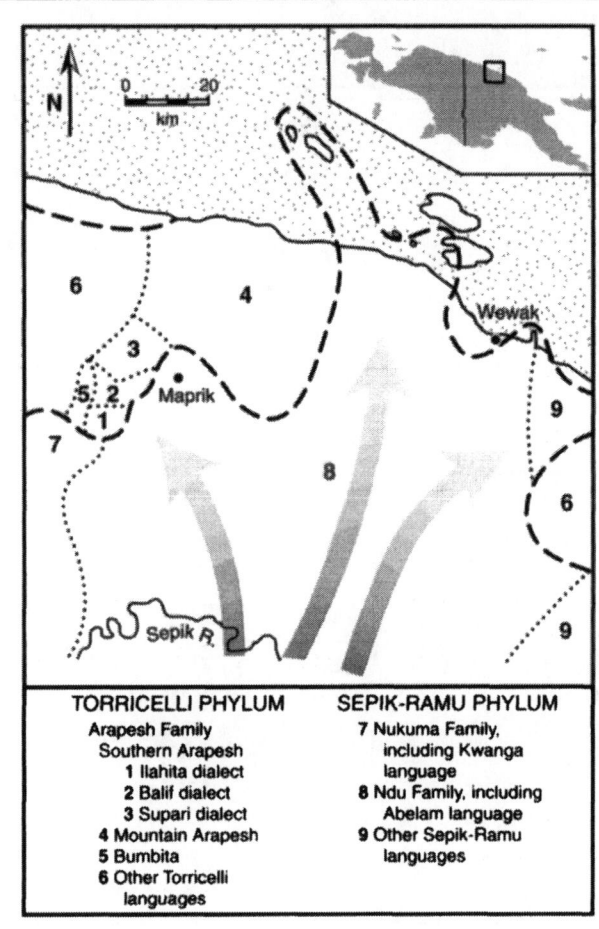

Figure 2.2. Languages of the Maprik-Wewak area (after Laycock 1973).

Those Arapesh and Abelam who were displaced fled north in search of land and sanctuary. Arapesh villages of the boundary area, seeing these refugees as the vanguard of an encroachment directly threatening to them, inhospitably sent them on their way. Ilahita, however, located well behind the lines and buffered from direct Abelam pressure by the border villages, several of which were Ilahita's traditional enemies, accepted these displaced groups. Some refugees were allowed to settle in Ilahita proper; others were established as defensible outliers of the main village or as independent villages. In the latter cases, residence sites and garden lands were given at little or no cost to Ilahita, either because they were seized for the purpose from enemy Arapesh villages, or they were too far from the village to be safe or practical to use.

Within one or two generations, Ilahita's policy produced something akin to a local empire: an immense, unassailable main village, with two colonial outliers and two tributary villages[4] situated to interrupt raids or territorial encroachments by enemy Arapesh villages to the south. As regards the Abelam, applying the principle that 'the enemy of my enemy is my friend,' Ilahita from the start established alliances with the foreign interlopers, while the southern Arapesh border villages were caught uncomfortably in the middle; that was the state of affairs when Australian control was established in early 1950s.

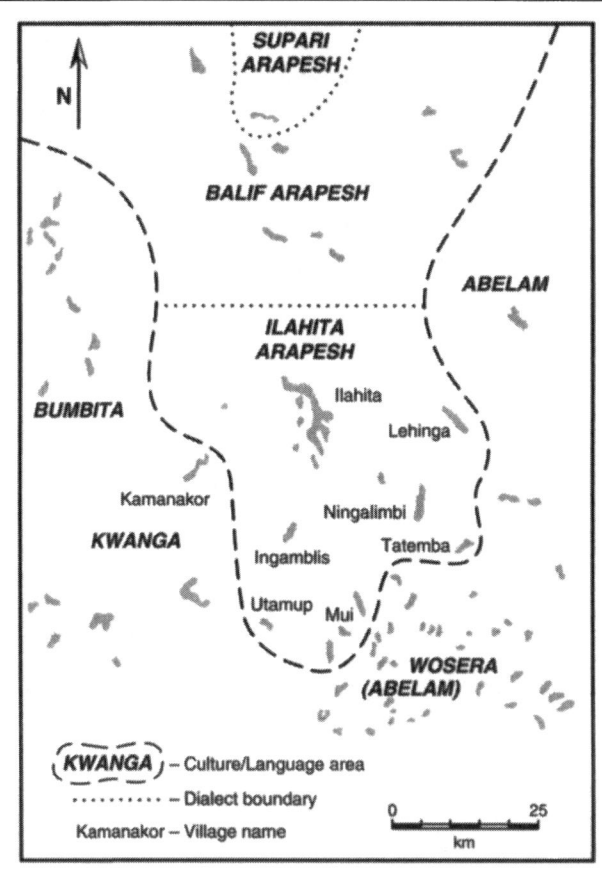

Figure 2.3. Language—Culture Areas of Ilahita Village and its Environs.

The scale and complexity of Ilahita's operations rendered that village unusual in the area; but the general pattern of sedentary, nucleated villages pushing and shoving against one another in a shifting patchwork of enmities and alliances was commonplace throughout the East Sepik, except where mountainous terrain decreed a more dispersed, hamlet-based, and, it would appear, more peaceable political geography. Across this social landscape, travel was very restricted. Trade and exchange relationships tended to be quite local,[5] and hinterland villages knew little of the world beyond the horizon; indeed, the people of Ilahita formerly believed that the world ended at the horizon. These barriers did little to obstruct the circulation of objects and ideas through the region, however, thanks mainly to the workings of the Tambaran.

The Tambaran and Regional Integration

In many local versions, the Tambaran is an institution specializing in ritual exchange, feasting, the initiation of youths and men into a series of grades roughly corresponding with life stages, social control, and war. But perhaps the most striking feature of Tambaran ceremonialism—one that has made the East Sepik region famous among the world's art connoisseurs—is the prolific manufacture of paintings, carvings, flutes, other decorated paraphernalia, and lofty, magnificent spirit houses. When a village is planning a major initiation ceremony for the dry-weather ritual season, the men busy themselves during the preceding rainy months, when male gardening duties are light, in producing artistic paraphernalia. Different villages coordinate their ceremonial calendars, such that those close enough to engage in cooperation or competition do not schedule major ritual events during the same year. Thus, even if one's own village has nothing planned, another village within its ritual-exchange orbit very well might, and therefore the rainy-season artistic endeavors go forward, only geared to contributing to the splendor of the other village's ceremony. It does not matter that the other village may be an enemy: just as the Tambaran rules over the conduct of war, accruing all kills and battle trophies to its own credit, so it prescribes and, under the threat of cult-sponsored sorcery, enforces periods of truce in accord with its ritual calendar.

More than any other form of transaction, the circulation of goods and services under ritual auspices was the principal mechanism of East Sepik regional integration. Ritual localities were distinctive, but not entirely so, for their ideas and practices were clearly cognate with those of other localities within their orbit of ritual exchange. Although from any arbitrary point of inertia, these 'family resemblances' became attenuated across the matrix of overlapping orbits, even localities at opposite ends of the Sepik basin—say the Ilahita Arapesh and, far to the southeast, the Banaro (Map 2.1)—possessed ritual systems that would have been partly intelligible to each other, and distinctively 'Sepik.'

The term ritual 'locality' is deliberately vague, in order to leave open the question of what type of local group is served by the cult shrines found in many parts of the East Sepik. In general, a group defines itself, ritually, by identifying with a particular cult house, upon which are focused various ceremonial activities, especially initiation. Lower-grade initiations of young boys are relatively modest affairs, with small cult houses and participation by little more than the celebrants' neighbors and extended family. In contrast, the higher-grade initiations require a large house, with participation in the building and use of it by everyone in the locality, as well as guests from other ritual localities.

The form and function of these great cult houses varies across the region (Newton 1971). Among the riverine Iatmul, the house is a large stilted structure, with open sides and majestic twin gables at front and rear. Among the Abelam, the house stands on the ground, and its main architectural feature is a soaring—up to 80–90 feet in height—triangular facade, with a steeply sloping ridgepole (Forge 1966). The facade consists of a mass of sago-palm spathes stitched together, on which are painted dramatic 'spirit' faces with large, staring eyes; this graphic design surmounts a lintel decorated with relief-carved faces of ancestor or spirit figures. Unlike the Iatmul version, which is the ritual center of the entire village, the Abelam house is commissioned by, and associated with, particular big men or clans. Accordingly, an Abelam village may have several such houses at a time.

Plate 2.2. An Abelam spirit house.

Plate 2.3. Abelam spirit-house façade.
(Note the row of 'heads' carved on the lintel near the bottom of the picture.)

**Plate 2.4. The Ilahita Nggwal Bunafunei spirit house.
(Photograph courtesy of Malcolm Kirk.)**

Among the Ilahita Arapesh, the cult house is adapted from the Abelam style, but with a shorter facade and a more gently sloping ridgepole, creating a much larger interior space. The painted facade features several rows of full-body spirit figures, while the lintel is carved with Ilahita's mythic 'first family'—a recumbent male and female at each end, respectively, with alternately-sexed children arrayed upright, paper-doll fashion, between them (see below). Like its Iatmul congener, the Ilahita house is the spiritual center of the entire village, and there is only one of them in the village at a given time.[6] But unlike the Iatmul and Abelam houses (or the shrine center of Telefolip), the Ilahita house is not meant to be long lasting. No effort is made to keep it in repair; after the 3-year initiation season for which the house is built, it is emptied of ritual paintings, sculptures, and other secret paraphernalia, and is allowed to deteriorate. When the ritual season returns—some twenty to twenty-five years later, in the case of the two highest grades—a new house is built. One such project observed in Ilahita village in 1971–72 consumed vast quantities of building materials and feast foods, and approximately 10,000 man-days of labor—a tribute, indeed, to the practical effectiveness of Tambaran ritual organization, and to the potency of Tambaran ideology in unifying disparate, often fiercely contentious, groups and individuals.

Shifting from the perspective of the village, where each has its own cult shrine, to the perspective of the local region, it can be seen that each Arapesh village is a shrine *center* during its moment in the rotation. Like the royal progresses of medieval Europe, the Tambaran seemingly moves in a circuit about his realm, creating as a shrine 'center' whichever village and cult house he is residing in for that multi-year season.[7] Any village may mount lower-grade initiations and *ad hoc* Tambaran activities at any time, according to its own practices and schedules; but as a regional system at the level of the higher grades, the Tambaran operates through this orderly rotation of shrine centers.

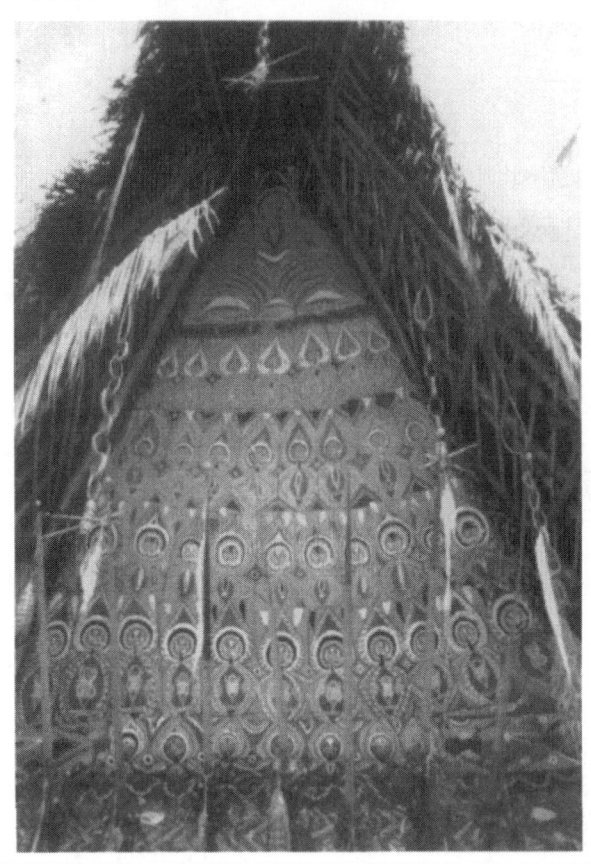

Plate 2.5. Spirit-house façade, Ilahita Arapesh.
(Note the linked 'children' and recumbent 'parents' carved on the lintel,
near the bottom of the picture.)

I hasten to say that the term 'orderly' should not be taken to mean that the exact sequence is fixed, or even that the actors are fully cognizant of the rotational character of the regional cult. What produces orderliness is, first, the understanding that different villages within the same ritual orbit should not plan major Tambaran activities in the same season, so as not to reduce the amount of labor or resources available for any one of them; and, secondly, the mixture of competitiveness, emulation, reciprocity, and demographic timeliness which causes the rotational sequence to be triggered by the launching of a major Tambaran event by any one of the villages in the circuit. This is an important point, for it is a nice Popperian instance of how a higher systemic property ('orderliness') having evolutionary consequences ('regional ritual coordination') may emerge unintentionally from lower-level operational understandings and practices ('avoidance of resource depletion').

While the rotational and reciprocal characters of the regional Tambaran tend to draw villages into the ritual 'queue,' these features interact synergistically with a behavioral dynamic occurring *within* the villages; together, these account for how villages actually come to participate in the system. The fact is, higher-grade Tambaran initiation ceremonies are expensive undertakings, requiring huge commitments of labor and resources. The collective will to mount such an affair does not come easily—and probably never has. Once the Tambaran has been 'fed' to its limit on yams, pigs, and two human sacrifices, and has been 'chased back to the forest,' the men are quite content to enjoy the masculine camaraderie and spiritual vigor that are the fruits of their collective accomplishment. Among those to whom the ritual debt has now passed, repayment seems a distant prospect, and there are even some who privately hope that it will never have to happen; *their* side, after all, is now safely initiated.

**Plate 2.6. Close-up of spirit-house lintel, showing recumbent 'father'
and three 'children' of alternating sex. Ilahita Arapesh.**

As the years pass, however, the village unity achieved under the Tambaran gradually but ineluctably declines. Amid growing fractiousness and incivility, disputes increase between descent and residence groups. Eventually, the elders of the cult decide that this spiritual malaise is a symptom of Tambaran 'hunger,' and that the time has come to mount an initiation ceremony. Their diagnosis is all the more credible because, by this stage, a new cohort of uninitiated men will have grown up, and much of the discord in the village stems from their fathers' angry impatience at junior partners who are slow in moving to build the spirit house, fashion the art, gather the feast foods, and mount an initiation ceremony. In the end, only the Tambaran can save the village from itself—and that is what it does.

This pattern of social decline leading to rejuvenating action by the Tambaran, occurs, of course, in all the villages of the ritual orbit, but on a staggered schedule corresponding to their place in the regional rotation. In other words, regularities at the regional level of the cult interact systemically with regularities at the local level of the cult. Just as Roy A. Rappaport (1984) described in his classic study of ritual and ecology among the Tsembaga Maring, the Tambaran is the 'transducer' that converts energy and information from one level (or subsystem) to the other. What is striking in the Arapesh case is that, whereas the cyclical regularities at both levels are spontaneous and uncognized, the process of transduction unites these levels into an institutional whole that is highly cognized and profoundly permanent—in a word, sacred.

The Region in Search of a Center

The image of the Tambaran as a creature of the *region* needs further explication, for it is a necessary (though not sufficient) condition for the emergence of a shrine center; it also contradicts the predominantly *village*-based character of this ritual system. Among the Ilahita Arapesh, each patriclan has a named, patron spirit—a *tambaran*—which moves back and forth between the clan's two component subclans at each turn in the initiation cycle. The art of the cult is magical, for it performs as the material embodiment of these spirits—the vehicle of their revelation and transmission.[8] As spiritual guardians, these tambarans look after their separate clans; but when they come together in the cult house at the time of the great ritual conclaves, they comprise a kind of parliament that is greater than the sum of its parts. It is this totality that is the unitary, capitalized Tambaran: the apotheosis of the village as a spiritual entity; a personification that can move about and interact with others of its kind; and the intellectual precursor to a monolotrous or 'High God' abstraction which, under the right political circumstances, could transcend village systems and become embodied in a *permanent* shrine center.[9]

To return to the present system of rotating centers: One effect of this arrangement is to propagate regional ritual culture by sharing ideas on a relatively frequent basis. A related effect is that secret ritual knowledge and techniques are preserved from extinction by being distributed across a supralocal ritual collective. If restricted to the village level, much Tambaran lore would be forgotten during the quarter-century separating major initiations, especially in view of the fact that the supreme knowledge is held by the oldest men in the cult. As it is, the exchange of ritual gifts and services causes cult members to invoke secret ideas and practice secret techniques far more frequently than the long-duration cycle would imply. Compared with the situation among the Mountain Ok, ritual sharing in this East Sepik area more effectively prevents the loss of ritual knowledge, and, because it is more systematic, probably yields greater doctrinal homogeneity and coherence among villages within a regional exchange orbit which, in Ilahita's case covers about ten villages scattered over an area of about 1200 square kilometers.

Until the 1970's, when exogenous changes finally made serious inroads into traditional life,[10] the Tambaran of Ilahita village appeared to be on its way to becoming a permanent shrine center. More than being merely a larger version of the other ritual centers (i.e., villages) in the area, Ilahita had developed certain characteristics that were categorically distinct. To begin with, we have seen that this village had emerged as dominant and special in various ways. Ilahita's size, and history of military and diplomatic effectiveness across the local region and beyond, gave it a degree of visibility and importance unapproached by other villages in the region. Indeed, in calling the dialect group 'Ilahita Arapesh' after Ilahita, largest of the seven co-lingual villages, I am borrowing from the people's own usage. Thus, when visiting elsewhere in the larger Maprik region, persons from this area tend to identify themselves as 'Ilahita,' regardless of which of the seven villages they actually come from.[11]

Ilahita was not only exceptionally large and militarily dominant, its size sustained an internal 'critical mass' of diversity, competition, and talent, such that the village was a center of *cultural* creativity, as well. Margaret Mead (1938) described the Mountain Arapesh as an 'importing culture.' The same was true of Ilahita and, as indicated earlier, most Sepik cultures, to one extent or another. But Ilahita village was also an exporter of culture. Thus, the late Anthony Forge, the anthropological authority on Abelam art and society, was the first to observe (Forge 1973:175) that Ilahita had developed a distinctive graphic-art style, which the Abelam—cultural exporters *par excellence* of the Maprik area, and the immediate source of the Ilahita Tambaran—condescended to import and to use in their own cultic projects.[12]

Further proof of Ilahita's cultural centrality comes from its leadership role in a Christian 'Revival' movement that swept the region during the early 1980's (Tuzin 1989, 1997). Ilahita became a virtual pilgrimage site, attracting folks from distant parts of the Sepik area to participate in the miracle-working and spiritual happenings going on in this village. One visitor, a Supari Arapesh man from the mountains to the north, summed up Ilahita's ritual preëminence in a way which also indicates that the village's current ritual centrality has precedence in traditional times: 'In the old days,' the visitor recalled, 'we used to come to Ilahita to learn new things about the Tambaran; now, we come to learn about the Revival.'

To be sure, some of what Ilahita taught, the village had acquired from elsewhere and was redistributing to, in this instance, the mountain-dwellers. But two points should be noted. First, Ilahita was not simply a conduit for ideas and images; rather, materials reaching it from outside were reworked, redefined, in a word 'naturalized' to the Ilahita cultural system, before diffusing onwards by means of the ritual-exchange practices mentioned earlier. Secondly, the mere fact that persons from distant villages—persons semi-distant in cultural and linguistic practice—looked to that village for guidance in spiritual matters, is a kind of ontological proof that Ilahita acted as a regional ritual center.

Ilahita as an Incipient Shrine Center

One structural feature indicating Ilahita as an incipient shrine center was that village's unique provision of a ritual rank specifically for old men, that is, beyond the age of about fifty. Known as *Nggwal Walipeine*, this was the class of Tambaran elders, greybeards past their political prime, who nonetheless enjoyed paramount ritual importance by virtue of their closeness to the ancestors and their mysterious understanding of the will of the Tambaran.

Other villages in the region did not have such a ritual category, possibly because there would not have been enough old men around to perform the requisite artistic, architectural, and ceremonial work of the grade. For Ilahita, however, the functioning of *Nggwal Walipeine* was crucial in maintaining village solidarity in the face of divisive behavior by young men and those in their political prime. Thus, for example, whenever a (natural) death occurred in the community, sorcery beliefs and accusations were liable to ignite disaffections that could (and in other places *did*) tear the village apart. In Ilahita, however, uniquely among villages of the region, the class of cult elders usually intervened with divinations indicating that the death, while proximally the work of a human sorcerer, was more significantly an event willed by the Tambaran, who was punishing the deceased, or someone close to him or her, for remembered offenses against ritual, or simply masculine, authority (Tuzin 1974, 1980).

If such claims had been made by men of lower grades, political rivals would have immediately challenged them. By lodging the authority for such claims with men who were seen to be ritually supreme and politically disinterested, whose prolix, non-partisan rhetoric exalted the glory of the Tambaran and the prosperity of the village, the legitimacy of the cult hierarchy was upheld, with the old men securely at the top, and village solidarity was renewed. Considering that, at their stage in life, Tambaran custodianship was the *raison d'être* of these cult elders, not to mention the source of their power and prestige, their élite occupational standing bore hints of a priesthood. And, to repeat, no other village in the region designated the old men as a separate ritual class.[13]

Another distinctive aspect of the Tambaran in Ilahita village was its degree of reproductive self-sufficiency. As previously observed, the distributive cycling of cult knowledge helped to prevent the loss of esoteric material during the long intervals between local initiations. Like the other villages in its ritual orbit, Ilahita was a beneficiary of this arrangement; but its large size enabled it to exercise another precaution, as well. Explicitly recognizing the risk inherent in entrusting supreme knowledge to the oldest hands, there was a practice that accelerated a certain few young men, called *umbaisi*, to a cult rank one initiation degree higher than that of their age cohort (Tuzin 1976:280–85)—on a par, that is, with their own oldest brothers, a promotion equivalent to half a generation in ritual time. Based on the blank looks I received upon asking visitors about the practice, my impression is that the six other villages in Ilahita's dialect area did not possess this safeguard for the transmission of secret knowledge. Nor would it have been feasible for the other villages to operate such a system, for the reason that their ritual cohorts had too few members to allow some young men to be promoted, without thereby blurring the categories of ritual hierarchy. In Ilahita, the cohorts were large enough that the practice had no structural effects of this kind.

Ilahita's gravitation toward ritual *cum* political hierarchy may be specified even further, by noticing that the young men chosen for promotion were nearly always the sons of master artists (Tuzin 1980). The Tambaran's heavy reliance on artistic and architectural expressions rendered the master artists especially important, with relatively generalized political authority. In 1971–72, there were about a dozen such adepts in Ilahita, and they come closest to performing the role of 'high priest' to the cult of the Tambaran. Strictly speaking, master artists ought not to be able to teach their craft to their own sons, for the latter would be too junior in initiation standing even to see, let alone participate in the manufacture of, secret ritual paraphernalia. Under the rules of ritual transmission, such knowledge should be passed to the master artist's junior initiation partner, who would normally be a distant younger agnate in the opposite subclan. The promotion of the artists' own sons obviated this problem of ritual eligibility; at the same time, it introduced a novel element of heritable rank and knowledge into a system that seems otherwise structured to prevent the consolidation of privilege within particular descent lines.

I mentioned at the start of this chapter that non-ancestral shrines in New Guinea are typically associated with anomalous landscape features. In addition to having the most elaborate ritual system in the vicinity, Ilahita village happens to be the site of a large, spring-fed pool, a highly unusual feature in this part of the country. Moreover, this pool is famous among villages of the area for being the scene of a creation myth having universal implications. In brief, the story of '*Nambweapa'w*' is about the First Man, who espies a group of cassowaries bathing in this pool.[14] Having doffed their avian skins, the bathers are beautiful (human) women. First Man secretly steals one of the skins, trapping its owner—*Nambweapa'w*—in her human form. He persuades her to come home with him, where they take up domestic life together. She gives birth to many children, alternating in sex (see Plates 2.5, 2.6), who later in the story intermarry and become the ancestors of all of the world's peoples—from the Ilahita and nearby cultural-linguistic groups, to more distant New Guinea groups, to white-skinned, English-speaking Americans.

Nearby villages know the story as belonging to Ilahita, and, from my limited observations, they appear to accept its claim to historical truthfulness.[15] That the Water of *Nambweapa'w* potentially qualifies Ilahita as a 'shrine center' or pilgrimage destination was indicated on my very first day in Ilahita, in early September, 1969. A group of hospitable villagers had taken me to the pool, where they told me the story of *Nambweapa'w*. Later, as we were leaving the site, one woman wondered out loud how they would feed and house the many visitors who would come from all over the world, once they learned that Ilahita was the origin place of all humanity. Ilahita, in this woman's proud opinion, was to be a shrine center not just for the immediate region, but for the whole wide world!

Conclusion

In his analysis of the distribution, variation, and propagation of ritual knowledge among Mountain-Ok groups, Fredrik Barth (1987:78) identifies four features of the social organization that are instrumental in producing the observed pattern:

(1) The segmentation of the population into small, localized and mutually rather suspicious local groups. (2) The differentiations of gender and initiation step within each such group. (3) The specialized role of initiator as the authoritative knower and revealer of secrets. (4) The pulsation in the modality of cosmological knowledge between long periods of secrecy and non-communication, and concentrated bursts of public manifestation and revelation.

The Ilahita Arapesh also fit this description, with the exception of the first element listed. Settlements in this part of the East Sepik region are very large by New Guinea standards, and we have seen that this element of size produces major differences in the way sacred knowledge is distributed and propagated in the two regions, respectively.

With regard to Ilahita village, the Telefolip, and Kelote as shrine centers, parallel appeals to cosmogonic myths or figurations indicate a tendency for ideology to precede infrastructural integration in the development of these systems. Of course, symbols and actions evolve in interaction with one another, and one must avoid arguing for unilateral causation in the formation of institutions such as shrine centers. But given the tendency among scholars (the present one, at least) to favor materialist explanations, evidence of even a slight precedence of centrist *ideology* is surprising and significant. From the examples presented here, it would seem that while most localities have myths to account for themselves, some localities aspire to an account placing them at the center of a wider universe. As with the Ilahita woman who contemplated a cosmo-touristic stampede, lack of worldly sophistication (in individuals or in cultures) yields a kind of narcissism which asks the question: why *wouldn't* the world be compellingly interested in what happens here?

This said, the observer must ask why certain localities (or, *mutatis mutandis*, individuals) think of themselves as important in this way. The materialist answer must be that something in their early experience—a doting parent, a string of successes, a streak of good luck, or a felicitous geographical placement—nudged them into the habit of believing they stand for a whole larger than themselves —sometimes much larger, even to where the eyes of the whole wide world are imagined to be upon them. Every locality—every ego, individual or collective—possessing a metaphysical account of itself is a kind of shrine. But when, on rare occasion, circumstances bring others to believe and to include themselves in that larger accounting, then a center is born—a larger metaphysic—and the pull of pilgrimage begins.

Notes

1. For a compendium of studies dealing with scores of Sepik-area societies, see Lutkehaus *et al.* 1990.

2. Fieldwork was conducted in Ilahita village for twenty-two months during the period 1969–72, and for eleven months during the period 1985–86. Funding for the first fieldwork was provided by the Research School of Pacific Studies, Australian National University, and by a grant-in-aid from the Wenner-Gren Foundation for Anthropological Research; the second fieldwork was funded by the National Science Foundation. Grateful acknowledgment is made to all of these organizations for their generous support.

3. The next-largest village in the dialect area numbered fewer than 700 persons, while the combined population of all seven villages, in 1969–70, was probably less than 4,500. Official census figures for the 1960–61 period (the most recent figures available at the time of my own census) show Ilahita's population to have been 1,282, which was 37% of the total dialect population at that time (N = 3,437). See Tuzin (1976:54) for specific village population figures for this area. By 1985, when I returned for further fieldwork, Ilahita's population had grown to 2,085, representing a forty percent increase in fifteen years.

4. The tribute in question was more symbolic than material. In ceremonies involving Ilahita and these dependent villages, cult elders from Ilahita would dance a greeting wearing netbags on their back, female-fashion, to signify their role as 'mother' in the relationship; the 'children' would reciprocate with token food gifts. By such means, the parties reconfirmed Ilahita's precedence and the permanent debt of military and political support she was owed by virtue of having given the others their existence in the area.

5. An exception were the trading paths connecting the plains and the beach, across the Prince Alexander mountains. According to Mead (1938), travelers depended upon hereditary partners living along the route, with whom they could stop for the night while traversing the mountains. Along these paths came various kinds of shell valuables, items treasured by the Ilahita, who, living far to the west and unaware of the ocean just beyond their northern horizon, did not know of their true nature or origin. My impression is that similar transmontane paths did not exist in the mountains directly north of Ilahita; at any rate, if they did exist, Ilahita did not know of them.

6. To be precise, Ilahita village has five grades, entered into in (1) early childhood; (2) late childhood; (3) adolescence; (4) early adulthood; and (5) late adulthood. Initiations and other ceremonies associated with the two most junior grades tend to concern only the residential ward, of which there are six in the village; the third grade features a lengthy initiation seclusion in a symbolic ritual 'village' erected in the forest. The two most senior grades each require the kind of major cult house discussed in the text, with the penultimate grade being somewhat the grander of the two. Because the ceremonies of initiation belonging to these highest grades occur in quick succession—albeit for men entering middle and late adulthood, respectively—it is usual for their houses to co-exist in the village, though on sites in different village wards. See Tuzin (1980) for an ethnography of the Ilahita Tambaran.

7. This idea of an itinerant Tambaran was captured in a remark made by one man when I commented that the spirit house in his village, Ningalimbi, was regrettably dwarfed by a gigantic fig tree next to which it had been constructed. The man laughed dismissively. 'Oh, no,' he replied, 'when people from a great distance see the tree [on the horizon], they will say, "Ah, yes, the Tambaran lives now in Ningalimbi!"'

8. Among the Abelam, from whom the Ilahita cult was originally acquired, these spirits are more explicitly ancestral. For the Ilahita, Tambaran spirits and ancestral spirits, as well as yam spirits, occupy and mutually interact on the same metaphysical zone; but they are understood to be separate entities. For more information on the way in which the Ilahita historically modified cultural ideas acquired from the Abelam, see Tuzin 1995.

9. A similar abstraction, with similar semiotic implications, is described by Barth (1987:3) for the Baktaman, one of the Min peoples. Barth reports that ancestral skulls are stored in the central 'ancestor-house' temple. But, 'For the last twenty years at least, only *one* complete skull has served as the focal relic....Though this skull is known to be of a particular clan, it symbolizes and represents the category of all ancestors; cult observances are directed towards this ancestor for all different ritual purposes....There is no necessary connection between the clan of the presiding ritual leader and that of the relic, and the members of all other clans, despite their descent from ancestors deriving from separate events of creation, address their prayers to ancestors to this common relic and share their sacrificial meals with him.

10. In Ilahita village, the Tambaran died on a Sunday in September, 1984, when the men voluntarily revealed the cult secrets to the women. See Tuzin (1997) for a discussion of this extraordinary event, and its unhappy aftermath. It may be noted that the Tambaran—at any rate, the two highest grades of the cult—was not ancient in Ilahita, but was acquired from the Abelam during the third quarter of the nineteenth century, by my estimate.

11. Likewise, in segmentary fashion, when persons from somewhere in the Maprik region are speaking to someone in Wewak, the self-identifier is 'Maprik'; to someone from another province it is 'Sepik.'

12. This would be like a panel of French chefs coming to Peoria in search of recipes.

13. By the logic of the system, men who lived long enough eventually advanced out of the 'top' of the hierarchy. Such men were truly retired and devoid of ritual or political power—a social death which anticipated, and seemed to hasten, physical oblivion.

14. 'Nambweapa'w' is demonstrably a version of the 'swan maiden' story, which is found throughout much of the Old World, from Ireland to Central Polynesia. For the full text of the story, see Tuzin (1980:1–8). For an extended analysis of the story, one that includes comparative reference to Afek, the abovementioned, mythic daughter of a cassowary, see Tuzin (1997: Chaps. 4–6).

15. On the other hand, their affirmation may be more a matter of courtesy than of conviction. I never actually heard someone from a different village claim co-descent from Ilahita's First Lady; neither, however, do I know whether other villages have universalistic creation stories of their own. When it comes to mythic claims and realities, logical contradictions or incompatibilities rarely present problems for the believer.

References

Barth, Fredrik (1987) *Cosmologies in the Making: A Generative Approach to Cultural Variation in Inner New Guinea.* Cambridge: Cambridge University Press.

Biersack, Aletta (1995) Introduction: The Huli, Duna, and Ipili peoples yesterday and today. In *Papuan Borderlands: Huli, Duna, and Ipili Perspectives on the Papua New Guinea Highlands*, edited by Aletta Biersack. Ann Arbor: University of Michigan Press, pp. 1–54.

Brumbaugh, Robert (1990) 'Afek Sang': the old woman's legacy to the Mountain-Ok. In *Children of Afek: Tradition and Change Among the Mountain-Ok of Central New Guinea*, Oceania Monograph 40, edited by Barry Craig and David Hyndman. Sydney: University of Sydney, pp. 54–87.

Craig, Barry and David Hyndman, eds. (1990) *Children of Afek: Tradition and Change Among the Mountain-Ok of Central New Guinea.* Oceania Monograph 40. Sydney: University of Sydney.

Flannery, Kent V. (1986) A Visit to the Master. In *Guilá Naquitz: Archaic Foraging and Early Agriculture in Oaxsaca, Mexico*, edited by Kent V. Flannery. Orlando: Academic Press, pp. 511–519.

Forge, Anthony (1966) Art and Environment in the Sepik. *Proceedings of the Royal Anthropological Institute, 1965*, pp. 23–31.

— (1973) Style and meaning in Sepik art. In *Primitive Art and Society*, edited by Anthony Forge. London: Oxford University Press, pp. 169–92.

Gewertz, Deborah B. (1983) *Sepik River Societies: A Historical Ethnography of the Chambri and Their Neighbors.* New Haven: Yale University Press.

Goldman, Laurance R. (1979) 'Kelote', an important Huli ritual ground, Southern Highlands. *Oral History* 7(4):14–18.

— (1983) *Talk Never Dies: The Language of Huli Disputes.* London: Tavistock.

Jorgensen, Dan (1990) Placing the past and moving the present: myth and contemporary history in Telefolmin. *Culture* 10(2):47–56.

Laycock, Donald C. (1973) Sepik languages: checklist and preliminary classification. *Pacific Linguistics*, Ser. B, no. 25.

Lea, David A.M. (1964) Abelam Land and Sustenance: Swidden Horticulture in an Area of High Population Density, Maprik, New Guinea. Unpublished Ph.D. thesis, Australian National University, Canberra.

Lutkehaus, C., Kaufmann, W.E. Mitchell, D. Newton, L. Osmundsen, and M. Schuster, eds. (1990) *Sepik Heritage: Tradition and Change in Papua New Guinea.* Durham, NC: Carolina Academic Press

Mead, Margaret (1938) The mountain Arapesh: I. an importing culture. American Museum of Natural History, *Anthropological Papers* 36(3):137–349.

Newton, Douglas (1971) *Crocodile and Cassowary: Religious Art of the Upper Sepik River, New Guinea.* New York: Museum of Primitive Art.

Rappaport, Roy A. (1984) *Pigs for the Ancestors: Ritual in the Ecology of a New Guinea People.* New Haven: Yale University Press.

Roscoe, P. (2000) New Guinea leadership as ethnographic analogy: A critical review. *Journal of Archaeological Method and Theory* 7:79–126

Tuzin, Donald (1972) Yam symbolism in the Sepik: an interpretative account. *Southwestern Journal of Anthropology* 28(3):230–54.

— (1974) Social Control and the *tambaran* in the Sepik. In *Contention and Dispute: Aspects of Law and Social Control in Melanesia*, edited by A.L. Epstein. Canberra: Australian National University Press.

— (1976) *The Ilahita Arapesh: Dimensions of Unity.* Berkeley: University of California Press.

— (1980) *The Voice of the Tambaran: Truth and Illusion in Ilahita Arapesh Religion.* Berkeley: University of California Press.

— (1989) Visions, prophecies, and the rise of Christian consciousness: a case of religious imagination. In *The Religious Imagination in New Guinea*, edited by Michele Stephen and Gilbert H. Herdt. New Brunswick, NJ: Rutgers University Press, pp. 187–208.

— (1995) Art and procreative illusion in the Sepik: comparing the Abelam and the Arapesh. *Oceania* 65(4):289–303.

— (1997) *The Cassowary's Revenge: The Life and Death of Masculinity in a New Guinea Society.* Chicago: University of Chicago Press.

3 Tribal Pilgrimages to Saints' Tombs in South Sinai

Emanuel Marx

I.

Every year towards the end of summer, members of each of the Bedouin tribes in South Sinai congregate at a saint's tomb in their tribal territory. There are about 20 well-known saints' tombs in the southern half of the peninsula, all located at major crossroads and not far from water sources. Some are found close to centers of population, while others are far from habitation. Throughout the year, individual Bedouin visit tombs in various parts of South Sinai, to request various saints to intercede with God (Fig. 3.1) for location of sites mentioned in the text). At some of these tombs annual tribal gatherings take place. I intend to look closely at the annual pilgrimages of three tribes: the Muzenah, who meet for three consecutive days and make the round of three holy tombs; from the tomb of their founding ancestor Faraj, they move to that of the prophet (*nabi*) Saleh, and thence to the tomb of *Nabi Harun* (identified with Aaron, the brother of Moses); the Awlad Sa'id, who gather once a year at the tomb of 'Ali Abu Taleb, the fourth Khalif; and the Jebaliyah, sections of whom gather on separate occasions at the tomb of Sheikh 'Awad, a holy man whose antecedents are unclear, but may have been a member of the tribe.

Other saints' tombs at which tribal gatherings take place are: Sheikh Qra'i for the 'Aleqat, Sheikh Suliman Nfe'i for the Qararshah, al-Hashash for the small Hamadah tribe, and the female saint Sheikhah Swerhah for the Sawalhah. All these major shrines are classified by Bedouin as *maqam* (literally 'place') a term widely used in the Islamic world to denote an important holy place, mostly, but not always, associated with a saint's tomb.[1] Here, in Sinai, the maqam is a shrine whose patron saint is definitely not buried in it. It is contrasted with the *turbah*, a lesser shrine supposed to enclose the remains of a holy man. Cemeteries surround the shrines, for it is assumed that the deceased are thus nearer to their God. Some of the tombs at the two major shrines, Nabi Saleh and Nabi Harun, have themselves become shrines of a kind. The ancestors of some Muzenah descent groups buried at Nabi Saleh, and of Jebaliyah groups at Nabi Harun, are visited by their descendants on *'id al-adha*, the Feast of Sacrifices, one of the two major holy days of Islam. All the major shrines are surmounted by domed buildings, crowned with a crescent, the emblem of Islam. Near each shrine, an assembly-hut has been erected, which throughout the year serves as a resthouse for weary travelers. It is always equipped with cooking utensils, and a small supply of tea and sugar left by each traveler for the next one. Tribesmen attend these gatherings for a number of reasons; they intend to meet friends, relatives and visitors from other tribes, to fulfill a religious duty, and to reaffirm their membership of the tribe and the right to use its territorial resources. For the greater part of the year tribesmen are dispersed in small groups and many men work for long periods outside their tribal area and even outside South Sinai. The tribal reunions are the culmination of their continuous efforts to maintain ties with other Bedouin. The variations in the reunions of the three tribes are connected to their different habitat and economies. Attendance at the tribal gatherings also fluctuates from year to year. This raises such questions as why the tribes celebrate an annual reunion, why the reunions of each tribe follow a different pattern, and why the attendance at the gatherings fluctuates from year to year. Another intriguing problem is why tribal gatherings should take place at saints' tombs. Some of these questions were raised over a century ago in Robertson Smith's *Lectures on the Religion of the Semites* (1889) and in Goldziher's essays on the cult of saints (1967–71). Most of their arguments have withstood the rigors of time remarkably well, but it will be seen that certain points require revision.

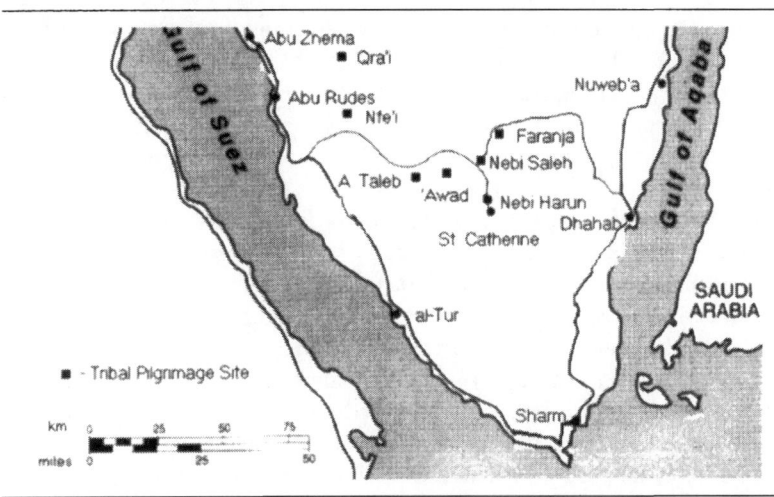

Figure 3.1. Bedouin tribes of south Sinai (c. 1970–72)

The cult of saints is found not only in Islam, but also in Judaism and in many parts of the Christian world. In his study of cults in Spain, Christian argues that saints respond to the unrequited needs of people. One of his informants put this very eloquently, when explaining why people visit a famous image of the Virgin Mary: 'God is simply not involved in our everyday activities, either because he chooses not to be involved, or because he does not have the power to act...[but the Virgin] actively helps us, whether this is by intervention with God, or whatever. She is closer to us, does things for us in this world' (Christian 1972: 147–8). This man's God is so distant that he even doubts his power to intervene in the concerns of individuals. But most adherents of the world religions believe in a middle range God,[2] one who is close enough to care for humanity, but not close enough to concern himself with the humdrum affairs of men. He is not too distant to become inaccessible, but too distant to be approached by living human beings, distinguished and saintly as they may be. Therefore men take recourse to the mediation of saints, whose proximity to God is assured, and who continue to maintain an interest in the people whose life they shared in the past.

Saints' cults are prevalent in many parts of Islam (Levy 1962: 258), but Islamic leaders and scholars of Islam disagree about whether they are a legitimate part of Islam or whether they are an aberration or accretion. Some scholars approve wholeheartedly of the practice; for instance, Linant de Bellefonds (1974: 355) claims that 'the permissibility of visiting tombs was admitted very early on by *idjma'* [consensual canonical law]: all the [law] schools...even went so far as to recommend the practice'. Goldziher (1967–1971 II: 259) disapproves of the practice, but at the same time clearly perceives its causes: 'The believers sought to create, through the concept of saints, mediators between themselves and an omnipotent Godhead in order to satisfy the need which was served by the gods and masters of their old tradition... Here too applies what Karl Hase says of the cult of saints in general: that it "satisfies within a monotheistic religion a polytheistic need to fill the enormous gap between men and their god".' Many writers have followed Goldziher's lead in rejecting the cult, sometimes without understanding that it fulfils a vital function. Thus von Grunebaum (1951: 67) views the cult of saints as 'a striking deviation from the genuine prophetic tradition', and Lazarus-Jaffé (1976: 2–3) describes even the pilgrimage to Mecca as a 'pagan heritage'. Geertz (1968: 48) too follows Goldziher's lead in interpreting the worship of saints as an 'expression of that necessity...for a world religion to come to terms with...a multiplicity of local forms of faith and yet maintain the essence of its own identity'. Other authors treat the cults as a more or less legitimate alternative or complement to official Islam. When Gellner claims that it is practiced in regions where 'official, genuine literate Islam...is present only in a minimal form' (1972: 59), he treats the cult as a less genuine, but nevertheless acceptable form of Islam. Waardenburg (1979: 363) even goes further by arguing that the worship of saints is part of popular Islam, which has local currency, as distinct from 'normative', universally recognized Islam.

All these critical evaluations start out from the position that genuine Islam is a strictly monotheistic religion; accordingly, they treat the cult of saints as either a pagan survival, as an aberration from orthodox religion,[3] or as a local custom, a small tradition. However, the cult of saints is found throughout Islam, and not only in places that are off the beaten track. It is practiced in cities, villages, and even associated with mosques (Canaan 1927: 2; Eickelman 1976: 112). There is no difference between centers and their periphery; the cult is essentially the same throughout the domain of Islam. Therefore one must view orthodox Islam and the cult of saints as the two sides of a coin; the distant omnipotent God and the cult of saints simply complement each other. For a distant God can be approached only through holy mediators. Individuals in need, who are unable to obtain the aid of their fellow men, or whose problems are beyond remedy, commune with God through the saint. This is the practice throughout Islam, although here and there it is periodically repressed by zealous governments or by 'official' representatives of Islam, who view it as an infringement of their monopoly of temporal or spiritual power.

The individual Muslim's belief in the efficacy of saintly mediation also underlies the communal pilgrimage. I shall argue that people perform the pilgrimage to a tribal sanctuary both as individuals and as members of a larger entity, whenever they face a series of problems that the authorities of this world either caused or cannot remedy, such as the men's extended absences from their homes and the failure of the authorities to provide even a modicum of social security. The tribal gatherings are designed to revitalize the tribe and to reinforce other relationships supporting the Bedouin's basic security.

However widespread the cult of saints, there are some Bedouin who do not practice it. Musil states categorically: 'The Bedouins know of no communion with the saints. In the whole inner desert there is not a single holy grave or shrine erected in honor of a saint... When they make short sojourns in the settled territory, where by every village the dome of a shrine rises above the real or imaginary grave of some man or woman whom public opinion considers to be a saint, they never pay attention to these domes' (1928: 417). The Bedouin he refers to are the great camel-raising Ruwala of Syria. But among the Bedouin of South Sinai and, incidentally, among those of Cyrenaica (Evans-Pritchard 1949: 66-67; Peters 1976), and Morocco (Berque 1955: 268 ff.) the visiting of shrines and pilgrimages are an important feature of social life. By gaining some insight into the cult of saints in Sinai we may improve our understanding of such cults elsewhere and, perhaps, explain their absence from the Ruwala and some other nomadic pastoralists.

II.

South Sinai is the mountainous southern part of the Sinai Peninsula bounded in the north by the Tih Plateau. It covers an area of about 17,000 square kilometers. Most of its interior is bare and rugged; high plateaus, interspersed with mountains, build up to the Mount Sinai massif at the center. The highest peak in the peninsula is Jebel Katarina, at 2,642 m, while several other peaks rise to nearly 2,000 m. Asphalted roads follow the seashore around the peninsula. In the interior of the country there were, during the period of fieldwork, only mud tracks, mostly lying on an east-west axis. Some of these are suitable for trucks and other roadworthy vehicles. During the 1970s there was no regular public transport, besides the daily flight between Lydda (now Ben Gurion International Airport) and Santa Katarina airfield, but the Bedouin car fleet of over a hundred vehicles, mostly American and Russian jeeps, pickups and a few trucks, generally in a bad state of repair, were fully used. Parts of the peninsula are inaccessible to motorcars, and can be reached by camel or donkey, often only by circuitous routes.

The region is arid, with small amounts of rainfall in the cool winter months, between November and March. In the coastal region, the annual average precipitation is about 10 mm, and in the high mountains about 60 mm (Ganor *et al.* 1973: 35). Rainfall is very irregular, and all parts of Sinai, with the exception of the region of high mountains, often experience two to three consecutive years without any rain. The spatial distribution of rains is also very changeable, and in consequence there are few reliable pastures. Any sizable rain causes floods (*fayadan*) in the lower reaches of wadis, which often cause serious damage to Bedouin property. Occasionally most of a year's rainfall comes in a single torrential downpour, sometimes outside the rainy season. In May 1968 such a flood destroyed hundreds of palm trees, houses and gardens, and ruined several major motor tracks. Other floods occurred in February 1975 and October 1979, with results almost as disastrous.

The winter months are usually cool. In the mountains there are each year cold spells with temperatures occasionally dropping to -10°C (14 F). Summer temperatures are uniformly high, and in the low-lying areas often reach 40°C (105 F) during the day, and in the mountains around 30°C. The vegetation is adapted to the harsh climate, and relies largely on ground water. During the long dry summer most plants wither, and only the ubiquitous artemisia (*ba'tharan*), anabasis (*ajram*) and some other shrubs seem to withstand the heat successfully. But after rains colorful annuals appear. Some plants come to life even in the absence of rain; milder weather following a cold spell entices them out of the ground. There are few sources of surface water in the region, except immediately after rains. Water is mostly obtained from wells dug by enterprising Bedouin. In recent years the authorities have sunk several deep wells to which all Bedouin have equal access.

Permanent settlements were few until the 1950s. There was the little port of al-Tur on the Red Sea with a population of about 500, mostly sailors and fishermen. Some of the inhabitants were Bedouin. Near al-Tur there was a quarantine station for Egyptians returning from the annual pilgrimage to the holy places of Islam in Mecca, which provided seasonal work for many Bedouin. During the Israeli occupation both al-Tur and the quarantine were deserted. Between 10 and 12 Greek monks inhabit the other permanent settlement, Saint Catherine's monastery on Mount Sinai. Founded in the sixth century and continuously occupied since, it is rightly viewed by the Bedouin as the most enduring institution in the region, more stable and reliable than ephemeral states. In the 1950s, the Egyptian authorities decided to develop the region. They set up a civilian administration based on Abu Znema, north of al-Tur, built army camps and an airfield, constructed roads along the Red Sea coast, and began the commercial exploitation of the oil fields, and the gypsum and manganese deposits near the Red Sea coast. These installations recruited most of their workers from the Nile valley; they hired only a small number of Bedouin for menial work.

South Sinai is inhabited by over 6,000 Bedouin, giving a population density of less than one person to two square kilometers. A considerable part of this population lives close to the main east-west passage through the mountainous interior, from Wadi Firan to Saint Catherine to Wadi Nasb. Although every Bedouin has a defined area, and a place in it that he considers his home ground, there are only a few permanent settlements of Bedouin. These have been established in recent years as local employment opportunities improved, and new wells were put in operation. The trend began in mid-1950, when smuggling of narcotics accelerated and Bedouin invested some of the profits in wells and orchards. Some of these settlements, such as Bir Zrer and Bir 'Oqdah, were set up in relatively inaccessible places, which could serve as hideouts in slack seasons. Wadi Firan is a different type of settlement: the copious supply of ground water allows Bedouin to cultivate fruit and vegetables and to remain there for many months on end. The permanent employment found in Saint Catherine's monastery in the mountains gave rise to a Bedouin village in its vicinity. These trends were intensified during the Israeli occupation, from 1967 to 1982. Though smuggling became almost extinct, more jobs became available locally and new wells were dug. As a result, Bedouin households tended to spend much longer periods in their home grounds.

In the distant past, a small and highly mobile pastoral population could maintain themselves in South Sinai, provided they had access to all parts of the peninsula. It appears that some Muzenah and Awlad Sa'id households even now subsist exclusively on their flocks. But while most Bedouin keep a few goats and sheep, as well as a camel or two, they do not generally view them as sources of income. No grain is grown in South Sinai, and the fruit and vegetables grown laboriously in small orchards scarcely supply the needs of a household during a few weeks in summer. Practically all the food consumed in Sinai is imported from outside the region. In the past, when employment was scarce and communications slow, Bedouin devoted more attention to their gardens. Some households, especially among the Jebaliyah, relied on the sale of garden produce for their livelihood. But for several generations now the main source of the Bedouin's income has been wage labor, mostly in the cities outside the region. Since the early 1970s, wage labor became widely available and the incomes of Bedouin rose rapidly. In consequence, Bedouin spend less time in their gardens, but still maintain them in fair condition.

III.

When the Bedouin of South Sinai talk about the tribe, they may refer to three separate, partly overlapping entities. First, they consider the tribe a territorial organization, whose members control certain resources in that territory, and obtain rights to exploit resources in a larger area of subsistence. Membership of the tribe confers the following rights: to 'build a house' anywhere in the tribal territory, which in practice means in oases or valleys where water can be tapped; preferential access to pastures and to employment in the territory; and to participate in smuggling caravans passing through it. This last is a recent transformation of the former monopoly on conducting travelers through the territory (Niebuhr 1799, I: 141,153). The tribe claims not so much to control a clearly bounded territory, but defined points in it and paths leading through it. When asked to describe their tribal territory, Bedouin come up with a list of salient points, such as oases, wells and pastures, but there is much disagreement between their statements about boundaries and even considerable overlap between tribal territories. This is to be expected in a country whose practical value to the Bedouin is located in particular tracts and where the population is very mobile. At any moment a considerable proportion of the men may be working outside the territory, and their flocks herding in the grounds of other tribes. Of course, this never deterred administrators and travelers from sketching tribal maps that neatly apportion all of South Sinai to the various tribes (Murray 1935: 247; Israel Army 1962: map 3; Glassner 1974: 35).

The tribesmen are united by the joint ownership of territorial resources, and when necessary some of them join forces to prevent outsiders from encroaching on their land. Thus I was told that some years ago an Awlad Sa'id man had constructed a stone house near a route, which the Jebaliyah claimed as their own. One of the Jebaliyah elders warned him that he was welcome to set up a tent in that place, but not a house. The Awlad Sa'id man moved away, and the house was then torn down.

Bedouin often migrate relatively short distances in their tribal territory. But they claim that 'membership of the tribe also gives them access to all the pastures of South Sinai'. They consider their tribes to belong to an alliance, which 'in the past elected a common leader and moderator', and together they are called the people of Mount Sinai (*Tawarah*, s.*Turi*). An apical ancestor does not represent the confederation in the genealogies. The authorities occasionally appointed one of the tribal chiefs as paramount chief, but this appointment was mainly ceremonial and the chief never exercised control over the population. Members of several tribes frequently share pastures; whenever this happens, the herdsmen may camp together, irrespective of their tribal affiliation. Without this sharing of pastures, pastoralism in South Sinai would be unthinkable.

Six tribes are usually considered members of the alliance of Tawarah: the Muzenah and 'Aleqat who together constitute one moiety, the Sawalhah, Qararshah and Awlad Sa'id—the other; and the Jebaliyah, who are slightly inferior members of the alliance. The Bedouin view the two other small tribes, the Hamadah and the Beni Wasel, as remnants of the ancient inhabitants of the country who lost their land, but tacitly accept them as belonging to the Tawarah. Only the Huwetat tribesmen are thought to be intruders without right to land; and indeed most of them appear to have entered the area as late as after the First World War. They only do not perform the annual tribal pilgrimage.

Second, the Bedouin view the tribe as a political organization, as an alliance of numerous patrilineal descent groups, whose purpose is to defend individual members and to protect the territory and its resources against intruders. The political tribe is made up in this manner: each Bedouin is born into an agnatic descent group. The group is called a family (*'eleh*), is named after an ancestor who lived two to four generations ago and bears either his name or his nickname (*naqbah* or *nabadh*). Some people cannot trace the details of their connection to this patronym. Bearers of the patronymic do not necessarily camp together or own joint property, or obey a formal leader. Some of the bearers of the patronymic, often close agnates may, in company with cognates or even non-relatives, engage in joint economic ventures, such as smuggling partnerships. Others, and even the members of the economic partnership themselves, may then consider this as an activity of the agnatic descent group, oblivious to the fact that not all its members participate in the joint activity and that some non-members are involved.

Several patronymic groups are affiliated to a large unit, which is at one and the same time considered a large descent group and a sub-unit of the tribe. It is believed to be associated with a not too clearly defined part of the tribal territory. This unit is called a quarter (*ruba'*, pl. *rubu'*), or branch (*fara'*, pl. *furu'*), both terms implying that it is a sub-division of a larger unit, the tribe. Tribesmen freely admit that their patronyms are not necessarily descendants of the ancestors of the ruba' and that some tribesmen originated outside the tribe and joined the ruba' within living memory. The members of the ruba' do not all reside in the territory associated with their ancestor. A respected member of one of the constituent groups—not necessarily of a large or wealthy one—is elected as elder, and his home becomes a meeting-place for members. This man distributes resources allocated to the group by external agencies, such as work supplied by the state, and in this context acts as representative of the tribal chief. He also makes the arrangements for periodical reunions of the group. The tribe is conceptualized as a group founded by a single eponym, whose sons—and as the term ruba' implies, there are often four—are the ancestors of the ruba'. This tribe, as distinct from the administrative tribe headed by a chief, exists exclusively as an organization for the control of territory and initiates few joint political or economic activities. Bedouin often argue that the tribe as a whole pays blood-compensation (*diyah*), but no one can recall any concrete instance. But a few respected old men, who are usually not in the limelight, and often not known to the authorities, act as mediators in disputes and exert great influence. It is they who make the arrangements for the tribal pilgrimage.

And third, the Bedouin endorse the authorities' conception of the tribe as an administrative unit, headed by a chief and by ruba' headmen. These men are chosen by the tribesmen, and confirmed in office by the authorities, which deal with the tribe through these representatives. The chiefs provide the authorities with well-sifted information, often taking into consideration their personal interest, and distribute the limited resources allocated by the authorities according to their light. In an economy based largely on wage labor outside the tribe, and with government services few and far between, the Bedouin do not attach great importance to these chiefs. They do, however, realize that the chiefs act as liaison officers between the authorities—and in the case of the Jebaliyah also between the monks of Saint Catherine's—and the tribesmen, and that their potential for causing harm is considerable. Bedouin usually describe them as 'government chiefs, who really represent only their personal interest'.

Bedouin are well aware that the term 'tribe' refers to different things, but often consider these to be several aspects of one entity. They do so by conceptualizing the tribe as a segmentary political organization, flowing out of joint descent, and summarized in genealogies. In this manner they explain under one head the territorial organization, the descent groups, political alliances and the administrative set-up. The segmentary theory is not the only one held by the tribesmen. Other theories account for various aspects of social organization, such as relations with the authorities, the nature of leadership, co-operation between members of different tribes, for instance in smuggling, the far-flung networks of kinship ties, or the organization of wage labor in towns.

In the annual tribal pilgrimage the three kinds of tribe merge and, what is more, for once the 'tribe' becomes a living reality. Its various aspects are represented in the ebb and flow of gatherings at the pilgrimage site, in the detail of the ritual, and in the form of the saint's tomb itself. Here not only the aspects covered by the theory of segmentary organization are reflected, but also other aspects of Bedouin life. Especially salient are the perennial problems of uncertain political conditions, the changing employment situation, and the hazards of life in a desert where drought and natural disasters are common occurrences.

I shall now briefly introduce the three tribes whose pilgrimages will be discussed: Muzenah, Awlad Sa'id and Jebaliyah. Each tribe differs from the others in size, territorial resources and economic activities. Table 3.1 presents a list of all the Bedouin tribes of South Sinai, arranged by size. The figures are based on Ben-David (1972: 113), who used a census carried out by the Israeli authorities in 1968. As later information largely confirms these figures, I made only slight corrections.

Tribe	Population	Population
Muzenah	1,700	East, Center and South West
Jebaliyah	1,100	High mountains
'Aleqat	1,050	West coast
Qararshah	900	From Wadi Firan to West coast
Awlad Sa'id	450	High mountains
Huwetat	390	Lower reaches of Wadi Firan
Hamadah	250	North West
Sawalhah	160	North West
Beni Wasel	100	Around al-Tur
Total	*6,100*	

Table 3.1. Bedouin tribes of south Sinai (c. 1970–72).

The Muzenah are the largest tribe and also occupy the largest territory. Murray (1935: 265) describes them as camel and sheep breeders, many of whom 'have lately taken to fishing'. Their control of the east coast and part of the west coast put them in an ideal position for receiving narcotics from Saudi Arabia, and passing them on to other middlemen in Sinai. The final destination was usually Egypt. Smuggling thrived until about 1970, when it was stopped almost completely by the Israeli authorities. Some of the best-known organizers of smuggling bands stem from this tribe, and Bedouin estimate that about 30% of its income was derived from smuggling. There are some fishermen and sailors among the Muzenah, but only few tribesmen own flocks of goats and sheep large enough for subsistence. Bedouin claim that 50-60 animals are the minimum needed. One of the few men I met who owned a flock of that size claimed that he obtained an average monthly revenue of IL 400, in addition to which National Insurance paid him IL 200. Altogether he had a monthly income of IL 600 (approximately £40). Most households live on the wage labor of one or more males, who earn IL 40 a day or more (nearly £3). While almost every household raises five to six goats or sheep, most people claim that they do not expect to make a profit on animals. For part of the dry season the animals are fed millet or corn, imported from outside Sinai. Women and girls herd the small flocks. This seems to have been the situation for a long time, since H.S. Palmer (1906: 69–72) found in 1869 that flocks were tended exclusively by girls, that men earned their living away from home (though not as wage laborers, but as caravaneers), and that they bought corn with the money earned (see also E.H. Palmer 1871: 81–2; Keller 1900: 26).

Even when Bedouin rely on their flocks, their movements are not so much influenced by the needs of the animals as by other requirements. Women and girls are expected to return home in the evening and to perform household chores. Therefore they do not venture too far afield with their flock. Camps must remain close to water, but not too close so as not to destroy the pasture prematurely. Therefore camps are usually set up at a distance of 2–3 km from a water source. They should be close to sources of firewood, such as broom (*ratam*), acacias (*seyal*), or tamarisks (*tarfah*), and not too far from public amenities, such as shops and roads. Because of these considerations Bedouin cannot provide the most favorable herding conditions for the animals, and therefore the flocks do not pay their way.

The Awlad Sa'id live in the mountains west of Saint Catherine's monastery. They straddle all the east-west routes across the mountains, and control some of the best pasture in the high mountains, leaving only a small area to the Jebaliyah. They rely to a much greater extent than the Muzenah on flocks, and not a few of them possess small and relatively neglected orchards in the mountains. In the past their camels carried pilgrims from Egypt and supplies from al-Tur to the monastery. They also used to engage in smuggling. Now they too depend largely on wage labor.

The habitat of the Jebaliyah is the high mountain. Their flocks are even smaller than those of the other two tribes, and some households do not raise animals. As their small territory includes no major mountain pass, they are more or less excluded from smuggling activities. They specialize in horticulture. Nearly every family owns one or more orchards in the high mountains, which it waters and cultivates regularly, even when it resides elsewhere. Before the Israeli occupation the Jebaliyah used to market their fruit in al-Tur and with the proceeds they bought a year's supply of grain. That did not leave enough money for other items, such as tea, sugar and clothing, so the men sought employment wherever available, in Sinai or in the Nile valley. Saint Catherine's monastery traditionally employs between 20 to 30 Jebaliyah men and also a few Awlad Sa'id. While it pays its workers much lower wages than the open labor market, it can offer them two advantages: work close to home and relatively secure employment. The monastery's employees often remain in their jobs throughout their working life, and even after retirement the monastery supplies them with small but regular food rations. Tribesmen complain about the meager pay, but remain in their jobs, for they know that the future is uncertain. The Jebaliyah also used to supply guides for pilgrims who wished to visit the many sites associated with the works of Moses in the vicinity of the monastery.

Jebaliyah explain that their close ties with the monastery go back into history. Their ancestor was a Greek slave, named Constantine. When the monastery was established, he was one of a number of slaves sent out to serve the monks. Procopius, the Byzantine chronicler, indeed reports that the emperor Justinian supplied the monastery with Vlach slaves. The story both supports the Jebaliyahs' claim for a special link to the monastery and their assertion that the tribal territory 'is owned by the monastery', and therefore cannot be touched by the authorities. While individual tribesmen admit to various origins, their attachment to one of the tribe's four sections gives them a right to enjoy the advantages of being 'children of the monastery' (*subyan al-der*), as they often call themselves.

As their territory was too small for herding on a large scale and as the monastery could employ only a few men, the Jebaliyah were among the first Bedouin to engage in wage labor. Some of them became skilled builders and well-diggers, whose services were in demand all over the peninsula. They still rely heavily on wage labor and most men work regularly in the towns of Sinai or in the Abu Rudes oil installations. Between 30 to 50 men are usually employed by the Israeli administration.

Jebaliyah households alternate as a rule between two locations: for most of the year, and especially during the cooler months, they stay in the 'low-lying' areas at an elevation of about 1,600 meters; during the hot summer months they move into the mountains to enjoy the cool air and the fruit of their orchards. The Awlad Sa'id observes a similar transhumance, but it takes place at a lower altitude. Their cool summer-sites are at about the same height as the 'sheltered' winter sites of the Jebaliyah.

All three tribes, then, depend on wage labor for their living, and most men stay for long periods away from home. At the same time, they tend their orchards and flocks of goats and sheep, while admitting that they either make little money, or even lose money, on their flocks and gardens. Why, then, do the Bedouin behave as if they were gardeners and herdsmen, and not move their families nearer to the places of work? The answer is twofold. First, when Bedouin obtain secure jobs, they often settle in the towns and cities of Egypt, and are then followed by their households and by other kin. Many 'Aleqat and Qararshah, and some members of other tribes, have become townsmen. While these people rarely return to live in South Sinai, they maintain the fiction that they are always drawn back to their homeland; they do not allow kinship ties to lapse and some of them still own orchards in the mountains. Second, the majority of Bedouin keep a secure foothold in the mountains of South Sinai because their employment is insecure. While most of their income is derived from wage labor, they know this to be of limited duration. They could lose their work at any time, through political upheavals and economic fluctuations, or because of illness, death and accidents. They expect these mishaps to occur and know they must prepare for them. Therefore they maintain a second economy (I use the term 'economy' in the most inclusive sense), on which they can fall back in time of need. In order to operate the second economy, they leave the households behind, tend their orchards and maintain the small flocks. In addition, they keep the tribe intact, and foster kinship and other ties. If anything should go wrong, they could always fall back on the resources of their country. By some serious effort they could increase their garden produce, and migrate with their flocks so as to make the best use of the available pasture. In this way they could build up an alternative, if less lucrative, market economy. Men keep their homes in the tribal area, and leave their gardens and flocks in the care of close kin. Should the need arise; kinsmen can be relied upon to supply all their needs. Bedouin often express this utilitarian behavior as a sentimental attachment to their land. A Jebaliyah man put it thus: 'Our country is arid, nothing grows in it. Last night the dew froze and burnt [sic!] my tomato plants. The same happens to the almond and apple blossoms.

It is not even a good country for goats, for you always have to supplement their food and you lose money on them. Only the landscapes are beautiful and in summer the climate is good, but we obtain our livelihood (*rizq*) outside the country. Yet I always return to it, because my family lives here. And I do not leave because my country is dear to me. I am tied to it by my navel-string. For when a child is born, the father buries the navel-string and the placenta deep in the ground.' Attachment to the land thus symbolizes both the secure base established on the ground and the social security provided by the people living on it. It indicates that the system is all of one piece, and that it is well worth preserving.

When the going is good, Bedouin do not balance the two economies very carefully. They feel secure, and put less work into their orchards and flocks. But they never neglect or abandon the second economy. When they feel threatened, they increase their efforts. Thus the input of work and effort varies with the news. This became evident in the 1973 war between Egypt and Israel, and once more late in 1975, during the negotiations between Egypt and Israel over an 'interim agreement' in Sinai. It happened a third time, when it became clear in 1979 that Israel would evacuate the Mount Sinai region. On each occasion there was a sudden flourish of activity in the basic economy. Bedouin stopped the sale of animals and showed a renewed interest in gardens. Some people acquired existing gardens; others dug wells and planted new gardens. These arrangements, they hoped, would enable them to compensate for the expected loss of employment.

Smuggling is to be viewed as a secondary accommodation to prevailing conditions. This wild and mountainous country is well suited to clandestine activities. The inhabitants eke out a bare living, and are therefore ready to do any gainful work that offers itself. In spite of high risks and the not extravagant pay, numerous people viewed smuggling as a business just like any other, as an accepted and respectable way of making a living, one that furthermore had many advantages over migrant labor. While only a handful of entrepreneurs made fortunes out of smuggling, it permitted the rank and file to stay at home for much longer periods, and did not expose them to the humiliating treatment of the city dwellers. Smuggling reinforces tribal allegiance, as the control over routes is a precondition for entering the game. It is also predicated on peaceful relations between the tribes located along the smuggling routes. Therefore the Bedouin of South Sinai shun violent disputes and, quite justly, refer to themselves as 'peaceful people'.

IV.

Wage labor, then, is the main source of the Bedouin's income. It takes many men for months on end away from their families and kin and out of the tribal area. The families they leave behind converge on the relatively large villages, where services and shops are located, and do not give the flocks and gardens all the attention they merit. While the men often work in the company of relatives, most of the people on whom they depend for mutual assistance and reassurance are located in the tribal area. Relationships with these people also require maintenance, for if one does not interact regularly with them, the relationship can no longer be relied upon. One cannot be certain whether it will hold in time of need. Therefore each Bedouin strives to visit his relatives and friends, whenever he takes time off from work. The opportunity to see many relatives at once presents itself in late summer, when the Bedouin congregate in the oases for the date harvest. These large concentrations, in turn, form the basis for the organization of the even more encompassing tribal gatherings.

Those Muzenah and Awlad Sa'id who do not become labor migrants go through annual migrations. Their pastoral year begins in *rabi'* ('spring'), the season when the weather becomes a little warmer and verdure springs up. This usually happens around February. In the mountains spring comes round every year, but in the lower areas only if there has been some rain in winter.

Then the Bedouin leave their winter quarters, relatively large stationary hamlets of tin shacks and tents, and some of them divide up into small camps of two to three tents in order to exploit the pasture wherever it is available. These movements are largely determined by the requirements of the larger flocks, but even households owning few animals may join in because they wish to stay close to relatives. Spring pasture does not last long and once it is exhausted the flocks move into the few reliable early summer pastures, such as Wadi Rahabah and Wadi Slaf. Some of the larger encampments remain almost immobile. They are made up of households whose income depends on wage labor, and who put little emphasis on herding. In spring these camps just move a short distance from the sheltered winter camping site to one that allows in the refreshing breezes.

The annual migratory cycle reaches the point of maximum concentration in summer, when the pasture is exhausted and water sources dry up. Then people converge on the remaining wells in the oases or on the seashore and harvest their dates or, in the case of the Jebaliyah, repair to their gardens in the mountains. Here people gather in larger concentrations; some of the men have already returned from work in order to enjoy the conviviality and the exchange of visits. On moonlit nights the young, unmarried Muzenah men organize dances. After the fruit has been picked and the time comes to move, the elders of the tribe call for a tribal gathering. The gathering not only fits into the seasonal pattern of maximum concentration of tribesmen, but also enhances it. It is the only occasion when the 'tribe' visibly becomes a group. At other times it does not operate as a united political group; there are not even constant reminders of its existence, such as tribal identification marks. Even the tribal camel brands are rarely applied these days. It is only when people plant gardens, build houses or engage in smuggling that they are reminded of being tribesmen.

What is it that makes a considerable number of tribesmen participate in the pilgrimage? There is very little persuasion involved; the organizers of the pilgrimage are respected elders, who exert a strong hold on people. There is no tribal chief or economic entrepreneur among them. Their main duties are to fix the date of the pilgrimage and to collect from their neighbors contributions for the tribal sacrifice, which are eventually returned to the donors in the form of boiled meat. A basic attraction of the pilgrimage is that each individual considers it as a beneficial activity. People all over the region acknowledge the reputations of the major shrines, not only the people in whose territory they are situated. All the saints attract individual pilgrims from all over the region, and the fame of some shrines has spread beyond the borders of South Sinai. Monday and Friday eves are considered as propitious for pilgrimage. On these days, throughout most of the year, individual households make their way to a shrine of their choice. In many instances this will be a saint's tomb, but there are also a few other pilgrimage sites. One of these, and the one most venerated, is the summit of Jebel Musa (where Moses is said to have received the Tablets of the Law). Others are Jebel Muneja' in Wadi Firan, and the uninhabited monastery of the Forty Martyrs in Wadi Lejah, a branch of Saint Catherine's monastery (Levi 1977: 175, 1978: 18–19). In these pilgrimages people either redeem vows made in times of trouble or request the saint's intercession. As the saint only mediates requests to almighty God, and cannot himself grant prayers, a visit to any holy tomb, perhaps the closest one, should do. Yet people are slightly skeptical, and trust their own and their relatives' experience, which shows that some saints intercede more effectively, while others are more efficacious in some matters than in others. While individual experience varies widely, some specialization has developed among the saints. Therefore each holy tomb attracts visitors from all parts of South Sinai, often coming from distant places. Thus members of one patronymic group of the Jebaliyah visited at various times during a five-year period the following sites: a woman who had not conceived for two years ascended Jebel Musa with her family; a man wished to protect the well-being of his family by taking them on an outing to Sheikh 'Awad; two men took their flocks by car to Sheikh Habus in order to safeguard their health; one man carried his family by camel to Nebi

Saleh, on recovering from an illness; and throughout the period an old lady reiterated her wish to make the expensive pilgrimage to Mecca 'next year', so far without success. In similar fashion, people from all over South Sinai visit close and distant shrines, thus covering the whole region with a dense network of pilgrimages, and reaffirming their respect for, and recognition of, all the saints of the region.

This situation affects tribal gatherings in two ways. First, the commonly shared belief in saints' tombs, and in saints as intercessors with God, is one of the foundations of the tribal pilgrimage. Each of the individuals who participate in the gathering believes that he or she obtains a spiritual benefit. It must be added, however, that he may also expect material advantages, such as encountering a debtor or getting an opportunity to offer a car or a camel for sale. Bedouin see nothing incongruous in seeking spiritual and material benefits at the same time. They do not conceive of purely spiritual occasions, or purely material exchanges, that are so typical of more specialized social forms.

Second, all the participants in the gathering, whether belonging to the celebrating tribe or not, respect the saint's tomb, and consider it the equal of the saints' tombs of other tribes. Even Nebi Saleh, whose tomb is the recognized center of the tribal gatherings, is not considered superior to the others. Individual pilgrims do not prefer him in any way to other saints, and there are weeks when no one visits the site. This equality among saints expresses an important facet of the gatherings: that they are not held exclusively for the members of one tribe, but that people from other tribes can also attend. Indeed, people say explicitly that the gatherings are expected to attract visitors from other tribes. Thus, the meeting-place of the Bedouin of South Sinai shifts periodically from one site to another. At each gathering one tribe slightly dominates because of its numerical preponderance, but never becomes superior to the others. Still, until recently there was one preferred site for tribal gatherings. People say that up to 1965, at least five tribes, the Sawalhah, Awlad Sa'id, Qararshah, Muzenah and Jebaliyah, held their separate annual tribal gatherings at Nebi Saleh. I surmise that the location turned this tomb into the central meeting place of the Mount Sinai Bedouin: it is situated at the intersection of the major east-west and north-south mountain passes, close to the main pastures, in an area frequented by Muzenah, Awlad Sa'id and Jebaliyah. In view of the great importance of smuggling in those days, and of caravan traffic in earlier times, each tribe attached great significance to its rights of passage through the mountains, as well as to the co-ordination of activities and the maintenance of peaceful relations with other tribes.

Today each tribe has its own meeting-place, in its tribal territory. There are two clusters of such sites. In the west, not far from the sea, are the pilgrimage centers of the 'Aleqat, Qararshah and Hamadah tribes. They are located close to the main concentrations of the homes of labor migrants employed in the towns in and around Sinai. Before the Israeli occupation, some men were employed in the mines and industries of the region, but the majority worked all year round as migrant laborers, and approximately half of them eventually settled in Egypt proper. For these geographically mobile people, the saint's tomb must be located close to home, as it refers to their attachment to the territory. The other cluster of pilgrimage centers includes those of the Muzenah, Awlad Sa'id and Jebaliyah, and will be examined in greater detail. They are located in the mountains, the former at the center of the tribe's large territory, and the other two at the outskirts of their tribal territory. Here pilgrimage requires most people to leave their homes and to travel some distance. They go through a rite of passage, 'beginning in a Familiar Place, going to a Far Place, and returning, ideally "changed", to a Familiar Place' (Turner 1973: 213). These tribesmen are intimately tied to the land, where their basic economy lies. Here the attachment to the land is a given, and Bedouin use their pilgrimages to forge or maintain relationships in and outside the tribe. The individual is drawn away from his round of daily life and its circumscribed field of relationships, and brought to another place where he meets people from a wider region.

The elders who set the date of the tribal gathering take into account all the relevant factors. A Bedouin explained what these are: 'The date of the gathering is fixed perhaps two months in advance, so that the news will get around to all tribesmen. Conditions of work are taken into account, as well as the end of the date harvest (*masif*) in Wadi Firan (where the dates ripen later than in other oases) and the position of the stars. Only after canopus (*thraiyah*) and other stars rise to the firmament, the mutton becomes suitable for eating. Before that the goats are too lean and their meat is hard to digest.' To complicate matters further, the feasts are held on Thursday afternoons, the eve of the Muslim weekend, and at full moon. The dates of the tribal gatherings vary but little over the years. The earliest reported date is the end of July (Burckhardt 1822: 489). The gatherings I attended, or for which I obtained the dates, all took place between the end of June and the beginning of September. In this respect there was no difference between the Muzenah, the Awlad Sa'id and the Jebaliyah.

My data on attendance are incomplete, but they do show that in recent years it varied considerably. Thus for the Muzenah gathering at Nebi Saleh in 1970, 100–150 men are reported (Meshel 1971: 95). In following years the numbers declined sharply, until in 1973 only 50 men were reported to be present. In 1975 the figure again rose to nearly 200 men.

The Awlad Sa'id attended their tribal meet at Abu Taleb more regularly. In July 1973 I attended a meeting of about 70 men, gathered in the rectangular open-sided hut opposite the saint's tomb. In the following year Kapara (1975: 193) reports 40-50 men in the big hut, with others still arriving. In contrast to the Muzenah, whose attendance declined up to 1973, and went up again in the following year, the Awlad Sa'id pattern was stable. Most of the men attended year after year.

The Jebaliyah's pattern of attendance differed again. Tribesmen claimed that in the past they had had annual tribal gatherings lasting three days. They used to start at Nebi Saleh, the major site for tribal gatherings, moved on to Nebi Harun (the reputed tomb of Aaron, the high priest), near Saint Catherine's monastery, and from there on to the monastery itself. This gathering was held for the last time in 1965. After that there were no more gatherings of the whole tribe, but in August 1973 I attended a gathering of about 65-70 men of the Awlad Jindi sub-tribe at Sheikh 'Awad, and in August 1975 another one at the same place attended by nearly all Awlad Jindi men. A month later another sub-tribe, the Wuhebat, held a gathering of their own at Sheikh 'Awad. While I was told that previously they had not had such gatherings, the pilgrimages of sub-tribes now became a regular annual feature.

A clear pattern emerges here: though the gatherings never ceased, attendance declined when plenty of work was available and when it was expected that the favorable economic and political conditions would continue. This was particularly true for the Muzenah and Jebaliyah, who largely depended on wage labor. People who regularly turned up at the gatherings were those who had a predominant interest in herding, as well as the former smugglers, who presented themselves as keepers of tradition: they were waiting for better times, when they would be able to resume operations. When I asked why others did not participate, I was often told that they were away working and would not jeopardize their jobs. So the men who had an interest in maintaining the tribe showed up at all the meetings while those whose employment was secure did not. After 1973, the employed people also took part in the gatherings. This was the result of a new kind of uncertainty. At that time, work was plentiful and well paid, but the political future of Sinai was uncertain. The Egyptians and Israelis were negotiating under the aegis of the American Secretary of State, Henry Kissinger, the Israelis were giving up territory in Sinai and no one knew where this was going to end. While elsewhere in the Middle East the extended negotiations raised hopes that peace would come to the region, they only spelled doubts and insecurity for the Bedouin. An Awlad Jindi man employed as driver by the Israeli administration had often told me that he never attended tribal gatherings. These were suited for the old people, he thought. In 1975 he attended for the first time, explaining that his wife had begged him to go and that he could not refuse her wish. He did not admit, perhaps not even to himself, that the future was uncertain and that he might have to rely to a larger extent than hitherto on the help of agnates and tribesmen. At the time he was toying with the idea of setting up a repair shop for motorcars. Relatives and neighbors could thus become more important, even if only as customers. He has attended the pilgrimage every year since.

The two levels of the individual's involvement in the pilgrimage are shown in the eating arrangements. At each gathering there is a communal meal. Several sheep or a young camel are slaughtered and all the men who contributed to the price attend the meal. The animals are bought, and cooking arrangements made, by an elder of the group. In the late afternoon or evening all the men gather for a festive meal. They pray together and then sit down in a large circle for a meal. Each man's name is announced for all to hear, as a tribesman who contributed to the tribal sacrifice. Then his portion of meat, wrapped in a flap of flat bread, is passed along a chain of servers up to the announcer who hands it to the man. There is no visible leader at these functions; no speeches and announcements are made. Visitors from other tribes are welcome. Their names are announced, and the epithet 'guest' added. They too are given portions of meat. Chiefs and notables mingle with other men and no special area is reserved for them. At one of the Muzenah gatherings the paramount chief of the tribe put in a short appearance, to pay respect to a gathering at which he did not preside. At the Awlad Sa'id gatherings the two tribal chiefs were present all the time and moved among the people. The Jebaliyah chief did not attend the Awlad Jindi meetings at all; but he was present at those of his own sub-tribe, the Wuhebat.

The chiefs' participation in the proceedings was largely determined by their position in the tribe. While all chiefs are considered to be the representatives of the administration, this does not count much where government is as distant and inactive as in South Sinai. The saint is treated as a mediator between the tribe and divine authority precisely because government is so distant and does not assure the Bedouin's basic requirements. Therefore there was no place for the 'government' chiefs in the ceremonies. Some of these men were however important in their own right, as organizers of smuggling rings and other economic activities, as powerful leaders of large groups of men, and as mediators in disputes between tribesmen. Such were the chiefs of the Awlad Sa'id and the headmen of the Muzenah sub-tribes, and they took their rightful place in the ceremonies. Others, like the chiefs of the Jebaliyah and the Muzenah, play less important internal roles, and do not need to be present.

The participants in the tribal gathering were at the same time individual pilgrims. All round the saint's tomb related families gathered in small circles. The women began to prepare food for a festive meal. In the late afternoon each man led his family and a sacrificial goat round the tomb, bearing a pan with burning incense and repeating the phrase *twakkal allah* (Rely on God). He then recited the *fatihah*, the opening chapter of the Quran, dedicating it to the saint, and offered a prayer for the health, well-being and livelihood of his family. Thereupon he slaughtered the animal; and while he prepared the meat, the women and children returned to their own family circle. The family and its guests, men, women and children, shared in a joint meal of meat and other dishes. For once, the order of precedence was dropped and all the members of the household ate together. The women in particular wore their finest dresses, embroidered with silver and gold thread. The atmosphere was relaxed and the women spoke up freely, even making jokes with sexual innuendos. There was much mutual visiting. The men most of the time made the rounds of friends, now and again returning to spend a few minutes with their families. At these gatherings people reaffirmed their friendly relations and, incidentally, settled debts and disputes and initiated commercial dealings, such as the sale of animals and cars, and other joint activities. Shopkeepers too had arrived and made brisk sales of cola bottles and sweets.

The significance of the tribal pilgrimages has gradually emerged. People attend at them for their material and spiritual well-being. They hope to meet their relatives and friends, to reaffirm old ties and to forge new ones. Throughout most of the year they do not meet many of these people. By participating in the annual tribal muster, and sharing the tribal sacrificial meal, they renew bonds with the tribe and its members, and assure themselves of access to territorial resources. The attendance of guests from other tribes emphasizes solidarity with the people of South Sinai for the preservation of peace, a precondition for access to pastures throughout the peninsula and for joint smuggling operations. Lastly, they supplicate the saint to forward their prayers to a distant God, in whom they put their trust. Without his help they could not survive in the wider world, on which they depend in so many ways and over which they exert no influence.

V.

The symbolism of the tribal pilgrimages must now be examined. I take a 'symbol' to be a sign replete with many interrelated meanings. In this working definition, which resembles Sapir's (1934: 493) characterization of the 'condensation symbol', I wish to stress the richness of meaning as identifying mark of the symbol, as opposed to the mechanical multiplication of mental associations that may attach to a particular sign. The meanings of the condensation symbol express, as Sapir (1934: 493) pointed out, 'a condensation of energy, its actual significance being out of all proportion to the apparent triviality of meaning suggested by its mere form'. To this I would add that much of the emotional impact of 'condensation symbols' derives from the fact that they evoke numerous, often contested and contradictory, meanings simultaneously. The secret of this immediate impact probably lies in the symbol's full integration in the daily routine of its users. Because of this, many students of society today agree that an external observer can tap the multiple meanings of symbols only through intimate knowledge of both native conceptions of society and of the social contexts in which the symbols are invoked. The whole gamut of a symbol's contextual uses, as well as the associated symbols and contexts, must be explored, before it can be properly understood. But once this is done, one may find that each element of a symbol's meaning has a precise referent and thus appeals directly to communicants.

Bedouin clearly distinguish between the meaning of the Mecca pilgrimage, which is made once in a lifetime, and the repetitive and regular pilgrimages to saints' tombs. The symbolism of the pilgrimage to Mecca centers no less on the journey than on the holy site itself. The route is often seen as a staging of the life course; it offers the pilgrim an opportunity to reflect on his or her past life, to make a clean break, and to formulate a plan for the future. The journey to Mecca is divided into stages of ever growing sanctity, culminating in the pilgrim's donning of two lengths of white cloth (*ihram*) on the outskirts of Mecca. The *ihram* is also the shroud he will be buried in, a reminder that his whole life is under review. Even in the sacred city, the pilgrim is obliged to continue the journey from one site to the next. He must thus consider the pilgrimage as a turning point in life and a preparation for death. The ultimate examples of this sacred journey are those Nigerian Muslims described by Bawa Yamba (1995: 181 ff.) whose pilgrimage may last a whole lifetime. They may interrupt it in the Sudan, in order to collect money for the onward journey, raise a family and die there. But no matter how long the sojourn in the Sudan, they will at all times view it as a way-station on the road to Mecca. This is emphatically not the case in the pilgrimage to saints' tombs, a repetitive performance whose main purpose is to maintain a useful relationship with the saint. Here the journey becomes less important and attention centers on the saint's tomb. The Bedouin even use different terms for the pilgrimage to Mecca and the pilgrimage to saints' tombs. For the tribal gatherings, as well as personal pilgrimages to saints' tombs, they employ the term used for visiting among friends and acquaintances (*ziyarah*, locally pronounced *zuwarah*). This usage is common in most Islamic regions. Only the pilgrimage to Mecca is called *hajj* (meaning precisely a 'sacred journey'). While Sinai Bedouin often compare the ascent to the summit of Jebel Musa to a pilgrimage to Mecca, they nevertheless call it a 'zuwarah'. There is only one place to which a Muslim pilgrimage is made, and that is Mecca. Every year a number of Bedouin men and women make the still arduous and costly journey there.

I shall now attempt to unravel the major strands in the mesh of meanings attached to the saint's tomb, concentrating on three major elements: the significance of the building erected over the tomb, the tomb itself, and the saint's person. I would argue that the building symbolizes the Bedouin's conception of the tribe's territorial rights, whose essence is the tribesman's exclusive right to build a house on tribal land. Geertz's (1968: 49) concise description of the Moroccan shrine fits that of South Sinai too: 'It is a squat, white, usually domed block-like stone building set under a tree, on a hilltop, or isolated, like an abandoned pillbox, in the middle of an open plain.' (See also Canaan 1927: 11). One might add that each shrine has a door, and usually also a small window. Only the dome,[4] often crowned with a crescent, and in a few shrines a prayer niche facing in the direction of Mecca, distinguish the shrine from an ordinary house, and indicate that it serves a religious purpose. We already know that Bedouin consider the building of a house as the exclusive right of tribesmen and do not permit outsiders to build houses on tribal territory. The shrine represents, among other things, the territorial claims of the tribe on whose land it is located. As they may not be the only tribe to visit the shrine, the rights of the owners of the land are as clearly defined as those of the members of other tribes: while they exercise exclusive rights to the construction of wells, orchards and houses, and the use of smuggling routes, the members of other tribes possess rights of pasture and of passage through the tribe's land. On another level, the use of the saint's tomb as a symbol of tribal ownership indicates that territorial rights are protected by supernatural sanctions, and not necessarily by the might of the whole tribe. Bedouin store property, such as tents and farming implements, inside or near saints' tombs, secure in the belief that the saint protects them. They recount stories about misfortunes that befell men who stole such property, until they restored it. Construction or repair of a saint's tomb is a pious act that gains the donors the respect of the community. They are also political acts: when Ghanem Jum'a, a wealthy Muzenah, built the shrine of Faraj, the tribe's ancestor, in the 1960s, he reasserted the tribe's sovereignty over an area which was at the time becoming the main supply center in South Sinai, and the major sales depot of the mobile merchants from al-'Arish who control nearly all the commerce in the region. Similarly, Jebaliyah elders every few years invite their tribesmen to subscribe money for repairs to the shrine of Sheikh 'Awad. This building activity reasserts a tribe's rights to the holy tomb, and through it, to territory; and incidentally, in this way all the shrines are kept in a good state of repair.

The saint's tomb occupies the center of the building, thus allowing visitors to circumambulate. The tomb rises to a height of about one meter. A shroud made of white or green cloth, on which sometimes the Islamic creed and the saint's name are embroidered, covers it. There are usually several layers of shrouds, for each time a shroud is worn out and torn it remains in place and a new one is placed on top of it. The old one is too sacred to be simply disposed of.

It is always doubtful whether the holy tomb actually contains a human body. While the tomb of Nebi Saleh is solidly built and one cannot therefore know whether anyone is buried in it, the tomb of 'Ali Abu Taleb consists of a flimsy wooden frame, just sufficient to carry several layers of embroidered shrouds. Canaan (1927: 22) remarks, with regard to Palestinian sanctuaries, that 'the tomb is often not in the shrine, but outside of it...it is not at all necessary that there should be a tomb...connected with the place to make it a shrine'. In South Sinai the Bedouin have gone a step further: they insist that no one is buried in a maqam. As proof they cite the 'well-known fact that Nebi Saleh is buried in Ramlah, in Israel, and has another tomb in Mada'in Saleh in Saudi Arabia, and that even the Sheikhs Habus and Abu Shabib have two holy tombs each. Only one of these holds a grave (*turba*), while the other is a place for gatherings of men (*maq'ad*).' The shrines at which tribes gather could not contain a body, even if the saint had been buried there. For it is common knowledge among Bedouin that the remains of good men dissolve into air (*hawa*) after some time, and only the bodies of ordinary persons remain in their tombs. This belief releases the saint from his earthly vestiges; he is removed from this world, and is therefore closer to the distant deity. He may be close enough to approach the deity and intercede on behalf of the Bedouin he associated with in life.[5]

The saint cannot be a named ancestor because the tribe is neither a corporate nor an agnatic group. For experience has shown that eponyms are generally reserved for agnatic descent groups. Most people cannot say anything definite about the saint's person, except that he was a holy man during his lifetime, as proven by instances in which he rescued individuals from various tribes in miraculous ways. Occasionally people hazard guesses about the antecedents of a saint. While some say that Nebi Saleh was a pre-Islamic Arabian prophet, others think that perhaps he was the ancestor of the Sawalhah. The same uncertainty seems to have prevailed over a century ago, when Robinson (1841, I: 215) reported: 'The history of the Saint is uncertain; but our Arabs held him to be a progenitor of their tribe, the Sawaliha.' Sheikh 'Awad is also said by some Jebaliyah to belong to their tribe, while others claim to know nothing about his origins. Some Muzenah consider Sheikh Abu Zaid to have been a Sawarkah Bedouin (from North Sinai), and others attribute Muzenah origins to him. The only saint who appears to be an acknowledged tribal ancestor is Faraj of the Muzenah. But his tomb is not reckoned among the maqams; it is named after a group, the Faranjah, and not after the ancestor Faraj; and only in recent years was a shrine built over the tomb. Yet the fact remains that Faranjah is one of the Muzenah's three pilgrimage sites, and one has to conclude that, in a sense, the saint is an emblem of the tribe.

The three holy tombs visited by the Muzenah allow us to define more clearly the symbolic significance of the saint, for the person of each of the three saints gives special emphasis to one aspect: Faranjah symbolizes the unity of the tribe, as well as its descent from the North Arabian Muzenah (Doughty 1937: II, 381). Nebi Saleh represents both the unity of the Tawarah of South Sinai as one region to which all inhabitants have access, and the inclusion of South Sinai in the Islamic world and, by extension, in the state controlling Sinai. Nebi Harun again stands for the connection with the monastery of Saint Catherine and the privileges associated with it on one hand, and on the other for the Islamic community, for Moses and Aaron are included in Islamic hagiography. I cannot fully explain this extended specialization of the three Muzenah saints, for in other tribes all the symbolic aspects merge today in a single saint. It may be connected with two facts: First, that the Muzenah have become the largest and most widely dispersed tribe (Lavie 1990). They control over half of South Sinai, including most of the east coast, and this encourages a tendency for the proliferation of smuggling rings, with the ensuing competition and strife. The elders of the tribe make special efforts to preserve unity, so as to keep the Muzenah predominant in the smuggling business. Therefore they stress joint descent and begin the pilgrimage at the tomb of Faraj. Yet in recent years the competition between rival smuggling rings has on several occasions erupted violently at the tribal gathering. Second, their exclusive use of the central sanctuary of Nebi Saleh expresses their political dominance among the tribes of South Sinai.

Whether the pilgrimage is made to one or three saints, it always symbolizes the Bedouin's solidarity with three social aggregates. If the saint is to represent all of them, his identity must be indeterminate. He is and he is not a tribesman, and he also is a son of Sinai, and an illustrious Muslim.

On a higher level of abstraction, the three Muzenah saints stand for ideologies that are deeply engrained in Bedouin thought and concern areas of their social life: agnation and territorial organization, kinship and the regionalism of South Sinai, and the universalism of Islam and, by extension, all the external world on which the Bedouin depend and which they do not control. All these ideologies are contained and, to some extent, integrated in a system of thought, in the Bedouin concept 'tribe'.

The tribal pilgrimage to saints' tombs is the Bedouin's answer to some fundamental problems; he came up with this answer because his view of reality is filtered through a theory of society that hinges on the tribe. The Bedouin participates as wage laborer in the wider economy and in a bureaucratic state. Both are distant and leave him an insecure outsider. But he has the tribe to fall back on. The tribe means to him several things: a territorial group owning resources from which he can make a living, land on which he can dig wells, plant orchards and build a house; a political group of agnates, whose members help and defend each other and their territory; and a group whose membership gives access to pastures all over South Sinai. All these together are the Bedouin's basic economy. The pilgrimage brings together the people who help to make this economy, and seeks to reunite them. At the same time it reflects the fears and uncertainties associated with the distant state, the vagaries of external wage labor, and the problems of life in general.

Thus the cult of saints refers not only to a regionalism more or less confined to the geographical boundaries of South Sinai and to the sharing of natural resources for the benefit of the Tawarah tribes. It also refers to a larger entity, to the world in which the Bedouin work, and from which they obtain most of their food and other supplies and services. This world is located chiefly outside the borders of South Sinai and, even more importantly, the Bedouin do not exert influence on its activities. A distant government and other external organizations determine much of their lives, but contact with, not to mention influence over, these forces is minimal. For the bureaucratic line of communication does not fully extend to the Bedouin, and their own appointed representatives, the sheikhs, do not greatly influence officials at the center. So the Bedouin place their reliance on a 'spiritual' representative, the saint, who is at least close to God and able to influence him. Two worlds are linked through the person of the saint, who is sometimes thought of as the patron of a tribe, perhaps even an ancestor, and at other times as a holy man of Islam. The saint represents both the tribe as conceptualized by the Bedouin, and the wide external world. His function is to mediate between the two worlds, which together sustain the Bedouin. I suggest that tribal reunions elsewhere also develop in response to similar situations: they will appear in tribal or other economically undifferentiated regions that depend on external forces (natural forces, or an external state and economy) over which they exert little influence. Such societies maintain a pastoral or farming economy on which they fall back in time of need, and maintain the tribe mainly in order to keep control over their territory. A society that is self-sufficient, or that can rely on economic alternatives and on government assistance, even when it is dubbed a 'tribe' does not need tribal reunions. The Syrian Ruwala, as described by Musil (1928), are so fully integrated in the state and in the market that they need neither personal nor tribal pilgrimages.

How does Robertson Smith's argument that there is a correspondence between social organization and religious representations, fare in the light of this discussion? Werbner (1977: XVIII) tends to reject the 'correspondence' theory, because 'the "community of the god" is a conception of boundedness'. True, Robertson Smith, like the Bedouin themselves, viewed the tribe as a bounded political and territorial entity, perhaps because he too considered agnation to be the backbone of the tribe. The ideology of agnation informs 'bounded' activities, such as the control over rights in land, the protection of life and property and the setting up of groups. To this kind of activity applies Robertson Smith's (1894: 150) dictum that holiness is 'a restriction on the license of man in the free use of natural things'. In the Arabian context, he believed that gods were associated with permanent sanctuaries, and that their powers were confined to a certain territory (*ibid.* 92). Therefore, 'at most sanctuaries embracing a stretch of pasture-ground, the right of grazing was free to the community of the god, but not to outsiders' (*ibid*. 144). This prescription did not fit the customary sharing of pastures. Although 'every tribe indeed has its own range of plains and valleys, and its own watering places...from which it repels aliens by the strong hand,...not only every tribesman but every covenanted ally has equal and unrestricted right to pitch his tent and drive his cattle where he will' (*ibid*. 143). The contradiction is immediately explained away: nomads did not claim private property in pastures, and for that reason the local god did not acquire ownership over them.

The material on saints' tombs in South Sinai shows that Robertson Smith was mistaken on two counts. First, the god or saint is not simply associated with one tribe and his influence not confined to a bounded territory. On the contrary, the 'local' god in ancient Arabia, like the saint in South Sinai, symbolizes the interdependence between the tribe and a wider region, particularly where pastures were concerned. Wellhausen shows that many sanctuaries in pre-Islamic Arabia had extensive spheres of influence. For instance, the sanctuary of the goddess Manat was located in Hudhail territory, but was frequented by Aus and Khazraj tribesmen and by others (Wellhausen 1961: 27–28). The sanctuary at Mecca too was not visited by the Quraish only, but attracted pilgrims from various tribes, while the Meccans must have visited other sanctuaries. In this manner, ties were forged between Bedouin stemming from different regions, links that facilitated transit and mutual access to the available pastures, even in the absence of a central government.

Second, for each restriction on the use of resources there must be a corresponding opening up of resources, as exemplified in the following quote, also taken from Robertson Smith (1894: 111): 'The Arabs regard rain as depending on the...seasons, which affect all tribes alike within a wide range; and so when the showers of heaven are ascribed to a god, that god is Allah, the supreme and non-tribal deity.' Evidently these tribesmen reserve certain rights in territory for themselves, but also grant rights to pasture on it to others, on a basis of mutuality. Robertson Smith cannot admit that the 'tribal deity' also stands for Allah; to imply that the same people believe in two gods, one tribal and one supreme, at the same time, is as far as he dare go. In South Sinai the saint is clearly associated with God. While he intercedes with God on behalf of his tribe, he also works on behalf of individuals from any tribe, and is thus never an exclusive patron of his own people. He represents both restrictions on the use of the country's resources in favor of some people, and access to the remaining resources to others. There is no paradox in this, for rights are always specific, so that every prohibition has its complementary permission. Thus in South Sinai certain rights in land, wells and roads are reserved for tribesmen, and other rights are expressly opened up to all Tawarah: land everywhere is available to anyone for pasture, drinking water for men and beasts may be drawn from any well, even when surrounded by a fence, and every Bedouin can travel freely anywhere in the peninsula, as long as he does not infringe local privileges of employment or uses another tribe's smuggling route.

Yet, after all is said and done, we are still left with a correspondence, between social reality and its symbolic representation. If the reality is more complex than Robertson Smith's, and if it has many dimensions, that is due to the more detailed ethnography available today. If, in addition to the tribe, we now see a variety of groups and networks of relationships, that is due to relatively new theoretical insights. The brilliance of Robertson Smith's original idea, and its eminent usefulness, remain undiminished: that symbols refer to a social reality, as seen and interpreted by people and that the symbols derive from ordinary daily life, so that they can be directly grasped and apprehended by people, in spite of their multiple meanings.

Acknowledgments

Work in Sinai was made possible by a grant from the Ford Foundation, through the Israel Foundation Trustees, which I gratefully acknowledge. An earlier version of this paper was presented at the ASA Conference on Regional Cults, University of Manchester 1976 (Marx 1977). It was revised for a conference on Religion in the Mediterranean, at Amsterdam's Free University (Marx 1985). The comments of Ernest Gellner, Raymond Firth, Don Handelman, Shuli Hartman, Smadar Lavie, Daan Meijers and Richard Werbner were of great help in preparing this further revision.

Notes

1.   The most famous maqam is *maqam Ibrahim* in the Mecca mosque, which is considered 'a place of prayer' (Kister 1980). Interestingly, it is not invoked by Muslim scholars in discussions of the worship of saints.

2.   I owe this insight to Daan Meijers.

3.   Scholars sometimes attribute their own Judeo-Christian ideas to Islam. How else can we understand Goldziher's claim that 'in ancient Islam an insurmountable barrier divides an infinite and unapproachable Godhead from weak and finite humanity' (1967–71, 2: 255), a statement he then modifies by saying that 'shortly after the spread of the new religion' (*ibid.* 259) saints were venerated.

4.   Goldziher (1967–71, 1: 233) argues that the term *qubbah* applies not just to the dome but to the whole building.

5.   By the same token the saint must be dead. Living saints cannot get close to the deity. Thus the living saints of North African Islam do not mediate requests to God. Instead, they are experts on such matters as scriptural learning, irrigation and law (Colonna 1980: 644).

References

Ben-David, J. (1972) Shivte ha-beduim bi-drom Sinai (The Bedouin Tribes of South Sinai). MA dissertation Jerusalem: Hebrew University, Department of Geography.

Bawa Yamba, C. (1995) *Permanent Pilgrims: The Role of Pilgrimage in the Lives of West African Muslims in Sudan*. Edinburgh: Edinburgh University Press for the International African Institute.

Berque, J. (1955) *Structures sociales du Haut-Atlas*. Paris: Presses Universitaires de France.

Burckhardt, J.L. (1822) *Travels in Syria and the Holy Land*. London: Murray.

Canaan, T. (1927) *Mohammedan Saints and Sanctuaries in Palestine*. London: Luzac.

Christian, W.A. (1972) *Person and God in a Spanish Valley*. New York: Seminar Press.

Colonna, F. (1980) Saints furieux et saints studieux ou, dans l'Aurès, comment la religion vient aux tribus. *Annales* 35 (3-4): 642–61.

Doughty, C.M. (1937) [1888] *Travels in Arabia Deserta*. New York: Random House.

Eickelman, D.F. (1976) *Moroccan Islam: Tradition and Society in a Pilgrimage Center*. Austin, Texas: University of Texas Press.

Ganor, A. *et al.* (1973) *Aklim Sinai* (The Climate of Sinai). Beth Dagon: Israel Meteorological Service (Hebrew).

Geertz, C. (1968) *Islam Observed; Religious Development in Morocco and Indonesia*. Chicago: University of Chicago Press.

Gellner, E. (1972) Political and religious organization of the Berbers of the central High Atlas. In *Arabs and Berbers: From Tribe to Nation in North Africa*, edited by E. Gellner and C. Micaud. London: Duckworth.

Glassner, M.I. (1974) The Bedouin of Southern Sinai under Israeli administration. *The Geographical Review* 64: 31–60.

Goldziher, I. (1967–71) On the veneration of the dead in paganism and Islam. In *Muslim Studies*, vol. 1, by I. Goldziher. London: Allen and Unwin, pp. 209–38.

Goldziher, I. (1967–71) Veneration of saints in Islam. In *Muslim Studies*, vol. 2, by I. Goldziher. London: Allen and Unwin, pp. 255–341.

Grunebaum, G.E. von (1951) *Muhammedan Festivals*. New York: Schuman.

Israel, Army (1962) *Beduei Sinai* (The Bedouin of Sinai). Israel: Army, Southern Command (Hebrew).

Kapara, Y. (1975) Ziarat Sheikh Abu Taleb (The Pilgrimage to the Abu Taleb Shrine). *Tevaʻ Waaretz* 17: 192–94 (Hebrew).

Keller, A. (1900) *Eine Sinai-Fahrt*. Frauenfeld: Huber.

Kister, M.J. (1980) Makam Ibrahim. In *Encyclopaedia of Islam*, New Edition. Leiden: Brill.

Lazarus-Jaffé, H. (1976) The religious problem of the Islamic pilgrimage: the Islamization of ancient rituals. *Proceedings of the Israel Academy of Sciences and Humanities* 5 (11):1–22.

Lavie, S. (1990) *The Poetics of Military Occupation: Mzeina Allegories of Bedouin Identity under Israeli and Egyptian Rule*. Berkeley: University of California Press.

Levi, S. (1977) An ancient tradition regarding the summit Menegat Musa in Sinai. *Tevaʻ Waaretz* 19,4: 173–6 (Hebrew).

Levi, S. (1978) Der Arbaʻin in Bedouin belief. *Bulletin of Field-School 'David Cliffs'* 12: 18–20 (Hebrew).

Levy, R. (1962) *The Social Structure of Islam*. Cambridge: Cambridge University Press.

Linant de Bellefonds, Y. (1974) Kabr. In *Encyclopaedia of Islam*, New Edition, Leiden: Brill.

Marx, E. (1977) Communal and individual pilgrimage: the region of saints' tombs in South Sinai. In *Regional Cults*, edited by R.P. Werbner. London: Academic Press.

Marx, E. (1985) Tribal pilgrimages to saints' tombs in South Sinai. In *Islamic Dilemmas*, edited by E. Gellner. Berlin: Mouton.

Meshel, Z. (1971) *Drom Sinai* (South Sinai). Jerusalem: SH.H.L.Y. (Hebrew).

Murray, G.W. (1935) *Sons of Ishmael: A Study of the Egyptian Bedouin*. London: Routledge.

Musil, A. (1928) *The Manners and Customs of the Rwala Bedouins*. New York: American Geographical Society.

Niebuhr, C. (1799) *Travels Through Arabia and Other Countries in the East*. vol. 1. Perth: Morison.

Palmer, E.H. (1871) *The Desert of the Exodus*. 2 vols. Cambridge: Deighton, Bell.

Palmer, H.S. (1906) *Sinai from the Fourth Egyptian Dynasty to the Present Day*. London: SPCK.

Peters, E.L. (1976) From particularism to universalism in the religion of the Cyrenaica Bedouin. *Bulletin of the British Society for Middle Eastern Studies* 3,1: 5–14.

Sapir, E. (1934) Symbolism. In *Encyclopaedia of the Social Sciences*. New York: Macmillan.

Smith, W. Robertson (1894) *Lectures on the Religion of the Semites*. London: Black.

Turner, V. (1973) The center out there: pilgrim's goal. *History of Religions* 12,3: 191–230.

Waardenburg, J.D.J. (1979) Official and popular religion as a problem in Islamic studies. In *Official and Popular Religion as a Theme in Religious Studies*, edited by P.H. Vrijhof and J.D.J. Waardenburg. The Hague: Mouton.

Wellhausen, J. (1961) [1887] *Reste arabischen Heidentums*. Berlin: de Gruyter.

Werbner, R.P. (ed.) (1977) *Regional Cults*. ASA Monograph 16. London: Academic Press.

4 The Rise of a New Negev Cult Center Today:

Baba Sali's Sanctuary in Netivot, Israel

Yoram Bilu

Introduction

Given the five to six millennia that separate the Gilat sanctuary from the adjacent contemporary cult center at Netivot, any attempt to ponder a direct linkage between them would appear dubious at best. The physical proximity between the two sites, which constituted the trigger for including the present essay in this volume, is hardly a clue for such a connection. After all, the concentration of many cult centers in a small space is a cardinal attribute of the area that has come to be known as the 'Holy Land'. Certainly, in the Eliadean vein, landscape and scenery may be endowed with extraordinary, awe-inspiring physical properties befitting hierophany (Eliade 1959). But this is hardly true for the monotonous, semi-desert area of the northern Negev in which the two sites are located.

In line with this reservation, one major lesson that the emergence of the shrine in Netivot may provide for archaeologists is a caveat. Working in the present makes one alert to the multiplicity of factors which conjointly contribute to the development of a particular cult center. Some of these factors may be inscribed in the land to form a durable physical evidence for future archaeologists; but it would be naive to assume that the complex tapestry of psychological motivations, religious sentiments, social associations, political constraints, and historical vicissitudes underlying the waxing and waning of cults could be fully reconstructed through excavations.

This introductory plea for caution notwithstanding, the dialogue on cults between archaeologists and anthropologists can be productive if it transcends the literal concreteness of place-bound resemblances on the one hand and contextualizes airy abstractions in the cast of Eliade's universal 'religious man' on the other hand. Specifically, processual observations in richly nuanced ethnographies may provide archaeologists with clues regarding the functioning and structural properties of ancient religious centers. While I do not intend to cull from my ethnographic notes on the sanctuary at Netivot a model for the working of its Chalcolithic neighbor from Gilat, in the concluding section I discuss some of the archaeological evidence for cultic activities at Gilat in the light of my fieldwork observations.

**Plate 4.1. Israeli postage stamp commemorating Baba Sali and the ritual center
in Netivot where he is buried. The Netivot complex is a major site
for contemporary pilgrimage in the northern Negev desert.**

In what follows I seek to explore the rise of Netivot into a contemporary cult center by situating it in the wider cultural and sociopolitical context of contemporary Israel (Fig. 4.1). While the constituting ingredients of this context are inextricably intertwined, I treat them here, for analytic purposes, as discrete themes or separable layers of meaning. It is my contention that the transformation of Netivot into 'the Benares of Israel', as a well-known Israeli writer and essayist has put it, cannot be fully realized without taking into account the character and functions of Jewish Maghrebi hagiolatry, the vicissitudes of Moroccan Jews in Israel, the particular strands of North African religiosity and ethnicity, the glowing 'lineage charisma' (Weber 1968) of the Abu-Hatseira family and the character and ambitions of its contemporary descendants, and the history of Netivot as an Israeli 'development town'. Unfolding these layers of meaning is the crux of this essay; but first, a short characterization of the new site is in place.

In January 1984 Rabbi Israel Abu-Hatseira, a renowned sage and scion of a virtuous Jewish family from Southern Morocco, passed away at the age of 94. He was buried in the southern development town of Netivot, where he spent his last years. In the years that have passed, the gravesite of Baba Sali, as the saint is rather affectionately known among his devotees, has swiftly become a pilgrimage center of national significance. Throughout the year, the grave is bustling with visitors who come in private cars or in organized busloads to pray, to ask for the saint's intercession in personal problems, to host meals in gratitude for requests granted, and to celebrate familial ceremonies, such as bar-mitzvahs.

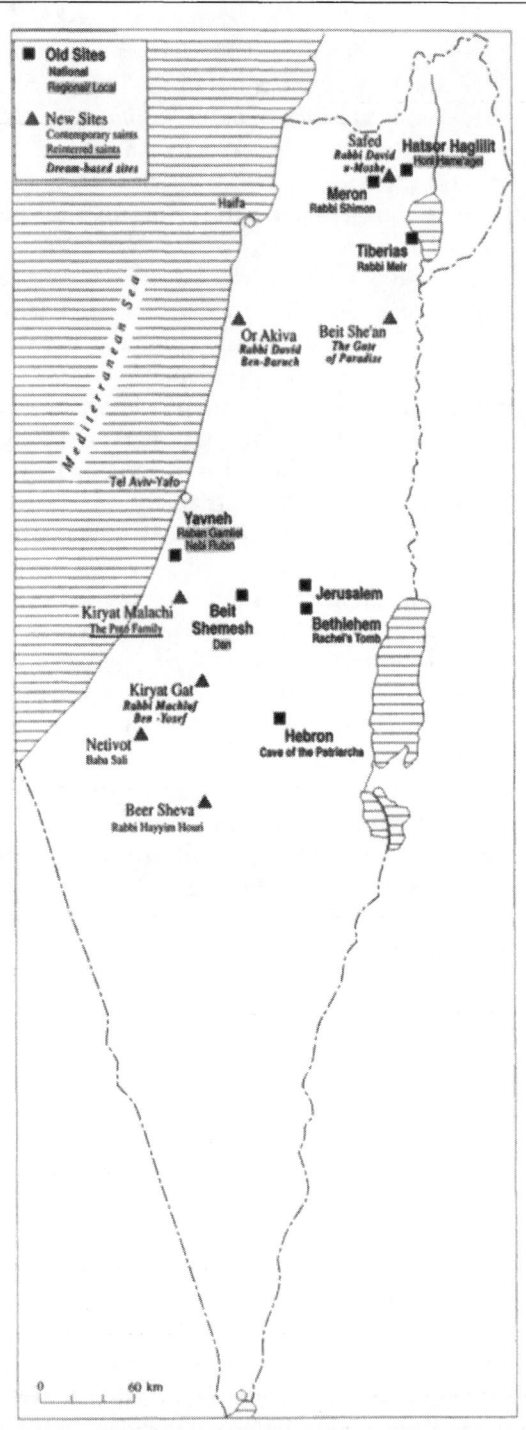

Plate 4.1. Pilgrimage sites in the Israeli periphery.

The celebration (Hebrew *hillula*) on the anniversary of the rabbi's death draws up to 150,000 adherents, a figure representing close to 3% of the country's Jewish population. In a country like Israel, which is replete with holy sites, such a crowd is at least impressive. It is second only to the sizable congregation assembled annually at the tomb of the legendary talmudic sage and mystic Rabbi Shimon Bar-Yohai at Meiron. In contrast to other *hillulot* (pl.), the festival in Netivot is the object of intense 'promotion campaigns', complete with media coverage, official invitations, special bus lines, organized markets and government backing. Moreover, the *hillula* also brings to it organized political interests and personages such as the prime minister and cabinet ministers, party leaders, and local officials, as well as representative of the chief rabbinate.

On regular days, the site is probably the most 'active' holy location after Jerusalem's Wailing Wall, the most cherished 'lieux de mémoire' (Nora 1989) in Israel's traditional and civil religions (cf. Liebman and Don-Yehiya 1983; Storper-Perez and Goldberg 1994). The comparison with the Wailing Wall and with Rabbi Shimon's sanctuary, pretentious as it may sound, is explicitly made by visitors to the Baba Sali's gravesite who refer to it as 'the Wailing Wall of Netivot' or 'the Southern Meiron' (Bilu and Ben-Ari 1996). The swiftly growing popularity of the site at Netivot has been informed by the meteoric rise of Baba Sali to the status of a national *tsaddiq*, the saint of Israel of the 1980s and 1990s. Today in almost any urban settlement one may find a street or synagogue bearing Baba Sali's name. His picture appears in more Israeli homes than any other Jewish figure, and his portrait adorns a surprisingly wide selection of holy and mundane objects, from prayer books to key chains. The intriguing qualities of this glorification process involve not only its course and direction but, no less important, its swiftness and pervasiveness. Charismatization of such magnitude is usually a lengthy historical process; but in the case of Baba Sali (as in the case of last leader of the Hasidic sect of Habad, the Rabbi of Lubavitch) a contemporary rabbi has transcended the bounds of historical reality and acquired a 'mythological' stature comparable with the most popular luminaries in Judaism (Bilu and Ben-Ari 1992).

As befits a 'national saint', the catchment population of the Netivot pilgrimage transcends narrow ethnic boundaries; but the strong presence of North African devotees and the style of celebration which resonates with the North African *ziara* (Arabic word meaning 'visit'), turns it, to some extent, into an 'ethnic renewal celebration' (Weingrod 1990). Hence, in order to understand the development at Netivot, the historical and cultural background of Jewish Maghrebi hagiolatry should be depicted.

Saint Worship in Morocco and in Israel

The folk-veneration of saints played a major role in the lives of the Jews in Morocco and constituted a basic component of their ethnic identity. In form, style and prevalence this cultural phenomenon clearly bears the hallmarks of indigenous saint worship, perhaps the most significant feature of Moroccan Islam (Crapanzano 1973; Eickelman 1976; Geertz 1968; Gellner 1969). At the same time, however, it was also reinforced by the deep-seated conception of the *tsaddiq* in classical Jewish sources (Goldberg 1983; Stillman 1982). In various Jewish groups outside North Africa, pious rabbis were accorded saintly attributes and their tombs became centers of popular pilgrimages. Saint worship was particularly developed in Jewish mystically oriented communities, given the central role accorded to the *tsaddiq* in *Kabbalah* (Scholem 1969). Moroccan Jewry was steeped in mysticism, as indicated by the popularity of the *Zohar* (the Book of Splendor), the canonical text of kabbalah mysticism, among the masses, unparalleled in other Jewish communities (Goldberg 1990). In the case of East European Hasidism the ideology of *tsaddiqim* crystallized into a religious movement that spawned many dynasties of venerated rabbis, each with its own organizational infrastructure and institutions (Scholem 1965). In the Maghreb, institutionalization of this scope did not take place. Yet the unique fusion of Jewish and Muslim traditions created a viable and pervasive folk-religious system.

The Jewish Moroccan saints were charismatic rabbis, distinguished by their mystical erudition and piety. These rabbis were believed to possess a special spiritual force, which did not fade away after their death. This force, akin to the Moroccan Muslim *Baraka* (Rabinow 1975; Westermarck 1926), could be utilized for the benefit of the saints' adherents. In contrast with their Muslim and Hasidic counterparts, most of the Jewish Moroccan *tsaddiqim* were identified as such only after their death. Therefore their miraculous feats were usually associated with their tombs. At the same time, however, the strong sense of inherited blessedness inherent in the notion of *zechut_avot* (literally, the virtue of the ancestors) allowed for the emergence of some dynasties of *tsaddiqim*. The Abu-Hatseira family, from which the protagonists of this presentation descend, is a noted example of such a holy succession, and so are the Pinto and Ben-Baruch families (Ben-Ami 1984:33–38).

Virtually every Jewish community, including the tiniest and most peripheral, had one or more patron saints (Ben-Ami 1984; Goldberg 1983). While the popularity of most of these saints was quite circumscribed, some of them acquired reputation and followings which transcended local, and even regional boundaries. Sainted figures like Rabbi Ya'aqov Abu-Hatseira, Rabbi David ou-Moshe, Rabbi Amram Ben-Diwan, Rabbi David Ben Baruch and Rabbi David Halevi Dra (Ben-Ami 1984) were venerated in many areas of the country. Some of the saints were well-known historical figures, while many others seemed to be legendary figures. The historical vacuum that envelops many *tsaddiqim* is congruent with the aforementioned fact that most of them were not known during their lifetime but were recognized as sainted figures after a posthumous apparition, most typically in dreams (Bilu 1990).

Generally speaking, the presence of the saints was a basic given in the social reality of Moroccan Jews, a central idiom for articulating a wide range of experiences (Crapanzano 1975). The main event in the veneration of each saint was the collective pilgrimage to his tomb on the anniversary of his death and the *hillula* there. In the case of the more renowned saints, many thousands of pilgrims from various regions would gather around the tomb for several days, during which they feasted on slaughtered cattle, drank *mahia* (an alcoholic beverage), danced and chanted, prayed, and lit candles. All these activities, combining marked spirituality and high ecstasy with mundane concerns, were conducted in honor of the *tsaddiq*.

In addition to collective pilgrimages, visits to saints' sanctuaries were made on individual basis in times of plight. As intermediaries between God Almighty and the believers, the problems which saints were considered capable of solving included the whole range of human concerns. The presence of the saint was also strongly felt in daily routine, as people would cry out his name and dream about him whenever facing a problem. At home, candles were lit and festive meals (*se'udot*) were organized in his honor; and male newborns were conferred his name. In many cases the relationship with the saint has amounted to a symbiotic association spanning the entire life course of the devotee.

The mass-immigration of Moroccan Jews to Israel during the 1950s and 1960s confronted the newcomers with a major challenge of maintaining cultural traditions rejected by the Israeli mainstream. Saint worship appeared particularly vulnerable in the new country, since it was linked to specific places now remote and inaccessible. Immigration to Israel meant, among other things, a painful dissociation from the *tsaddiqim*, and this loss exacerbated 'the predicament of homecoming' (Deshen and Shokeid 1974).

Clearly, the attractiveness of the saints' shrines, as centrifugal sacred sites located in the Diaspora, could not compete with the centripetal Messianic fervor generated by the establishment of the State of Israel (Cohen 1983). But the religious ascendancy of Zion *vis-à-vis* the peripheral shrines in the Maghreb did not mean that the saints were forgotten. Facing enormous difficulties after immigration, the support of the *tsaddiqim* was a cultural resource that their followers could not easily forgo. Yet the pressures exerted on the newcomers to shed off their ethnocultural heritage and to embrace the reigning ideology of secular-collectivist Zionism, together with the disengagement from the Maghrebi sites, contributed to the general diminution and decentralization of the *hillulot*. They had been reduced to domestic affairs, modestly celebrated at home or in the neighborhood synagogue (Ben-Ami 1981; Deshen 1974; Stillman 1995; Weingrod 1985, 1990).

Once the immediate difficulties of absorption were mitigated, however, Moroccan Jews responded to the separation from the saints by embracing various substitutes for the tombs that had been left behind. Apparently, the newcomers had to become more rooted in the local scene and more confident in their Israeli identity to start reviving their hagiolatric heritage. This dialectical pattern has underlain the resurgence of ethnic sentiments in many immigrant-absorbing countries ((Bennet 1975; Eisenstadt 1980; Holloman 1978). Contrary to a naive melting pot ideology, the massive trend of enculturation to the dominant culture that the newcomers have undergone facilitated rather than inhibited a proud assertion of their ethnic heritage. Given the central role of saint worship in the life-space of many Moroccan Jews before *aliya*, it is no wonder that this tradition in particular emerged as an emblem of ethnic pride. As an 'act of concentrated religious fervour, highly dramatic and fused with emotions' (Deshen 1974:139; see also Shokeid 1979, 1984), yet one which is quite undemanding in terms of the minutiae of religious observance, participation in *hillulot* was tailor-made for many Israelis of North African background, who remained believers at heart despite a growing distancing from strict ritual practice.

In what follows I outline the major hagiolatric avenues that Moroccan Jews have cultivated in Israel.

1. *Appropriating old time native pilgrimage sites.* Most accessible among the hagiolatric alternatives were the tombs of local, Eretz Israeli *tsaddiqim*, mainly from the Biblical and the Talmudic eras. The 'Moroccanization' of these old-time pilgrimage traditions has been particularly noted in the popular, all-Israeli *hillulot* of Rabbi Shimon Bar-Yohai (acronym: RaShBY) in Meiron near Safed and of Rabbi Meir Baal HaNess in Tiberias. For the mystically oriented Jewish communities in Morocco, the fact that Rabbi Shimon was the alleged author of the sacred *Zohar* granted him a particularly elevated stance among the *tsaddiqim*. His *hillula* on the festival of Lag Ba'omer (the 33rd day after Passover) brings together up to 200,000 celebrants—about 5% of the state's entire Jewish population. North African Jews and their descendants form the majority of the pilgrims in Meiron and Tiberias, and they imbue the pilgrimage with a distinctive Maghrebi style (Bilu and Abramovitch 1985).

2. *'Annexing' local, community-based pilgrimage sites.* Maghrebi Jews living in development towns throughout the country have adopted burial sites of native *tsaddiqim* in their vicinity. Although most of the pilgrimages thus created did not exceed local or regional boundaries, the resultant pattern of devotion seemed to reflect the Maghrebi tradition of a community with its own patron-saint. The creation of the *hillula* of Honi HaMe'agel ('the circle-maker'), a legendary Talmudic sage, in the northern town of Hatsor Haglilit, is perhaps the most well-known case among the regional *hillulot*. An old-time tradition has located the tomb of Honi in an ancient burial cave some 15 miles east of Safed, but the site was frequented only sporadically, in times of droughts (the termination of which was considered Honi's specialty).

Honi's finest hour came about after the development town of Hatsor Haglilit had been founded near the cave. His popularity mounted after the wars of 1967 and 1973, in which the town, situated not far from the border with Syria, did not suffer the slightest damage, ostensibly due to the *tsaddiq's* miraculous intercession. Consequently, Israel's Day of Independence was scheduled as the day of Honi's *hillula* (Ben-Ami 1981; Weingrod 1990).

The same Magharebi pattern of a community 'cultivating' its own patron saint has been witnessed in other towns such as Yavneh (Rabban Gamliel) and Carmiel (Rabbi Ishmael Cohen Gadol). In some places, a reappropriation of sites connected with the forebears of the tribes of Israel (Jacob's sons), but associated for years with Muslim saint worship, has been taking place. Examples are the sanctuaries of Dan (near the town of Beit Shemesh), Benjamin (near Kefar Saba), and recently Reuben (near Ashdod and Yavneh).

3. *Renewing past traditions of saint veneration.* As a compensatory rather than restorative mechanism, the 'Moroccanization' of local *hillulot* did not bring back the Jewish saints of Morocco who remained remote and not easily accessible. To cope with this loss, another more direct and daring accommodation had to be called for, namely, the 'symbolic translocation' of saints from Morocco to Israel (Bilu 1990). Here we deal with a seemingly spontaneous initiative of an individual who was inspired by a series of visitational dreams in which a saint urged him or her to erect a site for him at home. The same kind of dream-based initiative was also characteristic of the discovery of sacred sites associated with local saintly traditions (Bilu 1988).

The most well-known Jewish Moroccan *tsaddiq* to be transferred to Israel via dreams is Rabbi David ou-Moshe, with sites in Safed, Ashkelon and Ofakim. Other dream-based shrines of "migrant saints" have been erected in Beit Shean, Kiryat Gat, Yeru'ham and Or-Aqiva.

4. *Reinterring the remains of Jewish Moroccan saints in Israel.* In recent years, the option of digging the tombs of historical saints and bringing their remains to internment in Israel has begun to be realized. The most well-known case involved a distinguished scion from the noble Pinto family who brought the remains of four sainted ancestors of his to a reburial in the development town of Kiryat Mal'achi, where he figures as the chief rabbi.

5. *Creating new contemporary saints.* Rather than a frozen tradition from an archaic past, saint-veneration in Morocco was a very dynamic process with new *tsaddiqim* entering the scene all the time. In Israel, too, new sacred sites have been established around the tombs of contemporary rabbis. This is the hagiolatric avenue to which the shrine of Baba Sali in Netivot belongs. Another contemporary case of sanctification, which preceded that of Baba Sali (and was partly clouded by the latter's swift apotheosis) concerns Rabbi Hayyim Houri, a Tunisian Rabbi who died in 1957 in the southern town of Beer Sheva. The limited accessibility of the tomb, inconveniently located in the midst of a populated municipal cemetery, does not stop the crowds from transforming the cemetery into a scene of joy and ecstasy during the *hillula*. At the same time, in sheer contrast to the case of Baba Sali which we discuss presently, it points to the spontaneous, unplanned nature of Houri's emergence as a sainted figure, 'the saint of Beer Sheva' (see Weingrod 1990).

Against this review, the cult center in Netivot appears as but one manifestation of the burst of Maghrebi ethnocultural creativity which contributed to the shaping of Israel's sacred geography in recent years. Still, the exalted position of Baba Sali in the densely populated pantheon of native and imported sainted figures, and the unique features which have made its gravesite one of the most popular pilgrimage centers in the country, deserve a closer inspection.

The Making of Modern Saints: The Cult of Baba Sali

In terms of family background and lifestyle, Baba Sali lent himself easily to aggrandizement and mythologization. As the grandson of Rabbi Ya'aqov Abu-Hatseira (1807–1880), the first exponent of piety and holiness in the celebrated Abu-Hatseira family (Bar-Moha and Dor 1995),[1] Baba Sali's profound devotion and unswerving asceticism made him the present-day epitome of the family's *zechut*. Given his long life—born in 1890, he was still alive and accessible in the early 1980s—he could provide a focus for hagiolatric sentiments previously directed at Jewish saints whose tombs had been left behind in the Maghreb. Yet the mechanisms underlying his genesis as perhaps the holiest figure in present-day Israel are worth exploring. Here indeed the massive and effective recruitment of the 'modern' means of the media, the state, and large bureaucratic organizations appears to have played a decisive role in facilitating the rapid glorification

When the limelight turns from Baba Sali to his son and successor, Rabbi Baruch Abu-Hatseira (Baba Baruch), the prime mover behind the undertaking in Netivot, the question of sanctification becomes all the more intriguing. Unlike his virtuous father, Baruch has not devoted himself to scholarship and asceticism. Having spent much of his youth in Paris and capitalizing on the charisma attached to the name Abu-Hatseira, he decided to pursue a political career in Israel. He joined the Religious National Party and was elected deputy mayor of the town of Ashkelon.[2] During this period he was party to a much-publicized adulterous affair and, in his capacity as a deputy mayor, was accused of corrupt practices, found guilty, and sentenced to seven years in prison. On being paroled in at the end of 1983, after more than three years in prison, he joined his father for the last three months of Baba Sali's life.

Despite the corrosion of his public image and the existence of other, perhaps more worthy, contenders for the succession,[3] Baba Baruch has managed to take on his father's mantle. He took possession of his father's house in Netivot and arranged for Baba Sali's burial in the local cemetery. In a short time he transformed the informal network of his father's supporters in Israel and abroad into a very efficient organization. Relying on the generous financial aid of these adherents, he has built a magnificent sanctuary to cater to pilgrims around the burial site. Despite his notorious personal record as a former convict and adulterer, his claim for legitimacy garnered a widespread support, and he has been accepted by a wide circle of Moroccan Jews as his father's legitimate successor.

Since establishing himself as the possessor of the family's special blessing, Baba Baruch has embarked on his inextricable bond with his late father. We should now turn first to the image of Baba Sali as molded and propagated by his son. In a plethora of stories, Baba Sali is depicted as an ascetic and withdrawn figure, entirely free of mundane concerns. Reportedly, he seldom left his house, having his synagogue and ritual bath located within its confines. Devoting much of his time to solitary prayer and learning, often accompanied by week-long fasts, he radiated an image of humble self-sufficiency, constriction, introversion and 'invisibility'. While the rabbi's image was clearly shaped by his actual conduct, what is of importance is how his behavior has captured the imagination of the masses to produce a fertile matrix for mythologization.

Superimposed on the rabbi's passive image, in the eyes of the followers, is a representation at once complementary and antithetical to it. In this representation, which Baba Baruch took pains to promulgate and make known, each minor detail of the rabbi's most private behavior is portrayed as partaking of cosmic significance. For example, a popular story details how, just before the break of the Six Day War in 1967, the rabbi took to excessively penitent behavior which was interpreted as conducive to the swift military victory of Israel in that war. In a similar vein, each major occurrence in Baba Sali's life was 'mythologized'—rendered meaningful on an other-worldly level and linked to a historical or metahistorical event. Thus, people interpreted the fact that he changed residence many times, both in Morocco and in Israel, as a deliberate attempt to embody the collective Jewish experience of *galut* (exile). His final settlement in Netivot was accounted for as an emulation of Abraham the Patriarch, who erected his tent in nearby Gerar more than three millennia ago. Likewise, in oral accounts and written biographies, he is often straightforwardly compared with the greatest luminaries in Jewish history, from Moses and Rabbi Shimon Bar-Yohai to his namesake, the BESHT (acronym for Rabbi Israel Baal Shem Tov, the 18th founder of the Hasidic Movement). This transcendence of historical bounds was facilitated by the fact that Baba Sali is also said to have been a practicing kabbalist, deeply immersed in Jewish mysticism.

In order to bask in the glory of his mythologized father and enjoy the lineage charisma, Baruch had to reconcile his moral shortcomings with the familial aura of holiness. This he has managed to do by constructing an autobiographical narrative which creatively dwells on, rather than disregards, the dark aspects of his former life. Baruch's self-narrative seeks to convey three related messages. First, in emphasizing that he had lived in prison with murderers, rapists and drug addicts, he suggests that he is well-suited to deal with the human misery of those seeking his help. Second, in meticulously detailing his tribulations in prison, he claims that he had paid in full for his misconduct. And third, in pointing to his subsequent spiritual transformation, he asserts that his religious faith and moral commitment have been strengthened rather than weakened in prison. Furthermore, he presents the dire consequences of his short-lived political career as a heavenly trial, part of a mystical plan to test, purify and transform him into the worthy heir of his sainted father. In highlighting the role of prison as a penitentiary, he seeks to make a virtue out of his failings.

Taking advantage of the fact that he was alone with his father during Baba Sali's last hours, Baruch presents this critical time as the matrix for his self-transformation and symbolic rebirth. In fact, he argues that after his father's death, Baba Sali's soul found residence in his own body. Implicitly relying on both the Jewish mystical idiom of the transmigration of souls (see Scholem 1969) and the Maghrebi notion of inherited blessedness, he maintains that just before the departure of his soul, his father kissed him on his lips and thus, in resonance with the Maghrebi notion of holy grace as concrete and transferable (Crapanzano 1973; Eickelman 1976), endowed him with his spiritual gifts. Emphasizing the essential similarity and continuity between father and son has been one of Baruch's central rhetorical strategies. Since his position is clearly dependent on this perceived similarity, Baruch has been adamant to convey the notion that his every move is inspired and closely monitored by his father, mainly through visitational dreams. Moreover, he also hastened to wear his father's mantle and shoes, and to replicate his father's beard. The physical similarity, together with Baruch's adoption of the title 'Baba', has had a strong impact on many common believers, further reinforcing the idea that Baba Sali's soul now inhabits his son.

This is the background for the emergence of the thriving shrine in Netivot in terms of the *dramatis personae* involved. However, to account for the swiftness and scope of the sanctification of father and son, we have to shift our analytic lens from Baba Sali and Baba Baruch themselves to the means by which their stories have been passed on. We pass, in other words, from 'charisma' to its 'production'.

The conscious planning evident in the sanctification of Baba Sali and the development of his site in Netivot (Weingrod 1990:20), highlights the extent to which charismatic qualities can be actively promoted and propagated (Shils 1975:128). Indeed, the effective system for selling the saint that Baba Baruch set into motion is an ample manifestation of the extent to which charisma can be 'manufactured' (Glassman 1975) or 'synthesized' (Ling 1987).

Baba Baruch's organizational efforts capitalized on the proximity between his residence (formerly his father's) and the Baba Sali burial site in Netivot which enabled him to exert a close control over the shrine and to monopolize the intentional use of his father's 'assets'. The space between the house and the tomb, about half a kilometer long, was originally empty, so that each site could be extended toward the other. On the one side, the tomb was enclosed in a spacious white-washed sanctuary and an opulently decorated synagogue was erected next to it. This impressive edifice, visible from a distance (see Weingrod 1993), is now part of a larger, walled enclosure that includes a parking lot, a picnic area, a restaurant, vendors' booths and other facilities. On the other side, the father's (now his) residence was enlarged and the foundations for Kiryat Baba Sali, a big religious campus, were laid. Today the campus includes several buildings housing the headquarters of Baba Baruch's organization, a *yeshiva* (religious academy), a *Talmud Torah* (religious school), and a kindergarten. These were built in a distinctively Moorish style, sharply at odds with the plebeian neighborhood surrounding them.

In order to implement his plans, Baba Baruch has founded Amotat Baba Sali, a nonprofit, tax-exempt organization composed of public figures, rabbis, lawyers and accountants. The board of directors meets irregularly in the rabbi's house to discuss projects designed to 'cultivate and deepen Baba Sali's heritage', as one brochure puts it, but it usually just rubber-stamps Baruch's plans. Baruch also controls a small staff of executives, aides and secretaries who administer the institutions bearing Baba Sali's name. Complete with computers, fax machines and cordless telephones, the offices of this staff are marked by an atmosphere close to that of a quietly run, efficient business firm than to a center of religious zealots.

Clearly, the unparalleled sanctification of Baba Sali owes at least some of its success to the peculiar 'selling' of this saint. Recall how constricted, home-bound, and 'invisible' Baba Sali's actual life was. To achieve the power of a national myth, a private story had to go public; the invisible had to be placed under the spotlights, within the public eye. Thus, both the hidden, ineffable details of Baba Sali's life and the elaborate projects of Baba Baruch had to be highlighted and publicized. This publicity has gone far beyond anything that can be achieved by word of mouth, as Baruch has clearly taken advantage of the opportunities provided by the modern printing technology, the media and the Israeli state apparatus. A rich variety of literary products—periodicals, monographs and book series, using the latest types of graphic layout, printing and binding—recount the miraculous deeds and life story of the late patriarch. Some texts are specifically written for children, while others, translated into French, are designed for the Jewish Moroccan diaspora abroad. In addition, as the annual festival approaches, the country is subjected to a media blitz: special notices are published in major newspapers, and the day's program is posted on billboards all over Israel. By granting interviews to newspapers and journals and securing regular radio and television coverage, Baba Baruch achieves name recognition. Every year the big dailies carry color spreads of the *hillula*, complete with pictures of Baba Baruch, political dignitaries,[4] and 'typical' believers caught up in the ecstasy of the festival.

Like the media, the numerous objects—produced in modern workshops and factories throughout the country—that carry Baba Sali's image or that of his shrine also help to manufacture charisma. A partial list of these products, marketed on the site itself and around the country, include *mezuzot*,[5] prayer books, clocks, candles, cups, plates, pictures, postcards, photographs, key chains, tape cassettes with songs praising the saint, and videotapes of the *hillula*. While Baruch does not control the entire production and marketing of the sacred objects, he virtually monopolizes sales around the shrine, and he encourages the introduction of new products every year. Thus, the last few years have seen the introduction of holograms of Baba Sali's face, small carpets bearing his image, and miniature models of his sanctuary. The proliferation of the Baba Sali sacred 'industry' clearly reflects a creative and entrepreneurial spirit underlying the 'selling' of the saint. These mementos, souvenirs, postcards and photographs procured at Netivot help to propagate the saint's charisma in two ways: they are at one and the same time a means of 'bringing' the saint home, and icons of contemporary Jewish Maghrebi version of nostalgia (Stewart 1988).

Thus far, Baba Baruch's success in sanctifying his father and aggrandizing his burial site in Netivot has been mainly attributed to his skill in manipulating the Israeli media, commerce, industry and politicians to manufacture charisma. In this process of the 'selling of the saint' he managed to extend his own basis of legitimacy by propagating and highlighting his image as a physical and spiritual replica of his father. It should be noted, however, that behind the elaborate facade of similarity and identity lie striking differences, most obvious in the divergent lifestyles of father and son. These incompatible careers radiate distinct images of piety and virtuousness and emanate from altogether different sociocultural contexts. Unlike the purely spiritual image of Baba Sali, a man reportedly characterized by a constriction, asceticism and repugnance for mundane concerns, Baba Baruch radiates expansion, dominance and activity. Extroverted and energetic, his image is that of a strong-willed entrepreneur always seeking to expand his territory. Accompanied by a large entourage and ensconced in a spacious American-made gas guzzler, he travels up and down the country, to participate in festive meals, collect contributions and visit the religious institutions bearing Baba Sali's name he has established in various towns. Every three or four months he goes abroad to the big Jewish-Moroccan diaspora communities, mainly in France, but also in the US and Canada, which provide most of the support for his undertakings. Ambitious, opinionated and over-bearing, Baruch is deeply engaged with matters extending the religious realm, including municipal and national politics. Unlike his passive, humble father, Baruch is mobile, visible and involved. Even though he dresses like his father, he does not look like an ascetic. Full-bodied and unabashedly fond of alcohol, good food and imported cigarettes, he appears self-indulgent and even hedonistic—despite his spiritual reawakening.

Baruch's expansive style reflects a problem of which his father, the personification of piety and virtuousness, was altogether exempted. Unlike Baba Sali, Baruch has had to impress people by employing 'conspicuous creations, devices for mobilizing, attracting, focusing and ordering attention' (MacAloon 1987:262). Thus, the *hillula* and the invited guests, the American-made car and the entourage, the politicking and the public speeches about his father may all be seen as props, scenery and dramatic action in Baruch's play to appear powerful. In Glassman's (1975:618) terms, they are all part of 'stage-managing the charismatic process'.

Yet, Baba Baruch's entrepreneurial and expansive style is not merely a defensive maneuver intended to compensate for an initially inferior position in the pursuit of legitimation. Baba Sali's image as a sainted figure germinated in the Jewish society of southern Morocco and was sustained in Israel, frozen in time, as an exemplar of a lost and idealized past. In contrast, Baba Baruch, whose road to sacredness was paved in contemporary Israel, is a 'saint for our time'. As a 'child' of the Israeli political system, he seems to patently espouse and expertly employ the 'rules of the games'—the values, norms and symbols—that govern public life in Israel. Baruch's involvement with politics is particularly evident in Baba Sali's *hillula*. As against the spontaneous and apolitical spirit that dominates most of the other *hillulot* (cf. Weingrod 1990), the festival for Baba Sali includes a very tightly scheduled public event, replete with public addresses given by the most important figures in Israel. Baba Baruch uses the occasion to show politicians (from the two leading parties) his support and potential power, as well as to signify to his followers his centrality in the country's political life.

Unlike his father, then, Baba Baruch may be seen as representing something quintessentially Israeli. Beyond his general willingness to participate in state-regulated politics, he espouses specific models for actions derived from the Zionist ethos. Thus, he focuses his attention on the Jewish Moroccan diaspora as a potential source of financial support. In doing so he follows a path well-trodden by many political figures in Israel who look to the diaspora community as a source of support for projects promoting actualization of the Zionist dream (Kimmerling 1989:275). Like other leaders, Baruch sees that community as a 'mobilized diaspora' (Armstrong 1976) and an economic frontier, capitalizing on the Sephardi diaspora's growing sense of responsibility for their Sephardi brethren in Israel.

In addition, like many other public figures in Israel, Baruch constantly seeks to make his mark on the country's landscape, changing the actual physical topography of Netivot (and other places) by erecting and developing various institutions bearing his father's name. He uses contributions from abroad in accord with the Zionist ethos of nation-building, and this makes perfect sense to a following rooted in the reality of present-day Israel. Narratives about settlement can be seen as key scenarios (Ortner 1973) in Israeli collective life: they both formulate appropriate goals and suggest effective action for achieving them (see Katriel and Shenhar 1990). In this respect, Baba Baruch's excessive efforts to leave his mark on the land, although inspired by a traditional idiom, resonate with those of the early Zionists (Cohen 1977), *Gush Emunim*[6] (Aran 1991), and Jerusalem's ex-mayor, Teddy Kollek. All of them emphasized 'making' Israel by transforming the country's landscape: through building, constructing, assembling, expanding and creating 'facts'.

In conclusion, Baba Baruch's project in Netivot demonstrates how charisma can be 'manu-factured', how the saints can be 'sold', using modern means in order to achieve premeditated goals and in line with expectations in public life in contemporary Israel. These means include the media, which broadcast claims to charisma, the industry, which creates material objects for the sedimenta-tion of charisma, and the political machinery, which may render contested charisma legitimate by linking it to the society's symbolic centers and foci of power.

Netivot as a Holy Town

Thus far, the growth of Baba Sali to the level of a 'national saint' and the transformation of his grave site into a major pilgrimage center were discussed in terms of the Jewish Maghrebi folk-traditions of saint veneration and the personal characterizations and activities of the Abu-Hatseiras of Netivot. Using a dramaturgical imagery, the cultural idiom of saint worship may be likened to a storyline or a basic narrative structure which was then emplotted and enacted as a particular play, with Baba Sali and Baba Baruch as the *dramatis personae* or main actors. Having outlined the script and the performance, it is time now to turn the limelight to the third constituent theme in our account—the stage or arena in which the apotheosis of Baba Sali has been taking place. The fact that Baba Sali's sanctuary is situated in Netivot bears geopolitical implications pertinent to the contextualization of the renaissance of Maghrebi hagiolatry in contemporary Israeli society.

Founded in the mid-1950s, Netivot was one of a group of 'development towns' (*ayarot piuah*), hastily built to accommodate the massive flow of immigrants that poured into the country after the 1948 War of Independence. Moroccan Jews became particularly associated with the new 'planted' communities, since the peak of the population dispersion policy initiated by the Israeli government in the early 1950s coincided with the first massive waves of *aliya* (Immigration) from the Maghreb. As a result of this policy, pursued in response to pressing security, social-economic and demographic demands, many Moroccan Jews found themselves relegated to the periphery of Israel, where they were assigned pioneering roles which veteran Israelis were unwilling to assume (Inbar and Adler 1977). As the largest ethnic group placed in development towns, their partaking of the Zionist dream was marred by the many ills of these disadvantaged communities. These ills included limited occupational opportunities due to an underdeveloped infrastructure and reliance on one type of industry based on manual, low-paying jobs, an almost total dependence on government services, a poor educational system, and a high rate of population turnover in which the more resourceful, upwardly mobile inhabitants left the towns while the poor and the less able tended to stay (Aronoff 1973; Matras 1973; Semyonov 1981; Spilerman and Habib 1976).

Because of these chronic problems, developmental towns were depicted derogatorily as 'residual communities' or 'sinks' for the less resourceful immigrants (Cohen 1970; Kramer 1973; Spilerman and Habib 1976), and were viewed by mainstream Israelis with a mixture of condescension, mild disdain and paternalistic concern (Goldberg 1984:7). Against this stigmatic image, the optimistic goal-directedness and grand vision of early statist Zionism, inscribed in the appellations of such development towns as Netivot ('Pathways'), Ofakim ('Horizons'), and Sederot ('Boulevards') may appear sarcastically vain.

Built as a regional and commercial center for a cluster of *moshavim* (semi-cooperative agri-cultural settlements) east of the Gaza Strip, Netivot remained for many years one of the most back-ward and undeveloped 'development towns' in the country. The main factors underlying the town's socioeconomic ills were its remoteness from Israel's urban and industrial centers and the 'impover-ished assets' (Inbar and Adler 1977) of its original inhabitants, reflected in a paucity of professional skills, little formal education, and cultural norms favoring large families. These factors played a disruptive role in the growth of other development towns as well, but in Netivot they were particularly evident as the original population, 95% of which was from North Africa, was overwhelmingly traditional. For many years the local industry amounted to one single plant—an economically precarious carpet factory—and the town was characterized by a very high rate of population turnover and unemployment.

Netivot is still struggling with many of the problems that characterized its formative period, though in recent years it has fared better than all other developm
ent towns in the northern Negev. The population has grown to c. 18,200, and the recent influx of 3,000 newcomers from the ex-Soviet Union has significantly increased the professional manpower in town. The local industry has been expanded and diversified, the unemployment rate was reduced to 7.5%, and the potential of the town as a commercial center for its rural hinterland has begun to be more fully realized. Along with these changes, Netivot remained more religious than any other development town in Israel. 65% of the population are observant and 25% are ultra-orthodox. The latter include a large group of Ashkenazim organized around one of a several religious academies which the town now hosts. The special religious ambiance of Netivot brings us back to its role as a cult center for Baba Sali.

In 1952 Baba Sali made a first attempt to settle in Israel. As might be expected, he selected Jerusalem as his abode, but after a few months he decided to go back to Morocco, disappointed at the widespread secularization he had met in the Holy City. Baba Sali came back to stay 11 years later, when he was already 73-year-old. This time he settled in Yavneh, a development town 30 km south of Tel Aviv, where he had some relatives. In 1968 he moved further south to Ashkelon, where his son, Baruch served as the deputy mayor. In 1970 he completed his southward peregrination by settling in Netivot, where he spent the last 14 years of his life. Without going into the mystical accounts for Baba Sali's itinerary in Israel suggested by his followers, it is clear that the locomotion from Jerusalem through Yavneh and Ashkelon to Netivot indicates a centrifugal orientation, from Judaism's *axis mundi* to the epitome of peripherality. Given the systematic nature of this locomotion—each stop was further removed from the Holy City—it is hard to assume that it was taken unselfconsciously.

Baba Sali's ever-growing attraction to the southern periphery has been informed by his Moroccan roots. For many generations the Abu-Hatseiras had lived in the desert towns of the Tafilalt region, Rissani and Erfoud, located in the Ziz valley at the margin of the Sahara.[7] This inland, geographically peripheral location strengthened the image of the Abu-Hatseiras as pertaining to the indigenous and most traditional layers of Moroccan Jewry. Rabbi Ya'aqov, the cherished ancestor of the contemporary Abu-Hatseiras, was known in his lifetime as the avatar of conservatism (Manor 1982). Ascetic and moralist, he vehemently opposed any attempt to change the traditional way of life, from the religious novelties of the Jews expelled from the Iberian peninsula, the dominant force in Moroccan Jewry since the sixteenth century, to the modern European influence that began to be felt in the interior of the country toward the end of his lifetime. Is it not possible that in choosing the remote desert town of Netivot, Baba Sali followed and relived the old family ethos which he had imbibed in his youth in Tafilalt? If indeed he sought to emulate his venerated grandfather, then the town's 'backwardness' and traditional character were for him a virtue reminding him of the spiritual ambiance of strict observance and unyielding religious faith typical of his native town in Morocco.

Baba Sali's settlement in Netivot further strengthened the religious character of the town. This process was expedited after his death, with the emergence of his sanctuary as a popular pilgrimage center. A few modest shrines encasing the grave sites of recently deceased local rabbis have recently emerged in the Netivot cemetery. Though overshadowed by Baba Sali's adjacent majestic sanctuary, it seems safe to assume that their builders have sought to capitalize on the latter's success by basking in his glory. Moving from the dead to the living, Netivot has recently witnessed the rise of three charismatic rabbis who attract a wide following in their capacity as mystics and healers. Needless to say, Baba Baruch considers them usurpers and invests much effort in order to discredit them and dismantle their local bases. Ironically, they have been able to survive his assault up to now and to make themselves quite renowned partially due to the aura of sanctity and spirituality bestowed on Netivot by Baba Sali. It should be noted that the 'sanctification' of Netivot has not entailed a significant change in the town's economic situation. Most of the 'holy industry' related to Baba Sali is spread outside Netivot, and the major beneficiary of the money spent by visitors to the site is the organization erected by Baba Baruch to cultivate his father's heritage.

While the emergence of Netivot as a popular cult center is unparalleled in contemporary Israel, I noted earlier that other development towns have also become arenas for hagiolatric activities (see Ben-Ari and Bilu 1987; Bilu 1990). Many of the socioeconomic and political ills that characterized these towns in the 1950s and 1960s still haunted them in the 1990s. At the same time, the inhabitants who did stay in the towns, whether voluntarily or reluctantly, despite the social and economic difficulties, have slowly developed a genuine attachment to the locality. The growth of these 'natural' sentiments of belongingness and rootedness in one's own community finds expression in and is further enhanced by the presence of the saints in these towns. This presence grants metahistorical depth to places that were without a recognized and validated past, thus making them a more integral part of Israel. The *tsaddiq* accords the town an aura of sanctity, and the residents' sense of attachment is placed within a larger meaning-giving system, based on the idioms encoded in their Maghrebi traditions which they are now ready to proudly assert. Whether the 'Benares of Israel' or not, Netivot has clearly been the most impressive case in this process. Evaluating the changes in the town following the death and rapid sanctification of Baba Sali, one local inhabitant said with a modicum of pride: 'A town that was "outside" of Israel's map, is now not only "on" the map, thanks to Baba Sali it is also "above" it.'

Between Netivot and Gilat

In order to render the ethnographic observations from Netivot germane to archaeological investigations in a site more than 6,000 years old, these observations must be generalized and abstracted into the 'deep structure' of the cult complex. In what follows, I discuss some systematic processes and social patterns that constitute this structure in a comparative vein. But before that, I would like to dwell on one peculiar aspect of the regional significance of the shrines.

As noted in the introduction, it would be far-fetched to take Netivot's physical proximity to Gilat as a clue for an unbroken line of sacred heritage in this part of the Negev. Yet, one cannot ignore the attempts made by Baba Sali's followers to furnish Netivot with a mythic past by associating him with Abraham the Patriarch. Unlike the other mystical bonds with Jewish luminaries attributed to Baba Sali, this linkage is explicitly place-bound given Abraham's wanderings in the northern Negev and his settlement in the town of Gerar (Genesis 20:1). Tel Abu Hureira, identified as the site of biblical Gerar, is situated on Wadi Sharia (Nahal Gerar) near Netivot. This linkage reverberates with the strong national propensity to recover biblical and other ancient Jewish roots in the land of Israel in order to assert and legitimate Zionist territorial claims (Zerubavel 1995). The attempt to grant the peripheral town of Netivot a metahistorical depth by associating it with Abraham's Gerar draws us nearer to Chalcolithic Gilat. It should be noted, however, that no less than two millennia separate the cult center at Gilat and Abraham's Gerar.

Another significant point in the sacred geography of the region is the tomb of a Muslim sainted figure, Sheik Abu Hureira, whose name was conferred on the mound of ancient Gerar. The Bedouin tribes that lived in the area before 1948 depicted Abu Hureira, allegedly a friend of the Prophet, as one of their ancestors (Aref el Aref 1936). Hence, the 6,000-year interval which separates the shrines of Gilat and Netivot is dotted with two other places suffused with holiness, dating back to 2000 BCE and the seventh century CE. Suggestive as this cross-religious addition may be, it still does not amount to a narratively coherent 'sacred heritage' peculiar to the region.

Forsaking unsubstantiated transmillennial traditions of regional sacredness for processes and patterns of cultic activities, a possible point of departure is the characterization of both Gilat and Netivot as centers of regional cults (Werbner 1977, 1989). As middle range, personal security cults, regional cults are more far-reaching than any parochial religion of the little community, yet less inclusive in belief and membership than today's universal world religions. The waxing and waning of cults are based on a dynamic tension between inclusiveness and exclusiveness. Consequently questions regarding the permeability or effaceability of the boundaries between participants and strangers appear pertinent to both cults. The developmental pattern of the cult of Baba Sali has clearly been a growing boundary transcendence as the venerated *tsaddiq*, though emanating from a demarcated Jewish Maghrebi hagiolatric tradition, has gradually become the national saint of Israel. While Israelis of Moroccan extraction are still overrepresented among his followers, the latter also include many other adherents from a variety of Mizrahi (Sephardic) and, to a lesser degree, Ashkenazi backgrounds. These adherents are coming to the shrine from all over the country. Thus, cult participation gradually appears more inclusive in terms of ethnic and regional background.

The ethnocultural composition of the catchment population of the Gilat cult is less transparent. But, based on the material remains, it is possible to show that, although Palestine in the Chalcolithic period was a patchwork of different cultural groups, some cult objects (and, by implication, cult practices) transcended geographical and cultural boundaries. A notable example is provided by the violin-shaped stone figurines which were in use throughout the southern Levant, from Lebanon to the Sinai. In Gilat we may have evidence for the mass-production of these objects (see Commenge *et al.*, in this volume). Thus, in both cases, a process of greater inclusiveness is noted whereby the regional cult serves to integrate different geographic and cultural groups.

The cultic activities observed in the Baba Sali sanctuary may serve as clues for better linking the material remains excavated at Gilat to ritual patterns of pilgrimage and worship. The magnificent sacred complex built in Netivot has its Chalcolithic parallel in a special ritual center, architecturally well-demarcated, which includes many attention-focusing devices and special ritual facilities (see Levy *et al.* in Chapter 5 of this volume). These facilities, which included altars, benches, platforms, standing stones and basins of water, bring to mind the rich ritual paraphernalia in Netivot, from the gigantic candle-lighting stove near the tomb to the sacred artifacts in the adjacent synagogue and the selling booths. Worship at Gilat probably involved both conspicuous public display and hidden rites. A similar division is evident in Netivot, where the sanctuary is open to the public while the nearby house of the *tsaddiq* is less accessible, containing a synagogue and a ritual bath originally designed for the personal use of Baba Sali and now serving Baba Baruch and his family.

The iconic representations of omnipotent powers found in Gilat (like the aforementioned violin-shaped figurines) may be compared with the pictures of the saints and the other artifacts manufactured by the 'sacred industry' of Baba Sali. Under the uneasy monotheistic aegis of rabbinical Judaism, the ritual meaning of the wide array of objects on which the image of the saint or his shrine are inscribed is vague and subdued. And yet, many of the adherents would charge them with a spiritual or even magical significance. The eye-dazzling variety of these objects adds to the architectural grandeur of the sanctuary in amplifying and channeling the religious sentiments of the pilgrims. In addition, festive behaviors like dancing, chanting and alcohol consumption, which are part and parcel of the celebration at the site, no doubt contribute to the ecstatic and spiritual mood which shape the pilgrimage experience. The same combination of architectural wealth, conspicuous and redundant display of ritual objects, and devices for inducing and facilitating religious experience is assumed to have existed in Gilat.

Lastly, the ethnographic material from Netivot has emphasized the role of Baba Baruch as the prime mover behind the emergence of Baba Sali's sanctuary as a national pilgrimage center. I sought to show how charisma can be manufactured and how saints can be 'sold' using modern means which entail the media, the industry and the political apparatus. Through the astute employment of these means, Baba Baruch emerged as a classical case of 'Big Man' dominating an impressive political and economic power base. In Gilat, we have no direct access to the 'politics of the cult', and the cult specialists underlying the emergence of the sanctuary remain obscure to us. But, against the case of the Abu-Hatseiras of Netivot, the wealth and impressive presence of attention-focusing devices found in Gilat in the architecture and in movable facilities makes one wander who were the archaic 'Big Men' in the guise of priests or other ritual specialists who had been using the cult as an efficacious cover for satisfying their political and economic ambitions.

Notes

1. In the hagiographic literature on the Abu-Hatseira family, Rabbi Shmuel Elbaz is presented as the founder of the dynasty, but no historical markers exist to suport this claim. The authenticiy of the eight rabbinical figures presented as the successive link between Rabbi Shmuel and Rabbi Ya'aqov has not been verified either.
2. A southern town on the Mediterranean, 10 km north of the Gaza Strip and 30 km north-west of Netivot. Baba Sali had lived in Ashkelon before moving to Netivot.
3. Among other family members, Rabbi Elazar Abu-Hatseira, the son of Baba Sali's elder son (who died before his father), poses the major challenge for Baba Baruch. Having failed to stake a claim in Netivot, he established himself a stronghold in the southern town of Beer Sheva where he is frequented by many devotees from Israel and abroad (Bar-Moha and Dor 1995).
4. A special landing space near the site was prepared for the prime minister's helicopter. Prime Minister Shamir participated in the 1988 *hillulah* which I observed.
5. *Mezzuza* (singular), a small case attached to the doorpost in which a piece of parchment bearing a text from Deutronomy is rolled.
6. Hebrew: 'The Block of the Faithful'. A militant national-religious movement to which the hard-core settlers in the occupied territories belong. The first tenet of their political doctrine is the sacredness of the biblical land and a firm opposition to any notion of territorial compromise.
7. Note that the Alouite dynasty which has reigned in Morocco since the seventeenth century originated in the Tafilalt region. Is it a mere coincidence that the holiest families of the Jews and the Muslims in Morocco are coming from the same area?

References

Aref el Aref (1936) *The Bedouin Tribes of the Beer-Sheva Region*. Tel-Aviv: Bustantai (Hebrew).
Aran, G. (1991) Jewish Zionist fundamentalism: the bloc of the faithful in Israel. In *Fundamentalism Observed*, edited by M. Marty and R. Appleby. Chicago: University of Chicago Press, pp. 265–344.
Armstrong, J.A. (1976) Mobilized and proletarian diasporas. *American Political Science Review* 70:393–403.
Aronoff, M.J. (1973) Development towns in Israel. In *Israel: Social Structure and Change*, edited by M. Curtis and M.S. Chertoff. New Brunswick, NJ: Transaction, pp. 27–46.
Bar-Moha, J. and D. Dor (1995) *Saints LTD: The Abu Hatsera Family, Legend and Reality*. Jerusalem: Ma'ariv (Hebrew).
Ben-Ami, I. (1981) The folk veneration of saint among Moroccan Jews: tradition, continuity, and change. The Case of the Holy Man, Rabbi David u-Moshe. In *Studies in Judaism and Islam*, edited by S. Morag *et al*. Jerusalem: Magnes (Hebrew), pp. 283–345.
— (1984) *The Folk Veneration of Saints Among the Jews in Morocco*. Jerusalem: Magnes (Hebrew).

Ben-Ari, E., and Y. Bilu (1987) Saints' sanctuaries in Israeli development towns: on a mechanism of urban transformation. *Urban Anthropology* 16:243–72.

Bennet, J.W. (1975) Introduction. In *The New Ethnicity: Perspectives from Ethnology*, edited by J.W. Bennet. St. Paul: West Publishing, pp. 3–10.

Bilu, Y. (1988) The inner limits of communitas: a covert dimension of pilgrimage experience. *Ethos* 16:302–305.

— (1990) Jewish Moroccan 'saints impresarios' in Israel: a stage-developmental perspective. *Psychoanalytic Study of Society* 15:247–69.

Bilu, Y. and E. Ben-Ari (1992) The making of modern saints: manufactured charisma and the Abu-Hatseiras of Israel. *American Ethnologist* 19:29–44.

Bilu, Y., and E. Ben-Ari (1996) A saint at the crossroads of meaning: Israel, modernity, and the cult of Baba-Sali. In *Myth and Memory*, edited by D. Ohana and R. Wistrich. Jerusalem: Van Leer and Hakibbutz Hameuchad (Hebrew), pp. 290–303.

Bilu, Y., and H. Abramovitch (1985) In search of the *Saddiq*: visitational dreams among Moroccan Jews in Israel. *Psychiatry* 48:83–92.

Cohen, E. (1977) The city in Zionist ideology. *Jerusalem Quarterly* 4:126–44.

— (1983) Ethnicity and legitimation and legitimation in contemporary Israel. *Jerusalem Quarterly* 28:111–24.

Crapanzano, V. (1973) *The Hamadsha: A Study in Moroccan Ethnopsychiatry*. Berkeley: University of California Press.

— (1975) Saints, Jnun and Dreams: an essay in Moroccan ethnopsychology. *Psychiatry* 38:145–59.

Deshen, S. (1974) Political ethnicity and cultural ethnicity in Israel during the 1960s. In *Urban Ethnicity*, edited by A. Cohen. London: Tavistock, pp. 281–309.

Deshen, S., and M. Shokeid (1974) *The Predicament of Homecoming*. Ithaca, NY: Cornell University Press.

Eickelman, D. (1976) *Moroccan Islam*. Austin: University of Texas Press.

Eisenstadt, S.N. (1980) Introduction: Some Reflections on the Study of Ethnicity. In *Migration, Ethnicity and Community*, edited by E. Krausz. New Brunswick, pp. 1–4.

Eliade, M. (1959) *The Sacred and the Profane*. New York: Harcourt.

Geertz, C. (1968) *Islam Observed: Religious Development in Morocco and Indonesia*. New Haven: Yale University Press.

Gellner, E. (1969) *Saints of the Atlas*. Chicago: University of Chicago Press.

Glassman, R. (1975) Legitimacy and manufactured charisma. *Social Research* 42:615–36.

Goldberg, H.E (1983) The Mellahs of southern Morocco: report of a survey. *The Maghreb Review* 8 (3-4) 61–69.

— (1984) *Greentown's Youth: Disadvantaged Youth in a Development Town in Israel*. Assen: Van Gorcum.

— (1990) The *Zohar* in southern Morocco: a study in the ethnography of texts. *History of Religions* 29 (3): 233–58.

Holloman, R.E. (1978) The study of ethnicity: an overview. In *Perspectives on Ethnicity*, edited by R.E. Holloman and S.A. Artinov. The Hagues: Mouton Publishers, pp. 3–9.

Inbar, M., and C. Adler (1977) *Ethnic Integration in Israel*. New Brunswick, NJ: Transaction.

Katriel, T., and Aliza S. (1990) Tower and stockade: dialogic narration in Israeli settlement ethos. *Quarterly Journal of Speech* 76:359–80.

Kimmerling, B. (1989) Boundaries and frontiers in the Israeli control system: analytical conclusions. In *The Israeli State and Society: Boundaries and Frontiers*, edited by B. Kimmerling. Albany: State University of New York, pp. 265–84.

Liebman, C.S., and E. Don-Yehia (1983) *Civil Religion in Israel*. Berkeley: University of California Press.

Ling, R. (1987) The production of synthetic charisma. *Journal of Political and Military Sociology* 15:157–70.

MacAloon, J.J. (1987) Sociation and sociability in political celebration. In *Celebration*, edited by V. Turner. Washington DC: Smithsonian Institution Press, pp. 252–72.

Manor, D. (1982) *Kabbala and Ethics in Morocco*. Jerusalem: Ben-Zvi Institute (Hebrew).

Matras, I. (1973) Israel's new frontier: the urban periphery. In *Israel: Social Structure and Change*, edited by M. Curtis and M.S. Chertoff. New Brunswick, NJ: Transaction, pp. 3–14.

Nora, P. (1989) Between memory and history: les lieux de mémoire. *Representations* 26:7–25.

Ortner, S.B. (1973) On key symbols. *American Anthropologist* 75:1338–45.

Rabinow, P. (1975) *Symbolic Domination*. Chicago: University of Chicago Press.

Scholem, G. (1965) *Major Trends in Jewish Mysticism*. New York: Schocken.

— (1969) *On the Kabbalah and Its Symbolism*. New York: Schocken

Semyonov, M. (1981) Effects of community on status attainment. *Sociological Quarterly* 22:359–72.

Shils, E. (1975) *Center and Periphery: Essays in Macrosociology*. Chicago: University of Chicago Press.

Shokeid, M. (1979) The decline of personal endowment of Atlas Mountains religious leaders in Israel. *Anthropological Quarterly* 52:186–97.

— (1984) Cultural ethnicity in Israel: the case of Middle Eastern Jews' religiosity. *AJS Review* 9:247–71.

Stewart, K. (1988) Nostalgia: a polemic. *Cultural Anthropology* 3:227–41.

Stillman, N.A. (1982) Saddiq and Marabout in Morocco. In *Sephardi and Oriental Jewish Studies*, edited by I. Ben-Ami. Jerusalem: Magnes, pp. 489–500.

— (1995) *Sephardi Religious Responses to Modernity*. Harwood Academic Publishers.

Storper-Perez, D., and H. Goldberg (1994) The Kotel: toward an ethnographic portrait. *Religion* 24:309–32.

Spilerman, S., and J. Habib (1976) Development towns in Israel: the role of community in creating ethnic disparities in labor force characteristics. *American Journal of Sociology* 81:781–812.

Weber, M. (1968) *Economy and Society*. New York: Free Press.

Weingrod., A. (1985) The current state of ethnicity: a postscript. In *Israeli Ethnicity*, edited by A. Weingrod. New York: Gordon and Breach, pp. 341–52.

— (1990) *The Saint of Beersheba*. Albany: State University of New York Press.

— (1993) Changing Israeli landscapes: buildings and the uses of the past. *Cultural Anthropology* 6:370–87.

Werbner, R. P. (1977) *Regional Cults*. London: Academic Press.

— (1989) *Ritual Passage, Sacred Journey*. Washington D.C.: Smithsonian Institution Press.

Westermarck E. (1926) *Ritual and Belief in Morocco*. London: Macmillan.

Zerubavel, Y. (1995) *Recovered Roots: Collective Memory and the Making of Israeli National Tradition*. Chicago: University of Chicago Press.

II.
ARCHAEOLOGICAL FOUNDATIONS

5 The Sanctuary Sequence: Excavations at Gilat: 1975–77, 1989, 1990–92

Thomas E. Levy, David Alon[†], Yorke M. Rowan, and Morag Kersel

1. Introduction

The Gilat site is located on the eastern bank of the Nahal Patish (Israel Grid Coordinates 1153/ 0818), approximately 1 km east of the Ofakim development town in Israel's semi-arid northern Negev desert (Fig. 5.1; Plate 5.2). The site sits along the border between two distinct environmental zones that have bearing on the developmental history of the site. These ecological zones include the Negev coastal plain and the northern Negev inland foothill zone (see Chapter 1 for description). The size of Gilat is approximately 12 ha. The site is composed of two geomorphological segments: the main mound which incorporates c. 2.7 ha and the plain where cultural debris was found extending over an area of c. 9.3 ha (Fig. 5.1; Plate 5.2). Over the past 50 years the site has been damaged by continuous plowing resulting in the destruction of most of the archaeological remains from the last phase (Stratum I) of occupation at the site. Plowing activities brought numerous Chalcolithic artifacts to the surface, including a wide range of unusual objects such as stone pallets, massebot (Hebrew = standing stones), mace heads, special ceramic jars, violin-shaped figurines (Plate 5.1), and other finds. The importance of the site came to light in the early 1950s, when David Alon made his early surveys in the region and collected a large sample of these objects (Alon 1961).

In October 1975, Alon carried out the first trial excavations at Gilat in the northwest portion of the mound (and again in 1976, 1977). Additional small-scale excavations were carried out in the fall of 1987 under the joint direction of Alon and Levy (Levy and Alon 1993). In this study, the early work is referred to as the Phase I excavations. Large-scale inter-disciplinary excavations were carried out at Gilat during the spring and summers of 1990–92 under Levy and Alon and are referred to as the Phase II excavations (Figs. 5.1–5.7; 5.14–5.18). The Phase I excavations defined four main strata on the mound. Following the Phase II research, tighter stratigraphic control enabled us to sub-divide the stratigraphy into seven sub-strata (I, IIA, IIB, IIC, IIIA, IIIB, and IV). In this chapter, the Phase I investigations are incorporated into the general discussion of the excavations at Gilat. Table 5.1 presents a summary of all the excavation loci, their volume, context and other details. This 'master locus list' forms the basis of all the statistical and spatial analyses presented in this book.

The early excavations at Gilat carried out by David Alon (Plate 5.3) demonstrated the rich potential of this site for exploring the role of religion and ideology in fifth through fourth millenna BCE social evolution in the southern Levant (Plate 5.6–5.8). However, due to the small sample size of these excavations (N = c. 475m^2) and the elementary recording methods employed in 1975–77, new excavations were essential to gain a more representative picture of the sanctuary complex and its associated cult activities, enlarge the sample size of the artifact collections, and more fully explore the developmental history of the site. In 1987, to help clarify the stratigraphic history of the site, the Nelson Glueck School of Biblical Archaeology (NGSBA) of the Hebrew Union College-Jewish Institute of Religion, Jerusalem, sponsored a small-scale excavation directed by Levy and Alon, in which three 5 by 5 m squares (c. 80 m^2) were opened to the south of Alon's earlier work. The results of this work enabled Alon and Levy (1989) to publish the first systematic study of the archaeological evidence for ritual performance at Gilat; a study which has helped other researchers interested in the archaeology of cult (cf. Stoddart *et al.* 1993; Plates 5.9–5.13). While many of the archaeological correlates for cult activities were tested in that paper, it was clear that much larger excavations would be needed at the site to clarify the rise of this Chalcolithic ritual center and the emergence of one of the Levant's earliest regional cult centers (see Chapter 1 for an outline of the research goals of the Gilat project described here). From 1990 to 1992, thanks in great part to support from the C. Paul Johnson Family Charitable Foundation (Chicago and Napa; Plates 5.4–5.5), it was possible to carryout three field seasons in which an additional c. 1200 m^2 of the site were exposed (Plate 5.15). The new excavations focused on making broad-horizontal exposures primarily to the south (Areas Y and M) and west (Areas J and T) of Alon's work (Plate 5.6). As the work progressed, it was clear that preservation was best on the western side of the site. Thus, the largest exposures were made there. To achieve the other goals of the new work, intensive dry sieving was carried out for every pit, room floor and other material culture-rich context (locus) encountered. In addition, to facilitate spatial analyses in the Gilat sanctuary, great care was taken to record the location (in three dimensions) of each special find discovered during the course of the excavations (see various artifact tables in this volume). While the Phase II recording methods were superior to the earlier work at Gilat, they were still 'pre-digital' and carried out with dumpy levels and line levels. We would have to wait for the late 1990s and our work in Jordan before a truly 'digital archaeology' on-site recording program could be applied to our work (see Levy *et al.* 2001).

Most of the spatial, seriation and statistical studies presented in this volume are based on the 1990–92 excavations. The melding of empirical archaeological data and social theory has been a source of debate ever since the beginnings of the 'New Archaeology' in the 1960s. This issue was a source of great debate between the eminent French prehistorian, François Bordes, and Lewis Binford, one of the American prophets of the New Archaeology. In the 1970s, when Bordes discussed this problem around his breakfast table in the village of Carsac near the Dordogne river, home to numerous important French Middle Paleolithic 'Neanderthal' sites, he put it this way: 'Lew, he is interested in big beautiful theories, but I, I am interested in the ugly little facts.' In this book, we are certainly interested in both robust social theory and the more mundane archaeological facts. This is why we have devoted a considerable amount of paper in the presentation of dusty contextual field data on which all our beautiful theories rest (see Chapters 1–4 and 14–16 for extensive treatment of theoretical issues related to the anthropology of religion). This will allow other researchers to test our results and to take the research in new directions using the primary data published here. To build a developmental picture of the Gilat sanctuary, the four excavation areas (J, T, Y, and M) exposed in 1990–92 are presented in detail followed with an encapsulated view of the evolution of the site based on all the excavations carried out at Gilat to date. The main significance of Alon's earlier Phase I excavations are discussed below.

2. The Phase I Excavations

a. Area D (1975–77, 1987)

The Primary Sanctuary Remains. Alon's (1976, 1977) early excavations in Area D (Fig. 5.1, 5.31) brought to light the richest room assemblage of cult-related objects found at Gilat (Table 5.2; Fig. 5.12). As will be seen here, all subsequent excavations embellish the theme embedded in the architecture and artifacts found Area D (cf. Alon and Levy 1989; Plates 5.72, 5.74, 5.77). Based on the large area exposures made during the Phase II excavations (1990–92), it is now possible to link Alon's Area D excavations with all the new excavation areas. This was done primarily on the basis of elevation and tracing archaeological and sediment features across the site stratigraphically. What Alon referred to as Stratum II, is now identified with Stratum IIB and his Stratum III is equal to Stratum IIC in the new excavations. The Phase I investigations labeled rooms alphabetically (Room A, B, C, etc.) whereas in the Phase II excavations newly discovered rooms are labeled numerically (Room 1, 2, 3, etc.). The new stratigraphic divisions will be used throughout this book, while Alon's old room numbers are still employed. With the Stratum IIC excavations in Area D (Figs. 5.5, 5.16; Plate 5.21a-b), for the first time, the richness and complexity of cult-related activities came to light at Gilat and the evolution of the sanctuary can be studied through the local Chalcolithic sequence. In an earlier study of cult at Gilat (Alon and Levy 1989), the Stratum IIC data from Area D was shown to conform with many of Renfrew's (1985) test implications for identifying cult activities in the archaeological record. The following discussion and chapters outline in greater detail the nature of the architectural features from these key strata at Gilat and the finds associated with them. There are a number of architectural parallels between the building complexes in the Gilat sequence and the layout of Palestinian Chalcolithic and Early Bronze Age sanctuaries (Kempinski and Reich 1992). Like most Protohistoric sanctuaries in Palestine, the Gilat complex is situated at the highest point on the site (elevation = 127.80 amsl).

At Gilat, Stratum IIC, it is possible to distinguish an integrated architectural complex that we have defined as a sanctuary. This interpretation was based on our original study (Alon and Levy 1989) which utilized only the excavation data from Area D. As will be shown below, the Phase II excavations provide a much larger exposure of the cult complex at Gilat, enabling us to situate the Area D sanctuary remains within a much larger site-based socioeconomic context. (For a full discussion of the archaeological correlates used to identify Gilat as a sanctuary, see Chapter 1, this volume.) In Stratum IIC, the main Gilat sanctuary complex is composed of two main parts:

1. the central building whose interior measurements are c. 16.25 × 14.85 m; and
2. three exterior courtyards south and west of the central building (Figs. 5.5, 5.16, 5.21a-b).

The main structure (Fig. 5.6) is a single large, rectangular unit. The architectural complex is made up of broad rooms that comprise three sectors. These are:

1. the northern sector containing Rooms A and B,
2. the western sector with Room C,
3. the southern sector, which contains Rooms E and F; and
4. the eastern sector which consists of an open area including a large courtyard and small central Room D.

The orientation of the building is northeast; it was entered from the southwest through a number of passages that led in a straight line to Room A, where the now famous Gilat anthropomorphic (Plate 5.7) and zoomorphic (Figs. 5.8, 5.72) statuettes and numerous 'exotic' objects were found (Table 5.2; and see Chapter 15, this volume). The walkway begins through Room F and continues along the same line through Room E, and ends at the entrance to Room A (Fig. 5.16; Plate 5.6). This central entry divided the area into two primary sections: the western section made up of rooms and the eastern section consisting of a large courtyard with installations and a single small room (Room D). Outside this area in another courtyard a cache of large torpedo jar fragments was found clustered in a pit (L. 311; Plate 5.13).

All of the rooms in this complex were of the broad room type, whose length/width ratio changes from room to room. The broad room building seems to have its origin in the Chalcolithic period and continues into the subsequent Early Bronze Age when it was used for both domestic and public architecture (Levy and Holl 1987; Porath 1992; Kempinski and Reich 1992). The foundations of the Stratum IIC walls were made of rough wadi stones (usually flint, chalk and Kurkar sandstone). The area does not seem to have been utilized in the earlier Stratum III (Plates 5.52–5.53). A number of walls and silos were coated with mud plaster to seal and protect these architectural features (Figs 5.10 and 5.11). The absence of stone foundations for roof supports suggests that these buildings had no central posts. However, in the small courtyard in front of Room A (Fig. 5.5), a series of mud plastered depressions were found below the Stratum IIC surface which may represent an alignment of post bases or, alternatively, supports for pottery vessels. The general thickness of the walls varies from 0.5–0.6 m and only in rare cases exceeds 0.8 m; this suggests that they supported a single story building. In areas which required special support (near passages or corners of buildings), large wadi stones were added at different levels. The floors were made of stamped mud, earth fills with bands of ash, and in some cases out of mud-brick. Room A and E contained several additional features that seem to be characteristic of early sanctuaries. These include the presence of mud-brick 'benches' along the interior walls of the rooms. The width of the benches varies from 0.3 to 0.4 m. In the southwest corner of Room A, a small platform made of hard mud-brick that may have functioned as an altar (L. 8) was found. This platform, which was located near the interior walls of Room A (Fig. 5.5; Walls 3 and 5) measured 0.62 × 1.71 m and were preserved to a height of 0.30 m.

In terms of the general layout of Protohistoric Palestinian cult complexes, the most common trait is the location of a central cult room, which opens onto an enclosed courtyard (Fig. 5.5 and 5.16). These are known from Ein Gedi (Ussishkin 1980), Megiddo Stratum XIX (Loud 1948), Ai (Marquet-Krause 1949), Teleilat Ghassul (Seaton 2000) and Tel Arad (Amiran and Ilan 1996). Ironically, at Teleilat Ghassul where the most spectacular Chalcolithic wall paintings depicting 'cult' scenes have been found, only recently have scholars begun to suggest that sanctuaries existed at the site (Cameron 1981; Bourke 2001; Bourke et al. 2001; Lovell 2001). In an early paper, Hennessy (1982:55–8) proposes that Area E at the site is the 'sanctuary mound' enclosed within a stone and mud-brick wall. In terms of the general layout, he suggests that the Ghassul complex is very similar to the sanctuary at Ein Gedi. Seaton's (2000) analysis confirms this and adds richer details to our understanding of a Ghassul sanctuary. The fact that Rooms A and B in the Area D complex are linked together, may be a forerunner to the appearance of the later Early Bronze Age 'Twin Temples' that appear at Tel Arad and Megiddo XIX. Although Gilat follows a similar architectural pattern, as will be seen below, there are important difference that distinguish Gilat from the other Protohistoric Palestinian examples mentioned above—the wealth of portable cult related objects and the wide range of craft and domestic activities found in association with evidence of religious performance.

Another important common feature in Protohistoric Palestinian sanctuary architecture is the presence of a sunken basin or semi-subterranean circular feature in the courtyard of the complex. The best examples of this phenomenon come from Megiddo XIX, Ein Gedi and Arad. Some of the open-air sanctuaries discovered in the southern Negev and Sinai deserts by Avner (1984:120) and dated to the fifth–third millennia BCE also contain circular stone installations in the center of courtyards. At Gilat, Stratum IIC produced a well-built stone-lined (with 13 courses) circular installation (Fig. 5.11) which may have had a similar function. While it is possible that this facility may have functioned as a storage silo, its construction differs from all of the other silos in Gilat, which are usually made of mud-brick. Given the similarities between the general layout of the Stratum IIC complex excavated by Alon and the Protohistoric sanctuaries outlined above, we assume that the stone-lined installation also played a role in cult activities. While Alon's excavations do show a strong link between architecture and worship, it is the Phase II excavations and the large plaza, standing stones (Plates 5.12, 5.28–5.29), other architectural features and the wide range of 'cult' artifacts found in association with the architecture (cf. Table 5.2) which are essential in identifying the significance of the Stratum IIC sanctuary at Gilat. In the remainder of this chapter, the Phase II excavations are presented to help contextualize the full range of material culture studies presented in this volume.

3. The Phase II Excavations: 1990–92

a. Area J

Introduction. The Phase II excavations at Gilat contribute to the growing number of Chalcolithic excavations in the southern Levant (cf. Bourke 2001; Dollfus and Kafafi 1988; Eisenberg *et al.* 2001; Gilead 1995; Goren and Fabian 2002; Gopher and Tsuk 1996; Kerner 2001; Levy 1987; Lovell 2001; Perrot 1984; Schick 1998). In discussing the Phase II excavations, we begin with Area J (Fig. 5.17) because of the excellent preservation and stratigraphy record found here. Excavations in Area J provided us with the much needed stratigraphic to tie Alon's (1977) earlier fieldwork and cult complex discovery into the new exposures. Area J, opened in 1990 and expanded by the end of the 1992 season to cover 21 contiguous 5×5m squares (area = 525 m^2), lies southwest of Area D (Alon's excavation area, Fig. 5.17). Area J was excavated over a broad open exposure. By 1992, all of interior balks and remnant balk fragments (called 'balk islands' where four grid squares intersected) were systematically excavated (Plate 5.23). In total, c. 930 cubic meters of sediment were excavated from Area J.

Beneath the overlying layer of disturbed topsoil, Area J is comprised of seven main 'strata', each of which represents a different time period within the Chalcolithic period along the Nahal Patish. Each stratum is defined more precisely by a number of 'phases' (i.e. I, IIA, IIB, IIC, IIIA, IIIB and IV), and the phases are characterized by different 'loci'. The following describes in detail the four main strata, with a breakdown of the requisite sub-phases within each stratum, and a description of loci from an architectural standpoint. Surfaces, pits and walls, will be described together, and wherever possible, a phase will be described in the context of an associated 'room'. Second, loci will be considered in terms of the material culture. Stratum numbers will be listed, followed by the stratum's phase, and where necessary sub-phase. For example, IIBii denotes Stratum II, phase b, sub-phase ii. However, as the sub-phases could not always be identified across the entire site, for the purposes of quantitative and spatial analyses of artifacts, loci are ascribed only to stratum and phase (i.e. IIA, IIB, IIC, etc.; cf. Table 5.1)

Stratum I. Deep plowing carried out in the 1950s penetrated to a minimum depth of 0.4 to 0.6m, effectively destroying the last occupational phases in Area J (and the entire site; Fig. 5.2). At the bottom of the plow zone, a series of 0.1m wide furrows in parallel lines, c. 0.8m apart, running East–West were found across the area. At the extreme point of penetration, the plow occasionally left scour marks that were excavated as hard, metallic, very flat marks, easily mistaken for surfaces.

Topsoil. Although the topsoil loci produced vast amounts of artifacts, they are out of context and cannot be associated with architecture for spatial analysis. A rectangular-shaped cut in K3-K2 measuring about 6m wide and 2.5m long with a parabola-shaped bottom was recognized as a 'backhoe' cut probably made when a modern vineyard was established on the site in the early 1970s. This cut penetrated though to Stratum III.

Burials. In the Southeast aspect of J4, two burials were found directly below the limit of disturbed topsoil. These burials (L.822 and 802), since determined modern Bedouin graves, were cut through the topsoil and placed into IIA (see Chapter 8, this volume). Unfortunately, L.1032, also sunken into the topsoil, entered into the balk, and could not be excavated fully.

L.801 consists of a restricted area of very hard, compacted soil, which seems to have been compacted in the modern rather than ancient period. As peripheral material was found to contain disturbed topsoil, it is likely that L.801 was compacted from above during previous excavations of Area D.

Stratum II.

Stratum IIA (Figs. 5.3, 5.18). Stratum IIA is represented in large part by a surface more compact and homogenous than the topsoil above, a quantity of mud-brick tumble used as fill over the Room 1, 2 and 3 complex, a series of pits, various structures, an adult primary burial, and Room 9. In general, Stratum IIA seems to represent an ephemeral occupation were limited cult activities were carried out following the destruction of the Stratum IIB sanctuary.

Surfaces. Generally, the IIA surfaces represent a homogenous matrix less compact than the surfaces of the various phases of II and III below, and can be divided into two groups. The first are generally ephemeral 'caps' of light, thin and relatively soft material that covered earlier structures. The second are made from mud-brick of earlier structures and compressed into a very hard surface.

Soft surfaces. As will be discussed, IIB ended in a general destruction of architecture. Mud-brick walls seem to have fallen down in such a way that their courses created lines of mud-brick over the IIB surface. The IIA floor was set upon these mud-bricks and destruction ash. For example, this occurred in Sq. L1, where a IIA surface (L.1045) was set down over the tumble and ash of IIB L.1053, in K1, where IIA surface L.1030 was set down over IIB L.1189 tumble over the IIB surface, in J1, where IIA surface 1031 was laid over IIB L.1091 tumble and L.1028 ash, over IIB surface L.1097. Sediment 'caps' were constructed to cover the two concave mud-brick basins (CMB) of IIBi, in L1 and L2 (Plate 5.18; Fig. 5.20a-b). L.1122 was constructed of large, flat mud-bricks over the fill above L.1129 (CMB2) in order to level out the surface. This sequence was duplicated with the L.1166 cap over the fill above L.1120 (CMB1).

Mud-brick tumble. In at least four areas, mud-brick tumble from IIBi structures was collected, laid down and compacted to make a level IIA surface. The various walls of Rooms 1, 2 and 3 would have provided ample material. For example, in excavating L.819 in K3, much tumble was found lying in the vicinity of L.871, a IIBi wall. This tumble (L.848 and 849) had been scattered deliberately over both sides of L.871 in order to create a level surface. Similarly, the tumble of L.846 had been placed over the IIBi passage (L.1016) leading from Room 3 to Room 2 in the IIBi structure. This tumble would have afforded a level surface between IIBi W53 (L.875) and IIBi pit L.826.

Pits.

Ephemeral pits. The pits of IIA, as well as those of every other phase in Area J, are of two types. The first are simply cylinders or half spheres cut into a surface, with no provision for projecting a mud-brick aperture, mud-brick lining, or mud-brick/stone bottom. If used as storage facilities, these pits would presumably have functioned for one or two seasons only, after which they would have been used as rubbish tips and abandoned.

On numerous occasions, ephemeral IIA pits cut through earlier, better-constructed structures. For example, two pits (L.828b and 828c) of L3 were cut into the North aspect of an earlier, better-constructed pit (L.838a; Fig. 5.16). Likewise, L.810 of K4 cut into the IIA surface (L.818), through two IIC walls (L.1002, and L.1003), and through the East aspect of a IIBi-c storage silo (L.882). In L1, pits L.1160 and 1050 cut not only the IIA surface, but also IIB platform/surface 1162 below, as well as IIB wall L.1188.

Multi-season pits. The second type of IIA pit consists of those that required modification to allow at least some longer-term use. For example, IIA pit L.805 in J4 was dug through a IIA surface (L.804/824), through IIBi fill (L.890), and by chance into a IIBii pit (L.893). It appears that some stones were laid haphazardly around the outside of the rim. It is likely that these stones were found during the cutting of the pit through a IIBi architectural structure (perhaps L.877, 876, or 880), and used to line the aperture of pit L.805.

Rubbish receptacles. Regardless of their primary function, the ultimate use of most every pit was as rubbish 'tip'. Every IIA pit had at least some ash 'swept' from the surface above. As for domestic use, pits L.1160 and L.1050 in L1 contained much burnt pottery and ash, while pit L.1051 in L1–2 was filled with ash, burnt pottery and bags of bone (predominantly cow), but also of pig and sheep/goat.

Many IIA pit loci have some sort of shell, which may indicate some craft activity (see Chapter 7, this volume). In addition, various pits contained worked bone of some sort and three loci had spindle whorls. Almost all of the pits contained evidence of worked stone, and many for flint working. In J3, L.808 and L.807 contained hundreds of flint flakes and debitage, suggesting intensive flint knapping. L.813/962 contained two shell pendants and many shell fragments. L.806/958 contained a whole range of artifacts, although this may have something to do with the burial (discussed below). L.812 contained two spindle whorls, and bone artifacts. Such was also the case in L1 and L2, where flint and bone tool utilization (possibly for textiles) were being carried out. For example, L.1029 contained three bone awls, many flint cores, kilos of debitage, and many bladelets (see Chapter 11, this volume). In addition, the spindle whorls, pendants, beads and shell in L.1059 may also suggest craft activity.

The poorly preserved IIA structures as exemplified by L.1280 and 1281 in H4, and 1377 in H5 are constructed of mud-brick, blocks of Pleistocene material, and moderately large uncut stones in probably only one course, over the remains of the stone circle L.1360 of IIBi. They form a reasonable square enclosing Room 13.

Burial. In J3, situated in the bottom and west aspect of pit L.806 was found a primary burial (see Chapter 8, this volume). The skeleton was found lying in a flexed position, hands under its head, on its right side facing west (Plate 5.14). The skeleton, a fully articulate female, aged 35–40 years of age, was in perfect condition, save what appeared as a hole in the back of the skull. As our excavation did not create this hole, it is possible that it was the result of physical trauma (see Chapter 8, this volume). Only one offering can be attributed safely to the burial, an almost perfectly preserved 'V'-shape bowl of very fine fabric. Although the pit is filled at higher elevations with special artifacts, it seems unlikely that these artifacts are associated with the burial, as they are placed randomly in almost 1m of fill material above the skeleton. Whether a burial was the intended use for this pit is difficult to say. However, L.806/958 resembles very much the IIA pits of J3. As none of these pits contain burials, it is likely by association that L.806/958 served a secondary function as a burial. While a relatively large number of burials have been found at Gilat (n = 91), this example may reflect an almost haphazard placement of human burials at the site. Alternatively, the fact that so many bodies were buried around the sanctuary may be significant.

Room 9.

Walls. W55 (L.872), W52 (L.873), and L.1020 consist of oddly shaped and irregularly-sized stones set in lines one row thick. No mud-brick was used, even as fill. The walls do not meet, but because of their equally inferior construction, as well as their agreeable alignments and elevation, they are considered part of the same structure. The most ephemeral of the walls is W78 (L.1020). It consists of no more than ten stones set in a line, and abuts against W57, or L.871 of IIBi. It appears that construction of L.1020 included some excavation on the eastside of L.871 of IIBi, so that this wall could be used as a buttress for L.1020 on its west and outside flank.

Floor. The surface within the walls includes L.817 in L4, and L.816 in K4. The surface is similar to other IIA soft surfaces, and the material culture in Room 9 suggests seasonal craft production rather than domestic use.

Room 10. IIA Room 10 of J1-J2 consists of three and possibly four walls. During this phase Room 10 was more ephemerally constructed than during IIB. W85 (L.1109) was constructed obliquely over IIB wall 96 (1112), while IIA W80 (L.1071), running north/south was constructed over IIB mud-brick wall 90 (L.1108). Both IIA walls consist of one course of stone laid in one row, over the remains of the IIB mud-brick walls. On the southern aspect, the IIB wall 86 (L.1107) seems to have been reused in IIA. As for the east aspect of the room, it is possible that the IIB wall 93 (L.1106) was used to enclose this room, although this is uncertain. Unlike W86, which contains four courses of mud-bricks, only one course remains of W93, so that it is difficult to say whether the wall was reused into IIA.

Surface. The surface L.1052 in the south aspect of Room 20 is hard-packed mud-brick, possibly constructed at least in part by the mud-bricks from the fallen IIB walls. The structure resembles the IIA Room 9, and although c. 10 m apart, the structures share the same alignment.

Room 13. Room 13 is bounded by the walls, L.1280, L. L1281, L1413, and L.1414. Within this room, pits also cut a series of layers, including surface and fill. The upper surface (L.1238 in H4, 1407 in H5) is a patchy, pale yellow plaster, below which is a fill layer of light brown decayed mud-brick L.1261 in H4. Below this is a patchy, plaster surface L.1268, associated with the structures L.1280 and 1281. This sequence suggests that Room 13 contained at least two phases of IIA floors (Figs. 5.3, 5.18, 5.19a-b).

Associated with the earlier floor (L.1268) is a rectangular mud-brick structure (L.1356) in the extreme south aspect of H4. It is possible that this represents a step into the room, or perhaps a bench abutted to the south wall of Room 13. Furthermore, on the east aspect, and seemingly outside the room is a collection of limestone blocks, perhaps representing a structure abutting the outside of L.1377.

Stratum IIBi. The first well-preserved architectural remains found throughout the excavations appear in Stratum IIB (Figs. 5.4, 5.20a-b; Plates 5.15, 5.23). A well-planned sanctuary complex came to light characterized by a series of rectilinear broadrooms, courtyards, large circular platforms associated with human burials, storage silos, hearths, a well-constructed human mass burial facility and other features. Of particular interest is the evidence for ritual process revealed by the association of cult artifacts with these structures.

Surfaces.

Soft surfaces. The surfaces of squares H0, J0, K0, and L0 are all fairly soft and ephemeral, even though they are associated with various structures. Similar to IIA soft surfaces, it is likely that a formal surface was never laid down in IIBi in these squares, but that fill overlying the IIC surface was packed down by continued use. In H0, surface L.1244 was not recoverable in the west aspect of the square, while in J0 surface L.1272 was sketchy at best in the central aspect. In K0, surface L.1305 was recovered only because we identified L.1304 west of the W117 (L.1225), and because we had the elevation of the bottom of the wall on its east aspect. In L0, the surface L.1312 west of W120 (L.1314) is fairly certain, while the surface L.1311 was only recovered for a short distance east of the wall.

Hard surfaces. In H4 and H5, the IIBi surfaces were constructed of mud-brick and are considerably more substantial.

Pits. Square J0 has 7 pits in total, including four rubbish pits, two hearths and one depression.

Rubbish pits. The pits L.1262, 1264, 1267, and 1270 are no more than simple cuts into the surface L.1272. Whether constructed for such or not, the final function of the pits was as receptacles of rubbish, mainly burnt pottery, ash and bones.

Hearths. L.1263 and 1265 conform to other 'hearths' in Area J. Each are oval-shaped with the walls in the depression made very hard by intensely high heat, and contain hearth stones charred by fire (L.1265 contains 13 such stones), quantities of ash, burnt and broken pottery, and charcoal.

Structures.

Platforms. The platform L.879 (1.25m × 1.1m × 0.26m; Fig. 5.13) in K4 was constructed of mud-bricks (29 whole mud-bricks were excavated), over which stones were set (27 flat stones, including 5 querns). Most of the stones had been set flat, the others vertically around the outside of the structure. The structure is bell-shaped in plan, with two stones protruding from either side about halfway down the structure's length. Altogether, the structure resembles a 'frog' shape.

Preceding the construction of L.879, a trench was cut through the IIBi floor L.865, and through the IIC floor L.913. After construction, the trench was filled to the surface of L.865. However, the IIA floor was brought all the way up to the structure itself, suggesting that this floor superseded the platform's construction.

Platform L.878 (2.1m × 0.65m × 0.15 m) also of K4 seems contemporary with L.879 because it shares similar construction and elevation. L.878 lies at the southeast corner of L.860, and seems to abut W57. As the south/east aspect of this platform was removed before it was identified as a structure, only the top, bottom and part of the side of the 'bell' shape remains. Unlike L.879, this structure is contemporary and built upon the IIBi surface L.860, and does not penetrate the IIC level.

Platform L.877 (0.95m × 0.6m × 0.15m; Fig. 5.13) of J4 also shares the same elevation and construction, comprising flat stones laid horizontally in a rectangle. IIA pit L.805 most likely cut into this structure, so that the extant rectangle may not represent its original shape. Excavation revealed 4 boulders, 10 cobbles, and some broken mud-bricks. The platform is in a perfect line with L.879 and L.878, and the three lay about 3m apart. The foundation of this platform is curious: missing are the many mud-bricks found under L.878 and L.879. Rather, L.877 seems to have been constructed above a layer of fill (L.890), which was placed over IIC mud-brick surface L.904. Indeed, the material culture of L.890 forming the foundation of L.877 is rich, containing among other things part of an unarticulated human skeleton. It seems that in an attempt to raise the platform L.877 from the Stratum IIC elevation of L.904 to the elevation of L.878 and L.879, fill (L.890) was extracted from elsewhere and placed on top of L.904. This excavated fill may have come from a IIBii burial below.

Platform L.989 (1.1 m × 1.0 m × .37 m) is set at a right angle to the line L.879, L.878, L.877, about 6.5m southwest of L.877. Again, it is at about the same elevation, and shares the same general construction as the other platforms. The structure is made of flat rocks (14 stones, 3 of which were querns) laid horizontally. As with L.877, L.989 was truncated by a IIA pit (L.806/958), so that stones of L.989 project into the south aspect of L.806/958. After the pit was cut through the north aspect of L.989, a pit rim of mud-brick was placed around the top of the platform.

In H0, platform L.1243 consists of three rows of parallel stones sitting over a bed of mud-brick, and lies in a roughly straight line running east/west that includes structures L.993, 989, 877 (Fig. 5.4). This line also lies at right angles with platforms L.878, 879 and 1018. In addition, the platform L.1243 is also closely associated with a mud-brick circle in H0 (below) and a burial (L.1237, below), as was platform L.877 in J4.

It appears that great lengths were taken to set the five platforms at the same general elevation, and L.878 seems to be the elevation to which all others were constructed. Again, it is placed upon the floor of IIBi L.860, abutting L.871. In order to maintain this elevation, L.879 was set in a trench dug through two floors; L.877 was set upon fill which rested upon the hard IIC surface; L.989 was set upon fill (L.990) which ultimately rested upon a hard IIC surface (L.901/908); L.1243 rested upon mud-brick.

Stone circles. IIBi contains four stone circles which all share the general same size (c. 3m diameter) and construction: a line of flat stones, all about the same size, lying on the inside perimeter of the circle, enclosed within an outer circle of mud-bricks. As will be shown below, most of these circles are associated with infant burials implying that, whatever activities took place on these circular 'platforms', construction of the circles was associated with some rituals associated with death.

1.   *Circle 1* (Fig. 5.4): L.876, together with L.997 of J3 and H4 and L.876 of H4 make 3/4 of a circle 3.8m in diameter. The circle has been disturbed in various places. Pit L.807 cut through the middle of the line, obliterating both mud-brick and stones. Some of the stones were re-used in the pit rim. In addition, the construction of pit L.813/962 cut some stones of the inside circle of L.876. Further, L.805 may have disturbed the mud-bricks of the outside of the circle at its east aspect. This circle and associated ovals (below) sit upon fill L.905 that was placed over the pits and burials of IIBii. It is conceivable that this fill was laid down in order to raise the stone circle to the same elevation as the platforms, for which we have seen an effort to align their requisite elevations. Within the circle are two oval structures (L.890) abutting the circle in the northeast aspect. As many stones are missing from the circle in its north aspect, it is possible that L.890 was constructed at a later period from stones robbed from the stone circle of L.876.

2.   *Circle 2*: L.1360 (Fig. 5.4; Plate 5.17) and associated loci in H4-5 form a near perfect circle. This structure is composed of stones neatly placed in two concentric circles abutting each other and measuring together 3.5m diameter. In some places three courses of the circle remain, the stones of which, at least on the bottom row are fairly flat, and all are bonded with mud-brick. On the east aspect a digging stick weight has been incorporated into the structure. This circle overlies two burials of IIBii.

3.   *Circle 3*: Nearly half of a third circle (L.1292) was recovered in H0, about 3m in diameter. It is at the same elevation as the other circles and is associated with a platform and burial.

4.   *Circle 4*: L.993 of H2 may represent the remains of a fourth circle. As it has been truncated on the east aspect by pit L.966 and west side by pit L.985; it remains to excavate G2 before determining for certain whether this is merely a curved wall or indeed part of a circle.

Concave mud-brick basins (CMB). The enigmatic concave mud-brick basins were recovered in squares L1 and L2. IIBi CMB1 (L.1120) was quite large before it was cut by IIA pits L. 2051 and 1123. At its bottom was cut a pit, also severed by IIA L.1051. The section of L.1051 pit illuminates the stratigraphy beneath CMB1. It seems IIA cap L.1166 covered the basin, which overlaid a thick layer of ash, which in turn covered over another basin below, slightly larger than the CMB basin above. The line of the lower basin could be followed around, showing that the second basin sat within the confines of the lower basin. Beneath the lower basin again was a thick layer of ash. It appears that a deep pit was dug, into which ash was laid (or created by fire in the pit's bottom). After this, a large basin of clay or mud was molded into the ash and allowed to dry. After a certain period, more ash was laid into the basin, and another basin molded into the ash. A pit L.1118 was then dug in the middle of the upper basin. The function of this CMB may have been to catch and drain away fluids, such as the blood from the slaughter of animals or libations of some kind. As for CMB2, it was not yet possible to determine if there are in fact more basins beneath. This basin is smaller than the first, but its overall design suggests that it shared the same function. As the CMBs have no parallels in the archaeological literature, we have opted for the functional explanation presented above.

Burials. Stratum IIB produced the most impressive and only planned mortuary structure found in our excavations at Gilat (Plate 5.19). The human remains found in this mass burial are describe by Smith and others (Chapter 8, this volume). The mass burial (L.1237) in H0 can be described as follows.

Structure. L.1237 seemed at first glance an elaborately constructed silo, with several courses of finely crafted mud-bricks comprising its rim and walls. However, once completely excavated, it was discovered that its depth was only 0.6m, rendering it far shallower than any other known silo in Area J or other parts of the site. Therefore, it seems likely that it was built in the first place as a burial structure (and the only such example). Excavation revealed that the structure's base consisted of flat stones (L.1400) laid across a layer of fine silt (L.1404), which had in turn been laid over a mud-brick base (L.1409). After a circle was dug through a layer of ash, mud-brick was laid over the bottom of the feature, and then in several courses to the rim. Fine silt was then laid over the mud-brick bottom, so that the paving stones, having been laid over the silt, could be arranged on a fairly flat plane (Plate 5.20). While this structure was semi-subterranean, the preserved height indicates that its mud-brick superstructure rose above the plaza surface by at least c. 1–1.5 m.

Contents. The burial itself consisted of three parts. First, the human burials are represented by the inhumation of nine primary burials. However, the bodies were only semi-articulated, and it appears as if they had been moved within the pit on at least one occasion, apparently after the corpses had decomposed significantly. Indeed, the extreme east aspect of the structure's interior is devoid of remains, while the western aspect is more heavily concentrated. Beneath the human burials was found a layer of dark ash, lying upon a vast number of animal bones (L.1357; Plate 5.20). These bones were in turn lying upon a thin layer of silt, which covered the paving stones. After the burial had been constructed, the slaughter of mainly sheep/goat took place, with the carcasses dumped in the bottom of the pit. Ash was then deposited over the faunal remains, and the human burials placed over the ash. It is likely that this structure continued to be used as a burial for some time, as the bones were moved after they had undergone considerable decay. The pit was then covered.

Multi-use ritual pit. (L.1344b; Plates 5.21–5.22) Located in the southwest aspect of H0, this pit revealed evidence of production of a ritual act (Braudel's [1972] *evenement*) and possible craft activity related to certain artifacts over two phases.

Ritual. In the first and earlier phase, the pit was found filled with ash, as well as nine horn cores, two bone tools, an animal figurine (B. 4342;), and an almost complete basalt fenestrated stand (see Chapters 6, 12 and 15, this volume). A clay convex 'cap' fully covered the fenestrated stand (Plate 5.22) and stretched halfway across the pit, most likely originally sealing the first phase. The material remains support that this phase suggests ritual use. Indeed, the horn cores were unworked, with two of them still attached to the skull (Grigson, this volume). In addition, the cores were of gazelle, previously not found in Area J. Finally, this pit was almost devoid of pottery and flint so common to the pits of Area J.

Craft working. The second phase of the pit which was used above the clay 'cap' contained seven bone awls, all of which had been broken and charred by fire, fragments of another basalt fenestrated stand, and a tabular scraper splintered and bubbled by exposure to intense heat. In total, the evidence suggests that the second phase of this pit was associated with the production or internment of bone tools. The rich assemblage of bone tools (see Chapter 13, this volume) throughout the site indicates widespread craft activities (weaving, hide-work) in the sanctuary through time.

Room 1, 2, and 3 complex. These rooms and associated structures (5.6m north-south × 10m east-west, in K2 and K3; Fig. 5.4; Plate 5.23) will be described together, as they represent one structural complex.

Walls. A number of walls constitute this complex. The first is heavy mud-brick, represented by W58 (L.870), and W57 (L.871). These walls average .5m wide, and represent a high standard of construction. The mud-bricks lay perpendicular to the line of the wall, and are in an excellent state of preservation. The northeast section of W58 is shaved-off on an east-west alignment. As there was much evidence of the scoring of the deep plow at this elevation, it is likely that the wall was cut in the modern period by the deep plow. At the north end of W57, just south of the point where it meets W58, a threshold is visible in the mud-brick. This threshold is represented by very flat and smooth mud-brick laid at a lower elevation than the height of W57 on either side, and is of a reddish brown color, different from the more yellowish mud-brick of W57. In addition, on the southeast side of the threshold sits the door socket (L.1018). This threshold would have allowed access between Room 1 and Room 5 (Fig. 5.4).

Floors. The floor of Room 1 (L.841) is of very hard compact material, and is bounded on the north by W58, the east by W57, the south by floor L.839, and west in part by the mud-brick rim of pit L.826. The size of this room is small at 1.8m north-south × 1.6m east-west: given its size and the fact that it opens onto two rooms, it may have been a 'vestibule' or 'ante-room'. L.839 of Room 1 is defined by the proposed partition wall, W57 to the east, L.1013 to the south and west, and L.846 and L.1016 to the west. Again, this room had access to Room 1, and by the passageway L.1016, access to Room 3. L.996 represents the floor of Room 3. It is very hard and compact, and bounded on the west by W72, the south by W71 and the rim of pit L.965, the north by L.1014 and the rim of pit L.970, and the east by the back-hoe cut IIA L.811. The floor measures 2.5m north-south × 3.75m east-west, making it the largest room of this complex.

The material culture of the Room 1, 2, and 3 complex reflects domestic use. Upon the floors L.839 and L.841 were scattered and in place a great quantity of burnt animal bones, as well as flat lying broken pottery, including one partial 'V'-shaped bowl. In addition, a number of flint tools were recovered. In the southwest corner of Room 1, L.841 contained a limestone violin-shaped figurine fragment, flint axe, some broken pottery and a number of animal bones.

Pits. All six pits are constructed for permanent, perennial use, with mud-brick rims, lining and bottoms. They contained industrial, rather than domestic material. Although uncertain, these pits may have been reused in IIA when they were filled up with IIA industrial material. These pits certainly had potential to be used perennially, and long after their original functions had been fulfilled.

Hard-packed surfaces. Two areas of mud-brick are too densely compacted and contrived to be designated IIA fill, and are too irregularly shaped to be considered walls or floors. L.1013 stretches from W57, north of pit L.809, north of bench L.866, and south of W53. As it runs between the floor of Room 1 and the pit L.809, it seems reasonable that it functioned as some sort of hard landing in front of the pit. This same conclusion might be drawn for L.1014, which lies north of L.1007, and around either side of pit L.870.

Bench. L.866, lying south and at a lower elevation than L.1013, immediately west and east of the rims of pits L.809 and L.845/978 respectively, seem to have functioned perhaps as a 'bench'.

Room 5. Room 5 comprises 2 walls, a floor, two pits, a hearth and silo (Fig. 5.4; Plate 5.23).

Walls. W56 (L.868) runs along the same alignment as L.870 although it is constructed differently. The stones of W56 are irregular in size and shape, and follow no set pattern. In addition, the wall is truncated midway along its length. The wall was constructed over a completely filled IIIA pit L.859, and those stones in the middle of the pit's surface were mistakenly removed as 'floaters'. Six stones continued the line of the wall over the pit's surface, proving that the wall was built later than the pit.

Floor. The floor of Room 5, L.865/860 (6m northwest × 5m eastwest) consists of a very hard, smooth, fairly flat surface. Its boundaries are W56 (L.868) to the north, and W57 (L.871) to the west. The platform L.878 and silo L.882 bound the floor at least partially to the south, while the floor continues east into the balk. After the balk was excavated, the surface was found to continue: L.865 was mirrored by L.937 and L.860 by L.938 within the balk.

Pits. Pit L.862 was found in the southwest corner of Room 5, and is contemporary with the platform L.878. As it cuts into the very dense L.860 and IIC L.912 below, perhaps no extra provisions would have been necessary for this to be a permanent pit. However, it contained an almost complete ceramic fenestrated stand (Plates 5.24–5.25). The same can be said for pit L.973, which cuts through l. 937 in the balk, and into the hard IIC platform L.1017 below.

Hearth. L.867 (0.9m × 0.3m × 23m) is a hearth cut into L.865 and through the hard IIC surface of L.913 below. Again, mud-brick sides and bottom were unnecessary, as this hearth was cut into surfaces as hard as any in Area J. The hearth had scorched sides and was filled with ash.

Silo. Silo L.882 (2m × 2.07m; Plate 5.26) was constructed in IIC and used throughout IIC and IIBi. The floor of IIC (L.912) abuts its stone rim, as does the later IIBi L.860 floor. A mud-brick rim was found rising 0.25m above the height of the stone rim. This silo, its rim strengthened with stones and mud-brick, its sides constructed of several courses of mud-brick, and its bottom paved with mud-brick over paving stones, is of first-rate quality and designed for perennial use.

The extraordinary material wealth of silo L.882 reflects much craft work carried out on the floor of Room 5. As the IIA pit L.810 cut into the side of the silo L.882, the silo could not have been used after IIBi. Again, the silo was constructed in IIC and reused in IIBi, and it is likely that the silo would have been used continuously throughout IIC and into IIBi. Therefore, the fill within the silo would have come from a IIBi surface, and we can assume that the material in the silo came from, at least in part, the floor of Room 5. The following summarizes the special finds from this silo (L. 882):

2548	Pallet
2564	Worked bone
2566	Worked bone
2598	Shell
2599	Bone awl
2614	Shell
2618	Bone awl
2623	Malachite (sieved)
2631	Polished bone
2634	Flint chopper
2263	Flint chisel
2643	Malachite (sieved)
2643	Digging stick weight
2643	Mother of pearl shell
2652	Digging stick weight
2655	Carbon sample
2658	Micro end-scraper
2663	Digging stick weight
2665	Knobbed pot
2666	Mother of pearl shell
2682	Shell
2685	Horn core
2687	Charcoal
2688	Spindle whorl
2691	Worked bone
2694	Horn core
2698	Basalt bowl rim

Room 10.

Walls. Room 10 (Fig. 5.15) is contained by IIBi walls 96 (L.1112) to the north, 90 (L.1108) to the west, 86 (L.1107) to the south, and 93 (L.1106) to the east in K1, K2, G1 and G2. W96 runs along the same alignment as L.1014 to the east, situated on the northern aspect of Room 3. The doorway into this room is difficult to locate. However, it is possible that it lay somewhere in the SE aspect, and destroyed with the later IIA pit. The surface in this room consists of L.1052 in K1 and J1. It is made of mud-brick, and in some places is very hard. Over this surface lay much mud-brick tumble from the walls.

Courtyard. West of Room 10 in K1-J1 is a courtyard represented by the surface L.1097 in J1, (L.1028, 1091), as well as L.1052, all of which were covered with ash and tumble (L.1189). The surface L.1097 was cut by hearths L.1040, 1263, and 1265, and filled with much bone, ash, charcoal, burnt and broken cooking pots, and a cup-mark L.1043. The courtyard seems to be bounded by W87 L.1093 to the south, and W117 (L.1225) in K0 and measures c. 13m north-south. The artifacts suggest that domestic activities were carried out here.

Stratum IIBii. This phase is represented by a series of pits and burials set into and overlaid by fill. These structures were built after a penetration through a IIC hard surface, running comprehensively across this area and into IIIA architecture below. Fill was laid over this IIIA architecture, the pits and burials were set into the fill, fill was laid over top of the pits and burials, and IIBii architecture was built over this fill. In large part, this phase reflects the reorganization of the site following the destruction of the Stratum IIC sanctuary complex.

Pits. The pits of IIBii fall into three categories. First, in L1, K1, and J1, simple pits were cut into the IIB surface before structures and walls of IIBi were constructed. None of these pits have mud-brick rims, lining or bottom. The distinction between the second and third types of pits is that the second are not overlaid by IIBi architecture. The second series of pits, including L.821 and L.830–6, are placed on top of the surface/fill L.847, and are overlaid by L.803.

'Dump'. The presence of a 'dump' sheds additional light on the events occurring at the end of IIC, and prior to IIB. Following an arc stretching from Square H1, moving north through J1, east into J2, J3, and J4, it appears that in IIBii, the fill above and floor of IIC was cut down to almost the elevation of Stratum III architecture. Into this area was deposited much debris and fill, as well as the burials and related pits. The excavation of the arc for the purpose of dumping material would go a long way to explaining why the surfaces of IIC, IIIA, and IIIB have been cut in this area (discussed below).

Burials. The burials in IIBii seem to have been sunk into either the fill of the IIBii dump, or the layer of fill above the IIC surface (see Chapter 8, this volume). Often IIBi architecture was constructed immediately above the burials. It seems that the infant burials were placed as intentional deposits to mark the erection of three stone circles that characterize Stratum IIB.

Burials below Stone Circles.

Circle One. In Circle One, four infant burials were recovered (see Chapter 8, this volume, for skeletal details). L.886 in J3 consisted of an impression dug into the fill, containing a primary burial of an infant 0–11 months old. The skeleton was complete, lying on its right side, oriented to the west, and accompanied with no associated artifacts. The skeleton was compacted into a small area, with its femur and tibia/fibula thrust into its rib cage. It is possible the infant was 'bound' into this position. Less than 1m away, L.900 in J3 contained a primary, infant burial. Again, the body of an infant 0–11 months old was placed on its right side, facing south-west, within an impression cut into the fill (L.1021) overlying IIIA architecture. Again, this infant seems to have been bound, and was compacted even more so than the infant in L.886. In addition, the upper set of teeth (maxima) was facing upwards, with no lower jaw (mandible) present. It appears that the mandible must have been removed in antiquity, and that the head was swiveled upside-down before the body was buried. About 1.5m to the west is burial L.971 in J3. This burial was set into a depression cut through L.1021, and into the IIIA floor L.932, and placed in the corner of two walls, W61 (L.931), and W65 (L.1009). It consists of a complete fetus, perhaps stillborn, lying on its right side, and oriented to the southwest. IIBii burial (L.1301) was recovered at the bottom of the fill L.1246, and within what had been the balk island separating H4 and J4, in the extreme northwest aspect of H4. This infant burial consisted of a fetus in a large pot.

Finally, 2m west of L.971 and just outside the perimeter of Circle One was recovered infant burial L.894. This burial consists of an impression dug into the fill L.1021 overlying the architecture of 3c Room 8. It is a complete, primary, flexed infant skeleton of 0–11 months old, lying on its left side, facing northwest. The body was placed at an angle, probably along the side of the impression, so that the head was exposed fully before the rest of the body was excavated.

Circle Two. In Circle Two, two pits containing burials were found cut into the IIC surface, including L.1317, which contained an articulated neo-natal infant. The other pit, perhaps, although not certainly cut into pit L.1359, lies directly below the circle L.1360 (Plate 5.17), and contained the much-disturbed bones of another infant.

Circle Four. Under Circle Four was recovered an infant burial (L.1090) near the bottom of the IIBii dump, associated with at least one pit L.1085, and perhaps another, pit L.1075. Similar to the two burials above, this infant burial was found to be bound and headless.

Burials and domestic features. Burials also lie under the architecture of the IIBi complex in K3. Burial L.1169 lies under at least 0.6m of hard mud-brick of IIBi L.843 above, while its associated pit L.1119 lies under and is cut by IIBi pit L.826. Burial L.1103 lies partially under IIBi wall 57 (L.871). However, it is more difficult to be certain with Burial 2 (L. 1045), lying below IIBi floor 1015 of Room 1. The burial lies in the corner of the room, but does not actually lie under the nearby walls. It is possible that the burial was sunk into the floor after the floor was laid down. However, during excavation of this floor, no break appeared in the surface. In addition, a bone awl and conical cup (L.1045, B. 3418, 3419) were found underneath the adjacent wall 871, and it is possible that these artifacts were offerings associated with the burial. If so, the burial would have occurred before the wall was constructed.

Pits. It is typical that these infant burials are associated with an adjacent, contemporary pit. For example, pits L.902 and L.885 lie in the middle of an arc of burials L.886, L.900 and L.971. Although a little further away, pit L.911 nevertheless is reasonably close to burial L.894. Therefore, it is possible that the pits functioned somehow in conjunction with the infant burials. It does not appear that the offering of grave goods was considered a necessary rite for the IIBii infant burials. However, one function may have been as foundation deposits; alternatively, the architecture may have had a funerary function.

Burials in fill. Burials were recovered which comprised numerous human body parts spread across a 2m area in J3. L.1000 contains a human skull (cranium), L.887 a human hand (phalanges of four fingers intact), and L.897 a human lower arm (radius and ulna). The presence of these bones can be explained in the context of a general disturbance. As suggested above, fill was placed above the IIC surface L.904 to raise the elevation of the platform L.877. The hand and arm (L.887 and L.897) could have been excavated with the earth used as fill for the platform. As for L.1000, this skull was found within what might be construed as the 'rim' of L.850. After excavating a hole through the IIC hard layer, it appears that a rim was constructed around its aperture. In an effort to gain fill for the pit rim, it is possible that a burial was disturbed. L.898 of J3 also seems to contain the remains of a disturbed burial. Lying within the fill L.1021, L.898 contains an adult femur. Again, when the fill L.1021 was laid down into the bottom of the cut made through the IIC hard layer, it is possible that a burial was used in the excavation of fill.

Stratum IIc. Stratum IIC is characterized by very flat, hard surfaces covering large areas (Figs. 5.5, 5.16, 5.21a-b). Although rare, some IIC walls have been recovered in Area J, as well as various pits, and two rooms. In general, the Area J Stratum IIC exposure reflects part of an extensive 'plaza' where a wide range of craft, ritual and domestic activities took place that we interpret as having functioned as a public area associated with the IIC cultic complex first exposed by Alon in Area D.

Surface. The IIC 'hard surface' consists of very compact material, often underlain by mud-brick, as was found in Room 4 of K3. This surface has been cut either by individual pits, or *en masse* for the placement of burials and pits. One IIC surface stretches without a break across most of five squares, from K2 (L.1082), K1 (L.1111), J1 (L.1110), and part of H1 (L.1142), the eastern half of which is cut by the IIBii dump (Fig. 5.5). This dump also cut the south half of the IIC surface L.1061 in J2.

Pits. The pits of IIC are simply cylinders or half spheres cut into the various surfaces. Two small pits cut surface L.1111 in K1, while pit L.1128 and 1134 cut IIC surface L.1110 in J1. Pit L.1050 and 1105 cut IIC surface L.1061 in J2, while pits L.1135, 1124, and 1042 cut IIC surface L.1142 in H1. The exception to this rule is pit L.1081, which is constructed very carefully in five courses of finely crafted mud-bricks, cut later by IIA pit L.806, IIBii L.1075, and IIBii pit L.1085. The material culture of the pits sheds some light on the use of the surfaces adjacent to the pits. For example, pit L.1128 in J1 was filled with ash and animal bones, suggesting domestic activity, while the nearby pit L.1134 was packed full of pieces of flint and debitage, suggesting flint working. In H1, pit L.1127 had an extraordinary basalt grinder leaning across its rim. Also in H1, pit L.1042 was covered in a layer of dark ash, under which about 0.15m was a cup-mark resting on mud-brick which had been thrown into the pit. This feature may have supported a pot in a domestic, and/or industrial context. Activities took place on IIC surfaces, in domestic, industrial, and possibly religious contexts.

Standing stone with stone line. That the surfaces were used in a religious context is suggested by stone line L.1154, running east-west in K2 (Plates 5.28–5.29). This stone line sits on top of the best preserved, best quality surface on the site. In the middle of this line of 12 stones sits L.1083, what may have been a 'standing stone'. This stone is standing unsupported by the other rocks, about 0.33m high, near the middle of the line of rocks and may be considered as a massebah. The surface associated with this massebah feature was painted a light blue color.

Plaza. The main walls that delineate the IIC plaza form two roughly parallel lines—one running from K3 to H2 and the other northwest/southwest from L0 to J0 forming a well-defined partition wall (Fig. 5.5; Plate 5.30). The plaza is defined by these walls and walls 121 & 123 in Area T to the northwest forming a rough rectangular shape (Fig. 5.5). Thus, the IIC plaza covers an area of c. 360 m^2 (Fig. 5.21a-b). In the northeast aspect of the plaza in Square L4, a finely crafted violin-shape figurine was found. This sample which contains breasts but is missing the head, and was found on the surface (Plate 5.32, Square L4), Nearby in L. 1293 an unusually thick-walled (+ 2.5 cm) churn (L. 1293; Plate 5.33) was found on the same plaza surface. Most churns from Gilat have relatively thin walls (Plate 5.34; see Chapter 10, this volume). The very heavy (c. 20 kg) weight of this sample probably precludes its use in the daily production of milk products. In what is interpreted as a foundation deposit associated with the plaza, a cache of four well-preserved ostrich eggs (L. 1167) were found in a small pit sealed by the plaza surface in Square H2 (Plate 5.35). The pits associated with the Stratum IIC plaza contained a wide range of ritual related objects such as fenestrated stands, violin-shape figurine fragments, unusual pottery and other objects.

Silo. The silo L.882 (Plate 5.26) was constructed in IIC, and used in a secondary context in IIBi. Its superb construction (discussed above) fits well with the superlative quality of the mud-brick floors and plaza surfaces. It appears that the structures of this period were made to endure. This may explain the continued use of cult Room A in Area D from Stratum IIC to Stratum IIB.

Room 6. Room 6 (3m north-south × 1.5m east-west; Plate 5.37) in Area J and apsidal in shape in Area Y), is composed of walls, a platform, and a pit. Although the room stretches across both Area J and Y, only that part of the room within Area J is considered here.

Walls. The walls comprising Room 6 in Area J are W54 (L.1001), W67 (L.1002), and W68 (L.1003). As mentioned above W68 is constructed in the same manner as W69 and W70, and was built in conjunction with Room 4. In addition, it appears that the east-west walls of Room 6 may have abutted W70.

The relationship between W68 and W67 is difficult to determine, as the join was cut later by IIA pit L.810. While W67 is composed of three rows of mud-brick and stone, W68 consists only of mud-brick, just 2 rows in thickness. However, given their present alignments, W68 would have met W67 at a perfect right angle, and both walls share the same elevation. Therefore, it seems reasonable that W67 was used in a secondary context during the construction of Room 6, and that W68 abutted against the east side of W67.

The east extent of W68 continues into Area Y where the floor of Room 6 was shown to be level with the bottom course of the mud-brick walls of the room. An almost complete torpedo jar was found was found in the fill associated with this floor (Plates 5.39–5.40).

Platform. Abutted against the east side of W67, and constructed in conjunction with W54 and W68 of Room 6, a platform (1.7m north-south × 1.5m east-west) of mud-brick (L.1017) is situated in the west aspect of Room 6. The platform is made of a number of large mud-bricks (larger than those found in the floor of Room 4). Some of these mud-bricks are laid in rows, and represent much effort in construction.

Pit. Within this platform is set a circle of mud-brick, creating a perfectly round hole (0.35 × 0.31 m). The function of both platform and mud-brick pit is elusive; however, it may have served as a hearth.

Stratum IICi.

Surfaces. The surfaces of IICi are robust enough to suggest that they were purposefully laid down. Surface L.1303 in J0 is very strong, and the section afforded by its numerous pits suggests that it may be in places 0.1m thick. The surfaces L.1285 and 1276 in K0 are again very strong. The surfaces L.1388 in L0 and L.1351 in H0 are fragmentary. That in L0 has been cut by IIA feature L.1296, and by numerous large IIC pits, so that it appears only in a small area in the square's east aspect. As for surface L.1351, again it has been cut on the east and south-central aspect, as well as by the pit L.1237. However, what is left of the surface of IIC in these two squares is hard and substantial.

Pits.

Rubbish pits. Some pits were used at least in their final phase as receptacles for rubbish, and, given their character of simple cuts through surfaces, may have been constructed from the beginning to function as such. These can be divided into pits, which contained mainly ash, many cultural remains, and very few cultural remains. The ash pits include L.1307, which used W103 as its east aspect and L.1325 in J0, 1320 (a deep pit cut into the Pleistocene) and 1324 in K0, and 1401 in L0. Pit L.1277 in K0 contained many cultural remains, including faunal long bones, large amounts of sherds, cornets and ash. Finally, L.1319 and 1297 in J0 contained fairly sterile material. It may be that L.1297 had a bottom paved with mud-brick, although it is more likely that the pit was merely cut until a hard surface below was reached.

Silos. Square L0 seems to have contained two IIC silos (Fig. 5.5). L.1310 is very deep, at 1.63m from the IIC surface and 1.6m in diameter. Most of its depth is cut through the sterile Pleistocene, and it was filled almost entirely of ash. Adjacent and cutting into this pit is L.1322, a full 2m in diameter and 1.04m deep, which cuts not only the Pleistocene, but various pits of an earlier phase. Unlike L.1310, 1322 was filled with much jettisoned, used mud-brick. The lack of constructed rims, walls, and bases in these silos renders them different than others found in Area J; however, their great depth and diameter, as well as their incision through the extremely hard Pleistocene recommends them as silos.

Hearths. L.1298 in J0 was found full of hearth stones, ash, charcoal, burnt bones and pottery, with walls charred and hardened by fire.

Cup-marks. J0 contained two cone-shaped cup-marks, L.1302 and 1313 (Fig. 5.5). The former had a base lined with small stones set in a clay plaster, while the latter was merely a simple cut.

Container. L.1318 in J0, a ceramic churn set on end into the ground (Fig. 5.41), was used as a storage container and constructed as follows: a depression was cut, into which a churn was set on end with its top facing east. Clay was then poured around the churn, and the depression in-filled. The top third of the churn exposed above the surface was then removed. This storage receptacle should be viewed in conjunction with a range of domestic activities that were carried out west of the partition Wall 103 that helps to delineate the plaza area.

Stratum IICii.

Surfaces. The element, which sets IICi and IICii apart, are the different elevations of surfaces abutting the east aspect of W103. Surface L.1350, 1177, and 1178 in squares L1, K1 and J1, respectively, clearly pre-date those surfaces designated IICi.

Pits. Having excavated to the IIIA surface, it is clear that pits of L3 and L4 were cut before the IIC surface was laid down, and after the IIIA surface had fallen out of use. Such pits include L.861, 983, 84, 853, 856, 863, 855, 859, 863, and 927.

Walls. W103 (L.1140–1277) was uncovered in squares J0, K0, and L0, and totaled 13m in length. It was composed of stones or boulders, with three main breaks along the wall line. That this wall delineated a courtyard on its East aspect, and perhaps also on its West, is supported by its long curve to the southwest. Its curve and great length seem to suggest a delineation of space rather than a support for a structure's superstructure.

b. Stratum III

In Area J, Stratum III consists of a nucleus of buildings in the south of the area, well-built mud-brick silos, and an extensive plaza (Figs. 5.6, 5.7, 5.14, 5.15). Three different building phases can be defined within Stratum III. The phasing in Room 8 and Room 7 belong to IIIA, the second floor in Room 7 to IIIAi, and the remainder of IIIA to IIIAii.

Stratum IIIa.

Surfaces. IIIAi surfaces are very hard (Fig. 5.6). The best examples are those in squares L3 (L.1282), L4 (L.1423), and K4 (L.1424). In some places, the surfaces of these squares consist of mud-bricks laid down over a very flat plane. The surfaces of J0 (L.1334), K0 (1306) are also very hard. In addition, L.1306, especially within the southeast aspect, was exposed to an extremely hot fire; indeed, the surface was charred and overlaid by a very dark ash (L.1259). As for L0, although most of the surface has been cut away by IIC or IIIA pits, that which remains is very hard.

Pits. Squares L3 and L4 contain various pits sharing similar construction, and belonging to the same period. Before discussing their construction, it is important to define the time period. Pit L.859, as discussed above, had been filled in before IIBi W56 and IIA W55 were constructed over the top of the pit. In addition, pit L.853 of L3 and L4 also lies under W56. Accordingly, the pits of L3 and L4 must belong to at least IIC, if not earlier. However, pits L.854 and L.864 lie under IIC W70 in L3. Therefore, these, and by association, all of the pits in L3 and L4 must belong to at least IIIA. Similar to the first type of IIA pits, all of the IIIA pits in L3–4 were made for temporary use only. Mud-brick rims, sides and bottoms are not present, the pits merely being holes cut into the surface.

The material culture of the IIIA pits is very similar to that found in IIA pits, with one exception. A comprehensive and very dense quantity of ash was found throughout the three pits comprising L.853, suggesting that the complex be used for craft purposes. A great quantity of flint chips and debitage were sieved from the east pit, together with two scorched cores and other flint material. In addition, a large, cylindrical piece of ceramic, open at both ends, was recovered. This may represent part of a flue. As for the north pit, the sides of the pit are scorched, and a number of burnt mud-bricks were recovered within. In addition, a torpedo and two large jugs were found within the fill almost in perfect condition. The seemingly temporary construction of this complex of pits argues against an industrial context. However, its sides, especially in the north pit, have been fired, and although not lined with mud-brick, are very hard. It is conceivable that this complex was constructed originally for temporary use, and was later used in an industrial context.

Rubbish pits. Three types of rubbish pits were excavated: those filled with ash, those with ash and mud-bricks, and those containing many finds. By far the most prolific of the three are those containing mostly ash, a few sherds and bone. These include in J0 L.1353, 1352, 1345, 1343 and 1336; in L0 L.1362; in K0 1395, 1428, 1399, and 1398. L.1381 may have been such a pit, although its great depth and small diameter may recommend it as a very deep cup-mark. Those pits containing a significant number of mud-bricks were found in L0, and include L.1401, 1367, and 1363. Finally L.1337 contained an unusually large number of artifacts, including an extraordinarily high number of large sherds, as well as much ash.

Hearths. Of the two oval-shaped features in square K0, L.1403 and 1384, the former was filled with ash and charred stones, and therefore seems to have been a hearth. However, the lack of such evidence in L.1384 may recommend it instead as a peculiarly shaped pit.

Cup-marks. Two cup-marks, L.1342 in J0 and L.1402 in K0, were found with the bases of vessels *in situ* within the cup-mark. Also in K0, L.1379 was cone-shaped and appeared to have hardened walls, while L.1396 had merely a cone-shape.

Depressions. Square K0 contained two small depressions, L.1380 and 1383, the function of which is uncertain. However, similar to cup-marks, they may have held vessels.

Post-holes(?). L.1405 in K0 seemed at first to be a small cylindrical pit 0.25 in diameter. However, at the base of the pit 0.29m below the surface was a broken grinder stone. This grinder covered the bottom of the feature so perfectly that it seems likely that the pit was cut to accommodate the grinder. Although uncertain, it is possible that this grinder served as the base for a post.

Walls. Five walls belong to IIIAi. L.1386 (W124) running east-west in the north aspect of L0 seems associated with L.1388 (W122) running north-south on the East aspect of L0 and K0. That W124 is lower than W122 is explained by the formers' subsidence into the ashy fill of pit L.1371. Both walls are of mud-brick and of similar width. L.1388 (W122) runs parallel and sometimes under the IIC W103. This is due to the fact that L.1388 is straight, while, as mentioned, W103 curves to the southwest.

L.1228 (W118) in J1 belongs to IIIAi. The IIIA surface slopes west to east, and the surface associated with the arc L.1172 is the same as that associated with W118. The strongest link between the two surfaces is W113 (L.1430) in H1. Not only is this wall associated with the arc, it almost touches the south aspect of W118 as it curves around to the south west (see Fig. 5.6).

Structures. The function of two structures (L.1288 and 1289) recovered above the IIIA surface L.1423 in L4 is uncertain. Unfortunately, both have been much damaged by intrusive Stratum II pits. These structures may have comprised parallel walls: however, even given their considerable damage, they do not seem straight enough. Alternatively, they may have been platforms or other such installations.

Another structure L.1323 of IIIAi was found on the floor L.1306 of K0. It is a platform made of mostly spent grinders, all lying flat in a rough square 1 m × 0.8 m × 0.1 m. The platform has been severely burnt, and ash (L.1259) was found covering, as well as in between the stones. The large degree of ash in this area of L.1306, together with the adjacent pits, especially L.1337, which are filled with ash and pottery, together suggest that the platform L.1323 was used for cooking.

Room 7. Room 7 (1.5m north-south × 4.5m east-west; Plate 5.42) in J3 and J4 is comprised of walls and floors.

Walls. Two of the walls of IIIA Room 7 were reused from an earlier phase. Both W61 (L.931) forming the north aspect and W66 (L.1010) of the south aspect was constructed during IIIB, and therefore will be described below. However, W65 (L.1009) was constructed in IIIA.

W65 is a secondary wall constructed to redress the awkward angle of the west aspect of IIIB Room 7. The construction is as one would expect of a wall fulfilling a 'cosmetic' function. It has a base of mud-brick only one row wide upon which was constructed only one row of stones.

Foundation deposits. During the construction of W61, two deposits were made. In J4, in the East aspect and on the south side of the wall, L.959 was found. This locus consists of an Egyptian-style flint axe (see Chapter 11, this volume) 0.06 m wide by 0.1 m long. It is of excellent quality, and clearly was placed as an offering in the foundation of the wall.

At the west extreme of the wall, as it meets the later IIIA W65, a burial was found in the wall foundation. L.980 consists of a human fetus within a jar. Although the jar was crushed by the weight of the wall, the skeleton remained almost intact. That the burial is a foundation rather than an intrusive deposit is beyond question: in order to excavate the burial, we had to dismantle W61 in this section.

Floors. The floors of IIIA Room 7 consist of L.932 (1.5 × 1.5 m) and L.947 (1 m north-south × 2 m east-west). Floor L.932 occupies the west aspect of the room, and is bounded by W61 to the north, W65 to the west, W66 to the south, and it meets floor L.947 in the east. It is composed of a hard, compact material, with very little occupational material. It is likely that this floor was disturbed during the episode when the IIC hard surface was cut for the IIBii infant burials and pits. The floor contains one cup-mark (L.944).

The second floor (L.947), made of the same hard surface, and is joined on its south aspect by L.932, is bounded by W66 to the south, and is cut on its north and east aspect. More certainly than L.932, the cut to the north was made by IIBii pits and burials.

On the north aspect of L.947 there appears to be a 'patch' in the floor. This patch runs 0.9 m east-west × 0.4 m north-south, is at the same elevation, but is composed of a red and much harder material than the rest of L.947. This patch may be suggestive of a long occupational use of this floor.

It appears that a pot (L.998) was sunk into the IIIA floor L.947, through the IIIB floor L.916 and into the IV fill below (Plate 5.43). This pot lies against the inside of W61, and has been placed into a pit dug specifically for the purpose of holding the pot. The pit shows the section of the extant L.947, over L.916, and into the fill below.

The function of this pot appears to be a storage container in a domestic context, although the fabric of the pot seems at first glance too thin and delicate for use as a storage jar. Its size and state of repair are impressive. It stands 0.7 m in height, and has a rim diameter of 0.1 m and an actual diameter of 0.35 m. Although cracked in some places, it was fully restorable.

Pits. Three pits were cut into the floor of IIIB L.947 (Fig. 5.6), and appear contemporary with the use of the floor. Each of these pits is very small in diameter, but very deep. For example, pit L.953 has the largest diameter, at 0.3 m, and is a full 0.4 m deep. L.956 as a diameter of only 0.15 m, and is 0.84 m deep. Finally, L.955 is 0.18 m in diameter, and 0.49 m deep. The possibility exists that once penetrating first the IIIA floor and then the IIIB floor, the original pit bottom was reached, as very soft fill has been found in other areas below the IIIB floor.

Courtyard. The courtyard lying north of Room 7 is defined as such because there have been no walls delineating the space within. The IIIB W61 forms the south aspect and earlier 3c architecture the west aspect. However, later IIBi architecture of K3 and IIC architecture of K4 lie above the limits of this courtyard to the north, while IIBii pits truncate the courtyard on its east aspect. The extant dimensions are 2 m north-south × 6 m east-west.

Silos. L.1341 and L.1369 (Plate 5.45) represent two of the finest silos found in Area J. L.1369 was recovered in the extreme northeast quadrant of H2, and stretches across J2, J3 and H3. It was cut in IIC by pit L.1075, and 1085. In addition, a IIC silo L.1081, constructed in at least five courses of mud-brick, and cut by L.806 overlies L.1369. Thus, two mud-brick silos of different strata were constructed one on top of another almost perfectly.

Silo L.1369 was constructed of finely crafted mud-brick in several courses, and may have had at least three different floors, the last of which comprised paving stones. Much pottery, animal bones, and charcoal were excavated from this feature, and a very large amount of seeds were recovered by wet sieving. Interestingly, even though the pit penetrates the Pleistocene (this is known from the broad exposure of Pleistocene over H2 and directly adjacent to the silo), the inside of the walls was nevertheless lined in mud-brick from rim to base. Thus, the sterile Pleistocene was deemed insufficient material for the silo's walls.

L.1341 was found under the IICii surface, which acted as a 'cap' over the silo, in the north-east quadrant of L1, and north-west quadrant of L2. Similar to L.1369, this silo was constructed of many courses of mud-brick. This pit was excavated in section, the drawing of which indicates bands of ash between layers of greenish, clay-like material, with strong ash and charcoal in bottom of the north aspect. This section suggests moreover that the silo was used over a long period for distinctly different purposes.

Surface. L.917 in the west and L.929 in the east aspect make up the floor of the courtyard. The surface is generally hard-packed, overlying a reddish pebbly material. The elevation of both L.917 and L.929 correspond to the elevation of the IIIA floors within Room 7.

Cup-marks. Upon the floors are set numerous cup-marks. Most of these cup-marks follow the same general construction. They are set upon a large mud-brick, an impression is created out of the top 14–18cm in diameter, and sometimes as much as 10cm deep, although more often shallower. Presumably after hardening, the impression is worked until it is smooth. One exception is L.891, which is 0.25 m wide, 0.11 m deep, and lined with pottery sherds.

As for material culture, the IIIA surface L.917 contains many flint artifacts, and may have been used in an industrial context. If the cup-marks indeed held pots, they also may have served an industrial function. Indeed, it seems unlikely that so many cup-marks would have been lying on the floor of a domicile, given the sheer inconvenience that such a situation would produce.

Stratum IIIAii.

Surfaces. As with IIC, very hard, flat surfaces extend across the west aspect of Area J in IIIAii. In K2, the surface dips from on the east, south and west sides into the middle where lies pit L.1186. Above the floor was found a tremendous amount of animal bones within the fill L.1147, and below the IIC surface. The IIIAii surface in K2 recalls the CMB's, only on a much larger scale.

In K1 through J1, the surface is also very hard, cut by pits, and is bounded on the west by W103 L.1140. In J2, the surface is cut by the IIBii dump. This also occurs in H1, where the surface exists only in the west aspect, and plays host to the mud-brick arc described below.

Room 8. Room 8 (2 m × 2 m; Fig. 5.6; Plate 5.46) is comprised of walls, a floor and a large, flat stone.

As mentioned above, W74, running north-south forms the east aspect of Room 8. The wall is constructed of stone and mud-brick, much the same as IIIB W61. The north aspect of W74 joins these two walls. As for the south extent, the wall appears to continue south into H3, although this area has not been excavated fully. If so, the remaining walls of Room 8 would have abutted against an earlier constructed W74. This argument is supported by the construction of the remaining walls of Room 8. W77, running east-west, W76, running north-south, and W75, running east-west all are made of the same size of mud-brick, laid carefully in two rows. On the contrary (and as mentioned), W74 was made not only of mud-brick, but also of stone.

Unfortunately, the joins between these walls and W74 do not exist. W75 was cut by IIBii pit L.911. An opening exists between W77 and W74, which may represent the doorway, as no other area in the room serves as a better candidate.

Floor. The floor of Room 8 (L.982) (1 m × 1 m), is very hard and compact, harder in fact than any of the floors of Room 7.

Flat rock. Lying over this floor is a large flat rock (L.1022). It measures 0.49 m long and 0.42 m wide, 0.2 m deep, and sits in the southwest corner of Room 8. Its function is not readily apparent, but its flat nature suggests that it may have served as an 'anvil' or working area.

As for the material culture, no artifacts were recovered from the surface of the Room 8 floor. It is possible that the floor will produce more artifacts once excavated.

Pits. All of the IIIAii pits are merely cylinders cut into their requisite IIIAii surfaces. In K2, pit L.1186 is cut into IIIAii surface L.1180, while in K1, surface L.1177 contains three pits. Pit L.1184 is shallow and unremarkable, while the same can be said for pit L.1173. Pit L.1185 is interesting insofar as it penetrates an earlier surface containing a pit, L.1187.

Although pit L.1150 is very deep, we excavated it more deeply than its actual bottom. The mistake was discovered in the pit's section 0.8 m after the damage was done. Pit L.1348, clearly running below platform L.1323, but cutting L.1306, must belong to an earlier sub-phase of the surface L.1306. Pit L.1348, which contained many sickle blades, as well as L.1412, runs below IIIAi W122 (L.1387), and so must belong to an earlier sub-phase of IIIA.

Walls. The walls of IIIA are the most significant of the three strata. They have been found to be constructed with large pieces of masonry laid in sometimes several rows, as well as mud-brick. As discussed above, the foundation of IIC W69 in K3 appears rather to be of IIIA. The construction of the foundation, as well as its elevation, agrees with that of W61 on the north aspect of Room 7. Similarly, the foundation of IIC W62 L.1011 in J3 lies on a different alignment than the super-structure, and is therefore of an earlier construction. Its assignment to IIIA is by its association with the west wall of Room 8, which it abuts on the same elevation.

Structures. Below the fill covering the IIC surface in H1 was recovered a very delicately constructed arc of mud-brick, L.1161. This structure sits on top of the IIIAii floor, and is cut by IIC pit L.1168 on its east aspect, and later this pit was cut by the IIBii dump excavation. The arc is composed of three elements.

A half circle of mud-bricks made with ash and bounded by clay are set carefully on the IIIA surface. Within the circle are mud-bricks forming the infrastructure. On top of the circle was laid a thin plaster of clay. The function of this structure is unknown, but may have been some sort of platform.

In H3 north of W97 L.1190 lies a structure W98 L.1191. Although described as a wall, this structure, comprising two rows of both stones and mud-bricks, arcs in what would have been a very large circle if completed. It seems to be contiguous at its south aspect with W97, and so is contemporary. This structure is associated with a surface to the east L.1165, and west L.1164 of the IIIAii phase.

Stratum IIIb.

Surfaces. Stratum IIIB (Fig. 5.7) is represented by two pieces of surface running below surfaces of IIIAii. In J2, L.1175 surface, cut by the IIBii dump excavation can be found in the north aspect of the square. In H1, IIIB surface L.1183 is found in the extreme east of the square, below the IIIA surface holding the arc L.1161.

Pits. As the ash pit L.1371 lies under the IIIA W122 running east-west in L0, it must belong to IIIB. As with all of the IIIB pits in this area, it is cut well into the Pleistocene. Pit L.1371 also cut pit L.1354, relegating the latter to IIIB. That the latter pit does not belong to a phase earlier than IIIB is suggested by the height of its rim, which is located just 0.15 m under the IIIA surface, and by the fact that no surfaces between IIIA and the rim are discernible in section. That this section exists (on the east face of L0) is due to our method of digging the pits in this area: having excavated L.1322, it became apparent that L.1322 had been cut into much earlier pits whose rims were below the IIIA surface. We therefore began to excavate these pits 'horizontally' while standing at the bottom of pit L.1322.

Pit L.1361 lies not only under the IIIA surface L.1388, but also under the IIIA W122 and IIC wall (W103). The same is true for L.1366, cut by IIIAi cup-mark-shaped pit L.1367, and running under the IIIA W122. Finally, L.1385 was judged to be IIIB, as it was cut by L.1361. Only the impression of its bottom in the Pleistocene remains of this pit.

Courtyard. The boundaries of the IIIA courtyard will serve for those of the IIIB courtyard (Fig. 5.7).

The surfaces L.918 in the west and L.934 in the east are hard-packed, and on the same elevation as floors L.933 and L.916 of below IIIA Room 7. A hearth (L.956) was dug into the surface (L.918). Quantities of ash were saved for radiocarbon dating.

As for material culture, almost nothing exists, except for the ash in the hearth L.956. It is difficult to account for this almost complete lack of artifacts. However, continued excavation will allow penetration into, rather than merely over the floors L.918 and L.934, perhaps producing more artifacts. The absence of materials suggests a planned abandonment of the site during this occupation phase.

Stratum IV. In Area J, Stratum IV was exposed in a 'probe' covering the whole of H2, and includes a series of fills lying over, and pits penetrating into the Pleistocene sediment (Fig. 5.8; Plate 5.47).

Fill. Below the IIIA surface (L.1420) is a cultural in-fill of ash, pottery and bone (L.1273) which overlies a band of very dark ash running at a steep angle from west to east. As the IIIA surface is relatively flat, the in-fill L.1273 over the ash layer L.1274 overcame a significant slope. Indeed, it appears that the IIIA surface was made level by the deliberate in-filling of the cultural material of L.1273 over the sloping band of ash L.1274.

L.1274 heavy ash slopes from the west to east aspects of H2, and is readily visible in the east face section (Fig. 5.8; Plate 5.47) and south face section of H2 at 126.80 m OD (west) to 125.85 m MASL (east). As the in-filling (L.1273) above this ash bands belongs to the creation of a Stratum III floor, the ash band and that which lies below is considered Stratum IV. Indeed, the ash layer L.1274, recovered in all four sections of H2, seals the material below.

Directly beneath the ash band was found L.1275, characterized by cultural material, including much pottery, faunal bones, charcoal, flint and ash. It slopes at the same angle as the ash, beginning at 126.72 m OD (west), and sloping to the east to 125.30 m OD. It seems that this layer was a deliberate in-filling below the ash layer.

It also appears that this layer contained standing water for certain periods. As shown in the north aspect of the section (Fig. 5.8), distinct bands of colluvium were deposited directly beneath the ash layer L.1274. In order for these colluvial bands to collect, a continual source of water charged with sediment must have been introduced into this area over a long period of time. Most likely run-off water would bring in sediments, and once static, would discharge sediment in bands at the bottom of the sequence. That this area originally functioned as a water collection area is suggested by the clay cap found directly over the Pleistocene sediment, together with the sloping nature of the area to the SE corner of H2. Sometime later, pits were cut through the clay cap and into the Pleistocene material. Whether constructed as rubbish receptacles in the first place or not, their final function served as such: each contained material normally attributed to rubbish fill, which was then sealed by the clay covering L.1429. The lamination recovered in the north aspect of Section #2 above the clay cap L.1429, and below the ash layer L.1274 suggests that this area collected fresh water over a long period of time, and stored it in the SE corner of H2.

Pits. Below L.1429 clay layer were found various pits cut into the Pleistocene sediment, some containing substantial amounts of pit fill. The first cut (L.1294) was encountered in the west aspect of H2. Into this cutting was found various other pits, all sloping to the SE corner of the square. Cut into L.1294 was L.1308, within which was recovered much ash, bones and pottery. L.1326 was then cut into L.1308, and this pit also contained many cultural remains, most notably large amounts of charcoal. Cut into the east aspect of L.1326 was the most prolific pit of all in terms of cultural remains, L.1329. Cut into L.1308, and found at the extreme SE corner of the square and at the lowest elevation was L.1331. This again was filled with faunal bones, much ash and charcoal. In the north aspect of H2, L.1327 cut L.1294.

Area T. The Area T excavation covered an area of 12 5 × 5 m squares (c. 300 m²), immediately to the west of Area D and to the north of Area J. A one-meter-wide balk originally separated Area T in the south from Area J. Each square in Area T originally had a 0.50 m corner unexcavated, preserving a 1 m² 'balk island' to protect the site surveyor's grid stakes (Plate 5.15). In some cases, these cubes were removed to better understand features beneath the grid point.

Stratum I. Like other areas on the site, the upper 0.4–0.6 m of overburden in Area T was heavily plowed in the past, and thus no *in situ* architectural or cultural features remain. Though this disturbed zone is filled with Chalcolithic cultural material, the presence of historical and modern debris attests to the disturbance near the ground surface. Removal of this disturbed zone exposed an interesting feature that we believe is the result of this agricultural plowing. After removal of the very silty and loose upper disturbed level, the next level is a more compact, 'mud-brick-like' level. In some cases, the bottom of plow furrows seem to be visible; in one particular case, a decayed mud-brick level in squares M1 and M2 was cleaned thoroughly and linear plow furrows, spaced about 0.4 m apart, were visible running east-west at c. 127.70 m AMSL (c. 0.4–0.5 m below ground surface).

Stratum IIA. Though removal of the Stratum I disturbed sediments marks the end of most intrusive, later material, Stratum IIA (Figs. 5.3, 5.5, 5.18, 5.19) also suffered from post-depositional transformation of varying degrees. As mentioned above, the upper most levels of Stratum IIA are typically marked by a more solid, compact "mud-brick-like" matrix, which differs not only in density, but also in texture. In Area T, the majority of Stratum IIA features exposed are pits, many of which were probably truncated by post-depositional processes such as erosion and plowing. Only one wall (No. 81, sq. Ai1) was exposed, and may have been cut in two spots by plowing. Other cultural features include a platform (L. 632, sq. M1), a small stone installation or hearth (L.656, sq. N1-S1), and a 'cupmark' (small plaster-lined conical shaped pit, L.622, sq. Ai1), found near a flexed human burial (L.613, sq. Ai1; see Chapter 8, this volume). In the center of square S2, a collection of stones similar in construction and contours to other platforms may represent a partially destroyed platform (L.623).

Other Stratum IIA features (aside from fills) include primarily pits and hearths. Pit L. 620 (sq. Ai1), adjacent to wall 81, produced a highly polished and ground [amphibolite] votive axe (L.620, B.5082; see Chapter 12, this volume). The proximity of this pit, which appears to be shallow and directly under the wall, suggests a foundation deposit associated with the wall. To the south, in square S1, two large pits were exposed (L.639, L.643). South of those pits, pit (L. 618) clearly cut through circular mud-brick structure L.721. Also cutting this Stratum IIB structure (L.721) was pit L.703. South of this, in square N1, a series of pits (L.678/719, L.646, L.650) cut into the earlier, Stratum IIB surface of Room 11, where a tabular scraper (L.650, B.5176A) was found.

Next to those pits, straddling the line between squares N1 and M1, L.628 is a typical oval-shaped hearth, with burned beachrock fragments in a fine black ashy matrix. To the immediate southwest of this hearth, a series of four pits (L.696, L.710, L.714, L.713) in square M0 are designated as Stratum IIA primarily based on their relative contemporaneity with each other, and because L.710 cuts the earlier Stratum IIB wall 104. Also cutting wall 104 and its juncture with wall 87 was a large pit (L.700), which runs under the balk of square L0 on the south. This pit (L.700) produced an exceptional collection of artifacts, including two complete limestone spindle whorls (B.5322, B.5288), a pendant (B.5286) made of chlorite schist, a basalt fenestrated stand fragment

(B.5306), as well as a number of micro-endscrapers, grinders, and an un-worked hematite nodule (B.5281). The most exceptional artifact from this pit was a complete, polished, shallow granite bowl (B.5311) with rounded base.

To the west in square S0, a series of five hearths or shallow ashy pits were excavated (Fig. 5.3). The original contours of these as separate features could not be delineated; thus, these are known collectively as L.712. Contiguous to these hearths/pits, a deeper, larger pit (L.697) was cut into an even earlier Stratum IIB pit (L.709), but there was no clear distinction between these non-contemporaneous pits. The Stratum IIA pit (L. 697) contained a number of interesting artifacts, including a tabular scraper (B.5299), a bone awl (B.5304), a fenestrated basalt vessel fragment (B.5305), a violin-shaped figurine fragment (B.5294A), and a fragment of a ceramic figurine (B.5367).

Burials. Three complete human burials were exposed in Area T; a fourth burial (L.615) was only scattered human bone fragments found among the mud-brick collapse in square S2. These three were all discovered in Stratum IIA levels; the other burial (L.1510) is discussed in the section about Stratum IIC (see Chapter 8, this volume).

Burial L.613, in northern square Ai1, was an articulated complete flexed burial facing north. Age was estimated at 16–20 years old. No special finds were directly associated; though as mentioned previously, the votive axe (L.620, B.5082) was found nearby. The burial seemed to be placed in a shallow pit with a loose ash matrix.

Burial L. 648, in square S1, was also a flexed burial set on the right side, facing west. Preservation was not as good as L.613, but may be an older adolescent. No mortuary goods were found associated with this burial, which was along the edge of a pit (L.643; see Chapter 8, this volume).

Several other features were exposed during balk removals. Pit L. 760, exposed after the removal of the western balk of sq. MO, was clearly late, and may have been from the level of Stratum I originally. Within this pit, part of a vessel (B. 5443) was found. Another pit, L. 773, was discovered under the balk removal of squares, M0, M1, N0, N1 and may be the continuation of pit L.650. This pit appears later than, and cuts into, Stratum IIB pit L. 665, and is thus assigned to Stratum IIA.

Stratum IIB. Stratum IIB exhibits the best preservation of architectural elements and *in situ* features exposed in Area T (Figs 5. 4, 5.17, 5.20). The architecture in Area T provides important evidence of the restructuring of the cult complex at Gilat following the destruction of the Stratum IIC sanctuary. The following presents an overview of the main features exposed in Area T, Stratum IIB.

Room 11. Room 11 is defined by mud-brick walls 88 (N-S) on the east (sq. M1), wall 104 (N-S, squares M0, N0) on the west, and wall 87 (E-W, sq. M1) to the south. A small wall fragment (wall 105, E-W, sq. N1) we interpret as the northern wall to this room. In most cases, the mud-brick walls forming Room 11 are two rows with one course of well preserved mud-brick. The exception to this is wall 104, which was constructed of three rows. On the southern extent of wall 104, the later Stratum cuts the juncture with E-W Stratum IIB wall IIA-pit (L.700). The northern face of wall 104 has an additional row of stones, following the line of the wall further to the north. This is probably a slightly later, Stratum IIBi addition to the mud-brick wall, because the mud-brick continues no further than the line of wall 105, with which wall 104 probably originally formed a juncture. The stone row added was probably originally an attached wall to another room (associated with the room created by wall 102 just to the west), or part of a feature adjacent to the west side of room 11.

Within the confines of Room 11, a hard-packed, mud-brick surface (L.722) was exposed, with a contemporaneous pit (L.665). On the northern side of the room interior, L.723 is also a hard-packed, mud-brick surface probably associated with the room. Given that the preservation of the mud-brick extends no higher than one course, it is difficult to guess where the entrance to this room may have been, but the large gap in wall 89 on the northeast side of the room seems a likely possibility.

Platform/Porch (L.669). Just to the south of this gap in wall 89, abutting the exterior face of Room 11, a large stone platform was built in square M1. The platform/porch was built using flat, smoothed stones tightly placed and cemented using a mud-brick-like material. The platform/porch measures c. 3.5 m (N-S) and c. 1.1 m (E-W, maximum). Locus 669 is interpreted as a possible 'porch' because of its large size (Fig. 5.57) and the fact that the entrance to Room 11 seems to have been on the broadside of the room through wall 89. As such, the 'porch' sits on the well-constructed courtyard discussed below.

Courtyard. To the east of this 'porch', a hard-packed mud-brick surface (L.652) extends from its eastern edge across square M2 and into Area D. This surface also extends into Area J, abutting the concave mud-brick basin-like structures (Plate 5.18). The western-most hearth (L.654) is a typical oval-shaped hearth with a fine ash matrix and including burned angular beachrock fragments. About 0.5 m east of that hearth, the second hearth (L. 655) is smaller and more circular in shape, but is otherwise similar, with the same fine ash matrix and burned, angular beachrock fragments. To the east of these two hearths, along the western edge of square M2, an unusual hearth (L.647) was exposed (Plate 5.16). This hearth was exceptionally large (c. 1.5 m in diameter) and relatively deep (ranging from 0.7–0.9 m). The interior included the same type of fine ash matrix (of which many samples were taken, four full buckets floated, and the remainder sieved) as the other hearths, as well as the large, burned angular beachrock fragments. There was a large number of these burned beachrock fragments, and there seemed to be two concentrated piles, one on the west and one on the east. A large number of animal bone splinters were found in the ash associated with this large hearth.

Room 12. Room 12 is formed by mud-brick wall 100 (E-W, sq. M2-N2) on the south, wall 92 (E-W, sq. N2) on the north, and the remainders of a mud-brick wall 106 (N-S, sq. N1) on the west. Each of the walls consists of a double row of mud-brick, with a remaining height ranging from 0.25 to 0.35 m above the surface. Within the area defined by these walls, a hard-packed mud-brick surface (L.724, sq. N2) was exposed, similar to that of Room 11 and the 'courtyard' area with the three hearths. On the inner (northern) side of wall 100, a small stone installation was built into the wall. This installation was a semi-circular line of stones with a mud-brick center, possibly functioning as a small shelf or bench inside the room.

Mud-brick Circle. One of the most enigmatic and intriguing architectural features found in Area T was a well-built circular mud-brick wall (L.721, initially called wall 82). This circular installation extended across squares N1 and S1, but was cut in several places by Stratum IIA pits (L.618 to the east, L.703 on the west and L.639 to the north). Despite these destructive intrusions, it is clear that this was a circular double row of mud-brick, with only one course preserved. The inner diameter is 3.4 m, and the outer diameter is c. 4 m, which is only slightly larger than the stone circular structure found in Stratum IIA, Area J, in squares H4/H5. This mud-brick circle seems to represent the foudation of circular platform and served a similar ceremonial function to the ones discovered in Stratum IIB, Area J (see above).

Other walls, pits and hearths. A number of features were exposed which are not directly associated with the previously described larger architectural elements (Fig. 5.18). Directly north of the large circular mud-brick structure (L.721), in square S1, a number of wall fragments and hearths were uncovered. Adjoining the outer northeastern edge of L.721, a small stone feature (L.690) forms a three-walled installation. On the west side of square S1, a conglomeration of stone and mud-brick (L.691) appears to be the result of structural collapse. Just north of this, wall 95 is a small fragment of a stone and mud-brick course of indeterminate rows, cut by the later Stratum IIA-pit (L.639) just to the east. Directly north of wall 95, two well-preserved hearths were uncovered.

About 0.1 m to the north of wall 95, L.683 is a fairly typical hearth: oval, filled with fine black ash and burned angular beachrock fragments. The other hearth, L.681, touching hearth L.683, is equally typical of the hearths found at Gilat. Both hearths were dug into the Stratum IIB surface (L.663) that extends across the northern part of square S1 and into the southernmost part of square Ai1. About 1.5 meter to the east, a pit (L.661) was also contemporaneous with this surface (L.663). An additional double course mud-brick wall fragment, W94, running E-W, was uncovered just south of this pit (L.661) and seems contemporaneous with the surface joining these features. The large number of small hearths that are scattered throughout Area T contrasts markedly with domestic sites such as Shiqmim, Shiqmim South, Grar, Horvat Beter and other localities (cf. Porath 1992; Gilead 1995) where hearths are usually found in smaller numbers and in association with domestic houses.

In square S2, to the northeast of the large mud-brick circle (L.721; Pate 5.49), a single row, single course, small mud-brick arc (L.631) was exposed. The northern end of the arc abuts the southern end of stone wall 83. Contemporaneous with this mud-brick wall (L.631), a surface may have extended ca. .80 meters to the east. Against the stone wall 83, a hearth or pit (L.637) was built. Slightly further to the east an additional small pit (L.638) was exposed. This may represent an additional circular mud-brick platform adjacent and in the same courtyard as the larger L. 721 circular platform.

To the north, in squares Ai0, Ai1 and Ai2, preservation seemed to be poorer and stratigraphic relationships more difficult. Nevertheless, it is clear there was a great deal of building in this area, and thus some sub-phasing of Stratum IIB (i and ii) became necessary.

The previously mentioned Stratum IIB surface (L.663) extended into the southern section of Square Ai/1 for about 1.5 m. On the northern extent of square Ai1, a small mud-brick wall fragment (84) was exposed, unassociated with surrounding features and surfaces. Wall 84 is merely four mud-bricks and two stones. Immediately north of this wall, a hearth or pit (L.642) was excavated. The matrix of this pit was typical of a hearth (burned beachrock fragments and fine dark ash), but the boundaries of the feature were ambiguous and impossible to delineate in places, because of the soft, loose ash fill into which it was originally dug. Excavation of this feature was followed to a depth of approximately 0.5 m, but whether this was the actual original depth we remained uncertain.

Northwest of this pit, another pit (L.626) was discovered next to and slightly below the Stratum IIA pit (L.620). This pit (L.620) was about 1.5 m in depth, and was relatively rich, containing ochre (B.5105), a spindle whorl (B.5106), a basalt vessel fragment (B.5117) and a piece of quartz (B.5118).

Mud-brick walls 112 and 111 form a corner in the eastern center of square Ai0. Preservation was poor, and there is no more than one course of mud-brick preserved for either wall. Within (east of) the corner formed by the juncture of walls 112 and 111, an ash layer (L. 774) was excavated, exposing the contemporary surface (L.1585). Surface L.1585 matches in elevation (c. 127.00 m) the surface (L.662) to the east which was excavated in square Ai1, 1991. A hearth (L.1501) was placed in this surface near the east face of wall 111.

Mud-brick wall 101, running SW to NE, across squares Ai1 and Ai2 forms a corner with wall 111 in the 1m × 1m balk. Checking the elevations, it became clear that the western part of wall 101 was probably contemporary with walls 111 and 112. The eastern half, separate (by over 1 m) in square Ai2, was given a different wall number (126, Stratum IIC, see below), as the alignment is not the same as the western half, and the elevations are lower. Wall 91, in square Ai2, aligns better and the elevations are much closer, thus it is probably the continuation of wall 101. Preservation of both walls 101 and 91 were poor, with not even a complete single course of mud-bricks preserved in wall

91. The aforementioned surfaces (L. 662, L. 1585) and the hearth (L. 1501) seem to belong to the room formed by these walls (111, 112, 101 and 91).

Just south of the probable juncture of walls 111 and 101, on the opposite side of the 1m × 1m balk, a stone structure or collapse (L.795) seems to match in elevation those of walls 111 and 101. While it is not clear without removing the 1m × 1m balk between these walls and L. 795, it seems likely that L. 795 is either the remainder of a contiguous wall or the collapse from some contemporary feature.

To the west of the room formed by walls 111, 101 and 112, in square Ai0, a Stratum IIBi feature of a semi-circle of stones, wall 110, was built abutting the northern face of IIBii wall 112. It appears that these stones may have intruded upon the mud-brick of wall 112, thus the slightly later phase attribution. However, this is not certain, and the stones of wall 110 may have been a contemporaneous construction with wall 112.

Also in square Ai0, along the southern edge, pit (L.787) is assigned to IIBii, possibly slightly earlier than the mud-brick walls to the east. Within this pit, a dog cranium (B.5553) was found near the bottom. Also within this pit, two beads (B. 5529[amazonite], B.5535[flint]) were found in sieving. In the northwestern corner of this square, pit L. 775 (IIBii) was excavated according to the four major depositional layers. Three beads (B.5537, B.5469, B.5509), an ivory (?) half-ring (B. 5470) and part of a shell pendant (B.5470) were recovered from this pit. About 2 m to the southwest, a possible wall (109) runs N-S. Wall 102, a Stratum IIB wall, runs c. 2 m from the western balk of square N0. At this point, this possible mud-brick wall 109 forms a juncture and runs north c. 4.5 m. Despite careful excavation, this was never confidently determined to be a wall, and no contiguous features or floors were ever delineated.

In square S0, to the south of Stratum IIA pit L.697, another deeper pit (L.709) was uncovered. The distinction between these two pits (of different strata) was never entirely clear, but the greater depth of the upper rim of pit L.709 determined its earlier stratigraphic assignation. In order to excavate pit L.709, a hard burned mud-brick surface (L.727) was removed. A large amount of cultural debris was recovered from the pit (L.709), including a trapezoidal ferruginous sandstone token (B.5329), a bone awl (B.5341), the base of a conical vessel (B.5335A), a nearly complete ceramic fenestrated stand (B.5349; Plate 5.50), a complete tubular vessel and a mortar (B.5368A). The sides of this pit may actually have been constructed of mud-brick material, unlike the majority of other pits excavated in Area T. On the south side of pit L.709, two remaining features are Stratum IIB. In square N/0, a small stone and mud-brick wall runs E-W. Wall 102 is similar in construction technique to the stone section of wall 104 (discussed under Room 11, above) just to the east, with a double row, single course of mud-brick with a single line of stones on the northern face of the wall.

East of wall 102, a shallow pit or hearth (L.706) was filled with stone collapse that was probably part of the original pit/hearth superstructure. The matrix was typical fine, loose dark ash, but the stones found within do not seem burned to the degree evident in the large Stratum IIB hearth (L.647) in square M2. Hearth/pit (L.706) did not seem to cut wall 104 or wall 102, and because the rim of the feature is roughly the same as the base of the walls, we consider this contemporary.

In summary, Stratum IIB may be typified by the construction of the mud-brick circles, rectilinear rooms, relatively standardized hearths, and a variety of fairly amorphous pits. There is some evidence to suggest that surfaces were not simply earth beaten or trodden surfaces, but intentionally laid like "mud-brick plaster" surfaces. These surfaces, particularly L.724, L.652, L.722, and L.723, are hard and found with little cultural debris *in situ*. This fact, and the lack of associated ash (typically found with many surfaces, e.g., at Shiqmim) on the surface or just above, suggests a different attitude towards maintenance of the surfaces or may be a reflection of abandonment behavior at the site. Whether or not frequent cleaning or periodic intentional re-surfacing could be the explanation is unknown, however, consideration of site formation process points to the care and attention given to these surfaces and a concern with the notion of 'dirt' or cleanliness by the occupants of the site during this occupation phase.

Stratum IIC. Stratum IIC constitutes the major phase and broadest exposure in Area T during the 1992 season (Fig. 5.5; Plate 5.52). Removal of IIB walls 88, 89, 104 (forming Room 11), stone structure/platform (L.669), walls 100 and 92, and contemporary surfaces (L. 652, 722, 724, 723) from squares M1, M2, N1 and N2 exposed a broad plaza surface (L.1544; Figs. 5.5, 5.16, 5.21). This surface, c. 0.3 m below the IIB surfaces and associated architecture were hard-packed, flat and surprisingly devoid of features and pits across these squares. In square M2, L.788 was probably only an ash lens in an otherwise homogeneous fill (L.772, L.763) which further reinforced the impression of an intentionally built surface. Just south of the ash lens, in square M2, a shallow depression with an ashy matrix (L.1504) may be the remnants of a destroyed hearth. Across squares N2 to the north and M1 to the west, no other features were contemporary with the surface (L.1544). In square N1, two large pits contemporary with the surface (L.1544) were exposed. The southern pit (L.1508) was amorphous in shape, and was a simple cut (possibly two overlapping cuts) from the surface down into the sterile Pleistocene sediments. Half of a quartz ring (bead, B. 5611) was found. The other pit (L.1514), approximately 0.5 m to the north, was of typical cylindrical shape, quite deep (c. 1 m) and had an unfinished limestone bead (B.5654). To the west (c. 1.5 m) of this pit (L.1514), another pit (L.1505), was a large cylindrically shaped pit with a torpedo (B. 5614) with two spindle whorls (B. 5617, B.5618; see Plate 5.54), a flat-based vessel fragment (B. 5640), a beautiful complete red painted bi-conical vessel (B. 5639; Plate 5.55), and a worked sherd (token, B. 5651) (see Chapter 12, this volume, for an overview of the ground stone industry).

To the north, at the northern limits of squares N1 and N2, two walls seem to form a boundary for the northern limits of the surface (L.1544). In square N2, E-W wall 121 is a single row and course of stones extending c. 3.5 m, with occasional mud-brick preserved on top. Abutting wall 121 at its NW face, wall 123 was a single course of stone across the northern limit of square N1 and into square N2, with a single course of mud-brick preserved on top in some spots. Wall 123, c. 5 m long, appears to be a double row of stones in places, though not always clearly. On the south center face of wall 123 (NE corner of sq. N1), a double course of mud-bricks seem to be part of W123, but without any stone below. While both walls 123 and 121 appear to be contemporary with the large surface L. 1544, wall #123 may be slightly earlier, possibly built at the time of the surface. Wall 121, of much less robust construction, may have been a slightly later addition while the surface was in use. On the north face and covering the middle of wall 123, a mass of mud-brick was uncovered. It remains unclear whether this was a platform associated with wall 123, or simply collapse of the superstructure. Given the amorphous shape and shallow depth of the mud-bricks, we prefer the latter explanation.

North of these two walls, a series of surfaces, hearths and other features were assigned Stratum IIC both on the basis of relative elevations and stratigraphic relation to the removal of IIB features and surfaces. Directly north of walls 123 and 121, two hearths (L.1516 and L.1570) were of typical dimensions and construction. Both were oval in shape and had burned beachrock tightly packed in an ashy matrix, with occasional reddish brown burned earth lines demarcating the edge of the feature.

West of these three hearths, in square S1, a small (c. 0.35 m maximum diameter) pit (L. 793) was excavated from the first hard surface found under the removal of the IIB architecture. This pit was conical and quite deep (c. 0.5 m) for such a small pit, and it may represent a post-hole. The surface with which it was associated was difficult to follow, but the "post-hole" seemed to be on a rise or mound of hard-packed mud-brick material. About 1.5 m to the north, an amorphous ashy dump with a concentration of bones and stone (L.1512) appears contemporary with the remainder of a hard-packed surface (L.1559) in the NE of square S1. Another surface (L.1560) was found below and extending into square S2, suggesting repeated reuse of the area. Between the 'post-hole' (L. 793) and these surfaces, a large amount of mud-brick collapse was exposed. Lines of mud-brick could sometimes be discerned, but no structure could be delineated.

East of these features, in square S2, a number of hearths were exposed. L.1532 was actually two overlapping hearths; though neither had any stones within them, both had an ashy matrix, oval shape and burn lines at the rims. Slightly further to the west, L. 1538 was another hearth of typical dimensions and characteristics (Plate 5.56). Directly south of these three hearths, the removal of Stratum IIB stone wall 83 and curvilinear mud-brick wall (L. 631) exposed the continuation of the mud-brick-lined pit L.1511 (same as L. 682, 1991 excavations; Fig. 5.66). The southeast interior of this pit was excavated, and a large amount of artifacts and faunal remains was recovered. Among the more interesting finds were an unfired ceramic vessel base (B. 5700), a fenestrated basalt stand fragment (B.5720), and a violin-shaped figurine fragment (B. 5730). In addition, a geological sample of four exceptionally well-preserved and large mud-bricks were taken (B. 5782). Though a nice line of mud-bricks demarcated the rim and thus the dimensions of the pit, no such luck favored the interior of the pit. It remains unclear whether the bottom of the pit was found, gone through by our excavations, or not yet reached.

In squares Ai1 and Ai2, no further IIC features were revealed, but some changes in strata designations placed pits L. 675, 671, 668, and 679 in IIC. This change was effected for two reasons: first, the elevations of the tops of these pits is more closely commiserate with the elevations established for IIC levels in the southern squares, and secondly, the IIIA surface (L.1584) of square S2 is clearly below that of the tops of these pits. This same surface may be seen in the southern section (1991) of square Ai2, and is discussed more fully under Stratum IIIA.

In square Ai0, other than the fill (L.792), only one feature, pit L. 1507, was in Stratum IIC. To the south, on the border between squares S0 and S1, burial L. 1510 was assigned to Stratum IIC because it cut through the IIIA surface (L.1552). The burial was a flexed articulated adult male (?), which had been placed in a shallow cut in the earlier surface, oriented E-W, and facing north. Just 0.2 m southwest of the cranium, a vertical stone (B.5685, massebah) was standing upright. On the southwest side and touching the stone was the base of a vessel (B.5686) with very friable sherds of the same vessel. Though very close in proximity, the cranium and stone were not actually abutting. However, a large chunk of an unworked sandstone (B. 5683) was clearly associated with the burial directly under the ribcage of the skeleton. The sandstone has a brilliant blue mineral (copper bearing minerals?) acting as the binder, and is about 0.15 m × 0.1 m. No identification of the mineral has been made to date.

The previously mentioned hard-packed mud-brick and Pleistocene surface (L. 1544) extending across squares M1, M2, N1 and N2 does not extend into squares M0 and N0. Instead, a series of overlapping pits were cut from about the level of the IIC surface into the sterile Pleistocene sediments. While it is clear at a glance that pits such as L.781 and L.780 are later than pit L.771, this is only apparent once the sterile Pleistocene surface is fully excavated. While these pits could be divided into sub-phases of IICi and IICii, this would be arbitrary and unwarranted given the lack of contiguous features necessary to define later from earlier pits.

With the exception of one special find (half of a limestone mace head/loomweight, B. 5780) from pit L.1549, all of these pits are notable primarily for the paucity of artifacts and faunal remains, despite complete sieving of all of them. In addition, the utter futility of delineating many of the pits' contours prior to nearly complete excavation is due to the homogeneity of the pit fills.

These pits bear little resemblance to storage facilities, for they are not lined or constructed, nor are they deep. Yet, they certainly do not seem excavated for refuse dumps, as the low density of any artifact category will indicate in the future. The solution seems to be that the pits are primarily the result of quarrying activity for the hard sterile Pleistocene sediments, presumably used for the surfaces and probably for the mud-brick materials as well. It may not be coincidental that such a plethora of pits occurs in close proximity to the surfacing of L. 1544 (squares M1, M2, N1, N2) and continues into Area J.

Stratum IIIA. With the exception of the large surfaced area (L.1544), most areas of Area T were excavated at least to Stratum III, or even to the sterile Pleistocene basement levels of the site. Only a small amount of architecture was preserved from Stratum III, the majority presumably destroyed during the later stratum II rebuilding activity. In order to achieve a better understanding of the surface (L.1544) of squares M1, M2, N1 and N2, a section of this surface was excavated along the border of squares M0 and M1. Only c. 0.1 m below the IIC surface, another surface was exposed along a strip of c. 2–3 m (EW) by 5 m (NS) in squares M0 and M1. This surface (L.1586) differed from the later IIC surface; basically, the surface is flat sterile Pleistocene sediments with hard-packed 'mud-brick' material directly on it. Into this very hard surface, small shallow (c. 0.12–0.25 m) cuts, or pits (L.1521, L.1533) were cut. In addition, small shallow (c. 0.05 m) holes were cut (L. 1588), possible as supports for posts (or a stand with several legs?). This surface is missing where the later series of IIC pits cuts deeper in square M0, though a small portion was still preserved on the western center edge and the southwest corner of square M0.

To the north, in square N0, an unusual stone and mud-brick structure (L. 1567) was built directly on the Pleistocene sediments. Unfortunately some stones and mud-brick related to this structure were removed during its initial discovery. The function of this structure remains perplexing, but clearly was more substantial than a hearth or oven, because of the size and the lack of burning associated with it. Just to the west of this structure, a pit (L.1572) was dug into the Pleistocene sediments from the base of the structure; with only half of it exposed in square N0. At the top of the pit, a fine celt was found, and inside the pit, numerous fragments (including rims and the base) from a basalt vessel (B.5857) were recovered.

Further north, in square S0, a hard-packed mud-brick and reworked Pleistocene sediment surface (L.1552) was exposed, with contemporary pits (L.1536, L.1535 and L.1534). Within pit L.1534, a fenestrated basalt fragment (B.5727) and a bone awl (B.5746) were recovered. Just to the east, in square S1, two walls were exposed, though perhaps not absolutely contemporaneous. Running N-S (c. 2.2 m) along the western edge of square S1, wall 116 was a double row, single course of mud-brick about 0.4–0.5 m wide. Continuing directly south along the same alignment, wall 125 was a single row, double course, curvilinear mud-brick wall about 0.25 m in width. A shallow pit (L.1529) cut between these two walls, destroying any connection that may have existed. Though construction of the two walls is obviously not the same, the alignment fits well, as do the elevations at the base of the walls. Thus, whether wall 125 and wall 116 were built as one structure or not, they appear to be roughly contemporaneous.

A good stratigraphic connection was found via surface L.1552 in square S0, which runs up to the west base of wall 116. Another surface (L.1577), continues along the east side of wall 116 at a similar elevation, and continues in the northeastern area of square S1. This same surface continues into square S1 (L.1584) where a number of pits (L.1576, L.1565) and hearths (L.1575, L.1574 and L.1566) were cut from the surface or the same level. On the other side of later (IIC) pit (L. 682–1511), another pit (L. 1518) was also cut from the same level, though the same surface was not found to the east of the Stratum IIC pit (L. 682–1511). A scoria palette (B. 5862) was found in pit L.1576.

Further to the north, in the southwestern section of square Ai0, a rubbish dump (L.1530) directly over an ashy surface (L.1539) were at close relative elevations (126.71/.66 A.M.S.) to the base (126.68 A.M.S.) of a circular mud-brick feature (L.1525) directly to the north. These elevations are the same as that of the surface (L.1552, 126.65 A.M.S.) in the northern part of square S0, and thus the stratigraphic associations seem clear. The circular mud-brick feature (L.1525) was a single row and single course, and no depth below the base of the mud-bricks was found. The interior (L.1519) was relatively clean of any cultural artifacts, though the interior surface was preserved. The clean nature of the interior matrix and the small diameter does not resemble that of the silos known from other areas of Gilat (i.e. L.1341, L.1369, Area J 1992), nor was there evidence of burning.

In squares Ai1 and Ai2, there seems to be a major in-filling phase during IIIA, with no evidence of building activity. Other than the fills (L.716, L.676), only a few features were identified. To the east of Stratum IIIB pit L.640, a possible pit or hearth (L.707, square Ai1) was exposed originally dug into the fill (L.708) covering the sterile basal level. Walls of pit L.707 were never clearly defined, and a large amount of cores and rubble had been dumped into it.

In square Ai2, two pits were exposed in Stratum IIIA. L.675 was a pit in the northeastern corner of the square and running into the northern balk; about 1 m south of that, another pit (L 673) was exposed. Neither of these pits was lined or constructed in any way, and neither produced any exceptional finds. Across this area are numerous carved out depressions and pit bottoms (without any clear difference between the two), which seem to have been made at an earlier time. This is discussed further in the next section below, Stratum IIIB.

Stratum IIIB. Some of the best evidence for the Stratum IIIB occupation at Gilat was found in Area T. The 15 × 5 m area of squares Ai0, Ai1 and Ai2 were excavated to the sterile sediments. Across this exposure, almost all of square Ai2, and most of square Ai1, was excavated during the 1991 season. Square Ai0 and the completion of squares Ai1 and Ai2 was achieved during the 1992 year. The complete excavation of these three squares offers the broadest exposure of the sterile basement levels of the site. At this early level, there is virtually no flat ground; all of the 75 m² area consists of carved out, broad cavities in the natural sediments, with the bottom of smaller pits juxtaposed onto these broad depressions in the sterile sediments. The exception to the lack of cultural materials are found in three pits: L.640 (1991), pit (L.1579) on the border between squares Ai1 and Ai2, and the dog burial found in a large pit (L.698) in square Ai2.

Dog burial. The discovery of an unually well-preserved dog burial with grave offering provides an additional body of evidence concerning Chalcolithic ritual practice. In square Ai2, a thick (c. 1.7 m) ashy fill covered the square, into which the IIIA pits (L.673, L.675) were dug. Removal of this fill exposed two interesting features. One was the large pit L.692 in the northern aspect of the square, which a Stratum IIC pit (L.671) had cut into on the western side. Pit L.692 was about 2 m in diameter and IIC fill deposits and the aforementioned pit had clearly disturbed the upper portion of the pit. Within pit L.692, a complete dog-burial (L.698) was exposed facing south (see Chapter 6, this volume). At the hind end (east) of the dog, an unusual ceramic vessel (B.5383) was clearly associated with the dog. The vessel is a double-handled, cylindrical vessel with the exterior walls shaved. The dog and vessel were placed in a depression within the pit, surrounded by complete mud-brick that may have been either placed there or collapsed from the pit wall superstructure. Though other finds were recovered from within the same pit, such as a black stone bead (B.5258), a worked ceramic piece (B.5254A), and a limestone token (B.5384) and thus could be considered mortuary artifacts, only the vessel may be directly associated with the dog with absolute confidence (Plate 5.58).

An additional dog cranium was also found in the western part of the same pit (L.692) as the dog burial, and at the same relative elevation (c. 125.50 m AMSL) making it a 'double-dog' burial (Plate 5.58). In the northeastern aspect of pit L.692 and at the same elevation, a dog mandible was also found (originally given a new locus, L.702, but now considered the same as the interior finds of the larger pit L.692). (For a full discussion of this animal see Chapter 6, this volume.) Immediately south of this pit, removal of a thick layer of mottled ash, silt and mud-brick fill (L.676) exposed the hard sterile Pleistocene basement. On top of this sterile basal level, a layer of hard-packed mud-brick material (L.725) was found, though it is unclear whether this was intentional leveling by the inhabitants, or simply material dropped, trodden and packed without intentional construction.

In square N0, sterile levels were also exposed. Just to the north of the stone and mud-brick structure (L.1567), a small cylindrical pit (L.1569) was cut into the sterile sediments. In the matrix, the base and body sherds from the same vessel were found, and at the bottom of the pit, a large flat worked piece of limestone (B. 5827) probably served as the base to steady the vessel. About 0.5 m to the southeast of this pit, a similar pit (L.1583) was found, though without the limestone base or vessel fragments. It should be noted that designation of these features as Stratum IIIB is based on elevations, but these features may actually belong to Stratum IIIA—it is impossible to be certain. The sterile sediments on which Stratum IIIA structure L.1567 was built slopes down to the north where these small pits were found, but they may actually be contemporaneous with the structure (L.1567) and the pit to the west (L.1572). At these early levels, given the undulating, repeatedly carved and pitted nature of the hard Pleistocene sediments, absolute elevations are of little relevance.

In the southeast area of square S2, the bottom of Stratum IIIA pit (L.1565) was a hard-packed surface sloping down to the north. This seemed to be a beaten earth surface that became the bottom of the pit when originally excavated. A similar, but higher surface (L.1589) was discovered on the last day of excavation directly east of this pit. As both surfaces are clearly earlier than the Stratum IIIA pits (L.1575, 1576, 1565, 1566, and 1574) and surface (L.1584), they were assigned to Stratum IIIB.

Stratum IV. In square Ai2, two pits (L.705, L.718) and a surface (L.725) directly on the sterile level, just north of the pits, were all tentatively designated Stratum IV (Plate 5.59). This was because of the thick (c. 0.75 m) fill deposit (L.676) which overlay the pits and surface, into which Stratum IIIB pit (L.692, in which the dog burial was placed) cut. However, though these pits were very likely earlier than the dog burial (L. 698) and the pit in which it was placed (L.692), the isolated nature of these deep pits (L. 705, 718) demonstrate the difficulty of identifying Stratum IV at the site.

Area Y. Area Y is located due south of Alon and Levy's 1987 (1989) excavations in squares L5, L6, and L7 of Area D (Plate 5.60). Six 5 m × 5 m squares were opened in Area Y (Fig. 5.74). The east area was separated from the 1987 excavation area by a .50m. Balk on the north of squares K5, K6, and K7 (Fig. 5.10), creating a c. 1 m balk between the areas. To the west of the Area Y, another 1 m balk was established to separate it from Area J. In addition, to facilitate accurate drawings, two 1m × 1m balks were left in the center of the excavation block, one at the corner of Squares J5, K5, K6 and J6, and one at the corners of K5, K7, J6 and J7 (Fig. 5.11). This proved an excellent method of providing solid grid points for the survey team, yet obviated the necessity of balks (and balk removals). These square meter balks were taken into consideration for the computation of the loci volumetric data found on the loci sheets.

Some mention of methodology is warranted. As a matter of policy, all pits, surfaces and matrix associated with burials was sieved through 5 mm sieves, and all material from the sieving was kept for later separation by material type in the laboratory. While in rare instances this policy may have been overlooked, virtually all of these features were sieved, and thus sieving is only mentioned where it was overlooked or determined to be unnecessary. In addition, many flotation and fine screen (wet sieved) samples were taken.

Stratum I. Like other areas at Gilat, the surface in Area Y was disturbed through deep-plowing in the 1950s and until the mid-1970s when a vineyard was established on the site. The topsoil in Area Y was plentiful in Chalcolithic artifacts, but devoid of any *in situ* features, surfaces or architecture. In addition, the upper strata had some modern and historic material as well, such as glass, World War I bullet shells, Byzantine pottery, etc. It was quickly evident that the upper c. 0.3–0.4 m (below surface) was entirely disturbed, and this topsoil was removed with heavy tools. As a control, each topsoil locus had two guffa containers (Arabic = bucket made of old tires) of matrix sieved and all material was saved to provide an indicator of the potential amount of cultural material in the upper stratum.

Stratum II. Excavation of fills across the east area often exposed features such as pits (L. 523, 519, 520, 533, 522, 532) mud-brick 'platforms' or surfaces (L. 518, 540), and collapse (L. 508 B. 1085, L. 546, 544) which, due to their lack of clear association with each other and the absence of architecture, are difficult to assign to sub-phases as was possible in Areas J and T. Rather than rely solely on elevations to distinguish these sub-phases, some of these features are simply assigned to Stratum II without further distinction (see Table 5.1; Figs. 5.3–5.4).

In some cases, no clear distinction was discerned between the topsoil and the subsequent fills now assigned to this stratum. These fills were softer and less densely packed than the Stratum I topsoil that had been compacted from use as a road in recent times. While the removal of the Stratum I fills exposed the first signs of *in situ* Chalcolithic features and recovered a plethora of Chalcolithic cultural material, the fills themselves revealed little of interest with the exception of fill L. 515. This fill (sq. K6) was very loose silt and ash, and exposed IIA pits, L. 533 and L. 520, the latter of which may have been a hearth based on the burned flint cores and stones. Below the removal of this rubble pit/hearth L. 520, a violin-shaped figurine fragment (B. 1127; see Chapter 15, this volume) was found. Grigson (this volume) has suggested that some equid bones found in this fill (B. 1183) may be intrusive, however, horse remains were found at contemporary Shiqmim. As in the case with the first fill excavated in square J6 (L. 528, discussed below), the loose ashy deposits, without surfaces or features, indicates the possible disturbed nature of this context.

Stratum IIA. Removal of fills in squares J5 (L. 512), K5 (L. 507), and K6 (L. 509) exposed the first indications of architecture and features. In square K5, L. 518 was a c. 1.5 m × 1.5 m mud-brick feature, possibly a platform, was found. Just to the south of this mud-brick feature, what was probably the remains of a wall (51; Fig. 5.3) was delineated running in an east-west fashion and probably contemporaneous with the mud-brick feature (L. 518). Both features were largely mud-brick material, hard-packed, with some stones in the structure.

To the east of these features, in square K6, L. 510 was the exposure and removal of a human burial, possibly a juvenile. Placed in a shallow pit in fill L. 528, this burial was not well-preserved, but seemed to be partially articulated, probably facing southwest (see Chapter 8, this volume). No grave offerings were discovered with the burial, and no association with other features or surfaces could be postulated. It should be noted that Grigson (this volume) identified very probable intrusive animal bones (equid?) in the fill (L. 528) associated with this burial, which suggests the possibility that the burial itself may be intrusive. Given the large amount of ashy fill excavated in this fill (L. 528), it is entirely possible that some intrusive elements are not associated with other finds from the same fill.

In square J5, clearance of fill (L. 512) exposed a hard-packed surface (L. 516), with contemporaneous pit (L. 517) on the eastern aspect of the square. Clearance of the fill in L. 512 may have included material from the surface below, including artifacts such as a double-handled miniature (votive?) sherd (B. 1063), a tabular scraper (B. 1067), a granite palette (B. 1068), a ceramic hollowed 'pipe' or vessel base (B. 1070) and a rubber (B. 1071). These finds were at elevations 127.60 m–127.33 m AMSL) quite close to the top elevations (127.55 m–127.35 m) of the surface below (L. 516).

Exposure of this surface (L. 516) suggested the contemporaneity of the pit (L. 517) to the east, which contained some human bones, found in the sieving. On the surface, additional artifacts were recovered such as a fine chisel (B. 1086), a mortar (B. 1075) and some mother of pearl fragments

(B. 1087). The northern exposed area of the surface was along the division of squares K5 and J5, where a small stone feature (L. 511) was exposed. This feature was simply two small flat stones and a large sherd placed vertically around a horizontal and flat beachrock fragment, which may have functioned as a post-holder or vessel stand. Later, it became clear from both the western profile of square K5 and removal of the balk between K5 and K4 (see west Area J above, for further discussion) that this surface L. 516 almost certainly extended across square K5 as well.

Squares J5 and K5 represent the only area where sub-phases could be assigned to loci with any degree of confidence. Certainly pits L. 520 and L. 533, and collapse/structures L. 544 and L. 546 in square J6 could be assigned to Stratum IIA based on elevations, but the lack of association between the areas in squares J5 and K5 and the features of square J6 make the stratigraphic association speculative. Further east, the stratigraphic association is even hazier.

Stratum IIB. Removal of surface L. 516 in square J5 exposed a square (c. 1 m) platform (L. 521; Plate 5.61) constructed of flat, polished beachrock grinding stones, cores, beachrock fragments and a churn neck fragment, all placed tightly together in a single horizontal feature. The majority of stones used to construct this platform were grinding stones. Whether these were recycled or functioned as part of a large grinding installation is difficult to determine (Fig. 5.62).

To the north in square K5, removal of Stratum IIA wall 51 (L. 536), and fill removal (sq. K5: L. 527, L534; sq. J5: L. 525) exposed a series of contemporaneous features. Two pits (L. 529, L. 530) were exposed to the south of the grinding stone installation (L. 521; Fig. 5.13). Underneath and slightly to the south running into the 1 m × 1 m balk, a very dark, ashy pit (L. 537) was exposed with a fired limestone/chalk 'incense burner' (B. 1401) sitting directly on top. A pebbled surface (L. 538) was laid on a hard surface, extending c. 1 m to the south, and c. 3 m from the western balk of squares J5/K5 almost to the edge of ashy pit L. 537.

Stratum IIC. As in Stratum IIB, *in situ* features with the clearest association to Stratum IIC are concentrated in squares J5 and K5 (Fig. 5.5). Because an intriguing mud-brick oval structure (L. 582; Plate 5.64) had already been exposed (discussed in greater detail under Stratum IIIB), it became necessary to remove the grinding stone installation/platform (L. 521). Two features were exposed when this installation (L. 521) was dismantled and the fill (L. 588) exposed. One of these, L. 591, was a low EW wall, with a mud-brick 'buttress' or 'wing' running south perpendicularly off each end of this wall. The main wall L. 591 runs roughly EW c. 1.10 m, with the mud-brick protrusions extending off each end c. 0.75 m on the west, and c. 0.6 m on the east. The wall is constructed of mud-brick-like material with occasional flat stones within, forming no clear courses, and stands c. 0.5–0.55m in height, with a breadth of c. 0.3 m. The back (north) of the structure is built directly on top of foundation fill around the earlier oval mud-brick structure (L. 582).

Opposite this wall c. 1 m, L. 587 is a conglomeration of mud-bricks and stones. Removal of these exposed L. 589, three vertically placed rocks roughly parallel to the wall of L. 591. These rocks are of differing sizes, with the largest on the west (height: 0.37 m, width: 0.22 m, thick: 0.12 m), the smallest on the east (height: 0.2 m, width: 0.14 m, thick: 0.1 m), and the mid-sized in between (height: 0.3 m, width: 0.18 m, thick: 0.1 m). Abutting on the south of these three vertical rocks is a burned semi-circle which appears to support the stones, though whether this was a fortuitous occurrence or an intentional and integral part of the three stones standing alone is unclear. These three stones sit directly on top of the upper limits of a Stratum IIIB large circular pit (L. 586; Plate 5.64).

Two hypotheses have been suggested to explain the function of these two (L. 591, L. 589) structures. The first views these two features as interrelated, with the wall as a kind of altar or offering place associated with cultic ritual. The three vertical stones may represent standing stones, with parallel phenomena in the Sinai and western Negev that were also associated with cultic rituals (Avner 1984). The main problem with this hypothesis is that no finds of any type were found associated with either feature, thus neither supporting nor disconfirming the thesis.

The second hypothesis is based on some similarities with other platform features discovered in Area J (see above). Some of these platforms are built up with walls constructed of flat rocks underneath the final 'cap' of horizontally placed stones. The second hypothesis suggests that because some of the grinding stones are resting directly on the low wall L. 591, the dismantling of the horizontally laid grinders and beachrock simply exposed part of a single construction, the foundation so to speak, of a well-made single unit (Plate 5.64). This second hypothesis does not dispute the cultic possibilities of the structure. The inherent problem with this thesis is that of a single wall as support, that is, why is there not a similar wall on the southern side of the structure? Is this because the original wall L. 591 was simply reused to construct a different structure on top?

Other features in Stratum IIC are designated as such on a tentative basis. In square J6, an infant burial (L. 551) was exposed in the southeastern corner of the square. This burial, in such poor condition that no excavation was possible, was underneath L. 544 and L. 546, both collapse or rubble fill, and below the levels of pits L. 520 and L. 533. In addition, it was above the Stratum IIIA surface (L. 567) and the associated articulated burial (L. 579).

Stratum III. In Area Y, Stratum III suffers from the same stratigraphic problems as Stratum II; namely sub-phase assignments in this eastern portion of the site are exceedingly difficult. The possible exception to this is in square J5 where a well built oval mud-brick structure (L. 582, Fig. 5.72) was exposed.

Stratum IIIA. At the northern extent of square J5, and the southern edge of the pebbled surface (L. 538), two pits were exposed. On the west, pit L. 575 was excavated exposing burned beachrock fragments at the bottom, with a fine curved mud-brick lining forming all but the eastern wall 59, which was loose and ashy with negative impressions where mud-bricks had fallen out. L. 576 (Fig. 5.6) represents the eastern side of wall 59, that was filled with a similar ashy matrix. The eastern face of wall 59, forming the western wall of pit L. 576, that was constructed of mud-brick material and tabular sandstone placed vertically, some of which where burned or slightly scorched.

The decision was made to begin a probe (L. 580) to the east of pit L. 576 (Fig. 5.6). By following the mud-brick wall around, two discoveries were made: first, the two pits (L. 575 and L. 576) and wall 59 dividing them were later additions to the oval mud-brick structure (L. 583); and second, the oval mud-brick structure (L. 582) seems to have been originally constructed with the aid of a large foundation area. By scraping back the outer perimeter of the oval mud-brick structure, a clear distinction was visible in the area surrounding the oval structure

Surrounding the oval mud-brick structure was orange, virtually sterile sediment of a crumbly texture similar to the virgin Pleistocene clays. This suggests that in the early phases of occupation at Gilat, the Chalcolithic inhabitants originally excavated a large area. This is not unusual for this period given the abundance of 'earthwork' evidence from the subterranean settlements further south in the Nahal Beersheva (Levy *et al.* 1991; Witten *et al.* 1995). In this case, the mud-brick oval structure was built within this dug out area and the outer perimeter filled with Pleistocene clays as outer support of the oval mud-brick wall (L. 582). At a later date, the loose and very different wall 59 was placed inside the structure forming pits (L. 575 and L. 576). In addition, the foundation of Stratum IIC-wall feature L. 591 was later built on top of this foundation trench filled with Pleistocene clays. Similarly, the pebbled surface (L. 538; Plate 5.38), that covered the northern extension of the oval mud-brick structure (L. 582) was laid on top of all this and established later.

To the east in square J6, a pitted, hard surface (L. 567) was exposed in which a well-preserved flexed and articulated burial (L. 579) was placed, possibly in a very shallow pit similar to burial L. 510 (see Chapter 8, this volume). This surface is assigned to Stratum IIIA because it is earlier than the Stratum IIC pits (L. 548, L. 552) and because the relative elevation is only slightly lower than that of the oval mud-brick structure L. 582. In addition, as shown in Probe L. 553, the burial and its associated surface are well above a Stratum IV level seen in the profile of the probe.

Stratum IIIB. The oval mud-brick structure (L. 582) was first built in Stratum IIIB. With an interior of only 2 m (east/west) × 1 m (north/south), it presents a curiously small space that may have served as a storage facility.

A series of pits were observed in the profiles of probe L. 553 (Fig. 5.7). Two pits (L. 584 and L. 585) were cut into the hard sterile Pleistocene sediment. These pits were surrounded by a hard surface (L. 583) on which a hard-packed mud-brick-like material was laid. Removal of this material and excavation of the pits (L. 584, L. 585) revealed a much larger pit that probably functioned as a pit-house (L. 586; Plates 5.64–5.65). The diameter of the pit house measures c. 2.25 m. Near the center of the house floor, a large flat stone was found that might have functioned as a base for a roof support (Plate 5.64). Within the pit house, a virtually complete vessel, somewhat like an amphora was found leaning against the wall of the pit house (L. 586; B. 1412; Plates 5.65–5.66). This storage vessel was found resting in a very dark ash layer from which flotation recovered a large amount of burned twigs and stems that might represent fallen roof material. L. 586 represents the only complete pit house structure exposed at the site, however, some 5 m to the east, L. 548 may represent another pit house from Stratum IIIB. The contemporaneity of the oval mud-brick structure (L. 582) and the pit house (L. 586) seems certain based on the similar upper elevations of both features. How they functioned together is still unclear.

Stratum IV. A probe was made long the northwestern edge of square J6 at about the same elevation (c. 126.83 m–126.73 m AMSL) as a flexed human burial from Stratum IIIB (L.579; 126.50 AMS). The probe extended 1.7 m (eastwest) - 4 m (NS) in area. L. 553 excavated repeated layers of ashy silts, decayed mud-brick material, and a large quantity of cultural material. Nearly 1 m (c. 0.8–0.9 m) of mixed fills were found. Below this, at about 125.90 m AMSL, a hard mud-brick-like material was found extending across the entire probe. This mud-brick material (L.577) represented the western half of a large pit dug into the hard Pleistocene sediment during the Stratum IV occupation (Plate 5.63).

Area M. Area M, was opened c. 25 m to the south of the main excavation area (Plate 5.67).

The area included six 5 m × 5 m squares and was excavated without balks. Two 1 m × 1 m 'balk islands' were left in the center of the excavation block to facilitate recording. While architectural preservation was relatively poor in Area M, the majority of features were recovered in Strata IIA and IIB.

Stratum I. Area M exhibits the typical modern disturbed nature of the upper levels of Gilat. Although Area M seemed to contain less modern and historic cultural debris than the main excavation area to the north, no *in situ* architecture or features were found during the removal of the upper c. 0.5–0.6 m of loess.

Stratum IIA. The first visible feature exposed after the clearing of the upper 0.3 m of Stratum I loess was the remains of wall 60 in square C5. This wall consisted of nothing more than a single course running E-W. Wall 60, c. 2.5 m (Eastwest) × 0.3–0.5 m wide, had no clear mud-bricks, were only a single course high, and had no alignment of the stones typical of Chalcolithic walls. This feature may have been the collapse of a wall or a structure and had no other features associated with it.

To the west of wall 60, on the eastern side of square C4, a very large (c. 2.4 m max. diameter) pit (L. 014) was exposed at roughly the same level (127.68 m AMSL) as the base of wall 60 (c. 127.69 m AMSL). This pit was also quite deep; the bottom was c. 0.9 m from the top, and filled with a dark ashy matrix. Less than one meter to the southwest of that pit (L. 014), another pit (L. 027) of relatively equivalent elevation (127.64 AMS) was excavated. These two pits (L. 027, L. 014), and wall #60, are the sole features assigned to Stratum IIA in Area M. Based on the abundance of cultural material and the paucity of architectural features, it seems likely that Stratum IIA suffered from a great deal of disturbance, possibly the result of destruction.

Stratum IIB. Removal of the IIA fills in square B4 (L.015, L.018) and square C4 (L. 021) exposed a number of relatively ephemeral features and wall 64. In square B4, a surface (L. 032) and an almost completely eroded wall (W64). Wall 64 runs N-S about four meters in square B4, with an average width of c. 0.5 m. Wall 64 was extremely decayed or destroyed. Only the base of this eroded wall remained with the outlines of some complete mud-bricks

To the west of wall 64 in the southern extremity of square B4, a thin crust of mud-brick material (L. 032) was exposed at an elevation of about 127.62 m AMSL. Numerous embedded sherds, probably of the same vessel, lying flat marked this surface *in situ* on the surface. Exposure of the surface recovered a microlithic tool (B. 3108) and the rim of a basalt vessel (B. 3110; see Chapter 12, this volume).

To the north wall 64 (sq. C4) another surface (L. 044) was exposed with the base of a vessel (B. 3149) and the base of a basalt vessel (B. 3150) *in situ* on the surface. To the east of this surface (L. 044) and wall 64, two pits were uncovered, one on the north (L. 028), one on the south (L. 036). The pit on the north (L. 028) recovered two beads (B. 3109, B3113).

Removal of the Stratum IIA wall 60 (L. 011, sq. C5) exposed a small 'cupmark' (L. 042), a small post-hole sized pit (L. 029, 127.53 m AMSL) and an amorphous pit (L. 031, 127.47 m AMSL). To the east (sq. C5), two pits (L. 013, L. 009) cutting into one another had top elevations (127.55 m AMSL) equivalent to these features (cupmark and pits), represent Stratum IIB features. To the south (square B5), another pit (L. 016) had a roughly equivalent top elevation (127.48 m AMSL). This large (c. 2 m max. diameter) pit was capped with whole mud-bricks and a huge and restorable storage jar (B. 3148; Plates 5.68, 5.69). Excavations of this pit recovered three-quarters of a fine ivory or bone ring (B. 3055). Directly west of this pit (L. 016), another oval-shaped pit (L. 020; squares B5 and C5) was exposed in Stratum IIB.

Only pits, two partially destroyed or eroded surfaces (L. 044, L. 032) largely represent Stratum IIB, and the barely discernable remains of W64. The eroded and fragmentary nature of these features and the widespread distribution of scattered and burnt mud-brick suggest that this be destroyed at the end of the Stratum IIB occupation.

Stratum IIC. Features designated as Stratum IIC were found in only two squares (B4 and B5).

In square B4, removal of the Stratum IIB surface (L. 032) exposed a deep fill to the west of wall 64. Removal of the fill (L. 033) below that surface extended c. 0.5 m in depth. To the north of this fill removal (sq. B4) a rubbish dump (L. 040) was exposed. In addition to typical ceramic sherds and flint artifacts, a fenestrated stand fragment (B. 3144), a ceramic cylinder or pipe (B. 3143), and a spindle whorl (B. 3145) were all found on the upper levels of this dump. This dump may have actually been a section of a pit[s], the limits of which could not be delineated.

An additional pit (L. 035) was excavated (square B5) which may have originally been mud-brick lined, but destruction rendered the mud-brick extremely fragmentary, with no more than vague outlines. A shell bead (B. 3119), a piece of worked (inlay?) malachite (B. 3122), and a micro-endscraper (B. 3133) were recovered in this.

Stratum III. Stratum III was exposed in only two squares (B6 and C6). Due to the heavy disturbance in the area, it was not possible to sub-divide Stratum III. Excavation in squares B6 and C6 revealed more pits (L. 019, L. 022, L. 010, L. 023 and L. 025) at a greater depth than those of the western area. In square C6, removal of a fill (L.007) exposed another series of pits. In the NE portion of square C6, one, or possibly two pits (L.010) were contemporaneous with a thin crust of decayed mud-brick, possibly the remains of another disturbed surface. To the east of this pit(s), another pit (L. 019) was a shallow, with another intrusive pit within it, both running into the northwestern profile of the square. Three palettes, two of scoria (B. 3065, B. 3066) and a third of unidentified stone (B. 3064) were recovered in this feature of overlapping pits (L. 019; see Chapter 12, this volume). To the south of this pit, an oval-shaped pit (L. 022) was exposed with a rim of whole mud-bricks. The fill associated with this feature consisted of numerous mud-brick suggesting that L. 022 was collapsed silo.

Removal of a fill (L. 033, square B4) to the west of wall 64 exposed the most well-preserved feature (L. 043) in Area M (Plate 5.70). A well-built, curvilinear mud-brick wall, running from the south balk to the north forms the western wall of a pit or silo (L. 043). Like the silo L. 022, the fill in this silo consisted of numerous mud-bricks. When all these deposits and features from Area M are considered together it seems that at the end of its early occupation Stratum III suffered a destruction.

4. Conclusion—The Sanctuary

a. Sequence

In concluding this discussion of the developmental sequence of the Gilat sanctuary we follow Francois Bordes' dictum that it is essential to deal with the 'ugly facts' of the empirical archaeological record if we are to understand the processes that led to social change. Based on the data presented above, it is now possible to paint a very general picture of the 'rise and fall' of this prehistoric sanctuary in the northern Negev. This chapter does not attempt to deal with the cultural factors that promoted change or model the 'how and why' religion influenced social change (see Chapters 1, 6–10, 14–16 of the present volume). Instead, this chapter has focused on the architectural and stratigraphic record at Gilat. The relation between these features and the wealth of artifacts and ecofacts recovered at the site are discussed in the chapters that follow. The stratigraphic record discussed enables us to trace, in very broad strokes the developmental sequence of the sanctuary through time.

This developmental picture is provided by a total of 1,242 excavated loci at Gilat and the distributions of these contexts by archaeological strata are highlighted in Table 5.4. As noted earlier, all of the typological and spatial analyses presented in this volume are based on this master locus list. However, it is essential to bear in mind that after seven seasons of fieldwork at Gilat the excavation sample (N = c. 1,755 m^2) is relatively small when compared with other major Chalcolithic excavations in Palestine. For example, seven seasons of work at Shiqmim exposed c. 4,500 m^2 (Levy 1987; Levy *et al.* 1991), at Ghassul some 12 seasons of work revealed ca. 20,000 m^2 (Mallon *et al.* 1934; Bourke 2001 and pers comm.), and Perrot's (Commenge-Pellerin 1987, 1990) work at Bir es-Safadi (N = c. 8,000 m^2) and Abu Matar (N = c. 1500 m^2) produced similarly large excavation samples. It is in this context that the wealth of material culture, and especially cult related artifacts, should be considered. The summary begins with Gilat's earliest Stratum IV and moves forward in time to conclude with the modern disturbances encountered in Stratum I.

Stratum IV. As Sopher (1967:47-8) points out,

> Just as ecology is selectively ritualized in the simple ethnic religions, so are sacred places and territories in such religions a selective sanctification of tribal geography... It would appear that formal sanctification of a homeland reduces mobility...[and] Within a group's ecumene, particular places may be associated with a manifestation of sacred power.

What infused the Nahal Patish geographic locale as a sacred place where Gilat was first established may never be recognized. The rather non-descript hillock which forms the highest topographic point at Gilat was a small mound rising some two meters above the surround plain. This natural 'blip' on the plain markedly distinguishes Gilat for several kilometers over the northern Negev landscape. The mound was formed by redeposited loessial sediments typical of the northwestern Negev (Dan *et al.* 1976) that were deposited in the late Pleistocene period (Levy and Goldberg 1987). Just how much wind-blown loess covered this mound when the earliest settlers arrived at Gilat is open to question. However, there is evidence of Late Neolithic Wadi Rabah phase and early

Chalcolithic 'earthwork' in the basal layers of the site (Plate 5.71). The ceramic analyses presented by Commenge *et al.* (Chapter 10, this volume) shows Wadi Rabah ceramics in the basal layers of the site. From the beginning of settlement effort went into carving pits, storage facilities and pit houses into the Pleistocene sediment (Plates 5.59, 5.61). These simple construction activities continued into the following Stratum IIIB. However, as evidenced in the 1987 excavations at Gilat (Alon and Levy 1989), even in the earliest settlement phase the construction of cult related architecture, such as open-air platforms, took place.

Stratum IIIB. Although the excavation exposure is smaller for Strata IV and IIIB (Fig. 5.7), it is clear that the pit house tradition first observed in Stratum IV continues in IIIB. A series of occupation and abandonment episodes seems to have taken place between the two generic strata identified as IV and IIIB. However, in Stratum IIIB the first unequivocal evidence of cult activities can be documented. After the Stratum IV pit houses and related features were abandoned, some areas of the site seem to have been intentionally burned. In Area J, an ash layer was found sloping steeply from west to east across the whole of square H2 that sealed the features below. These features consisted of a layer of fill above a strong Stratum IIIB clay layer, which lay either directly upon the sterile Pleistocene, or over Stratum IV pits which still contained culturally rich fill. The function of this area alternated between a water collection point and rubbish tip. Finally, after a rubbish tip was burned, a strong band of ash was produced sealing the whole area. The possibility that these burnt deposits represent the residues of conflict cannot be ruled out in these early layers at Gilat (Fig. 5.14).

A larger exposure of Stratum IIIB was made in Area T (Fig. 5.7; Plate 5.53). Like other areas on the site, it is typified by pits and craters (L.1542, L.1527, L.1541, L.1558, L.716, L.1557 and L.1540) carved out of the sterile Pleistocene sediments. Most of these pits had relatively low concentrations of artifacts, and no structures or features are found manufactured from stone or mud-brick. These pits appear to be the result of quarrying activity, a deliberate 'excavation' of the sterile sediments for building and surfacing material. However, in this part of the site, the lack of bedded silts and laminated deposits indicates that water storage was not carried out here. Potable water would have been available in the nearby Nahal Patish where shallow wells (Arabic = *tha'mila*), c. 3–4 m in depth, could be dug.

In some areas, there appears to be a great depth of the site, attested to by the exposures in square Ai2, where the dog burial (L.698) was found in a deep IIIB-pit (L.692). That this is not merely an isolated case is confirmed in the small exposure to the south in square S2, where sloping surfaces (L.1589) are fairly deep (c. 126.35 m, c. 2 m AMSL below ground surface). The two dog burials in Area T and other parts of the site (discussed in greater detail in Chapter 6, this volume) are representative of ritual acts in the early strata at Gilat. While Natufian human burials have been found with puppies (Valla 1998), the Gilat dog burial (Plate 5.58) represents the earliest dog burial with a grave offering known thus far from the Levant. The fact that one of the dog's legs had been broken and left to heal points to the care given this animal. As shown by Goren's (this volume) petrographic study of the jar offering, its origin is in the region around Teleilat Ghassul in the lower Jordan Valley. As this is one of the furthest source areas for pottery imports found at Gilat, the association of this offering with the dog lends additional support to the ritual interpretation offered here. However, the dog burial ritual which takes off early on at Gilat is especially characterized by the removal of the skull from the dog's body and then ceremoniously buried. As Stager (1991) and others point out, there is a long ancient Near Eastern tradition of dog cults related to healing. This contextual parallel may shed light on the meaning of the Gilat dog burials and some of the earliest ritual activities at the site.

With the limited exposures made in IIIB, it is difficult to determine just how much ritual activity took place during this phase. As noted above, pit house architecture continued in use as evidenced in Area Y. Whether these dwellings represent a more ephemeral settlement of the site is still not clear. However, a new architectural phenomenon seems to emerge in Stratum IIIB—the planned in-filling of most of the pits and hollows of the excavation area in an effort to create a large open public area. Evidence for this process was found in Area J (squares J3). As will be seen below and in the studies of the small finds from Gilat, and the establishment of these plazas played a fundamental role in the later phases of ritual activities at the site. These public spaces provided the large areas needed to facilate *communitas* at the site.

Stratum IIIA. The establishment of public space, linked to ritual, is first documented in Stratum III. This is an important material signature for identifying the emergence of a pan-community ritual center in the Negev. In Stratum IIIA (Fig. 5.6) there is extensive evidence for the in-filling of the earlier Strata IV and IIIB pit houses, pits, and other features in order to create the first well-defined open plaza. The creation of this plaza played an important role in Stratum IIIA–IIC ritual and craft activities at Gilat. While the in-filling process may have already begun in IIIB, by Strata IIIA the plaza was well-defined for the first time and delineated by the remains of six small buildings that mark its perimeter (Fog. 5.15).

The majority of Area T was excavated specifically to expose Stratum IIIA (with the exception of the IIC surface L.1544). Pits, surfaces, hearths, walls and structures were all exposed at this level, including areas where the surface was directly on the sterile sediments (L.1586, squares M0-M1). Though this surface was of limited area exposure (c. 5 m × 3 m), it appears that the later IIC plaza surface (L.1544) used this as a base. As the plaza is the most dominant feature in Stratum IIIA in Area T there is lower concentration of cultural material here than in other excavation areas. A number of unusual structures were exposed at this level, including the circular mud-brick structure (L.1525) found in square Ai0 and a curvilinear mud-brick wall (W125) in square S1. It seems that the construction of circular platforms has its 'birth' in Stratum IIIA at Gilat (Fig. 5.87). These were fairly large open-air structures that all contained infant burials (foundation deposits?) and were probably used to facilitate group ritual.

In Area J, it was possible to trace differences in minor building phases at Gilat. Stratum IIIAii comprises two rooms (7 and 8), containing two consecutive floors, and three very substantial walls (Fig. 5.87). Room 8 may extend south into H3 with a similar cluster of stones and mud-brick perhaps providing the SE corner of a large rectangular room. West and north of this complex seems to be a courtyard of very hard surface. Two additional circles were found including a mud-brick arc in H1 and a stone circle in H3.

In Stratum IIIAi a series of pits, surfaces, walls and structures were added to the IIIA plan (Fig. 5.6). The pits fall into many categories, including simple rubbish pits which contained ash and sherds, and many finds; hearths, cup-marks, a post-hole and two superbly constructed silos. The plaza surfaces are often very hard and sometimes made of mud-brick. While the silo in square H2 may be linked to the Room 7 and 8 complex, the silo in the center of the plaza in square L2 seems to have had more general or public function. Additional evidence for the plaza construction in IIIAi is seen in the deliberate in-filling of the slope in H2, belonging to Stratum IV. Indeed, much effort seems to have been made to use whatever material was available; much of it very rich in artifacts, to level the area beneath what was to become the IIIA plaza.

There is no evidence for the destruction of the Gilat in Stratum IIIA. Instead, site formation processes (cf. Schiffer 1987), indicate that the site may have been abandoned and reoccupied sometime later when major building activities took place in Stratum IIC in preparation for the sanctuary that housed the Gilat Woman, Ram and a host of other ritual objects. While ritual acts such as the phenomenon of dog burials, foundation offerings and human burials are common in the earlier strata at Gilat, even by the time of Stratum III, there is no clear evidence for regional cult activities at the site. Tokens, which appear as early as Stratum IV, are finely crafted in Stratum III

(Plate 5.73). Simple care was invested in other groundstone artifacts such as spindle whorls (Plate 5.74). What differentiates Gilat Stratum IIIA from other Chalcolithic sites in Palestine (cf. Abu Hamid, Abu Matar, Bir-es Safadi, Horvat Beter, Shiqmim, Tuleilat Ghassul, the Golan and other localities) is the construction of a plaza capable of accommodating large numbers of people. As will be seen below, the plaza concept was integrated into the first regional cult center to appear in the Negev during the Stratum IIC occupation at Gilat.

Stratum IIC. Following the abandonment of the IIIA occupation at Gilat, the first sanctuary complex was established at the site. David Alon's fortuitous probes in 1975 landed directly on top of Room A where he discovered the Gilat Ram and Gilat Woman statuettes associated with a weath of other ritual paraphernalia. His 1976–77 excavations revealed a nexus of architecture in Area D where a series of small cult rooms, courtyards, silos and other features were built (Fig. 5.5; Plate 5.6). These small buildings housed a wide range of ritual paraphernalia including the now famous Gilat anthropomorphic and zoomorphic statuettes, violin-shape figurines, a host of cornet vessels (Plate 5.75; Table 5.2). A considerable number of fenestrated stands or incense burners were found in the small courtyards associated with the cult rooms (see Commenge *et al.*, Rowan *et al.*, in this volume). The 1990–92 excavations opened areas around Alon's early excavations revealing a large ritual complex where the plaza first built in earlier strata remained the focus of public ritual acts.

When the Stratum IIC plan is modelled in 3-D using ArcView's GIS program (Fig. 5.21a-b), it is possible to see how the cluster of rooms discovered by Alon were complemented by other room features to the west. These groups of rooms were integrated by a large public courtyard. The Stratum IIC plan (Figs. 5.5, 5.16) suggests that only a limited number of people could have entered the main cult rooms or participated in activities that took place in the enclosed courtyards. The large number of pits with cult objects, such as the cache of large torpedo jar fragments (Plates 5.13, 5.40), the large number of violin shape figurines, palettes (Plate 5.76) and other cult-related objects found radiating out from the main Area D cult rooms, demonstrate that access to the main cult room was limited. Besides the cluster of rooms associated with cult paraphernalia found in Area D (Plate 5.72), there is only one definitive room in Areas J and Y. Room 6 is unusual in that it contains an apsidal wall and well-built mud-brick hearth/installation. The torpedo vessel found *in situ* on the floor of this room suggests that it too is linked to the ritual activities that took place in Area D Rooms A, C and E (Fig. 5.21a-b).

The discovery of the well-surfaced plaza in Areas J and T suggests a divergent function where a large open area could have accommodated much larger numbers of people (Fig. 5.21b). The presence of standing stone features associated with painted surfaces, the cache of ostrich eggs (Plate 5.35), and other features found on this plaza suggest that some ritual acts took place here. However, sacred and secular activities appear well-delineated for the first time in Stratum IIC at Gilat. This is highlight by enclosure wall W103 that forms the western boundary of the plaza in Area J (Plate 5.30). The western side of this wall is characterized by numerous cooking hearths, faunal remains, cooking vessels and other domestic debris. It is difficult to determine the exact range of activities that actually took place on the plaza. Nevertheless, the considerable number of spindle whorls, bone tools, and tabular flint scrapers found on and around the plaza suggest that textile manufacture and hide working were important pursuits.

Stratum IIC ended in a massive destruction. In terms of site formation processes (cf. Schiffer 1987), the destruction is documented by thick ash deposits of fill found covering most of the architectural remains throughout the site. Although Hennessy (1969) suggested that the contemporary site of Tuleilat Ghassul suffered from at least one earthquake, at Gilat the lack of patterning in the mass of isolated mud-bricks found near building walls, in the pits of silos, and in other features point to a destruction rather than an earthquake. Just how important a role warfare played in this destruction will be discussed in the conclusion of this volume, however, the increase in mace heads found in IIC may point to an expansion in warfare at this time in the northern Negev (Fig. 5.77; see Chapter 12, this volume). Two hypotheses are suggested for the appearance of Predynastic Egyptian-style mace heads in this stratum: a) they were traded into Gilat; b) they may be linked to military activities of Egyptian polities in this part of southern Palestine.

Stratum IIB. Following the IIC destruction, the importance of Area D (Figs. 5.16, 5.20a) for occupation activities diminished. The presence of violin-shaped figurines (Plate 5.78), stone palettes, torpedo jars, fenestrated stands and other objects suggests that limited cult-related activities continued in Room A during Stratum IIB (Table 2). However, for the most part the complex of rooms and courtyards that were so central to the IIC-cult complex were left in disrepair (Fig. 5.4). This destruction and abandonment processes associated with the main cult room (Room A), which resulted in the presence of thick ash layers throughout the area, may explain the paucity of architectural remains in this part of the site during IIB. The ethnographic record is replete with examples of villages that were perfectly functional yet had large numbers of rooms, buildings, and even quarters in ruin (cf. Holl and Levy 1993). In Stratum IIB there is an increase in the density of architecture at the site coupled with a marked shift in the nexus of the cult complex to the west (Areas J and T, Fig. 5.4). In IIB, the entire sanctuary complex is more cardinally oriented and appears to involve a greater degree of planning. This is apparent from the architectural lay-out in 2-D and the 3-D representation (Fig. 5.20a-b).

For the most part, the new IIB-cult complex built in Areas T and J was established on the plaza. While exhibiting the same evidence of destruction, this IIC open public area provided a *tabula rasa* in which a new building complex could be established without having to remove old building debris. For the first time at Gilat, the architectural layout in Stratum IIB exhibits a greater degree of planning than in the earlier strata. As seen in Figs. 5.18 and 5.95, three building clusters were established and separated by courtyard areas. Unlike the nearby Beersheva valley sites of Shiqmim (Levy 1987), Bir es-Safadi (Perrot 1984) and Horvat Beter (Dothan 1959), the Gilat IIB courtyards are not enclosed but open to passage. In the center of the IIB excavation, one courtyard dominates the area and includes a number of atypical architectural features. These include the exceptionally large hearth in the center of the courtyard (L. 647; Plate 5.16), the Room 11 platform/porch (L. 669) facing east, and the two concave mud-brick basins (CMB; Plate 5.18) that may have been used in ritual activities.

While the CMBs are situated in the largest IIB, there are a series of some five circular mud-brick and stone-lined platforms surrounding the room complexes. As mentioned earlier, most of these circles are over 3 m in diameter and often associated with infant burials. The ritual act of infant burial in association with these platforms suggests that they were associated with scared rather than profane acts in Stratum IIB. Located outside the building compounds, these circular platforms would have been accessible to larger numbers of people than could have been accommodated in the buildings (Plate 5.17). Some infant burials were recovered directly below IIBi architecture (eight under stone circles, three under buildings). That these burials were offerings is suggested by the exclusivity of infant burials. Second, at least three of the bodies had been manipulated before their burial: compacted into a small area with femur and tibia/fibula thrust into the rib-cage, perhaps 'bound' into this position (see Chapter 8, this volume). Features that may or may not have been connected to ritual activities include six platforms in Area J that lie at equivalent elevations and in two lines meeting at right angles on the general alignment of IIBi architecture.

The mass human burial found in Stratum IIB represents the most impressive mortuary feature found at Gilat. As shown in earlier research, separate cemeteries are one of the new features that distinguish the Chalcolithic from earlier periods in the Levant (e.g., Levy 1986; 2003). Like earlier prehistoric periods, individual burials inside villages under house floors, in pits, and in association with other features continues during the Chalcolithic (cf. Levy 1987; Perrot 1955, 1984; Porath

1992). As Chapter 8 shows, at Gilat the majority of human burials are also found in what appear to be 'informal' contexts. However, the exception to this pattern is the mass human burial (L. 1237; Fig. 5.23) found in Area J between a platform and circle in H0 which contained the remains of nine bodies. They were found in what may have originally functioned as a silo, however, when compared with other well-built silos, its relative shallow depth suggests that it was specially constructed as a burial facility. Before the first bodies were laid to rest, a thick layer of animal bones (possibly the remains of meat offerings) were placed on the stone pavement of the burial facility. The burial facility seems to have been used for some time, as the bodies were moved after a significant period of decomposition had taken place, perhaps in order to make room for additional bodies. Nearby, a 'ceremonial' pit (L. 1344) was found containing one of the best preserved basalt fenestrated stands in association with a small animal figurine and nine gazelle horn cores (Plates 5.21 and 5.79). All of these objects were intentionally burned. Viewed together, the multiple burial and ceremonial pit are interpreted as examples of Braudel's *evenment* or 'historical' events linked to mortuary ritual. The fact that the mass burial facility was above ground and visible to the IIB occupants at Gilat marks a clear departure from other known Chalcolithic mortuary behaviors observed in cemeteries and intra-village human burials.

Summing up, while the Stratum IIC sanctuary reflects the birth of the earliest pan-regional ritual center, following its destruction, the construction of the Stratum IIB sanctuary offered an opportunity for reorganization and more deliberate planning. The sanctuary 'tradtion' had already been established in the northern Negev in IIC; by Stratum IIB, the Gilat ritual center was a well-established phenomenon in the Chalcolithic period (Fig. 5.20a-b), and well-oiled with imports of olive oil for use in the sanctuary (see Chapter 10, this volume). Finally, like Stratum IIC, the IIB-sanctuary suffered a destruction. Some insights concerning the abandonment processes that followed the IIB destruction are discussed below.

Stratum IIA. Following the destruction of the IIB-cult complex, there was a period of abandonment at Gilat before the site was reoccupied in Stratum IIA. However, the intensity of building, organization of ritual activities and general site occupation diminished by Stratum IIA. Site formation processes suggest that a relatively short period of time elapsed between the two phases. However, it is possible to discern that the IIA occupation did not occur immediately after the destruction of IIB. First, if abandoned for a long time, more sterile silts and windblown sediments would have covered the IIB stratum deposits, as was the case between Strata III and IIC. No such deposit of sterile sediments was observed between IIB and IIA. Second, often mud-brick from IIB architecture was prevalent enough to be used in the construction of floors or at least hard surfaces, indicating that very little of it was covered for a considerable amount of time following the IIB abandonment. Third, it is clear that the IIA occupation occurred after a IIB-destruction episode. This suggested by the large amounts of ash and charcoal found among the hard mud-brick 'tumble' of IIB architecture throughout the site, over which IIA soft surfaces were constructed. However, that some time had passed between the two occupation phases is suggested by the cutting through of IIB architecture by IIA pits. Had reoccupation occurred immediately after destruction, the IIA occupants would have known about the architecture below, and would not have cut into such hard material (Fig. 19a-b).

In general, the architectural remains associated with Stratum IIA are sparsely distributed and poorly preserved. The majority of features found during this occupation are pits (Fig. 5.16). However, at least six small stone platforms were found scattered over the excavation area. While this chapter does not focus on the small finds found through the stratigraphic sequence, it is significant that the largest number (n = 45 or 27%) of spindle whorls were found in Stratum IIA. The large number of tabular scrapers (Fig. 5.98) found in both Strata IIA and I indicate that hide-working or possibly wool-shearing activities (cf. Henry 1995:372) were more pronounced during the later occupation phases at Gilat (cf. Chapter 11, this volume). It seems that IIA represent a more ephemeral occupation during which a relatively small population lived at the site. The large number of IIA pits, spindle whorls, and other realms of material culture suggest that IIA craft activities at site use still went beyond the DMP. If this is correct, we can assume that more people continued to visit the site than actually lived there during the IIA occupation. Based on the paucity of rooms and other evidence for occupation in IIA (Figs 5.19a and b), it seems that Gilat did not rebound to its prior prominence as a regional ritual center. Instead, in Stratum IIB, Gilat was certainly a backwater in terms of the entire southern Levant Chalcolithic. Scattered ritual acts continued to take place, but there is no evidence for the centralized organization of those activities.

At the end of its occupation, Stratum IIA seems to have been abandoned. Unlike many of the earlier strata that show evidence of destruction activities, IIA do not appear to have ended in conflict. One of the most difficult questions is how Stratum IIA relates to the highly disturbed Stratum I. As noted here, Stratum I was totally disturbed by heavy modern plowing. However, it is possible that Stratum I was actually part of the IIA archaeological matrix at the site. If this is correct, then all of the artifact counts for both Strata IIA and I could be considered together. However, it is impossible to link these two strata because of the thorough disturbance of Stratum I and the absence of stratigraphic links to IIA. These site formation processes must be considered when discussing any of the archaeological sites found along the Nahal Patish and Nahal Grar.

Stratum I. Stratum I is represented by disturbed topsoil across the entire site that varies in depth from c. 0.4 m to 0.6 m below surface. Although a large amount of Chalcolithic cultural material was recovered from this stratum no architecture or *in situ* features were preserved. Some pits, such as L.639, L.653, L.678 and L.760, originally may have been cut from a higher elevation, but deep plowing has destroyed any traces of the upper portions of these features. In general, Stratum I included a mix of artifacts from the Chalcolithic, historic and occasional modern periods.

It is unfortunate that Stratum I suffered so much recent destruction. The rich assemblage of ritual artifacts recovered from this last occupation level at Gilat point to its importance in the developmental sequence at the site. Intriguing questions remain about how exactly Chalcolithic society collapsed in this part of the southern Levant and what the role of ritual and religion was in this process.

The remaining chapters in this volume focus on the spatial and analytical analyses of the artifacts and ecofacts recovered from the Gilat excavations.

Tables

Table 5.1. Master Locus List for Gilat Excavations
(1975–77, 1987, 1990–92)

Locus Code	Square	Field	Analysis	Volume (m3)	Description	#
1	Ai	1–2A	1	6.40	topsoil	1
2	Ai6	1–2A	1	6.40	topsoil	1
3	Ai6	1–2B	1	6.40	fill	6
4	S5	1–2A	1	6.40	fill	6
4B	S5	2B	2B	6.46	fill	6
5	Ai6	2C	2C	4.80	floor	11
6	Ai5	2C	2C	5.60	floor	11
7	Ai5	2C	2C	4.00	floor	11
8	S5	2C	2C	0.31	platform	7
9	Ai5	2C	2C	2.40	surface ash	4
10	N5	1–2A	1	0.40	fill	6
11	S5	2C	2C	4.50	floor	11
12	Ai7	2C	2C	0.60	pit	5
13	Ai5	3A	3A	2.45	floor	11
14	Ai6	3A	3A	3.76	floor	11
15	Ai6	3B	3B	0.06	pit	5
16	Ai5	3A	3A	1.80	fill	6
17	Ai6	2C	2C	0.01	pit	5
18	S6	2B	2B	6.40	topsoil	1
19	N5	2C	2C	4.00	floor	11
20	Ai5	3B	3B	2.69	surface	4
21	Ai5	3A	3A	0.14	pit	5
22	Ai7	2C	2C	4.00	floor	11
23	S5–S6	2C	2C	0.60	floor	11
24	S5	3A	3A	0.06	pit	5
25	Ai5	3A	3A	0.35	pit	5
26	N4–N5	2C	2C	2.45	floor	11
27	Ai7	3A	3A	3.50	fill	6
28	Ai7	3A	3A	1.68	fill	6
29	S4	2B	2B	1.71	fill	6
30	S5	2C	2C	1.71	floor	11
31	S5	3A	3A	0.60	floor	11
32	S6	3A	3A	4.50	fill	6
33	S5	3A	3A	1.44	fill	6
34	S5	3B	3B	1.54	surface	4
35	N5	2C	2C	1.80	floor	11
36	S4	2C	2C	0.85	floor	11
37	N6	2B	2B	4.64	floor	11
38	S4	2C	2C	1.71	floor	11
39	N4–N5	2B	2B	3.50	fill	6
40	S4–S5	2C	2C	1.71	floor	11
41	S4–S5	2C	2C	1.20	surface	4
42	S5	4	4	1.71	floor	11
43	S5	2C	2C	0.23	sterile pleistocene	15
44	S4–S5	2C	2C	1.71	floor	11
45	H2	U	U	–	surface	4
46	P7	U	U	–	surface	4
47	H2	dead locus	dead locus	–		
48	–	dead locus	dead locus	–	1.05	
49	–	dead locus	dead locus	–	1.35	
1976 Area DU=unknown						
50	Ai4	2B	2B	5.92	topsoil	1
51	N4–N5	2B	2B	8.00	topsoil	1
52	S4–S5	2C	2C	0.80	section, cleaning	13
53	N3	2C	2C	0.26	pit	5
54	N3	2A	2A	1.34	topsoil	1
55	Ai4	2B	2B	0.26	pit	5
56	S3	1–2A	1	13.12	topsoil	1
57	N4	2B	2B	3.20	pit	5
58	Ai4	2B	2B	1.54	topsoil	1
59	Ai4	2B	2B	0.00	surface	4
60	n4	2C	2C	0.80	floor	11
61	Ai4	2C	2C	0.48	floor	11
62	N3–N4	2C	2C	9.00	surface	4
63	N3–N4	2C	2C	2.70	surface	4
64	N4	2C	2C	1.76	pit	5
65	S4–S5	2C	2C	0.16	floor	11
66	N4	2C	2C	0.37	surface	4
67	M3–N4	2C	2C	0.42	surface	4
68	S7	1–2A	1	4.48	topsoil	1
69	N7	2C	2C	4.35	surface	4
70	N4	2B	2B	1.62	pit	5
71	N4	2C	2C	0.61	pit	5
72	S4	U	U	1.70	pit	5
73	S3	2B	2B	0.95	pit	5
74	S3	2C	2C	5.36	floor	11
75	S3	2C	2C	2.40	pit	5
76	SN-3/4	1–2A	1	11.03	pit	5
77	Ai6	2C	2C	1.12	floor	11
78	Ai4	3A	3A	1.12	fill	6
79	N4	3A	3A	3.52	fill	6
80	Ai4	2C	2C	1.12	floor	11
81	N4	2C	2C	3.52	floor	11
82	Ai4	3A	3A	5.12	fill	6
83	S3	2C	2C	2.68	floor	11
84	S7	2C	2C	4.00	surface	4
85	M6	2B	2B	7.04	surface	4
86	N3	2B	2B	4.96	surface	4
87	N3	1–2A	1	6.60	topsoil	1
88	N3	1–2A	1	6.96	topsoil	1
89	N3	1–2A	1	0.16	topsoil	1
90	N3	2B	2B	0.12	pit	5
91	N3	2B	2B	0.15	pit	5
92	N3	2C	2C	0.07	pit	5
93	N3	2C	2C	0.34	pit	5
94	N3	2C	2C	0.18	pit	5
95	M3	1–2A	1	0.38	topsoil	1
96	M6	2B	2B	4.16	floor	11
97	M3	2B	2B	0.28	floor	11
98	N3	2C	2C	0.30	floor	11
99	S3	2C	2C	0.22	floor	11
100	H2	dead locus	dead locus	–		
1977 Area DU=unknown						
110	M6	2C	2C	–	floor	11
111	M6	3A	3A	0.75	fill	6
112	M6–N6	3B	3B	1.60	surface	4
113	M4	2A	2A	0.16	pit	5

114	M4	2B	2B	0.53	pit	5
115	M4	2C	2C	0.22	pit	5
116	M4	2B	2B	0.64	surface	4
117	M3	3A	3A	0.14	pit	5
118	M3	2B	2B	0.86	fill	6
119	M5	2C	2C	0.81	pit	5
120	M5	2B	2B	0.52	pit	5
121	M5	2C	2C	0.10	pit	5
122	N7	3A	3A	3.42	surface	4
123	M5	2B	2B	0.84	pit	5
124	M5	2C	2C	0.18	pit	5
125	M6	2C	2C	0.29	pit	5
126	S7	3A	3A	2.56	floor	11
127	N6	3A	3A	0.14	pit	5
128	N6	2C	2C	1.31	pit	5
129	N3	3A	3A	0.81	pit	5
130	N6	2B	2B	1.41	pit	5
131	M/N–3/4	2A	2A	0.11	fill	6
132	N3	3A	3A	1.74	pit	5
133	M/N–3/4	2A–2B	2A	0.28	topsoil	1
134	M3	2B	2B	0.16	topsoil	1
135	N6	3A	3A	0.07	pit	5
136	S7	3A	3A	1.10	floor	11
137	M4	2C	2C	1.40	floor	11
138	M5	2A	2A	0.18	pit	5
139	N3	3A	3A	1.38	pit	5
140	M5	2C	2C	1.35	floor	11
141	S7	3A	3A	1.10	surface	4
142	M6	2C	2C	0.13	surface	4
143	M4	2C	2C	0.04	pit	5
144	N3	3A	3A	0.65	fill	6
145	S4	3B	3B	0.86	surface	4
146	S3	3A	3A	2.21	fill	6
147	S7	3B	3B	1.20	surface	4
148	M3–M4	2A	2A	0.68	surface	4
149	M4–M5	2A	2A	2.70	–	U
150	S4–S5	2B	2B	1.24	pit	5
151	M4–M5	2B	2B	0.78	pit	5
152	S7	3B	3B	1.15	surface	4
153	N3	3B	3B	0.12	pit	5
154	S7	3B	3B	1.35	floor	11
155	S5	4	4	2.30	pit	5
156	M3–M4	2C	2C	0.14	surface	4
157	SAi–4	1–2A	1	0.18	topsoil	1
158	M4	2C	2C	0.02	floor	11
159	M3	1–2A	1	3.90	pit	5
160	N5	3A	3A	–	surface	4
161	M3	2C	2C	0.01	pit	5
162	S5	3B	3B	0.13	surface	4
163	S5–S6	3A	3A	1.04	fill	6
164	S6	3A	3A	0.93	fill	6
165	S5	3B	3B	1.89	pit, fill	5
166	M/N–4/5	2C	2C	0.37	pit	5
167	M5–N5	1–2A	1	1.79	topsoil	1
168	S6	3B	3B	3.67	pit	5
169	S5	3B	3B	0.16	pit	5
170	N5–S5	1–2A	1	0.51	surface	4
171	M6	3A	3A	0.87	pit	5
172	N5	3A	3A	0.06	surface	4
173	N5–N6	2C	2C	1.54	silo	9
174	N5–N6	2C	2C	1.28	pit	5
175	M3	2B	2B	1.09	pit	5
176	S6	3A	3A	2.40	pit	5
177	N6	3A	3A	3.42	pit	5

1987 Area DU=unknown

70	N4	2C	2C	–	floor	11
92	N3	2B	2B	–	pit	5
110	M6	2C	2C	–	pit	5
128	M6	2C	2C	–	silo	9
172	N5	3A	3A	–	floor	11
64	N4	2B	2B	–	pit	5
250	L6	1	1	4.96	topsoil	1
251	L7	1	1	0.60	topsoil	1
252	M6	2C	2C	0.24	floor	11
253	L6	1	1	0.80	topsoil	1
254	L7	1	1	0.80	topsoil	1
255	M6	3A	3A	1.54	floor	11
256	M5	3A	3A	0.70	floor	11
257	N5	2C	2C	9.28	floor	11
258	L6	1	1	1.44	fill	6
259	L7	1	1	1.28	fill	6
260	M6	3A	3A	0.60	fill	6
261	M6	3A	3A	0.00	silo	9
262	M6	3A	3A	0.03	pit	5
263	M6	3A	3A	0.03	pit	5
264	L7	2B	2B	4.99	platform	7
265	L6	2B	2B	0.48	fill	6
266	L6	2B	2B	0.68	fill	6
267	M5–M6	1	1	2.97	topsoil	1
268	L7	2B	2B	0.33	platform	7
269	L6	2C	2C	0.46	oven	16
270	L6	2C	2C	0.27	pit	5
271	L6	2C	2C	0.38	fill	6
272	N7	3A	3A	20.64	floor	11
273	L6	2B	2B	0.56	fill	6
274	L6	2B	2B	0.69	fill	6
275	L5	1	1	3.84	topsoil	1
276	L5	1	1	–	fill	6
277	L5	2B	2B	0.40	fill	6
278	L5	2B	2B	1.10	fill	6
279	N4	3A	3A	–	pit	5
280	L5	2B	2B	2.24	floor	11
281	L5	2A	2A	1.12	pit	5
282	L6	2C	2C	0.24	pit	5
283	L5	2C	2C	0.36	fill	6
285	L6	3B	3B	0.18	pit	5
286	L6	1	1	0.60	fill	6
287	L5	1	1	2.11	pit	5
289	L6	2C	2C	0.47	pit	5
290	N7	3A	3A	0.96	fill	6
291	L6	2C	2C	2.79	fill	6
292	N7	3B	3B	1.47	pit	5
293	L6	2C	2C	0.82	pit	5
294	N7	4	4	3.60	fill	6
295	L7	2B	2B	0.66	platform	7
296	L7	2B	2B	0.66	platform	7
297	L7	2C	2C	4.44	fill	6
298	N7	3A	3A	0.75	pit	5
300	T7	U	U	–	cleaning	13
301	N5	3A	3A	0.98	cleaning	13
302	M7	1	1	2.90	topsoil	1

303	M7	1	1	4.70	topsoil	1
304	L7	1	1	0.21	pit	5
305	L7	2C	2C	0.53	pit	5
306	M7	2C	2C	0.18	fill	6
307	L7	2C	2C	1.76	fill	6
308	M7	2C	2C	1.95	fill	6
309	M7	2C	2C	1.95	fill	6
310	M7	2C	2C	1.22	fill	6
311	M7	2C	2C	1.22	pit	5
312	M7	2A	2A	0.74	pit	5
313	L5	2A	2A	2.13	pit	5
314	L5	2B	2B	1.13	fill	6
315	L7	3A	3A	1.17	pit	5
316	M7	3A	3A	1.15	fill	6
317	M7	3A	3A	0.17	surface	4
318	M7	3B	3B	0.35	fill	6

1992 Area DU=unknown

1050	M5	U	U	2.00	cleaning	13
1051	N5	U	U	3.00	cleaning	13
1052	M5	2Ci	2C	1.65	w#34,33, removal	10
1053	M5	2Ci	2C	0.50	w#36, removal	10
1054	N5	2Ci	2C	0.00	post-hole?	12
1055	M5	U	U	0.72	cleaning	13
1056	N5	2Cii	2C	0.30	pit	5
1057	M5	2Ci	2C	0.04	pit	5
1058	N5	2Ci	2C	0.92	probe	17
1059	M5	2Ci	2C	0.05	pit	5
1060	M5	2Ci	2C	0.03	pit	5
1061	N5	2Cii	2C	12.00	fill	6
1062	M5	2Cii	2C	4.13	fill	6
1063	M5	2Cii	2C	0.01	post-hole?	12
1064	N5	2Ci	2C	0.00	post-hole?	12
1065	N5	2Ci	2C	0.00	post-hole?	12
1066	M5	2Cii	2C	0.03	pit	5
1067	M5	2Cii	2C	0.04	pit	5
1068	M5	2Cii	2C	U	pit	5
1069	M5	2Cii	2C	U	sterile pleistocene	15
1070	M5	2Cii	2C	U	pit	5
1071	M5	2Cii	2C	U	sterile pleistocene	15
1072	N5	2Ci	2C	U	standing stone	18
1073	M5	2Cii	2C	0.28	pit	5

1990 Area YU=unknown

501	J5	1	1	4.49	topsoil	1
502	K5	1	1	3.47	topsoil	1
503	J6	1	1	6.85	topsoil	1
504	K6	1	1	5.24	topsoil	1
505	J7	1	1	8.83	topsoil	1
506	K7	1	1	5.08	topsoil	1
507	K5	1	1	5.30	fill	6
508	K7	1	1	8.33	fill	6
509	K6	1	1	5.85	fill	6
510	K6	2B	2B	U	burial	19
511	K5	2A	2A	U	cup mark	14
512	J5	1	1	5.63	fill	6
513	J7	1	1	7.68	fill	6
514/523	J7	2	2	0.05	pit/rubble feature	3
515	J6	1–2	1	16.66	fill	6
516	J5	2A	2A	2.31	surface	4
517	J5	2A	2A	0.57	pit	5
518	K5	2A	2A	0.81	m.b. platform	7
519	K7	2	2	0.68	pit	5

520	J6	2A	2A	0.46	rubble pit	5
521	J5	2B	2B	U	grinder platform	7
522	J7/K7	2	2	1.07	pit	5
524	K7	2	2	3.53	square probe	17
525	J5	2B	2B	11.52	fill	6
526	K6	2	2	0.38	fill under burial	6
527	K5	2	2	4.14	fill	6
528	K6	2C	2C	6.75	pit	5
529	J5	2B	2B	0.26	central pit	5
530	J5	2B	2B	0.32	pit	5
531	K5	3	3	U	fill below wall base	6
532	J7	2	2	0.84	pit	5
533	J6	2B	2B	0.58	small ash pit	5
534	K5	2C	2C	2.69	fill w/in small room	6
535	K5	2A	2A	0.34	w#51 removal	2
536	J7	2	2	1.54	fill	6
537	J5/K5	2B	2B	0.49	ash pit	5
538	J5/K5	2C	2C	U	pebble surface	4
539	K7	2	2	0.21	surface	4
540	K7	2	2	0.23	m.b. platform	7
541	K5/K6	2B	2B	U	burial	19
542	K7	3	3	1.32	fill	6
543	J7	2	2	0.22	pit	5
544	J6	2A	2A	0.17	structure in s.w. corner	3
545	K7	3	3	1.62	pit	5
546	J6	2A	2A	0.29	structure removal	10
547	K7	3	3	0.97	NE corner pits	5
548	J6	3	3	1.52	pit NE corner	5
549	J7	2	2	U	pit	5
550	K5/K6	2	2	0.70	fill	6
551	J6	3	3	0.01	burial	19
552	J6	3	3	0.82	pit	5
553	J6	3	3	2.07	probe 2x2	17
554	K6	2	2	0.32	pit NE	5
555	K6	3	3	0.95	pit NW	5
556	J7	3	3	0.93	pit	5
557	K6	2	2	0.19	pit	5
558	J7/K7	2C	2C	5.35	m.b. feature removal	10
559/560	K6	3	3	0.42	pit SW corner	5
561	J6	2	2	0.23	fill SE corner	6
562	J6/K7	2	2	0.16	pit	5
563	J7	2C	2C	U	human skull	19
565	K7	2C	2C	U	round stone/mb structure	3
566	K6	2	2	U	structure collapse	3
567	J6	3A	3A	1.16	surface?	4
568	J7	3	3	0.13	pit under st.II collapse	5
569	J5	2C	2C	1.54	removal of mb	10
570	K6	3	3	U	cupmark	14
571	J6	3	3	0.08	pit	5
572/574	K6	3	3	0.83	two pits	5
573	K7	3	3	0.02	pit under struct. L565	5
575	J5	3A	3A	0.40	pit	5
576	J5	3A	3A	0.58	pit	5
577	J6	4	4	1.42	pit in probe	5
578	J5	2B	2B	0.07	pit	5
579	J6	3A	3A	0.04	burial	19
580	J5	2A	2A	0.33	probe E. of L576	17

581	K7	2	2	2.45	pit under SW corner	5
582	J6/K5	3B	3B	U	mb oval struc	3
583	J5	3A–3B	3A	3.26	fill	6
584	J5	3	3	U	pit/section of probe	5
585	J5	3	3	U	2nd pit in W sect probe	5
586	J5	3B	3B	1.57	large probe	17
587	J5	2Bii	2B	0.24	mb stone structure	3
588	J5	2B	2B	0.47	fill under grinder plat	6
589	J5	2C	2C	U	3 standing stone	18
590	K5	2c	2c	U	Rm. 6 floor	11
591	J5	2C	2C	U	wall under grinder plat	2
592	J6	3	3	U	cupmark	14
593	K6	3	3	U	surface	4
594	K7	3	3	U	surface	4

1990 Area J U=unknown

800	J/K/L/ 3/4	1	1	122.40	topsoil	1
801	L4	1	1	0.89	mudbrick	20
802	J4	1	1	0.45	burial	19
803	J4	2A	2A	3.81	ash fill btwn plat. &pit	21
804	J4	2A	2A	4.10	ash fill, S. of platform	21
805	J4	2A	2A	3.53	pit-S	5
806	J3/H3	2A	2A	0.60	pit-SW	5
807	J3	2A	2A	0.40	pit-midwest	5
808	J3	2A	2A	0.55	pit-mideast	5
809	K3	2Bi	2B	0.31	pit SE corner	5
810	K4	2A	2A	1.07	pit SE corner	5
811	K3	1	1	2.39	pit SW corner	5
812	J3	2A	2A	0.26	pit NW corner	5
813	J3	2A	2A	0.64	pit SE corner	5
814	K4	1	1	1.89	fill	6
815	J3	2A	2A	7.75	fill	6
816	K4	2A	2A	0.95	floor	11
817	L4	2A	2A	5.76	fill over floor	6
818	K4	2A	2A	0.75	floor	11
819	K3	2A	2A	2.54	floor	11
820	L3	2A	2A	6.25	fill over floor	6
821	J4	2Bii	2B	0.84	pit-NW corner	5
822	J4	1	1	0.45	burial	19
823	J4	2Bii	2B	0.06	pit	5
824	J4	2A	2A	1.02	fill SW corner	6
826	K3	2Bi	2B	0.69	pit	5
827	L4	2Cii	2C	0.49	pit	5
828	L3	2Bi	2B	1.99	pit	5
829	L3/L4	2	2	U	mb wall	2
830	J4	2Bii	2B	0.35	pit	5
831	J4	2Bii	2B	1.52	pit	5
832	J4	2Bii	2B	0.00	pit	5
833	J4	2Bii	2B	0.01	pit	5
834	J4	2Bii	2B	0.00	pit	5
835	J4	2Bii	2B	0.02	pit	5
836	J4	2Bii	2B	0.00	pit	5
837	J4	2Bii	2B	1.12	pit	5
838	J4	2Bii	2B	0.26	pit	5
839	K3	2Bi	2B	0.65	floor	11
840	J3	2A	2A	0.88	mb collapse, over pit	20
841	K3	2Bi	2B	0.35	floor NE corner	11
842	J4	U	U	U	platform	7
843	K3	2A	2A	0.52	m.b. collapse	20

844	K3	2A	2A	0.20	m.b. collapse	20
845	K3	2Bi	2B	0.52	pit	5
846	K3	2A	2A	1.25	mb collapse	20
847	J4	2Bii	2B	0.45	fill below L803	6
848	K3/4	2A	2A	0.38	m.b. fill tumble	20
849	K3	2A	2A	0.39	m.b. fill w/tumble	20
850	J4	2Bii	2B	1.80	pit around burial L.822	5
851	L4	2A	2A	1.31	fill	6
852	L3-2/K3-4	1	1	0.13	topsoil	1
853	L3/4	2Cii	2C	1.94	pit	5
854	L3	2Cii	2C	0.06	pit	5
855	L4	2Cii	2C	0.16	pit	5
856	L4	2Cii	2C	0.08	pit	5
857	J3	2A	2A	0.04	pit	5
858	J3	2A	2A	0.04	pit	5
859	L4	2Cii	2C	0.23	pit	5
860	K4	2Bi	2B	U	surface, under 818	4
861	L3	2Cii	2C	0.66	pit	5
862	K4	2Bi	2B	0.06	pit	5
863	L4–L3	2Cii	2C	0.04	pit	5
864	L4–L3	2Cii	2C	0.02	pit	5
865	K4	2Bi	2B	1.51	surface? under L816	4
866	K3	2Bi	2B	0.29	bench/platform, L816	7
867	K4	2Bi	2B	0.13	hearth	22
868	L3/4	2Bi	2B	0.27	wall#56	2
869	L3	2Ci	2C	0.39	wall#70	2
870	K3-L3	2Bi	2B	0.15	W.58 m.b. E–W	2
871	L3-L2	2Bi	2B	0.44	W. 57 m.b. N–S	2
872	L4	2A	2A	0.22	W. 55 stone E–W	2
873	K4	2A	2A	1.90	W.52 stone E–W	2
874	K3	2Bi	2B	0.11	W.50 stone E–W	2
875	K3	2Bi	2B	0.05	W.53 stone	2
876	J3/4	2Bi	2B	1.43	m.b. & stone arch struct	8
877	J4	2Bi	2B	0.09	stone and m.b. platform	7
878	K4	2Bi	2B	3.98	m.b. platform	7
879	K4	2Bi	2B	0.36	stone & m.b. platform	7
880	J3/4	2Bi	2B	0.53	structure	7
881 dead locus						
882	K4	2Bi	2B	2.79	silo	9
883	J3	2Bi-ii	2B	4.88	fill, under L.815	6
884	J3-4/K3-4	1	1	0.98	topsoil, baulk island	1
885	J3	2Bii	2B	0.04	pit	5
886	J4	2Bii	2B	0.01	burial	19
887	J4	2Bii	2B	0.01	burial	19
888	J4	2C	2C	0.46	surface	4
889	J4	U	U	U	burial	19
890	J4	2Bi	2B	1.44	fill	6
891	J3	3A	3A	0.04	cupmark	14
892–893	J4	2Bii	2B	2.60	pit	5
894	J3	2Bii	2B	0.04	burial	19
895	J3	2Bii	2B	U	wall fill	2
896	J4	2Bii	2B	0.29	pit	5
897	J4	2Bii	2B	0.01	burial	19
898	J3	2Bii	2B	0.04	burial	19
899 dead locus						
900	J3	2Bii	2B	0.06	burial	19

Locus	Grid			Elev.	Description	No.
901/908	J3	2Bi	2B	1.16	surface	4
902	J3/4	2Bii	2B	0.20	pit	5
903	H3	1	1	14.50	topsoil	1
904	J4	2C	2C	0.13	m.b. platform	7
905	J3	2Bi	2B	0.70	fill	6
906	H2	1	1	12.75	topsoil	1
907–927	J2	1	1	17.00	topsoil	1
908/901						
909	J4	2Bii	2B	1.95	fill under 890	6
910(1104)	J3	3Aii	3A	0.25	fill	6
911	J3	2Bii	2B	0.07	pit	5
912	K4	2C	2C	0.32	surf. under 860	4
913	K4	2C	2C	1.02	surf. under 865	4
914	L4	2C	2C	U	surf. under 865	4
915	L4	2Cii	2C	1.08	pitted surface	4
916	J3/4	3A	3A	1.62	surf. with churn	4
917	J3	3Aii	3A	2.19	surf.w/cupmarks	4
918/934	J3	3Aii	3A	U	floor below cm	11
919	K4	1	1	1.10	baulk topsoil	1
920	J3	3Aii	3A	0.02	cupmark	14
921	J3	3Aii	3A	0.00	cupmark	14
922	J3	3Aii	3A	0.00	cupmark	14
923	J3	3Aii	3A	0.00	cupmark	14
924	K2	1	1	13.50	topsoil	1
925	H3	2A	2A	4.80	surface	4
926	H2	1	1	U	fill	6
927/(907)						
928	K2	2A	2A	2.25	surface	4
929	J4	3A	3A	3.29	surface? under 847	4
931	J3	3A	3A	0.60	wall #61	2
932	J3	3Aii	3A	0.63	surf. under1021	4
933	J3	3Aii	3A	U	floor under 932	11
934(918)	J4	3B	3B	U	floor under 929	11
935/816	K4	2A	2A	0.34	surface	4
936/818	K4	2A	2A	0.71	surface	4
937/865	K4	2Bi	2B	0.06	floor in baulk	11
938/860	K4	2Bi	2B	0.73	floor in baulk	11
940	J3	3A	3A	0.00	cupmark in 917	14
941	J3	3A	3A	0.00	cupmark	14
942	J3	3A	3A	0.00	cupmark	14
943	J3	3A	3A	0.00	cupmark	14
944	J3	3A	3A	0.00	cupmark in 932	14
945	J3	2C	2C	0.27	m.b. install	3
946	J4	2C	2C	0.74	surface? E.of wall	4
947	J4	3A	3A	U	surface	4
948	J4	3A	3A	0.30	fill under 916	6
949	H3	2Bi	2B	6.88	surface, under 847	4
950	H2	2A	2A	10.41	surface, under 926	4
951	J2	2A	2A	2.74	surface, under 927	4
952	K2	2Bi	2B	9.26	fill, under 924	6
953	J4	3A	3A	0.03	pit in 947	5
954	J4	3A	3A	0.02	pit in 947	5
955	J4	3A	3A	0.01	pit in 947	5
956	J3	3Aii	3A	0.09	pit in hearth	5
957	J2	2A	2A	0.45	pit NE	5
958/806	J2 H3/4	2A	2A	1.23	pit	5
959	J4	3A	3A	U	found deposit (axe)	23
960	J2	2A	2A	0.91	pit	5
961	H2	2A	2A	0.80	pit	5
962/813	H3	2A	2A	0.16	pit	5
963	H2	2A	2A	0.24	pit	5
964	J2	2A	2A	0.76	pit	5
965	K2	2Bi	2B	0.76	pit	5
966	H2	2A	2A	0.89	pit	5
967	H2	2A	2A	0.49	pit	5
968	K4	2Bi	2B	0.02	pit	5
969	J4	3A	3A	0.01	pit	5
970	K2	2Bi	2B	0.59	pit	5
971	J3	2Bii	2B	0.01	burial pit	19
972	H3	2A	2A	0.26	pit	5
973	K4	2Bi	2B	0.33	pit	5
974	J4	3Aii	3A	0.02	pit	5
975	H3	2A	2A	0.32	pit	5
976	H3	2A	2A	0.62	pit	5
977	K2	2A	2A	0.23	pit	5
978/845	K2-3	2Bi	2B	0.72	pit	5
979	K2	2A	2A	0.25	pit	5
980	J3	3Aii	3A	0.00	burial (baby)	19
981	K4	2C	2C	U	circle in m.bv.	8
982	J3	3Aii	3A	U	floor	11
983	L3	2Cii	2C	U	surface	4
984	K3	2C	2C	0.11	fill	6
985	H2	2Bi	2B	U	stone circle	8
986	H2	2Bi	2B	0.14	burner locus	5
987	J2	2Bi	2B	U	surface	4
988	H2	2Bi	2B	U	surface	4
989/999	H3	2Bi	2B	U	platform	7
990	H3	2Bi	2B	5.52	fill	6
991	J2/3 K2/3	1	1	0.35	topsoil	1
992	K2	2A	2A	0.44	pit	5
993	H2	2Bi	2B	U	wall	2
994	H2	2Bi	2B	0.19	pit	5
995	H2	2Bi	2B	0.14	pit	5
996	K2	2C	2C	U	floor	11
997	H3	2Bi	2B	U	stone circle	8
998	J4	3A	3A	U	large pot	28
1000	J4	2Bii	2B	U	burial	19
1001	K4	2C	2C	0.09	wall #54	2
1002	K4	2C	2C	0.24	wall #67	2
1003	K4	2C	2C	0.03	wall #68	2
1004	K3	3A	3A	0.08	wall#69	2
1006	K2	2Bi	2B	0.26	wall #71	2
1007	K2	2Bii	2B	0.22	wall #72	2
1008	H2	3A	3A	0.25	wall #73	2
1009	J3	3Aii	3A	0.30	wall #65	2
1010	J3/4	3Aii	3A	0.40	wall #66	2
1011	J3	3C	3C	U	wall #62	2
1012	J3	3B	3B	U	wall #74	2
1013	K3	2B	2B	U	surface	4
1014	K2	2B	2B	U	hard packed m.b.	4
1015	K3	2C	2C	U	floor	11
1016	K3	2Bi	2B	U	floor	11
1017	K4	2C	2C	U	m.b. platform	7
1018	K3	2Bii	2B	U	door socket	27
1019	K4	2C	2C	U	door socket	27
1020	K3/4	2A	2A	U	wall	2
1021	J3	2Bii	2B	U	fill	6
1991 Area JU=unknown						
1022	H1	1	1	17.50	topsoil	1
1023	J1	1	1	14.25	topsoil	1
1024	K1	1	1	13.00	topsoil	1

1025	L1	1	1	7.75	topsoil	1
1026	L2	1	1	7.25	topsoil	1
1027	K2	2C	2C	1.25	pit	5
1028	J1	2Bi	2B	3.75	ash	21
1029	L2	2Aii	2A	3.16	pit	5
1030	K1	2A	2A	2.45	surface	4
1031	J1	2Aii	2A	3.75	surface	4
1032	H1	1	1	0.03	burial	19
1033	K1	2A	2A	0.22	pit	5
1034	L2	2Aii	2A	2.19	surface	4
1035	J1	2A	2A	0.39	fill	6
1036	H1	2A	2A	11.50	ash	21
1037	H1	2A	2A	11.50	ash	21
1038	K1–L1	2A	2A	1.75	pit	5
1039	H1	2A	2A	11.50	ash	21
1040	J1	2Bi	2B	0.26	hearth	22
1041	L2	2A	2A	4.51	pit	5
1042	H1	2C	2C	2.37	pit	5
1043	J1	2Bi	2B	0.01	cupmark	14
1044	J1	2Bii	2B	2.06	pit	5
1045	L1	2A	2A	0.50	surface	4
1046	K3	2Bii	2B	0.01	burial #2	19
1047	H1	2A	2A	11.50	ash	21
1048 dead locus						
1049	J2	2C	2C	9.75	fill	6
1050	L1	2A	2A	1.77	pit	5
1051	L2	2A	2A	4.51	pit	5
1052	K1	2Bi	2B	0.30	surface	4
1053	L1	2Bi	2B	5.08	fill and tumble	6
1054	H3	3A	3A	1.43	fill	6
1055	J1	2Aii	2A	1.11	surface	4
1056	J2	2C	2C	0.44	pit	5
1057	J1	2Bii	2B	0.47	pit	5
1058	L2	1	1	2.00	topsoil	1
1059	L1–2	2A	2A	0.90	pit	5
1060	L1	1	1	2.28	topsoil	1
1061	J2	2C	2C	0.50	surface	4
1062	L3	1	1	2.48	topsoil	1
1063	L4	1	1	1.48	topsoil	1
1064	L3	2A	2A	0.72	surface	4
1065	K1	2Bi	2B	0.23	surface	4
1066	H2	2Bii	2B	5.25	fill	6
1067	K3	2Bi	2B	2.80	surface	4
1068	K3	2Bi	2B	3.75	removal	10
1069	L1–2	2Aii	2A	10.00	ash	21
1070	K1	2Bii	2B	0.24	pit	5
1071	J1–K1	2A	2A	0.08	removal	10
1072	K3	2Bi	2B	9.45	removal	10
1073	K2–K3	2Bi	2B	0.31	pit	5
1074	J1	2Aii	2A	0.37	heath	22
1075	J3–H3	2Bii	2B	0.67	pit	5
1076	K2	2Bii	2B	0.29	removal	10
1077	L2	2A	2A	0.22	surface	4
1078	L1	2Bi	2B	0.79	hearth	22
1079	K2	2Bi	2B	0.72	removal	10
1080	L3	2Ci	2C	0.04	surface	4
1081	J2–H2–H3	2C	2C	1.19	m.b. pit	5
1082	K2	2C	2C	0.75	surface	4
1083	K2	2C	2C	U	standing stone	18
1084	L3	2B	2B	0.57	removal	10
1085	H2–3	2Bii	2B	0.98	pit	5
1086 dead locus						
1087	K2	2Bi	2B	0.21	removal	10
1088	K1	2Bii	2B	0.02	pit	5
1089	K1	2Bii	2B	0.03	pit	5
1090	H3	2Bii	2B	1.76	burial	19
1091	J1	2Bi	2B	11.20	collapse	20
1092	K3	3A	3A	0.50	removal	10
1093	H1–J1	2Bi	2B	0.82	removal	10
1094	L3	2Ci	2C	U	removal	10
1095	K1	2Aii	2A	0.09	hearth	22
1096	K1	2A	2A	0.04	hearth	22
1097	J1	2Bi–ii	2B	3.33	surface	4
1098	K3	2C	2C	4.00	fill	6
1099	H3	3A	3A	0.90	fill	6
1100	K1–2	2A	2A	0.12	removal	10
1101	K1	2Bii	2B	0.26	hearth	22
1102	H1	2Bi	2B	1.80	surface	4
1103	K3	2Bii	2B	0.06	pit	5
1104	J3	2Aii	2A	1.12	fill	6
1105	J2	2C	2C	0.68	pit	5
1106	K2	2Bi	2B	1.10	removal	10
1107	J1–K1	2Bi	2B	1.06	removal	10
1108	J1–K1	2Bi	2B	1.40	removal	10
1109	K1–2	2A	2A	0.10	threshhold	29
1110	J1	2C	2C	0.50	surface	4
1111	K1	2C	2C	4.50	fill	6
1112	K1	2Bi	2B	0.50	removal	10
1113	K1	2C	2C	1.10	fill	6
1114	L1	2A	2A	0.01	pit	5
1115	L1	2A	2A	0.00	pit	5
1116	L1	2A	2A	0.73	structure	3
1117	H1	2A	2A	11.50	ash	21
1118	L2	2Bi	2B	0.02	pit	5
1119	K3	2Bii	2B	0.39	pit	5
1120	L2	2Bi	2B	3.05	CMB I	24
1121	L1	2Bi–ii	2B	1.58	surface	4
1122	L1–2	2A	2A	2.70	m.b. cap	20
1123	L2	2A	2A	0.10	pit	5
1124	H1	2Bii	2B	0.40	pit	5
1125	H1	2Bi	2B	7.72	ash	6
1126	K1	2C	2C	0.30	pit	5
1127	H1–J1	2C	2C	0.11	pit	5
1128	J1	2C	2C	0.84	pit	5
1129	L1–2	2Bi	2B	U	CMB II	24
1130	L1	2A	2A	0.06	platform	7
1131	K3	3A	3A	0.25	fill	6
1132	L1	2C	2C	U	surface	4
1133	L1	2Bii	2B	0.37	hearth	22
1134	J1	2C	2C	0.80	pit	5
1135	H1	2C	2C	0.26	pit	5
1136	K1	2C	2C	0.02	pit	5
1137	K2	2C	2C	0.01	pit	5
1138	L1	2Bii	2B	0.03	pit	5
1139	L1	2Bi	2B	U	wall	2
1140	J1–K1	2Cii	2C	U	wall	2
1141	L1	2Bii	2B	0.11	pit	5
1142	H1	2C	2C	0.25	surface	4
1143	K3	2C	2C	1.75	surface	4
1144	J2	2C	2C	4.32	fill	6
1145	J1	2C	2C	4.50	fill	6
1146	H1	3A	3A	10.75	fill	6

1147	K2	3A	3A	6.00	fill	6
1148	J3	3Aii	3A	0.54	removal	10
1149	H3	3A	3A	0.01	hearth	22
1150	H3	3A	3A	1.99	pit	5
1151	L1	2Bii	2B	0.01	hearth	22
1152	J3	2A	2A	0.04	pit	5
1153 dead locus						
1154	K2	2C	2C	0.62	wall	2
1155	J3	2A	2A	0.99	pit	5
1156	H3	3Aii	3A	1.05	fill	6
1157	K1	2C	2C	0.30	surface	4
1158	K1	2Cii	2C	3.25	fill	6
1159	H2	2C	2C	10.25	fill	6
1160	L1	2A	2A	1.23	pit	5
1161	H1	3A	3A	U	m.b. arc	3
1162	L1	2Bii	2B	U	platform	7
1163	H2	3A	3A	0.38	removal	10
1164	H3	3A	3A	U	surface	4
1165	H3	3B	3B	U	surface	4
1166	L2	2A	2A	U	cap over CMB	20
1167	H2	2C	2C	0.03	ostrich egg	30
1168	H1	2C	2C	0.78	pit	5
1169	K3	2Bii	2B	0.04	burial	19
1170	J2	3A	3A	4.32	fill	6
1171	J2	3A	3A	U	surface	4
1172	H1	3A	3A	U	cap over CMB	20
1173	K1	2Cii	2C	0.21	pit	5
1174	L1	2Bii	2B	0.02	pit	5
1175	J2	3A	3A	U	surface	4
1176	J2	3A	3A	0.15	pit	5
1177	K1	2Cii	2C	U	surface	4
1178	J1	2Cii	2C	U	surface	4
1179	H1	3A	3A	U	surface	4
1180	K2	3A	3A	U	surface	4
1181	H2	4	4	U	surface	4
1182	K3	3A–3B	3A	U	surface	4
1183	H1	3B	3B	U	surface	4
1184	K1	2Cii	2C	0.23	pit	5
1185	K1	2Cii	2C	0.09	pit	5
1186	K2	3A	3A	0.02	pit	5
1187	K1	3A	3A	U	pit	5
1188	L1	2Bi	2B	U	wall	2
1189	K1	2Bi	2B	0.75	collapse	20
1190	H3	3A	3A	U	wall	2
1191	H3	3Aii	3A	U	wall	2
1992 Area JU=unknown						
1200	L1	2Bi	2B	0.26	wall 1139, removal	10
1201	K4	2C	2C	2.40	floors (L.912,913) rem.	10
1202	L4	2Bi	2B	2.02	floor (L.865), removal	10
1203	K2	3A	3A	4.75	floor (L.1180), removal	10
1204	K2–L2	2Bi	2B	1.27	surface (L.1014), remov	10
1205	L1	2Bi–ii	2B	0.53	surface (L.1121) remov	10
1206	L3	2Ci	2C	1.46	surface (L.1080), remov	10
1207	L1	2Bi	2B	0.07	wall (L.1188), remov	10
1208	L1–L2	2Bi	2B	1.50	cmbII (L.1188), remov	10
1209	L2	2Bii	2B	1.15	surface (L.1034), remov	10
1210	L1–L2	2A	2A	0.28	platform (L.1130), remov	10
1211	L2	2Bi	2B	1.00	cmb I L.1120), remov	10
1212	H0	1	1	13.25	topsoil	1
1213	J0	1	1	12.50	topsoil	1
1214	H4	1	1	12.50	topsoil	1
1215	L3	2Bi	2B	0.27	wall#56 (L.868), remov	10
1216	L3	2Cii	2C	2.17	pit rim (L.853), remov	10
1217	L3	2Ai	2A	1.55	fill	6
1218	L3	2Bi	2B	3.06	pit rim (L.868a), remov	10
1219	L4	1	1	0.48	topsoil	1
1220	K0	1	1	12.25	topsoil	1
1221	L3	2Cii	2C	0.24	pit rim (L.856,855), remo	10
1222	L4	2Cii	2C	3.24	surface (L.915), removal	10
1223	L4	2A	2A	0.88	fill and surface	4
1224	K0	2A	2A	0.50	pit	5
1225	K0	2Bi	2B	0.50	wall #117, removal	10
1226	K0	2A	2A	9.90	surface and fill	4
1227	J1	2C	2C	U	wall #? and removal?	10
1228	H1–J1	3Ai	3A	U	wall #118	2
1229	L0	1	1	6.30	topsoil	1
1230	K4	2Bi	2B	0.00	cupmark	14
1231	L4	2Bi	2B	0.38	pit	5
1232	K4	2Bi	2B	0.04	pit	5
1233	K0	2B	2B	3.12	fill	6
1234	H4	2A	2A	0.63	hearth	22
1235	H4	2Bi	2B	0.69	pit	5
1236	K0	2B	2B	2.34	fill	6
1237	H0	2Bi	2B	0.38	(pit) burial	19
1238	H4	2A	2A	0.53	surface	4
1239	H4	2A	2A	0.38	pit	5
1240	H4	2A	2A	1.04	pit	5
1241	H4	2A	2A	0.46	pit	5
1242	H4	2A	2A	0.05	pit	5
1243	H0	2Bi	2B	U	standing stone	18
1244	H0	2Bi	2B	0.25	surface	4
1245	H4	2A	2A	2.14	surface	4
1246	H4	2B	2B	1.66	fill (baulk)	6
1247	H4	2B	2B	0.06	m.b. circle	8
1248	H4	2A	2A	U	m.b. &stone circle	8
1249	L4	2Bi	2B	0.13	pit	5
1250	H4	2Bii	2B	1.50	pit	5
1251	L4	2Bi	2B	0.10	pit	5
1252	L4	2Bi	2B	0.09	pit	5
1253	L4	2Bi	2B	1.19	pit	5
1254	L4	2Bi	2B	?????		U
1255	J0	2A	2A	0.30	pit	5
1256	J0	2A	2A	3.00	fill	6
1257	H4	2A	2A	1.86	fill	6
1258 dead locus ?		?	?	?	?	?
1259	K0	2C	2C	0.47	fill,ash	21
1260	J0	2A	2A	0.25	surface	4
1261	H4	2A	2A	U	fill	6

1262	J0	2B	2B	0.08	pit	5
1263	J0	2B	2B	1.81	hearth	22
1264	J0	2Bi	2B	1.45	pit	5
1265	J0	2Bi	2B	0.57	hearth	22
1266	L0	2A	2A	2.75	surface	4
1267	J0	2Bi	2B	0.51	pit	5
1268	H4	2A	2A	0.54	surface	4
1269	J0	2B	2B	0.54	pit	5
1270	J0	2B	2B	0.49	pit	5
1271	H4	2A	2A	U	pit	5
1272	J0	2B	2B	1.00	surface	4
1273	H2	4	4	2.50	fill	6
1274	H2	4	4	0.50	ash fill	21
1275	H2	4	4	3.75	fill	6
1276	K0	2C	2C	0.88	surface	4
1277	K0	2C	2C	0.15	pit	5
1278 dead locus						
1279 dead locus						
1280	H4	2A	2A	0.29	wall/structure-east	2
1281	H4	2A	2A	0.13	wall/structure-west	2
1282	L3	3A	3A	0.20	surface	4
1283	L4	2Bi	2B	0.01	surface	4
1284	J0	2B	2B	4.00	fill	6
1285	K0	2C	2C	0.80	surface	4
1286	H4	2B	2B	0.32	m.b. structure	3
1287	H4	2A	2A	0.58	surface	4
1288	L4	3A	3A	0.06	stone/m.b. structure	3
1289	L4	3A	3A	U	stone stucture	3
1290	L4	2Bi	2B	U	wall #115	2
1291	L4	2Bi	2B	U	wall#114	2
1292	H0	2Bi	2B	U	wall#119	2
1293	L4	2C	2C	2.00	fill	6
1294	H2	4	4	6.00	fill (pit)	6
1295	L0	2A	2A	2.80	fill	6
1296	L0	2A	2A	0.12	ash fill	21
1297	J0	2C	2C	0.86	pit	5
1298	J0	2C	2C	0.06	hearth	22
1299	K0	2C	2C	0.80	fill	6
1300	L0	2A	2A	0.89	fill	6
1301	H4	2Bii	2B	0.00	burial (baby)	19
1302	J0	2C	2C	0.02	cupmark	14
1303	J0	2C	2C	0.50	surface	4
1304	K0	2B	2B	0.20	surface	4
1305	K0	2B	2B	0.23	surface	4
1306	K0	3Aii	3A	U	surface	4
1307	J0	2C	2C	1.42	pit	5
1308	H2	4	4	2.41	pit	5
1309	L0	2C	2C	1.37	pit	5
1310	L0	2C	2C	10.31	pit	5
1311	L0	2B	2B	0.12	surface	4
1312	L0	2B	2B	0.04	surface	4
1313	J0	2C	2C	0.01	cupmark	14
1314	L0	2B	2B	0.10	wall#120, removal	10
1315	L0	2C	2C	0.20	surface	4
1316	J0	2C	2C	0.88	fill	6
1317	H4	2Bii	2B	U	burial pit	19
1318	J0	2C	2C	0.24	cupmark	14
1319	J0	2C	2C	2.21	pit	5
1320	K0	2C	2C	0.38	pit	5
1321	H0	2Bi	2B	1.75	fill	6
1322	L0	2C	2C	0.07	pit	5
1323	K0	3A	3A	0.08	stone platform	7
1324	K0	2C	2C	0.14	pit	5
1325	H0–J0	2C	2C	0.08	pit/1/2	5
1326	H2	4	4	0.79	pit	5
1327	H2	4	4	0.60	pit	5
1328	H3	3Aii	3A	1.65	fill	6
1329	H2	4	4	0.46	pit	5
1330	L0	2C	2C	1.20	fill	6
1331	H2	4	4	0.12	pit	5
1332	L0	2B	2B	2.85	fill	6
1333	K0	3Aii	3A	2.37	pit	5
1334	J0	3A	3A	1.00	surface	4
1335	J0	3A	3A	1.38	fill	6
1336	J0	3A	3A	0.51	pit (churn)	5
1337	K0	3A	3A	1.70	pit	5
1338	H4	2A	2A	0.00	surface	4
1339	H4	2A	2A	U	m.b./stone structure	3
1340	H4	2Bii	2B	0.64	pit	5
1341	L1–L2	3A	3A	3.57	silo	9
1342	J0	3A	3A	0.01	cupmark	14
1343	J0	3A	3A	0.00	pit	5
1344	H0	2Bi	2B	0.15	pit	5
1345	J0	3A	3A	1.74	pit	5
1346	H4	2Bii	2B	0.20	pit	5
1347 dead locus						
1348	K0	3Aii	3A	N.D	pit	5
1349	H4	2Bii	2B	U	surface	4
1350	L1	2Cii	2C	U	surface	4
1351	H0	2C	2C	0.25	surface	4
1352	J0	3A	3A	0.01	pit	5
1353	J0	3A	3A	0.17	pit	5
1354	L0	4	4	0.96	pit	5
1355	J0–K0	1	1	5.70	topsoil	1
1356	H4	2A	2A	U	mudbrick (step?)	3
1357	H0	2Bi	2B	0.20	U f. bone layer, bur pit	31
1358	H4	2Bii	2B	U	surface	4
1359	H4	2Bii	2B	0.01	pit, ash	5
1360	H4	2B	2B	U	stone circle	8
1361	L0	3B	3B	0.15	pit	5
1362	L0	3A	3A	0.21	pit	5
1363	L0	3A	3A	0.56	pit	5
1364	H0	2C	2C	U	stone circ. structure	8
1365	H5	1	1	9.10	topsoil	1
1366	L0	3B	3B	1.37	pit	5
1367	L0	3A	3A	0.09	pit	5
1368	L0	3A	3A	0.53	surface	4
1369	H2	3A	3A	3.51	silo	9
1370	J0–K0	2A	2A	0.20	surface	4
1371	L0	3B	3B	2.67	pit	5
1372	H5	2Ai	2A	U	pit	5
1373	J0–K0	2A	2A	0.34	pit	5
1374	H5	2Ai	2A	0.83	pit	5
1375	H5	2A	2A	0.31	surface	4
1376	H5	2A	2A	0.04	surface	4
1377	H5	2Ai	2A	U	M.B.wall (L.1280)	2
1378	H5	1	1	0.08	stones wall?	2
1379	K0	3Aii	3A	0.00	pit	5
1380	K0	3Aii	3A	0.02	pit	5
1381	K0	3Aii	3A	0.06	pit	5
1382	K0	3Aii	3A	0.96	pit	5

1383	K0	3Aii	3A	0.00	pit	5
1384	K0	3Ai	3A	0.15	pit	5
1385	L0	3B	3B	U	pit	5
1386	L0	3A	3A	U	wall, N. aspect #122	2
1387	L0	3A	3A	U	wall, E. aspect #122	2
1388	L0	3A	3A	U	surface	4
1389	H0	2Bi	2B	0.20	pit	5
1390	dead locus					
1391	J0–K0	2A	2A	1.50	fill	6
1392	H5	2Ai	2A	0.62	fill	6
1393	H0	2C	2C	2.39	fill, ash	21
1394	H5	2Ai	2A	0.12	fill	6
1395	K0	3A	3A	0.02	pit	5
1396	K0	3A	3A	0.00	pit	5
1397	H5	2Ai	2A	U	surface	4
1398	K0	3A	3A	0.02	pit	5
1399	K0	3A	3A	0.06	pit	5
1400	H0	2Bi	2B	0.23	stones, burial base(12.37)	19
1401	L0	2C	2C	0.56	pit	5
1402	K0	3A	3A	0.00	cupmark w/vessel frags	14
1403	K0	3A	3A	0.07	hearth	22
1404	H0	2Bi	2B	0.17	fill,silt, burial base	19
1405	K0	3A	3A	0.01	pit	5
1406	H5	2A	2A	U	pit	5
1407	H5	2Ai	2A	U	surface	4
1408	J0–K0	2C	2C	0.20	surface	4
1409	H0	2Bi	2B	0.43	m.b.layer in burial	20
1410	H5	2B	2B	0.74	fill	6
1411	H5	2B	2B	U	stone circle	8
1412	K0	3Aii	3A	0.15	pit	5
1413	H5	2Ai	2A	0.12	collapse	20
1414	H5	2Ai	2A	U	stone wall??	2
1415	J0–K0	2C	2C	0.05	pit	5
1416	J0–K0	2C	2C	0.27	pit	5
1417	H4	2Bii	2B	0.10	pit	5
1418	H4	2Bii	2B	U	m.b.structure?	3
1419	H2	2C	2C	0.50	surface	4
1420	H2	3A	3A	0.50	surface	4
1421	J0–K0	2C	2C	1.33	fill	6
1422	L2	2Cii	2C	U	surface	4
1423	L4	3A	3A	U	surface	4
1424	K4	3A	3A	U	surface	4
1425	H4	3A	3A	U	cupmark	14
1426	H4	3A	3A	U	cupmark	14
1427	J1	3Ai	3A	U	surface	4
1428	K0	3A	3A	U	pit	5
1991 Area TU=unknown						
600	Ai2	1	1	12.92	topsoil	1
601	Ail	1	1	12.96	topsoil	1
602	Sl	1	1	11.40	topsoil	1
603	S2	1	1	8.64	topsoil	1
604	M2	1	1	9.50	topsoil	1
605	N2	1	1	19.95	topsoil	1
606	M1	1	1	10.32	topsoil	1
607	N1	1	1	11.04	topsoil	1
608	S2	2A	2A	5.28	fill	6
609	dead locus					
610	dead locus					
611	Ail	2A	2A	1.44	fill	6
612	M2	2A	2A	2.27	fill	6
613	Ail	2A	2A	0.35	burial	19
614	Ai2	2A	2A	1.10	fill	6
615	S2	2A	2A	0.56	burial	19
616	N1	2A	2A	0.40	fill	6
617	M1	2A	2A	6.08	fill	6
618	S1	2A	2A	0.40	pit	5
619	Ai2	2A	2A	0.23	fill	6
620	Ail	2A	2A	0.26	pit	5
621	Ail	2B	2B	2.43	fill	6
622	Ail	2A	2A	0.01	cupmark	14
623	S2	2A	2A	0.50	stone feature	3
624	S1–N1	2A	2A	2.69	fill	6
625	S2	1	1	1.04	topsoil	1
626	Ail	2B	2B	0.20	pit	5
627	N2	2A	2A	8.10	fill	6
628	N1	2A	2A	0.15	hearth	22
629	N2	1	1	1.40	topsoil	1
630	M2	1	1	1.40	topsoil	1
631	S2	2B	2B	N.A.	mudbrick arch	3
632	M1	2A	2A	0.24	platform	7
633	M2	2B	2B	5.60	fill	6
634	Ai2–S2	2B	2B	9.51	fill	6
635	S2	2B	2B	0.23	fill	6
636	Ail	2B	2B	0.86	fill	6
637	S2	2B	2B	0.80	hearth	22
638	S2	2B	2B	0.08	pit	5
639	S1	2A	2A	1.57	pit	5
640	Ail	3B	3B	2.07	pit	5
641	Ail	2B	2B	0.10	pit	5
642	Ail	2B	2B	0.21	hearth	22
643	S1	2A	2A	0.84	pit	5
644	dead locus					
645	Ail	2A	2A	0.66	w81 removal	10
646	N1	2A	2A	0.08	pit	5
647	M2	2B	2B	1.41	hearth	22
648	S1–S2	2A	2A	0.06	burial	19
649	Ail	2C	2C	3.70	pit	5
650	Ni	2A	2A	0.32	pit	5
651	dead locus					
652	M2	2B	2B	0.03	surface	4
653	dead locus					
654	M2	2B	2B	0.02	hearth	22
655	M2	2B	2B	0.03	hearth	22
656	N1–S1	2A	2A	0.09	stone feature	3
657	M2–M3	2B	2B	0.11	pit	5
658	N1–S1	2B	2B	0.03	ash lens	21
659	Ai2	2A	2A	0.86	w91 removal	10
660	N2	2B	2B	0.21	w92 removal	10
661	S1	2B	2B	0.23	pit	5
662	Ail	2Bii	2B	U	surface	4
663	Ail–S1	2Bi	2B	U	surface	4
664	Ai2	2A	2A	U	surface	4
665	N1–M1	2B	2B	0.10	pit	5
666	S2	2C	2C	2.27	fill	6
667	Ai2	2C	2C	U	burial	19
668	Ai2	2C	2C	0.64	pit	5
669	M1	2B	2B	U	stone platform	7
670	Ail	2B	2B	0.03	pit	5
671	Ai2	2C	2C	0.85	pit	5
672	S3	3	3	U	fill	6
673	Ai2	2B	2B	0.52	pit	5

674	S1	2Bii	2B	1.24	pit	5
675	Ai2	2Bii	2B	0.40	pit	5
676	Ai2	2C–3A	2C	12.56	fill	6
677	S3–N3	1	1	0.35	topsoil	1
678	N1	2A	2A	0.12	pit	5
679	Ai2	2C	2C	0.21	pit	5
680	S1	2C	2C	9.80	fill	6
681	S1	2B	2B	0.15	hearth	22
682	S2	2C	2C	1.45	pit	5
683	S1	2B	2B	0.18	hearth	22
684	MO	1	1	11.16	topsoil	1
685	N1–M1	2B	2B	2.40	fill	6
686	N0	1	1	12.48	topsoil	1
687	S0	1	1	12.47	topsoil	1
688	Ai0	1	1	8.60	topsoil	1
689	M0	2B	2B	40.10	fill	6
690	S1	2Bi	2B	0.10	stone feature	3
691	S1	2Bi	2B	0.09	feature/collapse	3
692	Ai2	3B	3B	2.80	pit	5
693	M0–N0	2B	2B	U	fill (on wall)	6
694	S0	2A	2A	1.44	fill	6
695	N0–S0	2A	2A	5.04	fill	6
696	M0	2A	2A	1.21	pit	5
697	S0	2A	2A	0.71	pit	5
698	Ai2	3B	3B	0.03	dog burial	25
699	S1–N1	1	1	0.79	topsoil	1
700	M0	2A	2A	1.18	pit	5
701 dead locus						
702 part of L.6922A		2A				U
703	S1–N1	2A	2A	0.69	pit	5
704	N0	2B	2B	1.26	fill	6
705	Ai2	4	4	0.65	pit	5
706	S0–N0	2B	2B	0.31	hearth	22
707	Ail	3A	3A	0.07	hearth	22
708	Ail	3B	3B	0.93	fill	6
709	S0	2B	2B	1.68	pit	5
710	M0	2A	2A	0.85	pit	5
711	Ail	2Bii	2B	0.49	w101 remov.	10
712	S0	2A	2A	0.51	5 hearth	22
713	M0	2A	2A	0.86	pit	5
714	M0	2A	2A	0.73	pit	5
715	Ail	2Bi	2B	0.35	pit	5
716	Ail	3A–3B	3A	1.65	fill	6
717 dead locus						
718	Ai2	4	4	0.21	pit	5
719	N1	2A	2A	0.12	pit	5
720	S0	2A	2A	0.48	pit	5
721	N1–S1	2B	2B	U	circular m.b.	8
722	M1	2B	2B	U	surface	4
723	N1	2B	2B	U	surface	4
724	N2	2B	2B	U	surface	4
725	Ai2	4	4	U	surface	4
726	N0	2Bii	2B	U	surface	4
1992 Area TU=unknown						
750	Ai0–Ail	1	1	0.98	topsoil	1
751	M0	1	1	3.20	topsoil	1
752	M0–N0	2B	2B	U	wall cleaning	13
753	N2	2B	2B	0.75	w#92 removal	10
754	S0–S1	1	1	2.20	topsoil	1
755	M0	2B–2C	2B	22.20	fill	6
756	Ai0	2A	2A	4.58	fill	6
757	Ai1–Ai2	2B	2B	0.84	w#101, remov	10
758	M1	2B	2B	0.52	fill	6
759	M0–N0	2A	2A	0.08	ash lens	21
760	M0	2A	2A	0.65	pit	5
761	N2	2A	2A	7.26	fill	6
762	Ai0	2A	2A	3.06	fill	6
763	M1–N1	2B	2B	22.92	fill	6
764	M/N0/1	1	1	0.60	topsoil	1
765	M0–N0	2B	2B	2.44	w#104 , removal	10
766	S0–N0	2B	2B	U	w#109, defining	10
767	M1	2B	2B	0.66	w#88,89,L.669 removal	10
768 dead locus						
769	Ai0	2B	2B	0.73	fill	6
770	M/N1/2	1	1	0.38	topsoil	1
771	M0	2C	2C	2.30	pit	5
772	M2–3	2B	2B	20.51	fill	6
773	M1–N1	2A	2A	0.77	pit	5
774	Ai0–Ai1	2Bii	2B	0.08	ash layer (fill)	21
775	Ai0	2Bii	2B	4.20	pit	5
776	M/N1/2	2B	2B	0.16	fill	6
777	M0	2C	2C	2.48	pit	5
778	N2–N3	2B	2B	0.04	pit	5
779	S0–N0	2B	2B	2.25	fill	6
780	M0	2C	2C	0.44	pit	5
781	M1	2C	2C	0.50	pit	5
782	N1	2B	2B	0.06	w#105, removal	10
783	S1	2C	2C	11.70	fill	6
784	M1–N1	2B	2B	1.49	w#89, removal	10
785	N1–S1	2B	2B	1.05	w#82, removal	10
786	S0	2C	2C	16.20	fill	6
787	Ai0	2Bii	2B	1.85	pit	5
788	M2	2C	2C	0.05	ash lens	21
789 dead locus						
790	M/N0	2C	2C	0.59	pits	5
791 dead locus						
792	Ai0	2C	2C	0.24	surface, removal	10
793	S1	2C	2C	0.06	pit/post-hole	5
794	M/N0	2C	2C	0.79	pits	5
795	S0	2Bi	2B	0.51	rubble dump	6
796	Ai0–Ai1	2Bii	2B	1.75	fill	6
797	S1	2Cii	2C	0.03	fill	6
798	N1–S1	2A	2A	0.10	struct. (L.656), removal	10
799	N0	2B	2B	8.40	fill	6
1500	Ai0	3A	3A	0.08	pit	5
1501	Ai0	2Bii	2B	0.08	fill	6
1502	Ai0	2B	2B	0.26	w#110,111,112, removal	10
1503	Ai0	2Bii	2B	14.04	fill	6
1504	M2	2C	2C	0.10	fill	6
1505	N0–N1	2C	2C	0.88	pit	5
1506	S2–S3	2B	2B	0.67	w#83, removal	10
1507	Ai0	2C	2C	0.22	pit	5
1508	N1	2C	2C	1.02	pit	5
1509	N0–M0	2C	2C	U	pit	5
1510	S0	2C	2C	0.10	burial	19
1511	S2	2C	2C	3.47	pit (SE 1/2) = L.682	5
1512	S1	2C	2C	0.20	rubbish dump	6
1513	S2–3	2C	2C	0.75	fill	6
1514	N1	2C	2C	1.35	pit	5

1515	S1	2Cii	2C	0.07	pit	5
1516	S1	2C	2C	0.25	hearth	22
1517	M0–M1	2C	2C	3.68	fill	6
1518	S3	3A	3A	0.52	pit	5
1519	Ai0	3A	3A	0.02	surface, inside L. 1525	4
1520 dead locus						
1521	M0–N0	3A	3A	0.02	pit	5
1522	N0–S0	2Cii	2C	0.82	pit	5
1523	N0	2C	2C	0.02	pit	5
1524	N0	2C	2C	0.20	pit	5
1525	Ai0	3A	3A	U	mudbrick circle	8
1526	S2	2C	2C	8.36	fill	6
1527	Ai0	3B	3B	3.96	pit	5
1528	Ai0	3A	3A	0.12	M.B. circle, removal	10
1529	S1	2Cii	2C	0.29	cupmark	14
1530	Ai0	3A	3A	0.03	rubbish dump	6
1531	S0	2Cii	2C	U	cupmark	14
1532	S2	2C	2C	0.57	fills (2)	6
1533	M1	3A	3A	0.31	hearth	22
1534	S0–S1	3A	3A	1.22	pit	5
1535	S0	3A	3A	0.60	pit	5
1536	S0	3A	3A	1.14	pit	5
1537	S1–N1	2Bii	2B	0.31	surface removal	4
1538	S2–S3	2Ci	2C	0.08	fill	6
1539	Ai0	3A	3A	0.17	ash layer	21
1540	Ai0	3B	3B	0.68	fill	6
1541	Ai0–Ai1	3B	3B	0.52	pit	5
1542	Ai0	3B	3B	4.20	pit	5
1543 dead locus						
1544	M1/2–N2	2C	2C	U	surface	4
1545	S1–N1	2C	2C	0.32	m.b. collapse	20
1546	Ai1	3B	3B	0.27	pit	5
1547	S2	2Ci	2C	0.17	pit	5
1548	Ai1	3B	3B	1.26	pit	5
1549	N1	2Cii	2C	0.57	pit	5
1550	S1–N1	2Cii	2C	0.21	pit	5
1551 dead locus						
1552	S0	3A	3A	U	surface	4
1553	N1/2–S1/2	1	1	0.75	topsoil	1
1554	N0	2C–3A	2C	5.60	fill	6
1555	S1–S2	2A	2A	0.03	pit	5
1556	N0	2C	2C	0.70	pit	5
1557	Ai0	3B	3B	0.29	pit	5
1558	Ai1	3B	3B	0.12	pit	5
1559	S1	2Cii	2C	0.04	surface	4
1560	S1	2Cii	2C	0.35	surface	4
1561 dead locus						
1562	Ai1	3B	3B	0.52	pit	5
1563	S1	3A	3A	0.75	thru surface, fill	6
1564	S1	3A	3A	0.04	ash layer	21
1565	S2	3A	3A	0.89	pit	5
1566	S2	3A	3A	0.11	pit	5
1567	N0	3A	3A	U	stone structure	3
1568	N0	3B	3B	0.09	pit	5
1569	N0	3B	3B	0.02	pit	5
1570	S1	2Cii	2C	0.05	hearth	22
1571	S2	3A	3A	0.50	fill	6
1572	N0	3A	3A	0.38	pit	5
1573 (709)	S0	2Bii	2B	0.05	pit	5
1574	S2	3A	3A	0.06	pit	5

1575	S2	3A	3A	0.09	pit	5
1576	S2	3A	3A	0.75	pit	5
1577	S1	3A	3A	U	surface	4
1578(709)	S0	2Bii	2B	0.29	pit	5
1579	Ai1	3B	3B	0.40	pit	5
1580	S0	3A	3A	0.09	pit	5
1581	S1–N1	3A	3A	U	collapse	20
1582 dead locus						
1583	N0	3B	3B	0.01	pit	5
1584	S2	3A	3A	U	surface	4
1585	Ai0–Ai1	2B	2B	0.09	surface	4
1586	M0–M1	3A	3A	U	sterile pleistocene	15
1587	M0	3A	3A	0.04	pits	5
1588	M0–M1	3A	3A	U	pits	5
1589	S2–S3	3B	3B	U	surface	4
1990 Area MU=unknown						
1	C6	1	1	13.00	topsoil	1
2	C5	1	1	13.20	topsoil	1
3	C4	1	1	10.30	topsoil	1
4	B6	1	1	13.10	topsoil	1
5	B5	1	1	16.40	topsoil	1
6	B4	1	1	U	topsoil	1
7	C6	2	2	22.80	fill	6
8	B4	1	1	U	fill	6
9	C5	2B	2B	0.29	pit	5
10	C6	3	3	1.40	pit	5
11	C5	2A	2A	U	wall removal	10
12	C5	2C	2C	1.98	fill	6
13	C5	2B	2B	1.39	ashy area	21
14	C4	2A	2A	U	pit	5
15	B4	2B	2B	1.42	fill	6
16	B5	2B	2B	2.54	pit w/basin	5
17	B6	2	2	12.24	ashy fill	21
18	B4	2B	2B	1.32	m.b. collapse	20
19	C6	3	3	0.32	pit	5
20	C5/B5	2B	2B	0.45	pit	5
21	C4	2	2	2.34	fill	6
22	C6	3	3	1.02	pit	5
23	C6	3	3	0.02	pit	5
24	C4	2	2	0.60	pit	5
25	B6	3	3	U	pit	5
26	B5	2C	2C	U	pit	5
27	C4	2A	2A	U	pit	5
28	C4	2B	2B	U	fill	6
29	C5	2B	2B	0.01	post mold	12
30	B5	2	2	0.03	ash lens/pit	21
31	C5	2B	2B	0.02	pit	5
32	B4	2B	2B	0.20	surface removal	10
33	B4	2C	2C	8.10	fill	6
34	B5	2	2	3.17	fill	6
35	B5/B4	2C	2C	0.82	pit	5
36	C4	2B	2B	0.43	pit	5
37	C4	2B	2B	U	surface	4
38	B4	3	3	U	w. baulk pit	5
39	B5	2C	2C	U	cupmark	14
40	B4	2C	2C	0.68	rubbish dump	6
41	B4	3	3	0.02	pit	5
42	C5	2B	2B	U	cupmark	14
43	B4	3	3	0.39	inside silo?	6
44	C4	2B	2B	U	surface	4

Table 5.2. Inventory of Room 1, Area D, Gilat.

Violin shape figurines	2	3
Stone palettes	3	3
Torpedo vessels	2	3
Ceramic Fenestrated Stands	3	6
Stone Fenestrated Stands	–	2
Anthropomorphic Statuette	–	1
Zoomorphic Statuette	–	1
Female figurine	–	1
Animal figurine (broken)	–	1
Alabaster pendant (tear drop shape)	1	–
Massebot (Standing Stones)	1	1
Cornet vessels (minimum no.)	8	28
Number of items:	20	50

Table 5.3. Gilat 14C dates.

Sample	Stratum	Uncalibrated BP	Calibrated BCE (1-sigma)	Calibrated BCE (2-sigma)	Reference
OxA-3556	IIB	5790 +- 105	4774-4499	4902-4365	Burton and Levy 2001: 1244
OxA-3555	IIB	5700 +- 100	4688-4404	4777-4342	Burton and Levy 2001: 1244
Beta-131730		5730 +- 40	4669-4500	4705-4460	Burton and Levy 2001: 1244
RT-860A	IIC	5440 +- 180	4456-4042	4688-3816	Carmi and Segal 1992: 125
OxA-4011	IIIA	5540 +- 70	4455-4335	4516-4249	Burton and Levy 2001: 1244
Beta-131729		5560 +- 50	4455-4344	4494-4332	Burton and Levy 2001: 1244
RT-860B	IIA	4800 +- 135	3705-3377	3973-3141	Carmi and Segal 1992: 125
RT-2058	IIC	4530 +- 85	3367-3093	3515-2921	Burton and Levy 2001: 1244

Table 5.4. General distribution of contexts at Gilat by strata (all seasons).

Code #	Description	1	2	2A	2B	2C	3	3A	3B	3C	4	unknown	Total
1	topsoil	78	0	2	5	0	0	0	0	0	0	0	85
2	wall	1	1	6	14	7	0	10	1	1	0	0	41
3	feature	0	2	6	6	2	0	4	1	0	0	0	21
4	surface	1	1	30	38	39	2	30	10	0	2	2	155
5	pit	5	10	76	106	102	20	68	25	0	10	1	423
6	fill	16	8	27	54	43	4	32	3	0	4	0	191
7	platform	0	1	3	13	3	0	1	0	0	0	1	22
8	circular feature	0	0	1	7	2	0	1	0	0	0	0	11
9	silo	0	0	0	1	2	-0	3	0	0	0	0	6
10	removal	0	0	8	36	12	0	5	0	0	0	0	61
11	floor	0	0	3	9	34	0	12	2	0	1	0	61
12	post-hole	0	0	0	1	4	0	0	0	0	0	0	5
13	cleaning	0	0	0	1	1	0	1	0	0	0	4	7
14	cup-mark	0	0	2	3	6	2	14	0	0	0	0	27
15	sterile Plesitocene	0	0	0	0	3	0	1	0	0	0	0	4
16	oven	0	0	0	0	1	0	0	0	0	0	0	1
17	probe	0	1	1	0	1	1	0	1	0	0	0	5
18	standing stone	0	0	0	1	3	0	0	0	0	0	0	4
19	burial	3	0	3	18	3	1	2	0	0	0	1	31
20	mudbrick collapse	1	0	9	4	1	0	2	0	0	0	0	17
21	ash fill	0	2	10	4	3	0	2	0	0	1	0	22
22	hearth	0	0	6	16	3	0	4	0	0	0	0	29
23	found deposit (axe)	0	0	0	0	0	0	1	0	0	0	0	1
24	concave mudbrick basin	0	0	0	2	0	0	0	0	0	0	0	2
25	dog burial	0	0	0	0	0	0	0	1	0	0	0	1
27	door socket	0	0	0	1	1	0	0	0	0	0	0	2
28	pot	0	0	0	0	0	0	1	0	0	0	0	1
29	threshold	0	0	1	0	0	0	0	0	0	0	0	1
30	ostrich egg	0	0	0	0	1	0	0	0	0	0	0	1
31	bone cluster	0	0	0	1	0	0	0	0	0	0	0	1
	unknown	0	0	2	1	0	0	0	0	0	0	0	3
	TOTAL	105	26	196	342	277	30	194	44	1	18	9	1242

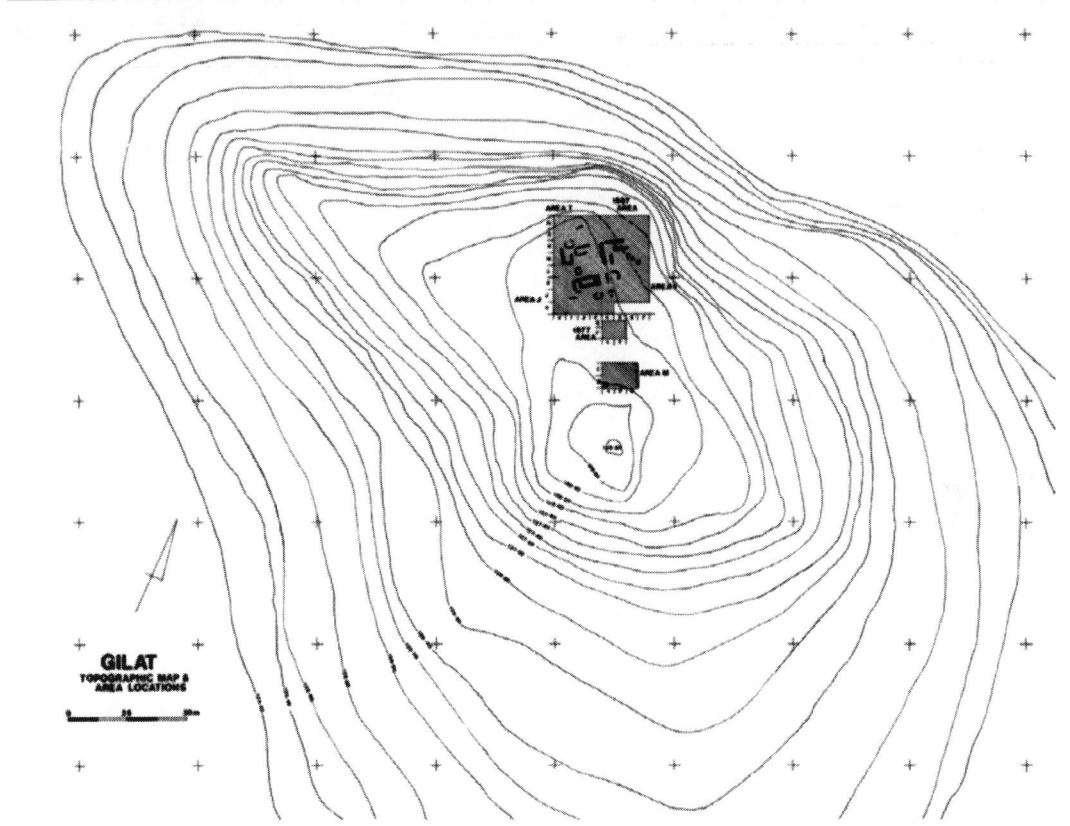

Figure 5.1. Topographic map of Gilat.

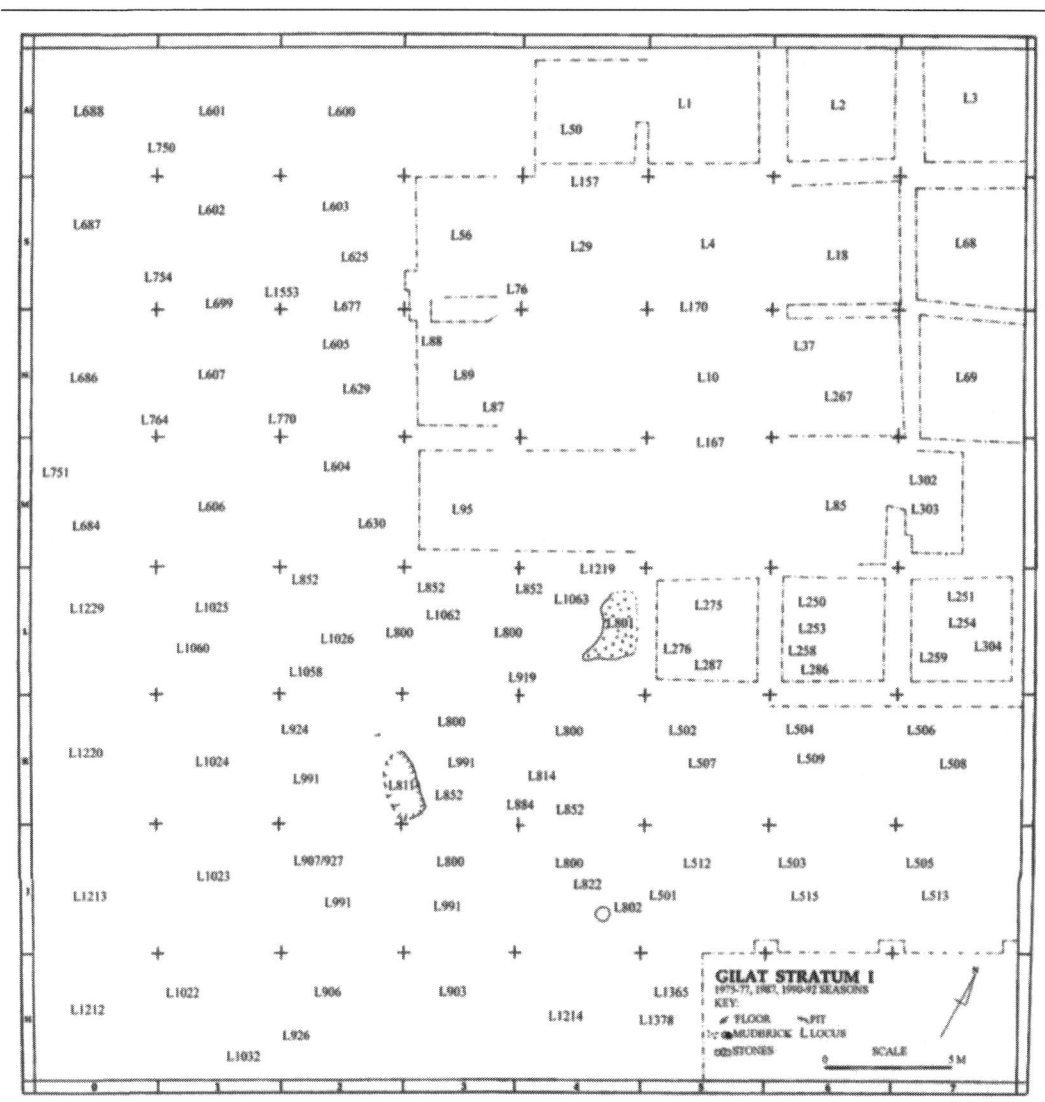

Figure 5.2. Stratum I general plan.

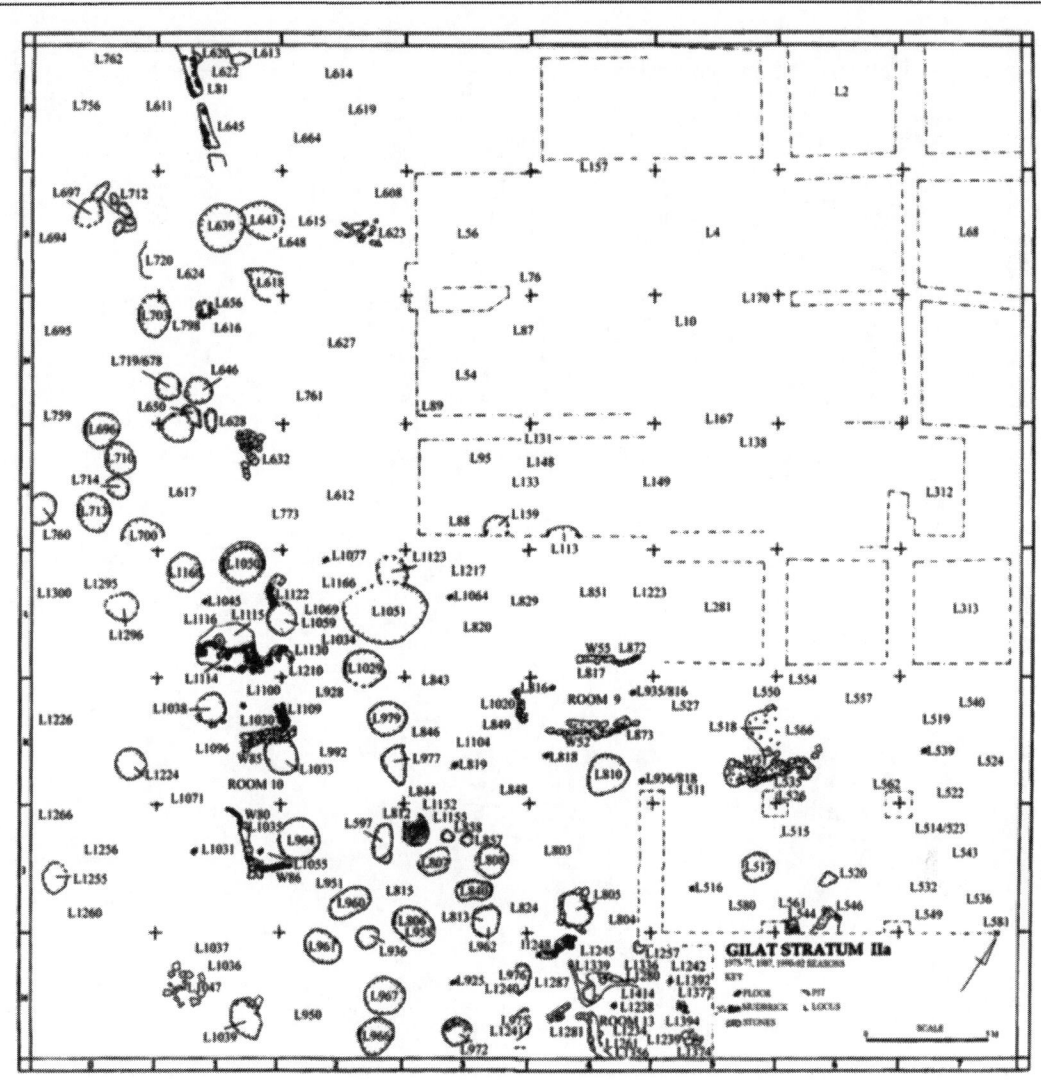

Figure 5.3. Stratum 2A general plan.

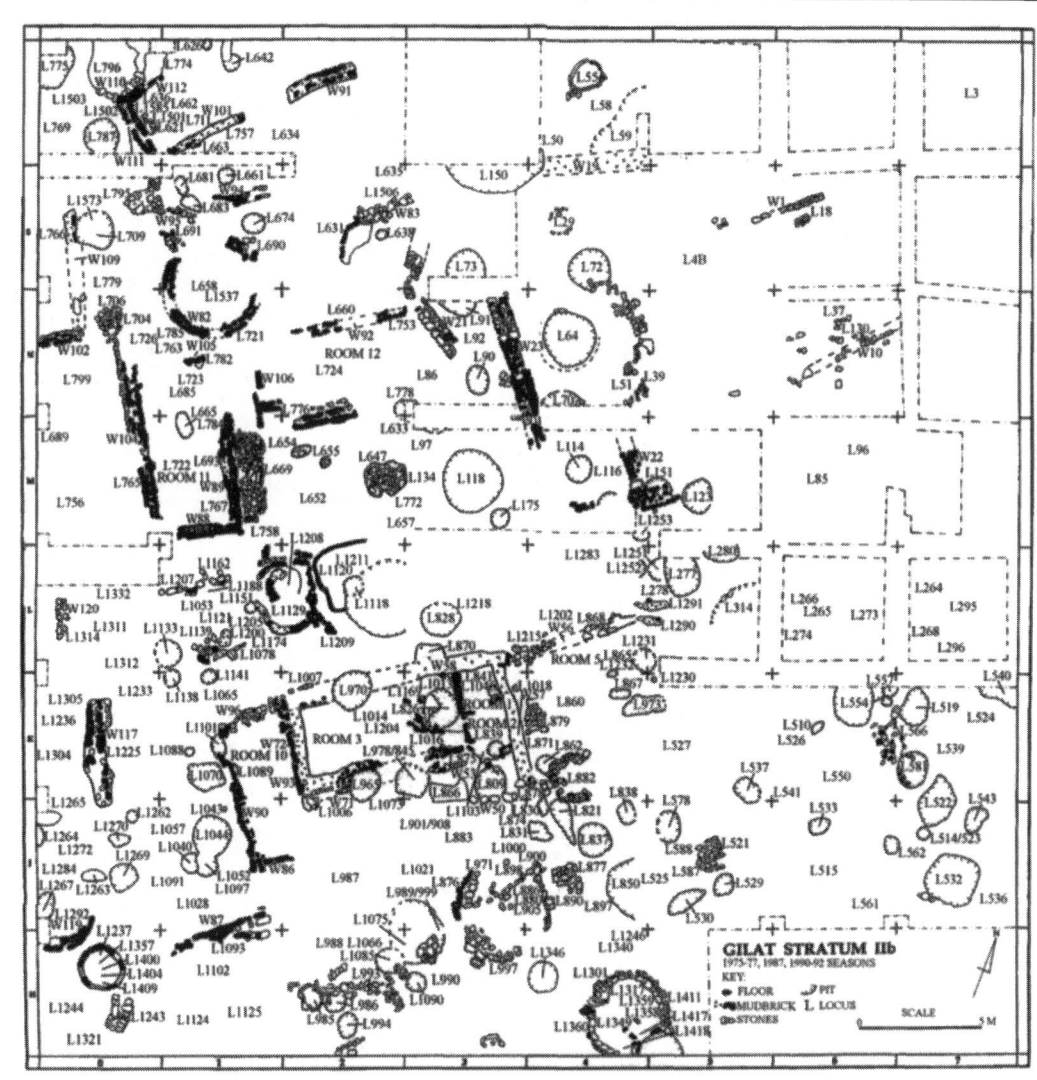

Figure 5.4. Stratum 2B general plan.

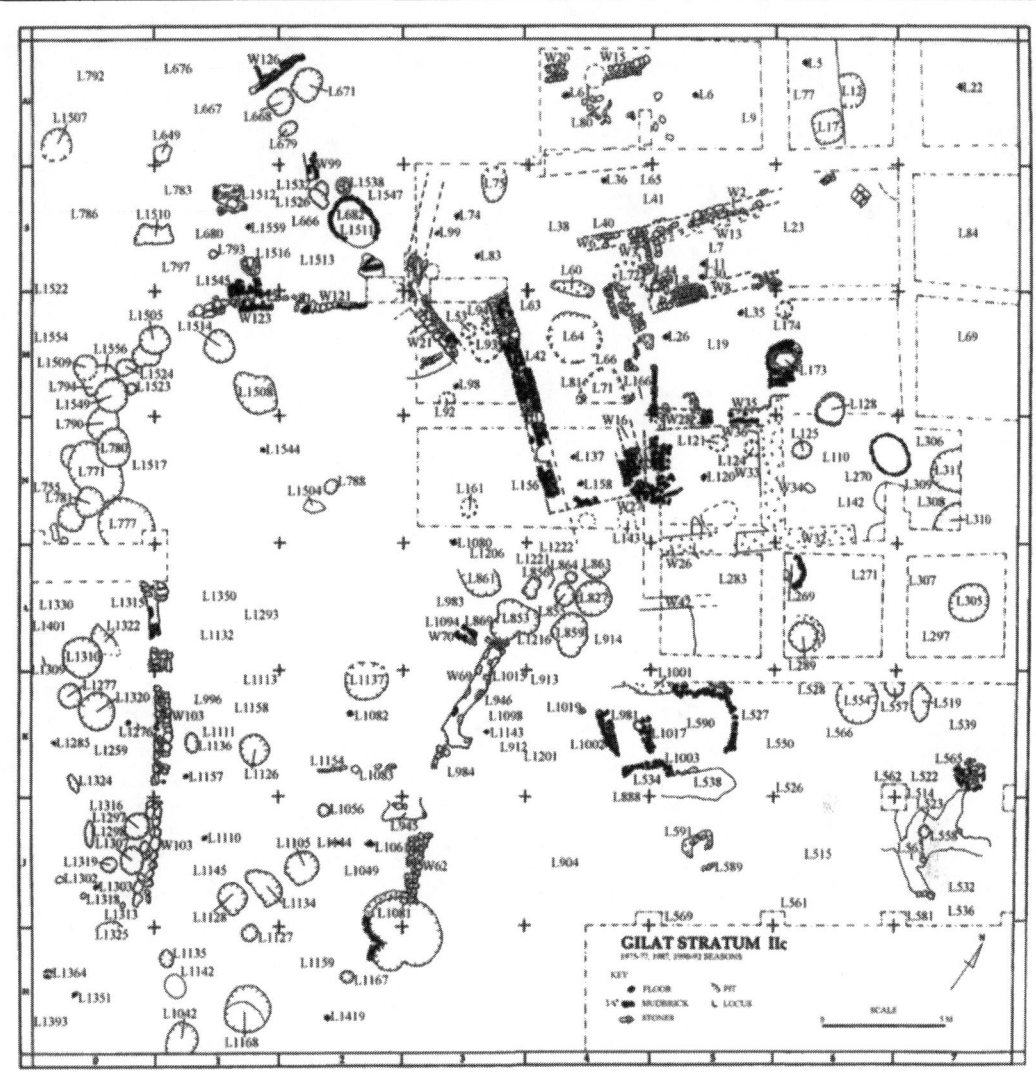

Figure 5.5. Stratum 2C general plan.

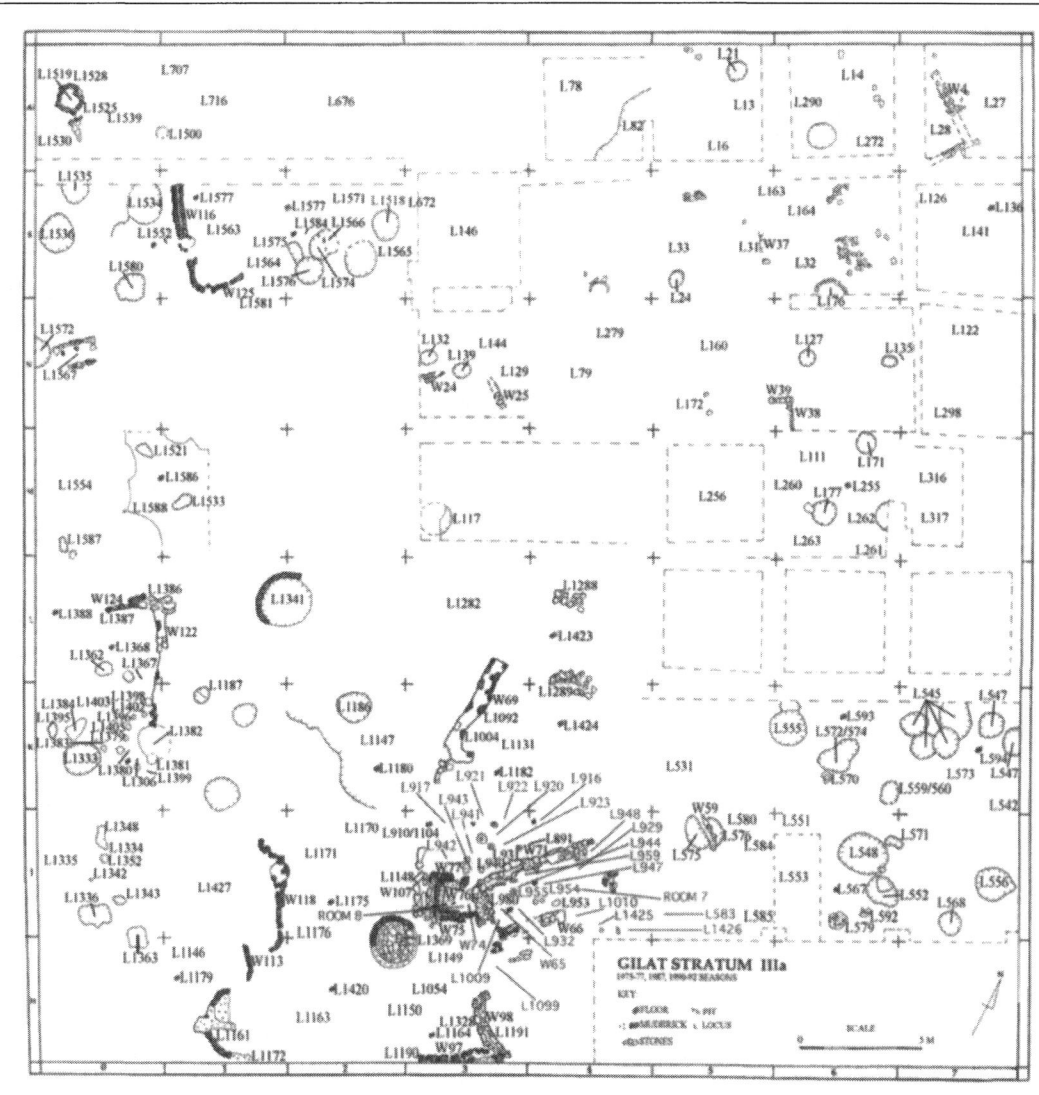

Figure 5.6. Stratum 3A general plan.

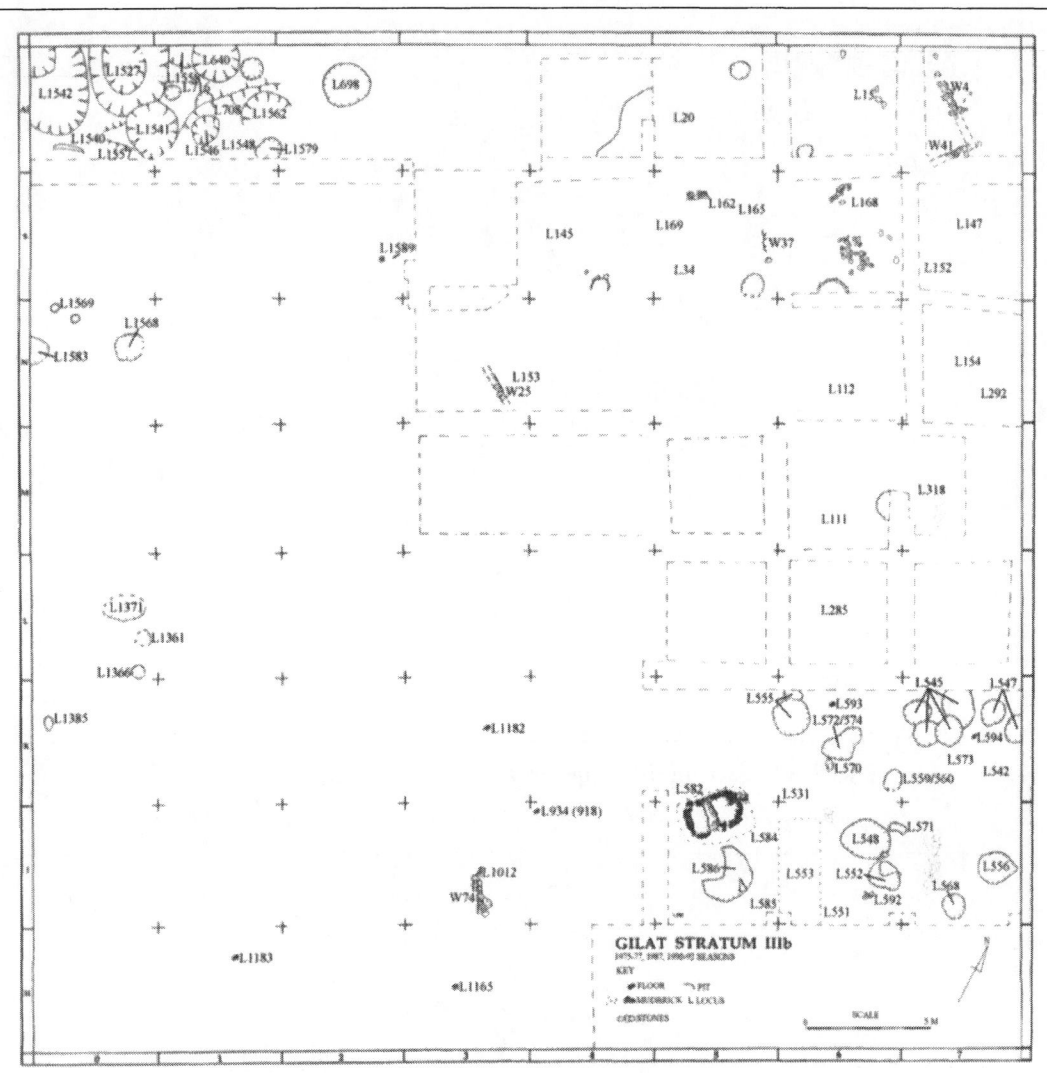

Figure 5.7. Stratum 3B general plan.

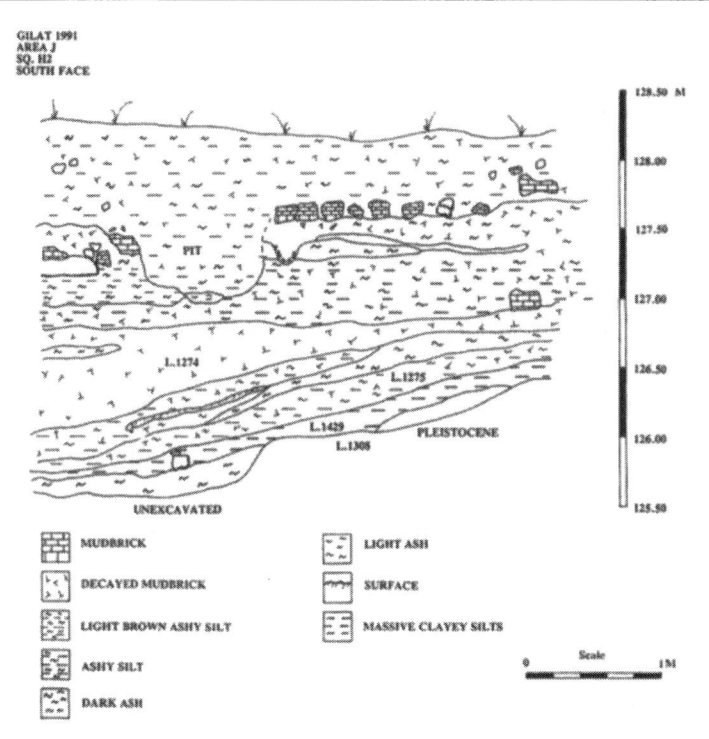

Figure 5.8. Section drawing 1991, Area J, Sq. H2, South Face.

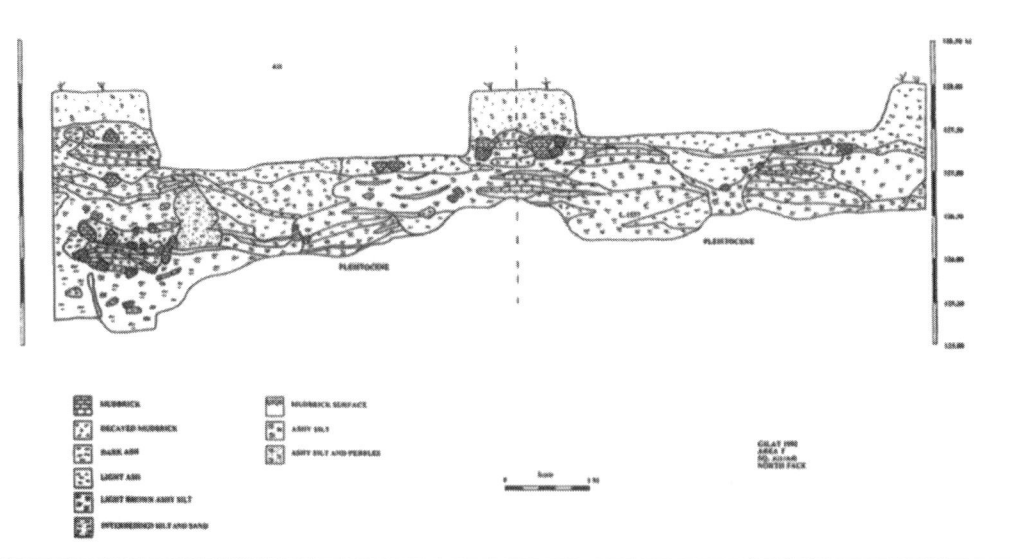

Figure 5.9. Section drawing 1992, Area T, Sq. Ai1/Ai0, North Face.

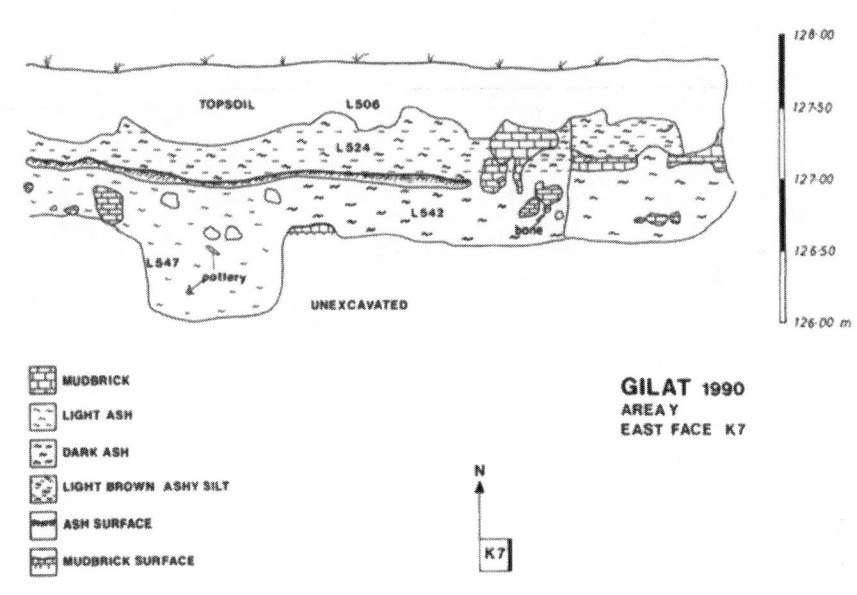

Figure 5.10. Section drawing, 1990, Area Y, Sq. K7, East Face.

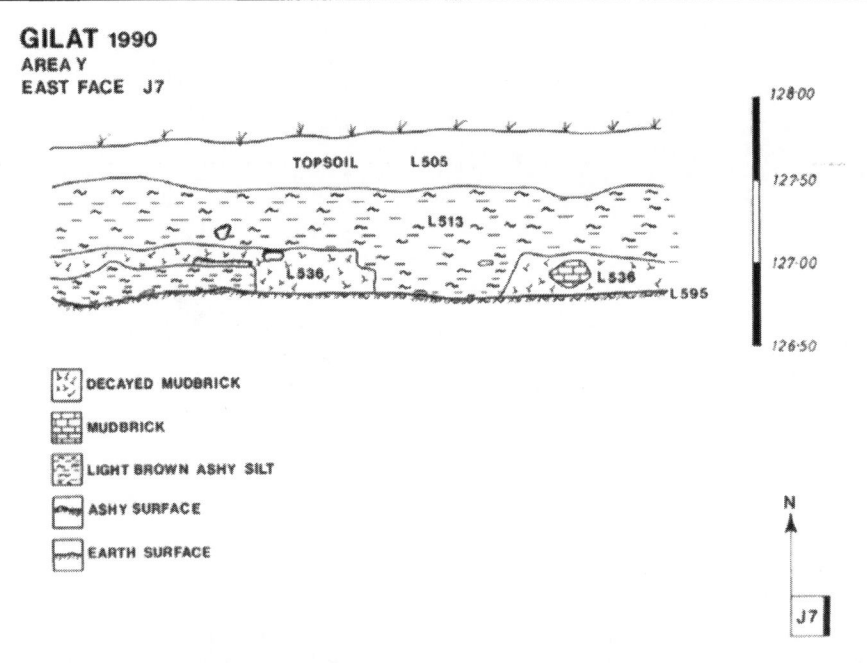

Figure 5.11. Section drawing, 1990, Area Y, Sq. J7, East Face.

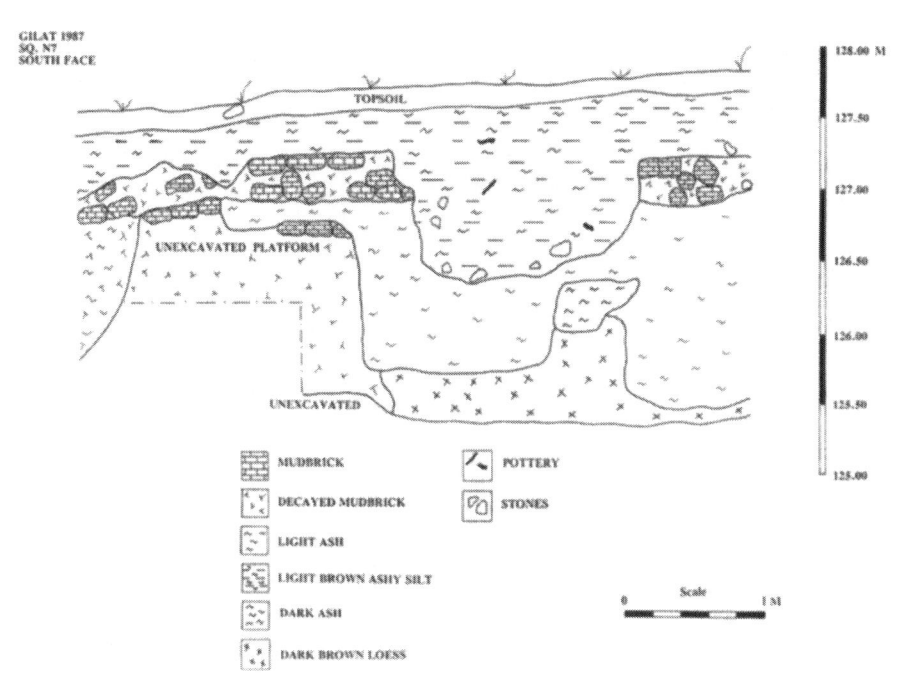

Figure 5.12. Section drawing, 1987, Area D, Sq. N7, South Face.

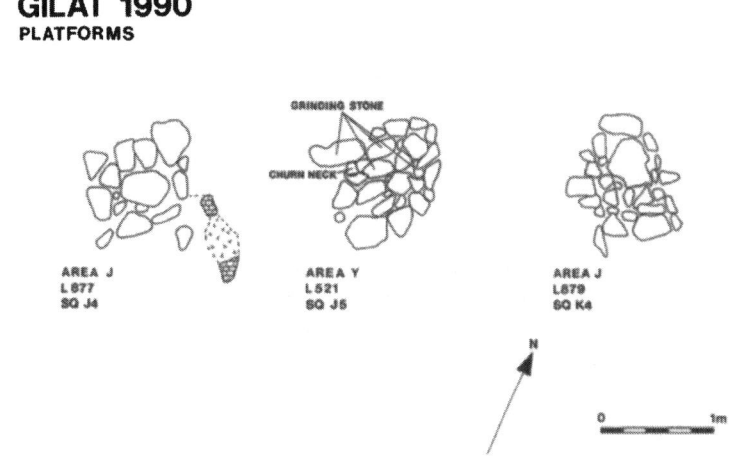

Figure 5.13. Platform drawings (Areas J and Y).

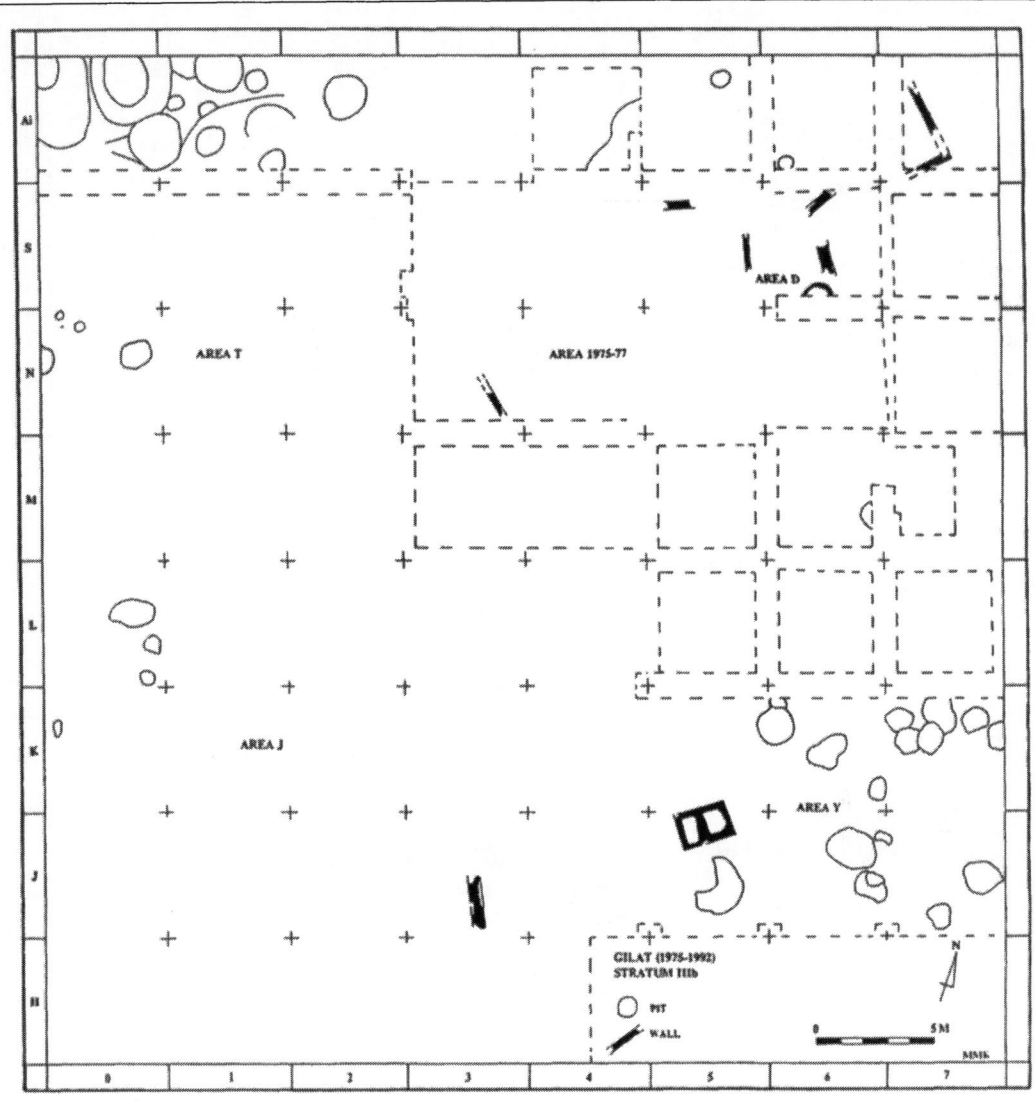

Figure 5.14. Stratum 3B schematic plan.

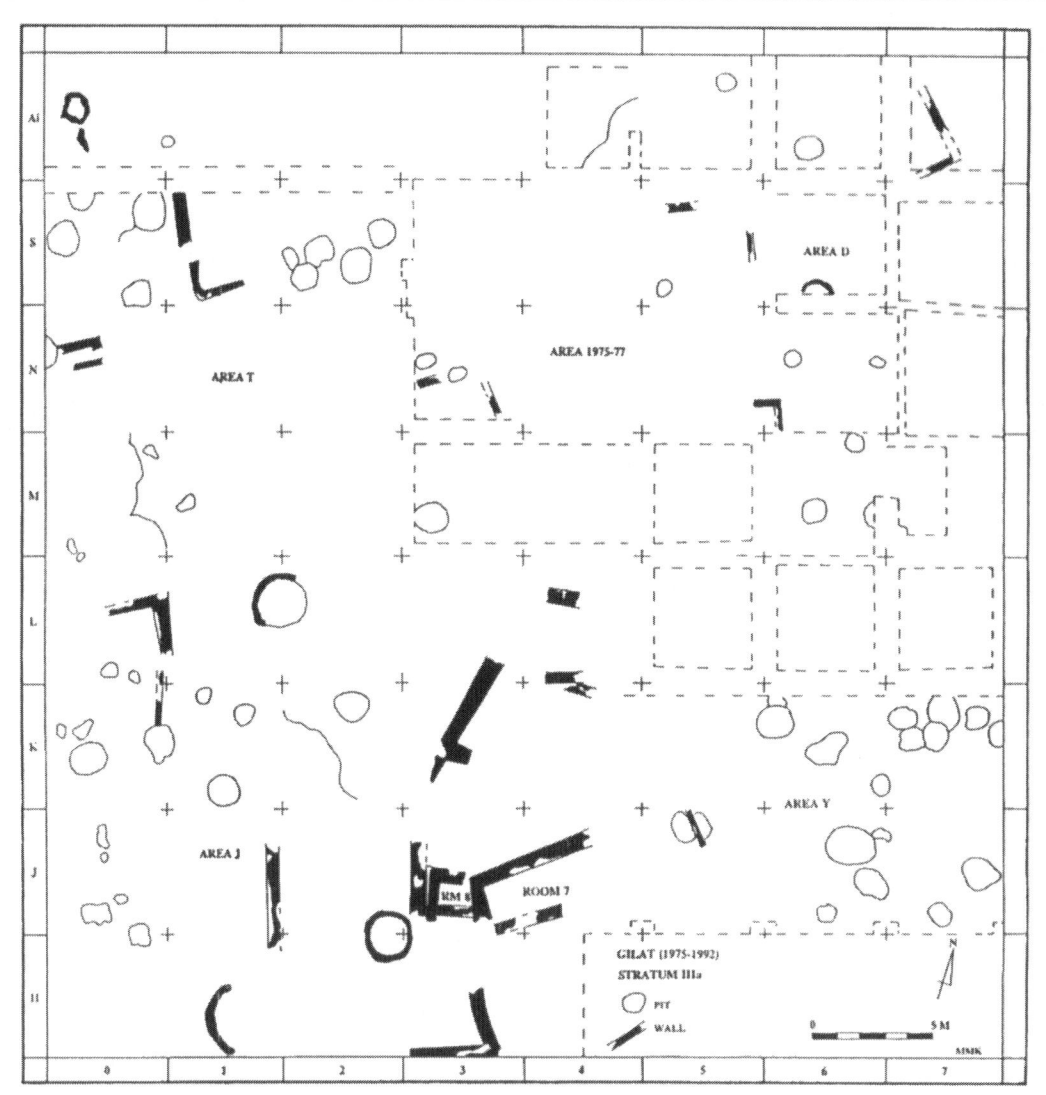

Figure 5.15. Stratum 3A schematic plan.

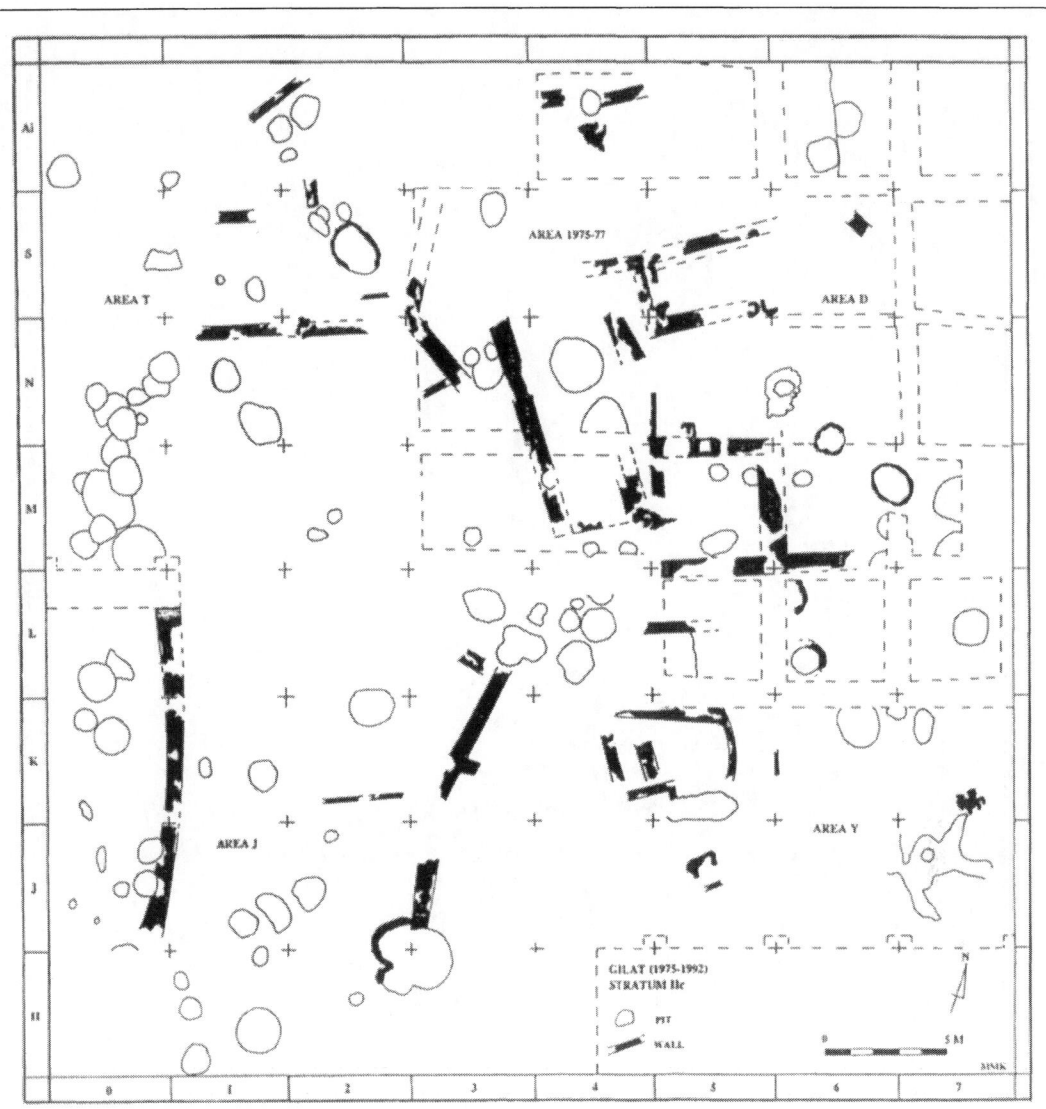

Figure 5.16. Stratum 2C schematic plan.

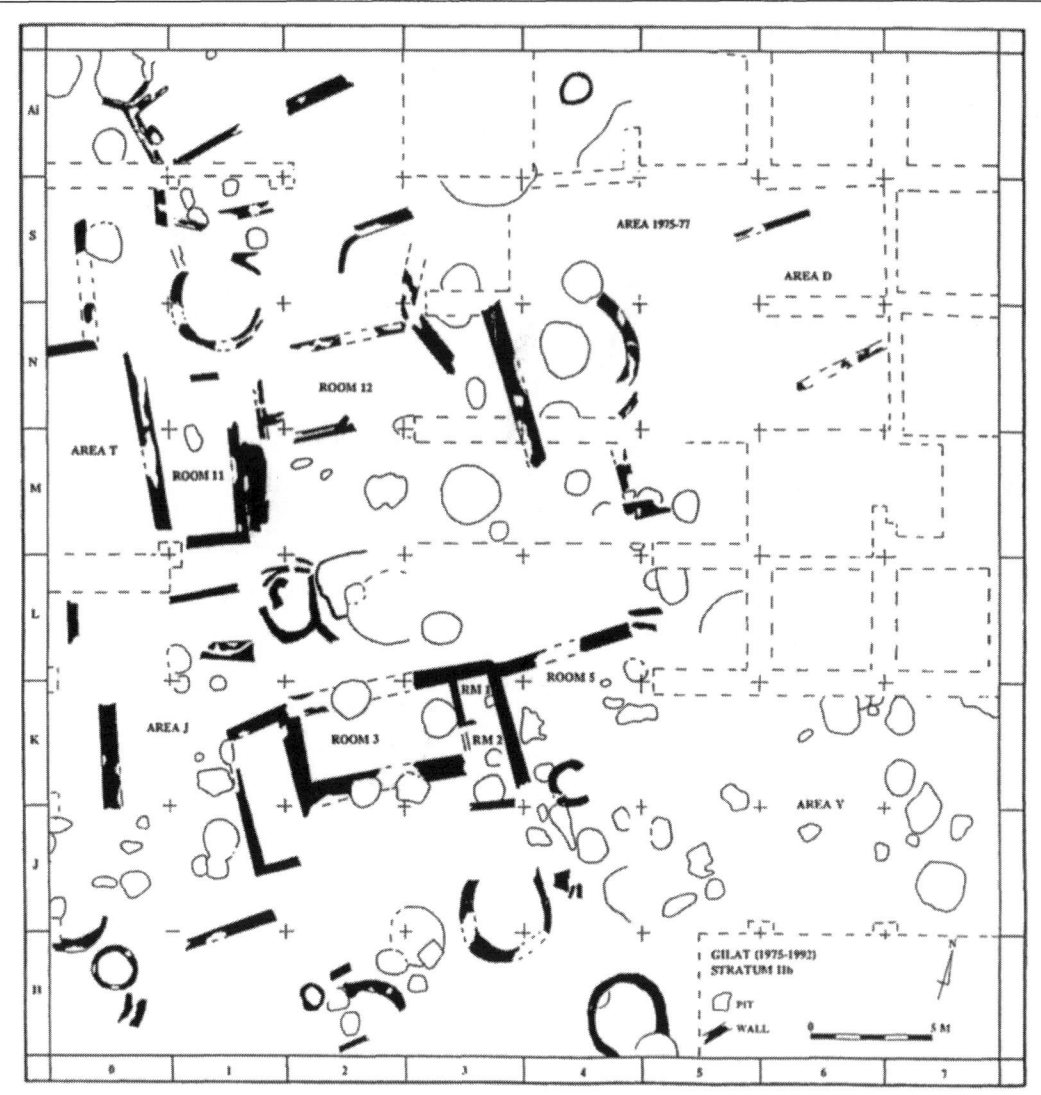

Figure 5.17. Stratum 2B schematic plan.

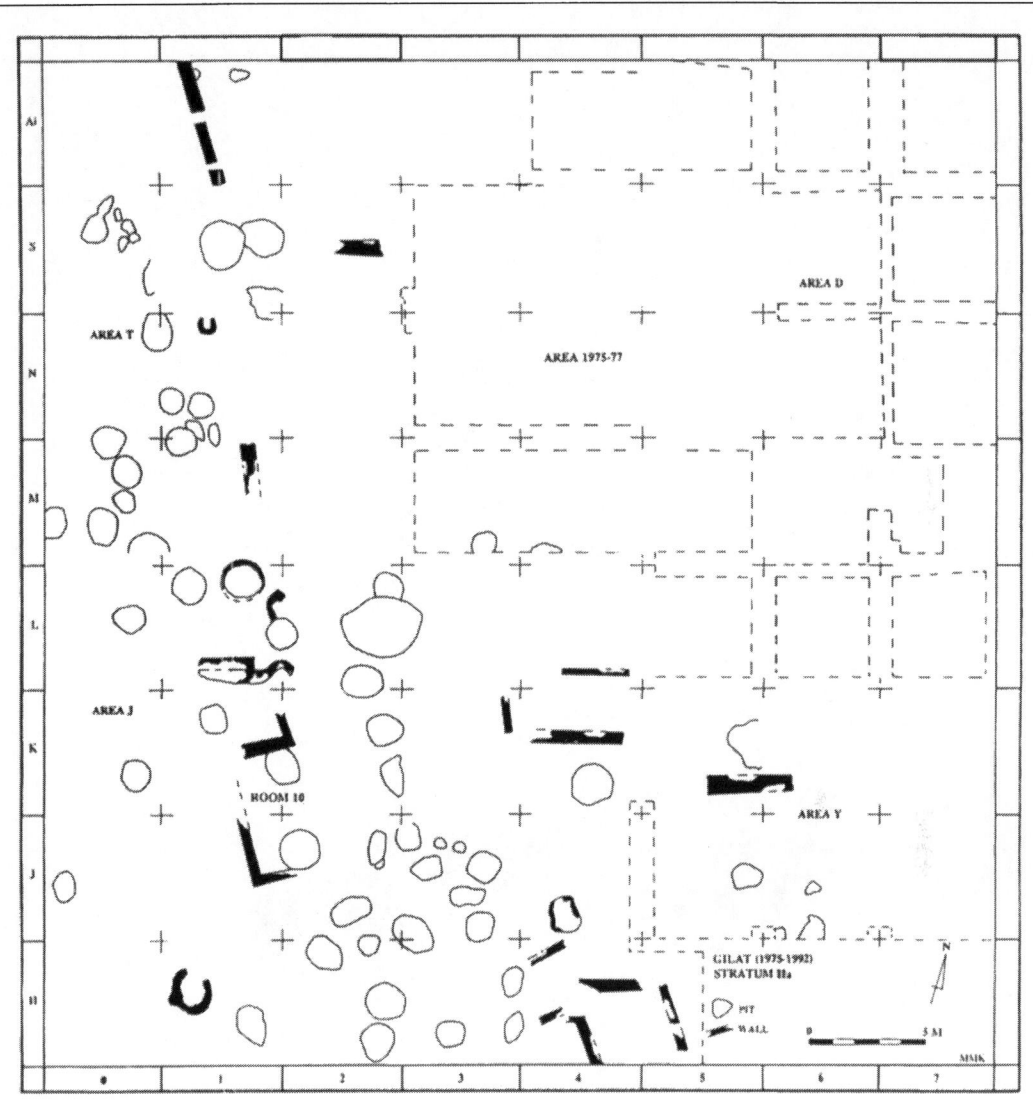

Figure 5.18. Stratum 2A schematic plan.

**Figure 5.19a. 2-D view (north) of Gilat sanctuary Stratum 2A;
(ArcView GIS project, Catherine Painter, UCSD).**

**Figure 5.19b. 3-D view (north) of Gilat sanctuary Stratum 2A;
(ArcView GIS project, Catherine Painter, UCSD).**

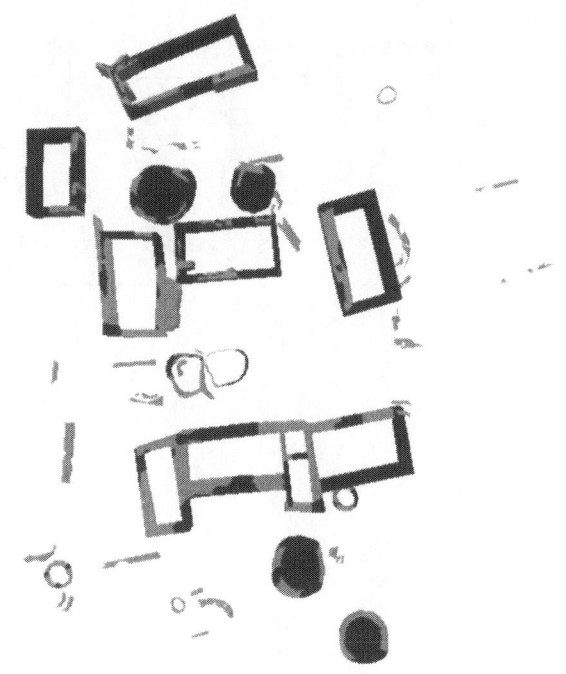

Figure 5.20a. 2-D view (north) of Gilat sanctuary Stratum 2B;
(ArcView GIS project, Catherine Painter, UCSD).

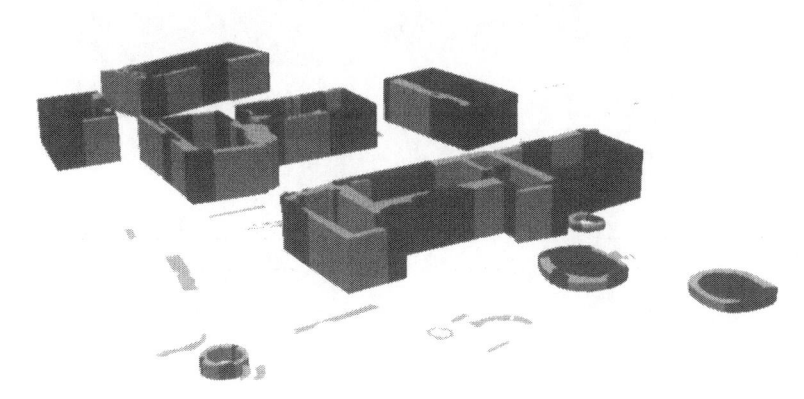

Figure 5.20b. 3-D view (north) of Gilat sanctuary Stratum 2B;
(ArcView GIS project, Catherine Painter, UCSD).

Figure 5.21a. 2-D view (north) of Gilat sanctuary Stratum 2C;
(ArcView GIS project, Catherine Painter, UCSD).

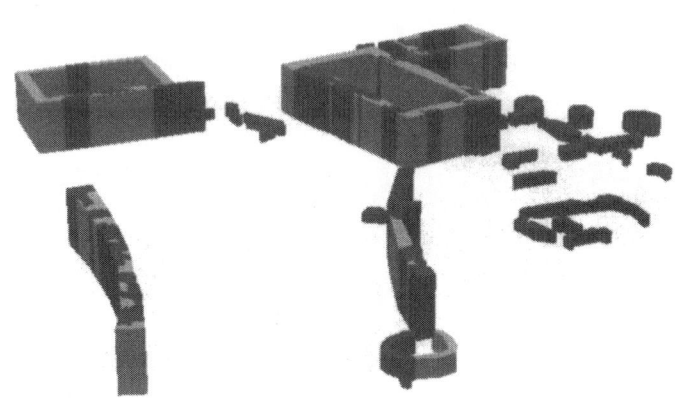

Figure 5.21b. 3-D view (north) of Gilat sanctuary Stratum 2C;
(ArcView GIS project, Catherine Painter, UCSD).

Plate 5.1. Violin shape figurine.

Plate 5.2. Overview of Gilat.

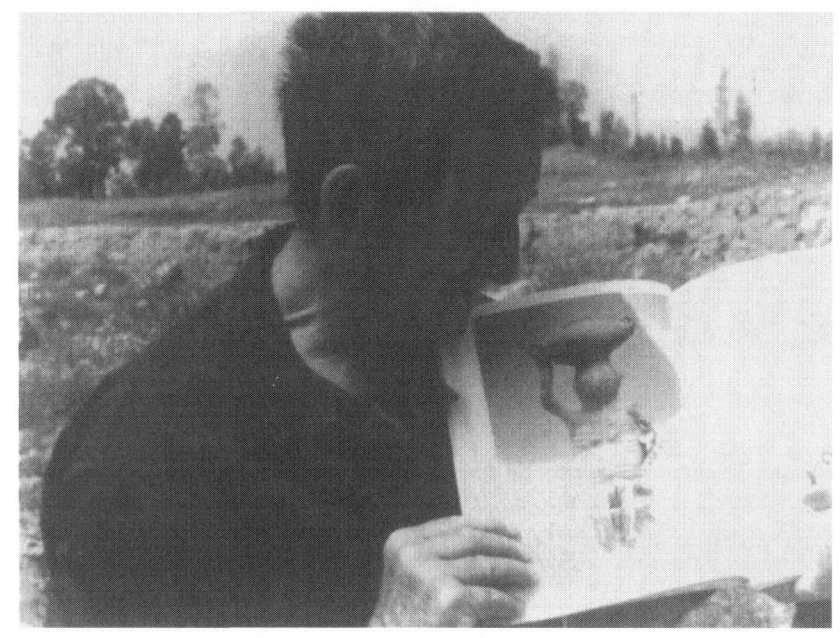

Plate 5.3. David Alon.

Plate 5.4. C. Paul Johnson and Thomas Levy.

Plate 5.5. Gilat excavations team.

Plate 5.6. Overview of Alon's excavation area after cleaning
at the end of the 1987 season.

Plate 5.7. Gilat Lady.

Plate 5.8. Gilat Ram.

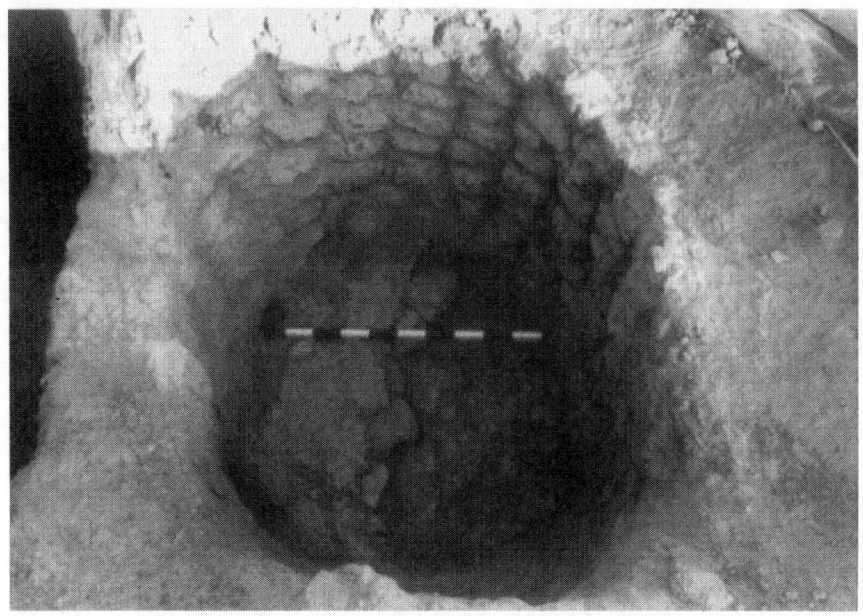

Plate 5.9. Mud-brick silo (L. 261) used for grain storage, Stratum III.

Plate 5.10. Detail of the mud-bricks used to line silo (L. 261).

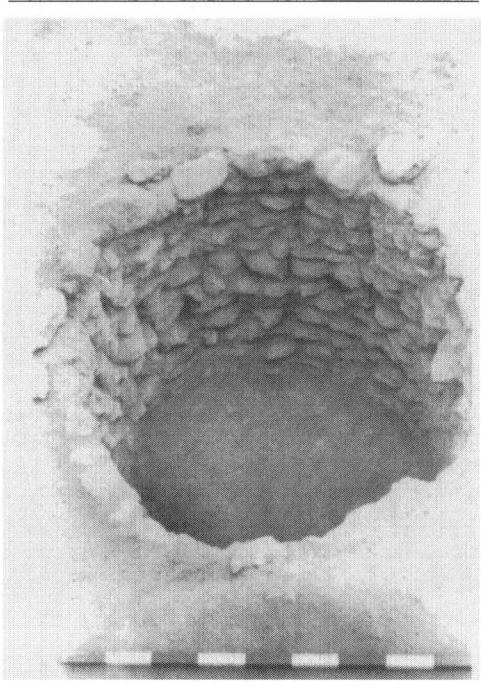

Plate 5.11. A stone-lined circular basin (L. 128) found in the courtyard
of the main Stratum III sanctuary.

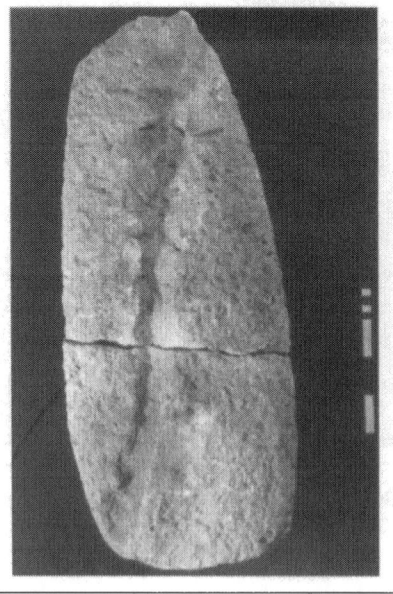

Plate 5.12. An incised standing stone (IAA 568-14) made of chalk (scale bar = 20 cm).

Plate 5.13. Collection of in-situ Gilat 'torpedo jars' from a pit (L. 310), main courtyard of Stratum III.

Plate 5.14. Human burial with V-shape bowl offering (Area J, L. 806, Sq. J3).

Plate 5.15. Overview (northeast) of the Stratum IIB sanctuary.

Plate 5.16. Large hearth found with numerous sandstone fragments
on a Stratum IIB courtyard.

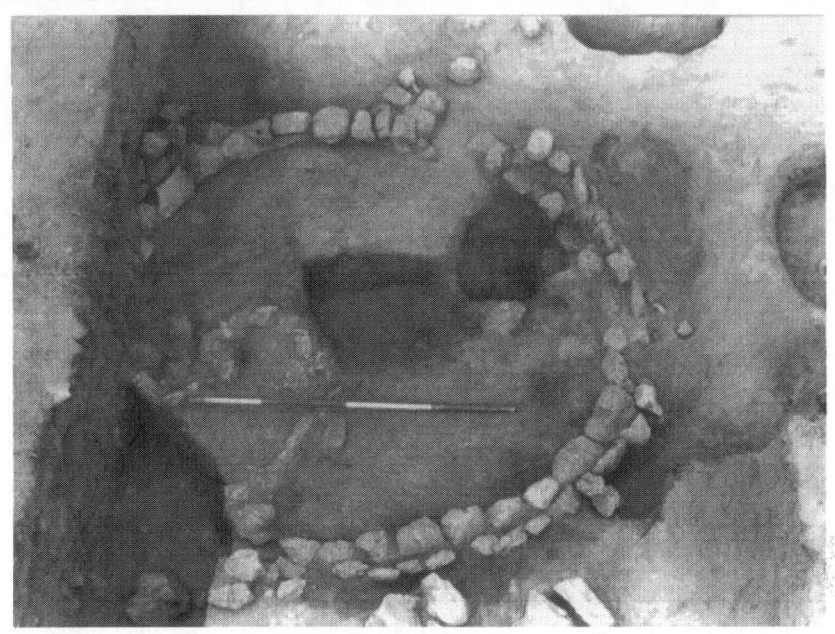

Plate 5.17. Stone-lined platform (L. 1360) found in Stratum IIB, Area J (view facing west).

Plate 5.18 Circular mud-brick basin (L. 1129, Sq L1/L2) found in Area J (view northeast).

Plate 5.19. Multiple human burial in mud-brick lined pit (L. 1237)
found in Stratum IIB, Area J.

Plate 5.20. Half of floor excavated in human burial structure (L. 1237).

Plate 5.21. Pit with ceremonial objects.

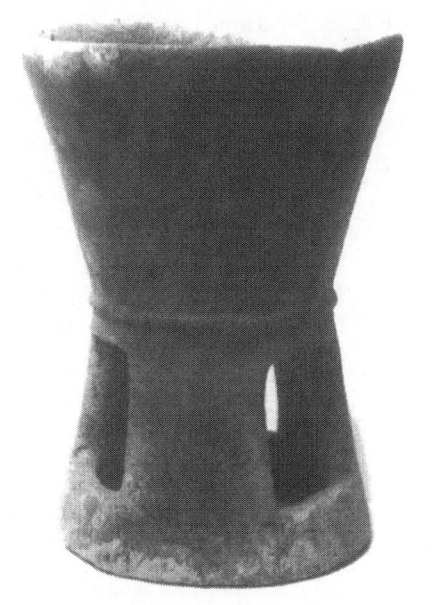

Plate 5.22. Complete basalt fenestrated stand.

Plate 5.23. Stratum IIB, Area J, Gilat.

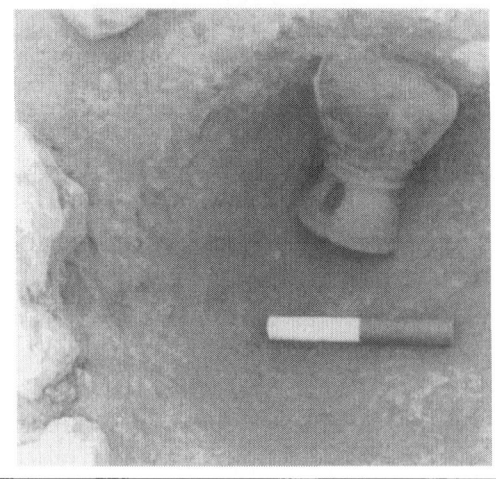

Plate 5.24. In situ fenestrated ceramic stand found in pit (L. 862), Stratum IIB.

Plate 5.25. Detail of ceramic fenestrated stand found in pit L. 862

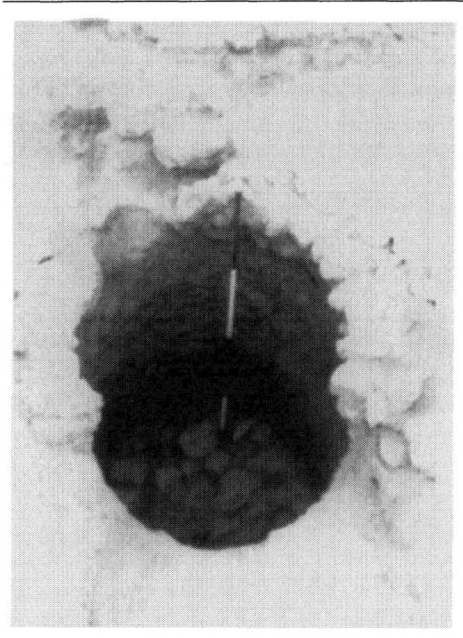

Plate 5.26. Deep silo (L. 882)

Plate 5.27. Overview (northeast) of the Stratum III plaza in Areas J and Y at Gilat.

Plate 5.28 Line of 12 stones (L. 1154) found on Stratum III plaza.

Plate 5.29. Detail of standing stone L. 1083, Stratum III plaza.

Plate 5.30. Sacred and profane—overview of Stratum III, western portion of Area J.

Plate 5.31. Overview (east) of the Stratum III plaza in Areas J and Y.

Plate 5.32. Asymmetrical violin-shape figurine with facetted breasts.

Plate 5.33. Large churn found in situ within shallow pit.

Plate 5.34 Selection of churns from Gilat.

Plate 5.35. Cache of ostrich eggs (L. 1167).

Plate 5.36. Ring-base large tulip bowl with three horizontal handles, Stratum IIB.

Plate 5.37. Room 6 associated with large silo in Area J.

Plate 5.38. Stratum IIC pebble surface (L. 538) adjacent to large ash pit (L. 537) containing torpedo vessel.

Plate 5.39. Detail of torpedo vessel found in situ in ash pit (L. 537).

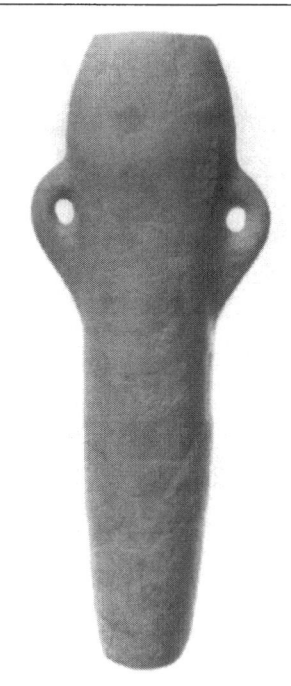

Plate 5.40. Reconstructed torpedo vessel found in situ in ash pit (L. 537)
from Stratum IIC.

Plate 5.41. Churn with mud plaster used in secondary context.

Plate 5.42. Overview (northeast) of Stratum IIIA, Areas J, T, and D.

Plate 5.43. Fragmentary churn and pithos found in Stratum IIB fill.

Plate 5.44. Selection of large vessels from Gilat.

Plate 5.45. Mud-brick silo (L. 1369) found in Stratum IIIA.

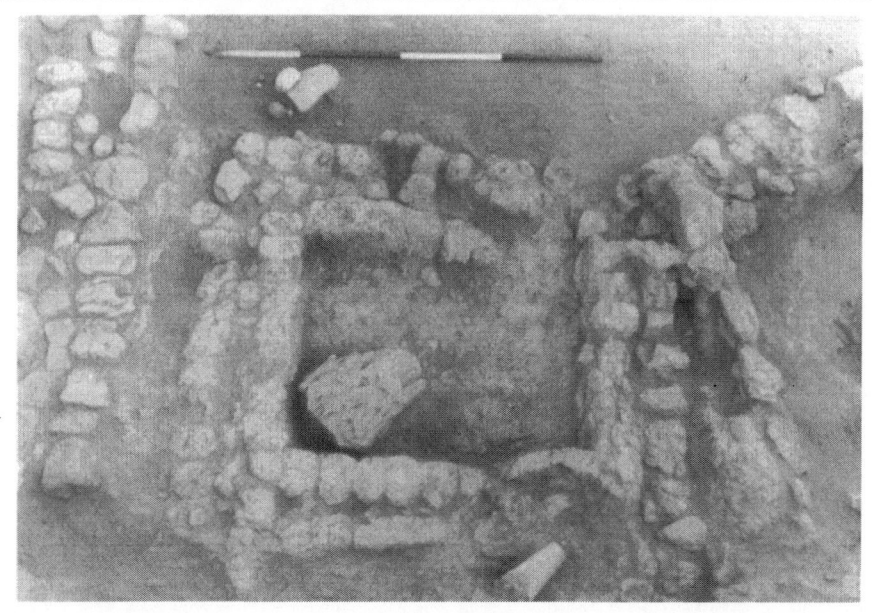

Plate 5.46 Small room (L. 910), possibly used for storage, found in Stratum IIIa.

Plate 5.47. South section of Square H2 in Area J.

Plate 5.48 Overview of Stratum IIB looking east.

Plate 5.49. Curvilinear structure (L. 721).

Plate 5.50. Pit (L. 709) with fenestrated stand.

Plate 5.51. Selection of small open vessels.

Plate 5.52. Overview (south) of the Gilat excavations.

Plate 5.53. Northwest corner of Stratum III plaza, Area T.

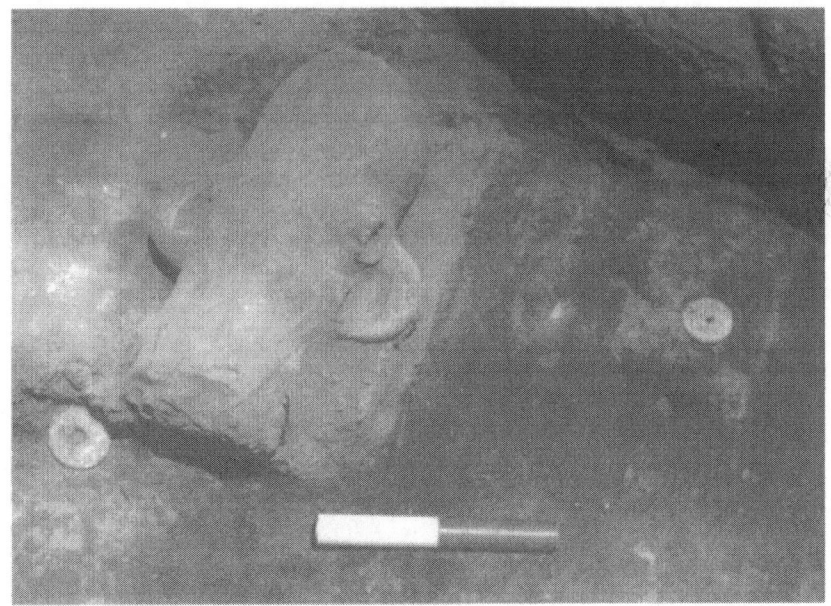

Plate 5.54. Large fragment of torpedo vessel found with two spindle whorls.

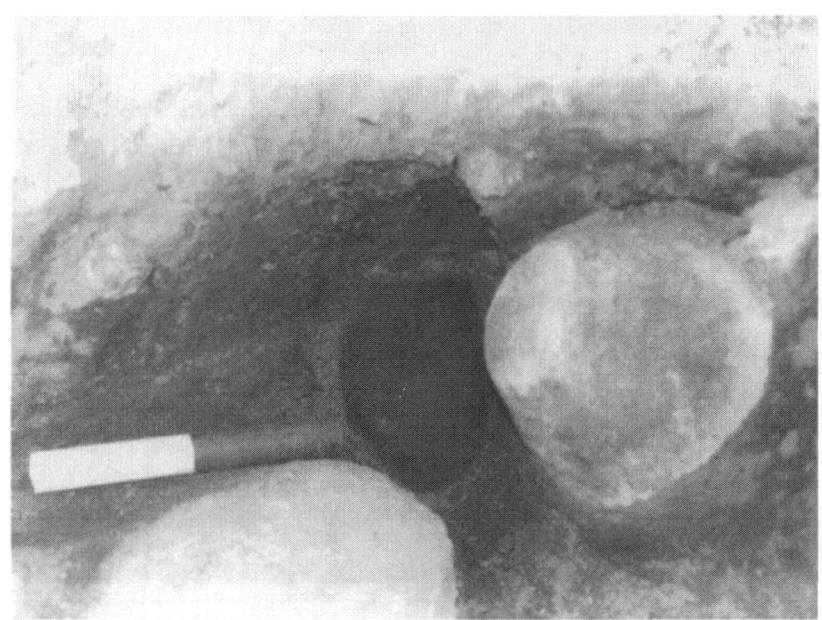

Plate 5.55. Small pit (L. 1505) found with V-shape pot.

Plate 5.56. Small hearth filled with grinding stones (L. 1538), Square S2, Area T.

Plate 5.57. Oval mud-brick lined pit (L. 1511) Square S2, Area T.

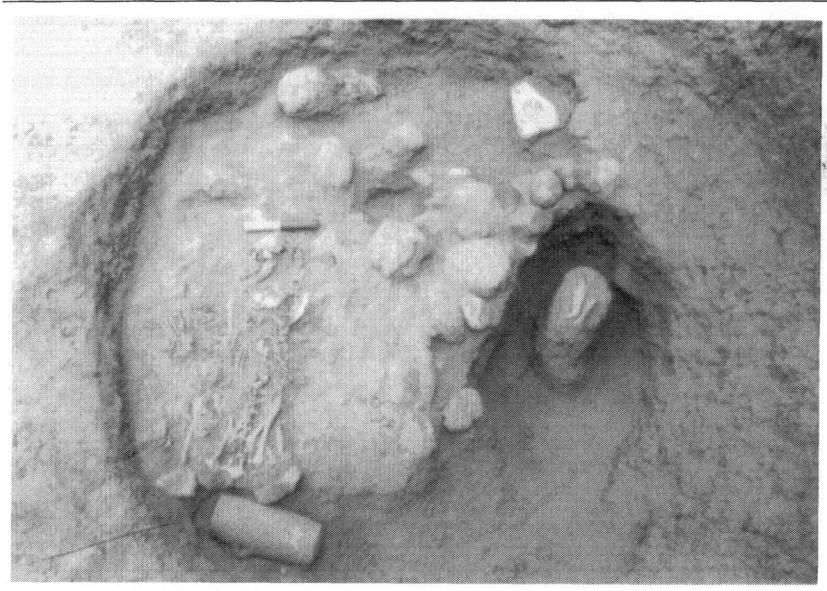

Plate 5.58. The dog burial (L. 698) found in Stratum IIIa pit (L. 692).

Plate 5.59. Exposure of basal Pleistocene layer, Stratum IV, in Area T

Plate 5.60. Overview (northeast) of the Area T excavations, 1990.

Plate 5.61. Overview of Stratum IIB platform made of grinding stones.

Plate 5.62. Oval mud-brick structure with partition (L. 582b), Square J5, Area Y.

Plate 5.63. Yorke Rowan admiring a pit (L. 577) dug into the virgin Pleistocene sediment.

Plate 5.64. Small wall feature facing three standing stones.

Plate 5.65. Detail view of spindle shaped torpedo vessel found in pit (L. 586).

Plate 5.66. Detail of spindle shaped torpedo vessel.

Plate 5.67. View looking south of Area M, Gilat.

Plate 5.68. Large pithos found in pit (L. 016), Square B5, Area B.

Plate 5.69. Reconstructed pithos with red painted decoration found in L. 016, Area M.

Plate 5.70. Mud-brick lined pit (L. 043) found in Area M.

Plate 5.71. Wadi Rabah sherds found at Gilat.

Plate 5.72. The Gilat Lady and Ram.

Plate 5.73. A series of 'tokens'.

Plate 5.74. Collection of spindle whorls.

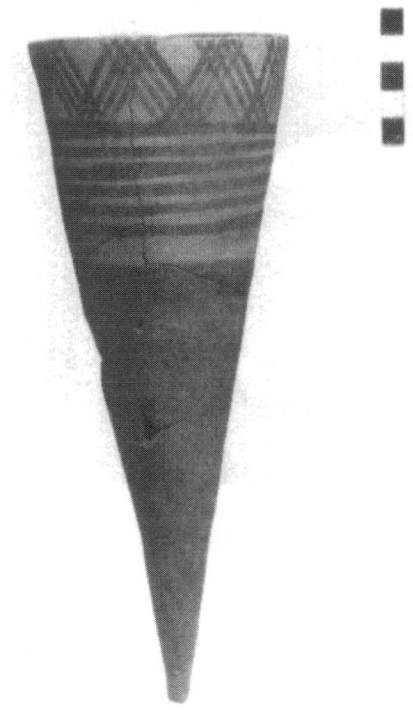

Plate 5.75. Complete cornet cup.

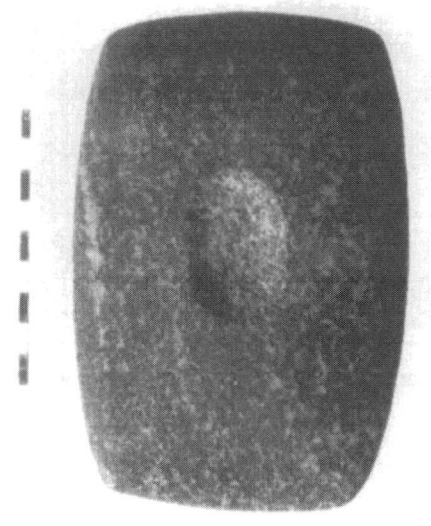

Plate 5.76. Palette made of granite.

Plate 5.77. Comparison of mace heads: Gilat vs. Shiqmim.

Plate 5.78. Violin shape figurines.

Plate 5.79. Assemblage of gazelle horn cores.

Plate 5.80. Sample of tabular 'fan' scrapers.

References

Alon, D. (1961) Early Settlements along the Nahal Garar and Nahal Patish. *M'befnim*.

— (1976) A Calcolithic site near Gilat. *Hadashot Arkheologiyot* 36–37:57–58.

— (1977) Gilat—1976. *Hadashot Arkheologiyot* 46:61–62.

Alon, D., and T. E. Levy (1989) The Archaeology of Cult and Chalcolithic Sanctuary at Gilat. *Journal of Mediterranean Archeology* 2:163–221.

Amiran, R., and O. Ilan (eds) (1996) *Early Arad II. The Chalcolithic and Early Bronze Ib Settlements and the Early Bronze II City: Architecture and Town Planning Sixth-Eighteenth Seasons of Excavations, 1971–1978, 1980–1984*. Jerusalem: Israel Exploration Society.

Avner, U. (1984) Ancient cult sites in the Negev and Sinai deserts. *Tel Aviv* 11:115–31.

Bourke, S. (2001) 'The Chalcolithic Period', in *The Archaeology of Jordan*. Edited by B. MacDonald, R. B. Adams, and P. Bienkowski. Sheffield: Sheffield Academic Press.

Bourke, S., E. Lawson, J. Lovell, Q. Hua, U. Zoppi and M. Barbetti (2001) The chronology of the Ghassulian Chalcolithic period in the southern Levant: New C-14 determinations from Teleilat Ghassul, Jordan. *Radiocarbon* V43:1217–22.

Cameron, D. O. (1981) *The Ghassulian Wall Paintings*. London: Kenyon-Dean Ltd.

Commenge-Pellerin, C. (1987) *La Poterie d'Abou Matar et de l'Ouadi Zoumeili (Beersheva) au IVe millenaire avant l'ere chretienne. Cahiers du Centre de Recherch Francais de Jerusalem 5*. Paris: Association Paleorient.

— (1990) *La Potterie de Safadi (Beersheva) au IVe millenaire avant l'ere chretienne*. Paris: Association Paleorient.

Dan, J., D. H. Ya'alon, H. Koyumdijsky, and Z. Raz (1976) *The Soils of Israel (with map 1:500,000): Pamphlet No. 159*. Bet Dagan: The Volcani Center.

Dollfus, G., and Z. Kafafi (1988) *Abu Hamid—Village du 4e Millenaire de la Vallee du Jourdain*. Amman: Centre Culturel Francais et Department des Antiquities de Jourdanie.

Dothan, M. (1959) Excavations at Horvat Beter (Beersheba). *Atiqot* II:1–42.

Eisenberg, E., A. Gopher, and R. Greenberg (2001) *Te'o : A Neolithic, Chalcolithic, and Early Bronze Age Site in the Hula Valley*. Jerusalem: Israel Antiquities Authority.

Gilead, I. (ed) (1995) *Grar : A Chalcolithic site in the Northern Negev*. Beer-Sheva: Ben-Gurion University of the Negev Press.

Gopher, A., and T. Tsuk (eds) (1996) *The Nahal Qanah Cave—Earliest Gold in the Southern Levant*. Tel Aviv: Monograph Series of the Institute of Archaeology Tel Aviv University.

Goren, Y., and P. Fabian (2002) *Kissufim road, a chalcolithic mortuary site*. Jerusalem: Israel Antiquities Authority.

Hennessy, J. B. (1969) Preliminary Report on a First Season of Excavation at Teleilat Ghassul. *Levant* 1:1–24.

Henry, D. O. (1995) *Prehistoric Cultural Ecology and Evolution : Insights from Southern Jordan*. New York: Plenum Press.

Holl, A. F. C., and T. E. Levy (1993) From the Nile Valley to the Chad Basin: Ethnoarchaeology of Shuwa Arab Settlements. *Biblical Archaeologist* 16:166–79.

Kempinski, A., and R. Reich (eds) (1992) *The Architecture of Ancient Israel—From the Prehistoric to the Persian Periods*. Jerusalem: Israel Exploration Society.

Kerner, S. (2001) *Das Chalkolithikum in der sudlichne Levante: Die Entwicklung handwerklicher Spezialisierung und ihre Beziehung zu gesellschaftlicher Komplexitat. Orient-Archaologie Band 8*. Rahden/Westf: Deutshces Archaeologisches Institut Oient-Abteilung, Verlag Marie Leidorf GmbH.

Levy, T. E. (1986) Archaeological Sources for the History of Palestine—The Chalcolithic Period. *Biblical Archaeologist* 49:83–108.

Levy, T. E. (ed.) (1987) *Shiqmim I: Studies Concerning Chalcolithic Societies in the Northern Negev Desert, Israel (1982–1984)*. Oxford: BAR International Series 356.

— (2003) 'The Chalcolithic of the Southern Levant', in *Near Eastern Archaeology: A Reader*. Edited by S. Richard, pp. 257–67. Winona Lake, Ind.: Eisenbrauns.

Levy, T. E., and D. Alon (1993) 'Gilat', in *The New Encyclopedia of Archaeological Excavations in the Holy Land*. Edited by E. Stern, pp. 514–17. Jerusalem: Israel Exploration Society.

Levy, T. E., D. Alon, P. Goldberg, C. Grigson, P. Smith, J. Buikstan, A. Holl, S. Shalev, S. Ben Izhak, and A. Ben Yosef (1991) Protohistoric investigations at the Shiqmim Chalcolithic Village and Cemetery: An interim report on the 1987 season. *BASOR Supplement*:29–46.

Levy, T. E., J. D. Anderson, M. Waggoner, N. Smith, A. Muniz, and R. B. Adams (2001) Interface: Archaeology and Technology—Digital Archaeology 2001: GIS-Based Excavation Recording in Jordan. *The SAA Archaeological Record* 1:23–29.

Levy, T. E., and P. Goldberg (1987) 'The Environmental Setting of the Northern Negev', in *Shiqmim I*, vol. 356. Edited by T. E. Levy, pp. 1–21. Oxford: BAR International Series.

Levy, T. E., and A. Holl (1987) 'Theory and Practice in Household Archaeology: A Case Study from the Chalcolithic Village at Shiqmim', in *Shiqmim I: Studies Concerning Chalcolithic Societies in the Northern Negev Desert, Israel (1982–1984)*. Edited by T.E. Levy, pp. 373–410. Oxford: BAR International Series 356.

Loud, G. (1948) *Megiddo II*. Chicago: University of Chicago Press.

Lovell, J. L. (2001) *The Late Neolithic and Chalcolithic Periods in the Southern Levant—New Data from the Site of Teleilat Ghassul, Jordan. Monographs of the Sydney University Teleilat Ghassul Project 1*. Oxford: BAR International Series 974.

Mallon, A., R. Koeppel, and R. Neuville (1934) *Teleilat Ghassul I, 1929–32*. Rome: Pontifical Biblical Institute.

Marquet-Krause, J. (1949) *Les Fouilles de 'Ay (et-Tell) 1933–1935*. Paris: P. Guethner.

Perrot, J. (1955) The Excavations at Tell Abu Matar, Near Beersheba. *Israel Exploration Journal* 5:17–41, 73–84, 167–89.

Perrot, P. (1984) Structures D'Habitat Mode de vie et Environnement. Les Villages Souterrains des Pasteurs de Beersheva, dans le sud d'Israel, au IVe Millenaire Avant L'ere Chretienne. *Paleorient* 10:75–96.

Porath, Y. (1992) 'Domestic architecture of the Chalcolithic period', in *The Architecture of Ancient Israel— From the Prehistoric to the Persian Periods*. Edited by A. Kempinski and R. Reich. Jerusalem: Israel Exploration Society.

Renfrew, C. Editor. 1985. *The Archaeology of Cult—The Sanctuary of Phylakopi*. London: The British School of Archaeology at Athens, Thames and Hudson.

Schick, T. (ed.) (1998) *The Cave of the Warrior—A Fourth Millennium Burial in the Judean Desert*. Jerusalem: Israel Antiquities Authority.

Schiffer, M. B. (1987) *Formation processes of the archaeological record*. Albuquerque: University of New Mexico Press.

Seaton, P. (2000) 'Aspects of New Research at the Chalcolithic Sanctuary Precinct at Teleilat Ghassul', in *Proceedings of the First International Congress on the Archaeology of the Ancient Near East, Rome, May 18th–23rd, 1998*. Edited by P. Matthiae, A. Enea, L. Peyronel, and F. Pinnock, pp. 1503–14. Rome.

Sopher, D. E. (1967) *Geography of Religions*. Englewood Cliffs, N.J.: Prentice-Hall, Inc.

Stager, L. E. (1991) Why Were Hundreds of Dogs Buried at Ashkelon? *Biblical Archaeology Review* 17:26–42.

Stoddart, S., A. Bonnano, T. Couder, C. Malone, and D. Trump (1993) Cult in an Island Society: Prehistoric Maltal in th eTarxien Period. *Cambridge Archaeological Journal* 3:3–19.

Ussishkin, D. (1980) The Ghassulian Shrine at En-Gedi. *Tel Aviv*:1–44.

Witten, A. J., T. E. Levy, J. Ursic, and P. White (1995) Geophysical Diffraction Tomography: New Views on the Shiqmim Prehistoric Subterranean Village Site (Israel). *Geoarchaeology* 10:97–118.

III.
BIOLOGICAL DATA
FROM GILAT

6 Farming? Feasting? Herding? Large Mammals from the Chalcolithic of Gilat

Dr
Hon Prof

Caroline Grigson

Introduction

Gilat is one of many sites of the Chalcolithic period on the north-western fringes of the Negev Desert which, because they are situated in a relatively small area and are broadly contemporary, provide a unique opportunity to assess inter-site and diachronic variability on a fine scale. With nearly 7000 identified animal bones Gilat has yielded one of the largest faunal assemblages so far studied for this period in the Middle East.

Levy (1983), who has been responsible for identifying and mapping Late Neolithic and Chalcolithic sites over the Beersheva Basin as a whole and carrying out major excavations in Abu Hof, Gilat and Shiqmim, has used the data he collected on settlement patterns to postulate that the area saw major changes in economic and social organization. He found that sites of the Late Neolithic were small and concentrated on the Negev coastal plain along wadis (especially the Nahal Besor) that transect the area (Levy 1983; Levy and Alon 1983; Levy and Alon 1987). The Chalcolithic sites were more numerous and tended to be spread out along Holocene terraces in the bottom of the major trough-shape valleys of the northern Negev inland foothill zone. Levy accounted for these differences by suggesting that primitive hoe agriculture continued the Late Neolithic cultivation tradition, but was supplemented by annual floodwater farming based on over-bank flow of the wadis providing some of the earliest evidence of irrigation farming in this part of the Middle East (Levy 1983). He envisaged that this was part and parcel of the initiation of specialized pastoralism based on the increasing use of secondary products, that is animal products which can be utilized without slaughter—milk, wool and traction, as proposed by Sherratt (1981, 1983). Given the small number of published faunal reports, Levy did not explore the importance of animal traction for ploughing in the emergence of the 'secondary products revolution' package in the Negev. The Chalcolithic period preceded the Early Bronze Age when the first cities arose and it is thought that the innovations outlined above were a necessary precursor to the economic and social changes which made that enormously important step in human history possible.

The site of Gilat poses particular questions of its own, because it appears to be a cultic centre of some sort. The excavated assemblage contained pottery derived from a large number of sources, suggesting that people came to it from a wide area across the northern Negev and southern Judean hills (Chapters 9 and 10, this volume). Among the finds were many cultic objects, including the now famous figurine of a woman with a Ghassoulian churn on her head (Fig. 5.7 and 5.72) and a sheep carrying three cornets (Fig. 5.8 and 5.72). Some of the architecture too can be interpreted as ceremonial in layout. However there were also signs of much day to day domestic activity such as cooking and spinning, and it is arguable whether such a cultic/domestic dichotomy is valid; there may have been a continuum between the two kinds of human behaviour. An additional and related fact which requires explanation is that some sites (including Gilat and Grar) have pig remains, whereas others do not (Grigson in prep.).

The analysis of the faunal remains from Gilat has been carried out with a view to shedding light on the origins of pastoralism, or at least on adaptation to arid conditions on the desert edge, as well investigating whether the cultic/domestic dichotomy is reflected in the excavated animal remains. Attempts will be made to inquire into human attitudes to live animals and to discern patterns of deposition. The composition of the fauna also has environmental implications.

This is the second very detailed faunal analysis of the Chalcolithic sites in this area to be published. The first, in which the same methodology was utilized, was the site of Grar, situated about 7 km away, on the Nahal Grar (Grigson 1995b; Gilead 1995). Other sites with faunal reports include Bir es-Safadi (Josien 1955; Ducos 1968; Grigson 1987b), Horvat Beter (Angress 1959; Grigson 1993a) and Bir Abou Matar (Josien 1955). Preliminary reports on the fauna from Shiqmim (Grigson 1985a, 1985b, 1987a, 1989b, 1989d, 1990; Levy *et al.* 1991; Whitcher, Grigson and Levy 1998), the Neolithic and Chalcolithic sites at Qatif (Grigson 1984) and the 1974–87 material from Gilat (Tchernov and Grigson 1990) have also been completed. Some comparisons will be made between Gilat and other sites, but a comprehensive comparative study cannot be made until further work on more of these sites has been completed.

Notes on Layout and Stratigraphy

The layout and stratigraphy of the site are discussed in detail in Chapter 5, but in order to understand the analysis that follows it is necessary to include a brief summary here. The total area excavated was about 1755 m².

Following the initial excavation of Gilat by David Alon in 1975–77 a small-scale excavation was carried out in 1987 by Tom Levy and Alon. Larger excavations took place in 1990, 1991 and 1992 in which the bulk of the faunal material discussed here was retrieved.

The main areas of excavation were designated Areas D, J, T, Y and M, but it must be remembered that these are artificial divisions of the site, used for convenience in excavation and recording. However, as they have been described individually in Chapter 5, an attempt was made to discover whether there were differences between their faunal remains (see below). Each of the excavation areas was subdivided into 5 m squares.

The unit for recording the finds was the locus, identified as some kind of cultural or natural feature within a particular area. Every locus was assigned to one of the 31 types of context recognized in the course of excavation, some relating to actual structures and others to fills of various types. A few, such as 'probe', 'removal' and 'cleaning' relate to excavation procedures, rather than archaeological features. A full description of the evolution of settlement at Gilat is presented in Chapter 5.

Animal Bone Retrieval

Most of the site of Gilat was excavated by trowel and all bones that were seen were retrieved, however parts of some bones were broken off in excavation and are missing from the collection. This is not surprising as much of the bone was extremely fragile. The bone element analysis shows that many of the smallest bones were missed.

Dry sieving, through a 5 mm mesh, was carried out on sediment from all pits, surfaces and any matrix associated with human burials, but even then retrieval was not 100% efficient.

Notwithstanding these problems the collection is far better than most of those made to date from Middle Eastern excavations, on many of which sieving has not been carried out at all and fragments thought to be unimportant or unidentifiable have been discarded on site.

Methods

Recording

Each bone was given a unique bone number, but, as two overlapping series of numbers were employed, the year of excavation has to be included in any reference to a particular bone, e.g. GIL91 4033. A description of each bone was entered into a *Lotus 123* spreadsheet under a large number of headings: site + year, area, square, locus, context, sieved or not, bone ID number, taxon, bone, bone part, states of epiphysial fusion, age, sex, pathology, utilized (?) and remarks, which included measurements. The analysis of the data involved sorting the spreadsheets on the basis of a wide variety of criteria using *Excel 5.0*. Additional manuscript notes were made on finds of particular interest.

Bone Counts

The quantification of the bones identified to taxon has been made on the basis of the *number of bone finds*. That is the number of identified specimens (NISP in the American literature), modified when it was clear that any one bone came from the same individual animal as another, when for example, bones from the same ankle were associated in the same locus or when one or more vertebrae were still in articulation. Numbers were used as a basis for quantification rather than weight because of the varying amounts of calcium carbonate coating the bones. Owing to constraints of time, the unidentified bones from Gilat were neither counted nor studied.

Although calculations of the minimum number of individuals (MNI) may be useful in small closed features, such as pits, both Gautier (1984) and Ducos (1983) have shown that the statistical chance that any one bone found on an open archaeological site belongs to the same individual as another is negligible, particularly on sites which were occupied for several hundred years. Therefore I have used MNI counts only in the bone element analyses (as a basis for estimating which elements are under-represented in the assemblage), I have *not* used them to quantify the relative contributions of the various taxa.

Measurements and Abbreviations

All measurements are in millimetres and are based on those defined by von den Driesch (1976). The measurements of the bones and teeth of each taxon at Gilat are listed in the appendices; the abbreviations used in tables, appendices and figures are explained in Appendix 6.1.

Spatial, Diachronic and Contextual Analyses

The faunal remains identified in the various strata and sub-strata are shown in summary form in Table 6.1. There were 219 bone finds identified to taxon in Stratum IV, 1,609 in Stratum III, 55 in a locus which could only be assigned to either Stratum III or Stratum II (III/II) and 5,408 in Stratum II, a total of 6,931. In addition Stratum I yielded 494 identifications, but as it included much modern material they have been excluded from the present study.

Before the fauna can be analysed in further detail it is necessary to decide what spatial and diachronic units the analysis should be based on and also to see whether the composition of the fauna is influenced by the type of context. Ideally each locus should be studied separately, however with 1,242 separate loci identified at Gilat, this would result in a large number of very small samples with a high degree of stochastic variation which would obscure the very patterns which we are trying to establish. Nevertheless certain loci were identified as differing from the general patterns and these are described below.

The main criterion used in the spatial, diachronic and contextual analyses was 'ungulate proportions', that is the relative numbers of domestic ungulates; the proportions of burnt to unburnt bone in different types of context were also calculated.

Spatial and Diachronic Analysis

In Area D only three of the sub-strata (IIIA, IIC and IIB) had large enough samples for analysis of the ungulate proportions. These are shown in the form of histograms in Fig. 6.1A and suggest that the proportion of sheep and goats was higher in sub-strata IIA and IIB than in the preceding IIC. This is interesting as it was IIC in which the main sanctuary was identified. In Area J (Fig. 6.1B) there is no such increase and in fact sub-stratum IIC has a higher proportion of cattle and pig bones than IIIA. However, there is an increase in sheep and goats in sub-stratum IIB, much of which is due to a high proportion of sheep and goat bones within the large burial pit (L. 1237 and 1357) (Plate 6.5b).

In Area T (Fig. 6.2A) the proportion of pigs in sub-stratum IIIB is slightly higher than usual, but there is no particular change from IIIA to IIC, nor is there in IIIB to IIA in Area Y (Fig. 6.2B). Sub-stratum IIB was the only sample in Area M large enough for analysis and it is not outstanding in any way (Fig. 6.2C).

When the ungulate proportions within the sub-strata are analysed for the site as a whole (Fig. 6.3A), no consistent overall pattern emerges, except for the increase in sheep and goats in sub-stratum IIB, which, as stated above, is largely due to the contents of the large human burial feature. Grouping the data according to the strata rather sub-strata blurs the pattern to an even greater degree (Fig. 6.3B).

Contextual and Diachronic Analysis

For the purposes of the faunal analysis, the contexts have been grouped into eight main types: fills, ash, pits, surfaces, dumps, features, hearths and burials, each of which was recognized in Stratum II. Figure 6.4A shows that in Stratum II hearths, and more particularly burials, tended to have more sheep and goats than the other types of context. The contents of both these types of context were sieved and this may account for improved retrieval of small sheep and goat bones. The fills, which were not sieved, had the lowest number of sheep and goats, with varying proportions in the other contexts. This slightly lower proportion in fills is echoed in Strata III and IV (Figs. 6.4B and C), but only a few types of context in these strata had large enough samples for analysis.

The proportions of burnt to unburnt bones in each of the strata are shown in Table 6.2, the figures for hearths and other ashy contexts were calculated separately from the contexts with no indications of burning. Both types of context contain both burnt and unburnt bone, with burnt bone never reaching more than 10.5% even in the ashy deposits. The presence of roughly 90% of unburnt bone in both ashy and unburnt deposits indicates that there has been a great deal of mixing of material. However in Stratum II the non-ashy deposits contain 7.6% of burnt bone, slightly but significantly less than the ashy deposits at 10.5%, suggesting that the presence of a small proportion of residual *in situ* material, lost within the general mixing. The data for the large burial pit (L. 1237 and 1357) were analyzed separately from the rest of Stratum II and contain only one burnt bone (0.3%) confirming that this material really is *in situ* (Plate 6.4).

Locational Analysis

As stated above, ideally, each locus should be studied separately, but with 1,242 loci this is clearly impractical. However, the behaviour of one parameter within all loci of one stratum was studied as an example. This was the relationship between sample size and the number of identified taxa in Stratum III (Fig. 6.5). It was found that there is a high degree of correlation between the two sets of figures (R=0.82), attesting to the homogeneity of the assemblages, presumably resulting from mixing. It is highly probable that the same holds true of the other strata. The mass burial pit L. 1237 and 1357 in Stratum II is an exception to this and there are also some other individual loci with 'special finds', which appear to be in primary deposition, which are described towards the end of this chapter.

Discussion and Results

It is not possible to discern any consistent spatial or temporal variation within the faunal assemblages of the various strata, sub-strata or contexts recognized at Gilat, except for the high proportion of sheep and goat remains in the burial pit (L. 1237 and 1357, sub-stratum IIB, Area J). The reasons for this blurring of probable differences seem to have been manifold and must be related to the fact that classification into units of space, time and context are to some extent artificial, having been imposed on the material in the course of excavation and analysis. This is particularly true of the division into areas. However, the most important consideration is that very few of the animal remains are in primary deposition, almost all have been redeposited with other types of rubbish during continued reworking of the site over several hundred years. As stated in Chapter 5 (this volume), even if most of the pits were initially used as storage facilities, they were in time abandoned and filled eventually with rubbish. The fills and most of the loose material within other contexts must also be regarded as recycled rubbish of mixed origin, as shown for the proportions of burnt to unburnt bone and the high degree of correlation between sample size and number of taxa within each locus. Only a few individual loci have 'special finds' which appear to be in primary deposition.

It was therefore decided that in general separate analysis of the fauna for different spatial or diachronic units would be meaningless, and so by and large the fauna has been considered as a single unit. This is unfortunate as it had been hoped to establish changes over time in the composition and other aspects of the faunal assemblage at Gilat and perhaps to establish general distinctions between secular and cultic activities.1[1]

Domestic Ungulates—Numbers

The numbers of domestic ungulates, sheep, goats, cattle, pigs and equids are shown in summary form in Table 6.1, with corrected totals for sheep/goats and pigs in Table 6.3 and for sheep and goats separately in Table 6.4. The following section give details of the numbers found with the reasons for considering them to be domestic rather than wild, with notes on their taxonomy, size and type.

Sheep (*Ovis aries*) and Goats (*Capra hircus*)

The total number of sheep and goat bones identified was 4,371; when the bones in the medium mammal category, most of which were fragmentary ribs, are dispersed proportionately amongst the sheep/goats and pigs the total for sheep and goats rises to 4,643.

The difficulties inherent in the separation of goat from sheep bones are well-known, and some of the criteria used are not always as obvious as they seem to be in the standard works (Boessneck

1969; Lawrence 1982). They are further compounded at Gilat, as on most Middle Eastern sites, by the presence of gazelle.

The basis for the quantification of sheep and goat bones are set out in Tables 6.3 and 6.4. The majority of the small ruminant bones at Gilat belong in the sheep/goat category, only 13% were further identified to taxon, that is, definite goat or definite sheep. A very small number of bones were assigned to a sheep/goat/gazelle category, but as the number of bones of sheep and goats out-number those of gazelle to such a great extent, they have all been included in the sheep/goat category.

There were 293 identifications of goats and 301 of sheep; clearly the numbers are virtually equal. If bones identified only as sheep/goat, plus the sheep/goat proportion of medium mammal bones, are dispersed amongst the bones identified to taxon the final total is 2290 goats and 2353 sheep. These figures have to be regarded as tentative; however it is of some interest that equal numbers were also found at Grar.

Cattle (*Bos taurus*)

As can be seen from Tables 6.1 and 6.5, 957 cattle bones and teeth were retrieved from Strata IV–II at Gilat. This number includes 86 bones identified as cattle/*equid* and *Bos?* and 63 large mammal bones (mostly fragmentary ribs) which on the basis of probability are likely to have been from cattle.

Pigs (*Sus scrofa*)

Table 6.1 shows that 854 bones were identified as domestic pig with one possible wild boar bone. When bones identified only as medium mammal (mostly rib fragments) are shared proportionately with sheep and goats the likely number of pig bones at Gilat rises to 916 (Table 6.3).

Equids (*Equus* spp.)

There were only 14 equid bones and teeth at Gilat, all in Strata III and II: two incisors, one upper cheektooth, three lower cheekteeth, one cervical vertebra, two distal radii, one lunate, one magnum, one astragalus, a proximal tibia and a distal tibia. The astragalus was probably from a domestic donkey and one of the distal radii, the distal tibia and two of the cheekteeth probably derive from domestic horses (see below).

Domestic Status and Type of the Ungulates at Gilat

Two criteria of domestication are invoked here—the presence of an animal outside the geographical range of its wild forbear and diminution in body size.

Despite the fact that a reduction in size is known to be one of the main effects of domestication in ungulates (see for example Zeuner 1963; Grigson 1969, 1978, 1989a; Davis 1982; Uerpmann 1979; Clutton-Brock 1981), there are extraordinarily few published data on their size in Middle Eastern archaeological sites. The main factors which are known to affect size in ungulates are domestication and sexual dimorphism. Statistical parameters of size such as the mean and standard deviation are not adequate, because it is necessary to know the pattern of the distribution of individual measurements within each size range.

Most of the work involving the study of size has been done by making comparisons with a standard animal—either an actual known museum specimen or the mean or a group of specimens. Various methods of doing this are used here following those devised by previous researchers. The advantage of this method is that it allows measurements of different bone elements to be plotted on the same histogram thereby helping to overcome the problems of small sample size which are so familiar in archaeological samples. However the results are not very precise as the degree of variability differs amongst different bone elements and if large samples are available it is preferable to plot measurements of each element separately.

As well as establishing the domestic status of goats, sheep, cattle, pigs and at least some of the equids at Gilat, it is necessary to investigate what type of each of these animals was present.

Goats

Uerpmann (1979) calculated the means from a male and female wild goat and used them as a standard for comparison of the size of goats of various periods (Table 6.6A). He showed that there was a major size change between the goats of what he calls the Proto-Neolithic (eighth millennium b.c.) and the Early Neolithic (about 7,000 b.c.). The diminution is really quite small, nevertheless it is definite enough to show that the goats in the Early Neolithic sites had already undergone morphological changes associated with domestication. Uerpmann also found that this was followed by a further reduction in the size of goats in the Pottery Neolithic of the sixth and fifth millennia. Figure 6.6A shows the size of the goats from Gilat compared with one of Uerpmann's (1979) histograms and indicates that the goats were from domestic animals. Measurements of the goat bones from Gilat are given in Appendix 6.2.

Apart from size the only valid osteological differences between different types of goat that are relevant to this study are in the morphology of the horncores. Wild goats have scimitar horns, but domestic goats have either scimitar or screw-shaped horns.

Screw horncores are absent from all the other Middle Eastern sites that predate 6,000 b.c. but seem to appear in the late fifth millennium. In some sites both scimitar and screw horns appear together, but scimitar horns seem to have disappeared during the Early Bronze Age. Clutton-Brock (1979, Fig. 4) plotted the frequency of screw horncores at Jericho, where they are present in quantity in the Early Bronze Age (late third millennium) with a few scimitar cores. Isolated examples occur among the numerous scimitar cores in the Pottery and Pre-pottery Neolithic levels, but it is possible that these were intrusive. It seems that screw horncores did not become common until the Chalcolithic in the late fifth or early fourth millennium b.c. At Gilat all the goat horncores whose shape was noted were twisted—seven of females and ten of males.

In a pioneering study Angress (1959) concluded that the goats from Horvat Beter (a Chalcolithic site close to Beersheva) were of dwarf animals. Analysis of his measurements suggests that he sometimes confused sheep and goats bones, which is not surprising as few of the osteological distinctions between the two species had been worked out in 1959, but he does seem to have identified some of the metacarpals correctly. Use of the withers height estimation factors worked out by Teicherdt (1975) on the measurements from Grar (Grigson 1995b), Horvat Beter (Angress 1959) and Bir-es Safadi (Ducos 1968) indicated rather short animals, with females ranging from 52 to 56 cm; female goats at Gilat range from 56–58 cm, with a single male at 68 cm.

Sheep

Uerpmann (1979) used a wild female sheep as a standard (Table 6.6B) for comparison of the size of sheep of various periods. He showed that there was a major size change between the sheep of what he calls the Proto-Neolithic (eighth millennium b.c.) and the Early Neolithic (about 7,000 b.c.). The change in size is really quite small, nevertheless it is definite enough to show that the sheep in the Early Neolithic sites had already undergone morphological changes associated with domestication. He found that this was followed by a further reduction in the size of sheep in the Pottery Neolithic in the sixth and fifth millennia. In the subsequent Chalcolithic, or Late Pottery Neolithic of Amuq (levels D-G—fifth millennium), there was a slight recovery in size.

Figure 6.6B shows the size of the sheep from Gilat compared with one of Uerpmann's histograms. The mean size of the Gilat sheep is a little larger than those of Uerpmann's Early Neolithic, apparently following the trend which he established for the Amuq sequence, so it would seem that the Gilat sheep are of the usual size for domestic sheep of the Late Pottery Neolithic/Chalcolithic in the Middle East. Measurements of the sheep bones from Gilat are given in Appendix 6.2.

A variant of the normal Ammon-curved horncore of sheep appears in Chalcolithic and later sites in which male horns can be horizontal at their base and tightly spiralled. Both Ducos (1968) and Angress (1959) noticed horncores of this type in the Chalcolithic of Israel and referred them to *Ovis longipes palaeoegypticus*. Only three sheep horncores survive at Gilat—all of the Ammon type.

Chaix and Grant (1987) compared the metapodials of sheep from Kerma in the Sudan with those from early sites in Europe and concluded that as the Kerma metapodials were so much longer than those in Europe the use of the term *longipes* was justified. There were only three adult sheep limb bones at Gilat which were complete enough for the length to be measured, they gave withers heights of 70–72 cm; their narrowness suggests that they were female. The equivalent at Grar was 64 cm for a female sheep, considerably less than the heights of the two sexes at Kerma (range 70–90, mean 80 cm). The Gilat sheep seem therefore to have had the unlikely combination of Ammon type horns and long legs of the *longipes* type. Perhaps at Gilat we are dealing with rather large sheep, but of the Ammon, rather than the *longipes* type.

It is worth noting that Garfinkel (1995) tentatively identified one of the figurines from the Wadi Rabah phase (Late Pottery Neolithic) at Munhata as a sheep with a wide tail. One of the animal figurines described in Chapter 15 of the present volume and illustrated in Plate 15.16 no. 7, also appears have a fat tail, although this does not seem to be the case with the statuette of the sheep carrying cornets (Plate 5.8).

If these identifications of fat tails are correct, it is likely that modern sheep of the area, which are of the fat-tailed variety, have an ancient origin.

Cattle

Buitenhuis (1985) used the complete skeleton of an aurochs cow as the standard animal for the comparison of sizes of cattle in the Middle East (Table 6.7A). Grigson (1989a) used the same standard animal for the comparison of sizes of wild and domestic cattle in the area, using log plots, and concluded that cattle were domesticated in the western half of the area during the sixth millennium (Fig. 6.7A). Comparison with the sizes of the Gilat cattle bones (Fig. 6.7B) shows clearly that the Gilat animals were smaller than both the wild and domestic cattle of the preceding millennia and therefore were domestic. Measurements of cattle bones are given in Appendix 6.3.

It is possible that the domestic cattle, or more probably some of the domestic cattle of the Levant in prehistory were not the familiar cattle, *Bos taurus*, but zebu or humped cattle, *Bos indicus*. Most of the criteria for their distinction on osteological material involve complete skulls and bones. However Grigson (1980) pointed out that the shape of the orbital rim below the eye which is flat in young cattle, in older taurine animals it becomes pointed as it approaches the lacrimal suture. This means that this character is only valid in cases were the skull is known to be of an elderly animal. No pointed rims were noted in the Gilat material, though flat rims were observed in three instances (GIL90 5032, GIL90 3489 and GIL92 3869) all were from young animals, that is animals in which the jugal/maxillary suture was still open.

The proximal metatarsal has characteristics which can be seen even on fragmentary material. In *Bos indicus* it has longer and more prominent surfaces for articulation with the navicular. The two metatarsals on which this character was studied were both taurine.

The bones of taurines tend to be shorter and broader than those of humped cattle. The only complete longbones were four metacarpals and two metatarsals and all of those fall outside the range of variation of *Bos indicus*.

Although the evidence is not overwhelming there seems no reason to believe tha
Gilat, or indeed at any of the other Chalcolithic sites, were anything other than domes

The only longbones complete enough for their length to be measured were four m
two metatarsals. Using Folk's data quoted by von den Driesch and Boessneck (1974) it is possible to
calculate the height at the withers in live animals from the lengths of their long bones. Three of the
complete metacarpals were of females so their length multiplied by Folk's factor for females of 6.0
gives heights of 1.2m for each of the cows, and his factor of 6.3 for males a height of 1.3m for the
bull or bullock. Thus the cattle at Gilat were very small.

Pigs

Comparison with Payne and Bull's 'standard pig'—the mean of a sample of modern wild boar from
Turkey (Table 6.7B)—shows that all the Gilat pigs with suitable measurements are definitely in the
domestic range (Fig. 6.8A). The dimensions of the teeth and bones are plotted separately and give
rather different results; the larger relative size of the teeth may be due to the fact that they come
from young animals and consequently have undergone very little interdental wear. Measurements of
the pig bones and teeth from Gilat are given in Appendix 6.4.

Little can be said about the type of pigs at Gilat, except that like the pigs from other Chalcolithic
sites in the Negev they were of very small stature. No complete skulls survive, but, as shown in Fig.
6.9, the teeth were not crowded so there is no reason to think that the jaws had shortened
disproportionately which some authors (Flannery 1983, Clutton-Brock 1981) consider to be a sign
of domestication.

Equids

Three species of equid have been found in the Chalcolithic of the Levant—onagers (*E. hemionus*),
domestic asses (*E. asinus*) and horses (*Equus caballus*). It has been suggested that wild asses (*E.
africanus* may also have been present. The difficulties encountered in the distinction of these species
have received much discussion in the various papers edited by Meadow and Uerpmann (1986,
1991).

It is possible to distinguish assemblages of bones of onagers, domestic donkeys and horses on the
basis of size, onagers being slightly smaller, or rather more slender, than domestic donkeys and
horses being markedly more robust (Grigson 1993b). It is probable that, like other ungulates,
donkeys underwent a reduction in size with domestication, but there are too few size data available
for this to be certain, and as yet no evidence that wild donkeys were present in the Negev in the
Chalcolithic. Although the horse (*Equus caballus*) was a member of the Pleistocene fauna of the
Levant, it died out before the end of the period, so any horse bones found in the area must be of
domestic animals.

The method utilized for size comparisons of the equids is that devised by Uerpmann (1982,
1986). He used the cumulative frequency of various indices to compare the sizes of the equid bones
from Shams ed-Din with those from Mureybet (Ducos 1978), where the equids were undoubtedly
wild and probably onagers. This method takes advantage of the fact that as the Mureybet equid
sample was large and the variability of the various dimensions can be utilized. The standard
measurements (means and standard deviations) are listed in Table 6.7C.

The formula used for calculating the size index of any particular dimension in an assemblage is:

$$SI = \frac{(a - X)}{4s} \times 100,$$

where *a* is the dimension of a particular element, *X* is the mean of that dimension at Mureybet, and *s* is the standard deviation of that dimension at Mureybet. The indices are set out in ascending order of magnitude and plotted on the X axis against the percentages of their cumulative frequency on the Y axis. In such plots the mean of the standard is at 0 on the index scale, the standard deviation *s* is 25 and its theoretical range (X +- 2s) is -50 to +50. The mean of each sample being compared with the standard can be read off from where the line connecting its points crosses the 50% level; *s* will be 25 and the range (X +- 2s). If the dimensions of the sample are larger than those of the standard, the mean will be to the right of the standard (i.e. +) and, if smaller, to the left (i.e. -).

The size indices calculated for Shams ed-Din and Mureybit (probably onagers), Tell Rubeidheh (almost certainly domestic donkeys—Payne 1988) and horses of the second millennium are plotted in Fig. 6.8B. The three suitable measurements from Gilat of a distal radius (GIL92 3578), a distal tibia (GIL77 207) and an astragalus (GIL 90 4599) have been added. The position of the radius suggests that it derives from a horse; it is far too broad for either donkey or onager and is similar in size to a radius at Shiqmim and another at Grar which have been identified as horse (Grigson 1993b). The tibia is probably from a horse and the astragalus could be from either a small horse or a large donkey. All three of these dimensions and those of the two measurable equid teeth (GIL90 3417 and GIL91 2089) are larger than those of the six equids excavated from Tell Brak in Iraq, which were positively identified as donkeys by Clutton-Brock (1989, 1993). Thus it seems that horses were definitely present at Gilat, and domestic donkeys probably so, whereas onagers may be excluded on the basis of size. The horses seem to have been rather smaller than those found in second millennium sites, lacking one would think the noble stature of those in Egyptian depictions. Measurements of the equid bones and teeth from Gilat are given in Appendix 6.5.

There are no other anatomical criteria for the distinction of wild and domestic equids which can be applied to the Gilat material, so it is uncertain whether any of the remaining equid bones are from small horses, or donkeys—they can only be listed as equids.

As so few domestic horses have been identified in the fourth millennium in the Middle East, outside Anatolia, one has to raise the problem of the possibility of intrusion. The intrusion of bones from later into earlier deposits of an archaeological site is something which can undoubtedly occur. The find localities for each of the equid bones at Gilat have been very carefully checked, all were from baskets in which there was no pottery other than Chalcolithic and all were from well below the surface. It would be desirable to test the fourth millennium assignation by obtaining direct radiocarbon accelerator dates, but attempts to date unburnt skeletal material from Near Eastern sites are usually unsuccessful due to the poor preservation of collagen.

The identification of domestic horses and donkeys at Gilat and other Chalcolithic sites is in direct conflict with the contention by Ovadia (1992) who claims, on the basis of their rarity on archaeological sites, that equids in the Chalcolithic had not been fully domesticated. However this is not a good criterion, since one would expect the remains of any domestic animal which was not a major producer of food to be present in only small numbers in any archaeological site, as indeed they are, almost invariably, in the succeeding Bronze Age and later periods when their domestic status is not in doubt.

The Management of the Domestic Ungulates at Gilat

Some idea of the way in which herds of domestic animals are managed can be gained by the study of their demography. This is also true of archaeological assemblages, when patterns of age and sex can be established they give information on the decisions made relating to the production of various commodities. The most important is of course the continuance of the herd that is herd security as discussed by Redding (1984). The main primary products obtained from the dead animal are meat, leather and sinew; secondary products, produced during life, include milk, hair and energy. That energy is utilised by people for their own purposes—pulling carts, ploughs or timber and carrying people or goods (Levy 1983; Sherratt 1981).

Two main methods of ageing animal remains used on archaeological assemblages are the eruption and wear of the mandibular teeth, sometimes simplified to comparisons of the total numbers of lower fourth deciduous molars (m_4) with lower fourth premolar (P_4) that succeeds it, and the state of fusion of the limb bones.

Survivorship curves, based largely or entirely on the state of fusion of long bones, have attracted attention because it is claimed that people would have killed hunted and domesticated animals at different ages, the theory being that in domestic populations more young animals would be killed, but that wild animals would be hunted randomly so that their kill-off patterns would reflect the natural age structure of the population in the wild (Hole, Flannery and Neely 1969; Hesse 1978, 1982; Hecker 1975). There are some difficulties here, one of which is that it has not been convincingly demonstrated that hunters do kill randomly, indeed some hunters are definitely selective (Binford 1978). Other difficulties more relevant to us here are that the criteria used for ageing are still not universally agreed upon, particularly the degree of variation in times of epiphysial fusion (see for example Bullock and Rackham 1982), and theoretically survivorship curves should fall with age, whereas sometimes they rise at two years (for example sheep/goat data based on the fusion of the distal tibia). Other difficulties include the facts that the less dense, younger bone may have been differentially destroyed, and most survivorship curves based on longbones only span the ages from birth to about early adulthood.

I have not been able to find data on the ageing of domestic ungulates in the Levant, but a very detailed and useful summary of demographic parameters relating to cattle, sheep and goats belonging to pastoral nomads in northern and eastern Africa have been published by Dahl and Hjort (1976) and will be referred to frequently below. Although their detailed conclusions relate to the diet of particular pastoralists, living in particular and mainly African environments are of doubtful relevance here, the basic information which they set out would seem to be applicable to the same species in different areas regardless of the different conditions.

Sheep and Goats—Age Distributions

Post-Cranial Bones. Despite the difficulties inherent in their construction, survivorship curves for sheep and goats from different sites do yield some very interesting information (for methodology - see Hole, Flannery and Neely 1969). The percentages surviving into adulthood increase progressively over time from the ninth or eighth millennium to Grar in the fourth millennium (Grigson 1995b).

Separate curves for the three main strata at Gilat where constructed (Table 6.8 and Fig. 6.10A), but are so similar that it is doubtful that they actually reflect any change over time. Figure 6.10B, in which the data for the three strata have been added together, shows that about 75% of the sheep and goats survived until the age of about 1 year, 64% to about 1½, 75% to about 2, 39.4% to 2½ and 27% to 3 years or more. The apparent recovery at the age of 2 years is based on the age of fusion of the tibia. As the same recovery occurs in Flannery's curves as well, there is clearly something intrinsically anomalous about it.

On the face of it the survival of so many animals into adulthood suggests a herding strategy directed at the use of secondary products, probably wool rather than milk, as Payne has shown that a high proportion of young males would be killed off in a specialized milk strategy. However a note of caution is needed here because the high level of destruction of softer bone discussed below must have biased the ageing pattern.

Mandibles and Lower Teeth. Figure 6.11A is a plot of the numbers of mandibles and loose teeth from Gilat which could be assigned to an age group expressed in two ways, as a histogram and as a curve of cumulative percentages subtracted from 100%. Figure 6.11B shows the same data adjusted to allow for the differential destruction of the bones of young animals and for 15% perinatal mortality. The calculations for the degree of destruction are based on the results of the bone element survival graph (Fig. 6.17C, below) which imply a rate of destruction of the mandibles aged 6 months of about 82%, and of about 77% at the age of 1 year 7 months.

Figure 6.11C is a plot on the same grid as Figs. 6.10A and B of Payne's (1973) three models of sheep/goat rearing strategies. These are (A) meat production, in which there is a high mortality of males at 2–3 years and only a few males reach adult life; (B) specialized milk production, in which there is a high mortality of males at 6–9 months, and only a few males reach adult life; from three years onwards these two curves are identical; and (C) specialized wool production, in which emphasis is on older animals of both sexes and most males are castrated and kept in a separate flock from the females and their young.

Figure 6.11D shows both the curves calculated from the raw data and the adjusted curve. The curve based on raw data mostly closely resembles Payne's wool strategy (C), but this is almost certainly unreliable. The adjusted curve is closest to Payne's model (A), implying a meat strategy. However the shape of the entire curve before three years of age depends largely on the degree of perinatal mortality. If, for the sake of argument, 50% of the lambs and kids had died or had been killed soon after birth, the resulting curve would be the same as Payne's specialized milk production curve (B).

Sheep and Goats—Sexual Attributes. Males of both sheep and goats tend to be larger than females, and in some periods at least, goats had a wider sexual dimorphism than sheep (Boessneck and von den Driesch 1979; Hesse 1978). Comparisons of the sizes of goat and sheep bones with standard animals are shown in Fig. 6.6. Although there is some skewness in the goats, there is none in the sheep; the same situation occurred at Grar. It may be that the sexual dimorphism in sheep is too small to be demonstrable in some or all of the measurements used in ratio diagrams. Another possibility is that the differences between the sexes of sheep have been obscured by the presence of castrates. However although there are few data on the relative sizes of rams and castrates it is likely that the width measurements, which are those used in the ratio diagrams, would bear more resemblance to each other than to ewes.

Figures 6.12A and B show the distribution of trochlear breadth of the humeri in adult goats and sheep and Figs. 6.12C and D the distal breadth of the astragalus. In both species the distributions are bimodal and skewed in favour of small, and presumably female, animals.

There are also some non-measurable differences between the sexes, particularly in the horncores and the pelvis. Horncores of both goats and sheep have been excluded from the sexual analysis because, as Boessneck and von den Driesch (1979) point out, they are unsuitable for quantification of sex as the heavier male horncores survive better than those of females and, in sheep, the females may lack horncores altogether. It is quite easy to determine both species and sex from complete pelves of adult sheep and goats, although damage can make specific identification difficult or impossible, but provided that the acetabulum is complete, sexing is usually possible (Lemppenau 1964). The sample of sexed sheep/goat pelves at Gilat is woefully small, but there were 6 female and 2 male pelves.

The predominance of adult females is a common pattern in prehistoric samples of domestic animal bones, suggesting that males were mostly slaughtered when young. The data from Gilat are too few for certainty, although in goats at least there are indications of a larger number of adult females than males.

Sheep and Goats Discussion. Dahl and Hjort (1976) have shown that in East Africa, when pastoral people keep goats and sheep as well as cattle, they tend to be kept as suppliers of meat, particularly as their slaughter does not involve the same degree of reduction in productivity, since goats are able to reproduce from 6 months of age and sheep at about 15 months. Sheep may give birth more than once a year, usually in the rainy season, whereas goats mate more continuously producing 2 or 3 young a year. As they say, 'Small stock are easy to slaughter for guests, minor ceremonies and meat', and the quantity of meat from a single animal is not too large for consumption by a single family.

Most male lambs are slaughtered at an early age. The ratio of entire rams to ewes is about 1:10 in Africa, 1:20 in Arabia and 1:5 for the Bassari in Iran. Some Somali sheep breeders castrate all male lambs at 5 months of age, only 2% of males being kept for breeding purposes. The proportion of breeding females in a flock varies from about 55% to 90%. Ewes produce 5–7 lambs in a lifetime, breeding until the age of 8 or 9 years.

Most male kids are also slaughtered early in life and breeding females comprise about 50% of the entire flock. Nanny goats are said to produce 6–8 kids before the age of about 5½–6, however much greater ages are also recorded with life expectancy extended to 8–10.

Mortality rates for both lambs and kids under the age of 6 months vary greatly, but seem to be about 25%; they can be as much as 70% during the first year.

The computer simulations of Dahl and Hjort (1976) suggest an annual slaughter of about 32% of both species if the herd size is to remain static and about 25% if the herd is to grow. This slaughter would be largely aimed at males of 1½–2 years, when they reach their mature size. Earlier slaughter of male sheep and goats, before they have reached their adult size is largely a response to insufficient grazing as it increases the survival chances of the females. However where pasture is more adequate young males may be castrated and reared for meat.

In both the adjusted and the unadjusted mandibular ageing curves for Gilat (Fig. 6.11A, B and D) the main period of slaughter is the second year. Although the figure for death at 6 years is also high it must be remembered that it covers a period of two years, not one.

In the unadjusted mandibular ageing curve for Gilat (Fig. 6.11A and D) about 22% of animals died in their first year and 30% in their second. In the adjusted mandibular ageing curve (Fig. 6.11B and D), in addition to 15% perinatal mortality, there was a further death rate of about 25% in the first year and 30% in the second.

Payne (1973) points out that flocks in subsistence economies are unlikely to be kept for milk or wool alone. When both milk and meat are required (but when meat is relatively more important) his strategy (A) might be followed, and similarly in strategy (B) the killed animals would still be eaten. I suspect, therefore, that in crude terms the age expectancy in a purely meat strategy would have a slightly younger emphasis than that illustrated by Payne's model (A). I also believe that in a specialized milk economy there would be slightly higher proportion of animals aged three years or more (mostly females, of course). Thus in unspecialized economies one can postulate three stages, each involving an increase in life expectancy, from meat production (which would still allow the use of other animal products such as skins), to meat + milk, to meat + milk + wool.

Despite the difficulties inherent in the separation of sheep from goat bones and the resulting small sample sizes when they are analyzed separately, it is possible to make some comparisons between the demographic parameters of sheep and goats. This was done for the Chalcolithic site of Bir es-Safadi, where it was found that a higher proportion of sheep than goats survived into old age (Grigson 1987b: Fig. 2); the data from Gilat have been arranged in the same way (Table 6.9 and Fig. 6.13A) and show a similar divergence with increasing age, although equal numbers appear to have been killed in the first year of life.

Separate survivorship curves can be constructed for the two sexes of each species using the fusion data of the distal metapodials and the distal humerus to determine age, and the size and shape of the bones to determine sex (Table 6.10). The results are tentative because the unfused, and therefore also the fused, bones identified only as sheep/goat have to be brought into the equation and assigned proportionately to the relevant group. The results are shown in Fig. 6.13B and suggest that as at Safadi a higher proportion of females, particularly female sheep, survives beyond the age of 2¼ years. Dahl and Hjort (1976), quoting from Staufer's (1965) work in Iran, say that in the Middle East goats give 50–100% more milk than sheep, nevertheless both species are milked. They also say that in Africa the breeding season of goats is less restricted than that of sheep so that milk can be obtained from them over a longer period of the year and they can be a reliable source of milk even in dry seasons. As goats breed faster than sheep, they can be killed off and eaten at an earlier age without endangering the survival of the flock, so perhaps the high rate of survival of female sheep is related to herd security combined with the production of wool in addition to milk. The presence of more sheep than goats is indicative of the same trend.

Exactly where Gilat fits on the continuum of meat, to meat + milk, to meat + milk + wool is difficult to ascertain, but what is clear is that the ageing and sexing analysis of sheep and goats does not indicate a highly specialised herding strategy. The most likely scenario, taking all the results together, is an unspecialized economy based primarily on meat production and herd security, but with secondary products such as milk and wool also being utilized.

Cattle—Age and Sex Distribution. The unusually large sample of cattle at Gilat has allowed both methods of ageing to be utilized in some detail.

There were 53 loose cheek teeth, or sets of cheek teeth, which could be roughly aged, though in some cases only 'less than' or 'more than' ages could be established. These were assigned to age group on two different bases, the first uses eruption dates for modern early maturing cattle as published by Silver (1969) and the second (see Table 6.11) using dates for early nineteenth century cattle, which were presumably late maturing, quoted by Meitinger (1983). Both also utilized some of the wear stages suggested by Grant (1982).

Figure 6.14A shows the results grouped on early maturation criteria and Fig. 6.14B the same data grouped on late maturation. The results for early maturing cattle indicate that almost all the animals at Gilat had been slaughtered by the age of 5 years. Higham (1967) using the same basic ageing criteria had a similar result at the Danish Neolithic site of Troldebjerg and concluded that, as the animals were not being kept into old age, they were not being used for ploughing or milking. However this is untenable for any assemblage, since in such a regime the cows would not live long enough to produce enough calves to replenish the herd, which would therefore gradually die out. It seems likely that the ageing criteria employed are not applicable to prehistoric populations.

One cannot be certain that all the results published by Dahl and Hjort (1976) for cattle kept by pastoral nomads in northern and eastern Africa are applicable to the Negev in the Chalcolithic, but they are the best guide we have. They give the age of four as the first year of calving by cows and state that only one offspring is produced at each calving. With a gestation period of nine months in practice this means one calf per year for each fertile female. In their baseline scenario in which cows calve each year from age 4 until 9 and there is a natural loss of calves of 20%, an average calving rate of 69% is just enough to keep the herd structure stable. If the calf mortality rate is reduced to 10% the herd can be maintained at a calving rate of 62%. With a 10% loss of calves or an extended breeding period (to 11 or 13 years) lower rates of calving will be adequate. The data at Gilat suggest calf mortality 10–20%, so it is clear that for an adequate supply of calves to be maintained it would have been necessary for most of the cows to have lived and continued to breed until at least nine years of age.

When the Gilat mandibles and lower cheekteeth are grouped according to the early maturation criteria (Fig. 6.14A), only about 2% survive beyond their fourth year and 50% were killed before their third year. From the information in the preceding paragraph this kill-off pattern is untenable, unless only a small proportion of the cattle herd was brought to the site for consumption. However in Fig. 6.14B, which uses late maturing criteria, at least 50% of the cattle survive until their fifth year. Two loose teeth which were not included in the analysis of age were a lower first or second permanent molar (M_1 and M_2 are difficult to distinguish—GIL92 2383) which was worn down well past the enamel islands and had a highly polished occlusal surface, and an incisor (GIL92 6398) in which the crown was almost completely worn away, these teeth testify to the survival into old age of at least two animals.

The supposition that the late maturation scenario is more likely to have been correct is given some support by the survivorship pattern based on the fusion of the epiphyses of long bones (Table 6.12 and Fig. 6.14C), which suggests that 50% of animals survived beyond their fourth year, even though fewer age groups can be recognized by this method. Unfortunately the information about ageing generated by a study of the teeth gives very little precision after the age of five, but only one of the late maturing teeth (P4 and M3) was worn severely enough to suggest an age of at least eight. Similarly with long bone fusion, as the last to fuse do so at 3½–4 years, information about age structures in older animals is lacking. This is something which can only be achieved when an adequate number of cranial fragments showing the state of fusion of the sutures is present; such sites are rare in the extreme (Grigson 1982a).

Using the simple method of dental age estimation indicates that there were 14 deciduous lower fourth molars (m_4) of cattle at Gilat and 25 permanent lower fourth premolars (P_4), that is 14 animals younger than 3½ years and 25 3½ years or more, suggesting that 64% survived into maturity. At Grar the equivalent figures were 7 and 17, that is, about 70% of the cattle were mature. The difference between Grar and Gilat is probably not significant.

As the sex ration for cattle at birth is roughly 1:1 and as it is the cows which need to survive into old age in order to achieve herd security, it follows that most of the animals killed before 4½ were bulls or bullocks, with only a few fertile mature males kept for breeding. Modern cattle, for example Jerseys, grow fastest in their first year, thereafter the growth rate gradually decreases until the age of six years when they reach their mature body weight. Thus when animals are utilized for meat, and other primary products, a balance has to be achieved between the cost of raising animals over a period of years, whether measured in terms of food supply, labour or money, and the amount of food and other materials supplied by a dead animal. The survival of so few males into old age makes one suspect that few, if any, were used for draught purposes. However, since females have to survive and have to suckle their calves, it would very surprising if milk were not also used for human consumption, and indeed this would help to mitigate the costs of rearing them into old age.

It is clear from the scenarios outlined by Dahl and Hjort (1976) that the majority of adult cattle have to be females, and indeed this seems to be the case in most archaeological assemblages of domestic cattle, including Gilat. Apart from the sexual dimorphism in the size of many of their bones, cattle can usually be sexed on the basis of non-metric characters of the pelvis and the shape and size of the skull, the horncores and the metapodials. None of the pelves at Gilat was complete enough for this to be done. The only horn core (GIL91 351) complete enough to be sexed was from a cow as were three of the complete metacarpals, a fourth metacarpal was from a male. The log ratio diagram (Fig. 6.7B), which uses almost only sexually dimorphic measurements, has a strong skew to the left, indicating a reliance on smaller animals: probably cows.

It is clear from the scenarios outlined by Dahl and Hjort (1976) that the majority of adult cattle have to be females, and indeed this seems to be the case in most archaeological assemblages of domestic cattle, including Gilat.

Pigs—Age and Sex Distributions. The mandibular ageing data were estimated on by combining the wear and eruption stages recognized by Bull and Payne (1982) for pigs' teeth, with the eruption ages proposed by Matschke (1967) and some additional wear stages taken from Grant (1982). It is possible to devise 10 stages and to assign approximate ages to them (Table 6.13). In cases in which estimates of age from the wear of two different teeth in the same mandible differed, that of the younger tooth was utilized as rates of wear are rather variable. The survivorship curve based on long bone diaphyseal fusion uses fusion dates given by Silver (1963). The results are set out in Fig. 6.15.

Figure 6.15A shows that over half the pigs were killed in their first year, nearly a half in the second year, with only 6% surviving into the third year or older. This pattern is very similar to that derived from the longbone fusion data (Table 6.14 and Fig. 6.15B) and indicates the usual slaughter pattern for domestic pigs, with the vast majority being killed before the end of the second year. Given the great degree of post-depositional destruction of bones of sheep and goats (see below), it is probable that the true figure for piglet mortality was rather more than 50%.

Pigs' jaws can be sexed by the size of the canines, or tusks, which are much larger in males. There were 11 jaws of adult sows at Gilat and 4 of boars, suggesting as one would expect a predominance of females. None of the pigs' pelves at Gilat were complete enough for sexing.

Pigs reproduce very fast, not only having very large litters, but sometimes breeding more frequently than once a year. Wild pigs in the Middle East sometimes give birth twice a year and this could also have been true of domestic pigs in the Chalcolithic. They yield little in the way of secondary products and would therefore have been raised for their meat alone.

Equids. There were too few bones of equids at Gilat to allow any analysis of ageing or sexing patterns which might throw light of the way in which they were managed. However the presence of a lower second premolar which is extremely worn

Pathology. There were 12 instances of encrustations of calculus on the cheekteeth of sheep/goats and, as often in the Middle East, the calculus had a shiny, metallic, gold-coloured appearance. It was usually sited at the gumline. It occurred most frequently in the dentition of elderly animals, but was present on a deciduous lower fourth molar. The teeth in seven mandibles had worn very unevenly perhaps indicating a degree of malocclusion with the opposing teeth and in 45 cases the roots of the cheekteeth were swollen and roughened, probably by infection, possibly actinomycosis. Such infections may result from overgrazing and were most common in the teeth of old sheep and goats. Two mandibles retained evidence of dental abscess around the root of the lower fourth premolar and this had resulted in the loss of the tooth. Three lower third molars had enlarged distal pillars.

Abnormalities in the dentition of sheep/goats are difficult to quantify as they are only obvious in loose teeth and in broken jaws in which the roots of the teeth are exposed. Although they appear to occur quite frequently the sample is so large that the proportion is really quite small and attests to a good standard of care of the sheep and goats at Gilat. Only six postcranial bones had any pathological condition - in one the navicular was fused to the proximal metatarsal, probably a case of spavin in old age, and there were signs of osteitis on six other proximal metatarsals.

Two of the 20 lower third molars of cattle at Gilat had unusually stout distal pillars. This is a lower incidence than at Grar where it occurred in three out of ten lower third molars of cattle (Grigson 1995b); it was conjectured on the basis of documentation by Miles and Grigson (1990) that its occurrence in a population of domestic animals at such a high rate could be due to inbreeding resulting from isolation. The teeth in two mandibles had worn very unevenly perhaps indicating a degree of malocclusion with the opposing teeth and the roots of two of the cheekteeth were swollen and roughened, probably by infection, possibly actinomycosis.

A distal humerus of an ox was slightly expanded laterally and there was slight medial expansion on two distal metacarpals. Five proximal phalanges showed slight proximal expansion, all were from the forefoot which carries more weight than the hindfoot, and one may have been from a wild ox. Two of the four phalanges of domestic size also had deep tendon insertions. Whether this is the result of old age or indicate use of cattle in traction is hard to say, but as the lesions are minor and for such a large sample, infrequent, age seems the more likely, especially as no abnormalities were observed in the metatarsals or middle phalanges.

Only one pig bone or tooth showed any sign of pathology, this was a lipping of bone around the fused epiphyses of the centrum of a dorsal vertebra. The low rate is probably related to the youthfulness of most of the pigs at the time of slaughter.

An equid upper second premolar, tentatively identified as horse, was extremely worn, either as a result of old age or of bit wear; this is described in more detail below. The equid distal radius had slight exostoses around the epiphysial suture line, probably related to age, but possibly due to load carrying or draft.

The low rate of pathology in the domestic animals at Gilat attests to a high standard of care in the management of herds and flocks and suggests that they had access to good grazing, and therefore were not confined within the settlement. However, there is some direct evidence for the presence, not necessarily continuous, of live domestic ungulates within the site. There were three upper fourth deciduous molars of sheep/goats and one of an ox, in which the roots had all been absorbed. This shows not only that the teeth had been shed from live animals, but that live animals were actually present *within* the confines of the site. They were retrieved from Strata III and II. There is no such direct evidence for the presence of living pigs in the site, but there is no reason to think that their treatment in this respect differed at all from that of cattle, sheep or goats.

Risk Management

Domestic animals at Gilat were maintained for a variety of purposes, but the chief preoccupation of their owners must have been with maintaining herds which were viable and self-renewing, and which could be used to minimize risk in times of shortage, particularly crop failure. It follows that keeping several different species with different nutritional needs and reproductive rates, would help to maximize the use that could be made of the different natural and man-made environmental niches in the locality, hence even if cattle are considered the most important animals in a particular society, it is an advantage to keep not only sheep and goats as well, as they can be taken away from settlements in order to graze, but also pigs which can scavenge offal and other rubbish in and around the site and which reproduce very fast. Storage of plant and animal food, particularly milk products, against hard times is an essential element in risk management and live animals can be seen as storage on the hoof.

The Utilization of Live Animals at Gilat

Milking

It was concluded in the section on animal management that the cattle, sheep and goats at Gilat were all probably milked. The presence of many large churns, that is Ghassulian churns (See Chapter 10, this volume and Plates 10.31:1–12, 10.32:1–5, and 10.33:1–7) which closely resemble the pottery and stainless steel churns still used in some parts of the Middle East today, suggests that milk was processed on the site. Animal skins are also still in use for churning (personal observation) and it may well be that the Ghassulian churn is a skuamorph of a skin. In most traditional Middle East societies today, milk products are produced from yoghurt, that is milk which has been fermented by the activity of various bacteria before churning. Milk is poured into a churn containing enough live yoghurt to start the fermentation process. The skin or churn containing the liquid milk is shaken about for some hours until the butter separates from the whey which is then processed into various form of cheese and other milk products (Martin 1980; Seeden 1982). This means that unlike meat, milk can be transformed into a non-perishable form which can be stored, and so provides not only immediate nourishment, but also food which can be kept against times of shortage. It seems probable that this fermentation process is the key to the efficient storage of milk products and that it was utilized in the past (Grigson 1995a).

The importance of the process of churning at Gilat is underlined by the statuette of the Gilat woman with a churn on her head (Fig. 5.7), and its relationship to cattle by that of a bull carrying a churn on its back from Ein Gedi (Ussishkin 1980; Grigson 1987a, 1995a). Another vessel commonly found on Chalcolithic sites which seems to be particularly adapted to the manipulation of liquids, is the cornet; the Gilat statuette of a sheep carrying three cornets (Fig. 5.8) may in fact refer to the use of milk in liquid form, perhaps fermented as yoghurt or even as alcohol. The incorporation of churns and cornets into figurines and statuettes of animals and people suggests that milk and the processes of its transformation into various forms may have had a particular ritual significance in the lives of the people of Gilat and other Chalcolithic sites in the Levant.

Surpluses produced for more prosaic reasons could have been used as food for non-productive members of society, perhaps a priestly elite, or in exchange for the acquisition of other goods without the erosion of capital which would be involved in bartering live animals. As stated above the preservation of milk products would have been an important element in risk management.

Bleeding
Blood is extracted from living cattle and other animals by some pastoral people in Africa. There is no indication that this was done in the Middle East, though it is certainly a potential source of food, particularly in times of shortage.

Fibres
Many spindle whorls made of pottery or stone (Chapters 10 and 12) and bone tools of kinds thought to be associated with weaving were excavated at Gilat (Chapter 14). Their presence not only attests to the production of woven fabrics, but also to the fact that the actual processes of manufacture, that is spinning and weaving, were being carried out at the site. Thus the site was definitely used for domestic as well as ritual activity.

Sheep and goats are not the only source of fibres. Fibres can be extracted from flax (*Linum usitatissimum*) and other plants, both wild and cultivated, so one cannot always be sure that any artifacts found on an archaeological site thought to be used for spinning or weaving are necessarily indicative of the use of sheep wool or goat hair.[2] Flax, from which linen fibres can be extracted, is one of the eight founder crops of Middle Eastern civilisations (Zohary 1992), so as carbonized seeds of flax have been found in some Chalcolithic assemblages, the use of linen cannot be ruled out. However the high proportion of adult sheep rather than goats suggests the importance of wool as a raw material.

Traction and Transport
It is possible that sheep and goats were used to carry loads, but any significant load bearing or traction would have to be carried out by larger animals, that is cattle or equids or both. Pigs and perhaps other domestic ungulates may have been used to trample in seeds at planting time, as attested by more recent Egyptian depictions.

The low number of adult bulls or bullocks at Gilat and the near absence of lesions associated with draft may indicate that cattle were little used for traction, or for ploughing or threshing. Indeed there is no direct evidence for either. However the bull with churns from Ein Gedi and the sheep with cornets from Gilat show that the idea of load-bearing animals was current.

As there were only a few equid bones at Gilat it is unlikely that donkeys or horses were bred for consumption, they were probably used in transport and perhaps draft. Their use as pack animals receives some support from the figurine of an ass loaded with two large vessels, or perhaps baskets, found with Late Chalcolithic material in a cave at Giv'atayim near Tel Aviv (Epstein 1985; Grigson 1987a, 1995a), though it is possible that it actually dates to Early Bronze Age I (Ovadia 1992). Both donkeys and horses move much faster than cattle, though their loads may have to be less. Also it must be remembered that the copper used in the manufacture of metal objects found in some Chalcolithic sites in the Negev (though not Gilat) was probably transported from far away, probably from Transjordan, as were some of the stone vessels (Chapter 12), so it is likely that it was carried by donkeys or horses rather than people or cattle.

The presence of domestic horses in the fourth millennium in the Middle East raises the question of the introduction of carts and chariots into the Levant. Pictograms show that solid-wheeled carts were in use in late fourth millennium (Uruk) times in Mesopotamia (Childe 1951), which may originally have been drawn by cattle (Piggott 1968, 1983) or donkeys (Littauer 1983). Almost all the depictions of horses from the second millennium onwards in both Mesopotamia and Egypt show them pulling light vehicles with two spoked wheels, that is, chariots as defined by Piggott (1968, 1983). So the presence of horses in the Levant in the fourth millennium raises the possibility that carts or chariots or both were already being used there.

One of the equid teeth, tentatively identified as horse because of its great length, was an upper second premolar, GIL91 2089, found in a pit (Sub-stratum 2bi, L. 1044 in Area J) (Plate 6.1b). The crown was worn down past the internal enamel patterns, the mesial face in particular was so worn that it sloped distally and was polished all over. It is possible that this is not merely the result of old age, but also of bit wear, or at least wear against a rope, signifying that the horse (or other equid) was under close control. The bevel on the mesial face is much like that produced by bit wear on the lower second premolar as described by Anthony and Brown (1991).

Prestige

Horses were and are to this day prestigious in most parts of the world and it is clear from second millennium depictions of magnificent horses that this was also true in the Middle East. Whether the smaller, humbler animals present in the Negev in the fourth millennium had such a high status is unknown as there are no depictions and no remains of horse trappings. However, horses are expensive animals to rear in terms of the nutrition and care which they need so it is probable that they had some special significance in Chalcolithic society.

It is well known that the possession of cattle imparts prestige amongst African pastoralists and indeed wealth, including bride-wealth, is usually measured in terms of the numbers of cattle owned. There is no way of knowing whether this was so in the Chalcolithic of the Negev, nor whether cattle and other domestic animals were owned by individuals, by families, by elite people or by a social group such as a tribe. Indeed cattle may have been part and parcel of the suite of farmyard animals and treated with no particular veneration. There is nothing in the faunal record at Gilat to suggest that cattle were held in high esteem.

The Utilization of Dead Animals at Gilat

Bone Element Analysis

The numbers of a selection of bone elements have been counted for each species represented by a large enough number of bone finds. The proximal and distal ends of most of the longbones (including loose epiphyses) have been counted separately, shafts lacking distal or proximal ends have been excluded and complete longbones have been counted twice—once for the proximal end and once for the distal end. Counts of mandibles and maxillae have been confined to fragments with teeth or alveoli. Scapula counts are confined to distal ends. All other bones used in element analysis have been counted on the basis of the total number of fragments.

Sheep and Goats

The representation of bone elements were calculated for all strata both separately and together (Table 6.15) and the results for all Strata together are shown in Fig. 6.15A. There was very little difference between the strata, but the bones from the burial pit (L. 1237 and 1357) differed from the remainder and have been plotted separately (Table 6.16 and Fig. 6.15B).

Figure 6.17A shows that all parts of the body are represented. The only sheep/goat bones to survive at a rate of more than 50% are the mandible, distal humerus and pelvis. There is a wide discrepancy in the numbers of the different elements. For example, there are 235 mandibular tooth-row fragments, but only 36 proximal tibiae. The difference between adjacent bones of the front limb is telling: 111 distal scapulas, 21 proximal humeri and 205 distal humeri, yet theoretically there should be the same number.

It is tempting to consider cultural reasons for this, such as butchery patterns and differential transport, but there are two simpler explanations. The first is that, despite sieving, there has been differential recovery with the smaller bones under-represented, for example only 135 middle phalanges of sheep/goats compared with 211 proximal phalanges. The second is that Fig. 6.18, which is a plot of the numbers of each element surviving plotted against its density (from Binford and Bertram 1977), shows that there is quite a close correlation (r=0.92), suggesting much differential destruction of the less dense elements.

The sheep/goat bones from the burial pit (L. 1237 and 1357) were plotted separately (Fig. 6.17B) as it was clear that several complete skeletons were, or had been, present. The distribution of survival rates is slightly more even than in the main body of data. Although there are still major discrepancies which can be accounted for by differential destruction and retrieval, the figure indicates a high proportion of bones of the feet and head, so it is possible that at least some of the material in the pit was deposited as feet and heads, that is, perhaps, as fleece or hide burials.

Cattle—Bone Element Analysis

The results of the bone element analysis of cattle are shown in Fig. 6.19A and Table 6.17. As the number of cattle bones in smaller diachronic or spatial units would have been too small for analysis, all bones from Strata IV-II were grouped together. All parts of the body are represented although in varying numbers. The only bones to survive at a rate of more than 50% are the mandible, distal humerus, proximal metacarpal, pelvis, calcaneum, astragalus and proximal and distal metatarsals. Although one would expect the distal scapulae, proximal humeri and distal humeri to be present in the same number, there were only two proximal humeri compared with 18 distal scapulae and 42 distal humeri. As distal humeri and scapulae are amongst the hardest bone elements and the proximal humerus is one of the softest, this suggests that the variations in number can be explained by differential destruction of the less dense bone elements of cattle. This means that there was no particular selection of body parts of cattle and the animals were probably killed at or near to the site. The same conclusion was reached in the analysis of the element distribution in sheep/goats and pigs.

Pigs

The most frequently occurring pig bones at Gilat are the bones of the skull, particularly the mandible (Table 6.18 and Fig. 6.19B). The only other bone elements to survive at a rate of more than 50% are the distal scapula and distal humerus. Again it seems likely that survival is related to density. The small numbers of the smaller bones may have been exacerbated by differential retrieval at excavation. If differential survival and retrieval did occur, virtually all parts of the body must have been represented, suggesting that the pigs were butchered at, or close to, the site.

As the sample consists largely of the bones of young animals it is probably not a coincidence that the most frequent long bone elements fuse at the age of about 12 months. It does seem that there has been large scale destruction of the softer bones and so the number of young pigs was probably rather greater than the numbers estimated from the surviving sample.

Conclusion—Bone Element Analysis

What we are looking for here is any suggestion that the pattern of representation is not related to normal taphonomic processes, but that particular parts of the body have been selected for deposition. Clearly this was not the case at Gilat where all parts of the body were originally deposited but have suffered varying degrees of post-depositional damage and attrition. It is probable that the sheep, goats, cattle and pigs were butchered at, or close to, the site.

Various factors can be surmised to have favoured the destruction of the less dense bone at Gilat: chewing by carnivores, especially dogs (Binford 1981), trampling by people, general disturbance of the deposits, destruction by humic acids, crushing by overburden, alternate drying and wetting, and alternate heating and cooling.

Body Part Analysis

A simpler method of investigating survival and representation of bones is to group all the bone finds into the area of the body from which they come and then to compare the results in the form of percentages for the taxon or stratigraphic unit being considered.

The body parts used are:

Cranial:	horncore, maxilla, other cranial parts, mandible
Teeth:	loose teeth
Trunk:	all vertebrae, sacrum, ribs
Forelimb:	scapula, humerus, radius, ulna
Hindlimb:	pelvis, femur, patella, tibia
Feet:	wrist, astragalus, calcaneum, navicular and other ankle bones, including fibula, metapodials and phalanges.

The results of grouping the bones of the three main domestic ungulates into body parts are given in Fig. 6.20. There seems to be no particular emphasis on one part of the body compared with another, but the high figures for loose teeth, particularly for sheep and goats, reflects the high degree of post-depositional damage established by the bone element analysis. The sheep/goat bones from the burial pit (L. 1237 and 1357) were counted separately from the remainder in Stratum 2 and show a much lower proportion of loose teeth and a higher proportion of bones of the feet, showing that there has been less damage than usual to the bones in the pit and suggesting that extra feet were deposited there. This is discussed further in the section on special finds below.

The Provision of Meat

Table 6.19 and Fig. 6.21 show the relative numbers of domestic ungulates at Gilat corrected in the manner already described. Equids have been excluded they would probably have been used for transport rather than food; however they are so few in number that their inclusion or exclusion makes very little difference to the proportions.

It can be seen that in terms of numbers the ungulate profile is dominated by sheep and goats, which together constitute 71% of the sample, followed by 15% of cattle and 14% of pigs. However when the relative numbers are translated into meat weights (Fig. 6.20), this situation is drastically altered with cattle contributing roughly 56% of the meat consumed at Gilat, with sheep and goat about 17.5% each and pigs 9%. It is not, of course, possible to quantify the contribution of each species' milk to the diet, but it must be remembered that if cows were milked, the yield per individual female would have been much greater than for sheep or goats, also as Dahl and Hjort (1976) point out the milk yield of cattle is more reliable than that of goats and considerably more so than that of sheep. Sheep and goats would also have contributed fibres, but the amount of leather from cattle would have been greater.

It was concluded above that cattle, sheep and goats almost certainly provided milk as well as meat and that sheep were also kept for wool. The contribution of pigs seems to have been minimal, perhaps they were kept for variety of taste and as providers of fat. Thus there was a truly mixed domestic animal economy at Gilat, in which cattle played the dominant role.

Feasting and Ritual?

The use of Gilat for secular activities is attested by the evidence of hearths, bone tools and domestic and craft items. However since Gilat appears to have had a cultic function as well, people may also have been taking part in ceremonial activity. Do the ungulates provide any support for this idea? In particular is there any evidence for feasting at Gilat?

It is often supposed that piglets raised on a large scale were an element in communal feasting, since they could so easily be replaced. However the counter argument, rather better documented in ethnographic studies (Dahl and Hjort 1976; Evans-Pritchard 1940; Russell n.d.), is that cattle were often kept not merely for prestige but also for feasting, since their large body size means that the meat has to be shared by a large number of people if it is not to be wasted. Nevertheless cattle remains are found in most periods on most archaeological sites even where there is no indication of ceremony, and of course the same is true of pigs. Analysis of the ageing patterns of pigs' jaws can sometimes be used to suggest periodicity of pig slaughter (Grigson 1989c), but the rather limited data from Gilat set out in Fig. 6.14B suggest year-round slaughter. The age profiles of all the ungulates correspond to what might be expected in terms of raising animals for economic purposes, so while feasting may indeed have taken place, the ageing profiles provide no evidence for it.

Another parameter that might be of significance here is the side of the body that the bones come from. In a few instances it has been shown that deposits have contained more bones of one side or the other and this is interpreted as having a ritual significance. Table 6.20 shows that there were nearly equal numbers of bones of each side for the main ungulate taxa and that there were no differences either between species nor within the main strata as a whole.

Cooking

That food was cooked at Gilat is suggested by the presence of so many hearths and animal bones, but there is no evidence as to how it was done. Table 6.21 shows that about 7% of the domestic ungulate bones were burnt, but in almost all cases the entire element was charred and this probably relates to the deliberate or accidental disposal of unwanted bone in fires. There is no indication that bones were partially burnt in the manner suggestive of roasting (Vigne & Marinval Vigne 1983), though such signs could have been obscured by later breakage and burning.

Butchery and Skinning

The bones at Gilat were so broken and so fragile that it was not possible to make a systematic study of patterns of dismemberment and deliberate breakage, although chopmarks were sometimes obvious. Transverse chopping of three axis bones of sheep/goats may relate to decapitation, but whether in slaughtering or in removal of the head in butchery is unclear. The vertical splitting of some of the longbones mentioned below may indicate the extraction of marrow.

As the surface of most of the bones was covered with concretions of calcium carbonate or gypsum or both, it was not possible to quantify cutmarks. However, they were occasionally noted and seem to be particularly prevalent on ankle bones where they may relate to skinning. Animal skins and leather must have been an enormously important resource at Gilat as indicated by the numerous flint scrapers described in Chapter 11 (this volume).

Hornworking

Horn does not survive on archaeological sites in the area around Gilat, but there is indirect evidence for the working of horns of goats and sheep and perhaps cattle at the site. Many of the cranial fragments and detached horncores of sheep and goats at Gilat had chop marks around the base of the cores suggesting that they had been deliberately removed, presumably for the utilization of the horn. As well as three horncore fragments there were three cattle horncore bases, all were damaged and showed no signs of horn removal, but their rarity in the assemblage perhaps indicates that cattle horns were processed away from the site. None of the gazelle horncores, including those in the cache in the 'multi-purpose pit' (L. 1344) which are described below, showed any sign of horn removal. Horns and horn itself as a raw material must have had a wide variety of uses which we can now only guess at. However it is likely that the famous Chalcolithic cornets were skuamorphs of horns and it is likely that both cornets and horns had a ceremonial function relating to the manipulation of liquids.

Bone Industry

Bone of certain elements, usually metapodials, radii, tibiae and ribs, is in itself a useful raw material for the manufacture of certain tools, particularly those employed in weaving. The bone tools from Gilat are described in Chapter 13 (this volume). But it is worth noting here that some of the bones from Gilat had been split vertically. This is not something that occurs in the natural processes of decay nor is it caused by dogs or scavengers; it may relate to the extraction of marrow, or an early stage in the manufacture of tools.

Conclusions—The Utilization of Dead Animals at Gilat

It is clear that as well as providing food the carcasses of domestic ungulates at Gilat were put to a wide variety of purposes, many of which we can only guess at, but which testify to the great importance of animals as multiple resources in the economy, and perhaps the ritual life, of the people of Gilat (see below).

Dogs

There were two spectacular finds of dog remains at Gilat, both in the same large pit (L. 698 and 692, Sub-stratum IIAi, Area T—see Plate), and include a skull and an articulated skeleton from a different animal. The cultural connotations of these finds are discussed with other special finds towards the end of this chapter and in different parts of this book (Chapters 1, 15, 16).

GIL91 139 was a complete skeleton from a dog burial; a very rare occurrence at such an early period. However, impregnation with gypsum crystals made it very fragile and consequently it was much damaged in excavation. Some of the bones, especially the smaller ones, were lost in excavation, but most of the missing bones were retrieved by sieving. It was from a very old animal, all the cranial sutures were fused (except the inter-nasal and interpalatal), and all the teeth were very worn with much exposure of dentine exposed. The cranium is shown in Plate 6.2a. As in most dogs the lower P4 and M1 overlapped slightly. The left ulna and radius (Plate 6.2b) were damaged in life by what appears to be an unhealed fracture with the marked osteitis. However the bones of the wrist and foot were still present. The survival of the animal after such trauma suggests that it received special care from the inhabitants of Gilat.

GIL91 138 was a nearly complete dog skull from the same locus. It was from a very old animal, all the cranial sutures were fused except the inter-nasal and inter-palatal. Although the mandible articulates with cranium, they were not in articulation when found. The posterior part of the mandible (Plate 6.2c) was damaged in antiquity. The lower P4 and M1 overlap. All the teeth in both jaws were very worn with much exposure of dentine.

As well as the complete skull and skeleton there were four other skulls which were probably complete when first exposed and about 55 other dog bones from various parts of the body were scattered through the deposits. The numbers found in each stratum are set out in Table 6.1 and all the dog bone and tooth measurements in Appendix 6.6.

Analysis of the absolute sizes of the various skulls (Appendix 6.6B and Table 6.22) at Gilat suggests that they were of dogs of medium size, similar to or perhaps slightly smaller than those from the Natufian studied by Tchernov and Valla (1997)—although the mean sizes are less, the differences are not statistically significant—and similar to Neolithic dogs at Jericho (Dayan 1994). Wapnish and Hesse (1993) in their excellent review of dog burials in Middle Eastern sites show that the same seems to have been true of Persian period dogs at Ashkelon and most dogs in other sites, for example Tell Brak in Iraq in the Akkadian (Clutton-Brock 1989).

Two craniometric indices based on those set out by Harcourt (1974), the 'snout index' (the length from the nasion to alveolare divided by the total length of the skull (that is von den Driesch's (1976) measurement no.8 x 100 / no.1), and the 'snout width index' (the width of the muzzle relative to its length (no.36 x 100 / no.8)), were calculated on the one complete enough skull (GIL91 138). They were 50.4 and 41.0 respectively and indicate an unspecialised dog with quite a broad snout of moderate length, similar in form to that of British dogs described by Harcourt as 'plain dog'.

An estimate of the shoulder height of the complete dog skeleton (GIL91 139) can be made using the indices employed by Harcourt (1974) in his study of early dogs in Britain (Table 6.23). The heights calculated from the lengths of the various longbones of this skeleton vary from 53.7–55.0cm with a mean value of 54.1cm.

Wing (1978) has established that it is also possible to estimate body weight from various mandibular measurements. The only suitable measurement for the Gilat material is the length of the lower molar row and the results shown in Table 6.24 indicate weights of 12.1 to 15.1 kg for GIL91 139.

Although Clutton-Brock (1989) believed that the Tell Brak dog had some affinity with the Saluki, it differed from it in not having widely spaced teeth and Wapnish and Hesse (1993) have shown that all the Middle Eastern dogs whose descriptions had been published differed in this and in other respects from the Saluki skeletons available for comparison. Neither the Gilat dog skulls, nor most of those from other archaeological sites in the Middle East, have any particular distinguishing characteristics and they probably resembled the ordinary pariah dogs still found around some villages in the Middle East, or in Harcourt's words, they were just 'plain dogs'.

No cutmarks were observed on the dog bones from Gilat, though they might have been obscured by calcium carbonate, and although many were broken the damage usually appears to be post-depositional, so it seems unlikely that dogs were eaten or butchered. The incidence of burnt dog bones rises as high as 8% in Stratum II, but is zero in Strata IV and III. However, the sample sizes are small so this is probably not significant. Whether the burning was post-depositional or deliberate is uncertain, but certainly none of the skulls was burnt.

Although gnaw marks were not quantified because the surface of most of the bones was obscured by deposits of calcium carbonate and other salts, they were recognized on many of the ungulate and other animal bones from Gilat. Similarly many of the longbones of the smaller ungulates had been reduced to bone cylinders, produced when the ends of the bones, which are softer than the shafts, had been chewed off. This indicates that dogs made a substantial contribution to the destruction of the softer bone elements as noted above.

As well as the bones affected by dog gnawing, at least ten small bones of sheep/goats had eroded surfaces, probably caused by passing through a dog's gut (Payne & Munson 1985), so dogs must have been allowed to scavenge around the site, feeding on discarded animal waste.

Whether dogs were simply scavengers like the pariah dogs of villages in the Middle East or whether they were used in hunting, herding or guarding is not possible to say. However dog burial and the heads suggest that some of the dogs had a ceremonial or totemistic role in the lives of the people at Gilat.

Wild Animals

Gazelles (Gazella sp.)

There were 116 gazelle bones at Gilat, including 23 less certainly identified. Two species of gazelle inhabit the southern Levant, the mountain gazelle (*Gazella gazella*) and the dorcas gazelle (*G. dorcas*). The dorcas gazelle is common in the vicinity of Gilat today, whilst the mountain gazelle lives further to the north. It is thought that *dorcas* was a relatively late immigrant to the Middle East from Africa, so it is of some interest to discover whether it was already present during the Chalcolithic. It has been claimed that the two species can be distinguished on the basis of their horncore morphology (Tchernov, Dayan, & Yom-Tov 1986/7). A very careful comparison of the many surviving horncores from Gilat with those of modern specimens of *Gazella gazella* and *G. dorcas* in the Department of Evolution, Systematics and Ecology of the Hebrew University in Jerusalem showed that the main distinguishing character, the presence and absence of vertical grooves in anterior and posterior surfaces of the horncores, are variable in both of the modern species and in those from Gilat. Another character which might be of some use is that the horncores of *dorcas* tend to be rounder in cross-section than those of *gazella*. Figure 6.23A shows that some of those from Gilat resemble *dorcas*, others resemble *gazella* and others are intermediate. This does not mean that both species were present at Gilat merely that there was a continuous range of variation in this character. A horncore of a male gazelle from Gilat is shown in Fig. 6.24A.

As the dorcas gazelle is smaller in the body than the mountain gazelle the size of the post-cranial bones might be a distinguishing feature, but with very few published measurements of dorcas gazelles, either past or present, it is not possible to apply this criterion to the Gilat bones. The gazelle bones from Gilat are of much the same size as those of modern mountain gazelles (data from Kolska-Horwitz, pers. comm.). The measurements the gazelle bones from Gilat are given in Appendix 6.7.

Table 6.25 and Fig. 6.22B show that although most parts of the body were represented, horncores were by far the most numerous, giving an MNI of 12. The mandible and the tibia are the next most frequent bone elements. The bias towards horncores was caused by one of the most spectacular of the animal bone finds at Gilat—nine burnt horncores of male gazelles retrieved from the 'multi-use pit' L. 1344 (Sub-stratum IIBi, Area J). Some were in the form of frontlets and all of them were probably deposited with intact hornsheaths; they may be the remains of complete gazelle heads. Their cultural connotations are discussed towards the end of this chapter. Many of the other gazelle bones in Strata III and II were also burnt and Table 6.21 shows that the total proportion of burnt bone of gazelles (19.1%) is much higher than that of the domestic ungulates (7.4%), a difference which is statistically highly significant. So it is probable that other parts of the body, as well as the heads, were deliberately burnt, but the charred remains have become dispersed in the various contexts at Gilat.

One gazelle bone, a middle phalanx showed signs of exostosis, probably due to old age.

Wild ox (*Bos primigenius*)

Six bone finds were identified as *Bos primigenius* on account of their very large size, a lower third molar, two distal humeri, a distal metacarpal, a middle phalanx, and a proximal and distal phalanx that appear to be from the same foot. Measurements are included with those of domestic cattle in Appendix 6.3.

Hartebeest (*Alcelaphus* sp.)

As well as two bones definitely identified as hartebeest there are three bones of large bovids which are too small even for domestic *Bos*. The definite hartebeest bones are a lumbar vertebra (GIL90 3786) and a distal phalanx. The less definite identifications are two more distal phalanges and the unfused distal condyles of a metacarpal. The measurements are given in Appendix 6.8.

Wild caprid—ibex? (*Capra ibex?*)

A very large proximal phalanx (GIL92 6413) was tentatively identified as that of an ibex or wild goat. If is from a wild animal, it is more likely to have been from an ibex since it is that taxon which is found today in the southern Levant, although now confined to a few isolated places—Ein Gedi in the Judean Desert and Avdat in the Central Negev. However, it may actually stem from a very large domestic male. A large upper third molar, which could only be identified as sheep/goat may have been from a wild animal.

Wild boar (*Sus scrofa*)

Only one bone was identified as wild boar and that only doubtfully on the basis of its very large size. It was a femur shaft cylinder (GIL90 1396) in L. 588, a fill in Stratum IIB, Area J. There was a population of wild boar in the marshes to the south of the Dead Sea and they are found further north. It is probable that they inhabited the lusher wadis of the Negev in the Chalcolithic, if and when shade and wallow were plentiful.

Hippotamus (*Hippopotamus amphibius*)

A small piece of tusk which had been both gnawed and cut was tentatively identified as hippotamus ivory. If correct this may well be of local origin since a bone of a hippopotamus was identified at Qatif Y2, a Chalcolithic site near the mouth of the Besor (Grigson 1984) and several finds along the coastal plain attest to their presence until the Iron Age (Horwitz & Tchernov 1990). [3]

Wild Canids

Although dogs (see above), jackals, red foxes and Ruppell's sand foxes have all been identified at Gilat, several bones could only be identified as canid. Measurements of canid bones are included in Appendix 6.8.

A proximal phalanx was identified as jackal (*Canis aureus*) bone on account of its size and the same is probably true of two other proximal phalanges.

Ten bone finds were identified as being from foxes: a pelvis and an articulating radius and ulna from Ruppell's sand fox (*V. ruppellii*) and at least two, a mandible and a distal humerus, of the red fox (*Vulpes vulpes*). It is probable that those identified only as *Vulpes* sp. also derive from the red fox. Both animals are widely distributed today, although Ruppell's sand fox is confined to desert environments.

Hyena (*Hyaena cf hyaena*)

There was one bone of a presumably striped hyena: the distal end of a scapula. Its measurement is included in Appendix 6.8.

Felidae

Several bones of cats were found at Gilat including four small fragments retrieved by sieving. They could only be distinguished on the basis of size. An ulna, a metatarsal and a middle phalanx probably derive from the wild cat (*Felis silvestris*) and two slightly larger proximal ulnae were probably of the same species. One much larger bone, a proximal tibia, may be of a caracal (*F. caracal*). Wild cats are or were common throughout the Levant in various habitats, but the caracal is a desert animal, found occasionally in the Negev and more rarely further north (Harrison and Bates 1991). Measurements of felid bones are included in Appendix 6.8.

Ostrich (*Struthio camelus*)

Two ostrich bones were found at Gilat—the distal half of a femur with the distal epiphysis fused (GIL90 4048) in L. 553 (a probe in Stratum III, Area Y), and a proximal phalanx in L. 1554 (a pit in Stratum IIC/3A, Area T) which had been gnawed. The measurements of the ostrich phalanx is included in Appendix 6.8.

As well as the bones there was a cache of four ostrich eggs, each with a drilled hole, in L. 1167 (Sub-stratum IIC, Area J)—a small pit sealed by the Stratum IIC plaza surface for which they may have been a foundation deposit (Fig. 5.40).

Although the presence of ostriches is quite frequently attested by fragments of their eggs in archaeological sites in the Negev, ostrich bones are very rare, although I identified one in a previously unopened box of animal bones from Bir es-Safadi. This is curious as ostriches make good eating and the bones of the legs and feet are extremely solid. The bone seems to be very fine-grained and dense and I suspect that it was sought after as material for tool making (Chapter 13, this volume).

Although one would assume that any ostrich in this area was of the small Syrian species *Struthio camelus syriacus*, Watson, Hesse and Wapnish (n.d.) have shown that ostrich vertebrae found in Late Bronze Age levels at Tel Jemmeh near the mouth of the Nahal Besor were so large that they probably derived from the larger North African form, *S. camelus camelus*. It is on record that the last known individual ostrich in the Middle East was drowned in a flood in Jordan in AD 1966 (Jennings 1986).

Other Wild Animals

The bones of other birds, small mammals, reptiles, amphibians and fish are noted in Table 6.1, but have not been studied further; the small mammals, reptiles and amphibians were probably accidentally incorporated into the deposits.

The Role of Hunting at Gilat

It is clear from Table 6.26 that with a total percentage of wild mammals of 2.2% and 0.03% of ostrich bones, hunting played a very minor role in the economy at Gilat, and with 0.8% of other birds and 1.3% of fish it is apparent that birding and fishing were also almost negligible. Preliminary investigations show that at least a few of the fish were marine and so could not have been caught in the vicinity of the site. Perhaps they were acquired along with marine molluscs (Chapter 7, this volume).

However, 116 of the 151 wild mammal bones were from gazelles and it was a cache of gazelle's horns, or heads, which received such special treatment in L. 1344. The ostrich eggs in L. would have been collected from nests, but they too represent some sort of obsequy to the wild.

Environmental Implications of the Gilat Fauna

The Modern Environment

The area around Gilat lies on the junction between three major climatic and vegetational zones: Mediterranean woodland to the north, Turano-Iranian steppe to the East and Saharo-Arabian Desert to the south and west. Small changes in rainfall produce wide latitudinal shifts in isohyets. Annual rainfall in the north western Negev is very variable, but averages about 220 mm at Gilat. The most significant environmental feature is Gilat's location at the interface between the Negev coastal plain and the northern Negev inland foothill zone (see Chapter 1, this volume).

The Gilat Fauna

Although it is uncertain whether the gazelles at Gilat were *G. dorcas* or *G. gazella*, their presence and that of ostriches and hartebeests together with the total absence of deer suggests quite a dry, open environment, not unlike that of today. The definite identifications of Ruppell's sand fox suggest dry and perhaps even desertic conditions.

However, the well-known Neolithic wet phase in North Africa of the fifth and fourth millennia almost certainly extended into the southern Levant. As well as the geomorphological evidence of Goldberg (1987) and Goldberg and Rosen (1987), there is some faunal evidence for wetter local conditions in the Chalcolithic (Grigson 1987a): catfish bones in the Besor site A (Roshwalb 1981) and soft-shelled turtle and hippopotamus at Qatif (Y2) near the coast (Grigson 1984); all of which require permanent fresh water. The fish bone assemblage at Gilat included catfish, perhaps caught in the nearby Nahal Patish.

On the other hand, it is the domestic animals in particular the pigs, that produce the most critical information about the local environment in the Chalcolithic. Pigs, both wild and domestic, have quite distinct environmental tolerances, they cannot take temperatures in excess of 35 degrees centigrade, unless they can compensate for their inability to sweat by wallowing in water or mud (Mount 1968; Hone and O'Grady 1980). Even when water and mud are available in hot climates pigs will seek the shade of trees, bushes or tall reeds during the heat of the day, emerging only in the early morning and evening to forage for food (Diener and Robkin 1978). Thus while wild pigs in the Middle East are most common in areas of moderate and high rainfall (Harrison 1968; Harrington 1977; Hatt 1959), they are also found in damp micro-climates in dry areas where there is lush vegetation. They are sometimes seen in open country (Hatt 1959; Harrison 1968; Hart 1891; Tristram 1866), but they soon return to shaded areas, so their presence at Gilat in the Chalcolithic indicates at least some dense vegetation in the vicinity, probably reeds and trees perhaps in the nearby Nahal Pattish, suggesting environment conditions moister than today. Today, wild pigs are quite common in the Jordan valley riverine microenvironment (Levy, pers. Observation).

It is of some significance that pigs are entirely absent from the Chalcolithic sites around Beer-sheva less than 16 km to the south at Shiqmim, and somewhat further at the Beersheva sites of Abu Matar and Bir-es Safadi (Grigson 1995a). Whether the explanation is a simple environmental one or whether social factors have played a part has yet to be decided, but it should be noted that in the fifth and fourth millennia most archaeological sites in the Middle East which are in areas with more rain than 350 mm a year have domestic pigs, whereas those in drier areas do not (Grigson, in prep).

Deposition and Disposal

'Special' Loci—Finds of Animal Skulls and Articulated Bones

Individual loci whose contents differ significantly from the general patterns may help to differentiate past activities at the site. It was not practical to carry out separate analyses on each individual locus, but all those with 10 or more bones which could be assigned to context, were tested for variations in representation. Although Table 6.27 shows that there was considerable variability, none of the differences were statistically significant.

Individual loci with 'special finds' which appear to be in primary deposition are perhaps indicative of special human behaviour, since it is reasonable to assume that they have been deliberately deposited. The criteria by which most special finds of bones are designated as such are a degree of completeness showing that the bone has not been broken before deposition (this applies particularly to skulls when separated from the rest of the skeleton) and when a group of bones within the same locus appears to be from the same animal or part of an animal, particularly when they were in articulation in the ground, indicating that they were held together by ligaments and probably also muscle and skin.

L. 698 and 692 (Sub-stratum IIIAi, Area T) together constituted a large pit (Chapter 5, this volume) which contained a complete, articulated skeleton of a dog (GIL91 139), the remains of a deliberately buried animal, as well as a complete cranium and mandible from another dog's skull (GIL91 138). The skeleton lay in a depression accompanied by a double-handled cylindrical ceramic vessel that was place near the dog's hind feet (Fig. 6.3B; see Chapters 9 and 10, this volume, for discussion of this vessel). The cranium and mandible lay nearby at the same level. Both the skull and the skeleton were from very old animals. In the skeleton, the left ulna and radius had been very damaged in life by what appeared to be an unhealed fracture which led to massive osteitis, but the ankle and the foot bones were present, suggesting that the animal had been well cared for from the time when its leg was broken until its death, months or even years later. A more detailed description of the bones themselves has been given above. It is likely that the skeleton was buried as a complete carcass of a dog and this skull, as well as those mentioned below, as a complete head severed from the body making it a 'double dog' burial.

L. 1167 (Sub-stratum IIC, Area J)—a small pit sealed by the Stratum IIC plaza surface—four entire ostrich eggs (Fig. 5.40) in what is thought to have been a foundation deposit associated with the Stratum IIC plaza. Other pits associated with the plaza contained a wide variety of ritual objects (Chapter 5, this volume).

L. 1237 and 1357 (Sub-stratum IIBi, Area J)—the mass burial pit. This pit which has already been mentioned several times contained the remains of at least 9 sheep/goats, including at least 6 individual goats and one sheep, as well as an unusually high proportion of bones of the feet of sheep and goats (see Fig. 6.15B) and some bones of cattle (Fig. 6.26). They were found in a shallow pit resembling a silo lined with mud-brick, paved with stone and used as a mortuary facility. The carcasses and feet were lying on a thin layer of silt overlying the floor and under a layer of ash. The contents of the pit are shown in Chapter 5 (Fig. 5.19, 5.20). The remains of nine human corpses were deposited on top of the ash.

L. 1344 (Sub-stratum IIBi, Area J)—the 'multi-use' pit near the mortuary facility mentioned abouve, contained one of the most interesting of the special finds of animal remains - a group of 9 horncores of male gazelles. They were situated at the base of the pit in an ash fill together with bone tools, a crude figurine of a sheep (see Chapter 15, this volume) and a fenestrated stand (Plate 6.5a–b), all sealed beneath a clay cap. They had all been burnt and some were still attached to the frontal bones, forming frontlets, it is likely that they were deposited with intact hornsheaths which were destroyed by fire, as well as skin. They might even be the remains of complete gazelle heads, the remainder of the skull having been destroyed by fire. Stordeur (1988) has established a sequence of colour change in bone when subject to different temperatures and she found that it burns black between 525–625°C—so these remains and the bone tools found with them must have been exposed to very great heat; one wonders how it was produced. Clearly as pointed out in Chapter 5 (this volume), these items represent a ritual or symbolic act, perhaps related to hunting. Bones of wild animals are infrequent at Gilat and although most parts of the body of the gazelle are represented their horncores outnumber all other types of bone element (see below).

Loci with other rather less spectacular special deposits of animal remains are listed below:

L. 13 (Sub-stratum IIB, Area M)—an ashy area—a damaged dog's cranium (GIL90 3868)—see Plate 6.6a.

L. 70 (Sub-stratum IIC, Area D)—a floor—a very damaged goat's skull (GIL87 704-707).

L. 553 (Stratum III, Area Y), a probe, contained the damaged remains of a dog's cranium (GIL90 3136 and 3143). The probe revealed two small pits cut into the fill of a much larger one, possibly a pit house, but the exact location of the skull was not recorded. The presence of an ostrich bone in the same locus is notable as they occur so rarely.

L. 671 (Sub-stratum IIC, Area T)—a small pit cut into the large pit (L. 698) with the dog's skeleton referred to above, contained what appears to have been the complete skeleton of a goat (GIL91 1039-1055).

L. 674 (Sub-stratum IIBii, Area T)—the skeleton of a very young lamb or kid (GIL91 2010-2014 & 2020-2022)

L. 773 (Sub-stratum IIA, Area T)—a pit—contained what was probably once an intact ox skull (GIL92 4211-4214), one of only two finds of cattle which might be considered special.

L. 787 (Sub-stratum IIBii, Area T)—a pit—a damaged dog's cranium (GIL92 2302) see Plate 6.6b.

L. 828 (Sub-stratum IIBi, Area J)—a pit—a damaged dog's cranium (GIL90 3232).

L. 1128 (Sub-stratum IIC, Area J)—a pit filled with ash and animal bones, contained the complete hindleg of an ox (GIL91 495-505).

L. 1168 (Sub-stratum IIC, Area J)—a pit—a complete, articulated skeleton of a piglet (GIL91 407) shown in Plate 6.7a and the skull in close-up in Plate 6.7b. Although this is only special find of a pig it indicates that pigs as well as other ungulates could have special significance.

L. 1369 (Sub-stratum IIIA, Area J)—a well-constructed silo—a damaged sheep's skull, GIL92 3383-3387.

L. 1522 (Sub-stratum IICii, Area T)—a pit—a very broken goat's skull (GIL92 3419-3421).

Totem, Cult, Ceremony

Although it is difficult to be certain of their significance the special finds may indicate some kind of formalised symbolic behaviour. As pointed out by Levy (1991) this must certainly have been true of the dog skeleton and dog skull as they were associated with a double-handled cylindrical ceramic vessel which probably had a ceremonial purpose.

The deposit of charred gazelle horncores and frontlets, which seems to represent the deliberate burning of a large number of gazelle heads and which were associated with a fenestrated stand, other loci with collections of sheep and goat bones probably the remains of entire skins, and the special cache of ostrich eggs must also be of ceremonial or ritual significance.

The complete ungulate skeletons were probably deposited as entire carcasses; they all seem to have been of young animals (sheep, goats and pigs) and it is possible that they simply represent the disposal and immediate burial of unwanted corpses. Whether such disposal would take place within the site is arguable. It may be by chance that the skulls listed above survive in their entirety through protection from damage by immediate burial of discarded animal heads, though the reasons for doing this are not obvious.

The special finds encompass several of the domestic animal species present at Gilat so they do not indicate veneration for any particular taxon and cannot be regarded as totemistic. However the animal figurines found suggest that this may not be the case for two of the wild animals.

Gilat produced a modest corpus of small, crude and damaged, zoomorphic figurines (see Chapter 15, this volume), of which two appeared to be of sheep, one of a bull and one probably of a pig; in addition two small clay horn fragments were identified as gazelle and ibex. A ram's head made from basalt was recovered at Gilat (Chapter 15, this volume). In such a small sample the absence of goats, dogs and equids cannot be taken as significant and, with one exception, the taxonomic composition of the figurine assemblage seems to correspond roughly with that of the animal bones, reflecting the importance of the living animals in the ritual, as well as the economic life of the inhabitants. The exception is the ibex horn, since only two bones could possibly have been from ibex. It is not possible to distinguish between the bones of ibex (*Capra ibex*) and wild goats (*C. hircus*), except for the horncores of males, but a few bones have been found on some sites in the Negev, which are identified as ibex rather than goat, since it is that taxon which is found today in the area, although now confined to a few isolated places such as Ein Gedi and Avdat. Nevertheless ibex certainly had a ritual or perhaps magic role in the Chalcolithic of the Southern Levant, as models of their heads and horns, and in one instance two complete animals joined together, decorate many of the ritual copper artefacts from the Cave of the Treasure (Nahal Mishmar) (Bar-Adon 1980). Ibex horns are also depicted on some of the Chalcolithic ossuaries found on the coastal plain (Perrot and Ladiray 1980:113). The presence of the small clay ibex horn at Gilat may reflect this connection with the Judean Desert sites as does the composition of some of the pottery (see Chapters 9 and 10, this volume).

The importance of gazelles in the Gilat ritual bestiary is manifest not only from the collection of burnt horns in the multi-purpose pit (L. 1344) but also by the presence of the small clay gazelle horn. As with ibex their importance seems to have been disproportionate to the number of their bones in the ordinary domestic assemblage. A gazelle's head is clearly depicted in the famous star fresco at Teleilat Ghassul near the Dead Sea excavated in 1932 and described in the report as 'un dragon' (Mallon et al 1934:139 and frontispiece). Also at Ghassul, but from the 1936 excavations, was a pot with two animal heads attached to the outer surface below the rim, believed by Koeppel to represent gazelles, although from the illustration they might equally be goats (Koeppel 1940: p. 84, plate 197).

Conclusions—Farming? Feasting? Herding?

It seems that secondary products were indeed utilized at Gilat, but the notion of a 'Secondary Products Revolution' (Sherratt 1981, 1983) depends on establishing whether animal management changed over time and whether it happened quickly enough to be termed revolutionary. In particular we need to know whether the herding practices in the Chalcolithic differed from those in the preceding Pottery Neolithic. Unfortunately there are only a few excavated sites of the Late Neolithic period in the southern Levant (Banning 1998; Garfinkel 1997, 1999) and none of them have large enough assemblages for the establishment of ageing or sexing profiles (Davis, pers. comm; Horwitz 1987, 1988; Ducos 1968; Jarman 1974; Grigson 1984).

It is necessary to heed Halstead's (1996) warning in his discussion of animal husbandry in the Neolithic and Bronze Age of Greece of the dangers of imposing modern patterns of husbandry on the distant past. As there is both direct and indirect evidence for the production and consumption of plant foods at Gilat and at Grar, and for the use of a wide range of both primary and secondary products derived from several different species of domestic animal, including pigs, it is clear that the economic system of the inhabitants of these sites cannot be described as 'specialized pastoralism', still less 'nomadic pastoralism', a conclusion also reached for Grar by the excavator (Gilead 1992, 1995). The discovery of many small transitory Chalcolithic sites in parts of the area (Gilead and Goren 1986) suggests a degree of movement of sheep and goats and some of the people around the local landscape. So the economy should be seen as mixed farming more akin to the agricultural system of the fellahin than the Bedouin. It may be that Levy's (1992) theory of 'specialized pastoralism' in the Chalcolithic will hold true of sites which are notable for the absence of pigs, such as Shiqmim and Abu Matar, Horvat Beter, Bir es-Safadi and Qatif Y2, but this still remains to be established.

Although one would expect a reflection of ritual as well as secular behaviour in the animal bone assemblage at Gilat in the form of inclusion or exclusion of particular species or bone elements in particular structures or areas of the site, none was found. What we have is a normal domestic assemblage representing the preparation and consumption of food, with the discarded remains being spread about the site in a haphazard manner. However in addition to this habitation debris, there were a few deliberate deposits which were still in primary deposition; most of these 'special finds' consisted of what were probably entire heads, though there were also some complete skeletons of very young sheep, goats and pigs. Only four finds were unequivocally special, and all were in Stratum II: the dog skeleton and dog skull associated with a double-handled cylindrical ceramic vessel, a deposit of charred gazelle horncores and frontlets, the collection of sheep and goat bones suggesting deposition of entire skins, and the cache of ostrich eggs. These apparent offerings represent brief individual episodes of human activity, *'evenements'* in Braudel's terminology (Levy and Holl 1995), or particular human behaviours in particular time and space. They were extraordinary events, probably of ritual significance, embedded within the vestiges of ordinary domestic activity. This dichotomy is also apparent in other classes of find at Gilat, for example the pottery assemblage with both domestic wares and ritual objects (Chapter 10, this volume) and the bone tools (Chapter 13, this volume). It is this combination of the ordinary and the extraordinary which characterises the site of Gilat.

Acknowledgments

All the faunal remains from Gilat are housed in the stores of the Israel Antiquities Authority in Jerusalem. I thank Tom Levy for giving me the opportunity to attend the excavations at Gilat, for allowing me to study the fauna and for his patience in awaiting the final typescript. My heartfelt thanks to Professor Eitan Tchernov (deceased), Dr Rivka Rabinovitz, Liora Kolska-Horwitz and many others whose inestimable kindness and support whilst I was studying the fauna in the Department of Evolution, Systematics and Ecology in the Hebrew University Jerusalem, made this work not only possible, but also immensely rewarding. My work in Jerusalem was also facilitated by the British School of Archaeology in Jerusalem.

Notes

1.   Editorial note: Diachronic studies of faunal assemblages are rare for Chalcolithic Palestine. Most studies treat the entire assemblage as one unit of analysis. Thus, the data presented here can more readily be compared with other sites. On the other hand, in the future, more elaborate statistical analyses of the fauna data presented here may yield new insights on the economy and use of animals at Gilat.

2.   Levy *et al.* in Chapter 14 distinguish 2 general sizes of spindle whorls which may reflect spinning of wool with the larger ones and spinning of flax with the smaller ones.

3.   Editor's note: It is also possible that the hippopotamus teeth were traded from the Nile valley/delta area.

Table 6.1. The vertebrate remains identified at Gilat.

	Stratum IV	Stratum III				Stratum III/II	Stratum II					Strata IV-II
		IIIB	IIIA	III	All III		IIC	IIB	IIA	II+IIB/C	All II	totals
domestic												
bos + bos? + lm	35	36	150	36	222	13	277	227	143	40	687	957
goat	5	11	39	17	67		70	109	41	1	221	293
sheep	14	19	46	11	76		90	73	44	4	211	301
sheep/goat	126	171	465	223	859	25	915	1090	650	112	2767	3777
pig + pig?	32	54	114	42	210	14	253	164	151	30	598	854
medium mammal	2	23	47	23	93		55	106	62	16	239	334
equid							4	2	3	1	10	10
donkey							1	1			2	2
horse			1	1	2							2
dog + dog?	1	5	11	6	22		12	14	7	4	37	60
total domestic	215	319	873	359	1551	52	1677	1786	1101	208	4772	6590
wild												
wild cattle		1	2		3		3	1	1		5	7
goat? wild?				1	1							1
sheep/goat wild?			1		1		1	4			5	6
hartebeest				1	1							1
gazelle+gazelle?	2	6	12	3	21	3	28	37	24	3	92	116
pig wild?								1			1	1
hippopotamus								1			1	1
jackal								1			1	1
fox		2	1		3			3	1		4	7
fox, red							1				1	1
fox, ruppell's							2				2	2
hyaena								1			1	1
Felis libyca			1	1	2			2	1	1	3	6
F. caracal?								1			1	1
ostrich											2	2
bird + bird?	1	0	2	5	7		23	14	12	0	49	57
fish + fish?		0	7	2	9		29	42	8	1	80	89
total wild	3	9	26	13	48	3	87	108	46	5	246	300
miscellaneous												
rodent								1			1	1
Meriones sp.									1		1	1
small mammal		1	1	1	3		2	7	8		17	20
reptile?			1	1			3	2	1	1	7	8
tortoise			1	1							7	2
Agama sp.							1		1			1
amphibian?				1	1		1				1	1
further study	1	2	3	4	4		7	3	3		7	2
Total miscellaneous	1	2	4	4	10	0	7	14	14	1	36	12
Grand total	219	330	903	376	1609	55	1771	1908	1161	214	5054	47
												6937

Table 6.2. Burnt and unburnt bone by context.

	burnt	not burnt	%burnt
STRATUM IV			
ash/hearth	-	-	-
others	23	196	10.5
STRATUM III			
ash/hearth	2	17	10.5
others	148	1436	9.3
STRATUM III/II			
ash/hearth	-	-	-
others	0	55	0.0
STRATUM II less burial pit			
ash/hearth	98	831	10.5
others	296	3584	7.6
STRATUM II burial pit *			
ash/hearth	-	-	-
others	1	351	0.3
STRATUM IV-II (all)			
ash/hearth	100	848	10.5
others	468	5622	7.7

Quantification by numbers of bone finds, except Stratum II pit where total numbers of bones are used.

Table 6.3. Corrected numbers of goats, sheep and pigs at Gilat.

	Strata IV-II		
	raw data	mm shared	shpgt shared
goat	293	293	2290
sheep	301	301	2353
sheep/goat	3777	4049	
pig	854	916	916
medium mammal	334		
totals	5559	5559	5559

Table 6.4. Sheep and goat identifications.

	Stratum IV	Stratum III				Stratum III/II	Stratum II					Strata IV-II
		3B	3A	3	All 3		2C	2B	2A	2+2B/C	All 2	totals
goat	5	11	39	17	67		70	109	41	1	221	293
sheep	14	19	46	11	76		90	73	44	4	211	301
goat?	1	2	13		15		6	6	1	2	15	31
sheep?	1		2		2		5	5	3	1	14	17
shpgt	124	168	446	220	834	25	884	1060	639	108	2691	3674
shpgt?		1	3	3	7		7	19	7	1	34	41
shpgt/gaz			1		1		13				13	14
shpgt totals	126	171	465	223	859	25	915	1090	650	112	2767	3777
med mamm	2	23	47	23	70		55	106	62	16	239	423

Table 6.5. Domestic cattle bones identifications at Gilat.

	Stratum IV	Stratum III	Stratum III/II	Stratum II	Totals
bos	33	173	12	590	808
bos/equid + bos?	2	27	1	56	86
large mammal		22		41	63
total bos	35	222	13	687	957

Table 6.6. Domestic cattle bones identifications at Gilat.

A: *Standard Wild Goat*			B: *Standard Wild Sheep*	
Means of recent female goat (BMNH 653M) and male goat (BMNH 653L) from the Taurus Mountains, taken from Uerpmann (1979)			Dimensions of recent female sheep (Field Museum of Natural History, Chicago, no 57 951) from western Iran, from Uerpmann (1979)	
			scapula SLC	19.5
humerus Bt	34.2	FORMULA	humerus Bt	29.5
radius Bp	35.5	index=	radius Bp	33.5
radius Bd	33.2	1/9*(1250*n/st-800)	radius Bd	31
metacarpal Bp	27.3	where	metacarpal Bp	25
metacarpal Bd	30.5	st=standard	metacarpal Bd	26.5
astragalus GL	32	n=measurement	astragalus GL	31.3
calcaneum GL	65.5		calcaneum GL	64
metatarsal Bp	23		metatarsal Bp	22.5
metatarsal Bd	28.5		metatarsal Bd	26

(Abbreviations from von den Driesch 1976)

Table 6.7. A: Cattle standard measurements; B: Pig standard measurements;
C: Equid standard measurements.

A: *Standard Wild Ox*		B: *Standard Wild Pig*	
Dimensions of female aurochs from Ullerslev, Denmark, from Degerbol and Fredskild (1970); after Buitenhuis (1985)		Means of wild boar from Turkey from Payne and Bull (1988)	
L lower M3	48.8	L upper m4	17.2
scapula SLC	69	L upper M1	20.3
humerus Bd	97	L upper M2	25.2
humerus Bt	89	L upper M3	38.8
radius Bp	100	L lower m4	22.7
radius Bd	92	L lower M1	20.4
metacarpal Bp	74	L lower M2	25.4
metacarpal Bd	73	L lower M3	41.5
femur Bd	116	astragalus GL	48.7
tibia Bd	78	calcaneum GL	95.2
astragalus GL	83	humerus Bd	50
calcaneum GL	165	humerus Bt	35
navicular GB	67	pelvis LAR	36.3
metatarsal Bp	62	radius Bd	41.3
metatarsal Bd	68	radius Bp	34.2
proximal phalanx anterior Bp	39	scapula SLC	29.8
proximal phalanx posterior Bp	35.5	tibia Bd	34.6
proximal phalanx mean Bp	37.25		
middle phalanx anterior Bp	36		
middle phalanx posterior Bp	34		
middle phalanx mean Bp	35		

(Abbreviations from von den Driesch 1976)

C: *Standard Equid*			
Equus hemionus/africanus at Mureybet, from Ducos (1986); after Uerpmann (1986)			
dimension (A)	mean (X)	s.d.	
astragalus GLm	47	2.06	
humerus Bt	60	1.77	FORMULA
metacarpal Bp	40	2.21	(A-X)*100/4*s.d.
metapodial Bd	37	1.50	
mid phalanx Bp	38	1.90	
prox phalanx Bp	39	1.89	
radius Bd	58	1.86	
scapula LG	44	1.98	
tibia Bd	55	1.84	

(Abbreviations from von den Driesch 1976)

Table 6.8. Age of sheep/goats, longbone fusion, Strata IV-II.

bone	part	age of fusion	fused?	Stratum IV no	% fused	Stratum III no	% fused	Stratum II no	% fused	Stratum IV-II no	% fused
m4 low	unworn	1 year	no	1		14		41		56	
radius	proximal	1 year	no	0		2		5		7	
humerus	distal	1 year	no	3		12		24		39	
pelvis	acetabulum	1 year	no	2		6		17		25	0
m4 low	worn or P4	1 year	yes	6		46		115		167	
radius	proximal	1 year	yes	2		18		39		59	
humerus	distal	1 year	yes	7		36		78		121	
pelvis	acetabulum	1 year	yes	0	71.4	12	76.7	22	74.5	34	75.0
proximal phalanx	proximal	1½ years	no	3		20		37		60	
middle phalanx	proximal	1½ years	no	0		2		21		23	0
proximal phalanx	proximal	1½ years	yes	1		16		62		79	
middle phalanx	proximal	1½ years	yes	6	70.0	23	63.9	41	64.0	70	64.2
tibia	distal	2 years	no	1		10		16		27	0
tibia	distal	2 years	yes	6	85.7	19	65.5	56	77.8	81	75.0
metapodial	distal	2½ years	no	4		26		84		114	0
metapodial	distal	2½ years	yes	3	42.9	23	46.9	48	36.4	74	39.4
femur	proximal	3-3½ years	no	3		20		27		50	
femur	distal	3-3½ years	no	3		6		12		21	
humerus	proximal	3-3½ years	no	1		3		8		12	
radius	distal	3-3½ years	no	1		5		22		28	
tibia	proximal	3-3½ years	no	2		10		15		27	0
femur	proximal	3-3½ years	yes	0		3		10		13	
femur	distal	3-3½ years	yes	0		1		5		6	
humerus	proximal	3-3½ years	yes	0		2		6		8	
radius	distal	3-3½ years	yes	2		3		12		17	
tibia	proximal	3-3½ years	yes	0	16.7	5	24.1	4	30.6	9	27.7
Total ageable bones				57		343		827		1227	

Table 6.9. Sheep and goat separate ageing, Strata IV-II.

	Raw		Corrected		% fused
	fused	*unfused*	*fused*	*unfused*	
radius prox (c5 months)					
sheep	10	0	38	4	90.4
goat	6	0	23	3	88.2
shpgt	44	7			
total	60	7	60	7	89.6
middle phalanx (c8 months)					
sheep	17	1	35	11	76.1
goat	16	1	35	11	76.1
shpgt	37	20			
total	70	22	70	22	76.1
humerus distal (c10months)					
sheep	35	0	77	25	75.5
goat	20	0	44	14	75.9
shpgt	66	39			
total	121	39	121	39	75.6
scapula distal (c15 months)					
sheep	14	1	22	10	68.3
goat	10	1	15	10	60.7
shpgt	13	18			
total	37	20	37	20	64.9
metapodials (c27 months)					
sheep	46	10	53	19	73.5
goat	17	15	20	29	40.6
shpgt	10	23			
total	73	48	73	48	60.3
femur prox + radius distal + tibia prox + humerus prox (c33 months)					
sheep	13	3	38	45	46.1
goat	4	5	12	74	13.7
shpgt	33	111			
total	50	119	50	119	29.6

Table 6.10a. Sheep and Goat, sex and age - 1 - distal humeri.

	Raw			Corrected			% fused+pt fused
	fused	part fused	unfused	fused	part fused	unfused	
sheep							
male	8	0	1	25	0.5	22	54.1
female	14	0	1	45	0.5	1	97.8
extra shpgt	48	1	21				
total	70	1	23	70	1	23	
goats							
male	6	2	0	10	7	20	45.9
female	9	0	0	15	0	0	100.0
extra shpgt	10	5	20				
total	25	7	20	25	7	20	
sheep/goat							
?sex	58	6	41				
totals	95	8	43	95	8	43	

Table 6.10b. Sheep and Goat, sex and age - 2 - distal metapodials.

	Raw			Corrected			% fused
	fused	unfused	total	fused	unfused	total	
sheep							
male	5	11	16	20	45	64	30.5
female	9	3	12	35	12	48	74.3
?sex	34	23	57				
extra shpgt	7	20	27				
total extra	41	43	84				
total	55	57	112	55	57	112	49.1
goats							
male	2	2	4	4	28	32	13.2
female	8	2	10	17	28	44	37.9
?sex	8	31	39				
extra shpgt	3	20	23				
total extra	11	51	62				
total	21	55	76	21	55	76	27.6
sheep/goats							
male	2	4	6				
female	2	1	3				
?sex	6	35	41				
total	10	40	50				
totals	76	112	188	76	112	188	40.4

**Table 6.11. A: Tooth eruption and wear in modern cattle, based on early maturation criteria.
B: Tooth eruption and wear in modern cattle, based on late maturation criteria.**

early maturing	late maturing			P2	P3	m4/P4	M1	M2	M3
age months	stage	age months	years						
M1 5-6m	1	0-6m				erupting *ab*	erupting		
	2	6m	6m			*cd*	*a*		
P2 24-30m	3	12m	1y	erupting		*ef*	*bc*		
	4	18m				*g*	*d*		
M2 15-18m	5	24m	2y			*h*	*e*	erupting *a*	
P3 18-30m	6	30m			erupting	*j*	*f*	*bc*	
	7	36m	3y			*kl*	*g*	*de*	
						mn/erupting			
M3 24-30m	8	42m				*a*	*h*	*f*	erupting
P4 28-36m	9	48m	4y			*bc*	*j*	*g*	erupting
	10	54m				*de*	*k*	*h*	erupting *ab*
	11	60m	5y			*f*	*l*	*j*	*cd*
	12	66m				*g*	*m*	*k*	*ef*
	13	72m	6y			*h*	*n*	*l*	*gh*
	14	78m				*j*	*o*	*m*	*jk*
	15	84+m	7y			*j*	*p*	*n*	*l*
	16	8y?	8y?			*j*	*p*	*o*	*m*
	17	9y?	9y?			*j*	*p*	*p*	*(n)*
	18	10y?	10y?			*j*	*p*	*p*	*(o)*
	19	11+y?	11+y?			*j*	*p*	*p*	*(p)*

Eruption:

1. Late maturing. The ages given by Girard 1807 (taken from Meitinger 1983) appear to relate to the completion of eruption, hence his relatively late age for the eruption of M3 compared with that of P4, which as Payne (1984) has pointed out, does not actually occur, since M3 begins to erupt slightly before P4. The dates above are based on those of Girard, but are all for the process of eruption, i.e. about six months before Girard's dates for all permanent cheekteeth, except M3, which appears to start erupting 3 or 4 months before P4, but to complete the process over a much longer period, perhaps as long as 18 months.

2. Early maturing. The ages are those given by Silver(1969). Those for the later erupting teeth (M2, M3 and P4) are earlier than those given for cattle of the early 19th century.

Wear:

The wear stages are those devised by Grant (1982) and their positions within the table are extrapolated from those observed in the cheektooth rows from Gilat.

Table 6.12. Age of cattle, longbone fusion, Strata 4-2.

bone	part	age of fusion	fused?	no.	% fused
pelvis	acetabulum	7-10 months	no	1	
scapula	distal	7-10 months	no	3	
pelvis	acetabulum	7-10 months	yes	4	
scapula	distal	7-10 months	yes	4	66.7
radius	proximal	12-18 months	no	1	
humerus	distal	12-18 months	no	7	
prox phalanx	proximal	c18 months	no	4	
mid phalanx	proximal	c18 months	no	1	
radius	proximal	12-18 months	yes	13	
humerus	distal	12-18 months	yes	15	
prox phalanx	proximal	c18 months	yes	40	
mid phalanx	proximal	c18 months	yes	15	86.5
tibia	distal	24-30 months	no	2	
metapodial	distal	24-36 months	no	7	
calcaneum	tuber	c36 months	no	6	
tibia	distal	24-30 months	yes	7	
mpodial	distal	24-36 months	yes	36	
calcaneum	tuber	c36 months	yes	5	76.2
femur	proximal	42 months	no	10	
radius	distal	42-48 months	no	2	
femur	distal	42-48 months	no	4	
tibia	proximal	42-48 months	no	3	
humerus	proximal	42-48 months	no	0	
femur	proximal	42 months	yes	2	
radius	distal	42-48 months	yes	8	
femur	distal	42-48 months	yes	4	
tibia	proximal	42-48 months	yes	4	
humerus	proximal	42-48 months	yes	2	51.3

(Based on Silver 1969)

Table 6.13. Tooth eruption and wear in modern pigs.

stage	Bull and Payne	age	m4	P4	M1	M2	M3
A		neo-nat	unerupted		in crypt		
B		5-6m	present		erupting/unworn	in crypt	
C	group 1	6-12m	present		sl worn	in crypt	
D		12-14m	present		worn	erupting/unworn	in crypt
E		14-18m	present		worn	sl worn	in crypt
F	group 2	18-23m		erupting	worn	worn	erupting
G		23-26m		unworn/sl worn	worn	worn	erupting
H		26-31m		worn	worn	worn	unworn
I	group 3	31-35m		worn	worn	worn	sl worn
J		36m+		worn	v worn	worn	worn
K		36m++		v worn	v worn	v worn	worn

(Age groups from Bull and Payne 1982)

Table 6.14. Age of pigs, longbone fusion, Strata IV-II.

bone	part	age of fusion	fused?	no.	% fused
humerus	distal	1 year	no	25	
pelvis	acetabulum	1 year	no	13	
middle phalanx	proximal	1 year	no	12	
radius	proximal	1 year	no	3	
scapula	distal	1 year	no	7	
humerus	distal	1 year	yes	10	
pelvis	acetabulum	1 year	yes	8	
middle phalanx	proximal	1 year	yes	15	
radius	proximal	1 year	yes	13	
scapula	distal	1 year	yes	2	44.4
metapodial	distal	2-2 1/4 years	no	26	
proximal phalanx	proximal	2 years	no	18	
tibia	distal	2 years	no	10	
calcaneum	proximal	2-2½ years	no	20	
metapodial	distal	2-2 1/4 years	yes	4	
proximal phalanx	proximal	2 years	yes	20	
tibia	distal	2 years	yes	14	
calcaneum	proximal	2-2½ years	yes	2	35.1
femur	distal	3½ years	no	6	
femur	proximal	3½ years	no	7	
humerus	proximal	3½ years	no	1	
radius	distal	3½ years	no	10	
tibia	proximal	3½ years	no		
femur	distal	3½ years	yes	1	
femur	proximal	3½ years	yes	1	
humerus	proximal	3½ years	yes	0	
radius	distal	3½ years	yes	1	
tibia	proximal	3½ years	yes		11.1

(Based on Silver 1969)

Table 6.15. Sheep/goat bone element analysis.

	stratum IV	stratum III	stratum II	all	no in skeleton	number expected	max % survival
			mni on mandibular toothrows = 126				
cranium, petrous	1	16	27	44	2	252	17.5
horncore	1	28	63	92	2	252	36.5
maxilla	1	12	23	36	2	252	14.3
mandible	11	59	165	235	2	252	93.3
upper teeth	19	128	370	517	12	1512	34.2
lower teeth	20	138	401	559	20	2520	22.2
hyoid		2	3	5	2	252	2.0
sternebra	1		3	4	6	756	0.5
atlas	4	7	16	27	1	126	21.4
axis	3	6	19	28	1	126	22.2
vert cervical	5	21	62	88	5	630	14.0
vert dorsal	6	27	82	115	13	1638	7.0
vert lumbar	18	17	62	97	6	756	12.8
sacrum	1	5	6	12	5	630	1.9
vert caudal		5	4	9	28	3528	0.3
scapula	3	25	83	111	2	252	44.0
humerus, proximal	1	5	15	21	2	252	8.3
humerus, distal	12	57	136	205	2	252	81.3
radius, proximal	3	21	50	74	2	252	29.4
radius, distal	3	8	36	47	2	252	18.7
ulna	2	22	46	70	2	252	27.8
carpals	5	4	59	68	20	2520	2.7
metacarpal, proximal	2	18	33	53	2	252	21.0
metacarpal, distal	2	23	56	81	2	252	32.1
pelvis	8	44	97	149	2	252	59.1
femur, proximal	5	22	36	63	2	252	25.0
femur, distal	3	9	29	41	2	252	16.3
patella		4	14	18	2	252	7.1
tibia, proximal	2	16	18	36	2	252	14.3
tibia, distal	7	28	77	112	2	252	44.4
fibula		1	2	3	2	252	1.2
astragalus	3	33	83	119	2	252	47.2
calcaneum	2	11	55	68	2	252	27.0
navicular	2	4	22	28	2	252	11.1
posterior cuneiform		2	7	9	2	252	3.6
metatarsal, proximal	7	14	82	103	2	252	40.9
mtarsal, distal	2	9	42	53	2	252	21.0
proximal phalanx	6	54	151	211	8	1008	20.9
middle phalanx	5	31	99	135	8	1008	13.4
distal phalanx	4	9	55	68	8	1008	6.7
metapodial, proximal		19	7	26	4	504	5.2
metapodial, distal		1	51	52	4	504	10.3
rib	3	86	225	314	26	3276	9.6

Table 6.16. Sheep/goat burial pit bone element analysis.

	mni on mandibular toothrows = 10			
	no found	*no in skeleton*	*number expected*	*max % survival*
cranium petrous	2	2	20	10.0
horncore	8	2	20	40.0
maxilla	18	2	20	90.0
mandible	18	2	20	90.0
upper teeth	18	12	120	15.0
lower teeth	7	20	200	3.5
hyoid		2	20	0.0
sternebra		6	60	0.0
atlas	3	1	10	30.0
axis	2	1	10	20.0
cervical vertebrae		5	50	0.0
dorsal vertebrae	1	13	130	0.8
lumbar vertebrae		6	60	0.0
sacrum		5	50	0.0
caudal vertebrae		28	280	0.0
scapula	7	2	20	35.0
humerus, proximal	1	2	20	5.0
humerus, distal	5	2	20	25.0
radius, proximal	7	2	20	35.0
radius, distal	4	2	20	20.0
ulna	2	2	20	10.0
carpals	23	20	200	11.5
metacarpal, proximal	11	2	20	55.0
metacarpal, distal	10	2	20	50.0
pelvis	11	2	20	55.0
femur, proximal	3	2	20	15.0
femur, distal	2	2	20	10.0
patella	3	2	20	15.0
tibia, proximal		2	20	0.0
tibia, distal	7	2	20	35.0
fibula	2	2	20	10.0
astragalus	11	2	20	55.0
calcaneum	9	2	20	45.0
navicular	9	2	20	45.0
posterior cuneiform	3	2	20	15.0
metatarsal, proximal	11	2	20	55.0
metatarsal, distal	16	2	20	80.0
proximal phalanx	36	8	80	45.0
middle phalanx	36	8	80	45.0
distal phalanx	23	8	80	28.8
rib	20	26	260	7.7

Table 6.17. Cattle bone element analysis.

	no in skeleton	number expected	number found	max % survival
		mni on distal humeri = 21		
horncore	2	42	6	14.3
petrous	2	42	19	45.2
maxillary toothrow	2	42	3	7.1
mandible toothrow	2	42	26	61.9
upper teeth	12	252	73	29.0
lower teeth	20	420	133	31.7
hyoid	2	42	1	2.4
atlas	1	21	6	28.6
axis	1	21	9	42.9
cervical vertebrae	5	105	14	13.3
dorsal vertebrae	13	273	27	9.9
lumbar vertebrae	6	126	12	9.5
sacral vertebrae	5	105	4	3.8
caudal vertebrae	28	588	9	1.5
scapula, distal	2	42	18	42.9
humerus, proximal	2	42	2	4.8
humerus, distal	2	42	42	100.0
radius, proximal	2	42	20	47.6
radius, distal	2	42	10	23.8
ulna	2	42	13	31.0
carpals	10	210	36	17.1
mcarpal, proximal	2	42	33	78.6
metacarpal, distal	2	42	14	33.3
pelvis	2	42	22	52.4
femur, proximal	2	42	11	26.2
femur, distal	2	42	12	28.6
tibia, proximal	2	42	8	19.0
tibia, distal	2	42	11	26.2
patella	2	42	2	4.8
navicular	2	42	20	47.6
post cuneiform	2	42	8	19.0
astragalus	2	42	33	78.6
calcaneum	2	42	30	71.4
fibula	2	42	1	2.4
mtarsal, proximal	2	42	33	78.6
mtarsal, distal	2	42	27	64.3
proximal phalanges	8	168	66	39.3
middle phalanges	8	168	30	17.9
distal phalanges	8	168	16	9.5
mpodial, proximal	4	84	2	2.4
mpodial, distal	4	84	17	20.2
rib	26	546	64	11.7

Table 6.18. Pig bone element analysis.

	no in skeleton	number expected	number found	max % survival
	mni on mandible = 35			
cranium frontal	2	70	18	25.7
cranium nuchal	1	35	11	31.4
cranium zygomatic	2	70	13	18.6
maxillary toothrow	2	70	36	51.4
mandibular toothrow	2	70	66	94.3
upper teeth	22	770	33	4.3
lower teeth	22	770	42	5.5
hyoid	2	70	0	0.0
sternebra	6	210	2	1.0
atlas	1	35	10	28.6
axis	1	35	8	22.9
cervical vertebrae	5	175	19	10.9
dorsal vertebrae	13	455	26	5.7
lumbar vertebrae	6	210	4	1.9
vert sacral	4	140	2	1.4
vert caudal **	23	805	4	0.5
scapula	2	70	38	54.3
humerus, proximal	2	70	1	1.4
humerus, distal	2	70	53	75.7
radius, proximal	2	70	16	22.9
radius, distal	2	70	8	11.4
ulna	2	70	12	17.1
carpals	10	350	5	1.4
pelvis	2	70	32	45.7
femur proximal	2	70	8	11.4
femur distal	2	70	7	10.0
patella	2	70	4	5.7
tibia proximal	2	70	8	11.4
tibia distal	2	70	24	34.3
fibula	2	70	3	4.3
astragalus	2	70	8	11.4
calcaneum	2	70	34	48.6
tarsals	12	420	8	1.9
metapodials	16	560	75	13.4
proximal phalanges	16	560	50	8.9
middle phalanges	16	560	32	5.7
distal phalanges	16	560	19	3.4
rib	26	910	16	1.8

Table 6.19. Relative meat weights.

	no of bone finds	% numbers	meat weight kg per individual	relative meat weight	% meat weight
cattle	957	14.7	625	598125	56.4
goats	2290	35.2	80	183235	17.3
sheep	2353	36.1	80	188238	17.7
pigs	916	14.1	100	91559	8.6
totals	6516	100.0	885	1061157	100.0

(meat weights from Clark and Yi 1983)

Table 6.20. Side of body by species and stratum.

	Stratum IV		Stratum III		Stratum III/II		Stratum II		Strata IV-II	
	L	R	L	R	L	R	L	R	L	R
cattle	5	3	14	5	2		86	88	107	96
goat	0	3	14	7			46	59	60	69
sheep			12	8			56	37	68	45
sheep/goat	20	17	47	61	5	2	360	342	432	422
pig	2	6	7	11	1	2	67	74	77	93
equid			1				4	1	5	1
horse							1		1	0
dog				4			4	4	4	8
gazelle			2			1	21	16	23	17
fox			1				1		2	0
hyaena							1		1	0
ostrich			1						1	0
total	27	29	99	96	8	5	647	621	781	751

Table 6.21. Burnt bone by species and stratum.

	Stratum IV			Stratum III			Stratum II			Strata IV-II		
	burnt	total	% burnt	burnt	total	% burnt	burnt	total	% burnt	burnt	total	%burnt
goat	0	5	0.0	7	67	10.4	9	221	4.1	16	293	5.5
sheep	1	14	7.1	2	76	2.6	13	211	6.2	16	301	5.3
sheep/goat	16	126	12.7	96	859	11.2	175	2767	6.3	287	3752	7.6
all sheep & goat	17	145	11.7	105	1002	10.5	197	3199	6.2	319	4346	7.3
cattle	4	35	11.4	6	223	2.7	28	687	4.1	38	945	4.0
pig	1	32	3.1	27	210	12.9	45	598	7.5	73	840	8.7
medium mammal	1	2	50.0	16	93	17.2	34	239	14.2	51	334	15.3
all dom ungulates	23	214	10.7	154	1528	10.1	304	4723	6.4	481	6465	7.4
equids				0	2	0.0	0	12	0.0	0	14	0.0
dog	0	1	0.0	0	22	0.0	3	37	8.1	3	60	5.0
gazelle	0	2	0.0	6	21	28.6	16	92	17.4	22	115	19.1
hyaena							1	1	100.0	1	1	100.0
cat				1	2	50.0	1	4	25.0	2	6	33.3
totals	23	217	10.6	161	1575	10.2	325	4869	6.7	509	6661	7.6

Table 6.22. Dog size at Gilat.

	Natufian	Neolithic*	Gilat
L M1 lower			
mean	22.17	21.50	22.06
standard deviation	0.873	1.01	1.63
standard error	0.33	0.31	0.61
N	7	7	7
L M1 upper			
mean	13.793	-	12.38
standard deviation	1.164	-	1.13
standard error	0.582	-	0.56
N	4	-	4
L lower molar row			
mean	37.82	-	33.93
standard deviation	2.655	-	1.21
standard error	1.328	-	0.70
N	4	-	3

Neolithic* = Prepottery and Pottery Neolithic at Jericho
Natufian data from Tchernov and Valla (1997)
Neolithic data from Dayan (1994)

Table 6.23. Dog height factors.

	factor	X	
humerus GL	3.43	-26.54	*formula* (GL x factor) +/- X = height
radius GL	3.18	19.51	
humerus + radius GL	1.65	-4.32	
ulna GL	2.78	6.21	
femur GL	3.14	-12.96	
tibia GL	2.92	9.41	
femur + tibia GL	1.52	-2.47	

GL = maximum length
from Harcourt (1974)

Table 6.24. Dog weight and height at Gilat.

	Gilat 90		Gilat 91
locus	859		692
stratum	2Cii		2Ai
bone no	3217	3219	138
L mand molar row (X)	33.0	33.5	35.3
log X	1.519	1.525	1.548
log y	4.084	4.105	4.179
weight gm (y)	12130	12740	15100
weight kg	12.1	12.7	15.1
mean shoulder ht	-	-	54.1 cm

formula log y = (3.2735*logX)-0.8873

y = body weight in gm;

X = L mandibular molar row (von den Driesch no. 10)

(formula for weight from Wing 1978)
(indices for height from Harcourt 1974)
(method from Wapnish and Hesse 1993)
(abbreviations from von den Driesch 1976)

Table 6.25. Gazelle bone element analysis.

	mni on horncores = 12			
	no found	*no in skeleton*	*number expected*	*max % survival*
horncore	22	2	24	91.7
cranium petrous		2	24	0.0
maxilla	1	2	24	4.2
mandible	9	2	24	37.5
upper teeth	10	12	144	6.9
lower teeth	11	20	240	4.6
hyoid		2	24	0.0
sternebra		6	72	0.0
atlas		1	12	0.0
axis	2	1	12	16.7
cervical vertebrae	2	5	60	3.3
dorsal vertebrae	1	13	156	0.6
lumbar vertebrae	1	6	72	1.4
sacrum		5	60	0.0
caudal vertebrae**		28	336	0.0
scapula	4	2	24	16.7
humerus, proximal		2	24	0.0
humerus, distal	5	2	24	20.8
radius, proximal		2	24	0.0
radius, distal		2	24	0.0
ulna		2	24	0.0
carpals		20	240	0.0
mcarpal, proximal	1	2	24	4.2
metacarpal, distal	2	2	24	8.3
pelvis	3	2	24	12.5
femur, prox		2	24	0.0
femur, distal		2	24	0.0
patella		2	24	0.0
tibia, proximal		2	24	0.0
tibia, distal	6	2	24	25.0
fibula		2	24	0.0
astragalus	5	2	24	20.8
calcaneum	1	2	24	4.2
navicular		2	24	0.0
post cuneiform		2	24	0.0
mtarsal, proximal	1	2	24	4.2
mtarsal, distal	2	2	24	8.3
proximal phalanx	9	8	96	9.4
middle phalanx	4	8	96	4.2
distal phalanx		8	96	0.0
mpodial, proximal		4	48	0.0
mpodial, distal	9	4	48	18.8
rib		26	312	0.0

Table 6.26. Wild and domestic animals at Gilat.

A: Numbers

	Stratum IV	Stratum III				Stratum III/II	Stratum II					Strata IV-II
		IIIB	IIIA	III	All 3		IIC	IIB	IIA	II+IIB/C	All 2	totals
Domestic mammals	215	319	873	359	1552	52	1677	1786	1101	208	4772	6590
Wild mammals	2	9	17	5	30	2	35	52	26	4	117	151
ostrich				1	1	1						2
bird + bird?	1	0	2	5	7		23	14	12	0	49	57
fish + fish?		0	7	2	9		29	42	8	1	80	89
total wild	3	9	26	13	47	3	87	108	46	5	246	300

B: Percentages

	Stratum IV	Stratum III				Stratum III/II	Stratum II					Strata IV-II
		IIIB	IIIA	III	All 3		IIC	IIB	IIA	II+IIB/C	All 2	totals
Domestic mammals	98.6	97.26	97.11	96.51	97.06	94.5	95.1	94.3	96	97.7	95.1	95.6
Wild mammals	0.9	2.7	1.9	1.3	1.9	3.6	2.0	2.7	2.3	1.9	2.3	2.2
ostrich	0.0	0.0	0.0	0.3	0.1	1.8	0.0	0.0	0.0	0.0	0.0	0.03
bird + bird?	0.5	0.0	0.2	1.3	0.4	0.0	1.3	0.7	1.0	0.0	1.0	0.8
fish + fish?	0.0	0.0	0.8	0.5	0.6	0.0	1.6	2.2	0.7	0.5	1.6	1.3
total wild	1.4	2.7	2.9	3.5	2.9	5.5	4.9	5.7	4.0	2.3	4.9	4.4

Table 6.27. Side of body by locus.

All loci containing >9 bones with side recorded											
Stratum IV			*Stratum III*			*Stratum II*			*Stratum II cont*		
locus	*L*	*R*	*locus*	*L*	*R*	*locus*	*L*	*R*	*locus*	*L*	*R*
294	3	6	261	6	5	13	8	6	786	9	10
1294	6	6	553	15	19	33	7	8	882	14	11
1354	15	8	556	6	2	270	16	11	1029	11	10
			567	8	6	297	12	5	1044	5	7
			586	14	16	528	16	11	1050	11	5
			692	5	5	649	5	8	1051	14	7
			1054	0	12	671	5	5	1057	4	7
			1131	5	9	696	12	12	1128	5	10
			1147	9	5	697	4	6	1159	12	5
			1369	6	9	703	6	3	1237	5	8
			1371	8	4	755	7	8	1322	6	3
			1562	6	4	772	6	7	1344	6	7
						773	6	5	1357	67	76
						783	11	6	1511	14	11

L. 1954 incl 11 R shpgt with 4 bits mandibles

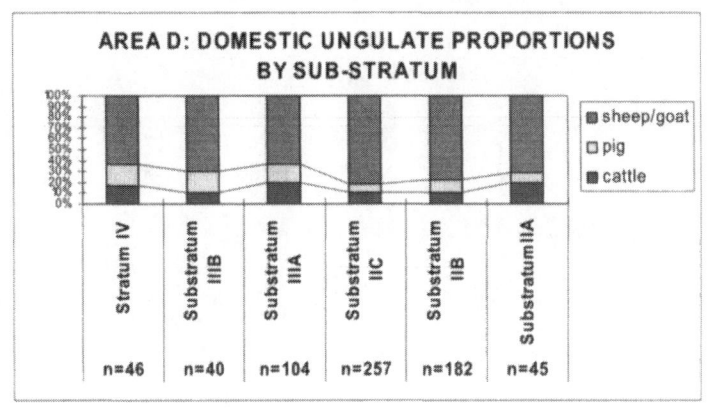

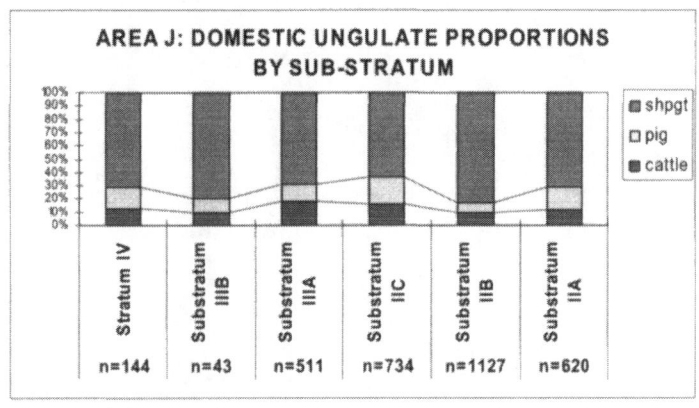

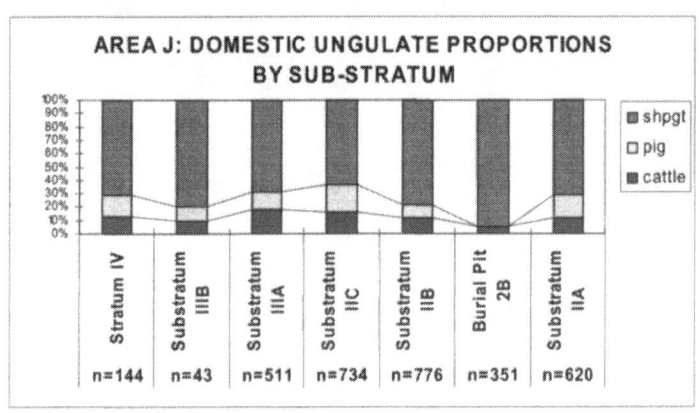

Figure 6.1. Spatial and diachronic analysis - domestic ungulate proportions by Sub-stratum - 1 - Areas D and J. A: Area D. B: Area J. C: Area J, with bones from the large burial pit (L. 1237 and 1357) counted separately. In Area D the proportion of sheep and goats is higher in Sub-strata 2B and 2A (the main sanctuary area) than in 3A. In Area J, Sub-stratum 2C has a higher proportion of cattle and pig bones than 3A, and the apparent increase in sheep and goats in Sub-stratum 2B is due to a concentration of their bones within the large burial pit.

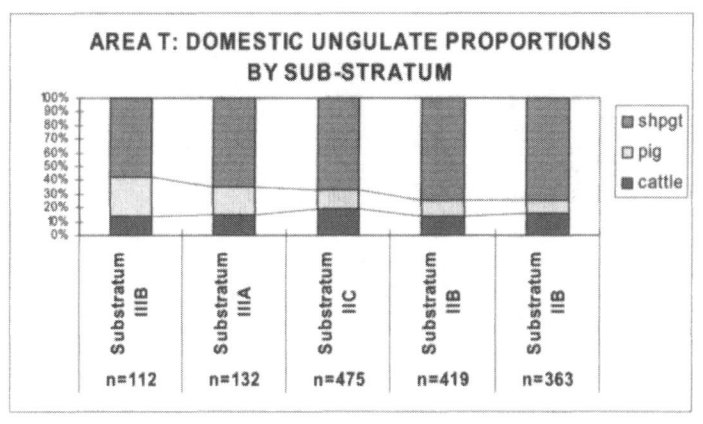

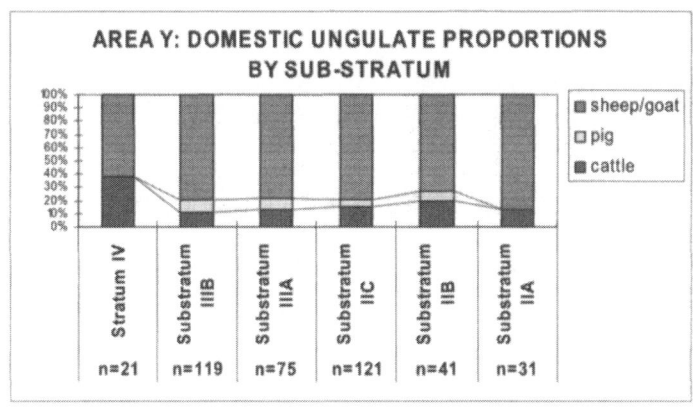

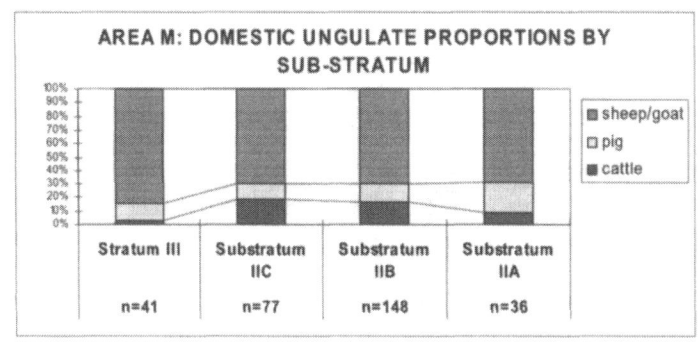

Figure 6.2. Spatial and diachronic analysis - domestic ungulate proportions by Sub-stratum - 2 - Areas T, Y and M. A: Area T; B: Area Y; C: Area M. In Area T the proportion of pigs in Sub-stratum 3B is a little greater than usual, but there is little change from 3A to 2C, or is from 3B to 2A in Area Y. In Area M, Sub-stratum 2B was the only sample large enough for analysis and has no particular features.

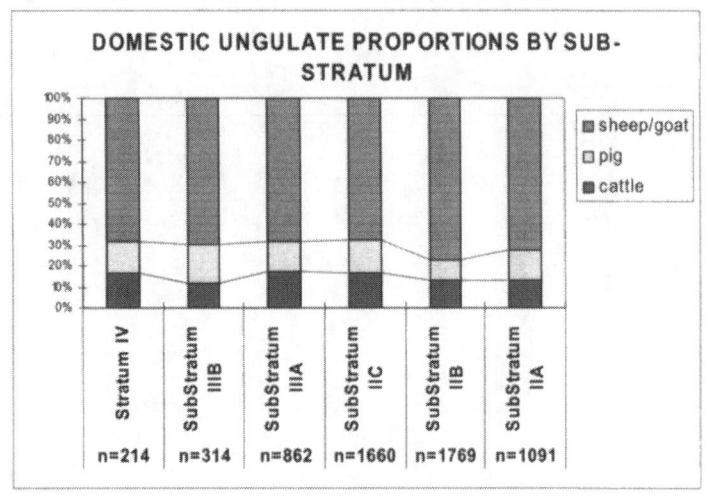

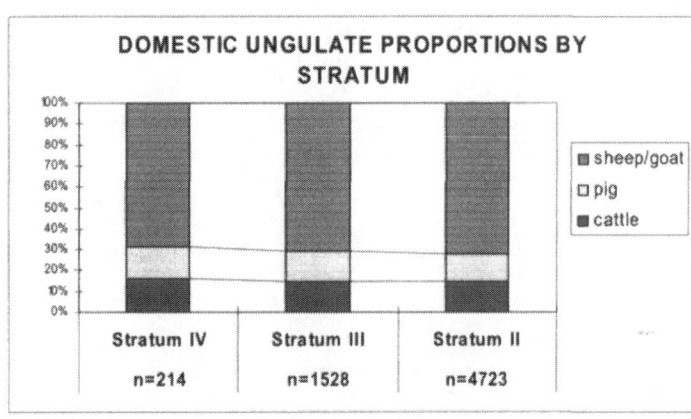

Figure 6.3. Diachronic analysis - domestic ungulate proportions for entire site. A: By sub-stratum; B: By stratum. There is no consistent overall pattern either within the individual sub-strata or when they are grouped by stratum, apart from the increase in sheep and goats in Sub-stratum 2B, due to the large burial pit.

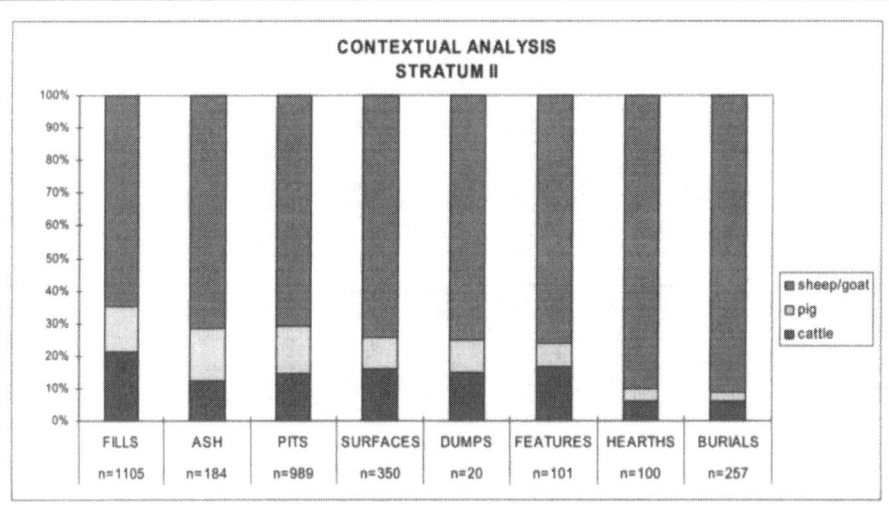

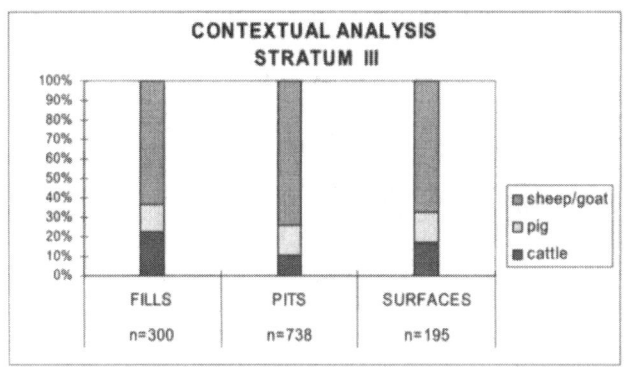

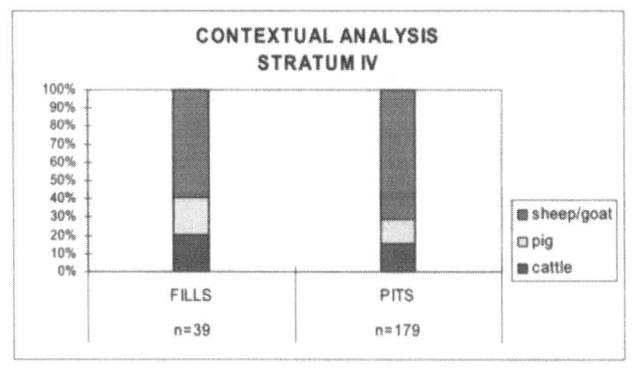

Figure 6.4. Contextual and diachronic analysis - domestic ungulate proportions by context. A: Stratum 2; B: Stratum 3; C: Stratum 4. In Stratum 2 the hearths and burials had more sheep and goats than the other types of context, probably as a result of sieving during excavation. The fills had the lowest number of sheep and goats, with varying proportions in the other contexts. The same is true in Strata 3 and 4, but here only a few types of context had large enough samples for analysis.

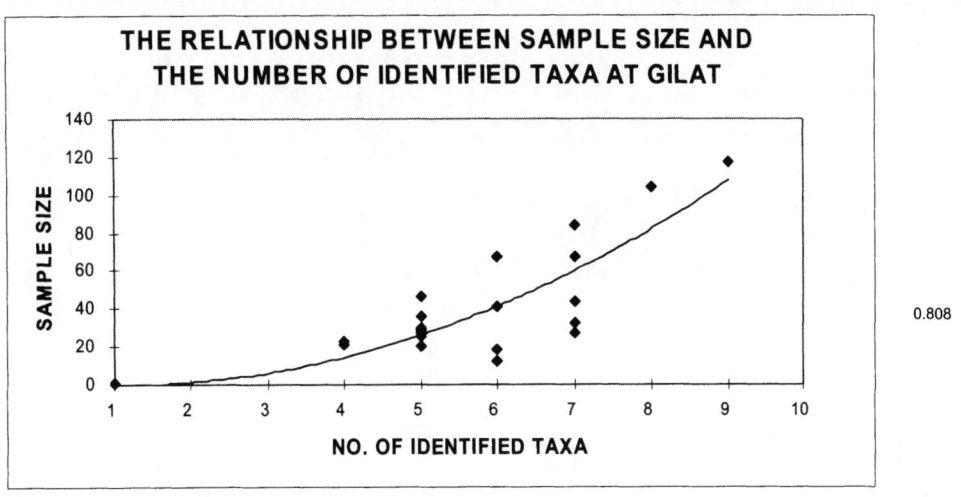

Figure 6.5. The relationship between sample size and the number of identified taxa in the Stratum 3 loci at Gilat. The two sets of figures are highly correlated, R=0.81, attesting to the homogeneity of the assemblages, due to mixing of the deposits.

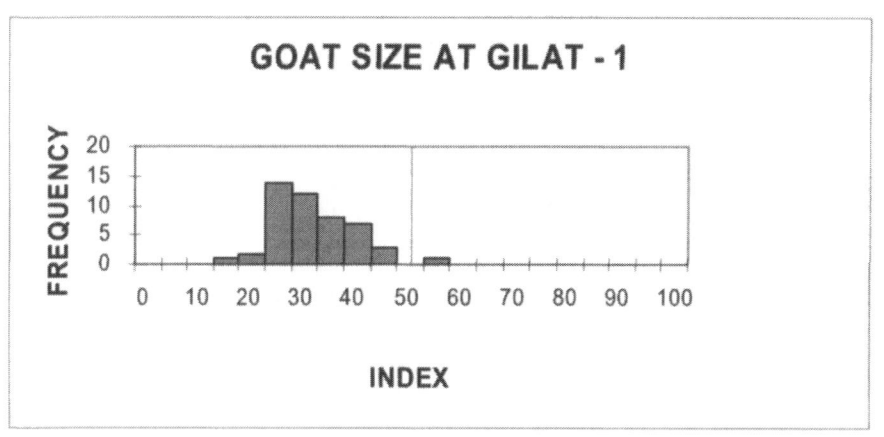

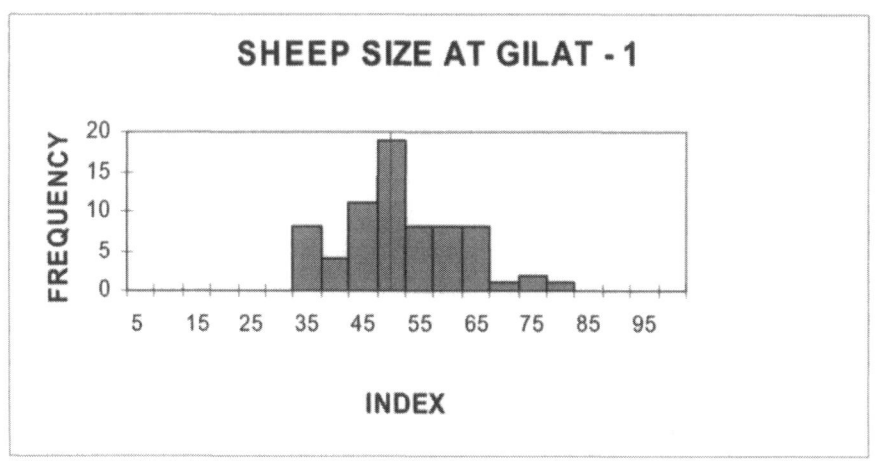

Figure 6.6. The size of goats and sheep at Gilat. A: Goat size - 1; B: Sheep size - 1. Comparison of the size of goats and sheep with those of domestic animals of the Early Neolithic shows that both were domestic; goats were even smaller than in the Early Neolithic and sheep were much the same size. Method and Neolithic data from Uerpmann (1979).

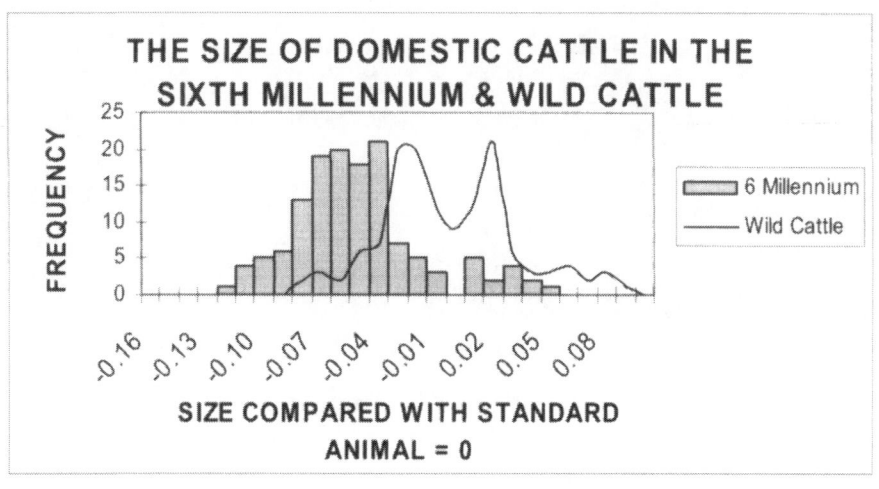

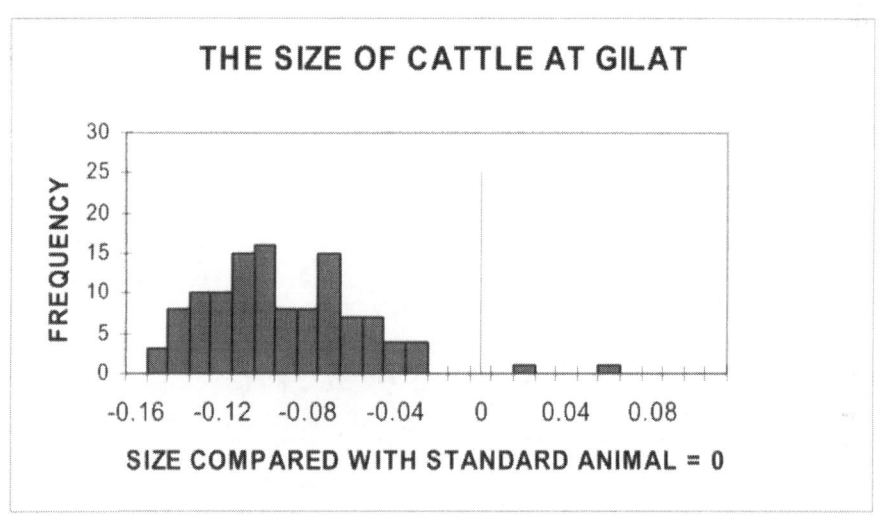

Figure 6.7. The size of cattle at Gilat. A: The sizes of wild and domestic cattle in the western part of the Middle East; B: Gilat cattle. The cattle at Gilat were much smaller than both the wild and domestic cattle of the sixth millennium and therefore were domestic.
Method and data from Grigson (1989a).

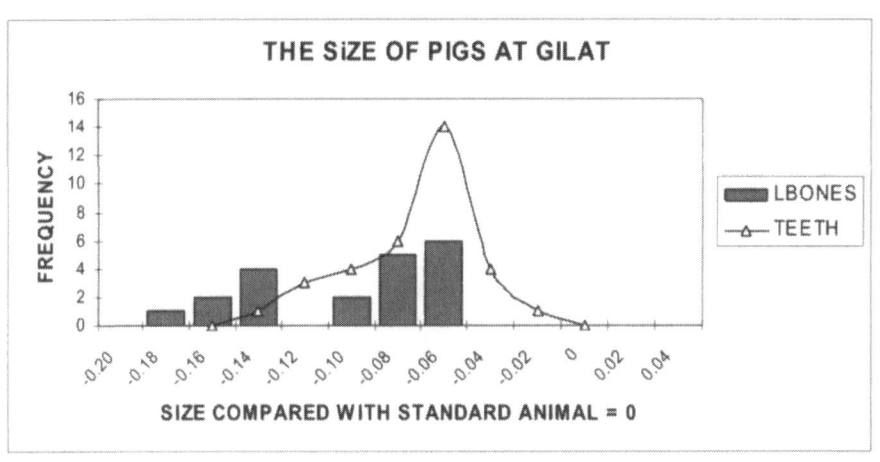

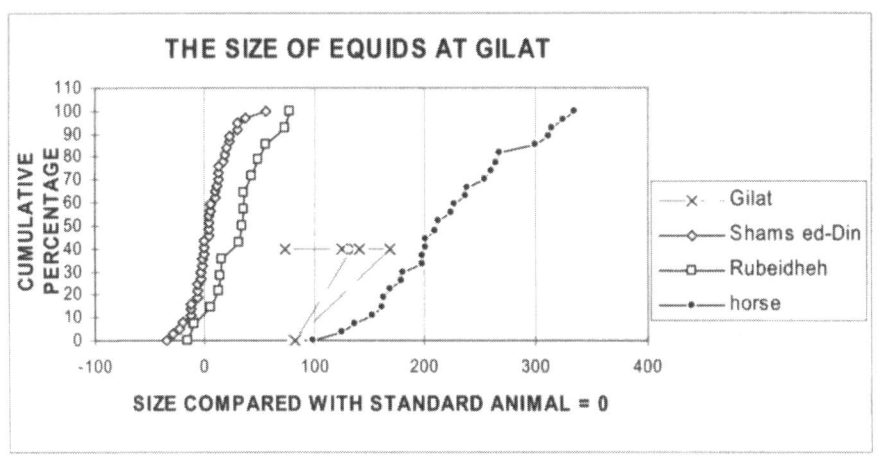

Figure 6.8. The size of pigs and equids at Gilat. A: Pigs; B: Equids. The Gilat pigs were much smaller than the standard Turkish wild pig of the Middle East and therefore domestic. The slightly larger relative size of the teeth may be due to the lack of interdental wear in these young animals. Standard animal from Payne and Bull (1988). The position of the size indices of the three equid bones from Gilat compared with the distribution of indices for Shams ed-Din and Mureybit (probably onagers), Tell Rubeidheh (domestic donkeys) and horses of the second millennium, indicates that the two largest (a distal radius and a distal tibia) probably derive from small horses. The smallest, an astragalus, could be from either a large donkey or a small horse. Method from Uerpmann (1982, 1986), additional data from Ducos (1978), Payne (1988) and Grigson (1993b).

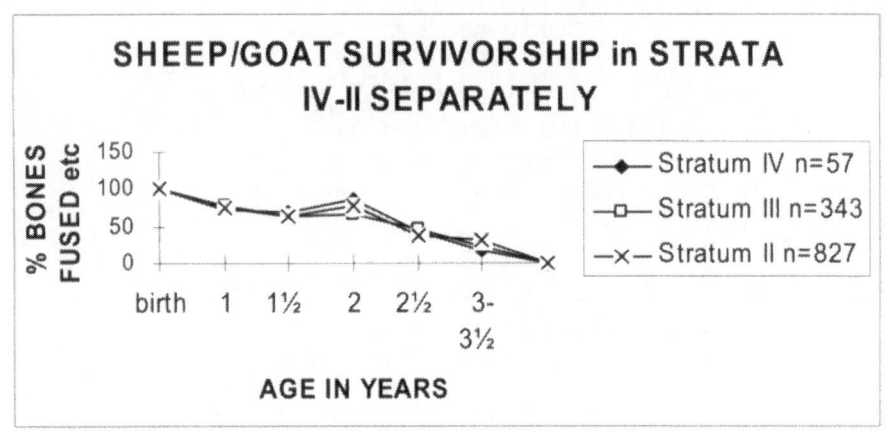

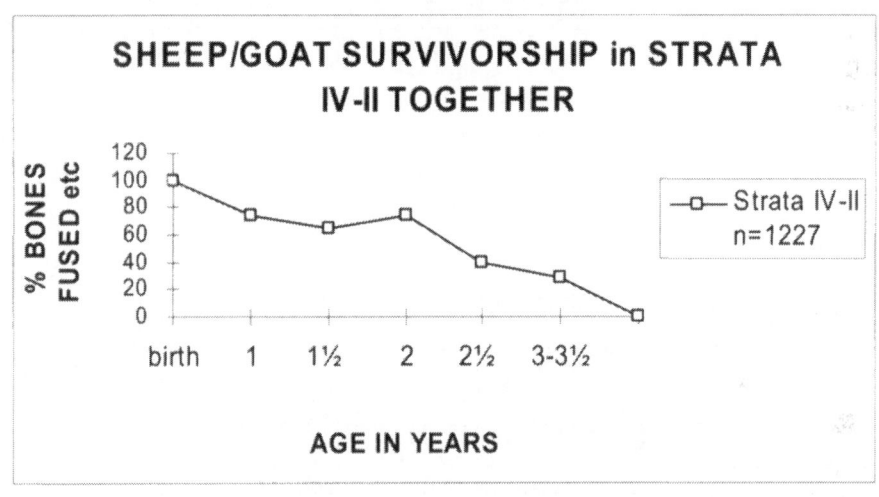

Figure 6.9. Sheep/goat survivorship at Gilat, based on longbone epiphysial fusion. A: Strata 4, 3 and 2 separately; B: Strata 4, 3 and 2 together. The separate curves for the three main strata are so similar that it is doubtful that they reflect any change over time. The curve for the three strata together shows that about 75% of the sheep and goats survived until the age of about 1 year, 64% to about 1½, 75% to about 2, 39% to 2½ and 27% to 3 years or more.

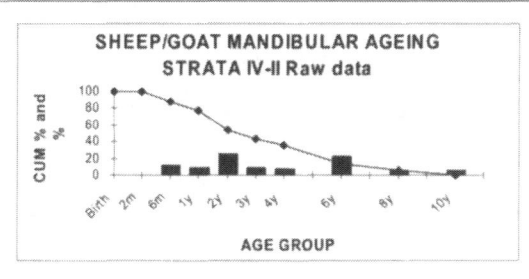

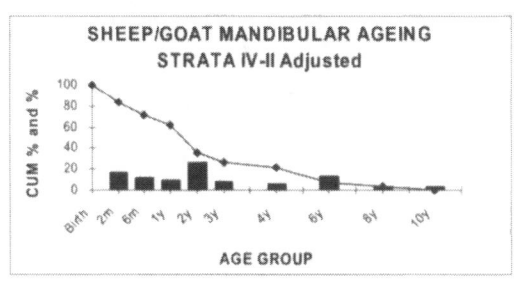

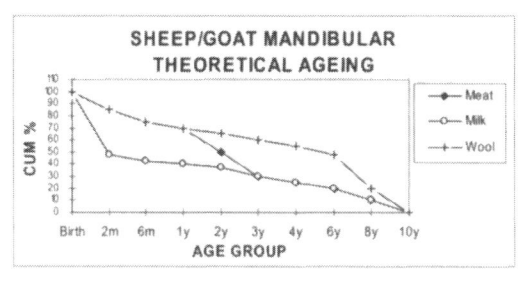

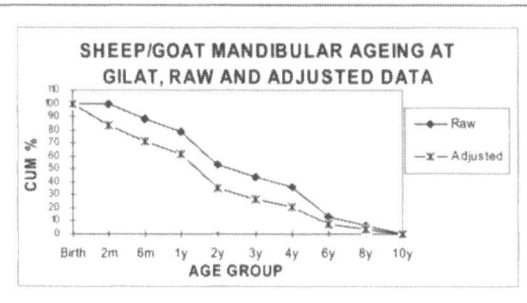

Figure 6.10. Sheep/goat mandibular ageing at Gilat. A: Raw data; B: Data adjusted for differential destruction and 15% perinatal mortality; C: Models for meat, milk and wool strategies (from Payne 1973); D: Raw and adjusted curves compared. A and B are plots of the numbers of mandibles and loose teeth from Gilat which could be aged expressed both as histograms and as cumulative percentages subtracted from 100%. The curves are compared with one another in D.
The raw data curve resembles Payne's wool model, although the adjusted curve is closest to the meat model, it is not identical and it is probable that sheep and goats were raised for meat, milk and wool.

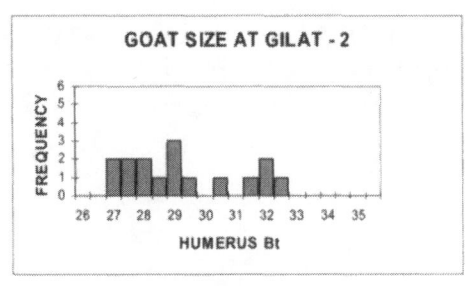

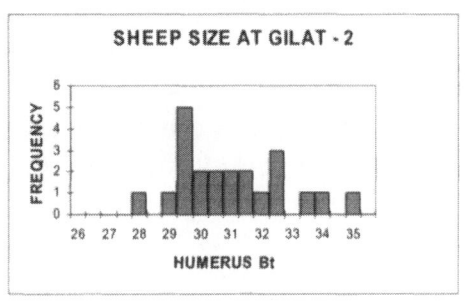

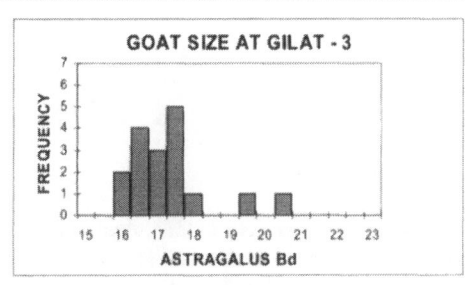

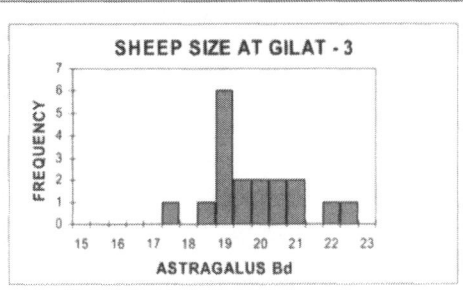

Figure 6.11. Sexual dimorphism in goats and sheep at Gilat. A: Goat size - 2. Trochlear breadth (Bt) of the humerus; B: Sheep size - 2. Trochlear breadth (Bt) of the humerus; C: Goat size - 3. Distal breadth (Bd) of the astragalus; D: Sheep size - 3. Distal breadth (Bd) of the astragalus. The distributions of these two breadth measurements in both sheep and goats are bimodal and skewed in favour of the smaller, and presumably female, animals.

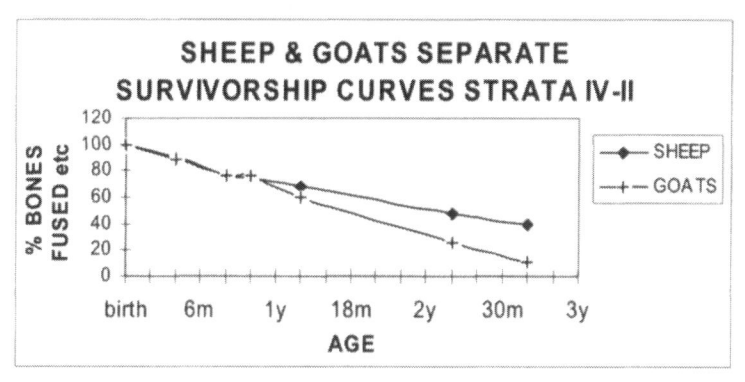

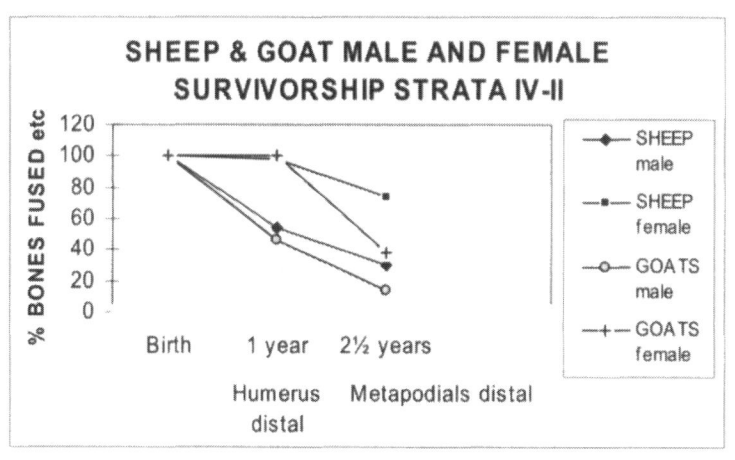

Figure 6.12. Survivorship curves for sheep and goats at Gilat, calculated separately. A: Based on longbone fusion of both sexed and unsexed bones. B: Based on sexed distal humeri and distal metapodials. Although equal numbers appear to have been killed in the first year of life, a higher proportion of sheep than goats survived into old age. In both species, but especially sheep, more females than males were older than 2¼ years, perhaps indicating a herding strategy aimed at the production of wool in addition to meat and milk.

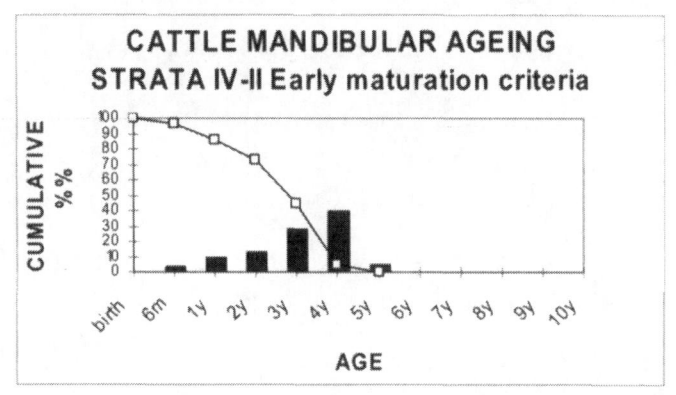

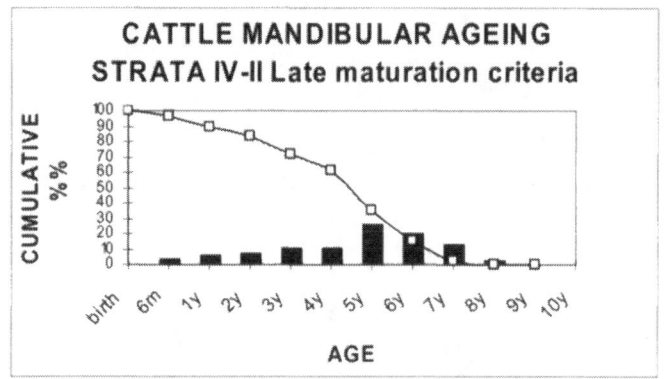

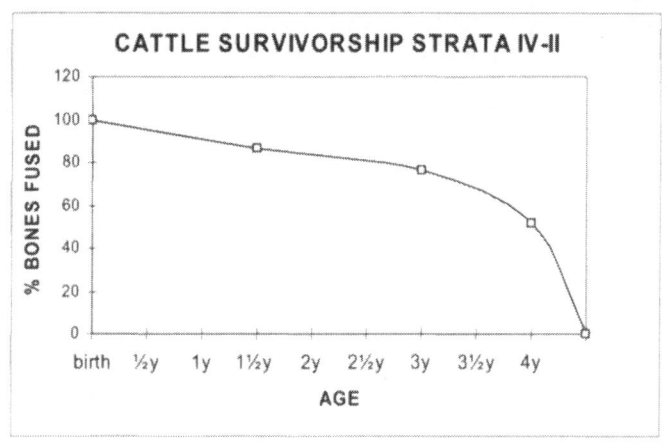

Figure 6.13. Cattle ageing at Gilat. A: Mandibular ageing, based on early maturation criteria; B: Mandibular ageing, the same data, based on late maturation criteria; C: Longbone epiphysial fusion. When early maturation criteria are used the plot shows that almost all the animals at Gilat had been slaughtered by the age of 5 years, but in such a regime the cows would not live long enough to replenish the herd. The same data based on late maturation criteria show that at least 50% of the cattle survive until their fifth year. Roughly the same conclusion can be drawn from longbone survivorship pattern.

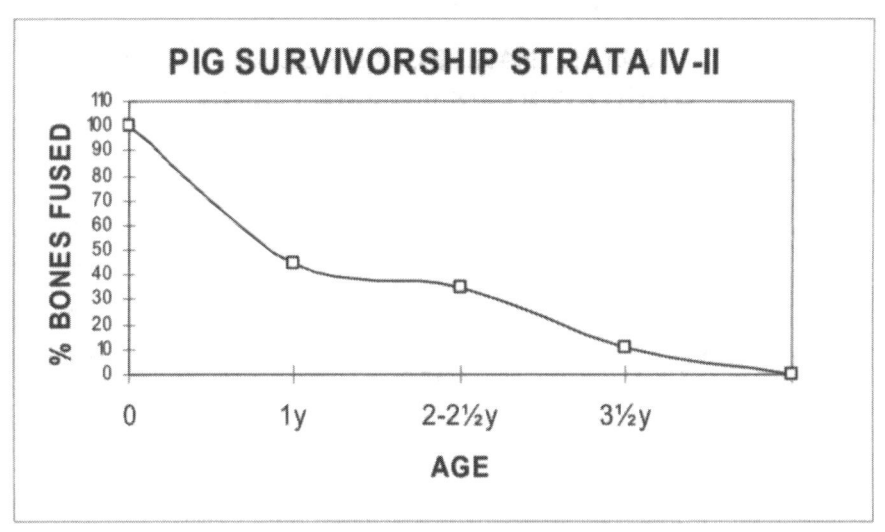

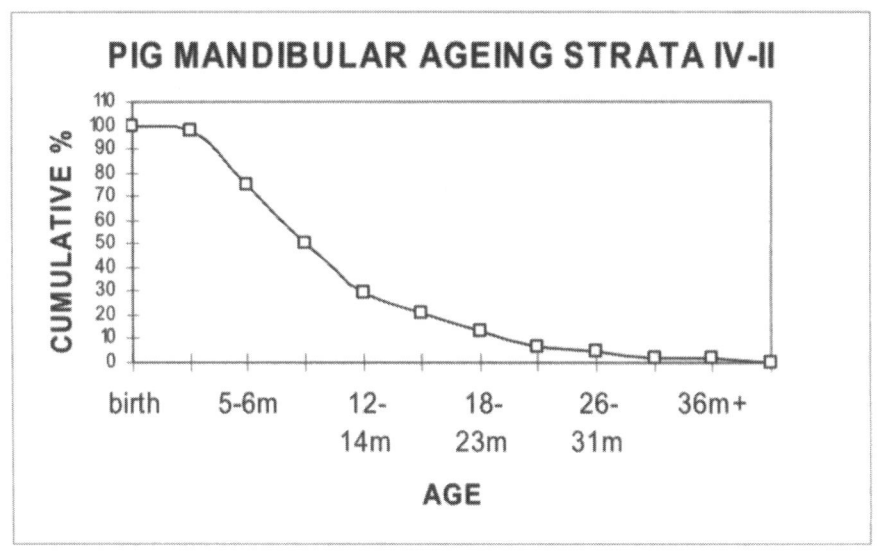

Figure 6.14. Pig ageing at Gilat. A: Mandibular ageing; B: Longbone epiphysial fusion. The mandibular data show that over half the pigs were killed in their first year, nearly a half in the second year, with only 6% surviving into the third year or older. A similar pattern is indicated by the longbone fusion data.

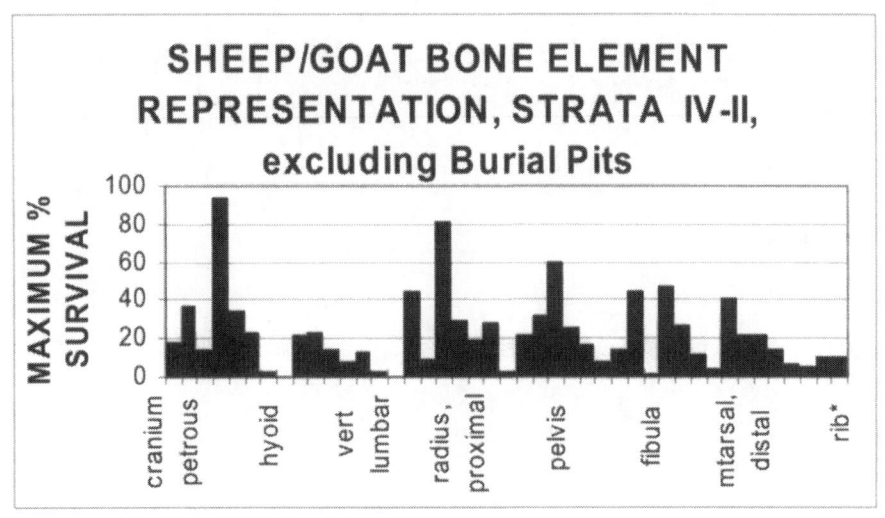

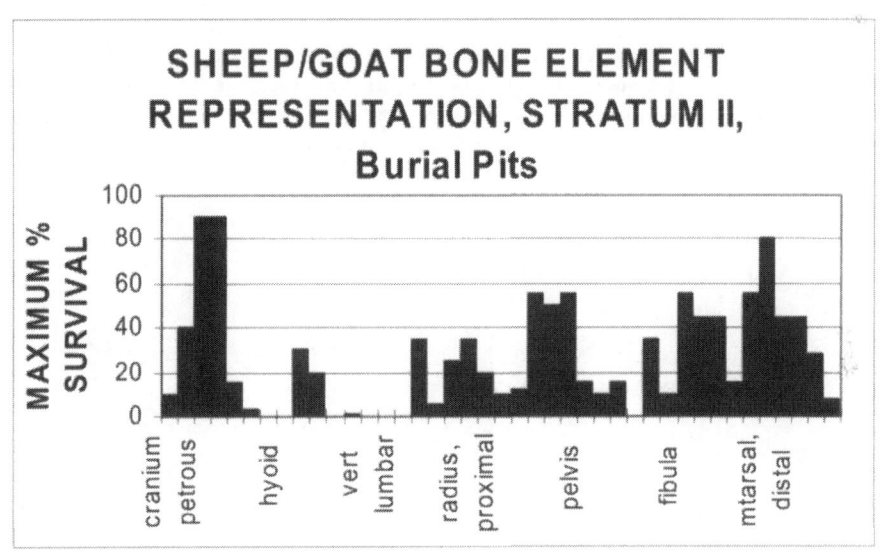

Figure 6.15. Bone element analysis in sheep/goats. A: Strata 4, 3 and 2, excluding the large burial pit; B: The large burial pit (L. 1237 and 1357). All parts of the body are represented, but there is a wide discrepancy in the numbers of the different elements. This can be explained by the differential retrieval of the smaller bones and the destruction of the softer elements (see Figure 6.16).

The distribution of survival rates in the large burial pit is slightly more even than in the main body of data, but there is a high proportion of bones of the feet and head, so it is possible that at least some of the material was deposited as fleeces or hides.

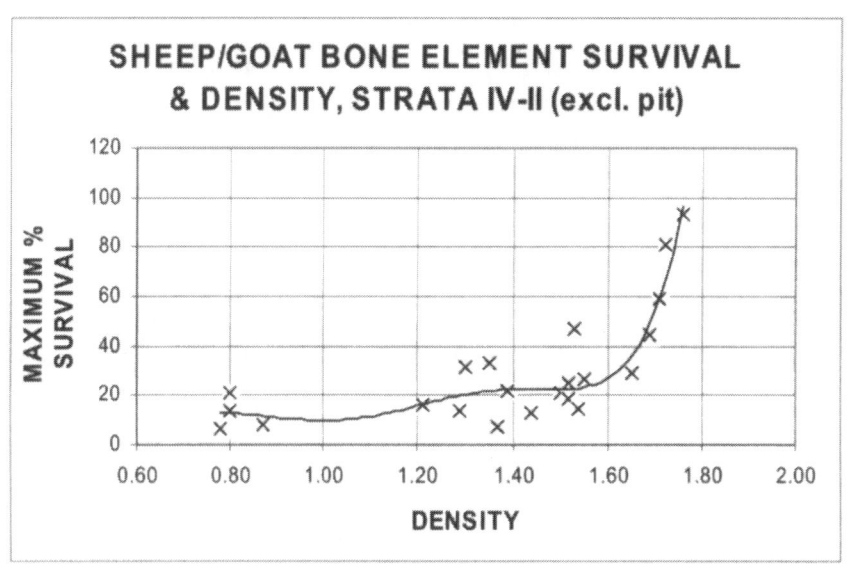

Figure 6.16. Sheep/goat bone element survival at Gilat, expressed as a percentage of expected numbers against density, in Strata 4-2 (excluding the large burial pit). There is a very close correlation (R=0.92) between the survival of each bone element and its density, suggesting much differential post-depositional destruction of the less dense elements. Density figures from Binford and Bertram (1977) for sheep aged 90 months.

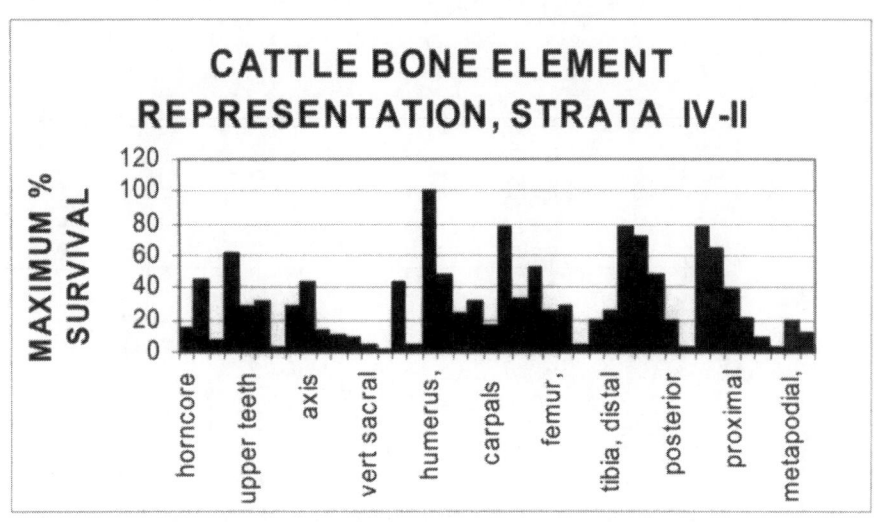

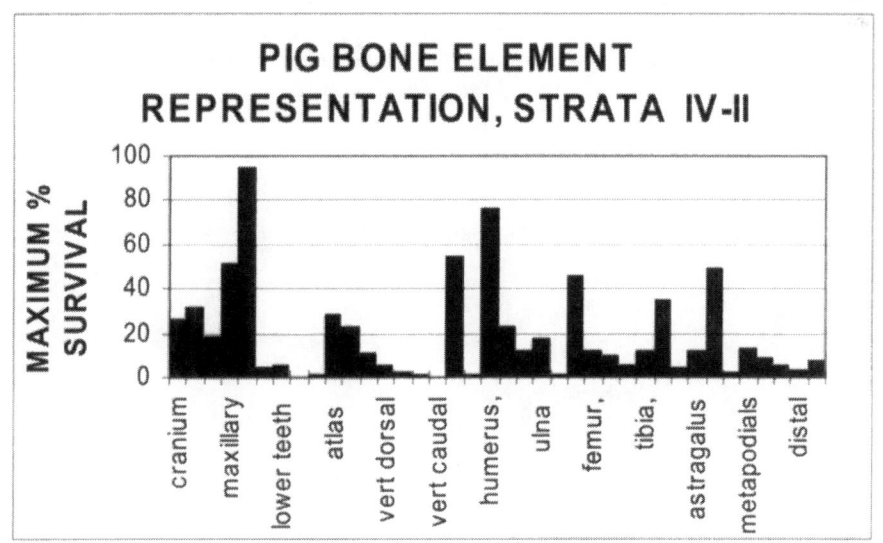

Figure 6.17. Bone element analysis in cattle and pigs. A: Cattle; B: Pigs. All parts of the body are represented in cattle and pigs, but as in sheep and goats (Figure 6.15) there is a wide discrepancy in the numbers of the different elements, probably due to the differential retrieval of the smaller bones and the destruction of the softer elements.

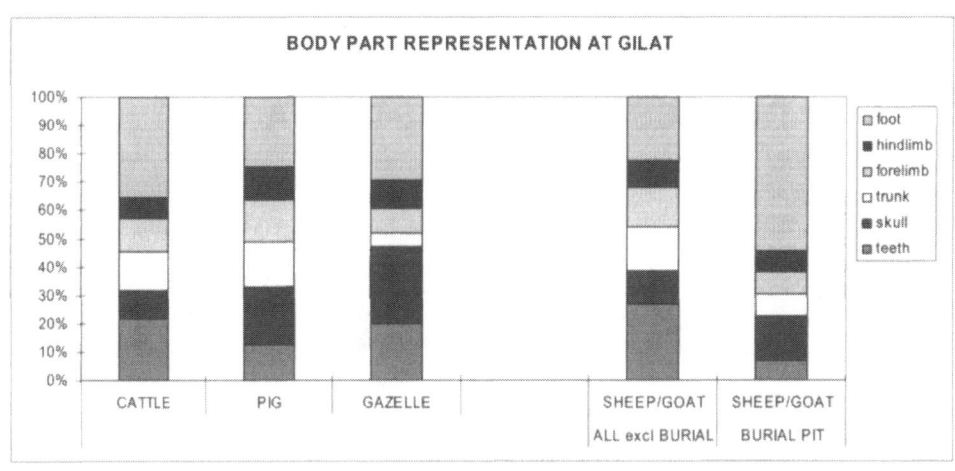

Figure 6.18. Body part representation in cattle, sheep/goats, pigs and gazelles at Gilat. There is no apparent emphasis on any particular one part of the body, but the large proportion of loose teeth reflects a high degree of post-depositional damage. The sheep/goat bones from the burial pit have a disproportionate number of footbones suggesting that entire feet, perhaps in fleeces or hides, were deposited there. Gazelle heads are relatively frequent due to the cache of horncores and frontlets recovered from L. 1344 (see Figure 6.20B).

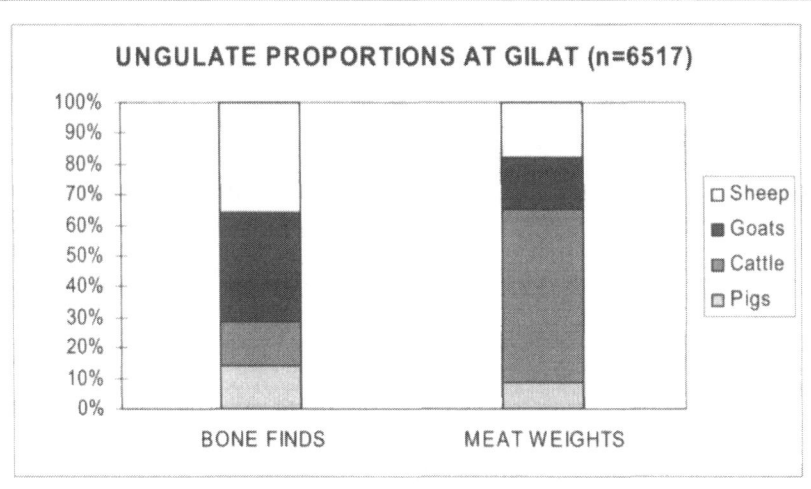

Figure 6.19. Domestic ungulate proportions at Gilat. Relative numbers of bones finds and relative meat weights. In terms of relative numbers the ungulate profile at Gilat is dominated by sheep and goats, which together constitute 71% of the sample, with 15% cattle and 14% pigs. But in terms of meat weight cattle contribute roughly 56%, with sheep and goat about 17.5% each and pigs 9%.

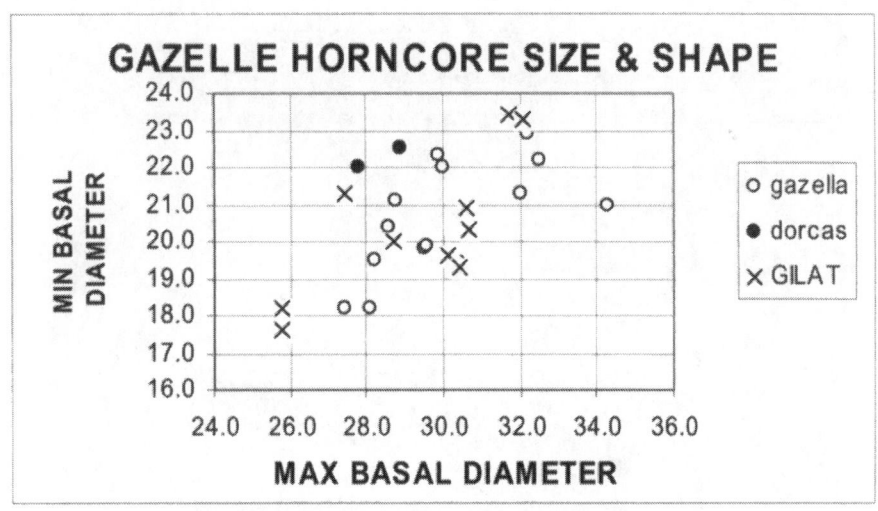

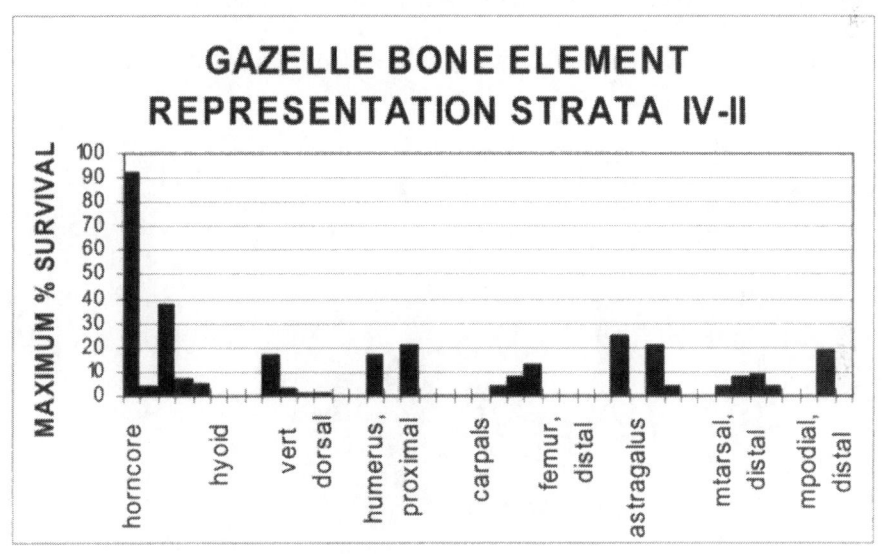

Figure 6.20. Gazelles at Gilat. A: Horncore shape and size; B: Bone element analysis. The plot shows that the two horncores of modern Gazella dorcas are rounder in cross-section than those of G. gazella, some of those from Gilat resemble dorcas, others resemble gazella and others are intermediate, probably indicating a continuous range of variation in this character. The bone element analysis shows that although most parts of the body were represented, horncores were by far the most numerous. This bias is largely due to the cache of burnt gazelle horncores in L. 1344.

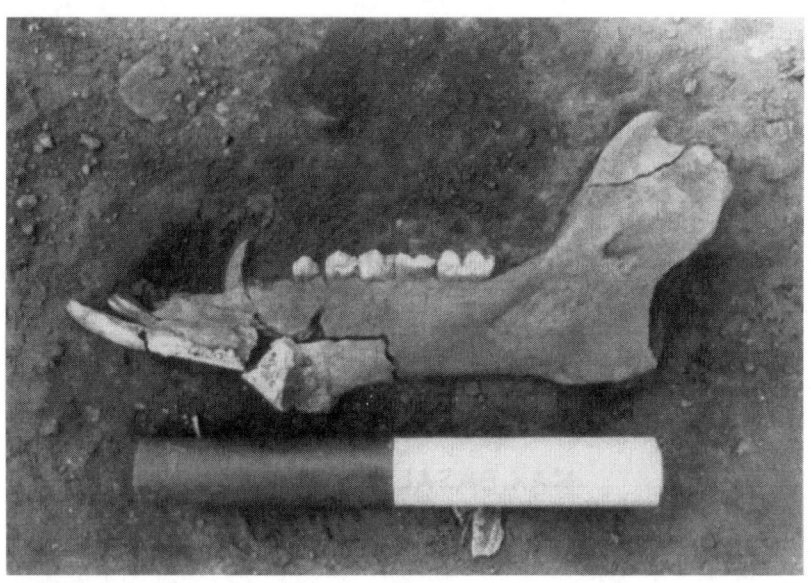

Plate 6.1a. Mandible of a young pig (GIL92 4209) showing the absence of crowding of the teeth.

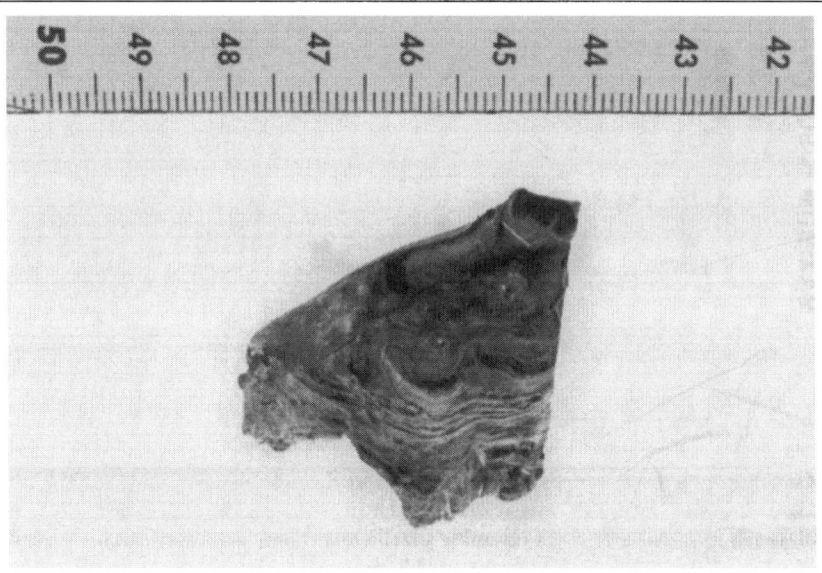

Plate 6.1b. Lower second premolar of an equid showing polish and excessive wear, possibly caused by a rope or a bit (GIL91 2089).

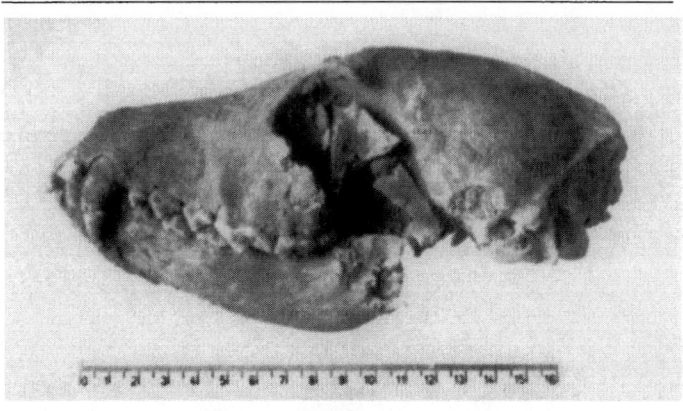

Plate 6.2a. The skull from the complete dog's skeleton found in L. 698/692 (GIL91 139).

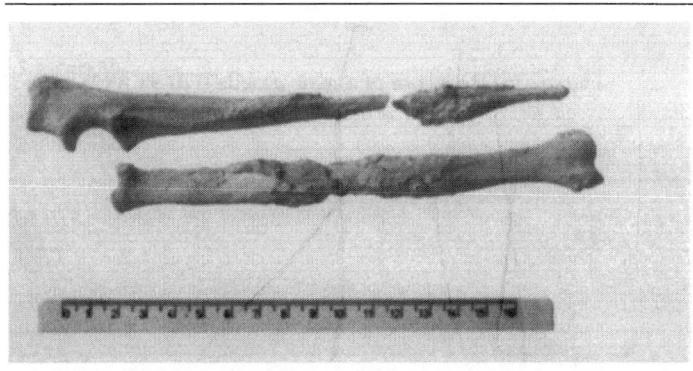

Plate 6.2b. Radius and ulna from the same dog skeleton as the skull above
showing a healed fracture (GIL91 139).

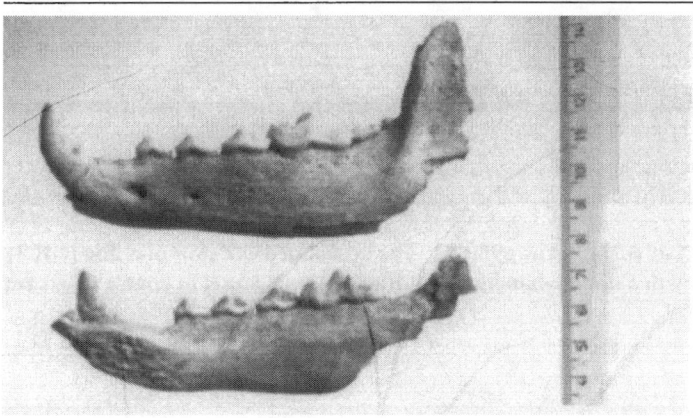

Plate 6.2c. Mandible from the second dog's skull found in L. 698/692 (GIL91 138).

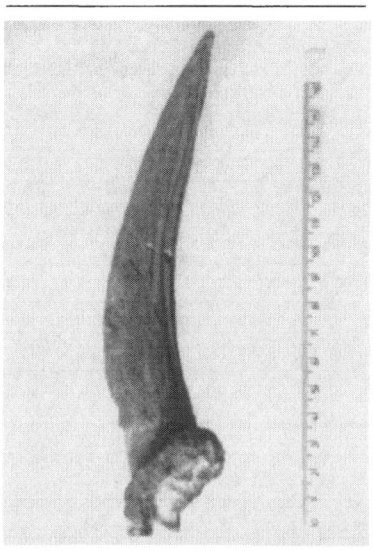

Plate 6.3a. Horncore of a male gazelle (GIL91 392).

Plate 6.3b. Locus 698/692. The articulated skeleton of a dog (GIL91 139)
with a double-handled cylindrical ceramic vessel in course of excavation.

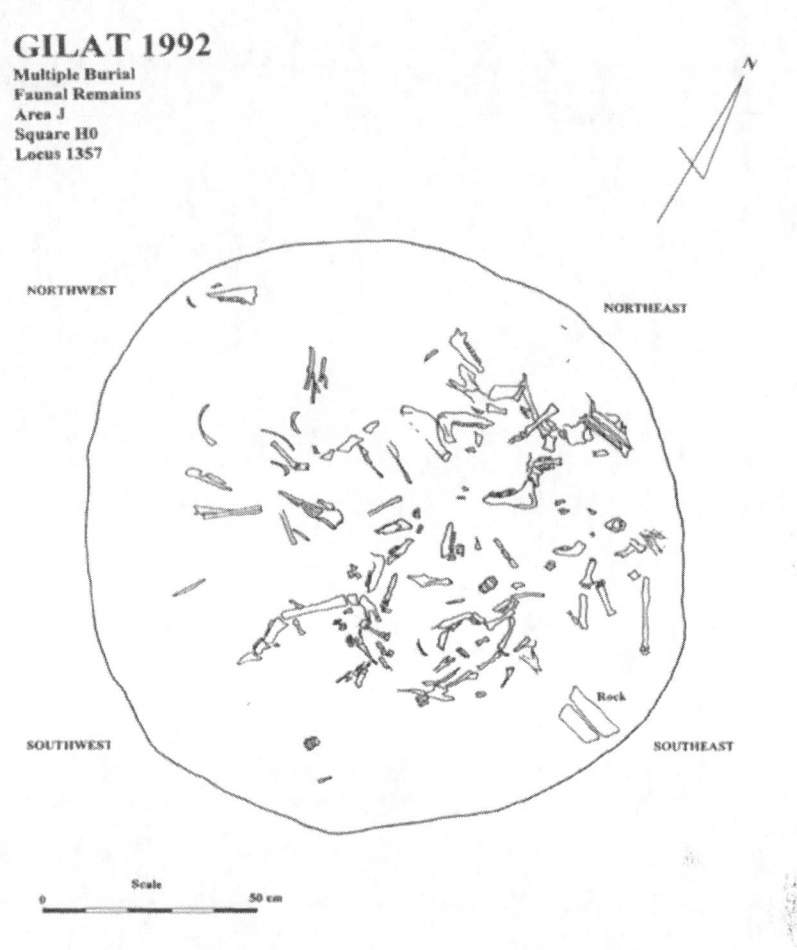

GILAT 1992
Multiple Burial
Faunal Remains
Area J
Square H0
Locus 1357

NORTHWEST

NORTHEAST

SOUTHWEST

SOUTHEAST

Rock

Scale

0   50 cm

Plate 6.4. Locus 1357. Plan of the animal bones in the burial pit.

Plate 6.5a. The multi-use pit (L. 1344). One of the gazelle horncores
and the fenestrated stand in course of excavation.

Plate 6.5b. The multi-use pit (L. 1344). Some of the gazelle horncores
and an animal figurine in course of excavation.

Plate 6.6a. Locus 013. Cranium of a dog (GIL92 3868).

Plate 6.6b. Locus 787. Cranium of a dog (GIL92 2302).

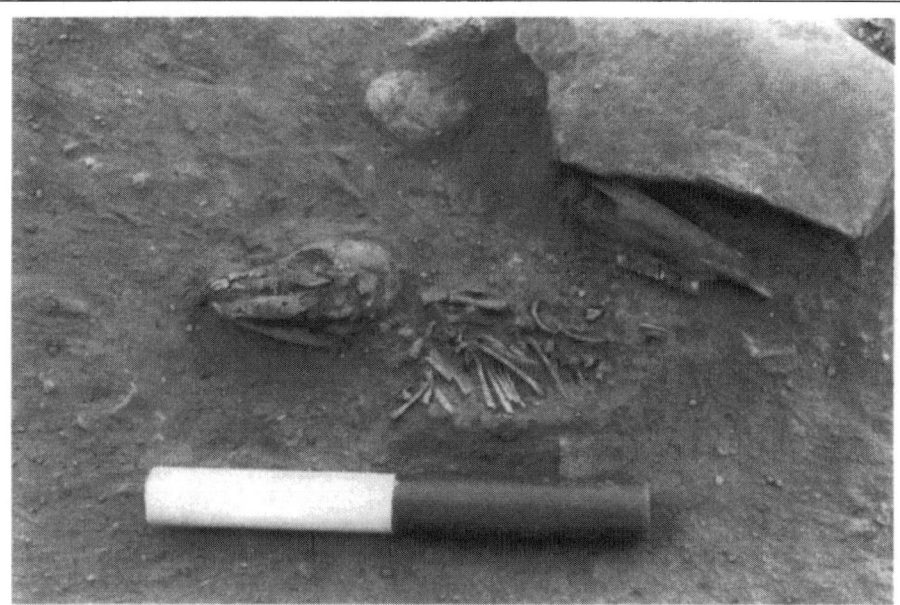

Plate 6.7a. Locus 1168. Articulated skeleton of a piglet (GIL91 407).

Plate 6.7b. Skull of the same piglet.

Appendix 6.1. Definitions of Measurements and Explanations of Abbreviations.

shpgt	sheep/goat
mcarpal	metacarpal
mtarsal	metatarsal
mpod	metapodial
art	articulate
L	left
R	right
F	female
M	male
prox ep	proximal epiphysis fused (y); unfused (n); partly fused (yn)
dist ep	distal epiphysis fused (y); unfused (n)
age	young (y); adult (ad); old (o)
ant	anterior
post	posterior
bnt	burnt
ident	identified
horncores	L=length (horncore length is along the anterior face)
	meas x meas=maximum cross section x minimum cross section at base
	circ=basal circumference
c	circa
e	estimated
phalanges	phal mid middle phalanx
	phal prox proximal phalanx
	phal dist distal phalanx
	ai=anterior inner
	ao=anterior outer
	pi=posterior inner
	po=posterior outer
teeth	alv=alveolus
	a letter after a tooth symbol indicates the wear stage after Grant (1982)

Appendix 6.2. Measurements of Sheep and Goat Bones and Teeth at Gilat.

site	locus	stratum	bone no	species	bone	prox ep	dist ep	age	measurement	notes
GIL91	1150	IIIA	595	goat	astragalus			y	GL 27.6; Bd 17.1	594 595 same ankle?
GIL92	1505	IIC	3719	goat	astragalus				GL 25.2; Bd 15.9	Female?
GIL92	1241	IIA	3848	goat	astragalus				GL 25.5; Bd 15.9	Female?
GIL92	1241	IIA	3851	goat	astragalus				GL 27.6; Bd 17.1	3850 3851 art?
GIL92	1221	IICii	3880	goat	astragalus				GL 26.5; Bd 16.5	Female?; burnt
GIL90	555	III	3969	goat	astragalus				GL 30.2	
GIL90	841	IIBi	4281	goat	astragalus			old	GL 25.5; Bd 16.4	Female?
GIL90	961	IIA	4321	goat	astragalus			old	GL 25.6; Bd 16.6	Female?
GIL90	548	III	4630	goat	astragalus				GL 29.2; Bd 20.2	Male?
GIL90	525	IIB	4754	goat	astragalus				GL 26.4; Bd 17.7	
GIL91	633	IIB	49	sheep	astragalus				GL 31.8; Bd 20.9	
GIL91	1103	IIBii	114	sheep	astragalus				GL 27.2; Bd 17.2	
GIL91	647	IIB	232	sheep	astragalus				GL 32.1	
GIL91	1159	IIC	467	sheep	astragalus				GL 30.8; Bd 19.5	
GIL91	649	IIC	647	sheep	astragalus				GL 28.5; Bd 18.6	
GIL91	1168	IIC	694	sheep	astragalus				GL 29.4; Bd 19.1	
GIL91	1159	IIC	833	sheep	astragalus				GL 30.9; Bd 20.2	833-835 art
GIL91	1050	IIA	1967	sheep	astragalus				GL 32.0; Bd 21.8	Male?; 1966 1967 1970-1974 same foot?
GIL92	1273	IV	2455	sheep	astragalus				GL 32.7; Bd 20.2	
GIL92	1572	IIIA	2589	sheep	astragalus				GL 30.7; Bd 20.0	
GIL92	773	IIA	2978	sheep	astragalus				GL 32.8	Male?
GIL90	826	IIBi	3504	sheep	astragalus				GL 30.4; Bd 19.0	
GIL90	586	IIIB	3611	sheep	astragalus				GL 28.2; Bd 18.8;	Female?
GIL92	1526	IIC	3691	sheep	astragalus				GL 27.9; Bd 18.6	
GIL92	775	IIBii	3765	sheep	astragalus				GL 29.5; Bd 18.9	Female?
GIL90	567	IIIA	3827	sheep	astragalus				GL 32.5; Bd 22.4	Male
GIL92	771	IIC	4323	sheep	astragalus				GL 29.1; Bd 18.7	Male?
GIL90	33	IIC	5034	sheep	astragalus				GLpe 30.4; Bd 18.5	
GIL90	586	IIIB	6321	sheep	astragalus				GL 30.5; Bd 20.8	
GIL92	1259	IIC	6537	sheep	astragalus				GL 25.8; Bd 16.5	Female?; burnt
GIL87	270	IIC	513	sheep	astragalus				GL 29.5	Female?
GIL92	1320	IIC	6233	sheep?	astragalus				GL 29.7; Bd 19.9	
GIL91	649	IIC	648	shpgt	astragalus				GL 34.3; Bd 22.3	
GIL87	281	IIA	720	shpgt	astragalus				GL 30.0	
GIL91	1144	IIC	879	shpgt	astragalus				GL 31.4; Bd 21.1	
GIL91	709	IIB	1172	shpgt	astragalus				GL 26.0; Bd 16.8	
GIL91	1125	IIBi	1185	shpgt	astragalus				GL 26.6; Bd 17.7	
GIL91	1028	IIBi	1853	shpgt	astragalus				GL 26.9; Bd 16.7	burnt
GIL91	1072	IIBi	1898	shpgt	astragalus				GL 28.2; Bd 18.1	
GIL91	1051	IIA	2000	shpgt	astragalus				GL 30.0; Bd 19.5	
GIL91	1044	IIBii	2098	shpgt	astragalus				GL 29.9; Bd 20.4	
GIL92	1351	IIC	3366	shpgt	astragalus				GL 26.0; Bd 16.3	Female?
GIL90	824	IIA	3515	shpgt	astragalus			y	GL 27.2; Bd 16.7	burnt
GIL90	949	IIBi	3728	shpgt	astragalus			y	GL 28.2; Bd 17.8	
GIL90	7	II	3854	shpgt	astragalus				GL 26.5; Bd 17.1	burnt

GIL90	528	IIC	3894	shpgt	astragalus				GL 36.3??; Bd 17.2	
GIL90	21	II	4512	shpgt	astragalus				GL 27.1; Bd 17.2	
GIL92	1309	IIC	6095	shpgt	astragalus				GL 31.8; Bd19.1	burnt
GIL92	1241	IIA	3850	goat	calcaneum	y			GL 56.9	3850 3851 art?
GIL91	1159	IIC	835	sheep	calcaneum	y			GL 61.9	833-835 art
GIL91	1050	IIA	1966	sheep	calcaneum	y			GL 65.4	Male?; 1966 1967 1970-1974 same foot?
GIL91	1037	IIA	814	shpgt	calcaneum	y			GL 52.0	
GIL92	1307	IIC	2766	shpgt	calcaneum	y			GL 66.7	
GIL92	763	IIB	3823	shpgt	calcaneum	y			GL 64.7	burnt
GIL92	1542	IIIB	3337	sheep	femur	y			Bp 49.4	
GIL76	68	I-IIA	170	goat	horncore				32.9 x 20.9	Male; twisted
GIL87	70	IIC	704	goat	horncore				23.3 x 15.3	Female
GIL91	703	IIA	1136	goat	horncore			ad	30.6 x 16.9; L in front c140 (>130)	Female; sl twisted
GIL92	1522	IICii	3419	goat	horncore				29.4 x 20.1	Female; twisted
GIL90	824	IIA	3700	goat	horncore			ad	c32.5 x 17.4	Male; sl twist
GIL92	1505	IIC	3702	goat	horncore			ad	c27 x 17.0; L in front c130	Female; sl twist
GIL92	783	IIC	3748	goat	horncore				29.5 x -; L in front 117	sl twist
GIL90	882	IIBi	3783	goat	horncore			y	34 x 18.5	Male; sl twist
GIL90	528	IIC	3881	goat	horncore			ad	>42 x 27	Male; massive, twisted
GIL92	772	IIB	4236	goat	horncore			ad	27.1 x 15.4; L in front 105	Female; sl twist
GIL92	772	IIB	4239	goat	horncore			ad	>49.8 x 27.2	Male; massive, v twisted
GIL90	025	III	4721	goat	horncore			old	26.5 x -	Female; twisted
GIL91	671	IIC	184	sheep	horncore				37.5 x 28.5	frontal//& front/par open
GIL91	649	IIC	353	sheep	horncore			old	L in front >121	Female
GIL91	1066	IIBii	444	sheep	horncore			ad	27.4 x 43.1	Male
GIL91	1053	IIBi	1462	sheep	horncore				25.4 x 16.3	Female; Ammon curve
GIL92	1572	IIIA	2590	sheep	horncore				20.3 x 15.6; L in front 60	Female
GIL92	1369	IIIA	3383	sheep	horncore				23.1 x 17.5; L in front 32	Female; Ammon curve; sutures open
GIL92	1511	IIC	3787	sheep	horncore			ad	59 x 41	Male
GIL90	882	IIBi	6051	sheep	horncore			ad	e53.6 x 36.1	Male
GIL90	558	IIC	6299	sheep	horncore				57.8 x 40.8	Male
GIL91	1147	IIIA	429	goat	humerus		y		Bt 28.7; Bd 29.8	
GIL87	281	IIA	719	goat	humerus		y		Bt 27.5; Bd 28.8	
GIL87	312	IIA	747	goat	humerus	n	yn		Bt 30.1; Bd 30.9	
GIL87	297	IIC	812	goat	humerus		y		Bt 31.4; Bd 33.1	
GIL92	1322	IIC	2503	goat	humerus		y		Bt 31.6; Bd 33.1	Male?
GIL92	1300	IIA	2784	goat	humerus		y		Bt 31.7	burnt
GIL92	1201	IIC	3247	goat	humerus		y		Bt 27.6	
GIL92	1371	IIIB	3348	goat	humerus		yn		Bt 32.3	
GIL92	1369	IIIA	3376	goat	humerus		y		Bt 29.5	
GIL90	946	IIC	3446	goat	humerus		y		Bt 27.5	

GIL92	1354	IV	3660	goat	humerus		y		Bt 28.0	
GIL92	1381	IIIAii	3973	goat	humerus		y		Bt 26.6	
GIL90	559	III	4194	goat	humerus		y		Bt 27.0; Bd 27.9	
GIL92	773	IIA	4219	goat	humerus		y		Bt 28.6	
GIL90	18	IIB	4455	goat	humerus		y		Bt 28.1; Bd 30.9	
GIL90	548	III	4562	goat	humerus		y		Bt 28.8; Bd 31.2	
GIL87	282	IIC	540	sheep	humerus		y		Bt 31.8; Bd 32.6	
GIL87	295	IIB	639	sheep	humerus		y		Bt 29.8	
GIL91	1168	IIC	698	sheep	humerus		y		Bt 31.3	
GIL91	1168	IIC	699	sheep	humerus		y		Bt 32.4	
GIL87	257	IIC	917	sheep	humerus		y		Bt 34.0	massive
GIL91	704	IIB	1119	sheep	humerus		y		Bt 28.9	
GIL91	1128	IIC	1696	sheep	humerus		y		Bt 27.6 (26.9 in front)	
GIL91	707	IIIA	1712	sheep	humerus		y		Bt 29.3	
GIL91	1092	IIIA	1731	sheep	humerus		y		Bt 31.3	
GIL91	1105	IIC	1801	sheep	humerus		y		Bt 30.5	
GIL92	1321	IIBi	2538	sheep	humerus		yn		Bt c30	Male?
GIL92	1316	IIC	2801	sheep	humerus		y		Bt 33.1	
GIL92	1548	IIIB	3331	sheep	humerus		y		Bt 30.6	
GIL92	1371	IIIB	3346	sheep	humerus	y			Bp 47.8	
GIL92	1371	IIIB	3347	sheep	humerus		y		Bt 35.0	
GIL90	586	IIIB	3593	sheep	humerus		y		Bt 29.1; Bd 29.3	
GIL90	528	IIC	3892	sheep	humerus		y		Bt 30.9; Bd 33.3	
GIL92	755	IIB/C	3898	sheep	humerus		y		Bt 29.2	
GIL90	40	IIC	4119	sheep	humerus		y		Bt 30.3; Bd 32.5	
GIL90	804	IIA	4209	sheep	humerus		y		Bt 29.1; Bd 30.1	
GIL92	1294	IV	4254	sheep	humerus		y		Bt 32.3	
GIL90	882	IIBi	4471	sheep	humerus		yn		Bt 29.1; Bd 30.0	
GIL90	025	III	4728	sheep	humerus		y		Bt 32.3; Bd 33.5	
GIL87	274	IIB	542	shpgt	humerus		y		Bt 30.8; Bd 33.5	
GIL91	1150	IIIA	583	shpgt	humerus		yn		Bt 29.6	
GIL87	292	IIIB	831	shpgt	humerus		yn		Bt 30.9; Bd 32.6	
GIL91	1049	IIC	1780	shpgt	humerus		y		Bt 30.4	
GIL91	674	IIBii	2023	shpgt	humerus		y		Bt 31.2	
GIL90	834	IIB	4999	shpgt	humerus		y		Bt 34.0; Bd 36.4	Male?
GIL90	33	IIC	5038	shpgt	humerus		y		Bt 27.9; Bd 29.0	
GIL90	581	II	5078	shpgt	M3 low			GH	LM3 25.5	large dist pillar
GIL87	270	IIC	500	shpgt	M3 low				LM3 23.0	
GIL87	311	IIC	760	shpgt	M3 low				LM3 23.4	
GIL87	272	IIIA	809	shpgt	M3 low				LM3 24.9	
GIL87	295	IIB	641	shpgt	mandible			GH	L trow 67.2	
GIL92	1319	IIC	2793	shpgt	mandible			I	L trow 67.2	
GIL90	517	IIA	3330	shpgt	mandible			G	L trow 83.6	large dist pill M3
GIL90	837	IIBii	4220	shpgt	mandible			F	L trow e82.6	
GIL92	1503	IIBii	4226	shpgt	mandible			G	L trow c77.5	
GIL90	961	IIA	4298	shpgt	mandible			H	L trow 71.5	
GIL90	1510	IIC	6011	shpgt	mandible			G	L trow 72.6	
GIL77	122	IIIA	5	goat	mcarpal		y		SD c12.0; Bd 24.5	
GIL77	141	IIIA	79	goat	mcarpal		n		Bp 24.4; GL -ep 86	burnt
GIL75	7	IIC	125	goat	mcarpal		n		SD 13.9; GL-ep	

c86;

						R	n	y	Measurements	Comments
GIL87	294	IV	857	goat	mcarpal		n	y	Bp 20.7; SD 11.7; GL-ep c67	
GIL87	257	IIC	914	goat	mcarpal		n		Bp 23.2; SD 13.3; GL-ep 81.2;	
GIL91	1125	IIBi	1187	goat	mcarpal	R		y	Bp 21.5; SD 17.7; Bd 30.1; GL 117.7	Male?
GIL91	1029	IIAii	1585	goat	mcarpal		n		Bp 20.6; SD 13.8; Bd shft 24.8; GL-ep 78.3	Male?
GIL91	694	IIA	2142	goat	mcarpal				SD 16.3	Male?
GIL90	542	III	3388	goat	mcarpal				Bp 23.0; SD 16.4	
GIL90	960	IIA	3404	goat	mcarpal		n		Bp 20.6; SD 11.7; GL-ep 65.8	
GIL90	949	IIBi	3723	goat	mcarpal		n		Bp 22.2; SD 13.1; GL-ep 74.1;	
GIL92	1511	IIC	3795	goat	mcarpal			y	Bp 24.5; SD 15.3; Bd 26.5; GL 100.9	Female?
GIL92	1369	IIIA	3803	goat	mcarpal			y	Bp 23.8; SD 17.4	tool sawn distally & polished
GIL92	1382	IIIAii	3929	goat	mcarpal			y	Bp 22.2; SD 15.8; GL e101.3	Female?; burnt distally
GIL90	938	IIBi	4365	goat	mcarpal			y	Bp 23.0; SD 15.6; Bd 27.4; GL 101.4;	
GIL90	13	IIB	4899	goat	mcarpal		n		Bp 22.5; SD 14.4; GL-ep e78.5	
GIL92	1328	IIIAii	3614	goat?	mcarpal		n		Bp 22.5; GL-ep e77.9	
GIL92	1354	IV	3658	goat?	mcarpal		n		Bp 23.6; SD 14.9; Bd-ep 28.7; GL-ep 90.4	Male?
GIL90	535	IIA	4686	goat?	mcarpal				Bp 23.4; SD 15.9	
GIL91	671	IIC	186	sheep	mcarpal		n	y	Bd 28.5 held tog	Male?
GIL87	92	IIB	664	sheep	mcarpal			y	Bd 26.2	
GIL91	696	IIA	1427	sheep	mcarpal			y	Bd 24.7	
GIL90	916	IIIA	3102	sheep	mcarpal			y	Bp 24.4; SD 14.0; Bd 25.4; GL 147.1	3102 3112 art
GIL92	1203	IIIA	3212	sheep	mcarpal			y	Bd 29.0	Male?
GIL90	586	IIIB	3603	sheep	mcarpal				SD 11.6	
GIL92	763	IIB	3826	sheep	mcarpal			y	Bd 24.5	burnt
GIL90	574	III	4526	sheep	mcarpal			y	Bd 25.0	
GIL90	547	III	4802	sheep	mcarpal			y	GL 135.5; SD 13.2	
GIL92	1277	IIC	4270	sheep?	mcarpal		n		SD 11.9; GL-ep c97	Female?
GIL87	295	IIB	646	shpgt	mcarpal				Bp 23.5	
GIL87	92	IIB	668	shpgt	mcarpal				Bp c25	
GIL87	261	IIIA	884	shpgt	mcarpal				Bp 23.0	burnt
GIL91	1028	IIBi	1847	shpgt	mcarpal				Bp 21.4	
GIL90	33	IIC	3273	shpgt	mcarpal		n		Bd 26.3 condyles held together	
GIL90	13	IIB	4912	shpgt	mcarpal				Bp 22.2	

GIL90	33	IIC	3284	sheep	mpodial		y	old	Bd 25.4	Female?
GIL87	92	IIB	666	shpgt	mpodial		n	?y	Bd-ep 28.0	
GIL87	92	IIB	672	shpgt	mpodial		n		Bd-ep 24.5	burnt
GIL91	697	IIA	1067	shpgt	mpodial		n		Bd 28.2	
GIL75	7	IIC	114	goat	mtarsal			y	GL 105.5; Bp 17.5; SD 11.0; Bd 22.1	
GIL91	1029	IIAii	1584	goat	mtarsal			y	GL 106; Bd 22.8	Female?
GIL91	695	IIA	2130	goat	mtarsal			M	Bp 23.5	v solid
GIL90	567	IIIA	3815	goat	mtarsal			y	old	Bp 19.5; SD 11.3; Bd 23.0; GL 105.6	Female?
GIL90	961	IIA	4288	goat	mtarsal			y	Bp 20.8; SD 13.8; Bd 23.8; GL 108.3	
GIL90	19	III	4372	goat	mtarsal		yn	y	Bd 27.2	Male?
GIL91	647	IIB	204	goat?	mtarsal		n	vy	GL -ep 69.0	204 205 a pair?
GIL91	647	IIB	205	goat?	mtarsal		n	vy	GL -ep 68.2	204 205 a pair?
GIL92	786	IIC	3581	goat?	mtarsal		n		Bp 18.3; SD 11.1; Bd 22.6 GL-ep 92.4	Female?
GIL91	671	IIC	187	sheep	mtarsal		n	y	Bd c28 held tog	Male?
GIL91	647	IIB	207	sheep	mtarsal		n	y	Bd 28.5 held tog	Male?
GIL77	124	IIC	328	sheep	mtarsal		n		Bp 18.5; SD 11.9; GL-ep c110	
GIL87	297	IIC	566	sheep	mtarsal		yn		Bd 23.1	
GIL87	295	IIB	647	sheep	mtarsal		n		Bp 19.9; SD 11.6; Bd 24.0; GL+ep 144;	
GIL87	257	IIC	916	sheep	mtarsal		n		Bp 17.3; SD 13.3; GL-ep 71.8;	
GIL91	1051	IIA	1324	sheep	mtarsal		y		Bd 27.0	burnt
GIL91	1050	IIA	1970	sheep	mtarsal		y		SD 13.4; GL 162.3	Male?; 1966 1967 1970-1974 same foot?
GIL92	761	IIA	3039	sheep	mtarsal		y		Bd 25.0	
GIL90	553	III	3173	sheep	mtarsal				SD 12.3	
GIL90	528	IIC	3871	sheep	mtarsal		n		SD 10.8; GL-ep 128.9	Female?
GIL92	786	IIC	4018	sheep	mtarsal				GL-ep c.132	
GIL90	13	IIB	4911	sheep	mtarsal		y		SD 13.2	
GIL92	1322	IIC	6383	sheep	mtarsal		n		Bp 20.3; SD 11.2; GL-ep 89.1	
GIL90	813	IIA	3120	sheep?	mtarsal		n		Bp 17.4; SD 9.8; Bd-ep 21.0; GL-ep 81.7	
GIL90	532	II	4687	sheep?	mtarsal				Bp 20.9; SD 10.6	
GIL87	270	IIC	516	shpgt	mtarsal				Bp 16.3	burnt
GIL92	772	IIB	2315	shpgt	mtarsal		y		Bd 23.6	Female?
GIL92	1354	IV	3674	shpgt	mtarsal		n	vy	Bp 18.5 SD 9.1 Bd-ep 21.7 GL-ep 73.1	
GIL91	671	IIC	1054	goat?	navicular				GB 26.0	
GIL91	1159	IIC	834	sheep	navicular				GB 25.1	833-835 art
GIL87	70	IIC	701	shpgt	navicular			y	GB 21.2	

GIL87	312	IIA	752	shpgt	navicular		GB 24.6	
GIL91	1105	IIC	315	shpgt	phal mid	y	Bp 14.0; GLpe 23.7;	Male?
GIL87	270	IIC	515	shpgt	phal mid	yn	Bp 10.6; GLpe 19.6	
GIL87	292	IIIB	846	shpgt	phal mid	y	Bp 13.2; GLpe 20.5	844-846 same foot
GIL87	294	IV	859	shpgt	phal mid	y	Bp 12.3; GLpe 20.5	
GIL91	671	IIC	1050	shpgt	phal mid		GLpe 24.3	1049 1050 art
GIL91	1128	IIC	1699	shpgt	phal mid	y	Bp 10.8; GLpe 22.4	
GIL91	1054	IIIA	1878	shpgt	phal mid	y	Bp 11.0; GLpe 20.6	
GIL92	777	IIC	2903	shpgt	phal mid	y	Bp 12.5; GLpe 25.2	
GIL90	916	IIIA	3097	shpgt	phal mid	y	Bp 11.1; GLpe 23.7	
GIL92	1511	IIC	3258	shpgt	phal mid	y	Bp 11.6; GLpe 19.7	burnt
GIL90	946	IIC	3450	shpgt	phal mid	y	Bp 12.1; GLpe 20.6	3450 3451 art
GIL90	946	IIC	3451	shpgt	phal mid	y	Bp 11.7; GLpe 33.3	3450 3451 art
GIL90	567	IIIA	3810	shpgt	phal mid	y	Bp 12.1; GLpe 21.0	
GIL90	971	IIBii	4067	shpgt	phal mid	y	Bp 12.5; GLpe 23.1;	
GIL92	1389	IIBi	4398	shpgt	phal mid	y	Bp 12.9 GLpe 23.0	Male?
GIL90	25	III	6055	shpgt	phal mid	y	Bp 11.2; GLpe 24.5	
GIL90	580	IIA	6173	shpgt	phal mid	y	Bp 12.2; GLpe 20.3	5092 6170-6176 same coll feet
GIL90	580	IIA	6174	shpgt	phal mid	y	Bp 12.4; GLpe 20.6	5092 6170-6176 same coll feet
GIL90	580	IIA	6175	shpgt	phal mid	y	Bp 12.3; GLpe 20.9	5092 6170-6176 same coll feet
GIL90	580	IIA	6176	shpgt	phal mid	y	Bp 12.0; GLpe 20.6	5092 6170-6176 same coll feet
GIL92	1393	IIC	6332	shpgt	phal mid	y	Bp 13.6; GLpe 22.8	Male? burnt
GIL92	1320	IIC	6443	shpgt	phal mid	y	Bp 13.0; GLpe 23.7;	large
GIL91	618	IIA	1654	shpgt	phal mid	n	Bp 12.9; GLpe 23.2	
GIL90	567	IIIA	3835	shpgt	phal mid	y	Bp 11.9; GLpe 21.6;	burnt
GIL90	567	IIIA	3841	shpgt	phal mid	y	Bp 11.5; GLpe 20.6;	burnt
GIL90	580	IIA	6181	shpgt	phal mid		Bp 10.6; GLpe 20.8	
GIL75	7	IIC	161	shpgt	phal mid	y	GLpe 24.6 Bp 12.4	
GIL91	1119	IIBii	383	shpgt	phal mid	y	Bp 14.0; GLpe 22.7	
GIL87	270	IIC	594	shpgt	phal mid	y	Bp 12.4; GLpe 23.5	Male?

GIL87 270	IIC	595	shpgt	phal mid	y	Bp 11.3; GLpe 22.8	Female?
GIL91 1037	IIA	825	shpgt	phal mid	y	Bp 12.1; GLpe 22.8	824 825 art
GIL87 292	IIIB	848	shpgt	phal mid	y	Bp 11.5	
GIL91 1050	IIA	1973	shpgt	phal mid pi	y	Bp 12.8; GLpe 23.5;	Male?; 1966 1967 1970-1974 same foot?
GIL91 1050	IIA	1974	shpgt	phal mid po	y	Bp 12.8; GLpe 24.5	Male?; 1966 1967 1970-1974 same foot?
GIL91 1066	IIBii	2227	shpgt	phal mid	y	Bp 12.1; GLpe 23.4	
GIL92 1260	IIA	2487	shpgt	phal mid	y	Bp 13.4; GLpe 28.3	Male?
GIL92 1307	IIC	2781	shpgt	phal mid	y	Bp 12.7; GLpe 25.5	
GIL92 1307	IIC	2782	shpgt	phal mid	y	Bp 12.6; GLpe 25.3	
GIL92 771	IIC	2991	shpgt	phal mid	y	Bp 10.8; GLpe 21.7	
GIL90 828	IIBi	3017	shpgt	phal mid	y	Bp 14.1; GLpe 26.7	
GIL90 16	IIB	3584	shpgt	phal mid	y	Bp 12.6; GLpe 26.5;	burnt dist
GIL90 925	IIA	4370	shpgt	phal mid	y	Bp 12.1; GLpe 24.3	
GIL92 1354	IV	4372	shpgt	phal mid	y	Bp 13.1 GLpe 27.2	Male?; burnt
GIL92 1354	IV	4373	shpgt	phal mid	y	Bp 11.3 GLpe 18.3	Female?
GIL92 1389	IIBi	4400	shpgt	phal mid	y	Bp 10.5 GLpe 21.8	
GIL90 882	IIBi	4492	shpgt	phal mid	y	Bp 11.3; GLpe 19.4	
GIL90 950	IIA	4588	shpgt	phal mid	y	Bp 14.5; GLpe 25.3	Male?
GIL92 1416	IIC	6120	shpgt	phal mid		Bp 11.1; GLpe 21.2	
GIL92 1354	IV	6347	shpgt	phal mid	y	Bp 13.3; GLpe 27.8	
GIL92 1371	IIIB	6414	shpgt	phal mid	y	Bp 12.0; GLpe 24.5	
GIL91 1044	IIBii	2118	shpgt	phal mid	y	Bp 11.1; GLpe 18.9;	
GIL92 1321	IIBi	2536	shpgt	phal mid	y	Bp 11.5; GLpe 20.6	
GIL92 756	IIA	2754	shpgt	phal mid	y	Bp 13.5; GLpe 23.9	
GIL90 828	IIBi	3032	shpgt	phal mid	y	Bp 29.9; GLpe e21.6	
GIL90 946	IIC	3436	shpgt	phal mid	y	Bp 12.2; GLpe 21.9	burnt
GIL90 580	IIA	5089	shpgt	phal mid	y	Bp 11.6; GLpe 23.0	burnt
GIL77 153	IIIB	11	shpgt	phal prox	y	GLpe 37.3; Bp 12.5	
GIL87 92	IIB	686	shpgt	phal prox	y	Bp 12.9; GLpe	

40.6

						Measurements	Notes
GIL87 292	IIIB	844	shpgt	phal prox	y	Bp 12.7; GLpe 36.8	844-846 same foot
GIL87 292	IIIB	845	shpgt	phal prox	y	Bp 13.1; GLpe 36.6	844-846 same foot
GIL91 1159	IIC	846	shpgt	phal prox	y	Bp 14.3; GLpe 38.4	burnt; massive
GIL91 671	IIC	1048	shpgt	phal prox	yn	Bp 12.3; GLpe 43.2	
GIL91 671	IIC	1049	shpgt	phal prox	yn	Bp 13.0; GLpe 43.4	1049 1050 art
GIL91 1051	IIA	1326	shpgt	phal prox	y	Bp 11.5; GLpe 33.1	
GIL91 1049	IIC	1779	shpgt	phal prox	y	Bp 14.7; GLpe 45.8	massive
GIL91 1105	IIC	1802	shpgt	phal prox	y	Bp 11.5; GLpe 32.2	
GIL91 695	IIA	2134	shpgt	phal prox	yn	Bp 12.0; GLpe 39.5	
GIL92 1536	IIIA	2353	shpgt	phal prox	yn	Bp 10.4; GLpe 33.4	
GIL92 1284	IIB	2465	shpgt	phal prox	y	Bp 12.3; GLpe 40.0	
GIL92 773	IIA	2988	shpgt	phal prox	y	Bp 12.4; GLpe 34.8	Male?
GIL92 760	IIA	3031	shpgt	phal prox	y	Bp 10.1; GLpe e31.8;	v narrow, but not gazelle
GIL90 828	IIBi	3036	shpgt	phal prox	y	Bp 12.8; GLpe 35.9	
GIL92 761	IIA	3040	shpgt	phal prox	y	Bp 11.8; GLpe 38.5	
GIL90 828	IIBi	3238	shpgt	phal prox	y	Bp 11.9; GLpe 34.6	
GIL90 586	IIIB	3612	shpgt	phal prox	y	Bp 12.8; GLpe 40.4	burnt
GIL90 528	IIC	3655	shpgt	phal prox	y	Bp 11.2; GLpe 33.6	Female?
GIL92 1526	IIC	3690	shpgt	phal prox	y	Bp 14.3; GLpe 40.5	Male?
GIL90 865	IIBi	3691	shpgt	phal prox	y	Bp 13.5; GLpe 35.2	Male?
GIL92 775	IIBii	3751	shpgt	phal prox	y	Bp 10.8; GLpe 30.8	burnt
GIL92 1391	IIA	3966	shpgt	phal prox	y	Bp 11.9; GLpe 33.8	
GIL92 799	IIB	3995	shpgt	phal prox	n	GLpe 38.6 ep held on	
GIL92 1206	IICi	4188	shpgt	phal prox	y	Bp 12.1; GLpe 36.0	
GIL90 534	IIC	4263	shpgt	phal prox	y	Bp 10.9; GLpe 32.0	burnt
GIL92 1389	IIBi	4397	shpgt	phal prox	y	Bp 12.2 GLpe 37.4	Male?
GIL90 553	III	4614	shpgt	phal prox	y	Bp 10.9; GLpe 32.2	Female?; 4614 4615 same foot?
GIL90 553	III	4615	shpgt	phal prox	y	Bp 10.9; GLpe 20.9	4614 4615 same foot?
GIL90 882	IIBi	4780	shpgt	phal prox	y	Bp 15.1; GLpe	

						e39.5	
GIL90 547	III	4796	shpgt	phal prox	y	Bp 11.6; GLpe 36.0	burnt
GIL90 528	IIC	4875	shpgt	phal prox	y	Bp 12.8; GLpe 35.9	
GIL90 556	III	4889	shpgt	phal prox	y	GLpe 31.5; Bp 10.8	
GIL90 580	IIA	6170	shpgt	phal prox	y	Bp 11.8; GLpe 32.8	5092 6170-6176 same coll feet
GIL90 580	IIA	6171	shpgt	phal prox	y	Bp 12.2; GLpe 33.3	5092 6170-6176 same coll feet
GIL90 556	III	6219	shpgt	phal prox	y	Bp 11.0; GLpe 31.6;	
GIL91 1131	IIIA	2070	shpgt	phal prox	yn	Bp 12.6; GLpe 40.5	
GIL92 1536	IIIA	2355	shpgt	phal prox	y	Bp 14.5; GLpe 42.1;	Male?
GIL90 580	IIA	5092	shpgt	phal prox	y	Bp 11.2; GLpe e32.8	Female?; 5092 6170-6176 same coll feet
GIL92 1371	IIIB	6413	goat? wild?	phal prox	y	Bp 13.4; GLpe 47.0	v big
GIL91 1159	IIC	479	shpgt	phal prox	y	Bp 11.7; GLpe 36.1;	burnt
GIL91 1150	IIIA	599	shpgt	phal prox	y	Bp 13.7; GLpe 39.0	burnt
GIL91 1150	IIIA	604	shpgt	phal prox pi	y	Bp 14.2; GLpe 43.1	
GIL87 92	IIB	687	shpgt	phal prox	y	Bp 12.2; GLpe 40.5	
GIL91 624	IIA	778	shpgt	phal prox	y	Bp 13.8; GLpe 39.5;	
GIL91 1037	IIA	824	shpgt	phal prox	y	Bp 14.1; GLpe 43.3	824 825 art
GIL91 1045	IIA	999	shpgt	phal prox	y	Bp 12.6; GLpe 39.6	
GIL91 696	IIA	1437	shpgt	phal prox	y	Bp 11.3; GLpe 36.8	
GIL91 696	IIA	1487	shpgt	phal prox	y	Bp 12.2; GLpe 36.8	
GIL91 1050	IIA	1971	shpgt	phal prox pi	y	Bp 13.9; GLpe 40.4	Male?; 1966 1967 1970-1974 same foot?
GIL91 1050	IIA	1972	shpgt	phal prox pi	y	Bp 13.1; GLpe 41.5	Male?; 1966 1967 1970-1974 same foot?
GIL92 1276	IIC	2474	shpgt	phal prox	yn	Bp 12.1; GLpe 38.6	
GIL92 1260	IIA	2486	shpgt	phal prox	y	Bp 14.2; GLpe 46.1	Male?
GIL92 1321	IIBi	2535	shpgt	phal prox	y	Bp 12.2; GLpe 36.1	burnt white
GIL92 1316	IIC	2805	shpgt	phal prox	y	Bp 13.2; GLpe 40.8	
GIL90 828	IIBi	3037	shpgt	phal prox	y	Bp 11.2; GLpe 34.5	
GIL90 916	IIIA	3112	shpgt	phal prox		Bp 12.6; GLpe 36.7	3102 3112 art
GIL92 775	IIBii	3760	shpgt	phal prox	y	Bp 12.3; GLpe	Female?

					pi				38.4	
GIL92	1222	IICii	3866	shpgt	phal prox	y			Bp 12.5; GLpe 40.4	
GIL92	1389	IIBi	4399	shpgt	phal prox	y			Bp 12.3 GLpe 37.9	
GIL90	986	IIBi	4935	shpgt	phal prox	y		old	Bp 12.2; GLpe 33.7	Female?
GIL92	1366	IIIB	6446	shpgt	phal prox	y			Bp 10.5; GLpe 32.6	burnt sl
GIL92	1241	IIA	3852	shpgt	phal prox	y			Bp 13.6; GLpe 37.2	
GIL91	1150	IIIA	573	shpgt	phal prox	yn		y	Bp 13.3; GLpe 40.7	v big
GIL91	685	IIB	738	shpgt	phal prox	y			Bp 13.1; GLpe 43.6	massive
GIL91	1073	IIBi	137	shpgt	phal prox	y			Bp 13.3; GLpe 40.2	
GIL87	297	IIC	621	shpgt	phal prox	y			Bp 12.7; GLpe 36.1;	burnt
GIL91	697	IIA	1090	shpgt	phal prox	yn			GLpe 43.2; Bp 13.0	
GIL91	1040	IIBi	1102	shpgt	phal prox	n			Bp ep 13.5	big
GIL92	783	IIC	2339	shpgt	phal prox	y			Bp 12.5; GLpe 35.3	burnt
GIL92	771	IIC	4324	shpgt	phal prox	y			Bp 12.3 GLpe 35.6	burnt
GIL87	270	IIC	926	goat	radius	y	n		Bp 25.1; SD 13.4; Bd 24.5; GL 122.3	ep held on
GIL92	1369	IIIA	3804	goat	radius	y			Bp 27.9	
GIL92	1416	IIC	6117	goat	radius	y			Bp 31.6	
GIL91	1147	IIIA	442	sheep	radius		y		Bd 35.6	big
GIL91	1159	IIC	466	sheep	radius		y		Bd 30.3	
GIL91	1140	IICii	513	sheep	radius	y			Bp 33.0	
GIL91	1168	IIC	696	sheep	radius		y		Bd 31.9	
GIL91	1159	IIC	844	sheep	radius	y			Bp 34.8	
GIL91	1125	IIBi	1189	sheep	radius	y			Bp 28.7	
GIL92	1310	IIC	2818	sheep	radius	y	y		Bp 33.3; SD 17.2; Bd 31.4; GL 173	
GIL92	1203	IIIA	3223	sheep	radius	y			Bp 29.3	
GIL90	586	IIIB	3463	sheep	radius	y	y		Bp 34.4; SD 17.4; GL c179;	
GIL90	567	IIIA	3796	sheep	radius	y			Bp 31.6	
GIL92	783	IIC	4060	sheep	radius	y			Bp 29.5	
GIL90	526	II	4976	sheep	radius	y			Bp 29.0	
GIL91	633	IIB	54	shpgt	radius	y	n		Bp 32.5; GL -ep 133	
GIL91	1103	IIBii	108	shpgt	radius	y			Bp 31	
GIL87	270	IIC	571	shpgt	radius	y			Bp 30.0	
GIL87	92	IIB	675	shpgt	radius		n	?y	Bd 31.1 loose ep	
GIL87	92	IIB	676	shpgt	radius		n	?y	Bd 27.0 loose ep	
GIL91	1038	IIA	1110	shpgt	radius	y			Bp 29.6	burnt
GIL91	696	IIA	1442	shpgt	radius		y		Bd 28.0	
GIL91	1051	IIA	1999	shpgt	radius	y			Bp e33	
GIL92	1517	IIC	2416	shpgt	radius		y		Bd 35.4	

GIL90	810	IIA	3313	shpgt	radius	y			Bp 28.7	
GIL91	716	IIIA/B	238	goat	scapula		y		SLC 23.5	
GIL91	1147	IIIA	625	goat	scapula		y		SLC 19.8	
GIL91	1057	IIBii	1233	goat	scapula		y		SLC 23.7	v big
GIL91	1158	IICii	2166	goat	scapula		y		SLC 17.1	
GIL90	538	IIC	3395	goat	scapula		y		SLC 16.4	
GIL92	1309	IIC	3635	goat	scapula		y		SLC 18.2	
GIL92	1205	IIBi-ii	4193	goat	scapula		yn		SLC 17.4	
GIL92	1259	IIC	6533	goat	scapula		y		SLC 19.6	
GIL91	1159	IIC	420	sheep	scapula		y		SLC 22.8	
GIL87	257	IIC	906	sheep	scapula		yn	y	SLC 19.8	Male?
GIL91	697	IIA	1063	sheep	scapula		y		SLC 16.3	
GIL91	1094	IICi	1645	sheep	scapula		y		SLC 21.8	
GIL92	1307	IIC	2767	sheep	scapula		y		SLC 17.5	
GIL90	537	IIB	3362	sheep	scapula		y		SLC e22.4	
GIL92	1309	IIC	3634	sheep	scapula		y		SLC 21.7	
GIL92	1223	IIA	3860	sheep	scapula		y		SLC 18.7	
GIL90	14	IIA	3919	sheep	scapula		y		SLC 22.8;	
GIL92	1416	IIC	3950	sheep	scapula		y		SLC 22.0	
GIL92	1372	IIAi	3984	sheep	scapula		y		SLC 21.0	
GIL91	1097	IIBi-ii	1526	shpgt	scapula		y		SLC 19.4	
GIL91	1150	IIIA	594	goat	tibia		n		Bd ep 25.2	594 595 same ankle?
GIL87	70	IIC	710	shpgt	tibia	n	n		Bd 21.3 -ep T481	
GIL87	294	IV	850	shpgt	tibia		y		Bd 24.5	
GIL91	692	IIIB	917	shpgt	tibia		y		Bd 23.9	
GIL91	612	IIA	1030	shpgt	tibia		y		Bd 26.0	
GIL91	697	IIA	1085	shpgt	tibia		y		Bd 24.2	burnt
GIL91	1038	IIA	1109	shpgt	tibia		y		Bd 27.3	
GIL91	704	IIB	1122	shpgt	tibia		y		Bd 26.1	
GIL91	1125	IIBi	1186	shpgt	tibia		y		Bd 25.2	
GIL91	1124	IIBii	1200	shpgt	tibia		y		Bd 21.4	burnt
GIL91	1057	IIBii	1235	shpgt	tibia		y		Bd 26.5	
GIL91	1051	IIA	1325	shpgt	tibia		y		Bd 23.0	burnt
GIL91	1029	IIAii	1572	shpgt	tibia		y		Bd 29.0	v big
GIL91	1029	IIAii	1577	shpgt	tibia		y		Bd 26.5	
GIL91	1029	IIAii	1586	shpgt	tibia		y		Bd 26.4	
GIL91	1128	IIC	1690	shpgt	tibia		y		Bd 28.1	
GIL91	1051	IIA	1996	shpgt	tibia		y		Bd 27.5	
GIL90	819	IIA	3514	shpgt	tibia		y		Bd e 28	
GIL90	949	IIBi	3720	shpgt	tibia		y		Bd 27.5	
GIL90	834	IIB	5007	shpgt	tibia		y		Bd 23.4	
GIL90	33	IIC	5039	shpgt	tibia		y		Bd 24.7	awl

Appendix 6.3. Measurements of Cattle Bones and Teeth at Gilat.

site	locus	stratum	bone no	species	bone	ant ep	post ep	measurements	notes
GIL91	1098	IIC	2079	cattle	astragalus			GL 58.8; Bd 38.2	Female?
GIL91	1098	IIC	2078	cattle	astragalus			GL 69.5; Bd 45.0	Male?
GIL91	1158	IICii	426	cattle	astragalus			GL 63.8; Bd 41.2	
GIL91	709	IIB	1158	cattle	astragalus			GL 65.4; Bd 42.5	
GIL92	756	IIA	2753	cattle	astragalus			GL 70.3; Bd 45.4	
GIL92	786	IIC	3266	cattle	astragalus			GL 66.1; Bd 44.6	
GIL91	1128	IIC	1688	cattle	astragalus			GL 70.1; Bd 46/5	
GIL90	14	IIA	3909	cattle	astragalus			Bd 39.6	
GIL91	1128	IIC	498	cattle	astragalus			GL 63.2; Bd 43.5	496-503 same limb
GIL92	1562	IIIB	2636	cattle	astragalus			GL 58.9; Bd 38.6	
GIL92	1201	IIC	3236	cattle	astragalus			GL 68.7; Bd e47	
GIL90	21	II	4503	cattle	astragalus			GL e68.6; Bd 47.4	
GIL92	783	IIC	4228	cattle	calcaneum	y		GL 135	
GIL91	1057	IIBii	1234	cattle	calcaneum	yn		GL 129	
GIL91	1147	IIIA	440	cattle	femur		yn	Bd c90; Dd 124	large
GIL91	1029	IIAii	351	cattle	horncore			43.4 x 35.5; circ c127	Female?
GIL92	1563	IIIA	2977	cattle	horncore			49.9 x -	
GIL90	820	IIA	5146	cattle	humerus		y	Bt 64.7; Bd 73.8	slight lateral expansion
GIL92	783	IIC	2341	cattle	humerus		y	Bt c81	
GIL90	583	IIIA/B	4098	cattle	humerus		y	Bt 74.5; Bd 79	
GIL92	1391	IIA	3969	cattle	M3 low			LM3 36.6	M3 distal pillar high; M3K
GIL92	1344	IIBi	3399	cattle	M3 low			LM3 35.2	M3K
GIL92	1511	IIC	3883	cattle	M3 low			LM3 37.9	M3G
GIL91	1150	IIIA	413	cattle	mandible			LM3 37.0; Ltrow 134	M3 dist pillar prominent
GIL92	1294	IV	4271	cattle	mandible			LM3 38.1	M3K
GIL90	956	IIIAii	3967	cattle	mandible			L alv M3 39.5	
GIL92	772	IIB	3846	cattle	mandible			LM3 38.2	M3C
GIL87	277	IIB	742	cattle	mandible			LM3 34.9	
GIL92	786	IIC	2436	cattle	mandible			LM3 37.1	M3C
GIL92	773	IIA	4214	cattle	mandible			LM3 35.3	M3C
GIL87	294	IV	821	cattle	mandible			Lm4 30.8; LM1 28.1	
GIL92	1277	IIC	4268	cattle	mcarpal			Bp 53.2; SD 29.1	Female?
GIL92	1206	IICi	4186	cattle	mcarpal		y	Bp 58.2; SD 36.3; Bd 61.2; GL 191.5	Female?
GIL92	1357	IIBi	3777	cattle	mcarpal		y	Bp 58.0; SD 28.5; Bd 56.3; GL 189.6	Female?; 3777-3782 same foot
GIL92	1372	IIAi	3971	cattle	mcarpal		y	Bp e67 SD 40.3 Bd 66.5 GL 206.3	Male?
GIL91	656	IIA	409	cattle	mcarpal		y	Bd 59.2	slight medial expansion
GIL91	1128	IIC	1683	cattle	mcarpal		y	Bd 52.6	slight medial expansion
GIL90	988	IIBi	4933	cattle	mcarpal??		y	Bd 48.0??	
GIL90	529	IIB	3669	cattle	mcarpal		n	Bd loose ep 58.9	
GIL91	1145	IIC	872	cattle	mcarpal			Bp c62	
GIL91	1147	IIIA	2204	cattle	mcarpal			Bp c57.5	
GIL90	34	II	3794	cattle	mcarpal			Bp 56.0	
GIL90	21	II	4206	cattle	mcarpal			Bp 55.6 Plate ?	
GIL91	624	IIA	456	cattle	mcarpal		y	SD 38.3	

GIL92	1320	IIC	6231	cattle	mcarpal		y	Bp 57.0; SD 28.9; Bd 61.5; GL e198	Plate ?
GIL92	1511	IIC	3800	cattle	mcarpal			Bp c66	
GIL91	1131	IIIA	395	cattle	mtarsal			Bp 52.7	spavin?
GIL91	1128	IIC	1684	cattle	mtarsal		y	Bd e58	1684-1686 articulate
GIL91	1072	IIBi	1899	cattle	mtarsal		y	Bp e53.5	
GIL91	1074	IIAii	1949	cattle	mtarsal		y	Bd 52.4	1949 1950 articulate
GIL90	895	IIBii	6016	cattle	mtarsal			Bp 48.5; SD 30.3	
GIL90	527	II	4971	cattle	mtarsal			Bp 51.2	
GIL90	528	IIC	3869	cattle	mtarsal		yn	Bp 43.8; GL e222	
GIL91	649	IIC	652	cattle	mtarsal		y	Bd 60.3	
GIL91	703	IIA	1142	cattle	mtarsal		y	Bd 62.1	
GIL92	1277	IIC	2467	cattle	mtarsal		y	Bd 51.3	
GIL90	882	IIBi	4766	cattle	mtarsal		y	Bd 53.3	
GIL90	577	IV	4832	cattle	mtarsal			Bd 53.6	
GIL90	13	IIB	4893	cattle	mtarsal		y	Bd 53.2	
GIL90	895	IIBii	6014	cattle	mtarsal		y	Bp 48.6; GL e243; SD 28.9; Bd 60.1	inner mpod shorter than outer
GIL92	1277	IIC	4269	cattle	mtarsal			Bp 46.9	
GIL90	577	IV	4831	cattle	mtarsal			SD 25.1	
GIL91	1128	IIC	499	cattle	navicular			GB 56.4;	496-503 same limb
GIL91	1074	IIAii	1950	cattle	navicular			GB 52.2	1949 1950 articulate
GIL91	1051	IIA	2003	cattle	navicular			GB 56.8	
GIL92	1319	IIC	2792	cattle	navicular			GB 57.7	
GIL91	1103	IIBii	401	cattle	pelvis	y		LA 74.0	massive
GIL90	586	IIIB	3480	cattle	phal mid	y		Bp 25.2; GLpe 35.8	
GIL92	1526	IIC	3696	cattle	phal mid	y		Bp 26.9; GLpe 39.2	
GIL91	680	IIC	896	cattle	phal mid	y		Bp 28.8	
GIL91	1042	IIC	1820	cattle	phal mid	y		Bp 29.3;	
GIL91	674	IIBii	2017	cattle	phal mid	y		Bp e29.2	burnt
GIL92	772	IIB	3845	cattle	phal mid	y		Bp 31.1; GLpe c42	
GIL91	1128	IIC	503	cattle	phal mid	y		Bp 29.9	496-503 same limb
GIL91	1029	IIAii	1576	cattle	phal mid ae	y		Bp 32.8; GLpe 40.0	
GIL92	775	IIBii	3750	cattle	phal mid ai	y		Bp 37.1	proximal expansion+osteitis
GIL92	1357	IIBi	3780	cattle	phal mid ai	y		Bp 27.3; GLpe 39.9	3777-3782 same foot
GIL92	1368	IIIA	3361	cattle	phal mid ao	y		Bp 33.4; GLpe 50.1	slight proximal
GIL92	1357	IIBi	3781	cattle	phal mid ao	y		Bp 27.6; GLpe 38.2	3777-3782 same foot
GIL87	301	IIIA	794	cattle	phal mid p	y		GLpe 30.4	
GIL92	1344	IIBi	3409	cattle	phal mid p	y		Bp 24.9	
GIL91	1128	IIC	1686	cattle	phal mid po	y		Bp 28.6; GLpe 40.8	1684-1686 articulate
GIL92	1294	IV	4265	cattle	phal prox	y		Bp 28.6; GLpe 51.6	
GIL92	1526	IIC	3695	cattle	phal prox	y		Bp e32	
GIL92	1509	IIC	3564	cattle	phal prox	y		Bp 26.4; GLpe 56.1	
GIL92	773	IIA	4220	cattle	phal prox	y		Bp 29.2	
GIL87	280	IIB	731	cattle	phal prox	y		Bp 30.1 GLpe 56.9 anterior	
GIL90	528	IIC	3891	cattle	phal prox a	y		Bp 28.5	
GIL92	772	IIB	3837	cattle	phal prox a	y		Bp 31.6 GLpe 62.0	
GIL92	772	IIB	2321	cattle	phal prox a	y		Bp e32.8	
GIL91	1135	IIC	703	cattle	phal prox ae	y		Bp 29.1; GLpe 54.9	

GIL87	301	IIIA	793	cattle	phal prox ai	y		Bp 32.1; GLpe 55.7	old; slight expansion; deep tendon inserts
GIL91	1147	IIIA	627	cattle	phal prox ai	y		Bp 33.1; GLpe 56.7	
GIL92	1284	IIB	2458	cattle	phal prox ai	y		Bp 31.1; GLpe 58.4	burnt
GIL92	755	IIB/C	3004	cattle	phal prox ai	y		Bp 30.4; GLpe 60.1	
GIL90	917	IIIAii	3301	cattle	phal prox ai	y		Bp 28.8; GLpe 53.8	
GIL92	1300	IIA	2788	cattle	phal prox ai	y	y	Bp 29.8	
GIL92	1357	IIBi	3778	cattle	phal prox ai	y		Bp 28.8; GLpe 56.1	3777-3782 same foot
GIL92	772	IIB	2303	cattle	phal prox ao	y		Bp 34.7; GLpe 56.1	Distal osteitis?
GIL90	577	IV	4245	cattle	phal prox ao	y		Bp 30.0; GLpe 57.7	
GIL92	1357	IIBi	3779	cattle	phal prox ao	y		Bp 28.8; GLpe 57.3	3777-3782 same foot
GIL91	1128	IIC	502	cattle	phal prox hi	y		Bp 30.1; GLpe 64.4	496-503 same limb
GIL91	1128	IIC	1685	cattle	phal prox po	y		Bp 30.2; GLpe 63.9	1684-1686 articulate
GIL91	1068	IIBi	1895	cattle	phal prox po	y		Bp 28.0; GLpe 57.5	
GIL92	772	IIB	2320	cattle	phal prox po	y		Bp 27.3; GLpe 60.1	burnt
GIL90	559	III	4133	cattle	phal prox post	y		Bp 27.8; GLpe 59.0	
GIL92	1357	IIBi	3782	cattle	phal term ai			GL 74.9	3777-3782 same foot
GIL91	1131	IIIA	394	cattle	post cuneif			GB 59.4	navicular & cuneif fused
GIL90	553	III	3146	cattle	radius		yn	Bd 80.8	
GIL92	1209	IIBii	4180	cattle	radius		y	Bd 81.1	
GIL92	1322	IIC	2507	cattle	radius	y		Bp e75	
GIL92	1511	IIC	3254	cattle	radius	y		Bp e72	
GIL90	33	IIC	5023	cattle	radius	y		Bp 72.7	
GIL92	773	IIA	4216	cattle	scapula		y	SLC 51.2 GL 60.6	
GIL92	1369	IIIA	2300	cattle	scapula		y	SLC 53.1; GLP 65.8	
GIL91	1159	IIC	415	cattle	scapula		y	SLC 50.9	
GIL92	786	IIC	4210	cattle	scapula			SLC 40.3	
GIL91	674	IIBii	2025	cattle	tibia		y	Bd 57.2	
GIL92	1511	IIC	3885	cattle	tibia		y	Bd 61.8	
GIL91	1150	IIIA	579	cattle	tibia		y	Bd 62.7	
GIL91	1128	IIC	496	cattle	tibia		y	Bd 59.1	496-503 same limb
GIL87	261	IIIA	879	wild? cattle	M3 low			LM3 39.5	
GIL91	1147	IIIA	422	wild? cattle	humerus		y	Bt e81	massive
GIL90	853	IICii	3998	wild? cattle	humerus		y	Bt e82; Bd 88	
GIL90	33	IIC	3276	wild? cattle	mcarpal		y	Bd e82.1	
GIL91	680	IIC	895	wild? cattle	phal mid ae	y		Bp 33.2; GLpe 42.8	
GIL87	297	IIC	611	wild? cattle	phal prox ao	y		Bp 32.6; GLpe 66.9	611 and 612 same foot?
GIL87	297	IIC	612	wild? cattle	phal dist ao			GL 69.5	611 and 612 same foot?

Appendix 6.4. Measurements of Pig Bones and Teeth at Gilat.

site	locus	stratum	bone no	species	bone	prox ep	dist ep	measurements	notes
GIL90	853	IICii	4658	pig	astragalus			GL 31.4	
GIL92	780	IIC	4347	pig	astragalus			GL 33.2 ?y	
GIL92	1565	IIIA	2603	pig	astragalus			GL 38.9; Bd 23.3	
GIL91	1051	IIA	2001	pig	astragalus			GL 41.4	
GIL92	1511	IIC	3562	pig	astragalus			GL e37 Bd	
GIL92	1237	IIBi	4179	pig	astragalus			GL e39.9	
GIL92	1374	IIAi	6157	pig	calcaneum	y		GL 65.0	
GIL91	611	IIA	1383	pig	calcaneum	y		GL 66.4	
GIL92	772	IIB	3819	pig	mandible			LM1 15.0	Female
GIL90	528	IIC	4980	pig	mandible			LM1 15.7; LM2 19.2	
GIL92	1511	IIC	3818	pig	mandible			LM1 16.0; LM2 21.7	Female
GIL92	786	IIC	4209	pig	mandible			LM1 16.2; LM2 22.0	Female
GIL87	297	IIC	811	pig	mandible			LM1 16.6; LM2 20.1	
GIL92	1394	IIAi	3956	pig	mandible			LM1 16.8; LM2 21.6	
GIL92	761	IIA	3036	pig	mandible			LM1 17.0	
GIL92	1548	IIIB	3326	pig	mandible			LM1 17.2	
GIL92	1511	IIC	3557	pig	mandible			LM1 17.4	
GIL92	1511	IIC	3533	pig	mandible			LM1 18.3	
GIL91	1037	IIA	798	pig	mandible			LM1 18.5	
GIL91	1131	IIIA	410	pig	mandible			LM1 18.5; LM2 22.6	
GIL91	1051	IIA	452	pig	mandible			LM2 20.1; LM3 e33.9	Female
GIL91	1125	IIBi	1194	pig	mandible			LM2 20.5	
GIL91	696	IIA	449	pig	mandible			LM2 21.1; LM3 34.6	
GIL90	904	IIC	4703	pig	mandible			LM2 21.3	
GIL91	1081	IIC	1617	pig	mandible			LM2 21.5	
GIL92	1511	IIC	3796	pig	mandible			LM2 22.1	
GIL91	1081	IIC	1624	pig	mandible			LM3 33.2	
GIL91	1034	IIAii	2185	pig	mandible			M2 20.9; LM3	
GIL90	528	IIC	3875	pig	mandible			Lm4 18.6	
GIL90	555	III	3977	pig	mandible			Lm4 18.6; LM1	
GIL91	696	IIA	451	pig	mandible			Lm4 19.0	
GIL91	1037	IIA	821	pig	mandible			Lm4 19.6	
GIL91	703	IIA	1124	pig	mandible			LP4 14.1; LM1 15.3; LM2 21.4	
GIL92	1277	IIC	2469	pig	maxilla			LM1up 17.7	
GIL92	1511	IIC	3534	pig	maxilla			LM1up 18.5; LM2up 21.7	
GIL90	519	II	4675	pig	maxilla			LM2up 20.9	
GIL91	1051	IIA	1989	pig	maxilla			LM2up 20.0	
GIL87	261	IIIA	878	pig	maxilla			LM2up 23.2	

GIL91 1159	IIC	493	pig	maxilla			LM3up 28.3
GIL91 639	IIA	1360	pig	maxilla			LM3up 27.8
GIL90 803	IIA	4214	pig	maxilla			LM3up 30.6; Male LM2up 21.2
GIL91 1059	IIA	414	pig	pelvis		y	int ht acet 19.0; LFo 41.5; LS c61; LAR 31.2
GIL92 1354	IV	6362	pig	phal mid central	y		Bp 14.7
GIL91 1044	IIBii	2108	pig	phal mid central	y		GLpe 22.2; Bp14.6
GIL90 574	III	4529	pig	phal mid central	y		GLpe 24.2; Bp 13.8
GIL90 567	IIIA	3842	pig	phal mid central	y		GLpe 20.4; Bp 13.8
GIL91 1147	IIIA	621	pig	phal mid central	y		GLpe 21.0; Bp 14.6
GIL92 1310	IIC	6526	pig	phal prox central	y		GLpe 20.7; Bp 15.7
GIL92 775	IIBii	6130	pig	phal prox central	y		GLpe 39.3; Bp 14.9
GIL91 1054	IIIA	1921	pig	phal prox central	y		GLpe 24.2; Bp 14.3
GIL90 896	IIBii	4335	pig	phal prox central	y		GLpe 29.6; Bp 16.5
GIL91 1050	IIA	248	pig	phal prox central	y		GLpe 30.6; Bp 14.2
GIL90 025	III	4730	pig	phal prox central inner	y		GLpe 30.1; Bp 15.5
GIL91 1054	IIIA	1922	pig	phal prox central outer	y		GLpe 18.7; Bp 10.7
GIL87 297	IIC	613	pig	radius	y		Bp 24.4
GIL87 265	IIB	604	pig	radius	y	n	Bp 24.7
GIL91 676	IIC/IIIA	1388	pig	radius	y		Bp 24.7
GIL92 1203	IIIA	3209	pig	radius	y		Bp 28.4
GIL91 689	IIB	730	pig	radius	y		Bp 29.7
GIL90 586	IIIB	6216	pig	scapula		y	SD 18.3; Bd 30.4
GIL91 1037	IIA	794	pig	tibia		y	Bd 26.8
GIL91 1034	IIAii	2186	pig	tibia		y	Bd 27.8
GIL91 692	IIIB	918	pig	tibia		y	Bd 28.4
GIL90 13	IIB	4900	pig	tibia		y	Bd 28.9
GIL91 1068	IIBi	1890	pig	tibia		y	Bd 29.5
GIL91 703	IIA	1134	pig	tibia		y	Bd 30.1

Appendix 6.5a. Measurements of Equid Bones at Gilat

site	locus	stratum	bone	species	on size	bone	dist ep	index	measurements	notes
GIL90	553	III	4599	equid	ass/horse	astragalus		74.03	GH e53.2; GB 51.4; BFd 48.2	
GIL92	786	IIC	3578	equid	horse?	radius	y	170.7	Bd 70.3; BFd 58.3	sl exos at suture line
GIL77	137	IIC	207	equid	horse?	tibia		125.0	Bd 64.5; Dd 44.6	

Appendix 6.5b. Measurements of Equid Teeth

bone no	GIL90 3417	GIL91 2089
locus	925	1044
stratum	2A	2Bii
tooth	M3 low	P2 up
occlusal length	31.9	36.1
occlusal breadth	12.3	21.3
notes	no penetration of silla by buccal sulcus: asinus/ hemionus. V shaped lingual sulcus: asinus	very worn, bit wear?

Appendix 6.6a. Measurements of Dog Skulls from Gilat

	Gilat 90				Gilat 91		Gilat 92			
locus	553	859		913	692	698	787	1571	1204	773
stratum	III	IICii		IIC	IIAi	IIAi	IIBii	IIIA	IIBi	IIA
bone no	3136	3217	3219	4020	138	139	2302	2582	4198	4223
cranium										
18 P4 LxB	17.7x10.3	-	-	-	20.2x11.0	20.7x10.8	-	-	-	-
20 M1 LxB	11.5x17.1	-	-	-	13.3x16.8	13.4x16.3	11.3x13.9	-	-	-
21 M2 LxB	-	-	-	-	7.5x11.7	7.5x11.2	-	-	-	-
1	-	-	-	-	195	188	-	-	-	-
2	-	-	-	-	182	178	-	-	-	-
3	-	-	-	-	172	167	-	-	-	-
7	-	-	-	-	-	c89	-	-	-	-
8	-	-	-	-	-	94.7	-	-	-	-
9	-	-	-	-	-	108.2	-	-	-	-
12	-	-	-	-	83.1	78.1	-	-	-	-
13	-	-	-	-	97	-	89.8	-	-	-
13a	-	-	-	-	96.8	88.5		-	-	-
13	-	-	-	-	-	-	89.8	-	-	-
15	-	-	-	-	70.4	69.1	-	-	-	-
16	-	-	-	-	20.5	21	-	-	-	-
17	-	-	-	-	-	53	-	-	-	-
23	-	-	-	-	66.8	-	-	-	-	-
24	-	-	-	-	63.8	60.6	-	-	-	-
25	-	-	-	-	38.6	35.8	-	-	-	-
27	-	-	-	-	18.2	-	-	-	-	-

28	-	-	-	-	17.5	-	-	-	-	-
29	-	-	-	-	-	59.1	-	-	-	-
31	-	-	-	-	-	33.7	-	-	-	-
32	-	-	-	-	-	51.1	-	-	-	-
33	-	-	-	-	-	37.1	-	-	-	-
34	-	-	-	-	65.2	62.5	-	-	-	-
35	-	-	-	-	36.7	35.8	-	-	-	-
36	-	-	-	-	38.4	38.8	-	-	-	-
37	-	-	-	-	-	26.8	-	-	-	-
38	-	-	-	-	-	52	-	-	-	-
39	-	-	-	-	-	48	-	-	-	-
40	-	-	-	-	44.6	-	-	-	-	-
mandible										
P4 LxB	-	-	-	11.3	-	-	-	-	-	-
13: M1 LxB	-	20.1x8.1	20.0x8.1	22.0x8.4	23.0x9.5	23.2x9.7	-	24.4x-	21.7x-	-
15: M2 LxB	-	-	-	9.4x6.8	8.7x6.8	10.0x7.4	-	-	-	-
16: M3 LxB	-	-	-	-	4.1x4.5	-	-	-	-	-
4	-	105.7	106.0	-	-	-	-	-	-	115.8
7	-	71.5	70.7	-	80.1	-	-	-	-	-
8	-	67.5	67.0	-	73.7	-	-	-	-	-
9	-	62.2	61.9	-	70.5	-	-	-	-	-
10	-	33.0	33.5	-	35.3	-	-	-	-	-
11	-	36.0	36.1	-	40.6	39.0	-	-	-	-
12	-	31.3	31.3	-	36.6	35.9	-	-	36.6	32.2
14	-	20.5	20.7	-	21.4	22.4	-	-	-	20.4
18	-			-	-	-	-	-	-	50.8

note 3217 (left) and 3219 (right) are from the same individual

Appenix 6.6b. Measurements of Dog Skeleton Gil91 139

site	locus	stratum	bone no.	bone	L/R	prox ep	distal ep	measurements etc
GIL91	698	3B	139	skull				see Appendix 5A
GIL91	698	3B	139	scapula	L		y	SLC 24.6; GLC e28.3
GIL91	698	3B	139	humerus	R	y	y	GL 165
GIL91	698	3B	139	radius	L	y		unhealed fracture; osteitis
GIL91	698	3B	139	radius	R	y		GL 167
GIL91	698	3B	139	ulna	L	y	y	osteitis; lower end oblit
GIL91	698	3B	139	metacarpal I	R	y	y	GL 20.7
GIL91	698	3B	139	metacarpal II	R	y	y	GL 55.1
GIL91	698	3B	139	metacarpal III	L	y	y	GL 61.7
GIL91	698	3B	139	metacarpal III	R	y	y	GL 61.6
GIL91	698	3B	139	metacarpal IV	L	y	y	GL 60.7
GIL91	698	3B	139	metacarpal V	L	y	y	GL 51.8
GIL91	698	3B	139	femur	L	y	y	GL 175.3
GIL91	698	3B	139	femur	R	y	y	GL 175.2
GIL91	698	3B	139	tibia	L	y		GL 180.7
GIL91	698	3B	139	astragalus	L			GL 24.8
GIL91	698	3B	139	calcaneum	L	y		GL 43.0
GIL91	698	3B	139	metatarsal II	R	y	y	GL 59.9
GIL91	698	3B	139	metatarsal III	R	y	y	GL 67.0
GIL91	698	3B	139	metatarsal IV	R	y	y	GL 69.5
GIL91	698	3B	139	metatarsal V	R	y	y	GL 62.2

Appendix 6.6c. Measurements of Other Dog Post-Cranial Bones

site	locus	stratum	bone no.	bone	L/R	prox ep	distal ep	measurements etc
GIL92	760	2A	3017	scapula				SLC 21.8
GIL91	716	3A/B	234	scapula	L		y	SLC 23.8; GLP 28.8
GIL87	261	3A	880	scapula	R		y	SLC 19.2; Bd 23.2
GIL90	528	2C	3653	tibia	R		y	Bd 20.1; burnt
GIL76	85	2B	E7	tibia				Bd 17.6

Appendix 6.7. Measurements of Gazelle Bones at Gilat.

site	locus	stratum	bone	bone	prox ep	dist ep	age	sex	measurements	notes
GIL91	1059	IIA	1218	astragalus					GL 27.8; Bd 16.9	
GIL92	777	IIC	2891	astragalus					GL 26.3; Bd 17.7	
GIL92	1259	IIC	6257	astragalus					GL 28.0; Bd 17.2	burnt
GIL90	33	IIC	5027	astragalus					GLpe 26.6; Bd 16.3	
GIL91	1145	IIC	874	astragalus					GL 26.8; Bd 16.1	
GIL92	1321	IIBi	2543	horncore				F	9.0 x 8.0	
GIL91	1085	IIBii	392	horncore				M	L c160; 21.7 x-	
GIL92	1344	IIBi	2912	horncore				M	L 175; 30.7 x 20.3	?pair 2907; mod groove inside post
GIL92	772	IIB	3841	horncore				M	30.6 x 20.9	deep anterior groove
GIL92	1344	IIBi	2914	horncore				M	L e190; 31.7 x 23.4; base-midline 13.9	anterior groove; v curved; burnt
GIL92	1393	IIC	2906	horncore				M	25.8 x 17.6	anterior grooves; burnt
GIL92	1393	IIC	2906	horncore				M	25.8 x 17.6	anterior grooves; burnt
GIL92	1344	IIBi	2910	horncore				M	27.4 x 21.3 L 152	deep grooves ant+post; v curved;
GIL92	1344	IIBi	2913	horncore				M	32.1 x 23.3; base-mid 10.3	deep grooves ant+post; v curved; bnt
GIL92	1344	IIBi	2909	horncore				M	L 171; 28.7 x 20.0; base-midline 5.4	grooves v deep outer side; part bnt
GIL92	1344	IIBi	2907	horncore				M	L e170; 30.1 x 19.6; base-midline 7.5	grooves v shallow; ?pr 2912; part bnt
GIL92	1344	IIBi	2916	horncore				M	L 160; 30.4 x 19.3; base-midline 12.5	no real grooves, except at tip; v curved; bnt
GIL92	1344	IIBi	2911	horncoresx2				M	25.8 x 18.2; b between bases 27.7	deep groove post; mod curved; part bnt
GIL90	528	IIC	3562	humerus		y			Bt 22.0; Bd	
GIL90	7	II	3861	humerus		yn			Bt 23.5 Bd 23.9	
GIL91	1041	IIA	1096	mcarpal		y			Bd 18.3	

site	locus	stratum	bone no	bone	prox ep	dist	measurements	notes
GIL90	846	IIA	4381	mcarpal			Bp 26.4; SD 13.5;	
GIL91	692	IIIB	916	mtarsal		y	Bd 19.8	bnt
GIL92	1554	IIC/IIIA	3519	mtarsal			Bp 21.3; SD 11.7	
GIL90	808	IIA	3352	phal mid	y	y	GLpe 20.3; Bp 8.2	3346 3352 art
GIL90	574	III	4533	phal mid	y		GLpe 23.7; Bp 10.6	bnt
GIL90	896	IIBii	3762	phal mid	y	old	GLpe 25.3; Bp 12.2	v big; posterior exostosis
GIL90	808	IIA	3346	phal prox	yn	y	GLpe 37.1; Bpe10.8	3346 3352 art
GIL90	555	III	3973	phal prox	y		GLpe 37.3; Bp 10.6	
GIL91	700	IIA	1280	phal prox	y		GLpe 41.7; Bp 11.2	
GIL90	828	IIBi	3024	phal prox	y		GLpe 42.4; Bp 10.8	
GIL90	847	IIBii	4923	phal prox	y		GLpe 36.0; Bp 10.0	bnt
GIL90	826	IIBi	3503	tibia		y	Bd 23.2	bnt
GIL92	1344	IIBi	3403	tibia	n	y	Bd 23.4	
GIL91	700	IIA	1276	tibia		y	Bd 23.7	
GIL91	613	IIA	1024	tibia		y	Bd 23.9	

Appendix 6.8. Measurements of Bones and Teeth of Minor Wild Animals at Gilat

site	locus	stratum	bone no	species	bone	prox ep	dist	measurements	notes
GIL92	1505	IIC	3700	hartebeest	phal dist			GL 47.2	
GIL76	86	IIB	335	hartebeest?	mcarpal		n	Bd 30.4 (condyles held together)	
GIL77	122	IIIA	266	hartebeest?	phal mid	y		GLpe 31.8; Bp	burnt
GIL91	1111	IIC	385	Vulpes vulpes	mandible			L M1 14.1	
GIL92	1307	IIC	2769	Vulpes ruppelli	radius	y	y	GL 94.6	
GIL90	586	IIIB	3458	fox	humerus	y	y	GL 104.9; Bd 17.4	
GIL92	1371	IIIB	6422	fox	radius		y	Bd 13.5	
GIL92	799	IIB	3991	jackal	phal prox	y	y	GL 21.6	ident on size
GIL92	799	IIB	3992	hyaena	scapula		y	SLC 28.5	
GIL90	7	II	3865	Felis lybica	mtarsal III			GL 46.9	ident on size
GIL92	1554	IIC/IIIA	3515	ostrich	phal prox post	y		GL 101.6; Bp 42.2; SD 25.7	

References

Angress, S. (1959) Mammal remains from Horvat Beter (Beersheva). *Atiqot* 2: 53–71.

Anthony, D.W. and Brown, D.R. (1991) The origins of horseback riding. *Antiquity* 65: 22–38.

Banning, E.B. (1998) The Neolithic Period: Triumphs of Architecture, Agriculture and Art. *Near Eastern Archaeology* 61: 188–237

Bar-Adon, P. (1980) *The Cave of the Treasure*. Jerusalem: Israel Exploration Society.

Binford, L.R. (1978) *Nunamiut Ethnoarchaeology*. New York: Academic Press.

— (1981) *Bones: Ancient Men and Modern Myths*. London: Academic Press.

Binford, L.R., and Bertram, J.B. (1977) Bone frequencies and attritional processes. In *For Theory Building in Archaeology*, edited by L.R. Binford. London: Academic Press, pp. 77–193.

Boessneck, J. (1969) Osteological differences bewteen sheep (*Ovis aries* Linné) and goats (*Capra hircus* Linné). In *Science in Archaeology*, edited by D. Brothwell and E.S. Higgs. 2nd ed. London: Thames & Hudson, pp. 331–58.

Boessneck, J., and von den Driesch, A. (1979) *Die Tierknochenfunde aus der Neolithischen Siedlung auf dem Fikirtepe bei Kadiköy am Marmarameer*. Munich: Institut für Palaeoanatomie, Domestikationsforschung und Geschichte der Tiermedizin der Universität München.

Buitenhuis, H. (1985) Preliminary report on the faunal remains of Hayaz Hüyük from the 1979–1983 seasons. *Anatolica* 12: 61–74.

Bull, G., and Payne, S. (1982) Tooth eruption and epiphysial fusion in pigs and wild boar. In *Ageing and Sexing Animal Bones from Archaeological Sites*, edited by B. Wilson, C. Grigson and S. Payne. British Archaeological Reports, British Series 109: 55–71.

Bullock, D., and Rackham, J. (1982) Epiphysial fusion and tooth eruption of feral goats from Moffatdale, Dumfries and Galloway, Scotland. In *Ageing and Sexing Animal Bones from Archaeological Sites*, edited by B. Wilson, C. Grigson and S. Payne. British Archaeological Reports, British Series 109: 73–80.

Chaix, L., and Grant, A. (1987) A study of a prehistoric population of sheep (*Ovis aries* L.) from Kerma (Sudan). *Archaeozoologia* 1 (1): 77–92.

Childe, V.G. (1951) The first wagons and carts - from the Tigris to the Severn. *Proceedings of the Prehistoric Society* 17: 177–94.

Clark, G., and Yi, S. (1983) Niche-width variation in Cantabrian Archaeofaunas: a diachronic study. In *Animals and Archaeology: 1. Hunters and their Prey*, edited by J. Clutton-Brock and C. Grigson. British Archaeological Reports, International Series 163, pp. 183–208.

Clutton-Brock, J. (1979) The mammalian remains from the Jericho Tell. *Proceedings of the Prehistoric Society* 45: 135–57.

— (1981) *Domesticated Animals from Early Times*. London: Heinemann & British Museum (Natural History).

— (1989) A dog and a donkey excavated at Tell Brak. *Iraq* 51: 217–24.

— (1993) Monre donkeys from Tell Brak. *Iraq* 55: 209–21.

Dahl, G., and Hjort, A. (1976) *Having Herds: Pastoral Herd Growth and Household Economy*. Stockholm Studies in Social Anthropology 2. Stockholm: University of Stockholm.

Davis, S. (1976) Mammal bones from the Early Bronze Age City of Arad northern Negev, Israel: some implications concerning human exploitation. *Journal of Archaeological Science* 3: 153–64.

— (n.d.) The animal bones from two fifth millennium BC sites in the Menashe Hills, Israel: 1990 excavations.

Davis, S.J.M. (1982) Climatic change and the advent of domestication: the succession of ruminant artiodactyls in the Late Pleistocene-Holocene in the Israel regions. *Paléorient* 8: 5–15.

Dayan, T. (1994) Early domesticated dogs of the Near East. *Journal of Archaeological Science* 21: 633–40.

Degerbøl, M., and Fredskild, J. (1970) The urus (*Bos primigenius* Bojanus) and neolithic domesticated cattle (*Bos taurus domesticus* Linné) in Denmark. *Det Kongelige Danske Videnskabernes Selskab Biologiske Skrifter* 17: 1–177.

Diener, P., and Robkin, E.E. (1978) Ecology, evolution and the searh for cultural origins: the question of lamic pig prohibition. *Current Anthropology* 19:493–540.

Ducos, P. (1968) *L'Origine des Animaux Domestiques en Palestine*. Publications de Préhistoire de l'Univsersité de Bordeaux 6. Bordeaux: Imprimeries Delmas.

— (1978) *Tell-Mureybet (Syrie, IX-VII millennaires), Étude Archaeozoologique d'Ecologie Humaine 1*. Paris: CNRS.

— (1983) La contribution de l'archéozoologie a l'éstimation des quantités de nourriture: évaluation du nombre d'individus. In *Animals and Archaeology: 3. Early Herders and their Flocks*, edited by J. Clutton-Brock and C. Grigson, British Archaeological Reports, International Series 202, pp. 13–23.

Epstein, C. (1985) Laden animal figurines from the Chalcolithic period in Palestine. *Bulletin of the American Schools of Oriental Research* 258: 53–62.

Evans-Pritchard, E.E. (1940) *The Nuer*. Oxford: Oxford University Press.

Flannery, K.V. (1983) Early pig domestication in the fertile crescent a retrospective look. In *The Hilly Flanks: Essays on the Prehistory of Southwestern Asia*, edited by L.S. Braidwood. Studies in Oriental Civilization, 36. University of Chicago: Institute Publication 105, pp. 163–87.

Garfinkel, Y. (1995) *Human and animal figurines of Munhata*. Les cahiers des missions archéologiques Francais en Israël 8. Paris: Association Paléorient.

— (1997) Sha'ar-ha-Golan, 1997. *Israel Exploration Journal* V47: 271–73.

— (1999) *Neolithic and Chalcolithic Pottery of the Southern Levant*. Qedem 39. Jerusalem: The Hebrew University of Jerusalem.

Gautier, A. (1984) How do I count you, let me count the ways? Problems of archaeozoological quantification. In *Animals and Archaeology: Husbandry in Europe*, edited by C. Grigson and J. Clutton-Brock. British Archaeological Reports, International Series 227, pp. 237–51.

Gilead, I. (1988) The Chalcolithic period in the Levant. *Journal of World Prehistory* 2: 397–443.

— (1989) Grar: a Chalcolithic site in the Northern Negev, Israel. *Journal of Field Archaeology* 16: 377–94.

— (1990) The Neolithic-Chalcolithic transition and the Qatifian of the northern Negev and Sinai. *Levant* 22: 47–63.

— (1992) Farmers and herders in southern Israel during the Chalcolithic period. In *Pastoralism in the Levant*, edited by O. Bar-Yosef and A. Khazanov. Monographs in World Archaeology No. 10. Madison, Wisconsin: Prehistory Press, pp. 29–41.

— (1995) *Grar, a Chalcolithic Site in the Northern Negev*. Ben-Gurion University of the Negev Press.

Gilead, I., and Goren, Y. (1986) Stations of the Chalcolithic period in Nahal Sekher, northern Negev. *Paléorient* 12/1: 83–90.

— (1989) Petrographic analyses of fourth millennium B.C. pottery and stone vessels from the northern Negev, Israel. *Bulletin of the American Schools of Oriental Research* 275: 5–14.

Goldberg, P., and A. Rosen (1987) Early Holocene palaeoenvironments of Israel. In *Shiqmim I*, edited by T.E. Levy. British Archaeological Report, International Series 356: 23–34.

Grant, A. (1982) The use of tooth wear as a guide to the age of domestic ungulates. In *Ageing and Sexing Animal Bones from Archaeological Sites*, edited by B. Wilson, C. Grigson and S. Payne. British Archaeological Reports, British Series 109: 91–108.

Grigson, C. (1969) The uses and limitations of differences in absolute size in the distinctions between the bones of aurochs (*Bos primigenius*) and domestic cattle (*Bos taurus*). In *The Domestication and Exploitation of Plants and Animals*, edited by P. Ucko and G.W. Dimbleby. London, Duckworth, pp. 277–94.

— (1978) The craniology and relationships of four species of *Bos*. IV. The relationship between *Bos primigenius* Boj. and *Bos taurus* L. and its implications for the phylogeny of the domestic breeds. *Journal of Archaeological Science* 5: 123–52.

— (1980) The craniology and relationships of four species of *Bos*. V. *Bos indicus* L. *Journal of Archaeological Science* 7: 3–32.

— (1982a) Sexing Neolithic cattle skulls and horncores. In *Ageing and Sexing Animal Bones from Archaeological Sites*, edited by B. Wilson, C. Grigson and S. Payne. British Archaeological Reports, British Series 109: 24–35.

— (1982b) Sex and age determination of bones and teeth of domestic cattle: a review of the literature. In *Ageing and Sexing Animal Bones from Archaeological Sites*, edited by B. Wilson, C. Grigson and S. Payne. British Archaeological Reports, British Series 109:7–23.

— (1983) Mesolithic and Neolithic animal bones. In Excavations at Cherhill, north Wiltshire, 1967, edited by J.G. Evans and I.F. Smith. *Proceedings of the Prehistoric Society* 49: 64–72.

— (1984 unpublished) Preliminary report on the mammal bones from Chalcolithic Qatif, site Y2 (including Ya), on the Sinai coastal plain (excavations of 1979, 1980 and 1983).

— (1985a) Archaeozoology. In Early farming societies in the Negev Desert, edited by T.E. Levy, P. Goldberg, C. Grigson and A. Rosen. *National Geographic Research Reports* 21: 256–57.

— (1985b) Shiqmim animal bones, 1984. *Bulletin of the Anglo-Israel Archaeological Society 1984–5*: 36.

Grigson, C. (1987a) Shiqmim: pastoralism and other aspects of animal management in the Chalcolithic of the Northern Negev. In *Shiqmim I*, edited by T.E. Levy. British Archaeological Report, International Series 356: 219–41, 535–46.

— (1987b) Different herding strategies for sheep and goats in the Chalcolithic of Beersheva. *Archaeozoologia* 1 (2): 115–25.

— (1989a) Size and sex—morphometric evidence for the domestication of cattle in the Middle East. In *The Beginnings of Agriculture*, edited by A. Milles, D. Williams and N. Gardner. British Archaeological Reports, International Series 496: 77–109.

— (1989b) Shiqmim I—archaeozoological aspects. *Mitekufat Haeven, Journal of the Israel Prehistoric Society* 22: 111–14.

— (1989c, in press) Animal husbandry in the Late Neolithic and Chalcolithic at Arjoune—the secondary products revolution revisited. In *Arjoune: Chalcolithic Sites beside the Orontes*, edited by P.J. Parr.

— (1989d, in press) Interim report on the vertebrate remains from Shiqmim village, excavations of 1988. In Protohistoric investigations at the Shiqmim Chalcolithic village and cemetery: interim report on the 1988 season, edited by T.E. Levy, D. Alon, P. Goldberg, C. Grigson, P. Smith, J. Buikstra, A. Holl, Y. Rowan and P. Sabari. *Bulletin of the American Schools of Oriental Research Supplement*.

— (1990) Interim report on the vertebrate remains from Shiqmim village, excavations of 1987. In Protohistoric investigations at the Shiqmim Chalcolithic village and cemetery: an interim report on the 1987 season, edited by T.E. Levy, D. Alon, P. Goldberg, C. Grigson, P. Smith, J. Buikstra, A. Holl, Y. Rowan and P. Sabari. *Bulletin of the American Schools of Oriental Research. Supplement* 27: 29–46.

— (1993a) The mammalian remains from the Chalcolithic site of Horvat Beter; excavations of 1982. *'Atiqot* 12: 28–31.

— (1993b) The earliest domestic horses in the Levant? New finds from the fourth millennium of the Negev. *Journal of Archaeological Science* 20: 645–55.

— (1995a) Plough and pasture in the early economy of the southern Levant. In *The Archaeology of Society in the Holy Land*, edited T.E. Levy. Leicester: Leicester University Press, pp. 245–68, 573–6.

— (1995b) Cattle keepers of the northern Negev: animal remains from the Chalcolithic site of Grar. In *Grar, a Chalcolithic Site in the Northern Negev*, edited by I. Gilead. Ben-Gurion University of the Negev Press, pp. 377–452.

— (in prep.) Culture, ecology and pigs, from the fifth to the third millennium in the Middle East.

Halstead, P. (1996) Pastoralism or household herding? Problems of scale and specialization in early Greek animal husbandry. In *Zooarchaeology: new approaches and theory*, edited by K.D. Thomas. *World Archaeology* 28, no. 1, pp. 20–42.

Harcourt, R.A. (1974) The dog in prehistoric and early historic Britain. *Journal of Archaeological Science* 1: 151–75.

Harrington, F.A. (1977) A Guide to the Mammals of Iran. Tehran: Department of the Environment.

Harrison, D.L. (1968) *The Mammals of Arabia. Vol 1. Carnivora, Hyracoidea, Artiodactyla*. London: Ernest Benn.

Harrison, D. L., and Bates, P.J.J. (1991) *The Mammals of Arabia*. 2nd ed. Sevenoaks: Harrison Zoological Museum Publication.

Hart, H.C. (1891) *Some Acount of the Flora and Fauna of Sinai, Petra and the Wady 'Arabah*. London: Palestine Exploration Fund.

Hatt, R.T. (1959) *The Mammals of Iraq*. Miscellaneous Publications of the Museum of Zoology 106. Ann Arbor: University of Michigan.

Hecker, H. (1975) *The Faunal Analysis of the Primary Food Animals from Pre-Pottery Neolithic Beidha (Jordan)*. Ann Arbor, Michigan and London: University Microfilms International.

Hesse, B. (1978) *Evidence for Husbandry from the Early Neolithic Site of Ganj Dareh in western Iran*. Ann Arbor, Michigan and London: University Microfilms International.

— (1982) Slaughter patterns and domestication: the beginnings of pastoralism in western Iran. *Man* (N.S.) 17: 403–17.

Higham, C.F.W. (1967) Stockrearing as a cultural factor in prehistoric Europe. *Proceedings of the Prehistoric Society* 6: 84–106.

Hole, F., K. Flannery and J. Neely (1969) *Prehistory and Human Ecology of the Deh Luran Plain*. Memoirs of the Museum of Anthropology 1. Ann Arbor: University of Michigan.

Hone, J., and O'Grady, J. (1980) Feral pigs and their control. Sydney: New South Wales Department of Agriculture.

Horwitz, L.K. (1987) Animal remains from the pottery Neolithic levela at Tel Dan. *Mitekufat Haeven, Journal of the Israel Prehistoric Society* 20:114–8.

— (1988) Bone remains from Neve Yam, a pottery Neolithic site off the Carmel Coast. *Mitekufat Haeven, Journal of the Israel Prehistoric Society* 21: 99–108.

Horwitz, L.K., and E. Tchernov (1990) Cultural and environmental implications of hippopotamus bone remains in archaeological contexts in the Levant. *Bulletin of the American Schools of Oriental Research* 280: 67–280.

Jarman, M.R. (1974) The fauna and economy of Tel 'Eli. *Mitekufat Haeven, Journal of the Israel Prehistoric Society* 12: 50–70.

Jennings, M.C. (1986) The distribution of the extinct Arabian ostrich *Struthio camelus syriacus* Rothschild, 1919. Fauna of Saudi Arabia 8: 447–61.

Josien, T. (1955) La faune chalcolithique des gisements palestiniens de Bir es-Safadi et Bir Abou Matar. *Israel Exploration Journal* 5: 246–56.

Laufer, B. (1926) *Ostrich egg-shell cups of Mesopotamia and the ostrich in ancient and modern times*. Anthropology Leaflet 23. Chicago: Field Museum of Natural History.

Lawrence, B. (1982) *Principal Food Animals at Çayönü*. In *Prehistoric Village Archaeology in South-Eastern Turkey*, edited by Linda S. Braidwood and Robert J. Braidwood. BAR International Series 138. Oxford: British Archaeological Reports, pp. 175-199.

Lemppenau, U. (1964) *Geschlects- und Gattungsunterschiede am Becken mitteleuropäischer Wiederkäuer*. Dissertation, Institut für Palaeoanatomie, Domestikationsforschung und Geschichte der Tiermedizin der Universität München.

Levy, T.E. (1983) The emergence of specialized pastoralism in the southern Levant. *World Archaeology* 15: 15–36.

— (1991) Dogs and healing. *Biblical Archaeological Review* 17(6): 14–18.

— (1992) Transhumance, subsustence, and social evolution. In *Pastoralism in the Levant*, edited by O. Bar-Yosef and A. Khazanov. Monographs in World Archaeology No. 10. Madison, Wisconsin: Prehistory Press, pp. 65–82.

Levy, T. E., and Alon, D. (1983) Chalcolithic Settlement Patterns in the Northern Negev. *Current Anthropology* 24: 105–7.

— (1987) Settlement Patterns Along the Nahal Beersheva—Lower Nahal Besor: Models of Subsistence in the Northern Negev. In *Shiqmim I*, edited by T.E. Levy. BAR International Series 356. Oxford: British Archaeological Reports, pp. 45–138.

Levy, T.E., Alon, D., Grigson, C., Holl, A., Goldberg, P., Rowan, Y., and Smith, P. (1991) Subterranean Negev settlement. *National Geographic Research, November 1991*: 394–413.

Levy, T.E., and Holl, A.F.C. (1995) Social change and the archaeology of the Holy Land. In *The Archaeology of Society in the Holy Land*, edited by T.E. Levy. Leicester: Leicester University Press, pp. 2–8.

Littauer, M.A. (1982) Les premiers véhicules a roues. *La Recherche* 142: 334–45.

Mallon, A., Koeppel, S. and Neuville, R. (1934) *Teleilat Ghassul, 1*. Rome: Pontifical Institute.

Martin, M. (1980) Pastoral production. Milk and firewood. *Expedition* 22(4): 24–28.

Matschke, G.H. (1967) Ageing European wild hogs by dentition. *Journal of Wildlife Management* 31: 109–13.

Meadow, R.H., and Uerpmann, H.-P. (eds.) (1986) *Equids in the Ancient World*, Vol. 1. Beihefte zum Tübinger Atlas des Vorderen Orients. Reihe A (Naturwissenschaften), 19/1. Wiesbaden: Ludwig Reichert.

— (1991) *Equids in the Ancient World*, Vol. 2. Beihefte zum Tübinger Atlas des Vorderen Orients. Reihe A (Naturwissenschaften), 19/2. Wiesbaden: Ludwig Reichert.

Meitinger, B. (1983) *Die Zahnaltersbestimmung beim Rind in ihrer Bedeutung für die Osteoarchäologie*. Munich: Institut für Palaeoanatomie, Domestikationsforschung und Geschichte der Tiermedizin der Universität München.

Miles, A.E.W., and Grigson, C. (1990) *Colyer's Variations and Diseases of the Teeth of Animals*. Cambridge: Cambridge University Press, p. 114.

Mount, L.E. (1968) *The Climatic Physiology of the Pig*. London: E. Arnold.

Ovadia, E. (1992) The domestication of the ass and pack transport by animals. In *Pastoralism in the Levant*, edited by O. Bar-Yosef and A. Khazanov. Monographs in World Archaeology No. 10. Madison, Wisconsin: Prehistory Press, pp. 19–28.

Payne, S. (1973) Kill-off patterns in sheep and goats: the mandibles from Asvan Kale. *Anatolian Studies* 23: 281–303.

— (1988) Animal bones from Tell Rubeidheh. In *Tell Rubeidheh, an Uruk Village in the Jebel Hamrin*. Iraq Archaeological Reports 2. Warminster: Aris & Phillips, pp. 98–135.

Payne, S., and Bull, G. (1988) Components of variation in measurements of pig bones and teeth, and the use of measurements to distinguish wild from domestic pig remains. *Archaeozoologia* 2: 27–66.

Payne, S., and P.J. Munson (1985) Ruby and how many squirrels? The destruction of bone by dogs. In *Palaeobiological Investigations*, edited by N.R.J. Fieler, D.D. Gilbertson and N.G.A. Ralph. British Archaeological Reports, International Series 266: 31–40.

Piggott, S. (1968) The earliest wheeled vehicles and the Caucasian evidence. *Proceedings of the Prehistoric Society* 34: 266–318.

Piggott, S. (1983) *The Earliest Wheeled Transport*. London: Thames & Hudson.

Postgate, J.N. (1986) The equids of Sumer, again. In *Equids in the Ancient World*, Vol. 1, edited by R.H. Meadow and H.-P. Uerpmann. Beihefte zum Tübinger Atlas des Vorderen Orients. Reihe A (Naturwissenschaften), 19/1. Wiesbaden: Reichert, pp. 194–206.

Redding, R.W. (1984) Theoretical determinants of a herder's decision modeling variation in the sheep/goat ratio. In *Animals and Archaeology*. Vol. 3. *Early Herders and their Flocks*, edited by J. Clutton-Brock and C. Grigson. Oxford: British Archaeological Reports, International Series 202, pp. 223–41.

Roshwalb, A. (1981) Protohistory in the Wadi Ghazzeh. Unpublished PhD thesis, University of London.

Russell, N. (n.d.) Cattle as wealth in Neolithic Europe: where's the beef?

Seeden, H. (1982) Ethnoarchaeological reconstruction of Halafian occupational units at Shams ed-Din Tannira. *Berytus* 30: 55–95.

Sherratt, A.G. (1981) Plough and pastoralism: aspects of the secondary products revolution. In *Patterns of the Past: Studies in Honour of David Clarke*, edited by I. Hodder, G. Isaac and N. Hammond. Cambridge University Press.

— (1983) The secondary exploitation of animals in the Old World. *World Archaeology* 15: 90–103.

Silver, I.A. (1963) The ageing of domestic animals. In *Science in Archaeology*, edited by D.B. Brothwell and E.S. Higgs. London: Thames & Hudson, pp. 250–68.

Staufer, T.R. (1965) The economics of nomadism in Iran. *Middle East Journal* 19:284–302.

Stordeur, D. (1988) Outils et armes en os du gisement natoufien de Mallaha (Eynan) Israel. *Memoires et Travaux du Centre de Recherche francais de Jerusalem* 6: 135.

Tchernov, E., and Grigson, C. (1990, unpublished) Preliminary report of the vertebrate remains from Chalcolithic Gilat. Seasons 1974–1987.

Tchernov, E., and Valla, F.F. (1997) Two new dogs, and other Natufian dogs, from the Southern Levant. *Journal of Archaeological Science* 24: 65–95

Tchernov, E., Dayan, T., and Yom-Tov, Y. (1986/7) The paleogeography of *Gazella gazella* and *Gazella dorcas* during the Holocene of the southern Levant. *Israel Journal of Zoology* 34: 51–59.

Teicherdt, M. (1975) Ostemetrische Untersuchungen zur Berechnung der Widerristhöhe bei Schafen. In *Archaeozoological Studies*, edited by A. Clason. Amsterdam: Elsevier, pp. 51–69.

Tristram, H.B. (1866) *The Land of Israel*. London: Society for Promoting Christian Knowledge.

Uerpmann, H.-P. (1979) *Probleme der Neolithisierung des Mittelmeeraums*. Wiesbaden: Ludwig Reichert.

— (1982) Faunal remains from Shams ed-Din Tannira, a Halafian site in northern Syria. *Berytus* 30: 3–48.

— (1986) Halafian equid remains from Shams ed-Din Tannira in northern Syria. In *Equids in the Ancient World*, Vol. 1, edited by R.H. Meadow and H.P. Uerpmann. Beihefte zum Tübinger Atlas des Vorderen Orients. Reihe A (Naturwissenschaften), 19/1. Wiesbaden: Ludwig Reichert, pp. 246–65.

Uerpmann, H.-P. (1987) *The Ancient Distribution of Ungulate Mammals in the Middle East*. Beihefte zum Tübinger Atlas des Vorderen Orients. Reihe A (Naturwissenschaften), 27. Wiesbaden: Ludwig Reichert.

Ussishkin, D. (1980) The Ghassulian shrine at Ein Gedi. *Tel Aviv* 7: 1–44.

Vigne, J.-D., and Marinval-Vigne, M.-C. (1983) Methode pour la mise en evidence de la consommation du petit gibier. In *Animals and Archaeology*. Vol. 1. *Hunters and their Prey*, edited by J. Clutton-Brock and C. Grigson. British Archaeological Reports, International Series 163, pp. 239–42.

Von den Driesch, A. (1976) *A Guide to the Measurement of Animal Bones from Archaeological Sites*. Peabody Museum Bulletin 1. Cambridge, MA: Peabody Museum of Archaeology and Ethnology, Harvard University.

Von den Driesch, A., and Boessneck, J. (1974) Kritische Anmerkungen zur Widerristhöhenberechnung aus Längenmassen vor- und frühgeschichtlicher Tierknochen. *Säugetierkundliche Mitteilungen* 22: 325–48.

Wapnish, P., and Hesse, B. (1993) Pampered pooches or plain pariahs? The Ashkelon dog burials. *Biblical Archaeologist* 56(2): 55–80.

Watson, G.E., Hesse, B. and Wapnish, P. (n.d.) Ostrich remains in archaeological excavations in Israel.

Wheeler Pires-Ferreira, J. (1975/6/7) Tepe Tula'i: faunal remains from an early campsite in Khuzistan, Iran. *Paléorient* 3: 275–80.

Whitcher, S.E., Grigson, C., and Levy, T.E. (1998) Recent faunal analysis at Shiqmim, Israel: a preliminary analysis of the 1993 assemblage. In *Archaeozoology of the Near East III*, edited by H. Buitenhuis, L. Bartosiewicz and A.M. Choyke. ARC Publicaties 18. Gröningen: Centre for Archeological Research and Consultancy, pp. 102–14.

Wing, E.S. (1978) Use of dogs for food: an adaptation to the coastal environment. In *Prehistoric Coastal Adaptations*, edited by B.L. Stark and B. Voorhies. New York: Academic Press.

Zeuner, F.E. (1955) The goats of early Jericho. *Palestine Exploration Quarterly*, April 1955: 70–86.

— (1963) *A History of Domesticated Animals*. London: Hutchinson.

Zohary, D. (1992) Domestication of the Neolithic Near Eastern crop assemblage. In *Préhistoire de l'Agriculture, Nouvelles Approches Experimentales et Ethnographiques*, edited by C. Anderson. Monograph du CRA 6. Paris: CNRS, pp. 81–6.

7 Marine and Riverine Shells at Gilat

Daniella E. Bar-Yosef Mayer

Introduction

The Chalcolithic site of Gilat in the northern Negev yielded a total of 1,142 mollusc shells and shell fragments (NISP) which are included in the following report. Most of them are of marine origin from the Mediterranean and Red Sea. One hundred and five of those shells are of freshwater origin: 103 shell fragments belong to *Aspatharia rubens*, a bivalve living in the Nile River. These shells are assumed to reflect socioeconomic activities, which will be discussed below. In this report it is assumed that snails and freshwater snails were not part of the cultural activities at Gilat and, therefore, are not included in this report. Thus, the mollusc shells and shell fragments reported on here are biological (ecofact) data that played a role in exchange networks that linked Gilat beyond its local geographic setting.

The malacological definitions below are based primarily on Tornaritis (1987) for the Mediterranean fauna and on Sharabati (1984) and Oliver (1992) for the Red Sea fauna. The taxonomic order follows Vaught (1989). In the shell description, a 'broken' shell is one where more than half the shell is present, and a 'fragment' means that less than half the shell is present. RS stands for Red Sea and M stands for Mediterranean. The following is a complete description of the shell assemblage at Gilat.

Description

Gastropods

Patella sp.—One fragment.

Trochidae (RS)—The columella of a shell from this family was found, probably belonging either to the genus *Trochus* sp. or *Tectus* sp.

Nerita sanguinolenta (RS)—Two complete specimens, one fragment, five shells with an artificial hole opposite the aperture (Fig. 7.1.1)

Nerita polita (RS)—One complete shell, three shells with an artificial hole opposite the aperture (one of them is broken).

Cerithium vulgatum (M)—Two complete shells, four broken shells and one with a hole in the body whorl (Fig. 7.1.11).

Cerithium scabridum (RS)—Two specimens in which the last whorl is broken.

Strombus gibberulus (RS)—One specimen, broken (Fig. 7.1.10).

Strombus taeniatus (RS)—One specimen, its outer lip broken and apex eroded (Fig. 7.1.9).

Strombus mutabilis (RS)—One specimen with a hole near the aperture (Fig. 7.1.8).

Lambis truncata (RS)—Two fragments of bracelets made of Lambis sp. were found (see discussion) (Fig. 7.1.15–16).

Cypraea cf. *turdus* (RS)—One fragment of the outer lip (Fig. 7.1.2).

Cypraea grayana (RS)—One fragment of the inner lip (Fig. 7.1.1).

Phalium granulatum (M)—One complete shell, one broken shell consisting of most of the shell without the lip, and 7 specimens which are 'cassid lips' (Reese 1989): These are usually naturally eroded lips of *P. granualtum*. Two of them are broken (Fig. 7.1.3).

Charonia tritonis (M)—One fragment (Fig. 7.1.6).

Murex trunculus (M)—One naturally eroded shell where only the aperture is present.

Chicoreus virgineus (RS)—One fragment, burnt (Fig. 7.1.7).

Thais haemastoma (M)—One broken shell.

Columbella rustica (M)—One complete specimen with the apex naturally eroded and two shells with an artificial hole in the body whorl (Fig. 7.1.14).

Cyclope neritea (M)—One broken specimen.

Nassarius gibbosulus (M)—One complete shell, naturally abraded.

Ancilla sp. (RS)—Two shells with a hole in the apex. The holes seem to be a result of natural abrasion yet could be used as beads (Fig. 7.1.5).

Conus parvatus (RS)—Two shells: One has a hole in the apex as well as a hole in the body whorl; the other has a hole in the apex and the base of the shell has been removed.

Conus mediterraneus (M)—Two shells. One has a hole in the apex; the other has a hole in the body whorl (Fig. 7.1.13).

Conus sp.—Three fragments.

Phos roseatus (RS)—One shell with a hole in the body whorl and the apex naturally abraded (Fig. 7.1.12).

Figure 7.1. Shells found at Gilat.

Figure 7.2. Shells found at Gilat.

Bivalves

Glycymeris violacescens (M)—A total of 333 shells: 56 are complete, 19 are broken, 150 are fragments, 2 are naturally abraded all around, 100 shells have a hole in the umbo, probably a result of natural abrasion (17 of them are broken) and six have a human-made hole in the umbo (Fig. 7.1.19–20).

Ostrea cf. *sentina* (RS)—One complete shell (Fig. 7.2.6).

Ostrea sp.—Twelve specimens which could not be identified at species level, but seem to originate in the Red Sea. Six are complete, five are broken and one is a fragment[1] (Fig. 7.2.9).

Hyotissa cf. *numisma* (RS)—Two broken shells and one fragment.

Plicatula cf. *plicata* (RS)—Two complete specimens (Fig. 7.2.7).

Unio cf. *terminalis* (local freshwater)—Two complete valves and one fragment.

Aspatharia rubens (Nile River)—A total of 103 specimens: 10 broken shells, 91 fragments and two worked fragments (Fig. 7.3.1–4).

Chama cf. *asperella* (RS)—One complete specimen.

Cerastoderma glaucum (M)—A total of 463 shells: 94 complete, 40 broken, 158 fragments, one naturally abraded all around, 149 with a natural hole in the umbo and 21 with a human-made hole near the umbo. A few specimens in this group might belong to the species *Acanthocardia tuberculata*. Due to their great similarity they were combined with the *Cerastoderma* sp (Fig. 7.1.21–23).

Tridacna maxima (RS)—Two complete valves (Figs 7.2.10 and 7.3.5).
Tridacna sp. (RS)—Nine fragments and one worked fragment (Fig. 7.3.6).
Solen sp.—One fragment (Fig. 7.2.4).
Asaphis deflorata (RS)—One fragment containing the umbo (Fig. 7.2.5).
Donax trunculus (M)—A total of 117 specimens: 46 complete shells, 22 broken, 48 fragments, and one with a natural hole near the umbo (Fig. 7.2.1–3).
Venus gallina (M)—One complete and one broken shell (Fig. 7.2.8).
Mother of pearl—21 fragments. Due to their fragmentary condition, there fragments were unidentifiable. However, they probably belong to either the Nilotic *Aspatharia* sp. or to the Indo-Pacific *Pinctada margaritifera*.
Bivalvia—Nine unidentifiable bivalve fragments were also found.

Figure 7.3. Shells found at Gilat.

In addition to the identified molluscs there was one artifact made of shell (Fig. 7.1.17).
Nine fragments of ostrich egg shell were also found in the mollusc collection. However, hundreds of other ostrich egg shell fragments were retrieved at the site (see Chapter 5 for discussion of the complete ostrich eggs found in Stratum IIC).

Discussion

From over 1,000 marine and freshwater mollusc shells and shell fragments, about 95% are bivalves and 5% are gastropods. *Dentalium* sp. (scaphopds), which are known from some Chalcolithic sites, were not found at Gilat.[2] Of the identified marine molluscs, 94% originate in the Mediterranean. and 6% are from the Red Sea.

All 105 freshwater shells included in this report were bivalves. One hundred and three belong to the species *Aspatharia rubens* and originated in the Nile River. This species is known from many sites of various periods (Reese *et al.* 1986), including a number of Chalcolithic sites: Tuleilat Ghassul, Abu Matar, Horvat Beter, Ben Shemen, Shiqmim and Gerar (Lee 1973:307; Perrot 1955:84; Dothan 1959:31; Mienis 1980; Bar-Yosef 1995). In the site of Kissufim, and in the caves of Nahal Mishmar, they were found as trapezoidal and/or engraved pendants (Bar-Yosef Mayer, in press a; Bar-Adon 1980: Ill. 24). Lee (1973:312) suggested that the presence of *Aspatharia rubens* is evidence for contact between the Chalcolithic inhabitants of Israel and the Nile Valley. It is worth mentioning, however, that at this period the Pelusiac branch of the Nile reached the area of northern Sinai (Butzer 2002; Stanley 2002; Tchernov 1988:231–32). This means that the Nile was only c. 100 km away during that period.

Among the marine shells, *Glycymeris* sp. and *Cerastoderma* sp. were the most abundant species. It is interesting to note that these two Mediterranean bivalves are usually found side by side, with larger quantities of *Glycymeris* sp. than *Cerastoderma* sp. (e.g. Bar-Yosef 1995). In this site, however, there is almost 1.4 times more *Cerastoderma* sp. than *Glycymeris* sp.

The two specimens of *Lambis* sp. deserve special attention: One fragment of a 'Lambis bracelet' was found in a fill under a burial in Stratum II (basket 1103, locus 526). Bracelets of this type are abundant in the *nawamis*—burial structures in Sinai (Bar-Yosef *et al.* 1977, 1986). Other parallels were found at Azor (Bar-Yosef Mayer in press b), in Shiqmim (Levy 1987: Pl. 13.2b: 1–2), and Bab edh-Dhra (Schaub and Rast 1989:311, and see further parallels there).

Some of the marine species present in Gilat are common to other Chalcolithic sites, especially *Glycymeris* sp., *Aspatharia* sp. and to a lesser degree *Nerita* sp., *Tridacna* sp. and *Phalium granulatum*. Those are present in most Chalcolithic sites including the Beersheva sites and Teleilat Ghassul (e.g. Lee 1973). Others, such as *Chicoreus* sp., *Phos* sp., *Solen* sp. and others, are very rare in Chalcolithic sites and in the archaeological record altogether (Table 1). The presence of uncommon species enhances the interpretation of the site as a place of worship. However, this conclusion should be taken with caution. The sample size at Gilat is much larger than that of most other sites mentioned above, and that might account for larger species diversity (Grayson 1984).

Conclusion

Assuming that Alon and Levy (1989) are correct, and Gilat is indeed a sanctuary, and if 'cult services performed at the Gilat sanctuary seem to have been the major item of exchange' (Alon and Levy 1989:211), then the shells retrieved in the site and described above may represent ritual acts or exchange activities of people who came to worship at Gilat from as far away as the Nile Valley, and the Red Sea and the Mediterranean coast. Alternatively, the shells could have been traded through 'down-the-line' exchange relations (cf. Renfrew 1975), but also with the ultimate goal of linking these materials to ritual needs. Those people exchanged shells (and other items) for participation in cult activities. Two other plausible explanations are: 1) that the inhabitants of Gilat (or visitors at the site) may have exchanged some of the shell items with other contemporaneous populations at the site when gathering there as noted above; 2) that they exchanged these items before coming to Gilat and left the shells there, either accidentally or as offerings. The shells might have been part of a broader economic exchange network before they reached Gilat. However, when considered along with other portable finds at Gilat such as non-local ceramics (Chapters 9, 10), groundstone fenestrated stands and other objects (Chapter 12), and figurines (Chapter 15), the Red Sea and Mediterranean shells seem to have played a more important role within religious, rather than economic, activities.

Notes

1.   Oliver (1992) relies on the color of shells for the description of this family. Since color is absent from the Gilat archaeological specimens, it was impossible to make an accurate identification. However, it is our impression that most, if not all, of the *Ostrea* sp. in Gilat originated in the Red Sea.

2.   Other Chalcolithic sites where *Dentalium* sp. was found include: Horvat Beter (Dothan 1959 fig 11:22), Grar (Bar-Yosef 1995), Tuleilat Ghassul (Mallon *et al.* 1934:79), Ein Hudra and Gebel Gunna (Bar-Yosef *et al.* 1977; 1986) and Shiqmim (Levy 1987: fig 6:11:9). It should be noted that they were found in very small quantities except at the *nawamis* sites.

Acknowledgments

I wish to thank H.K. Mienis (Curator, Mollusc Collection, Hebrew University of Jerusalem) for his assistance in shell identification.

References

Alon, D. and T.E. Levy (1989) Archaeology of Cult and the Chalcolithic Sanctuary at Gilat. *Journal of Mediterranean Archaeology* 2 (2):163–221.

Bar-Adon, P. (1980) *The Cave of the Treasure.* Israel Exploration Society, Jerusalem.

Bar-Yosef, D.E. (1995) The molluscs from Grar. In *Gerar : A Chalcolithic site in the Northern Negev*, edited by I. Gilead. Ben Gurion University of the Negev Press, Beer Sheva, pp. 453–62.

Bar-Yosef Mayer, D.E. (2002) The shell pendants of Kevish Kissufim. In *Kisufim: A Chalcolithic site*, edited by Y.P. Goren, R. Fabian, R. Rabinovich, F. Lemort, D.E. Bar-Yosef. Israel Antiquities Authority Monograph Series, pp. 49–52.

— (in press b) Azor: The shells. *Atiqot*

Bar-Yosef, O., A. Belfer, A. Goren and P. Smith (1977) The *nawamis* near 'Ein Huderah (Eastern Sinai). *Israel Exploration Journal* 27 (2–3):65–88.

Bar-Yosef, O., A. Belfer-Cohen, I. Goren, O. Hershkovitz, O. Ilan, H.K. Mienis and B. Sass (1986) *Nawamis* and Habitation sites near Gebel Gunna, Southern Sinai. *Israel Exploration Journal* 36 (3–4):121–67.

Butzer, K.W. (2002) Geoarchaeological Implications of Recent Research in the Nile Delta, in *Egypt and the Levant: Interrelations from the 4th through the Early 3rd Millennium B.C.E.*, edited by E.C.M. van den Brink and T.E. Levy. London: Leicester University Press (Continuum).

Dothan, M. (1959) Excavations at Horvat Beter (Beersheba). *Atiqot* 7.2.1–71.

Grayson, D.K. (1984) *Quantitative Zooarchaeology: topics in the analysis of archaeological faunas.* Orlando: Academic Press.

Lee, J.R. (1973) *Chalcolithic Ghassul: New Aspects and Master Typology.* PhD thesis, Hebrew University of Jerusalem. Hebrew University of Jerusalem

Levy, T.E. (1987) *Shiqmim I. Studies concerning Chalcolithic societies in the northern Negev desert, Israel (1982–1984).* British Archaeological Reports International Series 356. Oxford: British Archaeological Reports.

Mallon, A., R. Koeppel and R. Neuville (1934) *Teleilat Ghassul I.* Institut Biblique Pontifical, Rome.

Mienis, H.K. (1980) Mollusca. In *Tombes à ossuaires de la région cotière Palestinienne au IVe millénaire avant l'ère chrétienne*, edited by J. Perrot and D. Ladiray. Paris: Association Paléorient, pp. 94.

Oliver, P.G. (1992) *Bivalved seashells of the Red Sea.* Verlag Christa Hemmen, Wiesbaden.

Perrot, J. (1955) Excavations at Tell Abu Matar, near Beersheba. *Israel Exploration Journal* 5:73–84; 167–89.

Reese, D.S. (1989) On Cassid lips and helmet shells. *Bulletin of the American Schools of Oriental Research* 275:33–39.

Reese, D.S., H.K. Mienis and F.R. Woodward (1986) On the trade of shells and fish from the Nile River. *Bulletin of the American Schools of Oriental Research* 264:79–84.

Renfrew, C. (1975) Trade as Action at a Distance: Questions of Interaction and Communication, in *Ancient Civilization and Trade*, edited by J.A. Sabloff and C.C. Lamberg. Albuquerque: University of New Mexico Press, pp. 3–59.

Schaub, R.T. and W.E. Rast (1989) *Bab edh-Dhra: Excavations in the Cemetery Directed by Paul W. Lapp (1965–67)*. Winona Lake, Indiana: Eisenbrauns for the American Schools of Oriental Research.

Sharabati, D. (1984) *Red Sea Shells*. London: KPI.

Stanley, D.J.S. (2002) Configuration of the Egypt-to-Canaan Coastal Margin and North Sinai Byway in the Bronze Age, in *Egypt and the Levant: Interrelations from the 4th through the Early 3rd Millennium B.C.E.*, edited by E.C.M. van den Brink and T.E. Levy. London: Leicester University Press (Continuum).

Tchernov, E. (1988) The paleobiogeographical history of the southern Levant. In *The Zoogeography of Israel: The distribution and abundance at a zoogeographical crossroad*, edited by Y. Yom-Tov and E. Tchernov. Dordrecht: Dr. W. Junk, pp. 159–250.

Tornaritis, G. (1987) *Mediterranean Sea Shells, Cyprus*. Nicosia: G. Tornaritis.

Vaught, K.C. (1989) *A Classification of the Living Mollusca*. Melbourne, Florida: American Malacologists.

8 Death and the Sanctuary:
The Human Remains from Gilat

Patricia Smith, Tania Zagerson, Pamela Sabari, Jonathan Golden, Thomas E. Levy, and Leslie Dawson

Introduction

Gilat has been identified as one of the three earliest, permanent public ritual centers identified in the southern Levant (Alon and Levy 1989; Levy 1998), and the only one so far identified in the Northern Negev during the Chalcolithic period. It is one of a select group of sanctuaries that include Ein Gedi in the Judean Desert overlooking the Dead Sea (Ussishkin 1980) and Teleilat Ghassul located near the northeast coast of the Dead Sea (Bourke *et al.* 2001, Hennessy 1982, Seaton 2000). Occupation of the site both predated and postdated the period in which the sanctuary was built and functioned, and human skeletal remains have been recovered from burials dug into each of the three Chalcolithic strata identified. Altogether they number some 91 individuals, of whom half this number originated from the two strata associated with the sanctuary (Strata IIA and IIB).

In this chapter we describe their bio-anthropological characteristics and relationship with other contemporaneous populations of the Negev. We also suggest some hypotheses for understanding the meaning of mortuary practices within the confines of the formative Chalcolithic sanctuary at Gilat. In view of the unique status of Gilat as discussed elsewhere in this volume, we have also examined the bones for signs of differences in phenotype, disease or function that would indicate any special status or prestige for those buried in the vicinity of the sanctuary. The presence of 91 human burials in the relatively small excavations exposure at Gilat highlights the importance of mortuary practices for understanding some aspects of ritual practice at the site. It should be remembered that during the Chalcolithic, the southern Levant was witness to the first widespread occurrence of cemeteries (Levy 1998). Prior to this, during the Neolithic period (Banning 1998), human corpses were usually interred as inter-mural burials. The symbolism behind this practice has usually been interpreted to reflect ancestor worship (Bar Yosef 1998; Gopher 1998; Hershkovitz, Galili and Ring 1991; Hershkovitz *et al.* 1995; Kuijt and Goring-Morris 2002) which can be linked to autonomous village, tribal social organizations. With the establishment of cemeteries separate from settlements, the concern with territoriality can also be linked to the emergence regional settlement systems (Shennan 1982). The large assemblage of human burials within the Gilat sanctuary setting is a real puzzle when considered in relation to the large number of contemporary cemetery sites that were established on the nearby coastal plain (Perrot and Ladiray 1980; van den Brink 1998) and especially the Wadi Beersheva less than 16 km to the south of Gilat (Levy and Alon 1982, Levy and Alon 1985a, Levy and Alon 1985b). By using ethnographic and ethnohistoric source materials (see especially, in this volume, Bilu [Chapter 2] and Marx [Chapter 4]), the significance of the human remains for understanding dimensions of formative Levantine cult and religion can be postulated.

Human Remains by Strata

In all three Chalcolithic strata, primary burials were found in pits, silos, mortuary structures and fills (Plates 8.1–8.3). Many of them had been disturbed by building activities in later phases of settlement, leaving two or more bones still in articulation. In addition, isolated bones were found in fill and seem to have been accidental inclusions. For the site as a whole, bone preservation was poor, but were possible age and sex were determined. Each individual identified was assigned a Homo number (H), and the various burials are described by strata. They are summarized in Table 8.1.

Stratum I. Stratum 1 consists of topsoil that had been disturbed by deep plowing activities in the 1950's. From this stratum the remains of 6 individuals were identified from single and double primary burials, as well as one adult male (H4/L.802) identified in the field as an intentional secondary burial. However, because of the disturbed nature of this stratum the classification of this burial as secondary is open to question.

   Homo 4/L.802. This was a male, aged approximately 35 years of age represented by both cranial and post-cranial remains. The skull appeared to have been placed on top of the piled long bones.

   Homo 17/L.1032. H17 is an infant of approximately 3 months of age. Only the cranium was found. However, the post-cranial remains may be in the unexcavated baulk. The orbits exhibit cribra orbitalia.

   Homo 39/L.822. H39 is an infant found in a pit with an adolescent (H55).

   Homo 53/L.800. H53 is an adult represented by cranial fragments and long bones.

   Homo 55/L.822. H55 is an adolescent female of 16–18 years, represented by cranial fragments and post-cranial remains. The upper teeth show severe attrition with dentine exposed on the occlusal surface of the incisors and first molars. All teeth have hypoplastic defects. This individual was found in a pit with an infant (H39).

   Homo 60/L.508. H60 is an adult male represented by several cranial fragments. It was found in fill.

   Homo 77/L.13. H77 consists of the foot bones (tarsals, metatarsals and phalanges) of an adult recovered from fill.

Stratum IIA. Like Stratum I, Stratum IIA was also disturbed by plowing and was relatively poorly preserved in some areas. As outlined in Chapter 5 (this volume), this stratum is characterized by ephemeral architectural remains. However, the presence of platforms which may have served as alters, and numerous ritual paraphernalia point to the continued range of cult related activities at this time. Stratum IIA yielded 17 individuals, of which 9 were in fills, 6 were recovered from pits and 2 from mud-brick collapse. There was no discernible association between the burials and any of the architectural features. Most were located within the southeast area, but three adult burials were found to the west of the site in 'open areas'. All appeared to be primary single or double burials in shallow pits that were dug from the site surface in antiquity.

Hominid No.	Age	Sex	Cranial	Mandible	Teeth	Post Cranial
H1/L.613	17	F	+	+	+	complete
H2/L.615	adult	M	-	-	-	lower limbs
H3/L.648	adult	M	+	-	-	complete
H4/L.802	40+	M	+	+	+	up/lower limbs
H5/L.515	adult	?	+	-	-	-
H6/L.806	35-40	M	+	+	+	complete
H7/L.840	infant	?	+	-	-	-
H8/L.510	35+	F	+	+	-	complete
H9/L.541	infant	?	+	+	+	complete
H10/L.1046	neonate	?	+	+	+	complete
H11/L.536	adult	M?	-	-	-	tibia
H12/L.886	3	?	+	+	+	complete
H13/L.894	3 mos.	?	+	+	+	complete
H14/L.900	3-4	?	-	+	+	ribs, scapula, vertebra
H15/L.971	0-1 mo.	?	+	+	+	complete
H16/L.1103	18 mos.	?	+	+	+	complete
H17/L.1032	3 mos.	?	+	-	-	-
H18/L.1090	13	F	-	-	-	complete
H19/L.1169	4	?	+	+	+	complete
H20/L.887	infant	?	-	-	-	vertebrae, hand
H21/L.563	35-40	M	+	+	-	-
H22/L.551	3-4 mos.	?	-	-	-	ribs, pelvis, vertebrae
H23/L.551	18-20	F	-	-	+	complete
H24/L.980	3 mos.	?	+	+	+	complete
H25/L.528	6	F?	-	-	-	femur
H26/L.1237	19	F	+	+	+	complete
H27/L.1237	12	M?	+	+	+	complete
H28/L.1237	20	F	+	+	+	complete
H29/L.1237	9	?	+	+	+	complete
H30/L.1237	40+	F	+	+	+	complete
H31/L.1237	6	?	+	+	+	complete
H32/L.1237	14	M	+	+	+	complete
H33/L.1237	12	F	+	+	+	complete
H34/L.1237	4	?	+	+	+	complete
H35/L.1301	neonate	?	+	+	+	complete
H36/L.1317	infant	?	+	+	+	upper limbs
H37/L.1510	30	F	+	+	+	complete
H38/L.579	adolescent	F	-	-	+	complete
H39/L.822	infant	?				
H40/L.1000	adult	?	+	-	-	-
H41/L.1369	child	?	+	-	-	-
H42/L.33	adult	?	+	-	-	vertebrae, ribs, long bones, feet
H43/L.33	child	?	+			
H44/L.34	neonate	?	-	-	-	(postcranial)
H45/L.950	infant	?	-	-	-	limbs
H46/L.988	neonate	?	+	-	-	limbs
H47/L.962	adult	F?	-	-	+	limbs
H48/L.951	adult	?	-	-	-	limbs
H49/L.883	infant	?	+	+	+	complete
H50/L.938	infant	?	+	-	-	radius
H51/L.847	infant	?	+	-	-	-
H52/L.946	neonate	?	-	-	-	femur, pelvis
H53/L.800	adult	?	+	-	-	limbs
H54/L.1246	7	?	-	-	-	limbs
H55/L.822	16-18	F	+	-	-	limbs
H56/L.1090	8	?	-	-	-	vertebrae, pelvis, scapula
H57/L.962	infant	?	+	-	-	pelvis, limbs
H58/L.510	infant	?	-	-	-	vertebrae, pelvis
H59/L.528	6 mos.	?	-	-	-	femur
H60/L.508	adult	M?	+	-	-	-
H61/L.524	adult	?	-	-	-	femur
H62/L.813	child	?	+	-	-	-
H63/L.588	child	?	-	-	-	hand, ribs
H64/L.837	adult	?	+	-	-	ribs, patella
H65/L.862	infant	?	-	-	-	right/left femur
H66/L.862	adult	?	-	-	+	foot bones
H67/L.890	adult	?	-	-	+	foot bones
H68/L.970	adult	?	-	-	-	ulna
H69/L.995	adult	?	-	-	-	radius, phalanges
H70/L.548	adult	?	-	-	-	humerus
H71/L.553	9-10	?	-	-	-	tibia
H72/L.555	child	?	-	-	-	radius
H73/L.567	child	?	-	-	-	axis, ribs
H74/L.279	child	?	+	-	-	vertebrae, phalanges
H75/L.889	child	?				
H76/L.?	20	F	+	+	-	-
H77/L.13	adult	?	-	-	-	foot bones
H78/L.17	adult	?	-	-	-	left ulna and and radius
H79/L.34	adult	?	-	-	+	foot bones
H80/L.517	adult	?	-	-	-	hand bones
H81/L.910	adult	?	-	-	-	foot bones
H82/L.834	adult	?	-	-	-	hand bones
H83/L.834	child	?	-	-	-	femur
H84/L.835	adult	?	-	-	-	foot bones
H85/L.838	adult	?	+	-	-	-
H86/L.905	adult	?	-	-	-	hand bones
H87/L.771	adolescent	?	+	-	-	-
H88/L.786	adult	M?	+	-	-	-
H89/L.583	adult	?	-	-	-	hand bones
H90/L.542	infant	?	+	-	-	-
H91/?	adult	-	+	-	-	-

Table 8.1. Hominid inventory from Gilat.

Homo 1/L. 613. H1 is a female of 15 years of age with unfused epiphyses and unerupted third molars. This was a complete primary burial in pit fill. The skeleton was flexed and lay on its right side, facing north-north-west.

Homo 2/L. 615. H2 was an adult male. Only the lower part of the body was recovered (pelvic fragment, left femur, tibia, and the right and left fibula) with the leg bones articulated in a flexed position. A polished bone awl was found in this locus, however due to the disturbed nature of the burial and the burial context (mud-brick collapse) it is difficult to determine if these artifacts are associated with the burial.

Homo 3/L. 648. H3 is represented by the poorly preserved remains of an adult male. The skeleton was complete except for the mandible. This primary burial was found at the base of a pit, in a flexed position, on its right side, facing west.

Homo 5/L. 515. H5 is represented by the fragmented cranium of an adult recovered from fill.

Homo 6/L. 806. H6 is probably female and aged 35–40 years based on the degree of cranial suture closure and dental attrition. This individual was placed in a flexed position on its right side and oriented to the west. The burial was in a large pit which contained typical Chalcolithic artifacts. A ceramic v-shape vessel was found next to the cranium. Other artifacts in this pit included a tabular scraper, a violin-shape figurine, and a possible palette. However, no clear association was found between the artifacts and the burial since the pit was ca. 58 cm deep and 1m in diameter, and the artifacts were found throughout the fill.

Homo 7/L.840. H7 is an infant aged 0–3 months, represented by cranial fragments, a mandible and a number of long bones. This disturbed, incomplete burial was found under mud-brick tumble.

Homo 44/L.34. H44 represents an infant of approximately 3 months, found with H 79. The remains of this individual were greatly disturbed and only post cranial remains were recovered.

Homo 45/L.950. H45 is an infant of 0–3 months represented only by the limbs. It was found in fill covering an earlier surface.

Homo 47/L.962. H47 is an adult, possibly female, represented by teeth and limb bones. These remains were found in a pit together with an infant (H57).

Homo 48/L.951. H. 48 was an adult, represented by fragmented long bones recovered from the fill above a surface.

Homo 57/L.962. H57 is an infant. This burial is incomplete in that only the cranium, pelvis and limbs were recovered. This individual was found in the fill of a shallow pit in association with H47.

Homo 61/L.524. Locus 524 consists of a femur of an adult which was recovered during the excavation of a square probe.

Homo 62/L.813. H62 is represented by cranial fragments of a child. These remains were found in a pit.

Homo 78/L.17. H78 is an incomplete/disturbed burial of an adult, consisting of a left ulna and radius recovered from a pit.

Homo 79/L.34. Locus 34 contained foot bones (tarsals, metatarsals and phalanges) and a tooth of an adult. These remains were found in fill together with H44.

Homo 80/L.517. H80 is represented by the carpals, metacarpals and phalanges of an adult recovered from a pit.

Homo 81/L.910. Locus 910 yielded foot bones (tarsals, metatarsals and phalanges) of an adult in the fill.

Stratum IIB. Stratum IIB is perhaps the best preserved occupation layer at Gilat (see Chapter 5, this volume). A network of well-preserved buildings, courtyards, circular platforms and other features are associated with a wide-range of ritual objects (see Chapters 10, 12, and 15. Evidence for production activities involving textile manufacture and hide-working are prevalent here. Stratum

IIB yielded nearly half the burials recovered from Gilat. Like those in other strata they were mainly primary flexed burials, located in pits or fill. They were primarily situated in the southern part of the site, and included three infant burials lying against walls within rooms. Two of the infants (H10 and H 15) were lying on potsherds, while the third was in a complete pot (H 35). At least 6 other infant burials in the same age range (birth–3 months) were recovered from open areas but were not associated with potsherds. Four of these were by themselves, 2 were found with older individuals, and one was found above a pit containing an adult. In addition one large collective burial, with 9 individuals was found in the southwest corner of the site.

Homo 8/L. 510. H8 is the complete, primary burial of a female. The cranium was fragmentary but degenerative changes in the vertebrae indicated an age of some 35 years. This individual was buried in a flexed position, on its left side, with a northern orientation. Also found within this locus were the vertebrae and pelvis of an infant (H58).

Homo 9/L. 541. H9 is a child of approximately 3 years of age. The complete skeleton of this individual was found in a semi-flexed position on its right side, oriented toward the west.

Homo 10/L. 1046. H10 is an infant less than one month old. This was a complete primary burial found in Room 1 near a wall, lying on its left side in a flexed position, facing south. Several potsherds were found adjacent to the skeleton; however there appears to be no direct association between these sherds and the burial.

Homo 11/L.536. H11 is represented by an adult tibia, probably of a male individual. It was recovered from fill.

Homo 12/L.886. H12 is an infant of 18 months. The post-cranial remains of this individual are generally well preserved, however the upper limbs had suffered post-mortem damage. The mandible is present but the cranium is represented by only a few small fragments. It was found in a tightly flexed position, suggesting that it had been bound for burial. It lay on its left side and oriented to the north.

Homo 13/L.894. H13 is an infant of 3 months of age. The skeleton was complete, lying on its left side in a flexed position facing south.

Homo 14/L.900. H14 is a child of age 3–4 years. The post cranial remains were complete, however the cranium was missing. The skeleton was very tightly flexed, indicating that it had been bound. This individual was lying on its right side and was facing southeast.

Homo 15/L.971. H15 is a neonate less than one month old. The skeleton was in a flexed position lying on its right side facing southwest. It was lying on a number of potsherds and situated to the north of an incomplete mudbrick and stone arc structure.

Homo 16/L.1103. H16 is a complete skeleton of an infant of eighteen months. The skeleton was complete and had been placed in a flexed position on its right side. It faced west.
This burial was located in a pit cut into fill and was found in association with faunal remains.

Homo 18/L.1090. H18 is an adolescent of approximately 13 years of age, most probably a female. The skeleton was tightly flexed, lying on its left side and facing north-north-west. The post-cranial remains are complete, but the cranium, mandible and cervical vertebrae are missing. No teeth were recovered from the burial fill. There is no evidence of trauma on the remaining vertebrae to suggest decapitation or intentional removal of the skull before burial. Also found within this locus were the skeletal remains of a child aged 7–8 years old (H56), represented by scapula, vertebrae and pelvis. Artifacts retrieved from L.1090 include a bone awl and a flint ax/tool; however, their association with the burial is unclear.

Homo 19/L.1169. H19 is a child aged 4 years old. The skeleton is complete and well-preserved. It was lying in a semi-flexed position, on its right side, with a southwest orientation.

Homo 20/L.887. H20 is an infant represented by several vertebrae and a hand (carpals, metacarpals and phalanges).

The Collective Burial (L. 1237). The most remarkable burial feature found at Gilat was associated with Stratum IIB. During the 1992 season, a free-standing, circular mudbrick structure (L.1237) containing the complete skeletal remains of nine individuals were discovered (Plate 8.3; see also Chapter 5, this volume). They included three adults (H26, H28 and H30), three adolescents (H27, H32 and H33) and three children (H29, H31 and H34). They were lying on top of and alongside one another. The majority was extended on their backs, but one was laying face down (Plate 8.3). Beneath them was a layer of animal bones and broken potsherds that probably represent the remains of offerings placed in the mortuary structure before the dead were interred. Locus 1237 resembles other silos found at Gilat in size; however, it is different because it was not sunken in the ground, but rather free-standing on the edge of a large courtyard. It consists of concentric layers of mud-brick, and a base constructed of large flat paving stones leveled on a layer of fine silt. Below the layer of fine silt is a hard mud-brick base. The diameter of this structure (1.9m) is typical for silos at Gilat; however the sunken depth (0.6m) is relatively shallow. The shallow nature of this pit may be due to disturbance: the rim of this structure was found only 5cm below topsoil. Thus, the original rim may have been higher but removed by plowing. Thus, this was a free-standing small 'monument' established on the edge of a Stratum IIB plaza.

The order of deposition of the individuals into the silo is as follows: H33 was found disarticulated at the lowest level. The next individuals interred were H30 and H32; the upper body of H30 is mostly articulated, but the lower limbs were quite separate from the trunk probably dislodged by the weight of the bodies lying above him. H32 was articulated, but in a rather atypical position, probably due to the position of other bodies above it. H32 lay above H33. H26, H27 and H28 were all interred at the same level, H27 first and H26 last. They lay side by side along the north-south axis of the silo. H28 lay above H30, while H34 lay across the legs of H26. The last individual to be interred was H29 who was also lying across the legs of H26.

Homo 26/L.1237. H26 is a female aged approximately 19 years, with some epiphyses, such as the medial epi-condyle of the humerus, only partially fused. The skeleton was found in a semi-flexed position lying on its right side, facing east (Plate 8.4a, 8.6a, 8.6b). Despite the young age, arthritic changes were noted in some of the joints, specifically in the right elbow, neck and lower back region. The proximal region of the right ulna was arthritic and deformed, as were the bodies of most of the cervical vertebrae. A cystic lesion was found in one of the lumbar vertebrae. Additional evidence of inflammatory changes was found in the form of periostitis of the femur and tibia shafts. There is a markedly anterior slope to the mandibular condyles which is also reflected in the facets of the occipital bone. Some suture closure was noted internally at the base of the skull. The sloping of the mandibular condyles and the endocranial suture closure may be due to cultural influences (e.g. head binding) or may reflect individual variability. Attempts at restoration of this fragmentary cranium have not yet yielded sufficient detail for cranial measurements to be taken or to evaluate the probability of head binding. The dentition contains a supernumerary tooth, a peg-shaped incisor-in the upper jaw, and markedly asymmetric first premolars. The first molars in both jaws show less wear on the left side than on the right. This may be related to the early loss of the lower left second molar and is associated with alveolar resorption lingually (Plate 8.14–8.15). The dentition is hypoplastic.

Homo 27/L.1237. H27 is a child of 12 years probably male (Plate 8.7) with a supramastoid ridge on the temporal bones and a squarish mandible. The orbits of the cranium exhibit pitting indicative of cribra orbitalia. The inner surface of the frontal bone shows a roughened area of porous new bone growth extending posteriorly to bregma (Plate 8.9a–8.9b). This condition has been reported as indicative of meningo-encephalitis (Schultz 1987) and may have been the cause of death. The teeth are stained orange, and also show a green discoloration which appears as a 2 mm band at the neck of the tooth. This discoloration is also seen on unerupted teeth. The teeth are hypoplastic with dentine exposed on the central incisors. Some of the cervical vertebrae have slightly compressed vertebral bodies and the axis exhibits spina bifida. There are some circular cavities noted on some of the long bones which appear to be post-mortem in nature - probably due to roots or insect activity (Plate 8.5). The skeleton was found lying on its left side in a semi-flexed position, facing west.

Homo 28/L.1237. H28 is an adult female in her early twenties. Many of the cranial features are robust but other bones, such as the clavicle, exhibit features characteristic of females and this is borne out by measurements of the long bones which are gracile. There is asymmetry in the size of the facets and the transverse foramina of the atlas and one other cervical vertebra has a Shmorl's node and lipping. A second cervical vertebra exhibits an ante-mortem cavity and some lipping. There is post-mortem tunneling in the tarsals, probably from roots or beetle activity.

Homo 29/L.1237. H29 is a child aged 9 years old (Plate 8.12). The mandible is masculine in form with a square chin. The teeth show severe hypoplasia, as well as orange staining and green bands. The orbits of the cranium are cribrotic. There are circular holes in the bodies of several vertebrae which appear to have occurred post-mortem. This individual was lying on its left side in a flexed position, facing north.

Homo 30/L.1237. H30 is an adult female aged approximately 40 years old. The teeth exhibit severe hypoplasia and the lower left third molar is carious (Plate 8.11). This individual is the only one from Gilat with caries. Both the right and left lower second molars have been lost ante-mortem, possibly from caries or periodontal disease since the first molar which is commonly the most severely worn shows only moderate attrition, with limited exposure of dentine on the occlusal surface. The dentition shows orange staining, but no green bands. There is some lipping of the vertebral bodies. The cranium of H30 was oriented southeast and lying approximately 10cm south of the body. The lower part of the body was flexed and lying on its left side some distance away from the upper part of the body.

Homo 31/L.1237. H31 is a child aged 6–7 years. The teeth are hypoplastic and exhibit orange staining with green bands. The orbits exhibit cribra orbitalia (Plate 8.10). The skull was found with the face against the mudbrick wall of the silo. The post-cranial remains were extremely disturbed, but it appears as though the body originally lay in a supine position.

Homo 32/L.1237. H32 represents the complete skeleton of a 14 year old male with pronounced areas of muscular attachment on the long bones (Plate 8.8). The teeth show orange staining and green bands (Plate 8.13). The mandibular first premolar has a bifid root, and there is some shoveling of the maxillary incisor. There is marked bowing of the femurs. The cranium of H32 was found upside down and approximately 12 cm from the upper part of the body.

Homo 33/L.1237. H33 is the complete skeleton of a female aged 11–12 years. The upper second deciduous molar was still present, and the second premolars just erupting. Sex was determined from the gracile form of the bones and the slender pointed chin of the mandible (Plate 8.4b). The teeth are hypoplastic. H33 was found underneath H32 and H34. The cranium faced south but the post-cranial remains were dispersed; the femurs were set apart with the tibias folded underneath and the upper body lying over the legs. The arms were extended on the right side (see Plates 8.5a–8.5c).

Homo 34/L.1237. H34 is the complete skeleton of a child aged 4–5 years. The teeth show orange staining and the orbits are cribrotic. The cranium of H34 was extremely fragmentary but appears to have been upside down. The mandible was separate and found nearby. The post-cranial remains were fragmentary but indicate that the body was lying in a semi-flexed position on its left side.

Homo 35/L.1301. H35 is a neonate. It was found inside a ceramic vessel in association with the base of a wall of a domestic structure.

Homo 36/L.1317. H36 is an infant found in the fill of a shallow pit. Bones recovered include cranial fragments, mandible, unfused vertebrae, the right and left clavicle, the right and left scapulae, metacarpals, phalanges and a pelvis fragment. This individual was lying in a flexed position on its left side, facing north.

Homo 40/L.1000. H40 is represented by cranial fragments of an adult found within fill over a surface, adjacent to a wall.

Homo 46/L.988. H46 is a neonate found within fill above a surface. Bones recovered include cranial fragments and upper and lower limbs

Homo 49/L.883. H49 is the disturbed burial of a neonate recovered from fill. Skeletal remains recovered include fragments of the cranium (zygoma, occipital, petrous), mandible fragments, unfused vertebrae, ribs, metacarpals/metatarsals and phalanges.

Homo 50/L.938-860. H50 is an infant, aged 0–3 months, represented by cranial fragments and a radius. This individual was recovered from a surface area in the baulk.

Homo 51/L.847. H51 is represented by the fragmentary remains of an infant cranium. It was found in ash fill below a platform, together with the foot bones (tarsals, metatarsals and phalanges) of an older individual. The latter bones may belong to the disturbed burial of an adult found in a pit (H64) situated some 50 cm below H51.

Homo 56/L.1090. H56 is a child of 8 years of age found within fill. This individual is represented by a scapula, vertebrae and fragments of the pelvis. Also found within this burial context were the skeletal remains of an adult (H18).

Homo 58/L.510. Locus 510 contained the vertebrae and pelvis of an infant. Also found within this pit were the skeletal remains of an adult H8.

Homo 63/L.588. H63 is a child represented by hand bones (carpals, metacarpals and phalanges) and ribs. These remains were recovered from fill under a mudbrick platform.

Homo 64/L.837. H64 is an incomplete burial of an adult, consisting of cranial fragments, ribs and a patella. These remains were found in a pit beneath ash fill containing an infant and adult foot bones. The latter possibly belong to H64.

Homo 65/L.862. H65 is an infant represented solely by the right and left femurs. These bones were found in a pit together with the remains of an adult (H66).

Homo 66/L.862. H66 comprises metatarsals and phalanges, and a tooth of an adult. They were found in a pit with the fragmentary remains of H65.

Homo 67/L.890. H67 represents the disturbed remains of an adult (metatarsals, phalanges and a tooth) and was recovered from fill.

Homo 68/L.970. H68 consists of an adult ulna recovered from a pit.

Homo 69/L.995. H69 is represented by a radius and phalanges of an adult. These remains were recovered from a pit.

Homo 82/L.834. H82 is an adult represented by hand bones (carpals, metacarpals and phalanges). These remains were recovered from a pit. Also found within this pit were the skeletal remains of a child, H83.

Homo 83/L.834. H83 is a child represented solely by a femur. It was found in a pit and in association with the remains of the adult, H82.

Homo 84/L.835. H84 consisted of the foot bones (tarsals, metatarsals and phalanges) of an adult recovered from a pit.

Homo 85/L.838. H85 is represented by cranial fragments of an adult recovered from a pit. Some of the fragments were burnt to a dull black color. There was no evidence for shrinkage or fissuring to suggest that the bones were burnt when fresh.

Homo 86/L.905. Locus 905 contained hand bones (carpals, metacarpals and phalanges) of an adult recovered from fill.

Homo 90/L.542. H90 is represented by cranial fragments (zygoma, petrous) of an infant recovered from fill.

Homo 91/L.264. H91 was represented by the corpus of an adult mandible. The first molars exhibited severe attrition and both second molars had been lost ante-mortem.

Stratum IIC. Stratum IIC contained the mud-brick and stone foundation remains of the main sanctuary occupation identified at the site. The Gilat Woman and Zoomorphic statuettes were found in this stratum along with a host of violin-shape figurines and other ritual objects (see Chapter 5 for summary of this stratum; for figurative object see Chapter 15). Eight individuals were recovered from pits and fill in the western and eastern areas. In contrast to the other strata, this stratum shows no concentration of burials in the southern Area (Area J; see Chapter 5 for maps of the excavation areas).

Homo 21/L.563. H21 is represented by a cranium and part of a mandible. These remains belong to an adult male of approximately 35–40+ years of age. The skull was found in a mudbrick collapse.

Homo 25/L.528. H25 yielded the femur of a child of approximately 6 years old.

Homo 37/L.1510. H37 is an adult female aged approximately 30 years old. This individual was found in a pit in a tightly flexed position, lying on its right side, facing north-north-west. A V-shaped bowl was found adjacent to the head and a sheep/goat mandible was found alongside the trunk. Due to the tightly flexed position of the skeleton, it is likely that this was a bundle burial.

Homo 42/L.33. H42 is the incomplete remains of an adult found in fill. Bones recovered include; cranial fragments, scapula fragments, vertebrae, ribs, femur, shaft fragments, tarsals, metatarsals and phalanges.

Homo 43/L.33. H43 consists of cranial fragments of a child recovered from fill. Also found within this context were the incomplete remains of an adult (H42).

Homo 87/L.771. H87 is an adolescent represented by several cranial fragments recovered from a pit.

Homo 88/L.786. H88 is represented by fragmentary cranial remains of an adult recovered from fill.

Stratum IIIA. Stratum IIIA burials were primarily located in the eastern part of the site. They were found in an area of pits and fill, with no architecture. Many of these burials were disturbed, possibly due to the subsequent digging of new pits. Eleven individuals were identified and included two infants that were found in rooms (H24/L.980 and H52/L.946). No burials were found in any of the other large open areas of stratum IIIA.

Homo 22/L.551. H22 is an infant of 3–4 months in age. The skeletal remains are incomplete consisting of several ribs, fragments of the pelvic girdle, and several vertebrae.

Homo 23/L.579. H23 is an adult female aged 18–20 years old. Only the post-cranial remains were recovered but several loose teeth were recovered from the burial locus. This suggests that the cranium and mandible were originally present in the grave.

Homo 24/L.980. H24 is an infant of approximately 3 months of age. The skeleton is complete and was interred in a tightly flexed position in a large ceramic vessel, at the base of a wall in Room 7.

Homo 38/L.579. H38 is an adolescent female. This individual was found in fill overlying an earlier surface. It was placed in a flexed position on its right side, facing northwest.

Homo 41/L.1369. H41 is a child. Only the cranium was recovered. It was found in a silo.

Homo 52/L.946. H52 represents the incomplete remains of an infant approximately 0–3 months of age. Only the femur and pelvis were recovered. They were found on the floor of a room abutting a wall. This is the only instance of infant remains from Gilat found in association with a building without potsherds.

Homo 70/L.548. H70 is the right humerus of an adult found in a pit.

Homo 71/L.553. H71 is a child aged approximately 9–10 years old, represented by a right tibia recovered from a 2 x 2 m probe.

Homo 72/L.555. H72 is a child represented by a left radius.

Homo 73/L.567. H73 represents the incomplete remains of a child. The fragmentary skeletal remains were recovered from fill above a surface and include the axis vertebra and several ribs.

Homo 89/L.583. H89 is represented by the hand bones (carpals, metacarpals and phalanges) of an adult. These remains were found in fill.

Human Remains from Undetermined Strata

Homo 74/L.247. H74 is a child represented by the basiocciput, vertebrae and phalanges.

Homo 75/L.889. H75 is a child represented by fragmentary remains.

Homo 76/(locus unknown). H76 is an adult female aged 20 years old. This individual is represented by a cranium and a mandible. The burial context is unknown.

Additional Human Remains Allocated to a Scatter Context:
Stratum II/IIA.
L.522 adult phalange in a pit.
L.532 adult phalange in a pit.
L.14 adult right capitate in pit.
L.976 adult phalange in a pit.

Stratum IIB.
L.18 adult phalange in mud-brick collapse.
L.525 adult metatarsal in fill.
L.999 adult tooth from a platform.

Stratum IIC.
L 1206/1080 part of adult robust mandible with ant-mortem loss of M1.
L.40 adult rib in a pit.
Adult phalange in a pit.
L.569 adult phalange in mud-brick removal.
Adult tooth in mud-brick removal.

Stratum IIIA
L.542 left temporal bone of an infant from fill.
L.545 adult phalanges in a pit.
L.552 adult phalange and rib of an infant in a pit.
L.917 adult phalange from a surface.
L.587 adult incisor from a mud-brick structure.
L.1147 adult M1, M2 in fill. Attrition M1=4/5; M2=3/4.

DISCUSSION

Mortuary Practices

Burials were found in all the Chalcolithic strata excavated at Gilat, attesting to its use for mortuary activities over many generations (Fig. 8.1). As can be seen in Table 8.1 most of the burials at Gilat were concentrated in open (plaza) areas in the southeast area of the site (Areas J and Y) and most were attributed to stratum IIB (48.8%). Thus, based on the distribution of burials through time (Strata I–IV) at the site, the popularity of Gilat for mortuary related rituals was highest during the Stratum IIB occupation.

One burial was identified in the field as a secondary burial, but this is derived from the very disturbed most superficial level (Stratum I), and may represent an accidental disturbance. Primary burial then appears to have been the norm. The many incomplete skeletons and scattered bones uncovered probably result from accidental disturbance of burials rather than intentional secondary burial. This may be related to the absence of a defined cemetery area or grave markers (with the exception of the multiple burial) and re-use of different areas at the site over time. Individuals were for the most part interred in shallow pits or in fill associated with open, plaza, areas. The burials in pits probably express secondary usage of the pits since they contain much debris, usually potsherds and animal bones. This may also be the case for the collective burial (L.1237) which is, however, unique in several aspects. It is the only mass burial at the site. The pit /silo feature that was used is large and it contained numerous faunal remains as well as nine individuals. It is also situated in close proximity to the sanctuary building and a cache of burnt gazelle horns as well as other artifacts found in within the pit (see Chapter 5 for a description of the burial structure and Chapter 6 for the archaeozoological remains). On these grounds it is possible to identify two main burial rituals: 1) the internment of individuals in shallow pits linked to open areas in the sanctuary and 2) the establishment of a well-built free-standing mortuary 'monument' (Levy 1995:237) for a multiple human burial – linked to a public area.

The burials found within fill are often located in shallow pits in the fill above earlier floors or surfaces suggesting burial in an abandoned area. Burial position and orientation could be determined for 22 individuals, excluding those from the collective grave. As can be seen from Table 8.2 (next page), individuals were interred on either the right or left side, with the head oriented in every direction with the exception of the east. With the possible exception of infant burials, there is no period/age/gender distinction in burial type. Neither do natural features (e.g. the wadi) nor architectural features, appear to account for burial orientation. In all the double burials at least one of the interred was an infant or young child. The sex of the adult could be determined in four of these double burials and was female. However in at least one double burial the similarity in age precludes a mother-child relationship.

There were only two individuals definitely buried with artifacts. These were the adult male (H6) from stratum IIA, and an adult, probably female (H37) from stratum IIC. The former was interred in a large pit, and was lying on his right side in a flexed position with a western orientation. A V-shaped ceramic bowl was found next to the head. Other artifacts (tabular scraper, a violin-shape figurine and a palette) were recovered from the fill but at higher elevations than the burial context. H 37 was also buried in a pit in a tightly flexed position on its right side facing north-north-west. A V-shaped bowl was found adjacent to the head and a sheep/goat mandible was found alongside the trunk. Due to the tightly flexed position, it is likely that this was a bundle burial. No other burial contexts were specifically associated with artifacts, but a number of gazelle horns were found next to the mass grave, which contained the skeletons of 9 ungulates as well as nine humans. Based on the sample of 91 human burials, it can be stated that with the exception of one individual found with a V-Shape bowl, no burials showed evidence of burial goods.

West
   H3 male/right
   H6 male/right
   H9 infant/right
   H16 infant/right
   H23 female/right

Northwest
   H37 female/right *
   H38 female/right
   (H29 male?/left)

North-north-west
   H12 child/left *
   H18 child/left *
   H1 female/right

North
   H8 female/left
   H36 neonate/left

Northeast
   H26 female/right

Southeast
   H14 child/right *

South
   H13 infant/left
   H10 neonate/left
   H22 infant/left
   (H28 female/left)

Southwest
   H15 neonate/right
   H19 child/right
   (H27 male?/left)

*bound

Table 8.2. Positioning and orientation of the body, Gilat.

The occurrence of both semi-flexed or tightly flexed primary burials and disturbed burials in disused pits is known from many other Chalcolithic sites in the northern Negev. These include Grar (Gilead 1995), Bir es-Safadi (Perrot 1955), Abu Matar (Perrot 1955), and Tuleilat Ghassul (Mallon et al 1934) while at Shiqmim both this type of burial and other more elaborate burials have been identified from the village (Levy 1982; Levy and Alon 1985; Levy *et al.* 1990, 1991, 1993). At Grar, mention is made of both semi-flexed and tightly flexed burials (Locus 716 in Area C (Gilead 1995), while the collective burial from Gilat is partially paralleled by collective burials at Bir es-Safadi (Perrot 1955).

The only sub-distinction made in burial type at Gilat, is that relating to infant burials. Some infants were buried in jars or with potsherds in domestic installations while other infants of the same age were buried without jars, either singly or with older individuals in fill or pits in open areas. The jar burials from Gilat appear to have been buried above the floors in fill rather than beneath them and in close proximity to the walls of buildings, like those described from Ghassul (Mallon *et al.* 1934). However at Ghassul, in contrast to the situation at Gilat, many rooms contained more than one jar burial. Furthermore, these included the remains of children aged up to 8 years as well as infants. This differs from the situation at Gilat where all the jar burials were of neonates, or very young infants. Other indications of special treatment of infant remains in the Chalcolithic were found by Perrot (1955) at Bir es-Safadi (Perrot and Ladiray 1980). He reported that there were at least two ceremonial infant burials in domestic installations at Bir es-Safadi associated with hearths.

Mortuary practices have been interpreted as a communal expression of beliefs and practices regarding the dead, as an expression of territorial rights, and also, in the case of monumental tombs, as an expression of organized activity within a society. A second expression of social differences within a society is evidence of status-related differences in burial patterns, in terms of location, burial type and or grave. Ian Morris (1987: 29) wrote that 'the dead are one of our most fertile sources for ancient social systems', but considered them to provide no evidence of religious beliefs. On the other hand Hodder (1982) and Ucko (1969) have argued that mortuary practices reflect social attitudes to the phenomenon of death, rather than recognition of an individual's status during life. Drawing on ethnographic data from the Negev (Bilu, Chapter 4, this volume) and the Sinai (Marx, Chapter 3, this volume), it is possible that the evidence for repeated human burial in the sanctuary relates to the significance of the site as a place of pilgrimage and sanctity. While it is not possible to identify the elaborate tomb of an individual that could be interpreted as an individual with a chiefly, priestly, saintly, or other high ranking social personae, the repeated use of public space for human burial links the buried individuals to the sanctuary as a sacred space – what Harold Turner (Turner 1979) refers to as *domus ecclesiae*. As seen in the ethnographic data from the Negev and Sinai, the holy tombs (which can also be interpreted as holy space) of both Bedouin and Jewish saints often become the foci of repeated burial by devotees of these cult leaders. A similar process may have operated at Gilat.

In the Southern Levant the earliest type of burial is simple primary inhumation within living sites and grave offerings have been found in graves of even early hominids, such as an adolescent from Qafzeh (Vandermeersch 1970). In the Natufian Period some settlements have hundreds of burials, from different phases, that include single and multiple graves, primary and secondary burial and occasional grave goods. Wright (1978) claimed that such differences in burial pattern and associated grave goods in the Natufian site of El Wad were evidence for the existence of chieftainships at this time. However, it now seems that most of the differences in burial type reported by Wright reflect chronological trends rather than status differences within the group, while the presence or absence of grave goods seems sporadic rather than ceremonial (Belfer-Cohen 1995; Byrd and Monahan 1995). In the late Natufian and for much of the Pre-Pottery Neolithic period, secondary burial and skull removal and decoration, primarily of adult male skulls occurred at many sites (Hershkovitz and Gopher 1990). There are also a number of ritual sites, such as Nahal Hemar (Bar Yosef and Alon 1988) and Kfar Ha-Horesh, with many burials of different type at the latter site (Goring Morris *et al.* 1994–95; Kuijt and Goring-Morris 2002). In the Pottery Neolithic (PN) of the 5–6th millennium B.C.E. which immediately precedes the Chalcolithic, occasional intra-mural primary flexed burials, with infants interred in pots occur, (Gopher and Orelle 1995), but cemeteries outside of settlements are also found towards the end of this period-for examples at Eilat (Avner *et al.* 1994).

The intra-mural inhumations, in the Chalcolithic Period, which are often apparently found in disused rooms, pits or silos of settlements from the Negev to Galilee, then continue the traditional form of intra-mural burial practiced in the earlier PN. They continue, although in low frequencies, through to the Iron Age. This burial pattern differs from the complex and elaborate funerary treatment associated with the Chalcolithic cemeteries which contain hundreds of skeletons. These are situated at some distance from the settlements, and contain many secondary burials, often in ossuaries, in caves and in monumental tombs (Hanbury-Tennison 1986; Levy *et al.* 1993). At least in some sites, such as Shiqmim (Levy et al 1990) and Ben Shemen, such secondary burial seems to have been preceded by defleshing (Le Mort and Rabinovich 1994), rather than simply collection and concentration of skeletal elements after decomposition of the soft tissues.

Levy (1982, 1995; Levy *et al.*1990) and Gopher and Tsuk (1996), have interpreted the large scale of cemetery complexes in the Southern Levant during the Chalcolithic as evidence of organized group activities at the regional, rather than individual village level at this time. At least 6 distinct cultural units have been defined within the relatively small area of the southern Levant (Levy 1998). The size of these regions seems to have been small, approximating 40 km in length (Levy *ibid.*). These regional distinctions are to some extent maintained in ossuary types and/or associated items found in cemeteries.

Both monumental tombs and individual high status burials have been reported at Shiqmim to the east of Gilat (Levy *et al.* 1982), but these appear to be isolated instances. The spotty distribution of grave goods recalls the pattern of sporadic variation in grave size and decoration reported in the Natufian period (Belfer-Cohen 1995), rather than the distinctive pattern reported for the Badrian tombs in Egypt (Anderson 1992) where consistent differences and gradients were evident between tomb types. In this instance, the presence of a concentration of tombs with exceptional funerary goods was considered evidence of an elite group and hence a hierarchical society (Anderson 1992). Despite the obvious accumulation of wealth documented in many Chalcolithic sites (Levy 1995), mortuary patterns for this period do not display uniform patterns of inequality similar to that found in Egypt at the end of the Chalcolithic and beginning of the Early Bronze Age cf. (van den Brink and Levy 2002). This may be changing as more Chalcolithic cemeteries are excavated in the country cf. van den Brink 1998. For example, Gopher's (Gopher and Tsuk 1996) excavations in the Nahal Qana cave in Samaria yielded an adult male with high status grave goods including gold rings and Gal (Gal, Smithline, and Shalem 1997) interprets the Peqi'in Chalcolithic Cave in Galilee as representative of a rank society. Finally, the rich assemblage of beautiful textiles recently found in the Cave of the Warrior in the Judean desert has been interpreted by Tamar Schick (Schick 1998) as indicating a high status Chalcolithic burial.

The burial situation at Gilat is markedly different from 'normative' Chalcolithic burial caves, open-air cemeteries and human burial contexts found in village settlements throughout the region. At Gilat, where only two individuals are associated with grave goods of any kind, and these individuals can not be linked to the wide range of prestige ritual paraphernalia represented at the site (see Chapters 12 and 15, this volume). The burials at Gilat are among the poorest and simplest known for the Chalcolithic period in the Southern Levant. They resemble those found in sites such as Grar, which Gilead (1995) thinks may have been occupied by only one or two families at any one time, Bir es-Safadi and the village of Shiqmim and possibly even Ghassul, where the excavators refer to but do not detail, adult intra-mural burials. Despite its importance as demonstrated both by the scale of buildings and the wealth of objects found, there is no evidence at Gilat of special selection for burial or ceremonial treatment of the dead, that is characteristic of so many sites in the Chalcolithic period in this region.

Paleodemography

The age distribution by stratum appears in Fig. 8.1. It is likely that each stratum includes individuals from different generations, and the sample sizes are too small for the construction of life expectancy tables. However the data clearly show that all age groups and both sexes are represented in all strata. There is nothing in the paleodemographic profile to suggest selection based on age or gender in respect of burial location or type at Gilat. Indeed, the paleodemographic profile resembles that of other Chalcolithic and later villages from this region, where primary burial was practiced (Fig. 8.2). Like them, Gilat has high infant and juvenile mortality and few individuals surviving beyond 40 years. In contrast, the sites with secondary burial such as Ben Shemen (Perrot and Ladiray 1980), Mezad Aluf (Levy *et al*. 1993) and Kissufim (Zagerson and Smith 2002), contain a low frequency of sub-adults. However, this is due to the exclusion of infants and young children less than 3 years of age from burial in these cemeteries. In this context the high frequency of sub-adults identified from Nahal Qaneh (Gopher and Tsuk 1996) can be explained as due to the fact that the skeletons identified are those from primary burials in the cave and not from the ossuaries.

The age distribution at Gilat and other Chalcolithic village sites is similar to that currently found in many 'Underdeveloped' countries in terms of the ratio of adults to children, but contains an even lower percentage of older adults (Fig. 8.3). The age distribution of the sample from Gilat falls within the range found at contemporaneous sites with none appearing to have survived beyond 50 years of age. This is not just a bias in underestimating age, since in later periods some adults do show skeletal and dental changes consistent with an age estimation of over 50.

It has been argued that age assessments in skeletal remains consistently underestimate the age of older adults (Bocquet-Appel and Masset 1982), but this seems unlikely at Gilat, in view of the high morbidity, expressed in dental and skeletal characteristics of even immature individuals. Moreover, dental attrition rates were extremely high, yet only one individual showed dental attrition that was more pronounced than that found in the 20 year olds.

Using conventional anthropometric criteria (Bass 1971; Krogman 1962; Saunders and Katzenburg 1992), sex could be determined for 23 of the 46 adults and adolescents. The results were as follows:

Males; adult n=8, adolescent n=2

Females; adult n=8, adolescent n=5

For the remaining individuals sex could not be determined due to poor preservation or immaturity. When allowance is made for the differences in sample sizes between strata it seems that at no period was any age group or sex excluded from burial at the site. There is then nothing in the paleo-demographic profile to suggest selection or restrictions based on age or gender in respect of burial location or type at Gilat. Furthermore, there is no evidence of any development or change in burial patterns between the different occupation phases at the site. Differences between strata are primarily seen in the distribution of burials through time, with Stratum IIB the most 'popular' stratum for mortuary activities.

Population affinities

Renfrew (1992) has questioned the validity of both morphometric analyses of skeletal populations and extrapolation from modern population genetics for determining the affinities and movements of past populations. His criticism of the first is based on the fact that environment, as well as genes may affect body size and shape. However this criticism ignores the fact that most cranio-facial measurements are little affected by environmental factors (Keita 1988). Moreover most modern bio-anthropological studies include an assessment of the prevalence of and severity of environmental factors and their effect on growth, development and function, (Saunders and Katzenberg 1992; Smith 1989; Smith 1995a). The application of aDNA of course overcomes the second criticism, in that it permits direct genetic comparison of long dead and living populations and is the method of choice under ideal circumstances. However, the expense, the limitations imposed by degradation and contamination, as well as the difficulty of obtaining specimens from all the sites needed for detailed comparative analyses, have led us to focus here on conventional morphometric studies.

The number of measurements that could be taken on the Gilat bones was limited because of their poor condition. They are given in Tables 8.3 – 8.8 and indicate that all fall well within the range of variation previously reported for other Chalcolithic sites in the southern Levant (Smith 1989, 1995b). The crania were dolichocranic, the faces were short and broad and mandibles short but extremely robust (Plates 8.5- 8.6). Individuals were short with average stature estimated at 157 cm in females and 169 in males. The long bones were slender but had pronounced areas of muscle attachments in both sexes, indicating that all engaged in activities requiring considerable muscular exertion. These were most pronounced on the humeri, femurs and tibia and less pronounced in the radius, ulna or fibula. Cortical thickness (CCT) measured from radiographs of the humerus more closely resembled a Middle Bronze Age I sample than earlier Natufian populations (Table 8.9). Since CCT values are affected by both diet and function (Smith *et al.* 1984a), this reinforces arguments put forward elsewhere (Smith *et al.* 1984b; Smith 1989) proposing that the level of environmental stress affecting populations in the Southern Levant shows little change over the past 6,000 years or so.

Notes to Tables
1. Data for Byblos after Ozbek 1975
2. Data for Ben Shemen after Lacombe 1980
3. Data for Nahal Mishmar after Haas and Nathan 1973
4. Data for Wadi Makkuk-unpublished data Hebrew University
5. Data for Horvat Hor: Smith and Sabari 1995

Table 8.3. Cranial measurements from Gilat.

	H30	H.Hor[5]	W.Makkak	N.Mishmar[3]	Byblos[1]
Glabella -occipital length	182	183	(9)173.9	(4)181.3	(6)183.5
Breadth (max.)	128	130	(9)134.1	(4)136.8	(6)126.5
Minimal frontal width	84				
Bizygomaxillae breadth	85				
R. Orbital breadth	37				
R. Orbital height	51				
Nasal breadth	(18)				
Nasal height	(51)				
Bizygion	107				
Maximum circumference	497				

Table 8.4. Mandibular measurements, Gilat.

	H23	H26	H28	Byblos	B.Shemen	N.Mishmar	H.Hor	Arad
Max. l.	-	100	95	-	-	-	-	-
Body l.	-	74	72	-	-	-	-	-
Bicondylar b.	-	-	105	-	-	-	-	-
Bicoronoid b.	-	-	88	-	-	-	-	-
Bigonial b.	-	-	86	95(3)	96(2)	89(5)	85(2)	-
Bimental b.	-	-	45	43(5)	47(2)	-	43(2)	-
Ramus w.	-	30	33	30(7)	33(3)	-	31(2)	33(3)
Ramus ht.	-	53	57	-	-	-	-	-
Symph ht.	30	-	29	28(7)	30(3)	-	30(2)	32(1)
Ment f. ht	30	-	29	-	-	-	30(2)	-
Pm2-M1 ht.	28	-	28	27(8)	-	-	30(2)	-
M1-M2 ht	-	-	27	25(7)	30(8)	-	27(2)	30(3)
M2-M3 ht	-	-	26	24(4)	-	-	25(2)	-
Ment f w.	11	-	11	-	-	-	10(2)	-
M1-M2 w.	14	-	10	16(4)	13(7)	-	12(2)	12(2)
Gonial angle	-	135	128	-	-	-	-	-
Symphyseal w	-	-	13	-	-	-	15(1)	-

Key to Tables 8.5–8.8
   Side - l - left; r - right
   Sex - m -male;   f - female un; - unknown.
   Age - in years, un - unknown.
   Max l - maximum length.
   Phys l - physiological lenght.
   Ap- anterior-posterior diameter of the midshaft.
   Ml - medio - lateral diameter of the midshaft.
   Mc - circumference of the midshaft.
   Hd - maximum diameter of the head.
   Pmi - platymeric index.
   Pci - platycnemic index.

Stature could be calculated for arm bones of three females (after Bass 1971). No long bones of males were intact, so stature calculations could not be made, but may assumed to have been 10–12 cms greater than than that of females.
   H.23 - 155.41 ± 4.45 cm (for humerus); H.28 - 159.21 ± 4.24 cm (for radius);
   H.30 - 158.26 ± 4.24 cm (for radius).

Table 8.5. Femur measurements.

ID	Side	Sex	Age	AP	ML	MC	HD	PMI
H.6	R	M	35	22	27	91	42	
H.28	L	F	20	27	25	84		
H.30	L	F	40	27	24	81		
H.28	R	F	20	26	25	83		89.3
H.30	R	F	40	26	24	79		
H.37	R	F	?	27	23	77		

Table 8.6. Tibia measurements.

ID	Side	Sex	Age	AP	ML	MC	PCI
H.6	L	M	35	32	21	84	65.6
H.6	R	M	35	34	21	87	61.8
H.30	L	F	40	34	20	86	65.6
H.28	R	F	21	34	23	89	67.7

Table 8.7. Humerus measurements.

ID	Side	Sex	Age	Max L	AP	ML	MC	HD
H.6	L	M	35		20	16	62	
H.6	R	M	35		21	19	65	
H.28	L	F	20		20	18	62	
H.30	L	F	40		19	21	94	
H.28	R	F	20		19	17	61	
H.23	R	F	20	290	16	18	51	37
H.30	R	F	40		19	18	90	
H.37	L	F	UN		17	17	55	

Table 8.8. Radius measurements, Gilat.

D	Side	Sex	Age	Max L
H.28	L	F	20	220
H.30	R	F	40	218

Table 8.9. Mean measurements (in mm) and ratios calculated
for cortical bone thickness (cct) in humeri from different periods and from Gilat.

Period	Sex	Side	Shaft Diameter			CCT			CCT?Diameter		
			No.	X	S.D.	No.	X	S.D.	No.	X	S.D.
Natufian	M	R	10	18.5	1.2	10	12.1	1.2	10	65.9	0.07
	M	L	11	18.1	1.3	11	11.3	1.9	11	62.1	0.08
	F	R	9	16.3	1.3	9	10.0	1.7	9	61.0	0.09
	F	L	12	16.3	1.0	12	8.9	1.7	12	54.1	0.09
Gilat	M	R	2	17.3	0.2	2	9.8	0.5	2	58.0	0.3
	M	L	2	16.9	0.5	2	8.2	1.2	2	46.0	0.5
	F	R	1	16.0	-	1	7.9	-	1	48.5	-
	F	L	2	17.5	0.5	2	7.5	0.2	2	43.5	0.5
MBI	M	R	8	19.9	1.9	8	9.6	1.8	8	47.8	0.11
	M	L	13	19.1	1.2	12	9.8	1.2	12	50.8	0.05
	F	R	12	18.1	1.5	12	9.0	2.0	12	49.8	0.11
	F	L	11	17.2	1.8	11	7.6	2.2	11	45.0	0.14

Table 8.10. Mesio-distal dimensions (in mms) of upper teeth from four Chalcolithic sites.

Tooth	Site	No	Mean	SD	Minimum	Maximum
M3	Shiqmim	2	8.1	0.9	7.4	8.8
	W. Makkuk[4]	2	9.2	0.6	8.5	10.3
	Ben Shemen[2]	2	9.0	0.3	8.8	9.3
	Gilat	4	9.2	0.7	8.2	9.9
M2	Shiqmim	1	10.8	---	10.8	10.8
	W. Makkuk	25	10.1	0.4	9.2	10.9
	Ben Shemen	2	10.4	1.4	9.4	11.4
	Gilat	12	9.6	*0.5*	8.8	10.6
M1	Shiqmim	3	10.7	0.9	10.5	10.8
	W. Makkuk	29	11.2	0.9	10.2	12.3
	Ben Shemen	3	11.0	1.4	9.8	12.5
	Gilat	12	10.9	0.3	10.2	11.3
Pm2	Shiqmim	3	6.7	0.3	6.3	7.0
	W. Makkuk	11	6.5	0.4	5.6	7.0
	Ben Shemen	2	7.1	0.8	6.6	7.7
	Gilat	12	6.8	0.5	5.6	7.4
Pml	Shiqmim	2	6.9	0.3	6.7	7.2
	W. Makkuk	9	7.1	0.3	6.6	7.8
	Ben Shemen	1	6.4	0	6.4	6.4
	Gilat	12	7.1	0.4	6.5	7.8
C	Shiqmim	4	7.0	0.3	6.7	7.4
	W. Makkuk	7	7.8	0.2	7.3	8.1
	Ben Shemen	3	7.9	0.2	7.7	8.1
	Gilat	12	7.4	0.5	6.6	8.2
I2	Shiqmim	8	6.9	0.1	6.7	7.1
	W. Makkuk	2	7.3	0.2	7.1	7.5
	Ben Shemen	--	---	---	---	---
	Gilat	15	6.5	0.5	5.7	7.8
II	Shiqmim	5	8.6	0.4	8.2	9.4
	W. Makkuk	3	8.7	0.3	8.4	9.1
	Ben Shemen	--	---	---	---	---
	Gilat	11	8.6	0.5	7.9	9.8

Table 8.11. Bucco-lingual dimensions (in mms) of upper teeth from four Chalcolithic Sites.

Tooth	Site	No	Mean	SD	Minimum	Maximum
M3	Shiqmim	2	9.5	0.8	8.9	10.1
	W. Makkuk[4]	10	11.2	0.7	9.7	12.1
	Ben Shemen[2]	2	11.5	1.2	10.7	12.4
	Gilat	4	10.4	0.8	9.3	11.0
M2	Shiqmim	1	12.5	---	12.5	12.5
	W. Makkuk	25	11.4	0.6	10.1	12.7
	Ben Shemen	2	12.0	1.2	11.2	12.8
	Gilat	12	11.4	0.9	10.4	12.8
M1	Shiqmim	3	11.5	0.6	10.9	12.2
	W. Makkuk	29	11.5	0.5	10.7	12.5
	Ben Shemen	3	11.7	0.6	11.2	12.4
	Gilat	12	11.7	0.5	11.1	12.5
Pm2	Shiqmim	3	8.9	0.7	8.0	9.5
	W. Makkuk	9	8.7	0.6	7.9	10.2
	Ben Shemen	2	9.5	1.2	8.7	10.3
	Gilat	12	9.1	0.6	7.8	10.0
Pml	Shiqmim	2	8.1	0.5	7.7	8.5
	W. Makkuk	9	8.9	0.4	8.3	9.8
	Ben Shemen	1	8.3	0	8.3	8.3
	Gilat	12	9.1	0.4	8.6	9.9
C	Shiqmim	4	7.4	0.8	6.4	8.3
	W. Makkuk	7	8.4	0.4	7.9	9.2
	Ben Shemen	3	8.3	0.3	8.0	8.5
	Gilat	12	8.4	0.4	7.7	8.9
I2	Shiqmim	8	6.5	0.4	5.8	7.1
	W. Makkuk	2	6.3	0.2	6.2	6.5
	Ben Shemen	--	---	---	---	---
	Gilat	15	6.3	0.3	6.0	6.8
I1	Shiqmim	5	7.5	1.	7.4	7.7
	W. Makkuk	3	7.3	0.5	7.2	7.4
	Ben Shemen	--	---	---	---	---
	Gilat	12	7.3	0.3	6.9	7.8

Table 8.12. Mesiodistal dimensions (in mms) of lower teeth from four Chalcolithic sites.

Tooth	Site	No	Mean	SD	Minimum	Maximum
M3	Shiqmim	6	10.8	0.5	10.0	11.3
	W. Makkuk[4]	11	10.5	1.0	9.0	13.1
	Ben Shemen[2]	6	10.4	0.9	9.0	11.3
	Gilat	2	9.4	.04	9.4	9.5
M2	Shiqmim	6	11.2	0.6	10.0	12.0
	W. Makkuk	13	10.6	0.8	9.6	12.4
	Ben Shemen	9	10.7	0.8	9.3	11.6
	Gilat	7	10.6	0.5	9.8	11.2
M1	Shiqmim	5	11.6	0.6	10.7	12.3
	W. Makkuk	12	11.2	0.3	10.1	12.3
	Ben Shemen	7	11.0	0.6	10.1	12.0
	Gilat	11	11.0	0.7	10.3	12.0
Pm2	Shiqmim	8	7.4	0.3	7.0	7.9
	W. Makkuk	11	7.1	0.4	6.5	7.9
	Ben Shemen	2	7.5	0.3	7.50	7.55
	Gilat	6	7.2	0.5	6.6	8.1
Pm1	Shiqmim	8	7.1	0.2	6.5	7.4
	W. Makkuk	10	6.8	0.5	6.1	8.0
	Ben Shemen	3	7.3	0.8	6.5	8.1
	Gilat	10	7.1	0.4	6.4	7.8
C	Shiqmim	5	7.6	0.4	6.7	8.0
	W. Makkuk	4	7.1	0.1	6.9	7.4
	Ben Shemen	2	7.1	0.02	7.12	7.15
	Gilat	13	6.7	0.4	6.1	7.5
I2	Shiqmim	3	6.6	0.8	5.8	7.6
	W. Makkuk	7	5.8	0.4	5.2	6.5
	Ben Shemen	1	6.5	0	6.5	6.5
	Gilat	12	6.0	0.4	5.3	6.5
I1	Shiqmim	2	6.0	0.1	6.0	6.1
	W. Makkuk	3	5.8	0.3	5.5	6.1
	Ben Shemen	--	---	---	---	---
	Gilat	6	5.3	0.4	4.6	5.9

Table 8.13. Bucco-lingual dimensions (in mms) of lower teeth from four Chalcolithic sites

Tooth	Site	No	Mean	SD	Minimum	Maximum
M3	Shiqmim	5	9.6	0.2	9.4	10.8
	W. Makkuk[4]	11	9.8	0.8	8.7	12.0
	Ben Shemen[2]	6	10.0	0.7	8.9	10.7
	Gilat	2	9.0	0.3	8.9	9.2
M2	Shiqmim	6	10.4	0.4	9.7	11.1
	W. Makkuk	13	9.9	0.5	9.4	11.2
	Ben Shemen	9	10.3	0.5	9.3	10.9
	Gilat	7	10.0	0.7	9.2	11.1
M1	Shiqmim	5	11.0	0.6	10.0	11.9
	W. Makkuk	12	10.3	0.3	9.8	10.9
	Ben Shemen	7	10.4	0.2	10.1	10.8
	Gilat	11	10.5	0.4	9.4	11.2
Pm2	Shiqmim	8	8.5	0.6	7.6	9.3
	W. Makkuk	11	8.2	0.4	7.7	9.0
	Ben Shemen	2	8.8	0.5	8.5	9.2
	Gilat	6	8.4	0.5	7.6	8.9
Pml	Shiqmim	8	7.9	0.2	7.7	8.4
	W. Makkuk	10	7.6	0.5	6.9	8.8
	Ben Shemen	2	7.5	1.6	6.4	8.7
	Gilat	10	8.0	0.4	7.5	8.4
C	Shiqmim	5	7.6	0.4	6.7	8.0
	W. Makkuk	4	7.7	0.4	7.2	8.1
	Ben Shemen	2	7.5	1.5	6.4	8.5
	Gilat	13	7.8	0.4	7.2	8.6
I2	Shiqmim	3	6.6	0.8	5.9	7.5
	W. Makkuk	7	6.4	0.3	6.1	6.9
	Ben Shemen	1	7.2	0	7.2	7.2
	Gilat	12	6.4	0.2	6.1	6.7
Il	Shiqmim	2	6.5	0.2	6.3	6.6
	W. Makkuk	3	6.0	0.3	5.7	6.4
	Ben Shemen	--	---	---	---	---
	Gilat	6	6.0	0.2	5.7	6.2

Tooth size could be measured from a relatively large number of individuals, and was similar to that of other Chalcolithic populations in the region (Tables 8.10–13). The teeth were intermediate in size between those of the earlier Neolithic and later Bronze Age populations. They were broad bucco-lingually in relation to their length and this probably accounts for the obesity of the mandibles found at Gilat and in other Chalcolithic samples examined. Although the teeth were smaller than those of preceding Neolithic populations, they showed similar morphological traits, indicating population continuity. Upper first molars had large Carabelli cusps and additional marginal cusps were frequent (Plate 8.7).

Conclusion: Pathology
Skeletal. Due to the fragmentary condition of the skeletal remains, the overall prevalence of pathological lesions could not be estimated. Examination of bones that were sufficiently complete for examination indicates however, that disease prevalence was high. Periostitis was observed in two individuals; H6 and H27 and the femur shafts were markedly bowed (Plate 8.8). The distribution of the periostitis involved the right femur and the right and left tibiae in the first individual and all long bones in the second. In addition H27 exhibited inflammatory changes in the internal surface of the cranium, on the frontal bone, probably the result of meningo-encephalitis (Plate 8.9a–8.9b).

This may be an early example of tuberculosis, a condition already present in the Neolithic (Schulz 1987; El-Najjar *et al.* 1997).

Arthritis was noted in two of the sixteen individuals. It was present in the form of lipping in cervical and lumbar vertebrae (H6 and H26), and a distal humerus (H27). H6 exhibited prominent muscle markings, arthritic lipping of the cervical and lumbar vertebrae and periostitis of the lower limbs. Other skeletal pathologies noted included cribra orbitalia (Plate 8.10) in four individuals with part of the roof of the orbit present; spina bifida (H18); an ante-mortem cavity in a cervical vertebra (H28); and arthritic lipping of vertebrae (H28, H30). Mandibles of two females (H26 and H28) recovered from the collective burial (L.1237) had asymmetric mandibular condyles, as well as asymmetric occipital condyles. In H26, there is a markedly anterior slope to the mandibular condyles which is also reflected in the facets of the occipital bone. The mandibular teeth reveal an asymmetrical wear pattern with less wear on the left first molar than on the right.

Dental. Enamel hypoplasia (Plate 8.11) was present in all individuals and frequently severe. Blue/green and or orange-brown discoloration of the teeth was noted in a number of individuals. It affected both children and adults and was found on the root and as a discrete band on the crown, approximately 2 mm above the cemento-enamel junction. An orange/brown discoloration of the teeth was noted on six of the individuals from the collective burial; H27, H28, H29, H30, H32 and H34. This orange staining may be due to fluorosis from drinking water since many of the wells in the Negev today (and presumably past water supplies) contain high concentrations of fluorides.

Attrition was extremely severe at Gilat, with dentine exposed on the first permanent molars by the age of 12 years. This high rate of attrition continued in later life as shown by the marked difference in attrition of the three permanent molars (Plates 8.12–14). These erupt at 6 year intervals but if attrition proceeds slowly they show little difference in attrition scores. If the rate of attrition is high, then the first molar can show considerable wear by the time the second molar erupts and similarly the second molar wears down before the third molar erupts. Caries was present in molars of only two individuals, and in one of them the second molars had been lost ante-mortem, probably also from caries since this was a young individual with relatively little attrition. In another two individuals the lower first molars had been lost ante-mortem, but here it was unclear whether caries or attrition exposing the pulpal cavity was the cause. Other pathologies and abnormalities noted included: the divided root of a lower first premolar (H32); periodontal disease (H30); alveolar resorption (H32); a supernumerary tooth (H26); and dental abscesses (Plates 8.11, 8.15).

There is a marked trend towards increased severity and frequency of skeletal and dental pathology from the Neolithic through the Chalcolithic and Early Bronze Age (Smith *et al.* 1984b; Smith 1991). The severity of the bony pathology and hypoplastic defects of the teeth seen at Gilat appears to be even more severe than that reported from contemporaneous sites such as Shiqmim (Levy *et al.* 1993). Specifically the endocranial irregular new bone formation and arthritic changes in the knee and elbow of the juvenile from the mass burial, is indicative of an acute and virulent infection affecting both the meninges and joints. While the pathology seen in this individual is exceptionally severe, Gilat shows a high incidence and severity of enamel hypoplasia, while periostitis, cribra orbitalia and arthritic changes in the joints of even young individuals are common and indicate a high level of infectious disease at this site.

In the teeth and jaws the main change seen in the Chalcolithic period is in the increased frequency of ante-mortem tooth loss, primarily of lower first molars. In pre-Neolithic periods in the southern Levant, ante-mortem tooth loss rarely occurs except in individuals in whom the teeth are worn down to the roots. In Neolithic and later populations from this region, ante-mortem tooth loss also occurs in young individuals in whom the teeth that are present show only moderate attrition. This suggests that infectious conditions-caries or periodontal disease-and not attrition, are the agents responsible, and this seems to be the case for the three individuals from Gilat with ante-mortem tooth loss. If anything, dental status at Gilat as measured in terms of severity of enamel hypoplasia and attrition rates, appears to be worse than that documented to date for other Chalcolithic sites in the region (Smith 1989; Smith *et al.* 1984b). This may be the result of even poorer health and a coarser diet than that of Chalcolithic groups elsewhere in the southern Levant. However high fluoride levels are known to exacerbate both conditions through their effect on enamel formation and in view of the orange-brown staining found on the teeth, this may have contributed to the severity of both conditions at Gilat.

Phenotypically the people from Gilat show no differences from other Chalcolithic populations in the region. They were slight in build, with long dolichocranic heads and short broad faces with relatively large teeth. Their health status, like that of the other Chalcolithic samples referred to here was poor and again gives no grounds for assuming that the people at Gilat enjoyed any special privileges in terms of nutrition or freedom from physical effort.. There was a high prevalence of enamel hypoplasia, periostitis, cribra orbitalia and arthritic changes in the joints of even young individuals as well as meningo-encephalitis in one juvenile associated with joint destruction.

The biological data then provide no evidence to suggest that the individuals at Gilat belonged to any special caste or enjoyed any special privileges. However, the study of biologic diversity within the Chalcolithic is still in its infancy. The application of new techniques, such as isotopic analyses of paleodiets and DNA analyses of their genetic make-up, may yet enable us to obtain more detailed information as to the pattern and extent of biological diversity and socio-economical ranking in the Chalcolithic populations of this region.

Figures

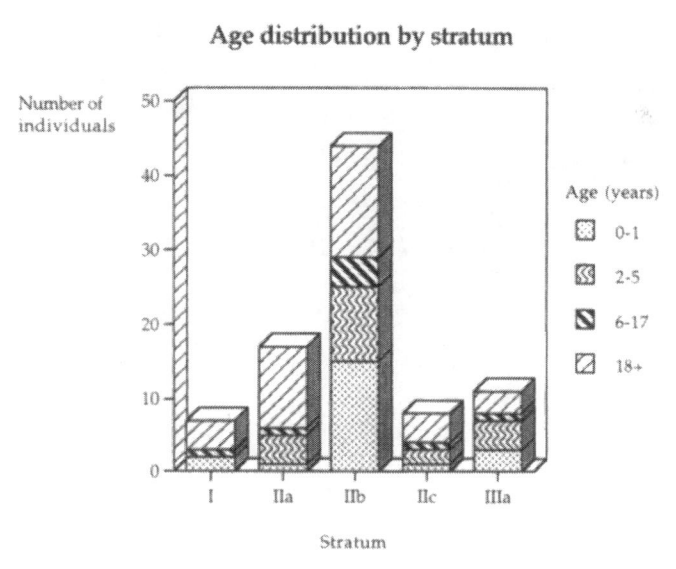

Figure 8.1. Age Age distribution by Stratum at Gilat.

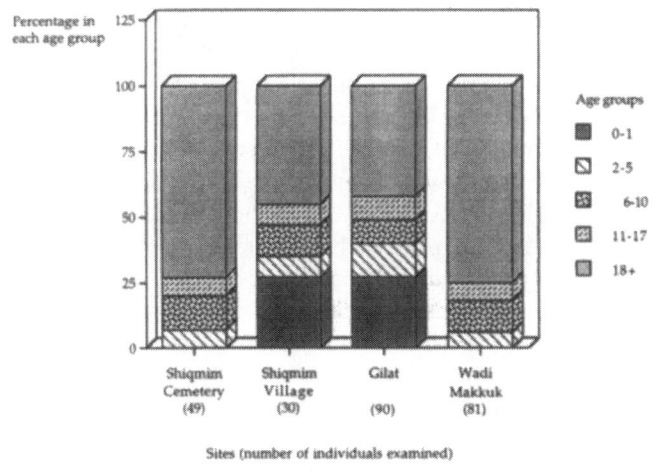

Figure 8.2. Age distribution at two sites with primary burial:
Gilat and Shiqmim village[4] and two sites with secondary burials: Shiqmim cemetery (Mezad Aluf)
and Wadi Makkuk. Note difference in percentage of individuals aged less than 18 years.

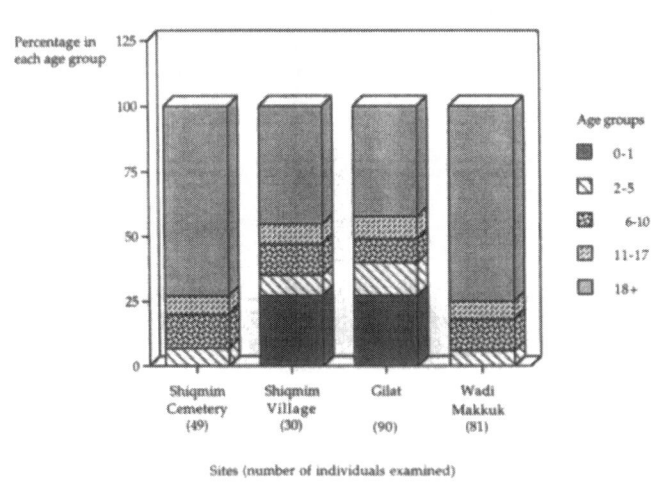

Figure 8.3. Age distribution of human skeletal remains from Chalcolithic sites.

Plates

Plate 8.1. Bundle burial with V-shaped bowl and sheep or goat mandible
(Stratum IIC, L. 1510, Sq S0—view east).

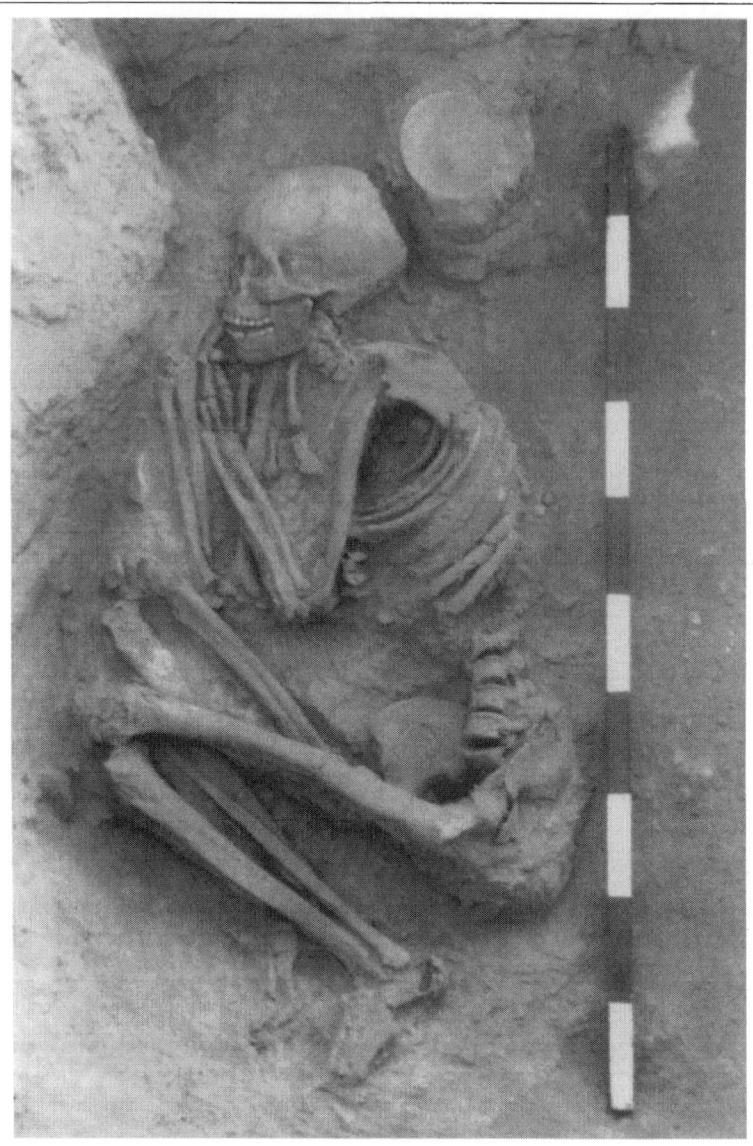

Plate 8.2. Flexed burial on side with V-Shape bowl
(L. 806, Sq J3, Stratum IIA—view north).

Plate 8.3. Overview of collective burial L.1237,
note the skulls of three individuals aligned in parallel.

Plate 8.4a. Skull of H26 in situ, note hypoplastic teeth and beetle holes in the zygoma, L.1237.

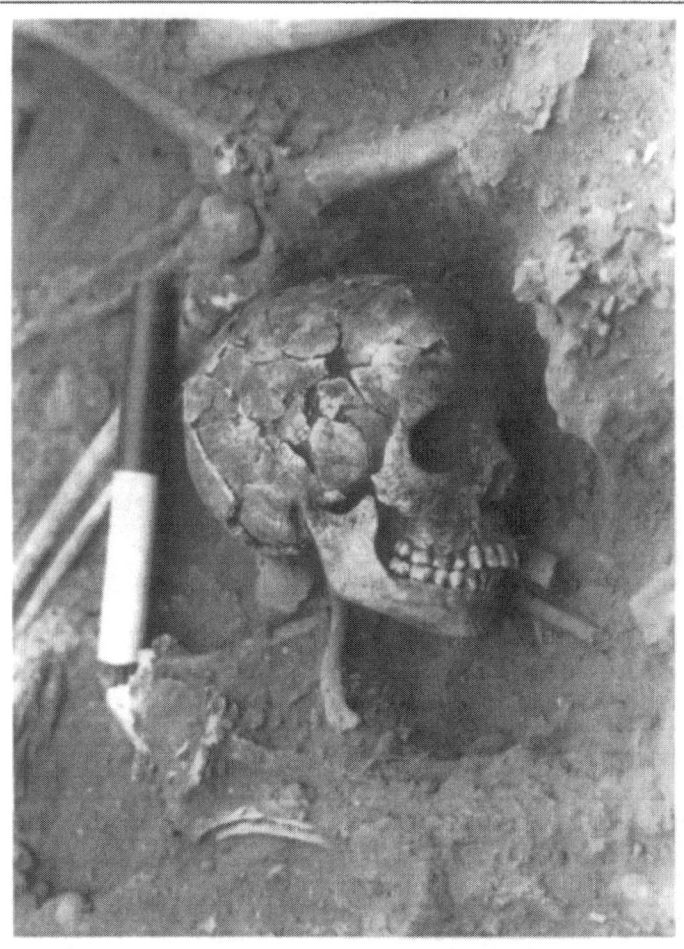

Plate 8.4b. Skull of H33 in situ, L.1237.

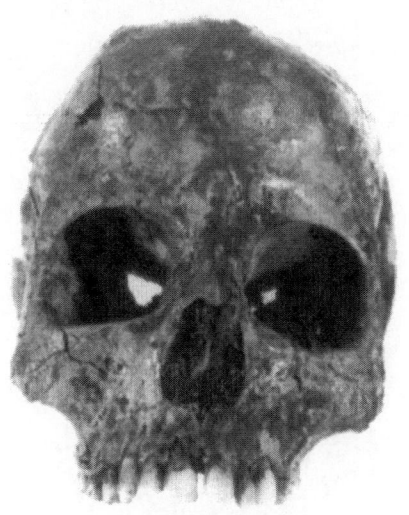

Plate 8.5a. Frontal view of H33, L.1237.

Plate 8.5b. Lateral view of H33, L.1237.

Plate 8.5c. Superior view of H33, L.1237.

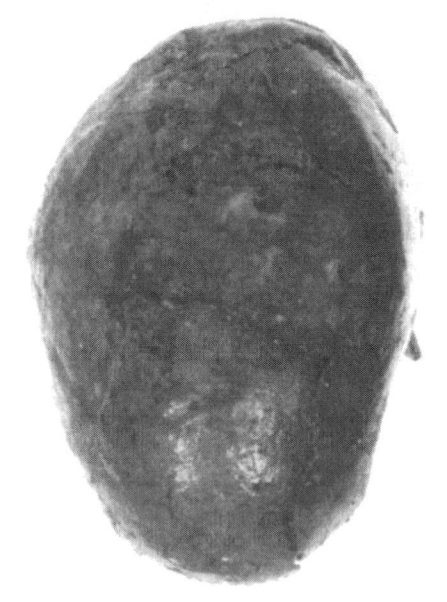

Plate 8.6a. Lateral view of H26, L.1237.

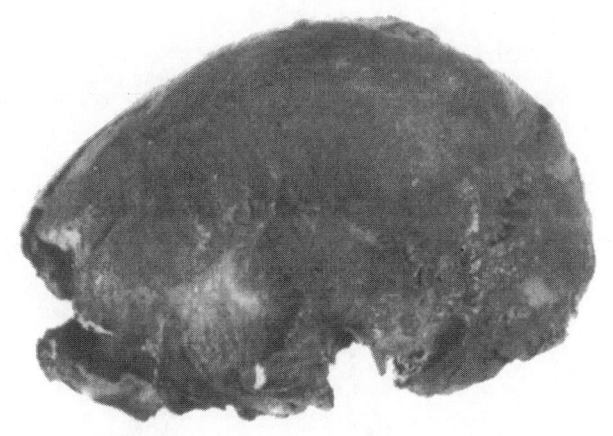

Plate 8.6b. Superior view of H26, L.1237.

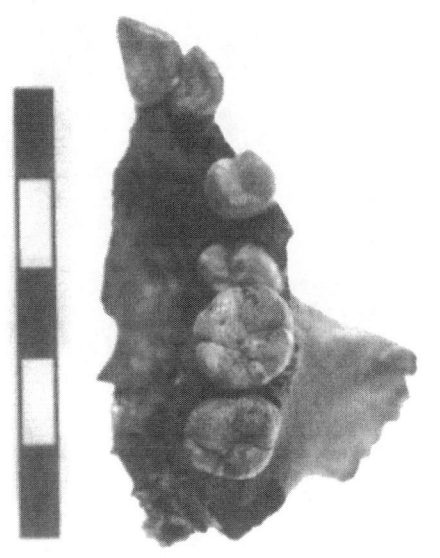

Plate 8.7. Occlusal view of upper teeth in H27,
note large Carabelli'cusp and distal marginal cuspules, l.1237.

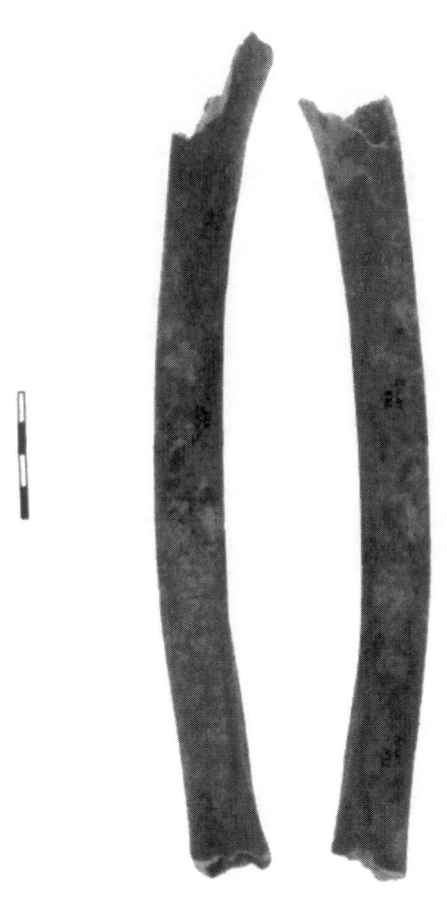

Plate 8.8. Femur shafts of H32, L.1237. They are slender and bowed.

Plate 8.9a. Inner (endocranial) surface of frontal bone of H27, L.1237, with irregular new bone formation in the midline. This may be due to meningo-encephalitis.

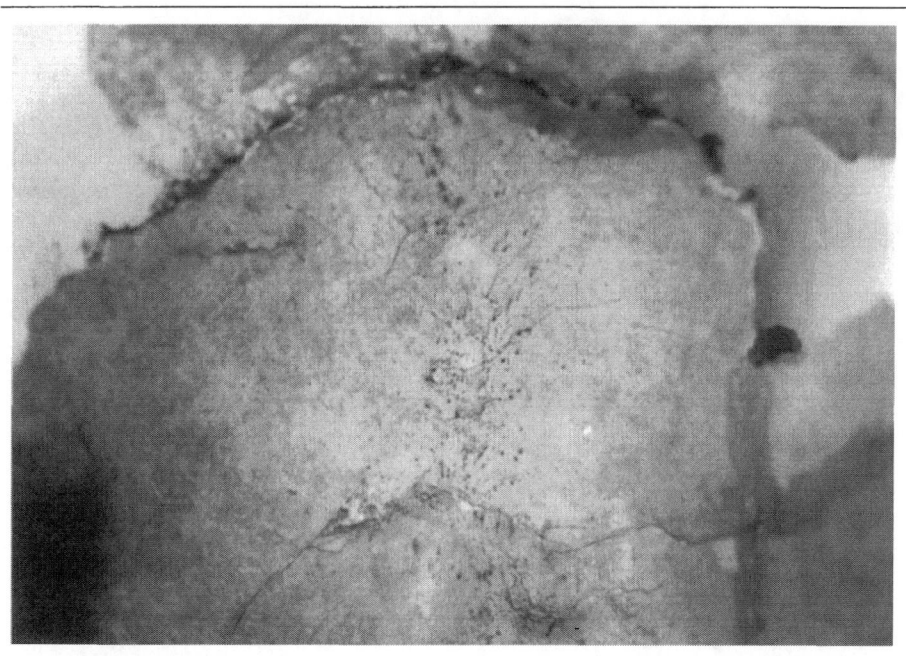

Plate 8.9b. Magnification of area of irregular bone formation, H27 (L.1237).

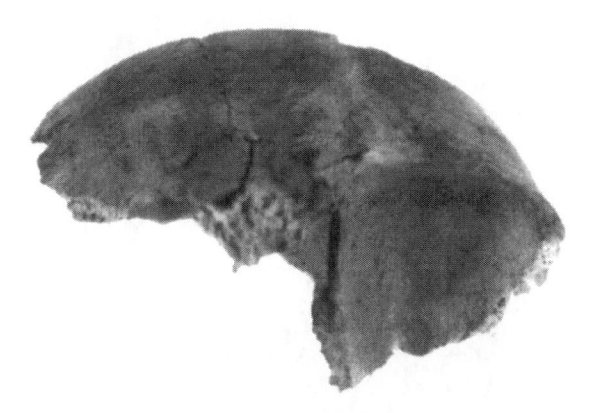

Figure 8.10. Part of frontal bone of H31, L.1237, with cribra orbitalia on left orbital rim.

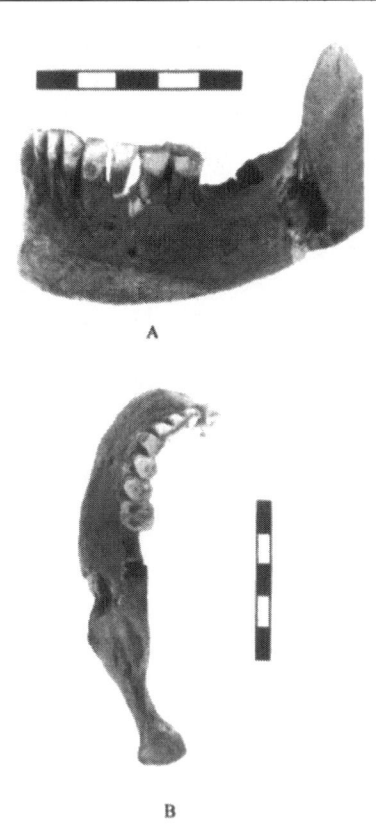

A

B

Plate 8.11. Left side (A) and occlusal (B) views of mandible of H30 (L.1237)
showing severe hypoplasia in the cervical region of all teeth.
Note also healed socket from second molar lost ante-mortem and empty socket
of third molar lost post-mortem.

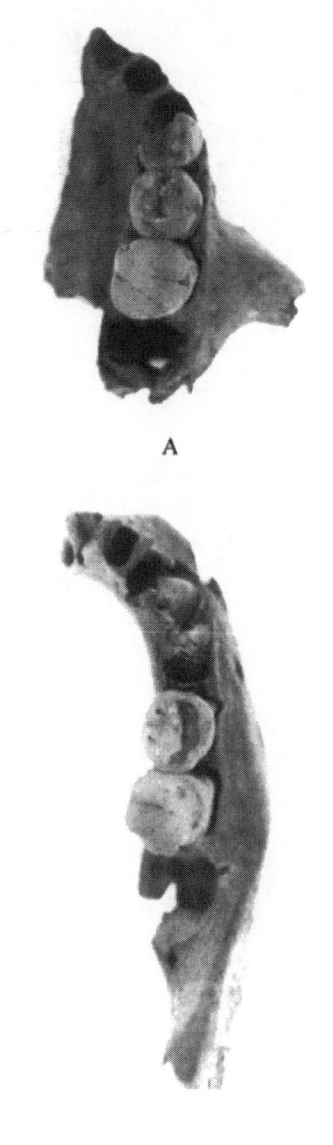

A

B

Plate 8.12. Occlusal view of upper (A) and lower (B) molars in H29 (L.1237),
note severe attrition in deciduous molars and exposed dentine
on the first permanent molars of this 9 year old child.

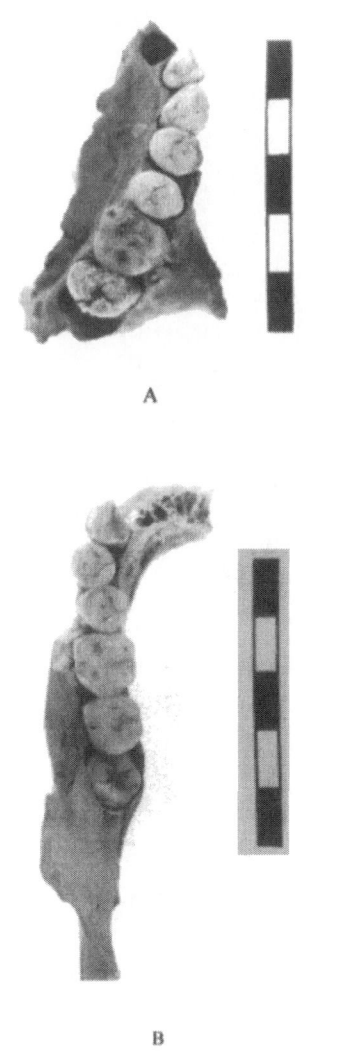

A

B

Plate 8.13. Occlusal view of teeth in H32 (L.1237), note exposure of dentine from attrition in premolars and first molars in this adolescent.

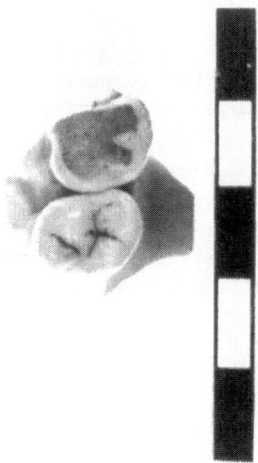

Plate 8.14. Upper second and third permanent molars of H26 (L.1237),
note the amount of difference of severity of attrition between them.
This indicates rapid wear since the two molars emerge at six year intervals.

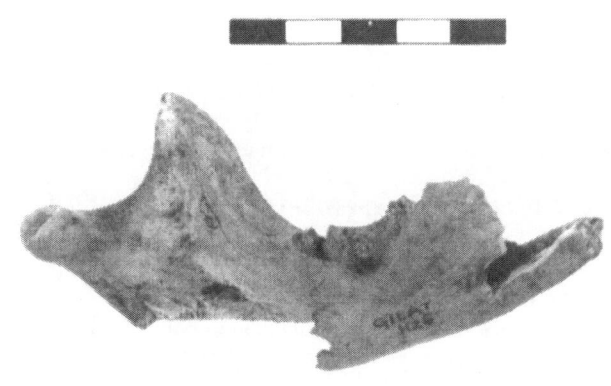

Plate 8.15. Lateral view of mandibular fragment of H26 (L.1237)
showing abscess cavity in the second molar region.

References

Alon, D., and T.E. Levy (1989) The archaeology and cult and the Chalcolithic sanctuary at Gilat. *Journal of Mediterranean Archaeology* 2:163–22

Anderson, W. (1992) Baderian Burials: Evidence of Social Inequality in Middle Egypt During the Early Predynastic Era. *Journal of the American Research Center in Egypt* 29:51–66.

Avner, U., I. Carmi and D. Segal (1994) Neolithic to Bronze Age settlement of the Negev and Sinai in light of radiocarbon dating: a view from the southern Negev. In *Late Quaternary Chronology and Paleoclimates of the Eastern Mediterranean*, O. Bar Yosef and R. S. Kra (eds), pp. 265–300.

Banning, E.B. (1998) The Neolithic Period: Triumphs of Architecture, Agriculture and Art. *Near Eastern Archaeology* 61:188–237.

Bar Yosef, O. (1998) 'Earliest Food Producers—Pre-Pottery Neolithic (8000–5500 BCE)', in *The Archaeology of Society in the Holy Land*. edited by T.E. Levy. London: Leicester University Press, pp. 190–204.

Bar-Yosef, O., and D. Alon (eds.) (1988) Nahal Hemar Cave. *Atiqot* 18, English Series. Jerusalem.

Bass, W.M. (1971) A Laboratory and Field Manual of the Human Skeleton. 2nd Edition. Missouri Archaeological Society Columbia Missouri.

Bocquet-Appel, J.P. and C. Masset (1982) Farewell to Paleodemography. *Journal of Human Evolution* 11:321–33.

Belfer-Cohen, A. (1995) Rethinking Social Stratification in the Natufin Culture: The Evidence from Burials. In *The Archaeology of Death in the Ancient Near East*, edited by S. Campbell and E. Green. Oxbow Monograph 51, pp. 9–16.

Bourke, S., E. Lawson, J. Lovell, Q. Hua, U. Zoppi and M. Barbetti (2001). The chronology of the Ghassulian Chalcolithic period in the southern Levant: New C-14 determinations from Teleilat Ghassul, Jordan. *Radiocarbon* V43:1217–22.

Byrd, B., and C.M. Monahan (1995) Death Mortuary Ritual and Natufian Social Structure. *Journal of Anthropological Archaeology* 14:251–87.

El-Najjar, M., A. Al Shiyab and I. Al Sarie (1997) Cases of Tuberclosis at 'Ain Ghazal, Jordan. *Paleorient* 22:123–28.

Gal, Z., H. Smithline and D. Shalem (1997) A Chalcolithic burial cave in Peqi'in, Upper Galilee. *Israel Exploration Journal* 47:145–54.

Gilead, I. (1995) *Grar. A Chalcolithic Site in the Northern Negev*. Beer-Sheva Vol 17, Ben Gurion University Monographs.

Gopher, A. (1998) Early oottery-bearing groups in Israel—The pottery neolithic period. In *The Archaeology of Society in the Holy Land*, edited by T.E. Levy London: Leicester University Press, pp. 205–25.

Gopher, A., and E. Orelle (1995) New Data on Burials in the Pottery Neolithic Period (Sixth-Fifth Millenium BC) in Israel. In *The Archaeology of Death in the Ancient Near East*, edited by S. Campbell and E. Green. Oxbow Monograph 51.

Gopher, A., and T. Tsuk (1996) *The Nahal Qanah Cave. Earliest Gold in the Southern Levant*. Monograph Series of the Institute of Archaeology Tel Aviv University No. 12.

Goring-Morris A.N., Y. Goren, L.K. Horwitz, I. Hershkovitz, R. Lieberman, J. Sarel and D. Bar-Yosef (1994–95) The 1992 season of excavation at the Pre-Pottery Neolithic B settlement of Kfar Hahoresh. *Journal of the Israel Prehistoric Society* 26: 74–121.

Haas, N., and H. Nathan (1973) Chalcolithic burial in the Nahal Mishmar Cave. In *Excavations and Studies, Essays in Honor of Professor Shmuel Yeivin*, edited by Y. Aharoni. Tel Aviv: Institute of Archaeology, pp. 145–53.

Hanbury-Tennison, J.W. (1986) *The late Chalcolithic to Early Bronze I transition in Palestine and Transjordan*. BAR International Series: 311.

Hershkovitz, I., and A. Gopher (1990) Palaeodemography, Burial customs and food producing economy at the beginning of the Holocene. *Journal of the Israel Prehistoric Society* 23:9–27.

Hodder, I. (1982) *The Present Past: an introduction to anthropology for archaeologists*. New York, pp. 144–45

Hershkovitz, I., E. Galili, and B. Ring (1991) Human skeletons 8000 years under the Sea—Indications on social and economical life of the inhabitants of the south coast in the Levant during the preceramic neolithic. *Anthropologie* V95:639–50.

Hershkovitz, I., I. Zohar, I. Segal, M.S. Speirs, O. Meirav, U. Sherter, H. Feldman and N. Goringmorris (1995) Remedy for an 8500 year-old plastered human skull from Kfar Hahoresh, Israel. *Journal of Archaeological Science* V22:779–88

Krogman, W.M. (1962) *The Human Skeleton in Forensic Medicine*. Springfield Illinois: Charles C. Thomas.

Keita, S.O.Y. (1988) An analysis of crania from Tell-Duweir using multiple discriminant functions. *American Journal of Physical Anthropology* 75:375–90.

Kuijt, I., and Goring-Morris, A.N. (2002) Foraging, farming, and social complexity in the pre-pottery Neolithic of the Southern Levant: a review and synthesis. *Journal of World Prehistory* 16: 361–440.

Lacombe, J-P. (1980) Les ossements humains. In *Tombes a ossuares de la region cotiere Palestinienne au IVe millenaire avant l'ere Chretienne*, edited by J. Perrot and D. Ladiray. Memoire et Travaux du Centre de Recherche Francais Jerusalem, No. 1, pp. 80–94.

Le Mort, F., and R. Rabinovich (1994) L'Apport de l'etude taphonomique des restes humains a la connaissance des pratiques funeraires: Exemple du site Chalcolithique de Ben Shemen (Israel). *Paleorient* 20 (1): 69–98.

Levy, T.E. (1982) The Chalcolithic mortuary site near Mezad Aluf, Northern Negev Desert. A preliminary study. *Bulletin of the American Schools of Oriental Research* 248:37–59.

— (1998) Cult, metallurgy and rank societies—Chalcolithic period (ca 4500–3500 BCE). In *The Archaeology of Society in the Holy Land*, edited by T.E. Levy. London: Continuum, pp. 226–44.

Levy, T. E., and D. Alon (1982) The Chalcolithic Mortuary Site Near Mezad Aluf, Northern Negev Desert: A Preliminary Study. *Bulletin of the American Schools of Oriental Research* 248:37–59.

— (1985) The Chalcolithic mortuary site near Mezad Aluf, Northern Negev desert: Third preliminary report, 1982 Season. *Bulletin of the American Schools of Oriental Research, Supplement No.* 23:121–35.

— (1985) Shiqmim: A Chalcolithic village and mortuary center in the Northern Negev. *Paleorient* 11:71–83.

Levy, T.E., D. Alon, P. Goldberg, C. Grigson, P. Smith, J. Buikstra, A. Holl, S. Shalev, S. Ben Itzchak and A. Ben Yosef (1990) Protohistoric investigations at the Shiqmim Chalcolithic village and cemetery: an interim report on the 1987 season. *BASOR* 27:29–46.

Levy, T.E., D. Alon, P. Goldberg, C. Grigson, P. Smith, J. Buikstra, A. Holl, and P. Sabari (1993) Protohistoric investigations at the Shiqmim C9halcolithic village and cemetery: an interim report on the 1988 season. *AASOR* 51: 87–106.

Levy, T.E., D. Alon, C. Grigson, Y. Rowan, A. Holl and P. Smith (1991) Subterranean settlement, village planning and adaptation at the Desert Edge: New Archaeological Perspectives from Chalcolithic Shiqmim. *Research and Exploration* 7: 394–413.

Mallon, A., R. Koeppel and R. Neuville (1934) *Teleilat Ghassul* 1, Rome: Pontifical Biblical Institute.

Morris, I. (1987) *Burial and Ancient Society*. Cambridge: Cambridge University Press, pp. 29–43.

Ozbek, M. (1975) *Hommes de Byblos. Etude comparative des squelettes des ages de metaux au Proche Orient*. Unpublished Ph.D. dissertation, Universite de Paris.

Perrot, J. (1955) The excavations at Abu Matar, near Beersheba. *Israel Exploration Journal* 5: 17–41, 73–84, 167–89.

Perrot, J., and D. Ladiray (1980) *Tombes a ossuares de la region cotiere Palestinienne au IVe millenaire avant l'ere Chretienne*. Memoire et Travaux du Centre de Recherche Francais Jerusalem, No. 1.

Renfrew, C. (1992) Archaeology, genetics and linguistic diversity. *Man* 27:445–78.

Saunders, S.R., and M.A. Katzenberg (1992) *Skeletal Biology of Past Peoples: Research Methods*. New York: Wiley-Liss.

Schick, T. (ed.) (1998) *The Cave of the Warrior—A Fourth Millennium Burial in the Judean Desert*. Jerusalem: Israel Antiquities Authority.

Schulz, M. (1987) Human skeletal remains. In J. Nissen, M. Muheisen and H-G. Gebel, Report on the first two seasons at Basta. *Annals of the Department of Antiquities, Jordan* 31:95–98.

Seaton, P. (2000) Aspects of new research at the Chalcolithic sanctuary precinct at Teleilat Ghassul, in *Proceedings of the First International Congress on the Archaeology of the Ancient Near East, Rome, May 18th–23rd, 1998*, edited by P. Matthiae, A. Enea, L. Peyronel and F. Pinnock. Rome, pp. 1503–14.

Shennan, S.J. (1982) The emergence of hierarchical structure. In *Ranking, Resource and Exchange—Aspects of the Archaeology of Early European Society*, edited by C. Renfrew and S. Shennan. Cambridge: Cambridge University Press, pp. 9–12.

Smith, P. (1989) The skeletal biology and paleopathology of Early Bronze Age Populations in the Levant. In *L'urbanization de la Palestine a l'age du Bronze Ancien*, edited by P. de Miroschedji. Oxford: Bar International Series 527(ii). Oxford: British Archaeological Reports, pp. 297–316.

— (1991) The Dental Evidence for Nutritional Status in the Natufians. In *The Natufian Culture in the Levant*, edited by O. Bar-Yosef and F. Valla. Ann Arbor: International Monographs in Prehistory, Archaeology Series 1, pp. 425–34.

— (1995) Skeletal remains. *American Journal of Archaeology* 99: 127–32.

— (1998) People of the Holy Land from prehistory to the recent past. In *The Archaeology of Society in the Holy Land*, edited by T.E. Levy. Leicester University Press, pp. 58–74.

Smith, P., and P. Sabari (1995) The Chalcolithic Skeletal remains from Horvat Hor. *Israel Exploration Journal* 45: 128–35.

Smith, P., R.A. Bloom and J. Berkowitz (1984a) Diachronic trends in humeral cortical thickness of Near Eastern populations. *Journal of Human Evolution* 13: 603–11.

Smith, P., O. Bar-Yosef and A. Sillen (1984b) Archaeological and skeletal evidence for dietary change during the Late Pleistocene /Early Holocene in the Levant. In *Paleopathology at the Origins of Agriculture*, edited by M.N. Cohen and G.J. Armelagos. Orlando: Academic Press, pp. 101–36.

Turner, H.W. (1979) *From temple to meeting house: The phenomenology and theology of places of worship.* The Hague and New York: Mouton.

Ucko, P. (1969) Ethnography and Archaeological Interpretation of Funery Remains. *World Archaeology* 1: 273–74.

Ussishkin, D. (1980) The Ghassulian Shrine at En-Gedi. *Tel Aviv*:1–44.

van den Brink, E.C.M. (1998) An index to Chalcolithic mortuary caves in Israel. *Israel Exploration Journal* V48: 165–73.

van den Brink, E.C.M., and T.E. Levy (eds.) (2002) *Egypt and the Levant—Interrelations from the 4th Through the Early 3rd Millennium BCE. New Approaches to Anthropological Archaeology.* London and New York: Continuum.

Vandermeersch, B. (1970) Une sepulture mousterienne avec offrandes decouverte dans la grotte de Qafzeh. *Comptes Rendus de l' Academie de Science* 270.D: 298–301.

Wright, G. A. (1978) Social differentiation in the early Natufian. In *Social Archaeology, Beyond Subsistence and Dating*, edited by C. Redman, M. J. Berman, E. V. Curtin, W. T. Langhorne Jr., N. M. Versaggi and J. C. Wanser. New York: Academic Press. pp. 201–23.

Zagerson, T., and P. Smith (2002) Human Remains from Kissufim Road. In *The Chalcolithic Mortuary Site at Kissufim Road, Israel*, edited by Y. Goren and P. Fabian. *Atiqot Monograph Series.*

IV.
THE EMERGENCE OF GILAT
AS A REGIONAL CULT CENTER:
PRODUCTION AND EXCHANGE

9 The Technology of the Gilat Pottery Assemblage:

A Reassessment

Yuval Goren

Introduction

In a previous publication, entitled 'Shrines and ceramics in Chalcolithic Israel: The view through the petrographic microscope' (Goren 1995), I attempted to investigate the nature of Chalcolithic ceremonial contexts through a provenance study of their ceramic assemblages. That study was part of a research project that attempted to investigate the nature of proto-historical social and economic traits through provenance studies of Late Neolithic, Chalcolithic and Early Bronze Age ceramic assemblages from the southern Levant (Goren 1987; 1991). The pronounced differences in the nature and the provenance of the ceramic assemblages of three important sites which bear clear indications for religious activities, namely En-Gedi, Nahal Mishmar and Gilat, had suggested to me that these sites represented different idiosyncrasies of cult that co-existed in the Developed Chalcolithic milieu. In context, this interpretation aimed to clarify at least some of the problems that were raised by the new information that came from the renewed excavations at Gilat (Alon and Levy 1989; Levy *et al.*, Chapter 5, this volume), as well as the increasing interest in the social and economic dimensions of the inhabitants of the southern Levant during the late fifth–fourth millennia BC (cf. Gilead 1989; Levy 1983, 1986, 1998; Levy and Alon 1987; Perrot 1984; Rosen 1986).

The interpretation of the nature of cult through the complex, sometimes unrelated, aspects of pottery typology, technology, and distribution, is undoubtedly a very ambiguous task. Patterns of pottery production, utilization and transportation can be related to numerous other functional, cultural and/or economic motives (e.g. Rice 1984). It is therefore very risky to link directly ceremonial activities and occurrences within one or more ceramic assemblages in a given time and space. Moreover, despite the 'theistic' approach in Near Eastern archaeology that tends to reduce religion to the worship of deities in shrines or sanctuaries, it should be realized that cult in proto-historic societies (as well as in later epochs) must have had many more expressions that may have left different patterns of archaeological remains. Nevertheless, since Near Eastern archaeology has always tended to interpret cult as activities restricted to shrines, it has attempted to concentrate on the location of sites and artifacts concerned with the worship of deities in communal *loci*, such as central or oversized buildings, or other installations of this nature. In this context, it is very tempting to attribute cultic activities to any location in which symbolic or 'precious' artifacts from an abundant aspect of the material culture. This approach, which led to my previous interpretations concerning Gilat, En-Gedi and Nahal Mishmar, may be justified in particular cases. However, it is merely intuitive and needs to be supported by other sources of evidence.

Cult, no doubt, was a predominant issue in the life of the inhabitants of the southern Levant during the Chalcolithic period. Of the several archaeological sites and features in the southern Levant that have been interpreted as elements of religion (Elliot 1977), the sanctuary at En-Gedi, the site of Gilat and the 'shrine' at Teleilat Ghassul (Seaton 2000)—the latter as yet fully published —are best known. To these we may add the Nahal Mishmar hoard which, although hidden in a cave, may have originated from some ceremonial center (Ussishkin 1971, 1980). In a previous study of the ceramic assemblages of these sites (excluding the Teleilat Ghassul shrine), I attempted to interpret their diversity on the basis of contemporaneous hierarchies in ritual activities. However, a closer look at the Gilat material, together with the current typological data that must be considered in this context, indicates that this interpretation was over-simplified.

In the present chapter, the role of cult in Gilat will be re-examined on the basis of a comprehensive petrographic study of the pottery assemblage. For the sake of this report, the petrographically examined sample was increased considerably in collaboration with C. Commenge (this volume, Chapter 10) who directed the social and cognitive study of the Gilat ceramic assemblage. Based on the typological and technological results, it was decided to slightly extend this report beyond the scope of the Gilat assemblage alone, and include in it comparisons with other assemblages that seem now to be relevant to it on a chrono-typological basis. Based on these revelations, a modified picture will be suggested for the questions concerning production and distribution of pottery in the Chalcolithic northern Negev, formerly discussed in some previous publications (Gilead and Goren 1989; Goren and Gilead 1987; Goren 1995).

History of the research and previous interpretations

The history of the petrographic research of the Gilat pottery has some important methodological implications, and thus it will be surveyed below in some detail.

A first attempt to investigate the technology of the pottery, excavated by Alon (1976) during the first seasons, was made in the early 1980s as part of a MA thesis (Goren 1987). From the beginning, the petrographic study of the Gilat assemblage featured many interesting aspects. The results of this very preliminary study of Chalcolithic ceramic assemblages, restricted mainly to the southern part of Israel (the northern Negev and the Judean Desert), have demonstrated that the Gilat assemblage was far more diverse than that of any other site in this region in terms of petrographic groups and their provenance. These results have been incorporated in Alon and Levy's (1989, 1990) previous discussions on the interpretation of Gilat as a regional center. In this preliminary study, the composite nature and the variability of groups in the assemblage was briefly delineated and compared to other Chalcolithic assemblages in the northern Negev and the southern Judean Desert. That study was based mostly on the petrographic examination of the outstanding vessels (e.g. the 'Gilat Torpedo jars' and other unique forms), revealing a remarkable variability incomparable with any other ceramic assemblage in the study area. At that stage, no regulated typological study was made on the material, and therefore the samples were selected with no regard to their stratigraphic or architectural context. Nevertheless, even at this preliminary stage, it became obvious that the provenance of most of the Gilat vessels did not extend beyond the limited research area of the northern Negev and the southern Judean Desert. Indeed, there was one Egyptian ('Nilothic') body sherd, but such a sherd is also known from site Y-2 at Qatif and from the small hamlet R-48 in northeastern Sinai (Oren and Gilead 1981; Goren 1987). Another vessel from Gilat was made of paste rich in *Orbitolina* fossils, common in the marine Lower Cretaceous formations of Samaria and the Galilee. Yet a jar with *Orbitolina* fossils was also observed in the assemblage of Abu Matar near Beer Sheva (Commenge-Pellerin 1987: Pl. I: 4) and another one was found in Wadi Makukh cave 6 nearby Jericho (Goren 1991: Appendix 2). Alon and Levy (1991:34) declared that the petrographic evidence was unequivocally in line with the conclusion that Gilat was an inter-regional center whose influence was lively and discernible in the southern Levant throughout the entire Chalcolithic period. However, this conclusion was somewhat overstated since the petrographic evidence suggested that Gilat was a center only for the northern Negev, or a part of it, the southern Shephela and the Judean Mountains. The sherds of vessels that were produced further away were too few and similar pieces were also found in regular habitation sites.

An extended study was made in the early 1990s, concurrently with preliminary attempts, made by T.E. Levy and his team, to study the typology of the then re-excavated Gilat assemblage. The petrographic sample was increased significantly in order to cover the entire range of shapes and variants. Accordingly, more petrographic thin-sections were prepared from the Gilat assemblage to form an overall number of 170 samples (Goren 1995). The previously observed petrographic variability was confirmed. Nevertheless, about half of the assemblage consisted of group 'loess-quartzitic sand', representing the lithology of the immediate vicinity of the site (*ibid*. Fig. 11). The related group 'loess-calcareous sand', whose distribution overlaps that of the former group at Gilat (*ibid*. Fig. 10), formed about 8% of the assemblage. Additional groups which might have been classified as local were those related to the 'Cream Ware' (Gilead and Goren 1989), usually composed of Taqiya marl. These formed about 15% of the total. Therefore, about 70% of the Gilat pottery assemblage had been defined as local or nearly local.

Amongst the foreign groups, about 9.5% of the assemblage was composed of groups 'Moza clay-dolomitic sand' and 'Moza marl-calcareous sand' attributed to the Judean Mountains. The remaining groups did not reflect any specific geological environment, yet they were extremely rare in the other assemblages of the northern Negev and more common in the assemblages of central Israel.

Other conclusions were the following:

1. Of the total of 19 bowls included in the petrographic sample (based on a preliminary examination of the assemblage), 15 (79%) belonged to the local loessial groups. The remaining groups are all related to the 'Cream Ware' class (mostly of the 'Taqiya marl' group). Consequently, it seems that most of the bowls were not imported to the site from distant localities.

2. In the case of the basins, churns and holemouth jars, though most of them are considered as local (40% of the basins, 63% of the churns and 54% of the holemouth jars), relatively high proportions of imported vessels occur. In most cases these belong to groups 'Moza clay-dolomitic sand' and 'Moza marl-calcareous sand'.

3. Twelve (92%) of the 13 examined 'fenestrated stands' (Alon and Levy 1989:198–200) relate to the local loessial groups. The remaining vessel is of the Moza clay category, thus Judean in origin.

4. The so-called 'Gilat Torpedo Jars' (Alon and Levy 1989:200–204) represent another enigma. Eight vessels of this type have been studied petrographically, providing a surprisingly high variability of raw materials. One vessel (no. 233) belongs to group 'loess-calcareous sand', containing mostly chalk sand as temper. This vessel was certainly produced in southern Israel, yet its pure chalk temper hints to the southern Shephela as its preferable provenance (Gilead and Goren 1989: Fig. 2). Two other jars (nos. 236 and 112) were produced of Taqiya marl and calcareous sand temper, implying an unknown origin which may or may not be local to the northern Negev. Yet the remaining five were produced of

Moza marl or clay with either calcareous sand or crushed calcite as temper, revealing a foreign (Judean) origin of these unique vessels as yet unknown from any other site (excluding one as yet unpublished fragment from Wadi Zeita and another one from Qatif Y-2.). None of these vessels was found to be produced of the dominant petrographic group at the site, namely 'loess-quartzitic sand'.

In the present research, the petrographic sample was increased again, and an attempt made to relate it to the newly made socioeconomic and cognitive analysis of the Gilat ceramic assemblage (Chapter 10, in this volume). Considering the apparent Early Chalcolithic nature of a major segment of the assemblage, it was compared with other Early Chalcolithic assemblages in the same geographical region (northern Negev–northern Sinai), and not only to Developed Chalcolithic sites as done before. Consequently, for the first time the technology of the Gilat pottery assemblage can be seen now in context and can provide a set of conclusions that take into account a wider range of cultural and chronological affinities. Although the interpretations of the petrographic groups remained as before, their relations with other sites in the Chalcolithic arena can be suggested more precisely. From a methodological point of view, this demonstrates that in every analytical method these aspects should be carefully thought about while planning the sampling strategy. Moreover, it warrants against any attempt to 'tie the chariot in front of the horses', and make the analyses prior to a thorough and careful typological work.

Method

Of the various techniques that are employed for analyzing the composition of pottery, petrography was chosen. Petrographic analysis is particularly useful for examining coarse, poorly fired, locally made pottery since it permits large numbers of samples to be handled at a low cost and provides valuable information relatively quickly. Moreover, our large collection of comparative material from many major sites in the southern Levant allows us to relate many fabrics to their geological context, thus facilitating provenance determinations.

The petrographic examination of the pottery assemblage was carried out in stages. In the preliminary stage, freshly broken sections of all the typologically identified vessels were inspected with the aid of a stereomicroscope (at magnifications up to ×20) and broadly grouped according to the characteristics of the fabrics, as suggested by Stienstra (1986). In the second stage, samples for petrographic thin section analysis were chosen on the basis of both the typology of the vessels and their raw materials and examined under a petrographic (polarizing) microscope (a detailed inventory of the thin-sections is presented in Appendix A).[1]

During the petrographic analysis, the samples were divided into petrographic groups. A 'petrographic group' encompasses vessels which share similar petrographic affinities in both clay and temper. This classification is determined according to the qualities of raw materials alone, regardless of variables such as typology, chronology and geographic location of the site. Therefore, this classification may serve as an independent technical criterion for a comparative assortment of ceramic assemblages. The application of this method for archaeological assemblages has been explained elsewhere (Porat 1984, 1987, 1989a, b; Goren 1987, 1991, 1992, 1995, 1996; Gilead and Goren 1989). In these previous studies we managed to define many petrographic groups and to correlate them with specific lithological environments. The 'key petrographic groups' to be described have typical attributes which enable a reasonable assessment of their geographical origin, and thus may be used for provenance studies. Since only a limited number of petrographic groups were traced in the pottery assemblage in question, their provenance could have been determined on the basis of these comparisons and the typical lithological 'fingerprint' of each one of them.

Results

A. Summary of the results

The lithological and technological properties of the major petrographic groups are presented here in summary for the convenience of the reader.

'Loess-calcareous/quartzitic sand' group. This group is characterized by a silty, moderately calcareous clay loam (loess) and sand of either quartz or calcareous rock fragments as temper. Its main occurrence is in the ceramic assemblages of sites located in the northern/northwestern Negev and the southern Shephela regions, that is, broadly speaking within the rectangle formed by Lachish, Gaza, Ashkelon and Beer-Sheva.

'Moza clay-dolomitic sand' group. This group is characterized by a mixture of fine clay, somewhat carbonatic and rich in iron oxides, and coarse dolomitic sand. It originates in the vicinity of the Judean hills, especially around Jerusalem.

'Taqiya marl' group. This group is characterized by a light, rather foraminiferous marl derived from the Taqiya formation. Outcrops of the Taqiya formation are widely distributed and therefore cannot be used to define particular provenance. It was widely used in sites located in the Shephela region of Israel.

'Lower Cretaceous' group. This group is characterized by the use of argillaceous, ferruginous, shale-rich clay, with high contents of silt, 'mature' quartz sand and typical ferruginous ooliths. It is identified as originating from the Nubian Sandstone series of the lower Cretaceous section. In the southern Levant it outcrops mostly east of the Jordan, and in few meager zones in the central Negev craters and in eastern Samaria. In the case of the Chalcolithic pottery assemblages, its most feasible origin is southeastern Jordan Valley (between Wadi Zarqa and Faynan), including the surrounding of Teleilat Ghassul.

'Nile mud' group. This group is a term used here for pottery produced in Egypt from the Nile river sediments.

B. The major petrographic groups of the Gilat assemblage
'Loess' group

Characterization. This group is characterized by silty, rather carbonatic clay matrix, and sand of mostly spherical quartz grains as inclusions. The silty component contains mainly quartz but also a recognizable quantity of other minerals including hornblende, zircon, minerals of the mica group, feldspars, tourmaline, augite, and more rarely garnet, epidote and rutile. Ore minerals are abundant too in this fraction. The silt is relatively well sorted and comprises about 10%–20% of the matrix.

The non-plastic components includes dense, well sorted, spherical sand-sized quartz grains with the occasional addition of other 'heavy' minerals (feldspars, hornblende, zircon, augite). The other minerals appear in similar or slightly smaller grain sizes as the quartz. They are also spherical and usually show no breaks or cavities resulting from chemical or physical weathering. In several cases they are accompanied by calcite cemented quartzitic sandstone ('*Kurkar*').

Interpretation and references. Based on a bulk of published data (Porat 1987:112–15, 1989a: 50–2; Goren 1987, 1988, 1991: 101–4, 1991c, 1996; Goren and Gilead 1987; Gilead and Goren 1989:7; Goldberg *et al.* 1986; Rognon *et al.* 1987) the matrix is readily identified as the loess soil which occurs in the southern Levant mainly in the northern Negev and the southern Shephelah regions. To the best of our knowledge, the overall distribution of Levantine workshops that produced pottery of the loessial petrographic groups in all periods does not extend significantly beyond the limits of the northern Negev-southern Shephelah zones (in the rectangle formed between Lachish, Ashkelon, Gaza and Beer-Sheva) in any of the periods we investigated.

Previous studies of ceramics assigned to the loess petrographic group (*ibid.*) demonstrated that the composition of the inclusions used in it varied with the geographic location of each site and could be correlated with sands occurring naturally in its vicinity (Gilead and Goren 1989: Fig. 2; Goren 1991a: 118–20, Fig. 13; 1995: Figs 3-8). The use of loess with inclusions in which limestone is the dominant component is prevalent mainly at sites northeast of the Beer-Sheva Valley and the southern Shephelah, whereas in the inner southern Shephelah region, chalk sand is commonly the sole non-plastic component. In the northwestern Negev sites quartz is the major constituent (Gilead and Goren 1989: Fig. 2). When quartz sand dominates the inclusions, it is usually accompanied by sand-sized grains of accessory minerals including hornblende, zircon, feldspar and augite. These hint at a littoral origin, since sandstone-derived quartzitic sands of other origins (such as the sandstones of the Lower Cretaceous formations) are devoid of all of these. To this evidence we should add the high proportions of the unstable minerals (like hornblende, pyroxene, rutile, garnet, etc.) that appear with the quartz as spherical sand-sized grains. These also hint at a littoral origin since they tend to weather very rapidly in sands of coastal origin that are swept inland by aeolian activity (Slatkine and Pomerancblum 1959; Pomerancblum 1966). This point is important because sands of coastal origin appear as far inland as the central Beer-Sheva Valley.

Provenance in the Gilat assemblage. In a previous study of Chalcolithic ceramic assemblages from southern Israel (Gilead and Goren 1989; Goren 1995; Goren and Gilead 1987), it was proved that the matrix to inclusion variants within the loess groups varied geographically and could be isolated and defined petrographically. In light of these results, the inner northwestern Negev should be regarded as a possible origin for this group in Gilat. Therefore, it can be generally defined as the local group of the Gilat area.

'Moza clay-dolomitic sand' Group

Characterization. This group is readily identified even with the naked eye by its very typical fabric. The clay color is yellowish, altering through pink as the firing temperature increases to dark gray at high temperatures. Its most characteristic feature is the non-plastic component, that is readily identified even by the naked eye by its very typical fabric. It is composed of homogenous, densely spread, well sorted whitish sand-sized particles, that under a magnifying glass exhibit rhombic shapes. In thin-section they appear as sand-sized inclusions of euhedral dolomite crystals. The typical rhomboid shape of the particles indicates the use of an 'immature' sand that was not subjected to any significant processes of translocation. This implies an *in-situ* development of this sand due to the dissolution of the cementing matrix of coarse crystalline dolomite aggregates. Such phenomena are quite common in the Cenomanian section of the Judean Mountain ridge (Bentor 1945; Arkin *et al.* 1965).

Interpretation. This well-defined petrographic group was previously published in detail (e.g. Goren 1995, 1996). Based on an extensive body of reference material (to be discussed below), it is identified as originating from clay of the upper member of the Moza formation, mixed with dolomitic sand that was quarried from the overlaying 'Amminadav formation. The non-plastic component was probably sieved to isolate the desired grain size, since in nature the dolomitic sand of the 'Amminadav formation appears to be much less sorted than in the pottery belonging to this group.

Chemical analyses of raw Moza clay pottery of this petrographic group from the Early Bronze Age IV (EBIV) site Nahal Refaim, and EBIV pottery belonging to this group from the central Negev (Goren 1996: Fig. 10), revealed that they all clustered well. This, together with the following petrographic data, strongly support the identification of this group as being purely Judean or Samarian in origin.

References. This petrographic group is well known from pottery assemblages from sites of different periods spread throughout the Judean-Samarian hills. In the Chalcolithic period it apparently typifies the Judean sites (Goren 1987, 1991a, 1995), but is rare in other regions. It has been recorded from Early Bronze Age I sites in central Israel extending from the Beer Sheva valley to Aphek (Porat 1989a:47–8; Mæir et al. 1992).

In the EBIV this group dominates sites in the vicinity of Jerusalem. In several assemblages, including the large habitation sites of Nahal Refaim (Eisenberg 1993; 1994), Minhat and Wadi Zimra (Meitlis 1991), it constituted a major part of the material (Goren 1996). Petrographic examination of the EBIV-MBA pottery collected in the Central Hill Country between Jerusalem and the Jezreel Valley (Finkelstein 1991) revealed that this group dominated the ceramic assemblages of sites located around Jerusalem (N. Shaharon, pers. comm.). At the EBIV-MBA site of Nahal Refaim, an ancient quarry of dolomitic sand was discovered (Eisenberg 1994:86). The quarry is located in an outcrop of the lowermost unit of the 'Amminadav formation, immediately above the uppermost member of the Moza clay. The use of this quarry during the EBIV is confirmed by the discovery of EBIV burials within it, providing a *terminus ante quem* for its use. MBA jar, filled with this sand, was found at the site together with numerous potters' wheels, confirming its use for some purpose, presumably for pottery production (Eisenberg 1993:1280). At Jebel Qaᶜaqir (London 1985:146) this group forms a minor component in the ceramic assemblage.

In the Middle and the Late Bronze Ages it again became one of the common raw materials of the Judean ceramic assemblages (Glass et al. 1993; N. Shaharon, pers. comm.). Moza clay, especially with dolomitic sand inclusions, dominates the ceramic assemblages of several burial cave sites around Jerusalem that were examined by us: Ma'ale Hahamisha, 'Efrat and Zova. In the as yet unpublished excavations at the tell of Moza (A. de Groot and Z. Greenhot, pers. comm.), it dominates the MBA ceramic assemblage.

This group is also known from the Iron Age I assemblages of Tell en-Nasbeh and Radana, as well as from the 'collared-rim' pithoi from the site of Giloh (all as yet unpublished) and the pottery assemblage of Shiloh (Glass et al. 1993:78). This group was found to be common in the Iron Age II assemblage from the City of David (Franken and Steiner 1990:79–85) and the contemporary sites of Ramot 06 and Moza (as yet unpublished).

Although dolomite rocks, and hence the dolomitic sand derived from them, can be found in other parts of the southern Levant, it seems that its use as an inclusion was restricted to the Judean hills. This was confirmed also by the results of Neutron Activation Analysis (NAA) study that attributed pottery of this petrographic group to the Jerusalem area even when it was found in the Negev and Sinai (Gunneweg et al. 1985: 273). Many of the vessels from Kuntillet 'Ajrud, Beer-Sheva, and Giloh mentioned in this article were examined by us petrographically and proved to belong to this petrographic group.

Provenance in the Gilat assemblage. The rich body of analytical data presented here clearly indicates that the 'Moza clay-dolomitic sand' petrographic group may be related directly to the Judean and Samarian hill sites, and more specifically to the Jerusalem area.

'Moza marl-calcareous sand' Group

Characterization. In this group the clay matrix is usually burnt into very light pinkish colors. It is rich in tiny (below 50 microns) rhombohedral dolomite crystals, perhaps altered into calcite after firing, which can be identified only under the microscope. This clay, in fact, may be classified as marl. Except for the dolomite rhombs, this marl contains many tiny concentrations of ore minerals. The non-plastic component includes a variegated calcareous sand. This sand originates in deposits of wadis which drain an area dominated by micritic and sparitic limestone, dolomite, chalk and chert. Quartzite and chalcedony particles are also characteristic of this assembly. Gypsum cleavage fragments appear sometimes as secondary elements in the coarse non-plastic assemblage. Their majority, especially close to the surface of the sherds, were dissolved and thus left cavities. Some of the samples contain fragments of fossils or grains of biogenetic limestone.

Interpretation. The lithic assemblage represented in this group points to a geological environment which is dominated by marl, a series of verified limestones and lesser dolomites, with occasional quartzite nodules, chert and gypsum. Such an assemblage agrees with the Moza marl, and the limestone and dolomite formations which are exposed in vast areas on the Judean-Samarian anticline. The Moza marl, located underneath the clay unit of this formation, contains about 18% of carbonate minerals compared to about 4% in the higher clay unit (Bentor 1966:48). Being the sole significant clay/marl formation in this region, it had been used extensively for the aim of pottery production.

Provenance in the Gilat assemblage. By its distribution, origin and general geology this petrographic group should be attributed to sites located along the Judean-Samarian mountain ridge. Its distribution overlaps that of the 'Moza clay-dolomitic sand' group which represents a more restricted phenomenon within the broader occurrence of ceramic production in the Chalcolithic Judean Mountains sites.

'Taqiya marl' Group

Characterization. This group is discernible by the naked eye because of its whitish or yellowish color which turns greenish-gray at higher firing temperatures. The inclusions include chalk (sometimes nummolithic), limestone, chert and quartz. Microscopically it is characterized by a light, highly calcareous marl containing sparse microfossils and iron oxides. The microfaunal assemblage within the matrix, when identified, is usually of Pliocene-Eocene age. When fired in an oxidizing atmosphere, the clay takes on a light tan color in thin section. Fine, fibrous carbonate crystals which sometimes exhibit weak optical orientation are abundant in the matrix. Well sorted, sparsely distributed silty quartz appears in many cases.

Interpretation. Based on its mineralogical and palaeontological affinities, this clay is usually identified as marl of the Taqiya Formation of Paleocene age (Porat 1984:63–73; 1989a:177–8) which is exposed in the northern and central Negev and central Sinai (Bentor 1966:72–3). It also outcrops in the Judean Desert and along the western slopes of the Judea-Samaria anticline. This formation is almost constant in its stratigraphic position and even in details of its composition. Equivalent beds appear in Egypt (Esna shales) and even in Morocco and Turkey (Bentor 1966:73). However, the use of Esna shales for pottery production was never recorded in Egyptian assemblages (P. Nicolson, pers. comm.). In the southern Levant, the use of this combination (Taqiya marl with chalk, limestone and chert with some quartz sand derived from the coastal plain) is very typical of sites located in the Shephela region (see below).

References. The use of Taqiya marl with the addition of various non-plastic materials was observed by Porat (1984:63–73; 1989a:177–8) in the Early Bronze Age II assemblages of the Negev, especially at Arad, for the production of jars and holemouth jars. Despite the widespread distribution of the Taqiya formation, it seems that in most periods its use as a ceramic raw material was restricted mainly to southern Israel.

Firing experiments were carried out on samples of the Taqiya marl collected from an outcrop near the Negev Junction on the Beer Sheva to Sde Boqer road (Goren 1996). They revealed that the Taqiya marl briquettes provided good quality ceramics even at 600°C. Of the raw material selected from the section, the more marly units produced ceramics with superior qualities to those prepared from the greenish shales, since the latter are richer in gypsum and montmorillonite. The former were also petrographically closer to the archaeological ceramics.

In EBIV contexts this group dominates the assemblage of Har Yeruham (Goren 1996), the only site in the central Negev where it proved to be the primary group. At other sites it appears as a secondary group with its weight in the assemblage decreasing roughly in inverse relationship to the distance from Har Yeruham Site. Given the fact that this is the sole site in the central Negev where a potter's workshop was found (Kochavi 1967:44–6), it may be regarded as being the locally produced fabric of this region, although this may not be stated categorically on petrographic grounds alone. On the contrary, examinations carried out by Glass (London 1985:145–7) on the pottery from Jebel Qaᶜaqir revealed that similar material (also identified by him as belonging to the Taqiya marl) forms 64% of the assemblage. The Taqiya formation also outcrops in the immediate neighborhood of Jebel Qaᶜaqir, thus it is conceivable that pottery was produced there.

Provenance in the Gilat assemblage. Although Taqiya marl is rather widespread, the inclusions that accompany this clay type in Gilat (as well as other Chalcolithic assemblages) usually contain Eocene chalk, chert and *nari,* suggesting that the upper Shephela region should be recognized as its most possible origin.

Minor groups
'Lower Cretaceous shales/clay' Group

Characterization. This petrofabric is characterized by argillaceous, ferruginous, shale-rich clay. The matrix has a relatively high content of typical ferruginous ooliths. As in most cases in this group, quartz sand is present as sub-spherical grains. These include rounded quartz grains (derived from sand or weathered sandstone), oolitic limestone, and spheroids of iron oxide (sometimes with an internal concentric structure). Other indicators of this group are diversified shale fragments, some of which are ferruginous while others tend to be more clayey. Pellets, tuff and weathered basalt fragments, and typical rhombohedral limonitic pseudomorphs after dolomite occasionally occur in this case. The coarser inclusions include angular grains of flint, and spherical grains of limestone.

Interpretation. This group has been described in detail by Greenberg and Porat (1996), and Goren (1992, 1995, 1996). A large body of comparative data enables us to determine that in this case, the lower formations of the Lower Cretaceous lithological section were used as a source for both clay and inclusions. These formations outcrop widely in the Transjordan, between the southern Dead Sea and Wadi Zarqa, but also in the eastern upper Galilee and southern Lebanon. Smaller outcrops appear in Wadi Malikh and Wadi Farᶜah in eastern Samaria and in the northeastern Negev craters. Similar outcrops appear also in Jebel Mghaᶜra in northern Sinai (the relevant references appear in Greenberg and Porat 1996, and Goren 1992, 1995, 1996).

References. The use of Lower Cretaceous shales and highly ferruginous marl for pottery production has been recorded in several cases. This clay is usually considered to be of superior quality for pottery production since its high iron content made it possible to achieve a high degree of sintering at lower firing temperatures due to the fluxing properties of the iron. Therefore, Lower Cretaceous ferruginous shales were often used to produce vessels which needed to be strong, especially liquid containers such as pithoi, jugs and storage jars. At the Chalcolithic site of Teleilat Ghassul, for example, most of the locally made pottery is formed of this iron-rich clay (Goren 1987:48–53, 1991a: Appendix 2), the typical pithoi being sintered to a surprisingly high quality (Edwards and Segnit 1984). Similar raw materials were used during the Early Bronze Age II-III in order to produce the high quality 'Metallic Ware' as well as other superior vessels (Porat 1989a:71–4; Greenberg and Porat 1996). In the EBIV this petrographic group is frequent at all the EBIV sites of the central Negev, and at some (Har Dimon, Beer Resisim) constitutes a major part of the assemblage (Goren 1996: Table 9.2). Recent examination of Iron Age I 'collared-rim' and 'Galilean' pithoi from several sites in the Samaria and Galilee regions (Glass *et al.* 1993; Cohen-Weinberger and Goren 1996) demonstrated that in several cases such clays were preferred by the potters in order to produce high quality vessels. The adoption of this clay for the manufacture of such vessels obliged the potter to carefully select a shale layer rich in clay minerals and poor in carbonates, since the latter may cause mechanical damage to the highly fired pottery due to the process of decalcination which occurs at 700°C and above. Nevertheless, at sites located near outcrops of these formations, these clays were used for producing most of the ceramic repertoire (Goren 1991a,b).

Provenance in the Gilat assemblage. The closest location to Gilat where Lower Cretaceous shales expose nearby known Chalcolithic sites is the eastern Jordan Valley, including Teleilat Ghassul. Similar formations also outcrop near Tell Far'ah North. Archaeological considerations suggest that pottery of this group should be attributed directly to Teleilat Ghassul.

'Nile mud' Group

Characterization. Silty, non-carbonatic matrix, exhibiting clear optical properties under crossed polarizers. The matrix contains abundant mica minerals. The inclusions are characterized by high contents of poorly sorted sand to silt sized quartz, in varying quantities and size ranges (i.e. badly sorted sediment). In both the silt and the sand fractions there are high proportions of accessory and heavy minerals including mainly minerals of the mica, pyroxene, amphibole, and the feldspar groups. Plant tissues and other vegetal remains (phytoliths) are frequently visible in the clay body.

Geological interpretation. This group is readily identified as being produced of the so-called Nile silt (the term Nile mud seems to us to be more precise). This term refers to pottery manufactured in Egypt from local Nile sediments. Petrographically, it is easily distinguished by its typical characteristics from Canaanite materials (Amiran and Glass 1979; Goldberg *et al.* 1986; Porat 1989b; Bourriau 1990; Goren 1991a). The results of the detailed technological research of Egyptian pottery assemblages, as well as the increasing data on Egyptian ceramic raw materials (cf. Arnold and Borriau 1993) facilitate identification of this raw material.

References. Nile mud was widely used in Egypt for pottery production during all periods. See Arnold and Borriau (1993) for the relevant references.

Provenance in the Gilat assemblage. Pottery of this group is an import from Egypt.

Discussion

Components of the Gilat Assemblage

The results of the petrographic analysis of each examined vessel are presented in Appendix A. The final examination of the Gilat pottery assemblage still indicates that a considerable component within it is alien and imported from notably remote regions, especially from the Judean Mountains and the Upper Shephela hill country. However, few vessels are imported from the even more distant locations of the Jordan Valley and Egypt. Although the locally produced component within the assemblage cannot be overlooked, about half of the examined vessels should be considered imported. This situation is incomparable with any other major Chalcolithic site in the northern Negev, namely Abu Matar, Beer Safadi, Hurvat Beter, Shiqmim, Nevatim and Grar (Gilead and Goren 1989; Goren 1991: Appendix 1).

However, a closer look at the ceramic assemblage reveals that this comparison neglects the typological and chronological traits of a main part of the Gilat assemblage. Therefore, before coming into any sweeping conclusions, we need to examine closely the cultural and chronological location of Gilat within the proto-historical sequence of the northern Negev.

The Gilat Assemblage in Context

During the last two decades, the cultural sequence from the Late Neolithic through the Chalcolithic period have been largely defined through extensive fieldwork (e.g. Gopher and Gophna 1993) as well as a richer body of radiocarbon dates (e.g. Burton and Levy 2001; Gilead 1994; Joffe and Dessel 1995). Within this sequence however, the Pre-pottery Neolithic and Developed Chalcolithic cultures have benefited from the most research, and the intervening Pottery Neolithic of the southern Levant has not been as extensively studied and is hence still relatively poorly understood.

The Pottery Neolithic period of Israel and Jordan is one of the least well known and investigated periods in Levantine archaeology. This can be seen on a map showing all the sites from this period which have been systematically studied, as well as from the list of radiometric dates presented. After the discovery of the key sites from this period during the 50s and 60s (Sha'ar Hagolan, Munhata, Jericho, Wadi Raba, Lod, Teluliot Batashi, Tell 'Ali, Kabri and Ein Jerba), interest in the Pottery Neolithic period subsided, and it is only in the last decade that this period has received new attention. Thus relatively many scholars now dedicate their research to studying the Pottery Neolithic, and several key sites, which have never been properly published, have been re-excavated (e.g. Sha'ar Hagolan, Lod, Tell 'Ali and Kabri). Moreover, new sites have been discovered and excavated. A renewed interest in the Pottery Neolithic is evident also in Jordan, where several important sites are currently under study (Ein Ghazal, Wadi Shueib, Abu Tawwab).

This renewed research brought about immense progress in the study of the Late Pottery Neolithic/Early Chalcolithic 'Wadi Raba culture'. Being the dominant culture in the southern Levant in the first half of the fifth millennium BC, it is now clear that this cultural phase consists of several variations which are evident in the material characteristics, particularly in the flint and pottery assemblages (Gopher 1995). First attempts to define and understand such variations are currently under way (see Gopher and Greenberg 1987; 1996; Gophna and Sadeh 1989), and it may very well be that in the future a comprehensive analysis of pottery assemblages will enable the understanding of the nature of this variability. However, it is becoming clear that all these cultural variations share a large number of characteristics. The common traits are demonstrated in the pottery assemblages by the appearance of red and black burnish and slip, the exploitation of chalky, light-colored and well-lavigated clay, and extensive use of the bow rim, of ribbon handles and of incised and impressed decorations.

The state of the research into the Late Pottery Neolithic/Early Chalcolithic of the Levant is not homogenous. Although in the northern and central parts of Israel and Jordan the chronological and cultural traits are somewhat understood (e.g. Gopher and Gophna 1993), in the southern parts of Israel and Jordan the cultural sequences are still not as clearly defined.

About a decade ago, a new cultural entity, dated approximately to the early to mid-fifth millennium BC, has been classified (Gilead and Alon 1988). Based on the results from their excavations in the Besor sites, as well as those of Epstein (1984) and Gilead (1990; 1993) at site Y-3 near Tel Qatif, Gilead and Alon (1988) concluded that the new culture prevailed in the northern Negev and northern Sinai prior to the establishment of the Developed Chalcolithic Ghassulian culture. The term 'Qatifian Culture' was coined after the key site of Qatif Y-3. The dating of this cultural phase was based on a single and rather dubious ^{14}C dating of burnt bones from Qatif Y-3, yielding a date of 5052–4836 BC (calibrated,[2] Pta 2968). The assemblages are characterized by trapezoidal, elongated or elliptical axes, broad flat sickle blades, and rough pottery vessels. All the pottery is very rough in appearance, made by hand and is characterized by a dark core, due to poor firing and a high content of vegetal components in the body of clay. The majority of vessels do not bare any decoration whatsoever, but in some cases there appear bowls with a red or reddish-brown paint (Gilead and Alon 1988:115–27).

In a later publication, Gilead (1990) suggested another cultural phase for the Early Chalcolithic of the northern Negev area, which he termed as the 'Besor stage'. This chronological and cultural entity was discovered mainly in the lower Besor area, but recently also at the site of Ramot Nof near Beer-Sheva (to be discussed later). In terms of ceramic typology, this phase is characterized by jars and holemouth jars with loop handles and thick bases (the 'Beth-Pelet jars'). Another common type is the bowl with straight walls, a precursor of the 'V-shaped bowls' of the Ghassulian Chalcolithic. An additional type is the large basin with a vertical thumb decoration and a rim similar in thickness to the wall. Similar finds were reported long ago by Macdonald (1932), from sites A, B, D and M of Nahal Besor. These finds were later assigned to the Pottery Neolithic\Early Chalcolithic by Wright (1937), and later by Moore (1973:59) Gophna (1979) and Roshwalb (1981, 1987). Wright (1937:4–21, 81) attributed sites A, B, D1 and M to a 'Sub-Chalcolithic' stage, earlier than the assemblages of sites E and O in the Besor, Teleilat Ghassul and Umm Qatafa which he considered as 'Lower Chalcolithic'. In this sequence, the northern assemblages which contained Gray-Burnished Ware represented, in his view, a 'Late Chalcolithic' phase. Within the 'Sub-Chalcolithic', Wright distinguished between an earlier stage, represented by the coarse, straw-tempered pottery of sites D1 and M, and a later stage represented by the finer, sand tempered pottery of sites A, B and D2. This model is basically similar to the one suggested later by Gilead and Alon (1998) and Gilead (1990; 1994). The latter referred to the earlier cultural entity (sites D1, M and Qatif) as the 'Qatifian', and to the later (sites A, B and D2) as the 'Besorian'.

Recent excavations at the site of Ramot Nof, in the northern part of Beer-Sheva (Nahshoni *et al.* 2002), yielded more evidence for the sequence suggested by Gilead (*ibid.*). In that site, ceramic and lithic assemblage similar to that of the 'Besorian' sites of the Wadi Besor was found, together with few typical Qatifian sherds. One ^{14}C date: 4681–4464 BC (calibrated, ETH-8828/51) places the 'Besorian' phase later then the Qatifian and slightly earlier than the emergence of the Developed Chalcolithic at the site of Shiqmim (Gilead 1994).

Commenge was the first scholar to identify a Wadi Raba component to the earliest occupation at Gilat. The detailed analysis of the Gilat ceramic assemblage, carried out by Commenge *et al.* (Chapter 10, this volume), together with the controlled stratigraphy of the current excavations at the site, suggest that the initial (and perhaps main) phase of occupation at the site should be considered earlier than the 'Developed Chalcolithic' phase of the northern Negev. This is portrayed by the presence of decorations and shapes which resemble Wadi Raba traits, the abundance of the loop-handled jars and holemouth jars comparable to the so-called 'Beth-Pelet jars' of the Besor sites and Ramot Nof, as well as other attributes that are nonexistent in the well-defined Developed Chalcolithic ceramic repertoire. This new aspect, not noticed by me in the earlier stages of the study, requires a new approach of petrographic comparisons with sites that have similar typological features. The Gilat pottery cannot be treated any more as a homogenous whole. It should be separated into early and late, or at least compared with contemporaneous assemblages within the same part of the southern Levant. In this sense, the one-to-one comparison of the Gilat assemblage with the Developed Chalcolithic 'cultic' assemblages of En-Gedi and Nahal Mishmar that was done before (Goren 1995) is seemingly meaningless. Such is also the comparison with Developed Chalcolithic habitation sites such as the Beer-Sheva sites, Grar and Shiqmim.

Of the several ceramic assemblages that are comparable with the 'Besorian' or early Chalcolithic aspect of the Gilat assemblage, it was imperative to select the ones that were already thoroughly examined by us petrographically. Since at the present stage of research little work has been done on the relevant assemblages from the Besor sites (apart of site DII, to be discussed later), it was decided to concentrate on four other assemblages that were already studied to some detail:

1. *Ramot Nof*: This site was mentioned above. Besides few Qatifian sherds, most of its pottery bares typical 'Besorian' attributes (Nahshoni *et al.* in press).

2. *Sites R-48 and A-301 in northern Sinai*: These two rather small hamlets, located in north-eastern Sinai, were surveyed, surface collected and partially excavated by Oren and Gilead (1981). As the authors had noticed, certain shapes within the ceramic assemblages were comparable only with pottery of the Besor sites, especially the abundant 'Beth-Pelet jars'. In their own words: 'The Neolithic appearance of this class (of jars, Y.G.) is enhanced by large arched loop handles of oval section. The survival of such Neolithic traits into the Chalcolithic tradition is almost unknown at the Beer-Sheva sites but was noted at Teleilat Ghassul and perhaps best exemplified in the prehistoric Far°ah sites and along the lower reaches of Nahal Besor' (Oren and Gilead 1981:30). A more detailed examination of the pottery presented in the publication reveals that most of the shapes belong to the 'Besorian' sphere.

3. *Wadi Zeita*: This site is referred to by Commenge (Chapter 10, this volume). The as yet unpublished ceramic assemblage includes mainly 'Besorian' traits.

4. *Site DII*: This site represents the 'Besorian' component of the Besor sites (Gilead and Alon 1988). A preliminary publication of the petrographic examinations of the ceramic assemblage appeared a decade ago (Goren 1988). Already there it was noticed that technologically the assemblage differs from the ceramic assemblages of the Beer-Sheva sites, especially in the use of marls and crushed calcite for the 'Beth-Pelet' jars and other vessel types.

The petrographic examination of these four contemporaneous sites (Appendix B) draws a surprisingly similar picture to that of Gilat. Of the identified petrographic groups in all of these sites, a considerable amount of pottery belongs to the Moza or the Taqiya petrographic groups, indicating substantial import of ceramic vessels from Judea and the Upper Shephela regions. Also noteworthy is the relatively significant presence of Egyptian pottery, a feature that has not even a single parallel in the later Developed Chalcolithic assemblages that were extensively examined by us (Goren 1987, 1991, 1995; Goren and Gilead 1987; Gilead and Goren 1989). The presence of the Lower Cretaceous shales group is also outstanding, since in the Developed Chalcolithic sites of the northern Negev this group rarely, if ever, appears. In conclusion, 'Besorian' pottery assemblages from northeastern Sinai, the northern Negev and the lower Shephela all illustrate a petrographic situation that is similar to that of Gilat, but differs significantly from the composition of the later Developed Chalcolithic assemblages in the same area.

This new picture is intriguing and requires a new look at the origin and the evolution of the northern Negev Developed Chalcolithic. Technologically, the 'Besorian' pottery assemblages are strongly influenced by foreign regions, as opposed to the 'closed up' nature of the Developed Chalcolithic northern Negev ceramic assemblages. In this sense, the outstanding feature of the Gilat ceramic assemblage should be conceived as the common feature of a certain cultural entity, in which the site of Gilat plays a pivotal role being the richest, largest and most extensively studied site.

C. Conclusions

The renewed petrographic examination of the Gilat pottery assemblage, coupled together with the new typological data, outlines a new picture that requires some fresh interpretations. As in the case of the Yarmukian, Jericho IX and Wadi Raba cultures of central and northern Israel, the detailed petrographic study of numerous assemblages can differentiate now between the technological characteristics of ceramic complexes of the various stages within the sixth–fourth millennia BC sequence. When accompanied by typology, these attributes provide fixed categories for the definition of each stage. Table 9.1 (next page) summarizes the chrono-cultural sequence for the northern Negev and southern Jordan, as suggested in light of the latest research including the results of this study.

	5500	5000	4500	4000	3500	3000	
Northern and central Israel and Jordan	Yarmukian	Jericho IX (Lodian)	Wadi Raba (Jericho VIII)	'Proto-Ghassulian' phase		Ghassulian and Golanian cultures, Hula Ware	Early Bronze Ia
Southern Israel and Jordan	Aceramic Neolithic	Qatifian		Besorian		Developed Chalcolithic Ghassul - Beer-Sheva culture	Early Bronze Ia
Sites: southern Israel and Jordan	Nahal Issaron, Qadesh-Barnea, Biq'at 'Uvda, Wadi Fidan C	Qatif Y-3, Tell Wadi Faynan, Machtesh Gadol, Ramot Nof (early).		Gilat (early), Besor A, B, D2, M, sites R-48 and A-301 in Northern Sinai, Ramot Nof (main), Wadi Zeita (early), Tell Wadi Faynan		Abu Matar, Safadi, Hurvat Beter, Shiqmim, Grar, Besor E, O, Qatif Y-2, Nevatim, Tel Beer-Sheva, Arad V, Abu Hoff, Gilat (late), Tell Halif terrace, sites R-48 and A-301 in Northern Sinai, Kissufim Road, En-Gedi, Nahal Mishmar	Besor H, Nizanim, Tur Ikhbeina, Ashkelon, Palmahim, Wadi Fidan 4
Pottery: 'leading fossils'		Coarse, hand-made pottery, loop handles, discus bases with spiral mat impressions, no paint		'Beth-Peleh' jars, proto-cornets, hybrid bowl-cornets, straight rimmed churns, plastic decorations		V-shaped bowls, cornets, developed churns, closed-rim holemouth jars, red painted decorations	Typical EBIa shapes (not surveyed here)
Technological traits of pottery		Coarsely formed vessels regularly made of local soils with high proportions of straw temper, formation on spiral mats, local production at each site		Marly clays, calcite temper is common, many imports from Judea and the Shephela, Egyptian imports appear (though extremely rare).		Local production at each site. In the northern Negev: regularly loess soil used as clay, sieved wadi sand for inclusions. Few imports from outside the northern Negev, no Egyptian wares.	Adjustment of the raw materials to the desired vessel shape, Egyptian imports & local imitations
Calibrated ^{14}C dates		Qatif Y-3: 5206, Tell Wadi Faynan Profile B: 5292-5060		Ramot Nof: 4572, Gilat Stage III: 4338, Tell Wadi Faynan square A: 4625-4247		Shiqmim BPIII (?): 4520-4399, Shiqmim BPII: 4240-3990, Shiqmim BPI: 3941-3833, Safadi: 4288-3954, Horvat Beter: 4130-3833, Nahal Mishmar: 4243-3569 (see Gilead 1994)	

Table 9.1. Petrographic groups and the Late Neolithic–Early Bronze Ia sequence in the southern Levant.

The earliest ceramics that appear in the northern Negev belong to the Qatifian culture, which, although not represented in Gilat, is essential for our further discussion. Already in their contention about the geographical extent of the Qatifian culture, Gilead and Alon (1988: 129) suggested that pottery finds from Wadi Fidan 4 near Faynan (Hauptmann *et al*. 1985, 1987) should be included in this cultural milieu. The site yielded several pottery types reminiscent of the Besor-Qatif assemblages, but their description in the original site report is cursory and unsatisfying (*ibid*.; Hauptman *et al*. 1989). Several surface collected sherds, apparently from Tell Wadi Faynan and Wadi Fidan 4, examined later (Goren 1991), supported the impression of a close technological and typological similarity between the Faynan area and the Qatifian ceramic assemblages. Thus, the existence, in a remote region, of pottery finds with characteristics similar to those of the northwestern Negev, raised the possibility that the distribution of the Qatifian culture was indeed larger than originally suggested. A similar (though very small) assemblage from the site of Machtesh Gadol in the eastern Negev (Cohen 1986), attributed there to the Chalcolithic period provides another location between the Faynan area and the northern Negev where this culture is represented.

Recent research in Faynan suggests that the Qatifian culture, as defined by the sequences at Qatif itself, is now clearly seen as being the margins of a broader southern culture whose heartland can now be clearly demonstrated to have its origins in southern Jordan. In the northern Negev the Qatifian culture appears after a very long sequence of Pre-pottery and Aceramic Neolithic. At the same time, it appears to be largely unrelated to the northern Neolithic developments, namely the Yarmukian, Jericho IX, and Wadi Raba cultures, in most of its characteristics (largely pottery, but also lithics and architecture where applicable). On the other hand, the Qatifian pottery of the Negev looks very similar to the Faynan area ceramics. In Faynan this pottery repertoire appears to span the entire Pottery Neolithic through the Early Bronze Age, as is seen from excavation of sites in the region, especially Wadi Fidan 4 (Adams and Genz 1994; R.B. Adams, M. Najjar, H. Genz and T.E. Levy, pers. comm.).[3] It is possible to draw the conclusion that the relatedness of the ceramic traditions of Qatif and Faynan are not coincidental, but rather that the Qatifian culture represents a western penetration of the local 'Feinanian' culture which occurred in the fifth millennium BC, perhaps as a result of the trade in exotic minerals (malachite, chrysocolla), many of which have been found in the Qatifian sites of the northern Negev.

At Faynan there is no evidence to date of a genuine Ghassulian Chalcolithic culture, while in the northern Negev there seems to be a local evolution of the later Besorian culture which develops towards the Beer-Sheva pattern of the Ghassulian culture. These facts seem to be indicative that there is a clear dichotomy between the development of the south Jordanian 'Feinanian' culture, which remained pure in the core area of Faynan itself well into the terminal fourth millennium and the EBI, and the entities which occurred in the northern Negev after the cease of the Qatifian-Feinanian episode. The Besorian entity, with its clear Judean–Shephela orientation in terms of ceramic provenance, may be considered a pioneering stage in which a Proto-Ghassulian element from these regions settled along the Nahal Patish and lower Nahal Besor and established a large center at Gilat, where cultic activities took place. This entity maintained contacts with its source area, as well as weaker relations with affiliated groups in remoter areas (like Teleilat Ghassul), then gradually crystallized to form the rather closed, well-defined 'Beer-Sheva Culture' of the Developed Chalcolithic. Still at this stage, ritual activities were performed at the site of Gilat but the importation of goods was now restricted to non-ceramic artifacts.

This diffusionistic interpretation of the development of the Chalcolithic cultures of southern Israel still needs to be tested by further research. First and foremost, though the petrographic data strongly suggests that Gilat and other 'Besorian' sites were strongly associated with late Wadi Raba entities in central Israel (the Judean Mountains and the Shephela), the research of the latter have yielded little if any evidence about the nature of contemporaneous sites within them. Enigmatic features, like the uniqueness of the Gilat torpedo jars in Gilat as opposed to their suggested provenance from the Shephela, the Judean Mountains and even Teleilat Ghassul or its area, need to be further investigated in order to tie the ends of the theories suggested here. Therefore, only future research will yield more information that may shed light on these unsolved problems.

Appendix A. Inventory of the Gilat petrographic thin-sections

No	Type	Art. No.	Matrix	Inclusions	Comments
1	Urn, large	1044	Loess	Chalk sand	
2	Jar	1086	Moza clay	Dolomitic sand	with limestone, dolomite, *terra rosa* mixed in matrix
3	Churn	110-CH	Taqiya	Crushed calcite	
4	Cornet	110-CO	Moza clay	Calcareous sand	
5	Varia	111-CO	Moza clay	Calcareous sand	
6	Varia	112-CO	Taqiya	Calcareous sand	
7	Jar, bi-convex	1135	Moza clay	Crushed calcite	
8	Urn, large	1269	Taqiya	Crushed calcite	
9	Churn, small	1397	Taqiya	Chalk sand	
10	Torpedo	1505	Moza clay	Dolomitic sand + quartz	
11	Torpedo	1509	Moza marl	Limestone + chert	
12	Urn, large	1536	Taqiya	Chalk sand	
13	Basin	1-BA	Taqiya	Quartz, limestone, chert + *kurkar* sand	
14	Pedast. bowl	212-IN	Moza marl	Crushed calcite	
15	Basin	229-BA	Moza marl	Calcareous + quartz sand	
16	Basin	232-BA	Moza clay	Calcareous + quartz sand	
17	Varia	233-CO	Rendzina	Chalk sand	
18	Churn	236-CH	Taqiya	Calcareous sand	
19	Varia	236-CO	Taqiya	Chalk sand	
20	Churn	2557	Moza clay	Calcareous sand	
21	Body sherd	25-BS	Taqiya	Calcareous sand	
22	Pot	2656	Loess	Quartz + chalk sand	
23	Beaker, globular	2682			
24	Pedast. bowl	26-IN	Loess	Quartz sand	
25	Bowl, tulip	2893	Taqiya	Chalk + quartz	
26	Holem. jar	309-HO	Taqiya	Quartz, calcareous + chert sand	
27	Basin	312-BA	Taqiya	Crushed calcite	
28	Varia	312-CO	Taqiya	Crushed calcite	
29	Cornet	314-CO	Loess	Quartz sand	
30	Holem. jar	329-HO	Taqiya	Crushed calcite	
31	Body sherd	339-BS	Taqiya	Calcareous sand	
32	Holem. jar	343-HO	Moza marl	Crushed calcite + some dolomitic sand	
33	Bowl, tulip (conical)	3456	Taqiya	Limestone + quartz sand	
34	Bowl	347-BO	Loess	Quartz, calcareous + chert sand	
35	Bowl, ring-base tulip	3528	Moza marl	Limestone, chert + quartz sand	
36	Basin	361-BA	Moza marl	Calcareous sand	
37	Holem. jar	361-HO	Moza clay	Crushed calcite + limestone	
38	Holem. jar	383-HO	Moza marl	Calcareous, chert + *nari* sand	
39	Body sherd	389-BS	Nile silt	Quartz sand	
40	Holem. jar	391-HO	Moza marl	Calcareous, quartz + chert sand	
41	Holem. jar	399-HO	Taqiya	Chalk sand	
42	Holem. jar	411-HO	Taqiya	Crushed calcite	
43	Holem. jar	426-HO	(?)	Quartz, chert + *kurkar* sand	
44	Cornet	428-CO	Taqiya	Calcareous sand	

45	Jar	438-JA	Moza clay	Calcareous sand	
46	Body sherd	438-JA	Taqiya	Calcareous sand	
47	Body sherd	441-BS-1	Moza clay	Calcareous sand	
48	Body sherd	441-BS-2	Taqiya	Calcareous sand	
49	Cornet	502.11	Loess	Quartz sand	
50	Body sherd	502.3	Taqiya	Calcareous sand	
51	Body sherd	509.2	Loess	Calcareous sand	
52	Holem. jar	511.1	Loess	Quartz, chalk, chert, *nari*, travertine + kurkar sand	
53	Pedast. bowl	511.7	Loess	Quartz + chalk sand	
54	Holem. jar	512.16	Moza marl	Calcareous sand	
55	Cornet	512.18	Loess	Quartz sand	
56	Cornet	512.19	Loess	Quartz sand	
57	Body sherd	512.29	Moza clay	Dolomitic sand	
58	Bowl	512.3	Loess	Calcareous sand	
59	Churn	512.34	Moza marl	Limestone, chert + quartz sand	
60		512-17	Taqiya	Calcareous, quartz + *nari* sand	
61		512-17	Taqiya	Quartz, limestone, chalk + *nari* sand	
62	Churn	512-35	Taqiya	Crushed calcite	
63		513-35	Taqiya	Crushed calcite	
64	Pedast. bowl	514.1	Loess	Calcareous + quartz sand	
65	Cornet	517.7	Taqiya	Quartz sand	Silty matrix
66	Cornet	517.8	Loess	Quartz sand	
67	Varia	518.7	Taqiya	Calcareous sand	Limestone and chert sand temper
68	Basin	519.3	Moza marl	No temper added	
69	Body sherd	520.3	Loess	Quartz + chalk sand	
70	Torpedo	5219-CO	Moza marl	Calcareous sand	
71	Body sherd	522.15	Taqiya	Calcareous sand	
72	Body sherd	522.26	Taqiya	Calcareous sand	
73	Cornet	522.27	Loess	Quartz sand	
74	Body sherd	522.34	Loess	Quartz + chalk sand	
75	Body sherd	522.6	Loess	Quartz, chalk + kurkar sand	
76	Torpedo	522.7	Taqiya	Crushed calcite + chalk	
77	Urn, large	5222	Moza clay?	Crushed calcite + chalk	
78	Urn, large	5223	Moza clay	Crushed calcite + limestone	
79	Body sherd	524.2	Loess	Quartz + calcareous sand	
80	Torpedo	5247	Taqiya	Chalk sand	
81	Body sherd	525.1	Loess	Quartz sand	
82	Bowl	526.1	Loess	Quartz + chalk sand	
83	Beaker?	526.11	Loess	Quartz + limestone sand	
84	Body sherd	526.16	Loess	Quartz, chalk + chert sand	
85	Body sherd	526.19	Loess	Quartz + calcareous sand	
86	Holem. jar	526.3	Loess	Quartz, calcareous + chert sand	
87	Jar	529.2	Taqiya	Chalk sand	Or rendzina soil
88	Bowl	531.4	Loess	Quartz + chert sand	
89	Body sherd	533.7	Loess	Quartz sand	
90	Churn	535.12	Taqiya	Calcareous sand	Chalk sand with some crushed calcite
91	Pedast. bowl	535.17	Loess	Quartz + chalk sand	
92	Churn	535.4	Taqiya	Calcareous sand	Chalk sand temper
93	Varia	535.9	Loess	Quartz + chalk sand	
94	Bowl, tulip	5354	Moza marl	Limestone sand	
95	Cornet	536.1	Loess	Calcareous sand	Chalk and *nari* tempered
96	Bowl	536.3	Loess	Quartz sand	
97	Holem. jar	536.7	Taqiya	Calcareous + chert sand	

98	Torpedo	5382	Moza marl	Limestone sand	
99	Holem. jar	542.5	Taqiya	Quartz, calcareous + chert sand	
100	Cornet	543.14	Loess	Quartz + chalk sand	
101	Cornet	543.2	Loess	Quartz sand	
102	Body sherd	543.5	Loess	Calcareous sand	
103	Bowl, tulip	543-30	Taqiya	Quartz + limestone sand	
104	Body sherd	545.9	Moza marl	Crushed calcite	
105	Body sherd	547.1	Taqiya	Calcareous + quartz sand	
106	Holem. jar	548.1	Moza clay	Calcareous sand	
107	Basin	550.6	Loess	Quartz + calcareous sand	
108	Pedast. bowl	550.7	Loess	Quartz sand	
109	Cornet	551.1	Loess	Quartz sand	
110	Body sherd	551.14	Moza marl	Limestone + quartz sand	
111	Cornet	551.15	Loess	Quartz sand	
112	Body sherd	553.1	Loess	Quartz sand	
113	Churn	554.5	Loess	Quartz + limestone sand	
114	Holem. jar	555.3	Taqiya	Calcareous + quartz sand	Very foraminiferous matrix
115	Pedast. bowl	555.5	Loess	Quartz + calcareous sand	
116	Torpedo, small	5568	Moza marl	Limestone, chert + quartz sand	
117	Pedast. bowl	558.15	Loess	Quartz, limestone, calcite + chert sand	
118	Holem. jar	558.2	Loess	Quartz sand	
119	Jar	558.4	Loess	Quartz sand	
120	Bowl	558-10	Taqiya	Calcareous sand	Chalk and *nari* sand temper
121	Pedast. bowl	559.5	Loess	Quartz + limestone sand	
122	Torpedo	5610	Moza clay	Dolomitic sand	
123	Pot	5644	Loess	Quartz + limestone + chert sand	
124	Cornet	565.1	Loess	Quartz, calcareous + chert sand	
125	Cornet	565.1	Loess	Quartz + calcareous sand	
126	Bowl	565.16	Loess	Calcareous sand	
127	Bowl	565.3	Loess	Calcareous sand	
128	Body sherd	565.31	Loess	Quartz + chalk sand	
129	Body sherd	566.12	Loess	Quartz + chalk sand	
130	Body sherd	568.3	Rendzina soil	Limestone, *nari* + dolomite sand	
131	Body sherd	568-BS	Taqiya	Calcareous sand	
132	Varia	568-CO	Taqiya	Calcareous, quartz, *nari* + chert sand	
133	Cornet	569.1	Loess	Quartz sand	
134	Cornet	569.19	Taqiya	Calcareous sand	Nari tempered
135	Basin	570.1	Loess	Quartz + calcareous sand	
136	Bowl	571.1	Loess	Calcareous + quartz sand	
137	Beaker, medium	5713	Taqiya	Limestone sand	
138	Churn, miniature	5739	L.C. clay	Ferruginous shales, limestone	
139	Holem. jar	574.12	Loess	Quartz, chert + limestone sand	
140	Cornet	574.18	Loess	Calcareous + chert sand	
141	Cornet	574.19	Taqiya	Calcareous + chert sand	
142	Jar	574.2	Loess	Quartz sand	
143	Holem. jar	574.5	Loess	Quartz sand	
144	Bowl	580.1	Loess	Calcareous sand	
145	Body sherd	580.11	Loess	Calcareous sand	
146	Body sherd	580.27	Taqiya	Calcareous sand	Chalk and *nari* tempered
147	Body sherd	580.31	Loess	Calcareous sand	
148	Varia	582.25	Loess	Quartz sand	
149	Bowl	582.3	Loess	Quartz, limestone + chert sand	

150	Body sherd	582.31	Loess	Quartz sand	
151	Body sherd	583.5	Loess	Quartz + chalk sand	
152	Churn	586.1	Loess	Quartz + chalk sand	
153	Base, ring	589.1	Taqiya	Limestone, chert + quartz sand	
154	Body sherd	589.1	Taqiya	Calcareous sand	
155	Pedast. bowl	590.2	Loess	Calcareous sand	
156	Churn	590.6	Moza clay	Calcareous sand	Chalk and *nari* sand temper
157	Holem. jar	592.3	Loess	Quartz + calcareous sand	
158	Body sherd	593.1	Taqiya	Calcareous + chert sand	
159	Bowl	593.13	Loess	Quartz sand	
160	Bowl	593.3	Taqiya	Calcareous, quartz + chert sand	
161	Bowl	593.9	Taqiya	Calcareous sand	Spherical *nari* wadi sand + travertine
162	Varia	594.13	Loess	Quartz + chalk sand	
163	Churn	594.2	Loess	Quartz + chalk sand	
164	Churn	595.12	Moza marl	Limestone, chert + quartz sand	
165	Basin	595-19	Taqiya	Calcareous + quartz sand	
166	Basin	595-19	Taqiya	Calcareous + quartz sand	
167	Pithos	595-3			
168	Pithos	595-3	Moza marl	Limestone, chert, chalk + travertine sand	Silty matrix
169	Pithos	605-1	Loess	Chalk, quartz, calcite + kurkar sand	
170		605-1	Loess	Chalk, quartz + kurkar sand	
171		607-8	Loess	Nummolitic chalk + quartz sand	
172		607-8	Loess	Chalk + quartz sand	Nummolitic chalk
173	Basin	608.24	Loess	Quartz sand	
174	Body sherd	608.5	Taqiya	Calcareous, chert + quartz sand	
175	Cornet	608.9	Loess	Quartz + limestone sand	
176	Pithos	608-20	Rendzina soil	Calcareous + chert sand	Bone fragments
177	Pithos	608-20	Rendzina soil?	Chalk, limestone + chert sand	Bone fragments
178	Body sherd	613.22	Loess	Quartz, chert + limestone sand	
179	Holem. jar	614.1	Moza clay	Dolomitic sand	
180	Body sherd	614.4	Loess	Quartz + chalk sand	
181	Spoon	620.2	Loess	Quartz + chalk sand	
182	Cornet	622.1	Loess	Quartz sand	
183	Pedast. bowl	622.11	Loess	Quartz + *nari* sand	
184	Pedast. bowl	622.15	Loess	Quartz + calcareous sand	
185	Basin	622.19	Moza clay	Calcareous sand	
186	Bowl	622.2	Loess	Quartz sand	
187	Bowl	622.7	Loess	Quartz + limestone sand	
188	Pithos	622-16	Taqiya	Limestone, chert + quartz sand	
189	Pithos	622-16	Taqiya	Limestone, quartz + chert sand	
190	Body sherd	623.16	Loess	Calcareous + quartz sand	
191	Bowl	623.2	Loess	Quartz + limestone sand	
192	Holem. jar	623.34	Loess	Quartz + limestone sand	
193	Pithos	623-5	Moza clay	Calcareous, *nari*, quartz, chert + calcite sand	
194	Pithos	623-5	Moza clay	Chalk, limestone, chert, *nari* + quartz sand	
195	Cornet	625.4	Loess	Quartz sand	
196		626-10	Taqiya	Limestone + chert sand	
197	Varia	627.7	Loess	Quartz + calcareous sand	
198	Cornet	628.7	Loess	Quartz, calcareous sand	
199	Holem. jar	628.8	Moza clay	Calcareous, quartz + chert sand	

200	Beaker?	628.9	Moza marl	Limestone, quartz + dolomite sand	
201	Varia	641.1	Loess	Quartz + chalk sand	
202	Body sherd	643.3	Loess	Calcareous + quartz sand	
203	Bowl	644.2	Loess	Quartz + limestone sand	
204	Body sherd	651.4	Taqiya	Calcareous sand	
205	Holem. jar	664.22	Moza clay	Dolomitic sand	
206	Body sherd	674.17	Moza clay	Dolomitic sand	
207	Churn	787	Moza clay	Dolomitic sand	
208	Beaker or urn	787	Loess	Quartz, chert + chalk sand	
209	Bowl	80-BO	Taqiya	Quartz sand	
210	Body sherd	82-BS	Loess	Quartz sand	
211	Beaker, large	888-2586	Taqiya	Limestone, quartz + travertine sand	
212	Cup	8-CU	Moza clay	Calcareous, quartz + chert sand	
213	Churn	91-CH	Moza clay	Dolomitic sand	
214	Pedast. bowl	91-IN	Loess	Quartz sand	
215	Body sherd	B-619	Loess	Quartz sand	
216	Torpedo, tubular	Dog burial	L.C. shales	Limestone sand	
217	Figurine: ram with cornets	Ram	Taqiya	Quartz sand	
218	Figurine: woman with churn	Woman	Taqiya	Quartz sand	

Appendix B. Inventory of the Gilat petrographic thin-sections

Site	Reg. No.	Type	Matrix	Inclusions	Comments
Ramot Nof	2		Taqiya, silty	Chalk, nari + quartz sand	
Ramot Nof	3		Taqiya	Chalk sand	
Ramot Nof	4		Loess	Quartz + limestone sand	
Ramot Nof	5		Taqiya, silty	Limestone, chalk + nari sand, grog	
Ramot Nof	6		Moza clay	Crushed calcite	
Ramot Nof	7		Moza marl	Crushed calcite	
Ramot Nof	8		Taqiya	Limestone + chalk sand	
Ramot Nof	9		Taqiya, silty	Limestone + chalk sand	
Ramot Nof	10		Taqiya, silty	Limestone + chalk sand	
Ramot Nof	11		Taqiya, silty	Limestone + chalk sand	
Ramot Nof	13		Taqiya, silty	Limestone + chalk sand	
Ramot Nof	14		Taqiya, silty	Limestone, chalk + nari sand	
Ramot Nof	15		Taqiya, silty	Limestone, chalk + nari sand	
Ramot Nof	16		Taqiya, silty	Limestone, chalk + nari sand	
Ramot Nof	17		Taqiya, silty	Limestone, chalk + nari sand	
Ramot Nof	18		Taqiya	Crushed calcite	
Ramot Nof	19		Taqiya, silty	Limestone, chalk + nari sand	
Ramot Nof	23		Taqiya, silty	Limestone, chalk, chert + nari sand	
Ramot Nof	25		Taqiya, silty	Limestone, chalk + nari sand	
Ramot Nof	26		Taqiya, silty	Limestone, chalk, chert, quartz + nari sand	
Ramot Nof	27		Foraminiferous marl	Limestone, chalk + nari sand	
Ramot Nof	28		Moza marl	Limestone, chalk + nari sand	
Ramot Nof	30		Taqiya, silty	Limestone, chalk + nari sand	
Ramot Nof	31		Taqiya	Chalk sand	
Ramot Nof	32		Taqiya, silty	Limestone, chalk + nari sand	

Ramot Nof	33		Moza clay	Crushed calcite	
Ramot Nof	34		Taqiya, silty	Limestone, chalk + nari sand	
Ramot Nof	35		Taqiya	Limestone, chalk + nari sand	
Ramot Nof	36		Taqiya, silty	Limestone, chalk, chert + nari sand	
Ramot Nof	37		L.C. shales	Biogenetic limestone fragments	
Ramot Nof	39		Taqiya, silty	Limestone, chalk + nari sand	
Ramot Nof	42		Taqiya, silty	Limestone, chalk, + nari sand	
Ramot Nof	47		Taqiya, silty	Vegetal matter, limestone, sand	
Ramot Nof	48		Moza clay	Vegetal matter, sparitic limestone sand	
Ramot Nof	50		Taqiya, silty	Limestone, chalk, quartz + nari	
Sinai R-48	10301	Holm.jar	Loess	Limestone + quartz sand	
Sinai R-48	10316	Holm.jar	Moza marl	Crushed calcite	
Sinai R-48	10349	Holm.jar	Moza clay	Dolomitic sand + calcite	A mixture of dolomitic sand with crushed calcite.
Sinai R-48	12060	Holm.jar	Loess	Quartz sand	
Sinai R-48	12061	Holm.jar	Loess	Quartz sand + vegetal matter	
Sinai R-48	12066	Holm.jar	Loess	Quartz sand + vegetal matter	
Sinai R-48	12083	Churn	Moza clay	Crushed calcite	
Sinai R-48	12084	Churn	Loess	Limestone + quartz sand	
Sinai R-48	12085	Churn	Loess	Quartz sand + vegetal matter	
Sinai R-48	12101	Jar	Loess	Quartz sand	
Sinai R-48	12925	Churn	Nile silt	Quartz sand	Rather untypical clay!
Sinai R-48	12932	Holm.jar	L.C. shales	Quartz sand	
Sinai R-48	21217	Amphoris	Ferruginous shales	Chert	Unknown in Israel. Similar to vessels from Abydos tomb Uj.
Sinai R-48	22223	Holm.jar	Nile silt	Quartz sand + vegetal matter	
Sinai A-301	11470	Amphoris	Loess	Quartz sand	
Sinai A-301	11478	Bowl	Loess	Vegetal matter + quartz sand	A Qatifian mixture?
Sinai A-301	11486	Holm.jar	Moza marl	Limestone, chert, quartz + quartzite sand	A rather silty matrix (uncommon in this petrographic group)
Sinai A-301	11504	Bowl	Loess	Limestone + quartz sand	
Sinai A-301	11508	Bowl	Loess	Limestone + quartz sand	
Sinai A-301	11514	Jar	Moza clay	Dolomitic sand	
Sinai A-301	11524	Body sh.	Moza clay	Dolomitic sand	
Sinai A-301	11988	Cup	Nile silt	Quartz sand + vegetal matter	
Wadi Zeita	63-567	Holm.jar	Taqiya	Chalk sand	
Wadi Zeita	63-550	Bowl	Loess	Quartz + limestone sand	
Wadi Zeita	63-536	Cup	Loess	Quartz, limestone + chert sand	
Wadi Zeita	63-535	Ped.bowl	Taqiya	Chalk + nari sand	
Wadi Zeita	63-526	Cornet	Taqiya, silty	Quartz + limestone sand	
Wadi Zeita	63-524	Cornet	Taqiya, silty	No temper added	
Wadi Zeita	63-516	Churn	Taqiya	Limestone, chalk + nari sand	
Wadi Zeita	6	Cornet	Taqiya	No temper added	
Wadi Zeita	31-9	Body sh.	Loess	Limestone, chalk + quartz sand	
Wadi Zeita	101-1	Cornet	Taqiya	No temper added	
Wadi Zeita	240-3	Krater	Taqiya	Limestone, chalk + nari sand	
Wadi Zeita	242-3	Jar	Loess	Quartz + limestone sand	
Wadi Zeita	63-528	Jar	Moza clay	Crushed calcite	
Wadi Zeita	289-17	Body sh.	Moza clay	Dolomitic sand	
Wadi Zeita	63-518	Body sh.	Nile mud	Vegetal matter	Egyptian sherd
Wadi Zeita	309-1	Bowl	Taqiya	Limestone, chalk + nari sand	

Acknowledgments

The previous petrographic study of the pottery assemblages was made as part of a PhD dissertation carried out in the Hebrew University of Jerusalem, supervised by P. Goldberg and I. Gilead. The present study was made with the kind collaboration of D. Alon, T.E. Levy and C. Commenge. I wish to thank P. Nahshoni and J. Ustinova for their permit to study the pottery from Ramot Nof. The pottery from northern Sinai was studied as part of the Sinai publication project organized by the Israel Antiquities Authority. I wish to thank E.D. Oren for his permit to study the ceramics from R-48 and A-301, and Y. Yekutieli for the collaboration in selecting the samples. The present study was carried out in the Petrographic Laboratory of the Institute of Archaeology, Tel-Aviv University, with the dedicated help of N. Halperin.

Notes

1. The examinations were made in the Petrographic Laboratory of the Institute of Archaeology, Tel-Aviv University, using a Zeiss Axiolab Pol petrographic microscope.
2. Calibration following Joffe and Dessel 1995; see Chapter 16, this volume for a discussion of the Gilat dates compared with other Chalcolithic sites.
3. For an alternative view, see T.E. Levy, R.B. Adams, A.J. Witten, J. Anderson, Y. Arbel, S. Kuah, J. Moreno, A. Lo and M. Waggoner (2001) Early metallurgy, interaction, and social change: the Jabal Hamrat Fidan (Jordan) research design and 1998 archaeological survey: preliminary report. *Annual of the Department of Antiquities of Jordan* 45:1–31.

References

Alon, D., and Levy, T.E. (1989) The archaeology of cult and Chalcolithic sanctuary at Gilat, *Journal of Mediterranean Archaeology*, 2: 163–221.
— (1991) The Gilat sanctuary its centrality and influence in the southern Levant during the late 5th–early 4th millennium B.C.E. (Hebrew), *Eretz Israel*, 21: 23–36.
Arnold, D.E. (1985) *Ceramic Theory and Cultural Process.* Cambridge: Cambridge University Press.
Bar-Adon, P. (1980) *The Cave of the Treasure* (English edn). Jerusalem: Israel Exploration Society.
Bender, F. (1974) *Geology of Jordan.* Berlin-Stuttgart: Gebruder Borntraeger.
Bentor, Y.K. (1945) *Petrographic investigations of the Upper Albian - Lower Cenomanian near Jerusalem and contribution to the problem of dolomitization and quartzification*, unpublished PhD dissertation, The Hebrew University, Jerusalem.
— (1966) *The Clays of Israel.* Jerusalem: The International Clay Conference.
Burton, M., and Levy, T.E. (2001) The Chalcolithic radiocarbon record and its use in Southern Levantine archaeology. *Radiocarbon* 43: 1223–46.
Commenge-Pellerin, C. (1987) *La Poterie d'Abu Matar et de l'Ouadi Zumeili (Beershéva) au IVe millénaire avant l'ére Chrétienne.* Paris: Association Paléorient.
— (1990) *La poterie de Bir Safadi (Beershéva) au IVe millénaire avant l'ére chrétienne.* Paris: Associacion Paléorient.
Edwards, W.I., and Segnit, E.R. (1982) Pottery technology at the Chalcolithic site of Teleilat Ghassul (Jordan). *Archaeometry* 26: 69–77.
Elliot, C. (1977) The religious beliefs of the Ghassulians c. 4000–3100 BC. *Palestine Exploration Quarterly* 109: 3–25.
Epstein, C. (1978) Aspects of symbolism in Chalcolithic Palestine, in *Archaeology in the Levant, essays for Kathleen Kenyon*, edited by P.R.S. Moorey and P. Parr. Warminster: Aris and Phillips, pp. 23–35.

Franken, H.J., and Steiner, M.L. (1990) *Excavations in Jerusalem 1961–1967*, Volume II: *The Iron Age extramural quarter on the South-East Hill*. Oxford and New York: Oxford University Press.

Gilead, I. (1989) The Chalcolithic period in the Levant. *Journal of World Prehistory* 2, 397–443.

— (1990) The transition Neolithic-Chalcolithic and the Qatifian of the northern Negev and Sinai. *Levant* 22: 47–63.

Gilead, I. and Goren, Y. (1989) Petrographic analyses of fourth millennium bc pottery and stone vessels from the Northern Negev, Israel. *Bulletin of the American Schools of Oriental Research* 275: 5–14.

Gilead, I., Rosen, S. and Fabian, P. (1991) Excavations at Tell Abu-Matar (the Hatzerim neighborhood), Beer Sheva. *Journal of the Israel Prehistoric Society* 24: 173–9

Glass, J., Goren, Y., Bunimovitz, S., and Finkelstein, I. (in press) Petrographic analyses of Middle Bronze III, Late Bronze and Iron Age I pottery assemblages from Shiloh. In *Shiloh I*, edited by I. Finkelstein. Tel-Aviv University Monographs in Archaeology, Tel-Aviv: Tel-Aviv University.

Gopher, A., Sadeh. S., and Goren, Y. (1992) The pottery assemblage of Nahal Beset I: A Neolithic site in the Upper Galilee. *Israel Exploration Journal* 42: 4–16.

Goren, Y. (1987) Petrography of Chalcolithic Period Pottery Assemblages from Southern Israel (Hebrew). Unpublished MA dissertation. The Hebrew University, Jerusalem.

— (1988) A petrographic analysis of pottery from sites P14 and DII. *Journal of the Israel Prehistoric Society* 21: 131–37.

— (1991) The Beginnings of Pottery Production in Israel: Technology and Typology of Proto-Historic Pottery Assemblages (Hebrew, English summary). Unpublished PhD dissertation. The Hebrew University, Jerusalem.

— (1992) Petrographic study of the pottery assemblage from Munhata, in *The Pottery Assemblage of the Sha'ar Hagolan and Rabah Stages of Munhata (Israel)*, edited by Y. Garfinkel. Paris: Association Paléorient, pp. 329–60.

— (1995) Shrines and ceramics in Chalcolithic Israel: The view through the petrographic microscope. *Archaeometry* 37: 287–305.

Goren, Y., and Gilead, I. (1987) Petrographic analyses of pottery from Shiqmim, a preliminary report. In *Shiqmim I. Studies concerning the 4th millennium societies in the Northern Negev Desert, Israel*, edited by T.E. Levy. BAR International Series 356. Oxford: British Archaeological Reports, pp. 411–17.

Hanbury-Tenison, J.W. (1986) *The Late Chalcolithic to Early Bronze I transition in Palestine and Transjordan*. BAR International Series 311. Oxford: British Archaeological Reports.

Hauptmann, A., Weisgerber, G., and Knauf, E.A. (1985) Archaeometallurgische und bergbauarchaologische untersuchungen im Gebiet von Fenan, Wadi Arabah (Jordanien), *Der Anschnitt* 37: 163–90.

Hauptmann, A., and Weisgerber, G. (1987) Archaeometallurgical and mining-archaeological investigations in the area of Feinan, Wadi 'Arabah (Jordan). *Annal of the Department of Antiquities of Jordan* 31: 419–37.

Heskel, D.L. (1983) A model for the adoption of metallurgy in the ancient Middle East, *Current Anthropology* 24: 362–6.

Ilan, O., and Sebbane, M. (1989) Copper metallurgy, trade and the urbanisation of southern Canaan in the Chalcolithic and Early Bronze Age. In *L'urbanisation de la Palestine a l'age du Bronze ancien, bilan et perspectives des recherches actuelles*, edited by P. de Miroschedji. BAR International Series 527(i). Oxford: British Archaeological Reports, pp. 139–62.

Kempinski, A. (1987) 'Temples in the Chalcolithic and Early Bronze Age'. In *The architecture of Ancient Israel from the Prehistoric to the Persian Periods* (Hebrew), edited by H. Katzenstien, E. Netzer, A. Kempinski and R. Reich. Jerusalem: Israel Exploration Society, pp. 49–53.

Key, C.A. (1980) The trace-element composition of the copper and copper alloy artifacts of the Nahal Mishmar hoard. In *The Cave of the Treasure*, edited by P. Bar-Adon. Jerusalem: Israel Exploration Society, pp. 238–43.

Levy, T.E. (1983) The emergence of specialized pastoralism in the southern Levant, *World Archaeology* 15: 15–36.

— (1986) The Chalcolithic period. *Biblical Archaeologist* 49: 82–108.

— (1998) Cult, metallurgy and rank societies: Chalcolithic period (ca. 4500–3500 BCE). In *The Archaeology of Society in the Holy Land*, edited by T.E. Levy. London: Leicester University Press, pp. 226–44.

Levy, T.E. and Alon, D. (1987) Settlement patterns along the Nahal Beersheva-Lower Nahal Besor, models of subsistance in the northern Negev. In *Shiqmim I: Studies Concerning Chalcolithic Societies in the Northern Negev Desert, Israel*, edited by T.E. Levy. BAR International Series 356, Oxford: British Archaeological Reports, pp. 45–138.

Levy, T.E. and Menachem, N. (1987) The pottery from the Shiqmim village: topological and spatial considerations. In *Shiqmim I: Studies Concerning Chalcolithic Societies in the Northern Negev Desert, Israel*, edited by T.E. Levy. BAR International Series 356, Oxford: British Archaeological Reports, pp. 313–31.

Levy, T.E. and Shalev, S. (1989) Prehistoric metal working in the southern Levant, archaeometallurgical and social perspectives. *World Archaeology* 20: 352–72.

Maeir, A.M., Yellin, J., and Goren, Y. (1992) A re-evaluation of the red and black bowl from Parker's excavations in Jerusalem. *Oxford Journal of Archaeology* 11: 39–53.

Mimran, I. (1969) *The Geology of the Wadi Malikh Area* (Hebrew). Unpublished MSc dissertation, The Hebrew University, Jerusalem.

Moorey, P.R.S. (1988) The Chalcolithic hoard from Nahal Mishmar, Israel, in context. *World Archaeology* 20: 171–89.

Nahshoni, P. *et al.* (2002) A Chalcolithic site at Ramot Nof, Be'er Sheva. *Atiqot* (Hebrew) 43: 1–24.

Notis, M.R., Moyer, H., Branisi, M.A. and Clemens, D. (1991) A mace head from a cave in N. Seelim. *Institute for Archaeo-Metallurgical Studies* 17: 4.

Oren, E.D. and Gilead, I. (1981) Chalcolithic sites in northeastern Sinai. *Tel-Aviv* 8: 25–44.

Perrot, J. (1957) Les fouilles d'Abou Matar prés de Beershéba. *Syria* 34: 1–ff.

— (1984) Structure d'habitat, mode de la vie et environnement les villages souterrains des pastures de Beershéva dans le sud d'Israel, au IVe millenaire avant l'ere chretiénne. *Paléorient* 10: 75–92.

Porat, N. (1984) Petrography and Mineralogy of Pottery from Archaeological Sites from Southern Israel. Unpublished MSc dissertation. The Hebrew University, Jerusalem.

— (1987) Local industry of Egyptian pottery in Southern Palestine during the Early Bronze I period. *Bulletin of the Egyptological Seminar* 8: 109–29.

— (1989a) Petrography of pottery from southern Israel and Sinai. In *L'urbanisation de la Palestine a l'age du Bronze ancien, bilan et perspectives des recherches actuelles* I, edited by P. de Miroschedji. BAR International Series 527(i). Oxford: British Archaeological Reports, pp. 169–88.

— (1989b) *Composition of Pottery: Application to the Study of the Interrelations between Canaan and Egypt during the 3rd millennium B.C..* Unpublished PhD dissertation, The Hebrew University, Jerusalem.

Potaszkin, R. and Bar Avi, K. (1980) A material investigation of metal objects from the Nahal Mishmar treasure. in *The Cave of the Treasure*, edited by P. Bar-Adon. Jerusalem: Israel Exploration Society, pp. 235–37.

Rabikowitz, S. (1981) *The Soils of Israel* (Hebrew). Tel-Aviv: Hakibbutz Hameukhad.

Rosen, S. (1984) The adoption of metallurgy in the Levant: a lithic perspective. *Current Anthropology* 25: 504–505.

— (1986) The analysis of trade and craft specialization in the Chalcolithic period, comparisons from different realms of material culture. *Michmanim* 3: 21–32.

Rye, O.S. (1981) *Pottery technology, Principals and Reconstruction*. Washington: Taraxacum.

Seaton, P. (2000) Aspects of New Research at the Chalcolithic Sanctuary Precinct at Teleilat Ghassul. In *Proceedings of the First International Congress on the Archaeology of the Ancient Near East, Rome, May 18th–23rd, 1998*, edited by P. Matthiae, A. Enea, L. Peyronel, and F. Pinnock. Rome, pp. 1503–14.

Shalev, S., and Northover, P. (1987) The Chalcolithic metal and metalworking from Shiqmim. In *Shiqmim I: Studies Concerning the 4th Millennium Societies in the Northern Negev Desert, Israel*, edited by T.E. Levy, BAR International Series 356. Oxford: British Archaeological Reports, pp. 357–71

Shalev, S., Goren, Y., Levy, T.E. and Northover, J.P. (1992) A Chalcolithic mace head from the Negev, Israel: Technological aspects and cultural implications, *Archaeometry* 34: 63–71.

Shalev, S. and Northover, P. (1993) The metallurgy of the Nahal Mishmar hoard reconsidered. *Archaeometry* 35: 35–47.

Shaliv, G. (1972) The geology of the Wadi Far'ah area (Part I: geology) (Hebrew). Unpublished MSc dissertation, The Hebrew University, Jerusalem.

Shoval, S., Gaft, M., Beck, P., Kirsh, Y. and Yadin, E. (1992) The preference of monocrystalline calcite tempers upon limestone ones in preparation of Iron Age cooking pots. In *Israel Geological Society Annual Meeting*, edited by B. Polishook). Jerusalem, p. 137.

Tadmor, M. (1989) The Judaean Desert treasure from Nahal Mishmar: a Chalcolithic traders' hoard? In *Essays in ancient civilization presented to Helene J. Kantor*, edited by A. Leonard and B.B. Williams. Chicago: The Oriental Institute of the University of Chicago.

Ussishkin, D. (1971) The 'Ghassulian' temple in En-Gedi and the origin of the hoard from Nahal Mishmar, *Biblical Archaeologist* 34: 23–9.

— (1980) The Ghassulian shrine at En-Gedi. *Tel-Aviv* 7: 1–44.

10 Gilat's Ceramics:
Cognitive Dimensions of Pottery Production

Catherine Commenge

with a contribution by T.E. Levy and E. Kansa

Introduction

The richness of Gilat's material culture, and its abundant ceramics set Gilat at the edge of several worlds. Situated of the edge of the arid Negev desert, the site had important interrelations with neighboring Mediterranean areas in Judea Mountains and the rolling hills of the Shephela that provided pottery vessels and perhaps olive oil for this formative sanctuary. Gilat emerged when dairying economies took root in Levantine societies for the first time during the Chalcolithic period. Thus, while Gilat's pottery assemblage was still embedded in a 'Neolithic tradition' it reflects technical innovations that characterize the pottery made somewhat later at the well-know Beersheva Chalcolithic sites. Finally, unlike most other Chalcolithic settlement sites, the ceramic assemblage from Gilat provides evidence for the segregation and coalescence of the profane and the sacred.

Assuming Gilat's ritual function, the systemic analysis of Gilat's ceramics presented here aims to enlarge, the nature of knowledge representation embedded in Gilat's material remains. It discriminates among different factors—from conceptual and technical schemes to the organization of production, and the nature of demand and use of the vessels. In this context, the many dimensions of this pottery assemblage reflect *social production* during the late fifth–early fourth millennium BCE. As any part of the material culture, this pottery assemblage was one of the loci of transformative forces and social relations of production as well as collective representations. From this dynamic perspective, an empirical rather than theoretical approach of the ca. five tons of pottery recovered at the site has been set forth in this study. It is primarily founded on inferences drawn from the thorough study of other Chalcolithic assemblages in the Northern Negev (cf. Commenge 1987, 1990; Gilead 1995). To this extent, it also allows a wider concern for the regional context of Gilat's pottery assemblage in a diachronic perspective.

The pottery assemblage at Gilat is representative of an industry that was a result of an instrumental chain of behavioral choices and events, which can assist in identifying through techniques, scale and organization of production, the dynamics of change or the resistance to innovation that took place during the Chalcolithic period in the Negev. In framing the extent of our problematic, a number of relevant elements emerged that help outline the complexity of Gilat's pottery assemblage. Although they are crucial in determining the place of Gilat at an early stage of the Chalcolithic period, they contrast with the situation observed at Late Chalcolithic sites such Abu Matar and Safadi, that have been evaluated as primarily domestic in nature and locally made. Source characterization indicates that almost 40% of the vessels used at Gilat were made off-site but at production centers located not far away from the site (Chapter 9). Dynamic inter-regional patterns of exchange appear limited to the southern fringe of the Mediterranean zone, however, some rare vessels indicate meaningful but tenuous interrelationships with remote, long distance exchange with Transjordan and the Nile Delta. As will be shown here, against all expectations, most 'imported vessels' comprise open shapes such as bowls or basins rather than closed storage vessels, and their inventory is not restricted to only fine, ceremonial wares.

Techniques of pottery manufacture recorded at Gilat almost exhaust the range of pre-wheel techniques. It provides evidence for diverse ceramic traditions that coexisted at all pottery production centers as seen in the co-variation between different vessel shapes and different technical processes. In addition it testifies for the coexistence of different ceramic production systems both on-site and at off-site production centers. A major innovation at Gilat was the introduction and use of the wheel. However, this technique, was applied as a secondary procedure, marginally concerned the making of V-shaped bowls but is best illustrated with the making of narrow beakers.

The typological classification of Gilat's pottery identified 22 types of vessels and as such, it doubles the list of vessel types registered in the Beersheva Chalcolithic sites assemblages. Significantly, the additional identified shapes present morphological elements that limit the extent of their functionality. For example, pointed base vessels, represent almost 20% of Gilat's assemblage—in contrast with what is observed in other Chalcolithic assemblages. Additional figurative elements increase this even more. Moreover, recurrent dimensional patterns are observed for most vessels that either present a tri-modal range from small, medium and large size, or range from regular to miniature types. Lastly, the notion of fine and coarse wares usually construed as ranking modalities of utilization of vessels is, in this assemblage, thoroughly challenged.

Spatial patterns of pottery distribution observed at other Chalcolithic sites are either undifferentiated, or point to specific domestic use. At Gilat, functional and significatory roles of vessels do not appear as mutually exclusive concepts (Mahias 1993:167 and cf. Lemonnier 1983:18). Recurrent patterns show a dual clustering of vessels that divides ceremonial and domestic wares yet also suggests their complementary interactive role on the social stage at Gilat.

By emphasizing these aspects in which Gilat's pottery assemblage is anchored, this information will help determine questions relating to social context and function presented below. Formal analysis is here privileged as the surest avenue to evaluate within this assemblage, the conceptual constructs and the plausible impact of ceremonial use on its whole structure in terms of demand and consumption at the site.

Quantitative and Qualitative Inventory of the Pottery Assemblage

Contextual Evaluation

A general, objective definition of the term *assemblage* gives it as (an) 'aggregate of artifacts collected at an archaeological site'.[1] But what does an archaeological assemblage represent? It can be assumed that elements of the assemblage have some intrinsic coherence that, however distorted, discloses information and optimistically, provides evidence concerning modes of production and consumption. However, channels of inferences can only be drawn with preliminary consideration of the qualitative and quantitative features of the assemblage, taken as a sample. Here quantitative evaluation is brought together with qualitative and contextual information, primarily obtained within the site (in observing the taphonomic complexity of deposits) and between sites—in relating the assemblage to any parent population and pondering the very nature of the sites where it was collected.

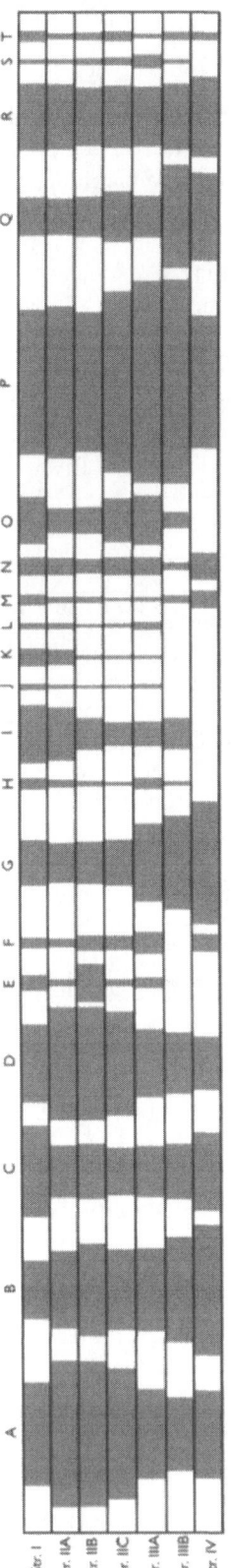

A   =   V-Shape   K   =   Cornet
B   =   Bowl   L   =   Urn
C   =   Basin   M   =   Tubular
D   =   Tulip Bowl   N   =   Fenestrated
E   =   Tulip Bowl (Ring) O   =   Pithos
F   =   Small Beaker   P   =   Holemouth
G   =   Medium Beaker   Q   =   Jar
H   =   Small Pointed-Base Beaker   R   =   Churn
I   =   Medium Pointed-Base Beaker S   =   Small Churn
J   =   Large Pointed-Base Beaker   T   =   Torpedo

Figure 10.1. Seriograph for the Gilat pottery assemblage.

Counting pots

Over five tons of pottery has been recovered at Gilat. This assemblage represents a minimal number of 10,429 diagnosed vessels, whose general inventory is presented in Table 10.1. A grand total of 11,031 vessels is more likely as some undiagnosed vessels bases complete this inventory. All fragments of pottery—229,300 sherds—have been kept and recorded. Following Cogwill (1970), it is here optimistically assumed that the large pottery assemblage of Gilat may, statistically, include examples of rare types.

Evidence for the relative contingency of taphonomy dynamics on the rate of pottery breakage must be taken into consideration at the Negev Chalcolithic sites. The index of pottery breakage in Gilat's assemblage is 20.3. As already stated for other Chalcolithic assemblages (Commenge-Pellerin 1990:4), this index, obviously simplistic, aims to provide an indication of the rate of pottery breakage that can be conveniently use for any assemblage. It does not speculate upon the life span of vessels, but it provides an *arbitrary* ratio of the number of sherds on the minimal number of individual vessels. The nature of archaeological deposits at Bir es-Safadi and Bir Abu Matar, sites that present similar underground architectural structures and stratigraphy evolution, is quite different from Gilat's (see Chapter 5, this volume). Safadi and Abu Matar respectively give indices of 16.8 and 31.9. The index of Gilat's pottery assemblage falls in-between. At Grar, a site whose taphonomic structure (and probably period of occupation) is closer to Gilat, the index of pottery fragmentation has been evaluated as 'hundreds of times higher' (Gilead 1995:142 and 197). On the one hand, the complex taphonomic structure of Gilat (Chapter 5) might not be reflected in the relatively low breakage rate of the pottery assemblage. On the other hand, the procedure of counting vessels bases similarly applied to the assemblages of Safadi, Zumeili, Abu Matar and Gilat might realistically secure a minimal number of individual vessels as pots and not rims were made and used.

The quantity of pottery recovered at Gilat is impressive. However, reconstruction of complete vessels was only possible within well-defined loci, with consideration of the site's intricate deposits. Thus, in relatively rare cases: 21% of the vessels present a complete profile against, for example, 52% at Bir es Safadi.[2] Counting bases certainly reduced the minimal number of individual vessels. to its simplest expression. This option has already been tested on other Chalcolithic assemblages (Commenge-Pellerin 1987, 1990). However simplistic, it anchors a common foundation to compare the composition of the sites respective inventories that range from heavy storage jars to fragile small beakers and pedestal vessels. Statistical and elaborated techniques (cf. Shennan 1988; Orton and Tyers 1990, 1991) offer some interesting tools in estimating the minimal number of vessels in any assemblage with regard to the completeness index of pots (Schiffer 1987:282) and/or the elaboration on the stratum of pots 'brokenness' (Orton *et al*.1993:169). However, counting bases finds its *raison d'être* within the assemblage of Gilat. Accurate diagnostics that relate rim sherds to specific vessels fails in numerous cases, such as, for example, the relation of rims to specific—either pointed, ringed or flat—bases of small beakers (see below). Moreover, in the specific context of Gilat, one cannot exclude intentional breakage of selected vessels.[3]

Bases are generally reinforced and are the better preserved parts of vessels. Other morphological elements intervene to corroborate the accuracy of bases counting in determining the minimum number of individuals in Gilat's assemblage. There include the inventory of necks of jars, necks and handles of churns, and handles of hole mouth jars. In the case of churns, the minimum number of individuals is determined by pairs of handles as their number overrates the number of bases. 37% of 229,300 fragments of pottery recovered at the site are diagnostic sherds, i.e., rims of vessel mouths, bases and other morphological secondary elements such as spouts, necks, pedestals, ring-bases or handles. Another 18% is composed of oriented fragments whose inflection and direction towards the vessel axis of revolution can be determined. Decorated fragments—this includes all types of decoration as the same pot can present different techniques of decoration or be partially or completely painted, elements that cannot be accurately diagnosed from fragments—represent over 45% of the assemblage.

With open shapes prevailing over closed shapes, Gilat's inventory of vessels seemingly follows a characteristic, recurring pattern observed at Chalcolithic sites (Table 10.1, Fig. 10.1 and Fig. 10.3 and cf. Commenge-Pellerin 1987:27, 1990:3). However, many idiosyncratic elements distinguish the Gilat ceramic inventory: the long list of small vessels, the frequency of pointed bases, the dimensional range of some open shapes, the introduction of new shapes such as torpedo jars, the outstanding number of miniature churns.

The following analysis is constructed step by step, with each particular case scrutinized in order to address the next, in an attempt to secure inferential schemes of interpretation and—partial—conclusions. The quantity and quality of the Gilat pottery assemblage provide a reasonably reliable framework for this enterprise. Analysis is achieved on large and coherent sequences. Our approach is more or less selective as sampling is securely operated on the largest and more monotonous series of vessels or rim fragments. Spatial and stratigraphic evidence offer sufficient reliability to effect contextual and chronological evaluation and to eventually test the assumed function of the site as a sanctuary. A seriation analysis of the Gilat assemblage is presented here by Kansa and Levy in Fig. 10.1.

Table 10.1. Frequency of vessels (m. n. i.) in the pottery assemblage of Gilat.

		N= 10,429 minimal number of vessel individuals (m. n. i.)	
types of vessels	m.n.i*.	% in the whole assemblage N=10429	% of m.n.i. in the open-shape category n1=6598
v-shaped bowls	1582	15.1	23.9
large bowls	992	9.5	15
basins	759	7.2	11.5
tulip-bowls	1217	11.6	18.4
Ring-based tulip-bowls	212	2	3.2
small beakers	162	1.5	2.4
medium beakers	594	5.7	9
small pointed-base beakers	88	0.8	1.3
med. pointed-base beakers	502	4.8	7.6
large pointed-base beakers	47	0.4	0.7
cornets	112	1	1.6
tubular goblets	73	0.7	1.1
urns	58	0.5	0.8
pedestalled bowls	200	1.9	3
n1: total of open shapes =	6598	n1/N= 62, 7%	-
types of vessels	m. n. i*	% in the whole assemblage N=10429	% of m. n. i. in the closed-shape category n2= 3831
pithoi	429	4.1	11.1
hole mouth jars	1943	18.6	50.7
necked jars	527	5	13.7
churns	765	7.3	19.9
miniature churns	71	0.6	1.8
torpedoes	96	0.9	2.5
n2: total of closed shapes =	3831	n2/N=36, 5%	-
Total (n1+n2)= N	N=10429		

*m. n. i: = minimal number of individuals. 102 undiagnosed vessels' bottoms can be added to this long inventory, 39% belong to large and closed shapes, either pithoi or jars. Sub-categories that include less than fifty vessels are not listed, (for example: small, medium and large tubular beakers). Saucers and small pots comprise one dozen of individuals, mostly incomplete.

Table 10.2a. Distribution of vessels types (m. n. i.) per stratum
(see also seriograph at Fig. 10.1).

m.n.i	V-s	bowl	Bas.	TB	TBR	Bks	Bkm	PBs	PBm	PBl	Ct	Urn	Tube	FPB	total
stratum I	264	151	237	199	41	27	118	29	152	16	46	15	25	44	1364
stratum IIA	408	217	149	312	20	24	111	21	149	11	41	17	16	48	1544
stratum IIB	481	306	184	370	124	51	140	17	109	9	13	10	17	45	1876
stratum IIC	314	195	115	249	17	36	111	9	59	7	9	9	8	41	1179
strat. IIIA	87	82	51	66	10	22	77	11	25	4	3	7	3	17	465
strat. IIIB	18	26	14	15	-	-	23	1	8	-	-	-	2	2	109
stratum IV	10	15	9	6	-	2	14	-	-	-	-	-	2	3	61
Total	1582	992	759	1217	212	162	594	88	502	47	112	58	73	200	
stratum I	120	370	96	169	10	27	792								
stratum IIA	68	421	103	180	12	17	801								
stratum IIB	85	458	130	187	18	24	902								
stratum IIC	104	431	122	146	17	21	841								
strat. IIIA	48	198	41	58	13	4	362								
strat. IIIB	4	50	25	16	1	2	98								
stratum IV	-	15	10	9	-	1	35								
Total	429	1943	527	765	71	96	MNI=10429								

Table 10.2b. Distribution of vessels types (m. n. i.) per stratum
(see also seriograph at Fig. 10.1).

M.N.I															Total
stratum I	264	151	237	199	41	27	118	29	152	16	46	15	25	44	1364
stratum IIA	408	217	149	312	20	24	111	21	149	11	41	17	16	48	1544
stratum IIB	481	306	184	370	124	51	140	17	109	9	13	10	17	45	1876
stratum IIC	314	195	115	249	17	36	111	9	59	7	9	9	8	41	1179
strat. IIIA	87	82	51	66	10	22	77	11	25	4	3	7	3	17	465
strat. IIIB	18	26	14	15	-	-	23	1	8	-	-	-	2	2	109
stratum IV	10	15	9	6	-	2	14	-	-	-	-	-	2	3	61
TOTAL	1582	992	759	1217	212	162	594	88	502	47	112	58	73	200	

							Total
stratum I	120	370	96	169	10	27	792
stratum IIA	68	421	103	180	12	17	801
stratum IIB	85	458	130	187	18	24	902
stratum IIC	104	431	122	146	17	21	841
strat. IIIA	48	198	41	58	13	4	362
strat. IIIB	4	50	25	16	1	2	98
stratum IV	-	15	10	9	-	1	35
TOTAL	429	1943	527	765	71	96	MNI=10429

Table 10.3. Frequency of pottery shapes per stratum.

	I		2A		2B		2C		3A		3B		4		total	
	n=	%	n=	%	n=	%	n=	%	n=	%	n=	%	n=	%	N=	% of N (10234)
v-s bowls	37	17.3	581	27.1	654	30.5	340	15.9	14.6	6.8	31	1.4	16	0.7	2138	20.8
tulip bowls	88	16	132	24	145	26.4	127	23.1	44	8	9	1.6	3	0.5	548	5.3
ring-base tulip bowls	24	38	11	17.4	12	19	8	12.6	3	4.7	5	7.9			63	0.6
small	13		6		7		5		1		2					
large	11		5		5		3		2		3					
beakers	45	15	80	26.6	110	36.6	43	14.3	7	2.3	14	4.6	1	0.1	300	2.9
small	5		28		28		12		5		4		1			
large	40		52		82		31		2		10					
pointed-base beakers	190	31.5	171	28.4	121	20	70	11.6	38	6.3	10	1.6	2	0.3	602	5.8
small	91		80		43		33		16		6		1			
medium	53		56		47		20		12		2		1			
large	46		35		31		17		10		2					
cornets	46	43.4	41	38.5	9	8.4	7	6.6	3	2.8					106	1
tubular beakers	25	31.6	16	20.2	19	24	8	10.1	3	3.7	6	7.5	2	2.5	79	0.7
small	8		12		10		6		2		2		2			
medium	10		2		6						2					
large	7		2		3		2		1		2					
urns	15	30.6	9	18.3	10	20.4	9	18.3	6	12.2					49	0.4
pedestal vessels	72	30.7	48	20.5	46	19.6	43	18.3	20	8.5	2	0.8	3	1.2	234	2.2
large bowls	221	16	310	22.5	397	28.8	296	21.4	108	7.8	25	1.8	20	1.4	1377	13.4
basins	229	32.6	142	20.2	163	23.2	99	14.1	49	6.9	13	1.8	7	0.9	702	6.8
cups			16	41	11	28.2	12	30.7							39	0.3
cylindrical basins	8	13.5	9	15.2	21	35.6	16	27.1	2	3.3	1	1.7	2	3.3	59	0.5
pithoi	40	37.7	15	14.1	15	14.1	24	22.6	8	7.5	4	3.7			106	1
hole mouth jars	376	18.3	439	21.4	527	25.7	437	21.3	202	9.8	44	2.1	25	1.2	2050	20
jars	176	20.7	156	18.3	200	23.5	202	23.7	81	9.5	25	2.9	10	1.1	850	8.3
churns	169	22.1	180	23.6	187	24.5	146	19.1	58	7.6	16	2	9	1.1	765	7.4
small churns	10	14	12	16.9	18	25.3	17	23.9	13	18.3	1	1.4			71	0.6
torpedoes	27	28.1	17	17.7	24	25	21	21.8	4	4.1	2	2	1	1	96	0.9
Grand total	2131		2385		2689		1925		795		208		101		N=10234	

* Subcategories of less than fifty vessels are not listed (for example, small, medium and large tubular beakers). In some under-represented typological categories (saucers and pots) the m.n.i. is liable.

Pottery Making—from Sources to Production

A composite nature characterizes this pottery assemblage, as tradition and innovation in technical procedures, off-site and on-site centers of production, domestic and ceremonial vessels merge to reflect its place at the interface of the Late Neolithic and Chalcolithic periods. The socioeconomic framework of ceramic production, the identification of technological systems and the degree of specialization need to be documented as the emergence of complex societies in the northern Negev sets Gilat at the threshold of major innovations that include the advent of the secondary products revolution, metallurgy and the use of the potter's wheel.

These perspectives are explored for this assemblage and fundamentally understood as social production. In an anthropological perspective, physical efficiency, technical features and processes are systems of meaning (Lemonnier 1986, 1993) as techniques cannot be reduced to a group of constraints (Van der Leeuw 1993). The pioneer work of Balfet initiated interest in pottery making techniques in the Late Prehistory of the Southern Levant (Balfet 1962). Crucial studies have compounded the developmental, historical and social dimensions of Middle Eastern traditions in pottery technology (Vandiver 1987). Recent case studies have concerned the emergence of wheel use in the southern Levant (Roux and Courty 1997, 1998; Roux 2003). However, this latter question needs to be set within a chronological perspective that documents techno-systems in their context of production (Commenge 2002) and reconstitutes steps toward innovation as processes, as the Chalcolithic period cannot not be cloaked into a broad and immobile single—Ghassulian horizon (cf. Bourke 1997, 2001; Lovell 1999).

The study of the Gilat assemblage aims to demonstrate that the impulse toward technological development, set in the midst of ancient tradition, was fueled by social concern to supply prestigious new commodities (Renfrew 1986; Hayden 1995). Innovation, as wheel shaping was used as a secondary procedure, concerns mostly beakers, that are small vessels of restrictive use in seemingly ceremonial contexts (Stratum IIC) and that were later completely integrated into the group of ceremonial vessels (Stratum IIB). Wheel shaping also concerns, marginally, V-shaped bowls that are always found in concentrations of vessels related to domestic activities. The output of V-shape bowls may have been meant for exchange at an early phase of the Chalcolithic period, as a new manufacturing technique (wheel-shaping) may have emphasized their exotic value (Commenge 2002).

Table 10.4. Distribution of sources (%).

types	total m. n. i	sample	loess	moza	taqiya	lower Cretaceous.
V-s bowls	1582	395	89%	-	11%	-
Tulip bowls	1217	404	70%	7.2%	22.8%	-
R-B tulip b.	212	53	-	100%	-	
P-B beakers	637	260	50.1%	19.8%	30.1%	-
Beakers	756	289	48%	12%	40%	
Pedestalled bowls	200	50	91.9%	8.1%	-	-
Basins	759	190	58%	32%	10%	-
Cornets	112	40	61.2%	7.5%	31.3%	-
Tub. vessels	58	20	47%	35%	13%	5%
Goblets/urns						(1.7% of N)
Pithoi	429	130	79.6%	**	20.4%	-
Hole mouths	1943	590	79%	8.3%	12.7%	-
Necked jars	527	170	79.7%	17.6%	2.7%	-
Torpedoes	96	50	-	69%	31%	-
Churns	765	240	51.3%	27%	21.7%	-
Small churns	71	37	5.4%	-	93.6%	1
Total	9396	2882	59%	11.5%	29.5%	0.07%
Body sherds	-	53	28	6	19	-

* tubular urn from the dog burial; ** occurrences

Raw Materials

The location of sources of clay deposits, their distances to the site, modes of access and the characterization of their properties are crucial elements in documenting the conditions of pottery production. Goren presents (Chapter 9) petrographic evidence concerning the nature of this assemblage. The spatial range of inter-regional 'trade' is limited.[4] It concerns off-site, but not too distant sources, localized within a minimal radius of ca. 70 km from Gilat (Judea) and even closer in the southern Shephela. Off-site production involved vessels meant for transport such as torpedo jars and churns, yet also small open vessels and basins. Torpedoes and churns are vessels whose contents were probably meant as offerings or trade (see Burton and Levy, Appendix 1). Local production appears centralized as loessic resources are found in the vicinity of the site, at a radius that does not exceed 5 kilometers (cf. Arnold 1985:51–2). However, off-site ceramic-products primarily involve types of vessels already produced locally at Gilat. Thus, *demand*, documented by specific modes of consumption, is central in our understanding of the assemblage of Gilat.

Sample. Petrography was used to identify the materials and locate their sources. Goren had under-taken a previous, random investigation (Goren 1995) of samples selected from the Gilat excava-tions. For the current study, additional samples were added and the results are presented in Chapter 9 (this volume). The new petrographic sample is larger and comprises vessels from all the excavated areas and strata. This sample includes all categories of vessels found in the ceramic assemblage (Chapter 9 and Table 10.4).

Distribution of clay matrices in the assemblage. The utilization of sources varies according to distance range from Gilat. Local resources of loess were primarily exploited (59%). Taqya sources, most probably located in the Upper Shephela at a distance of over 25 km from Gilat, comprise 29.5% of the assemblage, whereas Moza sources, probably located in the Judean mountains ridge, comprise 11.5%. This latter location, favored by Goren, seems corroborated by evidence issued from the site of Titorah at Modi'in, near Jerusalem, that provided one torpedo jar and small jars similar to Gilat (Lass pers.com). Besides Gilat, where torpedo vessels are common, to date, the only other locales where they have been recorded are at Titorah, and at the Chalcolithic site of Wadi Zumeili, located upstream from Gilat on the Nahal Patish. Two single vessels from Gilat and seemingly used in ceremonial activities (see below), include a cylindrical vessel found with a dog burial (Levy 1992) and one rare miniature churn are made from Lower Cretaceous clays—both probably from the lower Jordan Valley. Evidence for a few Egyptian, Nile Delta sherds has been commented on elsewhere (Commenge 2002). Thus, petrography is a key tool for identifying exchange patterns.

On the one hand, the nature of demand indicates contrasting patterns with dispersed clay sources and production centers for, in most cases, similar types of vessels. On the other hand typo-logical evidence and patterns of distribution (see below) converge to underline two main groups of vessels, that are respectively confined to either domestic or ceremonial activities. Modalities of use clearly prevail over manufacturing differences based on coarse and fine wares, as a majority of ceremonial vessels can be ascribed to a fine ware group (cornets, tulip bowls, pointed-base beaker). On the other hand, torpedo jars and urns for example, share similar patterns of spatial distribution, as fine wares but are made of coarse ware (see below).

Loessial clays were used to make almost all vessel categories in the Gilat ceramic assemblage. In general, loessial clays were exploited for either domestic or ceremonial vessels but in different proportions. For domestic vessels, the use of loessial clays ranges from 89% (basins) to 51.3% (churns). Some ceremonial vessels made locally are either over-represented (pedestalled vessels) or under-represented (miniature churns: 5.4%). The exploitation of loessial clay sources for making other ceremonial vessels ranges from 70% to 47%. 82% as seen in the large pointed-base beakers (93% of the cornets and almost 100% of the tulip bowls are made from local, fine white clay referred to as 'cream ware' by Ruth Amiran (Amiran 1955).

Taqya sources, located at a medium range distance, were seemingly exploited for the production of either domestic or ceremonial vessels, whose inventory, to the notable exception of tubular goblets, pedestalled bowls and torpedoes, duplicate those observed for loessial clays. Vessels meant for domestic activities (basins, holemouth jars, churns and necked jars) are moderately represented with percentages that range from 32% to 12.7%. The situation for ceremonial vessels is, as for loessial sources, highly contrasted, with a production that comprises over 90% of the miniature churns, 40% of the beakers and 30% of the pointed-base beakers, cornets, and torpedoes.

Moza sources, the most distant sources from Gilat (besides the lower Jordan valley and Delta sources that are poorly represented), still comprise a large inventory of either domestic or ceremo-nial vessels. Basins, churns and necked jars are moderately but still well represented (32% to 17%). Again the situation is contrasted for ceremonial vessels. Ring-based tulip bowls are exclusively made from Moza clay, as torpedo vessels are largely represented (69%). The representation of other ceremonial vessels ranges from 19.8% to 7.2%, with urns reaching as large as 35%.

A different situation characterizes some categories of ceremonial vessels as pedestalled bowls and chalices are mostly made from local loessial local clays (91.9%) and of ring-based tulip bowls and torpedo jars are all produced at off-site production centers. Moreover, the distribution of vessels (meant either for domestic or ceremonial activities) issued from off-site production centers favored either Moza or Taqiya sources areas. 'Upstream' patterns of specialization and 'downstream' patterns of demand intervene to compose the structure and more specifically the nature of exchange. The nature of production and its degree of specialization may be scrutinized by evaluating the technical input involved at each production center, as a plausible discriminative component.

Pottery manufacturing techniques

Manufacturing techniques in the assemblage of Gilat pertain from different conceptions of pottery making by the Chalcolithic potter. They illustrate different traditions of know-how, and possibly different systems of production. Vessels are shaped from a single lump of clay, pinched or coiled, thrown, or built from segmental pieces of clay, slabs, coils or strips. Some types of vessels are the result of composite techniques. The plasticity of the wet clay allows the obliteration of earlier procedures and primary or secondary procedures may not be easily identified (Rye 1981:62).

At the reduced scale of inter-regional distribution of sources and production centers, only the innovative use of the wheel as a secondary procedure of manufacturing suggests some patterns of differentiation between production centers, as more traditional techniques seem widespread with undifferentiated patterns of distribution. The structure of inter-regional production is remarkably homogenous, as similar but identifiable techniques are used at local or off-site production centers to form vessels of similar shapes.

The inventory of techniques and their distribution at production centers

Pinching-drawing. This technique is reserved to small vessels with either narrow or flaring profiles. Tubular goblets are the least elaborate of this technique. A roughly cylindrical lump of clay was drawn, perhaps first along a thumb, next around some kind of stick, then the rough-shape was stretched and thinned. The goblet was then rolled between the hands in order to perfect is cylindrical shape. The same basic process was used in the making of tulip bowls, but their construction required a high level of expertise. The stretched lump of was worked and shaped by regular paddling as the rough-shape was regularly turned, held upside down by the tapered end, until the walls were thinned to the required, extreme thinness. All the tulip bowls show a characteristic pinched, wrinkled inside base on the inside but the inner and outer surfaces of the vessels are thoroughly smoothed. With consideration of the high-skill needed for 'pinching', the molding of tulip bowls is a plausible technical alternative. Within the corpus of tulip bowls, conical vessels of regular if not standardized dimensions are so perfectly smoothed and regularly thinned that they could have been molded. The pinching-drawing technique was applied to cornets, 'with a twist'. A thin slab was thinned diagonally and rolled over. The opposite opening was then shaped and thinned. Pinching and drawing is a technique with undifferentiated patterns of distribution among local and off-site production centers.

Sequential slab building. This technique represents a resilient tradition of pottery making in the Near East. 'A common production technology, sequential slab construction was the main forming technology over a 3500 years period over a geographic range from Egypt to Pakistan, Turkey to Mesopotamia...' (Vandiver 1987:28, based on a study of 40,000 pots). Sequential slab building is easily identified on fractures that often occur between two slabs. The edge of the slab is a slightly rounded element that can be seen on the stepped fracture line (cf. Vandiver 1987:Pl. 1). In Gilat's assemblage, carinated necked jars are built with slabs. Fragmented bases evidence a two-fold slabs section (Fig. 10.2:1–3). Complete bases show, on the inside, a slightly plump, convex surface (Fig. 10.2:4). These 'cushioned' bases are also characteristic of many Palestinian Neolithic jars, more specifically from the Sha'ar Hagolan phase, at Munhata in the Jordan Valley, for example. Sequential slab construction was also used in an intricate fashion to shape high and narrow vessels, such as torpedo jars and urns. The fractured zones give evidence for complex patterns of overlapping 'walls' that pertain from different techniques applied to shape and join the slabs. Void of joints, indented patterns of overlapping slabs, ensconced between supplementary, inside and outside layers of slabs are regularly observed. Moreover, some urns and open shapes (all incomplete) with a slightly rounded bottom and a short ring-based illustrate a bandage technique. Strips of clay are added to the slab built wall, outside and sometimes inside and outside, in order to thicken the wall. Bases were shaped with one coil fashioned as a ring, then enveloped outside and inside with a sheet of clay, that gave bases their definitive shape.

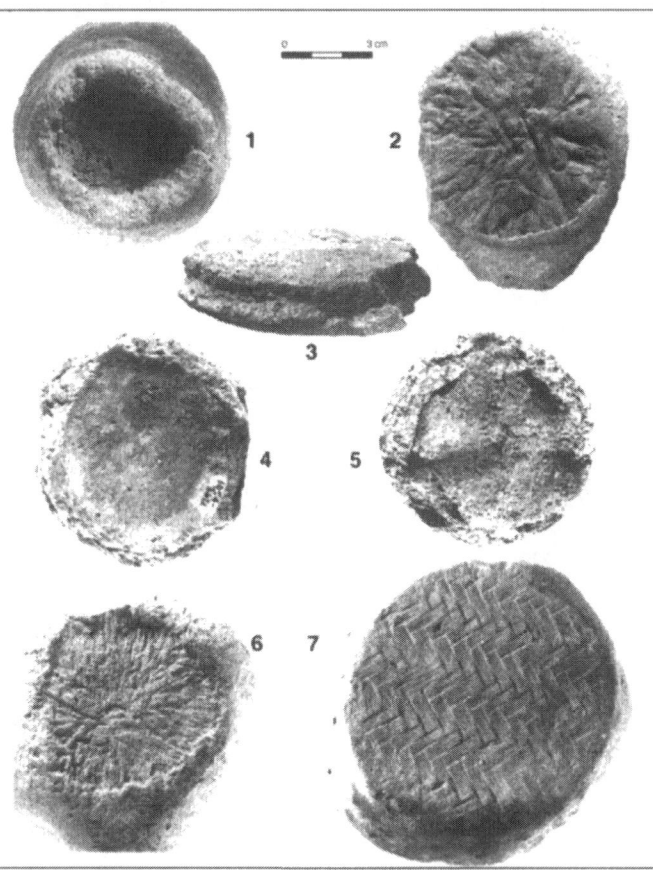

Figure 10.2. Gilat pottery bases (all viewed from the outside, 3 excepted).
1: 'triangular' deep imprint on the base of a tubular urn;
2: Vegetal(?) impression on a jar bottom;
3: base of a jar made with to slabs;
4 and 5: thick and irregular ring protruding around the bottom of jars;
6: wood or vegetal impression on the bottom of a jar;
7: woven matt impression on the bottom of a jar.

In considering the topology of manufacture, the primary and secondary procedures must be ascertained for high, narrow vessels (torpedoes and urns). The thickened, narrow bases may have first been shaped, perhaps resting inside some cylindrical hollow device or hole in the ground, used as a mold and fixing device. Reference to the manufacturing of the pointed ends of the churns may also provide evidence concerning the shaping of urns from top to bottom. The making of the tubular, open shapes may have proceed from the opening to the base, formed and closed with overlapping slabs (Plate 10.27:4–5). Similar techniques may have been used to shape pointed-base beakers. Some thick, pointed bases show an angular, flatten inside profile. It suggests that molding operated as the rough-shape was fixed to a cylindrical, flat-ended support. Molding would thus have been used as a technical step, either in positive of negative procedures, inside concave or convex devices. One base of a tubular urn shows a deep, triangular and probably deformed imprint that may give evidence for such cylindrical devices. These may also be related to the axis head of *tournettes* or wheels on which bases were affixed (Plate 10.23:1, 4–5). In the assemblage of Bir es-Safadi, for example, some bases of thrown or coiled made vessels show a similar imprint on the bases that may suggest the prevalence of devices used such as tournettes, and occasionally wheels (Fig. 10.2:6–7; Commenge-Pellerin 1991:12 and Plates II–III). Sequential slab construction also shows undifferentiated patterns of distribution at local or off-site production centers. Most carinated jars and a large majority of torpedo jars were made in Judea (Moza sources). However, tubular or flaring urns that were made, in contrasting proportions, from different production centers were all made by sequential slab construction as is one single tubular urn of Transjordan origin (Plate 27.5).

Coiling. Coiling was generally a technique that was favored to built up churns, hole mouth jars, basins, and necked jars. It is also evidenced on beakers and V-shaped bowls, either large or small, made from finely tempered clays. Churns are vessels that seemingly revolve around a horizontal axis of revolution, but are built up vertically, as jars are. The flatten end is primarily conceived as a base. The body of the jar is coiled up to the opposite end as the diameter is reduced to shape the pointed end. The last spire is left open to introduce a short coil that will was secured outside to form the handle. This closed jar is then placed horizontally, and an opening was cut through the body, at the point where the neck was fixed. Again, all vessels belonging to these different typological groups are made with similar technical procedures, at either local or off-site production centers. However, coiling is the only manufacturing technique applied to V-shaped bowls issued from off-site production centers (see below).

Throwing. In many respects, technical procedures found in the Gilat assemblage contrast with what has been observed at the Beersheva sites (Commenge-Pellerin 1987, 1990). In the Gilat assemblage, throwing is a secondary procedure applied primarily to coil-made beakers (63.4% of the beakers are thrown and this proportion is constant at any source production). The same sequential two-fold procedure is used to form 18.7% of the V-shaped bowls, in a fashion already illustrated at Abu Hamid, in the Jordan Valley (Roux and Courty 1998). The stratigraphic distribution of wheel-shaped beakers clearly insists on the increase of production during the occupational sequence at Gilat. The rate of bowls shaped on the wheel appears constant (Table 10.5a and 10.5b).

Secondary wheel shaping of beakers and bowls (Plate 10.1:1). This technical procedure underlines the importance of taking all fragments of vessels into consideration in any assemblage. 63.7% of the beakers were coiled from base up to two-thirds of their slightly flaring profile. Throwing is only applied to the rims that show a very apparent relief of 'rilling', slightly protruding off the beaker profile (Plate 10.1:1). The deep grooves of throwing may have intentionally been spared thorough smoothing, but they appear suggestive of the conditions of throwing. The thickness of the walls and the base is remarkably even, the outside angle of the base is rounded as by thorough, smooth abrasion in self-slip, as if the coiled shape was 'molded' by the hands that gave it a bilateral support on the tournette that was used as a wheel. Roux has pointed out that the smaller the diameter of the bowl, the faster the wheel would have rotated (Roux 2003:20). Thus, the rotating device involved in the partial wheel shaping of beakers may have been a highly specialized device.

The quantity of thrown V-shaped bowls in the Gilat assemblage is considerably lower than other Chalcolithic assemblages (Table 10.5a). 90% (N= 106) of the V-shaped bowls of Abu Matar and 100% (N= 1,865) in the assemblage of Bir es-Safadi were thrown (Commenge-Pellerin 1987:35; 1990:11). The use of thrown V-shaped modules to shape other types of vessels, such as large bowls or basins and even churns made from a basic module enlarged by coiling that characterize the assemblage of both Abu Matar and Safadi, do no occur at Gilat. The making of beakers, charac- terized by their narrowness, suggest that gestures, and perhaps specialized devices, involved in throwing procedures were different to those used, later, at the Beersheva sites. Evidence for one single, complete wheel proceeded V-shaped bowl that has been curiously enlarged by thorough paddling is perhaps significant but needs to find parallels in other assemblages (Plate 10.1:2). However, the bases of either beakers or V-shaped bowls give no evidence for any significant imprint of the device fixing them on the tournette, as observed in other, seemingly later assemblages (cf. Commenge-Pellerin 1990). Rare V-shaped bowls show a slightly concave bottom, sometimes partially edged by a protruding 'ring' (Plate 10.5) Thread-cut striations are observed on rare bases of V-shaped bowls (less than 0.04% of the thrown bowls at Gilat) and never on the bases of beakers. This technique is moderately documented in larger samples from other northern Negev Chalcolithic sites (Commenge-Pellerin 1990). Different patterns of regional distribution character- ize this technique. It is applied to beakers in similar proportions at local or off-site production centers. But no evidence for wheel-shaping, either as a primary or secondary procedure, has been recorded on V-shaped bowls made at off-site production centers in Judea from Taqya sources (demand for V-shaped bowls was seemingly not a concern regarding Moza sources.)

Techniques of Decoration

Techniques of decoration involved partial or total modification of the surface of vessels.[5] In the Gilat assemblage different decorative treatments were recorded that either proceeds with the application of matter, clay or paint, or alter the surface of plastic clay. These techniques are not exclusive and can be applied on the same vessel. Most were applied before firing. Burnishing and painting were aesthetical treatments applied to the surface of vessels (and sometimes combined). They are here recorded as surface types of decoration.[6]

Slip. The application of slip is a surface treatment distinct from the self-slip effect obtained by smoothing vessels with wet hands or cloth as a finishing operation. A thin fluid suspension of clay and color pigments in water coats the vessel. The slip is usually red to dark-brown red (Munsell 10R 4/6, 4/8). The coating is uneven in thickness and seems to be spread with a spongiest bundle. This slip, applied in particular on the outside of tulip bowls or large pointed-base beakers, is either mat or of a dull luster. Absence of evidence for burnishing traces on the surface of vessels, especially on the thin-walled cream ware of some tulip bowls or large pointed-base beakers may imply that luster was eventually imparted by the type of clay minerals used in slip solution. Rare examples of light brown (Munsell 7. 5YR 5/6, 5/8), thick and burnished coating of slip is found on vessels fragments that all bear delicate impressed designs, as some large pointed-base beakers (see for example Plate 10.26:5).

Paint. Paint often coats the whole surface of vessels or was used for more elaborate designs contrasting on the buff or white surface of vessels. A large majority of vessels displays painted designs, applied with a brush. Burnished painted surfaces or designs also occur and were applied in a fashion that stems from Late Neolithic traditions. Large pointed-base beakers but is also found on some large bowls, all made from local cream ware, and show thick layered and glossy red painted designs (Munsell 10R5/8, 2,5YR 5/8) that enhance the reserved bands of designs impressed on the white background. Approximately a dozen rims show evidence of burnished painting applied on the inside and outside. Slightly concave in profile, two of these rims are red burnished outside (Munsell 10R 4/6) and grey burnished inside. Oxidation of the outside may have occurred while the vessel was fired upside down—the grey inside of the pot resulting from firing reductive conditions. However, one fragment is black burnished inside out. All sherds show horizontal burnishing strokes when placed under slanting light. These painted and highly burnished rims derive from loci L.762 (Stratum IIA, fill), L.1135 (Stratum IIC, pit) and L.1351 (Stratum II C, surface).

Impressed designs. Impressed designs are made with finger tips or the blunt end of a tool on wet, soft clay. The tool, held vertically, was used to stamp discontinuous designs of varied shapes. The tip of (half) a reed or a straw may have been used for moon-shaped impressions (*lunulae*, see for example Plate 10.30:11, 14, 22). Some narrow, deep impressed lunulae may result from fingernail impressions (Plate 10.30:10). The blunt tip of a small pebble, or a bone or wood stick may also have been used for circular to oval impressions (Plates 10.10:8; 10.24:4). Tear-shape designs were made with similar tools, but the point was held obliquely and gently slid over the wet clay (Plate 10.30:4). Some impressed designs, displayed on horizontal bands, are so regular that they suggest the use of a stamp and perhaps a rolling stamp. Unfortunately, registered fragments are too small to ascertain this mode of design duplication—stamped (?), impressed designs include palmettes, horseshoe motifs or chevrons (Plates 10.30:8, 9).

Incised designs. Incised designs are made on leather-hard vessels. A sharp tool (a flint flake, a feather tip?) was used to penetrate into the surface. The edges of the incision generally bear small lumps of clay. Designs are rather stiff and linear (Plates 10.24:14; 10.30:21).

Appliqué *designs.* Molded and narrow bands of clay were fixed to the surface of vessels, in a rope-like fashion. Finger impressions run on the band (Plate 10.30:20). On some (rare) examples, the band of clay is scalloped with the blade of a tool, that was used obliquely, or the band of clay was folded to overlap finger impressions creating a scalloped effect (Plate 10.30:19).

Table 10.5a. Distribution and frequency of wheel-shaped V-shape bowls
per stratum (complete profiles, secondary procedure on the wheel).

Strata	TOTAL M. N. I.	N wheel shaped=	% thrown
III A	87	30	18.1
II C	314	109	19.6
II B	481	168	18.3
II A	408	130	18.7

Table 10.5b. Distribution and frequency of beakers with thrown rims
(complete profiles, partial wheel-shaping).

Strata	TOTAL M. N. I.	N thrown rims=	% thrown rims
III A	99	26	27
II C	147	101	68.9
II B	191	146	76.4
II A	135	110	81.3

Table 10.6. Distribution of clays and techniques.

	Loess	*Taqya*	*Moza*
Pinching	Tubular goblets	Cornets	Cornets
	Cornets	Tulip bowls	Tulip bowls
	Tulip bowls	Pointed beakers	Pointed beakers
	Pointed-beakers		
Slab construction	Urns	Urns	Urns
		Torpedoes	Torpedoes
			Carinated jars
Coiling	Beakers	Beakers	Beakers
	V-shaped bowls	V-shaped bowls	Basins
	Basins	Basins	Necked jars
	Necked jar	Necked jar	Hole mouth jars
	Hole mouth jars	Hole mouth jars	Churns
	Churns	Churns	Pedestalled bowls
	Pedestalled bowls		
Wheel shaping	Beakers	Beakers	Beakers
	V-shaped bowls	V-shaped bowls	

Production Systems and the Dynamics of Tradition and Innovation

Tradition in pottery making has been characterized by its limits defined by the choices that may not have been made (Van der Leeuw *et al.* 1991). The technical background of pottery Neolithic production systems in the southern Levant is scarcely documented by thorough investigations. To the exception of sequential slab construction, the lack of coherent contextual information on pottery making and production systems at Late Neolithic sites fail to provide an historical background to the emergence of the potter's wheel in the southern Levant. However, the assemblage of Gilat, at the interface of the Neolithic and Chalcolithic periods, gives evidence for diversified but highly compartmented production systems. Sequential slab construction, a deep-rooted tradition and widespread technique of pottery making in the Middle East, competes with coiling and pinching that are techniques that were already involved in the making of a large inventory of vessels (Table 10.6). It is certainly relevant that sequential slab construction was applied either to one single type of necked jars—carinated necked jars—that are associated with the earlier Wadi Rabah tradition or to torpedoes jars and urns that are, so far, found only in large quantities at Gilat (as two single torpedoes are reported elsewhere). As carinated necked jars anchor the assemblage of Gilat in the preceding Late Pottery Neolithic period, torpedoes and urns are 'temporary' by-products, as these vessels were not produced any more at a later phase of the Chalcolithic period. At an early phase of the Chalcolithic period, Judean production centers may have supplied Gilat with almost 70% of torpedo jars, constructed out of older traditions of slab building. This 'ephemeral' but abundant type of production also applies to beakers that were the major avenue of technical innovation in all Chalcolithic production centers.

The kinetics of innovation introduced with wheel shaping, *at an early phase of the Chalcolithic period*, as illustrated at Gilat, do not seem related to efficiency in production or to efficient rationalization of production as documented later by the throwing of modules at the Beersheva valley sites. Wheel shaping operates as a time-consuming, secondary procedure (Courty and Roux 1995; Roux and Courty 1998; Roux 2003) applied to beakers and bowls made by coiling. Coiling is a technique whose history has still to be investigated in earlier assemblages. To the difference of either sequential slab construction used for the making of large, robust closed shapes or pinching, used for the making of small, narrow open vessels, the inventory of coiled-made vessels encompass open and closed shapes of all sizes, as, in the case of churns and large pointed base beakers, they give evidence for flexibility in topological procedures. Coiling starts or ends with shaping the pointed end of the churns and beakers, and churns are first conceived with a vertical axis of revolution. Versatility that may pertain from the structural capacity of coiling to release the making of constrained forms, characterizes the category of coiled made vessels in the assemblage of Gilat. As spiraling in coiling and rotation in wheel shaping share some obvious conceptual affinity, coiling appears, in the *milieu technique* suggested by the assemblage of Gilat, as the most suitable technical system to support if not initiate innovation.

Technical constraints may have limited wheel shaping to small vessels like beakers and, marginally, V-shape bowls but the application of innovation to *individual serving sized vessels*, a category of vessels whose prominent role is emphasized by a variety of shapes used in restricted areas, may be underscored as significant of potent materialization of social identity. In the assemblage of Gilat, the inventory of individual serving sized vessels comprises a long list of ceremonial vessels. Cornets, tubular goblets, pointed-base beakers, tulip bowls and beakers are all recovered in large concentrations, in specific areas (see below). Beakers, which are small vessels meant for individual serving in ceremonial if not cultic activities, have been primarily invested with the added value of a new technology. Demand for beakers was high at Gilat, as much as 50% of the consumed beakers were supplied by off-site production centers. But a similar high demand for off-site produced urns or torpedoes jars, all meant for ceremonial, communal consumption, storage and/or transport, suggests that innovative technical in-put was not an exclusive stimulus to trade. As one can stress that the impetus for innovation may have sprang from and been promoted by religious authorities (see Chapter 15), and consumption fuelled by competition for prestige, demand for vessels issued from conservative techniques was still competitive. However, the rationale of production systems seems to encompass other categories of vessels and intricate patterns of distribution. The nature and the level of the demand, as defined by on-site patterns of consumption, have to be pondered.

*Organization, distribution and context of production.*It will be argued here that the nature of ceramic demand is closely related to the function of Gilat as a sanctuary site. Consumption of local and off-site produced ceremonial vessels *and* domestic vessels seem to fit complementary patterns of consumption, discriminated by mutually exclusive patterns of spatial distribution in the midst of Gilat's domain of cultic activities (see Chapters 15 and 16, this volume). Interaction between Gilat and other production centers may have operated at a relative small inter-regional scale, along partnerships that involved social affiliation and distance as kinship may still have been a crucial structure in developing complex societies (McGuire 1983) and as physical and social distance frequently operated as countervailing forces (Douglas and Kramer 1992).

Off-site production. At regional production centers located either in Judea or in the Upper Shephela, craft specialization seems to follow different patterns. Specialization has been defined by Costin (1991:4) as follows: *'specialization is a differentiated, regularized, permanent, and perhaps institutionalized production system in which producers depend on extra-household exchange relationships at least in part for their livelihood, and consumers depend on them for acquisition of goods they do not produce themselves'*. Distance can be considered as one discriminative factor that may explain the quantitative variations of 'exported' wares from different sources of production, but it applies only to small ceremonial vessels: cornets, beakers, pointed base beakers and tulip bowls. It is notable that the bulk of the output of Moza production center(s) primarily encompass closed shapes, storage containers meant for transport as churns, necked jars, small to medium sized hole mouth jars yet also large domestic containers (basins) or one kind of ceremonial vessel not produced elsewhere—ring-based tulip bowls. These contrasting patterns suggest that the demand for Moza by-products may have been of a different nature for each group of 'imported' by-products. High demand for small ceremonial vessels at Gilat may have been fulfilled through the channels of exchange. One cannot exclude that ceremonial, individual or communal serving sized vessels may have been brought to the site for *social exchange*, such as participation in feasting, or for any occasion (seemingly) where religious figures receive and/or bestow tribute to a selected crowd. This latter assumption may find some corroboration with basins that are large, open types of vessels. Basins are found in large concentrations in specific locations, often at the vicinity of large structures of combustion (see below). Basins are meant for short-time storage and/or communal food preparation and consumption (Commenge-Pellerin 1987, 1990). Their role as domestic vessels seems complementary to small, ceremonial and highly individualized small vessels and their spatial distribution suggest their utilization as food containers at feasting occasions. Torpedoes are narrow jars built up in apparent over-protective fashion that indicates a precious content, seemingly the actual focus of trade or tribute (see below). Production centers, either in the Shephela or in Judea, are located at the threshold of the Mediterranean zones. There is a high probability for an early trade of olive oil from production areas adjacent to the Northern Negev (see Burton and Levy, this volume) that may have been stimulated by strong demand and consumption at Gilat. Churns, generally understood as containers related to dairy by-products (see below) might have follow similar yet less intense patterns of trade as 50% of exogenous churns are almost equally traded from the two main off-site productions centers that supplied Gilat (privileged?) consumers. Exotic olive oil but also dairy by-products complementing the local, nascent exploitation of animal secondary by-products are issued from high-skilled, innovative techniques of subsistence production at this early stage of the Chalcolithic period. Carol Palmer (2002) shows a wide range of ethnographic associations between different food types, vessels and eating utensils, and ritual behaviors associated with both traditional farmers and herders in the southern Levant today that may have implications for the archaeological record at places like Gilat.

Production centers in the Shephela also supplied Gilat with large quantities of small vessels in particular cornets, pointed-base beakers and tulip bowls. The skill-laden regional technical trend for producing wheel shaped beakers may have been linked to the competitive value of other objects made from exotic materials from the Shephela, as some 40% of the beakers used at Gilat were issued from the Shephela production centers. Demand for necked jars (and their exotic contents?) made at those production centers is relatively high (21.7%). Small churns made from Taqiya clays were almost exclusively produced in the Shephela. This production-source appears to favor evocative, cultic vessels as small churns (see below) and vessels-effigies (see Chapter 15, this volume). It should be noted that, thus far, off-site production centers have not been identified, either in Judea or in the Shephela. Specialization is evaluated along terms defined by the level of demand at Gilat as counterparts for exchange stay immaterial. However, there seems little doubt that materials and objects from the Shephela were highly valued at Gilat.

Local production center(s). Three main components characterize local production. *Primo*, it duplicates a large part of the inventory of 'imported' vessels. As the *milieu technique* is fairly equivalent at all production sources, demand for exogenous vessels at Gilat reflects quantity rather than quality. Demand for churns, and probably their contents, suggests a situation of intense consumption as does demand for small open vessels. *Secundo*, the finest vessels, made of delicate cream ware are local by-products and not exotic, imported wares (pointed based beakers, cornets whose burnished and reserved, impressed designs emphasized value, yet also precious tulip bowls). So far, the archaeological record makes it impossible to establish whether Gilat, or any other northern Negev site traded 'cream ware' vessels. *Tertio*, the assemblage of Gilat gives evidence for a low output of wheel-shaped V-shaped bowls, which contrasts with the production of local wheel-shaped beakers —a type of vessels for which there was also a high demand from other inter-regional production centers. It has been suggested elsewhere that Gilat could have be one of the northern Negev possible source-production centers in trading V-shaped bowls to the Jordan Valley, at Abu Hamid, for example (Commenge 2002 and cf. Roux and Courty 1997). Time-consuming, innovative techniques might have added 'exotic' value to a type of vessels whose output was meant for long-distance trade—an assumption that might explain the low amounts of wheel-shaped, V-shaped bowls consumed locally, at Gilat, and their apparent indiscriminate spatial distribution at the site, that contrasts to the distribution patterns of other individual serving sized vessels (see below). I suspect that the output of V-shaped bowls is under-estimated, at least at the Beersheva sites (in Roux 2003, note that the extent of the excavated area disregards narrow, bowel-shaped, underground dwellings at Safadi, for example—see the introduction by Perrot in Commenge-Pellerin 1990 and Perrot 1984). On the one hand, mass-production may appear as an unsuitable, perhaps anachronistic term to define wheel shaping or later, throwing, in the context of southern Levantine late Prehistory. On the other hand, a low output of by-products that require high-skilled techniques, long apprenticeship and regular practice makes individual, occasional production improbable (Clark 1987). The modular structure of the assemblage of Safadi demonstrates that at least part of the output was re-integrated into other types of vessels as modules and may have been used to shape other types of vessels such as large bowls, basins and even churns (Commenge-Pellerin 1990). However, on the chronological horizon of the Beersheva sites, throwing was already a widespread technique that might have made long-distance trade redundant as it may have lessened the prestige value of V-shaped bowls (Commenge 2002). At all production centers, the primary stimulus and/or aim of technical innovation may have been prestige, insofar as interaction between sites were concerned, at interregional medium-distance range. As it initiated innovation at an early phase of the Chalcolithic period, the production system of Gilat emphasizes through its inventory of varied small vessels, the importance and legitimating of *individual status* as the *focus* of prestige. Apparently, wheel-shaped beakers were not integrated into the ceremonial paraphernalia before Stratum IIB. In the preceding Stratum IIC, these vessels were seemingly situated at intermediary locations, between domestic and ceremonial concentrations of vessels (see below, spatial distribution of vessels).

The production of pedestalled vessels has a number of implications. Large pedestalled vessels were almost all produced locally. Conversely, small pedestalled vessels, ring-based tulip bowls are all imported from Judean production centers. In addition majority of miniature, 'figurative', churns were imported from Upper Shephela production centers. This situation suggests control of the distribution and the consumption of high-status, ceremonial vessels, and plausibly attached specialization (Earle 1981; Brumfiel and Earle 1987; Costin 1986). The case of high value goods, such as olive oil and probably dairy by-products are types of goods with a seemingly low output at this early stage of the Chalcolithic period, suggests more than independent source production meant to meet economic needs (Brumfiel and Earle 1987). The nucleation of the production of vessels *and* goods seems probable. Whether it concerned restricted or unrestricted consumption (Costin 1991), and thus the control by the seemingly religious authorities of Gilat over interregional production is an open question. The highly discriminative and intense context of ritual consumption at Gilat may have entailed control over production and distribution, in order to secure the exclusive distribution of prestige commodities.

Petrographic evidence recorded in pottery assemblages from apparently modest Early Chalcolithic settlements like Wadi Zeita on the Nahal Patish, or site R-48 in the northern Sinai (Goren pers. com.), indicates exogenous sources for pottery production, located either in the northern Negev, the Upper Shephela or Judea. Off-site products appear to be part of the assemblage of Early Chalcolithic sites (Goren this volume), but in proportions that may suggest occasional trade. On the same chronological horizon, the demand for off-site production is remarkably amorphous in the pottery assemblage of Grar (Gilad 1995). This information tends to underline, as do the other material culture assemblages (see Chapter 15, this volume), that the nature of demand at Gilat promoted a centripetal flow of exogenous commodities. Contextual evidence of consumption will further document the nature of consumption and possibly, the nature of the intra-site and inter-site social relations involved at the sanctuary of Gilat.

The Structure of the Assemblage

This investigation aims to try and capture the integrative organization of this assemblage of vessels. The complexity of the *milieu technique* already sets this pottery production system at the interface of tradition and innovation. Beyond typo-chronological prerequisites, the conceptual space of this pottery production system, as defined by formal variation of vessel, has some intrinsic coherence that orders, divides and hybridizes several basic types of volumes and modes of decoration (Table 10.7, decoration). Morphological characters are prevalent, significant constants and variables that structure the typological grid in the pottery assemblage of Gilat. This particular structure of the pottery production system has already been identified in other Chalcolithic assemblages such as the Beersheva sites (Commenge-Pellerin 1987, 1990). Although not exhaustive, information on vessel decoration is part an assemblage structure even as an adjunct component (cf. Sackett 1990:33, 42). It is here integrated as related to the nature and the function of vessels.

To what extent do the distinctive components of this pottery assemblage provide evidence, in a functional and/or symbolic perspective, of profane and/or ceremonial consumption at Gilat? To answer this, all intra-site contextual information is explored here along with pottery assemblages from other sites that may indicate 'parent populations' for Gilat.

Typological classification

In the repertoire of the prehistoric pottery of the Southern Levant, some generic terms have been coined by different schools. As new shapes here supplement the inventory of Chalcolithic pottery, some terms have been introduced while others have been circumspectly avoided. Terms like *V-shaped bowls* or *holemouth jars* are quite evocative of the vessels they refer to and have become basic idioms in the Levantine archaeological literature. *Pithos*, is innocuous enough as a generic or specific term to single out large jars. The introduction of *beakers* fits into the broader context of Middle Eastern archaeology, where it generally refers to high and narrow open vessels, such as Susa or Nuzi beakers, (cf. Hole 1984; Kantor 1958). Numerous small vessels from Gilat can be set into this generic category. This designation applies to vessels of similar volume but of variable sizes. Its use introduces some coherence within a generic beaker category as it allows its division in sub-categories defined by secondary morphological attributes (e.g. pointed-base, lug-handles, ring base). Following Mallon and, more recently, Goren, the term goblet is reserved for small pots with no flaring profile (cf. Mallon *et al.* 1934; Goren 2002). *Krater* is a protean designation for vessels of various shapes in the very context of Greek archaeology (Yon 1981). Although it has recently been favored for some south Levantine Chalcolithic vessels that range from large basins to jars (cf. Garfinkel 1999:226–7), it is here avoided. The term *churn* is kept because it is so commonly used in the Chalcolithic literature (it is, so far, inadequate as it refers to the assumed function of spindle-shaped with necked vessels *see* Commenge-Pellerin 1987:44).

The following classification of vessels does not fulfill all the standards of a *stricto sensu* typology. Although long, the list of vessels with a complete profile does not encapsulate all the categories identified at Gilat. As an example, numerous large fragments belonging to vessels with biconvex or carinated profile have been recovered yet no complete vessel can help in reconstructing at least one reference type (see Plates 10.25; 10.26). The same goes for urn vessels, whose fragments and rims were easily identified but whose complete profile, are—with a narrow margin for inaccuracy—only reconstituted (Plates 10.27; 10.28; 10.29). The analytical framework concerns generic categories with recurrent morphological components and dimensional proportions. The broadest series of vessels, such as beakers or bowls, demonstrate that no two of them are identical, in shape, dimension or design. The category of necked jars introduces the most relevant evidence against the elaboration of rigid types. Complete necked jars show that a variety of neck shapes fit the same profile while jars of different profiles have identical necks. However, it seems prudent to define empirical sub-categories rather than types within a generic category of vessels. To facilitate summarizing the Gilat ceramic assemblage, two figures have been produced. Fig. 10.3 presents a graphic summary of the morphological structure of the Gilat ceramic assemblage illustrating both formal modules and hybrid shapes. Figure 10.4 is a graphic summary of the orientation of lug handles on the Gilat vessel assemblage.

The descriptive vocabulary used here follows standards elaborated for the morphological analysis of both Near Eastern and Mediterranean pottery (Yon 1981:176–7). Vessels are taken as volumes that revolve around a vertical axis, to the exception of 'churns' that present a horizontal axis of revolution (this last remark does not apply to churns in terms of the technical topology, see above). The profile of vessels is consequently determined by two combined shape criteria: the rectilinear, convex or concave nature of the walls, or segments of walls, from the base to the rim, and their orientation to the vertical axis, parallel, convergent or divergent.

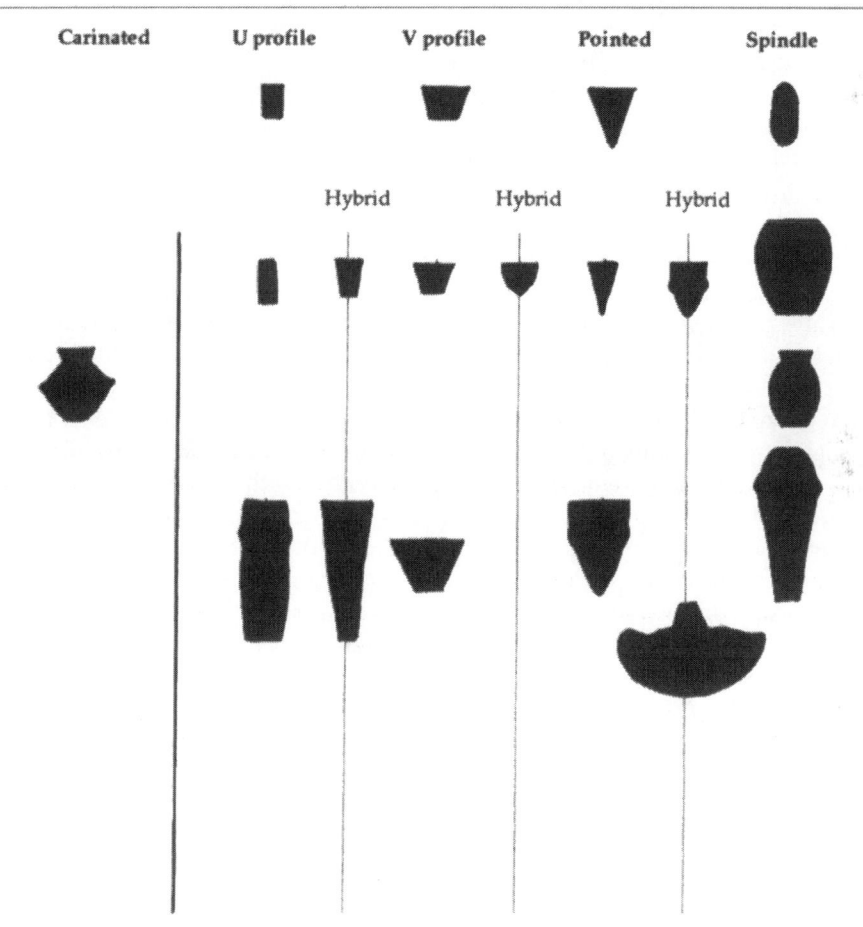

Figure 10.3 Morphological structure of the assemblage of vessels:
basic formal modules and hybrid shapes.

A. Open shapes

V-shaped bowls (Plate 10.1:1–4). V-shaped bowls have flat, circular, even bases with slightly convex flaring sides. The opening diameter ranges from 9 to 12.5 cm, the base diameter 3 to 4.2 cm and the height 6.9 to 10.5 cm. A light, uneven red slip covers the outside of 68.5% of the bowls or the inside and the outside (2.1% of complete shapes) of these vessels. In the Gilat assemblage, V-shaped bowls don't have the thin red painted band on the rim that characterizes so many bowls at other Chalcolithic sites. Red paint covers the outside and, eventually, a large band is painted around the internal rim of 15.2% of the bowls (Plate 10.5:4, 7). Designs are rare: horizontal dashes run below the rim (0.3% of the bowls, Plate 10.5:5) or lattices, designs characteristic of cornets, are painted on the outside of the bowl (0.01% of the bowls, Plate 10.5:2). Geometrical, red painted designs all derive from convex rims of bowls.

Only some of the V-shaped bowls (7.1%) present straight, flaring walls that notwithstanding discrepancy in proportions and techniques of production made them similar in profile to the Beersheva sites (Plates 10.1:1 and 10.5:1; see: Commenge-Pellerin 1987, Fig. 17:1–3; 1990, Fig. 18:1, 3, 4, 9–11). The opening diameter varies between 8.1 to 10.5 cm, the base diameter between 4.2 and 5.1 cm and the height between 6.6 and 8 cm. Only 2.3% of these V-shaped bowls are red painted, inside-out, base included (Plate 10.5:1).

Large V-shaped bowls (Plates 10.5:10; 10.6:2, 4–5, 9–10, 11. Variations in the diameter of the opening define three dimensional classes of narrow range: 15.3 to 17.2 cm, 19.7 to 21.4 cm and 22.9 to 24.8 cm. These statistical peaks refine and extend the dimensional grid established at Safadi, for example, where a large sample of bowls fits into two categories (see Commenge-Pellerin 1990:3).[7] Large V-shaped bowls have an opening diameter twice as large as their height (Fig. 10.5**:10). Large bowls have flaring, convex (54%) or straight (42.8%) walls. In contrast with large bowls in assemblages deriving from the Beersheva sites, bowls with flaring concave walls are rare (3.2%), while sinuous profiles (concave base—convex body) seem absent. Rims are thinned and rounded. Rare everted rims belong to large bowls with flaring and straight walls (less than 2% of the rims, Plate 10.6:3). Some rare rims are carinated (0.7% of the rims, Plate 10.6:6).

With reference to other southern Levantine assemblages, the frequency of decorated vessels is surprisingly high for this category of V-shaped bowls. Moreover, red painted decoration on large V-shaped bowls displays some designs that find only parallels with some small bowl decoration. 70.54% of the large bowls are decorated. They are red-painted, inside and outside (46.9%) or red painted and burnished (5.1%, see Plate 10.6:4). They are red-painted outside with a red painted, geometrical, design inside (16%). Several patterns of decoration can be recognized according to the position of the design on the bowl: multiple horizontal bands (72% of designs, Plate 10.6:12), vertical zigzags (16.3% of designs, Plate 10.6:1), and multiple pendant triangles (Plate 6:2, 9).

Impressed designs are also associated to red-painted decoration. Large bowls are red painted inside out with a row of impressed lunulae below the rim (0.02%, Fig. 10.6:10)). One complete large bowl is red painted with an incised design of vertical, elongated dashes (Plate 10.6:8). This incised design is found on 0.02% of red-painted sherds of large bowls. All carinated rims are red painted and slightly burnished.

The most remarkable design shows horizontal, alternate burnished red-brown painted bands and reserved bands of cream ware background (2.5% of the decorated large-bowls). The white-reserved band is filled up with (four) horizontal lines of small crescent-shaped impressions (*lunulae*) (Plate 10.2:1; Plate 10.5:3). As many other designs of Gilat, this type of decoration is clearly related to the Late Neolithic Wadi Rabah phase in the Southern Levant (Plate 10.30:12 and 17, and cf. Hennesey 1969, Fig. 8b:3; Kaplan 1969, Fig. 8:14; Garfinkel 1992, Fig. 139:2). Seven sherds show a thick coat of lime (?) on the outside (cf. supra). One large fragment of a large bowl, uncovered at Wadi

Zeita (Gat Govrin) presents the same crust of lime.[8] Similar lime coating has been observed on vessels from Teleilat Ghassul (Lovell 1999: Fig. 4; 1:3).

Basins (Plates 10.7, 10.8 and 10.35:4). The largest of the V-shaped vessels are basins whose opening varies between 27 to almost 43 cm (with two peaks, one at 28.2–30.5 cm and one at 40 to 42.1 cm (these latter large basins always have a thickened oblique rim). 11% are very large basins with an opening diameter between 45 and 48 cm (see Plate 10.35:4) The height of basins varies accordingly between 12 to 24 cm; the diameter of the base is between 8.5 to 13 cm. Flaring, slightly convex walls characterized 74% of the basins (Plate 10.7:1–4). The rim is rounded, everted with a flat, outward oblique ledge (Plate 10.8:6–7). Flaring, slightly concave walls are less common (7%, Plate 10.7:5). The rim is always rounded and sometimes slightly everted. 19% of the basins have convex, parallel walls (Plate 10.7:8). One complete, very large basin of this type has two vertical handles, triangular in section, that are not perfectly symmetrical (Plate 10.35:4). It presents a unique, rather sloppy red-painted design of running chevrons below the rim. The thickened, flat rim protrudes inward. It is decorated with irregular finger impressions. Diagnosed rims indicate that basin handles, as well as tubular spouts (Plate 10.8:5) are very rare. Counting two handles and one tubular spout per basin to establish a m.n.i of large basins with secondary features, one can consider that they represent only two vessels out of a total of 759 basins (0.2%). 66.4% of the basins are decorated: red painted inside and outside (31%), outside with a large band on the inner rim (12.7%), with a large band covering the outside and the inside rim (11.4%). Finger impressions creating a 'rope-like' design on either everted or carinated rim comprise 8% of the basins. 3.3% of the finger impressed designs are combined with painted decoration (Plate 10.8:2–8).

Pedestalled vessels. Only two complete pedestalled vessels were found. Numerous large fragments deriving from defined loci made it possible to identify and illustrate different types of this vessel. Many sherds were uncovered in fill context, and complement or enlarge the inventory of each category type as they exemplify details of decoration or ranges in dimensions. However, it seems prudent to leave the category of pedestalled vessels open as it is certainly more composite than in the following analysis.

Fenestrated pedestal bowls (Plates 10.9 and 10.10). Fenestrated pedestal bowls display the morphological trend to narrowness that characterizes so many profiles of vessels in Gilat's assemblage. 32% of the pedestalled vessels belong to this shape. The bowl has flaring, straight walls. The pedestal has slightly flaring, convergent straight walls with an everted base rim, meant to stabilize the stand. Two to three oblong, vertical 'windows' were cut into the pedestal. Windows are usually curved. The stand of one complete vessel shows three non-equidistant windows (Plate 10.10:3). Fenestrated pedestal bowls have a total height that varies from 17 to 20 cm, the bowl's opening diameter range from 11.2 to 13.9 cm; the pedestal is shorter than the bowl whose height varies between ca. 10.5 and 13 cm. However, some fragments show pedestal vessels of larger dimensions (Plate 10.10:1). 46% of the fenestrated pedestal bowls are red painted. The outside ridge that links the bowl to the pedestal is either sharply carinated (53.2%, Plate 10.10:3) or rounded and decorated with finger impressions in the rope-like fashion (36.3%, Plate 10.10:6), or with impressed dots (0.3%, Plate 10.10:8) or lunulae (9.9%, Fig. 10.10:1). One unique sherd with wavy impressions is orange and highly burnished, in the Wadi Rabah technique of pottery burnishing (Plate 10.10:7).

Chalices on fenestrated stem (Plate 10.9:5–8). Only fragmentary profiles can be identified. 43% of pedestal and rim sherds can be related to this shape. The chalice-shaped bowl is shallow with short, straight flaring walls. The cylindrical stand seems to be high and narrow with slightly flaring, convergent straight walls. Two symmetrically opposed curved head windows are cut in the stem. General proportions for chalices on stem can only be estimated. The shallow bowl has an opening of ca. five to ten times larger than its height; the stem is four times higher than the chalice bowl (Plate 10.9:6–7). No decoration is recorded for chalice on stem vessels.

Chalices on fenestrated bow stand (Plate 10.9:1–4). One complete vessel illustrates this category. From fragments of bases, one can estimate that 2% of the pedestalled vessels belong to bow stand chalices. The bowl is large but shallow, corollaceous, with flaring, straight walls. This type of vessel is a good illustration of the limited or confusing diagnosis that can be made from rim fragments: although the complete vessel can be used as a reference to consider that flaring rims belong to chalices, some basin rims are quite similar in shape and dimensions (Plate 10.8:2). The stand considered here represents the diagnostic part. It is a squat stand with slightly convex, parallel walls; the rim of the base is flattened or thinned (diameter: 12.7 to 15.6 cm, height: 6.4 to 7.7 cm). The most complete example indicates evidence for equal height of stand and chalice. Symmetrical and narrow circular windows are cut immediately below the top of the stand. 3.4% of the vessels with an identified profile have finger impressions on the outside of the everted rim.

Pedestalled plates. Shallow chalices or plates with flaring, convex walls represent 19% of the pedestalled vessels. 53% of them are red painted on the outside with a red painted inner rim (Plate 10.10:2 and 9).

Strainers on stem (Plate 10.10:5). A minimum number of 11 fragments of strainers on stem are recorded in the Gilat assemblage. All are thin walled and made of pinkish, rather gritty cream-ware. The perforations in the base of the bowl are very narrow and multiple. Strainers are not painted.

Tulip bowls (Plates 10.1:5–10; 10.2:7). The term tulip-shaped is coined in reference to the cup-like blossom shape of these delicate bowls. These small bowls have flaring, convex walls and a very narrow, tipped base, if any. The most delicate tulip bowls (8%) are perfectly conical; a light tip at the apex allows the bowl to stand in a precarious state of equilibrium (Plate 10.1:10). More generally, tulip bowls have an extremely narrow, pointed oval base (73%, Plate 10.1:7) or a slightly raised, protruding base (Plate 10.1:8; 19%). The opening diameter of tulip bowls varies from 8.5 to 9.2 cm, the base diameter from 0.3 to 1.1 cm, and the height from 7.3 to 8.5 cm. 79% of tulip bowls are painted red, of which 61% are also burnished (in the *luster* technique described above). The inside of some tulip bowls (12.3% of the decorated ones) is covered by a thin film of whitish slip, enhancing the pale color of the clay below; the red paint of the outside surface lines it up along the internal rim (Plate 10.1:7). The delicacy of shape and design of one fragmented bowl seems to fit it into the tulip bowls' category: a design of red-brown latticed rhombs shows off the cream-ware clay (Plate 10.2:7). Undecorated tulip bowls are extremely smoothed in a fashion that enhances the fine and light clay they are made from.

Ring-based large tulip bowls (Plate 10.2:2–5, 8). Two complete shapes illustrate this type of vessel. Their dimensions and identical features could make them twin pots, and argue rather, as do recurrent observations on identified sherds, for a trend to standardization. The bowl has convex, slightly divergent walls and a short rim that slightly narrows the opening (diameter: 17cm, height of the bowl: 13.5 cm). The rim is upright and thinned from both sides. The bowl base, conical, is set in a flattened ring that forms a short pedestal (diameter: 4 cm, height: 1.4 cm). Six small horizontal lug handles embellish the bowl. They are symmetrical and set in three—two are placed below the rim, one placed in their interval, 6 cm below. Bulging out of the convex wall of the bowl, these lugs seem to feature a face (with two eyes and one mouth) on both sides of the bowl (Plate 10.2:5). These ring-based bowls have no painted decoration. One unique fragment shows a kind of spout placed on the rim (Plate 10.2:3).

One fragment of a conical base set in a ring-based foot belongs to a tulip bowl of smaller dimensions that could be correlated to rare rim sherds of reduced diameter (6.2 to 7.3cm) (Plate 10.2:8). Similarly, one fragment with two horizontal, perforated lugs could belong to a small version of a ring-based tulip bowl (Plate 10.2:6). However, it is red painted and this more equally fits it into the 'tradition' of cornets from Teleilat Ghassul (Mallon *et al*. 1934: PL. 47:82–III)

Other ring-based, open vessels (Plate 10.2:9–11). The inventory of ring-based vessels is completed with a dozen other fragmented vessels. All have a convex bottom set on a rather cylindrical, short base. As with many types of vessels in the Gilat assemblage of large and small vessels the inside received the same smoothing as the outside of the vessels, and it is here assumed that they all belong to open shapes (Plate 10.2:9–11). One unique ring-base can belong to a very large vessel of this type (see Fig. 10.10:4). A small vessel on a ring base has convex and parallel walls (Fig. 10.2**:8); although fragmentary, this vessel also seems to find parallels with Teleilat Ghassul (Mallon *et al*. 1934, Pl. 49:95/IV; Blackman 1999).

Beakers (Plate 10.1:12–20). Beakers relate to the generic category of V-shaped vessels, coined as characteristic of the Chalcolithic period. However, they do represent a separate type that is relevant in terms of technology and chronology in the southern Levantine context. In contrast with V-shaped bowls, the height of beakers is always more important than is the opening diameter (see above Table 10.8a). It is a narrow shape, with straight, flaring walls. The flat base tends to be oval, as observed on some tulip bowls. Like many other shapes in the assemblage of Gilat, beakers range in three dimensional classes. *Small beakers* have an opening between 6 and 6.7 cm, a base between 2.1 and 2.9 cm and a height between 6.6 and 7.9 cm. They are very rare in the assemblage (less than 2% of the beakers—they are comprises with medium-sized beakers in Table 10.1). *Medium-sized beakers* have an opening between 8.1 and 8.7 cm, a base between 2.7 and 3.3 cm and a height between 9.2 and 9.4 cm (this is the most 'standardized' category). *Large beakers* have an opening between 12.2 and 14.5 cm, a base between 4.3 and 4.7 cm and a height between 10.8 and 13.3 cm. The flaring of the rim of large beakers results from different technical processes (see above; Fig. 10.1:17, 20). 39% of the beakers are decorated with a light red paint or slip, unevenly spread on the outside (small beakers 38.8%, medium-sized beakers: 39.1%, large beakers: 39%). Some beakers (0.3%) are also decorated around the base with horizontal rows of incised *lunulae* (Plate 10.24:13). One wheel-shaped beaker has two vertical lug handles symmetrically set above the base and a row of oblique impressed dots running from one lug to the other (Plate 10.24:12). One unique vertical lug is set rather low on one (fragmentary) base of a beaker (Plate 10.3:16).

Cornets (Plate 10.4). Two categories of cornets are documented, although the lack of a significant sample of complete profiles may bias this classification:
-*Elongated pointed-base cornets*, (Plate 10.4:4) comprise 56% of the cornet inventory. The long pointed base, circular in section, has a rounded tip. The base is full, with an average thickness of 2.5 cm on its upper part (height: 4.5 cm). The chalice is deep and narrow, with slightly flaring, straight walls. The rim is tapered and/or slightly flaring. Some rare chalices show slightly convex, flaring walls (Plate 10.4:6). The height of these cornets is more than four times the opening diameter.
-*Truncated pointed-base cornets* have a squat base, circular in section (height: 3.3 to 3.7 cm) with a flatten, circular tip, sometimes crooked (Plate 10.4:14, 16–17).
A large majority of cornet rims (91%) have an opening diameter comprises between 8.9 and 9.6 cm. Smaller cornets have a diameter that averages 5 cm. This suggests that cornets at Gilat come in two sizes like the cornets in the assemblage of Grar (Gilead 1995: Fig. 4.9:1–2; 14–15). Cornets with a corollaceous, flaring upper part, seem absent at Gilat (see Commenge-Pellerin 1990: Fig. 36:6).

However fragmentary, the Gilat cornets are all decorated. The bases of each type are always red painted. Fragments of rims are often more decorated, although the fragility of the ware has scattered them to minute pieces across the site. They display multiple chevrons or hatched triangles below the rim, always underlined by several horizontal lines. A large painted band decorates the inside of the rim. Geometric painted design decorate the inside of many cornets (Plate 10.4:8); reserved bands of the cream ware background are impressed with lines of delicate, vertical dashes

(10.7%, Plate 10.4:11). Some fragmentary, red-painted cornets have horizontal, twin lugs, symmetrically opposed below the rim,[9] in a fashion illustrated at Teleilat Ghassul (at Gilat—Plates 10.3:10; Plate 10.13, cf. Mallon *et al.* 1934, Pl. 47:82/III, Koeppel *et al.* 1940, Fig. 76:21).

Pointed-base beakers (Plates 10.3:1–5; 10.25; 10.26). Pointed base beakers have convex and divergent walls up to mid-profile, straight and parallel till the rounded and slightly tapering rim. Two symmetric vertical lug-handles are set above mid-profile. These lug handles are rounded—the section is roughly circular or semi-circular, the profile semi-circular—or elongated—the section and profile are triangular-. This last type belongs to the large pointed base beakers: the profile of the lug handle elegantly follows the profile of the beaker (No. 787.2). All lug handles actually fit the Chalcolithic fashion of ear lug handles (*anses oreillettes*). The conical base is rounded or finely pointed, light and hollow or heavy and full. This last type of bases has either rounded or flat inner bottoms (Plate 10.3:2, 4).

Three main dimensional categories of pointed-base beakers are identified: *Small pointed base beakers* have an opening between 4.9 to 5.7 cm and a height between 9.9 to 10.5 cm. Miniature pointed-base beakers are exceptional (M.n.i: 5, Plate 10.3:5). *Medium-size pointed base beakers* have an opening between 8.1 to 11 cm and a height between 13.7 to 15.1 cm. *Large pointed base beakers* are either globular (44.6%) or elongated (55.4%)(Plates 10.25; 10.26). While no complete profile is preserved, one can reconstruct *globular pointed-base beakers* with convex and parallel wall, maximal diameter at mid-profile and a rather squat pointed base, sometimes flattened at the tip (Plates 10.25:2, 4; 10.26:5). The opening is slightly smaller than the maximal diameter. The total height of the beaker can be estimated as twice the opening diameter. Numerous large fragments allow an estimation of 12.1 to 15.4 cm for the opening and a height of 22 to 28 cm. Vertical lug handles and more frequently twin lug handles (82%) are set slightly above the maximal diameter of the beaker. One unique, over-sized globular beaker (opening: 20 cm see Plate 10.25:1) has large, vertical lug handles placed rather low on the profile. All globular beakers are slipped and burnished, and among those 62% are decorated with a double row of impressed *lunulae* that runs around mid-profile and on the handles lower part (Plates 10.25:4; 10.26:5). *Elongated pointed base beakers* have parallel, slightly convex walls. The rim is rounded and in some cases, upright. The maximal diameter is slightly above mid-profile. Vertical, single lug handles, triangular in profile and section, are symmetrically opposed in the upper part of the beaker (Plate 10.26:1–2). Loop handles, circular in section, are the exception (see Plate 10.27:6). The opening of the beakers is between 9.4 and 11.6 cm, its maximal diameter is slightly larger (12 to 14 cm). The height of the beakers can be estimated between 27 and 36 cm (more than three times the opening diameter). All elongated beakers are red painted or slipped and burnished. 65.7% bear impressed designs. Most are lunulae but some beakers exhibit delicate impressions of stamped palmettes (2.1% of impressed designs, Fig. 10.26:4). Both designs are also found in the cream-ware reserved technique (on 6.4% of beakers). In the whole assemblage, only one sherd shows some linear designs with black paint (No. 553.3, not illustrated). Underrepresented in the inventory of Gilat are large, perhaps pointed base beakers, with convex, slightly flaring walls (see Plate 10.29:1). Some beakers present an everted, almost horizontal rim (Plate 10.29:6). More remarkable are rims with an inner short ledge (Plate 10.29:2, 4). One can suggest that at least two ledges were symmetrically set below the inner rim in a fashion already proposed for some deep basins at Safadi (Commenge-Pellerin 1990, Fig. 31:1–5).

Tubular goblets (Plate 10.3:11–15, 17–21). These cylindrical and narrow goblets are, in equal proportion, either crudely made or well shaped on the tournette (Plate 10.3:17, 19 and 10.2:1). Tubular goblets have a flat base and parallel, straight walls. The rim is slightly flaring. 58% of goblets have a heavy, thick base probably meant to secure a better balance for standing goblets. Its height averages 25% of the goblet's total height (Plate 10.3:18, 21). Two sizes of tubular goblets can be determined from complete shapes and fragments. However, they all fit the category of small, vessels. The smallest tubular goblets (24%) have an opening diameter of 3 to 3.4 cm, a base diameter of 2.4 to 2.7 cm and a height of 8 to 8.8cm high (Plate 10.3:20). The largest tubular goblets have an opening diameter of 5.2 to 5.6 cm, a base diameter of 3.4 to 3.8 cm, and height of 9 to 9.6 cm (Plate 10.3:11, 19). Some tubular goblets are unusually tall and narrow (Plate 10.3:21) or larger than average (Plate 10.3:15). Tubular goblets are never decorated.

Tubular Urns (Plates 10.27:2–5; 7–8; 10.28; 10.29:1–3, 6–7). This category of narrow, deep, almost cylindrical vessels also borders the line between open and closed shapes. To the difference of the open-shaped vessels described above, only large containers can be listed in the inventory of urns. However, as many vessels listed above, high, thickened narrow bases are here the rule. Two sub-categories of urns are identified: *Flaring urns*—92% of tubular urns are *flaring urns,* tall and narrow containers, with a high thickened base and slightly flaring walls. The walls are thick (2.5 to 3.2 cm). The rim is rounded (Plate 10.28:1) rounded and everted (Plate 10.28:2, 6), or thinned and everted (Plate 10.28:5). The opening diameter is between 15.4 and 18.3 cm, the estimated height is between 42cm to more than 50 cm. Thick lug handles, sub-triangular in profile and section, are symmetrically set above mid-profile. Flaring urns are not decorated. *Cylindrical urns* are best represented by one complete vessel found with the dog burial at Gilat (Plate 10.27:5). The thick walls are slightly convex and the base is double layered (see above). Cylindrical urns have rounded or pinched and everted rims, always much thinner than the wall (Plate 10.29:3, 7). Two vertical lug handles, triangular in section, were placed above mid-profile height. The opening diameter is between 9.3 and 13.2 cm, the height averages 30 cm, and the base 10 cm. Cylindrical urns are not decorated, with the exception of one fragmentary vessel, with large, horizontal red painted stripes (Plate 10.27:1).

The inventory of open shapes is completed by three other categories of rare vessels (m.n.i less than twenty) in the Gilat assemblage:

Dishes (Plate 10.5:17). They are shallow containers with flaring, straight walls, and a flat, rather thick base. The opening ranges 17.6 to 20 cm, the height of 6.5 to 8.2 cm and the base of 10.5 to 12.5 cm.

Cylindrical basin (Plate 10.5:20). One unique complete vessel was recorded. The rim of the basin is rounded, pinched horizontally by place and the base is flat. The walls and the bottom are rather thick: 1.3 cm. The most interesting feature of this cylindrical basin is a circular perforation set immediately above the base. The perforation was made into the wet clay, before firing. Opposite on the outside, there is a circular cup mark of similar diameter. The clay is saturated with charred seeds.

Cups (Plate 10.5:13, 16). Two small vessels fit this category. Both are of heavy fabric (clay III). One, complete, is almost cylindrical, with slightly concave walls. The inside of the thick base is convex (diameter: 8.1 cm, base: 6 cm, height: 4.6 cm).

Saucers (Plate 10.5:11–12, 14–15). These very small vessels are shallow. The base is roughly flatten and protruding. The short walls, rather shaped like a *marli*[10]) are straight and flaring, the rim is rounded, the base is flat and thick. In contrast to the crudeness of the outside, the inside is thoroughly smoothed. The opening diameter tends to be oval (7.5 to 10.8 cm), the height is between 1.5 to 2 cm, and the diameter of the base varies from 5.1 to 6.9 cm. The re-used, oval base of a beaker fits the category of saucers (Plate 10.24:11).

B. Closed shapes

Pithoi (Plates 10.11 and 10.12). These large containers also indicate an intermediary category between open shapes and closed shapes. They are large jars generally identified by the relative wideness of their opening. This and the frequent thickening of squared and horizontal rims are morphological characters that single them out in the category of large jars. Rims rather than complete shapes order the dimensional range of pithoi. The smallest have an opening diameter between 28.7 to 33 cm. The maximal diameter is between 30 to 35.6 cm. 82% of these pithoi have a rounded rim (Plate 10.11:2). Other display all the types of rims registered for large pithoi (Plate 10.11:5, 8). The largest pithoi have an opening diameter between 40 and 44 cm and a maximal diameter between 43 and 49 cm. 92% of the rims have an angular, square section. They are horizontal and flat rims (Plates 10.11:10; 10.12:4), with an inner pinched edge (Plates 10.11:9; 10.12:3), or oblique and flat rims (Plates 10.11:6; 10.12:1–2). Rounded and rolled out rims are less frequent (6.2%, Plate 10.11:5). Simple, rounded rims are rare (1.8%, Plate 10.11:2). 76.7% of the rims have a finger impressed decoration running on the edge of the external rim (61.3% (Plates 10.11:5, 9–10; 10.12:2–4, 6) or on the external and internal rim (15.4%, (Plate 10.11:6). In a dozen samples, rounded rims have finger impressions. 6% of pithoi are red-painted outside with one painted band covering the inside of the rim (Plate 10.12:5). Red paint is also associated to finger impressions on the rim (5.3%, Plate 10.12:3). Red painted designs occured on small and thin-walled pithoi (2.2%). Designs of large lattices or chevrons run inside and outside the rim, but many sherds suggest more complex—and unfortunately undecipherable—patterns (Plate 10.11:8). A vertical line of four large impressed dots, set below the rim can be interpreted either as a decoration or as a potter mark (Plate 10.12:1). However, it belongs to a fragmentary rim. One complete holemouth jar from Wadi Zoumeili has three impressed, large dots set in a triangle pattern on its shoulder (Commenge-Pellerin 1987: Fig. 49:5).

Holemouth jars (Plates 10.13 to 10.17 and 10.35:2). Narrow and large openings divide the assemblage of holemouth jars. In contrast to jars from the Beersheva sites, hole mouth jars at Gilat have characteristic ovoid, rather than globular, profiles (Plate 10.13 and cf. globular jars at Safadi: Commenge-Pellerin 1990, Figs 38:3, 6–7). The maximal diameter is slightly above mid-profile. The mean ratio between maximal diameter and height averages 0.61 for hole mouth jars with a wide opening and 0.76 for jars with a narrow opening (this ratio averages 1 for holemouth jars from Safadi, for example see Table 10.8b). Holemouth jars with a wide opening are more frequent (68.2%). However, size classes are similarly distributed among hole mouth jars with a wide opening and hole mouth jars with a narrow opening (see Table 10.8b).

Holemouth jars with a wide opening. The base is rather high and flaring, body walls are convex and parallel. This morphology finds parallels elsewhere, in assemblages with some other features matching Gilat's (Oren and Gilead 1981, Gilead and Alon1988 and see Plates 10.13 and 10.15). The rim is rounded or tapering and, in a few samples, slightly upright (Plates 10.15:4; 10.10, 10.35:2). Rare examples of small holemouth jars show upright rims are almost shaped as short necks (Plate 10.22:12, 1–15). Carinated rims, whose profile marks a sharp angle, are also rare (Plate 10.17:7). These carinated rims have parallel at Safadi (Commenge-Pellerin 1990, Fig. 41:5). The largest jars have two vertical lug handles diametrically opposed on the upper third of profile, at the maximal diameter of the jar (Plates 10.13:1; 10.15:4; 10.35:2). Lug handles have a sub-triangular profile and a triangular section. Rare examples of jars with two horizontal, plain lugs set below the rim are recorded (Plate 10.14:4, 7). Small jars have an opening between 10.1 and 12.5 cm, a maximal diameter between 16.3 to 18.1 cm, a base diameter between 7 and 8.1 cm; the height is between 18.4 and 22.3 cm. Medium size jars have an opening between 13.5 and 14.4 cm, a maximal diameter between 19 to 21.7 cm, a base diameter between 9.1 to 10.6 cm; the height is between 27.4 and 31.2 cm. The largest jars have an opening between 17.9 to 23.8 cm, a maximal diameter between 26.3 and 32 cm, a base diameter between 11.7 to 13.4 cm; the height is between 45.8 and 53.3 cm. All these jars are thin-walled, even the largest ones. Only 9% of this category of holemouth jars is red-painted and they are all small jars. Paint covers the entire outside surface and the inside of the rim (Plate 10.16:2).

Holemouth jars with a narrow opening. The mouth diameter is slightly larger than the base. The shoulder marks a continuous convexity to the rim. 81% of the rims are rounded and 32% of those have a characteristic 'snake head' profile (Plates 10.14:11; 10.16:4, 6–7). 7.3% of the rims are thinned (Plate 10.14:8) or thinned and slightly upright (Plates 10.14:9; 10.16:5, 9). 6.2% of the rims, that all belong to the largest jars, show an inner, oblique and flatten face (Plate 10.17:4) or an outer, oblique and flatten face (5.5%, Plate 10.17:10). Rims marked by a sharp convexity are rare and always observed on the largest jars (Plate 10.17:4). This also applies to rims of some larges jars whose inward, raising ledge has a rounded extremity (Plate 10.17:5 and cf. Commenge-Pellerin 1990, Fig. 41:1). The smallest jars have an opening between 6.4 and 7.9 cm, a maximal diameter between 16.7 and 18.5 cm, a base between 7.4 and 8.3 cm; the height averages 20 cm. Medium-sized jars have an opening between 9.4 and 11.1 cm, a maximal diameter between 19.7 and 23.1 cm, a base between 7.8 and 9.3 cm; the height averages 30 cm. The largest jars have openings between 12.4 to 14.9 cm, a maximal diameter between 26.7 to 33.9 cm, a bases ranging from 8.9 to 12 cm; the height averages 50 cm. Observations on complete vessels suggest that medium sized jars have lug handles set slightly above the maximal diameter. These vertical handles are triangular in profile and section. 30% of these holemouth jars are red-painted. This percentage rises to 45.5% for small-sized jars. 3.2% of small jars have painted designs. The jar is red-painted up to the shoulder. Wavy, horizontal designs decorate the shoulder (Plate 10.16:5). 2% of incomplete profiles show only impressed designs that may or may not have been associated with red paint. Broad holemouth jars are decorated with either horizontal rows of finger impressions on the rim (0.9% of the jars, Plate 10.16:12) or lines of lunulae (1.1%, Plate 10.16:13). 5.3% of the jars show red paint associated with impressed patterns, either horizontal lines of lunulae (3.2%) or dots below the rim (1%, Plate 10.14:11). 1.1% of shoulders have impressed patterns of dotted chevrons on a red painted background (Plate 10.15:3).

Small pots (Plate 10.24:2, 4–5). Only two complete vessels are recorded. Convex, parallel walls define elliptical profiles. One pot is shaped as a small holemouth jar and is red-painted at mid-profile (Plate 10.24:2). Impressed designs of dashes and dots belong to rim sherds (Plate 10.24:4).

Small necked pots (Plates 10.20:5; 10.22:13). Only two large fragments document this category of vessels. One is a globular vessel with a short, everted rim. The other one is a narrow, small jar with a short and everted rim. These two vessels are red-painted.

Pot with multiple lugs (Plate 10.24:8). One unique, fragmentary vessel illustrates this type. However characteristic, this type is always rare in other Chalcolithic assemblages (Commenge-Pellerin 1990: Fig. 53 and see Amiran 1955). The shoulder is convex, the rim short and upright. A double set of three and four vertical lug handles alternates on the upper part of the pot.

Necked jars (Plates 10.20; 10.21; 10.22:1–11). Complete jars do not exhaustively illustrate the inventory of necked jar shapes suggested by numerous fragmentary profiles. The inventory of necked jars is ordered here from continuous profiles to composite profiles, whose neck is a distinctive feature of the architecture of the vase. As already observed in other Chalcolithic assemblages, necked jars have versatile profiles.

Necked jars with a sloping shoulder (Plates 10.20:4, 6; 10.22:1). 9% of necked jars fit this category. The profile is elliptical, with a characteristic sloping, shoulder line that almost shapes a truncated cone neck. The rim is slightly flaring and rounded (Plate 10.20:4), pinched and rolled outside (Plate 10.20:6) or flat, oblique and shaped outward as a ledge (Plate 10.22:1). 87% of these jars are medium-sized, with a neck opening between 10.8 to 12.3 cm, a maximal diameter between 23.1 and 26.4 cm; (estimated) height averages 27 cm. Some are large jars with a neck opening ca. 12.2 to 14 cm, a maximal diameter ca. 28.2 to 31 cm; the (estimated) height averages 35 cm. Red slip is applied on the upper part of less than 1% of these jars.

Ovoid jars with a large neck and lug handles (Plates 10.19; 10.21:6). Many complete profiles illustrate this category, which comprises 35% of the necked jars. These jars are elliptical, with profiles elegantly balanced with a flat base almost as large as the neck opening. The junction to the neck is outlined by a continuous, vertical concavity, till the rounded or tapered rim. The inner bottom is convex in a cushion fashion described above (see, technological discussion above). Two pairs of vertical, small lug handles are symmetrically opposed on the shoulder. Dimensions are remarkably homogenous for this category of medium-sized jars. The neck opening is between 17.1 and 17.6 cm, the maximal diameter always reaches 26 cm, the base diameter is between 12.5 and 13.8 cm and the height is between 34.6 and 39.2 cm. Although sherds suggest a wealth of designs, decoration on complete vessels indicates recurrent patterns on this type of necked jars. Rather than asserting that all jars of this type are decorated, this study of the numerous large body sherds has not recorded any undecorated fragment. 21% of these jars are decorated with a double, horizontal row of impressed lunulae running around the maximal diameter, below the lug handles. On 79% of these jars, decoration associates large red-painted designs to impressed lunulae. A large band is found under the rim of the neck. Festooned painted patterns or large painted hoops decorate the shoulder around the lug handles and sometimes the base. A large, red-painted band always covers the impressed designs (Plates 10.19:2; 10.21:6).

Biconvex jars with a flaring neck (Fig. 10.21:1, 5). Carinated, biconvex profile jars at Gilat represent a 'new' type of necked jars to the Chalcolithic inventory. Jars with a carinated profile are found in assemblages of the Wadi Rabah phase (see: Garfinkel 1992, Fig. 128, Eisenberg 2001: Fig. 5.1:18). The neck is built as a distinct part of the profile, with rectilinear and vertical walls, flaring outward. The upper part of the jar has convex walls. Two pairs of vertical lug handles are diametrically opposed at mid-profile, enhancing the carination line. This category comprises 31.7% of the necked jars while all carinated profiles are considered (see below carinated jars). Only 9.3% of these jars are completely painted red or red-slipped, and in most cases, the paint also covers the inside of the neck (Plate 10.21:1).

The following jar types are illustrated by large fragments and/or incomplete profiles:[11]

Carinated jars (Plate 10.18). Numerous fragments have been recorded (1,012 sherds). They belong to large jars whose maximum diameter averages 30 cm. The lower part of the profile has slightly convex, flaring walls, the upper part has convex and convergent walls. The carination is underlined with impressed designs: lunulae (Fig. 10.18:5, 7) or dots (Fig. 10.18:6, 9). One fragment combines a design of vertical dashes and dots on the shoulder (Fig. 10.18:3). All carinated sherds are red-slipped.

Ovoid jars with a flaring neck (Plate 10.22:2–4, 6–7). Necks have concave profiles, with an everted, rounded or slightly thinned and facetted rim (Plate 10.22:7). This type of neck is found on jars of varied dimensions. The opening of the neck varies from 11.8 to 18.8 cm. This type comprises 4.9% of necked-jars.

Cylindrical necks (Plates 10.21:3–4; 10.22:5, 10). Necks are cylindrical with vertical walls and rounded rims (7.8%, Plate 10.21:4). Only two red-painted neck fragments have been registered. Some cylindrical, rather narrow necks have everted, rounded rims (Plate 10.21:3). 36% are painted red. Neck openings have rather regular dimensions, of ca. 8.9 to 9.9 cm. Two large necks (diameter 16.5 cm) with finger-impressed decoration were recorded (Plates 10.21:12; 10.22:10).

Bow necks (Plates 10.22:9; 10.24:3). Parallel, convex walls characterize the bow necks. They are rare in the assemblage of necked jars (3.8%). Some fragments of jars shoulders are decorated with impressed dots. Small jars with twin lug handles (Plate 10.24:3) find a parallel at Titorah in Judea whose assemblage comprises at least one torpedo jar, beakers and one violin shaped figurine (Lass, pers. com.). One complete profile from Titorah suggests a reconstruction of flat bases to with these jars whose height averages 20 cm.

Large jars with a short neck (Plate 10.20:8–11). These jars are not frequent (5.9%) but present at the site from Stratum IIIB onward. Large sherds and shoulder fragments give evidence for jars of elliptical profile. The neck is short, built in a 'pithos' fashion with a thick rim whose inner face is flattened and oblique (Fig. 10.20:8). The neck is simply everted (Plate 10.20:9) or everted with a stretched and horizontal rim (Plate 10.20:10). In one case, the short neck has rectilinear, slightly flaring walls and finger impressions on the outside of its everted rim (Plate 10.20:11). No decoration has been recorded for these jars.

Small jars with a flaring neck and twin lugs (Plate 10.24:1). There is no complete example of these rare small jars. They are narrow vessels, elliptical in profile with an angular shoulder and a rather high, flaring and concave neck (Plate 10.24:1). Two pairs of vertical lug handles, sub-triangular in profile and triangular in section, are set on the shoulder. The reconstructed height averages ca. 15 cm. The maximal diameter is between 7.2 and 7.9 cm and the neck opening between 3.8 and 4.9 cm. There is no evidence for decoration.

Small jars with a bow neck and twin lugs (Plate 10.24:3). Profiles are semi-elliptical for these small jars. A continuous convex line marks the shoulder. The bow neck has a thinned rim. Two pairs of vertical lug handles, sub-triangular in profile and triangular in section, are set on the shoulder. With regard to the relative thickness of the walls, a heavy, plain (pointed?) base is sometimes found. Small jars comprise 0.8% of the assemblage of necked jars. There is no evidence for decoration

Miniature necked jars (Plate 10.24:9). Two incomplete jars fit this category. The body is elliptical and the neck is rather high, cup-like with convex and flaring walls. The restituted height averages 8 cm, the opening is between 3 and 3.6 cm and the maximal diameter between 4.1–4.9 cm. All examples are red-painted, including the inside of the neck.

Torpedo jars (n = 96). This term was coined by Alon and Levy (1989). The term fits the oblong profile of these jars whose height is at least six times more prominent than the width. Thus far, sporadic samples of similar jars have been found, not far from Gilat, at Wadi Zeita (Gat Govrin, Perrot pers. com.) and in Judea, at Titorah (Lass, pers.com.). A number of 'torpedo' sub-types can now be defined based on the 1990–92 ceramic assemblage:

Tubular torpedo jars (Plates 10.34:3; 10.29:14; 10.35:3). This generic term, that applies to 81.3% of the 'torpedoes', refers to the almost tubular profile of the jar. In fact, the walls, rectilinear and imperceptibly flaring up to the second third of the profile, mark a characteristic concave-line at the point where the large lug handles have been fixed. The upper part is slightly bulbous. In most cases the rim is a simple extension of the wall but 23% of these jars have an everted rim that forms a short, oblique brim around the opening (Plate 10.35:3). The base is flat. Lug handles are heavy, triangular in profile and section (Fig. 10.35:3) or sub-circular in profile and circular in section (Fig. 10.34:3). Thorough examination of the assemblage contradicts the preliminary study of Gilat Torpedo jars that suggested all contained twin handles (Alon and Levy 1989). The present study shows only 7.7% of the tubular torpedoes have twin handles. The opening diameter varies between 9.8 to 12.5 cm, the maximum diameter between 10.5 to 14 cm, the height between 58.5 and 65.5 cm, and the base between 7.2 and 8.1 cm. Walls are thick and vary from 2.4 to 3.3cm.

Spindle-shaped torpedoes (Plate 10.35:1). Spindle-shaped torpedoes represent 19% of the assemblage. The base is elongated, with rectilinear and flaring walls up to mid-profile. The upper half of the profile is globular to half-elliptical. Spndle-shaped torpedoes have short necks shaped like a vertical brim at the opening (Plate 10.35:1). Walls are generally thinner than observed with tubular torpedoes. Lug handles are semi-circular in profile and triangular in section. They are rather small handles, smaller than handles set on tubular torpedoes. Twin handles seem absent on this type of torpedo. The opening diameter varies between 9.8 to 10.3 cm, the height between 59 to 68.3 cm, the maximum diameter between 15.6 and 16.2 cm, the base from 7.8 to 8.5 cm.

None of the 96 torpedoes recorded at Gilat are decorated, but all have been skillfully smoothed and tubular torpedoes made of Moza clay are all burnished.

Churns (Plates 10.31 to 10.34). These containers should rather be referred to as 'spindle-shaped vessels with a neck' (*vases fusiformes à goulot*) as the generic name of *churn* introduces a functional nomenclature in a morphological inventory. However, these vessels are also characterized by one flat extremity (flat end) and one conical extremity (ogival end) and as noted above, since the term is embedded in the archaeological literature we will use it here. The neck is set right above the maximal, vertical diameter of the churn and thus not exactly at mid (horizontal) profile (Plate 10.32:5). In this assemblage, the shape of the neck and/or the size of the churn was used to define churn sub-types. While this sub-division applies to the churns of Safadi for example (see Commenge-Pellerin 1990: Plate X:1–2), the absence of churns with a huge, globular neck is notable at Gilat (cf. Commenge-Pellerin 1987, Fig. 37:3 and 5; 1990, Fig. 56:8, 10–11; Gilead 1995, Fig.4.13:1). Miniature churns define another sub-category at Gilat.

Large thin-walled churns. (Plates 10.32; 10.33:1–4, 6; 10.34:2)
These churns, characterized by a large capacity, have remarkably thin walls (0.75 cm). This category comprises 81.7% of the churn assemblage. Large and thin-walled churn have a full volume as the distended goatskins they may duplicate. Complete vessels have a maximal diameter that varies between 27 to 29.3 cm and a length between 52.3 to 55 cm. Handles have a characteristic triangular section and sub-triangular profile (Plate 10.32:5 is an exception). The handle is usually set on the ogival part of the churn extends from the ogive (Plate 10.31:12) or more frequently, is set upright (Plate 10.31:10). Some rare examples have two or three large finger impressions on the top (Plate 10.31:10). The neck is set right above the vertical axis (maximal diameter) and thus, with consideration to the spindle-shape of the vessel, not exactly at mid-profile. Some churns (all made at Moza production centers) show a rather lengthy profile toward the flat end (Plate 10.34:2). This morphological particularity may be related to the general trend of these pottery production systems to make vessels remarkable for elongated, narrow profiles. However, there is a lack of complete jars of this type to thoroughly corroborate this point. In contrast with churns from the Beersheva sites, most churns in Gilat's assemblage have necks with 'truncated cone' profiles. Different profile are recorded: the neck is narrow with high, rectilinear and convergent walls (Plate 10.32:2, 8%), or with an upright rim (Plate 10.32:3, 2.3%). The neck is either short (Plate 10.32:5, 41%) or high (Plate 10.33:1–2, 21.4%) with slightly convex, convergent walls. 27% of the churns, were imported from Judean production centers (Moza sources), and are burnished as are torpedo jars from the same source area. The rare, red-painted necks of this assemblage belong to specific types. The neck has high, with slightly convex and vertical walls (Plate 10.33:6, less than 1%) or short, concave and slightly convergent walls (Plate 10.33:4, less than 1%). Necks with a sinuous profile, shaped like a small jar with a sloping shoulder that characterized churns from Safadi or Grar, are here exceptional (less than 1% of the necks). These necks always have a large base, and parallel vertical walls with an everted rim (see Plate 10.32:1 and 4). Although none of the complete vessels have decorated, necks, handles and bases and large body sherds seem to indicate that less than 10% of the churns were decorated. There is no evidence for painted designs but for the overall red painting of the churns.

Small, thick-walled churns (Plate 10.33:3, 5–7; 10.34:1). As stockiness characterizes profiles, these churns have thick, sturdy walls (2.5 to 3 cm). One can estimate that the dimensions of these churns are 20% less than the ones of the large, thin-walled churns. The most complete specimens suggest a large and high neck of truncated cone profile (Plates 10.34:1; 10.33:5) with an everted rim (Plate 10.33:3). The base diameter of the neck is only one third smaller than the churn's maximal diameter. Handles are thick, with sub-triangular profile and triangular section. No evidence for decoration is registered. However, rare traces of red paint have been observed on some fragments.

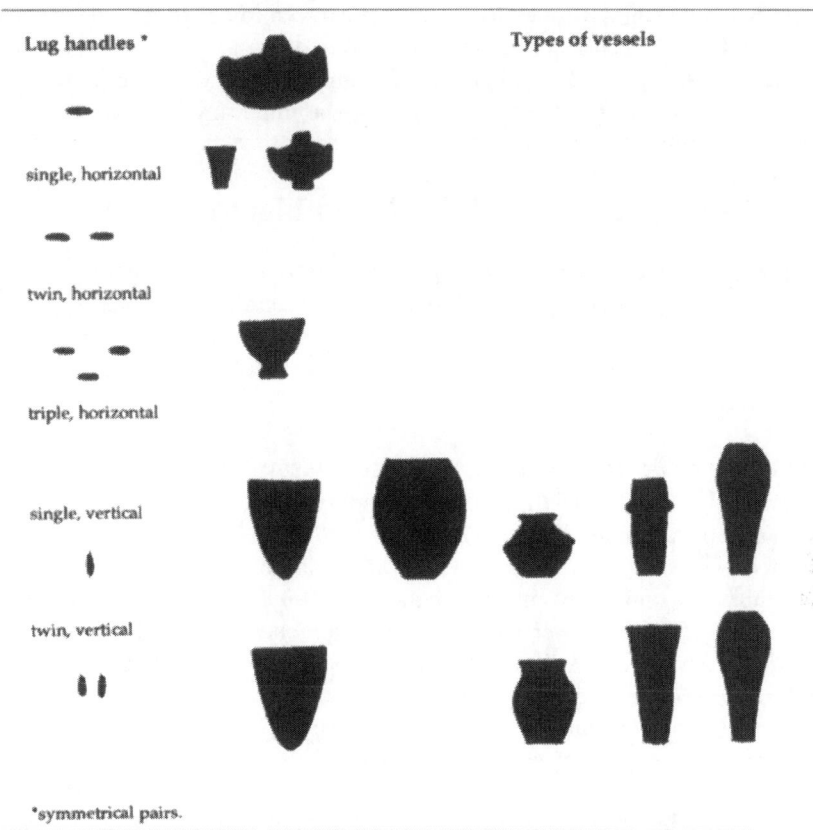

Figure 10.4. Orientation of lug handles on Gilat vessels.

Miniature churns (Plate 10.31:1–9 and 11). Over 70 miniature churns were identified, none of them complete. Recurrent observations on their morphological characters give a reasonable indication for partial description of some their idiosyncratic features. The body is spindle-shaped with a horizontal axis of revolution. Miniature churns have a flat end and an ogival end, either pinched or rounded. The maximal diameter appears standardized: it varies ca. 11.2 to 11.6 cm. The length can be estimated at ca. 21.5 to 24.5 cm. 160 handles were collected at Gilat. Among those, it has been possible to identify 71 ogival end handles and 71 handles set on the flat end of miniatures churns (hence 71 as the m.n.i. for miniature churns, corroborated by 69 complete ogive parts). Only 3.3% of the ogive end handles are of 'regular' shape. The handle is set on the upper part of the ogive, and sub-triangular to sub-circular in profile and triangular in section (Plate 10.31:1 and 5). 12.2% of the ogival end handles are horn-shaped handles, with a high triangular horn-like appendix on the top, and a triangular section (Plate 10.31:3). 84.5% of the ogival end handles are double handles. The large handle shows a medial groove that shapes two horns if seen from a frontal view. The profile of the handle is either sub-circular, or sub-triangular, the section is a double triangle (Plate 10.31:4, 7–9). It is notable that all the flat end handles are double-horned handles. In contrast to the ogival end double handles, flat end handles have a characteristic triangular profile shaped by a slightly protruding horn appendix (Plate 10.31:11). Unfortunately, no definitive miniature churn neck fragments were found. Indications of necks with rectilinear and convergent walls and a rounded rim are recurrent on the most complete fragments and on tiny fragments found with them or identified by sediments sieving (see for example Plate 10.31:11).

32 ring bases belong to miniature churns. Every preserved lower part of the miniature churns collected from Gilat has a ring base. This evidence tends to demonstrate that miniature churns, like large tulip bowls, have a short stand. All ring base, some more oval than circular, have a square section, with a flatten rim (Plate 10.31:9). 78.9% of the miniature churns are red-slipped and sometimes have a light burnishing.

The Integrative Organization of the Assemblage

Detailed classification of vessels for typological purposes tends to itemize the formal structure of the assemblage. The following integrative perspective aims to relate types into consonant, dissonant, complementary units that may possibly combine to disclose how they fulfilled patterns of consumption at Gilat. It underlines fundamental, idiosyncratic components in the assemblage yet also its roots in the Palestinian pottery tradition.

The Basic Structure of Formal Variation in Gilat's Assemblage

Different rhythms order formal variation in this assemblage:

1. *open* shapes prevail over closed ones, and *small open shapes*—that include at least six different types—over open vessels of medium or large size (Table 10.1).
2. the assemblage is composed of *basic* shapes and of *hybrid* shapes (Tables 10.1, 10.2a-b)
3. *Size* is a major factor of discrimination that intervenes at several levels. *Tri-modality* or *bimodality* characterize the size of vessels, in particular open shaped vessels. Moreover, *miniaturization* applies to specific shapes (Table 10.3).
4. profiles tend to be *high and narrow* and this morphological trademark is even perceptible in the V-shaped category of vessels as compared to later Chalcolithic assemblages (Table 10.8a).
5. decoration that involves time consuming techniques and add value to vessels, is not a primary criterion in segregating high-valued vessels at Gilat. In any event, decoration sets Gilat on the edge of two traditions in pottery making, as a southern outpost of the Wadi Rabah Pottery Neolithic tradition and as a forbearer of the Chalcolithic one.

A formal distinction between open and closed shapes, the first group significantly overrating the latter, was observed in other Chalcolithic assemblages (Commenge-Pellerin 1987, 1990). The same trend applies to the pottery of Gilat (see Table 10.1). Although hole mouth jars (18.6%) prevail over other categories of vessels, small open vessel are scattered into several categories. According to Yon (1981), an open vessel has an opening diameter slightly equal to its maximum body diameter. This definition concerns all the V-shaped vessels, which maximum diameter coincide with the opening of the bowl, yet also narrow and high vessels, ranked by size, such as pointed-base beakers and tubular vessels. Among the open shaped category, small vessels comprise 53.6% and more than one third (35.5%) of the whole assemblage. These small containers may be described as individual serving vessels, as containers one can hold in one hand and whose maximal volume capacity can reach 50 centiliters (Table 10.7).

Life expectancy of movable, small vessels frequently handled in daily use is estimated to have been shorter than the ones used for heavy storage (Foster 1960; Longacre 1981; Arnold 1985 and for an overview Mills 1989: Table 4).[12] It may reasonably be argued that thin-walled tulip bowls, or fragile cornets have not been used daily. However, evidence for documenting how the restricted use of vessels compensates for breakage propensity is considerably hampered by available contextual information at Gilat, but the correlation between high manufacture cost and low replacement rate of vessels has been amply demonstrated by ethnographic evidence (Mills 1989: Table 6). The frequency rate in the assemblage ranges (in descending order of frequency): V-shaped bowls, tulip bowls, beakers, pointed-base beakers, cornets and tubular goblets. The nature of their utilization involves functional and social parameters that implies the momentum of their use and may or may not be related to the degree of ware sturdiness.

Ranking in terms of functionality, from domestic to ceremonial activities, may be appraised by testing the morphological adaptability or inadaptability of eclectic, small vessels to fit patterns of utilization such as their size and frequency in the assemblage.

The typological grid has been screened to extract basic morphological modules (Table 10.1). These are represented by geometric projections of the profiles that define the module in space (in fact, in two dimensions): rectangular for tubular, cylindrical shapes, trapeze for the so-called V-shaped vessels, triangular for cornets, ellipse or semi-ellipse for spindle-shaped vessels Small, medium or large categories are relative as they apply within each category of vessels. Hybrid types of vessels are placed on border edges, between two reference types: beakers between tubular beakers and V-shaped bowls, tulip bowls between V-shaped bowls and cornets, pointed-base beakers between cornets and spindle-shaped vessels. Fenestrated pedestal bowls (32% of the pedestalled vessels) illustrate more a composite shape than a hybrid one as it is made from two V-shaped parts, mirror-like opposites from the base. The elliptic group is the most versatile one. Hydrid shapes with pointed-bases (and this is the case for churns) are all semi-elliptic volumes while semi-elliptical (torpedoes) to elliptical volumes are used in the making of closed shapes (jars).

The technical, modular, fluidity in the making of V-shaped vessels at other Chalcolithic sites is absent at Gilat and not characteristic other categories of open shapes. With the exception of beakers (that are characterized by the hybridizing of techniques, see above), small shapes were not meant as technical modules, or as basic morphological segments of the *chaîne opératoire* in the making of larger ceramic vessels. However, the formal structure of the assemblage that generated the hybridizing of shapes confirms that, in Gilat's assemblage, fluidity of techniques marks formal variation in the assemblage.

In the 'open shapes' category, the typological grid is structured with three basic shapes and their emanations, as three types out of six are hybrid types. Moreover, the hybrid category of semi-elliptic vessels with a pointed base is the best represented with small to large beakers and churns. Basic, V-shaped profiles comprise one half of the open shaped vessels (50.4%) as tubular vessels and cornets remains marginal (less than 2%). However, hybrid profiles are numerous (42.6% of the open shapes). Only fenestrated, pedestalled bowls that will remain a 'classical' shape in the repertoire of all Chalcolithic assemblages fits in this chart. It represents less than 1% of the open shapes category. Pedestalled chalices and bow stems are anchored in early traditions (Garfinkel 1992, Figs 45 and 102) and endured later (Commenge 1987, Fig. 22:13).

In the 'closed shapes' category, carinated, biconvex jars are single out and appear dissonant to the intricate harmony of the whole assemblage. Although well represented in the jar category (31.7%), they seem absent from later assemblages, at the Beersheva sites, for example. They are absent at Grar, in a pottery assemblage that shares some features with Gilat's (beakers, impressed lunulae on reserved stripes, cornets). Carinated jars may be indicative of a 'morphological archaism' as they may originate from the Wadi Rabah tradition (Garfinkel 1992, Fig. 128, Eisenberg 2001: Fig. 5.1:18).

In a broader perspective, Table 10.1 demonstrates that, to the exception of churns, hybrid types of vessels are absent in other recorded Chalcolithic pottery assemblages. Cornets are present at many sites, in extremely variable quantities that range from apparent absence to relative frequency (cf. Gilead 1995:162–3). The structure of Gilat's assemblage, as translated in Table 10.1, suggests that cornets represent a basic module, a fundamental component in the structural organization of the assemblage. As such—and most certainly as any particular vessel in any context—cornets cannot be singled out as *insulae per se* as one tries to define their function. Further questions have to be addressed prior to the examination of the functional patterns in Gilat's ceramic assemblage.

Dimensional categories have been elaborated in the typological grid, whose nominal range is relative to each type of vessel. An evaluation of the capacity of vessels may provide a better mediation for our understanding of the structure of the assemblage and further, of its function. The general chart of capacities allows a relative calibration of vessels, with classes meant as standards for the assemblage (Table 10.8a and 10.8b). All dimensions, taken at significant points of vessels' profile, have been logged into an Excel program meant for multiple volumes calculation (Capaci-XLS 2). Capacity is here expressed in decimal centiliters.

Table 10.8a brings open vessels in a focus as less complete, closed vessels are available. The variability that characterizes the category of open vessels is emphasized by patterns of mean capacity ranking. The smallest vessels can now be ascribed to a miniature group (6.7 cl to 7.5 cl, note that some pointed-base beaker have a capacity of less than 5 cl). With the exception of large bowls, characterized by size variability, there is a gap between medium-sized vessels and large ones. The very large capacity of large basins with handles challenges the storage capacity of some of the holemouth jars.

All open shapes are set in a hierarchical pattern that calls for comment. Small, very small and medium categories comprise at least three types of vessels, which include basic and hybrid shapes. Beakers are represented in all three categories as v-shaped vessels fit only the small category and are further represented in large and very large categories. Vessels of small capacity overshadow other categories. They represent almost one third of the total assemblage (m.n.i.) of vessels at Gilat and 45% of the open shapes. Pointed-base beakers and beakers of medium capacity comprise more than 10% of Gilat's assemblage, and are respectively more numerous than necked jars and pithoi, for example (cf. Table 10.8b). Very large containers are rare in the assemblage of closed shapes. However, the category of vessels of small capacity (less than five liters) includes all the registered closed shapes in the assemblage to the exception of pithoi. Heavy containers but not capacious torpedo jars fall into this category.

The hierarchical range in the capacity of vessels introduce a discriminative ordering:

a. Two types of vessels, one open—V-shaped vessels—and one closed—holemouth jars with a wide opening—fan out an extended range of capacities. Holemouth jars, rooted in south Levantine tradition and V-shaped vessels, focus of technical innovation, share two other characteristics: a high rate frequency in the assemblage and a shape defined as basic in the structure of the assemblage (Table 10.1).
b. Tri-modality in size is the rule for five types of vessels: beakers, pointed-base beakers and tubular vessels in the open shapes category, churns and necked jars in the closed-shapes category. Tri-modal in size necked jars appear complementary in all types considered, with only biconvex jars in the small capacity group. However, one should remain prudent on this view, as the relative scarcity of complete profiles is challenged by the many types of necks not related to any specific type of jars.
c. Tulip bowls and cornets illustrate bimodality in size. Tulip bowls and ring-based tulip bowls have standardized dimensions: small tulip bowls are six times less capacious than the pedestalled ones. The capacity of cornets is mostly estimated on a large sample of fragments. Cornets seem to fit either the very small capacity group or cluster with medium-sized beakers or pointed-base beakers.

This ordered inventory of capacity challenges the notion of miniaturization of vessels. Vessels of very small capacity—less than 10 cl—belong to the bottom scale of tri-modal in size open-shapes. They are actually *miniaturized* containers. By contrast, 'miniature' seems somehow inappropriate when applied to the smallest of the churns (that are only 8 times smaller than the largest ones, while for example, small pointed-base beakers are 42 times smaller than the largest ones). It is the morphological elements that appear not to be directly linked to functional purposes—horned handles, a short pedestal—that single out 'miniature' churns in this typological category.

Table 10.7. Mean capacity of vessels.

type	Open Shapes				
	very small <or = 15cl	small <or = 25cl	medium < or = 50	large >150cl	very large >300cl
Cornet	12-14cl**	-	44 cl	-	-
Tubular goblet	6.7cl	21.2cl	-	-	-
Tubular urn	-	-	-	176cl**	-
Beaker	7.4cl	17.2cl	50.8cl	-	-
V-shaped bowl	-	25.8cl	-	93-116-137cl**	-
Basin	-	-	-	-	390cl
Large handled basin	-	-	-	-	-3080cl-
Tulip bowl	-	19.7cl	-	117cl	-
Pointed-base beaker	7.5cl	-	37cl	300cl	-
%on M. N. I. **	1.8%	28.2%	11.2%	12.4%	7.2%

* for large bowls, average capacity is meant per dimensional category, ** estmated

type	closed shapes			
	small <or =500cl	medium >500cl	large >1000cl	very large =or >2000cl
Hole mouth jar**	440cl	710cl	1490cl	2070cl
Necked jar	-	630cl	1010cl	-
Carinated necked jar	360cl	-	-	-
Tubular torpedo	370cl	-	-	-
Spindle-torpedo	-	710cl	-	-
Churn (thin-walled)	-	-	1300cl	-
Churn (thick-walled)	-	700cl	-	-
Miniature churn	150cl**	-	-	-
% on M. N. I.**	9.9%	6.7%	12.7%	3.1%

*capacity of miniature churns is evaluated **estimated,:pedestalled vessels, pithoi and hole mouth jars with a small opening are discarded samples as tprofiles do not cover the whole size or type range.

Height/Width Ratio as a Significant Morphological Marker[13]

The propensity to form elongated shapes is idiosyncratic in this assemblage of vessels. Keeping in mind the diversity of sources of production, this recurrent morphological pattern generated more eclectic trends. Beakers, torpedoes and tubular vessels are 'generic' examples, but the stamping of the trend is eloquent as it permeates V-shaped vessels, hole mouth or necked jars. Narrow bases and pointed bases are fit to either small or large vessels. Although statistical comparative evidence is not (yet) available in the southern Levant, this 'morphological marker' appears to have parallels in the assemblage of Teleilat Ghassul (as illustrated in Mallon *et al.* 1934 or Koeppel *et al.* 1940).[14] However, some rare vessels from either Safadi or Abu Matar, all locally made, may stand for 'cultural remainders' in those assemblages (Commenge-Pellerin 1987: Fig. 30:7; 1990: Fig. 46:1),

Table 10.8a*. Dimensional ratios modifying profiles of small, open-shaped vessels/

type	sample	site	O/H*	_/_ °
V-shaped bowls (thrown)	n= 50	Gilat	1.27–1.32	= or > 70°
V-shape bowls	n= 50	Gilat	1.23–1.42	= or> 72°
V-shape bowls (thrown)	*n= 50*	*Safadi*	*1.5–2*	*= or > 60°*
V-shaped bowls	*n= 50*			*= or > 60°*
Tulip bowl	n= 33	Gilat	1–1.3	= or > 75°
Beakers	n= 50	Gilat	0.9–1	= or> 80°

*O= opening diameter; H= height. For meaningful co-variations, only complete profiles were sampled. _/_°: outside angle between base plane and the wall.

Table 10.8b: Dimensional ratios modifying profiles of closed shapes

type	sample	site	max. O/H*
Hole mouth jars (wide opening)	n= 27	Gilat	0.59–0.63
Hole mouth jars (small opening)	n= 29	Gilat	0.74–0.78
Hole mouth jars	*n= 22*	*Safadi*	*0.81–1*
Hole mouth jars	*n= 18*	*Abu Matar*	*0.82–0.96*
Necked jars	n= 31	Gilat	0.65–0.76
Necked jars	*n= 30*	*Safadi*	*0.86–1.14*
Necked jars	*n= 22*	*Abu Matar*	*0.79–1*

* O=maximal body diameter/H= total height. Jars with a short neck have been considered at Abu Matar and Safadi.

Secondary Morphological Elements

Some morphological elements are added to certain vessels—pedestals, lugs, lug handles, spouts, strainers—and some are, somehow, subtracted from vessels—pointed-bases. It is assumed here that, as 'actors' in formal variation, secondary morphological elements are sequatorial to the function of vessels—a view that does not derogate their role in emphasizing 'the style' of vessels.

Bases, as secondary morphological elements, are of critical importance in this assemblage that includes 18.9% pointed-base vessels and 3% of either ringed bases or pedestalled vessels. Moreover, churns, that are made with one flat and one pointed extremities, awkwardly stand on the side of their body. They comprise 7.3% of the vessel assemblage. High, narrow and plain bases (that can represent one eighth of the vessel's height, as for some torpedoes or urns) comprise 2.17% of the vessels. More than one third (31.32%) of the vessels in this assemblage were not conceived with a stable, flat base suited for 'practical and orthodox' use, for easy stacking up and eventually, for avoiding risks of breakage.

Footed vessels give evidence for different morphological conceptions. Pedestals and stems, mostly fenestrated, are affixed to containers with flaring profiles and flat bases. A large majority of ring bases are set on vessels with either pointed bases (tulip bowls) or no actual bases (miniature churns). Some rare examples that are not documented by complete profiles, illustrate ring bases on rounded bottom, open shapes (Plates 10.2:9–11; 10.23:2, 5 and 10.3:1). Ringed bases affixed to close-shapes with a flattened inner base (probably small jars) are exceptions (Plate 10.23:7, 9). Disk bases are exceptional features, observed either on closed or open vessels with a rounded base (Plate 10.23:3, 4).

As generic components of Chalcolithic pottery assemblages, lug handles are ubiquitous in the Gilat assemblage. Most have characteristic triangular profiles and sections. Their orientation on the body of the vessel is either horizontal or vertical (the latter averages 90% of the lug handles). To the exception of one (unique) pot with multiple lug handles (Fig. 10.24:8), single, twin and in some cases triple lug handles are symmetrically opposed. Obviously, lug handles set on capacious containers such as large basins, holemouth jars, necked jars or torpedoes were used as grips to help in filling, emptying, moving the vessels around. Suspension can even have been meant for some of vessels (pointed-base beakers, ring-based tulip bowls and perhaps churns) and suspension around one's neck is not excluded for small pointed-base beakers. However appropriate or satisfactory seems this one-sided functional interpretation, it may reduce the integration of lug handles as constituent units to formal variation of Gilat's vessels.

Over 33% of vessels have lug handles, of which 4.7% are twin handles and 2% triple handles. Although small enough to be held in one hand, small pointed-base beakers, that comprise almost 3% of the individual, small sized, open vessels, have diametrically opposed single lug handles. This percentage reaches 15.8% if pointed-base beakers of medium capacity (37 cl) are added. Twin and triple lug handles appear as specific features to either one type of vessel, or to the major part of vessels inside one typological category. Twin, vertical lug handles are set on all ovoid jars with a large short neck and on 82% of the large pointed-base beakers. Horned lug handles, single or more generally double (84.5%) seem exclusive to miniatures churns. Triple lug handles are always small and fit either horizontally or vertically on the body.

Ring-based tulip bowls represents the only category of vessels with horizontal lug handles whose pattern—two lugs above one single lug—amazingly alludes to the features of a human face (two eyes, one mouth, Plate 10.2:4). These lug handles are semi-circular in profile, with rather large and circular perforations meant to enhance the human face effect, disconcerting when light and shade play on the vessel. One can already note that horned, single or twin handles and triple, horizontal lug handles are exclusively associated *to ring-based vessels*. Observations on decorative designs also suggest one tight correlation between designs of impressed lunulae and vessels with twin lug handles (pointed-base beakers and necked jars, and to the exception of torpedoes). Vertical, triple lug handles with horizontal perforation belong to one single fragmentary pot, isolated in the assemblage (Plate 10.24:8). However, on larger samples issued from later Chalcolithic assemblages, one can observe that versatility in the number, location and orientation of the lug handles on these kinds of pots is the rule (cf. Commenge-Pellerin 1987, Fig. 34:9–11; 1990, Fig. 36:22, Fig. 53:1, 3, 5, 7).

Loop handles only comprise 0.03% of the handles in the assemblage. Profiles and sections of loop handles are sub-circular to circular. They belong to large jars fragments (pithoi or hole mouth jars, and to some rare, large pointed-base beakers). The only complete shape with vertical and diametrically opposed loop handles is a large pointed-base beaker (Plate 10.27:6).

Other secondary elements are diversely affixed to vessels:

Three fragments of vessels have horizontal inner ledges, roughly sub-triangular in profile which are placed immediately below the inside rim. Two belong to narrow open vessels (Fig.10.29:2, 4), with a narrow opening (10cm). Similar inner ledges are found on larger vessels at Safadi. A possible function was proposed for those devices, which, if diametrically opposed, might have helped to set a lid, or a (basketry?) sieve into the opening of the vessel (Commenge-Pellerin 1990:20, Fig. 31:1–5).

Nine fragments of spouts were recorded. Only one can be identified as part of a large basin (Plate 10.8:5). This record is actually low if compared to examples in the assemblage of Safadi that comprises 205 spouted vessels (large basins and small hole mouth jars) that include 4.17% of the registered complete vessels at Gilat. Less than one dozen of strainers fragments are diagnosed as perforated bases of pedestalled or ring-based vessels (Plate 10.10:5). With consideration to Gilat's large sample of pottery vessels, this tends to confirm that strainers, if commonly used, where mainly made of vegetal materials. However, the fact that some pedestal bowls are perforated tends to valorize the intended sieving function of these devices.

Formal Variation and Decoration

The formal conception of shapes extends to decoration, as decoration is not haphazardly added on vessels. Decoration studied *per se* may entail a rather unorthodox view of the assemblage. The definition of formal patterns in the composition and the organization of decoration allow the identification and integration of more consonant components into the typological grid, as it elaborates correlations and co-variances between designs and morphological characters. This perspective in investigating pottery designs has already been applied to some other Chalcolithic assemblages (Commenge-Pellerin 1990:29). A dichotomy between undecorated and decorated vessels seems efficient only when one group can challenge and counter-balance the other. *Meaning, in terms of social or symbolic value, cannot be predetermined as exclusive to decorated pots in this assemblage, as contextual evidence will demonstrate.*

The intricate distribution of decoration types among the different shapes that compose this assemblage appears to follow patterns that call for comment. It reveals that the shape and/or the size of vessels are, as augured above, crucial elements in determining this distribution.

53.36% of the vessels are decorated in the assemblage of Gilat. The major portion (40.5%) are red-painted, from mouth to bottom and in most cases red-paint largely daubs the inner opening. Impressed designs (8.52%) almost double painted designs (4.99%). They encapsulate different techniques and motives and are generally combined to painted surfaces, reserved, burnished painting or even painted designs. Incised designs remain very discrete.

Tables 10.9a to 10.9c records the distribution of undecorated and decorated vessels and sherds in Gilat's assemblage. Complete profiles provide valid information on the composition and organization of designs. Pottery sherds demonstrate a wealth of designs and provide a measure of our loss of information in the archaeological record due to the paucity of complete vessels at Gilat. Information deriving from the large inventory of sherds slightly modifies the proportion of undecorated *versus* decorated vessels. Techniques of decoration are roughly similar in percentages to those registered for complete vessels. The most significant raise concerns red-painted designs as a fair number of painted vessels are made from fragile and highly breakable cream ware (over 15% of painted designs are recorded on sherds collected by sediments sieving).

The Distribution of Decorative Techniques (Table 10.9c)

Morphological discrimination. Distribution of red-painting decoration spans seventeen types of vessels (that cluster into twelve categories; Table 10.9a–10.9c). For several categories of vessels, red paint is the only mode of decoration. In each category of vessels, it accounts for either very low frequency (less than 10% for churns and hole mouth jars with a large opening), to moderate (39% for beakers) or very high frequency (78% up to over 90% for miniature churns, tulip bowls or small to medium-sized pointed-base beakers). Proportions of red-painted vessels can be contrasted inside the same typological class: the frequency of red-painted churns is almost inverse to the frequency of miniature churns (Table 10.9b).

Burnishing and painting are aesthetic treatments applied to the whole surface of vessels (and sometimes combined see Table 10.9a and 10.9b). These techniques have been recorded as surface types of decoration. Combined, they are exclusive either to some vessels per category (for example, 5.1% of the large bowls are red-painted and burnished), or to all the vessels of one category (all the decorated large pointed-base beakers). They also comprise all the vessels that are painted with reserved and impressed designs on a cream ware back ground (cornets and large bowls). Burnishing is applied alone on the self-slipped surface of churns and tubular torpedo jars issued from Moza production center. The burnishing creates a pale ochre, shining surface.

The combination of painting with other techniques of decoration is characteristic of Gilat's assemblage: paint overlaps rows of finger impressions, stamped impressions are covered with paint, painted zones alternate with reserved, impressed ones.

A relatively large spectrum of decorative techniques applies to diverse categories of vessels. Red-painted background and impressed designs, red-painted, geometric designs are applied on necked jars, on holemouth jars with a narrow opening and on large V-shaped bowls. This short list adds relevance to morphological discrimination of vessels insofar as two types of vessels belong to categories that comprises either similar shapes coming in different sizes (V-shaped category) or vessels of the same generic category that differs by one morphological character (hole mouth jars). *Size* is also a determinant component in the mode of decoration of vessels. Over 70% of the large pointed-base beakers are decorated (painted and impressed, painted and impressed in the reserved cream-ware technique) as most of the medium or small sized pointed-base beakers are undecorated. Cornets monopolize elaborated techniques of decoration (painted designs or painted and impressed designs on reserved cream-ware bands). The case of cornets refutes practical considerations that consider decoration of easier making and display on large vessels (as, for example, suggested with the V-shaped category of vessels or the large pointed-base beakers).

Structure of design patterns. However varied the distribution and types of designs, constant patterns of organization emerge. All painted vessels, open or closed, small or large, and display similar patterns of horizontal registers, from simple horizontal bands to linear rows of more intricate designs. One complete cornet illustrates the horizontal organization of different registers of overlapping multiple chevrons, horizontal, parallel thin bands below and thorough, plain red paint to the tip of the base (Plate 10.4:4). Pendants or even vertical motives set below rims follow similar horizontal pattern but designs radiate inward to the centers of the base (Plate 10.6:1, 9). Discontinuous motifs, either painted or stamped, prevail on continuous ones (as bands or stripes) but linear, horizontal compositions are the rule. Like all rules there are exceptions, illustrated a few examples. Some fragments of pots or small holemouth jars seemingly bear unorganized, wide-spread tear-shaped impressions in a fashion that suggests running drops of water (Plate 10.30:4 and see, for example, Garfinkel 1992: Fig. 139:10). *Lunulae,* horse-shoe, nails, dots, dashes, palmettes and other impressions are designs shared by Gilat and the Nahal Zehora II assemblages (Orelle 1993: Appendix C).

Combined versus complementary design techniques. Geometric designs are painted on either closed or open shapes, but their distribution clearly favored the latter (4.22% *versus* 0.77%). The list of designs is not exhaustive. Recorded designs are simple bands, wavy lines or running chevrons (Plates 10.16:5; 10.35:4), but a large majority comprises more complex motifs of festoons, overlapping hoops, hatched triangles, latticed rhomboids (Plates 10.7:3; 10.19:2; 10.4:5, 9; 10.2:7). In opposite fashion, reserved, geometrical designs are created between geometrical painted motives of opposed triangles or festoons (Plates 10.4:6, 8; 10.7:3). More intriguing, stylize figurative designs derive from tiny pottery sherds (Plate 10.30:3).

Impressed motifs range from simple dots or dashes to *lunulae* and more elaborated palmettes. *Lunulae* and palmettes are always set in horizontal rows, sometimes wavy, as on necked jars. Dots express more complex, geometrical designs of multiples chevrons (Plate 10.16:3), or angular to triangular figures (Plate 10.30:16, 21). A major part of impressed motifs are horizontally displayed around the mid-profile of large pointed-base beakers and necked jars, or organized in multiple horizontal rows running around shoulders of holemouth jars (Plate 10.14:8, 9). However, the characteristic rupture in profile of carinated jars is always underlined by a row of impressed *lunulae* or dots (Plate 10.18:5–7). Over 10% of the pedestalled bowls bear impressed lunulae, or sometimes dots, set on the thickened junction line between the bowl and the pedestal. In these two latter cases, impressed designs are placed, in the same fashion as finger impressions, to emphasize the strong, protruding points of the profiles. Impressed designs are more frequently stamped on painted (or painted and burnished) surfaces. The technique of linear finger impressions is applied in a rather 'opportunist' fashion on vessels with thicken rims (the largest basins, pithoi, hole mouth jars, large necks) or on angular features such as protruding ridges between bowls and pedestals or in some cases, on the back of lug handles. These remarks also apply to the rare appliqué finger impressions (Plate 10.10:6, for example). However, finger impressions do not occur on the thick rims of either urns or torpedoes that are radical, plain types of vessels.

As illustrated with necked jars (Plates 10.19:2; 10.21:6), painting is meant as a background for impressions, but its eventual convolutions of designs are not related to the development of impressed ones. The apparent lack of correlation between painted and impressed designs finds its best illustration with a small goblet. Painted, intricate *rinceaux* are overlapped with triple rows of dotted chevrons (Plate 10.24:6). By contrast, complementary correlation of designs is illustrated with reserved, impressed fields and red paint surfaces. Horizontal, painted registers define reserved zones of impressed cream-ware on evenly burnished vessels. Wavy, impressed stripes of reserved cream-ware are rare but seem characteristic of cornets (Plate 10.4:11). Associated to this reserved tecnique, brownish to light orange paint contrasts with the dark red paint that covers the outside of cream-ware tulip bowls. In this last case, painting deliberately masks the cream-ware on the outside surface and sets off the creamy, white self-slip inside surface of the tulip bowls.

Time-consuming in terms of technical investment, painted-burnished wares with reserved and impressed registers remains discrete in the assemblage. It is also exclusive. This technique is only applied on selected open vessels: rare large V-shaped bowls with convex, parallel walls, large pointed-base beakers and cornets. Evidence from numerous, large or small fragments converge to suggest a similar organization of designs on the large bowls and cornets as the reserved, impressed band is placed right above mid-profile. The reserved, impressed band is placed below mid-profile on large pointed-base beakers. Again, recurrent observations on rims, bases and large sherds made from orange-painted and burnished cream ware, suggest that only one narrow, impressed stripe decorates these beakers. However, some rare sherds suggest that intricate, perhaps 'free style' painted designs do occur (Plate 10.24:6).

Decorated Versus Undecorated Vessels: The Means of Value

Social added value is generally—and reasonably—bestowed upon decorated vessels, a status that seems challenged at Gilat. Ring-based tulip bowls, tubular goblets, urns, torpedoes jars are not decorated, a characteristic that they seemingly share with one type of pedestalled vessels, chalices on stem. This short inventory obviously does not include 'pots and pans' but elaborated, fine vessels (to the exception of a rare, crudely made goblets) that comprise over 4% of the total assemblage, and 10% of the total undecorated vessels (Table 10.9a and 10.9b). These vessels are singularized either by morphological characters or by time-consuming techniques involved in their making. Pedestals (either stems or ring bases) are meant to set off containers of particular shapes. Tubular vessels and torpedoes are at least double-walled or double-bottomed vessels. Moreover, a large majority of these vessels are not locally made and have been imported to the site. This is the case for all the burnished churns and all the torpedoes jars, and for almost 50% of the tubular urns and all the ring-based tulip bowls. Contextual evidence and restrictive patterns of spatial distribution emphasize the status of these undecorated vessels, to the exception of churns. For example, one tubular urn whose surface is roughly scrapped with a knife is part of one unique dog burial deposit. Torpedoes and ring-based tulip bowls compound with complex and/or decorated vessels in loci of intense, seemingly ceremonial activities at the site as necked jars, V-shaped vessels or holemouth jars with elaborated designs cluster in areas devoted to seemingly domestic activities (see below).

Specific patterns of decoration cannot be assigned to specific sources of production, to the exception of decorated cream-ware vessels, that show the most intricate patterns of painted and/impressed designs. In categories of vessels that comprise undecorated and decorated vessels, some contradictory patterns emerge. One third of the V-shaped vessels are undecorated (Table 10.9a). Local bowls and large bowls, issued from either local or off-site (in the upper Shephela) production centers) are decorated in similar proportions but, wheel shaped V-shaped bowls are undecorated (the technique seems sufficient for increasing the bowls' value). Imported basins are all decorated. However, the most delicate vessels, cornets and some of the large pointed-base beakers, made from cream ware and adorned with complex geometrical designs, or painted and burnished with impressed designs set on a reserved band are local by-products.

Table 10.9a. Distribution of designs on open shapes.

Vessels	Designs (% per category)									
undecorated			3		5			8		n/N**=
31.2%	68.5	0.3	-	-	-	-	-	-	-	15.1
	(5.1)									
29.46%	52	16	-	0.02	2.5	-	-	-	0.02	9.5
	(5.1)			(100)	(100)					
33.6%	31	23.7		-	-	8	3.3	-	-	7.2
7.5% ped. bowl	46	-	10.2	-	-	36.3	-	-	-	0.65
	(#)	-	-	-	-	-	-	-	-	0.83
100% chal./stem	-	-	-	-	-	34	-	-	-	0.039
66.7% chal./bow*	-	-	-	-	-	-	-	-	-	0.38
47% ped. plate	53									
21%	79	#	-	-	-	-	-	-	-	11.6
	(61)									
100%	-	-	-	-	-	-	-	-	-	2
60.6%	39.1	-	#	-	-	-	-	0.3	-	1.5
61%	39	-	-	-	-	-	-	-	-	5.7
16%	84	-	-	-	-	-	-	-	-	0.8
9.6%	90.4	-	-	-	-	-	-	-	-	4.8
2%	29.7	-	-	63.8	6.4	-	-	-	-	0.4
	(100)			(100)	(100)					
0%	-	89.2	-	-	10.7	-	-	-	-	1
					(100)					
100%	-	-	-	-	-	-	-	-	-	0.7
100%	-	#	-	-	-	-	-	-	-	0.5
%/N** 21.84%	35.32	4.22	0.06	0.3	0.38	0.82	0.23	0.009	0.019	62.7

**N=10429 vessels

*chalice on bowed stem represent 2% of the pedestalled vessels, yet counting is made according to fragmented stems and associated sherds, making alleatory the actual frequency of decoration on this type of vessel. # — very rare, on fragmented profiles. (-) burnished vessels per type.

Table 10.9b. Distribution of designs on closed shapes.

Vessels	Designs (% per category)								n/N**=
undecorated									n/N**=
9.79% pithoi	6	2.2	-	-	-	76.7	5.3	-	4.1
91%	9	-	-	-	-	-	-	-	11.5
52.1%	37.7	3.2	1.1	5.3	-	0.9	-	-	7.1
41.25%	9.3	10.2	10.8	27.7	-	0.75	-	-	5
90.2%	9.8	-	-	-	-	-	-	-	7.3
(27%)									
21.1%	78.9								0.6
(#)									
100%	-	-	-	-	-	-	-	-	0.9
(31%)									
%.N** 24.8%	5.3	0.77	1.57	1.7	-	3.24	0.22	-	36.7

**N=10.429 vessels; (-) burnished vessels per type

Table 10.9c. Distribution of decoration technique in the whole assemblage (M.N.I) versus sherds.

All vessels N= 10429	Types of designs									
46.64% undecorated	40.5%	4.99%	1.63%	2%	0.38%	4.06%	0.45%	0.009%	0.019%	53.36% decorated
All pottery sherds N= 229.300	Types of designs									
36.18% undecorated	42 9%	7.29%*	3.01%	1.82%	3.9%	4.16%	0.69%	0.02%	0.03%	63 82% decorated

*42% are sherds with painted designs on the inside—meaning that at least 42% belong to open shapes.

The Structure of Gilat's Assemblage with References to Late Prehistory Regional Assemblages

The complex structure of Gilat's assemblage should be understood in its historical context by defining what it encompasses, upstream, in terms of genealogy and what it generates, downstream, in terms of innovation. However, available southern Levantine assemblages are paradoxical and inadequate fields of comparison and inter-site significance is largely impaired by the lack of contextual information. Differences in the inventory of vessels but also in techniques and patterns of decoration narrow the field of comparison with assemblages deriving either from Chalcolithic or from Late Neolithic assemblages (the term 'assemblage' is perhaps unsuitable with regard to published ceramics materials, mostly composed of selected pottery sherds with the exception of a few sites).

Dimensional ranking within the open-shape categories is a trend that is perceptible—notwithstanding differences in morphology that mark cultural origins—in some Neolithic assemblages. Deep bowls and seemingly pedestalled chalices in the Yarmukian assemblage, at Munhata IIB, and at least one open shape (deep carinated bowls) in the Wadi Rabah assemblage, at Munhata IIA, range from small and medium size (cf. Garfinkel 1992). However, in contrast with the prevalence and variety of small, open shapes at Gilat, small containers are less numerous in Munhata' assemblages (2% to 2.5%) than the medium-sized vessels (8.7 to 14.6% of the total assemblage—the highest percentage belongs to the Sha'ar Hagolan phase).[15] The impetus to make and use small vessels appears as an innovation in Gilat's assemblage that is still permeated by Wadi Rabah core components such as impressed designs (see below), carinated vessels and holemouth jars with a wide opening.

Hybridizing of morphological basic types shows manifest affinities to the corpus of (only small-sized?), varied, *'exceedingly common horn-shaped cups'* from Teleilat Ghassul (Koeppel *et al.*:55 and Pl. 76:3–26, from stratum IV, or A–D, cf. Hennessy 1969:23) as might the trend to form vessels with high and rather narrow profiles (for rare complete profiles see Koeppel *et al.* 1940: Pl. 78:11, 79:11). Torpedo jars and urns stand out unique in both Late Neolithic or Chalcolithic assemblages. They find parallels in rare examples from Wadi Zeita (Gat Govrin, along the Nahal Patish excavations by Jean Perrot, Commenge pers. obs.), and at Titorah in Judea (Lass, pers.com.).

Complex types of decoration, that might be meaningful references in terms of chronology, find many parallels in assemblages assigned to the later phase of the Neolithic period in Israel, namely the Wadi Rabah phase, coined by Kaplan's excavations at the eponymous site (Kaplan 1958). The most striking parallels encompass impressed designs (with many similarities in designs and patterns) at Gilat and, for example, at Munhata IIA (4.2%; Garfinkel 1992:80–1). The genealogy, from the Yarmukian phase onward, of impressed, reserved bands of cream ware on red burnished background has been documented by the comprehensive 'grammatical' analysis of decoration at Nahal

Zehora (Orelle 1993:154–5).[16] Impressed designs, most of them stamped *lunulae,* can be traced from western Galilee to the Jordan Valley. The assemblage of Gilat marks the extent of the Wadi Rabah tradition to the south, as Serabit el-Khadim may represent the southernmost, remote outpost of this 'Early Chalcolithic' culture in Western Sinai (Beit-Arieh 1980; Commenge 2002:140–1). This latter site and Wadi Zeita (Gat Govrin) provide Pointed-base beakers with red burnished and impressed designs on reserved cream ware, closely correlate Gilat's assemblage with sites located along the Nahal Patish (Wadi Zeita, where one violin-shaped figurine was recovered) or in the Sinai (Serabit el-Khadim). Along the coastal terraces of Northeastern Sinai, site R-48, located west of Yamit, have yielded *fossiles directeurs* of the Early Chalcolithic phase illustrated at Gilat (associated with one violin-shaped figurine), as did site Y2, on the Khan-Yunis coast, near Qatif (Oren and Gilead 1981; Oren 1993:1387).

At other Chalcolithic sites, notably in the northern Negev, fields of comparison for impressed designs are narrow to non-existent. One impressed sherd from Shiqmim may be part of a large (pointed-base?) beaker, a type of vessel not recorded at the site (Levy 1987, Fig. 12.19:12). The assemblage of Grar offers decoration apparently well related to other northern Negev sites production, but some impressed lunulae and dots designs stand for attention (Gilead 1995, Fig. 4.20:4, 7). Impressed lunulae on either closed or open shapes have been recorded at Ghassul (Hennessy 1969: Fig. 8a:2, 8b:3, respectively assigned to phases D and E).

From a broad, general perspective, the frequency of decorated vessels in the assemblage of Gilat is roughly similar to observations made, for example, on the assemblage of Bir es-Safadi (Commenge-Pellerin 1990:31). Observations on smaller assemblages, Abu Matar or Zumeili, for example, show higher proportions of decorated vessels (up to 82%, but these assemblages have been sorted and 'the best part' selected...see Commenge-Pellerin 1987). No records on decoration frequency are published for Grar (Gilead 1995) or Shiqmim (Levy 1987). With consideration on the non-exhaustive records on Chalcolithic pottery assemblages, it can perhaps be stated that structural differences in decorative patterns between Gilat and the Beersheva sites' assemblages opposes a 'filled' conception of design to a 'framed' conception of design. The decoration of vessels at Gilat aims to fill space and/or to cover large zones (and, frequently, even the inside of open shapes). The decoration of vessels in the assemblage of the Beersheva sites soberly emphasizes the 'architecture' of the vessels in underlining rims, necks bases, shoulders, mid-body circumferences and handles. The quasi absence on Gilat's V-shaped vessels of a red-paint band running around the vessel rim openings—colloquially coined as 'lipstick' design amongst specialists-, that is a characteristic, ubiquitous feature in other Chalcolithic assemblages compounds the gap (cultural and most certainly chronological) between Gilat and the Beersheva sites (Fig. 10.6:3 is an exception). However, these two opposed conceptions of pottery designs are not estranged: they converge in dividing space and volumes horizontally and in the linear composition of motifs.

The Nature of Consumption: Versatility and Specificity of Functional Means and Meaning

'*Were pots made first for foods?*'—this crucial question was addressed by Vitelli (1989) in the context of nascent Aegean Neolithic pottery production. In the following approach, this view is taken as a lead, in a broader perspective and in a less literal sense, I shall consider that the functional analysis of vessels should not be restricted to material necessity but rather should also include its social, primary value. The integrative organization of Gilat's assemblage entails intricate and articulate components whose strata and contextual significance must be evaluated.

At Gilat, contexts of discard provide, in most cases, the setting for intense consumption of vessels. Patterns of production systems have already suggested the complex nature of demand as

41% of vessels are obtained at off-site production centers. Demand for commodities has been proposed as *'a function of a variety of social practices and classifications rather than a mysterious emanation of human needs'*...(Appadurai 1986:29, cf. Douglas and Isherwood 1980). The nature of demand—and thus of consumption—of vessels at Gilat points to a 'centripetal' flow of vessels (and most probably for part of them, their contents) to the sanctuary.

Many idiosyncratic features of Gilat, as demonstrated in this volume (Chapters 6–9, 12–16, this volume), emphasize the possible ceremonial character of consumption for this assemblage. In the perspective of vessel consumption, ceremonial and profane functions are not, *a priori*, mechanically, different functions. Ceremony can add value to modest artifacts just as elaborate artifacts may be used in secular but nonetheless socially significant endeavors. *Singularization* and/or *commodization* in the lifespan of vessels, as defined by Kopytoff, are not immobile (Kopytoff 1986:73). However, the potter has in view 'the first use to which vessels will be put' (Sterner 1989:453), either secular or ceremonial.[17]

Investigation of the integrative organization of this assemblage is intended as an introduction to its behavioral context. With optimism and boldness, it tries to identify some grammatical rules inside the structure of the assemblage, whose syntax still needs some elucidation. In order to trace and document the nature of demand at Gilat, the plausible significance of—at least—some of the assemblage's components must be ascertained and its interpretation screened through contextual evidence. It has been suggested that consumption aims at sending and receiving social messages (Appadurai 1986:31). More specifically, these 'messages' as signified by pottery vessels, are not meant for outsiders but for the users (Sterner 1989:458; Leach 1976:45). This observation may provide a safeguard to secure this investigation on intra-site activities, and in defining the functional nature of the site of Gilat. Sites, whether they are villages, sanctuaries, seasonal stations or cemeteries fulfill a function. Accordingly, sites may be defined as circumscribed social spaces whose activities isolate or link them to other sites in a regional network of similar, complementary or opposed activities. The determination of prehistoric, Middle Eastern sites function through the variability of pottery assemblages has already yielded seminal results. For example, functional comparison of ceramic assemblages from Tepe Sarab and Seh Gabi (Mount C) in Central western Iran, based on thorough theoretical and empirical foundations, has established the seasonal use of the former by special-task groups and the year-round, home-base occupation of the latter (Henrikson and McDonald 1983). In the southern Levant, a pioneer approach by Kangas focused on ceramics at Shiqmim's upper and lower villages and at the nearby cemetery of Mezad Aluf (Kangas 1994, and see Levy and Alon 1985). Intra-settlement variability of vessels, related either to primary (household, storage facilities) or secondary deposit contexts (sealed structures) has been evaluated for the occupational sequence at Bir es Safadi (Commenge-Pellerin 1990:33–5, 172–5 and Fig. 7). Intra-site variability based on pottery rims has been undertaken at Grar and compared to other assemblages (Gilead 1995:197–214 and Figs 4.23–9). The sanctuary site at Ein Gedi in the Judean desert (Ussishkin1980) or funerary sites along the coastal plain and the Shephela (Perrot and Ladiray 1980: Van den Brink forthcoming: Commenge forthcoming), in the north-western Negev (Goren and Fabian 2002) or in the Galilee (Gal *et al.* 1997), provide other, specific or eclectic, sources of comparison.

The meaning of any artifact is fundamentally encapsulated in the way it is comprehended and used (Sterner 1989:459; Chippendale 1992:274). Some methodological lines are here proposed in investigating formal organization and contextual inferences. Although sometimes recalcitrant in the field of meaning *per se*, recurrent information sketches out the complexity of modes of consumption as it points out its versatility during the occupational sequence of Gilat.

Basic Function Versus Primary Value

Morphological characteristics of vessels combine aspects of geometry and physical possibilities with functional classes of vessels to meet a specific frame of morphological conditions. Pots are made to fulfill basic functions—consumption, storage and transformation of edible, solid or liquid matters (eventual storage of non edible goods can also be added to this non-exhaustive list). As such, implications imposed by function upon form have been thoroughly tested and corroborated, and even universally documented (Ericson *et al*. 1972; Henrickson and McDonald 1983). But how basic is the intent behind needs and why? Any adaptive determinism to human needs fails to address this question. To stretch the point, one can suggest, with some reasoning, that all small open vessels at Gilat were meant for individual consumption, either drinking or eating. However, the variety of shapes of these small vessels obviously stem from protocols of behavior and social considerations. I shall propose that degrees in functionality that refer to primary value in use can be assigned to 'intermediary' *degrés du fait* (with reference to stylistic, cultural choices ascribed to the '*derniers degrés du fait*' (Leroi-Gourhan 1945:30–36; Lemonnier 1993:24). As it is often the case with the wealth of evidence collected in the northern Negev, demonstration is available *in situ*. The simplification of the inventory of pottery shapes to a basic, domestic kit of the later Beersheva sites' assemblages cannot reasonably be related to limitation in basic needs in the mere context of the advent of specialized pastoralism and the eventual raise of complex societies.

It is assumed here that significant, functional, ranking can be drawn from the 'anatomical' particularities of vessels. This systemic approach, inferred from the integrative organization of the assemblage, is meant to track a plausible 'ceremonialization' of vessel function. It is corroborated by data issued from investigation into intra-site spatial distribution. Kansa and Levy (below) have derived information from the localization of vessels in the most secured loci in areas of architectural preservation (that yielded 40% of the ceramic assemblage), and plotted some selected shapes, along criteria defined below. Results substantiate discrimination in the spatial distribution of vessels. Moreover, patterns of utilization show a shift in the nature and extent of ceremonial activity through time, in particular from the earlier Stratum IIC to Stratum IIB. This investigation of patterns of spatial distribution suggests highly differentiated and specific functions. Functional ranking that most probably indicates primary, selective areas of profane and ceremonial activities, also points to more segregated endeavors that may involve kinship and/or gender or age. The import of vessels content may also have been an essential vector in the restricted utilization of materials by these social groups.

Morphological Boundary Conditions in Ranking Vessels' Function

Different morphological parameters were identified to interpret patterns that may reflect specific vessel use in Gilat's assemblage. Interweaving correlations of several criteria among the different ceramic groups may reveal their assignation to specific functions. This selection aims to define degrees in functionality and a plausible ceremonial functional of some types besides other major functional categories. In addition to size, some morphological elements have been recognized as discriminative components in the structure of the assemblage. Although basic functional classes can be broadly defined as consumption—for serving and/or storage—either fixed or meant for transport—and transformation, the contextual conditions and circumstances of vessel utilization may vary. Some morphological elements point to the modification of vessels from their primary function of consumption (storage, transformation etc.) to their use in ceremonial activities. This may be seen with the pointed bases, the plain, narrow bases of heavy containers, the pedestals fixed to vessels already set with either pointed bases (ring-based tulip bowls) or vessels with no proper base (small churns). The figurative lug handles may also point to ritual use as they are affixed to vessels with either pointed bases or pedestals. Moreover, the miniaturized versions of generic types occur with vessels that present at least one of the selected morphological elements (tubular goblets, pointed-base beakers, small churns). One can observe that a large part of these special vessels were chosen to construct the effigy vessels presented in Chapter 15: churns (by the means of the ram's body and as the vessel carried on the Lady's head), pointed-base beakers carried on the back of the ram effigy, and pedestalled vessels, one placed under the Lady's arm and one meant as her seat (Chapter 15, Fig. 15.1–6).

The Means and Meaning of Ranked Consumption within Open Shapes for Individual and Communal Serving

The multiplicity of small shapes in the Gilat ceramic assemblage highlights the importance of individual serving. This is seen in the bi- or tri-modality in size that reflects variation in modes of utilization. Proposed modes of utilization, corroborated by spatial distribution, must be explicated. To this end, two more parameters should be added to the parameters listed above that introduce, *de facto*, distinct treatment of flat based V-shaped vessels *versus* other open vessels. The first one is derived from the range of vessel capacity, as V-shaped vessels overextend their inventory to vessels of very large capacity, and the difference of other open shapes (Table 10.7). The second one derives from the spatial analysis that tends to differentiate locations of use and/or discard of V-shaped vessels and other open vessels that fit the pre-defined parameters for possible ceremonial function. The beakers, built up with a flat base (and indicative of technical innovation), are frequently found in association with 'ceremonial vessels' or in concentrations in restricted areas that do not include V-shaped bowls. Whereas V-shaped bowls, as demonstrated below, are found with clusters of vessels seemingly used in domestic activities (Table 10.2a-b).

Tri-modal sized vessels are frequent in other Prehistoric assemblages. For example, Early Neolithic Ertebølle but also later assemblages from southern Scandinavia provide information on tri-modal sized, pointed-bottom vessels[18] (Gebauer 1995). These vessels are meant for cooking and serving and their capacity range presents some analogies with open vessels at Gilat. The smallest Ertebølle vessels have a maximal capacity of 70 cl that fits in Gilat's medium capacity range and medium-sized Ertebølle vessels have a maximal capacity of one liter (100 cl) that may parallel large V-shaped bowls and large ring-based tulip bowls. The largest Ertebøolle vessels have a capacity of 3.5 liters (3500 cl) equivalent to the capacity of the large pointed-base beakers at Gilat or V-shaped basins. The ethnographic record is more suggestive on social behavior as it documents circumstances of vessels utilization. Cooking and non-cooking vessels come in three sizes, for example in the Shipibo-Conibo assemblages of eastern Peru, as some other types of vessels comprise only one size (DeBoer and Lathrap 1979). Observations on the primary use of tri-modal sized vessels in household context give evidence for formal/functional class divisions, but vessels of different sizes have the same basic function. *Ollas* are used for transformation, jars for storage, transportation and serving, and beer mugs for serving. The communal use of the largest vessels and the individual character and mobility of the smallest vessels is observed for all types of vessels. Large beer mugs are used for communal drinking during feasts (as it is passed around), medium-sized mugs are daily used for drinking beer and small mugs are carried on trips (DeBoer and Lathrap 1979:105–6). *Ollas* (open V-shaped vessels with a vertical, concave upper part) are most commonly used for brewing alcoholic beverages but medium-sized *ollas* are also used daily as cooking pots as small *ollas* are reserved to heating medicines. Necked jars are also tri-modal in size. The largest are used for serving beer, the medium-sized jars are used for carrying water and storage, and the smallest are gourd-shaped flasks. Tri-modal in size beer mugs shows that circumstances—ordered by social behavior and protocol—intervene to rank a similar function. One can also note that large jars, as occasional 'punch bowls', and large *ollas* are communally used during special social events. By contrast, medium-sized food bowls (a unique size for this category of vessels), are communally but selectively used, according to gender and age (male/children *versus* women).

This latter example underlines correlations of size patterns and covariance in different functional classes. It may shed some light upon the meaning of size range in Gilat's assemblage of open vessels, but it does not explicate the formal variation of an assemblage that encapsulates tubular goblets and urns, pointed-base beakers, tulip bowls and cornets. All these shapes, in particular the smallest, point to one basic function—serving (as cooking is improbable—there are no cooking pots evidenced at Gilat—, storage and transport are impractical). Material expression may entail many possible explanations that involve temporality—with functional classes determined by the ceremonial agenda?—and/or social identity—with functionnal classes determined by gender and/or age or rank?—and/or specific content.[19] Indexical, self-referential information is necessary for ceremonial performance as its variability counter-balances invariant, canonical sequences (Rappaport 1999:328). Robust, thick-bottomed beakers and goblets contrast with delicate cornets and tulip bowls as basic shapes juxtapose with hybrid shapes. Moreover, internal ranking, in each or all of the functional classes, may be induced, in subtle intricate scales, by decoration, ware, or emphasized by the exogenous provenance of vessels.

The relative narrow openings of the largest vessels (up to 18 cm for the largest urns or pointed-base beakers) make them inappropriate for serving by scooping. Their capacity ranges from 1.7 to almost 3.0 liters. Large pointed-base beakers may have been used for communal drinking. 70% (of which 6.4% are made of cream-ware) of these vessels are painted, burnished and delicately impressed with palmettes. This may also suggest communal drinking for either high status consumers and/or precious, consecrated content. Thick-rimmed urns may have been used for short term storage and pouring rather than drinking. Libation, especially for flaring urns, may have been instrumental in merging value of contents and containers (see below and cf. Chapter 15). Urns and tubular goblets cluster with other ceremonial vessels. This tends to demonstrate that fine, thin-walled vessels mingle with well made but coarser ones in a seemingly unobtrusive fashion. One tubular urn was meant as an offering in the dog burial in Stratum 3B (Locus 698 and see Fig. 10.27:5; Levy 1992). The bottom portion of the vessel was double-walled—a regular feature for urns, and the lower part was neatly, perhaps intentionally, broken. In considering the way the elements join and overlap with slab construction, the 'cap' at the bottom may have simply been worn and damaged. Dog burials appear as a cultural echo of an Epipaleolithic Levantine tradition anchored in the Natufian culture. The privilege relationship between humans and dogs, the first animal ever domesticated, is illustrated by ceremonial burials of humans and dogs at several Natufian sites (Valla 1990; Tchernov and Valla 1997). Valla's comments concerning the protocols of deposition in Natufian burials—and other circumstances—strike a chord at Gilat: '*In a way, symbolizing thought appears to have assimilated dogs to humans, or in other words, the domestication of dogs seems to be understood as their introduction into the humanized side of the world*' (my translation, Valla 1990:174–5). In the context of Chalcolithic agro-pastoralist societies, dogs appear, beyond shepherds' substitutes or congenial companions, as actual *alter ego*(s). Confirmation of common status may be expressed and affirmed in similar if not more ostentatious funeral ceremonial. The tubular urn associated with this dog burial is a (single) vessel imported to Gilat from Transjordan (Goren this volume). This case is not isolated at Gilat as the cranium of a dog was topped by a cluster of vessels (L 787, Stratum IIB2), most defined as ceremonial, and here all contextually ritualized: two (one complete, one incomplete) fenestrated chalices (Plate 10.9:4 and 6), one red-painted beaker (Fig. 10.1:16), two large beakers and one large pointed-base beaker (Figs 10.26:1; 10.29:1; 10.27:6), and one (fragmented) bow rim jar with twin handles. For a discussion of the dog burials at Gilat, see Grigson (this volume).

Ubiquitous, small V-shaped bowls are the simplest vessels in the open-shape category. They are also, marginally the focus of technological innovation as discussed above. V-shaped bowls have been assigned to elementary yet polyvalent functions (Commenge-Pellerin 1987:49). Recurrent observations in the ethnographic record point to serving and eating functions for open bowls with flat bottoms whose dimensions encompass small to large bowls in the assemblage of Gilat (Henrickson and McDonald 1983:632). In the mainly domestic contexts at Safadi, small V-shaped bowls are also found near large basins or large storage jars, a location that suggest their use as scoops. At this latter site, the lack of evidence for standardization fails to document their utilization as measures of volume.[20] Spatial attribute analysis of V-shaped vessels has been considered at Shiqmim Upper and Lower Village and at the nearby cemetery of Mezad Aluf (Cemetery). The narrow size range of V-shaped bowls at Cemetery I led Kangas to propose a special function for the smaller bowls (Kangas in Levy 1985:78 and Fig. 5). The emphasis of personal ownership and/or offering meant for an individual, singularized adult male is evidenced in burial L. 806 at Gilat Stratum IIA, Area J. In this burial, one V-shaped bowl was associated with the deceased. Crucial information is also expected from the burial cave at Peqi'in, in Upper Galilee. The concomitance at the site of V-shaped bowls and 'goblets is reminiscent of the more elongated cornets' (pointed-base beakers?) (Gal *et al.* 1997:150)[21] and seems highly promising to complement this discussion.

Basins may be considered as 'family sized' containers, meant for communal preparation and consumption (Commenge-Pellerin 1987, 1990). The correlation between consumption and 'unrestricted' vessels (Henrickson and McDonald 1983:532) may confirm that basins with thickened rims (Plate 10.8:2, 6–7) introduce a morphological boundary between consumption and storage. Dry-storage vessels, whose openings are wide enough for scooping, were used for temporary or medium term storage. However, the range of dimensions proposed by Henrickson and McDonald (opening diameter of 22 to 52 cm) span large bowls to large basins in the inventory of Gilat. The (two) spouted, large basins of Gilat (Plates 10.8:5, 10.35:4), obviously meant for storing liquids, challenge the predetermined attribution of dry-storage to squat, low vessels with low centers of gravity as derived from ethnographic data (Ericson *et al.* 1972:89). A fair number of large basins with spouts (vats or kraters) are recorded at Chalcolithic sites in the Golan Heights. Claire Epstein has suggested that they were connected to oil production (by decantation) and storage (Epstein 1981:79; 1998:164). In contrast with the Golan, olive oil consumption rather than production is probable at Gilat (see below and Appendix 1—Burton and Levy, this volume). But this process of cleaning or separation may have been duplicated for dairy by-products such as cream that may have been collected through the spout after settling of the milk. In any event, the spout was placed near the rim to allow the vessel to be used at full capacity, and not, as suggested elsewhere, specific to its decanting function.

Extensive information on the interregional distribution of cornets has been summarized by Gilead (Gilead (1995:162–3). The author claims 'a more profane function' for cornets recovered at sites like Grar or Ghassul *versus* the large assemblage of cornets found at the sanctuary of Ein Gedi (Ussishkin 1980:38). Notwithstanding the absence of chronological perspective (Grar *versus* the Beersheva sites' assemblages) or the liberal assignation of 'domestic context' to Teleilat Ghassul (Gilead 1995:163), it appears that the very presence, however discrete, of elaborate cornets in 'domestic assemblages' may argue in favor of valorization and not trivialization of their function. Contextual evidence for centralization—at Gilat or Ghassul—or specialization—at Ein Gedi—of ceremonial activities does not rule out their presence in household contexts, at other types of settlements. Moreover, Chalcolithic settlement-sites also give evidence for some ceremonial and/or ceremonial activities, centered on specific architectural features—buildings, sealed rooms, caches (Levy 1987; Commenge Pellerin 1990). The multiplication of simple V-shaped bowls and the (consequential?) disappearance or recession in production of various, elaborate open shapes, notably at the Beersheva sites, may infer the functional polyvalence, in different realms of social behavior, of V-shaped vessels. It is necessary, in any comparative enterprise, to consider parameters that are, *de facto,* variables: contextual information that may identify the function of sites without ignoring the chronological indications that corroborate processual evaluation or interpretation. However, and this may significantly be the case with cornets, the residual appearance of vessels of symbolical, socially selective function, should not be ignored.

A minimal number of two hundreds pedestalled vessels have been collected at Gilat. This is, so far, the largest number of pedestalled vessels ever collected at any south Levantine Chalcolithic site. The addition of ring-based vessels, either large tulip bowls or small churns, emphasizes the privileged role of shapes literally 'put on a pedestal'. In contrast with other vessels segregated by exclusive parameters of formal variation, pedestalled vessels belong to a generic type, anchored in a Levantine pottery tradition from as early as Yarmukian times and whose posterity extends into the Early Bronze Age. As already observed with the V-shaped bowls, this 'permanence' in pottery assemblages (whose interregional widespread distribution is mitigated by discrepancies in frequency (see, for exhaustive references: Gilead 1995:163–4) is paralleled with the notable presence of pedestalled vessels at burial sites (in particular at Azor—Perrot and Ladiray 1980, or for example at Shoham, Van den Brink forthcoming, Commenge forthcoming). Pedestalled goblets with basket handles are part of the funerary deposit at the mortuary site of Kissufim (Goren and Fabian 2002: Fig. 4.2). One pedestalled globular vessel, adorned with painted designs of 'palm' leaves and basketry, was recovered at Shiqmim in a cache of thirteen vessels (Levy and Alon 1985; Levy 1987: Fig: 12.14). Fenestrated pedestal vessels are also frequent at the Ein Gedi shrine (Ussishkin 1980). At Gilat, fenestrated pedestal vessels are illustrated by various shapes (most of them of incomplete profiles). Fenestrated pedestal vessels cluster with other 'ceremonial' shapes. The large opening and the low wall of either pedestalled chalices or plates suggest display of the content, a function that may be denied to narrow, deep-welled bowls. Pedestalled vessels do not bear any superficial calcination that could document their use as 'incense burners'—a function often allotted to these type of containers. Fire clouding or soot has been observed one a few vessels at Grar (with no specification on the part of the vessel damaged by heating, Gilead 1995:165). More significant are soot deposits inside high pedestalled chalices on which were laid human skulls, in the burial cave at Peqi'in (Gal *et al.* 1997:150). The possible utilization of pedestalled vessels for processing (edible?) ingredients, may be inferred by one basalt, pedestalled vessel used as a mortar, an utilization identified for part of the large basalt bowls, in the assemblage of Safadi (Commenge forthcoming).

Ring-based tulip bowls plausibly double as attention focusing devices. The symmetrical position of three horizontal lug handles gives two 'faces' to the bowl. Placed on delicate ring-based vessels, allusive features to a human face and probable impersonation epitomize the importance of figurative display, by the means of pottery vessels, in ceremonial performance. In the impressive, largely figurative pottery materials from the Peqi'in burial cave, some bowls (on very high, fenestrated pedestals) are designed with painted human features with a nose in relief (Gal *et al.* 1997:150). Impersonation appears seems confined to Peqi'in, as it insists on the private destination of the dedicated vessel. More allusive, less skilled human representations are also remarked on some pithoi from the Beersheva sites. Large, vertical lug handles, generally finger impressed, stand for the prominent nose of a bearded face painted around it; symmetrical orifices of the lug figure the eyes (Commenge-Pellerin 1987, Fig. 29:2; Levy 1987, Fig. 12.15:9).

Multimodal Inferences of Storage, Transformation and Transport: Multifocal Inferences

The embodiment of small churns (another ring-based vessel) by the Ram as a mythical character (see Chapter 15, this volume) and/or by rams as an *ovis* species seems corroborated by twin horned handles set on this type of vessels. Miniature churns—with no horned handles or ring bases—are found at settlement-sites (Commenge Pellerin 1987, Fig. 36:8, with impressed designs of palmettes, 9–11) yet also at mortuary sites (Perrot and Ladiray 1980: Fig. 71:1; Goren and Fabian 2002, Fig. 4.5:3). I have argued (Chapter 15, this volume) that the recurrent allusion to rams that stems from the explicit interplay between morphological characters of vessels and animal attributes (barrel-shaped body, horns) could represent metaphors,[22] recondite in relating the function of spindle-shaped, spouted vessels that have been coined as 'churns' in the literature (Kaplan 1954). In the realm of more materialistic, chemical corroboration, tenuous but direct evidence for milk residues in churns can have been evidenced by Margie Burton (pers.com; Burton 2004). The use of elaborate, heavy vessels by Chalcolithic agro-pastoralist societies instead of light, easy pouring containers such as goat skins used by pastoralist Bedouin tribes in the ethnographic present has never been addressed (but Epstein underlined the lack of churns in the Golan and the plausible use of goat-skins, Epstein 1998:164). The weight of filled churns (even in considering that space should be allowed for churning) can be evaluated as well over ten kilos for medium-sized churns and over fifteen kilos for large churns. The horizontal axis of the body and the upright, triangular handles set at each end of the vessels, are highly adequate features for churning by lateral movement. Obviously, formal variation within this category of vessels indicates that different processes may have been involved for a functional class that can be meant for dairy by-products transformation. But what kind of by-products would have been induced by churning? The fat part of rested milk must be skimmed. It gains density through churning as buttermilk tends to form butter lumps. Thick-walled churns made from grainy white clay, with overlarge, globular spouts recovered at Grar or at the Beersheva sites thus appear the most suitable apparatus for milk churning (Commenge-Pellerin 1990: Fig. 56:8–11; Gilead 1995, Fig. 4; 12:2). Churns with broad, globular spout are absent at Gilat. Churns with 'regular' anatomical characters are by many means closed shapes with one, narrowed opening from which even milk curd and whey would have been uneasily extracted, forming eventually thick, fat deposits at the bottom (a goat skin is supple enough to be pressed for extraction and can be turned inside out). Fat deposits on the inside of jars reduce evaporation in a way that makes redundant the outside burnishing of the vessel. The jars used for making and storing 'lassi' in Nepal are not burnished, in contrast to milk jars (Birmingham 1975:377, 384). In Gilat's assemblage, only churns made from Moza clay are thoroughly burnished. As they are containers that were produced off-site, burnishing could be assigned to functional and/or value added to by-products issued from specialized production, and meant for trade (that also applies to torpedoes of the same provenance). The plausible processing of dairy by-products appears fastidious as it involves some 'culturally meaningful transformation' recently won in manipulating *nature*, in the plausible perspective of the advent of Secondary Products Revolution on this chronological horizon. In other words, one may consider that churns of 'regular shape' were meant as milk jars whose complex morphological characters had derived from the symbolic meaning of their plausible content. Small ringed—base churns with twin horned handles will thus encapsulate the clues to their—decipherable (?)—meaning (see Chapter 15).

Were churns used for transport? Churns in the Gilat assemblage offer the first evidence, in the Chalcolithic record, for off-site production. This information indirectly gives some weight to an old assumption that churns—and other jars—were transported (Kaplan 1969; Ussishkin 1980; Epstein 1985). The oblong, spindle-shaped volume of the churns and their narrow opening are features suitable for transport, either on peddlers' back or on beasts of burden. Carolyn Grigson has established the presence of domestic donkeys at Chalcolithic sites in the northern Negev as she has evidenced domestic horses at Shiqmim and Grar (Grigson 1993). Large, crossed painted bands that characterize churns at the Beersheva sites (Commenge-Pellerin 1990, Fig. 55:14) may reproduce rope or cord bounds fixing the vessels for churning but also 'pack-saddle' straps.[23] Jar stoppers made of raw clay can be fit to the spouts of churns (Commenge-Pellerin 1987, Fig. 31:1–2). Churns comprise 7.3% of the total M. N. I. of vessels in the assemblage of Gilat and at Grar, 5% of the total assemblage (Gilead 1995: Fig. 4.21). At Safadi, churns comprise 14% of the assemblage and rank as the most frequent vessels in the category of closed shapes. This information seems coherent with an early stage at Grar and Gilat of the advent of the Secondary Products Revolution and the subsequent choice of specialized pastoralism at the Beersheva sites in the northern Negev. However, another significant and relevant factor has to be taken into consideration. Grar and Gilat, located in an area above the present 250 mm isohyet, show different patterns of animal husbandry with higher figures for pig bones, and cattle (at Grar) than the agro-pastoralist sites in the Beersheva area (Grigson 1995). This may indicate a concern for 'importing' additional milk products to Gilat.

One dozen (fragmented) pedestalled strainers were found that add complementary information to the seemingly valorization of another device that may have been meant for food processing (of dairy by-products?). Strainers are mostly absent in Chalcolithic assemblages, but this kind of device fits vessels with complex morphological characters such as pedestalled vessels or miniature churns (Perrot and Ladiray 1980: Fig.71:1).

Concerning Olive Oil Routes...

Assignation of pottery to functional the classes of storage and transport can be securely proposed for torpedoes jars. In the perspective of off-site production that characterizes part of the Gilat assemblage, torpedoes stand out with high variability in raw materials (Goren pers.com) and centers of production were located either off-site in Judea or in the Shephela, at sources not too distant to the site (Chapter 9). All morphological elements—narrowness of profile, high plain base, thick double to triple walls (Plate 10.35:1, 3)—merge to indicate highly specialized containers. Gas chromatography of lipids extracted from torpedo jar walls reveals fatty acid profiles consistent with degraded olive oil (cf. Burton and Levy, this volume). The sample of Gilat pottery sherds studied by gas chromatography includes at least one urn fragment (568, loc. 39). Another tested fragment, unspecified, is thin-walled (0.8 cm) and belongs to another type of vessel (a churn? possibly a local, loessial specimen?).[24] Sources of pottery production are regionally circumscribed to geological deposits and are not definite sites on the map. Their location in the Judean Mountains coincides with an area where olive trees are part of the native arboreal vegetation. of the long-term macro-climate (Liphschitz 1988) suggests that the southern Shephela may be the southernmost border of this species. Perhaps more suggestive than olive stone distribution, are the distribution of remnants of olive wood at Early Holocene sites, from the PPNA onward, as they are found with relative frequency in the Judean Desert and in the Negev (Liphchitz et al., 447: Table 2). Olive oil production activities are documented as early as the Late Neolithic-Early Chalcolithic period along the Carmel coast in northern Israel, notably at Kfar Samir (Galili and Sharvit 1995). While the question of irrigated olive cultivation has been addressed for Teleilat Ghassul in the lower Jordan Valley, and olive stones have been recovered at other Chalcolithic sites (Abu Hamid, Tell esh Shuna North, Tel Tsaf, Qaliq—cf. Liphschitz et al. 1991: Fig. 1), evidence from Kfar Samir may suggest that 'large scale olive oil production preceded olive domestication by several centuries or even a whole millenia' (Kislev 1995:142). The sample of complete profiles suggests that (burnished) tubular torpedoes were made at Moza source-production centers and spindle torpedoes at Taqiya source production centers (in the southern Shephela). As it may be to speculative to draw firm conclusions from these observations, it remains that two different torpedo shapes reflect storage of olive oil and that the functional implications should have been a primary variable in the vessel selection for the gas chromatography study.

The frequency of torpedo jars at Gilat calls for comment. Approximately one hundred specimens were collected at the site. On the one hand, their relative scarcity at Gilat emphasizes functional specialization while their off-site provenance suggests social significance. However, torpedo jars are under represented in the storage class of vessels whereas holemouth jars are twenty times more numerous, and necked jars over five times more frequent. On the other hand, concerning the very limited of torpedo vessels recorded at other sites in this chronological horizon, torpedo jars appear 'concentrated' if not 'centralized' at Gilat. While a few torpedo bases have been found at Wadi Zeita (J. Perrot, pers. com., Goren pers.com.) and one (that may be a tubular urn) at Titorah in Judea (at location Modi'in near Jerusalem, Lass, pers.com.).[25] This type of vessels seems absent at Grar, in an assemblage that shows some significant similarities with Gilat's in both economy and material culture. Compared with churns, the spatial distribution of torpedo jars in close association to other specific shapes raises the question of their use in ceremonial activities. A row of standing torpedoes, lug handles akimbo, may have served as attention focusing devices as a display of exotic goods (cf. Chapter 5, Plates 5.65; 5.13).

The frequency of holemouth jars at Gilat (18.6%) is rather high with reference to other Chalcolithic sites (Grar, less than 15%, Safadi, 6.3%, Abu Matar, 8.2%). Mud-brick silos are frequently recorded at Gilat (see Chapter 5, this volume), as are bell-shaped silos at the Beersheva sites. Jars of medium and small sizes are more frequent than large, capacious jars at all those Chalcolithic sites. Evidence for storage facilities with concentrations of holemouth or necked jars are absent at Gilat as they are elsewhere (Commenge-Pellerin 1990:37). As necked jars and holemouth jars are generally recovered among clusters of basins, churns and bowls, torpedo jars are found in concentrations in selective areas.

Contextual details are provided in Chapter 5 (this volume) documenting a large holemouth jar with lug handles that was buried in previous occupational layers, with its opening set into the floor of Room 7, Stratum IIIA. The capacity of this jar averages 13 liters. The walls are thin, but not considerable if one considers one holemouth jar of similar proportions from Safadi (Commenge-Pellerin 1990, Fig. 40:7) or another large jar from Gilat (Plate 10.13:1). It is possible that this capacious holemouth jar was buried to secure its resistance to pressure when full, but other large jars at other sites seem to have been used in more usual storage locations. The use of one large storage pithos, interred in a pit, is documented at the early Chalcolithic site of Abu Hamid, in the Jordan Valley (Dollfus *et al.* 1988:577 and Fig. 7). The size of this pithos, ca. 1m in diameter and 1.50 m high—dwarfs the holemouth jar recovered at Gilat. At Abu Hamid, the opening of the pithos was doubled by a mudbrick ledge, built as the rim of a well, and the base of the pithos rests on a stone slab. Those buried, large jars may have been used as water storage containers. One can add that the burying of a jar meant for communal purposes, into either older occupational deposits or bedrock-sediments, may have also involved some symbolical processes with reference to foundation deposits. Those are immaterial in direct archaeological record, but one can note that Room 7 at Gilat, where the large holemouth jar was set, includes two walls with foundation deposits—one burial (L. 980) and one Egyptian-style flint axe (L.959) (cf. Chapter 5, this volume). Jars that contained secondary burials were unfortunately not available for the analysis presented here.

Gilat's Cooks...

Diet and cuisine are enlightening avenues to follow in the archaeological record as they document, eventually, food-processing innovation and new strategies in vegetal or animal food production (Sherratt 1997). One oven (Stratum 2A) and twenty-six hearths have been recorded at Gilat (Table 5.4). Hearths are pits whose walls are burnt and hardened, filled with ashes, charred stones and burnt fragments of pottery. However, there is no evidence for cooking pots in the assemblage of Gilat, insofar as cooking means heating the content of the vessel on ashes and ambers. This process induces thermal stress that may be tempered by adding a coat of sand and clay to protect the vessel's bottom (Rye and Evans 1976:25). Fire clouding and soot on, at least, the lower and bottom parts of vessels are generally indicative of their use as cooking pots (Rice 1987:235). The broad assemblage of vessels considered here—and the attention paid for counting or technological evaluation of vessels' bottoms—indicate that cooking ware is notably absent. In the assemblage of Bir es-Safadi for example, this function was only evidenced for small, spouted holemouth jars (Commenge-Pellerin 1990:34). Cooking pots come in many shapes, even as pointed-based vessels. This is the case of afore-mentioned pointed-bottom beakers at Neolithic Ertebølle. These vessels were found standing *in situ* in ashes deposits in the kitchen middens of Flynderhage (Denmark). These pointed-base vessels were used for food cooking as the inside base still show wear traces of heated crust. However, delicate, small or large pointed base beakers in Gilat's assemblage do not show, as any bases of *complete* vessels in the assemblage, inside or outside, traces indicative of heating. This includes all burnt fragments of pottery collected in hearth pits that are small calcinated sherds. Some large fragments included walls or half bottoms of jars or basins whose fractures were all calcinated, and indicate soot (they have explicitly been heated as broken vessels not as complete ones). This is the case for fragmented and charred vessels (mostly lower parts of jars or large bowls) recovered on the western side of Wall 103, Stratum II C. These larges sherds may have been used to scoop ashes and ambers, or as parts of refractory material to protect pieces of food and help in the heating process. One may argue that cooking pots, over used and charred by long use over ambers, may have been broken and their remnant parts, re-used. In any event, there are no vessels type that can be identified, with reasonable evidence, as cooking pots in the way that small complete spouted holemouth jars were in the smaller assemblage of Bir es-Safadi. One unique, complete vessel shows traces of overall heating. The clay seems saturated with seeds, perhaps incrusted in the wet clay before firing or heating the vessel (as this vessel is complete, observations on fractures could not be made). This vessel is perforated near its base and presents a symmetrical, concave mark on the outside wall (Plate 10.5:20). The orifice at the base may have been used as an internal draft or vent device. One large V-shaped bowl associated with this particular perforated vessel in ashy pit 1511 (Stratum IIC) shows no evidence of soot and two small saucers from the same pit fill are unbaked (Plate 10.5:10 and 20).

The Spatial Distribution of the Pottery Assemblage

Based on observations of the integrative composition of the ceramic assemblage described above to indicate 'ceremonial vessels' designed for special functions, the spatial patterns of aggregation and segregation of vessels at Gilat also point to the ritual significance of the pottery assemblage. Spatial analysis undertaken by Eric Kansa and Thomas Levy demonstrate that, however specialized, spatial organization evolved in time as did the background stage of protocols of behavior in a key-area at the site that can be defined here as 'the sanctum' (Areas J and D). The unique patterns of distribution of the ceremonial and domestic vessels at Gilat enable the interpretation of their complementary interaction at the site.

The extent of the probe into *Stratum IV* was too limited to provide significant patterns of distribution of vessels. Stratum III, which includes a larger exposure, comprises three sub-strata. Stratum IIIB and IIIC are somewhat disturbed layers of occupation, aggravated by an intricate network of pits.

Stratum IIIA
The main structural and spatial features of the site come into existence with Stratum IIIA (including the 'plaza', buildings, silos, pits, ritual burials, etc. see Chapter 5, this volume). There are no decisive patterns of ceramic distribution in Stratum IIIA. 'Surfaces' found on the large plaza. Similarly, the fill in pits offer the same amorphous assemblages that include both domestic and ceremonial shapes. A short period of abandonment of the site occurred before the building activities linked to Stratum IIC where the removal of the lightest vessels may have occured. Some erratic contexts are recorded in the frequency of some types of vessels. The rates of large pointed-base

beakers, basins and fenestrated chalices are (relatively) high as are the frequency of holemouth jars (torpedo jars are rather low). As is the case with Stratum IIA, the general conditions of deposition in Stratum III A offer no secure evidence for interpretation. Room 7, whose floor yielded only a very few sherds, contained two large hole mouth jars, one sunken into the floor (see above). Some structures, silos or stones circles, contained one, two at most, pristine ceremonial vessels: one large, red-painted pointed base beaker was recovered in the well-built silo L1369 in Square H2, one beaker and one tubular goblet were found in L1534 in Square Ai0, one torpedo and two large pointed-base beakers were recovered in silo 853. These finds are modest with reference to the fill of similar structures in Stratum IIB (see below). However, these patterns reinforce evidence for recurrent associations of ceremonial vessels in silos or selected pits. This type of association, indicative of ritual deposits, is a strong evidential thread to follow across levels of occupation.

With the exception of one human burials and silos, the spatial distribution of ceramics at Gilat essentially mirror patterns of discard in numerous fills of pits and structures. In order to sketch out some broad outlines of systemic configurations of vessel deposits in specific occupational areas, Kansa and Levy have presented statistical plots illustrated in Figs. 10.5 and 10.6. The contexts selected for these spatial distributions at Strata II B and IIC, both strata extensively excavated, are pits, silos, hearths, floors, surfaces (occupational floors with no obvious architectural boundaries), burials and installations. These loci provide relatively secure evidence from a stratigraphic perspective. However, interpretation of vessel distribution and association relies on the primary assumption, based on the excavators' observations, that vessels were recovered in their primary context of use or in secondary context as discarded in nearby pits. *De facto*, Strata IIC and IIB are reduced here to broad units of occupation as local observations—as described in Chapter 5, there is strong evidence for occupational evolution between these different strata. 18.80% of the ceramic assemblage was recovered from Stratum IIC and 26.2% in Stratum IIB.

Stratum IIC and IIB: …Plotting In and Around the 'Sanctum'. By Eric Kansa and Thomas Levy

a. *Stratum IIC (Fig. 10.5)*. Basins are concentrated in Squares J0, J1, S1 and Ai0 and are found mostly in pits. Their distribution is somewhat different from the other 'domestic' vessels. In general, they tend to be found to the west of the large courtyard in this building phase. 'Domestic' vessels (holemouth jars, necked jars, (fragmented) pithoi, churns and V-shaped bowls (small and large) have very similar distributions in Stratum IIC. They mostly concentrate in pits in Squares L3 and L4, on the eastern margin of the courtyard. Secondary concentrations occur in pits and on surfaces in Squares S0, S1, Ai0, Ai1 and M0 on the north-west margin of the courtyard. Beakers, either medium or small, show a different pattern of distribution. The vast majority of beakers concentrate in pits in Square Ai1, to the north of the courtyard.

The following 'ceremonial vessels'—cornets, pointed bases beakers of all sizes, torpedo jars, fenestrated pedestal vessels, tulip bowls and ring-based tulip bowls and urns cluster at the periphery of the buildings. Pointed-base vessels (beakers or cornets) were found only in Squares K5-7. They are associated with tubular beakers, urns and fenestrated pedestal bowls. Torpedoes are exclusively associated to pedestal bowls, or cluster in large areas. Tubular beakers and urns form several isolated clusters, in Squares H1 and L0. For all these 'ceremonial vessels' the greatest concentrations are found in Square K6, east of the courtyard and in the vicinity of the long curved wall in Squares J-K-L/0-1.

In two cases, ceremonial vessels are associated to violin-shaped figurines: fenestrated pedestal bowls in Square S0 and tubular beakers and large urns in Square L0. Violin-shaped figurines are also found scattered at the periphery of one of the major cluster of pedestal bowls, tubular beakers and pointed-base vessels in square K5-6.

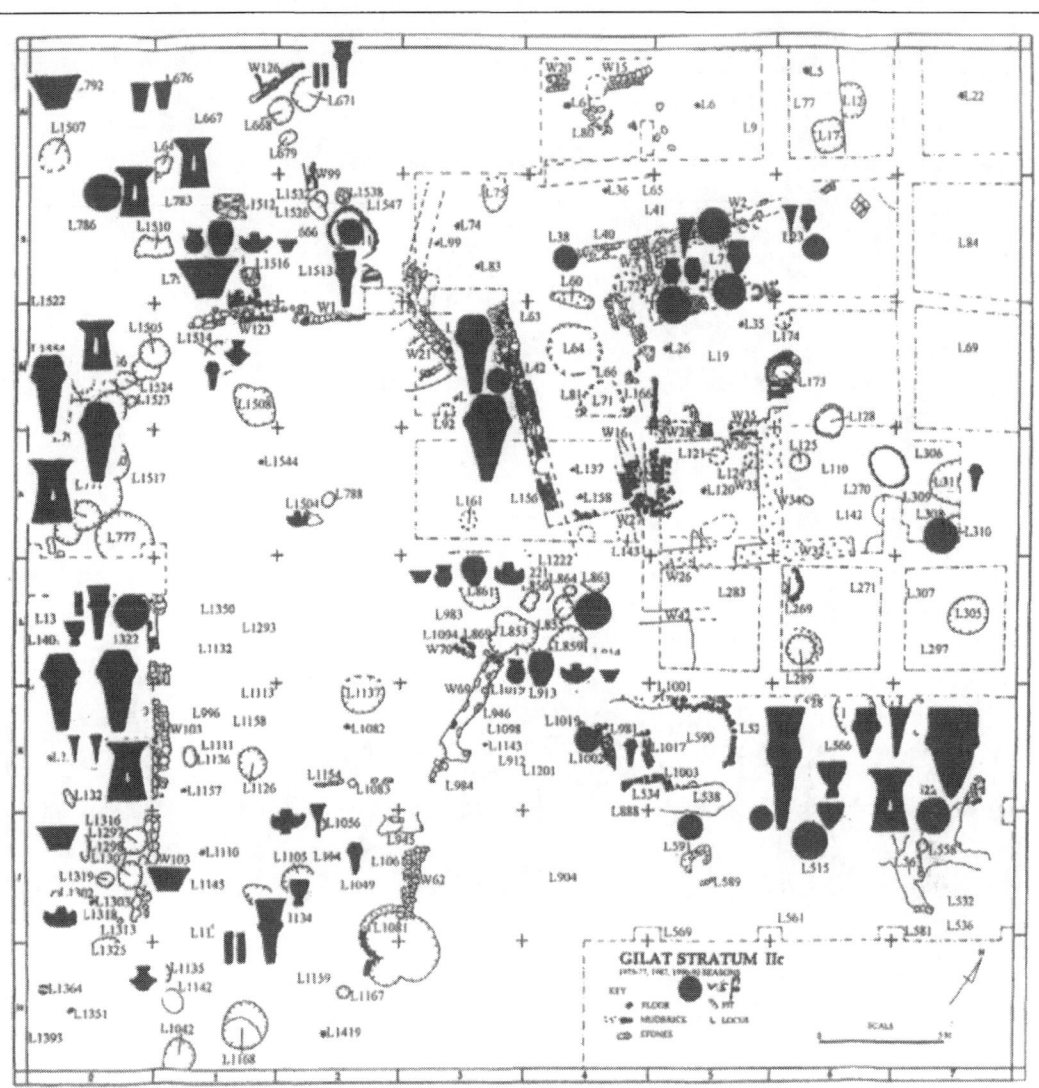

**Figure 10.5. Stratum IIC general plan showing distribution of vessels
(silhouettes indicate concentrations, not individual finds)**

Figure 10.6. Stratum IIB general plan showing distribution of vessels
(silhouettes indicate concentrations, not individual finds)

b. *Stratum IIB (Fig. 10.6).* Basins concentrate mostly in pits of Square J0. A few specimens were recovered in other contexts from the rest of the area exposed. In contrast with other 'domestic' vessels, there are no secondary concentrations of basins in Square J3. Holemouth jars, necked jars, pithoi (fragments), large and small V-shaped bowls and churns show similar patterns of distribution. They mostly concentrate in pits in Squares J0, J3 and Ai0. Scattered examples were recovered in other squares, notably in the vicinity of the rooms 10, 3 and 2 in the southern and south-western part of the building. As previously observed in Stratum IIC, beakers show different patterns of distribution. They are now found together with 'ceremonial vessels', and mostly concentrate in Squares K5, with secondary zones of concentration in Square K0. Cornets, pointed bases beakers of all sizes, torpedo jars, fenestrated pedestal vessels, tulip bowls and ring-based tulip bowls and urns, interpreted as 'ceremonial vessels', show parallel patterns of distribution with beakers. They concentrate in Square K5 and show lesser accumulations in Square K0. In Square K5, 'ceremonial vessels' and beakers are all found east of Rooms 10, 3, and 2 of the building.

Stratum IIA. Stratum IIA illustrates a decline in the momentum of occupation at Gilat, following a short period of abandonment (see Chapter 5, this volume). Numerous pits and disturbed structures make it difficult to investigate the spatial distribution of vessels in this stratum. Pit fills, elusive floors, and the rubble of structures yielded great amounts of pottery with no reliable contexts. However, this tends to contradict the interpretation proposed by the excavators (Chapter 5), as does the apparent dense evidence of craft activity that the population decreased in any significant way during this phase of occupation at Gilat. Based on the spatial layout of the Stratum IIA architecture (*ibid.*), the nexus of the site and the sanctuary may have shifted in this occupation phase.

Exploring Intra-Site and Across Strata (IIC-IIB) Patterns of Distribution in the Sanctum

An informative picture, like a chess-board with pawns of different value that all master strategic positions, emerges from the spatial distribution plots of ceramics against the background of the excavation. Statistical evaluation enhances the identification of the main trends of vessel distribution and types of associations or dissociations as the plots tend to ascertain spatial discrimination of vessel use. Can these restrictive *domains* of utilization be construed in terms of social activities in a ceremonial area?

Silhouettes of vessels have been added to the overall plots in Figs. 10.5 and 10.6 in order to record isolated complete vessels found in structures or pits (with the exception of vessels in the building W3-W2-W8 in Square S5, most are single vessels). All these vessels are of remarkable quality and their relative isolation may appear as meaningful in a context largely dominated by the plethora of vessels clustering in specific areas.

Stratum IIC (Fig. 10.5). Considered as a key area at Gilat, the compound of buildings, courtyards and plausible enclosure walls (north-south Wall 103 and Wall 62–69; see Fig. 5.21A) show contrasting patterns of vessel distribution that seem to delineate various *domains* of differentiated activities. It is perhaps judicious to first bring forward...negative evidence. Extensive zones, the so-called 'plaza' (see Chapter 5) that roughly covers Squares K-N/1-2, another broad open area in Squares J3-6, and one large building of NNW-SSE orientation and its immediate vicinity in Squares M-S/4 are remarkable for their lack of vessel deposits and low concentrations of pottery sherds in their subsequent fills. Ceremonial vessels aggregate in specific areas and their associations are far from uniform. Domestic vessels also give evidence for spatial differentiation.

Some valuable information concerns the apparent segregate distribution of basins. Basins were used and discarded in areas restricted to the west of the large courtyard (or 'plaza' see Chapter 5).

With the notable exception of Square K6, basins cluster at the periphery of areas devoted to 'ceremonial vessels', and in two cases are found only in high concentrations in the vicinity of low concentrations of holemouth jars, necked jars, pithoi, churns and V-shaped bowls, north of Wall 123 in Square S2 and in Square Ai0. In two cases, dozens of basins have been recovered in the vicinity of hearths (west of wall 103, not far away from hearth L. 1298 in Square J0) and north of wall 123, near hearth 1516 in Square S1. The inferred function of basins in communal food preparation—to the exclusion of cooking see *supra*—and consumption seems corroborated here. Their local, high concentration suggest frequency and/intensity in preparation and/or consumption, as the average capacity of basins is 390 cl (4 liters). I should argue that, with consideration of the numerous and various open shaped vessels of individual serving capacity in the assemblage of Gilat, communal serving from basins appears redundant, although it cannot be ruled out, in a way illustrated by the ethnographic record (see *supra*). A cluster of hearths, L. 1526, 1532, 1538, is located north of Square S2 without any associated vessels.

One can note that in Square Ai0/Ai1, one cluster of basins appears to be adjacent to one cluster of beakers. These adjacent domains of large open containers and small ones may be interpreted as complementary in terms of serving. What does the archaeological record suggest? At Chalcolithic Kissonerga in Cyprus, concentrations of earth ovens and cooking pits are considered as evidence of feasting in a ceremonial area (Peltenburg 1991:14). This situation is not duplicated Gilat, however, the concentration of basins, vessels whose anatomical features and capacity cannot be meant for storage, point to large if not considerable, disposable of amounts of food or liquids in specific areas.

Coherent and recurrent evidence documents the spatial distribution of 'domestic vessels' recovered by groups composed of small to medium sized open shaped and storage jars. These groups are similar to those regularly recorded in domestic contexts at subterranean or surface dwellings at Chalcolithic settlement sites (for example Safadi, Commenge-Pellerin 1990:156–70). As in settlement sites, churns are part of what can be ascribed to a 'domestic equipment' that may be ascribed to a 'normative kit' of Chalcolithic pottery assemblages. These clusters of domestic vessels are found in discrete concentration and extent compared to the patterns of distribution of 'ceremonial vessels'. The highest concentrations occur over a rather amorphous zone of pits in Squares L3 and L4, in an area that appears to span a large gap in the (enclosure?) Wall 69.

A wealth of artifacts was recovered in Room A in Square S5 (two vessels effigies and a violin-shaped figurines see, Chapter 15). Vessels found on floor 44, to the south-west of the room, include two decorated necked jars, and two small holemouth jars, one of them decorated (Plates 10.10:6; 10.16:5; 10.13:3). This is the only opportunity, in primary context, for evidence of the importance of decoration on vessels whose morphological characters signal practical use. Evidence of ranking in function and inherent symbolic meaning can be construed in different degrees. Painted designs seem the common denominator that adds 'supplementary' value and significance to one necked jar and one holemouth jar. Fragmentary vessels found on the same floor comprise brown burnished pointed-base beakers with delicate palmettes, impressed or in the 'cream ware reserved' technique, and rims of red painted, small holemouth jars. It should be added that one complete, exquisite and capacious cornet was recovered in the fill immediately above floor 44. Outside the northern wall of Room A, on Floor 40, one red-painted basin was surrounded by fragmentary large bowls, all red-painted outside and with painted designs inside (for example, see Plate 10.6:1). To the north-east of Room A, on Floor 23 in Square S5, some large fragments of cornets and pointed base beakers were laying near fragments of violin-shaped figurines.

The spatial distribution of small open shapes is highly discriminative. Small and large V-shaped bowls are largely confined to areas of seemingly domestic activities. Decorated specimens—as documented by rare, localized evidence—are sparsely found at the vicinity of areas restricted to ceremonial activities: around Room A, around Structure 682, in pit 1511 in Square S2, with fragments of violin-shaped figurines—see Chapter 15, this volume). The unique, wide spread but high concentration of beakers in Square Ai1, borders concentrations of basins to the west yet also pedestalled vessels to the south. The status of beakers appears to find here a functional definition that may rank them between V-shaped bowls and pointed-base vessels (cornets, beakers or tulip bowls). In Pit L 528 in Square K6, at the northern limit of a broad concentration of ceremonial vessels, several beakers were recovered. This information also seems to confirm the *intermediary* status of beakers.

The case of tubular vessels, tubular goblets or large tubular or flaring urns adds weight to relevant patterns of segregation and aggregation in the spatial distribution of open shapes. These vessels are always found together either in large pits (L 671 in Square Ai2, in and around L 1128 in Square J1,) or, in one case, in a broad concentration with ring-based tulip bowls, west of the enclosure—Wall 103. This information tends to confirm that generic vessels of the same typological class but of different capacity were used for closely related activities. The high concentration of ceremonial vessels in Square K6 comprises tubular goblets and urns recovered with pointed-base or pedestalled vessels. Pointed-base vessels, delicate cornets and tulip bowls, pointed-base beakers are recovered in large quantities in a wide spread cluster of ceremonial vessels that also includes pedestalled vessels (either fenestrated, pedestalled bowls and chalices or delicate ring-based tulip bowls) in Square K6. This situation tends to confirm the ceremonial function of open shape as ranked by size and profiles, but it fails to provide evidence for more specific information on their respective roles. Intensive and selective consumption and perhaps libation may have been staged in the open area in Square K6. Large open vessels, either large, frail pointed-base beakers or robust urns can be used as short-term storage containers providing individual serving to a systemic (and hierarchical?) range of small open vessels, or as communal containers for selected consumers. Specific ceremonial activity as libation and dedication may find some indirect corroboration with clusters of fragmented violin-shaped figurines recovered south of this remarkable open area (in Squares K5, J5 and J6). Consumption here comes with plausible presentation of offerings as suggested by multifarious pedestalled vessels, fenestrated pedestal chalices or bowls and ring-based tulip bowls. Storage vessels are absent in this particular assemblage of ceremonial vessels.

Pedestalled vessels (bowls, chalices or tulip bowls) are the most ubiquitous vessels that can be found with various tubular and pointed-base vessels, or with only torpedoes jars; they cluster with no other types of vessels. South of Square S Ai0-Ai, in two wide areas, pedestalled vessels cluster with torpedoes jars, west of the courtyard in Squares S-N0 and west of the enclosure—Wall 103 in Square K0. These two locations seem to stage highly specialized activities revolving around storage containers of precious content (possibly olive oil) and offering devices. By contrast with the high concentration of ceremonial vessels in Square K6, individual and/or communal serving vessels are oddly absent, with the exception of a few (incomplete) cornets discarded in pit L1277, north of Square K0. Torpedo jars are also found in one single cluster that spreads south and between Walls 123 and 21 in squares N2-3. One isolated torpedo vessel was recovered in pit L311, in the vicinity of pit L310 (in Square L7) that yielded fragmented violin-shaped figurines. Another torpedo was found lying close to a small circular structure of mud-bricks (L 981, in Square K5). Fragmented violin-shaped figurines were recovered nearby, east of Wall 1002. In a few cases, single, complete vessels were recovered in pits of various capacities. One complete ring-based tulip bowl was found lying in Pit L 1105. Two carinated, red painted jars were respectively found in small pits (L 1135 north of Square H1 and L 1514 in Square N1). Other isolated finds include a few cornets and one fragmented miniature churn in a small circular pit (L 1056, south of K2).

Stratum IIB (Fig. 10.6). Only one high concentration of basins is observed in Stratum IIB. It clusters in Square J0 and is surrounded by an assemblage of assorted domestic vessels: hole mouth jars, necked jars, churns and bowls. As observed elsewhere in Stratum IIC, basins were found in dense concentrations around two hearths (L 1265, L 1263). The assemblage of domestic vessels were recovered scattered in the vicinity of structures and less often discarded in pits. The composition of clusters of 'ceremonial' vessels is diversified. In Square K5, high concentrations of pedestalled vessels, small pointed base beakers and flaring urns, in an open area south-west of Rooms 10-3-2, can duplicate the situation in Squares K6-7 in Stratum IIC. Torpedo jars are know included to varied assemblages of small shapes (pointed base vessels, tulip bowls and beakers west of Wall 117 in Square K-J/0). In contrast to Stratum IIC, clusters composed of torpedoes or torpedoes and fenestrated, pedestalled chalices seem absent. There are no concentrations of beakers. The beakers appear now to mingle with pointed-base vessels and tubular goblets in the most remarkable concentrations of 'ceremonial' vessels either in open areas or in loci that provided a wealth of materials as silo 882 or pit 787 (see below). However, one can remark that Room 3, like floor L 44 in Stratum IIC (building in Square S5), yielded the most delicate pointed base vessels, either cornets, beakers or tulip bowls. Other individual serving sized vessels (beakers or tubular goblets) are excluded. In contrast to the situation at Stratum IIC, delicate, small, individual serving sized vessels, but also large pointed-base beakers are associated to clusters of vessels that comprise torpedoes jars. Evidence collected with the large and dense concentration of ceremonial vessels west of Wall 117 (Square KO) tends to confirm this situation. As violin-shaped figurines are still found associated with 'ceremonial vessels' (west of W117, in silo 882, in Room 3 and 5), those associations do not seem as systematic as they were at Stratum IIC.

Some specific locations of 'ceremonial' vessels call for additional comments: Silo 882, in Square K4 is a well-built, circular structure made of mud-brick that was used from Stratum IIC through Stratum IIB1 (Plate 5.26). In Stratum IIB, this silo is associated with Room 5. Silo 882 contained a wealth of artifacts and vessels. Flint tools, bone tools, one spindle-whorl, worked shells and bones, two digging stick weights, one horn core and one palette were recovered in its fill with an assemblage of fine vessels that comprises one ring-based tulip bowl, two tubular goblets, one large pointed-base beaker, three small beakers, one small hole mouth pot, the neck of a churn and two undecorated V-shaped bowls simply refined on the slow-wheel (Plate 10.1:4). This wealth of material buried in the fill of one silo has parallels at the Beersheva sites in the northern Negev, and more specifically at Bir-es Safadi (Commenge-Pellerin 1990:156–70 and Commenge forthcoming). At Safadi, some bell-shaped silos in underground houses, or cut into the surface of the site, have yielded assemblages of complete artifacts, stored or cached, sometimes at different times (those silos were not filled with discarded vessels and fill-soil). One silo (L. 408) was sealed. The inventory of those silos includes complete, 'brand new' vessels (all parts of the Beersheva ceramic 'kit' assemblages, sometimes including pedestalled vessels) in large quantities but also complete, engraved basalt vessels (in Silo 633, Commenge-Pellerin 1990: Fig. 6 by J. Perrot), limestone or granite maces, stone figurines and vessels (silo III in house 354), fine stone tools and palettes (double silo 305–6) palettes and notched pebbles (silo 408). At Gilat, complete ceremonial vessels and other complete artifacts certainly document an intentional, plausibly symbolic deposit (the fill is partially identified as discard from Room 5 by the excavators; see Chapter 5, this volume). Attention should be drawn to the single fragmented vessel found in silo 882: the neck of a churn that may seem innocuous enough in a context partially interpreted as of 'discarded' materials. Recycling of parts of vessels may indicate ceremonial behavior for vessels used for daily domestic purposes (Sterner 1989). The ethnographic record provides evidence for shattered pots whose parts were ceremonially hidden or buried, as *complete necks may be left at places designated as shrines* (Sterner 1989:458). Churns are usually found within assemblages composed of utilitarian vessels (bowls, basins, jars…). Their role in the processing of dairy products has still to be ascertained (see above), however, the presence of this neck in the remarkable inventory of vessels and other artefacts in silo 882 may be construed as intentional and meaningful. I have also tried to demonstrate (see above and Chapter 15) that by many means, from the way they are made to the way they have been twice selected in composing vessels-effigies, churns are involved in 'making social and symbolic statements'. The border between commoditization and singularization, between profane and sacred functions, shifts in the lifetime of artifacts (Kopytoff 1986:69) and the archaeological record rarely provides an opportunity to acknowledge this fact. In Area J, Square H0, pit 1334 has been described as a multi-use ceremonial feature. Fragmented cornets and tubular goblets are part of the inventory of its earlier phase (see Chapter 5). Complete and almost complete 'ceremonial' vessels were recovered in Pit 787 in Square Ai0 including two chalices on fenestrated pedestals, two large pointed-base beakers, one small jar with lug handles, two tubular goblets and one beaker.

Conspicuous Consumption: Collection and/or Distribution of Subsistence Goods?

Patterns of consumption, as documented by the pottery and violin-shaped figurine production systems, suggest that the nature of demand at Gilat promoted and probably monitored the interregional circulation of commodities. Demand for elaborate artifacts and vessels produced either on-site or off-site, including subsistence goods (olive oil and milk?) appears high at Gilat. Some insights on the evolution of modes of production and patterns of exchange, in the context of emerging social complexity in northern Negev Chalcolithic societies (Levy 1993, 1995), have already and partially set the stage for the socio-economical settings of Gilat as they have emphasized the crucial role of conspicuous consumption (Commenge 2002) in Chalcolithic society in the Negev. Within the limits of the data currently available for the Southern Levant, Gilat seems to have attracted commodities through a periphery to core flow that one can, thus far, ascribe to the propensity of intermediary societies to collect tribute, promote conspicuous consumption and/or exchange (Commenge 2002:144). The intra-site distribution of 'ceremonial' vessels, as far as the extension of the excavations allows interpretation, appears to duplicate this centripetal flow to the area defined as the sanctum of Gilat (Area J and D—Strata IIB, IIC) as it meets the restrictive distribution of violin-shaped figurines at the site. However, within the area of the sanctum, patterns of vessel distribution indicate a shift from the core to the periphery of the sanctum. This perceptible structure may indicate that distribution takes precedence over offering of subsistence goods in the enacted social ceremonial. This hypothesis should also be tested fully across Strata IIC and IIB.

The dynamics of intermediary societies, fuelled by the pursuit of prestige, generate social and political dependency through competitive collection and redundant distribution of goods—and subsistence goods—to the benefit of clients, kinfolk and/or other political actors (Earle 1978, 1991; Thomas 1986). Consumption does not generate destruction of goods and wealth *'but their reincorporation into the social system that produces them in some other guise'* (Gell 1986:112). To what extent do patterns of vessel distribution at Gilat mirror the plausible patterns of a *centripetal flow of tribute* (Wright 1994) and/or the redistribution of largesse?

The spatial distribution of vessels in and around the compound of buildings that defined the 'nexus of the sanctuary' (see Chapter 5) in Area J and D, Stratum IIC and recomposed at Stratum IIB, completes and modifies the eloquent image displayed by the concentrations of violin-shaped figurines (Fig. 15.15–23 and Chapter 15, this volume). High concentrations of ceremonial vessels in Area J that contrasts with situation in other investigated areas, underline an inward shift toward what could have been the core sanctum at Gilat. This situation that finds some parallels at later Middle Eastern sites either in religious or secular institutional contexts (Beale 1978; Nicholas 1987) appears reinforced by the presence of exogenous vessels, in particular torpedoes jars and their possible content of exotic olive oil. However, torpedoes are never found in locations that suggest storage capacities but rather, point to the conditions of their utilization or discard, with pedestalled vessels plausibly meant for offering, or in Stratum IIB in particular, with small, individual serving vessels and urns. Evidence for hoarding may be drawn from the accumulation of fines wares, concentrations of torpedoes jars and violin-shaped figurines. However, storage facilities (silos, pits) do not provide evidence for any accumulation of vessels that may be indicative of a formal trend for hoarding delicate vessels (as it may be illustrated by some specific features at Bir es-Safadi, for example, see Commenge 1990:37).

The dense patchwork of distribution patterns seems to illustrate social ritual in action, or with consideration of the numerous pit fills, in 'post-action'. *Discriminative distribution* of subsistence goods is suggested by the extreme variation in small vessels meant for individual-sized servings, yet also by the large pointed-base beakers meant for probable communal, 'passed around' servings. It seems to reflect social protocols of behavior that may induce the identification of the contents with the social identity of the consumers. As a supplementary indication, the size range of individual serving vessels may highlight social differentiation, in terms of gender, age and/or rank. The modest capacity of urns and their recurrent pairing with the crudest and low capacity tubular goblets suggest libation rather than collection. It appears to document a general context of conspicuous consumption. Protocols underlying patterns of distribution of artifacts and/or vessels may be induced by cosmology (of social order promoted as natural order?) in religious surroundings as evidenced by the distribution of violin-shaped figurines (see Chapter 15, this volume), adding legitimacy to the mediation of political and/or religious control.

How selective might have been access to the sanctum? In Stratum IIC, concentrations of ceremonial vessels are peripheral to the large courtyard (with exclusion to the clustering of ritual objects in Room A). Only two areas, in Squares K6 (urns, pedestalled and pointed-base vessels) and N3 (torpedoes only), located in the vicinity of the buildings, are enclosed in the 'sacred circle' defined by the distribution of figurines. Individual-sized serving, ceremonial vessels comprise 212 vessels including 127 tulip bowls, 70 pointed-base beakers (of which 17 are large beakers), 7[26] cornets and 8 tubular goblets. One may note that delicate tulip bowls are more than three times as frequent as pointed-based vessels. Cornets are relatively rare and are six times as frequent at Stratum IIA, with no spatial concentrations recorded, all excavated areas considered. From a general point of view, this situation underlines that vessels recovered in primary and secondary contexts (pits) are relatively scarce against the grand total of vessels per category collected at the site, mostly from fill. Although 'high concentrations' of clusters of ceremonial vessels are apparent, contingents of individual sized serving vessels seem relatively low in a context that suggests consumption and discard. One may consider that V-shaped bowls served as a normative, standard reference in evaluating the quantities of ceremonial, individual vessels. 340 V-shaped bowls were recovered in Stratum IIC (78% out of the sanctum area, others in concentrations of domestic vessels). A ratio of 1.7 bowls per ceremonial, individual serving sized vessel in Stratum IIC averages the ratio obtained for the whole assemblage. On the one hand, this situation makes more intriguing the 'semi-restrictive', intermediary distribution of the 47 beakers, in areas devoid of ceremonial or domestic vessels, with the exception of basins. On the other hand, it enhances the high rates of torpedo jars (20) and more significantly of fenestrated pedestalled vessels (42 fenestrated chalices and 8 pedestalled tulip bowls): an average ratio of one pedestalled vessel for four individual sized serving, ceremonial vessels seems the rule.

Clusters of domestic vessels do not indicate circumscribed residential areas inside the sanctum. Residential areas, modest or extended are part of many sanctuary or religious compounds. However, in Area J and D, concentrations of domestic vessels total 376 holemouth jars, 188 necked jars and 123 churns and 340 V-shaped bowls. There are no architectural features that materialize storage facilities or internal patterns of deposition that structure in ordered clusters the different types of storage vessels. In other locations, mostly peripheral, capacious structures of combustion and intense preparation and short-storage of food, in some 99 basins clustering in high concentrations zones, may lend support to ceremonial feasting at the sanctum. Precise chronological evaluation that may indicate the length of time of the use of the sanctum at Stratum IIC is beyond this study. Occasional, perhaps seasonal social gatherings are suggested. On the one hand, the variety of ceremonial vessels (pedestalled vessels and urns associated with small, individual sized serving vessels) in most concentration zones, indicate complex, recurrent ceremonial actions that involved (concomitant?) actions of offering (libation, presentation of pedestalled vessel content) and distribution from urns to individual vessels or locally, from torpedoes (in Squares L/K0). On the other hand, the assumption of the distribution of the collective content of basins, of large supplies of subsistence goods (staple, but also water and perhaps milk) stored in jars and churns, into individual, socially marked servings can be reasonably assumed. The ratio of capacious, storage vessels to individual-sized serving, ceremonial vessels is 3.2. If one considers that multi-functional purposes V-shaped bowls, restricted to domestic areas, may have got their share of the feast, this ratio goes down to 1.2 individual-sized serving vessels per large storage container. This situation tends to demonstrate the capacity to provide food surplus to sustain feast-giving. Again, the relative low frequency of individual-sized ceremonial vessels may underline extremely restrictive access to distribution. It may also demonstrate that individual serving sized vessels, that herald social status, were possessions precious enough for not being intentionally discarded at every event of the social ritual.

How expedient was the disposal of vessels at Gilat? Conditions of disposal of vessels at Gilat do not indicate banqueting—at least as models document it elsewhere in the archaeological record (Bradley 1991; Forest 1978). Punctual and massive disposal of vessels after banqueting, consequential, intentional breakage of vessels is not evidenced at Gilat. Moreover, conditions of discard, as illustrated by many pits fills, indicate that if intentional discard of vessels operated after ceremonial feasting, as expected with faunal remains systematically disposed of at the same locations. A large majority of the vessels were recovered in secondary contexts, in the numerous pits where they may have been discarded or in fills and rubble that may have resulted from the destruction of structures, eventually leveled for rebuilding (those vessels are not included in the spatial analysis, see also Chapter 5, this volume). Patterns of concentration indicate that clusters of vessels in primary and secondary contexts overlap, in a fashion that suggests that vessels were disposed of in pits near the vicinity of their use.

Comprehensive studies on the ubiquitous bevelled-rim bowls in Mesopotamia (Uruk period, until Uruk IV) have been scrutinized and discussed at length for their possible function of these molded vessels, always found in large quantities and concentrations. Bevelled-rim bowls have been, in different archaeological contexts and with reasonable weighted arguments, presented either as vessels used and discarded during banquets (Forest 1978), as offering bowls in a religious institutional context (Beale 1978), and as presentation bowls whose contents were meant for taxes to centralized, administrative institution (Nicholas 1987; Blackman et al. 1993). Coined as the simplest and least attractive of all near eastern pots (Millard 1978:49) bevelled-rim bowls are essentially coarse, mass-produced vessels, molded or in some cases ('flower pots') made on the slow wheel. Criteria selected to document ubiquity, density, structural position and condition of deposition (Nicholas 1987:63) seem irrelevant for the small, and varied ceremonial shapes of Gilat. For votive-offering bowls (in a religious context either centralized and/or domestic), ubiquity would be expected to be variable, density high in either temple or household contexts, and structural position would be expected to be regular and conditions of deposition would provide complete vessels with internal residues. For presentation, bowl ubiquity would be expected to be moderate, density high in most instances, low in household contexts, and whose structural position would be expected variable as would conditions of deposition, with either stacked vessel disposal or broken vessels in trash deposits. Elaborate, discriminative, individual sized serving vessels at Gilat do not agree with those models, neither does modalities of distribution, structural position or conditions of deposition. At Gilat, different types of ceremonial vessels appear expediently trashed in the same pits and are never stacked, or disposed in heaps. Evidence for the intentional breakage of particular vessels, defaced in extraordinary circumstances, is not obvious. No direct evidence of intentional breakage of vessels is recorded, as might suggest the smashing of the finest specimens (cornets or some large pointed-base beakers) or traces of deliberate strokes that damaged surfaces around fractures lines on robust vessels (torpedoes). The breakage rate of squat vessels (for example, basins), is not significantly lower than the breakage rate of fragile, large pointed-base beakers or heavy urns. Pointed bases' breakage, either from fine or thick-walled vessels, but also fenestrated pedestals split along the 'windows' or short pedestals neatly removed from the bases, simply show that breakage tends to intervene at the weakest constitutional parts of vessels when used or discarded.

In Stratum II C, one may suggest that occasional, ceremonial feasting in the sanctum entailed selected offerings (in pedestalled vessels), and distribution of subsistence goods for possible ranked social groups. Expedient and un-discriminate disposal of broken ceremonial vessels in pits appears to be the rule in the sanctum, within areas privileged by the social ritual. Whether disposal of all types of ceremonial vessels in pits was consequential to their use and systematic at ceremonial gatherings or concerns only inadvertently broken vessels remains an open question. One single pit (L 1514, in Square N1), that contained one torpedo jar, one biconical red-painted jar, two spindle-whorls and one token (a re-shaped pottery sherd) gives evidence for some ritual protocol of deposition.

Churns were clearly integrated into clusters of domestic vessels at Stratum IIC. But two exceptions conflict with this generalization. In one occurrence, a churn lies at the center of the courtyard, with no particular feature meant to enhance its position that can be construed as casual with regard to the conditions of destruction at this occupational stratum. Another churn is consecrated as part of a construction (L 1318). Six miniature churns on short pedestals, all fragmented, have been discarded around the sanctum. No churn, however fragmentary, was recovered around the compound of buildings in Squares M-S/4-5, where Room A enshrined the two effigy-vessels that appear impregnated by the symbolical meaning and social import of the churn (through its possible assimilation of the Ram entity see, Chapter 15 and Fig. 15.1 to 6).

In Stratum IIB, two concentrations of ceremonial vessels are distributed outside of the 'sacred circle' defined by the concentrations of violin-shaped figurines. One off-center deposit of figurines may consecrate one cluster of torpedoes and small vessels located to the west of wall W117, in Square K0. Individual serving sized, ceremonial vessels comprise 375 vessels (beakers included), of which 145 tulip bowls, 121 pointed-base beakers (of which 31 large beakers), 9 cornets and 16 tubular goblets. 84 beakers are now placed with other ceremonial vessels. V-shaped bowls, still restricted to domestic zones, are twice more frequent as they were at Stratum IIC (654, the ratio to other individual serving sized vessels is similar to what is observed at Stratum IIC). Concentrations of domestic vessels, yet also vessels collected in various fills over Squares M-N/0-2, duplicate in terms of frequency, the situation at Stratum IIC. 431 holemouth jars, 181 necked jars and 176 churns give a ratio of 2.2 jars to one individual sized, ceremonial vessel (beakers contribute to lower the rate reached at Stratum IIC). By contrast to the situation at Stratum IIC, if one takes into account V-shaped bowls, individual sized vessels are more numerous than large storage vessels (1.3 small vessels to one jar or churn). However, the rate of individual-sized vessels remains low (see supra). Concentrations of basins are less frequent than at the previous stratum of occupation (67 basins are recorded in the sanctum area, that represents only 41% of the basins at Stratum IIB). The largest hearth-platform (L 647 in Square M2) emphasizes shifts in the social ceremonial at Stratum IIB as no concentration of basins, or other domestic vessels, are observed around it. The apparent context of ashes and mixed faunal remains found in Rooms 3-1 (see Chapter 5) that also comprises ceremonial vessels (pointed-base beakers, some fragmented cornets and tulip bowls) and violin-shaped figurines contrast with the apparent ceremonial order in Room A, Stratum IIC. However, the limits of the excavated area cannot be taken for an unmovable framework where the sanctum has been spatially duplicated, from Stratum IIC to Stratum IIB. Occupation in Stratum IIB overlap layers resulting from the total obliteration of the previous sanctum (see Chapter 5). As observed in the excavation (*ibid*.), it may be suggested that the centers of the sanctum had eventually moved to the south. The remarkable Stratum IIB mass burial recovered in Square H0, in the vicinity of concentrations of ceremonial vessels to the south. Finally, different contextual information for Stratum IIB indicates differences with Stratum IIC. Protocols of deposition indicate that complete vessels and possibly ceremonially recycled parts of vessels were involved, locally, in votive deposits or to consecrate some pit deposits (L 787, 882, 1344 see supra and Chapter 5).

Concluding Remarks

How should one conclude an open case study? The composite structure of the pottery assemblage of Gilat has been presented in symmetrical but complementary terms of tradition and innovation, ceremonial and domestic domains, local and off-site productions. As social patterns related to intermediary societies tend to emphasized the role of authorities or elites and the play for power, it is, perhaps, commensality in consumption paired with personal, individual status as evidenced by the inventory and the spatial distribution of vessels at Gilat that etched the patterns of social relations, of social group identification and/or social boundaries at this early phase of the Chalcolithic period, in its most accurate and humanist dimension.

Notes

*   See section below—*Stratum IIC and IIB: ...plotting in and around the 'sanctum'*....By Eric Kansa and Thomas Levy. My warmest thanks to David Alon and Tom Levy for inviting me to undertake this study. My many thanks to Daniel Ladiray for the illustrations used here, his talent and his unfailing support - he brought me up as an archaeologist - and I could not have had a better field master.

1.   See 1989, *Webster Encyclopedic Unabridged Dictionary of the English Language*. New York: Gramercy

2.   The collection of Gilat includes 1,887 vessels with a complete profile that constitute the basis for most of the diagnostic repertoire.

3.   Paradoxically, it is the sherd totals that are usually given as indicative for the sorted assemblages of Safadi or Abu Matar (Commenge-Pellerin 1987, 1990) that have been selectively used elsewhere for varied purposes, while the totals of complete vessels have been inexplicably disregarded (e.g. Gilead 1995, Roux 1997).

4.   My warmest thanks to Yuval Goren, for a long and fruitful partnership concerning Northern Negev Chalcolithic pottery assemblages.

5.   Descriptive terms are those coined in the literature by Rice (1987) and/or Yon (1981).

6.   These techniques are referred to as 'primary', and impressed designs as 'secondary' (Orelle 1993). However convenient, these terms are, they are confusing insofar as ceramics were first impressed then painted and/or burnished. Besides they introduce ranking in value for different and combined techniques and designs.

7.   There is no apparent correlation between the distribution of sizes of large bowls and their provenance or contextual location at the site.

8.   Thoroughly studied by Y. Yiekutieli and myself, the assemblage of Wadi Zeita does not yield any vessel that can be related to an Early Bronze Age occupation.

9.   One beaker from Gilat, with twin horizontal lugs below the rim, has been published. This vessel was not available for my analysis of Gilat assemblage (cf. Alon and Levy 1989, Fig. 12:2).

10.   There is no word—as far as I know—in the English language for *marli* (Tellerand in German or *tesa* in Italian). A marli is, for example, the flatten edge, the 'brim' of some (modern) plates.

11.   The number of jars was recorded from complete bases corroborated by the number of necks. Carinated jars, identified from body sherds (see Plate 10.18) have no proper excavation record, cf. Table 10.1.

12.   The highest breakage rates come with cooking pots. However, cooking pots seem absent in Gilat's assemblage.

13.   The term 'style', often ambiguous in the literature, is scrupulously avoided. My investigation is purposefully based on a rather isochrestic vison of stylistic behavior as defined, with talent, by James Sackett (Sackett 1990).

14.   The best illustration of complete Chalcolithic vessels or profiles are to be found in the earliest publications (Mallon *et al.* 1934, Koeppel *et al.* 1940). While considerable and important stratigraphic evidence has been recently brought to our attention, it concerns rim sherds and not complete profiles(cf. Lovell 1999).

15.   Percentages are given as indicative—they are based of the quantities of rims (sources: Garfinkel 1992).

16.   Impressed and incised designs are discriminated according to either the traces of punctate or linear tool application on the surface of vessels at Munhata as all impressed designs are defined here are considered as incised designs by Orelle.

17.   Ceramics specialists tend to consider that prehistoric potters were women. They refer to the ethnographic record (for example, Vitelli 1993a) or to direct observations on vessels—Orelle for example relates finger impressions to small, woman-sized fingers (Orelle 1993). This last claim, however, could be indicative of gender hierarchy in the organization of production and to my opinion is not sufficient to corroborate that pottery production was actually undertaken by, and only by women (see also above).

18.   4600–3900 BC calibrated. The assemblages of the later Funnel beaker phase (3900–3100 BC). comprise tri-modal sized beakers of larger capacity that range from 75 cl for the smallest, 75–1000cl for the middle range, and 1000 cl to 3200 cl for the largest. The individual character of the smallest is only evidenced in burial deposits at the end of the period.

19.   Tradition, that edges to ceremonial protocole, order the drinking of specific wines in specific, elaborate glasses (at least in France!).

20.   Evidence for small bowls used as standard measures is found in the Pithos House at Kissonerga 4, in Cyprus, for example (Late Chalcolithic, Peltenburg 1993:15).

21.   My warmest thanks to Zvi Gal and his staff (Israel Antiquities Authority) for allowing me to see, many times, the wealth of the materials collected at Peqi'in.

22.   Small 'votive' churns are known as 'bird vases' (vases-oiseaux: Mallon *et al.* 1934: Pl. 50), in reference to their pointing ends, that may suggest spread wings.

23.   This interpretation has been proposed by Jean Perrot (pers.com.).

24.   The sample of vessels included in this gas chromatography were analyzed at UCSD.

25.   My thanks also to Edwin Van den Brink (IAA) for making the 'first hand connection' to the Titorah material mentioned here.

26.   The first report on Gilat gave higher figures for cornets but this category included all pointed-base vessels, with no internal distinction (Levy and Alon 1987).

Plates

Note: Catalogue of the pottery vessels
Figures with an asterisk represent drawings by Daniel Ladiray, Centre National de la Recherche; Scientifique, Centre de Recherche Français de Jérusalem
Key for references: TG: Teleilat Ghassul; TaH: tel Abu Habil Leonard; TeM: Leonard

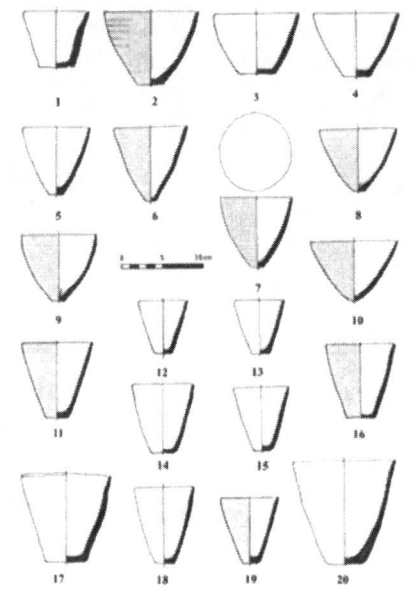

	basket	locus		level	description	references
1	4319	1361	pit	IIIB	small bowl, loessic matrix, smoothed on the tournette, smoothed circular axis 'imark	
2	5210				*V-shaped bowl, shaped on the wheel, lustrous red paint*	
3	4152	1321	fill	IIB1	small bowl, loessic matrix, coil-made,smoothed	
4	2614	882	silo	IIB1	V-shaped bowl, loessic matrix, wheel-made, 'axis' print on bottom slightly smoothed	
5	1099	522	pit	II	Tulip-bowl, loessic matrix, coil-made, slightly concave bottom	TG II, pl.41: 6, Leonard 1992, pl. 20: 1
6	3456	1079	hearth	IIB1	Tulip-bowl, molded, pinched base, red wash	
7	3327.3	1026	fill	IIA	Tulip-bowl, oval opening, molded, cream ware red burnished paint,	Mallon et al. 1932: fig. 42: 3 Koeppel et al. 1940, pl. 76: 7
8	3327. 1	1026	fill	IIA	Tulip-bowl, pinched base, red paint, white wash inside	Koeppel et al. 1940, pl. 76: 10
9	3327. 2	1026	fiil	IIA	Tulip-bowl, pinched base, red paint, white wash inside	Koeppel et al. 1940, pl. 76: 11
10	2893	806	pit	IIA	Tulip-bowl, molded, conical base, red paint	
11	5224	674	pit	IIB2	V-shaped beaker, red paint	
12	2626. 1	882	silo	IIB1	small V-shaped beaker, smoothed inside-out	
13	2626. 2	882	silo	IIB1	small V-shaped beaker, smoothed inside-out	
14	1153	528	pit	IIC	V-shaped beaker	
15	2527	882	silo	IIB1	small v-shaped beaker	
16	-	787	pit	IIB2	V-shaped beaker, slightly concave base, smoothed inside-out, red paint	Gophna & Sadeh 1989, fig. 9: 4
17	1145	528	pit	IIC	V-shaped beaker, *asymmetrical*	
18	-	570	cupmark	3	small V-shaped beaker	Oren & Gilead 1981, fig. 7: 18
19	4359. 1	1369	silo	IIIA	small V-shaped beaker, smoothed inside-out, red wash	
20	4359. 2	1369	silo	IIIA	large V-shaped beaker, thrown upper part, axis print on bottom	

Plate 10.1. V-shaped bowls, tulip bowls, beakers.

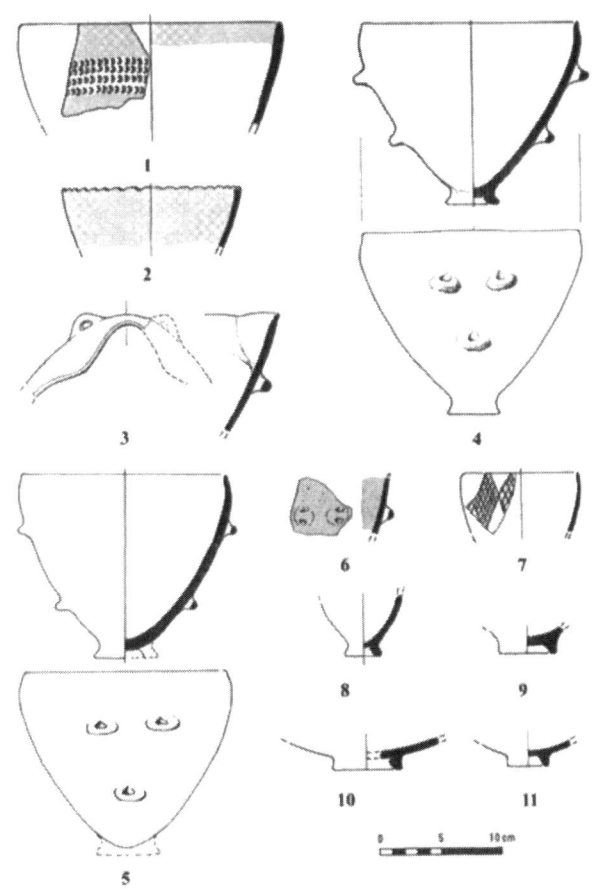

	basket	locus		level	description	references
1		558	structure	IIC	fragmented bowl, *cream ware*, red paint reserved for impressed lunulae design	
2	66.75	1097	floor	IIB1/2	fragmented bowl, impressed rim, red paint	
3	66.75	1077	floor	IIA	fragmented bowl, *clay*, (intentionally?) distended rim or spout, lug handles	
4	3528	1105	pit	IIC	Ring-based tulip bowl, clay, lug handles	cf. Garfinkel 1992, fig. 45: 13
5	2665	882	silo	IIB1	Ring- based (damaged) tulip bowl, clay, lug handles	
6	25. 3	13	floor	IIIA	fragmented bowl, lug handles and red paint	
7	3321.1	721	structure	III	fragmented bowl, cream ware, red-brown painted design	Gophna & Sadeh 1989, fig. 7: 3; Mallon *et al.* 1932, pl. 56: 1
8	4232	1322	pit	IIC	fragmented miniature ring-based tulip bowl, clay	Commenge-Pellerin 1987, fig. 22: 7
9	580.11	--	-	topsoil	ring-base, rounded bottom	
10	3818	1211	floor	IIB1	ring-base, rounded bottom	Gophna & Sadeh 1989, fig.12: 15
11	3545	1116	structure	IIA	ring-base, rounded bottom	

Plate 10.2. **Ring-based tulip bowls, fragmentary bowl, beaker, and ring-based vessels.**

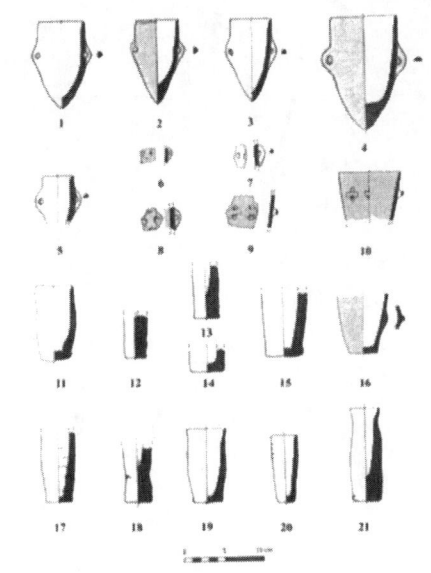

	basket	locus		level	description	references
1	3419.1	1068	structure	IIB1	small pointed-base beaker, vertical lug handles	Leonard 1992, pl. 2: 23,
2	3853	1217	fill	IIA	small pointed-base beaker, vertical lug handles, red paint	Koeppel 1940, TG,pl. 78: 2; Gilead & alon, 1988, Besor P 14, fig. 11: 6
3	3419.5	1068	structure	IIB1	small pointed-base beaker, vertical lug handles	
4	5713.6	1534	pit	IIIA	medium pointed-base beaker, vertical lug handles, red paint	Hennessy 1969, TG, Fig. 5: 2
5	3419. 7	1068	structure	IIB1	miniature pointed-base beaker, vertical lug handles	
6	3321.2	721	structure	III	vertical and small lug handle, red paint	
7	526.19	112	floor	IIIB	vertical and small lug handle	
8	522. 26	112	floor	IIIB	vertical and small lug handle, red paint	
9	213.4	69	hard soil	IIC	twin horizontal and small lug handles, red paint	
10	25 22	13	floor	IIIA	fragmented beaker(?), horizontal twin lug handles, red paint	Gilead 1995, Grar, fig. 4. 8: 4; Koeppel & et al 1940, pl. 76: 16; Sussman 1990, sheikh Ali, fig.V: 14
11	2682. 4	882	silo	IIB1	tubular beaker, protuding base	Gilead 1995, Grar, fig. 4. 18: 6
12	5713. 2	1534	pit	IIIA	high plain base, tubular beaker	
13	4359. 8	1369	silo	IIIA	high plain base, tubular beaker	
14	3575	1128	pit	IIC	base, tubular beaker	
15	4318.3	1344	pit	IIB1	fragmented tubular beaker, protuding base	
16	5281	700	pit	IIA	fragmented V-shaped beaker, vertical knob, red paint	Mallon et al. 1932, TG, fig. 56: 6
17	3749	1094	fill	IIC	fragmented tubular beaker, coil-made	
18	3818	1211	structure removal	IIB1	high and palin base, tubular (?) beaker	
19	2682.5	882	silo	IIB1	tubular beaker	
20	5351. 2	709	pit	IIB	tubular beaker, smoothed on the tournette	
21	5351.1	709	pit	IIB	tubular beaker, plain base	

Plate 10.3. Pointed-base beakers, tubular beakers and small lug-handles.

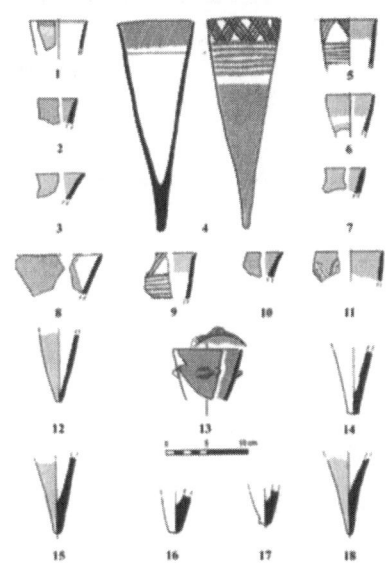

	basket	locus		level	description	references
1	3577	1125	ash fill	IIB1	fragmented cornet, cream ware, red painted design	
2	4318	1344	pit	IIB1	fragmented cornet, clay, red paint	
3	4281. 3	1339	structure	IIA	fragmented cornet, clay, red paint	
4	36. 87	647	hearth	IIB	cornet, cream ware, red painted design	
5	3251				fragmented cornet, cream ware, red painted design	Mallon et al. 1932, TG, pl. 65: 1-2; Koeppel et al 1940, TG, pl. 76: 12
6	3351	1056	pit	IIC	fragmented cornet, cream ware, red painted design	Koeppel et al 1940, TG, pl. 76: 24
7	4318	1344	pit	IIB1	fragmented cornet, clay, red paint	
8	3844	1274	fill	IV	fragmented cornet, cream: ware, red paint outside, red painted design inside	
9	3351.1	1056	pit	IIC	fragmented cornet, cream ware, red painted design	
10	4281.2	1339	structure	IIA	fragmented cornet, clay, red paint	
11	3416	1070	pit	IIB2	fragmented cornet, cream ware, red paint, redpaint reserved for fine incised design outside	
12	515.1	1076	floor removal	IIB1	pointed base, cornet?, red paint	
13	25. 22	13	floor	IIIA	fragmented beaker, twin horizontal lug handles, red paint	Mallon et al., TG, 1932, pl. 65: 7; Koeppel & et al 1940, TG, pl. 76: 21
14	4331	1374	pit	IIA	pointed base, cornet?	Koeppel & et al 1940, TG, pl. 76: 22
15	543.14				cornet base, red paint	
16	49	23	floor	IIC	pointed base, beaker?	
17	565. 10				pointed base, slightly flatten at the tip	Koeppel & et al 1940,TG pl; 48: 92; Sussman 1990, Sheikh Ali, fig. IV: 4
18	3351. 2	1056	pit	IIC	cornet base, red paint	Hennessy 1969, TG, fig. 7b: 2

Plate 10.4. Cornets, fragments and pointed bases.

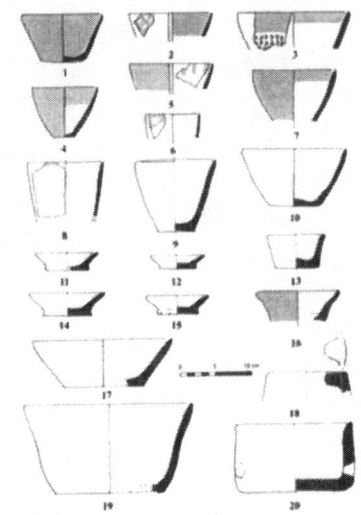

	basket	locus		level	description	references
1	46.13	24	pit	IIIA	V-shaped bowl, large circular concavity on bottom, red paint all over	
2	46.1	24	pit	IIIA	fragmented bowl, red paint and design	Lovell 2002, TG, fig; 4: 20; 2; Gophna & Sadeh 1989, Tel Tsaf fig. 8: 6
3	170.7	51	fill	IIB	fragmented bowl, cream ware, red paint reserved for impressed lunulae	Hennessy 1969, fig. 8b: 3
4	58.4	32	fill	IIIA	V-shaped bowl, narrow, clay, burnished red paint	Eisenberg et et al 2001, fig.52: 2
5	151.12	54	rubble soil	IIA	fragmented bowl, red paint and design inside	
6	193.1	61	floor	IIC	fragmented beaker, clay, red painted design	
7	170.15	51	fill	IIB	fragmented bowl, burnished red paint	
8	3352. 1	1057	pit	IIB2	fragmented beaker, cream ware, burnished red paint	
9	4359. 3	1369	silo	IIIA	Deep V-shaped bowl, concave bottom, coiled made	
10	5612. 2	1511	pit	IIC	large V-shaped bowl, coiled made, convexinside bottom	Commenge-Pellerin 1991, fig. 19: 6
11	3536. 3				saucer	cf. Garfinkel 1992, fig. 34: 7
12	565. 16				saucer	
13	-	-	topsoil	I	cup, convex inside bottom	cf. Koeppel & et al 1940, pl. 79: 6
14	571. 1				saucer	
15	3800	removal wall 1139		IIB1	saucer, finger prints on outside base	
16	11. 11	3	fill	I-IIB	fragmented large saucer, red paint	Commenge-Pellerin 1987, fig. 22: 8
17	62. 8	29	fill	IIB	large and shallow bowl, fragmented	
18	3051				fragmented cylindrical bowl? knob on the inside rim	
19	58.1	32	fill	IIIA	fragmented basin, circular imprint on bottom	
20	5612. 1	1511	pit	IIC	cylindrical bowl, clay saturated with carbonized seeds, perforation at the base and circular mark opposite	

Plate 10.5. Bowls, saucers, cups and basins.

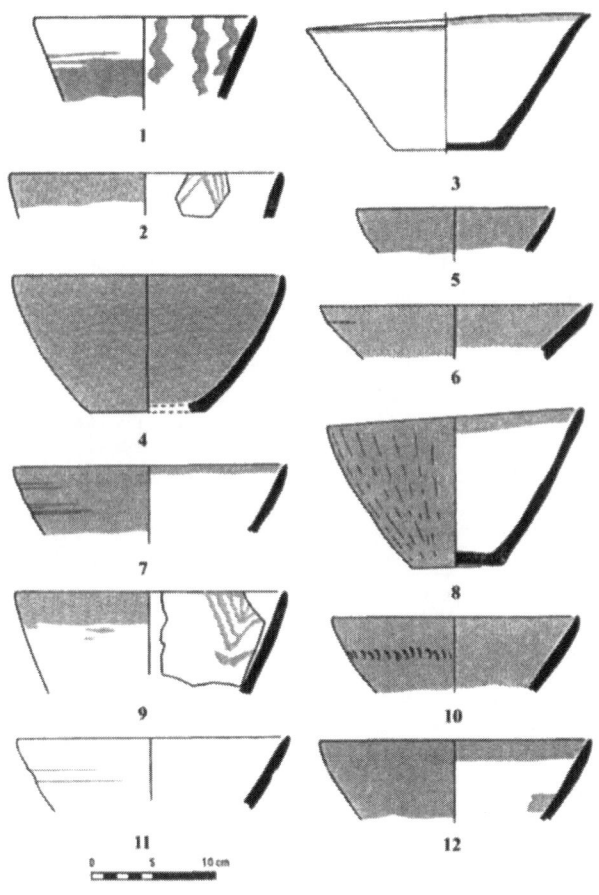

	basket	locus		level	description	references
1*	85. 20	40	floor	IIC	V-shaped bowl, fragment, red paint and design	
2*	201. 25	56	rubble soil	I-IIA	basin, fragment, red paint and design	
3*	3051				basin, red paint	Commenge-Pellerin 1991, fig. 19: 11
4*	55. 56	28	fill	IIB	basin, burnished red paint	
5*	177. 4	572	pit	III	large bowl, fragment, red paint	Lovell 1999, fig.4. 1: 7
6	177. 9	572	pit	III	basin, fragment, carinated rim, red paint	
7	223.8	54	rubble soil	IIA	basin, fragment, red paint and traces of tool	
8*	272. 1	90	pit	IIB	basin, concave bottom, red paint and impressed design	
9*	80. 21	40	floor	IIC	basin, fragment, red paint and design	Mallon et al. 1932, pl 42: 9 Hennessy 1969, fig. 8b: 3
10*	212. 3	68	rubble soil	I-IIA	large bowl, fragment, red paint and impressed lunulae	
11	14. 10	6	floor	IIC	basin, fragment, circular groove made by tool	
12	151. 15	50	fill	IIB	basin, fragment, red paint	

Plate 10.6. Large V-shaped bowls.

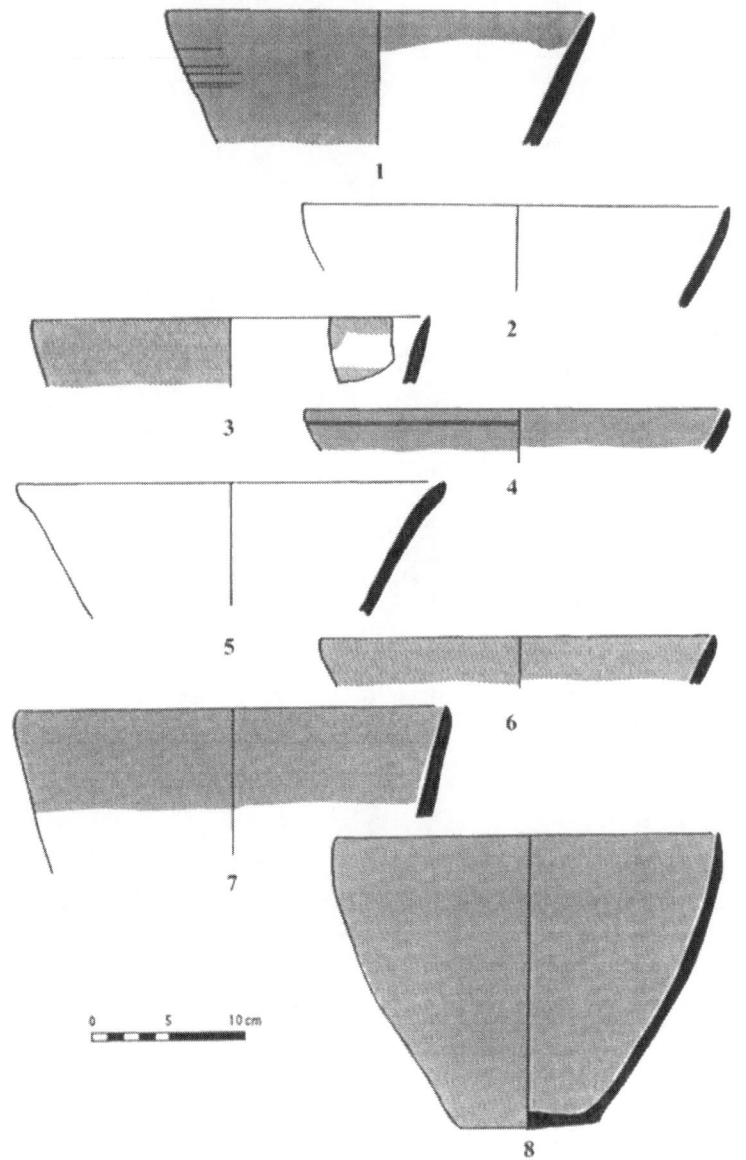

	basket	locus		level	description
1	82. 3	39	fill	IIB	basin, fragment, red paint
2	29. 18	13	floor	IIIA	basin, fragment
3	206. 2	64	pit	IIC	basin, fragment, red paint and design
4	188. 17	56	-	I-IIA	basin, fragment, red paint
5*	197. 1	58	rubble soil	IIB	basin fragment, everted rim
6	217.14	70	pit	IIB	basin, fragment, red paint
7*	36. 10	24	pit	II-IIIA	basin, fragment, red paint
8*	727. 3	141	floor	IIIA	deep basin, lightly burnished red paint

Plate 10.7. Basins.

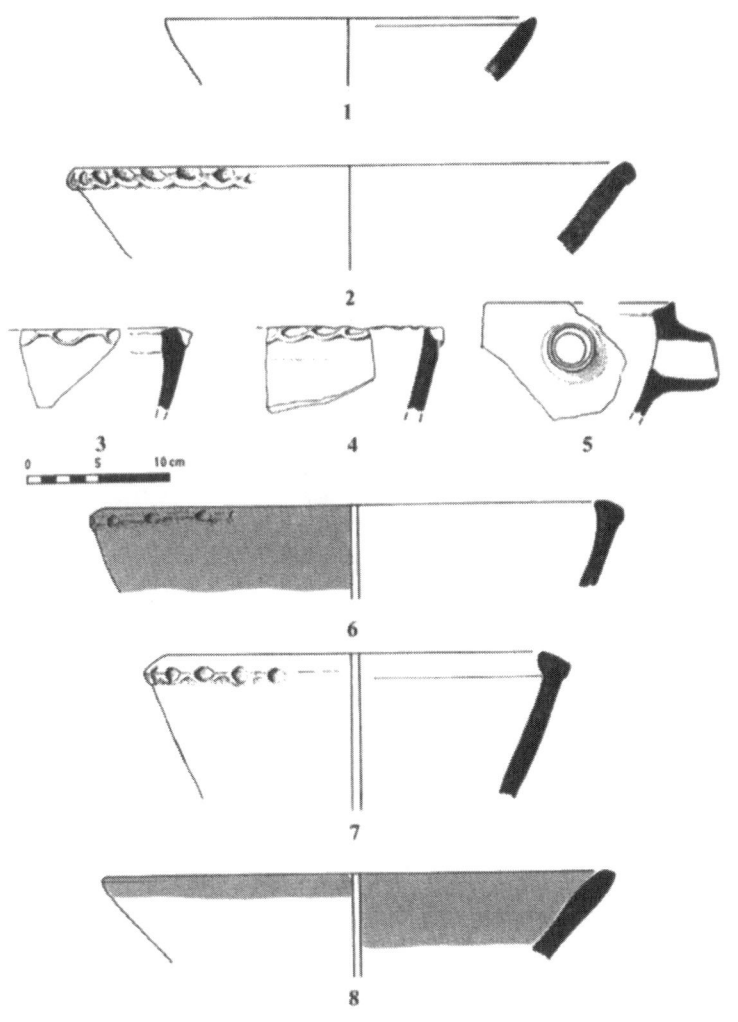

	basket	locus		level	description	references
1	151. 14	50	fill	IIB	basin, fragment, oblique rim	
2*	14. 23	6	floor	IIC	large basin, fragment, impressed design	Commenge-Pellerin 1991, fig. 24: 1
3*	3371				large basin, fragment, impressed design	
4*	3340				large basin, fragment, impressed design	
5	5208	671	pit	IIC	large basin, fragment, spout	Eisenberg et et al 2001, fig. 6. 2:1; ******TGII pl. 54: 3
6*	221. 6	69	floor	IIC	large basin, fragment, impressed design and red paint	Lovell 2002 fig. 4; 22: 4
7*	63. 4	38	floor	IIC	basin, fragment, impressed design on oblique rim	Commenge-Pellerin 1991, fig. 27: 8
8	3352	1057	pit	IIB2	large basin, fragment, red paint	

Plate 10.8. Basins and tubular spout.

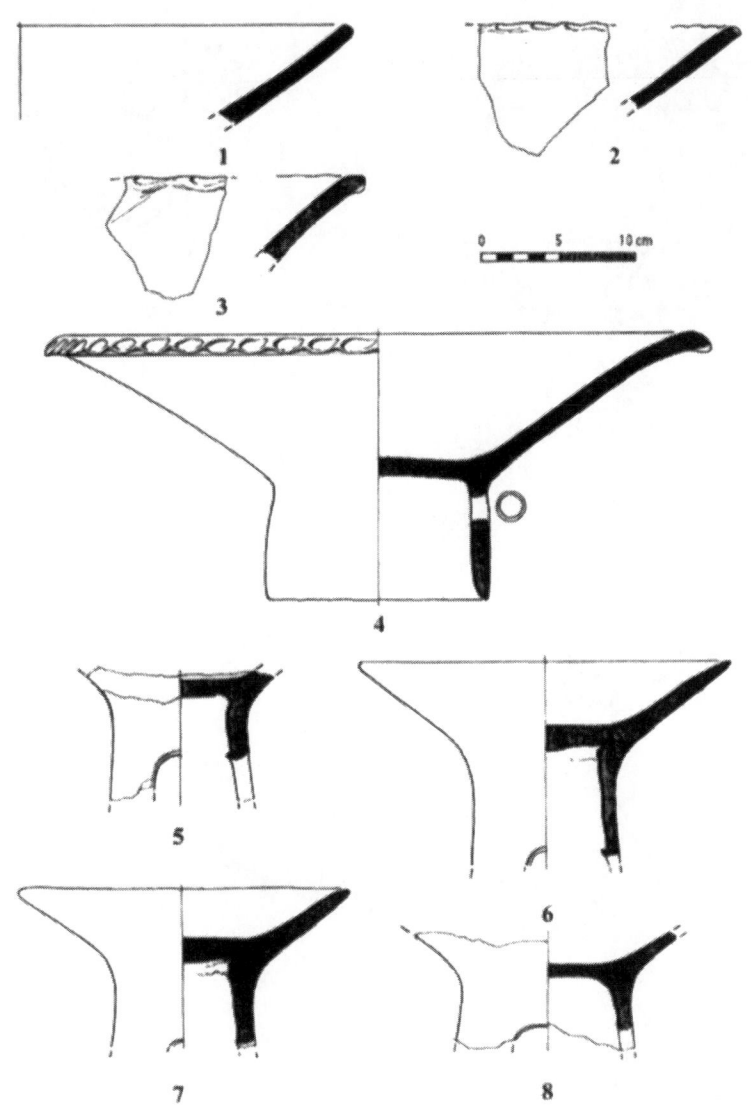

	basket	locus		level	description	references
1	1381	586	probe	IIIB	large bowl, fragment	
2*	3352	1057	pit	IIB2	large bowl, fragment, impressed design	
3*	3203				large bowl, fragment, impressed design	
4*	5537	787	pit	IIB2	fenestrated pedestal chalice, impressed rim and circular symmetrical opening in pedestal	Mallon et al. 1932, fig. 56: 9
5*	5139	636	fill	IIB	fenstrated pedestal vassel, fragment	
6*	5568	787	pit	IIB2	fenestrated pedestal chalice, fragment	Gilead 1995, fig. 4. 10: 4
7*	5349	709	pit	IIB	fenestrated pedestal chalice, fragment	Commenge-Pellerin 1991, fig. 20: 1
8*	3231	1026	-	I	fenestrated pedestal chalice, fragment	

Plate 10.9. Chalices on fenestrated pedestals and fragments.

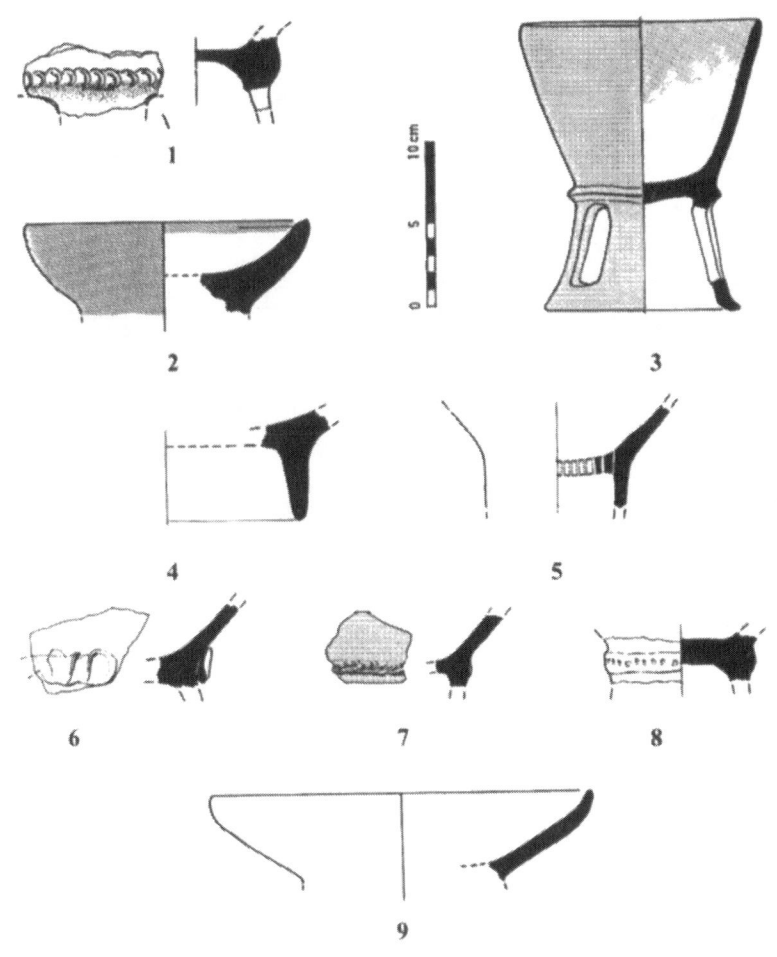

	basket	locus		level	description	references
1*	5308	699	-	I	incised lunulae on relief, fragment	
2	110	42	floor	IV	small chalice, fragment, lightly burnished red paint	Cf. Garfinkel (1992): fig. 45: 6 Koeppel *et al.* (1940): pl. 79: 2
3*	2475	862	pit	IIB1	fenestrated pedestal bowl, red paint, ridge around the bowl's base	Leonard (1992): pl. 3: 23
4*	5334	649	pit	IIC	large ring-base of an open vessel, fragment	Garfinkel (1992): fig. 102: 6–7
5*	3434	1075	pit	IIB1	pedestalled bowl, strainer, thin walls	Dollfus *et al* (1985): fig. 8: 6
6*	525. 2	112	floor	IIIB	fenestrated pedestal, fragment, impressions on ridge	Gilead (1995): fig. 4. 10: 2 Commenge-Pellerin (1991): fig. 20: 7
7*	525. 1	112	floor	IIIB	fenestrated pedestal, fragment, fine impressed design on ridge and red paint	
8*	5045	607	-	I	pedestalled bowl, fragment, impressed dots on ridge	
9*	26. 5	8	platform	IIC	pedestalled chalice, fragment	

Plate 10.10. Bowls on fenestrated pedestals and pedestalled plates.

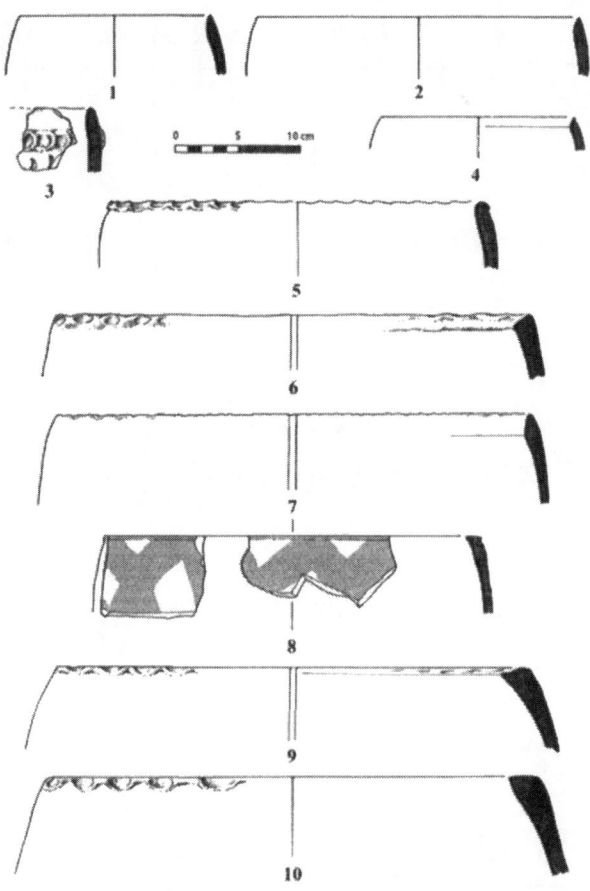

	basket	locus		level	description	references
1*	23	12	pit	IIC	small pithos, convex, rim, thinned from inside	
2	165.9	51	fill	IIB	convex, rim thinned from inside	
3*	201.35	56	rubble soil	I-IIA	pithos rim, finger impression on ridge and impressed lunulae	Mallon *et al.* 1932, fig. 60: 17
4*	24. 7	14	pit	IIA	small pithos, inside oblique rim	
5*	88.3	39	fill	IIB	large pithos, impressions outside the everted rim	
6*	-	-	-	-	large pithos, fimpressions on inside oblique rim	Commenge-Pellerin 1991, fig. 33: 5
7*	99. 1	43	red surface		large pithos, slighlty oblique inside rim impressions on rim's edge	
8*	192;2	56	rubble soil	I-IIA	painted desing and horizontal rim	
9*	150. 13	-	-	-	large pithos, impressions on horizontal, large rim	
10	82.	39	fill	IIB	large pithos, impressions outside the horizontal, large rim	

Plate 10.11. Pithoi.

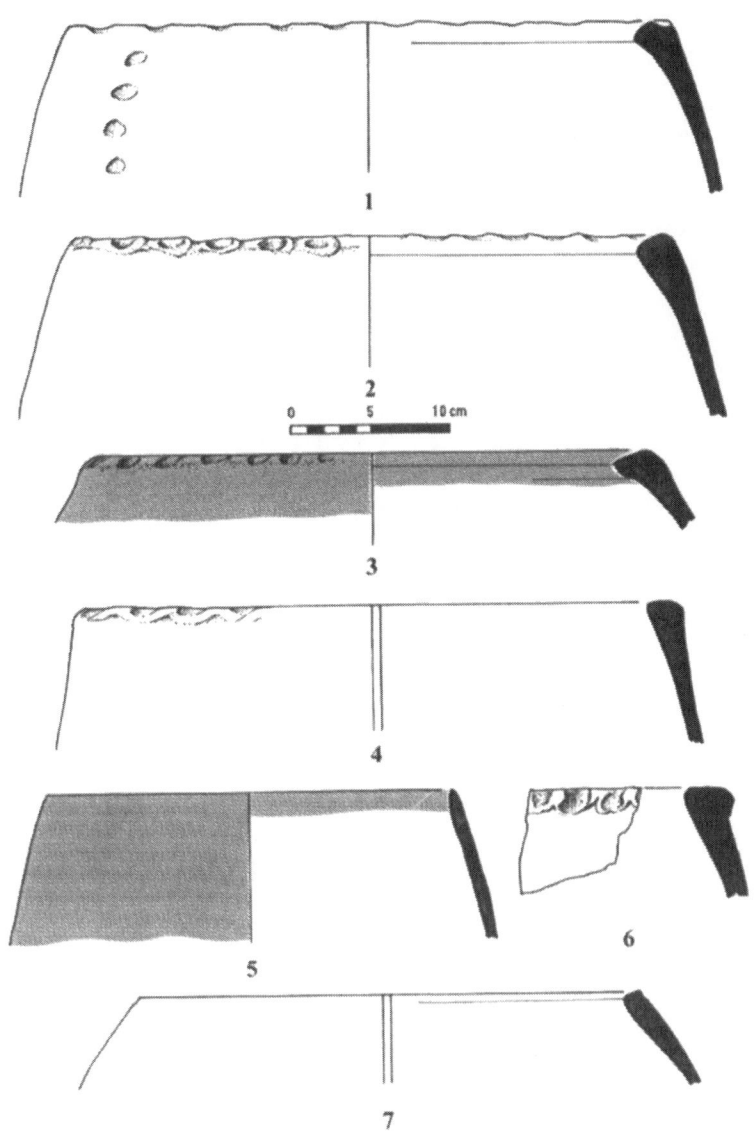

	basket	locus		level	description
1*	216.1	56	rubble soil	I-IIA	large pithos, thickened oblique rim, impressions on rim's edge, and vertical line of impressed large dots
2*	11.5	3	fill	I-IIB	large pithos, thickened oblique rim, impressions on rim's edge
3*	8. 10	6	floor	IIC	thickened rim forming an inside ridge, impressions on rim's edge
4*	24.64	14	floor	IIIA	horizontal rim, impressions on outside edge
5*	34;2	16	fill	IIIA	pithos, red painted
6*	82.39	39	fill	IIB	thickened horizontalrim; outside ridge with impressions
7*	213. 22	69	floor	IIC	inside oblique rim

Plate 10.12. Pithoi.

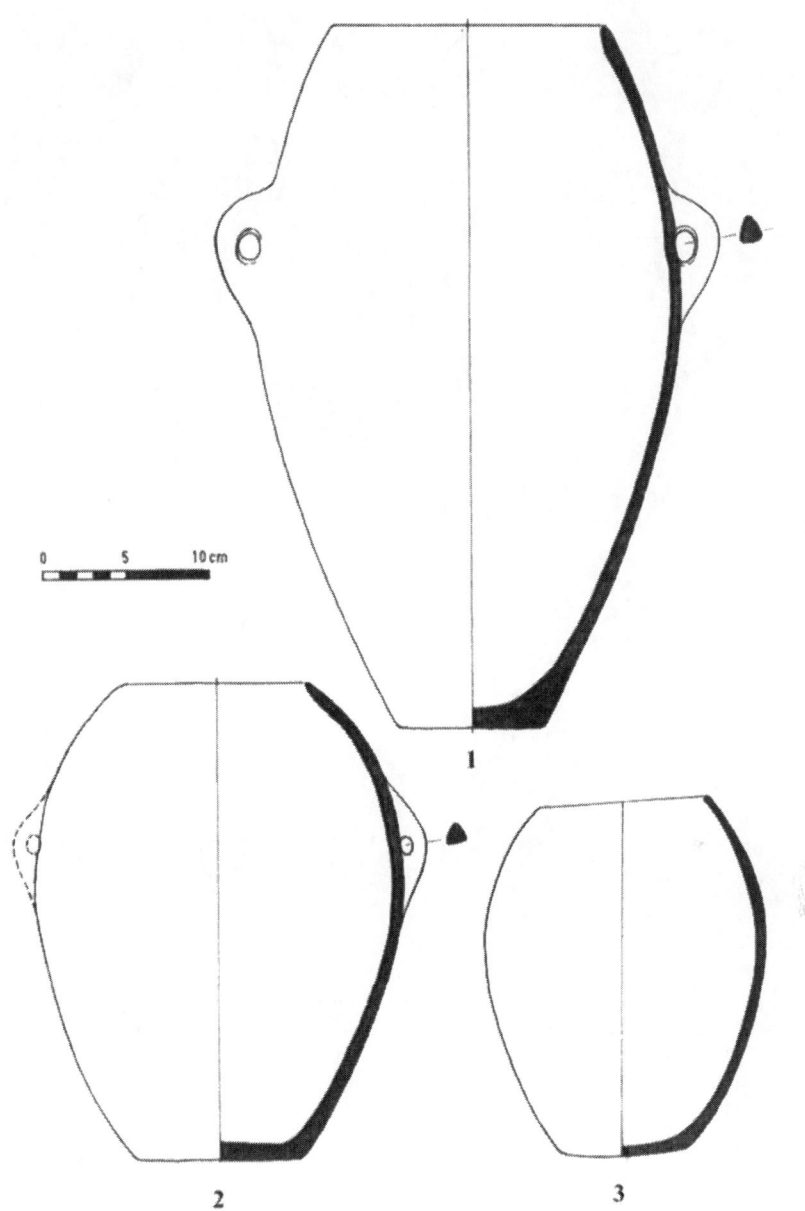

0   5   10 cm

	basket	locus		level	description	references
1*					Besor type, deep pithos, symmetrical handles with triangular profile	
2*	1260	548	pit	III	hole-mouth jar, symmetrical lug handles	
3*	97	44	floor	IIC	small hole-mouth jar	Gilead & Alon, 1988, Besor P14, fig. 11: 9

Plate 10.13. Holemouth jars.

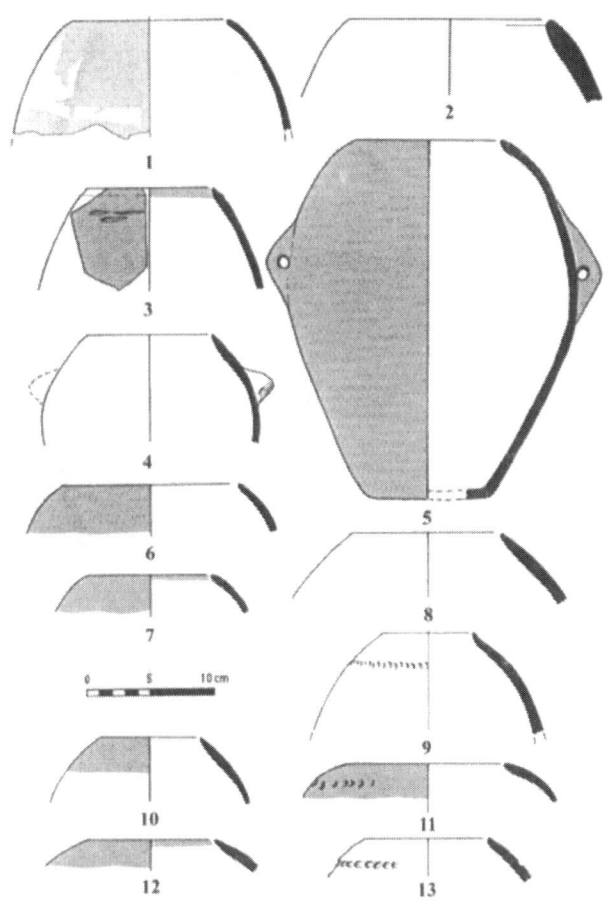

	basket	locus		level	description	references
1*	-	1064	surface	IIA	fragmented hole-mouth jar, red paint	
2*	21.89	9	hard soil	IIC	thick, 'snake' profile rim	
3*	51. 23	26	floor	IIC	painted and impressed fragment, thinned rim	
4*	164. 2	50	fill	IIB	pithos or pot, fragmented, symmetrical lugs	Koeppel & et al 1940, Pl; 77: 4
5*	172	50	fill	IIB	red painted, lightly burnished hole-mouth jar, lug handles	Mallon et al. 1932, fig. 47
6	92. 14	44	floor	IIC	red painted rim	
7	92. 14	44	floor	IIC	red painted rim	
8	36. 17	24	pit	IIIA	hole-mouth fragment, thinned rim	
9*	1175	542	fill	III	'hole-mouth' fragment with an upright rim, lunulae impressions	
10*	233. 1	73	pit	IIB	small jar, red paint	
11	71;.13	-	-	-	hole-mouth rim, sharply convex, red paint and lunulae impressions	
12	176. 2	55	pit	IIB	hole-mouth rim, red paint	Lovell 2002, fig. 4. 4: 1
13	62. 4	29	fill	IIB	hole-mouth rim, horizontal line of dots	

Plate 10.14. Holemouth jars and rims.

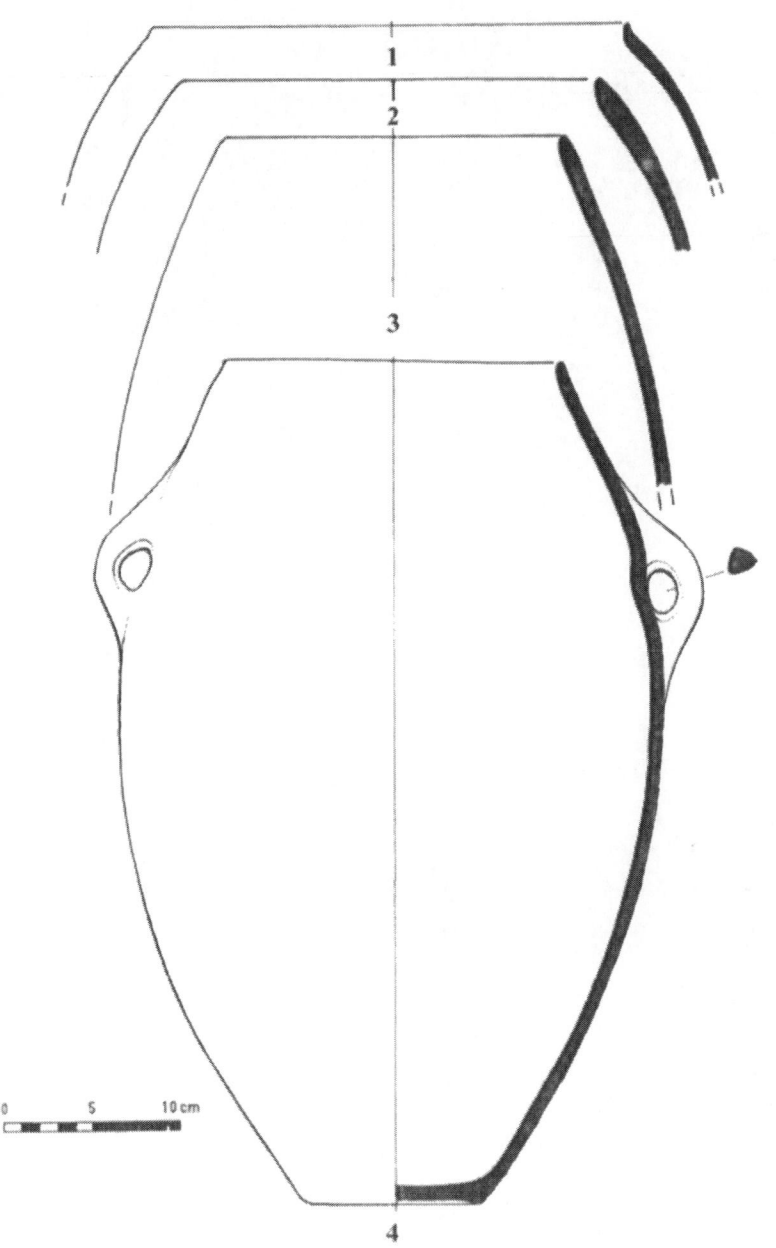

	basket	locus		level	description
1*	3712				upright rim of a large pithos
2	91.19	42	floor	IV	'snake' profile rim
3*	5567	796	fill	IIB2	large 'Besor type' pithos, fragment
4*	2894	998	********	IIIA	'Besor type' pithos, symmetrical handles with triangular profile, concave bottom

Plate 10.15. Holemouth jars.

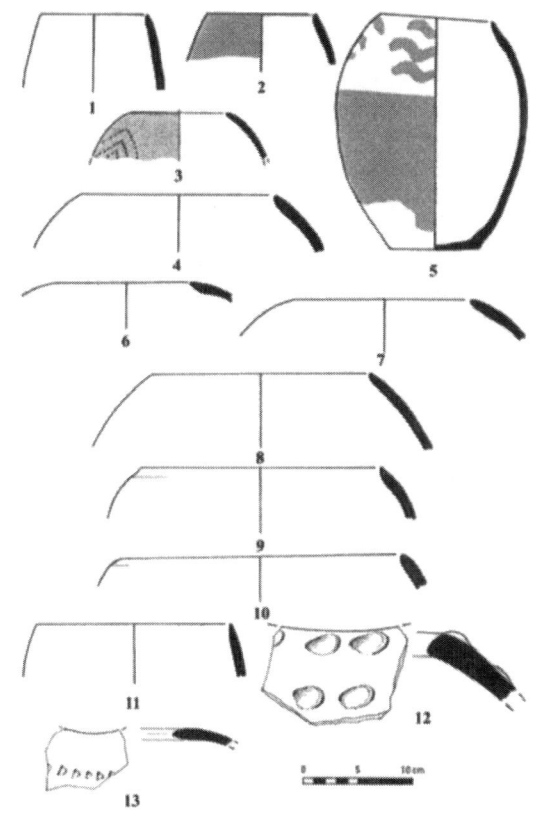

	basket	locus		level	description	references
1	29. 4	13	floor	IIIA	small pithos, fragment	
2	22.21	7	floor	IIC	small pithos, fragment, red paint	Garfinkel 1992, Munahata, fig. 115: 2 Sussman 1990, Sheikh Ali, fig.III: 5
3*	176. 3	55	pit	IIB	hole-mouth jar, fragment, red paint and incised design	
4	92.16	44	floor	IIC	hole-mouth jar, fragment	
5*	97. 12	44	floor	IIC	hole-mouth jar, upright rim and red painted design	
6	62; 1	29	fill	IIB	hole-mouth jar, 'snake' profile rim	
7	63. 8	38	floor	IIC	hole-mouth jar, 'snake' profile rim	
8	176. 4	55	pit	IIB	large hole-mouth jar, fragment	
9*	217 23	70	pit	IIB	upright rim	
10	67. 25	36	floor	IIC	rim of a large pithos	
11	40. 14	19	floor	IIC	pithos, fragment	
12*	-	771	pit	IIC	horizontal rim of a hole-mouth jar, incised lunulae	Lovell 2002, fig. 4. 24: 4
13*	3716				hole-mouth jar, very large rim with impressed dots design	

Plate 10.16. Holemouth jars, and rims.

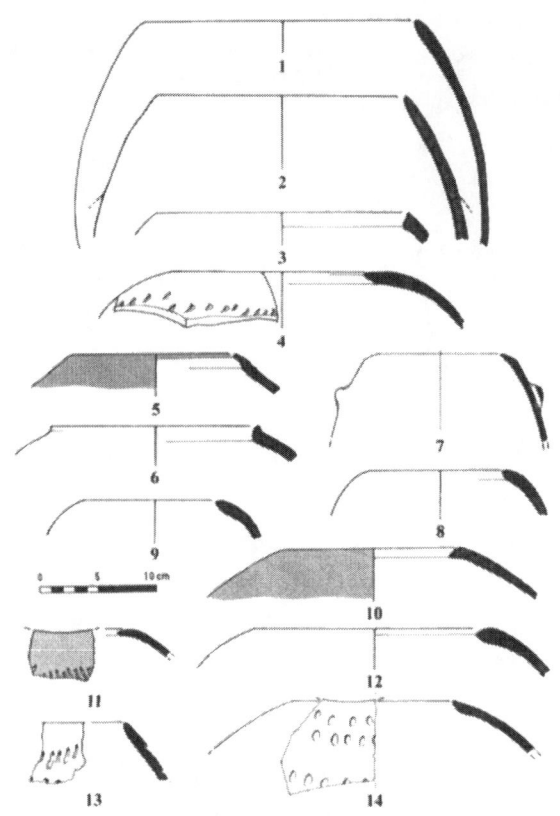

	basket	locus		level	description	references
1*	394;1	141	hard soil	IIIA	large 'Besor' type pithos, fragment	
2*	86; 3	43	red surface	IIC	large 'Besor' type pithos, fragment, symmetrical handles or lugs	
3*	52; 5	30	floor	IIC	thickened, oblique rim of a pithos	
4*	87; 39	42	floor	IV	large hole-mouth jar, horizontal pitched rim, oblique face inside	
5*	-	-	-	topsoil	hole-mouth rim, upright and pitched	
6*	3575	1128	pit	IIC	hole-mouth rim, upright	
7*	664. 22				pithos, fragment, horizontal rim, horizontal lug handles	Commenge-Pellerin 1991, fig. 41: 10 Lovell 2002, fig; 4. 5: 5
8	-	-	-	topsoil	'snake' profile rim	
9	-	-	-	topsoil	'snake' profile rim	
10	-	-	-	topsoil	hole-mouth rim, oblique insidei rim, red paint	Eisenberg et al 2001, fig. 5.7: 6
11*	3614				hole-mouth horizontal rim, incised design and red paint	
12	230. 8	55	pit	IIB	'snake' profile of a large hole-mouth rim	
13	664. 18				incised design, hole-mouth rim	
14	2816				hole-mouth rim, upright rim, large dots impressed	Commenge-Pellerin 1990, fig. 41: 8

Plate 10.17. Rims of pithoi and holemouth jars.

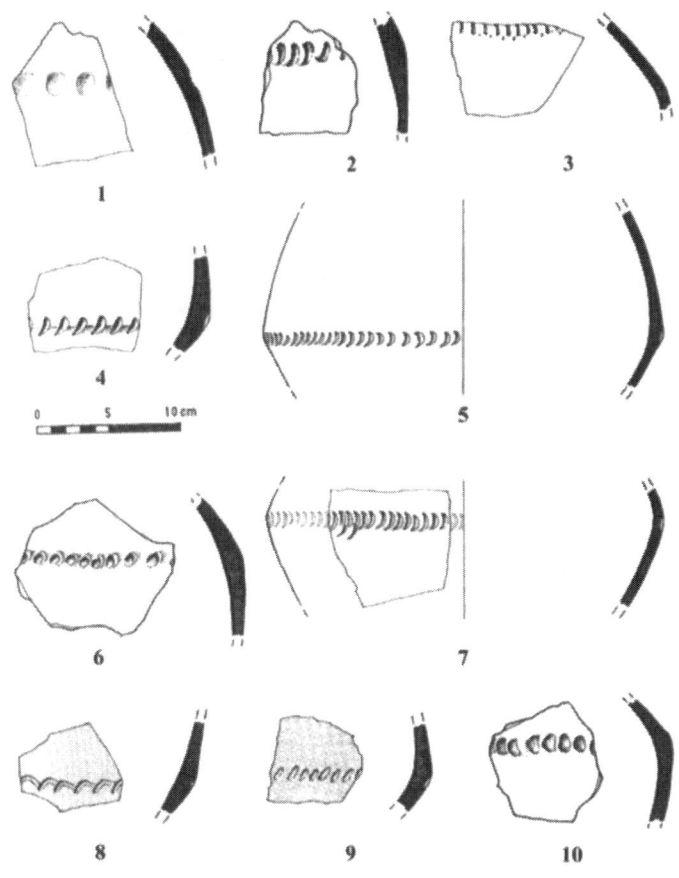

	basket	locus		level	description	references
1	2650				convex fragment, large finger impressions	
2	213. 27				fragment, impressed lunulae	
3	3575	1128	pit	IIC	carinated fragment, impressed lines and dots	
4	3371				carinated fragment, open shape, impressed lunulae	
5		1105	pit	II C	large carinated jar, fragment, impressed lunulae	Garfinkel 1992, fig.128: 3–5
6	40. 8				carinated fragment of a jar, impressed large dots	Oren & Gilead 1981, fig. 9: 11
7		1056	pit	IIC	large carinated jar, fragment, impressed lunulae	
8	80. 28	40	floor	IIC	carinated rim of a large bowl, impressed bows	
9		985	stone circle	IIB 1	carinated fragment, open shape, impressed elongated dots	
10	82. 6				carinated fragment, coarsely impressed lunulae	

Plate 10.18. Biconvex jars, fragments.

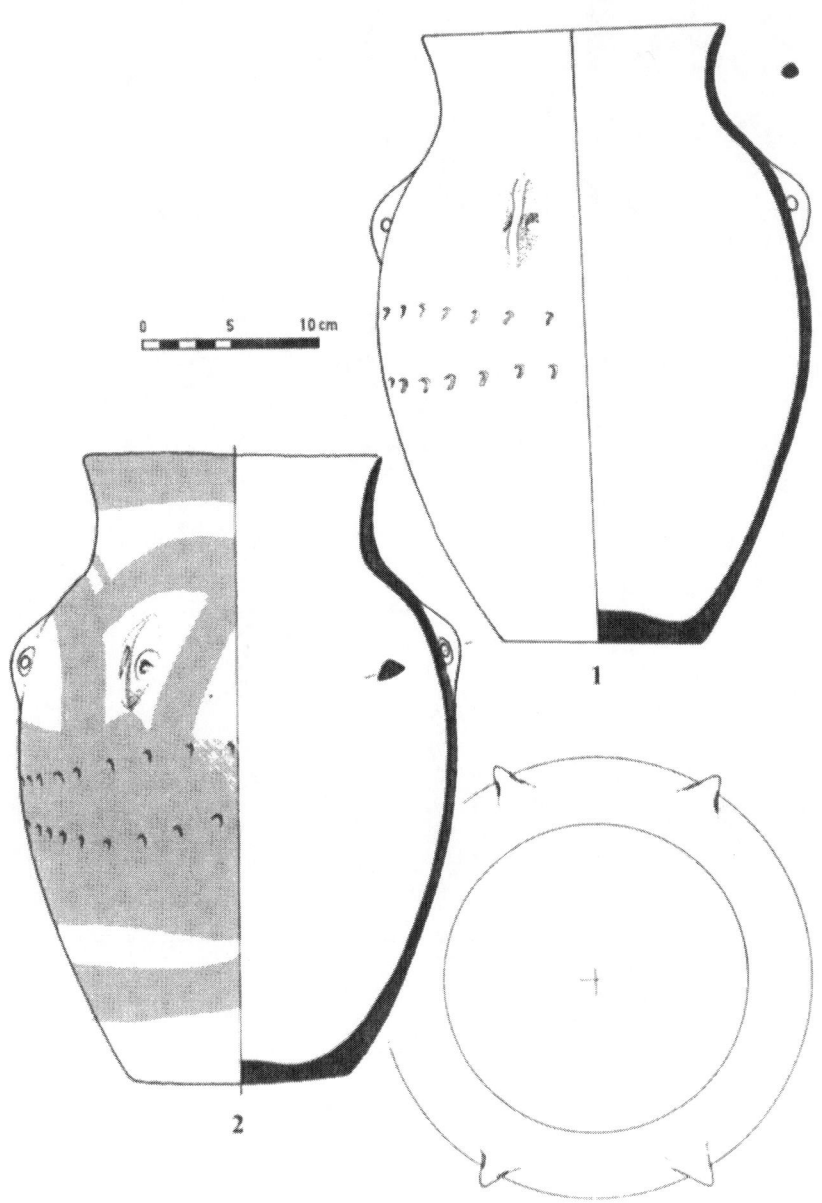

	basket	locus		level		description
1	97. 1	568?				necked jar, four symmetrical lug handles, impressed lunulae
2		568?				necked jar, four symmetriccal lug handles, red painted design and impressed lunulae

Plate 10.19. Necked jars.

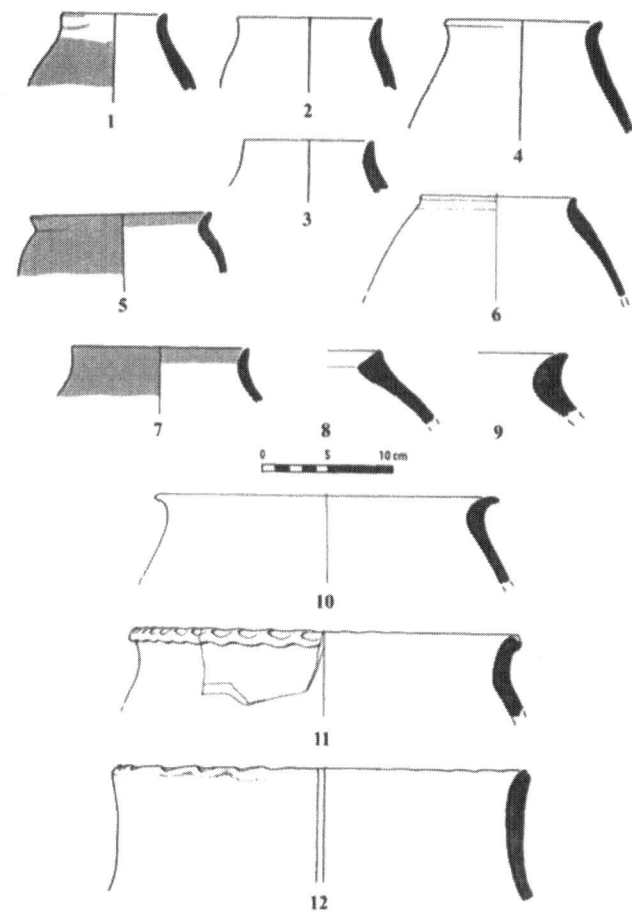

	basket	locus		level	description	references
1	217. 12	70	pit	IIB	neck, type, red painted	Commenge-Pellerin 1987, fig. 33: 3
2	14. 12			IIIA	neck, type	
3	205. 18				neck, type	Hennessy 1969, fig. 9a: 3
4	31. 4				neck, type, everted rounded rim	Commenge-Pellerin 1990, fig. 45 12
5	-	712	hearths	IIA	small pithos, everted rim and red painted	
6	512. 29				jar, everted rounded rim	
7	212. 21	68	rubble soil	I-IIA	neck, type, red painted	
8			zone T		inverted rim of a large jar, thickened and obliquely flatenned	
9		1105	pit	IIC	neck, thick everted and rounded rim	
10	5357	716	fill	IIAB	short and large neck, type	
11	3846	1214	topsoil	I	short and large neck, type, impressed rim	
12	25. 2	13			short and large neck, type, impressed rim	Koeppel & et al, TG pl. 77: 7

Plate 10.20. Rims of pithoi and necked jars.

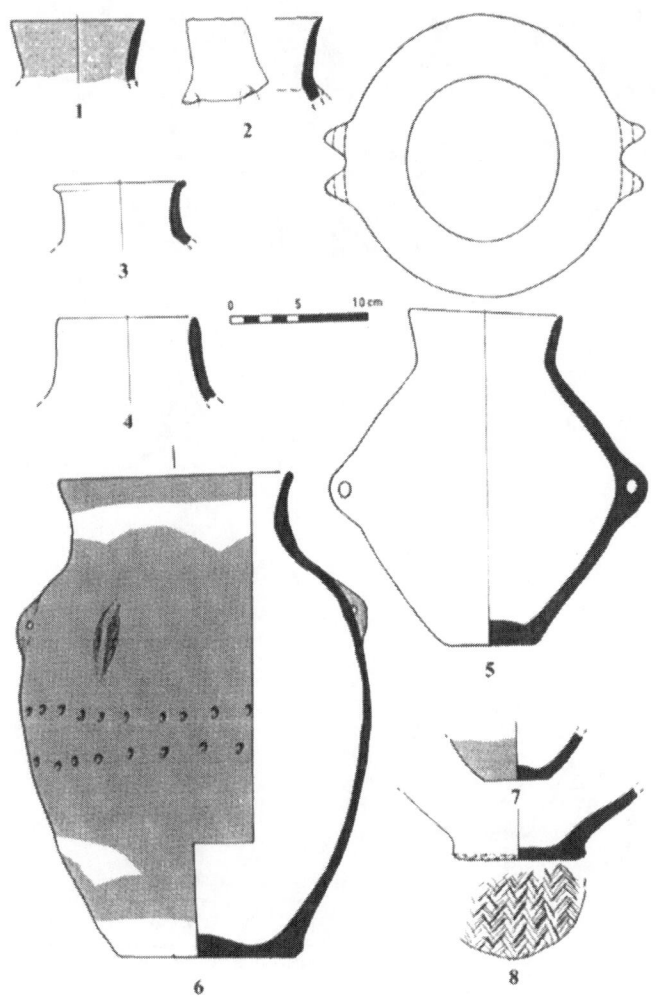

	basket	locus		level	description	references
1	1134.1	1351	surface	IIC	small neck, type, red painted	
2	-	611	pit	IIA	neck, type protuberances on shoulder (lugs?)	Commenge-Pellerin 1990, fig. 47: 1
3	-	606 I	topsoil		neck, type	
4	5323. 1	639	pit	IIA	neck, type	
5	-	1135	pit	IIC	Carinated neck jar, flaring neck and symmetrical lug handles	Garfinkel 1992, fig. 124: 11-12; Lovell 2002, fig. 4. 26: 1 (although smaller)
6	97. 2	44	floor	IIC	Necked jar, large neck, four symmetrical lug handles and red painted design	Hennessy 1969, fig. 6: 6
7	-	30	floor	IIC	bottom of a small jar or pot, convex inside bottom	
8	81.4	42	floor	IV	base of a jar, protuding, basketery impression outside	Garfinkel 1992, fig. 131: 5

Plate 10.21. Necked jars, necks and bases.

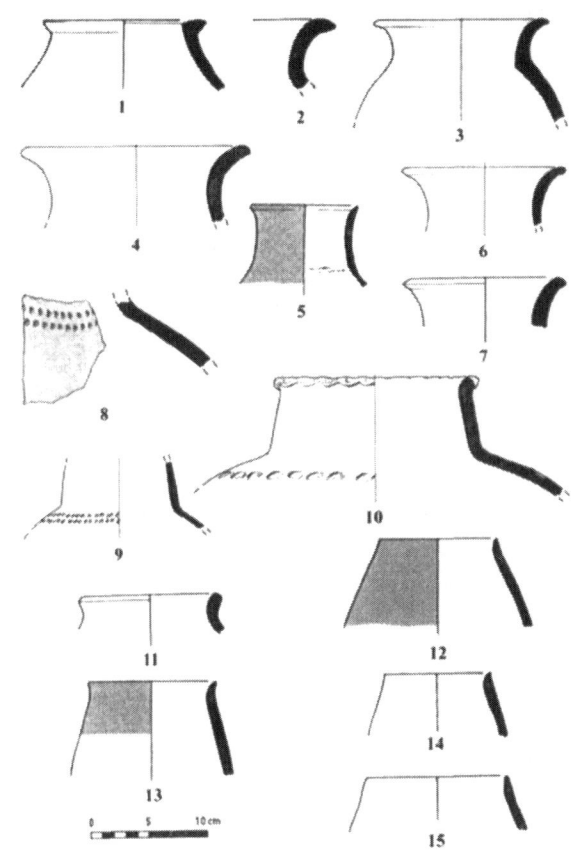

	basket	locus		level	description	references
1	85. 15	40	floor	IIC	short neck,type, horizontal everted rim	
2	-	755	fill	IIB-C	neck, type, everted rim	
3	5357. 7	796	fill	IIB2	necked jar, type	
4	3247. 3	688	topsoil	I	large neck, type, everted rim	
5	77. 7	38	floor	IIC	narrow neck, type, red painted	
6	-	1103	pit	IIB	neck, type	
7	-	--	-	topsoil	neck, type	Commenge-Pellerin 1990, fig. 45: 7
8	5245	1557	pit	IIIB	jar's shoulder, red painted z,d impressed lunulae	Hennessy 1969, fig. 8a: 9
9	81. 3	42	floor	IV	jar, bow neck, type, impressed dots	Eisenberg et a.l2001, fig. 5. 6: 12
10	4331	1374	pit	IIA	large jar, type, finger impressions	Koeppel & et al,1940 pl. 77: 7
11	164. 3	50	fill	IIB	neck, type	
12	-	755	fill	IIB-C	fragmented pot, red painted	
13	-	-	-	topsoil	fragmented pot, everted rim, red painted	
14	91. 18	42	floor	IV	fragmented pot, thinned everted rim	
15	63. 7	38	floor	IIC	fragmented pot, thinned everted rim	Lovell 2002, TG, fig. 4 6: 6

Plate 10.22. Necks and small holemouth jars.

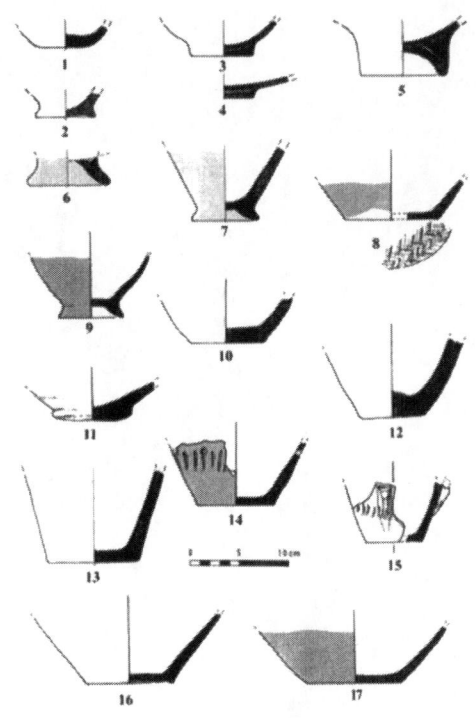

	basket	locus		level	description	references
1	3891. 52	725	surface	IV	jar's bottom, convex inside	
2	--	1076	structure	IIB1	open shape with ring, flaring base	Garfinkel 1992, Munhata, fig. 130: 16
3	--	725	surface	IV	disk base, closed shape	Garfinkel 1992, Munhatafig. 130: 2, 132: 4; Gilead and Alon 1988, Besor P14, fig. 11: 12
4	-	725	surface	IV	disk base, closed shape	
5	-	1534	pit	IIIA	open shape with ring, flaring base, red paint	cf. photograph, figure 10.**
6	522. 15	112	hard soil	IIIB	flaring ring base, red paint	
7	589. 1	151	pit	IIB	pot, flaring ring base, red paint	Lovell 2002, TG fig. 4. 18: 10
8	151. 8	51	fill	IIB	jar, red painted design, mat impression	
9	55. 1	28	fill	IIIA	open shape, flaring ring base, red paint	
10	67. 5	36	floor	IIC	jar's base, thick flatten angular bottom	Lovell 2002, TG, fig. 4. 18: 3
11	27. 7	8	platform	IIC	irregular disk base	
12	19. 12	6	floor	IIC	urn's base? convex inside	Beit Arieh verif
13	3649				high and narrow base, angular bottom	
14	62. 7	29	fill	IIB	narrow base, angular, red paint and impressed lunulae	Mallon *et al.* (1932): fig. 56: 5
15	-	-	-	-	beaker's base, angular, vertical lug and impressed lines	
16	99. 2	43	hard soil	IIC	large base, outside ridge	
17	192. 8	56	rubble soil	I-IIA	large base, red paint	

Plate 10.23. Bases.

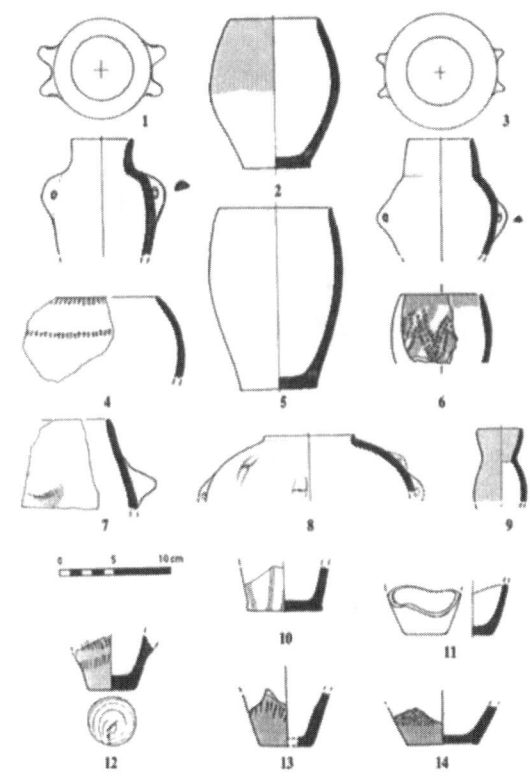

	basket	locus		level	description	references
1	5294. 2	697	pit	IIA	small jar, twin symmetrical lug handles	
2	5644. 1	1505	pit	IIC	small hole-mouth jar, red painted	Commenge-Pellerin 1991, fig. 38: 10
3	5537. 1	787	pit	IIB2	small jar, bow rim, twin symmetrical lug handles	Koeppel & et al 1940, pl. 78: 12
4	5739.3	1511	pit	IIC	rim of a globular pot, impressed design	
5	2656. 1	882	silo	IIB1	pot	
6	391. 34	725	surface	IV	small potor goblet, red painted and impressed dots	Goren 2002, fig. 4. 1: 15 Garfinkel 1992, fig. 95: 12
7	-	-	-	topsoil	pithos rim, plain horizontal lug handle	Garfinkel 1992, fig. 66: 1
8	-	sq. M6	-	topsoil	pot with two registers of small lug handles on the shoulder	
9	3345	1037	ashy lens	IIA	miniature pot, red painted	Koeppel et al. (1940): pl. 77: 6
10	-	1525	mudbrick circle	IIIA	base of a large tubular (?) vessel, red painted	
11	5253				re-shaped base of a beaker	
12	5423	755	fill	IIB	Thrown beaker's base incisions and light red paint, lug handles	
13	-	658	ashy lens	IIB	beaker's base, red painted and impressions	Beit Arieh (1980): fig. 7: 15
14	52. 1	30	floor	IIC	pot's base, red painted and impressions ridge around the base and red paint	

Plate 10.24. Small pots, miniature jars, cup and bases.

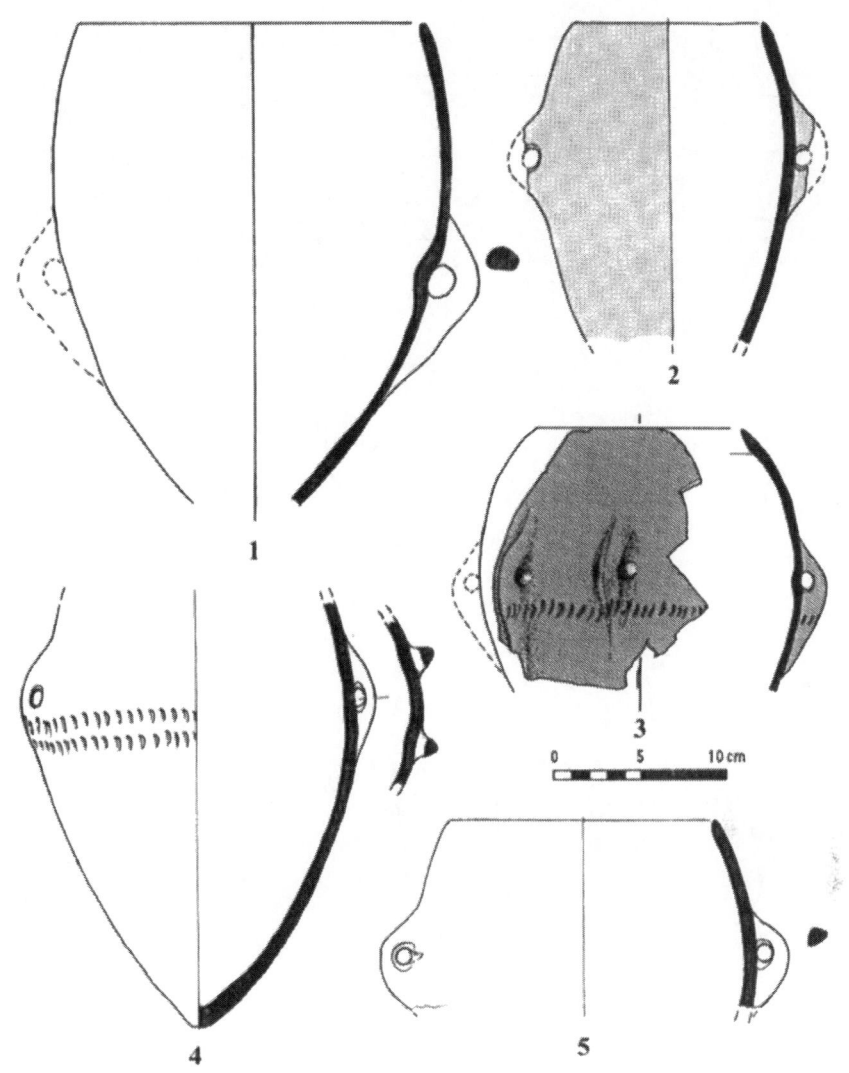

	basket	locus		level	description	references
1		727			large, open beaker, symmetrical lug handles	
2	2682	882	silo	IIB1	large and narrow beaker, symmtrical lug handles, red painted	
3	64. 5	28	fill	IIIA	globular large beaker, symmetrical lug handles, red painted and impressed lunulae	GarfinkelMEITAR in Qedem 273
4	3840	1217	fill	IIA1	pointed-base beaker twin symmetrical lug handles, impressed lunulae	Beit Arieh 1980, fig. 9: 1 Oren & Gilead 1981, fig. 6: 4
5	548. 1	-	-	topsoil	large, open beaker, symmetrical lug handles	

Plate 10.25. Large pointed-base beakers, pithos and torpedo.

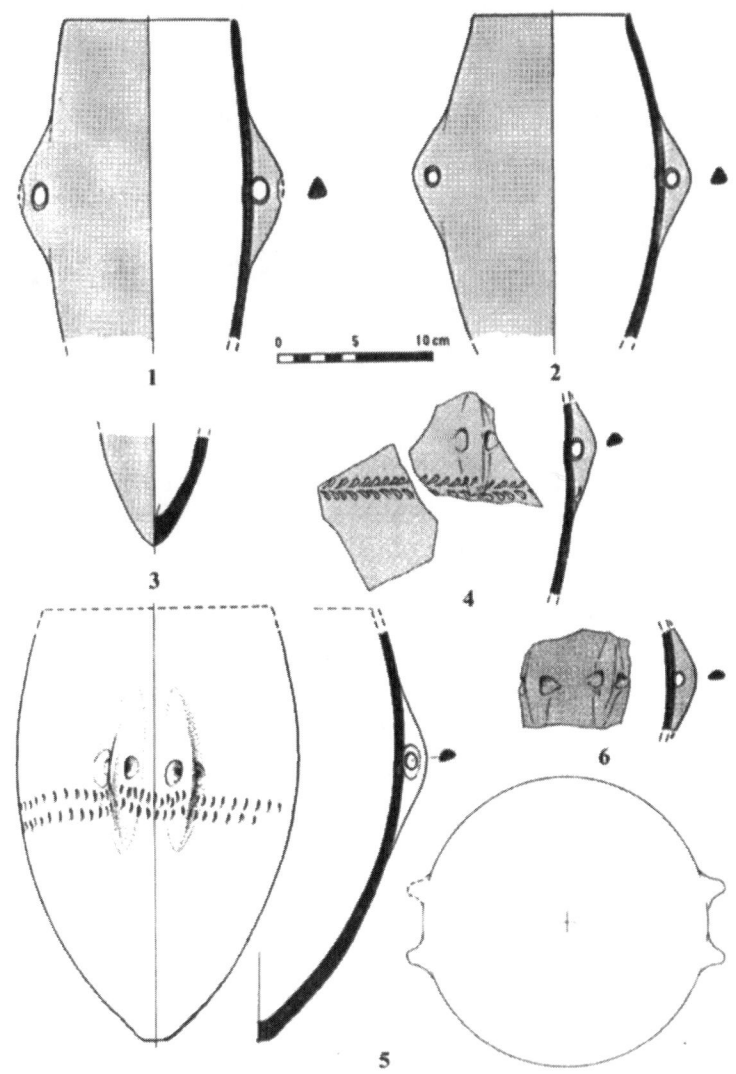

	basket	locus		level	description
1	5568. 1	787	pit	IIB2	large beaker, symmetrical lug handles, red painted and lightly polished
2	4389	1369	silo	IIIA	large beaker, symmetrical lug handles, red painted and lightly polished
3	5657	1522	pit	IIC2	pointed-base, red painted
4	94. 1/2	44	floor	IIC	fragments of a beakern lug handle, light brown painted, sheer polish, light impressions of palmettes
5	3840	1217	fill	IIA1	pointed-base beaker, slighltly flatten base, twin symmetrical handles, impressed lunulae
6	574. 20	-	-	topsoil	twin lug handles, red painted and polished

Plate 10.26. Large pointed-base beakers.

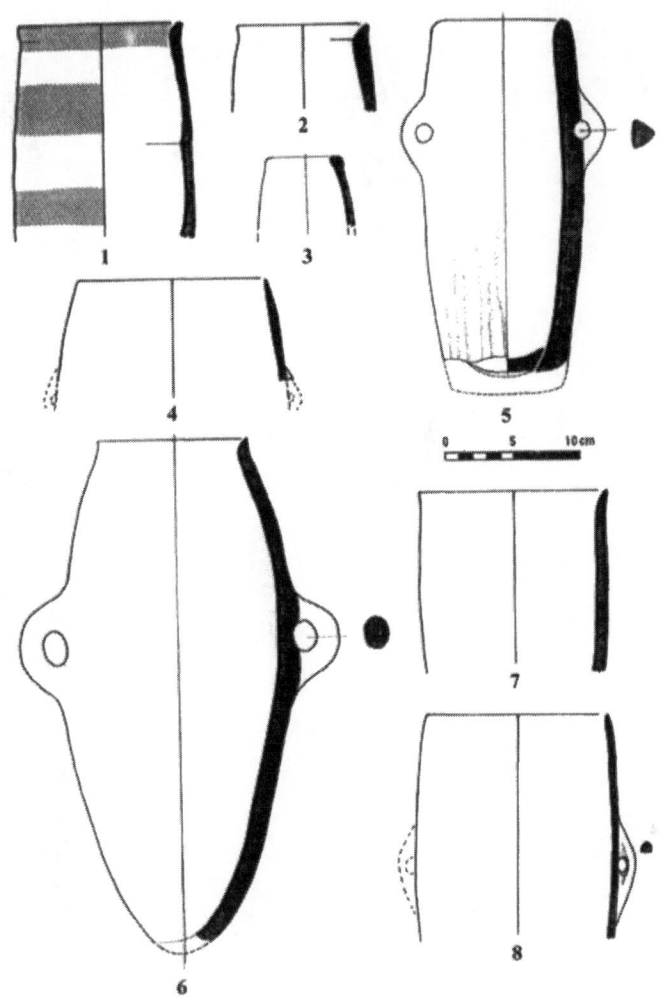

	basket	locus		level	description	references
1	217.4	70	pit	IIB	tubular beaker?, everted rounded rim, red painted	
2	221.2	69	hard soil	IIC	tubular beaker? oblique inside rim	
3	3659	1158	fill	IIC2	narrow, tubular vessel, thikened flat rim	
4	232. 36	56	rubble soil	I-IIA	large beaker, symmetrical lug handles	
5			dog burial		tubular beaker, symetrical lug handles, double-layered bottom	Koeppel & et al 1940, pl. 78: 6 (miniature)
6	5568. 2	787	pit	IIB2	pointed-base beaker, symmetrical loop handles	Mallon et al. 1932, fig.
7	-	-	-	topsoil	tubular beaker?, slightly flaring rim	Lovell 2002, fig. 4. 6: (presented as a neck); Oren & Gilead 1981, fig. 7: 9; Hennessy 1969, fig. 9b: 9
8	45. 21	31	fill	IIIA	large beaker, symmetrical lug handles	

Plate 10.27. Tubular urns, pointed-base beaker, fragmented urns.

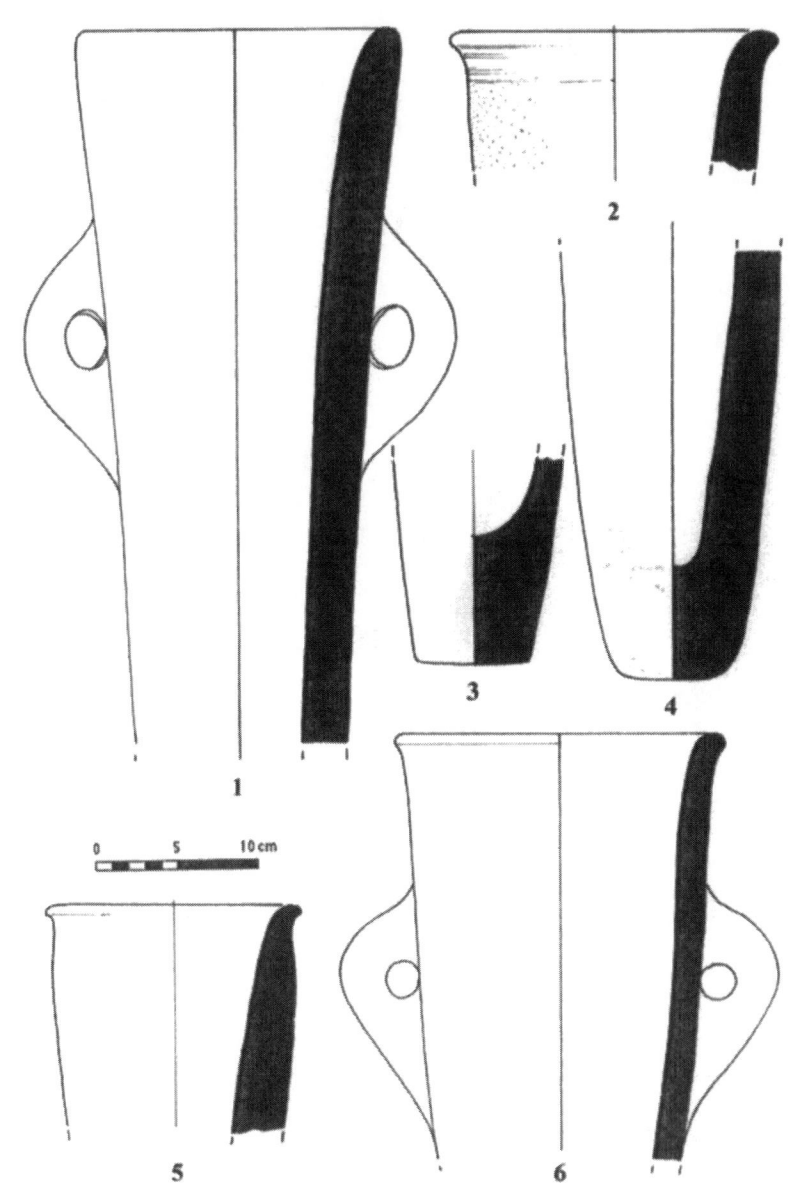

	basket	locus		level	description	references
1	568				urn, large lug handles	Cf. Garfinkel 1992, fig. 126: 17
2	-	1517	fill	IIC	urn, everted rim	
3	-	1513	fill	IIC	high thick base	
4	568				tubular base, thick bottom	
5	5222				urn, thin everted rim	
6					urn, everted rim and large lug handles	

Plate 10.28. Flaring urns and bases.

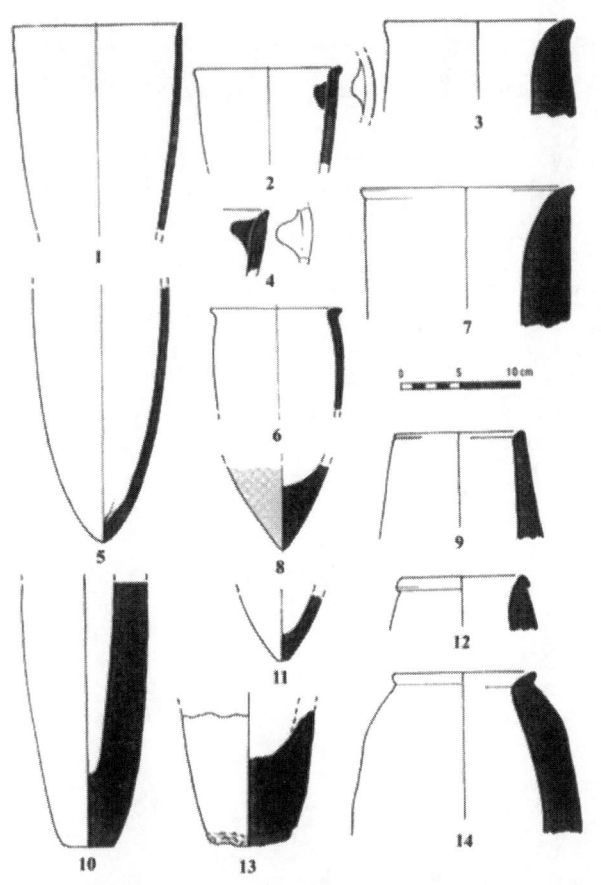

	basket	locus		level	description	references
1	-	787	pit	IIB2	large beaker	
2	5294.2	697	pit	IIA	large beaker, lug fit under inside rim	Commenge-Pellerin 1991, fig. 31 3; Levy 1987: fig. 12. 7: 5, 13. 6: 9
3	82;2	39	fill	IIB	thick tubular beaker rim	
4	590. 3				horizontal lug fit under inner rim	
5	2586	888	surface	IIC	pointed base of a large beaker	
6	3352	1057	pit	IIB2	large beaker, everted horizontale rim	
7	15.14	5	floor	IIC	thick tubular beaker rim, thinned and everted rim	
8	574. 19				thick pointed-base, red painted	Commenge-Pellerin 1987, fig. 36 6; Levy 1987: fig. 12. 19: 1
9	82; 3	39	fill	IIB	tubular beaker, rim	
10	-	-	-	-	high base of a tubular beaker, thick bottom	
11	3560				pointed base of a beaker	
12	31. 21	11	floor	IIC	tubular beaker's rim? rim rolled out	
13	688. 40				base of a tubular beaker, thick bottom	
14	53. 3	26	floor	IIC	torpedo jar, type, everted oblique rim	

Plate 10.29. Large beakers, pointed-bases, tubular urns and torpedoes.

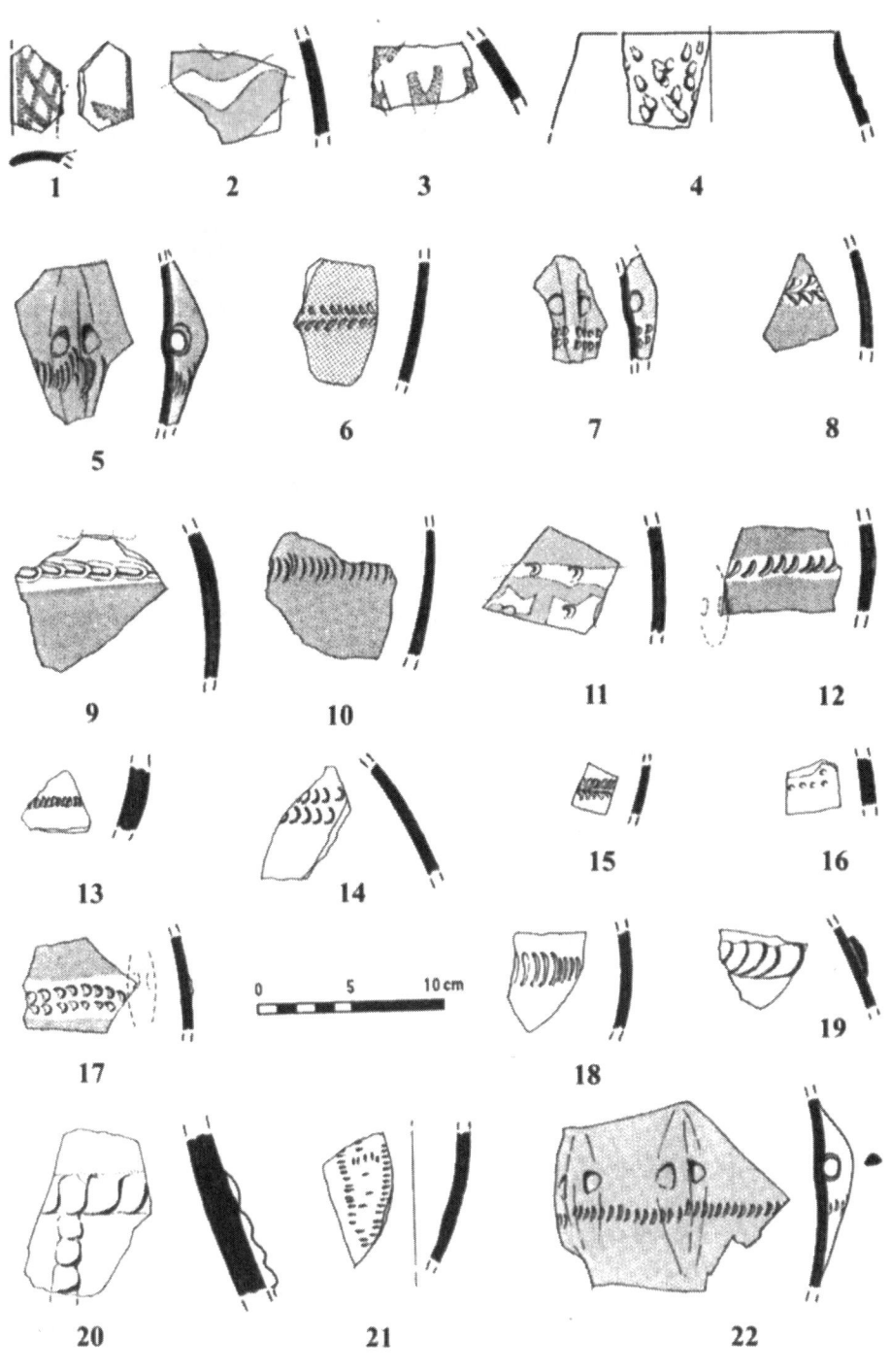

	basket	locus		level	description	references
1	3382				thin partof a spoon(?), cream ware, red painted design	Porath 1985, fig. 5: 8
2	-	1259	fill	IIC	wavy red painted design	
3	558. 1				organized red painted design	
4	5678	1510	burial	IIC	pot's rim, plastic design of drops	Garfinkel 1992, fig. 139: 10; Sussman 1990, Sheikh Ali, fig. IV: 38
5	46. 2	24	pit	IIIA	lug handle, red paintand nail impressed lunulae	
6	5411	756	fill	IIA	palmettes impressed on alight brown, burnisheded beaker	Mallon et al. 1932, fig. 60: 3
7	194. 2	62	hard soil	IIC	lug handle, red paint and impressed lunulae	
8	274.1	91	pit	IIB	impressed palmettes on reserved white clay background, lightly burnished red paint	Garfinkel 1992, fig. 137: 20
9	348. 38	122	hard soil	IIIA	red painted, reserved white background with impressed 'chain' design	
10	3397	1049	fill	IIC	nail impressed lunulae on a red painted beaker sherd	Mallon et al. 1932, fig. 60: 6
11	3844	1214	topsoil	I	red painted design, reserved zones with impressed lunulae (beaker's body sherd)	
12	3372				red painted, reserved stripes with impressed lunulae (beaker's body sherd)	Garfinkel 1992, fig. 139: 2
13	-	-	-	-	lunulae on slight carination	
14	3047				impressed lunulae on a jar's shoulder	Dofffus & et al 1986, fig. 10: 2
15	-	-	-	-	lightly impressed palmettes on a red polished sherd	
16	-	632	platform	IIA	impressed dots, geometric design	Garfinkel 1992, fig. 139: 7
17	261.1	86	hard soil	IIB	red painted beaker, reserved stripe of white clay impressed lunulae	de Contenson 1960, fig. 25: 20
18	5420	760	pit	IIA	impressed lunulae on a beaker fragment	
19	5841	1579	pit	IIIB	scalloped 'rope' on a shoulder fragment	Dofffus & et al 1986, fig. 10: 14; Sussamn 1990, Sheikh Ali, fig. VI: 21
20	3348	1044	pit	IIB2	large finger impressed rope designed on a shoulder fragment	Gophna & Sadeh 1988, fig. 12: 5
21	5354	1510	burial	IIC	blurred pointille design, small pointed-base beaker fragment	Garfinkel 1992, fig. 138: 14 Mallon et al. 1932, fig. 60: 19
22	64.5	28	fill	IIB	impressed lunulae on twin lug handles	

Plate 10.30. Designs.
(all drawings by D. Ladiray)

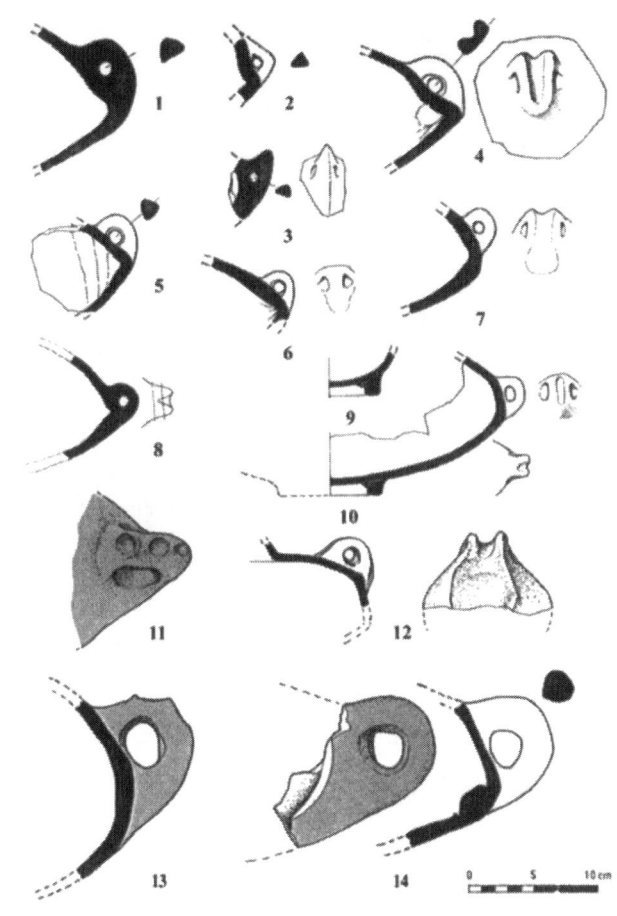

	basket	locus		level	description	references
1	-	1397	surface	IIA1	miniature churn, triangular handle	
2	-	-	-	topsoil	miniature churn, triangular handle	
3	-	-	-	-	miniature churn, horn handle	
4	3373	1056	pit	IIC	miniature churn, double 'horn' handle	
5	3261	1031	surface	IIA2	miniature churn, triangular handle	Lovell 2002, fig. 4. 23: 1
6	-	-	-	-	miniature churn, loop handle	
7	-	-	-	-	miniature churn, double 'horn' handle on heel side	
8	3878	1218	pit rim	IIB1	miniature churn, double 'horn' handle	
9	-	-	-	-	miniature chrun, on ring base	
10	5731	1536	pit	IIIA	miniature churn, double 'horn' handle on heel side, ring-based	
11	91.2	42	floor	IV	churn's handle, spindle side, red painted and finger impressions	
12	110. 3	42	floor	IV	miniature churn, double 'horn' handle on heel side	
13	213. 3	69	hard soil	IIC	churn's handle, thumb notch on top, red painted	
14		-	-	-	churn's handle, spindle side, red painted	

Plate 10.31. Miniatures churns, churns.

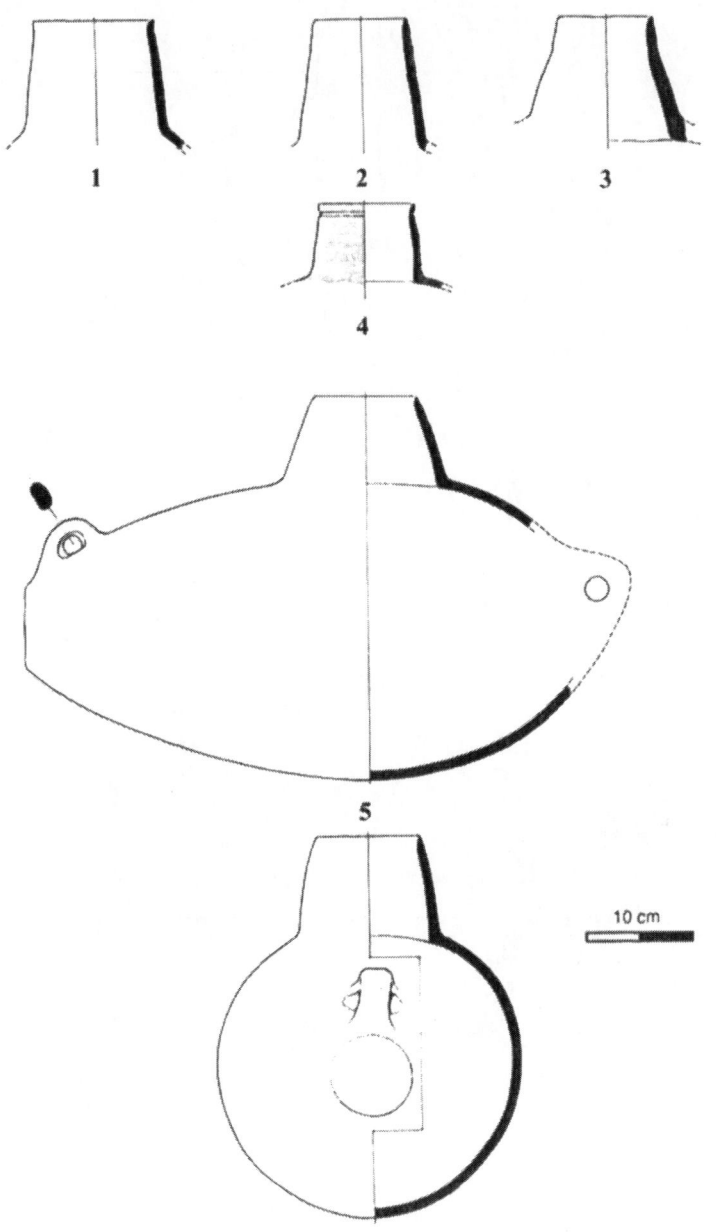

	basket	locus		level	description	references
1	2682	882	silo	IIB1	churn's neck, type	
2	3372				churn's neck, type	
3	615. 3				churn's neck, type	
4	3649				churn's neck, type	
5	4140	1318	cupmark on floor	IIC	churn, type	Commenge-Pellerin 1991, fig. 55: 7

Plate 10.32. Churn and necks.

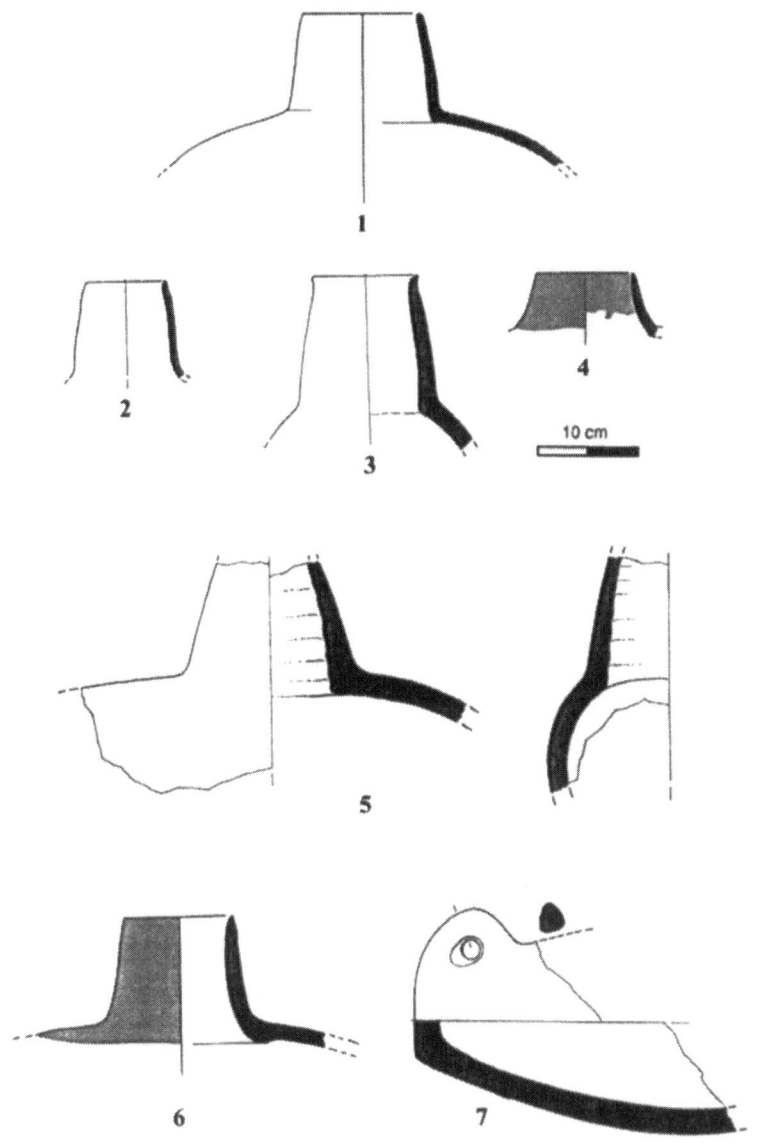

10 cm

	basket	locus		level	description
1	31. 1	11	floor	IIC	churn's neck, type
2	3340				churn's neck, type
3	5607	1511	pit	IIC	churn's neck, type
4					churn's neck, type, red painted
6	1385. 1	556	pit	III	churn's neck, type
7	77. 1	38	floor	IIC	churn's neck, type, red painted
8	1387	556	pit	III	heel-side of a churn

Plate 10.33. Churns, fragments.

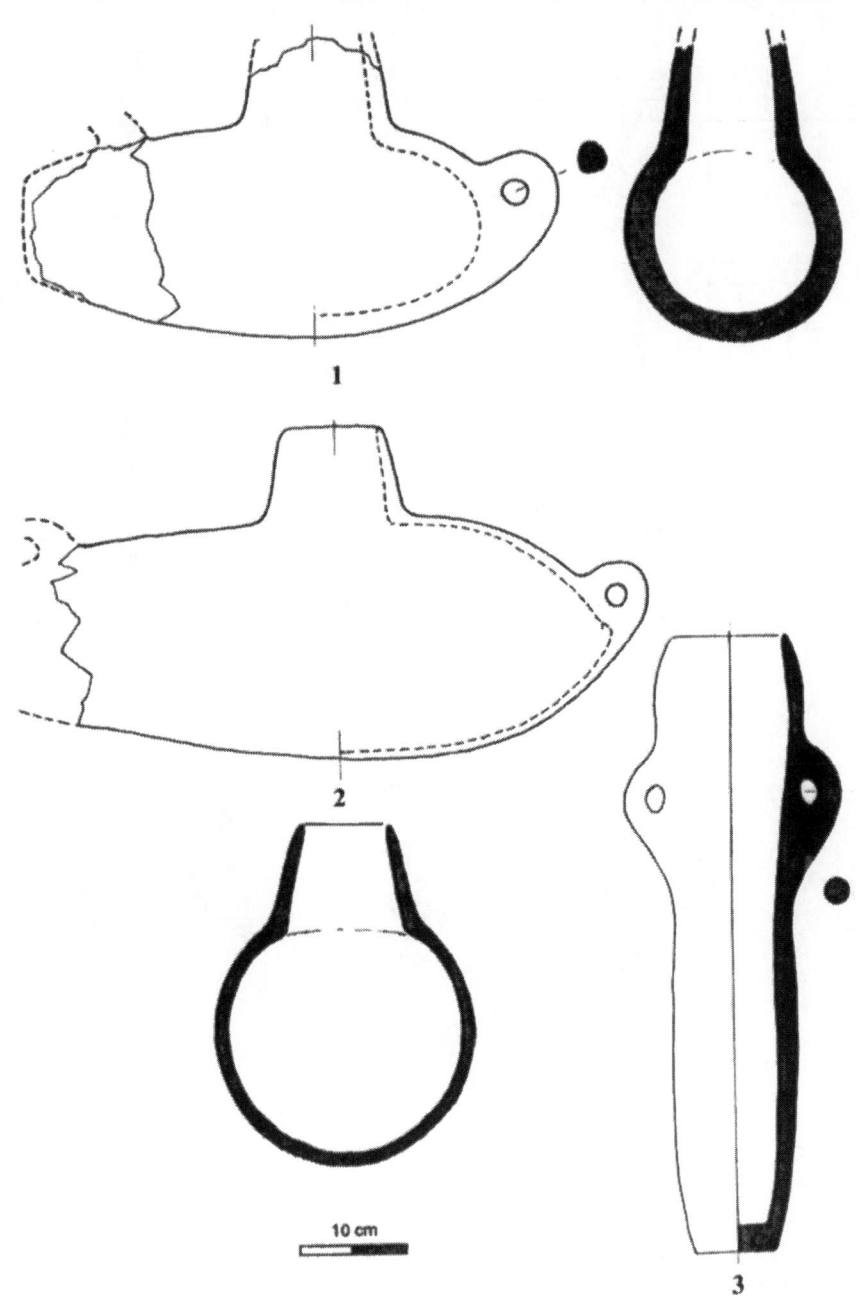

	basket	locus		level	description
1					churn, type
2					churn, type
3					torpedo, type

Plate 10.34. Churns and torpedo.

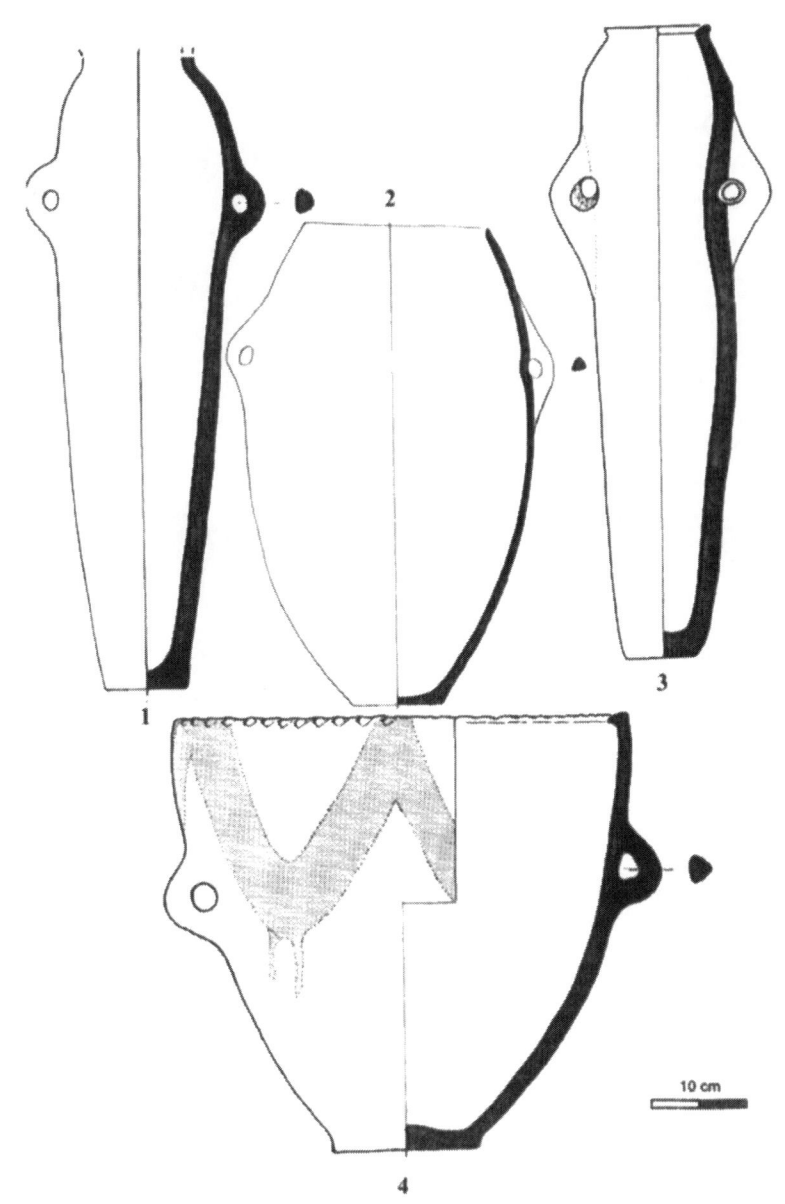

	basket	locus		level	description
1					torpedo, type
2	2894	998	stone ircle	IIIA	hole-mouth jar, symmetric lug handles
3	-	311	pit	IIC	torpedo, type, double symmetrical handles
4	3178	016	pit	IIB	large basin, symmetrical handles and red painted design

Plate 10.35. Torpedoes, holemouth jar and large basin.

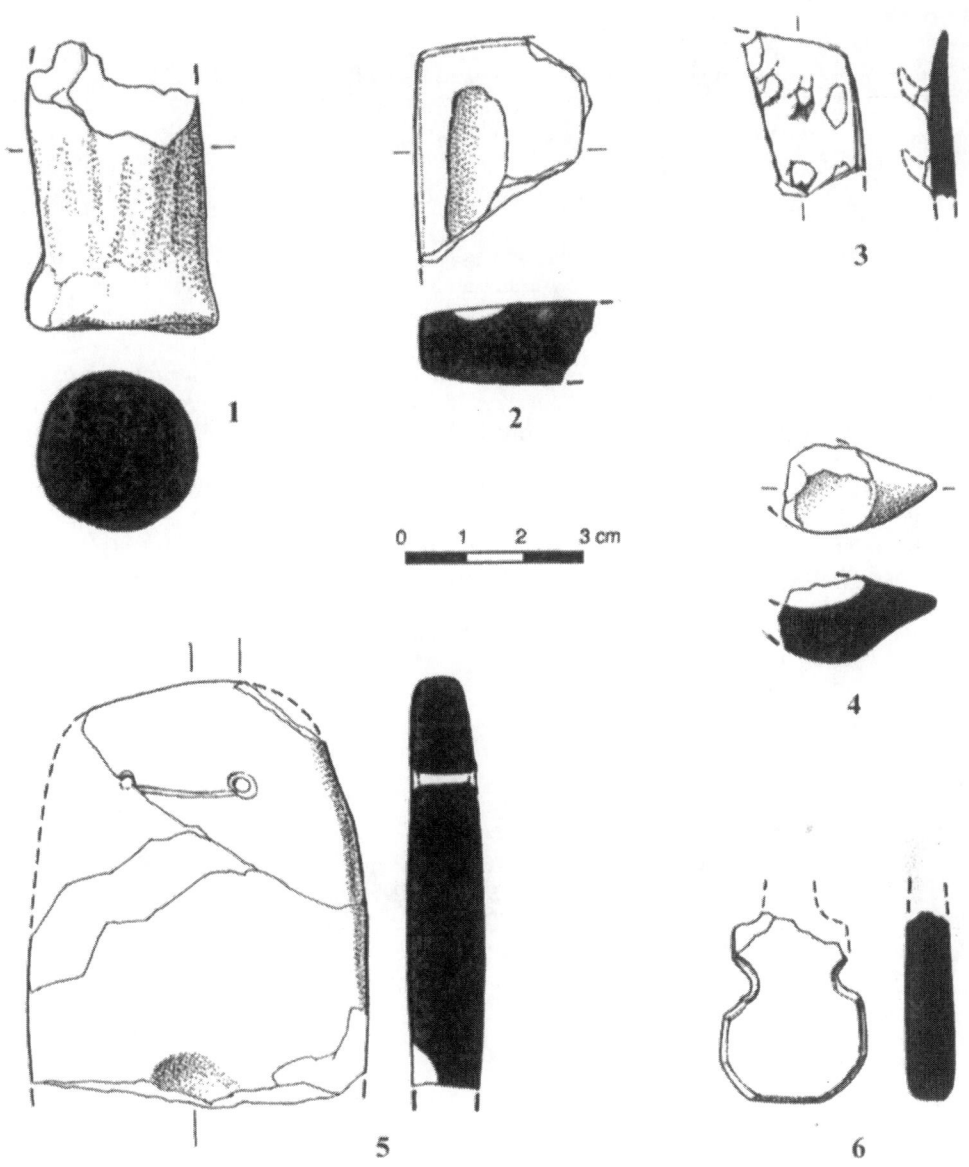

	basket	locus		level	description
1	3282	1039	ashy lens	IIA	'leg' of an artifact?
2	5254	692	pit	IIIB	'palette' with a groove, fragment
3	1240	542	fill	III	head part of an ossurary, protuding horns
4	5491	780	pit	IIC	spoon
5	3567	1124	pit	IIB2	loom weight?, tabulated, cup mark on front
6	3474	1064	pot-hole	IIC1	violin shaped figurine, cut out from a thick sherd

Plate 10.36. Baked clay artifacts and violin-shaped figurine.

References

Alon, D. (1961) Early settlement along the Nahal Garar and Nahal Patish. *M'befnim* 1: 87–96.
— (1977) A Chalcolithic temple at Gilat. *The Biblical Archaeologist* 40/2: 63–65.
Alon, D., and Levy, T.E. (1989) The archaeology of cult and the Chalcolithic sanctuary at Gilat. *Journal of Mediterranean Archaeology* 2: 163–221
Amiran, R. (1955). The 'Cream Ware' of Gezer and the Beesheba Late Chalcolithic. *Israel Exploration Journal* 5: 244–5.
Appadurai, A. (1986) Commodities and the politics of value. In *The Social Life of Things—Commodites in Cultural Perspective*, edited by A. Appadurai. Cambridge: Cambridge University Press, pp. 3–63.
Arnold, D.E. (1985) *Ceramics Theory and Cultural Process: New Studies in Archaeology*. Cambridge: Cambridge University Press.
Arnold, D.E., and Nieves, A.L. (1992) Factors Affecting Ceramic Standardization. In *Ceramic Production and Distribution*, edited by G. J. Bey and C. A. Pool. Boulder, CO: Westview Press, pp. 93–114.
Arnold, J.E. (1987) *Craft Specialization in the Prehistoric Channel Islands, California*. Berkeley: University of California Press.
— (1996) Organizational transformations: power and labor among complex hunter-gatherers and other intermediate societies. In *Emergent Complexity, The Evolution of Complex Societies*, edited by J. E. Arnold. International Monographs in Prehistory, Archaeological Series, 9. Ann Arbor, pp. 59–73.
Arnold, J.E., and Munns, A. (1994) Independent or attached specialization: the organization of shell bead production in California. *Journal of Field Archaeology* 21: 473–87.
Balfet, H. (1965) *Ethnographical Observations in North Africa and Archaeological Interpretation: The Pottery of the Maghreb*. In *Ceramics and Man*, edited by F. Matson. Chicago: Aldine Publishing Company, pp. 161–77.
Bar Adon, P. (1980) *The Cave of the Treasure*. Jerusalem: The Israel Exploration Society.
Barley, N. (1994) *Smashing Pots: Feats of Clay from Africa*. London: British Museum Press.
Beaudry, M., Cook, L. and Mrozowski, S. (1991) Artefacts and active voices: material culture as social discourse. In *The Archaeology of Inequality*, edited by R. McGuire and R. Paynter. Oxford: Blackwell, pp. 150–91.
Bell, C. (1992) *Ceremonial Theory, Ceremonial Practice*. Oxford and New York: Oxford University Press.
Beit Arieh, I. (1975) A Chalcolithic work station near Serabit el Khadem. *Qadmoniot* 8: 62–4 (Hebrew).
— (1980) A Chalcolithic site near Serabit el-Khadim. *Tel Aviv* 7: 45–65.
Beit Arieh, I. and Gophna, R. (1977) A note on a Chalcolithic site in Wadi Araba. *Tel Aviv* 4: 105–9.
Birmingham, J. (1975) Traditional potters of Kathmandu Valley: an ethnoarchaeological study. *Man* 10/3: 370–86.
Blackham, M. (1999) Tulaylat Ghassul: an appraisal of Robert North's excavations (1959–60). *Levant* 31: 19–64.
Blackman, M., Stein, G. and Vandiver, P. (1993) The Standardization Hypothesis and ceramic mass production: technological, compositional, and metric indexes of craft specialization at Tell Leilan, Syria. *American Antiquity* 58/1: 60–79.
Bourke, S.J. (1997) The pre-Ghassulian sequence at Teleilat Ghassul. In *The Prehistory of Jordan II*, edited by H. Gebel, Z. Kafafi and G. Rollefson. *Studies in the History and Archaeology of Jordan* 6, pp. 249–59.
— (2001) The Chalcolithic period. In *The archaeology of Jordan*, edited by B. Macdonald, R. Adams and P. Bienkowski. Sheffield: Sheffield Academic Press.
Braun, D. (1983) Pots as tools. In *Archaeological Hammers and Theories*, edited by A. Keene and J. Moore. New York: Academic Press, pp. 107–34.
Bromberger, C. (1979) Technologie et analyse sémantique des objets. *L'Homme* 19/1: 105–40.
Brumfiel, E.M., and Earle, T.K. (eds) (1987) *Specialization, Exchange and Complex Societies*. New Directions in Archaeology. Cambridge: Cambridge University Press.
Cameron. D.O. (1981) *The Ghassulian Walls Paintings*. London: Kenyon-Deane.
Chase, P.G. (1985) Whole vessels and sherds: an experimental investigation of their quantitative relationships. *Journal of Field Archaeology* 12:2: 213–40.

Clark, J.E., and Parry, W. (1990) Craft Specialization and Cultural Complexity. In *Research in Economic Anthropology*, Vol. 12, edited by B. Isaac. Greenwich, Connecticut: JAI Press Inc, pp. 289–346.

Cowgill, G.L. (1970) Some sampling and reliability problems in archaeology. In *Archéologie et Calculateurs: Problèmes sémiologiques et Mathématiques*, edited by J.-C. Gardin. Paris: Editions du CNRS, pp. 161–75.

Commenge-Pellerin, C. (1987) *La Poterie d'Abou Matar et de l'Ouadi Zoumeili (Beershéva) au IVᵉ millénaire avant l'ère chrétienne*. Cahiers du Centers de Recherche Français de Jérusalem, 3. Paris: Association Paléorient.

— (1990) *La Poterie de Safadi (Beershéva) au IVᵉ millénaire avant l'ère chrétienne*. Cahiers du Centers de Recherche Français de Jérusalem, 5. Paris: Association Paléorient.

— (2002) Competitive involution and expanded horizons: exploring the nature of interaction between northern Negev and Lower Egypt (ca. 4500–3600 b.c.e). In *Egypt and the Levant Interrelations from the 4th through the Early 3rd Millennium BCE*, edited by E.C.M. van den Brink and T.E. Levy. New Approaches to Anthropological Archaeology. London and New York: Continuum, pp. 139–53.

— (forthcoming) *The Chalcolithic Groundstone Assemblage of the Beersheva Sites, Israel*.

— (forthcoming) The pottery from burial caves 1, 2 and 4 at Shoham (north).

Contenson de, H. (1992) *Préhistoire de Ras Shamra—Les sondages stratigraphiques de 1955 à 1976*. Ras Shamra-Ougarit VIII (2 volumes). Paris: Editions Recherche sur les Civilisations.

Costin, C.L. (1991) Craft specialization: Issues in defining, documenting, and explaining the organization of production. *Archaeological Methods and Theory* 3: 1–56.

Courtois, L. (1992) Examen au microscope pétrographique de poteries néolithiques de Ras Shamra V et IV. In H. de Contenson: Préhistoire de Ras Shamra—Les sondages stratigraphiques de 1955 à 1976. Ras Shamra-Ougarit VIII (2 volumes). Paris: Editions Recherche sur les Civilisations, pp. 209–22.

Courty, M.A. and Roux, V. (1995) Identification of wheel throwing on the basis of ceramic surface features and microfabrics. *Journal of Archaeological Science* 22: 17–50.

D'Altroy, T., and Earle, T.K. (1985) Staple finance, wealth finance, and storage in the Inca political economy. *Current Anthropology* 26/2: 187–206.

David, N., Sterner, J. and Gavua, K. (1988) Why pots are decorated. *Current Anthropology* 29: 365–89.

Davis, S. (1984) The advent of milk and wool production in western Iran: some speculations. In *Animals and Archaeology 3. Early Herders and their Flocks*, edited by J. Clutton-Brock and C. Grigson. BAR International Series 202. Oxford: British Archaeological Reports, pp. 265–78.

DeBoer, W.R. (1984) The last pottery show: system and sense in ceramics studies. In *The Many Dimensions of Pottery Ceramics in Archaeology and Anthropology. Cingula VII*, edited by S. Van der Leeuw and A.E. Pritchard. Amsterdam: Universiteit von Amsterdam, pp. 526–62.

DeBoer, W., and Lathrap, D.W. (1979) The making and breaking of Shipibo-Conibo ceramics. In *Ethnoarchaeology—Implications of Ethnography for Archaeology*, edited by C. Kramer. New York: Columbia University Press, pp. 102–37.

Detienne, M., and Vernant, J.-P. (1979) *La cuisine du sacrifice au Pays Grec*. Paris: NRF/Gallimard.

Digard, J.-P. (1979) La technologie en anthropologie: fin de parcours ou nouveau souffle? *L'Homme* 19(1): 73–104.

Dollfus, G., Kafafi, Z., Rewerski, J., Vaillant, N., Coqueugniot, E., Desse, J. and Neef, R. (1988) Abu Hamid, an early fourth millenium site in the Jordan Valley: preliminary results. In *The Prehistory of Jordan: The State of Research in 1986*, edited by A.N. Garrard and H.G. Gebel. BAR International Series 396 (2 volumes). Oxford: British Archaeological Reports, pp. 567–601.

Dollfus, G., and Kafafi, Z. (1995) Représentations humaines et animales sur le site d'Abu Hamid (mi-7°–début 6° millénaire BP). *Studies in the History and Archaeology of Jordan 5*, edited by K. Amr, F. Zayadine and M. Zaghloul: 449–56.

Douglas, M., and Isherwood, B. (1981) *The World of Goods*. New York: Basic Books.

Douglas, E.J., and Kramer, C. (1992) Interaction, social proximity and distance: a special issue. *Journal of Anthropological Archaeology* 11: 103–10.

Dunand, M. (1973) L'Architecture, les tombes, le matériel domestique—des origines néolithiques à l'avènement urbain. In *Fouilles de Byblos*, tome V (2 volumes). Paris: Jean Maisonneuve.

Dunnell, R. (1971) *Systematics in Prehistory*. New York: The Free Press.

Earle, T. (1981) Comment on P. Rice: Evolution of specialized pottery production: a trial model. *Current Anthropology* 22/3: 230–31

Eisenberg, E. (1993) Kitan, Tell. In *The New Encyclopedia of Archaeological Excavations in the Holy Land, III*, edited by E. Stern. New York and Jerusalem: The Israel Exploration Society and Carta, pp. 878–81.

Epstein, C. (1978) A new aspect of Chalcolithic culture. *Bulletin of the American Schools of Oriental Research* 229: 27–45.

— (1981) More on the Chalcolithic culture of the Golan. *Eretz Israel* 15: 1–20 (Hebrew, 78*–79* English summary).

— (1982) Cult symbols in Chalcolithic Palestine. *Bolletino del Centro Camuno di Studi Preistorici* 19: 63–81.

— (1985) Laden animal figures from Chalcolithic Palestine. *Bulletin of the American Schools of Oriental Research* 258: 53–60.

— (1998) *The Chalcolithic Culture of the Golan*. Israel Antiquities Authority Reports 4. Jerusalem: IAA Publications.

Erikson, J.E., Reed, D.W. and Burke, C. (1974) Research design: the relationships between the primary functions and the physical properties of ceramic vessels and their implications for ceramic distribution in an archaeological site. *Anthropolgy UCLA* III(2): 84–95.

Féblot-Augustins J., and Perlès, C. (1992) Perspectives ethno-archéologiques sur les échanges à longue distance. In *Ethno-archéologie, Justification, Problèmes et Limites*, edited by F. Audouze, A. Gallay and V. Roux. Juan-les-Pins: APDCA, pp. 195–209.

Foster, G.M. (1960) Life expectancy of utilitarian pottery in Tzintzuntzan, Mexico. *American Antiquity* 25: 606–9.

Gal, Z., Smithline, H. and Shalem, D. (1997) A Chalcolithic burial Cave in Peqi'in, Upper Galilee. *Israel Exploration Journal* 47/3-4: 145–54.

Galili, E. and Sharvit, J. (1995) Evidence of olive oil production from the submerged site at Kfar Samir, Israel. *Mitekufat Haeven* 26: 122–33.

Galili, E., Stanley, D.J., Sharvit, J. and Weinstein-Evron, M. (1997) Evidence for earliest olive-oil production in submerged settlements off the Carmel Coast, Israel. *Journal of Archaeological Science* 24:1141–50.

Galili, E., Zohary, D. and Weinstein-Evron, M. (1989) Appearance of olives in submerged Neolithic sites along the Carmel coast. *Mitekufat Haeven* 22: 95–7.

— (1995) Shrines and ceramics in Chalcolithic Israel: the view through the petrographic microscope. *Archaeometry* 37(2): 287–305.

Gamble, C. (1982) Interaction and alliance in Paleolithic society. *Man* 17: 92–107.

Garfinkel, Y. (1983) *Local Knowledge: Further Essays in Interpretive Anthropology*. New York: Basic Books.

Gebauer, A.B. (1995) Pottery production and the introduction of agriculture in southern Scandinavia. In *The Emergence of Pottery—Technology and Innovation in Ancient Societies*, edited by W.K. Barnett and J.W. Hoopes. Washington and London: Smithsonian InstitutionPress, pp. 99–114.

Gell, A. (1986) New comers to the world of goods: consumption among the Muria Gonds. In *The Social Life of Things—Commodites in Cultural Perspective*, edited by A. Appadurai. Cambridge: Cambridge University Press, pp. 110–40.

Gilead, I. (1995) *Grar, a Chalcolithic Site in the Northern Negev*. Studies by the Department of Bible and Ancient Near-East 7. Beersheva: Ben Gurion University of the Negev Press.

Gilead, I. and Goren, Y. (1986) Stations of the Chalcolithic period in Nahal Sekher, Northern Negev. *Paléorient* 12/1: 83–90.

Gophna, R. (1976) Excavations at En Besor. *Atiqot* 14: 9–16.

Gille, B. (ed.) (1978) *Histoires des techniques. Technique et civilisation. Technique et Sciences*. Paris: Gallimard.

Godelier, M (1986) *The Mental and the Material: Thought, Economy and Society*. London: Verso

Goren, Y. (1987) *The Petrography of Ceramic Assemblages from the Chalcolithic Period of Southern Eretz Isarael*. M.A., The Hebrew University of Jerusalem.

Goren, Y. (1992) Technological study of the Late Pottery Neolithic ceramic assemblage from Kabri, area B. In *Excavations at Kabri, Preliminary Report n°6*, edited by A. Kempinski and W.D. Niemeier. Tel Aviv: Tel Kabri Expedition and Tel Aviv University, pp. 12–20.

Goren, Y. and Fabian, P. (2002) *Kissufim Road, a Cahcolithic Mortuary Site*. IAA Reports 16. Jerusalem: Israel Antiquities Authority.

Grigson, C. (1987) Pastoralism and other aspects of animal management in the Chalcolithic of the Northern Negev. In *Shiqmim I, Studies concerning Chalcolithic Societies in the Northern Negev Desert, Israel (1982–1984)*, edited by T.E. Levy. BAR International Series 356 (2 volumes). Oxford: British Archaeological Reports, pp. 219–42.

— (1988) Different herding strategies for sheep and goats in the Chalcolithic of Beersheva. *Archaeozoologia* 1/2: 115–25.

— (1993) The earliest domestic horses in the Levant? New finds from the Fourth millenium of the Negev. *Journal of Archaeological Science* 20: 645–55.

— (1995) Cattle keepers of the northern Negev: animal remains from the Chalcolithic site of Grar. In *Grar, a Chalcolithic Site in the Northern Negev*, edited by I. Gilead. Beersheva: Ben Gurion University Press, pp. 377–452.

Haudricourt, A.-G. (1968) La technologie culturelle: essai de méthodologie. In *Ethnologie Générale*, edited by J. Poirier. Paris: Gallimard, pp. 731–822.

Henrickson, E.F., and McDonald, M.A. (1983) Ceramic Form and Function: An Ethnographic Search and an Archeological Application. *American Anthropologist* 85: 630–43.

Hayden, B. (1995) The emergence of prestige technologies and pottery. In *The Emergence of Pottery: Technology and Innovation in Ancient Societies*, edited by W.K. Barnett and J.W. Hoopes. Smithsonian Institution in Archaeological Inquiry. Washington and London: Smithsonian institution Press, pp. 257–66.

Henrickson, R. (1991) Wheelmade or wheel-finished? Interpretation of 'wheelmarks' on pottery. In *Materials Issues in Art and Archaeology II*, edited by P. Vandiver, J. Druzik, and G. Wheeler. Pittsburgh: Materials Research Society. 185, pp. 523–41.

Hodder, I. (ed.) (1989) *The Meaning of Things*. London: Unwin Hyman.

Kafafi, Z. (1988) Jebel Abu Thawwab. A pottery Neolithic village in north Jordan. In *The Prehistory of Jordan: The State of Research in 1986*, edited by A. Garrard and H.G. Gebel. BAR International Series 396 (2 volumes). Oxford: British Archaeological Reports, pp. 451–71.

Kangas, S.E. (1994) Social and Economic Organization during the Chalcolithic Period in the Northern Negev, Israel: a study of ceramic variability. PhD Thesis: Brandeis University.

Kantor, H. (1958) The Pottery. In *Soundings at Tel Fakhariah*, edited by H. Kantor. Chicago, pp. 21–41.

Kaplan, J. (1954) Two Chalcolithic vessels from Palestine. *Palestine Exploration Quaterly* 76: 97–100.

— (1958) Excavations at Wadi Rabah. *Israel Exploration Journal* 8: 149–60.

— (1959) Excavations at TelutiotBatashi in the Vale of Sorek. *Eretz Israel* 5: 9–25 (Hebrew).

— (1969) Ein el Jarba. Chalcolithic remains from the Plain of Esdraelon. *Bulletin of the American Schools of Oriental Research* 194: 2–39.

Kaplan, F., and Levine, D.M. (1981) Cognitive mapping of a folk taxonomy of Mexican pottery: a multivariate approach. *American Anthropologist* 83: 868–84.

Kislev, M.E. (1995) Wild olive stones at submerged Chalcolitihc Kfar Samir, Haifa, Israel. *Mitekufat Haeven* 26: 134–45

Koeppel, R., Mallon, R. and Neuville, R. (1940) *Teleilat Ghassul II*. Rome: Pontifical Biblical Institute.

Kopytoff, I. (1986) The cultural biography of things. In *The Social Life of Things—Commodities in Cultural Perspective*, edited by A. Appadurai. Cambridge: Cambridge University Press, pp. 64–91.

Kramer, C. (1985) Ceramic ethnoarchaeology. *Annual Review of Anthropology* 14: 77–102.

Krause, R. (1984) Modeling the making of pots: a ethnoarchaeological aprroach. In *The Many Dimensions of Pottery*, edited by S. van der Leeuw and A. Pritchard. Amsterdam: Universiteit van Amsterdam, pp. 615–99.

— (1985) *The Clay Sleeps: An Ethnoarchaeological Study of Three African Potters*. Tuscaloosa: University of Alabama Press.

Lechtman, H. (1977) Style in technology-some early thoughts. In *Material Culture: Styles, Organization, and Dynamics of Technology*, edited by H. Lechtman and R. Merrill. New York: West, pp. 3–20.

Laudan, R (ed.) (1984) *The Nature of Technological Knowledge*. Dordrecht: D. Reidel

Leach, E.R. (1976) *Cuture and Communication*. Cambridge: Cambridge University Press.

Lee, R. (1973) *Chalcolithic Ghassul: New Aspects and Master Typology*. PhD thesis. Jerusalem: Hebrew University.

Lemonnier, P. (1980) *Les Salines de l'Ouest. Logique technique, logique sociale*. Paris: Editions de la Maison des Sciences de l'Homme.

— (1983) La description des systèmes techniques: une urgence en technologie culturelle. *Journal de la Société des Océanistes* 37 (70–71): 39–75.

— (1986) The study of material culture today: towards an anthropology of technical systems. *Journal of Anthropological Archaeology* 5: 147–86.

— (1991) De la culture matérielle à la culture? Ethnologie des techniques et Préhistoire. In *25 ans d'Etudes Technologiques en Préhistoire*. XI° Rencontres d'Archéologie et d'Histoire d'Antibes. Juan-les-Pins: Editions APDCA, pp. 15–20.

— (1992) *Elements for an Anthropology of Technology*. Anthropological Papers 88. Ann Arbor: The University of Michigan Museum of Anthropology.

— (1993) (ed.), *Technological Choices: Transformation in Material Cultures since the Neolithic*. London and New York: Routledge.

Leroi-Gourhan, A. (1945) (reprnted in 1973) *Evolution et Techniques: Milieu et Techniques*. Paris: Albin Michel.

— (1965) *Le Geste et la Parole. I. Technique et Langage. II. la Mémoire et les Rythmes*. Paris: Albin Michel.

Levi-Strauss, C. (1985) *La Potiere Jalouse*. Paris: Plon.

— (1988) *The Jealous Potter*. Chicago: University of Chicago Press.

Levy, T.E. (1983) The emergence of specialized pastoralism in the Southern Levant. *World Archaeology* 15: 15–36.

— (1992) The Gilat Sanctuary, Northern Negev Desert, Israel. *National Geographic Research and Exploration* 8: 372–4

Levy, T.E. (ed.) (1987) *Shiqmim I. Studies Concerning Chalcolithic Societies in the Norhern Negev Desert, Israel (1982–1984)*. BAR International Series 356 (2 volumes). Oxford: British Archaeological Reports.

Levy, T.E., Adams, R.B. and Najjar, M. (1999) Early metallurgy and social evolution: Jabal Hamrat Fidan. *ACOR Newletter* 11(1): 1–3

Levy, T.E., and Golden, J. (1996) Syncretistic and mnemonic dimensions of Chalcolithic art: a New human figurine from Shiqmim. *The Biblical Archaeologist* 59/3: 150–9.

Levy, T.E., and Alon, D. (1985) Shiqmim: a Chalcolithic village and mortuary centers in the northern Negev. *Paléorient* 11/1: 71–83.

Levy, T.E., and Shalev, S. (1989) Prehistoric metalworking in the Southern Levant: Archaeometallurgical and social perspectives. *World Archaeology* 20: 353–72.

Levy, T.E., and Holl, A. (1987) Theory and practice in household archaeology: a case study from the Chalcolithic village at Shiqmim. In *Shiqmim I. Studies Concerning Chalcolithic Societies in the Norhern Negev Desert, Israel (1982–1984)*, edited by T.E. Levy. BAR International Series 356 (2 volumes). Oxford: British Archaeological Reports, pp. 313–32.

Levy, T.E., and Menahem, N. (1987) The ceramic industry at Shiqmim: typological and spatial considerations. In *Shiqmim I. Studies Concerning Chalcolithic Societies in the Norhern Negev Desert, Israel (1982–1984)*, edited by T.E. Levy. BAR International Series 356 (2 volumes). Oxford: British Archaeological Reports, pp. 313–32.

Liphschitz, N. (1988) Dendroarchaeological and dendrochronological investigation in Israel as a mean for the reconstruction of past vegetation and climate. *PACT* 22: 133–46.

Liphschitz, N., Gophna, R., Hartman, M. and Biger, G. (1991) The beginning of olive oil (Olea europaea) cultivation in the Old World: a reassessment. *Journal of Anthropological Science* 18: 441–53.

Longacre, W. (1981) Kalinga pottery: an ethnoarchaeological study. In *Pattern in the Past: Studies in Honor of David Clarke*, edited by I. Hodder, G. Isaac and N. Hammond. Cambridge: Cambridge University Press, pp. 49–66.

Lovell, J. (2002) *The Late Neolithic and Chalcolithic Periods in the southern Levant: New data from Teleilat Ghassul, Jordan*. Doctoral dissertation, University of Sydney.

Lowenthal, D. and Bowden, M. (eds) (1976) *Geographies of the Mind*. New York: Oxford University Press.

Macdonald, E., Starkey, J.L. and Lankester-Harding, G.L. (1932) *Beth-Pelet II. Prehistoric Fara*. Series of the British School of Archaeology in Egypt 52. London: Bernard Qaritch and British Shool of Archaeology in Egypt.

MacGuire, R.H. (1983) Breaking down cultural complexity: inequality and heterogeneity. In M. B. Schiffer (de.): Advances in Archaeological Method and Theory (8): 91–142. New york: academic Presse.

McLeod, M. (1984) Akan terracotta. In *Earthen Ware in Asia and Africa*, edited by J. Picton. London: Perciaval David Foundation, pp. 365–81.

Mahias, M.-C. (1993) Pottery techniques in India: technical variants and social choice. In *Technological Choices. Transformation in Material Cultures since the Neolithic*, edited by P. Lemonnier. London and New York: Routledge, p. 157–80.

Mallon, S.J., Koeppel, R. and Neuville, R. (1934) *Teleilat Ghassul I, Compte-Rendu des Fouilles de l'Institut Biblique Pontifical 1929–1932*. Rome: Pontifical Biblical Institute.

Matson, F.R. (1974) The archaeological present: near eastern village potters at work. *American Journal of Archaeology* 78(4): 345–7.

Neef, R. (1990) Introduction, development and environmental implications of olive culture: the evidence from Jordan. In *Man's Role in the Shaping of the Eastern Mediterranean Landscape*, edited by S.G. Bottema, G. Entjes-Nieborg and W. van Zeist. Rotterdam/Brookfield A.A. Balkema, pp. 295–306.

Otron. C. (1982) Computer simulation experiment to assess the performance of measures of quantity of pottery. *World Archaeology* 14/1: 1–20.

Orton, C.R. and Tyers, P.A. (1990) Statistical analysis of ceramic assemblage. *Archeologia e Calcolatori* 1: 81–110.

— (1992) Counting broken objects: the statistics of ceramic assemblages. *Proceedings of the British Academy* 77: 163–84.

Orton, C.R., Tyers, P.A. and Vince, A. (1993) *Pottery in Archaeology*. Cambridge Manuals in Archaeology. Cambridge: Cambridge University Press.

Miller-Rosen, A. (1986) *Cities of Clay. The Geoarchaeology of Tells*. Chicago: University of Chicago Press.

Mills, B.J. (1989) Integrating functional analysis of vessels and sherds through models of ceramic assemblage formation. *WorldArchaeology* 21.1: 137–47.

Oren, E., and Gilead, I. (1981) Chalcolithic sites in Northeastern Sinai. *Tel Aviv* 8: 25–44.

Palmer, C. (2002) Milk and Cereals: Identifying Food and Food Identity among Fallahin and Bedouin in Jordan. *Levant* 34: 173–95.

Peltenburg, E. (1988) A Cypriot model for Prehistoric ceremonial. *Antiquity* 62: 289–93.

— (1993) Settlement discontinuity and resistance to complexity in Cyprus, ca. 4500–2500 B.C. *Bulletin of the American Schools of Research* 292: 9–24.

Perlès, C. (1990) L'outillage de pierre taillée néolithique en Grèce: approvisionnement et exploitation des matières premières. *Bulletin de Correspondance Hellénique* 114: 1–42.

— (1992) Systems of exchange and organization of production in Neolithic Greece. *Journal of Mediterranean Archaeology* 5/2: 115–64.

Perrot, J. (1955) The excavations at Abu Matar, near Beersheba. *Israel Exploration Journal* 5/3: 167–89.

— (1959) Statuettes en ivoire et autres objets en ivoire et en os provenant de gisements préhistoriques de la région de Beershéba. *Syria* 36:1–2: 7–19.

— (1964) Les ivoires de la 7°campagne de fouilles à Safadi, près de Beershéva. *Eretz-Israel* 7: 92–93.

— (1968) Préhistoire palestinienne. In *Supplement au Dictonnaire de la Bible, fascicule 43*. Paris: Letouzé & Ané

Umm qala'a, pp. 286–479.

Perrot, J. and Ladiray, D. (1980) *Tombes à Ossuaires de la Région Côtière Palestinienne au IV° millénaire avant l'ère chrétienne*. Mémoires et Travaux du Centers de Recherches Préhistoriques Francais de Jérusalem 1. Paris: Association Paléorient.

Pétrequin, P. (1995) North wind, south wind. In *Technological Choices, Transformation in Material Culture since the Neolithic*, edited by P. Lemonnier. London and New York: Routledge, pp. 36–76.

Pfaffenberger, B. (1988) Fetished objects and humanised nature: towards an anthropology of technology. *Man* NS 23: 236–52.

— (1992) The social anthropology of technology. *Annual Review of Anthropology* 21: 491–516.

Philip, G. and Williams-Thorpe, O. (2003) A provenance study of Jordanian basalt vessels of the Chalcolithic and Early Bronze Age periods. *Paléorient* 19/2: 51–63.

Philip, G., Williams-Thorpe, O. and Keynes, M. (2004) The production and distribution of ground stone artefacts in the Southern Levant during the 5th–4th milleniua BC: some implications of geochimical and petrographic analysis. In *Proceedings of the First International Congress on the Archaeology of the Ancient Near-East (Rome, May 18th–23rd 1998)*, edited by P. Matthiae, A. Enea, L. Peyronel and F. Pinnock. Rome, pp. 1380–96.

Rappaport, R.A. (1999) *Ceremonial and Religion in the Making of Humanity*. Cambridge Studies in Social and Cultural Anthropology. Cambridge: Cambridge University Press.

Read, D.W. (1982) Toward a theory of archaeological classification. In *Essays on Archaeological Typology*, edited

by R. Whallon and J. Brown. Evanston: The Centers for American Archaeology Press, pp. 56–92.

— (1989) Intuitive typology and automatic classification: divergence or full circle? *Journal of Anthropological Archaeology* 8: 189–211.

Renfrew, C. (1969) The development and chronology of the Early Cycladic figurines. *American Journal of Archaeology* 73: 1–32.

— (1972) *The Emergence of Civilization: The Cyclads and the Aegean in the Third Millenium B.C.* London: Methuen.

— (1979) Systems collapse as social transformation, in *Approaches to Social Archaeology*, edited by C. Renfrew. Cambridge, MA: Harvard University Press, pp. 366–89.

— (1984) Trade as action at distance. In *Approaches to Social Archaeology*, edited by C. Renfrew. Cambridge, MA: Harvard University Press, pp. 86–134.

— (1986) Varna and the emergence of wealth in Europe. In *The Social Life of Things: Commodities in Cultural Perspective*, edited by A. Appadurai. Cambridge: Cambridge University Press, pp. 141–68.

— (1993) Cognitive archaeology: some thought on the archaeology of thought. *Cambridge Archaeological Journal* 3/2: 247–70.

— (1994) Towards a cognitive archaeology. In *The Ancient Mind, Elements of Cognitive Archaeology*, edited by C. Renfrew and E.B.W. Zubrow. New Directions in Archaeology. Cambridge: Cambridge University Press, pp. 3–12.

Renfrew, C., and Scarre, C. (1998) *Cognition and Material Culture: The Archaeology of Symbolic Storage*. McDonald Institute.

Rice, P.M. (1981) Evolution of specialized pottery production: a trial model. *Current Anthropology* 22.3: 219–40.

— (1984) Change and conservatism in pottery-producing systems. In *The Many Dimensions of Pottery: Ceramics in Archaeology and Anthropology*, edited by S.E. Van der Leeuw and A.C. Pritchard. Amsterdam: Universiteit van Amsterdam, pp. 231–88.

— (1987) *Pottery Analysis, a Source Book*. Chicago: Chicago University Press.

— (1990) Functions and uses of archaeological ceramics. In *The Changing Roles of Ceramics in Society: 26,000 B.P. to the Present*, edited by W.D. Kingery. Westerville, OH: The American Ceramic Society, Inc, pp. 83–117.

— (1996a) Recent ceramic analysis: 1. ceramic function, style, and origins. *Journal of Archaeological Research* 4.2: 133–63.

— (1996b) Recent ceramic analysis: 2. composition, production, and theory. *Journal of Archaeological Research* 4.3: 165–202.

Richter, M. (1982) *Technology and Social Complexity*. Albany: State University of New York Press.

Rosen, S. (1983) The tabular scrapers trade: a model for material culture dispersion. *Bulletin of the American Schools of Research* 249: 79–86.

Roshwalb, A. (1981) *Protohistory in Wadi Ghazzeh: a typological and technological study based on the Macdonald excavations*. Unpublished PhD Dissertation, University of London.

Roux V. (2000). [Article] *Archaeometry* 43(Part 2): 281–85.

— (2001) Comments on 'Technological choices in ceramic production', *Archaeometry* 42(1), 1–76.

— (2003) A dynamic systems framework for studying technological change: application to the emergence of the potter's wheel in the Southern Levant. *Journal of Archaeological Method and Theory* 10/1: 1–30.

Roux, V., and Courty, M.A. (1998) Identification of wheel fashioning methods: technological analysis of 4th–3rd millennium B.C. Oriental ceramics. *Journal of Archaeological Sciences* 25: 747–63.

— (1998) Les bols élaborés au tour d'Abu Hamid: rupture technique au 4e mill. avant J.C. dans le Sud-Levant. *Paléorient* 23/1: 25–43.

Rowan, Y., and Levy, T.E. (1991) Use-wear analysis of a Chalcolithic scrapers assemblage from Shiqmim. *Mi'tekufat Haeven* 24: 112–34.

Rye, O. (1981) *Pottery Technology: Principles and Reconstruction.* Washington, DC: Taraxacum.

Rye, O., and Evans, C. (1976) *Traditonal Pottery Techniques of Pakistan: Field and Laboratory Studies.* Smithsonian Contribution to Anthropology 21. Washington DC: Smithsonian Institution.

Sackett, J.R. (1990) Style and ethnicity in archaeology: the case for isochrestism. In *The Uses of Style in Arxhaeology*, edited by M. Conkey and Ch. Hastorf. New Directions in Archaeology. Cambridge: Cambridge University Press., pp. 32–43.

Saraswati, B.N. (1978) *Pottery-making Cultures and Indian Civilization.* New Dehli: Abhinav Publications.

Schlanger, N. (1994) Mindful technology: unleashing the chaîne opératoire for an archaeology of mind. In *The Ancient Mind—Elements of Cognitive Archaeology*, edited by C. Renfrew and E.B.W. Zubrow. New Directions in Archeology. Cambridge: Cambridge University Press, pp. 143–151.

Schiffer, M.B. (1987) *Formation Processes of the Archaeological Record.* Albuquerque: University of Mexico Press.

Schiffer, M.B and Skibo, J.M. (1987) Theory and experiment in the study of technological change. *Current Anthropology* 28.5: 595–609, 614–22.

Senior, L. (1998) *Time and Technological Change: Ceramic Production, Labor, and Economic Transformation in a Third Millennium Complex Society (Tell Leilan, Syria).* Unpublished PhD Dissertation. Department of Anthropology, University of Arizona.

Senior, L., and Birnie, D.P., III (1995) Accurately estimating vessel volume from profile illustrations. *American Antiquity* 60.2: 319–34.

Sherratt, A. (1981) Plough and pastoralism: aspects of the secondary products revolution. In *Patterns of the Past: Studies in Honour of David Clarke*, edited by I. Hodder, G. Isaac and N. Hammond. Cambridge: Cambridge University Press, pp. 261–305.

— Diet and cuisine: farming and its transformations as reflected in pottery. *Documenta Praehistorica* XXIX.

— (1997) *Economy and Society in Prehistoric Europe—Changing Perspectives.* Princeton, NJ: Princeton University Press.

Sinopoli, C. (1988). The organization of craft production at Vijayanagara, South India. *American Anthropologist.* 90: 580–97.

— (1991) *Approaches to Archaeological Ceramics.* New York and London: Plenum Press.

Smith, C. (1975) Production in western Guatemala: a test of Von Thunen and Boserup. In *Formal Methods in Economic Anthropology*, edited by S. Pallner. Washington DC: American Anthropological Association Special Publication 4, pp. 5–38.

Sperber, D. (1979) La pensée symbolique est-elle pré-rationelle? In *La Fonction Symbolique. Essai d'Anthropologie:*, edited by M. Izard and P. Smith. Paris: Gallimard, pp. 17–42.

— (1992) Culture and matter. In *Representations in Archaeology*, edited by J.-C. Gardin and C. Peebles. Bloomington: Indiana University Press, pp. 56–65.

Stekelis, M. (1972) *The Yarmukian Culture of the Neolithic Period.* Jerusalem: The Hebrew University & Magnes Press.

Sterner, J. (1989) Who is signalling whom? ceramic, style, ethnicity and taphonomy among the Sirak Bulahay. *Antiquity* 63: 451–9.

Tilley, C. (1986) Interpreting material culture. In *Proceedings of the World Arcchaeological Congress, II. Material Culture and Symbolic Expression*, edited by I. Hodder. Southampton: University of Southampton, pp. 1–21.

Torrence, R. (1986) *Production and Exchange of Stone Tools: Prehistoric Obsidian in the Aegean*. Cambridge: Cambridge University Press.

Ussishkin, D. (1980). The Ghassulian shrine at Ein Gedi. *Tel Aviv* 7/1–2: 1–44.

Van den Brink, E. (forthcoming). *Shoam*.

Vander Leuw, S. and Pritchard, A.C. (eds) (1984) *The Many Dimensions of Pottery: Ceramics in Archaeology and Anthropology*. Cingula VII. Amsterdam: University of Amsterdam (Instituut voor Pre- en Protohistorie).

Van der Leeuw, S. (1977) Towards a study of economics in pottery making. In *Ex Horreo*, edited by L. Beek, R.W. Brandt and W. Grueman van Watteringe. Cingula 4. Amsterdam: Albert Egges van Giffen Institute voor Prae-en Protohistorie, University of Amsterdam, pp. 68–75.

Vitelli, K.D. (1989) Where pots first made for cooking? doubts from Franchti. *World Archaeology* 21: 17–29.

— (1995) Pots, potters, and the shaping of Greek neolithic society. In *The Emergence of Pottery: Technology and Innovation in Ancient Societies*, edited by W.K. Barnett and J.W. Hoopes. Smithsonian Institution in Archaeological Inquiry. Washington and London: Smithsonian institution Press, pp. 55–63.

Whallon, R. (1972) A new approach to pottery typology. *American Antiquity* 37: 13–33.

Whallon, R.J., and Brown, J.A. (eds.) (1982) *Essays in Archaeological Typology: Centers for American Archaeology*: Evanston, Illinois.

Yellin, J., Levy, T.E. and Rowan, Y.M. (1995) New evidence on Prehistoric trade routes: the obsidian evidence from Gilat, Israel. *Journal of Field Archaeology* 23: 361.

Young, D.E. (1985) The need for a congitive approach to material culture. *Culture* 5 (2): 53–67

Zohary, D. (1975) Beginnings of Fruit Growing in the Old World. *Science* 187: 319–27.

Zubrow, E.B. (1992) Formal Models of Ceramic Production. In *Ceramic Production and Distribution*, edited by G.J. Bey and C.A. Pool. Boulder: Westview Press.

11 The Chipped Stone Assemblage at Gilat

Yorke M. Rowan

Introduction

Of all the realms of material culture found at Gilat, the chipped stone assemblage probably represents the most profane dimension of material culture found at the site. At Gilat, the two most common forms of material culture are the ceramics and lithics. While ceramics played an important role in both domestic and ritual activities at the site, only limited aspects of the chipped stone assemblage can be linked to ritual activities. The vast majority of the tools and debitage recovered from Gilat were related to domestic activities. However, several types of flint artifacts indicate a role in activities beyond the domestic sphere. This includes the large number of tabular scrapers and their possible linkage to animal hide and wool processing (Chapter 14, this volume). In at least one example, axes were placed in ritual deposits as votive or foundation deposits. While these aspects of the lithic assemblage are discussed here, the major contribution of this chapter is the detailed presentation of the entire corpus of material found during the 1990–92 excavations to facilitate comparative studies with other Levantine and eastern Mediterranean sites. Thus, this chapter provides typological descriptions of the chipped stone assemblage and comparison with other published Chalcolithic chipped stone assemblages. As noted by other scholars (Gilead *et al.* 1995; Levy and Rosen 1987; Rosen 1997), earlier collections of chipped stone assemblages from Chalcolithic sites have ignored or discarded many components of the lithic assemblages, particularly the expedient flake tools and debitage, which creates problems for comparative studies. Compounding this issue, analyses of Chalcolithic chipped stone assemblages are still hampered by a lack of agreement on 1) typology, 2) field sampling methods, and 3) incomplete and disparate reporting and storage systems. Despite these drawbacks, beginning in the 1980s, all relevant chipped stone data began to be recorded from a number of northern Negev sites such as Shiqmim (Levy and Rosen 1987; Rowan 1990), Grar (Gilead 1995) and the Wadi Gaza sites (Roshwalb 1981). As this is the most intensively researched region of Chalcolithic settlement in Palestine, these assemblages provide important comparative material for Gilat. However, until systematically collected assemblages are published from other Chalcolithic settlement regions, the chronological, geographical and cultural potential of lithic analysis remains severely constrained.

Analytical Methods

Archaeological typologies are a complex issue, and debates over different approaches and their theoretical value are extensive (e.g. Brown 1982; Dunnell 1978, 1986; Hill and Evans 1972; Hodson 1982; Krieger 1944; Rouse 1960; Spaulding 1982). The literature on archaeological chipped stone typologies is also vast, and for brevity, the theoretical aspects of classification schemes will not be addressed here. The utility of particular typologies is frequently determined by their applicability, often with specific goals of a regional or chronological nature in mind. That is the case in the present description, where the typological schemes of Rosen (1987, 1989, 1997) and Levy and Rosen (1987) are followed based on applicability to late prehistoric assemblages and with the intention of providing some basis for future comparison of type frequency variability. Their methodology was recently criticized for the lack of distinction between primary elements and other classes of the debitage (Gilead *et al.* 1995:228). For the analysis of the chipped stone assemblage from Grar, a preference for the Bordesian system, based on tool analysis from French Paleolithic contexts, was stated (Gilead *et al.* 1995:225). However, the use of Bordes' (1961) system includes problematic factors affecting type variability, and in particular, confuses different aspects of function and technology (Dibble 1987; Rolland and Dibble 1990). In the end, the analytical scheme used to study Shiqmim (Levy and Rosen 1987; Rowan 1990), Grar (Gilead *et al.* 1995:223–80) as well as other sites (Rosen 1997) seem to require only minor adjustments to render the typologies comparable to Gilat.

Nomenclature of stone tools often includes a number of functional labels, which are rarely based on known tool functions. The goal of the present discussion is to describe the large chipped stone assemblage such that it may be of utility to future scholars, who in some cases may use the functional tool nomenclature (e.g. axe, adze, scraper, etc.) traditionally assigned these classes. Though each class is described separately, the detailed typological analysis of such a large and rich assemblage awaits future study. The distinction between stylistic and functional aspects of the stone tool assemblages during the late prehistory of the southern Levant remains relatively unexplored.

The flint tool production at Gilat may be viewed in seven separate technological spheres. These technologies are:

1. expedient tools, including a wide variety of retouched and utilized flakes and chunks, scrapers (with various sub-types), borers, awls, choppers, denticulates and notches;
2. celts, or core tools, including adzes, axes, chisels, and picks;
3. blade tools, including sickles, sickle blanks and retouched blades;
4. tabular scrapers and fragments;
5. bladelets, including micro-endscrapers and retouched bladelets;
6. prismatic blades;
7. micro-borers.

The limestone tools could be considered an eighth separate sphere, but the overwhelming majority of limestone tools are typologically and technologically similar to other chipped flint tools, particularly expedient flake tools. A similar observation was reported from the nearby site of Grar (Gilead and Fabian 1995; Gilead 1989). The greatest quantity of tools and debitage reflects the domestic manufacture of simple retouched and utilized flakes and other miscellaneous pieces (utilized or retouched chunks, cores and cobbles).

Waste

The manufacture of chipped stone tools produces a large quantity of residual debris, the classification of which is instrumental to the analysis of flint tool production. Thus, the emphasis at the excavations of Gilat was on the collection and permanent storage of all chipped stone material.[1] Waste categories reflect the presence or absence of the different flint production techniques, and in this manner assist the determination of what techniques were of local, on-site production, and which techniques were practiced off-site. Waste recovered from Gilat is broken into four major categories, three of which reflect the major types of core reduction strategies practiced at the site. These categories are debris, flakes, blades and bladelets. For instance, the absence of primary flakes, the first flakes removed from a cobble, may indicate flint was first reduced away from the site. In the case of Gilat, the high number of primary flakes indicates that the flaking technique, the most prevalent form of tool production, was practiced at the site with locally available flint cobbles, most likely from the nearby Nahal Patish. On the other hand, the complete absence of 'tabular' flint debris or prismatic blade cores suggests these tools were manufactured off-site. Both of these types are recognizable technologically and by the flint selected for those artifacts. Other flint recovered from the site reflects locally available wadi pebbles, which vary from brown to gray, with some banded flints of light and dark gray. These banded flints tend to be used primarily for blade production, which is also noted for the blades from Grar (Gilead *et al.* 1995:226) and Chalcolithic sites in the Beersheva Basin (Rosen 1997:45–46). Total debitage frequencies are presented in Table 11.1a, and summarized data for the entire assemblage are presented in Table 11.1b.

Debris (chips=26,914; chunks=35,589)
Debris includes chips and chunks, which are the amorphous shatter from reduction. Chips and chunks are arbitrarily divided on the basis of size; chips are less than 5 mm in maximum size, and may include fragments of flakes. Chunks are larger, blocky, and of uncertain origin in the reduction process. The arbitrary point at which chips are distinguished varies between analyses (Gilead 1995: 237), and the size limit here is smaller than that used at some sites, but is consistent with the analysis of the Shiqmim assemblage (Levy and Rosen 1987:238; Rowan 1990). Moreover, this distinction is not closely followed in laboratory separation, where rapid sorting was a necessity. It should be acknowledged that the utility of this category is limited, and counts of chips could be affected dramatically by other factors such as 'bag wear', sampling methods and sieve mesh size. Chips and chunks are too amorphous to determine what type of reduction strategy they result from. Chips from Gilat are 43.06% of the debris counts (Table 11.1b), similar but lower than that of Grar (Gilead *et al.* 1995: Table 5.3). Sieving methodologies from Gilat and Grar are comparable; hence this is probably a result of the smaller size limit of chips for the Gilat assemblage. Debris constitutes 54.5% of the total debitage counts, which is a higher frequency when compared to that of Grar (30% of total debitage, *ibid.* Table 5.3), as well as Bir es-Safadi and Qatif (*ibid:* Fig. 5.1).

Debitage (see Table 11.4)

Flakes (primary flakes=7,903; flakes=36,515)
Like most domestic Chalcolithic sites, the primary reduction technique practiced at Gilat is a simple flake technology. As mentioned above, primary flakes, defined here as those flakes with over 80% cortex remaining on the dorsal side, are the first flakes struck from a cobble. Flakes are the result of further reduction of the cobble, and the flakes may be used as expedient tools (see discussion of retouched flakes, below), retouched individually to form specific tools, or simply discarded. Flakes

from Gilat are highly variable in size, with numerous errors such as 'hinge' flakes and material flaws. These and the amorphous cores (discussed below) are probably the result of an expedient core technology (Parry and Kelly 1987), where flaking techniques are relatively uncontrolled and the cores are unprepared in most cases. The combination of primary flakes and all other unmodified flakes comprises 85% of the total debitage counts, roughly comparable to that of Shiqmim (Levy and Rosen 1987: Table 10.1), but much higher than that of Grar, Bir es-Safadi or Qatif (Gilead *et al.* 1995: Fig. 5.2). Though it is difficult to interpret this large difference, it may in part be a reflection of a much greater intensity (and probably duration) of occupation, and flint production, at Gilat and Shiqmim.

Flake Cores (n=1,935) and Flake Core Fragments (n=1,372)

Flake cores are the reduced cobbles from which flakes have been struck, and represent a wide variety of stages of manufacture, from tested cobbles which have only a few flakes removed, to exhausted cores (or core nuclei), which are too small to reduce further. Flake core fragments are often the result of striking platform removal or rejuvenation, to facilitate further core reduction. Flake core fragments are also the result of flake core breakage during the reduction process. Both flake cores and flake core fragments are occasionally found with evidence of their subsequent re-use as expedient tools. The absence of standardized elements highlights what Levy and Rosen (1987: 289) termed the *ad hoc* nature of flake production, or an expedient core technology (Parry and Kelly 1987). The debitage resulting from the flake reduction process, including all flakes, flake cores and flake core fragments, accounts for 41% of the total waste. If the debris counts (chips and chunks) are excluded, the flake technology (flakes, cores and core fragments) comprises 91% of the total debitage. This highlights the predominance of the unspecialized flake reduction technique to the local inhabitants.

Blades (n=2,403)

Blades are flakes removed from a core with far greater precision and standardization than that of flakes. Blades by definition are at least twice as long as they are wide, with relatively parallel lateral margins (Crabtree 1982:16), possibly produced through the use of a punch. At Gilat, blades appear to be primarily for the production of sickles; very few other tools are manufactured from blades. Blade production may represent a specialized technology, and may not have been produced entirely on-site. Some specialized production sites on the lower Nahal Besor (Wadi Gaza) exhibit much higher frequencies of blades and waste from blade production (though these data are unquantifiable), indicating a distinctive manufacturing process, if not craft specialization (Rosen 1987:298). Though a large number of blades were recovered, blades constitute under 5% of the total debitage assemblage (Table 11.1b), which falls in between the high range of Grar (Gilead *et al.* 1995: Fig. 5.2) and the low frequency (*c.* 1.1%) of Shiqmim (Levy and Rosen 1987: tab. 10.1). Though few unmodified blades were measured, the mean is substantially larger than that of other blade/bladelet types (Table 11.12).

Blade Cores (n=35, Figures 11.9:5, 7; 11.10:1-2; 11.11:1–4) and Blade Core Fragments (n=195, Figure 11.9:6)

The majority of the blade cores are made of a light to dark gray-banded flint, ranging in length from approximately 4 to 8 cm. The majority are single platform cores, worked on a single face, with cortex still evident on the opposed face. Blades, blade cores and blade core trimming elements combined constitute only approximately 2% of the total waste or 5% if counts of debris are excluded (Table 11.1b). The presence of blade cores at the site suggests that at least some blades were produced at Gilat; however, the numbers of blades, sickles, sickle blanks and retouched blades combined add up to over 3,000 blades, a disproportionately high number relative to the 35 blade cores recovered. This suggests that the majority of blades may have been imported to the site, possibly from specialized sites such as Wadi Gaza Site A (Roshwalb 1981; Rosen 1987). Whether or not these blades were produced by local specialists indigenous to Gilat, or were exchanged from outside specialists, remains unclear. However, the large quantity of other non-local materials found at Gilat supports the possibility that outside specialists manufactured the blades away from the site.

Bladelets (n=298)
Like the blades, bladelets may require greater skill to manufacture than flakes. Bladelets are also defined by their outline, with a length at least twice that of the width. In addition, bladelets are almost exclusively manufactured from a very fine, semi-translucent flint, usually a light brown color, but sometimes a very fine light gray flint. Bladelets form a statistically separate category from other blade types based on the average widths and thicknesses (see discussion, below) and are typically smaller (see Table 11.12), averaging about 25 mm (L) × 8.8 mm (W) × 2.9 mm (T).

Bladelet Cores (n=60, Figures 11.9:1–4) and Bladelet Core Fragments (n=1,439)
Bladelets, bladelet core and fragments constitute only 1.5% of the total waste assemblage or 3.5% if the debris counts are excluded (Table 11.1b). Bladelets seem to be produced almost exclusively for the manufacture of micro-endscrapers. Production of bladelets was clearly on-site, as indicated by the presence of all reduction stages (primary flakes, other flakes, bladelet core trimming elements and bladelet cores).

Mixed Cores (n=96)
A relatively small number of cores appear to have been used for both flake and blade production. It is unclear whether these were failed attempts to manufacture blades and subsequent re-use of the core, or if the occasional parallel flake scars are simply accidental.

Standardized Tools

Sickle Blades (n=389, Figures 11.14:2–13; 11.15:1, 5–7, 11–12; 11.16:2–7, 9)
Sickle blades are backed blades with a bright polish along the cutting edge which is probably the result of silica deposits from the harvesting of plants (Anderson 1980; Unger-Hamilton 1989) although alteration of the flint surface from reaping is also posited (Meeks *et al.* 1982). Typical sickle segments are backed, and either truncated on one end and snapped on the opposing end (Figure 11.4:3), simply snapped on both ends, or dorsally truncated on both ends (Figures 11.4:2, 5). Table 11.2 provides descriptive attributes of sickle blades; as can be seen, the majority of sickles has a trapezoidal cross-section (69%), is trapezoidal or rectangular in outline (75%), with dorsal backing retouch (95%). The mean metric measurements for sickles are length: 33mm (S.D. +10.7), width: 11mm (S.D. +2.0) and thickness: 4mm (S.D. + 1.2); further metric measurements are given in Table 11.2 according to types of proximal and distal end modification. The means presented here closely match those from Grar (Gilead *et al.* 1995: Table 5.9, 5.10), though the Gilat sickles tend to be slightly larger. Only 12% of the sickles are clearly serrated intentionally, and fewer are otherwise retouched along the edge (3.6%). Three of the sickles are made from the fine translucent brown flint usually used for the production of bladelets and micro-endscrapers.

Sickle Blanks (n=192, Figures 11.14:1; 11.15:8, 10; 11.16:8, 10–11)

Sickle blanks differ from sickle blades only in the lack of visible silica sheen, an indication that they were not yet used as intensively as sickle blades, if used at all. Like the sickle blades (see Table 11.2), the majority has a trapezoidal cross-section (68%) due to invasive, dorsal backing retouch (96%), and has a trapezoidal to rectangular outline (81%). Mean metric measurements are also very similar to sickles; 27mm long, 11mm wide and 4mm thick, confirming the observation (Gilead *et al.* 1995:255) that sickle gloss is an additional element in the definition of sickle blades. The range of sickle blank and sickle widths, as well as those of micro-endscrapers and retouched blades, are presented in Figure 11.2. The histogram indicates that the general widths of sickles and sickle blanks are similar, with a peak between 9–13 mm. Figure 11.2 presents the range of thickness measurements of the same blades where a similar pattern is evident. These similarities indicate that there is no real difference between sickle blanks and sickles, except the lack of a highly developed polish on the 'blanks'.

Core tools (n=133, Figures 11.26–11.36)

The category of core tools is also a broad term, encompassing all of the bifacial core tools (Levy and Rosen 1987; Rosen 1987), some actually made from flakes rather than cores. This includes axes, adzes, chisels, picks, fragments and those of unknown type. These terms have not been shown to relate to function, but are retained here because of their common usage. Fragments of these tools are a significant proportion (n=39) of this assemblage, and these fragments support Lee's suggestion (1973:248) that these tools were put to hard use. Debitage from celt manufacture has not been identified, and thus the absence of diagnostic cores does not necessarily imply off-site manufacture (Rosen 1997:106). Frequencies of descriptive attributes and mean dimensions are presented in Table 11.3.

Axes and adzes (n=56, Figures 11.28, 11.30:2, 11.31:2, 11.32). In the present analysis, the difference between axes and adzes is simply defined, following Levy and Rosen (1987) and Lee (1973), by the positioning of the bit (working edge) relative to the tool's profile and cross-section. Those with an asymmetrical bit relative to the profile and cross-section are defined as adzes (n=17), and those with a symmetrical bit are called axes (n=39). These sub-types of the core tools may seem of dubious value to analysis, and may be the result of bit rejuvenation or original manufacture idiosyncrasies, rather than a functional difference. However, there is a tendency for axes to have bi-convex cross-sections, while adzes more frequently have a plano-convex cross-section (Table 11.3). The difference between axes and adzes is strengthened by the co-variation with edge polish. While adzes occasionally exhibit polish on the edge (c. 30%), both axes and chisels are usually polished (85% and 92%, respectively). In addition, Table 11.3 shows the range of length means for axes, adzes, chisels and the unknown type. There is a tendency for the axes to be longer (Figure 11.18) and for axes and adzes to be larger in all respects compared to the chisels. Widths follow similar trends, as seen in Figures 11.3–5, where adzes and axes follow closely, though axes again tend to be larger, and chisels tend to be narrower. Finally, Figure 11.20 presents the range of core tool sub-type by thickness measurements. This provides the most distinctive characteristic because the axes are clearly thicker than other sub-types, while adzes and chisels are not clearly differentiated on the basis of thickness measurements.

Chisels (n=13, 11.26, 11.27, 11.29, 11.30:1, 11.31:1, 11.33, 11.34, 11.35). Chisels are easier to distinguish as a separate tool category, though the functional difference remains obscure. Lee (1973:249) postulated that chisels were reserved for the finer, finishing touches of woodworking. Chisels are narrower, with relatively parallel margins, and bits which are usually no wider than the body of the tool. As seen in Table 11.3, and discussed above, chisels tend to be narrower, thinner, with a slightly lower average edge angle, and exhibit a greater tendency towards square-like (trapezoidal to rectangular) cross-sections than the other core tool sub-types. Virtually all of the chisels show evidence of polish, and one example, tentatively classed as a chisel, is made of a re-worked tabular scraper fragment which is heavily ground and polished bifacially (Fig. 11.19:2).

Unknown (n=8). The unknown category is those core tools that have no clear bit edge, either due to fragmentation or an intention to re-sharpen the bit.

Picks (n=11, Figures 11.36:1–2). Picks do not resemble the other core tools beyond the use of a core reduction technique. These tools typically have cortex covered butts (proximal ends), with a distal end retouched to form a thick point, which is roughly trihedral in cross-section. Similar tools were noted from Tuleilat Ghassul and the Wadi Gaza sites (Lee 1973; Roshwalb 1981). While many core tools may have been hafted, it is unlikely the picks were, given the large and uneven bulk of the proximal end.

Preforms (n=7, Figure 11.33:1). These core tools are clearly unbroken, yet have no clear bit and are very rough. It is unclear whether these tools are in a finished form, requiring no further reduction for their purpose, or were unfinished core tools that were abandoned. These hint at the possibility that blanks or preforms were brought to the site, where they were later finished. A number of Wadi Gaza sites, particularly Site A, recovered large numbers of core tools, including many blanks (Roshwalb 1981), which are interpreted as specialized production sites (Rosen 1987:299).

Tabular Scrapers (n=39, Figures 11.20–11.22; 11.23.1) and Fragments (n=69)

Tabular scrapers, also referred to as 'Ghassulian fan scrapers' (Lee 1973; Mallon *et al.* 1934; McConaughy 1979), were originally thought to be produced from veins of flint. More recently this assumption has been discounted, and the flint is now thought to be from large nodules, possibly originating in the western Negev (Rosen 1983a) and Sinai (Kozloff 1972/73), though also known to occur in Jordan (Muheisen *et al.* 1988:482–3).[2] Characterized as non-local at most Chalcolithic and Early Bronze Age sites where recovered, the lack of residual by-products from their manufacture suggests that tabular scrapers were made off-site. Workshop sites are known from the western Negev (Rosen 1987), Har Qeren 15 (Rosen 1983a), and in the Sinai (Kozloff 1972/3). In addition, like those from Shiqmim, very few are 'fan' shaped (Table 11.4), a situation noted for southern Early Bronze Age sites as well (Rosen 1989:202); oval shapes are also common to the Maadi tabular scraper assemblage (Rizkana and Seeher 1988:30). The fine flint that is typically used, usually a dark to light brown, indicates greater selectivity in flint procurement. Preference for large cortical flakes is evident, the manufacture of which typically creates a pronounced bulb of percussion, probably as a result of manufacture using a block-on-block technique (Rosen 1997:71). The bulb of percussion is usually thinned with ventral flaking (Figures 11.20:2; 11.21:3; 11.22:1; 11.23:1–2), broken off before the tool is completed (Figure 11.20:1), or both. Cortical grinding is also evident on some artifacts. Circumferential dorsal retouch was preferred to achieve the desired finished product, and on some tools, heavy grinding wear and polish is evident on lateral margins (Figure 11.21:1) and ventral aspects (Figure 11.21:3). As seen in Table 11.4, the majority of tabular scrapers are transversally retouched to such an extent that the finished tool is usually wider than its length. Mean edge angles, though slightly lower, are comparable to those of normal flake scrapers. None of the Gilat specimens are inscribed on the dorsal, cortex side, a feature which does not begin until the Early Bronze Age (Rosen 1989).

Tabular scrapers have been associated with ritual contexts, particularly those from northern Early Bronze Age contexts (McConaughy 1979; Rosen 1989). This may prove true of Chalcolithic tabular scrapers as well; the association of a large tabular fan scraper with a burial context at the Shiqmim cemetery (Levy and Alon 1987:350, Table 13.3) provides one of the few flint artifacts associated with an interment at the cemetery. A tabular flint 'knife' is also known directly associated with the ritual structure found at Shiqmim (pers. obs, 1989 season). Tabular scrapers (and fragments) constitute a higher percentage (2.7%) of the overall tool assemblage at Gilat as opposed to that of Shiqmim (1.1%) or Grar (1.01%, Gilead *et al.* 1995: Table 5.8).

Prismatic (Canaanean) Blades (n=18; see Figures 11.12–11.13)[3]

These large blades are rare, forming the lowest quantity of any tool type (0.4% of the tool assemblage from the 1990–2 excavations). They are characterized by a wide flat outline with parallel margins, and usually two parallel dorsal flake ridges, the result of previous blade removals from the core. While prismatic blade manufacture can be achieved with direct percussion (Sollberger and Patterson 1976), the negative bulb of percussion on the dorsal aspect of the blade's proximal end suggests a punch may have been used (Rosen 1983b:16–17). Cross-sections are trapezoidal, but unlike the typical Chalcolithic sickles, the prismatic blades are usually symmetrically trapezoidal. Width measurements are on average at least 50% greater than average Chalcolithic sickle blades. The flint used to manufacture these blades is sometimes similar to that used for tabular scrapers, a similarity noted from later EB contexts as well (Seger *et al.* 1990:22).

The prismatic blades from the 1987, and 1990–1 seasons at Gilat have previously been described (Rowan and Levy 1994), but the 1992 excavations add five more prismatic blades to the Gilat assemblage, bringing the total number of these blades up to 18 (including one from the 1987 excavation). Three of these blades have silica sheen on one or both lateral margins. As Rosen (1987, 1989) noted, Early Bronze Age prismatic blades are typically used as sickle blades, replacing the less efficient Chalcolithic sickle blades, which only possessed one working edge. The majority of prismatic blades from Gilat do not appear to be sickle blades. Given the invasive retouch on both lateral margins and the distal aspect, and the lack of sickle sheen on the majority of the blades, these tools were probably utilized for some other function, perhaps as hand-held reaping knives, though Schick (1978:60–1) suggests that backing retouch and bitumen found on similar long harvesting knives recovered from Arad indicate hafting. Similar long blades, not modified into sickle blades, are also known from other EB sites such as En Shadud (Rosen 1985), Jericho (Crowfoot 1935) and others (cf. Rosen 1983b).

This technology, which later in the Early Bronze Age supplants the standard production technique of the Chalcolithic sickle blades, required a different fine-grained, quality flint not locally available at Gilat or other sites in the northern Negev desert. Future research will probably reveal more of these blades, and microwear analysis such as that by Shea (1989), Unger-Hamilton (1989) and Rowan and Levy (1991) may elucidate the function of these early proto-types of the Canaanean sickle blade.

Other investigators have claimed similar blades from Chalcolithic contexts, such as those from Qatafa cave in the Judean desert (Perrot 1992), the Jordan Valley site of Fasa'el (Milstein and Ronen 1985:13) and perhaps the Wadi Fidan sites A and F as well as sites in the Jerash region (Hanbury-Tennison 1986:146–50), but these claims are disputed on incorrect terminological or chronological grounds (Rosen 1989:207).

In retrospect, our previous term for these blades as 'proto-Canaanean' is probably a misnomer (Rowan and Levy 1994). Based on metrics, these blades clearly fall within the grouping of Canaanean sickle widths (*ibid.* Rosen 1989: Fig. 3), and though a few exhibit sickle sheen, the majority would appear to be functionally different from Canaanean sickles. Like the blades from Maadi, the complete blades resemble 'endscrapers' on blades (a functional label equally ill-defined); the fragments do not resemble sickle blades. Equally important, the early radiocarbon dates from Gilat (see Chapter 5) and the complete absence of EBI artifacts distances these pieces from the EBI chronologically. However, similar blades are also unknown from Wadi Rabah sites. Though technologically these blades are remarkably distinct from other blades at Gilat or other Chalcolithic sites, parallels are few.

The possibility that these blades either originated from Predynastic Egyptian contexts, or were manufactured at the same source, cannot be categorically discounted. Unfortunately, collection and publication of flint tools and debitage from Predynastic sites is only rarely representative of the assemblages of those cultures (Holmes 1989:22–32). Nevertheless, there are some parallels, such as from the cemetery excavations at Armant (Mond and Meyers 1937: Plate XX, lower left register) as well as Maadi (Rizkana and Seeher 1988). A number of blades from Maadi seem more similar to the Gilat blades than other blades from Palestinian contexts and the possible connections between Maadi and southern Palestinian Chalcolithic and EBI sites have been previously suggested. In addition, the probability that at least some occupations at Maadi were contemporaneous with the Palestinian Chalcolithic seems high (Joffe and Dessel 1995:513). A number of blades which are termed 'endscrapers on blades' at Maadi are similar to those from Gilat; one fragment with steep retouch, on a rounded distal edge and similar trapezoidal cross-section (Rizkana and Seeher 1988: pl.32.2) is similar to Gilat B.3555 (Figure 11.29:1). Also similar are the long, complete blades with bilateral retouch, and scraper retouch on at least one end (Rizkana and Seeher 1988: pl.36.1, 5), which are similar to another Gilat prismatic blade (Figure 11.12:3), with one important difference: the Maadi blades have ventral lateral retouch as well, which only one of the Gilat artifacts exhibits. However, other Maadi blades also lack significant ventral retouch. Also notable from both sites is the lack of silica sheen, and the presence of some low luster polish, on many of the artifacts from both Gilat and Maadi. Other similarities may also exist, but the important point is the increased probability of contact between these two sites. However, neither site produced cores from which these blades were manufactured, so their origins remain unknown.

Micro-Endscrapers (n=237, Figure 11.17:6–8)

These bladelet tools were first recognized by Neuville (1930:69) and Nasrallah (1936), and were the subject of analyses by Gilead (1984). Like the majority of the bladelets, the flint is a very fine, semi-translucent brown or gray. The distal end is lightly retouched on the dorsal aspect, usually forming a convex shape, and retouch often extends along the lateral margin as well. This light, 'nibbling' retouch suggests that the edges were intentionally dulled, perhaps to prevent cutting the user's fingers. Micro-endscrapers are, on average, less than 10 mm in width, and the length:width ratio of complete examples (with the bulb of percussion) is over 3:1 (see Table 11.5). As discussed below, micro-endscrapers are common at Gilat and the nearby site of Grar, as well as the Wadi Ghazzeh sites, particularly Site A (Roshwalb 1981:26–8, 58–73) but are virtually non-existent at Shiqmim, though bladelets are occasionally recovered. Because none of these tools are retouched bilaterally, it seems likely that the unmodified edge was utilized. However, the function of these tools remains unknown. At least one, and probably two, additional micro-endscrapers were found manufactured on obsidian from Anatolia, which are discussed elsewhere (Yellin, Levy and Rowan 1996).

Micro-Borers (n=21, Figure 11.17:2–3; 9–12)

Though few in number, the microliths form a clearly separate tool type. Though some are manufactured of the same material as the bladelets, others are made of whitish, soapy flint. These microliths were studied prior to Rosen's (1994–5) typological discussion, but an effort will be made to relate the present collection to that study.

These can be broken into three sub-types. Type 1 (n=12, Figures 11.17:9, 11, 12) is generally trapezoidal in both cross-section and outline, with bilateral, dorsal retouch. The proximal end is either the butt or is dorsally truncated; the distal end is usually a horizontally tapered end, giving the appearance of a tiny wedge or chisel. The average dimensions for this sub-type is: length, 13.3 mm; width, 5.8 mm; and thickness, 3.5 mm. Type 1 does not seem similar to any of Rosen's types, but the closest parallel would be the straight drill (1994–5:153). Sub-type 2 (n=7, Figures 11.17:3,

10) is typically trapezoidal in cross-section, elongate triangular in outline, with bilateral, dorsal retouch. The distal tip is pointed, giving the appearance of a miniature awl. The average dimensions for sub-type 2 are: length, 22.8 mm; width, 6.6 mm; and thickness, 3.2 mm. Type 2 resembles Rosen's triangular drills (Rosen 1994–5: Fig. 2.9). Types 1 and 2 are retouched along the entirety of the lateral margins. The third sub-type (n=2, Figure 11.17:2) resembles many of the larger borers typically made on flakes, with bilateral dorsal retouch to form a point, but without retouch on the entire piece, resembling closely Rosen's 'double-shoulder' drills, one in particular (Rosen 1994–5: Fig. 2:5). The points on these two pieces measure 7 mm and 11 mm. The extremely small size of all three sub-types suggests these tools were probably hafted (Burian and Friedman 1985), presumably for bead manufacture or incising and drilling ground stone artifacts such as pendants.

Retouched Blades (n=159, Figure 11.12:1-2, 4)

Like at Shiqmim, blade tools are rare at Gilat (Levy and Rosen 1987), and the majority appears to be in various stages of manufacture for sickle blades. As is evident in Table 11.6, most retouched blades have a trapezoidal cross-section, like sickles and sickle blanks (compare to Table 11.2). Where the blade is backed, backing retouch is typically dorsal and invasive like the sickles. The high degree of standardization typical of sickle blades is indicated by the low standard deviation of width means compared to other blades (with the exception of bladelets, which also have very low standard deviations, see Table 11.12), which is supported by comparisons of metric blade attributes from different sites (Gilead *et al.* 1995: Fig. 5.19). The uneven, irregular outline of most retouched blades is due to the discontinuous retouch, suggesting that many of the pieces were probably unfinished sickles. As seen already in Figures 11.1 and 11.2, retouched blades have a less pronounced peak, and a broader distribution of size, based on widths, yet this peak is still centered comparably to that of the sickles and sickle blanks.

Retouched Bladelets (n=108)

Like the micro-endscraper, retouched bladelets are manufactured from a very fine, semi-translucent brown flint of a glassy texture. Retouch is almost always a light, regular, direct dorsal retouch along one lateral margin, and because the majority of these are fragments, it is probably a safe assumption that these are primarily broken micro-endscrapers. Only two of these are ventrally retouched along one lateral margin. Retouched bladelets are common at both Gilat and Grar, but rare at most Beersheva sites such as Shiqmim (Rowan 1990; Levy and Rosen 1987) and Bir es-Safadi (Gilead *et al.* 1995: Fig.5.34).

Flake and Expedient Tools

As previously mentioned, the predominant flint tool production of flakes is reflected in the tools produced and the debitage, with only a small presence of other production types (blades and bladelets, core tools and limestone tools). However, though much of this production is of an unspecialized nature, there seems to be a (tripartite) scheme of production. One is the production of specialized tools, such as tabular scrapers, core tools (celts), prismatic blades, and perhaps blades and bladelets. Secondly is the *ad hoc* tool production (Levy and Rosen 1987), or an expedient tool use, with flakes and cobbles produced for use, or simply picked up, used or retouched for a task, and then discarded. However, it is not clear that all of the non-formal tools are of an expedient nature. Instead, some tools, particularly scrapers and borers seem fairly standardized in terms of the desired final product. This is reflected in a number of attributes. For instance, the borers are typically made on flakes, with the projection on the distal end of the flake, and typically retouched bilaterally on the dorsal aspect. This is not to suggest that these tools are the result of specialized manufacture, but that there may be an element of standardization in their production. Such standardization may reflect more functionally desired characteristics. Even if such a tripartite scheme is demonstrated, both standardized and *ad hoc* tools appear to be part of the domestic tool assemblage (Levy and Rosen 1987:289).

Notches (n=50)

Notches are small, invasively retouched indentations on flakes, blades or chunks, usually on the dorsal aspect of flakes. Two notches are on the lateral margins of blades, and eight are on chunks. The remaining 40 notches are on flakes; 22 are on the lateral margins of flakes (three of which are ventrally retouched) and 18 are on the distal aspect of flakes (three of which are ventrally retouched). Only three of these notches are on primary flakes, the remainder is on secondary or tertiary flakes. This distribution indicates little preference for reduction elements, beyond the use of flakes, for use as notches. The function of these tools is unclear, though perhaps they were used for shaving wood.

Borers/Perforators (n=385, Figures 11.17:1, 4, 13–16; 11.18:1–5)

These tools are points manufactured on a variety of elements, predominantly flakes (70%, Table 11.7). The points vary from short and slightly modified (`epin', Figure 11.32:3) to long, intensively and steeply retouched points along the extent of both lateral margins (awls, Figure 11.17:13; 11.18:1). Six of these tools are manufactured from the fine translucent flint usually used for bladelets and micro-endscrapers. Six of the borers are manufactured from re-worked sickle blades, identified by the sickle sheen still visible on part of the tool. Table 11.7 presents the descriptive attributes and mean dimensions of different borer/perforators. Figure 11.6 presents the length ranges of the borer points according to the different reduction elements on which they were manufactured.

Denticulates (n=26, Figure 11.24:1)

Denticulates are small 'teeth' created by retouch along the margins, creating small protrusions, which differ from borers by the lack of retouch on the protrusion itself. Denticulates are fairly rare, and represent a far less common tool type than at the site of Shiqmim. The majority of these may be repeated notches on the same element, while others may have functioned as cutting implements.

Side Scrapers (n=29, Figures 11.25:5, 11.23:3)

Side scrapers are retouched flakes, with the primary retouch occurring along one, or infrequently, both lateral margins. These tools differ from scrapers both by their larger size and by the location of the retouch; however, use-wear analyses also indicate that these tools were used primarily for cutting and other heavier activities than for the majority of scrapers (Rowan and Levy 1991). Nevertheless, just as scrapers are often multifunctional tools, side scrapers probably also functioned in a number of capacities.

Scrapers (n=183, Figures 11.24:2–4; 11.25:4–7)

Scrapers are a broad category of retouched elements, usually primary or secondary flakes. These tools are distinguished from retouched flakes by more intensive retouch, which is clearly not the result of simple utilization. As seen in Table 11.8, there is a clear preference for regularity in outline, from a roughly ovoid shape (Figure 11.24:4) to the 'simple' shape (resembling the outline of a thumbnail). Retouch is not as extensive along the margins as that of tabular scrapers, nor is the bulb of percussion removed or thinned. Edge angle of the working edge (usually the distal aspect) was typically measured 2–3 times with a goniometer, and the results averaged. Thus the averages as presented in Table 11.8 are not as precise as they appear, and there is no significant variation between the average edge angles of different scraper classifications.

Choppers (n=61)

Choppers are typically manufactured from wadi cobbles by trimming one edge, either unifacially or bifacially. Some choppers are manufactured by first splitting a cobble, creating a ready edge, which may be retouched as it dulls from use. Choppers commonly occur in relatively small numbers at southern Levantine Chalcolithic assemblages (e.g. Levy and Rosen 1987; Yeivin 1959).

Retouched and Utilized Flakes (n=1459)

Over one third (35%) of the tool assemblage is expedient tools - flakes with minimal retouch or edge damage from use. Table 11.9 shows the frequencies of flake types and the location of retouch or utilization damage. As in the debitage, primary flakes are defined by complete or near complete (< 80%) dorsal cortex, secondary flakes have some dorsal cortex, but less than c. 80%, and tertiary flakes have no dorsal cortex. These frequencies indicate a preference for secondary flakes as expedient tools because the primary flakes, fewer than 8% of the total retouched flakes, constitute c. 18% of the total debitage flakes. Nearly 90% of all retouched flakes exhibit retouch only on the distal or lateral margin, with no other modifications to the flake.

Miscellaneous Trimmed Pieces and Varia (n=377, Figures 11.25:1)

Miscellaneous trimmed pieces are those retouched or utilized elements that do not fit standardized categories. Frequencies of this category are presented in Table 11.10. Over half of these pieces are retouched or utilized chunks and retouched core (blade and flake) fragments. Varia includes all pieces that could fit into more than one standardized category, for example, scrapers with a perforator on the same piece. Also included in this category are possible fragments of tools which cannot be clearly identified, such as probable scraper edge fragments. Included in this category are two highly unusual fragments, both of them worked with a careful, flat retouch bifacially (Figures 11.19:1–2). Both have broken protrusions that look more like stems or tangs than the typical protrusions of the borer/perforators class. Without known parallels from Chalcolithic period contexts in the southern Levant, these odd pieces are more similar to Predynastic tools than any published illustrations. The closest parallels available again come from the site of Maadi, where fragments illustrated are somewhat similar (Rizkana and Seeher 1988: Pl.III: 1–2; Pl.69: 6).

Limestone Tools (n=193, Figures 11.25:1–2, 4–7)

Tools manufactured from limestone were first noted for the Chalcolithic only recently from the nearby site of Grar (Gilead 1989; Gilead and Fabian 1995). This appears to be a localized phenomenon, like that of the micro-endscrapers, both of which appear in far greater numbers at Gilat and Grar than at Shiqmim, though our knowledge of this phenomenon may be hampered by biased collection from other excavations. Grar is only about 7 km northeast of Gilat. Like Grar, the most common type of limestone tool at Gilat are retouched flakes, as seen in Table 11.11. Like retouched flint flakes, retouched limestone flakes are typically retouched along the dorsal aspect of the distal or a lateral edge (compare Tables 11.11 and 11.9), with only 20% (n=15) of the limestone flakes retouched on the ventral aspect of the flake.

The second most common form of tool manufactured from limestone is the scrapers, also of a similar proportion to the overall limestone assemblage to that from Grar (Gilead 1989: Table 3, p. 104).

The overall impression of the limestone assemblage is similar to that of the flint flake assemblage; the major tool categories are retouched flakes, scrapers and miscellaneous trimmed pieces (retouched chunks and cobbles). As noted from Grar, it is equally significant which tools are *not* manufactured from limestone. Tabular scrapers and celts, as well as blade tools such as sickles, prismatic blades, micro-endscrapers, are under-represented or non-existent in the limestone assemblage.

Discussion

Typological Considerations

Similar to most Chalcolithic sites, the majority of tools, debris, and debitage indicate the importance of a simple flake production technique. However, while expedient tools such as retouched and utilized flakes form an important component of this flake production, more standardized tools such as scrapers, borers and many of the limestone tools are perhaps not manufactured on the same *ad hoc* basis.

Blade technology has long been recognized as a significant feature of typical Chalcolithic lithic assemblages (Rosen 1987, 1997). Within Chalcolithic blade assemblages, a number of permutations have been suggested, but with few exceptions (e.g. Rosen 1983b; Roshwalb 1981), very little systematic study has been conducted on the variability of blades. This has resulted in varying terminology and different interpretations of blade types. At a subjective level, analysis of bladelets and other blades suggested that there is a difference in size between bladelets, blades and prismatic ('Canaanean') blades. Earlier research has suggested that the distinction of size between blades and bladelets was arbitrary (Rosen 1987; Tixier 1963).

To achieve a better understanding of the size differences between blade categories, a sample of the Gilat blade, bladelet and prismatic blades were analyzed on the basis of metric attributes (length, width and thickness). This sample included all sickles, sickle blanks, retouched blades, bladelets, retouched bladelets, micro-endscrapers, prismatic blades, and a few unmodified blades from the 1990–1 excavation seasons (N = 720 blades). Because the one overriding definition of all blade classes is that the length to width ratio be at least 2:1, the present analysis included only those blades with at least a 2:1 ratio. It is safe to assume that this includes many fragments, particularly of sickles (which can be identified exclusively by the sickle sheen, rather than by length to width ratio). The mean metric attributes with the standard deviation of these blade classes are presented in Table 11.12. Note that these mean measurements do not include the total of all blades recovered from Gilat, but by comparing the means of Table 11.12 with those of the different blade classes (Tables 11.2, 11.5 and 11.6), it is clear that a larger sample size would have little effect on the means and standard deviation values.

These metric data were subjected to a discriminate function analysis using SPSS-X. The discriminate function indicates that the strongest discriminating factors are primarily width, and secondarily, thickness. Given that many of the blades, especially the sickles and sickle blanks, are probably fragmentary, width and thickness measurements would seem the most reliable indicators of inter-group differences. Though there is no obvious metric correlation to each specific blade type, there may be significant correlations between each technological blade class: blades, bladelets and prismatic blades. For instance, as seen in Table 11.12, mean widths for sickles, sickle blanks and retouched blades range from 11.2 mm to 13.1mm, whereas mean widths for bladelets, retouched bladelets and micro-endscrapers range from 8.5 mm to 9 mm. Mean width for prismatic blades, at 25.3 mm, is double that of the next highest mean blade widths, that for retouched blades. Likewise for mean thickness measurements, significant differences are apparent. Mean thickness measurements for sickles, sickle blanks and retouched blades are all over 4 mm, whereas mean thickness for bladelets is all less than 3 mm. Prismatic blades are again far larger than any other technological class, with a mean thickness of 9 mm. It is clear that a discriminate function analysis only confirms the obvious fact that prismatic blades are far larger than any other blade class.

This suggests that rather than treating each of these blade types separately, the next analytical procedure should focus on determining whether the two major technological blade classes (blade and bladelet) are significantly different solely on the basis of metric data. These blade classes were combined into only three classes: sickles, sickle blanks and retouched blades were grouped into

Group 1; retouched bladelets, bladelets and micro-endscrapers were grouped into Group 2; and prismatic blades were left as they were, Group 8. Another discriminate function was run and, as in the first discriminate run, Group 8 (prismatic blades) is distinguished very easily from the other blade classes. Group 1 (blades) and Group 2 (bladelets) are separated better than on the first run, but the centroids remain very close. Thus the question remains, is this difference statistically significant? As seen in Table 11.13, two-tailed t-tests confirm that on the basis of *both* thickness and width means, Group 1 (sickles, sickle blanks and retouched blades) and Group 2 (bladelets, retouched bladelets and micro-endscrapers) differ significantly below the .001 level.

Though the Gilat means differ slightly, these results are similar to those of Roshwalb (1981:23, and Fig. 3) who found that the width limit between retouched blades and retouched bladelets fell at 12 mm. The means for the Gilat assemblage differ, of course, because the means for sickles and sickle blanks are included in the Group 1 means. Excluding these means would only increase the distance between Group 1 and Group 2.

Bladelets, whether retouched or not, differ only slightly in their width means, an observation paralleled in Roshwalb's conclusions. In fact, mean widths for retouched bladelets and unmodified bladelets from Wadi Ghazzeh Site A and Gilat are almost identical. In conjunction with the different materials and restricted geographic range, this emphasizes that bladelets are a different tool and debitage category that should be treated separately in analyses.

The majority of the flint knapping techniques is probably either hard hammer or soft hammer. The exception to this are the prismatic blades, which were manufactured using a punch (Rosen 1983b), and the tabular scrapers, which used either a block-on-block technique or direct percussion for initial flake manufacture and subsequent retouch by direct percussion (Levy and Rosen 1987; Rosen 1989). There is little or no evidence for pressure flaking, and the bladelets may have been manufactured using soft hammer percussion (Ohnuma 1993).

Stratigraphic and Spatial Observations

Total frequencies of chipped stone tools and debitage are presented in Table 11.1a. Total collection of chipped stone and sieving of all pit and floor loci resulted in a large proportion of debitage, which constitutes 96.5% of the total chipped stone collected during the seasons of 1990–2 at Gilat. Of this debitage, over half (56.5%, Table 11.1b) is amorphous debris (chips and chunks), of little utility to analysis. Examination of the debitage reveals a predominantly flake manufacturing technology, similar to that previously noted at other Chalcolithic sites (Levy and Rosen 1987; Rowan 1990; Rosen 1989; Gilead *et al.* 1995). Excluding the debris counts, flakes comprise 85% of the debitage, with blades and bladelets comprising just over 5%, and the remainder cores and core fragments, proportions which closely resemble those of Shiqmim (Rowan 1990: Table 1).

Figure 11.7 compares the frequencies of tool assemblages from Shiqmim (Rowan 1990: Table 1), Grar (Gilead *et al.* 1995: Table 5.8) and Gilat. In order to compare these assemblages, some adjustments were necessary to compensate for the slightly different typologies used for Grar and that of Shiqmim and Gilat. For instance, micro-borers (the relative frequency of which is negligible or absent from each site) are treated as a separate category in the Gilat analysis, but are included with borers at Grar (*ibid.* 245). Further adjustments were necessary for choppers, which, though a separate type for the Gilat assemblage, are included under the category of 'miscellaneous trimmed pieces/varia', presumably where the Grar choppers are included (they are not mentioned as tools). The Grar analysis includes all sickle blanks in the sickle category; thus the same is done for the Gilat assemblage. Finally, burins and truncations are not separate tool categories for the Gilat assemblage, and thus the Grar burin and truncation counts are included with the miscellaneous trimmed pieces and varia category. Finally, limestone tools were included with the general chipped stone assemblage frequencies, but are treated separately at Grar, hence those frequencies from Gilat are not included for the present discussion and percentages were adjusted accordingly.

Comparison of these frequencies highlights a number of interesting contrasts. One of the most striking is the much higher frequency of retouched and utilized flakes, from both the Gilat and Shiqmim assemblages in contrast to Grar. This is probably a result of different perceptions of what constitutes a used or retouched flake, but the possibility that there is another explanation (such as the greater intensity, or duration, of occupation at Gilat and Shiqmim) cannot be ruled out. Though the area exposures of these sites are comparable, the absolute counts of tools from Shiqmim and Gilat are far higher.

The presence of blade and bladelet cores and core trimming elements from each type indicates that at least some of the blade tools (sickles and sickle blanks) and bladelet tools (micro-endscrapers) were manufactured on-site. However, examination of tool frequencies for Gilat provides some interesting contrasts to the Shiqmim assemblage. One of the most striking differences is the significant presence of micro-endscrapers at Gilat, whereas at Shiqmim, though bladelets are found, almost no micro-endscrapers have been found. At Shiqmim, modified bladelets are less than 1% of the tool assemblage; at Gilat, retouched bladelets and micro-endscrapers combined comprise over 8% of the total tool assemblage. This difference between Beersheva and Besor sites is supported by Rosen's compilation of data for the Chalcolithic northern Negev, where the low frequency of bladelet tools (Rosen 1987: Tab.11–1b) and bladelet debitage (Rosen 1987: Tabs. 11–3a, c) from the Beersheva site of Horvat Beter is similar to those of Shiqmim, a trend also observed by Gilead (1984:9). Bladelet cores and blade core trimming elements form about 0.5% of the debitage at Shiqmim, which suggests those few retouched bladelets found at Shiqmim may have been manufactured on-site. At Gilat, the presence of all stages of manufacture (primary flakes, core trimming elements, cores) indicates that the micro-endscrapers and retouched bladelets were certainly manufactured on-site. Whether or not this is a chronological, geographical or functional difference will require more data from other comparable Chalcolithic sites, however, given the multi-strata occupation of both sites, and the long duration of Shiqmim, some overlap in chronology seems possible. The function of this tool also remains to be determined. However, the existence of micro-endscrapers appears to be a component more of the 'Ghassulian facies' (Perrot 1992) than one of the Beersheva region, given their presence at the Mediterranean coastal sites, such as the Wadi Ghazzeh sites (Roshwalb 1981), northeastern Sinai sites and Qatif (Gilead1984), and even to the north (Nasrallah 1936). General metric attributes of the Gilat micro-endscrapers are also more similar to these sites, particularly that of Qatif (compare Table 11.12 with Gilead 1984: Table 1), as well as Tuleilat Ghassul. Recovery of similar forms in obsidian from Tuleilat Ghassul (Lee 1973: 261, LB9a), like at Gilat, seems to support this hypothesis, as do other realms of the material culture, such as basalt vessel forms, violin-shaped figurines and scant evidence for copper metallurgy. Micro-endscrapers are also a significant component of Predynastic Egyptian sites such as Maadi (Rizkana and Seeher 1988:27, Pl.33).

Another significant difference between these two sites is the far greater number of borer/perforators from the site of Gilat. While this is probably the result of functional differences, the nomenclature of 'borers' is a broadly defined category with great diversity of sub-types and sizes (see Table 11.7). These tools represent a diversity of tasks, from bead and pendant manufacture (for the smallest artifacts) to leather working, incising of organic materials, and perforation of ground stone rings. However, there is a large difference, seen in Figure 11.7, between the frequency of borers from Gilat as opposed to Shiqmim and Grar. It seems likely that this is the result of a far larger corpus of spindle whorls, 'loom weights', beads and pendants at Gilat than the other sites (see chapter on ground stone, this volume). The correlation of these suggests that many of these perforated artifacts were made at Gilat with the borer/perforators found on-site.

Sickles and sickle blanks also form a much higher proportion of the tool assemblage from Gilat (c. 14%) than from Shiqmim (6%), but much less than Grar (Gilead et al. 1995: Table 5.8). This suggests that agricultural production was clearly a major component of daily subsistence activity at

Gilat, and may have played a more central role in daily subsistence practices at the Nahal Grar and Nahal Patish sites than at the Chalcolithic Nahal Beersheva sites, such as Shiqmim. However, it is also possible that inhabitants of more arid regions such as Shiqmim might have torn grasses out by the roots, a practice which is still preferred by Bedouin groups such as the Bedul (Simms and Russell 1997) and others (Kislev 1987). Alternatively, these more southerly sites might have exploited a greater diversity of resources rather than primarily agriculture. The higher proportion of sickles at Gilat compared to Shiqmim is confirmed by analysis of chipped stone tools from Grar (Gilead 1989:108) when compared to the Nahal Beersheva sites. At both Shiqmim and Gilat, only a very few blade cores were discovered (less than 0.05% of debitage assemblage for each site), which suggests that given the large number of sickles, sickle blanks and retouched blades recovered at both sites, most were manufactured off-site. Despite the blade cache discovered at Gilat (see discussion below), the presence of blade cores and blade core trimming elements in terms of relative frequency to the overall assemblage is not significantly different than that of Shiqmim. This is in marked contrast to Wadi Gaza Site A, where hundreds of blades, bladelets and cores from blade and bladelet production were found (Roshwalb 1981), suggesting a specialized production site (Rosen 1987).

Finally, the comparison of assemblages in this manner can be deceiving. The larger frequency of retouched flakes at Gilat 'mutes' the perceived frequency of other categories, such as borers and sickles, which, if the retouched flake category were equal to that of Grar, would increase the perceived frequency of borers, sickles and other types.

Intra-Site Variation

One of the remarkable discoveries of the 1991 season at Gilat was the excavation of a stratum 2A pit (L.1029) with a high density of blade components, including all stages of manufacture, (blades, sickles, sickle blanks and blade cores). This cache included 32 retouched blades (20% of all retouched blades); 281 unmodified blades (11.7% of all blades); 8 blade cores (22.9% of all blade cores); and 140 sickles and sickle blanks (24% of all sickles and sickle blanks). It seems that this 'cache' represents some form of specialized manufacture because all stages of blade production are represented, suggesting the remains of a workshop or storage area of craftsperson.

Tables 11.14 and 11.15 summarize the chipped stone assemblage by stratum designations. Although Stratum 1 is very disturbed and a rich assemblage of Chalcolithic flint tools and debitage were collected, there are no significant features on which to base spatial interpretations. Clearly, the major proportion of tools and debitage are found in the Strata IIA, IIB, and IIC (72.5% of all debitage is found in Stratum II; 65% of the tools were found in Stratum II), where the majority of architectural and cultural debris were exposed as well. Stratum 3 and its sub-phases were of a more limited exposure, with few surfaces, and only one room (Room #7, Stratum IIIA) associated with these phases. Only 5.6% of the total debitage were recovered from surfaces and floors; 5.2% of the total tools were recovered from floors and surfaces. In contrast, 55.3% of the debitage was recovered from pits, and an additional 23.7% was recovered from fills. A similar pattern for the tools is evident; with 41% of the tools recovered from within pits, and an additional 29.7 % from fills (a greater proportion of tools were recovered from topsoil than debitage, probably a combination of the larger size of tools, as well as selectivity on the part of excavators).

Given the limited number of surfaces and rooms on which to base interpretations, it is difficult to provide spatial analyses based on the tools and debitage (Tables 11.16–18). However, both site formation processes and behavioral patterns produced the predominant pattern of clean floors and high densities of tools and debitage in pits. It seems likely that room floors and perhaps even surfaces were periodically cleaned, with the refuse deposited in the pits. Clearly, the vast majority of lithic tools and debitage from Gilat, recovered from pits, fills and topsoil, are of limited utility to understanding activity areas related to lithic production, use and discard. Artifacts recovered from these contexts, and many found near floors and surfaces, are derived from secondary contexts unrelated to these patterns of production, use and discard. However, given the lack of *in-situ* lithic artifacts found on room floors, we may posit that at least some of this pattern is the result of human activity and not just the impact of site formation processes. This is not surprising because we would not expect flint knapping to occur inside of the rooms.

An interesting contrast is evident when compared with lithic density patterns from other sites. Studying the lithic assemblage distributions of Early Bronze desert sites (Biqat Uvda 16, Har Horsha, Nahal Mitnan), Rosen (1997) shows a trend for higher lithic densities in rooms, as opposed to courtyards. He suggests this may be the result, in part, of lithic production in the rooms, and notes that a similar distribution is evident in the much more intensively occupied site of Shiqmim. Unfortunately, though there are open, surfaced areas at Gilat, these plazas appear to be fundamentally different to those from Shiqmim or the EB sites. Without the boundaries created by courtyard walls and adjacent areas (i.e. rooms), it is difficult to compare the lithic densities with other spatially bound areas. Though our provenience units are generally too imprecise to isolate clusters of tools and waste, field observations generally support that this 'clean' nature of the Gilat room floors is accurate. However, the negative evidence precludes in-depth functional analyses based on the lithic assemblages.

Unfortunately, the pitted areas and constant cleaning, re-surfacing and re-building with mud-brick architecture constrain the potential of spatial analyses in the search for discrete activity areas. This does, however, represent the reflection of behavioral patterns in itself, and cleaning of rooms and surfaces may be typical of domestic Chalcolithic sites; the infrequent recovery of spatially discrete living surfaces such as that of Room #6 at Shiqmim (Levy and Holl 1987) may be the result of actual behavioral activity, as well as site formation processes, as much as it is the result of archaeological excavation techniques.

Conclusions

The overall chipped stone industry from Gilat represents a very diverse and large assemblage (N=118,882 pieces), with an array of tool types atypical thus far in the published literature from southern Levantine Chalcolithic sites. Just how unique this assemblage is remains difficult to judge, given the limited results published from other large Chalcolithic sites. Although aspects of the assemblage are typical of Chalcolithic domestic sites (e.g. predominance of flake production, presence of sickles, tabular scrapers and core tools), others are uncommon, such as the presence of prismatic blades and micro-borers, and the high frequency of borers and perforators. The presence of micro-endscrapers and other retouched bladelets, limestone tools, and the higher frequency of sickles, suggests a commonality between Gilat, the Wadi Gaza sites and Grar. This distinguishes them from lithic assemblages found at the Beersheva sites, a distinction recognized first recognized by analyses of the Grar collections (Gilead *et al.* 1995). However, it remains possible that these distinctions are not only regional, but also reflective of chronological changes in tool assemblages.

An additional problem is the poor state of knowledge concerning Late Neolithic flint assemblages in contrast to those from the Chalcolithic. This is particularly true of the Wadi Rabah/Qatifian phases, which are typified by amorphic cores and predominantly flake production. While arrowheads and denticulated sickle blades are features of Yarmukian lithic assemblages, these features virtually disappear by the end of the Late Neolithic in the Wadi Rabah phase (Gopher 1995:211). In a similar manner, pressure flaking and flat retouch are rare by Late Neolithic phases such as Wadi Rabah, attributes that are virtually absent from Chalcolithic lithic industries as well. Other aspects of Wadi Rabah and Chalcolithic lithic assemblages are also interchangeable. For instance, Roshwalb (1981) discovered no clear sub-types of celts between the Late Neolithic and Chalcolithic periods.

Nevertheless, there are a few indicators of possible Wadi Rabah elements in the lithic assemblage from Gilat. Bladelets are known from late Neolithic phases, such as the Qatifian (Gilead 1990), but are of limited distribution during the Chalcolithic. As discussed above, bladelet tools, in particular micro-endscrapers, are primarily found in the so-called 'Besorian' cluster of sites, including Gilat, Grar, Tuleilat Ghassul and the Wadi Gaza sites (Gilead 1984; Roshwalb 1981). The Beersheva sites such as Shiqmim, Bir es-Safadi, Abu Matar and Horvat Beter show far lower relative frequencies (Gilead *et al.* 1995: Fig. 5.34; Levy and Rosen 1987; Rosen 1987; Rowan 1990). This trend is also clear for microlithic tools. While there is clearly a distinction between these regions—the Besorian vs. the Beersheva—it is unclear if these are sub-cultural/regional distinctions or if they also have chronological significance. However, in light of other evidence supporting a chronological differentiation (i.e. presence/absence of copper), this is probably an additional important distinguishing factor.

Obsidian is present at Gilat (Yellin, Levy and Rowan 1996), one of the only material remains suggestive of trade contacts during the Wadi Rabah (Gopher 1995:218), but is extremely rare at other Levantine Chalcolithic sites. This also hints at an early Chalcolithic date, or Wadi Rabah phase occupation, for the earliest levels at Gilat. One published exception is a single obsidian bladelet from Tuleilat Ghassul (Lee 1973:261, LB9a), where late Neolithic levels are also attested (Bourke 1997). Whatever the chronological interpretation, the presence of this local tool type, made of an exotic material from very distant sources, once again underscores the long-distance ties exemplified at Gilat (see Chapter 12 for other examples).

Finally, the presence of two bifacial knife fragments is also unusual for the standard Chalcolithic lithic repertoire. Although the flint of these two fragments is not clearly non-local, they may be related to Egyptian types and they are otherwise unlike the 'tabular' scrapers in material, form or retouch. Similar artifacts do not appear in other published Chalcolithic assemblages, but it remains possible that their presence at Gilat is a reflection of sporadic Egyptian contacts and not necessarily chronological.

In fact, the richness of the lithic assemblage may even obscure some notable aspects hinting at important social ramifications. One such aspect may be the tabular scraper, which at an intuitive level seems far more numerous than from other Chalcolithic sites. While tabular scrapers are only 2.7% of the total chipped stone tool assemblage at Gilat (a notably higher frequency in contrast to Grar and Shiqmim, see Figure 11.37), this low frequency represents a large number (n=108) relative to the size of the excavation area, suggesting some greater importance. For instance, the excavated area from the 1990–2 excavations at Gilat is estimated at about 1200 m². In contrast, the excavated area from Shiqmim is estimated at about 4500 m², nearly four times that of Gilat. Nevertheless, the tabular scraper count at Gilat is two and a half times that of Shiqmim. Although this contrast between Gilat and Shiqmim is true of some other tool types as well (e.g. borers, sickles, micro-endscrapers and retouched bladelets) it is not true of all tool types. We can only speculate about the possible function(s) of tabular scrapers, but whatever their purpose, this large disparity supports a potentially important distinction between Gilat and other sites. Closer proximity to sources of the flint material would seem a logical explanation, but if this were true, we would expect to see a similar occurrence at the nearby site of Grar. The opposite is true of Grar however: only seven (c. 1 % of the total flint tool assemblage) tabular scrapers were found there (Gilead *et al.* 1995: Table 5.8), despite a roughly similar area of excavation.[4]

Based on the chipped stone assemblage, affinities are strongest to those from sites such as Tuleilat Ghassul, Grar and the Wadi Gaza sites. Given the poor contextual documentation and selective collection for assemblages from the older excavations at Tuleilat Ghassul and the Wadi Gaza sites, only Grar remains as a comparative assemblage. Major differences between assemblages from Gilat and Grar suggest very different activities at the respective sites. For example, the number of notched pieces and sickles found at Grar comprise 44% of the total assemblage. In contrast, at

Gilat these two tool types comprise only about 15% of the total tool assemblage, despite the much higher frequency of sickles from Gilat in comparison to Shiqmim. Thus, although Gilat exhibits some closer affinities to the 'Besorian' sites, there are nevertheless critical differences between Gilat and our limited knowledge of Besorian assemblages. The substantially higher relative and absolute number of tabular scrapers at Gilat was previously discussed. The presence of large prismatic blades made from non-local material is notable not only for their rarity, but also for possible connections to Predynastic Egyptian sites, particularly Maadi (Rizkana and Seeher 1988).

While some differences, such as high frequencies of sickle blades, micro-endscrapers and borer/perforators probably reflect particularly important functional activities at Gilat, other types are less clearly functional. Tool types such as prismatic blades, tabular scrapers, and the two bifacial tool fragments suggest tools that do not seem primarily functional. Thus, the flint assemblage from Gilat supports a number of overlapping features. A domestic assemblage, like most other Chalcolithic sites, is evident in the large number of retouched flakes and other expedient tools. At the same time, specialized activities are more prominent than at other contemporaneous sites, indicated most strongly by the large number of borers/perforators. Although borers, perforators and awls were used for a variety of tasks, these probably functioned in part to create the large variety of bored stone artifacts found at the site, including beads, pendants, spindle whorls, mace heads, as well as the other drilled objects of unknown function. Flint tool borers, perforators and awls formed an important component of specialized activities carried out at the site. It is probable that these tools were also used on other materials less likely to preserve well, such as wood and leather. Those specialized activities may relate to exchange activities at the site as well. The cache of blades and blade cores previously discussed may also relate to similar specialized activities and exchanges occurring at the site.

Finally, other artifact types made from non-local flint, such as the prismatic blades and tabular scrapers, may be important tools beyond a solely functional level. While perhaps still a hypothesis awaiting further comparative data from other contemporaneous sites, the flint assemblage apparently reflects the domestic realm, a specialized production realm which may be connected to exchange activities carried on with populations from different sub-regions, as well as a specialized/symbolic realm. The symbolic value of certain flint tools will probably remain difficult to test, but comparative analyses will first necessitate publication of other large assemblages from contemporaneous sites.

Acknowledgments

Much of the analysis for this research was conducted while a Fellner Research Scholar at the Hebrew Union College-Nelson Glueck School of Biblical Archaeology (NGSBA, Jerusalem). Thanks to Tom Levy for discussions concerning the chipped stone industry and for his financial and logistical support, for which I would like to express my sincere appreciation. In addition, I would like to thank Professor A. Biran, Hanni Hirsh and the staff of NGSBA for providing the logistical support and collegial atmosphere while conducting research at their institute. Preliminary sorting of debitage was conducted by Alison Jones-Nassar, without which this analysis would have been much more difficult. I would like to take this opportunity to thank Steven Rosen, from whom guidance and debate has encouraged my lithic studies over the years. Additional insights and discussions with David Ilan, Morag Kersel and Tamar Noy greatly improved this paper. Steven Rosen and Thomas Hester read earlier drafts of this paper, which benefited from their comments. The final result is of course my responsibility. Special thanks to Catherine Commenge for her support and Daniel Ladiray of the CNRS in Jerusalem for drawing the majority of the illustrations used here. Thanks also to Leonid from the IAA for his drawings.

Notes

1. The majority of the Gilat lithic collections are stored at the Israel Antiquities Authority in Jerusalem. Smaller samples are at the Hebrew Union College, Jerusalem.

2. Recent research in the Jabal Hamrat Fidan region (Faynan district) of southern Jordan by Levy's UCSD team identified one flint quarry for tabular scrapers (Levy, personal communication).

3. These illustrations were previously published (Rowan and Levy 1994), but are reproduced here with the scale omitted in the previous publication.

4. Grar is considered six different sub-sites, with a combined excavated area of 1200 sqm (Gilead 195: Table 3.1). The greater depth of most excavated areas of Gilat suggests either a longer occupational history, or less plowing disturbance, than at Grar. It is clear that Grar suffered the same cultural formation processes as Gilat (see Chapter 5, this volume, for discussion of site formation processes).

Tables

Debris & Debitage	n=	%	Tools	n=	%
Chips	26,914	23.40	Notch	50	1.20
Chunks	35,589	31.10	Borer/Awls	385	9.30
Primary flakes	7,903	6.90	Denticulates	26	0.60
Flakes	36,515	31.80	Sidescrapers	29	0.70
Blades	2,403	2.10	Scrapers	183	4.40
Bladelets	298	0.26	Tabular scrapers	39	1.00
Flake cores	1,935	1.70	Tabular scraper frags.	69	1.70
Blade cores	35	0.03	Sickles	389	9.40
Bladelet cores	60	0.05	Sickle blanks	192	4.70
Flake core frags.	1,372	1.20	Celts	133	3.20
Blade core frags.	195	0.17	Choppers	61	1.50
Bladelet core frags.	1,439	1.20	Retouched flakes	1,459	35.30
Mixed cores	96	0.08	Retouched blades	159	4.00
			Retouched bladelets	108	2.60
			Micro-endscrapers	237	5.70
			Miscellaneous trimmed pieces	377	9.10
			Prismatic blades	18	0.40
			Limestone tools	193	4.70
			Micro-borers	21	0.50
TOTALS	114,754	100.0	TOTALS	4,128	100.0

Table 11.1a. Gilat 1990–92, total lithic tool and debitage frequencies from all areas and strata.

Category	n=	%
Primary flakes	7,903	15.13
Flakes	36,515	69.88
Blades	2,403	4.60
Bladelets	298	0.57
Core-trimming elements	3006	5.75
Cores	2126	4.07
Subtotal (Debitage)	52,251	100.0
Chips	26,914	43.06
Chunks	35,589	56.94
Subtotal (Debris)	62,503	100.0
Debitage	52,251	43.95
Debris	62,503	52.58
Tools	4,128	3.47
TOTAL	118,882	100.0

Table 11.1b. Summarized frequencies of major flint categories, Gilat 1990–92.

	Sickles	(n=385)	Sickle blanks	(n=184)
	n=	%	n=	%
Cross-Section				
Trapezoidal	267	69.4	125	68.0
Triangular	74	19.2	47	25.5
Both (trap-tri)	44	11.4	12	6.5
totals	385	100.0	184	100.0
Outline				
Trapezoidal	291	75.6	149	81.0
Triangular	24	6.2	10	5.4
Irregular	69	17.9	25	13.6
Lunate	1	0.3	0	--
totals	385	100.0	184	100.0
Backing				
Dorsal	366	95.0	177	96.2
Ventral	8	2.1	6	3.3
None	6	1.6	0	--
Natural (cortex)	1	1.3	1	0.5
totals	385	100.0	184	100.0
Edge retouch				
Serrated	47	12.2	1	0.5
Ventral	8	2.1	3	1.6
Dorsal	6	1.6	0	--
None	324	84.1	180	97.8
totals	385	100.0	184	99.9
Truncation Type				
1) Dorsal truncation/snap	168	43.6	69	37.5
2) Ventral truncation/snap	22	5.7	4	2.2
3) Double dorsal truncation	56	14.5	18	9.8
4) Double snap	104	27.0	65	35.3
5) Double ventral truncation	3	0.8	1	0.5
6) Unmodified/snap	11	2.9	13	7.1
7) Dorsal truncation/butt	13	3.4	11	6.0
8) Dorsal & ventral truncation	8	2.1	3	1.6
totals	385	100.0	184	100.0

	Average Dimensions (mm)					
	Sickles			Sickle blanks		
Truncation type	Length	Width	Thickness	Length	Width	Thickness
1) Dorsal truncation/snap	29.3	10.8	4.2	25.0	11.2	4.1
2) Ventral truncation/snap	33.4	12.4	4.6	31.1	12.1	3.9
3) Double dorsal truncation	42.5	12.2	4.9	36.3	12.7	5.5
4) Double snap	24.3	10.1	3.8	23.8	10.4	3.8
5) Double ventral truncation	40.5	13.2	5.2	35.0	12.5	5.0
6) Unmodified/snap	43.8	20.6	4.8	29.1	11.7	4.0
7) Dorsal truncation/butt	40.7	11.6	4.6	33.3	10.8	6.6
8) Dorsal & ventral truncation	38.2	13.8	4.9	39.8	13.5	4.5

Table 11.2. Sickle and sickle blank attribute frequencies and mean dimensions.

	Axes	Adzes	Chisels	Unknowns
Cross Sections				
Trapezoidal/rectangular	14	4	9	3
Diamond	4	0	0	0
Convex	1	10	2	3
Bi-Convex	18	3	2	2
Triangular	2	0	0	0
totals	39	17	13	8
Outline				
Rectangular	3	2	2	1
Trapezoidal	22	9	1	2
Triangular	12	2	0	1
Irregular	2	1	4	4
Elongate	0	3	6	0
totals	39	17	13	8
Average Dimensions (mm):				
Length	88.5	81.5	77.6	65.8
Width	35.3	34.3	25.0	27.7
Thickness	22.3	21.4	17.7	16.6
# with polish	32	5	12	3
Mean edge angle	68	61	58	--

Table 11.3. Celt types and mean dimensions.

	Complete	Incomplete
Retouch location		
Distal-unilateral	1	3
Distal-bilateral	4	2
Circumferential	20	6
Dorsal and ventral	3	0
Bifacial	1	0
Distal only	1	0
total	30	11
Shape		
Oval	14	2
Irregular	6	6
Rectangular	1	1
Lunate	2	0
Fan	3	1
Elongate	3	0
Bi-convex	1	1
total	30	11
Dorsal aspect		
Cortex covered	19	9
Partial cortex	3	1
No cortex	8	1
total	30	11
Ventral aspect		
Bulb present	4	1
Bulbar thinning	12	2
No bulb	14	8
total	30	11

	Average Dimensions					
	Complete			Incomplete		
	Length	*Width*	*Thickness*	*Length*	*Width*	*Thickness*
Oval	63.2	70.8	11.2	n.a.	76.0	10.0
Irregular	63.7	64.5	11.7	52.0	44.0	6.5
Lunate	61.5	56.5	10.8	n.a.	n.a.	n.a.
Fan	42.7	76.0	6.3	n.a.	n.a.	n.a.
Elongate	89.0	38.7	11.2	n.a.	n.a.	n.a.

Table 11.4. Tabular scraper attributes and mean dimensions.

	with bulb	without bulb
Cross-section		
Trapezoidal	83	42
Triangular	53	29
Both	19	8
Totals	158	79
Retouch		
Distal only	34	16
Distal and unilateral	106	57
Distal and half unilateral	17	5
Distal-ventral	1	1
Totals	158	79
Average dimensions (mm)		
Length	30	23.3
Width	9.2	8.7
Thickness	2.7	2.7

Table 11.5. Micro-endscraper attributes and mean dimensions.

Blade attributes	n=	%
Cross-Section		
Trapezoidal	82	51.6
Triangular	39	24.5
Both (trap-tri)	38	23.9
totals	159	100.0
Outline		
Trapezoidal	34	21.4
Triangular	14	8.8
Irregular	111	69.8
totals	159	100.0
Backing		
Dorsal	70	44
Ventral	5	3.2
None	77	48.4
Natural (cortex)	7	4.4
totals	159	100.0
Edge retouch		
Serrated	5	3.1
Ventral	9	5.7
Dorsal	45	28.3
None	82	51.6
Bilateral-dorsal	15	9.4
Bilateral-ventral	3	1.9
totals	159	100.0
Truncation Type		
1) Dorsal truncation/snap	16	10.1
2) Ventral truncation/snap	1	0.6
3) Double dorsal truncation	0	-
4) Double snap	69	43.4
5) Double ventral truncation	0	-
6) Unmodified/snap	3	1.9
7) Dorsal truncation/butt	56	35.2
8) Dorsal & ventral truncation	0	-
9) No truncation	14	8.8
totals	159	100.0

Truncation Type	Average Dimensions (mm)		
	Length	Width	Thickness
1) Dorsal truncation/snap	31.1	14.1	5.1
2) Double snap	30.8	12.6	4.7
6) Unmodified/snap	22.0	10.0	2.8
7) Dorsal truncation/butt	41.1	15.1	5.4
9) No truncation	41.9	15.4	5.2

Table 11.6. Retouched blades and blade fragments, attributes and mean dimensions.

	Primary flakes	Flakes	Blades	Chunks	Others	Sub-totals
Retouch						
Bilateral-dorsal	14	151	17	33	21	236
Inverse-alternate	0	36	4	5	3	48
Unilateral-dorsal	0	12	1	5	4	22
Bilateral-ventral	0	6	0	3	1	10
Unilateral-ventral	0	2	1	0	0	3
totals	14	207	23	46	29	319
Point location						
Distal	11	126	6	3	2	148
Proximal	0	18	0	0	1	19
Lateral	2	33	0	1	0	36
No I.D.	1	30	17	42	26	116
totals	14	207	23	46	29	319
Average Point Length (mm)	20.9	14.2	39.9	15.9	20.1	

Table 11.7. Borer and perforator attributes and mean point lengths.

	Primary flakes	Flakes	Blades	Others	Sub-totals	Average Edge Angle
Retouch Location						
Distal only	18	29	0	4	51	71
Distal and unilateral	23	31	1	5	60	69
Distal and bilateral	18	28	0	3	49	69
Circumferential	9	5	0	2	16	72
Other	2	1	0	4	7	74
totals	70	94	1	18	183	70
Shape						
Oval	37	26	0	3	66	69
Irregular	21	35	0	10	66	71
Simple	1	24	0	0	25	68
Trapezoidal	4	4	0	2	10	68
Round	5	3	0	1	9	74
Elongate	0	1	0	1	2	72
Lunate	2	1	0	1	4	69
Triangular	0	0	1	0	1	-
totals	70	94	1	18	183	70
Polished	1	3	1	0	5	

Table 11.8. Scraper attributes and edge angles.

Retouch location	n=	%	%
Primary flakes			
Distal or unilateral			
dorsal retouch	99	6.8	
Ventral retouch	12	0.8	
Sub-total	111	7.6	7.6
Secondary flakes			
Distal or unilateral			
dorsal retouch	923	63.3	
Ventral retouch	87	6	
Bilateral-dorsal	17	1.2	
Alternating inverse	10	0.7	
Bilateral-ventral	1	-	
Proximal-dorsal	1	-	
Sub-total	1039	71.2	71.2
Tertiary flakes			
Distal or unilateral			
dorsal retouch	284	19.5	
Ventral retouch	17	1.2	
Bilateral-dorsal	6	0.4	
Bilateral-ventral	2	0.1	
Sub-total	309	21.2	21.2
GRAND TOTAL	1459	100.0	100.0

Table 11.9. Retouched flake frequencies and retouch location.

Miscellaneous pieces and varia	n=	%
Retouched or utilized chunks:		
Single edge retouch	181	48.0
Double edge retouch	11	2.9
Bifacial edge retouch	4	1.1
sub-total	196	52.0
Retouched or utilized core fragments:		
blade core fragments	20	5.3
flake core fragments	33	8.8
bladelet core fragments	37	9.8
sub-total	90	23.9
Varia and others:		
Denticulated scrapers	5	1.3
Double borers	11	2.9
Scraper edge fragments?	25	6.6
Multiple borers	2	0.5
Denticulated borer	3	0.8
Bifaces	2	0.5
Celt fragments?	7	1.9
Borer fragments?	6	1.6
Uniface	1	0.3
Borer on celt fragment	1	0.3
Retouched flake with notch	1	0.3
Scraper with borer	5	1.3
Notch with borer	2	0.5
Knives	3	0.8
Scraper with notch	1	0.3
Retouched cobbles	16	4.2
sub-total	91	24.1
Grand Total	377	100.0

Table 11.10. Miscellaneous trimmed pieces and varia.

Limestone tool type	n=	%
Scrapers	66	34.2
Sidescrapers	11	5.7
Denticulates	2	1.0
Notchs	2	1.0
Borers	2	1.0
Celts	1	0.5
Subtotal	84	43.4
Misc. trim. pieces		
Retouched chunks	19	9.9
Retouched cobbles	7	3.6
Retouched core frags.	5	2.6
Scraper edge frag.	1	0.5
Subtotal	32	16.6
Retouched flakes		
Dorsal retouch	59	30.6
Ventral retouch	12	6.2
Distal & bilateral dorsal retouch	3	1.6
Distal & bilateral ventral retouch	2	1.0
Inverse alternate	1	0.5
Subtotal	77	39.9
Grand Total	193	99.9

Table 11.11. Frequencies of chipped limestone tools.

Blade Type	n=	Length (mm)		Width (mm)		Thickness (mm)	
		Mean	S.D.	Mean	S.D.	Mean	S.D.
Sickles	204	33.1	10.7	11.4	2.0	4.4	1.2
Sickle blanks	113	30.0	8.7	11.2	2.2	4.3	1.7
Retouched blades	61	36.0	13.5	13.1	3.8	4.9	1.7
Retouched bladelets	45	23.4	7.2	8.5	2.1	2.6	0.8
Micro-endscrapers	131	28.2	7.5	9.0	1.8	2.8	0.9
Blades	10	48.8	19.0	15.8	5.3	6.6	2.4
Bladelets	147	25.6	6.4	8.8	1.7	2.9	1.0
Prismatic blades	9	65.3	25.1	25.3	3.9	9.0	1.3

Table 11.12. Metric data and standard deviations for blades (1990–91)
used for discriminant function and t-tests.

Variable	# of Cases	Mean	STD	Standard Error	F Value	2-tail Prob.
Width						
Group 1	378	11.6	2.55	.131	1.96	.000
Group 2	323	8.8	1.82	.101		
Thickness						
Group 1	378	4.47	1.47	.076	2.53	.000
Group 2	323	2.82	.93	.052		

Table 11.13. Results of two-tailed t-tests for Group 1 (blades)
and Group 2 (bladelets) types, from 1990–91 excavations.

Strata		Chip	Chunk	Prim. flake	Flake	Blade	Bladelet	Flake cores	Blade cores	Bladelet core	Flake core fg	Blade core fg	Bladelet core fg	Mixed core	Totals	%	Core wts.(kg)	Debitage wts.(kg)
I	n=	891	4382	1351	4717	276	27	387	6	13	222	40	124	21	12457	10.91	49.21	257.473
	%	7.15	35.18	10.84	37.87	2.22	0.22	3.11	0.05	0.1	1.78	0.32	0.99	0.17	100.0			
IIA	n=	7406	8912	1992	9487	777	68	385	14	11	327	70	327	26	29802	26.09	48.74	294.26
	%	24.85	29.9	6.68	31.83	2.61	0.23	1.29	0.05	0.04	1.1	0.23	1.1	0.09	100.0			
IIB	n=	5891	8934	1763	8677	564	60	430	8	8	323	31	281	10	26980	23.62	47.92	246.189
	%	21.83	33.11	6.53	32.16	2.09	0.22	1.59	0.03	0.03	1.2	0.12	1.04	0.04	99.99			
IIC	n=	7631	7502	1554	7773	421	47	408	3	6	304	29	265	21	25964	22.73	40.9	231.555
	%	29.39	28.89	5.99	29.94	1.62	0.18	1.57	0.01	0.02	1.17	0.11	1.02	0.08	99.99			
IIIA	n=	3809	4391	891	4250	249	74	213	2	22	136	22	378	9	14446	12.65	23.555	141.043
	%	26.37	30.4	6.17	29.42	1.72	0.51	1.47	0.01	0.15	0.94	0.15	2.62	0.06	99.99			
IIIB	n=	915	1013	229	1059	74	12	71	2	0	46	2	49	2	3474	3.04	7.255	32.385
	%	26.34	29.16	6.59	30.48	2.13	0.35	2.04	0.06		1.32	0.06	1.41	0.06	100.0			
IIIC/IV	n=	232	321	78	365	31	5	27	0	0	9	1	11	6	1086	0.95	3.265	14.36
	%	21.36	29.56	7.18	33.61	2.86	0.46	2.49			0.83	0.09	1.01	0.55	100.0			
totals		26775	35455	7858	36328	2392	293	1921	35	60	1367	195	1435	95	114,209	99.99	220.85	1217.27

Table 11.14. Debitage frequencies by stratum.

Strata		Notch	Borer	Dentic	Side-scrap	Scrap.	Tab. scrap.	Tab. scrp./g	Sick.	Sickle blank	Celt	Chop.	Ret. flake	Ret. blade	Ret. bidlet	Micro-end.	MTP-varia	Prism. blade	Lime-stone	Micro-borer	Tool totals	%
I	n=	17	76	1	8	52	11	20	40	10	21	19	387	19	12	16	66	2	28	1	806	19.75
	%	2.11	9.43	0.12	0.99	6.45	1.36	2.48	4.96	1.24	2.61	2.36	48.01	2.36	1.49	1.99	8.19	0.25	3.47	0.12	99.99	
IIA	n=	12	69	5	5	46	13	16	116	134	38	10	268	57	27	53	80	6	58	4	1017	24.92
	%	1.18	6.78	0.49	0.49	4.52	1.28	1.57	11.41	13.18	3.74	0.98	26.35	5.61	2.65	5.21	7.87	0.59	5.7	0.39	99.99	
IIB	n=	8	94	10	7	31	6	14	87	17	30	14	314	37	30	60	87	4	43	3	896	21.96
	%	0.89	10.49	1.12	0.78	3.46	0.67	1.56	9.71	1.9	3.35	1.56	35.04	4.13	3.35	6.7	9.71	0.45	4.8	0.33	100	
IIC	n=	7	87	5	4	30	5	11	73	14	28	7	268	21	14	55	77	4	39	4	753	18.45
	%	0.93	11.55	0.66	0.53	3.98	0.66	1.46	9.7	1.86	3.72	0.93	35.59	2.79	1.86	7.3	10.23	0.53	5.18	0.53	99.99	
IIIA	n=	6	47	5	4	16	3	6	58	14	10	3	149	23	15	39	42	1	18	4	463	11.34
	%	1.3	10.15	1.08	0.86	3.45	0.65	1.3	12.53	3.02	2.16	0.65	32.18	4.97	3.24	8.42	9.07	0.22	3.89	0.86	100	
IIIB	n=	0	2	0	0	5	0	0	10	0	1	5	46	1	5	6	7	0	6	3	97	2.38
	%		2.06			5.15			10.31		1.03	5.15	47.42	1.03	5.15	6.19	7.22		6.19	3.09	99.99	
IIIC/IV	n=	0	6	0	1	2	0	0	2	2	2	1	15	0	4	3	9	0	1	1	49	1.2
	%		12.25		2.04	4.08			4.08	4.08	4.08	2.04	30.61		8.16	6.12	18.37		2.04	2.04	99.99	
Total		50	381	26	29	182	38	67	386	191	130	59	1447	158	107	232	368	17	193	20	4081	100

Table 11.15. Tool frequencies by stratum.

Loci Type		Chips	Chunk	Prim. flake	Flake	Blade	Bladelet	Flake cores	Blade cores	Bladelet cores	Flake core fg	Blade core fg	Bladelet core fg	Mixed core	Totals	%	Core wt. (kg)	Deb. wt. (kg)
1	n=	732	3935	1213	4221	232	25	362	6	12	207	39	109	21	11114	9.68	47.65	237.42
	%	6.59	35.41	10.91	37.98	2.09	0.22	3.26	0.05	0.11	1.86	0.35	0.98	0.19	100.0			
2	n=	4521	8724	2266	9589	581	69	650	8	18	421	49	312	32	27240	23.74	77.04	387.18
	%	16.6	32.03	8.32	35.2	2.13	0.25	2.39	0.03	0.07	1.54	0.18	1.14	0.12	100.0			
3	n=	422	416	87	435	15	3	17	0	0	10	1	16	1	1423	1.24	2.68	11.81
	%	29.66	29.23	6.11	30.57	1.05	0.21	1.2			0.7	0.07	1.12	0.07	99.99			
4	n=	19014	18751	3523	18402	1292	167	671	20	24	578	87	853	30	63412	55.26	71.47	467.19
	%	29.98	29.57	5.55	29.02	2.04	0.26	1.06	0.03	0.04	0.91	0.14	1.35	0.05	100.0			
5	n=	426	907	232	1128	120	6	96	0	4	51	4	44	3	3021	2.63	8.97	38.21
	%	14.1	30.02	7.68	37.34	3.97	0.2	3.18		0.13	1.69	0.13	1.46	0.1	100.0			
6	n=	679	394	89	355	16	3	15	0	0	9	0	16	4	1580	1.38	1.72	9.511
	%	42.98	24.94	5.63	22.47	1.01	0.19	0.95			0.57		1.01	0.25	100.0			
7	n=	985	2328	448	2202	136	20	110	1	2	91	15	85	4	6427	5.6	11.3	65.94
	%	15.33	36.22	6.97	34.26	2.12	0.31	1.71	0.02	0.03	1.42	0.23	1.32	0.06	100.0			
No loci	n=	135	134	45	183	11	5	14	0	0	5	0	4	1	537	0.47	1.63	3.77
	%	25.14	24.95	8.38	34.08	2.05	0.93	2.61			0.93		0.74	0.19	100.0			
Total		26914	35589	7903	36515	2403	298	1935	35	60	1372	195	1439	96	114,754	100.0	222.48	1221.05

Table 11.16. Debitage frequencies by contextual (loci) types.

Table 11.17. Tool frequencies by contextual (loci) types.

Loci Type		Notch	Borer	Dentic	Side-scrap	Scrap.	Tab. scrap.	Tab. scrp.fg	Sick.	Sickle blank	Celt	Chop.	Ret. flake	Ret. blade	Ret. bl.let	Micro-end.	MTP-varia	Prism blade	Lime-stone	Micro-borer	Tool totals	%
1	n=	16	69	1	5	46	10	19	35	8	19	18	358	16	11	15	62	2	28	1	739	17.9
	%	2.17	9.34	0.13	0.68	6.22	1.35	2.57	4.74	1.08	2.57	2.44	48.44	2.17	1.49	2.03	8.39	0.27	3.79	0.13	100.0	
2	n=	16	127	11	10	67	11	21	106	21	60	20	470	35	23	46	106	6	65	3	1224	29.65
	%	1.31	10.38	0.9	0.82	5.47	0.9	1.71	8.66	1.71	4.9	1.63	38.4	2.86	1.88	3.76	8.66	0.49	5.31	0.25	100.0	
3	n=	0	5	0	0	0	0	1	5	1	2	0	18	1	1	6	4	0	4	0	48	1.16
	%		10.42					2.08	10.42	2.08	4.17		37.5	2.08	2.08	12.5	8.33		8.33		99.99	
4	n=	11	144	9	12	55	11	21	192	150	34	18	480	90	64	144	153	7	81	16	1692	40.99
	%	0.65	8.51	0.53	0.71	3.25	0.65	1.24	11.35	8.87	2.01	1.06	28.37	5.32	3.78	8.51	9.04	0.41	4.79	0.95	100.0	
5	n=	0	12	2	0	5	2	2	15	3	5	2	43	2	3	7	10	2	6	0	121	2.93
	%		9.92	1.65		4.13	1.65	1.65	12.4	2.48	4.13	1.65	35.54	1.65	2.48	5.79	8.26	1.65	4.96		99.99	
6	n=	1	2	0	0	0	0		5	3	3	0	13	2	0	4	9	0	0	0	43	1.04
	%	2.32	4.65					2.33	11.63	6.98	6.98		30.23	4.65		9.3	20.93				100.0	
7	n=	6	22	3	2	9	4	2	28	5	7	1	65	12	5	10	25	0	9	0	215	5.21
	%	2.79	10.23	1.39	0.93	4.19	1.86	0.93	13.02	2.33	3.26	0.46	30.23	5.58	2.33	4.65	11.63		4.19		100.0	
none	n=	0	4	0	0	1	1	2	3	1	3	2	12	3	1	5	8	1	0	1	46	1.11
	%		8.7			2.17	2.17	4.35	6.52	2.17	6.52	4.35	26.09	2.17	2.17	10.87	17.39	2.17		2.17	99.98	
Total		50	385	26	29	183	39	69	389	192	133	61	1459	159	108	237	377	18	193	21	4128	99.99

Locus	Locus type	m²	Tools (n=)	Waste (n=)	Tool/m²	Waste/m²
Rm #9			*Stratum IIA*			
817	fill	11.0	9	180	.82	16.36
816/935	surface		10	154	.91	14.09
			Stratum IIB			
Rm #1 841	Surface	1.56	0	120	0	76.92
Rm #2 839	surface	2.25	4	54	8.33	24.00
Rm #3 1014	surface	18.0	0	0	0	0
1204	surface removal		4	82	.22	4.56
Rm #11 685	fill	18.0	3	86	.16	4.78
722/723	surface		0	0	0	0
			Stratum IIIA			
Rm #7 847	fill	7.65	1	148	.13	19.35
947	surface		0	0	0	0
932	surface		5	251	.65	32.81
929	surface		1	37	.13	4.83
			Pits and Hearths			
Stratum IIA 964	pit	2.01	1	108	.50	53.73
Stratum IIA 967	pit	2.01	0	37	0	18.41
Stratum IIA 810	pit	2.01	5	255	2.49	126.87
Stratum IIA 628	hearth	.40	2	28	5.0	70.00
Stratum IIB 970	pit	1.76	5	322	2.84	182.95
Stratum IIB 1133	pit	.79	0	40	0	50.63
Stratum IIB 674	pit	.79	14	481	17.72	608.86
Stratum IIB 787	pit	1.54	30	984	19.48	638.96
Stratum IIB 681	hearth	.40	2	38	5.0	95.00
Stratum IIC 777	pit	3.04	14	533	4.61	175.33
Stratum IIC 1137	pit	2.27	1	64	.44	28.19
Stratum IIIA 1333	pit	1.77	6	335	3.39	189.27
Stratum IIIA 555	pit	1.77	9	285	5.08	161.02

Table 11.18. Flint tool and waste densities: selected rooms, pits, and hearths.

Figures

Figure 11.1. Range of widths of sickles, sickle blanks,
retouched blades and micro-endscrapers.

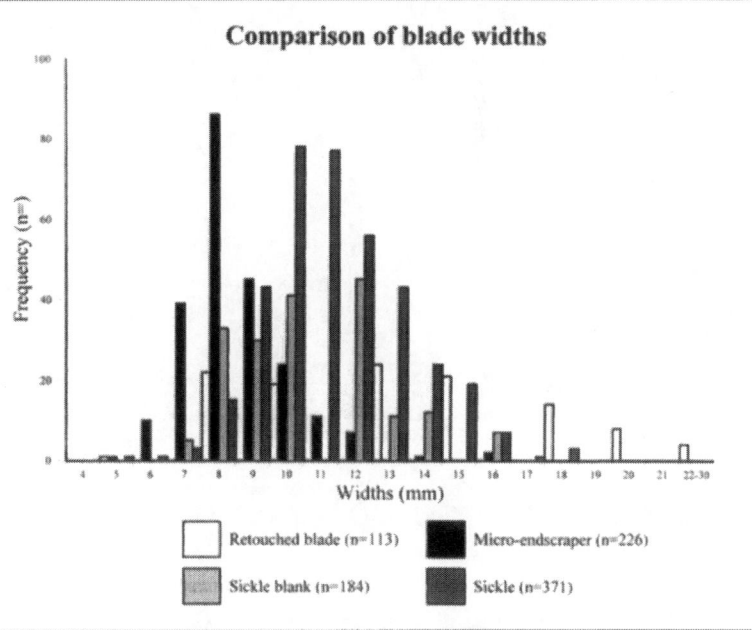

Figure 11.2. Range of thickness of sickles, sickle blanks,
retouched blades and micro-endscrapers.

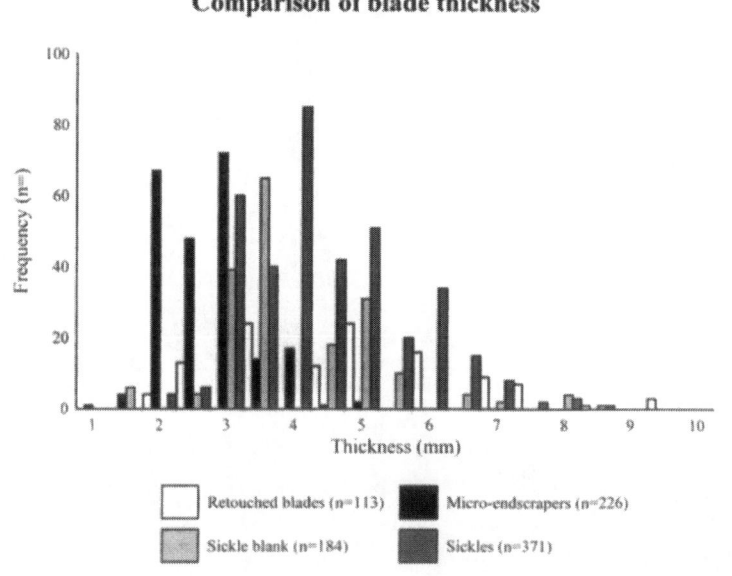

Figure 11.3. Range of lengths of celts (adzes, axes, chisels and unknowns).

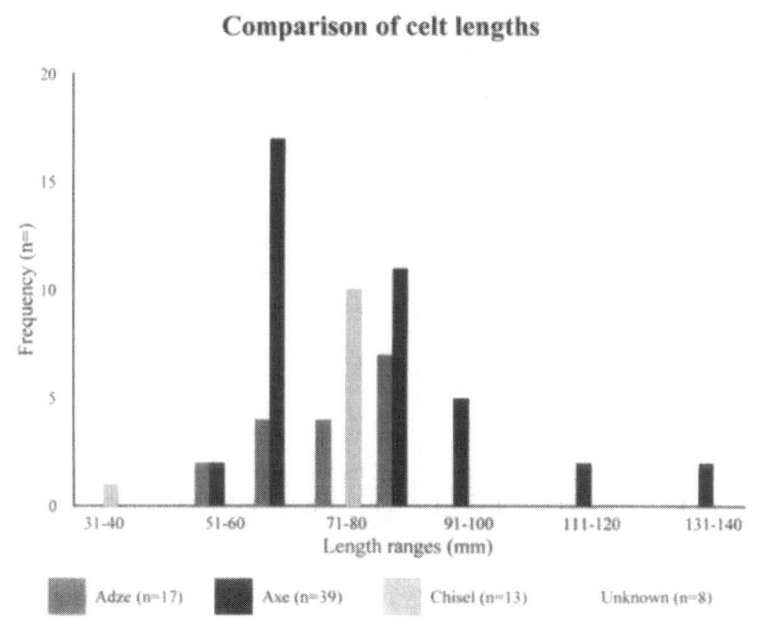

Figure 11.4. Range of widths of celts (adzes, axes, chisels and unknowns).

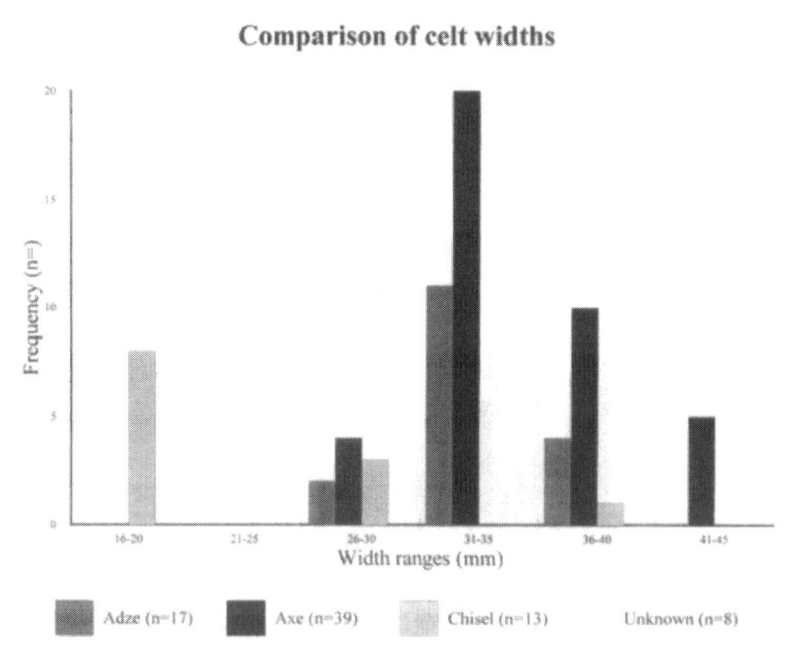

Figure 11.5. Range of thicknesses of celts (adzes, axes, chisels and unknowns).

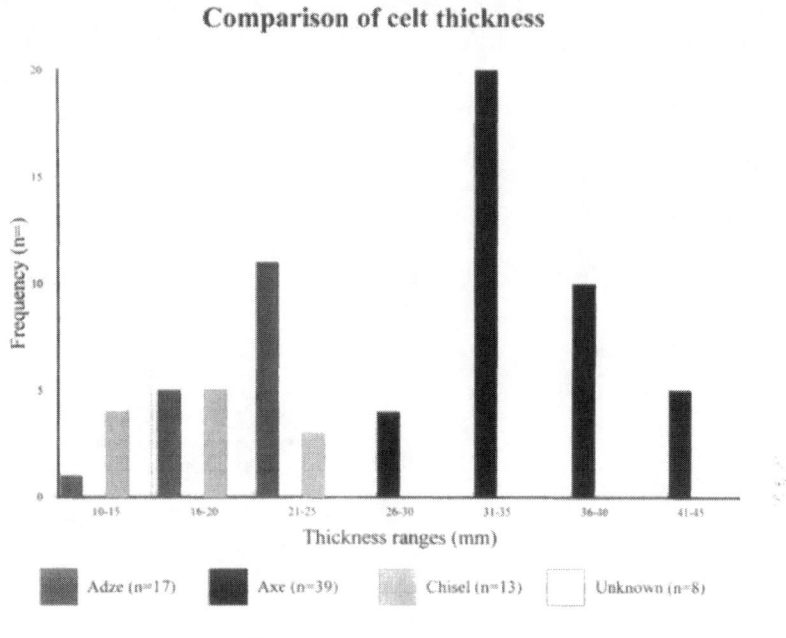

Figure 11.6. Ranges of length ranges of borer and perforator points according to reduction element.

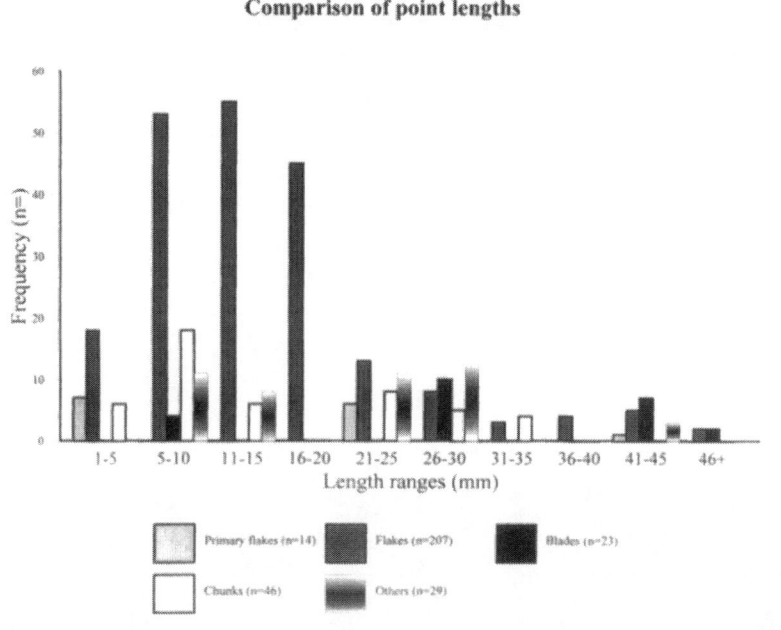

Figure 11.7. Tool frequencies from Chalcolithic sites of Gilat, Shiqmim and Grar.

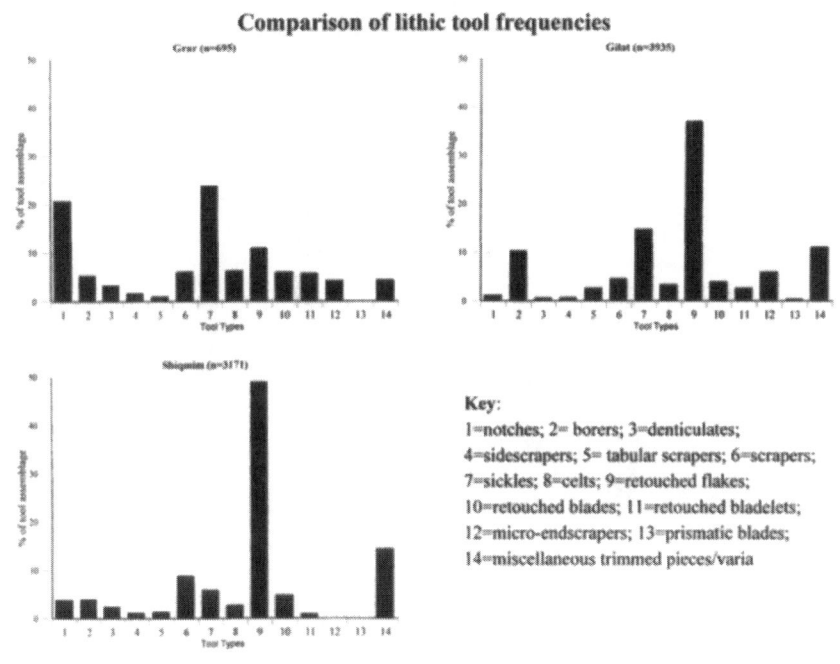

Figure 11.8. Scatterplot of tool versus waste densities of selected rooms, pits and hearths.

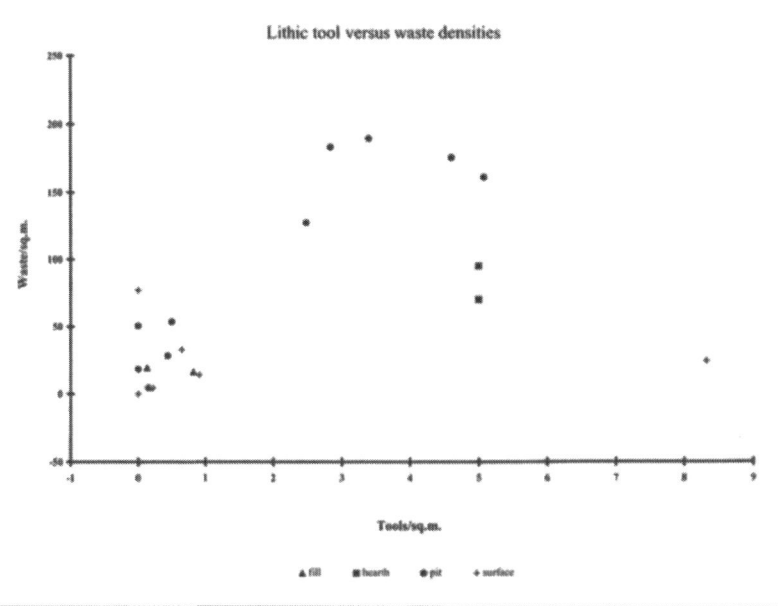

Figure 11.9. Blade and blade cores.

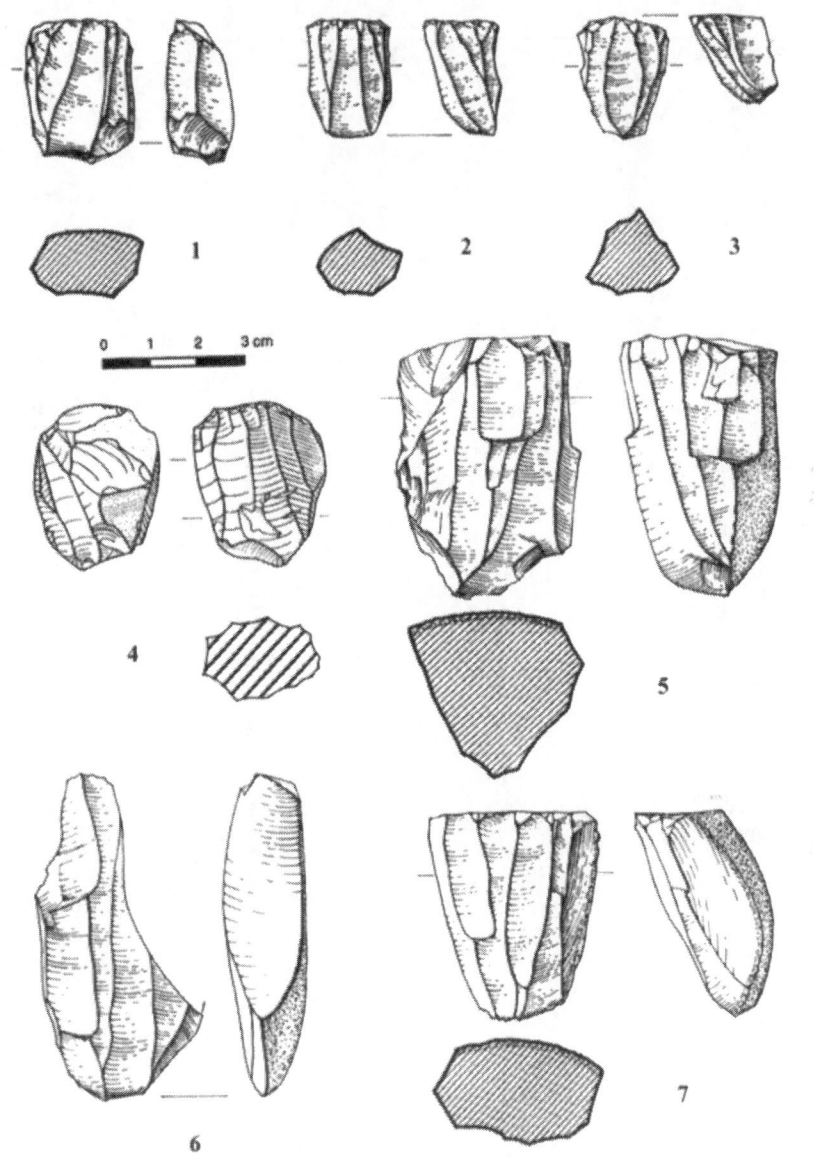

No.	Artifact	Reg. No.	Locus	Basket	Stratum	Description
1	Bladelet core	19/91	1150	3686	2B	fine, semi-translucent flint
2	Bladelet core	49/90	025	3096	3	fine, semi-translucent flint
3	Bladelet core	19/91	1029	3256	2A	fine, semi-translucent flint
4	Bladelet core	49/90	009	805/825	2B	fine, semi-translucent flint
5	Blade core	19/91	1029	3256	2A	single platform, fine, semi-translucent flint
6	Blade core fragment	19/91	1029	3256	2A	fine, semi-translucent flint
7	Blade core	19/91	1029	3256	2A	single platform, fine, semi-translucent flint

Figure 11.10. Blade cores.

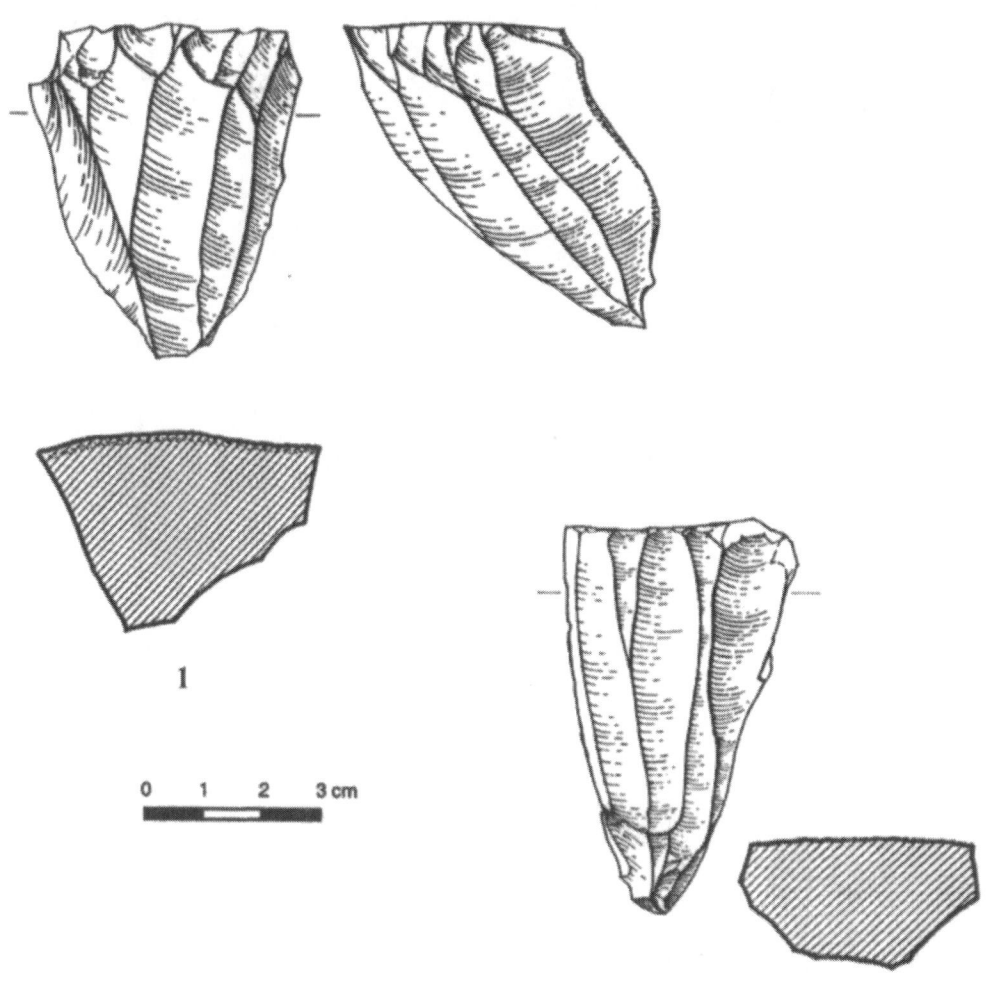

No.	Artifact	Reg. No.	Locus	Basket	Stratum	Description
1	Blade core	19/91	1029	3263	2A	single platform, fine, semi-translucent flint
2	Blade core	19/91	1029	3263	2A	single platform, fine, semi-translucent flint

Figure 11.11. Blade cores.

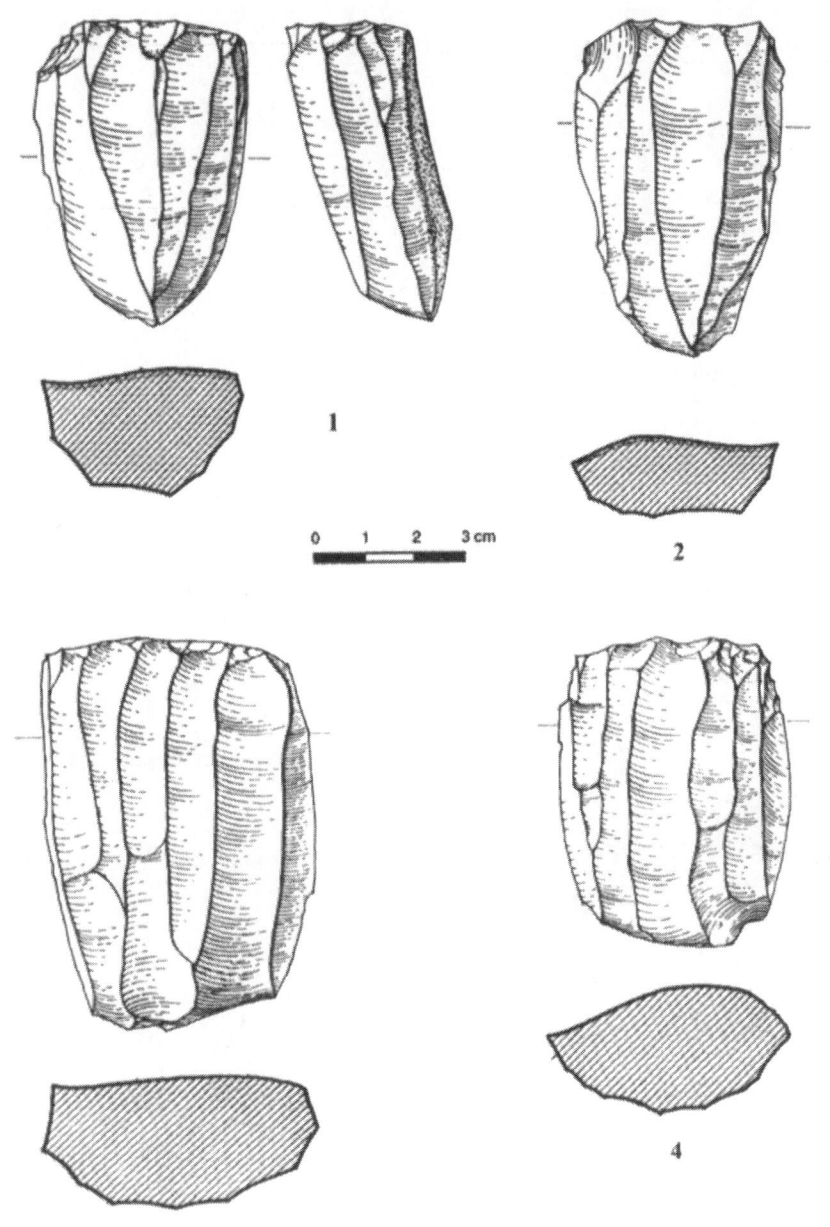

0 1 2 3 cm

No.	Artifact	Reg. No.	Locus	Basket	Stratum	Description
1	Blade core	19/91	1029	3263	2A	single platform
2	Blade core	19/91	1029	3256	2A	single platform
3	Blade core	19/91	1029	3256	2A	single platform
4	Blade core	19/91	1029	3256	2A	single platform

Figure 11.12. Prismatic blades.

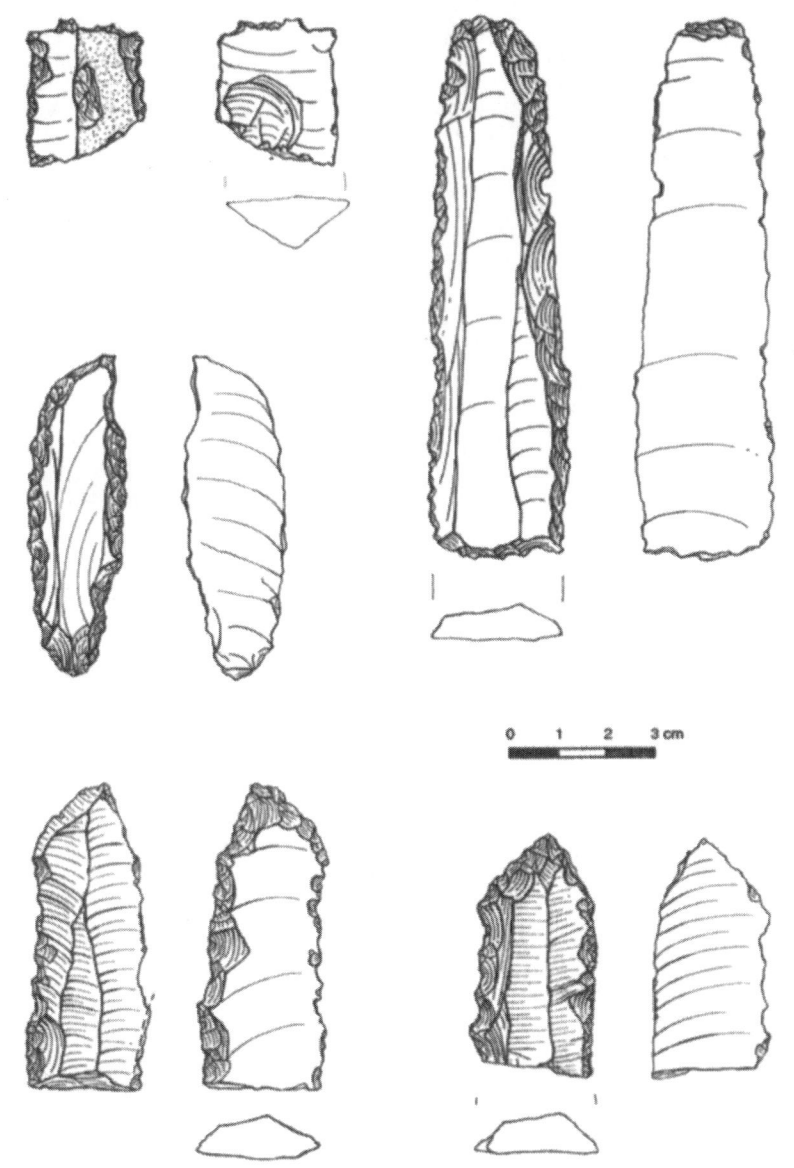

No.	Artifact	Reg. No.	Locus	Basket	Stratum	Description
1	Prismatic blade	49/90	034	3125	2	medial fragment; bilateral retouch
2	Prismatic blade	36/87	-	2226	1	steep bilateral and distal dorsal retouch
3	Prismatic blade	49/90	882	2557	2B	pronounced bulb, circumferential dorsal retouch
4	Prismatic blade	19/91	1022	3227	1	fragment; alternating bilateral retouch, distal ventral retouch
5	Prismatic blade	19/91	609	5040	2A	fragment; bilateral and distal dorsal retouch

Figure 11.13. Prismatic blades.

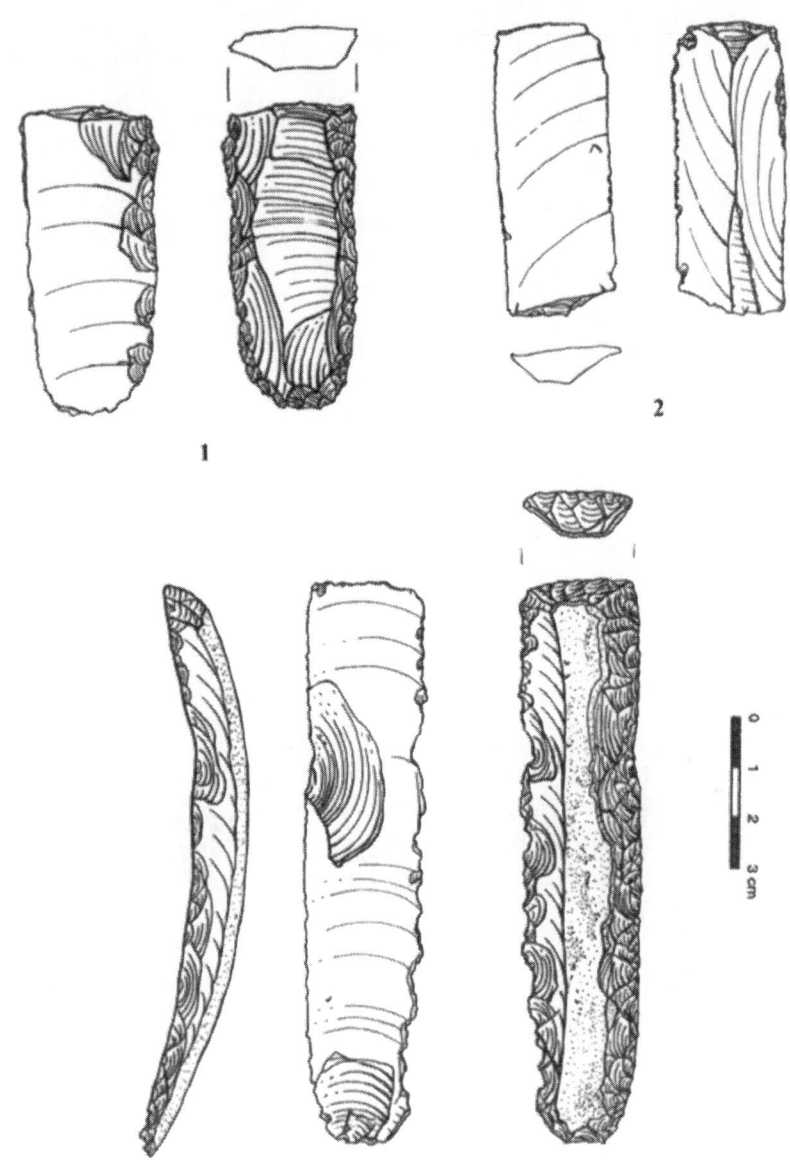

No.	Artifact	Reg. No.	Locus	Basket	Stratum	Description
1	Prismatic blade	19/91	1111	3555	2C	fragment, distal-bilateral dorsal retouch
2	Prismatic blade	49/90	999	2897	2B	slight unilateral dorsal retouch
3	Prismatic blade	19/91	695	5282	2A	arched, cortex, circumferential dorsal retouch

Figure 11.14. Sickles and sickle blank.

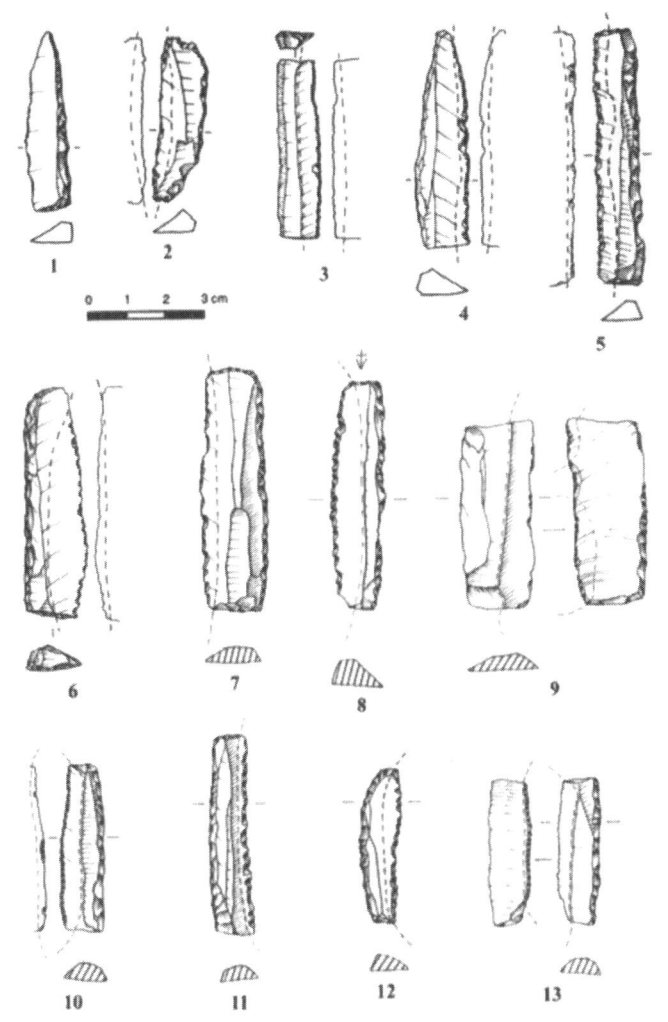

No.	Artifact	Reg. No.	Locus	Basket	Stratum	Description
1	Sickle blank	57/92	1368	4303	3A	tapered end, no sickle sheen
2	Sickle	57/92	1320	4197	2C	crescent-shaped
3	Sickle	57/92	1310	4149	2C	naturally backed
4	Sickle	57/92	1321	4158	2B	tapered end
5	Sickle	57/92	1259	4033	2C	arched, serrated
6	Sickle	57/92	1217	3840	2A	serrated
7	Sickle	568	6	5	2C	backed
8	Sickle	568	26	51	1-2	backed
9	Sickle	568	20	42	3B	no backing retouch,
10	Sickle	568	43	89	2C	backed
11	Sickle	568	2	4	1-2	serrated
12	Sickle	568	13	25	3A	backed
13	Sickle	568	15	30	3B	ventral edge retouch

Figure 11.15. Sickles, sickle blanks, blades, bladelets and micro-endscraper.

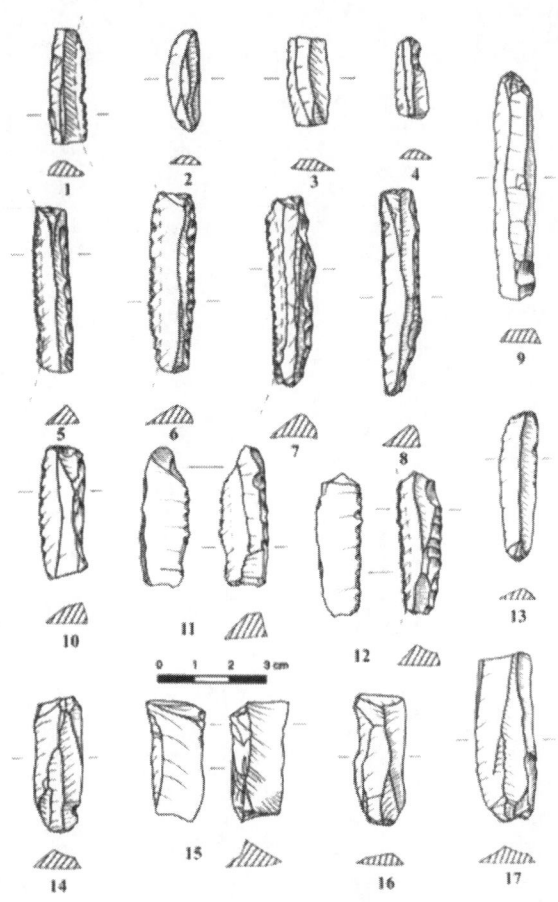

No.	Artifact	Reg. No.	Locus	Basket	Stratum	Description
1	Sickle	568	stray find			no backing retouch
2	Bladelet	568	stray find			no retouch
3	Blade fragment	655	stray find			no retouch
4	Bladelet fragment	655	stray find			no retouch
5	Sickle	655	70	217	2B	backed
6	Sickle	655	68	212	1-2A	
7	Sickle		stray find			
8	Sickle blank		stray find			
9	Blade	655	69	221	2C	no retouch
10	Sickle blank	655	50	150	2B	no sickle sheen
11	Sickle	655	68	212	1-2A	no backing retouch
12	Sickle	655	69	221	2C	slight ventral edge retouch
13	Micro-endscraper	655	69	221	2C	distal dorsal retouch
14	Blade fragment	655	70	217	2B	no retouch
15	Blade fragment	655	stray find			no retouch
16	Blade fragment	655	68	220	1-2A	no retouch
17	Blade fragment	655	50	159	2B	no retouch

Figure 11.16. Sickles, sickle blanks, and bladelet.

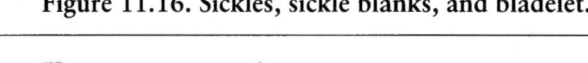

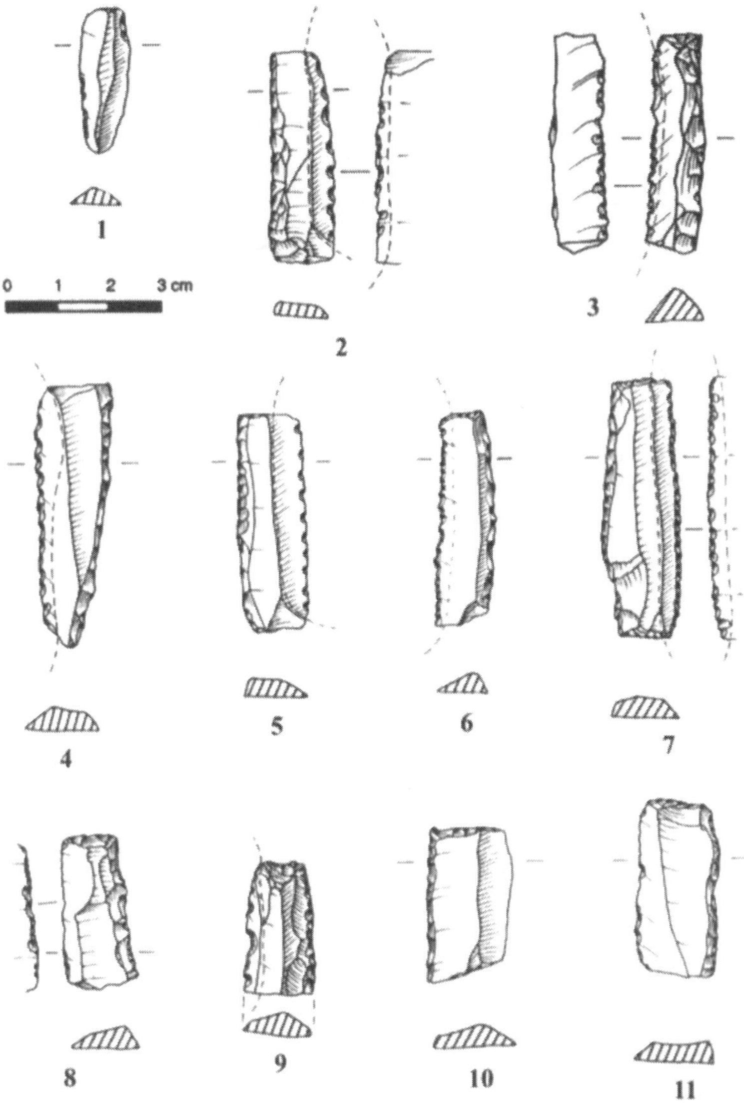

No.	Artifact	Reg. No.	Locus	Basket	Stratum	Description
1	Bladelet	568	18	39	2B	slight nibbling retouch
2	Sickle	568	11	32	2C	backed, serrated
3	Sickle	568	72	218	2C	backed, ventral edge retouch
4	Sickle	568	19	40	2C	backed
5	Sickle	568	26	51	2C	
6	Sickle	568	1	3	1-2	sickle
7	Sickle	568	7/8	26	2C	fine edge retouch
8	Sickle blank	568	11	33	2C	no sickle sheen, slight backing retouch
9	Sickle	568	2	2	1-2	backed
10	Sickle blank	568	11	31	2C	backing retouch, no edge wear
11	Sickle blank	568	43	89	2C	no sickle sheen

Figure 11.17. Borers, micro-borers, and micro-endscrapers.

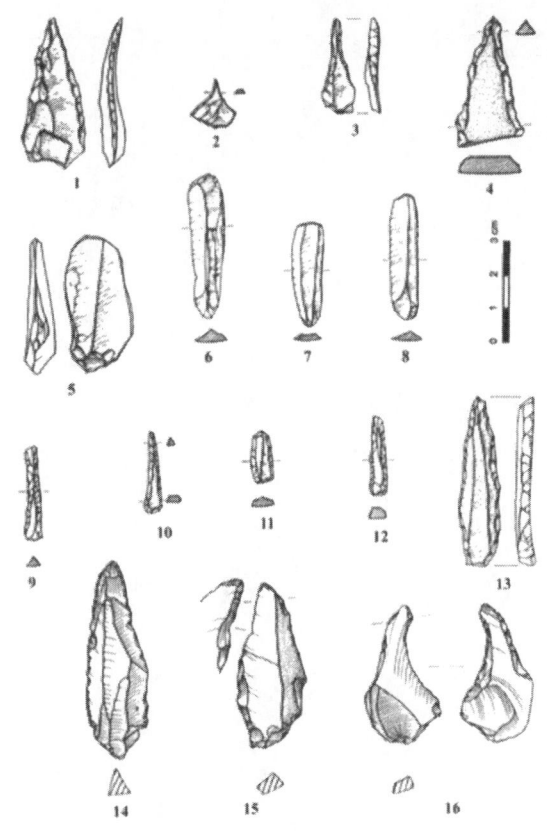

No.	Artifact	Reg. No.	Locus	Basket	Stratum	Description
1	Chisel	49/90	501	1003	1	bifacially polished
1	Borer	19/91	1023	3221	1	on flake, bilateral dorsal retouch
2	Micro-borer	57.92	775	5455	2B	double-shouldered, fine semi-translucent flint
3	Micro-borer	57/92	1354	4278	4	single shoulder
4	Borer fragment	49/90	509	1054	1	made from tabular scraper fragment
5						
6	Micro-endscraper	19/91	684	5249	1	distal and unilateral fine retouch
7	Micro-endscraper	19/91	650	5176	2A	distal and unilateral fine retouch
8	Micro-endscraper	19/91	677	5168	1	distal and unilateral fine retouch
9	Micro-borer	57/92	1322	4216	2C	straight drill, complete
10	Micro-borer	19/91	634	5192	2B	straight drill, bilateral dorsal retouch
11	Micro-borer	49/90	007	3057	2	straight drill, circumferential dorsal retouch
12	Micro-borer	49/90	003	3005	1	straight drill, circumferential retouch, complete
13	Awl	19/91	1033	3257	2A	made on sickle blade
14	Borer		33?			bilateral dorsal retouch, blade core fragment
15	Borer		20?			inverse bilateral retouch on flake
16	Borer		4?			bilateral retouch on core fragment

Figure 11.18. Awl and borers.

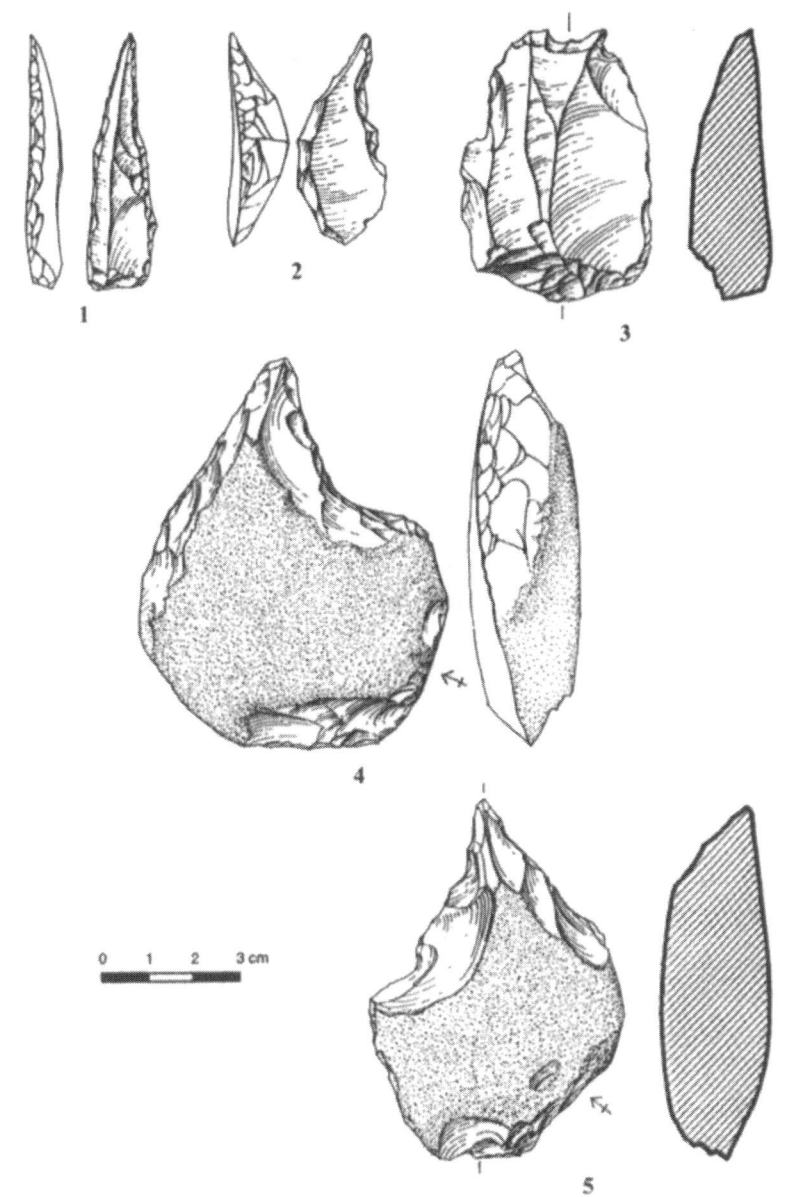

No.	Artifact	Reg. No.	Locus	Basket	Stratum	Description
1	Awl	19/91	1096	3499	2A	on blade, bilateral dorsal retouch
2	Borer	49/90	504	1026	1	on chunk, unilateral retouch
3	Borer	49/90	505	1027	1	on flake, bilateral dorsal retouch
4	Borer	19/91	1075	3467	2B	on large thick flake, bilateral retouch
5	Borer	19/91	676	5297	3B	on large thick flake

Figure 11.19. Bifacial fragments.

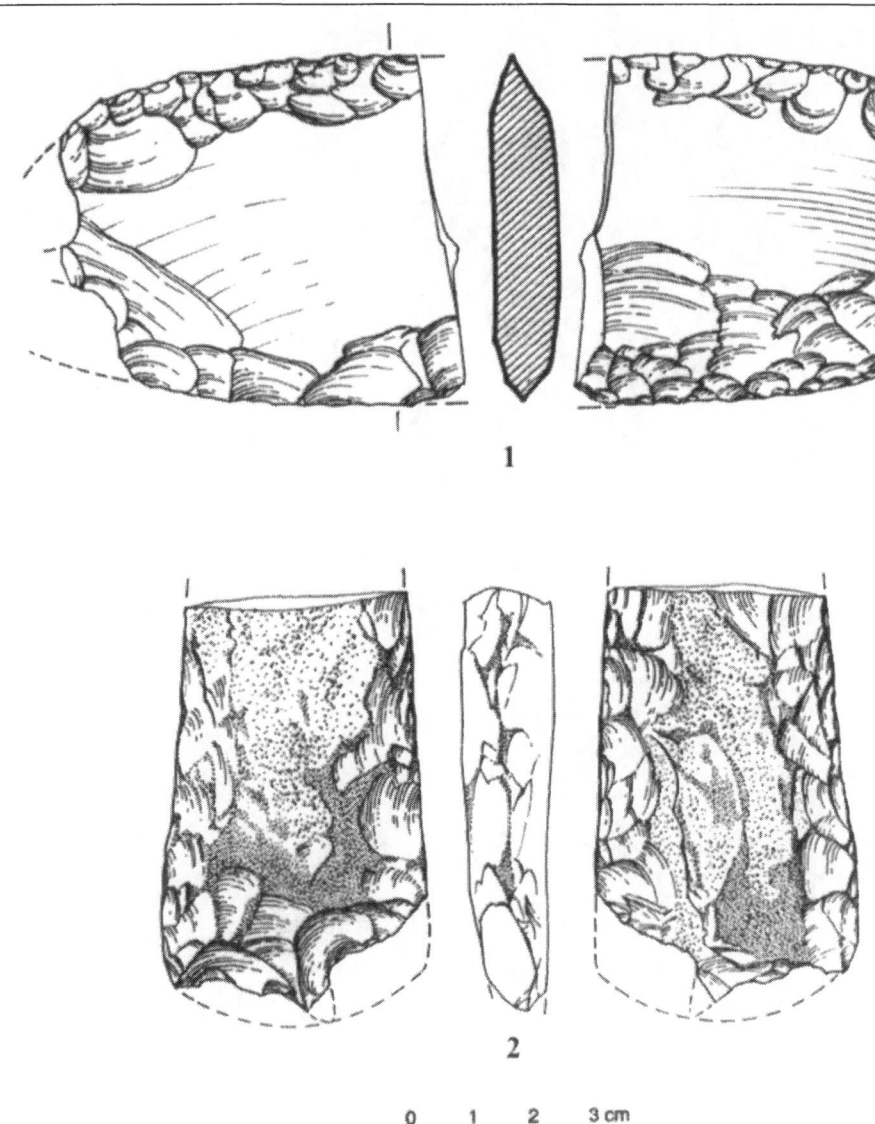

1

2

0   1   2   3 cm

No.	Artifact	Reg. No.	Locus	Basket	Stratum	Description
1	Biface	19/91	649	5364	3A	bifacial flat retouch, with broken stem?
2	Biface	19/91	1090	3510	2B	bifacial flat retouch and ground(?), with broken stem? associated with burial

Figure 11.20. Tabular scrapers.

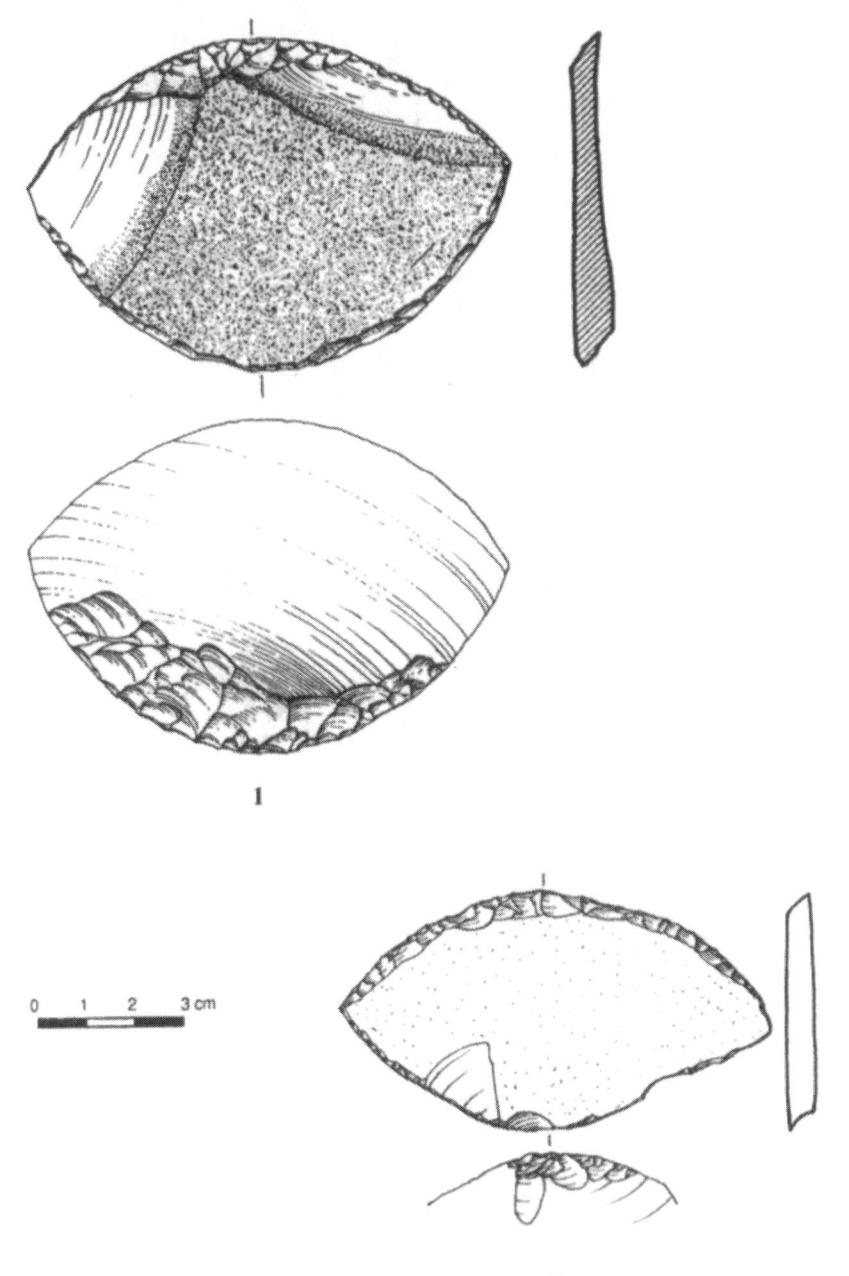

1

2

0   1   2   3 cm

No.	Artifact	Reg. No.	Locus	Basket	Stratum	Description
1	Tabular scraper	57/92	0	5029	none	ventral flaking, bulb removed
2	Tabular scraper	19/91	806	2363	2A	slight ventral bulbar thinning

Figure 11.21. Tabular scrapers.

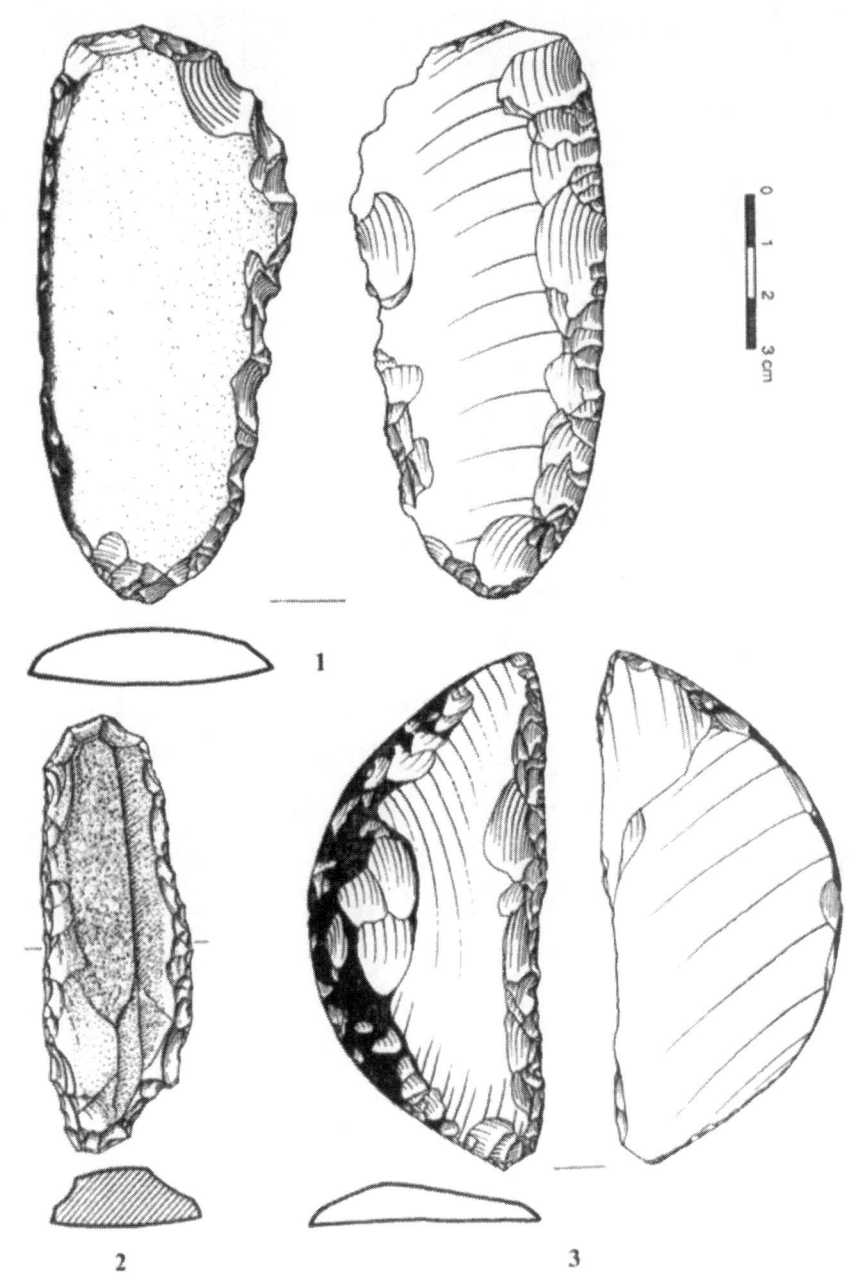

No.	Artifact	Reg. No.	Locus	Basket	Stratum	Description
1	Tabular 'scraper'	49/90	524	1121	2	knife?, lateral polish
2	Tabular scraper	19/91	686	5243	1	elongate, circumferential dorsal retouch
3	Tabular scraper	49/90	525	1108	2B	no cortex, pronounced grinding polish on ventral side

Figure 11.22. Tabular scrapers.

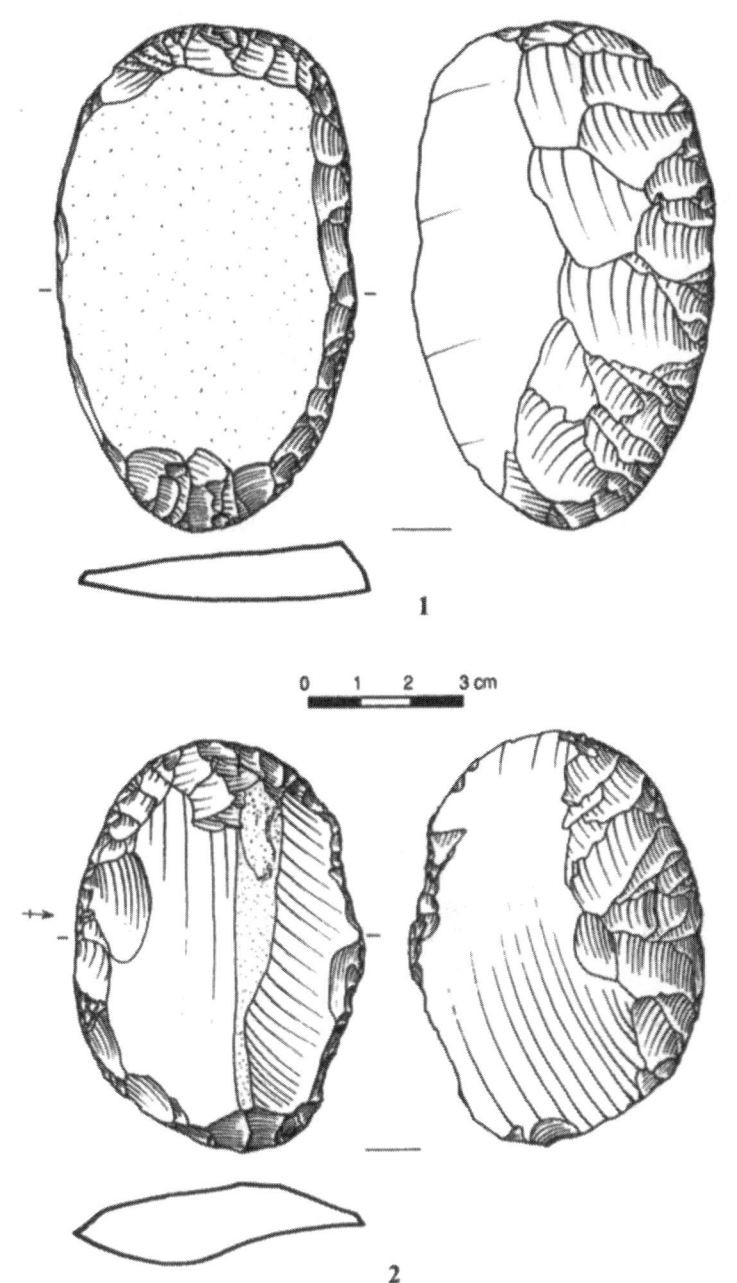

No.	Artifact	Reg. No.	Locus	Basket	Stratum	Description
1	Tabular scraper	49/90	800	2130	1	extensive ventral retouch
2	Tabular scraper	19/91	1026	3360	1	ventral bulbar thinning, little cortex remaining

Figure 11.23. Tabular scraper, retouched tabular flint blade/flake, and sidescraper.

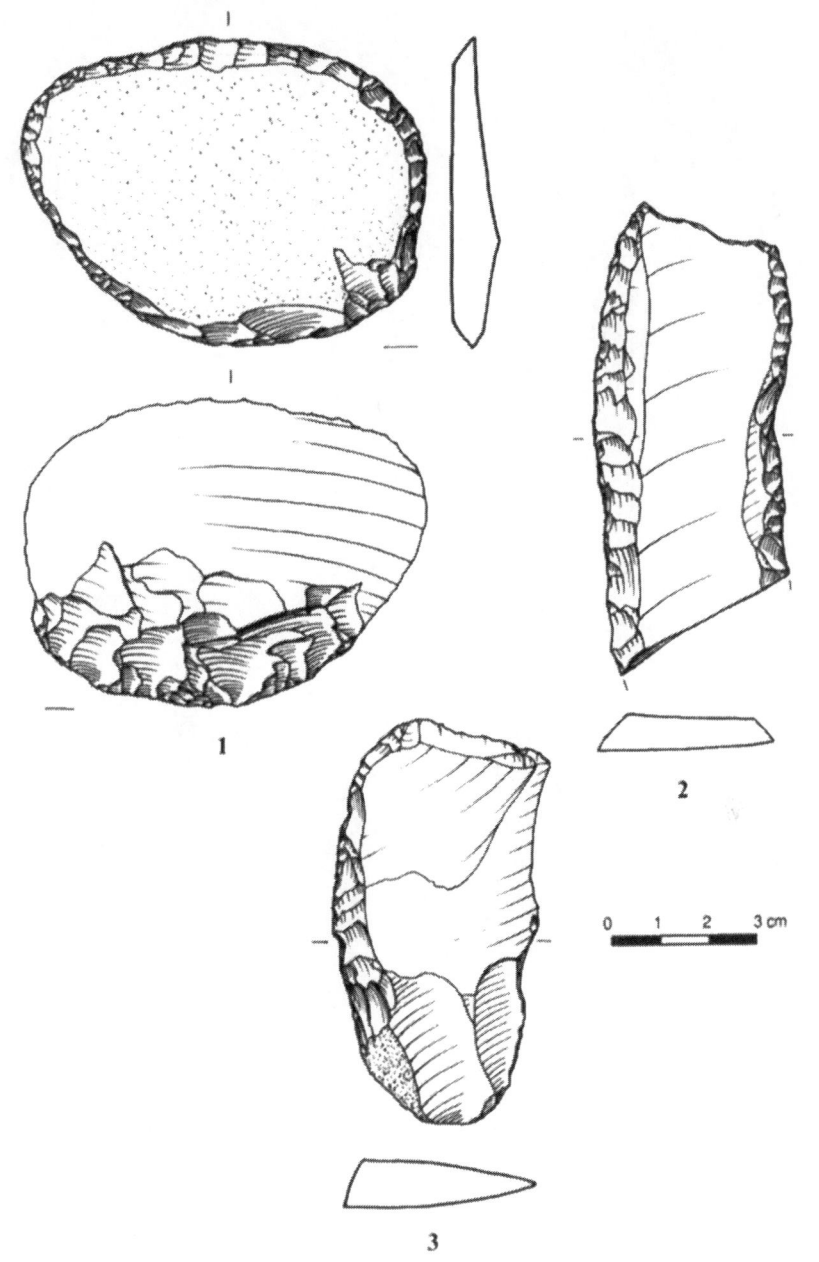

No.	Artifact	Reg. No.	Locus	Basket	Stratum	Description
1	Tabular scraper	49/90	507	1040	1	ventral bulbar thinning
2	Blade/wide flake	57/92	1289	4115	3A	fine brown flint, 'tabular flint' bilateral dorsal retouch
3	Sidescraper	49/90	503	1025	1	Flake, (fine brown flint?)

Figure 11.24. Endscrapers and denticulated scraper.

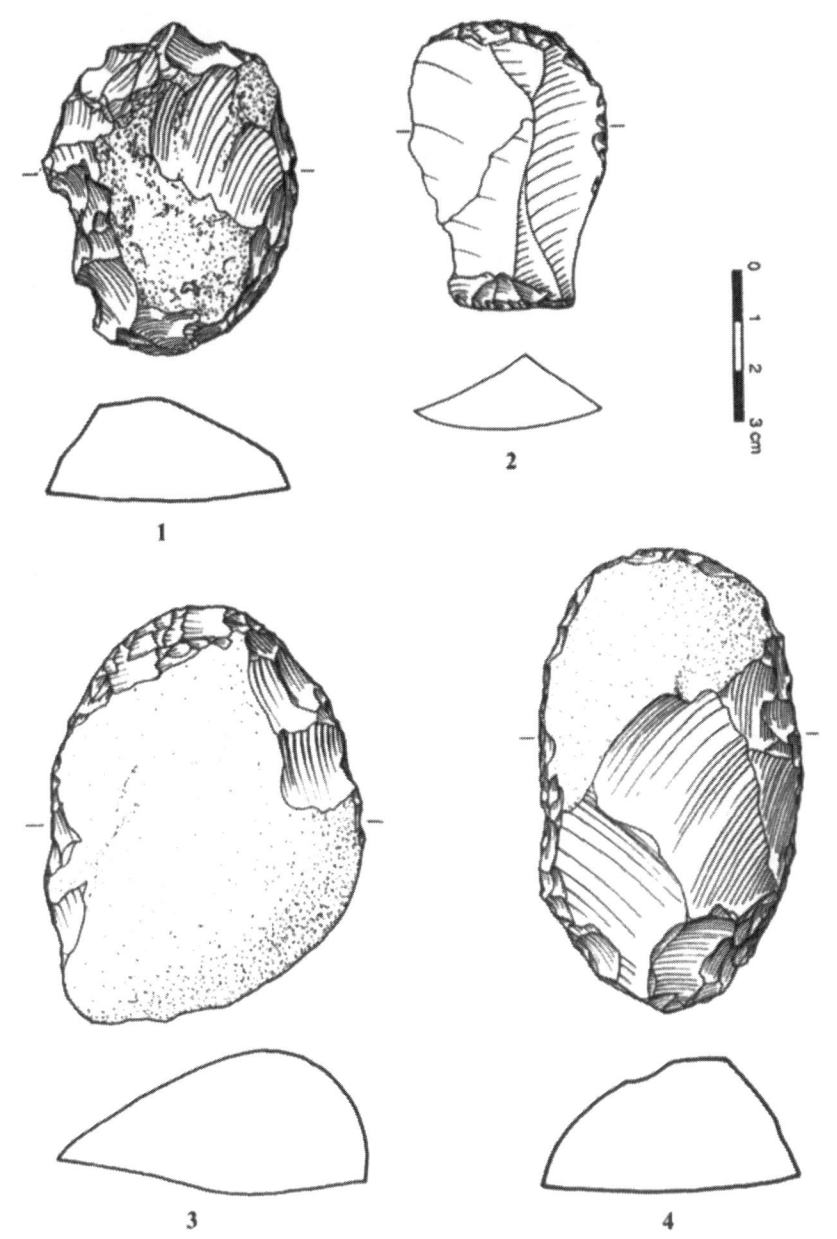

No.	Artifact	Reg. No.	Locus	Basket	Stratum	Description
1	Varia	19/91	606	5033	1	denticulated scraper
2	Endscraper	19/91	716	5362	3A	distal retouch on flake
3	Endscraper	19/91	1029	3263	2	distal retouch on primary flake
4	Endscraper	19/91	686	5241	1	distal, bilateral dorsal retouch

Figure 11.25. Limestone tools and blade.

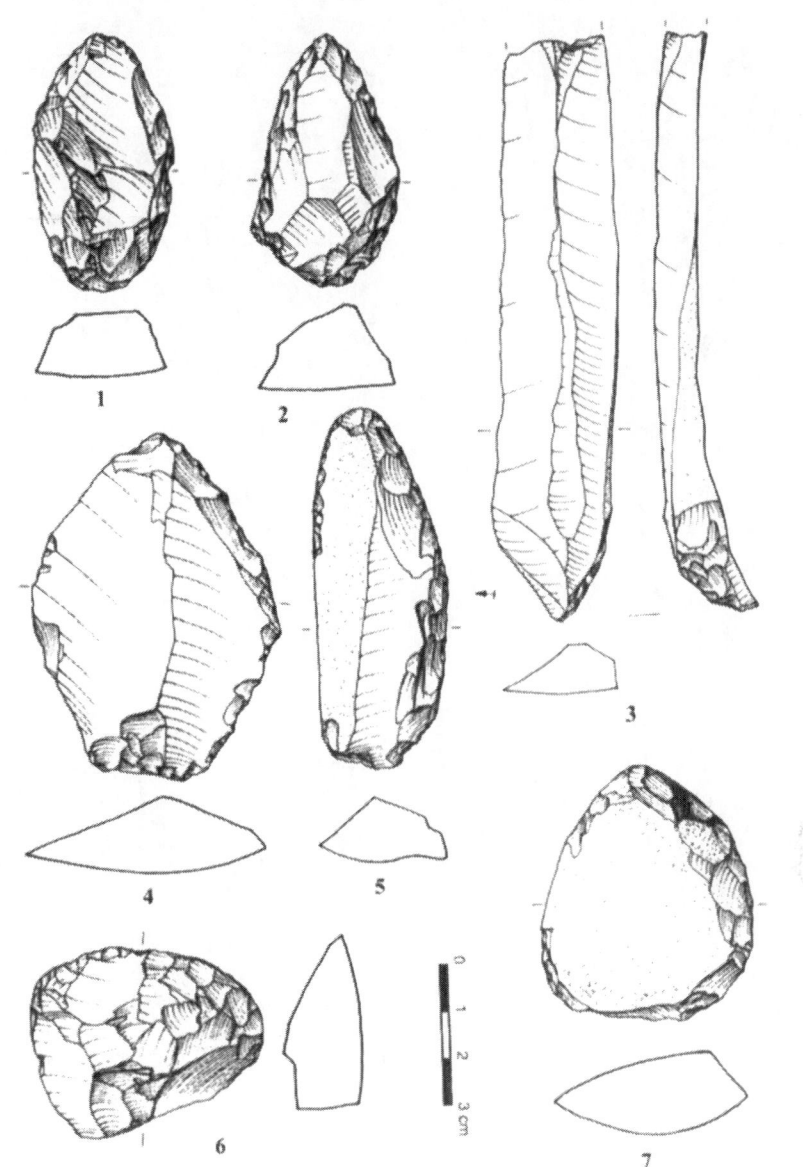

No.	Artifact	Reg. No.	Locus	Basket	Stratum	Description
1	Limestone scraper	49/90	800	2058	1	ovate, nearly circumferential dorsal retouch
2	Limestone scraper	49/90	828	2339	2A	pointed, circumferential dorsal retouch
3	Blade	49/90	877	2529	2B	fine brown flint, slight cortex
4	Limestone flake	49/90	528	1152	2C	unilateral dorsal retouch
5	Limestone scraper	49/90	560	1236	3	elongate, distal-bilateral dorsal retouch
6	Limestone scraper	49/90	014	3040	2A	steep retouch, worn from use
7	Limestone scraper	49/90	013	3037	2B	nearly circumferential retouch, lateral polish

Figure 11.26. Celts.

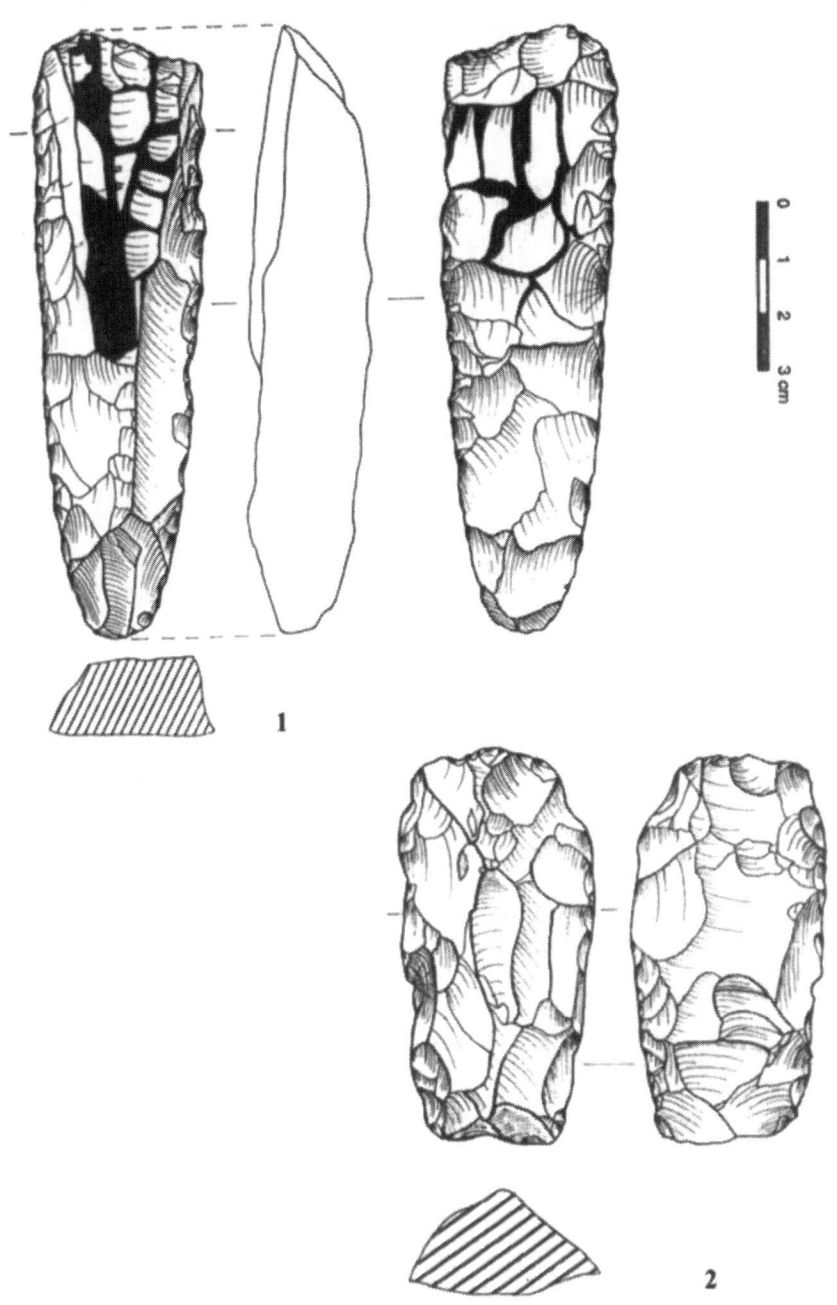

No.	Artifact	Reg. No.	Locus	Basket	Stratum	Description
1	Adze	568	stray			bifacial polish, trapezoidal cross-section
2	Axe?	568	stray			possibly restored, modified celt fragment

Figure 11.27. Celts.

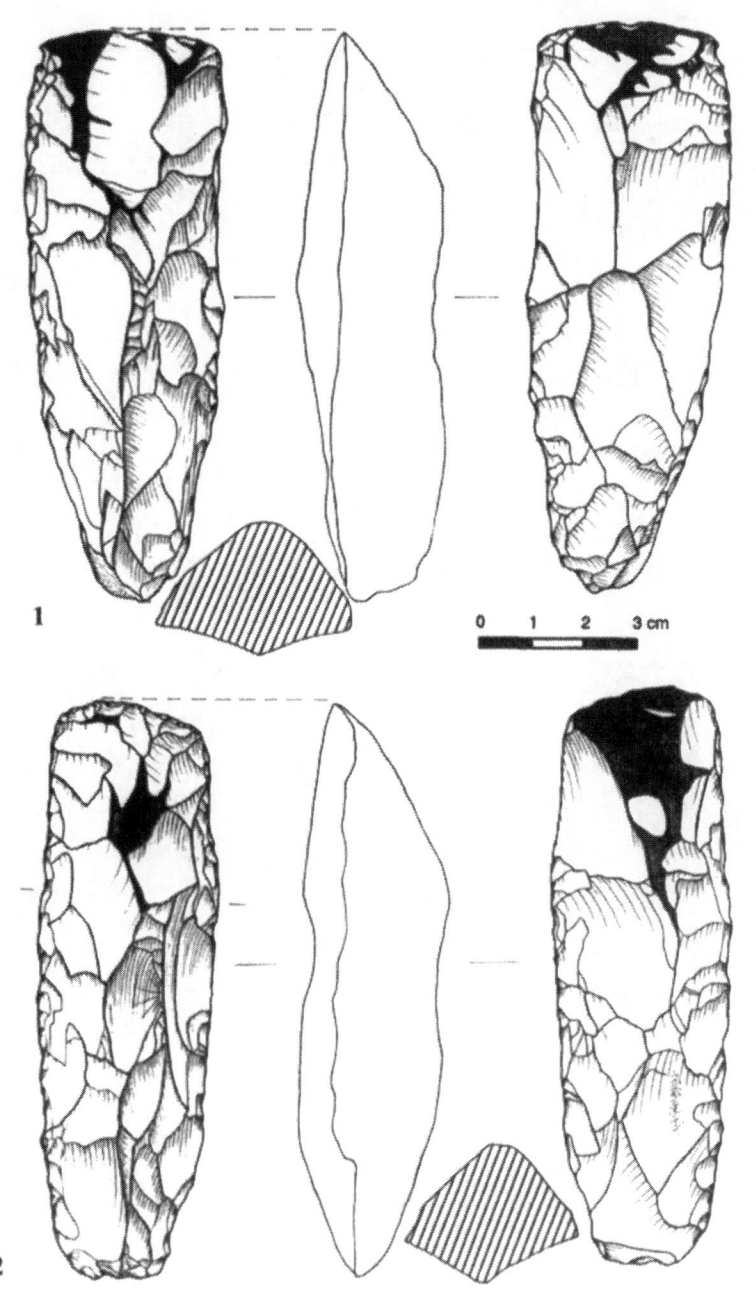

No.	Artifact	Reg. No.	Locus	Basket	Stratum	Description
1	Adze?	568	stray			bifacial polish near edge
2	Adze?	568	stray			bifacial polish

Figure 11.28. Celts.

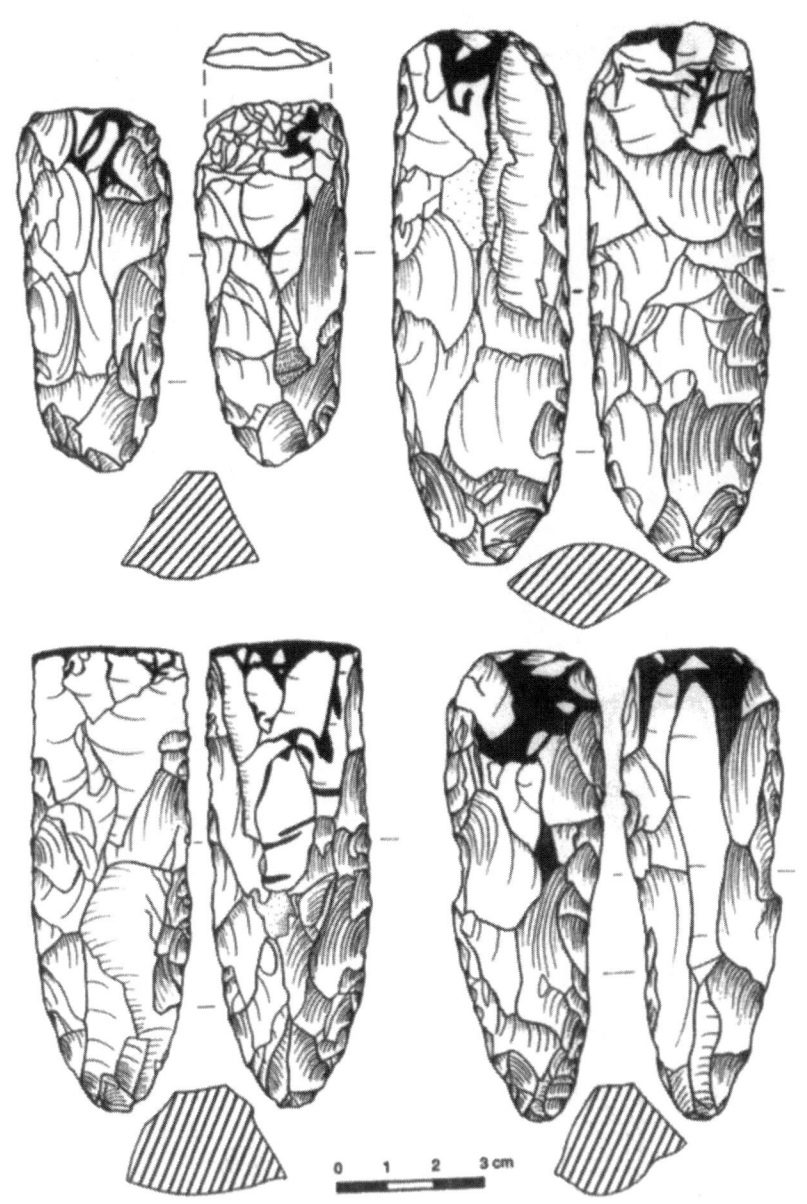

No.	Artifact	Reg. No.	Locus	Basket	Stratum	Description
1	Adze?		stray			bifacial polish near edge
2	Adze?		stray			bifacial polish
3	Adze?		stray			slight bifacial polish
4	Axe?		stray			pronounced bifacial polish

Figure 11.29. Celts.

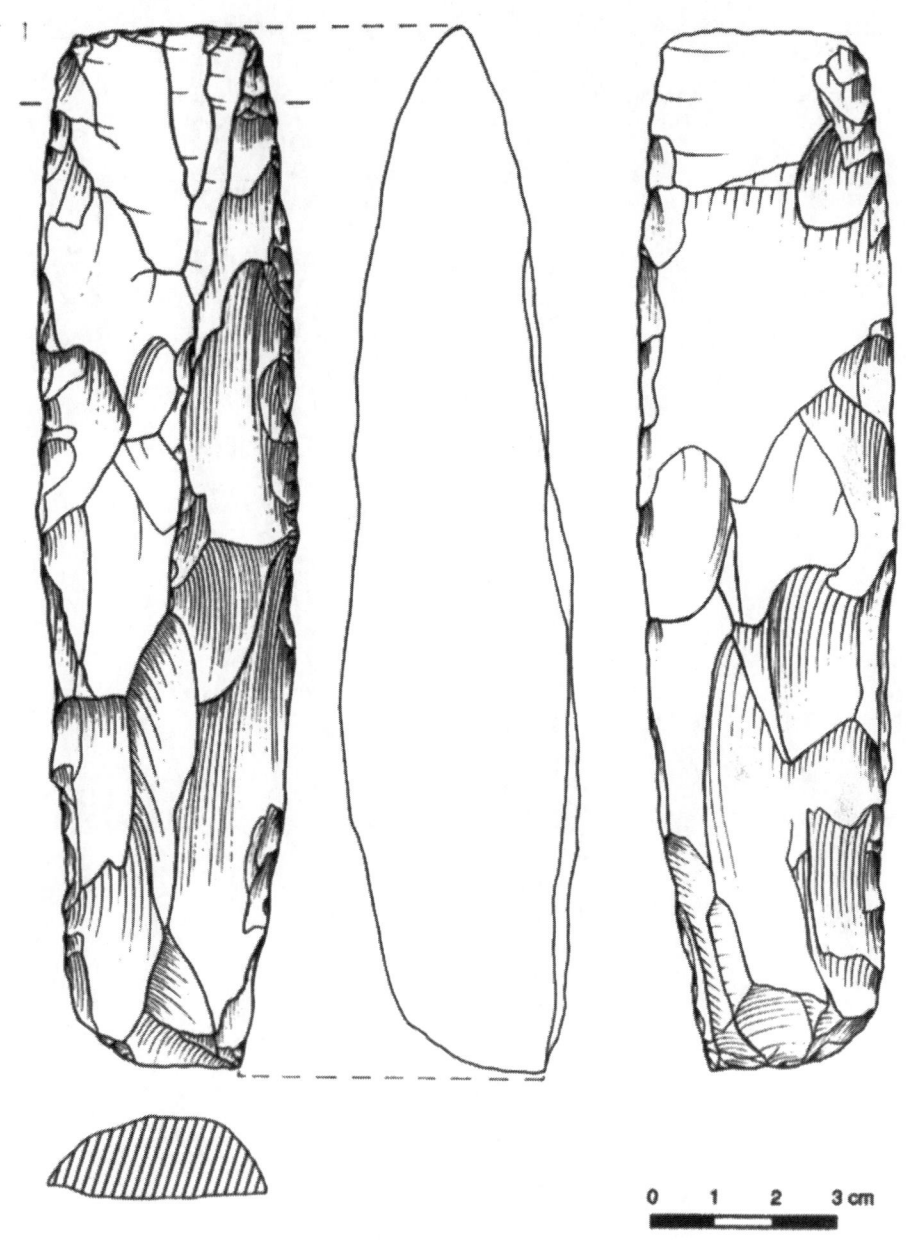

No.	Artifact	Reg. No.	Locus	Basket	Stratum
1	Axe?	568	34	75	3B

Figure 11.30. Celts.

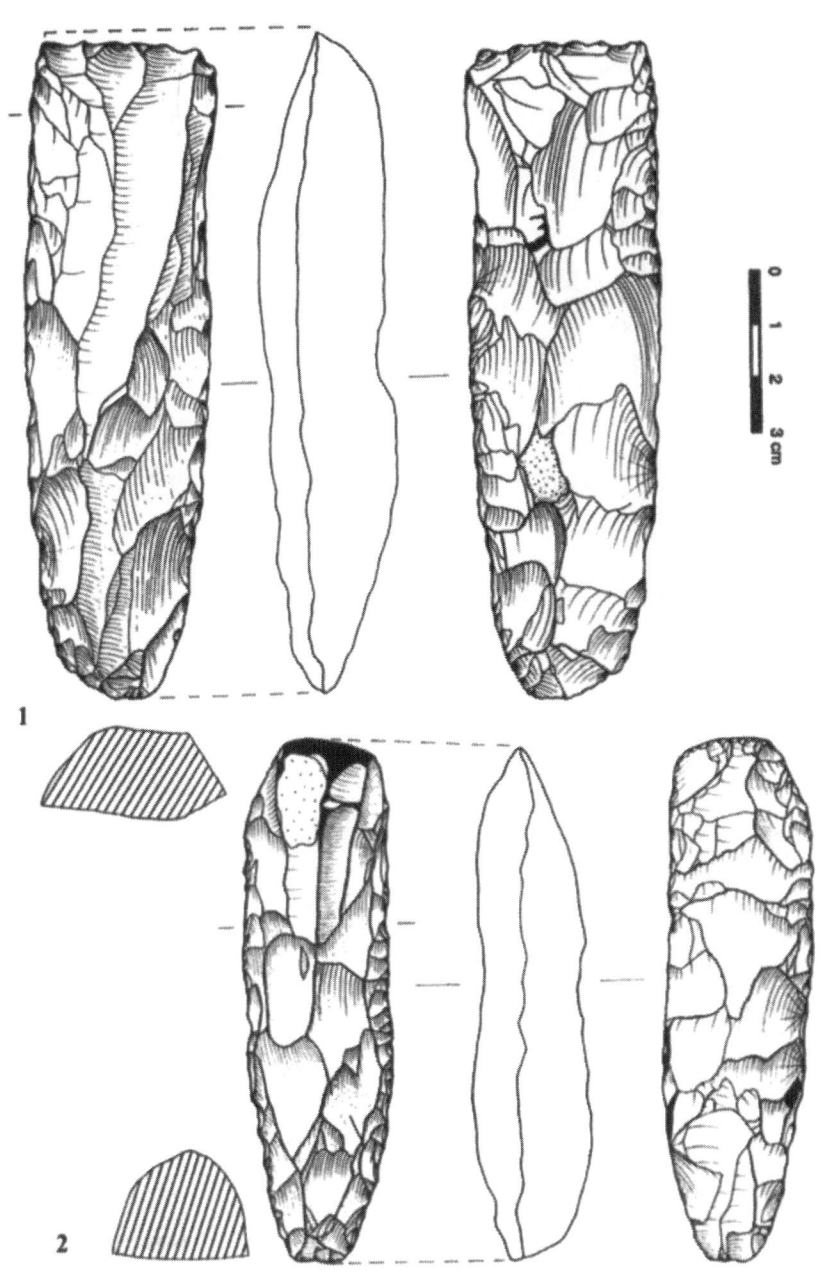

No.	Artifact	Reg. No.	Locus	Basket	Stratum	Description
1	Axe	568	11	31	2C	
2	Axe	568	29	56	2B	unifacial bit polish

Figure 11.31. Celts.

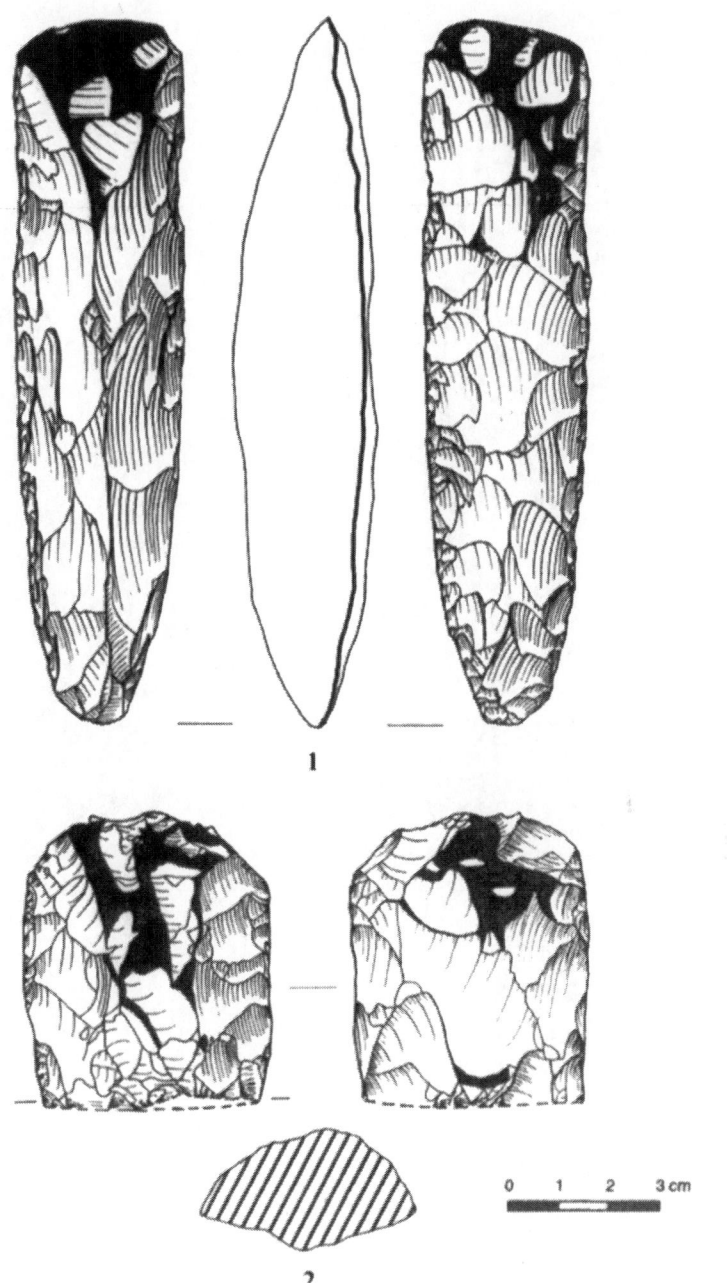

1

2

No.	Artifact	Reg. No.	Locus	Basket	Stratum	Description
1	Axe	57/92	1572	5791	3A	bifacially polished
2	Axe	568	240?	400?		fragment, bifacially polished

Figure 11.32. Celts.

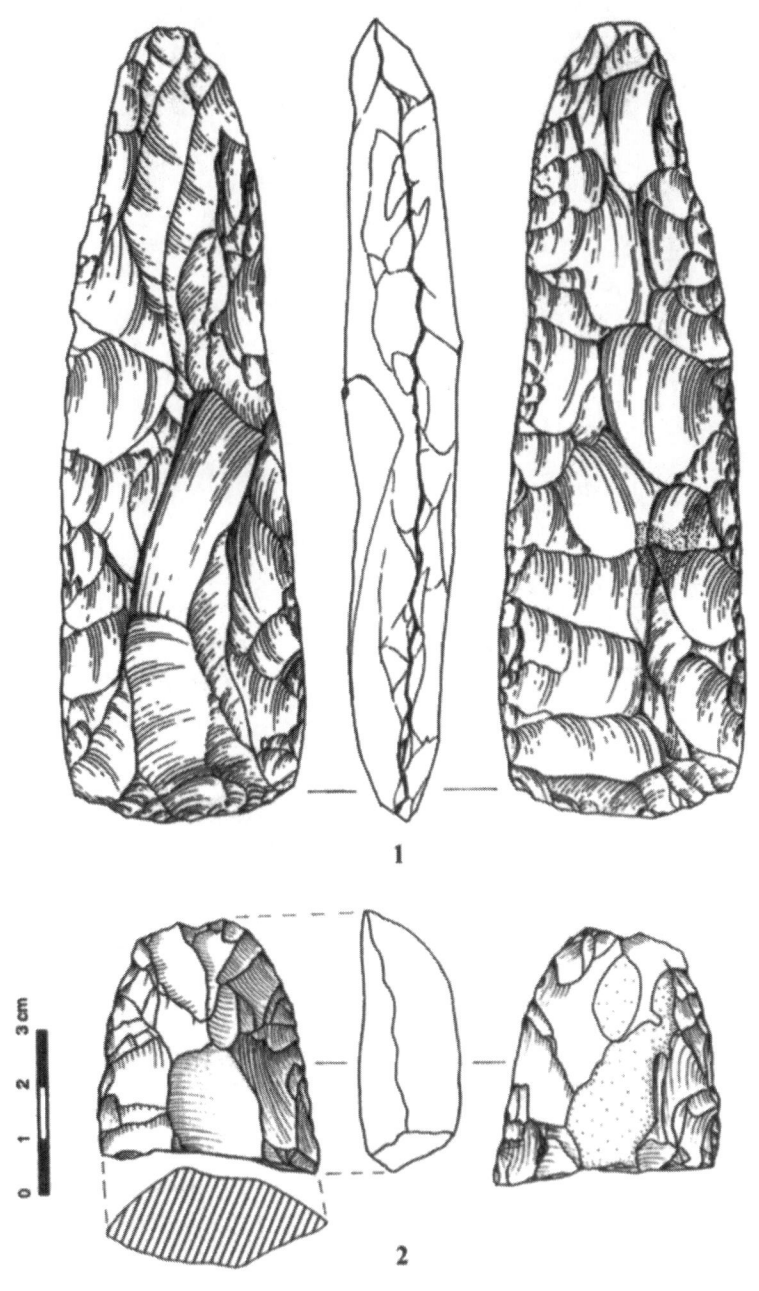

No.	Artifact	Reg. No.	Locus	Basket	Stratum	Description
1	Axe	49/90	957	2724	2A	large, from foundation deposit
2	Celt	568	2	4	1-2	fragment

Figure 11.33. Celts.

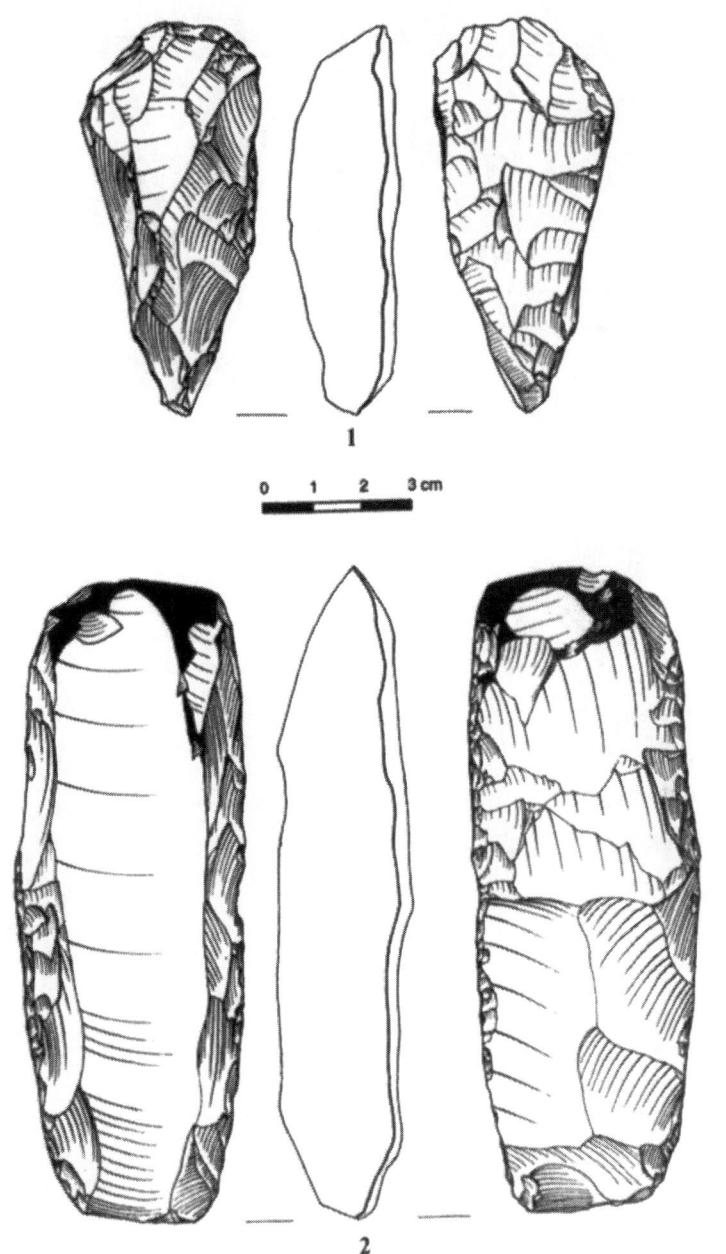

No.	Artifact	Reg. No.	Locus	Basket	Stratum	Description
1	Adze	49/90	001	3003	1	
2	Axe	19/91	627	5185	2A	single, long, unifacial flake scar bifacially bit polish

Figure 11.34. Celts.

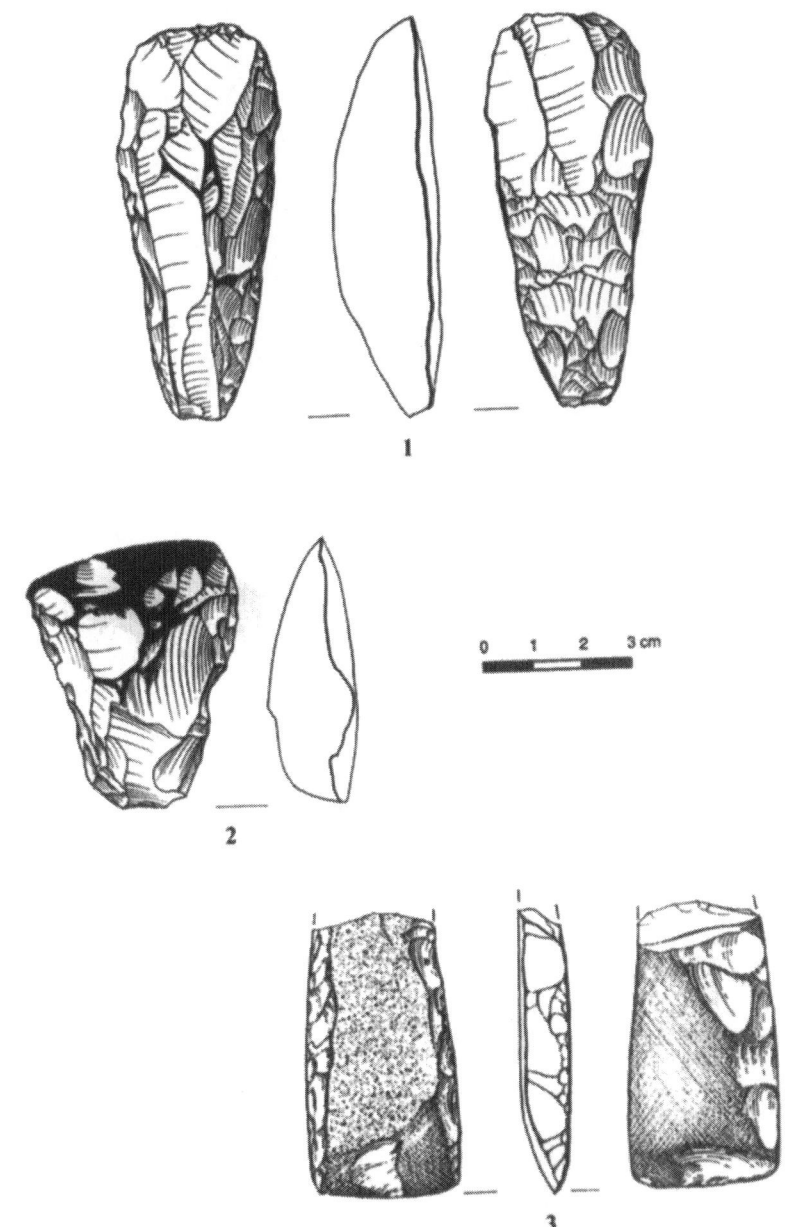

No.	Artifact	Reg. No.	Locus	Basket	Stratum	Description
1	Axe	19/91	601	3019	1	
2	Axe	19/91	600	5055	1	bifacially polished
3	Chisel/axe	19/91	689	5342	2B	bifacially polished tabular scraper fragment

Figure 11.35. Celts.

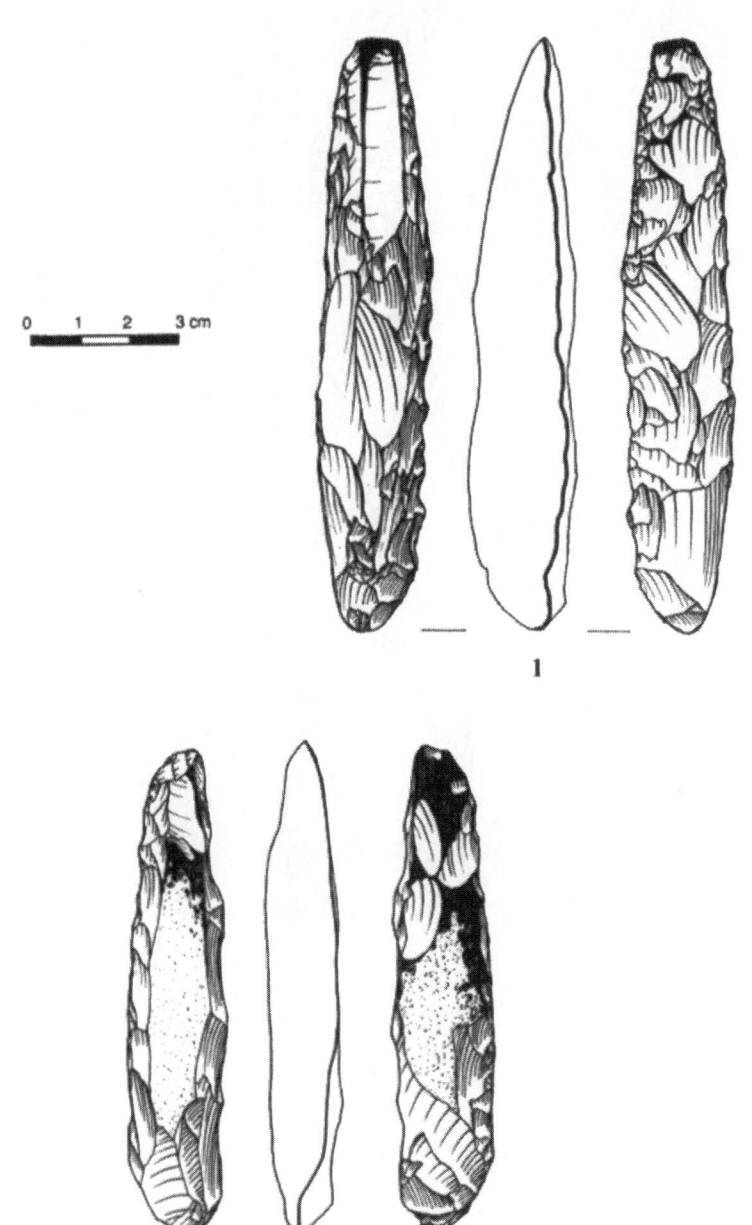

No.	Artifact	Reg. No.	Locus	Basket	Stratum	Description
1	Chisel	49/90	501	100	1	bifacially polished
2	Chisel	57/92	796	5555	2B	bifacially polished

Figure 11.36. Bifacial core tools.

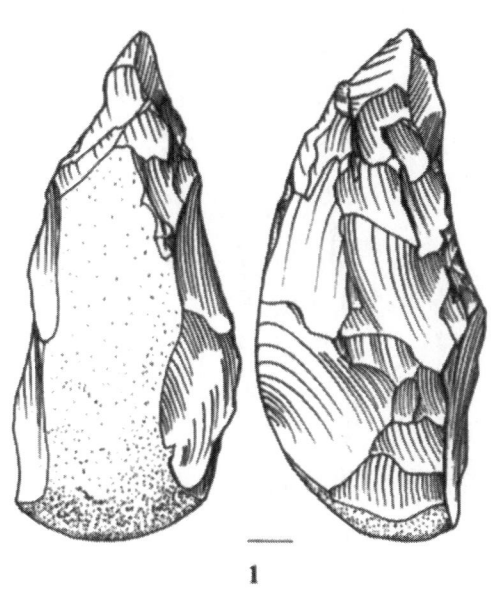

1

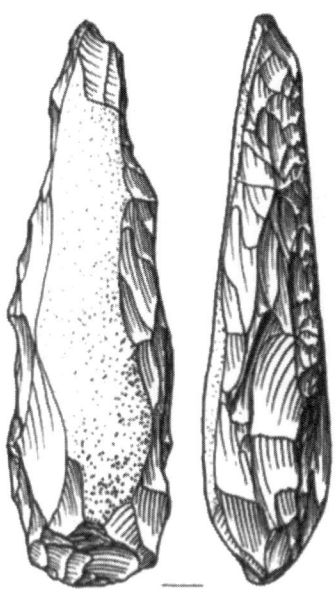

2

No.	Artifact	Reg. No.	Locus	Basket	Stratum	Description
1	Pick on cobble	57/92	771	5463	2C	trihedral cross-section
2	Pick	49/90	005	3016	1	bifacial cortex

Figure 11.37. Celt preform, scrapers and chopper.

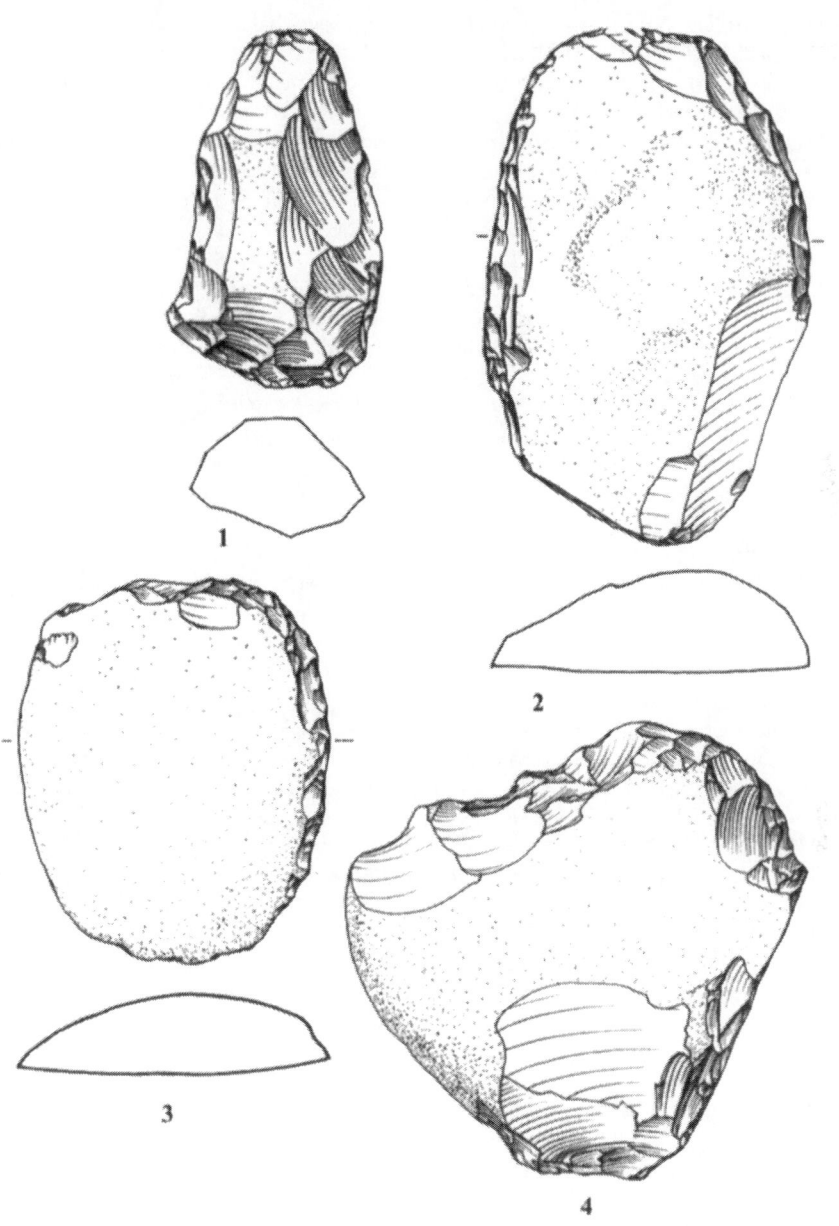

No.	Artifact	Reg. No.	Locus	Basket	Stratum	Description
1	Celt preform?	57/92	1526	5788	2C	unfinished core
2	Limestone scraper	57/92	775	5455	2B	primary flake, distal-bilateral dorsal retouch
3	Sidescraper	49/90	800	2163	1	primary flake
4	Chopper	57/92	762	5426	2A	retouched split cobble

References

Alon, D. and Levy, T.E. (1989) The archaeology of cult and the Chalcolithic sanctuary at Gilat. *Journal of Mediterranean Archaeology* 2:163–221.

Anderson, P.C. (1980) A testimony of prehistoric tasks: Diagnostic residues on stone tool working edges. *World Archaeology* 2: 181–94.

Bordes, F. (1961) *Typologie du Paleolithique ancien et moyen*. Publications de l'Institut de Prehistoire de l'Universite de Bordeaux Memoire No.1. Bordeaux: Universite de Bordeaux.

Bourke, S. J. (1997) The 'Pre-Ghassulian' sequence at Teleilat Ghassul: Sydney University Excavations 1975–1995. In *The Prehistory of Jordan II*, edited by H.G.K. Gebel, Z. Kafafi, and G.O. Rollefson. Berlin: Ex Oriente, pp. 395–417.

Brown, J.A. (1982) On the structure of artifact typologies. In *Essays on Archaeological Typology*, edited by R. Whallon and J.A. Brown). Evanston: Center for American Archaeology Press, pp. 176–89.

Burian, F. and Friedman, E. (1985) Flint borers: Methods of production and use. *Mitekufat Ha'even, Journal of the Israel Prehistoric Society*. 18:63–5.

Crabtree, D. (1982) *An Introduction to Flintworking, Occasional Papers of the Idaho Museum of Natural History* 28 (2nd edn). Pocatello, Idaho.

Crowfoot, J. (1948) Some flint implements from Affula. *Journal of the Palestine Oriental Society* 21:72–9.

Crowfoot-Payne, J. (1960) Flint implements from Tell al-Judaidah. In *Excavations in the Plain of Antioch. Oriental Institute Publication 61*, edited by R.J. Braidwood and L.S. Braidwood. Chicago: University of Chicago Press, pp. 525–9.

Dibble, H.L. (1987) The interpretation of Middle Paleolithic scraper morphology. *American Antiquity* 52: 109–17.

Dunnell, R.C. (1978) Style and function: A fundamental dichotomy. *American Antiquity* 43:192–202.

Dunnell, R.C. (1986) Methodological issues in Americanist artifact classification. *Advances in Archaeological Method and Theory* 9:149–208.

Gilead, I. (1984) The micro-endscraper: a new tool type of the Chalcolithic period. *Tel Aviv* 11:3–10.

Gilead, I. (1989) Knapped limestone series from the Chalcolithic period of the northern Negev, Israel. *Journal of the Israel Prehistoric Society (Mitekufat Haeven)* 22:98–110.

Gilead, I. (1989) Grar: A Chalcolithic site in the northern Negev, Israel. *Journal of Field Archaeology* 16: 377–94.

Gilead, I., Hershman, D., Marder, O. (1995) The flint assemblages from Grar. In *Grar: A Chalcolithic Site in the Northern Negev*, edited by I. Gilead. Beer-Sheva: Ben-Gurion University of the Negev Press, pp. 223–80.

Hanbury-Tenison, J. (1986) *The Late Chalcolithic to Early Bronze I Transition in Palestine and Transjordan*. BAR International Series 311. Oxford: British Archaeological Reports.

Hill, J.N. and Evans, R.K. (1972) A model for classification and typology. In *Models in Archaeology*, edited by D.L. Clarke. London: Methuen, pp. 231–73.

Hodson, F.R. (1982) Some aspects of archaeological classification. In *Essays on Archaeological Typology*, edited by R. Whallon and J.A. Brown. Evanston: Center for American Archaeology Press, pp. 21–9.

Joffe, A.H. and Dessel, J.P. (1995) Redefining chronology and terminology for the Chalcolithic of the southern Levant. *Current Anthropology* 36(3):507–18.

Kislev, M.E. (1987) Chalcolithic plant husbandry and ancient vegetation at Shiqmim. In *Shiqmim I: Studies Concerning Chalcolithic Societies in the Northern Negev Desert, Israel*, edited by T.E. Levy. BAR International Series 356. Oxford: British Archaeological Reports, pp. 251–79.

Kozloff, B. (1972–3) A brief note on the lithic industries of Sinai. *Museum Ha'aretz Yearbook* 15/16:35–49.

Krieger, A.D. (1944) The typological concept. *American Antiquity* 9:271–88.

Lee, J.R. (1973) Chalcolithic Ghassul: New Aspects and Master Typology. Unpublished PhD dissertation, Hebrew University, Jerusalem.

Levy, T.E. and Alon, D. (1987) Excavations in Shiqmim Cemetery 3: Final report on the 1982 excavations. In *Shiqmim I: Studies Concerning Chalcolithic Societies in the Northern Negev Desert, Israel*, edited by T.E. Levy. BAR International Series 356. Oxford: British Archaeological Reports, p. 333–55.

Levy, T.E. and Holl, A. (1987) Theory and practice in household archaeology: a case study from the Chalcolithic village at Shiqmim. In *Shiqmim I: Studies Concerning Chalcolithic Societies in the Northern Negev Desert, Israel*, edited by T.E. Levy. BAR International Series 356. Oxford: British Archaeological Reports, pp. 333–55.

Levy, T.E. and Shalev, S. (1989) Prehistoric metalworking in the southern Levant: Archaeometallurgical and social perspectives. *World Archaeology* 20(3):352–72.

Levy, T.E. and Rosen, S.A. (1987) The chipped stone industry at Shiqmim: Typological considerations. *Shiqmim I: Studies Concerning Chalcolithic Societies in the Northern Negev Desert, Israel*, edited by T.E. Levy. BAR International Series 356. Oxford: British Archaeological Reports, pp. 281–94.

Mallon, A., Koeppel, R. and Neuville, R. (1934) *Teleilat Ghassul I*. Rome: Pontifical Biblical Institute.

McConaughy, M. (1979) Formal and Functional Analyses of the Chipped Stone Tools from Bab edh-Dhra, Jordan. Unpublished PhD dissertation, University of Pittsburgh.

Milstein, S. and Ronen, A. (1985) Flint Implements. In Y.Porath, A Chalcolithic building at Fasa'el. *'Atiqot* 17:11–13.

Mond, R. and Meyers, O.H. (1937) *Cemeteries of Armant I*. London: Egypt Exploration Society.

Muheisen, M., Gebel, H.G., Hannss, C., Neef, R. (1988) Excavations at 'Ain Rahub, a Final Natufian and Yarmoukian site near Irbid (1985). In *The Prehistory of Jordan*, edited by A.N. Garrard and H.G. Gebel. BAR International Series 336 (ii). Oxford: British Archaeological Reports, pp. 473–502.

Nasrallah, R.P.J. (1936) Le gisement Ghassoulien de Tell es-Soma. *Journal of the Palestine Oriental Society* 16: 293–315.

Neuville, R. (1930) Notes de prehistoire Palestinienne: I-La grotte d'et-Taouamim. *Journal of Palestine Oriental Society* X:64–75.

Ohnuma, K. (1993) Experimental studies in the determination of manners of micro-blade detachment. *Al-Rafidan* 14:153–81.

Parry, W.J. and Kelly, R.L. (1987) Expedient core technology and sedentism. In *The Organization of Core Technology*, edited by J.K. Johnson and C.A. Morrow. Boulder, CO: Westview, pp. 285–345.

Perrot, J. (1992) Umm Qatafa and Umm Qala'a: Two 'Ghassulian' caves in the Desert of Judea. In *Eretz Israel* (Biran Volume), edited by E. Stern and T.E. Levy. Jerusalem: Israel Exploration Society, pp. 100–11.

Rizkana, I. and Seeher, J. (1988) *Maadi II: The lithic industries of the predynastic settlement*. Mainz am Rhein: P. von Zabern.

Rolland, N., and Dibble, H.L. (1990) A new synthesis of Middle Paleolithic variability. *American Antiquity* 55: 480–99.

Rosen, S.A. (1983a) The tabular scraper trade: a model for material culture dispersion. *Bulletin of the American Schools of Oriental Research* 249:79–86.

Rosen, S.A. (1983b) The Canaanean blade and the Early Bronze Age. *Israel Exploration Journal* 33:15–29.

Rosen, S.A. (1985) Appendix B: The En Shadud lithics. In *En Shadud: Salvage Excavations at a Farming Community in the Jezreel Valley, Israel*, edited by E. Braun. BAR International Series 249. Oxford: British Archaeological Reports, pp. 153–66.

Rosen, S.A. (1987. The potentials of lithic analysis in the Chalcolithic of the northern Negev. In *Shiqmim I*, edited by T.E. Levy. BAR International Series 356. Oxford: British Archaeological Reports, pp. 243–312.

Rosen, S.A. (1989) The analysis of Early Bronze Age chipped stone industries. In *L'Urbanisation de la Palestine a l'age du Bronze ancient*, edited by P. de Miroschedji. BAR International Series 527. Oxford: British Archaeological Reports, pp. 199–222.

Rosen, S.A. (1994–5) Microlithic drills from the Camel Site, Mitzpeh Ramon. *Journal of the Israel Prehistoric Society* 26:148–58.

Rosen, S.A. (1997) *Lithics after the Stone Age: a handbook of stone tools from the Levant*. Walnut Creek, CA: AltaMira Press.

Roshwalb, A. (1981) Protohistory in Wadi Ghazzeh: a Typological and Technological Study Based on the Macdonald Excavations. Unpublished PhD dissertation, University of London.

Rouse, I. (1960) The classification of artifacts in archaeology. *American Antiquity* 25:313–23.

Rowan, Y.M. (1990) A Chalcolithic Chipped Stone Assemblage from the Northern Negev Desert: Phase II (1987–1989) Investigations at Shiqmim. Unpublished MA thesis, University of Texas at Austin.

Rowan, Y.M. and Levy, T.E. (1991) Use-wear analysis of a Chalcolithic scraper assemblage from Shiqmim. *Journal of the Israel Prehistoric Society (Mitekufat Haeven)* 24:112–34.

Rowan, Y.M. and Levy, T.E. (1994) Proto-Canaanean blades from the Chalcolithic site of Gilat. *Levant* 26:167–74.

Schick, T. (1978) Flint implements. In *Early Arad: The Chalcolithic Settlement and Early Bronze Age City I. First Fifth Seasons of Excavations 1962–1966.* Jerusalem: Israel Exploration Society, pp. 58–63.

Seger, J.D., Baum, B., Borowski, O., Cole, D.P., Forshey, H., Futato, E., Jacobs, P.F., Laustrup, M., Seger, P.O., Zeder, M. (1990) The Bronze Age settlements at Tell Halif: Phase II excavations, 1983–1987. *BASOR Supplement* 26:1–32.

Shea, J.J. (1989) Tool use in the Levantine Mousterian of Kebara Cave, Mount Carmel. *Journal of the Israel Prehistoric Society (Mitekufat Haeven)* 22:15–30.

Simms, S.R., and Russell, K.W. (1997) Bedouin hand harvesting of wheat and barley: Implications for early cultivation in Southwestern Asia. *Current Anthropology* 38: 696–702.

Sollberger, J.B. and Patterson, L.W. (1976) Prismatic blade replication. *American Antiquity* 41:517–31.

Spaulding, A.C. (1982) Structure in archaeological data: Nominal variables. In *Essays on Archaeological Typology*, edited by R. Whallon and J.A. Brown. Evanston: Center for American Archaeology Press, pp. 1–20.

Tixier, J. (1963) *Typologie de l'Epipaleolithique du Maghreb. Memoire de centre de recherches anthropologiques, prehistoriques, et ethnologiques* 2. Paris: Aris et Metiers Graphiques.

Unger-Hamilton, R. (1989) The Epi-Palaeolithic southern Levant and the origins of cultivation. *Current Anthropology* 30(1):88–103.

Valla, F. (1978) Essai de typologie des objets de silex lustres de Susiane. *Paleorient* 4:325–35.

Yeivin, S. (1959) Flint implements from Horvat Beter. *'Atiqot* 2:43–47.

Yellin, J., Levy, T.E. and Rowan, Y.M. (1996) New evidence on prehistoric trade routes: The obsidian evidence from Gilat, Israel. *Journal of Field Archaeology* 23: 361–68.

12 Gilat's Ground Stone Assemblage:
Stone Fenestrated Stands, Bowls, Palettes and Related Artifacts

Yorke M. Rowan, Thomas E. Levy, David Alon†, and Yuval Goren

Introduction

This chapter describes the ground stone and related artifact assemblage from Gilat, one of the larger components of material culture found at the site. These objects encompass a wide diversity of forms, functions and materials ranging from domestic grinding implements to finely crafted mace heads and palettes. These tools, vessels and decorative objects epitomize the versatility of craftsmanship for which the Chalcolithic has become known throughout the southern Levant. A total of 2,038 artifacts are included in this study, representing the largest published southern Levantine ground stone assemblage from the Chalcolithic period (cf. Commenge in press; Gilead 1995; Lee 1973). Three primary objectives were the focus of this research; description, quantification and comparison to other late prehistoric assemblages. Though the function of many of these artifact classes is an intriguing question, and one about which we occasionally suggest hypotheses, no use-wear or residue analyses were attempted, and thus the function of many artifact types is not examined in a critical fashion. Included within this discussion are also some non-stone artifacts (e.g. shell, ivory, bone, ceramic) which belong to larger artifact classes primarily made of stone such as beads, pendants and other decorative objects.

Ground stone artifacts are a common feature of agricultural societies, and have been recognized by archaeologists as a typical feature of foraging and early farming communities for some time. In general, with the advent of increasingly sedentary societies beginning with the Natufian (Valla 1998) and into the Neolithic periods (Bar-Yosef 1998), there seems to be an increase in the number and types of ground stone tools and objects found in the archaeological record. Nevertheless, site reports from excavations in the southern Levant rarely present comprehensive, quantified data on the ground stone assemblages. In addition, the significance of ground stone tools is rarely discussed. This seems particularly true as one moves from earlier prehistoric sites to historic and 'biblical' periods. This is only slightly surprising because chrono-stratigraphic concerns were paramount in the past, and ceramic typologies were viewed as the most sensitive indicators of chronological changes and continuities. While in no way disputing the importance of ceramic analyses, which will probably remain more indicative of chronological and stylistic change, the potential implications of information derived from study of the more prosaic late prehistoric ground stone assemblages will always remain obscure if not included in the basic final reports of excavations. Admittedly, as research questions have shifted from the chronological to the more anthropologically oriented questions of archaeology, this bias is changing. Nevertheless, complete reports on Chalcolithic ground stone assemblages are still very rare, and without efforts to provide contextualized, quantified description of these assemblages, the potential information of these artifacts and their comparative value to other assemblages will remain unknowable. As archaeologists seek more information on the daily subsistence activities of past societies, the grinding and pounding implements, as mainstays of daily domestic life, provide potential information on subsistence economies, prehistoric technology, and in some cases, local exchange, which is only available through the study of the ground stone tools and their production.

This discussion is separated into two general sections. One section focuses on describing the grinding and pounding tool assemblage (though not all were used for these activities), which could be referred to as the 'domestic ground stone assemblage'. These artifacts manufactured of stone were probably utilized for the daily subsistence activities of the inhabitants of the site, and include the grinding slabs, hand-stones, mortars, pestles, hammer stones, large perforated stones, as well as various other miscellaneous ground stone artifacts, such as the polished pebbles, various modified cobbles and ground stone fragments.

The second section includes other artifact classes which are decorative (beads and pendants), rare or disproportionately made of non-local materials (mace heads, 'tokens', palettes), or not exclusively manufactured of stone (spindle whorls, beads, pendants). The stone vessels, most of which are made of basalt, are also described in this section. The function of these vessels is unknown, and it is not clear that they are part of the domestic assemblage, but for quantified comparison with other sites, they are included in the second section. In order to understand function, future excavations should establish protocols to sample ground stone objects for gas chromatography and other science-based analyses. These sections are presented in this manner primarily to facilitate comparison with other ground stone assemblages. Tool classes commonly reported from other sites are discussed in the first section. A section in which an artifact class is discussed is intended to facilitate comparison with other late prehistoric assemblages, most of which do not have comparable frequencies of artifacts from the second section. In this sense, we hope the ground stone assemblage from Gilat will help establish a systematic framework for this kind of study in future research.

Description of the artifacts included a number of factors for each object:

1. *Provenance*: The area, square, year, locus and basket number was recorded for each artifact. Artifacts collected from the site surface or from dubious contexts are considered 'stray' finds, and are not given a locus number or stratum designation, though some were assigned basket numbers for identification. Nevertheless, these artifacts are also considered part of the late fifth to fourth millennium assemblage, because there is nothing to suggest that any of the assemblage pre- or post-date the Chalcolithic at Gilat. As shown by Commenge *et al.* (this volume), ceramic evidence suggests some Wadi Rabah Late Neolithic occupation. While a few pit houses and isolated loci could be attributed to the Wadi Rabah phase, there are no strata or extensive areas that could be linked specifically to this occupation phase.

2. *Metric measurements*: Each artifact, whether complete or fragmentary, was measured for length, width and thickness. For descriptive statistical purposes, those artifacts that were complete or nearly complete are considered separately from fragments. Where relevant, measurements of perforation depths and hole diameters (minimum and maximum, if possible) are also included. Perforation diameter of spindle whorls is an important factor for interpretation (Barber 1991) and as a result we regard this as a potentially important

criterion for understanding the function of any perforated artifact. Weights were deter-mined for many artifact classes, usually accurate to $\pm$ 10 g. Smaller artifacts, such as mace heads and spindle whorls, were re-weighed with more precise instruments, accurate to $\pm$ 1 g. These data are presented in a series of tables included in this chapter.

3. *Morphology*: The primary descriptor was the object as viewed in plan view, which includes 8 primary shapes; rectangular, round, trapezoidal, ovoid, triangular, square, elongate (elliptical), and irregular (indeterminate). Transversal cross-sections were also included for many types, and are referred to simply as 'cross-section'. This includes the eight shapes discussed above, with the addition of plano-convex, concave-convex (U-shaped), bi-convex and irregular. Profiles (longitudinal cross-sections) were also recorded for many artifact types, but are discussed only when it seems an important discriminating factor in artifact classes.

4. *Raw material*: The general lithology composition of the stone artifacts was determined with a hand lens and macroscopically. A wide variety of rock types were identified includ-ing limestone, chalk, flint, beach-rock, basalt, scoria, hematite, chlorite schist, granite, as well as numerous other rarer materials. Where lithology composition was difficult, identifi-cation was made with petrographic thin-sections. This was necessary with only a few mace heads, palettes and the ground 'votive' axes. These data are of central importance for identifying interaction patterns at Gilat.

The Grinding and Pounding Assemblage

The ground stone artifacts from Gilat are divided into 19 general artifact groups, based on analyses begun soon after the final (1992) excavations. These classes were first defined based on observations of common types from late prehistoric sites. This analysis was conducted before Wright's (1992a, 1992b) typological studies were available, but in general, the definitions of most types follow hers, including the primary morphologically derived attributes of the classifications. In some cases, our terminology differs or additional categorical refinement was necessary, and where possible, these differences are noted.

Ground stone artifacts are defined as those in which abrasive wear is the primary feature of the final lithic reduction process. The distinction between ground stone artifacts and chipped stone technology is not always clear-cut, and both technologies share some parallels and contrasts (Wright 1993:93). Many of the ground stone artifacts from Gilat, like other Chalcolithic sites, were first roughly shaped by chipping the general morphology of the desired product, which may or may not have been further reduced or finished through grinding or abrasive wear.

Throughout much of this discussion, three general categories are used for the different types. *Complete* artifacts are those which seem unbroken, or have virtually no apparent broken sections significantly altering the morphological outlines. *Incomplete* artifacts are those missing some portion of the original morphology, but which may still permit interpretation as to the original morphology and hence typological category. *Fragments* may still permit interpretation of the typological category, but are generally too small to guess the original morphology.

At Gilat, the two major materials utilized for the manufacture of the domestic ground stone implements are the locally available sedimentary beach-rock and a variety of limestone and chalks. Within the latter, there is a range of materials, including siliceous limestone and soft chalks. Other materials, such as basalt, sandstone and flint are uncommon, with the exception of the hammer stones/pounders and the smoothed pebbles, which are commonly made of flint nodules. As we discuss, this distinction is primarily limited to the domestic assemblage, with a much greater lithology diversity among non-domestic ground stone artifacts.

Grinding Slabs (complete = 68; incomplete = 22; fragments = 441; TOTAL = 531; Total weight = 1083.53 kg).

These are the lower, stationary stones that represent the surface on which grains, minerals and other materials were placed for crushing and grinding. Wright (1993:94–5) distinguishes between two types; stones with lateral grinding striae which are called 'grinding slabs' and 'querns' which exhibit elliptical grinding striae. However, given the lack of macroscopically visible striae on most of the specimens, and the lack of artifacts exhibiting rotary or elliptical grinding wear, this distinction was not considered viable for the Gilat assemblage. Hence, all of the present examples are classed as grinding slabs, called *metates* in the New World. Ethnographic information indicates that similar types of artifacts may be reused for other grinding activities, which may obscure the original traces of wear, or otherwise alter the interpretation of the primary use (Roux 1985).

Grinding slabs constitute the largest category of ground stone implements from Gilat, if fragments (n=441) are included. One of the reasons for such a large number of samples is the fact that grinding slabs were often recycled and used to build walls, silo bases, and other features. This is a very large number of fragments, but the thickness and the unifacially ground aspect are recognizably similar to the grinding slabs. Table 12.1, which lists only the complete and incomplete grinders, summarizes the contextual information and dimensions. Shapes of the complete grinders are predominantly oval (n=42, 62%), while the second most common shape is 'loaf-shaped', a roughly elongate, elliptical shape (n=18, 26%). Table 12.2 shows that the average dimensions of complete specimens are c. 25 cm (length), 17 cm (width) and 6.5 cm (thickness). Profiles of these are typically plano-convex (n=39, 57%) with the planar face well-ground to a flat face, which has become slightly convex in some cases. Others (Figure 12.20:3) are flat in profile (n=25, 37%); for both types of profiles, thickness generally increases with overall length and width dimensions. Within the fragments, plano-convex profiles are also the most common. As seen in Table 12.2, an additional 26 fragments (49.41 kg) are probably also grinding slabs. The majority of grinding slabs are not substantially concave on the working face, suggesting the rock used was easily obtainable and neither utilized until exhausted nor curated over long periods of time.

Beach-rock was the preferred material for these implements. All complete and incomplete examples were made of beach-rock, with the exception of one large, complete vesicular basalt grinding slab.[1] Fragments are also primarily made of beach-rock, but one fragment is of limestone and another of sandstone. Grinding slabs are probably recovered from most domestic Chalcolithic assemblages, though not always illustrated or quantified. Similar artifacts are known from Grar (Gilead 1995: Fig. 7.4:3–5), Horvat Beter (Dothan 1959a: Fig. 19.9) and others of basalt are illustrated from Tuleilat Ghassul (Lee 1973:268, LB21a), En Shadud (Braun 1985: Fig. 39:3; 40:1–9), a variety of materials at Jericho (Dorrell 1983: Fig. 230:11), and flint and basalt grinding slabs at Arad (Amiran *et al.* 1978: Pl.79:1–7).

Hand-Stones (complete = 19; incomplete = 3; fragments = 24; TOTAL = 46)

Hand-stones, or *manos* as they are referred to in the New World, are the upper, mobile grinding stone used against the planar face of the grinding slabs and querns. Attempting to distinguish between these two artifact types can sometimes be difficult, where sizes fall in between the intuitive categories, a problem encountered in other studies of ground stone as well (e.g. Hovers 1996:173). Like that study, we were sometimes able to resolve this problem through close examination of the working surface. Grinding slabs tend to develop concave working surfaces through use, and hand-stones tend to remain flat or even become convex. Where size was an insufficient variable to determine the category of an artifact, those with convex working faces and a size acceptable for one- or two-handed locomotion were considered hand-stones.

As seen in Table 12.3, the average length of hand-stones (12 cm) is less than the average width of grinding stones (c. 17 cm), which accords well with their possible identification as different tools used together in a pair. Hand-stones are far less numerous, constituting less than 5% of the total identifiable assemblage; however, there is an even greater number (discussed below) of possible hand-stones. Shapes are more commonly round to oval, and the profiles are more often flat rather than plano-convex, unlike the stationary grinding slabs. Like grinding slabs, hand-stones are only occasionally discussed and illustrated, but some hand-stones are illustrated from Grar (Gilead 1995: Fig. 7.4:1–2), Arad (Amiran *et al.* 1978:58, Pl.80:9–11, 13–15), Neve Ur (Perrot *et al.* 1967: Fig. 13:11–13), and Tuleilat Ghassul (Lee 1973:270, LB25:a–d).

Table 12.4 lists the hand-stones and the summarized contextual and metric information for each. Three materials were used for hand-stones; beach-rock, scoria, and basalt. For the present discussion, scoria and basalt are considered as one group because they are similar rock types of non-local, volcanic origin. Judging by the morphological attributes of the hand-stones made of the two different materials; these may be functionally distinct types. While beach-rock hand-stones are often flat or plano-convex in profile (Table 12.3), the scoria and basalt hand-stones often have a slightly concave working face, suggesting that they were used in a different manner. Descriptive statistics of the two groups (Table 12.5) also suggest distinctive types. Comparison of the complete and incomplete examples of hand-stones from these two different materials indicates that the beach-rock hand-stones are longer, wider and thicker than those of scoria and basalt.

Probable Hand-Stones (complete = 15; incomplete = 7; fragments = 23; TOTAL = 45)

As noted above, the identification of these artifacts is difficult because of the overlap in the range of sizes between stationary grinding slabs and hand-stones. This category refers to those which are assumed to be hand-stones, but are indeterminate. Mean dimensions (Table 12.6) support the suggestion that some are hand-stones; length, width and thickness are only slightly larger than that for the hand-stones (Table 12.3) discussed above, and much smaller than for the grinders (see Table 12.2). Like the grinding slabs, most are made from beach-rock, only one of limestone and one of *kurkar* were found. All fragments are manufactured from beach-rock.

Grinding Slabs or Hand-Stones (Complete = 9; incomplete = 5; fragments = 8; TOTAL = 22)

It is unclear whether some artifacts are grinding slabs or hand-stones (manos). Both means and dimensional ranges (Table 12.7) indicate that these fall in between those of grinding slabs and hand-stones. As the comparative frequencies of the dimensions and weights of these indicate, this category straddles the division between the larger, heavier grinding slabs and the smaller, lighter hand-stones.

Unidentifiable Ground Stone Fragments (n = 68; 32.23 kg)

These are primarily flat (n = 60) fragments, none of which could be placed confidently in any category. Those with flat profiles are almost all made of beach-rock; four are limestone, one is made of *kurkar*, and one is made of granite. Four fragments have plano-convex profiles (one of which is scoria), while one, made of limestone, is concave on the dorsal face and flat on the opposite face. The remaining fragments have irregular profiles, and are made of beach-rock. It is not certain that all of these were artifacts, but it seems likely most were at least collected with the intention of use, possibly for the creation of other artifacts or for grinding other materials. The dimensions of these fragments (Table 12.7) are similar to those of the grinding slab/hand-stones (Table 12.7) as well as the hand-stones (Table 12.3), which suggests it is possible that some of these unidentified fragments are also hand-stones. These may have been used on an *ad hoc* basis for other light grinding tasks, such as the creation of other ground stone artifacts (such as pendants, beads, tokens, etc.). Some fragments could have served for the grinding necessary in bead production (Foreman 1978:21–2, Fig. 10).

Perforated stones (large stone rings) (Complete = 21; incomplete = 3; fragments = 42; TOTAL = 66)

Stone rings are bifacially chipped, drilled, and ground such that the cross-section of the hole is bi-conical (Figure 12.17:3–6). Table 12.8 gives mean dimensions. All of the complete and incomplete specimens are roughly round to oval, though symmetry and form were clearly not of primary importance in some cases. Most are only roughly chipped to shape the exterior, though many were abraded on at least one face. Six have a plano-convex profile; the other 17 are all relatively flat in profile (the opposing faces are roughly parallel). Of the fragments, 21 are flat in profile, eight are plano-convex, three are bi-convex, and two are very irregular.

Table 12.9 lists summarized contextual and metric information for the complete, incomplete and fragments of large stone rings. Both limestone and beach-rock were used for the stone rings, indicating that the selection of material was probably not as important as for the grinders and hand-stones. Only one was made of soft chalk and two of basalt, while the remainder were made of either limestone (n=23, Figure 12.17:3, 5) or beach-rock (n=35, Figure 12.17:4, 6). At least three (two complete and one incomplete) rings were originally grinders, and were later drilled and reused as stone rings. Three additional fragments were also grinders, becoming stone rings in secondary use. All of those which were originally grinders and later refashioned for use as stone rings are made of beach-rock. Alternatively, it is possible that the ground face of the examples were intentionally created for use as the lower segment of a potter's wheel (e.g. Figure 12.17:6). However, the upper section should have a protuberance, and no artifacts of that type were recovered. There are two perforated stones with similar grooves from the lateral margin to the perforation, which appears to have held rope or twine in place (Figure 12.17:4, 5). Similar pierced stones are commonly recovered from a variety of sites, including Arad (Amiran *et al.* 1978:57, Pl. 77:12–23), Horvat Beter (Dothan 1959a: Fig. 19:15–18), Tuleilat Ghassul (Mallon *et al.* 1934: Pl. 34:1; Lee 1973:274, LB42h-j), Abu Matar (Perrot 1955:78, Pl.13:B), Shiqmim (Grigson 1987:227; Levy and Holl 1987:403, Fig. 15.51:1, 15.16:1–2), Jericho (Dorrell 1983:554, Fig. 230:19–20), Meser (Dothan 1959b: Fig. 8:16), Tel 'Eli (Stekelis 1970: Fig. 32.2) and Grar (Gilead 1995: Fig. 8.1:1–3).

The function of these artifacts is unknown, though they are routinely referred to as digging stick and counterpoise weights (there are good ethnographic analogies for the former (Goodwin 1947:8–12; Van der Merwe 1987:68; Waldron 1987:69–71)). Perforated stones could also have served in a similar capacity to those used in hand drilling (Hartenburg and Schmidt 1969). However, a stone ring weighing over eight kilograms, such as the largest example from Gilat, may be too heavy to serve as a digging stick weight or drilling weight, suggesting these artifacts were used in more than one capacity.

Hammer Stones (pounders) (n = 21)[2]

These are large, battered cobbles of flint (n=16) or limestone (n=5) which are roughly round. Though probably spherical when selected, as some still are (n=5), many are ground and pecked such that the profile varies (see Table 12.10). Mean dimensions, shapes and profiles are presented in Table 12.11, which indicates that most are spherical, or round with one side which is faceted or battered. Comparison of length measurements (Figure 12.1), widths (Figure 12.2), and weights (Figure 12.3) indicate that hammer stones are typically larger and heavier than the smoothed pebbles, confirming the intuitive observation that these represent functionally distinct classes. However, there is overlap of the larger smoothed pebbles with some hammer stones, and the visible pecking, grinding and battering remains the defining characteristic of the hammer stones. Hammer stones and cobble pounders are commonly recovered from prehistoric and historic contexts (Rosen 1997), and were probably utilized for a variety of purposes. Frequently they are reported with the chipped stone industries because of their presumed association with chipped stone manufacture, though this need not be the exclusive function (e.g. Adams 1989). Illustrated hammer stones include those from Tuleilat Ghassul (Lee 1973:260, LA41:a).

Pestles (complete = 10, fragment = 1; TOTAL=11)

Table 12.12 lists the summarized contextual and metric information for the few pestles recovered. A range of materials was used to manufacture these artifacts. Four of the pestles are made of limestone, three are flint, two are basalt, and one each is made of hematite and beach-rock. Working ends are ground and pecked, with flat to convex ends, sides are sometimes also ground smooth. Like the pestles found at Abu Hamid, most are conical to elongate in profile (Wright 1992a: Fig. 5:58a–d). Transverse cross-sections are roughly round; only two have roughly trapezoidal to rectangular cross-sections.

The low frequency of pestles suggests the possibility that wooden pestles may have been more commonly used, or that the classic elongate type of pestle has fallen out of use by the Chalcolithic period. A similar observation of low pestle frequency at the Chalcolithic site of Abu Hamid is suggested to support the former interpretation (Wright 1992a:253). However, given the very shallow depth of most mortars from Gilat, hammer stones and pounders could also have served as the hand-held tool (Commenge in press). Dimensions (Table 12.13) indicate a relatively broad range among the very small sample. Comparable artifacts are illustrated from Horvat Beter (Dothan 1959a: Fig. 11:12, 13), of basalt from Jawa (Helms 1991: Fig. 193.691–3), Arad (Amiran *et al.* 1978: Pl.80.12), and Jericho (Dorrell 1983: Fig. 230.6).

Smoothed Pebbles (n = 176)

During the 1990–91 excavations, numerous small stream-rolled pebbles were noticed, and the decision was made to collect all of these as artifacts. Clearly, this number represents only a sample of the total that could have been collected during all seasons of excavation. The majority of these have no apparent modification, and the possible functions are numerous (burnishing stones, game markers, counters, etc.). The most common shape is spherical, followed closely by oval shapes with relatively flat profiles. These and the other shapes represent the natural shapes of the pebbles. Although there is overlap in dimensions and weights (see Table 12.14 and Figures 12.1–3) between these and the hammer stones, the obvious modification of the hammer stones as opposed to the smoothed pebbles readily distinguishes the two in most cases. Similar artifacts have been noted from Arad (Sebbane n.d.). Though the pebbles are found in all contexts, there is a greater density in pits and silos, where almost half (47%) of all the pebbles are found. The second most common context for the pebbles is on surfaces, an atypical density compared to flint tool densities. Pebbles are commonly found associated with palettes in Predynastic Egyptian burials, often with minerals such as malachite and ochre still evident on their surfaces (i.e. Peet 1914:4; Petrie 1896:10; Baumgartel 1960:81). Such a clear association between palettes and these polished pebbles was not possible at Gilat.

Door Sockets/Pivot Stones (complete = 4, incomplete = 1; TOTAL = 5)

These are large, flat limestone blocks with shallow depressions incised on one face. A few remain in the field *in situ* as an integral part of the architecture. Summarized information is provided in Table 12.15. Unlike the mortars (discussed below), the interior of the depressions are generally round, with interior concentric grooves indicating heavy pressure in a circular motion. In addition, and also unlike the mortars, the incised concavity is much smaller in relation to the block. Dimensions range from 15–26 cm (length), 12–25 cm (width), and 6–13 cm (thickness/height), with a range in weight from 2.0–8.11 (kg). Circular depressions range in diameter from 7–11 cm, with a range in depth of 1–3 cm. These types of stones are probably commonly found at Chalcolithic sites, though reports of their discovery are rare, and sometimes referred to as 'cup-marks' (cf. Gilead 1995:325) or door sockets, for example at Arad (Amiran *et al.* 1978: Pl 80:20). Not all of these artifact types were collected at Gilat because they were embedded in walls or left *in situ*.

Mortars (complete = 26, incomplete = 5, fragments = 72; TOTAL = 103)

Mortars are made primarily of beach-rock and limestone, with a few small ones made of chalk (Table 12.16). These vary from small pebble mortars to bowl-mortars; no large 'boulder' mortars were found. The majority of the mortars are shallow pebble mortars, made on nodules or cobbles with well depth ranges of 1–5 cm (Figure 12.4). Most are short and shallow (Figure 12.18:3, 4, 7), with vertical height ranges primarily in the 2–10 cm range (Figure 12.5) and well diameter ranges of 13–19 cm. The small pebble mortars are often oval, made of softer materials such as chalk and non-siliceous limestone (Figure 12.6), and often striated on the interior (Figure 12.10:3–4). This suggests that many were not used in a vertical, up-and-down pounding motion, but were instead used as small hand-held grinding receptacles. Most of the mortars exhibit the natural, weathered exterior surface of the original nodule, or are sometimes pecked and roughly shaped. It is clear that in most cases, little attention was paid to the exterior finish or the overall symmetry of the utensil, an observation supported by on-going analysis of mortars from Arad (Sebbane n.d.) The assemblage from Gilat includes shallow indented objects, which do not fit a traditional notion of a 'mortar'; it is unlikely these were used for heavy pounding. Similar artifacts are sometimes called 'cup-marks' (e.g., Grar Gilead 1995:325, Fig. 7.3:13).

The marked decrease of mortars as part of ground stone assemblages during prehistory has been noted from the Natufian to the Late Neolithic (Wright 1994: Fig. 8), and this trend seems to continue into the Chalcolithic. In addition, the low frequency of pestles recovered from Gilat (not an anomalous occurrence, see Wright 1992a), should be viewed in light of the rarity of large, deep mortars at Gilat. It is possible that the low frequency of pestles reflects not only the use of wooden pestles, but also the decrease in large, deep mortars, and the increase of the small, shallow 'pebble' mortars. These small shallow mortars would not require a long, cylindrical pestle, because the shallow well would easily allow the use of any small cobble or hammer stone. A variety of stone vessels are termed 'mortars', including limestone examples from Horvat Beter (Dothan 1959a: Fig. 11:1–3, 5, 6; 19:6; 24, 26, 27), Arad (Amiran *et al.* 1978: Pl. 78: 5, 6, 10–16), Jericho (Dorrell 1983:553, Type H), the 'Silo Site' on the Tel Halif Terrace (Alon and Yekutieli 1995: Fig. 26:1, 3–4) and Gezer (Seger 1988: Pl. 6.7, 17; Pl. 40.P, R). From sites closer to basalt sources, mortars are commonly made of this rock, such as at Jawa (Helms 1991: Fig. 189.675–8) or both limestone and basalt as found at Tuleilat Ghassul (Mallon *et al.* 1934: Pl 34:1).

Low frequencies of pestles may relate to several factors. There are few deep mortars at Gilat, suggesting that the function of the numerous small pebble mortars are unrelated to the function(s) of the larger deeper mortars, and did not require use of a pestle. Moreover, based on ethnographic and epigraphic evidence, there is no reason to assume that different ground stone tool types correlate to specific foods (see Wright 1994 for discussion and references therein). In addition, wooden pestles are preferred to stone pestles because the latter crushes the seeds, rendering separation of bran from seeds difficult or impossible (*ibid.* 243). Increasing numbers of general grinding tools may reflect the effects of sedentism and rising populations, and a resultant effort to maximize the caloric intake from plant foods, despite the higher labor costs involved (Wright 1994). The increased number of small shallow mortars would suggest a function unrelated to food production intensification.

Multiple use tools (n = 9)

This category follows that of Wright (1992a:641), simply defined as any tool which could fall into more than one of the other ground stone categories. All of the examples from Gilat fall roughly into various types exhibiting both grinding and pounding types of wear (Table 12.17). Two (L.882, B.2643 and L.583, B.1389) exhibit use both as pestles and hand-stones (Wright 1992:641, Type L, No. 130). Another example from Gilat (L.527, B.1136) is similar to these, but more elongate.

Two tools are of particular interest, both unique to the Gilat assemblage. One closely resembles a ground stone ax (un-provenienced), such as those known from earlier prehistoric assemblages (cf. Roodenberg 1986; Wright 1992a:142, Type H 88) but made of vesicular basalt. The piece is roughly ovate in shape with bi-convex cross-section and profiles, ground on both sides, with relatively parallel margins tapering toward the butt. The 'bit' is flaked, but does not form a sharp, clear edge. The poorly defined bit edge and presence of pecking and battering on both the butt and bit leads us to suggest its multi-functionality. The other piece, made of granite, is classified as both a mano and pounder (un-provenienced). Two faces are flat and clearly ground, but there is also evidence of pounding and grinding on the ends. While there is clearly pounding and grinding wear on the piece, it may have been a 'rough-out' or blank intended for a mace head, which are the primary objects made of granite found at Gilat. However, the lack of drilling precludes positive identifycation as a tool type.

Miscellaneous (complete = 16, incomplete = 2, fragments = 50; TOTAL = 68)

The majority of artifacts that are not easily categorized are small chalk or limestone fragments with visible ground faces, often with striae, but which are probably too soft and small to be used as typical hand-stones (e.g. Figure 12.19:6). For brevity, summarized information and metric measurements are listed in Table 12.18. A number of artifacts are more unusual, including a very small and shallow chalk bowl fragment with striae (Figure 12.18:5), a complete, trapezoidal piece of finely ground chlorite schist, possibly used as an inlay for decoration or possibly a bead blank, and a corner fragment of finely ground and polished dark green rock (possibly gabbro) that may be the corner of a palette or a finely ground axe. Another unusual fragment (Figure 12.18:6) is made of finely ground pinkish limestone forming a right angle, similar to a siliceous limestone fragment from Abu Matar (Commenge in press). One small, complete chalk artifact (L.558, B.1287) is somewhat almond-shaped in profile, rather like the 'tags' of Predynastic Egypt (Petrie 1921: Pl. 33.42, 47–9). Similar artifacts are known from Horvat Beter (Dothan 1959a:30, Fig. 19:28, Pl. VII:7) and Abu Matar (Commenge in press); but the Gilat example, while well-ground and striated, is more trapezoidal in shape and the similarity may be fortuitous.

Two artifact fragments are made of scoria and are similar to each other. Each is concave on one face and convex on the opposed face. On one, the opposed face has a knob protruding from the surrounding surface c. 20 mm, and both are roughly c. 20–30 mm in maximum diameter, suggesting something like a pot lid with a knob, although scoria seems an unlikely material for such an implement. The protrusion on one is near the edge of the fragment, suggesting that this may have been a small 'knob' or foot on a short, shallow vessel. On the other the protrusion seems centered on the fragment, unlike the base of a vessel, more closely resembling a hand-stone or palette (Figure 12.29:10). Alternatively, these may have served as grinding devices, with the knobs serving as handles, and the concave faces the use-surface for grinding artifacts. No traces of ochre were found on either artifact.

Another finely ground limestone fragment (L.608, B.5038) may be the leg of a figurine, or possibly the leg of a small vessel. Roughly round in cross-section (c. 12 mm diameter), the piece forms a horizontal line for approximately 39 mm, then angles back up about 44 mm before the break.

Two incised stones are also included. One (Figure 12.20:4) is a roughly ovoid chalk nodule with a deep (c. 5 mm) incision extending the circumference of the piece longitudinally (lengthwise, Figure 12.20:4). Roughly bi-convex in cross-section, the entire piece is ground, with one lateral margin ground perpendicular to the faces. The other incised stone (L.48, B.104) is a large chalk nodule with a pronounced worn circumferential groove around the mid-section, possibly created to hold rope or twine in place, securing it to the stone. Artifacts similar in size and shape were found at Tuleilat Ghassul (North 1961: Pl. X: S8134; Lee 1973:275, LB44a). Both of these may have served as weights.

Two unusual ceramic pieces (L.567, B.1357; L.567, B.1363) were associated with each other. Both appear to be complete, bulbous unfired clay pieces that were formed intentionally. One (L.567, B.1357) is nearly piriform in shape, but flattened on the top. The opposite end has a perforation with diameter of 11 mm, 21 mm deep. Height of the piece is 44 mm, with a diameter of 60 mm. The other (L.567, B.1362) seems like the first, but with the perforated end crushed. The height is 47 mm, and the diameter is 48 mm. It is not certain there was a perforation, though the crushed appearance suggests that the end might have been hollow. The closest parallels are the clay mace heads known from a few Predynastic Egyptian contexts, particularly those from the cemetery at El Mahasna (Ayrton and Loat 1911:21, 33; Pl.XLI:2), the identification of which is doubted by Baumgartel (1960:111).[3] Another very similar piriform model with a ceramic handle was also recovered from Mostegedda (Brunton 1937:89, Pl.XL:13), and dated to S.D. 40-57. Other parallels are clay models of concave conical mace heads, dissimilar to the Gilat artifacts, but nevertheless they underscore the presence of clay imitations in Predynastic Egypt (Petrie 1901: Pl.V, bottom left; Baumgartel 1960:108). While the disturbed burial nearby is not directly associated, the close proximity suggests these may have been associated.

Other Materials

A variety of other materials were also recovered during excavation. Some of these are materials that show no evidence of modification, but were brought to the site for modification. Others are materials that were clearly the by-product or raw materials for the production of other materials or artifacts.

Ochre (n = 56)

A pulverulent and usually impure form of oxide, the ochre from Gilat is reddish and thus presumably consists of hematite (Baumgartel 1960:202). All ochre recovered from the 1990–92 excavations was kept (see Table 12.19). Just over half of the pieces found (n=29) show traces of grinding (Figure 12.21:2–3, 8–9, 12). While probably used as a pigment in paints for ceramic decoration, it may also have been used for body decoration, wall painting and other artifact coloring. Since the Mousterian, ochre is established as a material of symbolic significance, evident from use in burial customs and cultic artifacts (e.g. Fox 1995; Perrot 1955; Schick 1998; Schmandt-Besserat 1980).

Unworked Materials (n = 39)

A number of rock types appear to be unmodified, some of which were clearly intended for manufacture in the future, or may be the by-products or failures of manufacturing processes. These materials are listed in Table 12.20. Some pieces may have been used, but wear is not visible, a more likely possibility for the harder materials such as the pyrite and hematite nodules. Others are unusual materials not typically found in the ground stone assemblage at Gilat, and might have been collected or desired for their color. This seems likely with materials such as the sandstone (n=4) which are bonded with blue-green mineralization (probably copper minerals), the largest of which was found directly associated with a flexed adult burial (L.1510, B.5683). Others were probably intended for the manufacture of beads, such as the small nodules of amazonite (n=2), carnelian (n=1), turquoise (n=1), and jasper (n=1), or for pendants, such as the calcite (n=1). Still others could have been intended for a variety of artifacts, such as the chlorite-schist (n=2) and the chrysocolla (n=5). Finally, the recovery of two granite nodules, one of them possibly worked (surface find), may have been intended for manufacturing mace heads. Alternatively, the ground faces of one nodule of granite may indicate use as small hand-stone.

Section II: Mace heads, Palettes, Tokens, Fenestrated Stands and Decorative Artifacts

This section is devoted to the description and analysis of those artifacts linked to ideology, power, ritual and aesthetics that are less commonly found at late prehistoric sites, or found in more limited quantities. Included in this are decorative objects, such as pendants and beads, as well as other artifacts made of non-local rock types (e.g. basalt vessels, mace heads, ground stone axes) or recovered in uncommonly large numbers (tokens, spindle whorls, palettes). These are treated separately in order to provide more accurate comparative frequencies between the ground stone discussed in Section I and other late prehistoric site assemblages.

Tokens (complete = 29; incomplete = 3; fragments = 9; unknown = 5; TOTAL = 46)

This class of artifact is defined simply as small geometric artifacts, most of which are made of stone (Fig. 5.73). Table 12.21 presents summarized measurements, contextual data, and shapes for these artifacts. Three are made of clay, two of ceramic (probably worked pottery sherds), and three are made of bone. The remainder are made of a variety of rock types, of which the most common is limestone (n=17). The second most common material is chalk (n=9), followed by chlorite schist (n=4, Figure 12.21:4). The remainder are sandstone, including ferruginous sandstone (n=3, Figure 12.21:1), green sandstone (n=1, Figure 12.21:7) and plain sandstone (n=1). One additional piece was made of diorite, and no identification of lithology composition was made for the remainder.

The most frequent shape is trapezoidal (n = 10, Figure 12.21: 5, 7), with an additional six which are a roughly rounded trapezoidal shape. Rectangles are also common (n=6), with an additional rounded rectangular shape sample. It is unclear how these small geometric shapes functioned or what they represented, nor is it certain they all belong together as one class. Some types, such as the trapezoidal and rounded trapezoidal artifacts may be unfinished (not yet drilled for suspension) pendants. This also may be true of the conical artifact as well (L.761, B.5427), which is made of chlorite-schist, like many of the pendants (Figure 12.22:2–3). The triangular pieces could have been intended as pendants as well (Figure 12.21:6), however, this would be an atypical shape. Others, such as L.1097, B.3505 and L.0, B.1259 (fine reddish limestone), might have been intended as palettes, or as votive facsimiles of palettes. However, some of these small geometric artifacts may have simply served as game pieces or symbolic markers integral to exchange. While it is open to speculation, their presence seems marked in contrast to other late prehistoric sites.

Similar artifacts are rare in the literature from late prehistoric sites in Palestine and Transjordan, but where found, they are sometimes termed 'amulets' (Dothan 1959a:20; Bar-Adon 1980: Ill.24:2), or, simply, a 'smoothed limestone rectangle' (Lee 1973: LB9:d). They are also known now from mortuary contexts at Shoham [N] (Rowan in press b). Other tokens recorded from Palestine are generally earlier, usually from the seventh millennium BC, such as those from Beidha, 'Ain Ghazal and Munhatta (Schmandt-Besserat 1992: 405–15). Although tokens discussed by Schmandt-Besseratt are frequently ceramic, many from these three sites are also made of stone. It is interesting to note that three tokens from Jericho, dated to the sixth millennium BC, are also made of stone (*ibid.* 411). In addition, the single stone token recovered from Ktar Tell Kazarei is rectangular and dated to the fifth millennium BC (*ibid.* 412); however, that token has incised vertical and horizontal lines. Nevertheless, these two sites provide a tenuous chronological connection to the possibility that the tokens recovered from Gilat operated within a similar pan-Levantine sphere of interaction. However, the lack of punctuated or incised decoration on those from Gilat, like many of the others from Palestine, leaves this connection difficult to interpret.

Ground Stone Axes (n = 3)

Three complete ground stone axes all made of hard, highly polished igneous rock were recovered. Two (L.1147, B.3689 and L.620, B.5082; Figure 12.19:7, 8) are very similar in size (46 x 36 x 18 mm and 40.5 x 32 x 16 mm respectively) and morphology. The third (568-19-50) is similar in morphology, but larger (75 x 48 x 30 mm) than the other two. In addition, the large one has a clearly faceted bit, such that the edge is flat and non-functional. The two smaller ones are roughly triangular in shape, with lenticular profiles and cross-sections. The two smaller are made of amphibolite, while the largest (568-19-50) is made of dolerite. None of these seem likely to have been functional, not only because of the faceted edge on the largest, but also because the small size would not permit use as a hand-held cutting implement. At the same time, the small, highly polished nature would argue against hafting, of which there is no evidence.

Similar ground stone axes are known from prehistoric contexts, but seem rare from the Chalcolithic of southern Palestine. Two polished axes very similar in size, but of unknown rock (one blue, one green) were reported from the Wadi Rabah levels at Ein el-Jarba (Kaplan 1969:20, Figs 10:1, 2 and Pl. VI:3). From Wadi Gaza Site A, a 'syenite, conoid' axe was reported (Macdonald 1932: Pls XXVIII:5, XXVII:76) which appears similar. Site D (pit 7) also produced what was called a 'polished adze of green basalt' (*ibid.* Pls XXVIII:6 and XXVII:75), but this artifact is thinner and flatter than the Gilat and 'Ein el-Jarba examples. A 'votive' axe of polished basalt was also reported from Horvat Beter (Dothan 1959a: Fig. 19:31), and a diorite one was published from Tuleilat Ghassul (Mallon *et al.* 1934: Pl. 27.7). The pecked and flaked axe from the Pottery Neolithic contexts at Jericho does not seem similar (Dorrell 1984:547, Fig. 228:26).

While there seem to be few examples from southern Chalcolithic contexts, and perhaps a tendency for these to occur either in the late Neolithic or in the earlier phases of the Chalcolithic, Predynastic Egyptian contexts seem to commonly produce similar polished axes, often of hard, igneous materials. Two axes of granite and diorite, similar to our larger example, were recovered from El 'Adaima (Needler 1984: Figs 8.109, 110). Another, also of diorite, is known from the settlement at Kom el Ahmar (*ibid.* Fig. 22.86). Others are also known from Merimde (Hoffman 1991: 177, Fig. 48), and from the 'Tasian' at Mostegedda (Brunton 1937:32, Pl.XIII:1–3,6,10,11) as well as other contexts, though not always securely dated (Petrie 1921:24, Pl. XXVII.2, 5). Based on the equivocal information from Predynastic contexts and Wadi Rabah contexts, the origin of the finely polished axes remains unclear.

Pendants (Complete = 7; incomplete = 12; fragments = 40; TOTAL = 59)

A large number of artifacts were classed as pendants, 28 of which were from the 1975–87 excavations and no longer available for study (Table 12.22). Though we have contextual information for those from the earlier excavations, our discussion concentrates on those from the 1990–92 excavations, including two from the 1987 excavations. Pendants are defined as those artifacts modified such that the piece would be suspended and could not be interpreted as a tool. Most are perforated or drilled on at least one end. In most cases, these criteria easily distinguish them from the beads, which are drilled biconically or bifacially through the center. Only in a few cases do we find artifacts that could belong to either category.

Five pendants are very similar. All are small, ranging in length from 25–47 mm, with a single perforation at the narrow end. Three are cylindrical and are made of limestone, amazonite and calcite respectively (Figure 12.23: 1, 4, 5). Cylindrical pendants are infrequent from Chalcolithic contexts, though a similar type of calcite was recovered from Horvat Beter (Dothan 1959a: Fig. 19:29) and one of bone from the En-Gedi shrine (Ussishkin 1980: Fig. 10.26). Another (Figure 12.23: 3), made of green schist/chlorite, is slightly more conical, but is within the same size range (31 mm), with a round cross-section like the cylindrical examples. A similar example made of 'greenstone' was found recently in the burial cave of Nahal Qanah (Gopher and Tsuk 1996: Fig. 4.29:2 and 4.30). The fifth example from Gilat (L.1059, B.3399), also made of green chlorite-schist, is drilled at one end, 25 mm long, but is more trapezoidal and flatter than the others (Figure 12.23: 2).

Six pendants are roughly similar because of their trapezoidal shape, though some are fragments. One example (L. 798, B. 5566; Figure 12.20:1) is very similar to two others, each made of limestone or chalk and roughly the same size. One of these has four unfinished drill marks, two on each face of one end. Another is unusual because it is made of unfired clay with two small perforations on one end, as well as a concavity along the mid-section along the break.

Three pendants from Gilat are decorated. One (L.297, B.623) is trapezoidal in outline, with two perforations at one end. Both perforations were made with bifacial drilling, and both are broken. After breaking, the piece was reground around the holes and suspended from the remaining protrusion formed between the two holes. Decorated with faint chevron designs on both faces, those on one side are slightly obscured by subsequent wear that left striations along one edge. A similar, smaller fragment (L.786, B.5538) also made of chalk, exhibits the same protrusion, probably created by broken perforations. This reuse of pendants seems particularly common, as examples from Arad (Amiran *et al.* 1978: Pl. 67:2) and Horvat Beter (Dothan 1959a: Fig. 18:39, Pl.VII:6) bear similar evidence for repair. However, other pendants have this protrusion unrelated to repair and reuse but rather an intentional design for suspension (Figure 12.22:13–15). Another decorated pendant, roughly cylindrical, is also incised with chevrons (Figure 12.24:5). The last decorated pendant, made of shell, is very finely ground bifacially with chevrons incisions (Figure 12.22:15). Incised decorations on pendants are not common during the Chalcolithic but when found are typically made of shell, such as those from Bene Beraq (Kaplan 1963: Fig. 9:15) and Shiqmim (Levy and Alon 1987: Fig. 13.14:2, 3) or from stone, such as one made of schist from Abu Matar (Perrot 1955: Fig. 20:3) and one of limestone from Palmahim (Gophna and Lifshitz 1980: Fig. 4:12; Pl. I:6).

Shell pendants are primarily small, with a single hole drilled on one end. A general discussion of the shell assemblage is made in Chapter 7 (this volume). In some cases, the end where the hole is drilled has been prepared with grinding, making the end flat similar to a few from Abu Matar (Perrot 1955: Fig. 20:13–15). Two shell pendants are different from the other shells, and virtually identical to each other in size and manufacture. Both (L.552, B.1228 and L.909, B.2659; Figure 12.16:12) are a rounded trapezoidal shape, arched in cross-section, with four small holes (c. 1mm in diameter) drilled, two at each end. These might have been held on a bracelet or necklace rather than suspended as a pendant. Similar types of the same size (c. 20–25 mm in length), called 'bracelets', and were found at Tuleilat Ghassul (Hennessy 1969: Fig. 11.20) but with only one hole on each end. Pendants of mother-of-pearl are also common (Figure 12.22:8, 10–11, 13–14), sometimes simple discs with a single central perforation (Figure 12.22:11) to more elaborate designs with fine perforations laterally (Figure 12.22:13–14). Mother-of-pearl pendants are also illustrated from Abu Matar, both round types with central perforations (Perrot 1957: Figs 23:8–9, 11–12) and more trapezoidal or incomplete shapes (*ibid.* Figs 20:6–7).

Three pieces are classed as pendants, though their actual function is unclear. Two are similar in size, and each has a drilled hole on one edge, at an offset angle to the long axis of the piece. One (L.895, B.2597) is complete, triangular in cross-section, made of ferruginous sandstone, and has the hole at one end. The other (L.553, B.1307) is incomplete, made of chalk, trapezoidal in cross-section, and has a hole drilled on the very edge of the mid-section. The third is made of an unidentified hard black rock, highly polished, with a triangular cross-section and off-set drilled hole (Figure 12.24:6).

Three more pieces are not clearly pendants, but appear to be modified with the intention of suspending them from a thong or thread. All three are a rounded, trapezoidal shape, almost ovoid, and are similar in size, ranging from 36–45 mm (length), 18–26 mm (width) and 6–10 mm (thickness). Two (L.1221, B.3868 and L.1547, B.5767) are made of limestone and have bilateral fine incisions along the upper edges, possibly to hold a thread in place. A third, made of chalk, (L.961, B.2782) has an incision, or possibly the remains of a broken hole, along one edge, with an additional, unfinished hole on the opposite edge (Figure 12.24:7). This piece also has an unfinished bifacial drill mark in the center.

Two artifacts are complete, limestone objects with unfinished bifacial drill marks. One (L.040, B.3141) is flat, trapezoidal, with pronounced bifacial striations and is highly polished. The other (L.1321, B.4169) is flat, oval, and also has bifacial striations. If these central holes were completed, these would not have suspended easily, but because morphological they are more similar to pendants than beads, they are included here.

One other pendant is striking, and should be noted. This piece (L.800, B.2093; Figure 12.22:4) is a dome-shaped piece made of hippopotamus ivory, with four small (c. 1–2 mm diameters) holes drilled along the wide flat edge. A similar object is also made of ivory, a dome-shaped pendant with a single suspension hole and a punctuated line meandering across the surface from Bir es-Safadi (Perrot 1979: Fig. 72). Unfortunately the Gilat example is from topsoil, and thus has a calcareous concretion on the exterior. We know of no other parallels to this piece from prehistoric contexts in Palestine/Transjordan.

While there is a wide diversity of materials used to manufacture pendants, the majority of the pendants from Gilat are made of easily obtainable local materials such as chalk (n = 10), limestone (n = 9), clay/ceramic (n = 15) and bone (n = 2). Given the proximity of Gilat to the coast, the numerous shells (n = 7) could indicate local exchange or visits from the inhabitants of the site. Only a few may be non-local materials, such as those made of chlorite/schist (n = 4), gypsum/calcite (n = 4), amazonite (n = 1), ivory (n = 1) and possibly the ostrich shell (n = 1); ferruginous sandstone and ferruginous limestone (n = 2) may also be non-local.

Trapezoidal to rectangular pendants appear to be the most common type of pendants found at Chalcolithic sites, and similar types are known from Affula (Sukenik 1948: Pl.XIII:5,6), Ben Shemen (Perrot and Ladiray 1980: Fig. 134.1), Tuleilat Ghassul (Lee 1973: LB73:a–h; Koeppel 1940: Pl. 97:13; Mallon *et al.* 1934: Fig. 32, 33; Pl. 37; North 1961: Pl.X:S8345; Hennessy 1969: Fig. 11.21), Nahal Mishmar (Bar-Adon 1980: Ill. 24:3–5), Horvat Beter (Dothan 1959a: Fig. 11:23; 18:37, 38), Abu Matar (Perrot 1955: Figs 20:1–5, 10; Perrot 1957: Figs 23.1–5, 10; Perrot 1979: Pl.87), Shiqmim (Levy and Alon 1987: Fig. 13.14:1–3, 11; 6.12:1–2, 5), Wadi Gaza Site O (Macdonald 1932: Pl.XXI:15, Pl.XXVIII:11) and Grar (Gilead 1995: Fig. 8.7:1–6, 8–10). Only the site of Tuleilat Ghassul seems to have a comparable number of pendants as Gilat, however, an absolute count from Ghassul is not available. The trapezoidal shape and chevron motifs may represent a category of signs with intuitive meanings (Bernbeck 1999), found throughout the different possible sub-groups during the Chalcolithic.

Beads (n = 105)

A large variety, both in shape and materials, are evident in the collection of beads. Table 12.23 lists the beads recovered from Gilat, with summarized contextual information and measurements. This sample, in fact, is relatively small but comes from a variety of different contexts and materials. Such a dispersed spatial pattern suggests that this sample may represent a larger number of necklaces at Gilat.

The bead assemblage is divided into nine categories based on shape, profile and cross-section. These types are depicted according to morphological category in Figure 12.7, which includes three categories (shell, drilled nodules, and unknown/irregular) which are not classifiable based on morphology. Two beads (L.250, B.500; L.692, B.5258), with longitudinal scoring, are manufactured of glass and are thus considered intrusive. That such small objects could be found at any level in the site comes as no surprise given the clear presence of bioturbation in most areas of the excavations.

The range of length measurements for cylindrical beads (2–25 mm) is slightly more variable, but similar to that of the biconical and biconvex types (5–22 mm). The flat, disc- and oval-shaped beads are generally smaller, ranging from 4–14 mm, with two outliers of 25 mm. Flattened, spherical beads are similar in range of lengths (c. 5.5–25 mm), but are generally thicker than the other types.

As shown in Figure 12.18, the majority is flat, disc-shaped (n = 25, Figure 12.23:6–9, 13–16), generally similar to the oblate or barrel disc beads defined by Beck (1928: Pl.II). The second most common shape is the cylindrically-shaped beads (n = 16, Figure 12.23:11–12, 17), almost all of which fit Beck's long cylinder, round beads (*ibid*. Pl.II). The most common form from Wadi Gaza Site A were beads of disc shape (Roshwalb 1981:87). Comparison of the materials used to manufacture flat, disc beads and the cylindrical type shows distinct differences. Virtually the entire range of rock types are used to make the flat, disc-shaped beads, with the highest frequencies made of chlorite-schist (n = 4), amazonite (n = 5), jasper (n = 4) and limestone (n = 6). The remainder is made of almost all materials used for beads, with the exception of bone. Cylindrical beads, on the other hand, are predominantly made of limestone (n = 10), with some of calcite (n = 2), bone (n = 3) and one of gypsum. Based on the frequencies of materials used for the entire bead assemblage from Gilat, it is clear that the most frequent materials are chalk and limestone (c. 30%, Figure 12.8), but clearly there is a preferential use of materials for certain types of beads. The category of flat, oval-shaped beads (Figure 12.23:8) includes only four examples, and are similar to the flat, disc-shaped beads, differing only in a slightly asymmetric shape. Like the flat, disc-shaped beads, these are primarily made of finer materials; one each of amazonite, turquoise, ostrich eggshell, and chalk. This suggests greater selectivity for the more exotic or colorful materials for the round and oval disc beads than for the long, round, cylindrical beads. The third most common variety is the shell beads, which are not typified by any modification other than a drilled hole in at least one end, or the modification of a pre-existing hole in the shell.

Our category of bi-conical (n = 9; Figure 12.23:23–26, 29–30), similar to Beck's long truncated bicone (1928: Pl.II) and bi-convex shaped beads (n = 5; Figure 12.23:21–22, 27), similar to Beck's long truncated convex bicone (*ibid*.), differs only in the degree to which the central section is pronounced; the bi-conical beads have a more pronounced ridge. These two types are predominantly made of more exotic materials; the materials used for these two categories are amazonite (n = 5), chlorite-schist (n = 3), calcite (n = 1), chalk or limestone (n = 4) and one of an unknown material.

Finally, the flattened sphere beads (n = 11) are almost spherical, but have flattened aspects on the drilled ends (Figure 12.23:28). Beck's typology doesn't closely approximate this type, but may be described as round in cross-section, ellipsoidal in long section, but truncated. These are roughly divided between locally available materials such as limestone and chalk (n = 4) and flint (n = 2), and the more 'exotic' materials, such as calcite (n = 1), turquoise (n = 2), amazonite (n = 1) and agate (n = 1).

Roughly one third of the bead assemblage (c. 34 %; n = 34) is made of materials probably non-local to Gilat (amazonite, turquoise, agate/jasper, chlorite-schist and carnelian) and representing some form of exchange. The relative frequency could be higher if the counts of ostrich egg shell (n = 2), calcite/gypsum (n = 6) and some shells are included. It seems possible that the bead sample represents a higher number of necklaces that are under-represented because of site formation processes.

Other Decorative Objects (n = 4)

Several other artifacts are probably fragments of decorative objects. Two are ivory fragments; one (L.812, B.2415) is a very small (15 x 12 x 3 mm) edge fragment, which may be the top of a zoomorphic figurine. However, this fragment is too small to determine what the original artifact looked like. The other ivory fragment (L.1369, B.4319) is also quite small (27 x 21 x 6 mm), and is decorated on both sides with a zigzag design (Figure 12.22:5). One edge is smooth and worked, and probably represents the only original, unbroken edge. This may be a fragment from a small ivory palette, but there is no known parallel for such an object.

Another fragment (L.1056, B.7014) is a flat curving piece of polished shell measuring 34 x 11 x 3 mm, and is probably the remains of a Lambis bracelet (Figure 12.22:7). The final artifact is two pieces forming a complete ring of bone. This ring is quite small, but could fit on a child or small person's finger, and is quite delicate; it may have been a dangling bodily adornment.

Mace Heads (complete = 7, fragments = 9; unknown = 9; TOTAL = 25)

An unusually large collection of mace heads was recovered from Gilat, surpassed only by the enormous cache from Nahal Mishmar. The 25 mace heads from Gilat represent an unusual diversity in both form and materials. Of those available for study (n = 16), analysis included lithology identification (using petrographic thin sections in some cases), morphological classification, and measurements, which included exterior dimensions, as well as the minimum and maximum diameters of the drilled holes. Weights were also recorded, and where the size of fragments permitted, an estimate of the original complete mace head is also presented (Figure 12.10). These summarized data, with contextual information, are presented in Table 12.24.

The diversity of materials used to manufacture the mace heads from Gilat is atypical of other Chalcolithic examples. While hematite, smelted copper and limestone seem, subjectively, to be the most frequently utilized materials at most sites during the Chalcolithic, the Gilat assemblage includes not only hematite and limestone, but also other, less common rock types. Figure 12.9 presents the relative frequency of materials for the Gilat mace heads, which shows the most frequent material used for the Gilat examples is granite (n = 8), followed closely by hematite (n = 7). Limestone follows with only three examples, and the rest are one or two examples of the other variety of materials (dolerite, porcelenite, diorite, chrysocolla [?], basalt, and chalk).

A few observations are possible based on the materials. One obvious contrast to many Chalcolithic collections is the complete lack of copper mace heads at Gilat. It remains unknown whether this is the result of an early date for Gilat in the Chalcolithic chronology, or if it is the result of tightly guarded specialists' knowledge (Levy 1998), or both. Outside of the Nahal Mishmar hoard and the Beersheva basin sites, copper mace heads are rare, so this absence may not be unusual. However, the use of materials such as porcelenite, diorite, dolerite and chrysocolla for mace heads from the southern Levant mace heads is unusual, reflecting an early date as well as access to a diversity of non-local rock types.[4]

Morphology also suggests an atypical collection in comparison to the southern Levantine prehistoric mace heads (see Fig. 12.25). Similar to other late prehistoric sites, the predominant type at Gilat is the piriform shape (n = 6), which is made of hematite (n = 3), limestone (n = 1), porcelenite (n = 1), and chalk (n = 1). Others are also usual shapes, such as the flattened spheroid (globular) mace head (L.275, B.552) made of a limestone with iron oxides, which closely resembles a mace head from Bir es-Safadi (Perrot 1979: Fig. 88, lower right register). Another globular example is known from stratum XVIII at Beth Shean (Fitzgerald 1935: Pl. III: 27). In addition to piriform shapes, globular and barrel forms continue into the Early Bronze Age I period (e.g. Schaub and Rast 1989:289–94).

Other types are not typical of Chalcolithic contexts from southern Palestine, and the closest parallels are found in Predynastic Egyptian contexts. The remaining eight mace heads can be divided into two general types: disc-shaped (n=4) and carinated (n=4).

The carinated examples are not precisely similar to each other, and may be further sub-divided. One is more appropriately called bi-conical, because of the pronounced symmetrically placed carination which occurs at the center of the artifact (Figure 12.25:4), similar to a hematite fragment from Azor (Perrot and Ladiray 1980: Fig. 77:4) and others of copper from Nahal Mishmar (Bar-Adon 1980: Nos. 137, 142, 143). The other three are asymmetrical in profile, with the carination occurring nearer the top (Figures 12.25:1, 2). These three resemble early Predynastic Egyptian types, termed 'conical pear-shaped' by Cialowicz (1989:263, Fig. 1:4), and in particular resemble examples from the Fayum at Kom W (Caton-Thompson 1934: Pl.XXX:2). One of these three in particular (L.13, B.24), which is made of granite, very closely resembles the example from Kom W, both in shape and in size, though the Kom W mace head is made of limestone. A few similar mace heads are also illustrated by Petrie (1921: Pl.26.55, 57).

The other category, disc-shaped mace heads, includes four examples, all of them similar in size, ranging from 64 to 86 mm in maximum exterior diameter. Disc-shaped mace heads are termed 'convex-topped conical mace heads' by Cialowicz (1989:262, Fig. 1:1), which he suggests originated in Nubia, where the majority were found. Convex-topped conical mace heads are the antecedents to the varieties of conical mace heads typical of Naqada I-IIa (*ibid*. 263). His terminology stresses the bi-convexity of this type of mace head, which are not really flat like a disc.

The smallest of these from Gilat (L.1295, B.4084), made of limestone, is probably the only example that is questionable as a mace head, but the size, estimated original weight (c. 200 gm), and well-ground exterior suggest it belongs with this type. The other three vary in the degree of convexity as seen in profile. The least convex, which also exhibits the sharpest 'point' (carination) on the edge, is a basalt fragment (L.007, B.3027; Figure 12.17:1). This particular example is very similar in shape and size to the diorite mace head found on the surface of the Wadi Rayan divide in the Fayum (Caton-Thompson and Gardner 1934: Pl. 30.3), though the Gilat fragment is slightly (c. 10 mm) larger in diameter. The other two examples, of granite (L.92, B.588) and diorite (L.0, B.3210) are even closer in diameter to the Fayum example, but thicker. Outside of Gilat, only one example from Tuleilat Ghassul, made of hematite (Mallon *et al.* 1934: Pl. 35.1), resembles a convex-topped, conical form similar to those from Gilat and Predynastic Egypt.

Though parallels are strong, Cialowicz (1989:263) notes that both the conical, convex-topped (Type Ia) and the conical pear-shaped mace heads seem to be limited to the Fayum and Nubia, the latter a rather distant territory to propose connections with Gilat. In addition, he suggests the conical type, in general, originated on the Upper Nile. Similar types are not dated nor identified to origin (Petrie 1921: Pl.XXVI.49, 51). However, a few other examples of convex-topped, conical (discoidal, or bi-convex) mace heads are also known from southern Levantine contexts, such as one from Tuleilat Ghassul (Mallon *et al.* 1934: Fig. 27), Shiqmim (personal observation, made of copper), Neve Ur (Perrot *et al.*1967: Fig. 13.5) and a similar one from Bir es-Safadi (Perrot 1979: Fig. 88, center). However, all of these are disc-shaped, with very little evidence for convexity.

The origin of mace heads, particularly those of piriform shape, has been the subject of some debate (cf. Ward 1964; Baumgartel 1960). Petrie (1901:24) suggests that disc forms, primarily those made of syenite, porphyry and alabaster, are earlier, dating from S.D. 31-40 and ending by S.D. 53. Piriform types are primarily of hard white limestone, though basalt, hematite, breccia and alabaster are also known, and occur no earlier than S.D. 42, continuing until the IVth Dynasty. Ward (1964:15–16), in particular, has indicated the difficulties in chronologies when attempting to compare earliest examples of piriform mace heads from such vast territories where they are found, from Mesopotamia, Anatolia, Syria to Egypt. Though piriform mace heads were long recognized as characteristic features of Naqada II, piriform and spherical mace heads were both found at Merimde, suggesting they actually occurred earlier (Hoffman 1991:177, Fig. 48). Unfortunately, the relative chronology of Merimde is not clear, though current scholarly opinion places it earlier than Naqada I, probably equivalent to Fayum A and perhaps earlier or equivalent to the Badarian (Hassan 1985; *contra* Baumgartel 1955:16–18, who put Merimde and Naqada II contemporary). It has been suggested previously that Badarian, Fayum A and Merimde are all closely related (Kantor 1949:77). Current radiocarbon dating chronology indicate that there is probably significant overlap between the Neolithic communities of the Fayum and Merimde, both of which, based on the few dates, roughly correspond to the Wadi Rabah and early Chalcolithic of southern Palestine (Hassan 1985: 111, Fig. 2).

If this dating is correct, then piriform mace heads appearing in Merimde place its appearance in Egypt before Naqada I, as early as any known thus far from Mesopotamia and vicinity (Ward 1964:18). The fact that piriform mace heads are now known early[5] from the Chalcolithic sequence of Palestine, and with other varieties of mace heads, argues against a western Asiatic origin. This interpretation does not, however, preclude a common derivation between southern Levantine and Egyptian populations. Though the existence of disc-shaped and 'conical pear-shaped' are indicated early in the Egyptian chronological sequence, and the similarities of the Gilat parallels are compelling, these forms are perhaps too vague to assert that they, or the idea for their form, originated in Egypt. Our chronological synchrony between the two at this point may even allow the possibility that the idea for this mace head form was imported to Egypt from Palestine.[6] The persistence and development of disc-shaped and 'conical pear-shaped' morphologies only in Egypt would suggest, however, that this type originates in the region of Egypt/Nubia and was traded or exchanged into Palestine. The presence of such a potent symbol of warfare and ceremonial power hints at contacts between the growing power of Predynastic Egyptian chiefdoms and those of the southern Levant, possibly related to increasing martial expeditions

Spindle Whorls and Perforated Sherds (n = 163 [TOTAL])

Typologically, the perforated sherds and perforated small stone artifacts are one of the most difficult to classify (see Figs 12.30–12.31). Terms such as 'spindle whorl', 'loom weight', 'weight' and others are used with very little explanation for a particular artifact's classification (see Figure 12.16). Two factors probably contribute to this confusion: one is the poor understanding for the function of these classes of prehistoric artifacts, the other, the lack of consideration of what constitutes important attributes for a particular artifact class. Compounding these failings, we are only rarely presented with quantified data permitting inter-site assemblage comparisons. Levy *et al.* (this volume, Chapter 14) discuss the role of spindle whorls in textile manufacture at Gilat and the relation of this production activity to cult activities at the site.

Central to this problem is what criteria are the most important in order to identify spindle whorls. Two important attributes for functional spindle whorls are weight and the diameter of the perforation, factors which archaeologists routinely exclude from their reports (Barber 1991:52). An additional critical factor includes the symmetry of the perforation, which must be well-centered to avoid wobble (*ibid.* 52). Though we are aware that compilation of weight and perforation dimensions will not necessarily provide all the typological answers we seek, they may be considered the first step to establishing the foundations of a database for future late prehistoric assemblage comparisons.

A complete list of the artifacts considered in this category is presented with contextual and metric information in Table 12.25. The collection of 163 perforated sherds and stones from Gilat may be subjectively placed into three broad categories. One class (Figure 12.31:1–8) is the perforated ceramic sherds (n=52),[7] which are generally close to flat, many of which have ground edges (c. 63%, n=33). A second class is the well-ground, generally flat, but occasionally slightly bi-convex (cross-section/profile) perforated artifacts (n=59), most of which are limestone (Figure 12.30:1–8). The third class (n=39) is the perforated chalk and limestone artifacts, which range from bi-convex in cross-section to almost spherical, many of them fragments. The remaining artifacts are recorded from the earlier excavations, but the whereabouts of some of the objects are unknown. Perforated stone artifacts which are not symmetric or drilled in multiple spots are classed separately (discussed below as 'small perforated stones'). The second class, those of well-ground, flat, usually limestone artifacts are very likely to have functioned as spindle whorls. These artifacts closely fit Barber's (*ibid.*) criteria to qualify as spindle whorls; all have well-centered perforations ranging from 4 to 11 mm in diameter, and are heavy enough to sustain the momentum necessary to spin.

The other two categories, however, are not as clearly functional as spindle whorls. In order to examine the data for groups, we compiled the weight and estimated weight data for all of these artifacts and created the histogram presented in Figure 12.11. Based on the single attribute of weight, no clear groupings are evident, but some patterns may exist. Clearly, the perforated sherds are generally lighter than the perforated stones, the former contributing to the large predominance of perforated artifacts falling in the range of 10 to 25 gm. The majority of the perforated stones fall in a broad range, ranging from about 15 to 65 gm. Whether or not the separation between the groups of 10–25 gm and 30–55 gm of perforated stone artifacts is typologically meaningful (i.e. reflective of functional or intentional stylistic differences) is difficult to evaluate. However, if at least some of the heavier perforated sherds are also functionally similar to the perforated stones of the same weight, this bi-modality may be reflective of functional differences. This would suggest that the peaks represented by the range of 10–25 gm, and 30–55 gm may represent two different 'types' or general classes of spindle whorls (see Figure 12.16).

Spindle whorls as light as 8 gm have been observed ethnographically for spinning short, fine wool in Afghanistan (Ryder 1968, as cited in Barber 1991:52; see also Chapter 14, this volume). We should probably consider those few (c. n=14) perforated artifacts (primarily ceramic sherds) below 8 gm as functionally different (not for spinning) from the others. The data in these figures suggests that, if we accept that there may be bi-modality represented by the weights of these perforated artifacts, two different fibers may have been worked at the site. In fact, this parallels the ethnographic observations of Ryder in Afghanistan, where lighter spindle whorls (c. 8 gm) were used for lighter, shorter wool, and larger spindle whorls (c. 33 gm) were used for longer wool (or heavier thread). In addition, with the recent discovery of cotton fibers to the east (Betts *et al.* 1994) from contexts roughly coeval with Gilat or slightly later, the possibility that these were in use must also be considered. Even if we accept that some of the lighter, perforated sherds, as well as some of the poorer perforated chalk artifacts should be eliminated from this class, a rough estimate of over

100 spindle whorls would seem a conservative estimate. Given the range of whorl weights that could be used to spin thread of a particular weight or thickness, we would not expect to see two clear separate and distinct groups. In the end, we may at least tentatively suggest that the distribution of spindle whorls weight and size data suggest that a range of thread weights were spun, grouping into a lighter finer thread and a heavier, coarser thread.

Typologically, a category of 'loom weights' seems an unnecessary division, although this term is common. Loom weights are well-attested from later periods, perhaps as early as the Early Bronze, but there is thus far little to support this separate class for assemblages from the Chalcolithic, nor do artifacts called 'loom weights' bear any resemblance to those found later during the Bronze and Iron Ages. Loom weights are unnecessary when using ground looms, and thus far, at least from the southern Levant (or Predynastic Egypt), there is little evidence for vertical looms (see Barber 1991:83–113).

The overwhelming majority of these perforated artifacts are stone, primarily limestone (n = 67), a few of which are limestone with oxides or ferruginous limestone (Table 12.25). Perforated ceramics (n =5 2), as noted above, are all vessel sherds with one exception. The next most common type are perforated chalk (n = 26) artifacts, a few of which are chalks with oxides. A few exotic materials are also used for the finest examples of spindle whorls, including three of chlorite schist, one of gabbro, one of masonite (feldspar), and one of fine-grained, polished red flint. These six colorful spindle whorls, as well as the ferruginous limestone and limestone/chalks with oxides, all finely ground and well proportioned, suggest some preference for fine materials. Though this is not a large percentage of the overall assemblage, it suggests a possible distinction within the assemblage for material preferences. This in turn may reflect differential access and power within exchange networks supplying these non-local materials.

It is difficult to compare such a large assemblage to the few published examples from other sites. Observations based on the assemblage from Tuleilat Ghassul currently on display at the Pontifical Biblical Institute (Jerusalem) suggest the two are roughly similar. The collection from the early excavations at Ghassul includes finely ground spindle whorls, some of which are also made of chlorite schist and limestone and chalks probably selected for the coloring imparted to the materials with oxides (Mallon *et al.* 1934: Fig. 28:2–9; Pl.1–12; Lee 1973: LB512a, LB513a–g). Though we have no quantified information on the number from Tuleilat Ghassul, that collection is similar in the quality of well-ground examples, and even includes a few decorated examples.

Also striking is the absence of a ceramic type sometimes encountered in excavations, like those found at nearby Grar (termed 'loom weights', Gilead 1995: Fig. 8.4:5, 7–9). This type of perforated ceramic artifact, roughly bi-convex (or 'bi-conic') in cross-section, is also known from Horvat Beter (Dothan 1959a: Fig. 18.13–14), Meser (Dothan 1959b: Pl.37A), Tell Turmus (Dayan 1969: Fig. 9.7), Neve Ur (Perrot *et al.* 1967: Fig. 16:9,10; Pl.41:5, 6), Shiqmim (Levy and Holl 1987: 403, Fig. 15.51:1, 15.16:1–2), and Wadi Gaza Site H, House I (Macdonald 1932: Pl.23.36). Whether there is any significance to this is unclear.

The presence of exotic, non-local rock types may indicate a differential distribution of access to prestige materials. Similar materials are used to manufacture the finest of the violin-shaped figurines, as well as some pendants and palettes, suggesting spinning was not simply relegated to a household production. A more in-depth discussion of these 'tabular' stone objects is presented in Chapter 15 (this volume). Instead, creation of textiles appears to have moved beyond the domestic mode of production. Whether this was a function of the specialized nature of Gilat as a cultic site, or perhaps indicates production by or for a restricted number of individuals is not entirely clear. However, evidence of finer, non-local materials suggests the intertwined nature of production, exchange and cultic activities at Gilat (see Chapter 14, this volume).

Small Perforated Stones (complete = 12, fragments = 15; TOTAL = 27)

The distinction of the perforated small stones from the large stone rings is primarily one of size. While the sizes of the large perforated stone rings range from 90 to 380 mm, the small perforated stone rings range from 20 to 60 mm in maximum length (compare Table 12.8 and Table 12.26). Minimum diameters of the perforations also distinguish these two categories; small stone ring perforation minimum diameters range from 5 to 23 mm, while large stone ring minimum perforation diameters range from 18 to 60 mm (Table 12.26). These distinct classes between large and small were also recognized at Grar (Gilead 1995:335). In addition, while the majority of the large stone rings are made of beach-rock, the small perforated stones are made of chalk (n = 18), limestone (n = 8) and basalt (n = 1).

The perforated small stones are not a single type. Included are at least several different types. One broad category has multiple drill marks and perforations, which includes three artifacts. These (L.754, B.5410; L. 689, B5340; L. 60, B.222) are unusual chalk pieces with multiple perforations, excluding the possibility they were intended as loom weights, mace heads, beads or spindle whorls. Two of these (L. 754, B.5410 and L. 60, B.222) have more than one perforation. L.60, B. 222 is a chalk flake with at least three holes drilled on the edge, with the beginnings of a fourth hole. L. 754, B.5410 is a fragment, possibly of a disc with a central hole, with two additional holes in the body of the disc. The third piece is a flat, rectangular fragment with bifacial drill marks, incomplete, on the broken edge.

A second broad category is round, perforated artifacts which seem not to fit with any of the other perforated categories of mace heads, beads or spindle whorls. Two limestone fragments (L.1549, B.5780 and L.611, B.5061) are both roughly spherical. Though well-ground, they are made of softer limestone which, in addition to their small size and small projected weights (45 and 65 gm, respectively), do not seem likely to represent mace heads. These could be spindle whorl fragments, though they are quite unlike those found at Gilat (discussed above) or possibly a mace head (though the estimated weight of 90 gm also argues against this function).

A number of small perforated artifacts fall between the categories of beads and spindle whorls in size, weight and morphology. For example, some are bifacially drilled flattened spheres (Figure 12.22:8), while others are more ring-like, with pronounced biconical holes in cross-section (Figure 12.23:2).

One chalk fragment (L.851, B.2433) is unusual, and may represent an unfinished or broken decorative object (bead or pendant). It is a relatively well-ground trapezoidal shape, trapezoidal in cross-section, with visible bifacial striae, and the remains of a perforation on the fragmented edge of only one face.

The remaining artifacts are typical of many drilled stones found at Chalcolithic sites, but for which the function is unknown. Three of these are complete, but the perforations were unfinished. Each is bifacially drilled, but the holes do not meet. All are roughly ground and irregular in shape and cross-section. Similar roughly shaped and bifacially drilled chalk and limestone nodules are commonly recovered from Chalcolithic sites and sometimes called 'loom weights', such as those found at Grar (Gilead 1995: Figs 8.2:8,10; Figs 8.3:2, 7–9). Other similar small perforated ground stone artifacts are also reported from Arad (Amiran *et al.* 1978: Pl.76:7–27), En Shadud (Braun 1985: Fig. 38.1, 3), Jawa (Helms 1991: Fig. 196.704–708; 197.709–711, 713), and Megiddo (Guy and Engberg 1938: Pl. 76:5–6, 17).

Palettes (complete = 25; fragments = 16; TOTAL = 41)

Palettes are generally rectangular to trapezoidal finely ground stones, which range in cross-section from flat to slightly bi-convex (see Figures 12.26–29). Summarized contextual and size information for palettes is found in Table 12.27.

Rectangular shapes often have convex sides and slightly rounded corners (Figures 12.28:2, 12.30:1–3, 6 and Alon and Levy 1989: Fig. 10; Alon 1990: Fig. 2). Only one palette (L.545, B.1241) has an oval shape, though a few other rounded rectangular examples are close to ovoid (Figures 12.28:1, 3; 12.29:7). Another is probably a fragment of a palette, re-ground for continued use as a palette (L.261, reg. no. 36-87-637). Most of the palettes (n=19) exhibit a shallow unifacial concavity clearly from grinding wear, and a few, made of scoria, were recovered with ochre still retained in the vesicles. Two palette fragments are corner fragments where the central area of grinding is absent, and two others may be unfinished examples. The remaining nine examples, though finely finished in most cases, show no evidence of actual use for grinding of ochre or other materials.

Palettes are commonly recovered from Chalcolithic contexts, primarily from sites located in southern Palestine. Three palettes were recovered from Horvat Beter (Dothan 1959a: Pl.VII:3), one with malachite traces, and others are known from Tuleilat Ghassul (Lee 1973: LB24a). One, probably made of chlorite schist, was found at Wadi Gaza Site A (Macdonald 1932: Pl.XXIII:28, Pl.XXVIII:7). Southern Palestine's relatively close proximity to Egypt may point to the importance of Egyptian-'Canaanite' interaction during the Chalcolithic for the exchange of these objects of the idea for these objects.

Palettes are well-known from Predynastic Egyptians sites, from as early as the Badarian (c. 4500–3700 BCE). Typically, these are referred to as slate or schist palettes, though geologically, much of this is probably graywacke, or less frequently, slate (Needler 1984:319). Though the earliest Predynastic Egyptian palettes are often geometric, the Badarian types are frequently rhomboidal (Baumgartel 1960:81–84), and later types frequently have anthropomorphic designs. However, some types from the 'Tasian' and Badarian at Matmar represent the closest parallels to those from southern Palestine, which are often rectangular, sometimes with rounded corners, while others may be almost ovoid or elliptical (Brunton 1937: Pl.XIII:19, 20, 24, 25; Pl.XXII:17, 20, 30). Badarian types are not limited to the rhomboidal however, and similar flat, rectangular types with rounded corners, made of porphyry, are also known (Brunton and Caton-Thompson 1928:35). The diversity of lithology composition for the Gilat palettes is atypical of the palettes published from southern Palestine, which are usually siliceous limestone (i.e. Bir es-Safadi and Abu Matar, Commenge in press; Shoham [N], Rowan in press b). This highlights the selectivity and desirability of exotic and non-local rock types such as granite, scoria, mica schist, and chlorite schist (Figure 12.14) for the Gilat palettes. Great attention to detail for creating beveled edges and fine corners is not unusual (Rowan in press a).

Palettes from Predynastic Egyptian sites were often included with mortuary paraphernalia, and many clearly were used as small hand-held grinding surfaces on which pigments such as ochre and galena could be reduced to powder. It is clear that some of the palettes from Gilat, in particular those made of scoria, served a similar function. Scoria palettes all have at least a slight depression on one face created from repeated grinding wear, and some have ochre residues caught in the vesicles. Other palettes from Gilat also exhibit similar concavities of varying extents and depth, but their density is not as likely to retain traces of visible residues. A few, often finely worked and polished, seem to show little wear at all (Figure 12.28:3).

Predynastic Egyptian palettes are also evidently symbolically loaded artifacts. The most famous example is the later ceremonial Narmer palette, variously interpreted as a narrative detailing Narmer's unification of Lower and Upper Egypt, a generic motif for the unification process that culminated during Narmer's reign, the conquest of Nubia by Narmer and more (e.g. van den Brink and Levy 2002). Palettes apparently served functional, magico-medicinal and symbolic needs according to different contexts and probably changed in significance through time. Unless reporting from other sites was badly misrepresentative, Gilat seems to have a far higher concentration of palettes than other sites. Given the symbolic loading embedded in these objects, the large number of palettes found at Gilat add another dimension to the range of cult activities carried out at the site.

Stone Vessels (complete = 3; incomplete = 2; fragments = 298; TOTAL=303)

Stone vessels are an integral part of Chalcolithic assemblages, and basalt vessels are a well-recognized component of these assemblages, considered a hallmark of the Chalcolithic period (Amiran and Porat 1984:11; Levy 1986:95–96). Chalcolithic ground stone vessels are typically made of three materials; basalt, beach-rock, and limestone. Less common are vessels made of sandstone, phosphorite, calcite and granite. At many Chalcolithic sites, a fundamental distinction can be made between finer bowls made of basalt and those of other lithology (usually limestone).

While basalt vessel fragments are virtually ubiquitous at Chalcolithic sites in the southern Levant, the numbers recovered are generally fairly small. For example, 37 fragments were found at the site of Grar, representing an estimated 20–30 vessels (Gilead 1995:319).[8] Other sites produced similarly small numbers of basalt vessel fragments. Recent analysis of ground stone assemblages from Bir es-Safadi and Abu Matar (Commenge in press) report on some of the finest examples of basalt vessels from the northern Negev region. However, whether considered in terms of relative numbers of fragments or estimated minimum number of vessels (MNV), the Gilat assemblage seems to exceed all other sites. The possible exception to this is Tuleilat Ghassul, but the constraints of field selectivity and dispersal of the collection make MNV estimates very approximate for that site.

The definition of vessels requires some elaboration. The distinction between mortars and bowls is not always made clear in discussions of ground stone assemblages, though in the case of the Gilat artifacts, few fragments were difficult to categorize. Our definition, following Wright (1992a:75; 1993:95), distinguishes vessels (as opposed to mortars) as those with either a well-defined base or a well-defined uniform rim; a consistent or gradually changing wall thickness, and an exterior finishing. According to these criteria, pieces are rarely encountered that are difficult to classify. The most difficult to classify are thicker rim fragments.

Table 12.28 presents the frequencies of stone vessels and fragments, categorized to fragment type and material. A total of 303 pieces are included in the vessel category. Throughout this discussion, reference is made to the vessel typology recently completed for the late prehistoric stone vessels found in the southern Levant (Rowan 1998). For the sake of brevity, this discussion includes only the types relevant to those found at Gilat.

The Gilat collection includes three complete vessels, two nearly complete vessels, and 298 fragments. Vessel fragments are divided into six different types of fragments.

Fenestrated stands may be divided into three broad categories of identifiable fragments:
1. 'Ring base' fragments, the joining ring at the base of the fenestration or legs;
2. Leg fragments; and
3. Medial fragments, the central section where the legs join to the base of the bowl.

These fragment types are included in Table 12.28.

Plain bowls may be divided into three categories as well; rims, bases and wall fragments. Obviously, many rim and wall fragments could derive from fenestrated stands or bowls and the absence of any other distinctive element prevents further typological classification of these fragments. Thus, rims and wall fragments are classified separately ('unidentifiable type'), unless the specific fragment suggests some other basis for classification.

Pedestal vessels, distinguished only by the unusual elevated base, are only included if the base is recognizably different from that of a regular bowl or fenestrated stand.

By looking at the fragments, it is clear that the overwhelming majority of the stone vessels from Gilat are fenestrated stands. Only eleven pieces are clearly from bowls, while 111 fragments are from fenestrated stands, plus two more complete fenestrated stands. While estimation of minimum number of individuals (MNI) decreases this ratio of fenestrated stand to vessels from 10:1 to about 4:1, it is clear nevertheless that the majority are the remains of fenestrated stands.

A large number of rims are not characteristic of specific vessel types. Although these could arguably increase the number of bowl vessels, they could also be fenestrated stand fragments, because neither size nor profile of the rims permits determination of vessel type.

Fenestrated Stands (complete = 2; fragments = 111; MNV = 43)

Amiran and Porat (1984) distinguish two different types of pedestal, fenestrated basalt bowls. One, more aptly called 'fenestrated', is set upon a hollow 'foot' (pedestal), with 'windows' cut into this hollow pedestal. The other is an open form vessel with straight walls set upon a tripod, or sometimes on four legs (cf. Commenge in press; Rowan 1998), joined at the base with a narrow circular ring. For convenience, the present discussion identifies the 'fenestrated' examples as Type 4Ci, while the latter (the bowl on a tripod) is referred to as Type 4Cii.[9] A complete list of fenestrated stand fragments with summarized contextual and measurements are presented in Table 12.29.

The large number of Type 4Ci, fenestrated stand fragments seem, subjectively, to be standardized to some degree, which also seems distinct from the better known, larger Type 4Cii fenestrated stands best known from the Beersheva sites. The latter seem larger, with 'legs' as more clearly distinct elements, than the Gilat examples. The two complete basalt fenestrated stands from Gilat closely resemble one another, both in size and decorative elements. In height, they are close, with one (Alon and Levy 1989: Fig. 12.3) 185 mm, and the other, (L.1344, B.4301; Figure 12.33:1) standing 165 mm. Rim diameters are almost exactly the same, one is 135 mm and the other 136 mm, respectively. Base diameters differ by just over 2 cm, with one 89 mm and the other 117 mm. Both are decorated with a single, incised, raised band at the medial point, just above the top of the fenestrated stand. This raised band is a standard feature of many of Gilat fenestrated stands (Figure 12.33: 1–2, 7, 9).

A total of 55 fenestrated stand ring base fragments permitted estimation of the original diameter.[10] The ranges of these estimated diameters are depicted graphically in Figure 12.13, which indicates that the majority (c. n = 43, 78%) fall between 100 and 150 mm in maximum diameter, with none over 200 mm in diameter. Though there are relatively few comparative measurements of similar vessel types from other sites; those that are available indicate some potentially significant differences. For instance, the few fenestrated vessels on stands from the Beersheva sites of Bir es-Safadi (n = 11) and Abu Matar (n = 5) are substantially different (Commenge in press). Only a few have the ring base preserved; both measure roughly 200 mm in diameter, much larger than most of the Gilat examples. However, fenestrated stand base diameters measured from Grar (an unspecified number, but less than seven) suggest a range of 90 to 120 mm (Gilead 1995:314), similar to that of Gilat. This hints at greater affinities between the basalt vessel manufacturers serving Gilat and Grar than between those two sites and those of the Beersheva region.

The single chalk fenestrated stand (727-435-190; Rowan 1998: Fig. 39C) is unlike any of the other fenestrated vessel stands from Gilat, nor are there published parallels from late prehistoric sites in the southern Levant (or Egypt). This fragment appears originally to have had two thick supports or 'legs', but it is not possible to know if they were joined at the base or not. The upper section is constricted, above which the vessel section stood. It is also unclear how much of the vessel section is missing, though the tapering nature of the vessel walls suggests that the vessel did not extend much further than that which remains. Overall, this fragment seems to be battered, and the upper vessel section could be much damaged. The closest parallels seem to be the Late Neolithic pedestal vessels with a very high foot; however, the few documented are typically on a solid foot, such as those from Kabri (Prausnitz 1969: Fig. 6.1, 2, 4) and Kfar Galim North (Galili and Weinstein-Evron 1985: Pl.II.2) and do not closely resemble the Gilat example.

Only one fenestrated stand medial section indicates a vessel with four legs rather than the typical three legs originally. Of these fenestrated stand medial fragments, 11 have evidence for regrinding the broken legs on the base of the vessel (Figure 12.33:7), with an additional three that were probably also reground. Modification of broken basalt fenestrated stands is very common and apparently an effort to prolong their utility. Reground fragments are noted from Abu Hamid (Wright 1992a: Fig. 5–63a), Shoham [N] (Rowan in press b) and Tuleilat Ghassul (Mallon *et al.* 1934: Fig. 23.7), and are also known from other sites such as Abu Hof (unpublished), and Qiryat 'Ata (Rowan forthcoming a).

Basalt vessel fragments are also frequently re worked into other artifacts, such as spindle whorls or palettes at Shiqmim (unpublished), and Nahal Tillah on the Tel Halif Terrace (unpublished). This rejuvenation of broken vessels and modification of fragments further supports the interpretation that basalt, a non-local material, was valued more highly than other rock by the prehistoric inhabitants.

Plain Bowls (n = 13; complete = 1; incomplete = 1; fragments = 11; MNV = 12)

Relative to the high frequency of fenestrated stand fragments, fragments of simple vessels are few, limited to only one complete and one incomplete vessel, and 11 base fragments (Table 12.30). All of these are basalt bowls, with the exception of the complete vessel, which is made of granite.

The complete granite example (Figure 12.18:1) seems unique to prehistoric stone bowl assemblages from southern Palestine. It is unclear how to classify this artifact; by our own definition of vessels above, this does not fit the criteria, yet it is even more clearly not a mortar. Manufactured from pink granite, the ovoid vessel (Class 1, Type 1A) is finely ground to a polish in the interior, while the exterior is well-ground. In profile, the deep concavity of the piece is not deep enough to be called 'hemispherical', but has no flattened area representing a base, nor is the rim clearly defined. The lack of a flat base and the absence of interior pounding or other heavy use suggests that this vessel was either not functional or was only intended for serving or display purposes. This vessel most closely parallels one found at Maadi, also made of granite (Type 5c, Rizkana and Seeher 1988:64, Pl.108.16 and Pl. XII:3). This general vessel type was regarded as undatable by Petrie, probably owing to the rather general form, but exhibits parallels to one from Abadiyeh of alabaster (Petrie 1901: Pl.IX.11) and dated early to S.D. 33–41 (Rizkana and Seeher 1988:64). That example however is unlike the Gilat granite bowl. Parallels may also be made to the dishes with rounded base (Class XX, Pl.112, no. 4796 [Saqqara, Dyn. I, alabaster]) or bowls with rounded base (Class XI, Pl.92, no. 2610 [Abydos, basalt] or no. 2605 [Naqada, alabaster, see Petrie 1921: Pl.XLI, 144, p.35) in el-Khouli's stone vessel typology (1978). These examples date to the Predynastic and Dynasty I but the parallels are rather vague and none are made of granite. Moreover, similarities to such a vague shape are not surprising.

Turning to the other bowls, the single incomplete example (Class 3, Type 3A; Figure 12.32:8) is most similar to the upper bowl section of the fenestrated vessels in profile, though a bit larger (ht: 124 mm; rim diameter: 154 mm; base diameter: 75 mm). One side is broken off, and there is a hole (c. 20 mm in diameter) in the bottom of the base. It is very possible that this is the rejuvenated upper section of a broken fenestrated stand, but no traces of the legs remain.

The others are primarily small base fragments, ranging in estimated diameters from 60–120 mm. The seven examples of the smaller range (60–90 mm) are primarily deep, relatively concave bowl bases, though one is flat with a hole worn through the base (Figure 12.32:12). Only one of these is probably the base of the widely flaring bowls (Type 3B) commonly found at Chalcolithic sites. The larger base fragments (100–120 mm) are primarily flat bases (Figure 12.32:15); only one exhibits the rounded corners typical of the smaller range. Two of these are probably bases of the widely flaring bowls, one appears to have fairly straight walls, and the other two are much too fragmentary to determine the wall profiles.

Pedestal 'Footed' Vessels (n = 7; incomplete = 1; fragments = 6; MNV = 7)

These are differentiated from other classes of stone vessels by the pronounced thickness and extended height of the base, creating the effect of a stubby pedestal (Type 4, Rowan 1998:150–62). Very few fragments belong to this type, with great variety among these seven artifacts. Table 12.31 lists contextual and measurements of these artifacts. Parallels are relatively few, and come either from Late Neolithic contexts, or unclear contexts. Those from solid Neolithic contexts include one from Tel Dan (Gopher and Greenberg 1987: Fig. 5.8; 1996: Fig. 2.4:1), two from Tel 'Eli (Prausnitz 1970: Fig. 35:2, 3), and one from Yiftah'el (Braun 1997: Figs15.6:3–6). One of those from Tel 'Eli (Prausnitz 1970: Fig. 35.3) is notably similar in general shape and size to the pedestal fenestrated stands from Gilat and Tuleilat Ghassul, but without the fenestrations. From less certain or unknown contexts, fragments of pedestal vessels are known from Tell Abu Hamid (Wright 1992a: Fig. 5–63c; 5–64) and Kfar Galim North (Galili and Weinstein-Evron 1985: Pl.II.2), while a complete pedestal vessels is reported from Tell el-Mafjar (Leonard 1992: Pl.5.29). Finally, from Kabri, two very unusual pedestal vessels are dissimilar to most others (Prausnitz 1969: Fig. 6.1, 2), while the third (ibid. Fig. 6.4) is similar in shape.

The pedestal fragments from Gilat include six of basalt and one of chalk. The chalk example is very unusual, and it is unclear what the uppermost, bowl section would have looked like. This base fragment (Type 4Ai, L.294, B.609) is roughly chipped on the bottom, and portions of the base exterior are only roughly ground (Figure 12.33:8). The interior is well-ground, with a remaining depth of c. 31 mm (but originally deeper). It is unclear what the original profile of the walls would have been, though straight or globular seems more likely than flaring or concave. The profile of the base is constricted just below the well area, and the very bottom of the base is also slightly narrower.

While the vessels with high pedestals (Type 4A) may be further divided into solid (Type 4Ai) and hollow pedestals (Type 4Aii), only one is clearly solid (flat at the bottom, with no concavity). This base fragment tapers slightly toward the bottom, and the base is not quite symmetric, measuring 67 x 75 mm. The base is approximately 55 mm in height. Five base diameters range from 75 to 100 mm; the sixth, a fragment of a hollow pedestal, is 120 mm in diameter. This fragment is only the remains of the hollow pedestal section (Type 4Aii), and thus the identification of the vessel is not certain. This type of vessel is virtually unknown from Chalcolithic published assemblages, but a similar fragment is illustrated from Abu Hamid (Wright 1992a:605, Fig. 5–64).

The other four pedestal basalt vessels all have some degree of concavity on the base underside, ranging from 7 to 21 mm in depth. One of these is complete enough to reconstruct the original dimensions of the vessel. This is a pedestal vessel with a very shallow concavity (c. 7 mm) on the base underside. The original vessel was 112 mm in height, with a well-depth of c. 50 mm. The profile represents an open, slightly flaring straight walled vessel. Rim preservation is not substantial enough to allow an original diameter estimate.

One of these pedestal vessels (Figure 12.32:13) is constricted just above the base (Type 4Bi), then flares again upward, similar to a pedestal basalt base fragment from Abu Hamid (Wright 1992a:604, Fig. 5–63.c).

Rim and Wall Fragments (n = 170; wall s= 52; rims = 118)

As discussed above, while rim diameters are computed, this information tells us little without knowing the vessel type they represent. In most cases, there is little the rim and wall fragments can tell us, particularly because so few are decorated. Among the rims, the majority appear to be from straight-walled, open, flaring bowls and only a few exhibits deep profiles (Figure 12.32:5).

Two basalt vessel rims appear to have been ground on the rim; one of these is clearly faceted because of grinding, the other may have been ground (Figure 12.33:4). Neither of these bears any resemblance to the ground, beveled rims that become common during the EBI, which are ground flat on the top of the rim (Type IA, Braun 1990:87). Summarized contextual data and measurements for rims are presented in Table 12.32; information for stone vessel wall (body sherds) fragments is to be found in Table 12.33.

Decorative Motifs (n = 43)

A total of 43 basalt fenestrated stand vessel fragments, plus 2 complete basalt fenestrated stands, are decorated with the incisions creating at least one raised band around the medial section of the vessel (medial defined as the contracted central 'waist' of the vessel, where the bowl section meets the stand or leg section). The majority of these (n=39) are decorated with a single raised band in this section. Additional variants on this motif include two fragments with two or three raised bands; three fragments with three raised bands and one with four or possibly five raised bands. Only one, a fenestrated stand medial fragment, has no raised band, suggesting the importance of this decorative element to the producers of this assemblage.

Other evidence for decoration is scant. Only one fenestrated stand fragment has decoration other than the raised bands, a leg fragment with cross-hatching covering the exterior (unprovenienced). Comparable decorative elements are rare, but a similar example is illustrated from Grar (Gilead 1995: Fig. 7.1.8). Other fenestrated stand legs decorated on the exterior, although less elaborate, are known from sites such as Abu Matar (Commenge in press) and Tuleilat Ghassul (Mallon *et al.* 1934: Fig. 23.5, 6, 8). Elaborate incised decoration on the exterior of fenestrated stand leg and ring based fragments are also found at Shoham [N], a mortuary cave site (Rowan in press b).

Decoration on other vessel fragments is virtually nonexistent. Only two rims have incised chevrons, a typical design motif of many Chalcolithic assemblages (ceramic and stone). One chevron is faintly visible on the interior of the vessel rim, which is the only example of a rim from a widely flared large bowl found at Gilat, a bowl type common to the Beersheva sites of Bir es-Safadi, Bir Abu Matar and Shiqmim. Incised chevrons are the most commonly added decoration on these large flaring bowls, and are illustrated from Horvat Beter (Dothan 1959a: Fig. 19.1, 11.18), Jericho Layer VIII (Ben-Dor 1936: Pl. XXXIII.17), Meser (Dothan 1959b: Fig. 5:15), Palmahim (Gophna and Lifshitz 1980: Fig. 4.10), Tuleilat Ghassul (Mallon *et al.* 1934: Fig. 23.2; Lee 1973: 263, LB1a, b; a–f), Chalcolithic levels at Arad (Amiran *et al.* 1978: Pl.68.8,9), and Abu Matar (Commenge in press). The other rim fragment also has cross-hatching across the exterior of the rim fragment, an uncommonly detailed example, but a few comparably elaborate examples are known from Horvat Beter (Dothan 1959a: Fig. 19.1), Abu Matar and Bir es-Safadi (Commenge in press), Grar (Gilead 1995: Fig. 7.1.6), Shoham [N] (Rowan in press b) and Tuleilat Ghassul (Mallon *et al.* 1934: Fig. 23.1). None of the bowl bases from Gilat exhibit any traces of decoration.

In terms of the stone assemblage from Gilat, the stone vessels provide the most convincing stylistic parallels and contrasts to other sites. Basalt vessel fragments are virtually ubiquitous at Chalcolithic sites in the southern Levant, but the large number of fragments from Gilat is anomalous.[11] The predominance of fenestrated stands has been noted previously (Alon and Levy 1989), and is matched by a large number of ceramic fenestrated vessels. This sub-type of fenestrated stand is both quantitatively and qualitatively different than the more commonly recognized sub-type. This second sub-type (Type 4Cii, Rowan 1998) is typical of the Beersheva basin sites, such as Bir es-Safadi, Abu Matar, Shiqmim and Neve Noy; whereas the first (Type 4Ci, Rowan 1998) is common to Gilat, Tuleilat Ghassul, Wadi Zeita, Grar and the Wadi Ghaza, Site A (MacDonald 1932: Pl. 40.30, 34, 36), but is also known at least as far north as Meser (Dothan 1957: Pl. 37B), Qiryat 'Ata (Rowan forthcoming a) and Tel En-Assawir (Rowan forthcoming b). Is this difference a chronological or regional one? Or, in fact, is it the result of both chronological distinctions as well as regional differences?

One clue can be found in the basalt vessel assemblage presented thus far from Abu Hamid. Although published photographs (Dollfus *et al.* 1988: Pl. III:4) indicate a large, flared bowl typical of the Beersheva sites, as well as other sites, the fenestrated stands discussed by Wright (1992a) indicate some similarities with the sub-type of Ghassul, Gilat and the Wadi Gaza sites. In particular, the pedestal or 'footed' basalt vessel fragments, also known from Gilat, are more reminiscent of Late Neolithic types, and are unknown thus far from the Beersheva sites. This contravenes the implication that sub-variants are a reflection solely of cultural regional boundaries. Coupled with the large, more elaborate fenestrated stand variants recently discovered from the burial cave sites of Shoham (Rowan, in press b), Nahal Qanah (Gopher and Tsuk 1996), and Peqi'in (van den Brink in prep.), this may hint at a chronological distinction. However, these recently recognized new variants are associated with secondary burials in caves, and suggest specialized production for mortuary goods (van den Brink *et al.* 1999). To date, no basalt bowl workshop has been identified.

Conclusions

Ground stone artifacts such as the grinding slabs, hand-stones, pounding stones, and hammer stones, represent typical Chalcolithic domestic ground stone assemblages. Other artifacts such as pestles, mortars and the large pierced stone rings are difficult to compare quantitatively from other Chalcolithic and EBI contexts because of the lack of published data, but the Gilat assemblage seems to represent typical frequencies. Quantitative comparison is made more difficult by some of the unusual aspects of the Gilat assemblage, such as the large number of ground stone spindle whorls, mace heads, 'tokens' and palettes (Table 12.18). By excluding those categories, as well as excluding the artifacts of decorative adornment such as the beads and pendants, the relative frequencies of the overall ground stone assemblage may be compared to the assemblages from Abu Hamid and Grar. These frequencies indicate some differences, but the interpretation of those differences is still complex.

Comparison of the identifiable ground stone assemblages from these three sites is shown in Figure 12.15. In this study, the classification of the artifacts follow Wright's typology (1992a) and thus some adjustments were necessary to standardize the Grar ground stone collection to her typology. Data for Abu Hamid is taken from Wright (1992a: Table 5–35). The ground stone assemblage representing Grar is derived from different tables in Gilead (1995), in some cases combining different sources to fit Wright's typology. For instance, the category of 'pierced stones' from Grar includes six pierced stones (Gilead 1995:335), as well as the spindle whorls and loom weights (*ibid.* Tables 8.2, 8.4). These same categories were combined from Gilat as well, with the addition of mace heads. For the category of pounders from Grar, the limestone hammer stones (*ibid.* Table 6.1) were used, though it is unclear if there were other types of hammer stones, pounders or hard cobbles. Following Wright (1992a:626–7), artifacts called 'cup-marks' and 'pebbles with depressions' from Grar (Gilead: 325, Table 7.2) were classed with the mortars, as were those from Gilat. In addition, three artifacts called 'bowls' at Grar (*ibid.* Fig. 7.3:1–3) are classified as mortars, based on the illustrations, which are clearly types which would be considered mortars under the present typology for Gilat.

These assemblages exhibit strong similarities and a few striking differences. Tool categories such as the pestles, grooved stones, multiple use tools, and the mortars are very similar in the relative frequencies they represent from each site. Frequencies of pestles and multiple-use tools are very low from all three sites. While the classification of multiple-use tools is probably very subjective, the low frequency confirms the observed trend (Wright 1992a) for decreasing recovery of pestles from later prehistoric (late Neolithic and Chalcolithic) sites, in comparison to earlier prehistoric sites, such as the Natufian. This may reflect a preference for wooden pestles, which are functionally superior for de-husking when used in combination with mortars (*ibid.* 307); however, mortars could be used for a variety of other tasks, including crushing pigments and grog, softening skins, or pulverization of plants (*ibid.* 293).

Some other differences, though negligible in quantified terms, are nevertheless important for their contrasts with other Chalcolithic sites. For instance, the presence of highly polished, 'votive' axes made of non-local igneous rock is typical both of Predynastic Egyptian sites and Late Neolithic (Wadi Rabah) sites, but not well-attested from other Chalcolithic contexts in the southern Levant. The diversity and materials of the mace heads is also atypical of Chalcolithic sites in southern Palestine, with some shapes similar *only* to Predynastic Egyptian examples. Other mace head forms, such as the disc-shaped (bi-convex) are similar to a few examples from southern Palestine as well as Predynastic Egyptian artifacts. However, the poorly understood dating of the Predynastic Egyptian forms prevents a succinct understanding of the relationship between the mace heads from Gilat and those from Predynastic Egyptian contexts. It is possible that these forms, probably earlier, derive from the east or Palestine originally, and were copied or imported into Egypt. However, they strongly suggest some regularity in Egyptian-'Canaanite' interaction at this early period.

Ground stone artifacts from Gilat represent an unusually diverse assemblage, both in quantity relative to the excavated area, as well as lithology composition. This is most apparent when comparing the quantities of the most exotic artifacts such as the pendants, tokens, palettes, mace heads and stone bowls. At the same time, the abundance of domestic ground stone artifacts such as grinding slabs, hand-stones and mortars, suggest a substantial presence of inhabitants or visitors conducting domestic activities typical of any large Chalcolithic settlement site. Multiple occupations, rebuilding and dense artifact concentrations all attest to the intensive use of the site, despite the significant lack of obvious domestic architecture.

How then do we interpret such an anomalous abundance of exotic artifacts alongside the evidence from the grinding and pounding artifacts, the latter generally presumed to represent the tools of food production? Clearly, the high frequency of basalt vessels stand out as imports from non-local sources, and the absence of any production at the site suggest they were made elsewhere. At the same time, other exotic materials were imported to Gilat from non-local sources, located in either Sinai or the region of modern southern Jordan/Israel. Many of these may have been manufactured at Gilat. Particularly compelling evidence comes from the correlation of the high quantities of perforated artifacts, such as spindle whorls, pendants, mace heads, and beads with the large number of borers and other pointed types of flint implements (see Chapter 11). Some of these artifact classes, in particular the spindle whorls, argue for specialized production at Gilat beyond that of other domestic sites. Despite that compelling evidence, greater ambiguity is suggested when we attempt to interpret other artifact classes, such as the palettes, tokens and mace heads. These appear to represent evidence of both objects of prestige as well as symbolically important cultural representations, brought to the site and deposited or exchanged. Repeated use of the site seems to have destroyed the original context of many objects, but the overall quantities, when compared to other Chalcolithic sites, stand in unmistakable contrast.

Notes

1. It is interesting to note the similar occurrence of one basalt example, amid the predominantly beachrock grinding slabs, recovered at Grar (Gilead 1995:327, Fig. 7.4:4).

2. This is probably not an accurate representation of the hammer stone frequency from Gilat. We suspect that counts of hammer stones fell between the separate analyses of the chipped and ground stone assemblages.

3.   Ayrton and Loat did not propose a date for this burial, but Petrie (1920: Pl.LII) dates it to S.D. 36-43, a date which Baumgartel (1960:113) finds dubious because of the wide range of pottery represented.

4.   By the EBI, copper virtually disappears as a medium for mace heads, and the majority seem to be made of hard white rock types, such as limestone, chalkstone and alabaster (e.g. Schaub and Rast 1989:289–94).

5.   However, it should be pointed out that the earliest known mace heads from Palestine are not piriform or disc-shaped, but rather barrel-shaped to globular, as at Jericho IX (Ben-Dor 1936: pl.XXX:19) and Ein el-Jarba (Kaplan 1969: Pl.VI.11). At the same time, those of Gilat may also date quite early, given the presence of Wadi Rabah ceramics at Gilat.

6.   Recent excavations in the Nile Delta at sites such as Buto show the presence of imported and locally (Delta) made Negev Chalcolithic (albeit Beersheva style) pottery. See E. van den Brink, and T.E. Levy (eds) in prep.

7.   All of the ceramic perforated artifacts are vessel sherds, with the exception of one (L.558, B.1403) manufactured from ceramic material, which very probably served as a spindle whorl.

8.   This estimate is based on an additional five fragments made of phosphorite, superficially similar in color but very different in lithologic composition.

9.   For brevity, typological discussion is limited to those types relevant to Gilat. Greater typological details may be found in Rowan (1998).

10.   One of these is a ring base fragment with part of the leg remaining, and is made of siliceous limestone. Though of a different material, it otherwise closely resembles the other fenestrated stands. A similar fragment of limestone was also found at Grar (Gilead 1995:324, Fig. 7.3:14).

11.   In addition, none of the vessels fragments from Gilat were manufactured from phosphorite, a material similar in superficial appearance, but geologically quite different (Goren 1991).

Table 12.1. Summarized data for complete and incomplete grinder slabs, 1990–92 excavations.

	Stratum	Context	Locus	Basket	Square	Area	Length cm	Width cm	Thick cm	Wt kg	Profile	Shape	Condition
63		None	1278	4038	J0	J	27	16	9	3.8	Plano/convex	Oval	C
62		None	1278	4028	J0	J	25	13	8	2.32	Plano/convex	Oval	C
65	0	None	0	3820	H2-J1	J	26	15	11	3.5	Bi-convex	Irregular	C
64	0	None	0	3205	L3	J	28	17	8	3.95	Plano/convex	Oval	C
67	0	None	0	0		Y	22	18	5	2.85	Plano/convex	Oval	Inc
55	1	Topsoil	607	5035	N1	T	26	16	7	3.75	Plano/convex	Elongate	C
57	1	Fill	507	1046	K5	Y	16	14	4	2.24	Flat	Loaf	C
68	1	Topsoil	629	5119	N2	T	19	12	8	2.26	Plano/convex	Loaf	Inc
51	1	Topsoil	699	5308	S1-N1	T	19.5	17	5.5	2.5	Flat	Oval	C
61	1	Topsoil	1022	3220	H1	J	22	19	5	2.13	Flat	Oval	C
59	1	Topsoil	1026	3327	L1	J	30	22	8	5.24	Concave/plano	Oval	C
58	1	Topsoil	1553	5801	S2-N1	T	17	12	4	0.83	Flat	Oval	C
53	1	Topsoil	607	5035	N1	T	23	15	9	3.34	Plano/convex	Oval	C
66	1	Topsoil	1026	3230	L2	J	11	8	2	0.22	Flat	Oval	Inc
52	1	Topsoil	502	1002	K5	Y	22	14	5	2.35	Plano/convex	Oval	C
70	1	Topsoil	1026	3327	L1	J	20	16	5	1.85	Flat	Oval	Inc
54	1	Topsoil	1026	3230	L2	J	25	16.5	6	2.37	Plano/convex	Oval	C
76	2	Probe	524	1119	K7	Y	21	12.5	5	1.73	Flat	Elongate	Inc
27	2	Probe	524	1119	K7	Y	11	6.5	2	0.24	Flat	Rectangular	C
74	2	Fill	527	1125	K5	Y	16	18	5.5	1.76	Flat	Round	Inc
28	2 a	Pit	700	5318	M0	T	31	16	7	4.6	Flat	Elongate	C
71	2 a	Floor	816	2438	K4	J	17	18	8	2.82	Plano/convex	Irregular	Inc
34	2 a	Pit	1033	3259	K1	J	27	16	6	3.42	Flat	Loaf	C
33	2 a	Pit	700	5318	M0	T	22	18	9	3.91	Flat	Oval	C
37	2 a	Fill	1391	4369	J0-K0	J	25	16	3	0.96	Flat	Oval	C
35	2 a	Structure	1116	3547	L1	J	24	17	7	3.35	Plano/convex	Oval	C
36	2 a	Pit	805	2520	J4	J	25	13	7	3.15	Plano/convex	Oval	C
32	2 a	Pit	700	5318	M0	T	22	15	6	2.28	Flat	Oval	C
83	2 a	Pit	805	2269	J4	J	23	16	8	2.35	Plano/convex	Oval	Inc
69	2 a	Pit	517	1080	J5	Y	16	15	7	1.96	Plano/convex	Oval	Inc
84	2 a	Hearth	628	5156	N1	T	23	22	7	3.13	Plano/convex	Round	Inc
75	2 b	Fill	847	2518	J4	J	17	12	5	1.3	Plano/convex	Elongate	Inc
12	2 b	Structure	1072	3432	K3	J	43	22	15	13.49	Plano/convex	Elongate	C
11	2 b	Fill	1284	4070	J0	J	33	16	5.5	3.84	Flat	Elongate	C
77	2 b	Structure	876	2521	J4	J	20	18	5.5	2.48	Concave/conv	Irregular	Inc
8	2 b	Pit	965	2761	H3	J	25	15	7	2.95	Flat	Loaf	C

ID	Phase	Group	Type									Section	Shape	
24	2	b	Surface	1121	3664	L1	J	25	15	4	2.33	Flat	Loaf	C
7	2	b	Silo	882	2643	K4	J	23	13	10	4.03	Plano/convex	Loaf	C
14	2	b	Structure	879	2768	K4	J	23	14	6	2.51	Plano/convex	Loaf	C
3	2	b	Structure	876	2521	J4	J	42	25	8	8.05	Flat	Loaf	C
16	2	b	Structure	985	2887	H2	J	25	13	7	2.48	Plano/convex	Loaf	C
23	2	b	Platform	521	1388	J5	Y	32	19	9	5.34	Plano/convex	Oval	C
19	2	b	Pit	970	2791	K2	J	24	15	6	2.9	Plano/convex	Oval	Inc
72	2	b	Floor	841	2503	K3	J	17	19	6	2.5	Plano/convex	Oval	C
25	2	b	Surface	1052	3349	K1	J	24	17	5.5	2.91	Plano/convex	Oval	C
1	2	b	Structure	876	2521	J4	J	37	24	7	6.34	Plano/convex	Oval	C
21	2	b	Pit	850	2425	J4	J	27	17	5	3.39	Plano/convex	Oval	C
18	2	b	Fill	634	5166	Ai2	T	29	22	10	6.1	Plano/convex	Oval	C
20	2	b	Fill	1284	4070	J0	J	23	15	6	2.34	Plano/convex	Oval	C
15	2	b	Structure	879	2768	K4	J	26	17	5.5	2.42	Flat	Oval	C
6	2	b	Wall	993	2878	H2	J	29	23	5	4.15	Flat	Oval	C
10	2	b	Platform	521	1388	J5	Y	32	21	5	3.51	Flat	Oval	C
2	2	b	Pit	850	2425	J4	J	26	15	3	1.45	Flat	Oval	C
5	2	b	Fill	763	5560	N2	T	23	17	5	2.18	Flat	Oval	C
85	2	b	Surface	949	2851	H3	J	19	21	6	3.11	Concave/conv	Oval	Inc
13	2	b	Platform	521	1388	J5	Y	19	18	6	3.71	Flat	Oval	C
87	2	b	Removal	1112	3541	K1	J	27	21	7	4.55	Flat	Oval	Inc
9	2	b	Fill	1284	4070	J0	J	25	17	6	3.42	Plano/convex	Rectangular	C
4	2	b	Fill	890	2619	J4	J	20	18	6	2.41	Plano/convex	Round	C
73	2	b	Wall removal	711	5344	Ai1	T	19	19	4.5	2.1	Flat	Square	Inc
17	2	b	Wall	993	2878	H2	J	33	32	10	11.84	Flat	Square	C
22	2	b	Fill	763	5533	M1	T	20	13	5	1.67	Flat	Triangular	C
46	2	c	Pit	1297	4083	J0	J	25	25	6	2.83	Concave/plano	Oval	C
45	2	c	Pit	1505	5626	N0-N1	T	24	18	6	2.56	Plano/convex	Oval	C
30	2	c	Pit	1127	3597	J1	J	35	25	9	9.29	Concave/conv	Oval	C*
78	2	c	Fill	680	5263	S1	T	32	26	9	10.61	Plano/convex	Oval	Inc
86	2	c	Pit	1042	3523	H1	J	50	31	10	16.95	Concave/conv	Oval	Inc
48	2	c	Fill	680	5263	S1	T	23	15	5	1.97	Flat	Oval	C
31	2	c	Pit	1522	5668	N0-S0	T	28	15	9	3.31	Plano/convex	Oval	C
47	2	c	Pit	1184	3780	K1	J	24	17	8	3.23	Plano/convex	Oval	C
49	2	c	Pit	1509	5756	N0	T	26	14	6	3.33	Plano/convex	Oval	C
50	2	c	Hearth	1570	5835	S1	T	25	13	6	2.54	Plano/convex	Oval	C
38	2	c	Pit	1524	5662	N0	T	35	32	5	6.3	Flat	Oval	C
29	2	c	Surface	1222	3869	L4	J	24	16	6	2.39	Plano/convex	Oval	C
42	2	c	Fill	786	5521	S0-N0	T	29	20	6	4.67	Flat	Oval	C
43	2	c	Pit	861	0	0	J	29	17	8	4.87	Plano/convex	Rectangular	C
82	3		Probe	553	1272	J6	Y	20	17	8	2.58	Plano/convex	Oval	Inc

26	3		Pit	548	1248	J6	Y	23	15	5	1.8	Plano/convex	Oval	C
80	3	a	Wall removal	1148	3650	J3	J	36	26	9	9	Concave/conv	Elongate	Inc
79	3	a	Pit	1150	3732	H3	J	19	11	4	1.18	Flat	Elongate	Inc
44	3	a	Pit	1150	3732	H3	J	22	16	6	1.89	Plano/convex	Oval	C
41	3	a	Pit	1150	3740	H3	J	23	16	7	2.58	Plano/convex	Oval	C
40	3	a	Pit	1536	5750	S0	T	29	17	9	4.55	Plano/convex	Oval	C
81	3	a	Fill	1054	3374	H3	J	14	15	6	1.42	Flat	Round	Inc
39	3	a	Fill	1054	3374	H3	J	27	20	6	4.63	Flat	Triangular	C
60	3	b	Probe	586	1395	J5	Y	23	14	6.5	2.8	Plano/convex	Loaf	C
56	3	b	Pit	692	5253	Ai2	T	26	12	8.5	3.31	Plano/convex	Loaf	C

Table 12.2. Descriptive statistics for grinding slabs (complete, incomplete and fragments), and possible grinding slabs.

Grinders, complete (n=68)

	Length	Width	Thickness	Weight(kg)
Mean	25.56	16.93	6.56	3.6
SD	6.02	4.79	2.19	2.39
Range	34.1	27	13	13.33
Min.	8.9	5	2	0.16
Max.	43	32	15	13.49
Sum				245.07

	Shapes						Profiles
	Loaf/elong.	Oval	Triang.	Rectang.	Irreg.	Round	
	11	25	0	2	0	1	Plano-conv.
	7	15	2	1	0	0	Flat
	0	1	0	0	1	0	Concave-convex
	0	1	0	0	0	0	Concave-flat
	0	0	0	0	1	0	Biconvex
	18	42	2	3	2	1	Totals
						68	Total

Grinders, incomplete (n=22)

	Length	Width	Thickness	Weight(kg)
Mean	21.72	17.79	6.38	3.57
SD	8.41	5.39	1.9	3.83
Range	39	23	8	16.73
Min.	11	8	2	0.22
Max.	50	31	10	16.95
Sum				78.71

	Shapes						Profiles
	Loaf/elong.	Oval	Triang.	Rectang.	Irreg.	Round	
	3	6	0	0	1	1	Plano-conv.
	2	3	0	1	0	2	Flat
	0	1	0	0	2	0	Concave-convex
	0	0	0	0	0	0	Concave-flat
	0	0	0	0	0	0	Biconvex
	5	10	0	1	3	3	Totals
						22	Total

Grinders, fragments (n=441)

	Length	Width	Thickness	Weight(kg)		
Mean	15.45	13.22	5.92	1.64	Plano-convex	206
SD	5.07	4.28	1.7	1.48	Flat	187
Range	50	31	12	16.9	Concave-conv.	15
Min.	5	3	2	0.05	Concave-flat	14
Max.	50	31	12	16.95	Biconvex	1
Sum				759.75	Plano-irreg.	4
					Irreg.	11
					Total	438

Possible grinder fragments? (n=26)

	Length	Width	Thickness	Weight(kg)		
Mean	15.73	12.06	6.45	1.9	Plano-convex	5
SD	6.15	4.3	3.8	2.85	Flat	13
Range	25.3	18.3	18.3	14.4	Concave-conv.	0
Min.	7.7	6.7	1.7	0.1	Concave-flat	0
Max.	33	25	20	14.5	Biconvex	1
Sum				49.41	Plano-irreg.	2
					Irreg.	5
					Total	26

Table 12.3. Descriptive statistics, shapes and profiles of all hand stones, Gilat 1990–92.

Handstones, complete and incomplete (n=22)

	Measurements			
	Length (mm)	Width (mm)	Thickness (mm)	Weight (kg)
Mean	115.0	86.1	35.4	0.54
S.D.	35.5	20.5	13.1	0.51
Range	115.0	71.0	50.0	1.78
Min.	75.0	59.0	15.0	0.10
Max.	190.0	130.0	65.0	1.78
Sum.				10.35

	Shape					Profiles
	Round	Oval	Elongate/Loaf	Rectang.	Irreg.	
	4	3	-	4	1	Flat
	-	5	-	1	1	Plano-conex
	-	-	1	-	-	Bi-convex
	-	-	-	-	1	Irregular
	-	1	-	-	-	Concave-convex

Handstones, fragments (n=24)

	Measurements			
	Length (mm)	Width (mm)	Thickness (mm)	Weight (kg)
Mean	90.9	72.8	38.1	0.50
S.D.	41.1	25.0	26.7	0.54
Range	170.0	85.0	26.7	0.54
Min.	50.0	35.0	17.0	0.04
Max.	220.0	120.0	140.0	2.05
Sum.				8.03

Profiles	N=
Flat	15
Plano-conex	4
Bi-convex	1
Irregular	-
Concave-convex	2

Table 12.4. Summarized data for hand-stones, primarily 1990–92 excavations.

Stratum	Locus	Basket	Square	Year	Area	Length (mm)	Width (mm)	Thick (mm)	Wt. (kg)	Material	Condition
0	0	0		1975	D	83	69	30	0.23	Basalt	C
0	0	0		1975	D	97	74	27	0.33	Basalt	C
0	0	Silo		1991	D	81	81	45	0.37	Beachrock	C
0	0	0		1975	D	92	64	28	0.13	Scoria	C
0	0	0		1975	D	89	71	27	0.14	Scoria	C
0	0	0		1975	D	130	96	36	0.55	Scoria	C
0	0	0		1975	D	120	95	32	0.40	Scoria	Inc
0	0	0		1975	D	84	60	25	0.10	Scoria	C
0	0	0		1975	D	87	59	29	0.11	Scoria	C
0	0	0		1975	D	61	80	26	0.12	Scoria	F
0	0	0		1975	D	81	65	37	0.15	Scoria	C
0	0	0		1975	D	73	70	22	0.08	Scoria	F
0	0	0		1975	D	83	97	24	0.16	Scoria	F
0	0	0		1975	D	64	60	24	0.07	Scoria	F
0	0	0		1975	D	52	52	24	0.06	Scoria	F
0	0	0		1975	D	61	49	21	0.04	Scoria	F
1	907	2647	J2	1990	J	190	110	55	1.22	Beachrock	Inc
1	907	2647	J2	1990	J	150	80	55	0.88	Beachrock	F
1	607	5035	N1	1991	T	120	120	30	0.46	Beachrock	C
1	1062	7029	M5	1992	D	66	71	24		Scoria	F
2	515	1115	J6	1990	Y	50	41	140	0.06	Beachrock	F
2	524	1131	K7	1990	Y	130	100	25	0.43	Beachrock	C
2 a	962	2747	H3	1990	J	180	110	65	1.78	Beachrock	Inc
2 a	762	5426	AiO	1992	T	100	100	35	0.33	Beachrock	C
2 a	808	2341	J3	1990	J	190	130	50	1.41	Beachrock	C
2 a	517	1080	J5	1990	Y	80	110	55	0.86	Beachrock	F
2 b	1267	3998	J0	1992	J	75	75	15	0.11	Beachrock	C
2 b	18	3085	B4	1990	M	150	100	40	0.80	Beachrock	F
2 b	1044	3348	J1	1991	J	110	70	40	0.42	Beachrock	F
2 b	588	1391	J5	1990	Y	84	63	19		Scoria	F
2 b	879	2768	K4	1990	J	72	46	25		Scoria	F
2 c	1128	3611	J1	1991	J	132	88	24		Scoria	C
2 c	786	5579	S0	1992	T	60	47	17		Scoria	C
2 c	1052	7006	M5	1992	D	60	35	24		Scoria	F
2 c	1307	4161	J0	1992	J	59	55	24		Scoria	F
3	25	3126	B6	1990	M	115	120	70	0.98	Beachrock	F

							Length	Width	Thickness	Weight		
3	25		3126	B6	1990	M	120	90	40	0.61	Beachrock	F
3	25		3126	B6	1990	M	120	100	40	0.57	Beachrock	F
3	25		3126	B6	1990	M	130	80	45	0.28	Beachrock	F
3	553		1314	J6	1990	Y	150	100	45	1.08	Beachrock	C
3	1054	a	3398	H3	1991	J	220	120	70	2.05	Beachrock	F
3	567	a	1356	J6	1990	Y	105	90	60	1.04	Beachrock	C
3	1187	a	3784	K1	1991	J	117	75	39		Scoria	C
3	1576	a	5862	S2	1992	T	96	62	20		Scoria	C
3	1534	a	5713	S0-S1	1992	T	66	57	24		Scoria	F
3	708	b	5332	Ai1	1991	T	76	55	22		Scoria	F

Table 12.5. Descriptive statistics for beachrock hand-stones versus scoria hand-stones.

Beachrock handstones, complete and incomplete (n=10)

	Length (mm)	Width (mm)	Thickness (mm)	Weight (gm)
Mean	132.1	101.6	42.5	823
Median	125	100	45	750
S.D.	43.60	16.87	16.03	555.18
Range	115	55	50	1670
Minimum	75	75	15	110
Maximum	190	130	65	1780
Sum				8230

Scoria and basalt handstones, complete (n=9)

	Length (mm)	Width (mm)	Thickness (mm)	Weight (gm)
Mean	95.9	72.6	30.1	235.6
Median	89	69	29	150
S.D.	17.38	13.88	4.14	156.37
Range	49	37	12	445
Minimum	81	59	25	100
Maximum	130	96	37	545
Sum				2120

Table 12.6. Descriptive statistics, shapes and profiles of possible hand stones, Gilat 1990–92.

Handstones, complete and incomplete (n=22)

| | Measurements | | | | Shape | | | | | |
	Length (mm)	Width (mm)	Thickness (mm)	Weight (kg)	Round	Oval	Elongate/Loaf	Rectang.	Irreg.	Profiles
Mean	147.5	107.5	46.8	0.98	2	-	1	1	4	Flat
S.D.	56.8	24.2	15.6	0.61	1	4	2	1	3	Plano-conex
Range	162.0	80.0	62.0	1.86	-	-	-	-	-	Bi-convex
Min.	83.0	70.0	18.0	0.21	-	-	-	-	-	Irregular
Max.	245.0	150.0	80.0	2.07	1	-	-	-	1	Concave-convex
Sum.				19.67						

Handstones, fragments (n=23)

| | Measurements | | | | | |
	Length (mm)	Width (mm)	Thickness (mm)	Weight (kg)	Profiles	N=
Mean	90.9	72.8	38.1	0.50	Flat	11
S.D.	41.1	25.0	26.7	0.54	Plano-conex	8
Range	170.0	85.0	26.7	0.54	Bi-convex	2
Min.	50.0	35.0	17.0	0.04	Irregular	2
Max.	220.0	120.0	140.0	2.05	Concave-convex	-
Sum.				8.03		

Table 12.7. Descriptive statistics of grinders or hand stones, complete, incomplete, and unidentifiable ground stone fragments.

Grinders/Hand stones, complete and incomplete (n=14)

| | Measurements | | | |
	Length (mm)	Width (mm)	Thickness (mm)	Weight (kg)
Mean	196.4	133.6	63.9	2.02
S.D.	21.3	19.5	14.3	0.53
Range	70.0	60.0	55.0	20.9
Min.	150.0	110.0	35.0	12.6
Max.	220.0	170.0	90.0	33.5
Sum.				28.31

Grinder/hand stones, fragments (n=8)

| | Measurements | | | |
	Length (mm)	Width (mm)	Thickness (mm)	Weight (kg)
Mean	107.3	95.8	41.2	0.56
S.D.	29.2	27.6	13.5	0.34
Range	87.0	76.0	38.0	0.91
Min.	63.0	54.0	22.0	0.12
Max.	150.0	130.0	60.0	1.03
Sum.				4.44

Unidentifiable ground stone fragments (n=68)

| | Measurements | | | |
	Length (mm)	Width (mm)	Thickness (mm)	Weight (kg)
Mean	102.9	72.1	30.4	0.48
S.D.	47.5	25.9	23.4	1.31
Range	365.0	193.0	167.0	10.92
Min.	65.0	37.0	13.0	0.08
Max.	430.0	230.0	180.0	110.0
Sum.				32.23

Table 12.8. Mean dimensions of large perforated stones.

Large perforated stones, complete and incomplete (n=24)

	Length (cm)	Width (cm)	Thickness (cm)	Weight (kg)	Hole dia. min. (cm)	Hole dia. max. (cm)
Mean	15.30	13.37	5.15	1.58	2.36	3.79
Median	14.00	12.65	4.55	0.93	2.20	4.00
S.D.	6.16	4.14	1.75	2.06	1.23	1.62
Range	29	18	6.5	8.35	5	8
Minimum	9	8	3.5	0.37	0	0
Maximum	38	26	10	8.35	5	8

Large perforated stone, fragments (n=42)

	Length (cm)	Width (cm)	Thickness (cm)	Weight (kg)	Hole dia. min. (cm)	Hole dia. max. (cm)
Mean	13.67	11.05	5.56	0.85	2.51	3.46
Median	14.00	11.00	5.60	0.79	2.60	4.00
S.D.	2.90	3.53	1.22	0.49	1.90	2.67
Range	16	17	5.5	1.89	6	10
Minimum	7	4.7	2.5	0.19	0	0
Maximum	23	17	8	2.08	6	10
number=	41	40	41	41	39	39

Table 12.9. Summarized data for large stone rings, 1990–92 excavations.

Stratum	Locus	Basket	Length (cm)	Width (cm)	Thickness (cm)	Wt. (kg.)	Material	Hole dia. min. (cm.)	Hole dia. max. (cm)	Condition
	0	5007	17	15	8	1.46	Beachrock	4	7	F
	0	5000	11	11	3.9	0.35	Limestone	2.5	4.2	F
	0	0	12.8		5.6	0.82	Basalt	3.4	4.7	F
	0	0	9.3	8.3	4.9	0.46	Basalt	2.5	3.6	F
	0	0	13.3	12.3	4.2	1.00	Sandstone	2.4	4.4	C
	0	0	12.4	4.7	4.2	0.34	Sil. limest.	4	5.6	F
1	754	5408	15	15	5	0.92	Beachrock	6	6	F
1	800	2069	11	10	4	0.49	Beachrock	2.2	4	C
1	800	2075	15	6.5	5.5	0.66	Beachrock	0	0	F
1	800	2117	13	8	6	0.37	Beachrock	2.2	3	F
1	1023	3221	11	11	4	0.28	Beachrock	2	3.1	F
1	800	2259	14	11	4	0.79	Beachrock	2.2	4	C
1	1022	3245	17	13	3.5	0.90	Beachrock	2	5	Inc
1	1023	3221	14	9	5.5	0.58	Beachrock			F
1	1022	3214	14	11	5	0.92	Beachrock	3	4.5	F
1	607	5035	9	8	3.5	0.37	Beachrock	2	3.6	C
1	602	5054	14	16	6	1.84	Beachrock	3	5	F
1	1024	3216	11	7	4.5	0.34	Limestone	2.6	3.5	F
1	686	5241	15	10	6	1.08	Limestone	0	0	F
1	686	5241	17	14	5.5	1.05	Limestone	1.5	4	C
1	508	1083	12	11	5	0.94	Limestone	1.5	3.4	C
1	4	3036	13	7	6	0.69	Limestone	0	0	F
2	7	3012	11	11	5.5	0.41	Limestone	2.5	4	F
2 a	756	5411	16	16	6	1.47	Beachrock	6	6	F
2 a	1029	3263	17	8	6	0.79	Beachrock	6	6	F
2 a	808	2341	17	17	6	1.21	Beachrock	3	7	F
2 a	1031	3254	20	20	4.6	2.64	Beachrock	5	5	C
2 a	964	2764	38	18	10	8.35	Beachrock			C
2 a	808	2314	16.5	16.5	5.5	0.88	Beachrock	4	8	F
2 a	972	2846	10	9	4	0.60	Beachrock	1.6	3.5	C
2 a	817	2387	12	12	4.5	0.70	Beachrock	2.3	3.4	C
2 a	1036	3270	12	10	3.4	0.54	Chalk	2	2.5	F
2 a	624	5185	16	14	5	0.93	Limestone	2.5	4	C
2 a	1029	3263	14	13	6	1.07	Limestone	0	0	F
2 a	517	1080	11	6	4.5	0.50	Limestone	0	0	F
2 b	882	2663	17	17	6	2.08	Beachrock	3.3	6.5	F

2	b	1211	3818	17	11	6	1.55	Beachrock	0	0	F
2	b	1057	7015	14	14	7	1.29	Beachrock	3	3	C
2	b	785	5507	26	26	10	7.39	Beachrock	4	8	C
2	b	525	1123	15	14	5.5		Beachrock	4.4	5.6	C
2	b	634	5242	18	18	7	2.24	Beachrock	4.5	5	C
2	b	882	2652	12	11	4.5	0.63	Beachrock	2.8	3.6	C
2	b	1418	4415	14	14	5	1.18	Beachrock	2.2	3.7	C
2	b	965	2772	11	8	5	0.62	Limestone	2.3	4	C
2	b	1215	3830	17	17	5.3	1.20	Limestone	0	0	Inc
2	b	787	5568	12	12	6	0.71	Limestone	4	4	F
2	c	1511	5739	15	15	7	0.79	Beachrock	4	4	F
2	c	1105	3528	7	6	5	0.25	Beachrock	0	0	F
2	c	26	3093	15	13	8	1.44	Beachrock	0	0	F
2	c	786	5710	13	13	6	0.48	Beachrock	4	4	F
2	c	827	2314	13	11.5	4.5	0.63	Beachrock	1.8	2.5	C
2	c	1298	4086	9	9	4	0.43	Beachrock	2	4	C
2	c	783	5526	17	14	4	1.33	Limestone	0	0	Inc
2	c	827	2303	12	9	5	0.84	Limestone	0	0	F
2	c	680	5259	15	14	6.5	1.29	Limestone	5	10	F
2	c	827	2313	12	12	4	0.60	Limestone	2	3.5	C
3		552	1234	8.5	7	3.5	0.19	Limestone	2.7	3.3	F
3		10	3031	11	7	5	0.60	Limestone	2.3	4.5	F
3		60	222	10	5	2.6	0.16	Limestone			
3	a	1054	3374	14	15	5	1.31	Beachrock		0	F
3	a	692	5254	16	9	6	0.98	Limestone	0	0	F
4	b	1294	4075	13	13	5.5	0.62	Beachrock	3	3	F

Table 12.10. Summarized data for hammerstones and pecked cobbles, 1990–92 excavations.

Stratum	Locus	Basket	Square	Area	Length (mm)	Width (mm)	Thickness (mm)	Wt. (kg)	Material	Profile	Shape	Condition
1	927	2673	J3	J	50	49	30	0.08	Flint	Sphere		C
1	6	3052	B4	M	120	50	35	0.36	Flint?	Elongate		C
1	5	3025	B5	M	41	30	33	0.06	Limest.	Sphere		C
2 a	818	2458	K4	J	53	42	40	0.11	Flint?	Oblong	Round	C
2 a	1029	3263	L3	J	70	55	49	0.25	Limest.	Sphere		C
2 a	961	2740	H2	J	55	43	37	0.11	Limest.	Oblong		C
2 b	674	5210	S1	T	71	45	32	0.15	Flint	Elongate	Elongate	C
2 b	895	2595	J3	J	100	60	50	0.58	Flint	Sphere		C
2 b	18	3085	B5	M	48	48	43	0.12	Flint	Elongate	Elongate	C
2 b	16	3059	B5	M	83	35	27	0.10	Flint?	Ovoid	Ovoid	C
2 b	882	2683	K4	J	67	43	40	0.16	Flint?	Sphere		C
2 b	882	2683	K4	J	75	67	52	0.36	Flint?	Oval	Oval	C
2 b	882	2683	K4	J	98	74	67	0.65	Flint?	Irreg.	Irreg	C
2 b	882	2682	K4	J	49	33	39	0.10	Flint?	Flat	Round	C
2 b	16	3059	B5	M	55	44	16	0.06	Limest.	Round	Round	C
2 c	794	5551	M0-N0	T	62	55	35	0.13	Chalk	Oval	Oval	C
2 c	1509	5756	N0	T	80	60	45	0.30	Flint	Bi-conv	Cylinder	C
2 c	137	397	M4	D	76	52	43	0.26	Flint?	Oval	Oval	C
2 c	40	3141	B4	M	79	45	35	0.19	Flint?	Bi-conv	Oval	C
2 c	137	397	M4	D	45	36	33	0.08	Flint?	Bi-conv	Ellipt.	Inc
3	25	3126	B6	M	83	83	55		Chalk	Sphere		C
3	556	1385	J7	J	51	40	36	0.10	Flint?	Oval	Oval	C
3 a	917	2650	J3-J4	J	66	47	49	0.21	Flint	Irreg.	Round	C
3 a	917	2675	J3-J4	J	79	64	32	0.20	Flint	Plano-conv	Round	C
3 a	567	1375	J6	Y	55	42	26	0.08	Flint?	Plano-conv		C
4	155	413	S5	D	57	40	36	0.11	Flint?	Bi-conv.	Bi-conv.	C

Table 12.11. Descriptive statistics and shapes for hammerstones and pounders.

	Measurements			
	Length (mm)	Width (mm)	Thickness (mm)	Weight (kg)
Mean	66.0	48.6	38.7	0.19
S.D.	16.4	11.4	11.0	0.16
Range	59.0	44.0	51.0	0.59
Min.	41.0	30.0	16.0	0.06
Max.	100.0	74.0	67.0	0.65
Sum.				4.10

	Shapes					
Profiles	Round	Spherical	Oval	Elongate/Loaf	Irregular	Oblong
Oval	2	-	4	-	-	-
Spherical	-	5	-	-	-	-
Elongate	-	-	-	2	-	-
Plano-convex	1	-	-	-	-	1
Flat	1	-	-	-	-	-
Oblong	-	-	-	-	-	3
Irregular	1	-	-	-	1	-
Totals	5	5	4	2	1	4

Table 12.12. Summarized data for pestles, 1990–92 excavations.

Stratum	Locus	Basket	Square	Area	Length (mm)	Width (mm)	Thickness (mm)	Wt. (kg)	Material	Condition
0	0	0			126	49	38	0.34	Flint?	C
1	1213	3893	J0	J	200	85	55	1.03	Limestone	C
1	6	3011	B4	M	100	51	48	0.36	Flint?	C
2	527	1136	K5	Y	140	80	60	1.09	Flint	C
2 b	908	2633	J3	J	45	44	43	0.13	Limestone	F
2 c	8	26	Rm A	D	83	44	44	0.48	Hematite	C
2 c	783	5608	S1	T	80	50	25	0.25	Beachrock	
2 c	7	22	Rm A	D	90	58	46	0.34	Basalt	C
2 c	11	32	Rm A	D	75	48	30	0.17	Basalt	C
3 a	575	1337	J5	Y	70	55	30	0.18	Limestone	C
3 b	112	351	M/N6	D	66	35	35	0.14	Limestone	C

Table 12.13. Descriptive statistics of pestles (n=11) from Gilat excavations, 1975–92.

	Length (mm)	Width (mm)	Thickness (mm)	Weight (kg)
Mean	97.7	54.5	41.3	408.1
Median	83.0	50.0	3.28	102.5
S.D.	43.3	15.2	10.9	340.1
Range	155.0	50.0	35.0	960.0
Min.	45.0	35.0	25.0	130.0
Max.	200.0	85.0	60.0	1090.0

Table 12.14. Descriptive statistics and morphological attributes of smoothed pebbles from 1990–91 excavations.

	Measurements			
	Length (mm)	Width (mm)	Thickness (mm)	Weight (kg)
Mean	46.5	33.4	18.5	0.05
S.D.	20.9	14.0	7.2	0.05
Range	120.0	96.0	47.0	0.27
Min.	16.0	12.0	7.0	0.01
Max.	120.0	96.0	47.0	0.27
Sum.				7.28

	Shapes						
Profiles	Round	Spherical	Oval	Elongate/Loaf	Irregular	Oblong	Totals
Oval	1	-	7	-	-	-	8
Spherical	-	73	-	-	-	-	73
Elongate	4	-	-	3	-	-	7
Plano-convex	1	-	-	-	-	-	1
Flat	7	-	53	-	6	3	69
Oblong	1	-	-	-	-	4	5
Round	-	-	-	-	-	1	1
Bi-convex	-	-	1	-	-	-	1
Irregular	-	-	-	-	9	-	9
Totals	14	73	61	3	15	8	174

Table 12.15. Summarized data for door sockets/pivot stones.

Stratum		Locus	Basket	Length (mm)	Width (mm)	Thickness (mm)	Wt. (kg.)	Material	Hole dia. min. (mm.)	Hole dia. max. (mm)	Condition
1		800	2066	160	120	70	2	limestone	70	70	C
2	a	618	5076	170	150	80	2.79	limestone	80	90	C?
2	b	1066	3507	200	250	100	4.85	limestone	80	80	C
2	b	634	5179	260	210	130	8.11	limestone	110	110	C
3		556	1390	150	130	60	2.27	limestone	80	80	C

Table 12.16. Summarized data for mortars.

Strata	Locus	Basket	Length (mm)	Width (mm)	Thick. (mm)	Height (mm)	Wt. (kg)	Material	Diameter (mm)	Bowl depth	Condition
0	0	0	51	59	30		0.23	Basalt	145		F
0	0	0	102	51	30		0.23	Basalt	140-150		F
0	0	0	58	95	27		0.31	Basalt	60		F
0	0	0	115	155	95		2.29	Basalt			F
0	0	0	77	46	23		0.11	Basalt	80		F
0	0	0	115	155	95		2.29	Basalt	130		F
0	0	0	70	48		37	0.08	Chalk		17	F
0	0	0	105		36	84		Chalk			C
0	0	1311	98			66	0.57	Limestone	95	18	C
0	0	2604		85		60	0.34	Limestone		45	F
1	800	1044		95	44			Beachrock	140		F
1	507	2629		100		130	3.21	Beachrock	140	80	C
1	906	3866			33			Beachrock	150		F
1	1219	5011	135	115	20	72		Chalk			F
1	602	1054	95	60		45	0.16	Chalk			C
1	509	3212	65	56		29		Chalk			C
1	0	2010	130	90		65	1.20	Chalk		10	C
1	800	1026	41	36	19			Chalk			F
1	504	1054	117	79	52			Chalk			F
1	509	1061	123	97	24	35		Chalk			F
1	508	3005	135	101	39			Kurkar			F
1	3	3230	22	47	30			Limestone			F
1	1026	3002		90	41		0.47	Limestone	130		F
1	3	5043	70	69	23	25		Limestone		10	F
1	602		220	170		70	2.44	Limestone			C

1		907	2630	85	82	33		0.24	Limestone			F
1		903	2616	54	41	27		0.06	Limestone			F
1		1024	3239	129	90	27		0.23	Limestone	140		F
1		1214	3848	110	68	42		0.45	Limestone			F
1		1220	3921		60	24	24		Limestone	200	11	C
1		508	1041	87	150	42	39		Limestone			F
1		800	2071	90	77	39	34	0.42	Limestone		15	C
1		85	266		80		45		Limestone		29	C
1		1022	3225	86			39		Limestone	120		F
2	a	800	2220	93	61		68	0.59	Limestone		41	I
2	a	55	230	108		24	71		Beachrock	93		I
2	a	17	3073	130	90		110		Beachrock	150	55	F
2	a	57	261	31	130	14	32	0.42	Kurkar?			F
2	a	17	3073	89	28		110		Limestone			F
2	a	527	1132		72				Limestone			F
2	a	120	330						Limestone		15	C
2	a	532	1122	150	100			1.95	Limestone	180	70	F
2	a	1029	3263	140	85	90	90	1.23	Beachrock		28	F
2	a	1059	3378	120	90	65	100	0.22	Beachrock			F
2	a	1029	3263	220	130	60	18	0.86	Beachrock		30	F
2	a	1256	3963	110	120	90	43	2.19	Beachrock			F
2	a	1029	3256	120	100		45	0.29	Beachrock			F
2	a	1029	3263	160	29	21		0.07	Beachrock	120	45	F
2	a	516	1079	28		18	22	2.04	Beachrock			F
2	a	1266	4006	80	50				Chalk		9	F
2	a	1117	3551	90	60			0.13	Chalk		30	F
2	a	925	2705	100	52	40		0.24	Chalk		26	F
2	a	703	5293	56	150	22			Chalk			F
2	a	958	2746	170				0.14	Chalk			I
2	a	618	5076		100		80	2.79	Limestone	170	20	C
2	a	710	5348	150			50	1.66	Limestone	150	10	C
2	a	804	2317		90		90	1.62	Limestone	140	25	C
2	a	1033	3257	120	59	45		0.43	Limestone		30	F
2	a	1029	3263	69	100	45	50	0.48	Limestone			F
2	a	1223	3923	190			120		Limestone			C
2	a	544	1185						Limestone		10	F
2	a	1029	3263	74			34	2.00	Limestone			F
2	b	1091	3483				90	0.12	Beachrock	60	10	I
2	b	965	2773		50			3.91	Beachrock	180	20	C
2	b	838	2495	50	50		48		Chalk	50		C
2	b	1108	3532		40	30		0.08	Chalk			F

C1	C2	C3	C4	C5	C6	C7	C8	C9	Material	C11	C12	C13
2	b	16	3059	75	34	29	50		Limestone			F
2	b	755	5429	65	60		128	0.22	Limestone			C
2	b	537	1401			30			Limestone	96	70	C
2	b	16	3051		60				Limestone	210		F
2	b	879	2774	150	130	50	13	1.94	Limestone	15		F
2	b	706	5327	101	66	30		0.83	Limestone			F
2	c	786	5667	80	75	35			Basalt	180		F
2	c	1511	5690	55	50	30		0.30	Basalt			F
2	c	1056	3373					0.11	Chalk		45	F
2	c	528	1199					0.19	Chalk		20	F
2	c	783	5526	65	40	41	50		Chalk	160		C
2	c	676	5237	110	50		41	0.18	Chalk		11	F
2	c	1522	5659		53		66		Chalk			F
2	c	1310	4149	71	45	24	24		Chalk		17	C
2	c	569	1296	72	51	7	23		Chalk		75	F
2	c	1056	3366	180	140		90	1.16	Limestone			C
2	c	1513	5630	140	110		35	0.10	Limestone			C
2	c	676	5274	110	70	28	35	0.36	Limestone		10	F
2	c	1227	3975	52	43		61		Limestone			C
2	c	1549	5786	130	110			1.25	Limestone		30	F
2	c	946	2863	110	90			0.74	Limestone			F
3		548	1260	32	26	6.5	16		Chalk			I
3		124	338	160	103		58	0.62	Chalk		37	F
3		25	3135	70	80		50	0.17	Limestone			F
3		10	3031				65	0.55	Limestone		20	F
3		25	3116	140	70	25		0.69	Beachrock			C
3	a	548	1284	220	200	80	150	5.63	Beachrock		20	F
3	a	1337	4215	115	103		150		Beachrock	120	80	C
3	a	583	1383	120	80		55	1.34	Chalk		28	F
3	a	1131	3714	202	122	21	80	0.46	Felsic Porphyry			F
3	a	1328	4171	90	40	45		0.17	Limestone			F
3	a	1146	3661				70	0.81	Limestone	140	30	F
3	a	1170	3719	150	80	50		0.54	Limestone			F
3	b	583	1389	180	160	50	20	0.65	Chalk			C
3		1569	5827	95	97	50		0.66	Basalt			F
4		1275	4061	70	40		25	0.08	Chalk			C

Table 12.17. Summarized data for multi-functional ground stone tools.

Stratum	Locus	Basket	Square	Context	Type	Area	Length (mm)	Width (mm)	Thickness (mm)	Wt. (kg)	Material	Profile	Shape	Notes
0	0	0		None	Axe/pestle		98	49	32	0.24	basalt	bi-convex	ovoid	Bi-polar pecked, axe shaped body and edge
0	0	0		None	Pounder/mano		105	82	68	0.96	granite	irregular	ovoid	Bi-polar pecked, highly ground on at least one face
0	0	0		None	Incised/pounder		92	59	50	0.47	basalt	central groove		Bi-polar pecked, medial concave, longit. groove
0	0	0		None	Mano/hammer	D	81	81	45	0.37	beachrock	plano-convex		
2	527	1136	K5	Fill	Pounder/pestle	Y	140	80	60	1.09	flint	flat	elongate	
2 b	882	2643	K4	Silo	Mano/pestle	J	68	59	49	0.15	limestone	plano-conv	round	
2 b	86	292	N3	Fill	Rubber/pounder	D	68	41	37	0.13	limestone	cylinder	cylinder	Bi-polar pecked, 2 sides ground
3 a	567	1356	J6	surface?	Ground/battered	Y	78	64	21		chalk			Ground and battered
3 b	583	1389	J5	Fill	Mano/pestle	Y	62	62	45	0.23	beachrock	flat	round	

Table 12.18. Summarized data for miscellaneous ground stone artifacts.

Stratum	Locus	Basket	Square	Area	Context	Description	Material	Length (mm)	Width (mm)	Thick. (mm)	Condition
0	0	0			none	shallow, platter-like	unknown	80	71	23	F
0	0	0			stray	highly polished corner of palette/axe?	unknown	26	24	11.5	F
0	0	0			stray	bifacially ground with striae	chalk	54	42	23	F
0	48	104	J5-K5	D	baulk	incised stone	chalk	150	103	63	C
0	stray	1244	N5	Y		bifacially smoothed with striae	chalk	54	42	23	F
1	3	3005	C4	M	topsoil	flat, unknown	limestone	42	36	14	F
1	600	5009	Ai2	T	topsoil	shallow concavity, end chipped (chopper?)	limestone	129	79	47	Inc
1	602	5020	S1	T	topsoil	square, bifacially ground	limestone	66	63	14	F
1	630	5124	M2	T	topsoil	ground stone frag	mica schist	52	29	8.5	F
1	800	2091	J4	J	topsoil	knob on convex/concave fragment	scoria	95	91	33	C
1	800	2197	J3	J	topsoil	elongate pebble with striae	chalk	72.5	21	16	F
1	800	2242	K4	J	topsoil	flat	ferrug. sandstone	35	24	11	F
1	1212	3907	H0	J	topsoil	possibly ground	sandstone	43	34	5.5	C
1	1213	3967	J0	J	topsoil	roughly chipped disc	chlorite-schist	85	83	25	C
2	117	327	M3	D	pit	disc	beachrock	68	65	29	C
2	522	1099	J7/K7	Y	pit	flat, nodule, smoothed	chalk	90	53	14	C
2a	14	3139	C4	M	pit	flat, with striae, possibly perforated	chalk	50	35	13	F
2a	608	5038	S2	T	pit	acute angle, figurine fragment?	limestone	44	39	13	F
2a	628	5103	M1	T	hearth	cylindrical piece with ochre deposits	hematite	37	19		F
2a	806	2379	J3	J	pit	irregular shape, flat, edges ground	limestone/dolomite	49	51	11.5	C
2a	810	2319	K3	J	pit	bifacial striae, smoothed and flat	limestone	36	30	13	F
2a	813	2296	J3	J	pit	bifacial striae, with small 'rim'	chalk	21	20	6.5	F
2a	816	2394	K4	J	floor	flat, triangular, palette-like, w/striae	kurkar	127	88	19	C
2a	840	2560	J3	J	m.b.collapse	possibly ground	kurkar	75	78	18	F
2a	960	2739	J2	J	pit	ground stone frag	chalk	59	19	20	F
2a	1037	3367	H1	J	fill, ash	flat, with striae	chalk	35	29	12.5	F
2a	1050	3394	L1	J	pit	flat, very worn	chalk	27	24	11.5	F
2a	1051	3372	L2	J	pit	unifacial ochre deposits	kurkar	100	95	26	C
2b	525	1109	J5	Y	fill	limestone pebble, possibly ground, oval	limestone	116	72	24	F
2b	626	5118	Ai1	T	pit	flat, slight concave one side	gypsum-satinspar	38	23	4	C
2b	660	5196	N2	T	wall removal	flat, ground	chalk	36	16	15	F
2b	755	5441	M0	T	fill	knob on convex/concave fragment	scoria	80	67	35	F
2b	755	5539	N0-M0	T	fill	bifacial concavities, ca. 28 cm diameter	chalk	79	75	40	F
2b	772	5540	M2	T	fill	bifacially ground	chalk	33	26	9.5	F
2b	775	5476	Ai0	T	pit	flat	sandstone	35	25	14	F
2b	901	2641	J3	J	surface	bifacial striae, well-ground	limestone	78	40	25	F

2	b	965	2756	K2	J	pit	sphere, worn and ground	chalk	55	44	44	C
2	b	1028	3304	J1	J	fill, ash	mortar body frag?	chalk	31	28	13	F
2	b	1028	3391	J1	J	fill, ash	flat, bifacial striae, bowl?	chalk	18	15	6	F
2	b	1075	3447	H3	J	pit	flat	kurkar	12.8	58	8	F
2	b	1139	3618	L1	J	wall	flat, with striae	chalk	82	47	23	F
2	b	1236	3941	K0	J	fill	unifacial striae, small nodule	limestone	45	24	22	C
2	b	1236	3926	K0	J	fill	handstone?	quartzite	52	41	29	F
2	b	1503	5599	Ai0	T	fill	flat	limestone	34	17	4.5	F
2	c	6	9	Ai5	D	floor	disc	limestone				
2	c	35	3132	B4-B5	M	pit	trapezoidal outline and profile	chlorite schist	11	5.5	2	C
2	c	558	1287	J7	Y	m.b. feature	trapezoidal shape, bifacial striae	limestone	55	37	12.75	C?
2	c	777	-	M0	T	pit	'L' shaped fragment	limestone	119	160	42	F
2	c	1105	3528	S2	J	pit	slightly bi-convex, round, ground	limestone	58	30	9	F
2	c	1105	3528	J2	J	pit	flat, with striae	chalk	33	26	11.5	F
2	c	1213	3967	M5	D	floor	disc	scoria				F
2	c	1310	4149	L0	J	pit	chalk nodule with concavity	chalk	71	45	24	F
2	c	1511	5607	S2	T	pit	small, worked fragment	limestone	20	16	12	F
2	c	1511	5712	S2	T	pit	flat, slight unifacial concavity on cobble	limestone	125	67	26	F
2	c	1511	5712	S2	T	pit	abraded flat cobble frag	limestone	125	67	26	F
3	a	556	1390	J7	Y	pit	rectangular, with squared edges	limestone	50	39	13	Inc
3	a	567	1357	J6	Y	surface	clay with perforation; macehead model?	ceramic	62	58	44	C
3	a	567	1363	J6	Y	surface	clay, with perforation? macehead model?	ceramic	48	42		C
3	a	1131	3587	K3	J	fill	bifacially incised oval nodule	chalk	76	53	23	C
3	a	1146	3675	H1	J	fill	nodule, probably ochre traces	flint	75	44	38	C
3	a	1150	3747	H3	J	pit	disc, possibly re-worked vessel	basalt	121	121	45	C?
3	a	1170	3718	J2	J	fill	limestone nodule, poss ground, flat	limestone	56	52	14	C
3	a	1369	4407	H2	J	silo	smooth, bifacial striae, oblong	limestone	111	53	15	C
3	a	1528	5703	Ai0	T	m.b.circle	ring fragment?	chalk	30	17	12	F
3	a	1530	5687	Ai0	T	rubbish dump	bifacially ground	chalk	65	43	26	F
3	a	1535	5716	S0	T	pit	flat	sandstone	33	25	3	F
3	a	1565	5821	S2	T	pit	irregular shape	chalk	33	17	13	F

Table 12.19. Summarized data for modified and unmodified ochre.

Stratum		Locus	Basket	Context	Square	Year	Area	Description	Length (mm)	Width (mm)	Thickness (mm)
		0	3333		H2	1991	J	ground nodule	34	29	21
		0	1050		N7	1990	D	worked, trapezoidal	32	31	12
		264	531		L7	1987	D	ground, pyramid shaped	21.5	21.5	20
		294	609		N7	1987	D	unworked	26	24	10
		0	-	silo	B4	1987	M	stray find	24	16	5
1		1214	3912	topsoil	H4	1992	J	worked, trapezoidal	24	20	14
2		7	3039	fill	C6	1990	M	ground on one edge	33	25	11
2		21	3076	fill	C4	1990	M	ground nodule	10.5	10	3
2	a	608	5097	fill	S2	1991	T	nodule, unworked	18	12	7
2	a	656	5188	stone feature	N1-S1	1991	T	nodule, unworked	29	22	18
2	a	697	5294	pit	S0	1991	T	may be ground	18	14	11
2	a	1030	3312	surface	K1	1991	J	nodule, ground	16		
2	a	1095	3498	hearth	K1	1991	J	worked, trapezoidal	13	7	3
2	b	55	177	pit	Ai4	1976	D		-	-	
2	b	626	5105	pit	Ai1	1991	T	nodule, unworked	15		
2	b	674	5233	pit	S1	1991	T	nodule, unworked	10	9	5
2	b	763	5559	fill	N1	1992	T	worked, 1 face ground	35	18	11
2	b	772	5561	fill	M2-M3	1992	T	2 frags, unworked	-	-	
2	b	799	5574	fill	N0	1992	T	worked, 1 face ground	25	18	9
2	b	994	2876	fill	H2	1990		nodule, unworked	18	14	5
2	b	1028	3325	ash	J1	1991	J	nodule, unworked	18	11	11
2	b	1124	3586	pit	H1	1991	J	worked, 1 edge ground	21	13	5
2	b	1218	3878	pit	L3	1992	J	worked, 1 face ground	27	23	6
2	b	1246	4058	fill	H4	1992	J	worked, 1 face ground	26	23	9
2	c	26	3098	pit	B5	1990	M	nodule, unworked	15	2	4
2	c	35	3118	pit	B5-B4	1990	M	crumbs	-	-	
2	c	41	41	-	Rm A/B S4-S5	1975	D		-	-	
2	c	52	152	-	Rm.A/B S4-S5	1976	D		-	-	
2	c	125	365		M6	1977	D		-	-	
2	c	528	1154	pit	M0	1990	Y	ground nodule	31	23	11
2	c	777	5467	pit	M0	1992	T	2 frags, unworked	-	-	
2	c	783	5513	fill	S1	1992	T	nodule, unworked	75	68	41
2	c	783	5542	fill	S1	1992	T	worked nodule	38	21	11.5
2	c	786	5676	fill	S0	1992	T	worked, triangular	32	27	5
2	c	786	5759	fill	S0	1991	T	worked, triangular	42	20	9

2	c	792	5528	surface removal	Ai0	1992	T	worked, 1 face ground	29	26	11
2	c	1056	3373	pit	J2	1991	J	worked, 1 face ground	31	22	6
2	c	1131	3715	pit	K3	1991	J	ground nodule	17	16	7
2	c	1510	5858	burial	S0	1992	T	worked, 1 face ground	16	12	6.5
3		22	3080	pit	C6	1990	M	crumbs, unworked	-	-	-
3		560	1279	pit	K7	1990	Y	nodule, unworked	17	14	9
3	a	32	58	-	Rm. A S6	1975	D		-	-	-
3	a	127	369	pit	N6	1977	D		-	-	-
3	a	139	383	-	N3	1977	D		-	-	-
3	a	146	390	-	S3	1977	D		-	-	-
3	a	171	442	pit	M6	1977	D		-	-	-
3	a	1054	3388	fill	H3	1991	J	worked, trapezoidal	24	19	11
3	a	1131	3733	fill	K3	1991	J	nodule, unworked	51	35	10
3	a	1150	3755	pit	H3	1991	J	worked nodule	20	16	12
3	a	1170	3727	fill	J2	1991	J	worked, smooth	30	21	8
3	a	1534	5729	pit	S0	1992	T	nodule, maybe smooth	24	21	20
3	a	1535	5716	pit	S0	1992	T	worked, triangular	28	18	7
3	b	34	34	-	Rm. A S5	1975	D		-	-	-
3	b	1562	5838	pit	Ai1	1992	T	worked nodule	33	27	12
3	b	1562	5825	pit	Ai1	1992	T	worked, trapezoidal	52	24	19
4		1275	4063	fill	H2	1992	J	nodule, unworked	35	23	7

Table 12.20. Summarized data for unmodified rocks and minerals.

Stratum	Locus	Basket	Square	Area	Context	Material	Length (mm)	Width (mm)	Thickness (mm)	Description
	270	557	L6	D	none	clay	89		46	round clay lump, bi-convex
	293	604	L6	D	none	hematite	33	24	19	nodule
Stray		-	-	-	none	limestone/iron oxides				chunk
Surface		-	-	D	none	unknown	53	41	18	flat, oval, rounded & polished
Surface		-	-	D	none	granite	58	66		flat on 2 ends, ground? macehead blank?
1	504	1026	K6	Y	topsoil	pyrite	27	18		cylindrical
1	509	1055	K6	Y	fill	pyrite	16.5	7.5		pyrite
1	512	1070	J5	Y	fill	beachrock	205	87	65	elongate, with incisions, natural?
1	602	5020	S1	T	topsoil	limestone	66	63	14	nodule,square - ground?
1	800	2267	K4	J	topsoil	sandstone,copper minerals	70	42	43	sandstone w/copper minerals
1	800	2157	K3	J	topsoil	chrysocolla-azurite	26	20	6	2 conjoinable fragments
1	927	2673	J3	J	topsoil	hematite	27	18	10	nodule
2	21	3076	C4	M	fill	malachite				crumbs
2 a	627	5183	N2	T	fill	carnelian	11	10	7	nodule
2 a	628	5103	M1-N1	T	hearth	hematite	37	19	5	cylindrical with depression at top
2 a	700	5281	M0	T	pit	hematite	28	21		nodule prob. unworked,semi-sphere
2 a	806	2363	J3	J	pit	pyrite	27	8		cylindrical
2 b	674	5215	S1	T	pit	amazonite	15	6	4	nodule
2 b	693	5268	M0	T	fill	chrysocolla	7	5		chrysocolla
2 b	776	5468	M1/2-N1/2	T	fill	sandstone	43	32	20	blue-green mineral lump
2 b	882	2643	B4	J	silo	chrysocolla	-	-		crumbs
2 b	882	2623	K4	J	silo	chrysocolla-azurite	18	11	10	chunk
2 b	905	2622	J3	J	fill	hematite	16	10	6	nodule
2 b	905	2622	J3	J	fill	hematite	37	20	18	nodule
2 b	905	2622	J3	J	fill	hematite	36	18	12.5	nodule
2 b	1028	3325	J1	J	ash	chlorite schist	40	20	13	nodule
2 b	1028	3347	J1	J	ash	amazonite	24	19	15	nodule
2 b	1072	3436	K3	J	removal	hematite	68	57	46	nodule possibly worked
2 b	1246	3951	H4	J	fill	jasper	21	17	7.5	smoothed pebble
2 b	1246	4062	H4	J	fill	turquoise	13	12	9	turquoise
2 c	786	5521	S0-N0	T	fill	quartz				nodule
2 c	1062	7029	M5	D	fill	unknown	34	16	12	vitrified material
2 c	1168	3734	H1	J	pit	chrysocolla	17	9	4	nodule
2 c	1222	3867	L4	J	surface	sandstone	15	14	12	chunk green stone
2 c	1510	5683	S0	T	burial	sandstone, copper minerals	80	40	35	sandstone w/blue-green material
3	168	430	S5		pit	granite	48	45	36	nodule
3	547	1196	K7	Y	pit	pyrite	27	14		cylindrical
3 b	640	5315	Ai1	T	pit	chlorite schist	151	58	23	cylindrical
3 b	692	5253	Ai2	T	pit	calcite	15	10	8	trapezoidal crystal

Table 12.21. Summarized data for tokens.

Stratum		Locus	Basket	Length (mm)	Width (mm)	Width2 (mm)	Thickness (mm)	Wt. (gms)	Material	Shape	Condition
0		0	1259	58	45		9.5	40	fer. limestone	rectang.	Inc
0		0	0	42	28		12	24	limestone	rectang.	C
1		5	3016	44	27		10	18	chalk	ovoid	C
1		6	3052	30	15	23	11	11	green sandstone	trapez.	C
1		1025	3232	50	15	22	10	16	limestone	ovoid	C
2		34	3115	12	13		6	2	chlorite/schist		F
2	a	1160	3720	39	14.5		8	4	chalk	trapez.	C
2	a	961	2805	35	21		12	22	chlorite/schist	rectang.	F?
2	a	761	5427	42	11	23	18	28	chlorite/schist	conical	C
2	a	1382	4360	32	14		6	4	limestone	r.trapez.	C
2	a	1150	3737	42	39		8	18	limestone	irregular	C
2	a	608	5049	32	21		8	10	limestone	trapez.	C
2	a	1074	3433	50	20	26	10	21	limestone	r.trapez.	C
2	a	138	380						unknown		
2	b	838	2496	28	7.5	9	3	1	bone	trapez.	C
2	b	150	394						ceramic		
2	b	1344	4307	28	15		5.5	3	ceramic	r.trapez.	C
2	b	828	2452	39	30		10	14	chalk	rectang.	C
2	b	1236	3926	51	17	27	15	30	chalk	ovoid	C
2	b	633	5128	38	31		7	6	chalk	triang.	C
2	b	1207	3829	33.5	19	22	6	9	chlorite/schist	trapez.	C
2	b	709	5329	27	5	12.5	4	2	fer. sandstone	trapez.	C
2	b	882	2623	30	16		8.5	7	fer.sandstone	irregular	C
2	b	1057	3357	40	20.5		10		limestone	r.trapez.	C
2	b	1097	3505	54	40.5		10	29	limestone	r.rectang.	C
2	b	1057	3495	31	14	21	6	7	limestone		F
2	c	83	178						bone		C
2	c	864	2489	44	7	9	2	1	bone	trapez.	C
2	c	786	5615	26.5	18		6		chalk		F
2	c	1062	7029	44	20		12	14	chalk		F
2	c	1054	3374	33	31		12	15	chalk		F
2	c	1259	4069	29	15	22.5	10	9	chalk	trapez.	C
2	c	38	63						clay		
2	c	649	5172	53	48		12	46	fer.sandstone	round	C
2	c	1547	5767	43	28		10	17	limestone	r.trapez	C

2	c	1309	4118	50	32		15	27	limestone	irregular	C
2	c	1056	7009	42	22	29	9	8	limestone	r.trapez.	C
2	c	771	5463	30	23	28	5	8	limestone		F
3		560	1269	28	18		9	5	limestone	trapez.	C
3		585	1379	44	52		12	45	limestone		F
3	a	1334	4282	33	26		11	14	limestone	triang?	Inc
3	b	692	5384	34	23		12.5	16	clay	rectang.	C
3	b	702	5291	46	28		13	24	clay	rectang.	Inc
4		1354	4279	27	17		8	8	limestone	trapez.	C
4		1273	4116	32	30		10	21	sandstone		F
?		1153	3680	53	53		14	66	diorite	round	C

* Notes for abbreviations: r.trapez. = rounded trapezoid; r.rectang = rounded rectangular;

Table 12.22. Summarized data for pendants.

Stratum	Locus	Basket	Length	Width	Thick.	Hole 1, dia.	Hole 2, dia.	Material	Condition
	?	562	34	44	17	6	9	chalk	F
	1055	7008	15	15	2			ostrich shell	F
	0	0	35	27				shell	?
	0	0						shell	?
1	1214	3862	20	12	7			fer.limestone	Inc
1	800	2161	46	49	7			limestone	Inc
1	800	2093	37	32	24	1	2	ivory	Inc
2 a	54	161						gypsum	?
2 a	159	424						ceramic	?
2 a	700	5286	31	10	10	1		chlorite/schist	C
2 a	798	5566	52	35	14			chalk	Inc
2 a	14	3123	48	35	8			limestone	Inc
2 a	170	441						calcite	?
2 a	961	2782	41.5	26	7			chalk	Inc
2 a	159	424						ceramic	?
2 a	68	212						ceramic	?
2 a	138	380						ceramic	?
2 b	1321	4169	32	20	9			limestone	C
2 b	55	67						stone	?
2 b	18	38						ceramic	?
2 b	123	336						bone	?
2 b	1124	3567	71	58	14.5	3	3	clay	Inc
2 b	763	5629	26	9	9	2		calcite	Inc
2 b	37	68						ceramic	?
2 b	18	36						ceramic	?
2 b	895	2597	45	19	11.5	2		fer. sandstone	C?
2 b	909	2659	30.5	13	2	1	1	shell	C
2 b	1321	4208	27	21	7	2		limestone	F
2 b	150	394						ceramic	?
2 c	72	245						ceramic	?
2 c	1320	4173	18	8	6	2		chlorite/schist	F
2 c	1393	4379	38	23	1	1	1	shell	F
2 c	137	371						chalk	?
2 c	1393	4379	24	11	0.5	1		shell	F
2 c	1059	3399	25	13.5	5.5	1		chlorite/schist	Inc

2	c	8	26					ceramic	?
2	c	786	5538	34	28	17		chalk	F
2	c	7	22					calcite/gypsum	?
2	c	1221	3868	45	21	8		limestone	C
2	c	40	3141	25	20.5	6		limestone	C
2	c	36	67					ceramic	?
2	c	19	33					chalk	?
2	c	52	152					chalk	?
2	c	6	9					quartz	?
2	c	1062	7026	31	7	6	1	amazonite	C
2	c	1320	4151	16	19	7		chlorite/schist	F
2	c	38	63					?	?
2	c	1547	5767	36	18	10		limestone	C
2	c	297	623	80	45	14		chalk	Inc
3		552	1228	33	15	2	1	shell	C
3		552	1228	178	11.5	2	4	bone	F
3		553	1307	42	28	16	2	chalk	Inc
3	a	1131	3756	47	13	13		limestone	Inc
3	a	24	46					ceramic	?
3	a	14	29					ceramic	?
3	a	139	383					ceramic	?
3	a	14	29					limestone	?
3	a	171	442					chalk	?
3	b	1558	5805	26	12	1	3.5	shell	F

Table 12.23. Summarized data for beads, 1975–92 excavations.

Stratum	Locus	Basket	Square	Area	Material	Description	Length (mm)	Width (mm)	Thick. (mm)	Hole dia. (mm)	Condition
0	1050	7004	M5	D	limestone	flat disc	8	-	3	1.5	C
0	0	3837	K3-L3	J	shell	flat disc	26	26	1.5	2	C
0	1051	7001	N5	D	shell	one hole drilled	8.5	-	1	1	F
0	Stray	Stray	B4	M	chalk	flat, oval	14	8	-	3	C
1	1214	3885	H4	J	chlorite schist	flat disc	5	-	2	1.5	C
1	250	500	L6	D	glass/opaque	green, with long incisions	5	6	-	2	C
1	603	5022	S2	T	limestone	cylindrical	22.5	8	-	3	C
1	926	2737	J4	J	shell	one hole drilled	27	15	1	-	C
1	1229	3931	L0	J	limestone	cylindrical	18	10.5	-	3.5	C
2 a	1059	3387	L1-L2	J	amazonite	flat disc	11.5	-	2	-	F
2 a	761	5424	N2	T	amazonite	probably worked	9	6	5	-	F
2 a	1030	3321	K1	J	bone	cylindrical	25	11	-	5	Inc
2 a	1069	3459	L1-L2	J	bone	cylindrical	2	3	-	0.5	C
2 a	1217	3851	L3	J	bone	cylindrical	10	9.5	-	5.5	C
2 a	1037	3345	H1	J	chalk	perforated ground stone	22	20	12	-	F
2 a	1037	3357	H1	J	limestone	biconical	21	16	-	4	C
2 a	850	2550	J4	J	limestone	biconical	21	17	-	4	C
2 a	957	2726	J2	J	limestone	cylindrical	16	8	-	3	C
2 a	643	5158	S1	T	shell	shell	15	13	1.5	2.5	C
2 a	608	5062	S2	T	turquoise	oval	7	5	3	1	C
2 b	787	5529	Ai0	T	amazonite	biconical	11.5	7	-	2	C
2 b	16	3055	B5	M	bone	2 polished, conjoined frags.	15	-	2	13	C
2 b	637	5145	S2	T	calcite	cylindrical	15	8	-	3.5	C
2 b	150	394	S4-S5	D	ceramic		-	-	-	-	
2 b	150	394	S4-S5	D	ceramic		-	-	-	-	
2 b	938	2763	J3-J4	J	chalk	flattened sphere	24.5	-	16.5	7	C
2 b	1249	3954	L4	J	chalk	nodule w/ hole drill, unfinished	18	14	16	-	C
2 b	634	5179	Ai2-S2	J	chlorite schist	flat disc	25	-	3	5	C
2 b	787	5535	Ai0	T	flint	flattened sphere	9	-	4	1	C
2 b	529	1117	J5	Y	flint	flat disc	6	-	2.5	2	C
2 b	28	3109	C4	M	flint	flat, spherical	5.5	-	4	1	C
2 b	883	2563	J3	J	limestone	bi-convex	12.5	9	-	2	C
2 b	787	5565	Ai0	T	limestone	flat, rough, irregular	8	-	3	1.5	C
2 b	775	5537	Ai0	T	limestone	cylindrical	12.5	7	3	3	C
2 b	28	3113	C4	M	limestone	flat disc	7.5	-	1.5	1	C
2 b	1246	3984	H4	J	limestone	flat disc	5	-	1.5	1	C

2 b	18	3100	B4	M	limestone	cylindrical	13.5	7	-	2.5	C
2 b	835	2346	J4	J	limestone	flat disc	9	-	4	1	C
2 b	775	5509	Ai0	T	limestone	cylindrical	12.5	7	-	3	C
2 b	1053	3504	L1	J	limestone	cylindrical	14	9	-	3	C
2 b	985	2845	H2	J	limestone	flattened sphere	9	7.5	-	3.5	C
2 b	879	2770	K4	J	shell	one hole drilled	14	8.5	-	3	C
2 b	973	2842	K4	J	shell	one hole drilled	12	8	-	3	C
2 b	1057	3375	J1	J	shell	shell	16	8.75	-	4	F
2 b	775	5469	Ai0	J	shell	one hole drilled	19	10	2	-	C
2 b	755	5470	Ai0	T	ostrich egg	flat, oval	8	-	2	2.5	C
2 b/c	1514	5654	N1	T	Tridacoua shell	unfinished, no hole,cylind.	9	8	-	-	C
2 c	1127	3579	J1	J	agate	flat sphere	11	7.25	5	4	C
2 c	1159	3694	H2	J	amazonite	biconical; plano-convex profile	13	8.5	-	-	C
2 c	962	2834	J4	J	amazonite	bi-convex	10	5.5	-	2	C
2 c	574	1324	K6	Y	burned limestone	drilled pebble, oval	21	15	6	4	F
2 c	1508	5611	N1	T	calcite	flat disc	13	6	3	2	C
2 c	555	1246	K6	Y	carnelian	flat disc	10	-	5	2	F
2 c	Stray	5008	J6	Y	chalk	roughly spherical	31	31	-	7	C
2 c	11	31	S5	D	chalk	biconical	22	-	-	2	F
2 c	311	642	M7	D	chlorite schist	biconical	13.5	10	7	2	F
2 c	1322	4230	L0	J	chlorite schist	biconical	7	6	-	2	C
2 c	1056	7021	N5	D	chlorite schist	flat	6	-	3	1.5	C
2 c	1062	7025	M5	D	chlorite schist	flat disc	8.75	-	3	1.5	C
2 c	69	224	N7	D	flint?		-	-	3	-	C
2 c	1322	4231	L0	J	gypsum	cylindrical	12	7	-	3	C
2 c	1052	7002	M5	D	limestone	flattened sphere, 2 frags.	22	15	-	4	F
2 c	1056	7021	N5	D	limestone	flat,roughly round	14	-	5	3.5	F
2 c	270	565	L6	D	limestone	flat, disc	5	-	2.5	1	C
2 c	74	209	S3	D	limestone	cylindrical	13	-	-	-	C
2 c	572	1313	K6	Y	limestone	cylindrical	12.5	8	-	2.5	C
2 c	856	2601	J4	J	shell	one hole drilled	13	8.5	-	2	C
2 c	270	565	L6	D	shell	one hole	11.5	8.5	-	4.5	C
2 c	270	565	L6	D	shell	one hole drilled	9	6	-	1	C
2 c	35	3119	B4-B5	M	shell	one hole drilled	11	11	6.5	1	C
2 c	13	25	Ai5	D	stone		-	-	-	-	C
2 c	23	45	S5-S6	D	stone	biconical	22	-	-	-	C
2 c	13	25	Ai5	D	stone		-	-	-	-	C
3 a	916	2742	J4	J	amazonite	flattened sphere	9	-	4.5	2	C
3 a	1203	3816	K2	J	carnelian	trapezoidal w/ bi-convex x-sect	9	8.75	5	2	C
3 a	916	2800	J4	J	chlorite schist	perforated pebble, unshaped	13	10	3.5	1.5	C
3 a	1150	3735	H3	J	limestone	cylindrical	12.5	8	-	3.5	C

3	a	1147	3681	K2	J	limestone	flattened sphere	25	-	16.5	7	C
3	a	272	547	N7	D	shell	one hole	9	-	4	2	C
3	a	24	3112	C4	M	shell	flat disc	8	-	2	3	C
3	a	27	3095	C4	M	shell	one hole drilled	12.5	7	-	2.5	C
3	a	567	1362	J6	Y	shell,burned	one hole drilled	12	10	7	3	C
3	a	146	390	S3	D	white quartz	irregular, rough	30	23	7	6	C
3	b	34	3140	B5	M	calcite	cylindrical	12	8	-	3	C
3	b	1562	5824	Ai1	T	chlorite schist	biconical	7	6	-	1.5	C
3	b	692	5258	Ai2	T	glass	longitudinal ridges	9	9	3	3	C
4		294	617	N7	D	amazonite	flat oval	4	-	1.5	1	C
4		294	617	N7	D	amazonite	bi-convex, slightly flat	10	6.5	-	2	C
4		294	617	N7	D	amazonite	bi-convex	8	-	6	2	C
4		294	617	N7	D	amazonite	flat disc	4	-	1	1	C
4		294	617	N7	D	amazonite	uneven,rough,oval	4	-	1.75	1	C
4		294	617	N7	D	amazonite	flat disc	4	-	1	1	C
4		294	617	N7	D	amazonite	flat disc	3.5	5	-	1.5	C
4		294	617	N7	D	amazonite	flat disc	3.5	-	1.5	1	C
4		294	617	N7	D	calcite	bi-convex	5	-	3	1.5	C
4		294	617	N7	D	calcite	rough, flattened sphere	9	-	5	3	C
4		294	617	N7	D	jasper	flat disc	4	-	1.5	1	C
4		294	617	N7	D	jasper	flat disc	4	-	1.5	1	C
4		294	617	N7	D	jasper	flat disc	4	-	1.5	1	C
4		294	617	N7	D	jasper	flat disc	4	-	1.5	1	C
4		294	617	N7	D	ostrich egg	flat disc	6	-	2	2	C
4		294	617	N7	D	turquoise	flattened spheroid	8	-	3.5	2	C
4		294	617	N7	D	turquoise?	natural,oval	4.5	-	2.5	1	C
4		294	617	N7	D	turquoise?	flat disc	4	-	1.5	1	C
4		294	617	N7	D	turquoise?copper minerals	flattened sphere	7.5	-	4	2	C

Table 12.24. Summarized data for maceheads, 1975–92 excavations.

Stratum	Locus	Basket	Square	Year	Area	Description	Material	Ht. (mm)	Width (mm)	Hole max. (mm)	dia. min.	Thickness (mm)	Wt. (gm)	Wt (est.) (gm)	Condition
0	0	3210	L3	1991	J		diorite	38	79	23	12	38	310	310	C
0	0	5818	Ai1	1992	T	carinated	limestone	40	48	12		23	50	110	F
0	0	0	0	197?	0		?	32	54	21	12	-	115		C
1	275?	552?	L5	1987	D		hematite	36	45	10.5		-	160	160	C
1	275	552	L5	1987	D	barrel	limestone w/iron oxides	41	50	19	13	41	155	155	C
2	7	3027	C6	1990	D	disc	basalt	26	86	-		26	105	225	F
2 a	1223	3899	L4	1992	J	carinated	granite	33	69	28	13	33	210	210	C
2 a	2	4	Ai6	1975	D	biconical	granite	-	-	-		-	-		
2 a	618	5102	S1	1991	T		chalk	42	37.5	10.5		-	-		
2 a	1030	3454	K1	1991	J	piriform	porcelenite	37	42	11	9	37	40	100	F
2 a	818	2446	K4	1990	J	piriform	hematite	37	41	13		30	50	180	F
2 a	1295	4084	L0	1992	J		limestone	64	13	-		-	100	200	F
2 b	1215	3898	L4	1992	J	carinated	granite	28	66	25	13	28	170	170	C
2 b	763	5560	N2	1992	T	carinated	chalk	44	48	9		21	35	100	F
2 b/c	5	13	Ai6	1975	D		hematite	-	-	-		-	-		
2 c	859	2471	L4	1990	J		dolerite	56	42	12		56	55	125	F
2 c	11	32	Rm A S5	1975	D		granite	-	-	-		-	-		
2 c	129	370	N3	1977	D		hematite	-	-	-		-	-		
2 c	69	224	N7	1976	D		granite	-	-	-		-	-		
2 c	13	24	Ai5	1975	D		granite	-	-	-		-	-		C
2 c	293	600	L6	1987	D		hematite	27	40	10		26	45	180	F
2 c	?92	588	N3	1987	D	disc	granite	-	77	22	9.5	27	220	220	C
2 c	36	67	Rm B S4	1975	D		hematite	-	6.3	-		-	-		
2 c	31	57	Rm A S5-6	1975	D		hematite	-	-	-		-	-		
3 a	5	13	D	1975	D	carinated	granite?	32	74	23	13	32	200	200	C

Table 12.25. Summarized data for spindle whorls.

Strata	Locus	Basket	Square	Area	Context	Material	Description	Length (mm)	Width (mm)	Thick. (mm)	Hole dia (max)	Hole dia (min)	Wt. (gm)	Wt. Projected
0	0	0			none	ceramic	ground vertical edge	43	43	9	6	6	15	15
0	0	4394	H0	J	none	chalk	ovoid	57	48	33	12	-	80	107
0	0	5004	J6	J	none	chalk		36	25	14	8	8	17	34
0	0	0	M6	D	none	limestone	unfinished perfs.	54	45	19	5	-	50	50
0	0	0			none	limestone	ground vertical edge	49	49	14.5	12	8.5	50	
0	0	5779	Ai2	T	none	limestone	flat, polished	42	36	10	8	5	20	20
0	-	-		D	surface	sandstone		-	0.7		4.9		-	
0	-			D	surface	sandstone, red		-		5.5			
1	1025	3236	L1	J	topsoil	ceramic	sherd, rough	14	7	7	5	5	1	3
1	258	522	L6	D	fill	ceramic	sherd	40	30	8	5.5	5.5	15	15
1	800	2031	J3	J	topsoil	ceramic	sherd, rough	27	7	6.5	7	7	1.5	3
1	800	2232	K3	J	topsoil	ceramic	sherd, ground edges	37	6	10	6	6	8	16
1	503	1013	J6	Y	topsoil	ceramic	sherd, rough	46	46	10	4	4	26	26
1	506	1035	K7	Y	topsoil	ceramic	sherd, rough	37	4.5	9	4.5	4.5	11	22
1	802	2172	J4	J	burial	chalk		40	40	18	9	9	11	22
1	800	2017	J4	J	topsoil	limestone	flat	14		13	7	7	7	21
1	802	2165	L4	J	burial	limestone	flat, vertical edges	53	53	11.5	7	7	25	50
1	503	1015	J6	Y	topsoil	limestone	flat	43	43	11	9	9	33	33
1	601	5059	Ai1	J	topsoil	limestone	not round	45	45	6.5	8.5	8.5	10	20
1	1023	3244	J1	T	topsoil	limestone		37	40	10	5.5	5.5	20	20
1	684	5249	M0	D	topsoil	limestone	bi-convex	21	33	7	8	8	5	20
1	286	584	L6	T	fill	limestone		52	50	16.5	7	7	50	50
1	607	5031	N1	J	topsoil	limestone	flat	51	51	18	14		26	52
1	800	2170	L3	J	topsoil	limestone	unfinished, rectang	45	45	11	10	10	18	36
1	1022	3233	H1	J	topsoil	limestone	polished, smooth	38	26	17	-		22	29
1	751	5412	M0	T	topsoil	limestone	flat, vertical edges	43	8.5	10	8.5	8.5	30	30
1	501	1005	J5	Y	fill	limestone	flat	50	53	13	9	9	38	38
1	507	1042	K5	Y	fill	limestone		53	53	14	6	6	29	58
1	509	1054	K6	Y	fill	limestone	flat, vertical edges	50		20	-		21	63
1	800	2108	J4	J	topsoil	limestone	flat, vertical edges	46.5	46.5	11.5	6	6	18	36
1	509	1054		Y	fill	limestone	unfinish.perfs.	50	50	20	6	6	20.5	41
2	7	3039	C6	M	fill	ceramic	sherd, ground edges	35	6	5.5	6	6	4	8
2	21	3076	C4	M	fill	ceramic	sherd, ground edges	48	48	9	8	5.5	12	24
2	527	1148	K5	Y	fill	ceramic	sherd, rough	34	5	8	5	5	6	12
2	24	3090	C4	M	pit	ceramic	sherd, ground edges	48.5	7	8	7	7	10	20
2	556	1396	J7	Y	pit	ceramic	sherd, ground edges	40	5	7.5	5	5	6	12
2	30	3104	B5	M	ash	ceramic	sherd, ground edges	30	20	7	-	-	3	6
2	617	5075	M1	T	fill	ceramic	sherd, ground edges	48	9	9	5.5	5.5	12	12
2	519	1094	K7	Y	pit	chalk	plano-conv.	39	39	15	9	9	18	18

2		24	3082	C6	M	pit	chalk	bi-convex	36		15	12	5	8	24
2		21	3076	C4	M	fill	chalk	irreg. flat, sq. edges	35		17	12	5	14	19
2		527	1110	K5	Y	fill	chalk	irreg.	40	35	27	5	5	31	31
2		283	577	L5	D	fill	gabbro	flat, fine ground	58	9.5	11.5	12	7	63	63
2		278	278	L5	D	fill	limestone	flat	50	49	9	9	9	36	36
2		266	535	?	D	fill	limestone	flat	42	42	7.5	9	6	15	15
2		24	3090	C4	M	pit	limestone	unfinished perfs.	40	32	22	6		13	17
2		21	3076	C4	M	fill	limestone		61	61	17		5	60	80
2	a	1041	3305	L2	J	pit	ceramic	sherd	24		8.5	5	6.5	3	9
2	a	1029	3309	L2	J	pit	ceramic	rim sherd, angular	34	26	5	6.5	5	3	12
2	a	1050	3339	L1	J	pit	ceramic	sherd, ground edges	37		8	5	5	3	12
2	a	701	5292	S0	T	none	ceramic	sherd, ground edges	29		7	5	4	7	7
2	a	1029	3309	L2	J	pit	ceramic	sherd, ground edge	20	21	21	4		3	9
2	a	1039	3282	H1	J	ash	ceramic	sherd, ground edges	35		6.5		5	4	8
2	a	1074	3438	J1	J	hearth	ceramic	sherd, ground edges	38	32	7	5	6	10	10
2	a	1050	3339	L1	J	pit	ceramic	sherd, ground edges	20	5.5	7	6	5.5	5	20
2	a	1041	3305	L2	J	pit	ceramic	sherd, rough	46	42	8	5.5	5	11	22
2	a	696	5301	MO	T	feature/collapse	ceramic	sherd, ground edges	28		5	5	4	1	2
2	a	815	2352	J3	J	fill	ceramic	sherd, ground edges	37	5	6	4	5	4	8
2	a	618	5083	S1	T	pit	ceramic	sherd, rough	41	27	10	5	5	11	22
2	a	639	5146	S1	T	pit	ceramic	sherd, ground edges	35		7	5	6.5	2	4
2	a	1041	3305	L2	J	pit	ceramic	sherd, ground edges	31.5	17	5	6.5		9	9
2	a	1051	3365	L2	J	pit	ceramic	sherd, unperf, rough	53	54	6.5	7	7	20	20
2	a	806	2821	J2-3,H2-3	J	pit	ceramic	sherd, rough	30	6	6.5	6	6	2	4
2	a	958	2746	J2-H2-H3	J	pit	ceramic	sherd, rough	40	6	8	6	6	7	14
2	a	1029	3272	L2	J	pit	ceramic	sherd, ground edges	40		8	6	3	15	15
2	a	1050	3344	L1	J	structure	chalk	ovoid	54	54	24	13	4	45	90
2	a	1116	3549	L1	J	pit	chalk	unfinished perfs.	55	45	23	10	10	50	50
2	a	1374	4366	H5	J	wall	chalk	square	51	45	19	15		58	58
2	a	1160	3706	L1	J	ash	chalk		40	21	14	15		9	36
2	a	872	2766	L4	J	pit	ferrug. limest.	flat, vertical edges	48	45	22	18	7	48	48
2	a	803	2219	J4	J	surface	limest. w/ oxides		48	48	6	7	7	23	23
2	a	159	424	M3	D	pit	limestone								
2	a	700	5322	MO	T	pit	limestone	flat, well-ground	45	45	24	8	6.5	56	56
2	a	1064	3473	L4	J	pit	limestone	oval, well-ground	46	46	12	10	10	40	40
2	a	858	2469	J3	J	fill	limestone		61	48	18	11	6	61	61
2	a	1034	3275	L2	J	pit	limestone		40	19	18	15		12	24
2	a	697	5294	S0	T	pit	limestone	ground pebble, bi-convex	53		23	9	9	60	120
2	a	1223	3930	L4	J	fill	limestone	flat	45	45	14	9	7	36	36
2	a	812	2362	K3	J	pit	limestone	unfinish. perfs.	40	34	20	17		27	27
2	a	700	5288	MO	T	pit	limestone	flat, well-ground	53	53	19	14	5	71	71

2	a	639	5143	S1	T	pit	limestone	ground vertical edge	35	35	6.5	6	6	4	8
2	a	1266	4025	L0	J	surface	limestone	ground vertical edge	37	18	10	–	–	6	12
2	a	1223	3894	L4	J	fill	limestone		53	50	18	10	10	52	52
2	a	1037	3484	H1	J	ash	limestone	flat, ground	51.5	51	11	5	5	20	40
2	a	639	5143	S1	T	pit	limestone	sq. edges	39	18	16	–	–	10	30
2	a	616	5171	N1	T	fill	masonite (feldspar)	flat, vertical edges	37	37	6	6.5	6.5	16	16
2	b	1059	3408	L1-L2	J	pit	sandstone	ground vertical edge	22	–	9	–	–	6	24
2	b	1052	3386	K1	J	surface	ceramic	sherd, rough	55	–	7	5.5	5.5	12	24
2	b	1346	4298	H4	J	pit	ceramic	sherd, rough	28	27	6.5	5	5	6	6
2	b	1124	3564	H1	J	pit	ceramic	sherd, ground edges	42	–	8	9	9	8	16
2	b	1102	3520	H1	J	surface	ceramic	sherd, ground edges	40	–	8	6	6	5	10
2	b	675	5214	Ai2	T	pit	ceramic	sherd, ground edges	22.5	13	4	–	–	0.5	2
2	b	681	5226	S1	T	hearth	ceramic	sherd, ground edges	38	18	6	–	–	3	6
2	b	693	5337	M0	T	fill	ceramic	sherd, ground edges	40	36	6.5	6.5	6.5	10	10
2	b	882	2688	K4	J	silo	ceramic	sherd, ground edges	39	6	6.5	6	6	10	10
2	b	1057	3379	J1	J	pit	chalk	square, rough	45	45	15	9	9	21	21
2	b	900	2742	J3-J4	J	burial	chalk		44	35	20	–	–	33	132
2	b	880	2544	J3	J	structure	chalk		38	38	11	7.5	7.5	12	12
2	b	1028	3304	J1	J	ash	chalk	ground vertical edge	15	–	7.5	–	–	1.5	4.5
2	b	1052	3343	K1	J	surface	chalk	unfinished	25	27	12	5	5	1	1.33
2	b	1250	3978	H4	J	pit	chalk	unfinish.perfs.	44	35	23	10	10	30	30
2	b	626	5106	Ai1	T	pit	chlorite schist	bi-convex, smooth	56	51	11.5	11	11	52	52
2	b	1236	3938	K0	J	fill	flint	polished	53	53	9	6	6	52	52
2	b	1044	3316	J1	M	pit	limestone	flat, well-ground	43	39	9.5	8	8	25	25
2	b	16	3059	B5	D	pit	limestone	small	25	25	6	4.5	4.5	4	5
2	b	1052	7002	M5	M	surface	limestone		20	10	14	6	6	4	8
2	b	9	3030	C5	D	pit	limestone	flat	49	49	19	15	15	32	64
2	b	1121	3673	L1	J	surface	limestone	finely ground	55	55	10	9	9	40	40
2	b	150	394	Rm A/B	D	floor	unknown		–	–	–	–	–	–	–
2	b/c	5	12	Ai6	D	floor	limestone		–	–	–	–	–	–	–
2	c	1049	3342	J2	J	fill	ceramic	sherd, ground edge	40.5	40	10	3.5	3.5	20	20
2	c	1052	7006	N5	D	removal	ceramic	sherd	39	36	7	5	5	12	12
2	c	1056	7021	N5	D	pit	ceramic	ground vertical edge	50	6	11	6	6	36	36
2	c	1259	4066	K0	J	fill	ceramic	sherd, ground edges	37	31.5	7	4	4	8	8
2	c	853	2479	L3	J	pit	ceramic	sherd, ground edges	40	6	6	6	6	4	8
2	c	128	518	N6	D	pit	ceramic		35	16	6	7	7	10	10
2	c	257	515	N5	D	floor	ceramic		39	19	7	6	6	11	22
2	c	558	1403	K7-J7	Y	mb struc.	ceramic	NOT sherd, ground	63	63	16	7	7	71	71
2	c	1144	3654	H2	J	fill	ceramic	sherd, ground	44	21	6	6	7	6	12
2	c	1128	3592	J1	J	pit	chalk	bi-convex	60	60	18	9	9	37	49
2	c	1221	3857	L4	J	removal	chalk	bi-convex	50	50	21	17	9	11	33

2	c	1309	4118	L0	J	pit	chalk		30	19	16	-		5	15
2	c	1310	4128	L0	T	pit	chalk	bi-convex	39	18	25	7	7	18	36
2	c	1259	4069	K0	J	fill	chalk		20	-	6.2	-		-	-
2	c	786	5583	S0-S1	T	fill	chalk	plano-conv.	45	43	19	11	8	30	30
2	c	69	213	Rm A/B N7	D	surface	chalk w/ oxides		-	-	-	-		-	-
2	c	1064	3473	L4 or J2	J	surface	chlorite schist	flat, well-ground	54	52	11	7	7	41	41
2	c	1505	5618	N1-M1	T	pit	chlorite schist	flat, vertical edges	45	45	10	7	7	35	35
2	c	13	24	Ai5	D	floor	limestone		-	-	-	-		-	-
2	c	36	67	Rm B S4	D	floor	limestone		-	-	-	-		-	-
2	c	11	31	Rm A S5	D	floor	limestone		-	-	-	-		-	-
2	c	137	371	M4	D	floor	limestone		-	-	-	-		-	-
2	c	35	66	N5	D	floor	limestone		-	-	-	4.1		-	-
2	c	40	3145	B4	M	rubbish dump	limestone	flat	55	50	13	12	6	49	49
2	c	649	5175	2C	T	pit	limestone	flat, vertical edges	60	60	18	22	11	86	86
2	c	64	206	Rm C N4	D	pit	limestone		-	-	-	-		-	-
2	c	83	179	S3	D	floor	limestone		-	-	-	-		-	-
2	c	1105	3528	S2	J	pit	limestone		58	29.5	9	-		-	-
2	c	13	25	Ai5	D	floor	limestone		-	-	-	-		-	-
2	c	1111	3553	K1	J	fill	limestone	flat, smooth	45	45	10	8	8	31	31
2	c	1505	5617	N1-M1	T	pit	limestone	flat	56	56	14	11	11	47	47
2	c	946	2701	J4	J	surface (wall)	limestone	flat, polished	46	46	12	7.5	7.5	38	38
2	c	649	5324	Ai1	T	pit	limestone	flat, well-ground	50	50	7	6.5	6.5	21	21
2	c	649	5181	Ai1	T	pit	limestone		33	34	7	5.5	5.5	10	10
2	c	528	1182	K6	Y	pit	limestone	flat, vertical edges	46.5	46.5	11	7	7	36	36
2	c	1052	7006	N5	D	removal	limestone		36	14	8	14	10	5	15
2	c	29	56	Rm B 2C	D	fill	sandstone		-	1.1	-	5.3		-	-
2	c	35	72	N5	D	floor	sandstone		-	1.1	-	4.5		-	-
2	c	29	56	Rm B S4	D	fill	sandstone		-	-	-	4.4		-	-
2	c	19	33	N5	D	floor	sandstone		-	0.9	-	5		-	-
2	c	19	40	N5	D	floor	sandstone		-	1.1	-	6		-	-
2	c	23	45	Rm A S5-S6	D	floor	sandstone		-	1.4	-	1.4		-	-
2	c	19	40	N5	D	floor	sandstone		-	-	-	4.9		-	-
3		25	3089	B6	M	pit	ceramic	sherd, ground edges	38	21	6	21		3	6
3		548	1198	J6	Y	pit	limestone	ground vertical edge	48	21	11	21		17	34
3	a	1147	3736	K2	J	fill	ceramic	sherd, ground edges	51	-	9	-		12	24
3	a	1147	3679	K2	J	fill	ceramic	sherd, rough	37	5	5	5	5	5	10
3	a	301	622	N5	D	cleaning	chalk		32	14	14	6.5		13	13
3	a	1054	3570	H3	J	fill	limestone		45	10	8	10	10	30	30
3	a	144	388	N3	D	fill	limestone		-	-	-	-		-	-
3	a	14	29	Ai6	D	floor	unknown		-	-	-	-		-	-
3	b	112	351	M6-N6	D	surface	limestone		-	-	-	-		-	-
4		1294	4075	H2	J	fill	limestone		60	29	31	23		43	57

Table 12.26. Summarized data for small perforated stone artifacts.

Stratum	Locus	Basket	Material	Square	Area	Length (mm)	Width (mm)	Thick. (mm)	Hole dia. max/min (mm)	Wt. (gms)	Condition	Description
none	0	0	chalk			39	28	17	21/9	15	C	very rough, flat bottom
none	0	0	chalk			50	36	30	15/5	93	C	unfinished bifacial drilling
1	754	5410	chalk	S0-S1	T	35	27	14	8/5		F	minimum of 3 drilled holes
1	258?	528?	chalk	L6	D	68	70	32		190	C	shallow bifacial drill marks, modified nodule
2a	618	5102	chalk	S1	T	42	38		13/8	79	C	unfinished bifacial drilling, ground nodule
2a	695	5309	chalk	N0-S0	T	52		36	11.5/?	45	F	est. original wt. 90 grams
2a	611	5061	limestone	Ai1	T	34	21	25		15	F	macehead?, est. wt. 65
2a	851	2433	chalk	L6	J	22	21	18			F	unifacial drill mark, cube
2a	1029	3263	chalk	L2	J	30.5	18	11	11/?	10	F	unfinished bifacial drilling, ground nodule
2a	1033	3259	chalk	K1	J	32	32	23	12/5	25	C	bifacially drilled, irregular, roughly shaped
2a	820	2285	limestone	L3	J	43	43	27	15/9	50	C	bifacially drilled, irregular, dorsally rough
2a	992	2884	limestone	K2	J	36	36	27	13.5/7.5	40	C	bifacially drilled, hole askew
2a	1029	3256	basalt	L2	J	47	47	27	25/10	90	C	joins w/ L.508, B.1039, str. 1. pump drill?
2a	1037	3345	chalk	H1	J	22	20	12		5	F	bifacially drilled, squared,
2b	938	2763	chalk	J3-J4	J	25	24	16.5	?/7		I	bifacially drilled, flat sphere, spindle whorl?
2b	689	5340	chalk	M0	T	42	39	16			F	bifacial drill marks, flat
2c	1221	3857	chalk	L4	J	36		30		10	F	bifacially drilled, est. original wt. 20 gms
2c	1050	7004	chalk	M5	D	28	30	14	8	10	C	irregular, rough; bead? spindle whorl?
2c	119	329	limestone	M5	D	43	41	21	14/?	46	C	bifacially drilled, not ground, irregular
2c	60	222	chalk	N4	D	57	42	18			F	3 complete drill marks
2c	1259	4069	chalk	K0	J	20	9	3.5			F	small fragment
2c	1549	5780	limestone	N0	T	36	32		14/7	25	F	spherical, est. original wt. 45 grams
2c	1351	4358	limestone	H0	J	25	18.5		14/8		F	bifacial hole
3a	1147	3681	limestone	K2	J	25	25	16.5	7/4		C	bifacially drilled, flat sphere, spindle whorl?
3a	1563	5840	chalk	S1	T	33	21		14/8		F	bifacial hole
3a	1565	5860	chalk	S2	T	42	42	34	15/?	55	C	unfinished bifacially drilling, spherical
4	1294	4075	limestone	H2	J	60	29	31	?/23		F	very rough, irregular

Table 12.27. Summarized data for palettes, 1975–92 excavations.

Strata	Locus	Basket	Year	Square	Area	Material	Context	Length	Width	Thick.	Description
			568-6	Ai9	D	limestone	surface	97	35	12	F
	0	0	568-48	none	D	chlorite schist	surface	97.5	84.5	12.5	C
			71-5203		D	chlorite schist	surface	105	63	6	C
			568-5	Ai8	D	chlorite schist	surface	102	39	10	F
			568-5		D	mica schist	surface	58	40	12	F

1		0	0	568-114	none		surface	granite				
1		512	1068	1990	J5	D	fill	granite	108	93	16	C
1/2a		4	?	568-16	S5	Y	fill	sandstone	100	73.5	23	C
1/2a		4	?	71-5199	S5	D	fill	chlorite schist	123	93	11.5	C
2	a	1223	3900	1992	L4	D	fill	granite	129	85.5	21.5	C
2	a	1266	4000	1992	L0	J	surface	quartzite	98	64	21	C
2	a	1034	3269	1992	L2	J	surface	mica schist	78	66	17	F
2	a	1223	3933	1992	L4	J	fill/surface	limestone	81	114	16	F
2	a	817	2382	1990	L4	J	fill	granite	54	58	18	F
2	a	1224	3901	1992	K0	J	pit	limestone	95	63	24	C
2	b	92	?	36-87-597	N3	D	pit	chlorite schist	88	78	13	F
2	b	633	5153	1991	M2	T	fill	granite	114	92	19	C
2	b	134	?	727-328-50	M3	D	rubble feature	limestone	94	102	23	F
2	c	882	2548	1990	K4	J	silo	scoria	94	42	18	F
2	c	528	1162	1990	K6	Y	pit	limestone	91	107	25	F
2	c	8	?	568-41-8	S5	D	platform	granite	85	53	17.5	C
2	c	6	?	568-197-51	Ai5	D	floor	limestone	39	54	11.5	F
2	c	257	?	36-87-519	M5	D	floor	granite	61	42	5	F
2	c	5	?	71-5200	Ai6	D	floor	granite	157	109	25	C
2	c	7	?	568-25-51	Ai5	D	floor	chlorite schist	124	82.5	21	C
2	c	19	?	568-7	N5	D	floor	tuff[a]	120	91	11	C
2	c	1062	7029	1992	M5	D	fill	scoria	93	71	20	C
2	c	1511	5712	1992	S2-S3	T	pit	kurkar	99	65	27	C
3		545	1241	1990	K7	Y	pit	scoria	96	60	25	C
3		19	3064	1990	C6	M	pit	scoria	133	71	30	C
3		19	3065	1990	C6	M	pit	scoria	186	103	18.5	C
3		19	3066	1990	C6	M	pit	scoria	160	72	59	C
3	a	24	?	727-170-104	S5	D	pit	granite	153	87	20	C
3	a	122	?	727-348-122	N7	D	fill	chlorite schist	98.5	68	19	F
3	a	917	2660	1990	J3	J	surface	limestone	141	83	36	F
3	a	1337	4243	1992	K0	J	pit	scoria	86	63	20	C
3	a	126	?	727-443-50	N6	D	floor	limestone	29	40	5	F
3	a	261	?	36-87-264	M7	D	pit	ferrug. limestone	74	70	14.5	C
3	a	261	?	36-87-637	M7	D	pit	scoria	92	83	12	C
3	b	586	1381	1990	J5	Y	probe	limestone (crystal.)	94	64	11	C
3	b	168	?	727-435-189	S6	D	pit	granite	35	42	7.5	F

Table 12.28. Stone vessel fragments and estimated minimum number of individuals (MNI).

Fragment type	Basalt	Limestone	Chalk	Granite	No.	Total	MNV
Fenestrated stands							
Base/leg	19	1	0	0	20		1
Base/medial	0	0	1	0	1		1
Leg	8	0	0	0	8		0
Medial/rim	6	0	0	0	6		3
Medial	40	0	0	0	40		36
Ring base	35	0	0	0	35		0
Rim/base	1	0	0	0	1		0
sub-totals	109	1	1	0	111		41
Complete	2	0	0	0	2		2
Totals	111	1	1	0	113	(113)	43

Fragment type	Basalt	Limestone	Chalk	Granite	No.	Total	MNV
Plain Bowls							
Incomplete	1	0	0	0	1		1
Bases	11	0	0	0	11		10
Complete	0	0	0	1	1		1
Totals	12	0	0	1	13	(13)	12

Fragment type	Basalt	Limestone	Chalk	Granite	No.	Total	MNV
Pedastaled Vessels							
Incomplete	1	0	0	0	1		1
Bases	4	0	1	0	5		5
Base/rim	1	0	0	0	1		1
Totals	6	0	1	0	7	(7)	7

Fragment type	Basalt	Limestone	Chalk	Granite	No.	Total	MNV
Unidentifiable to Type							
Rims	115	3	0	0	118		0
Walls	52	0	0	0	52		0
Totals	167	3	0	0	170	(170)	0

Total stone vessels fragments 303

Total estimated number of vessels (all types) 62

Table 12.29. Summarized data for fenestrated, pedestaled vessel fragments (C = complete, F = Fragments).

Basket	Context	Material	Condition	Element	Length (mm)	Width (mm)	Thick. (mm)	Rim dia.	Base dia.	Med dia.	Wall thick.	Base thick.	Leg thick.	Band width	Decor	Modification
none	unknown	basalt	C		76	46	10	136	89					7	single band	
none	unknown	basalt	F	base/leg	69	54	22		100			22	16		none	
none	unknown	basalt	F	base/leg	52	70			100			20	16		none	
none	unknown	basalt	F	base/leg	75	77			120			16	29		none	
none	unknown	basalt	F	base/leg	82		21		120						none	base, part of leg
none	unknown	basalt	F	base/leg	60	73			140			20			none	
none	unknown	basalt	F	base/leg	61	64			80			14	18		none	
none	unknown	limest.	F	base/leg	80		26								none	
none	unknown	basalt	F	base/leg	87	72			140			20	25		none	
none	unknown	basalt	F	leg	52	52	16						16		none	
none	unknown	basalt	F	leg	68	55			100			18			none	incised
none	unknown	basalt	F	leg	57	45	20		100						none	mod. vesicular
none	unknown	basalt	F	leg	67	56	23		150						cross-hatching, covers ext. face	dense basalt
none	unknown	basalt	F	medial	50					77	13			10	single band crude	battered, poorly manufactured
none	unknown	basalt	F	medial	91	80	24								none	no foot, base re-ground?
none	unknown	basalt	F	medial	85	60	45					26		6	single band	band is wavy
none	unknown	basalt	F	medial	63	87	15			70	12			10	single band, pronounced	
none	unknown	basalt	F	medial	55	71								8	single band	legs re-ground
none	unknown	basalt	F	medial	113	94	20					10			3 distinct bands	massive, mod. vesicular
none	unknown	basalt	F	medial	52	40	15			80	15			6	single band	prob. re-ground leg, hole drilled thru bottom
none	unknown	basalt	F	medial	122	85	15	140						6	single band	broken leg re-ground; hole in base
none	unknown	basalt	F	medial	77	45	12								single band	broken legs re-ground smooth.
none	unknown	basalt	F	medial	42	55	10							8	single band	mod. vesicular, broken foot re-ground
none	unknown	basalt	F	medial	80	80				80		20			single band	base re-ground? broken rim re-ground

No.	Context	Material	Cond.	Part	d1	d2	d3	d4	Dia	x	y	z	band (mm)	Decoration	Comments
104	unknown	basalt	F	medial	99	92	16			61	10			single band	
none	unknown	basalt	F	medial	48	80				80	13	27		single band	
none	unknown	basalt	F	medial	52	89	55						8	single band, wavy and vague	
none	unknown	basalt	I	medial	102	70								none	
none	unknown	chalk	F	medial				100						single band	legs re-ground; base thin, worn
none	unknown	basalt	F	medial	60	72	30			90	15	6	6		base ground, prob. was fen. stand
none	unknown	basalt	F	medial	98	95								single band, vague	none
none	unknown	basalt	F	medial	48							28	8	single band, very pronounced	mod. vesicular
none	unknown	basalt	F	medial	55	70							8	single band	
surface		basalt	F	medial	45	78							8	single band	mod. vesicular
none	unknown	basalt	F	medial	59	90								3 bands, distinct	
none	unknown	basalt	F	medial	70	48							16	3 bands, 12, 15, 18mm	mod. vesicular
none	unknown	basalt	F	medial	60	87							5	4 bands, well made	
none	unknown	basalt	F	medial/leg	117	95	24				19		6	two bands	mod. vesicular
none	unknown	basalt	F	medial/rim	106	69	12				21			single band, pronounced	rim - medial section
none	unknown	basalt	F	base ring	55	44	16		110	15	16			none	trapez x-sect
none	unknown	basalt	F	base ring	85	44	20		120					none	
none	unknown	basalt	F	base ring	62	41			140					none	
none	unknown	basalt	F	base ring	86	74	26		100					single band	
none	unknown	basalt	F	base ring	72	30	21		120					none	
none	unknown	basalt	F	base ring	52	56	22		160					none	
none	unknown	basalt	F	base ring	68	64	21		200					none	
none	unknown	basalt	F	base ring	84	52	15		120					none	
none	none	basalt	F	base ring	75	29	16		140					none	
2647	topsoil	basalt	F	base/leg	47	59	16		100					none	
2018	topsoil	basalt	F	base/leg	65	47	14		140		14			none	
3234	topsoil	basalt	F	base/leg	45	30	22		140					none	leg frag
2053	topsoil	basalt	F	leg	35	47	30							single band	two holes drilled in base
5041	topsoil	basalt	F	medial	54	78								single band	medial frag.
3956	topsoil	basalt	F	medial	72	51	18							single band	
3401	topsoil	basalt	F	base ring	57	34	17		140					none	base ring
3230	topsoil	basalt	F	base ring	56	33	15		120					none	base ring
3238	topsoil	basalt	F	base ring	59	33	20							none	base ring
2161	topsoil	basalt	F	base ring	40	35	15.5		120					none	base ring frag
5234	topsoil	basalt	F	base ring	57	32	15		140					none	base ring

No.	Context	Material	Type	Part								Decoration	Notes
553	fill	basalt	F	base ring	54	36	16	130			12	none	hole drilled in leg
181	floor	basalt	F	base ring	61	60	12	120			18	none	none
185	floor	basalt	F	base ring	65	67		100			24	none	none
28	fill	basalt	F	rim/med	40	101	15				15	single band	
2301	fill	basalt	F	base/leg	46	40	16	100			8	none	base to leg frag
5306	pit / mb	basalt	F	medial	68	99						single band	
2350	collapse	basalt	F	base ring	40	26	14.5	85				none	ring base frag
1185	structure	basalt	F	base ring	56	29	15	120				none	ring base frag
4301	pit	basalt	C					117	135			single band	hole in bottom, slightly flared rims
4120	pit	basalt	F	base/leg	75	45	17	130				none	base to leg frag
3812	surface	basalt	F	leg	35	48	14					none	
5339	fill	basalt	F	med/rim	158	30	14		160		14	single band	medial frag to rim
404	unknown	basalt	F	medial	50	48	14				8	single band	
3960	fill	basalt	F	medial	51	50	18					single band	
5532	fill	basalt	F	medial	91	132	18					single band	
5305	pit	basalt	F	medial	62	100						single band	rim re-ground, no vessel depth left
3410	removal?	basalt	F	base ring	50	36	12	160				none	battered and thick, 4-legged
3150	surface	basalt	F	base ring	111		15	80			15	single band	ring base
1202	pit	basalt	F	base ring	27	23	10.5	100				none	re-worked on base
3370	fill	basalt	F	base ring	47	28	13	110				none	ring base frag
3375	pit	basalt	F	base ring	40	33	15	110				none	ring base frag
5340	fill	basalt	F	base ring	56	31	18	130				none	ring base frag
88	fill	basalt	F	base ring				130				none	ring base
2838	pit?	basalt	I	rim/med			15	200		102	15	single band	legs/ring gone, hole in base
2533	pit	basalt	I	rim/med			7	75		46	7	single band	small cup, re-ground f.stand?
4218	fill	basalt	F	rims/base	89	29	16	140	150		16	none	3 frags, all from same vessel
5791	fill	basalt	F	base/leg	59	40	15	120				none	base to leg frag
5502	fill	basalt	F	medial	96	75	16					single band	
5720	pit	basalt	F	medial	61	71	9					single band	legs and rim gone
3996	wall	basalt	F	medial	74		14					single band	wavy medial band
4112	pit	basalt	F	medial	114	102	8					single band	medial to rim frag
596	pit	basalt	F	base ring	85	95		120				3 bands	sampled by N. Porat
276	pit	basalt	F	base ring	74	46				19	18	none	
5635	fill	basalt	F	base ring	45	32	18	90				none	base ring

ID	Context	Material	F	Part								Decoration	Description
1306	pit	basalt	F	base/leg	109	70	35	140				none	base ring with leg frag, massive
3078	pit	basalt	F	base ring	43	36	20	180				none	ring base frag
1243	fill	basalt	F	base ring	31	22	10	80				none	base to leg frag
5832	pit	basalt	F	base/leg	60	63	15	120				none	base to leg frag
5381	fill	basalt	F	base/leg	73	35	22	100				none	base to leg frag
5727	pit	basalt	F	base/leg	55	50	12	90				none	base to leg frag
5731	pit	basalt	F	base/leg	97	58	31	160				none	base to leg frag
544	floor	basalt	F	medial	77	95	20					single band	dense basalt, prob. re-ground fenest.stand
348	fill	basalt	F	base ring	25	30	15	120			15	none	ring base frag
1356	surface	basalt	F	base ring	42			100				none	7 frags; 5 rims; all pieces prob. from 1 vessel
5857	pit	basalt	F	rims/media				130				single band	
519	baulk	basalt	F	leg	63	55					18	none	
4060	fill	basalt	F	leg	76	49	24					none	leg frag
515	floor/wall	basalt	F	medial	53				100	14	10	none	hole in base, intentional, legs poss. re-ground
513	surface	basalt	F	medial	68	70			70	12	8	single band	
423	floor	basalt	F	base ring				100			13	none	re-ground

Table 12.30. Summarized data for bowl base fragments.

Stratum	Locus	Basket	Material	Condition	Element	Length (mm)	Width (mm)	Thick. (mm)	Height (mm)	Rim dia.	Base dia	Wall thick.	Base thick.	Context type	Wt. (gms)	Modification
none	none	none	basalt	F	base	53					100		18	unknown	430	flat base
none	none	none	basalt	F	base	51					100	18	19	unknown	275	flat base
																rounded
none	none	none	basalt	F	base	51					60	12	20	unknown	110	base
none	none	none	basalt	F	base	85					121	23	40	g.surface	1345	flat base
none	none	none	basalt	F	base	60					80	20	24	unknown	275	flat base
2	91	297	basalt	F	base	43					60	9		pit	70	hole in base
2a	700	5311	granite	C		165	129	26						pit		round base
2b	016	3051	basalt	F	base	52	90	27			120			pit	235	bowl base
2b	860	2580	basalt	F	base	65	117				117			l.surface		flat base
2c	1554	5817	basalt	F	base	62	109				90	18	20	fill		flat base?
2c	270	567	basalt	I	rim/base	154		14	124	154	75			pit	1130	hole in base
3a	272	546	basalt	F				18	92	120	85			floor	540	bowl/mortar
4	1354	4280	basalt	F	base	105		16			82	16		pit	1020	deep bowl

Table 12.31. Summarized data for pedestalled vessel fragments.

Stratum	Locus	Basket	Context	Material	Condition	Element	Length (mm)	Width (mm)	Height (mm)	Base dia. (mm)	Med dia.	Wall thick.	Base thick.	Wt. (gms)	Modification
none	none	none	unknown	basalt	Inc		97	81	95	85				1030	pedestaled bowl/mortar, concave base (ext.)
none	none	none	unknown	basalt	F	base	91	63		100			21	380	concave base = 21mm
none	none	none	unknown	basalt	F	base/rim			112	80		15	65	485	concave ext. base, shallow and small
none	none	none	unknown	basalt	F	base	72			70		20	54	820	thick, footed base
2c	69	213	fill	basalt	Inc	base/med.	81			120			27	455	re-ground, prob. was hollow footed stand
4	294	609	fill	chalk	Inc	base/med.		98	119	99	83		99		thick, high base
4	155	413	pit	basalt	F	base	51			70		14	35	360	concave ext. base = 8mm

Table 12.32. Summarized data for stone vessel rim fragments.

Stratum	Locus	Basket	Context	Material	Length (mm)	Width (mm)	Wall thick.	Rim dia.ca.	Weight (gms)	Modification
?		604		basalt	28	56	19	115	83	straight
	none	none	unknown	basalt	72	66	13	160	88	flared
	none	none	unknown	basalt	75	73	25		170	thick, open, shallow mortar?
	none	none	unknown	basalt	120	55	16		195	flared
	none	none	g.surface	basalt	66	73	15	110	85	ground, facetted, flared
	none	none	unknown	basalt	75	73	20	160	245	open, thick, shallow mortar/bowl
	none	none	unknown	basalt	57	106	13	140	160	flared
	none	none	unknown	basalt	46	45	12	120	45	flared
	none	none	unknown	limest.	21	82	11		103	thin, closed, polished
	none	none	unknown	basalt	85	95	10	220	205	flared
	none	none	unknown	basalt	82	68	15	160	120	flared, 2 drilled holes
	none	none	unknown	basalt	27	99	20		310	open, thick, mortar/bowl
	none	none	unknown	basalt	71	67	19	150	135	flared
	none	none	unknown	basalt	43	49	16	280	37	flared, chevron
	none	none	surface	basalt	76	50	15	160	66	flared, rim ground?
	none	none	unknown	basalt	79	72	20	135	160	open, thick
	none	none	unknown	basalt	78	62	13	140	120	flared
	none	none	unknown	basalt	42	115	16	150	243	flared
	none	none	unknown	basalt	51	49	13	150	58	flared?
	none	none	unknown	basalt	42	34	15		35	flared
	none	none	unknown	basalt	85	107	23	140	335	straight, deep bowl
	none	none	unknown	basalt	46	77	22	80	114	straight wall, prob. mortar
	none	none	unknown	basalt	70	82	15	160	145	flared
	none	none	unknown	basalt	68	61	11	130	70	thin, flared
	none	none	unknown	basalt	58	65	12	180	78	open, straight
	none	none	unknown	basalt	68	82	13	140	130	flared
	none	none	unknown	basalt	106	110	15	160	260	flared, prob. fenest.stand
	none	none	unknown	basalt	88	65	16	180	112	flared
1	1	1	topsoil	basalt	48	46	10	100	45	thin, flared
1	4	10	topsoil	basalt	150		15	180	1390	3 rims; 1 body
1	76	259	pit	basalt	31	56	12		60	flared
1	1022	3214	topsoil	basalt	43	50	12	180	52	flared
1	1023	3215	topsoil	basalt	17	54	14		33	flared
1	1023	3288	topsoil	basalt	32	44	17		32	flared?
1	1025	3235	topsoil	basalt	52	53	20	70	71	straight, open form
1	1025	3232	topsoil	basalt	47	100	14	200	135	flared

1		1062	3383	topsoil	basalt	45	67	12	140	64	flared
1		1213	3826	topsoil	basalt	52	50	12	120	51	flared
1		1214	3919	topsoil	basalt	42	22	9		14	flared?
1		501	1001	topsoil	basalt	69	14	15		62	slightly flared
1		505	1027	topsoil	basalt	63	35	21	110	87	straight, squared rim edge
1		508	1053	fill	basalt	79	57	17		145	open, sinuous wall
1		600	5053	topsoil	basalt	38	63	17	120	75	open form
1		605	5034	topsoil	basalt	29	40	12		27	flared
1		677	5236	topsoil	basalt	30	62	8		40	too small
1		751	5405	topsoil	basalt	85	60	13	160	120	flared
1		800	2149	topsoil	basalt	92	81	24	160	220	flared
2		69	213	fill	basalt	43	38	11	140	30	flared?
2		91	297	pit	basalt	15	28	11	180	70	flared
2		94	304	pit	basalt	62	51	12	200	80	flared
2		94	304	pit	basalt	75	49	10	130	91	flared
2		017	3060	fill	basalt	83	55	18	200	285	flared
2		017	3083	fill	basalt	95	103	14	180	29	straight
2		021	3092	fill	basalt	44	40	15	160	43	slightly flared
2		032	3110	l.surface	basalt	43	66	12	200	200	open, deep bowl
2		550	1208	fill	basalt	50	102	21	160		
2		851	2428	fill	limest.	110	90				
2	a	1031	3254	l.surface	basalt	51	52	13	100	44	flared
2	a	1036	3299	fill	basalt	32	51	16	100	72	open form, shallow
2	a	1050	3351	pit	basalt	32	69	14	150	50	flared
2	a	1223	3890	fill	basalt	40	49	17		42	thick, straight wall
2	a	1266	4006	l.surface	basalt	95	25	14	200	100	flared
2	a	517	1080	pit	basalt	20	69	13	140	82	too small, straight?
2	a	611	5060	fill	basalt	70	51	15	120	72	flared
2	a	624	5178	fill	basalt	34	72	12	120	30	flared, polished
2	a	817	2371	fill	basalt	47		14	180	88	open form
2	b	39	88	fill	basalt	58	56	12		70	widely flared
2	b	118	360	fill	basalt	91	72	14	110	125	open, not flared
2	b	704	5313	fill	basalt	42	70	20	210		mortar?, open form, not flared
2	b	753	5407	wall removal	basalt	83	55	20	200		wavy wall, open, not flared
2	b	755	5423	fill	basalt	65	66	16			flared
2	b	1066	3490	fill	basalt	32	42	10	120	31	
2	b	1124	3563	pit	basalt	16	76	13		59	too small
2	b	1233	3922	fill	basalt	29	24	10	140	13	2 conjoin. frags, flared?
2	b	1284	4147	fill	basalt	64	73	10		80	too small
2	b	1301	4105	burial	basalt	14	17	9		4	
2	b	626	5117	pit	basalt	66	112	21		270	open, thick

2	b	634	5179	fill	basalt	67	81	14	160	104	flared
2	b	647	5163	hearth	basalt	62	61	14	150	103	flared
2	b	685	5328	fill	basalt	50	74	16	210	102	flared
2	b	689	5346	fill	basalt	17	52	15		41	flared
2	b	755	5539	fill	basalt	55	40	15	120	45	open/flared?
2	b	763	5541	fill	basalt	37	111	21	220	225	open, deep bowl
2	b	763	5582	fill	basalt	55	55	18	140	81	straight
2	b	772	5540	fill	basalt	95	63	10	140	120	open form
2	b	772	5561	fill	basalt	68	41	11		76	flared
2	b	796	5573	fill	basalt	93	58	11	130	85	flared
2	b	850	2538	pit	basalt	88	105	15	200	275	flared
2	b	850	2538	pit	basalt	46	33	12	180	27	open form
2	b	850	2536	pit	basalt	44	45	13	170	32	flared?
2	b	882	2698	silo	basalt	68	85	18	120	145	open form, shallow
2	b	901	2640	l.surface	basalt	72	114	14	180	230	2 joined frags, flared
2	c	22	44	floor	basalt	39	58	12	100	55	rim ground, flared?
2	c	033	3127	fill	basalt	15	70	23		57	straight
2	c	1128	3575	pit	basalt	17	97	13		94	too small
2	c	1159	3705	fill	basalt	101	88	12	160	210	flared
2	c	1297	4083	pit	basalt	55	33	10	120	29	flared
2	c	1322	4216	pit	basalt	58	61	18	100	64	flared
2	c	666	5206	fill	basalt	109	38	11	190	250	flared
2	c	676	5266	fill	basalt	25	63	8.5		21	too small
2	c	682	5228	pit	basalt	56	25	11	120	66	flared
2	c	777	5480	pit	basalt	67	94	13	140	32	flared
2	c	783	5526	fill	basalt	101	85	15	210	185	flared
2	c	786	5586	fill	basalt	41	82	15	120	67	flared
2	c	786	5688	fill	basalt	79	62	9	150	111	flared?
2	c	797	5803	pit	basalt	43	84	20	120	31	open form, small bowl?
2	c	25	3131	floor	basalt	112	53	11	160		open form, not flared
3		110	509	floor	basalt	42	65	11		40	flared
3	a	13	25	floor	basalt	90		14		125	flared
3	a	1170	3727	fill	limest.			26	140	120	2 rims, straight wall
3	a	1572	5852	pit	basalt	61	97	14	210	126	flared
3	a	272	543	floor	basalt	45	45	13	130	99	flared
3	b	34	65	fill	basalt	79	142	23	200	40	open, not fired
3	b	640	5147	pit	basalt	31	51	11	90	23	open form, small bowl?
3	b	692	5254	pit	basalt	51	45	6	120	40	thin, flared
4		42	95	fill/floor	basalt	45	30	15	120	45	flared
4		42	107	fill/floor	basalt						
4		126	358	floor	basalt	27	69	10	120	47	thin, very flared

Table 12.33. Summarized data for vessel wall fragments.

Stratum	Locus	Basket	Context	Material	Year	Length (mm)	Width (mm)	Wall thick.	Weight (gms)	Modification
none	none	none	unknown	basalt	75	55	32	15	50	
none	none	none	unknown	basalt	75	74	58	15	110	
none	none	none	unknown	basalt	75	55	50	16	85	
none	none	none	unknown	basalt	90	85	52	15	112	
none	none	none	unknown	basalt	75	77	70	18	180	
none	none	none	unknown	basalt	75	65	50	21	115	
none	none	none	unknown	basalt	75	43	42	14	50	
none	none	none	unknown	basalt	75	110	46	18	180	
none	none	none	unknown	basalt	75	66	41	14	85	
none	none	none	unknown	basalt	75	70	60	15	120	
none	none	none	unknown	basalt	75	61	30	16	55	
none	none	none	none	basalt	90					
1	005	3035	topsoil	basalt	90	68	55	14	109	
1	1023	3238	topsoil	basalt	91	37	30	16	29	
1	1024	3229	topsoil	basalt	91	62	50	14	81	
1	1025	3232	topsoil	basalt	91	65	54	28	111	
1	1062	7029	topsoil	basalt	92	42	38	16	32	
1	1213	3875	topsoil	basalt	92	63	53	10	55	
1	500	1000	topsoil	basalt	90	81	48	17	140	
1	505	1033	topsoil	basalt	90	36	20	18	21	
1	509	1038	fill	basalt	90	42	24	14	18	
1	684	5255	topsoil	basalt	91	95	50	12	88	
1	684	5249	topsoil	basalt	91	52	30	11	28	
2	017	3073	fill	basalt	90	94	57	18	160	
2	024	3082	pit	basalt	90	44	42	13	45	
2	527	1105	fill	basalt	90	51	24	20	32	ground
2	556	1386	pit	basalt	90	74	42	18	78	
2 a	1374	4362	pit	basalt	92	42	30	12	45	
2 a	1374	4362	pit	basalt	92	76	38	12	19	
2 a	515	1076	fill	basalt	90	113	60	19	310	
2 a	515	1128	fill	basalt	90	53	26	20	33	
2 a	535	1137	wall removal	basalt	90	49	51	21	64	
2 a	639	5148	pit	basalt	91	34	25	12	19	
2 a	760	5420	pit	basalt	92	68	60	18	76	
2 a	975	2803	pit	basalt	90	102	91	20	285	
2 b	018	3061	m.b.collapse	basalt	90	54	46	13	55	

2	b	1108	3532	removal?	basalt	91	48	41	11	37
2	b	1233	3932	fill	basalt	92	74	28	20	92
2	b	755	5422	fill	basalt	92	101	55	19	170
2	b	799	5593	fill	basalt	92	30	24	10	9
2	c	1307	4113	pit	basalt	92	58	38	10	37
2	c	1510	5625	burial	basalt	92	33	30	9	12
2	c	1516	5826	hearth	basalt	92	32	28	14	18
2	c	1517	5635	fill	basalt	92	47	35	15	35
2	c	783	5502	fill	basalt	92	52	41	10	41
2	c	792	5528	surface removal	basalt	92	57	41	18	48
2	c	797	5803	fill	basalt	92	51	37	9.5	24
3		025	3135	pit	basalt	90	35	23	15	16
3	a	1131	3745	fill	basalt	91	43	35	12	29
3	a	1147	3684	fill	basalt	91	53	38	15	60
3	a	1572	5852	pit	basalt	92			10	126
3	a	1572	5852	pit	basalt	92	50	43	14	36

5 drilled holes

Table 12.34. Frequency of ground stone artifacts from Gilat, 1975–92.

Artifact class	(non-stone) n=	Stone n=	Relative % of all ground stone	Relative % of identifiable ground stone
Grinding slabs		531	27.63	31.38
Handstones		46	2.39	2.72
Large perforated stone		66	3.43	3.90
Hammer/pounders		21	1.09	1.24
Pestles		11	.57	.65
Smoothed pebbles		176	9.16	10.40
Pivot stones (door sockets)		5	.26	.29
Mortars		103	5.36	6.09
Multiple use		9	.47	.53
Miscellany	(2)	66	3.43	3.90
Tokens	(8)	38	1.98	2.25
Axes		3	.16	.18
Pendants	(26)	33	1.72	1.95
Beads	(27)	78	4.06	4.61
Maceheads		25	1.30	1.48
Spindle whorls	(53)	110	5.72	6.50
Small perforated stones		27	1.40	1.60
Palettes		41	2.13	2.42
Stone vessels		303	15.76	17.91
Possible handstones/grinding slabs		67	3.49	
Unidentifiable fragments		68	3.54	
Ochre		56	2.91	
Unworked minerals and stones		39	2.03	
Totals	116	1922	99.99	100.0

Figures

Figure 12.1. Length of smoothed pebbles vs. hammerstones.

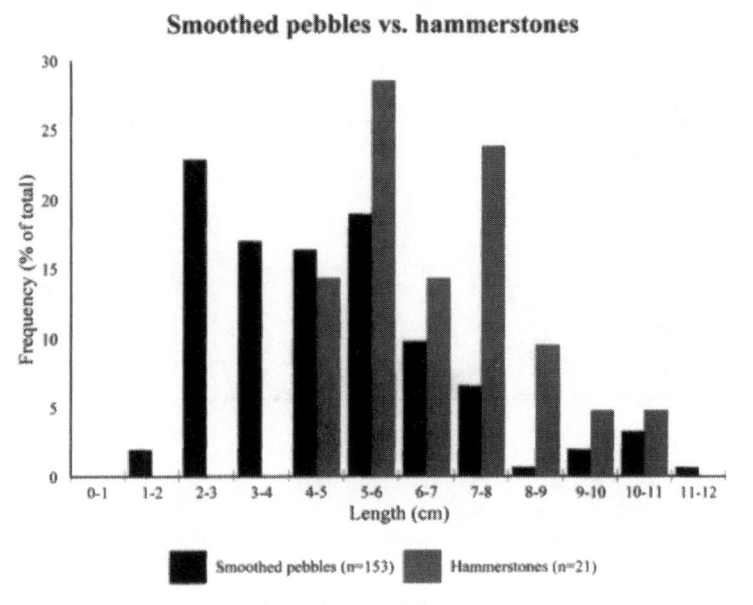

Figure 12.2. Width of smoothed pebbles vs. hammerstones.

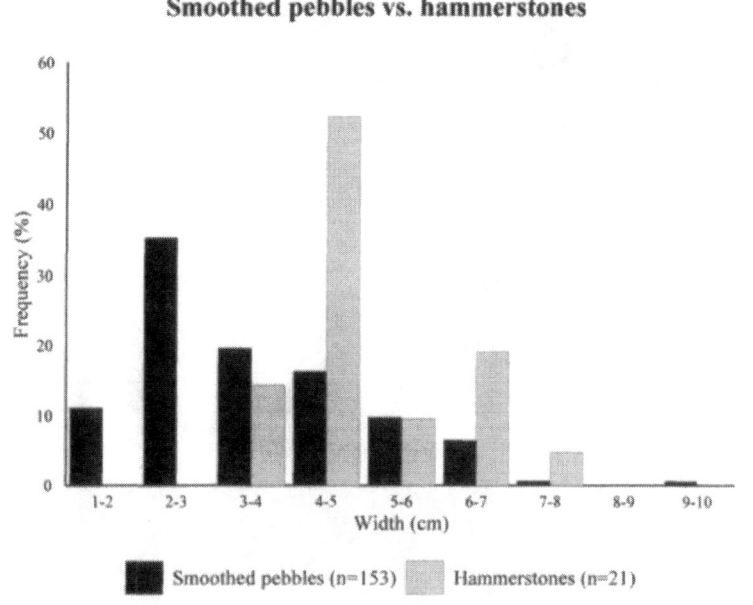

Figure 12.3. Weights of smoothed pebbles vs. hammerstones.

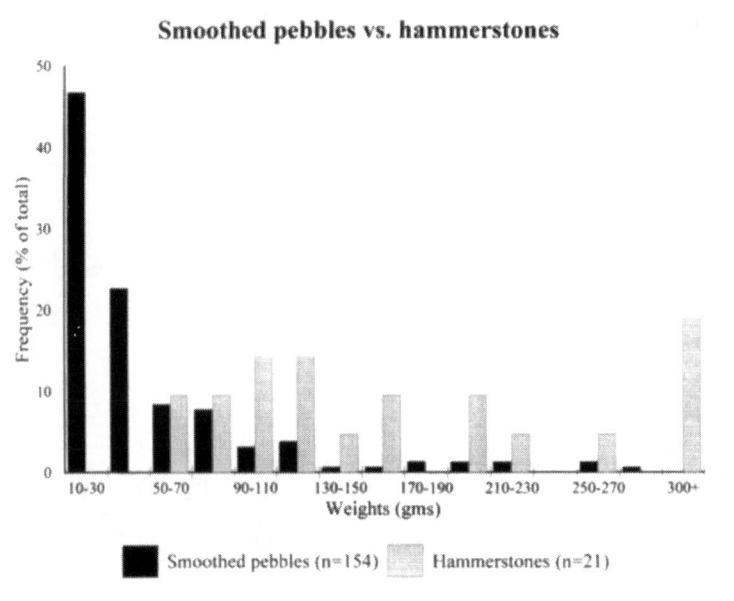

Figure 12.4. Range of mortar well depths.

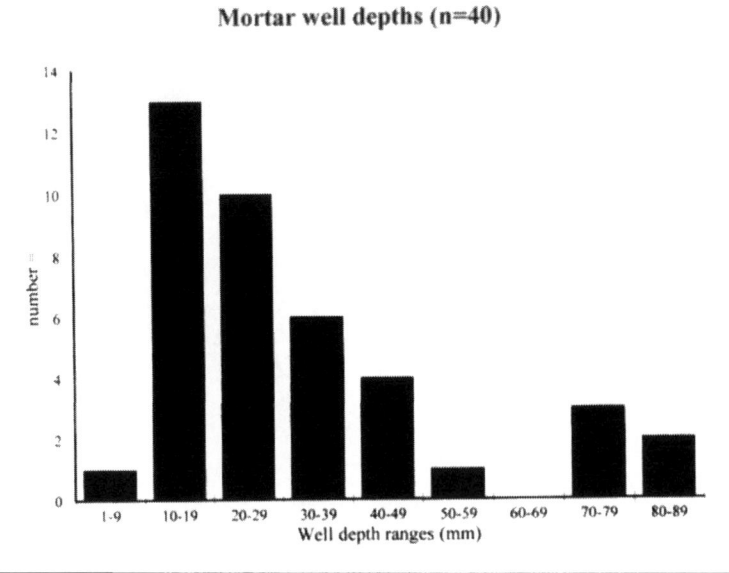

Figure 12.5. Range of mortar heights.

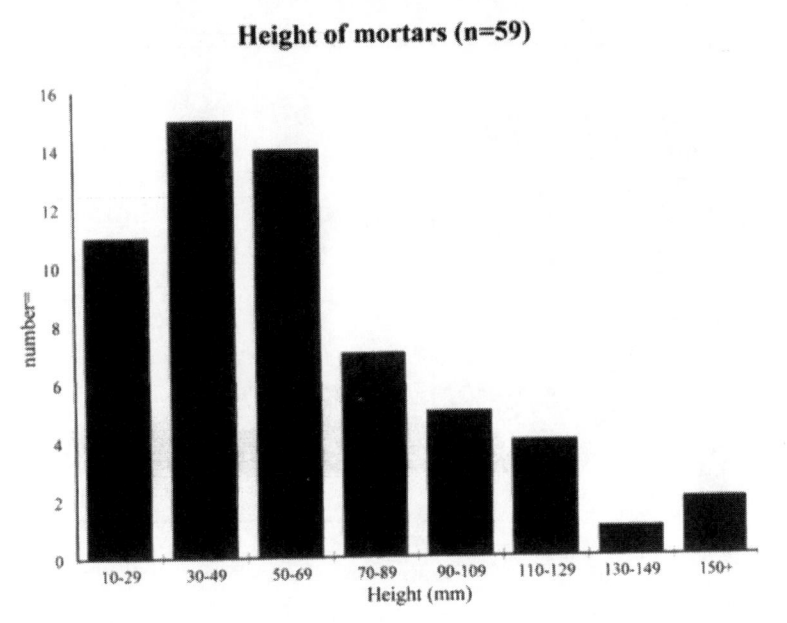

Height of mortars (n=59)

Figure 12.6. Frequency of rock types used to make mortars.

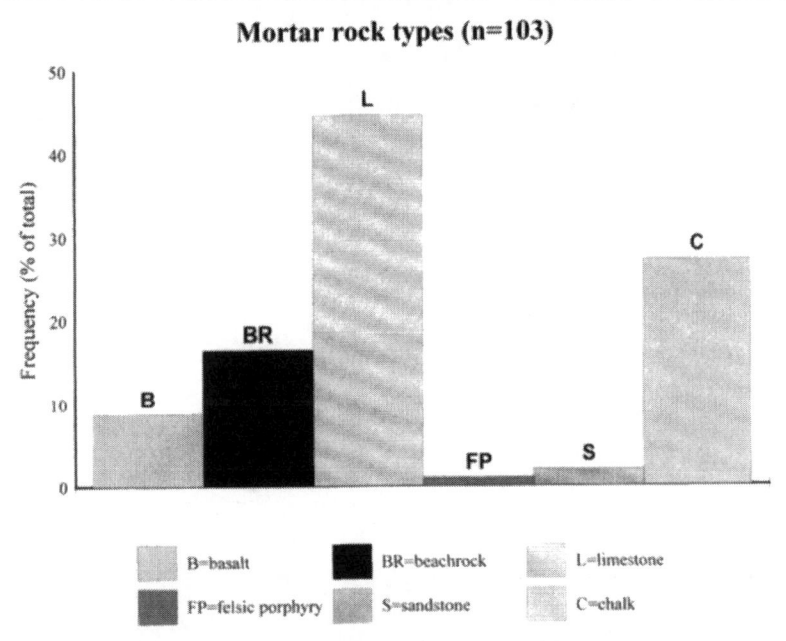

Mortar rock types (n=103)

Figure 12.7. Frequency of bead shapes.

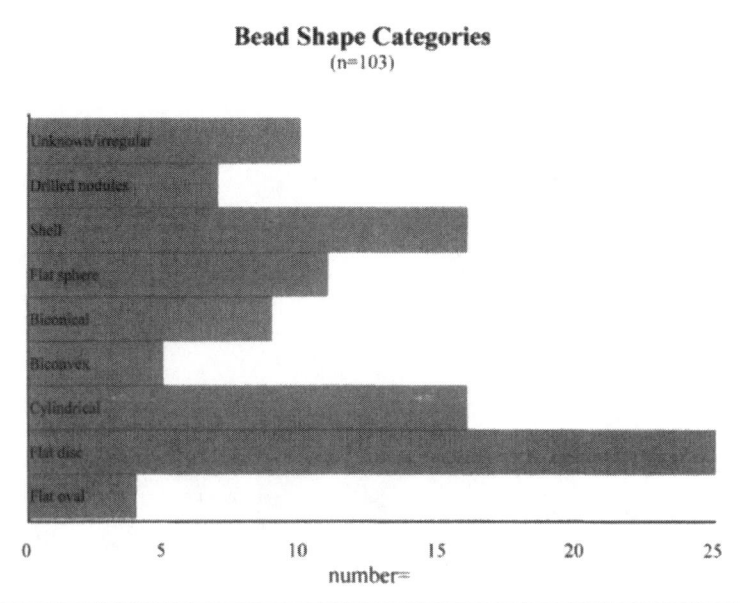

Figure 12.8. Frequency of materials used to make beads.

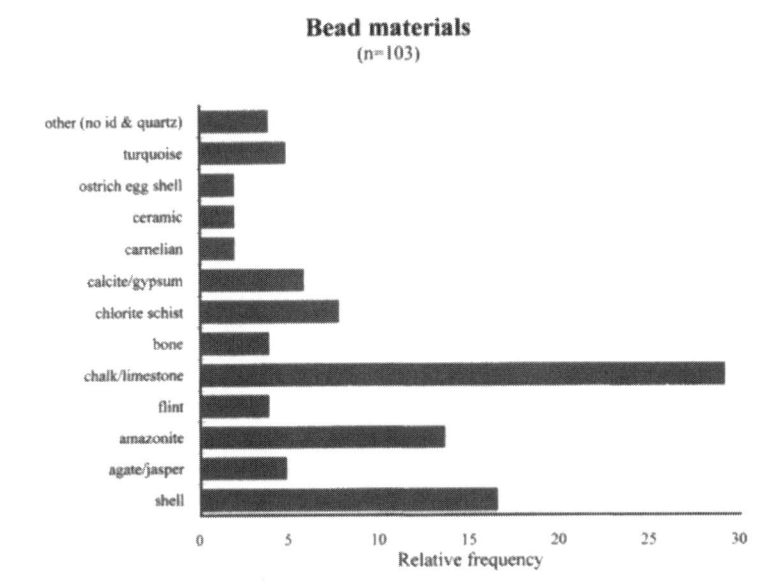

Figure 12.9. Frequency of rock types used to make maceheads.

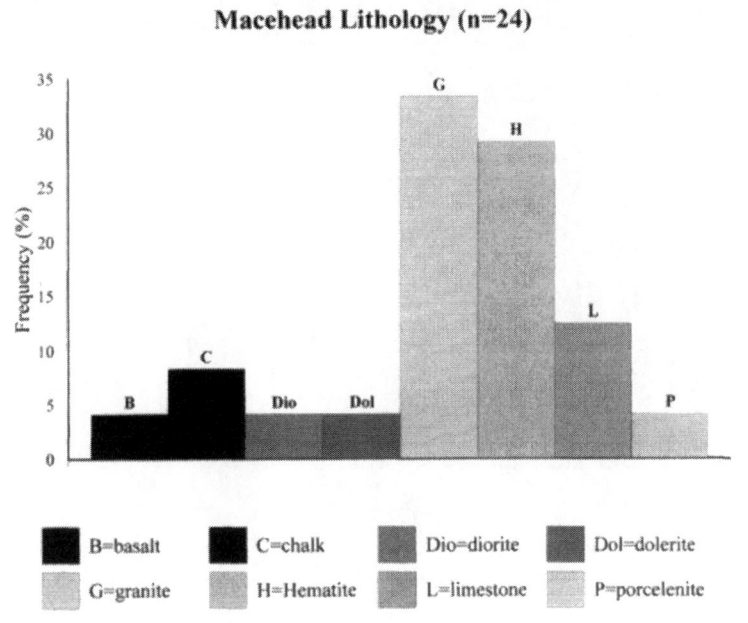

Figure 12.10. Estimated weight ranges of maceheads.

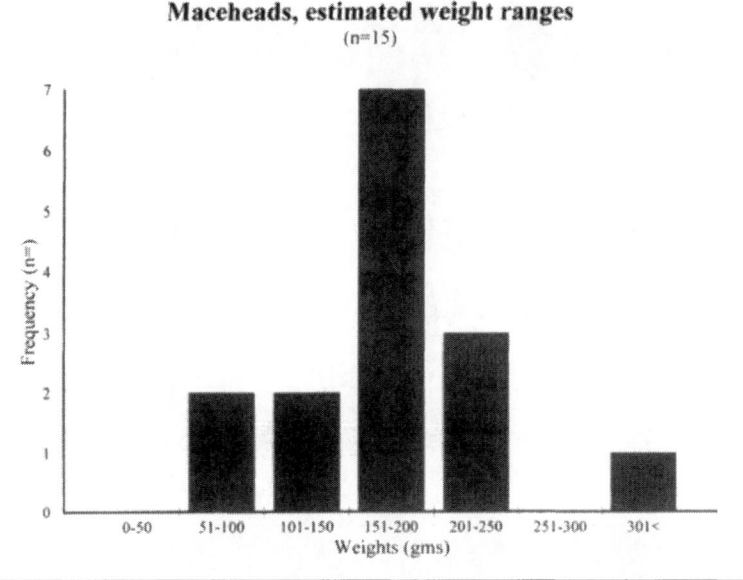

Figure 12.11. Frequency of weights of perforated sherds and stones.

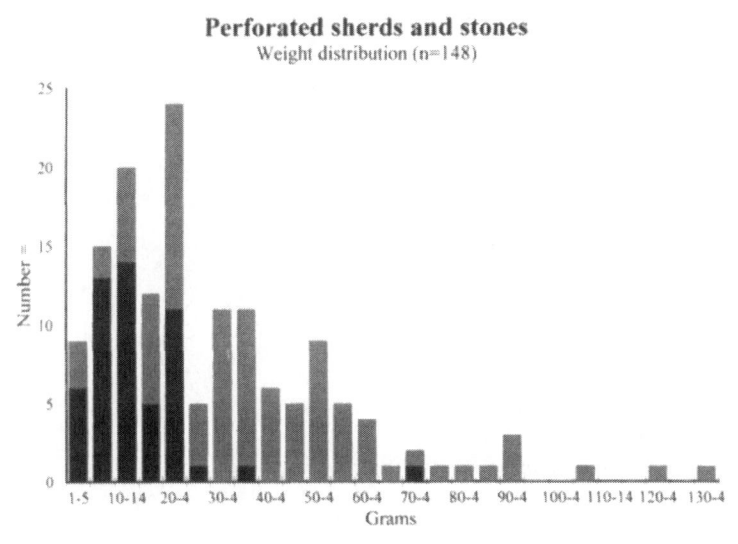

Figure 12.12. Palette lithology.

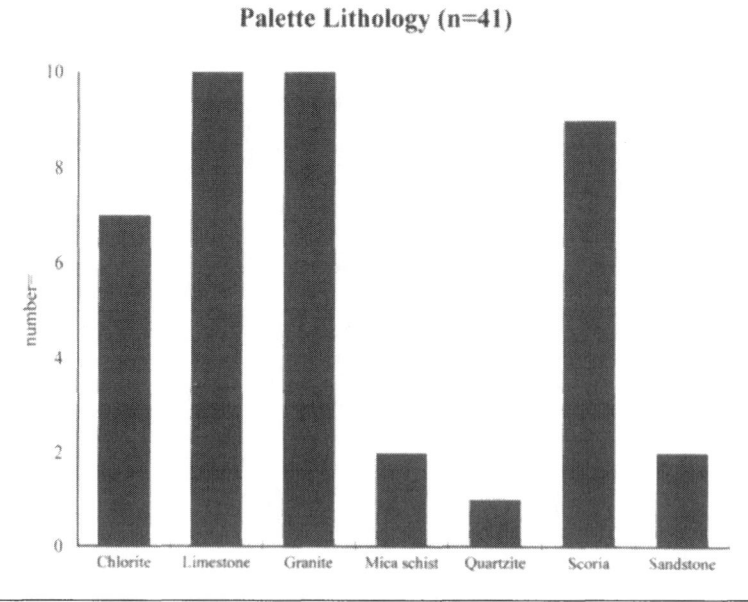

Figure 12.13. Ring base diameter frequencies for fenestrated stands.

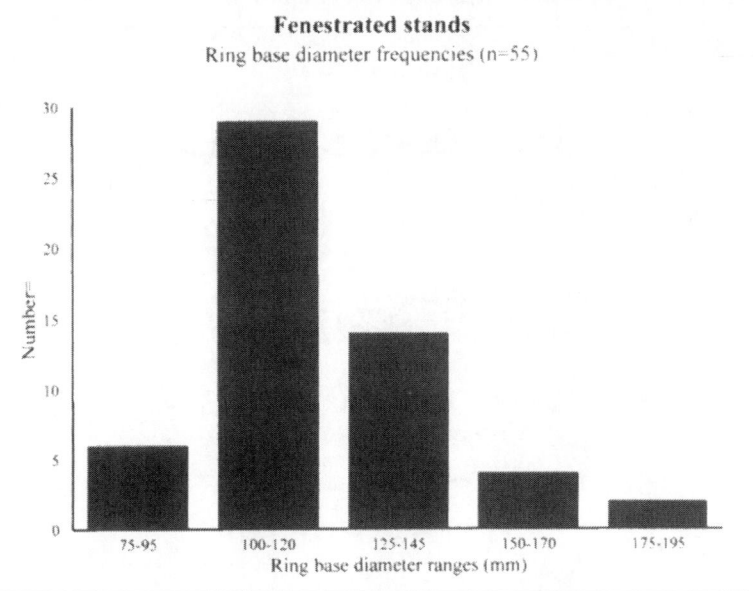

Figure 12.14. Range of estimated diameters of fenestrated stand ring base fragments.

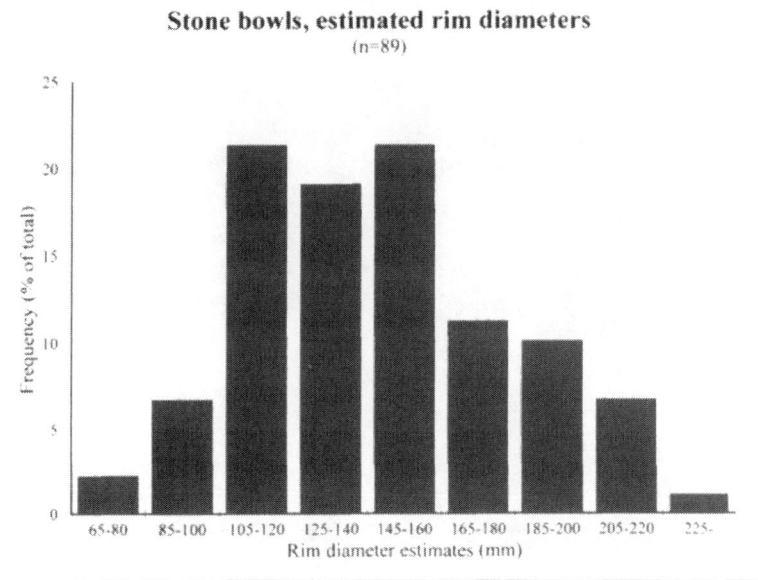

Figure 12.15. Comparison of identifiable ground stone frequencies from Gilat, Grar and Abu Hamid.

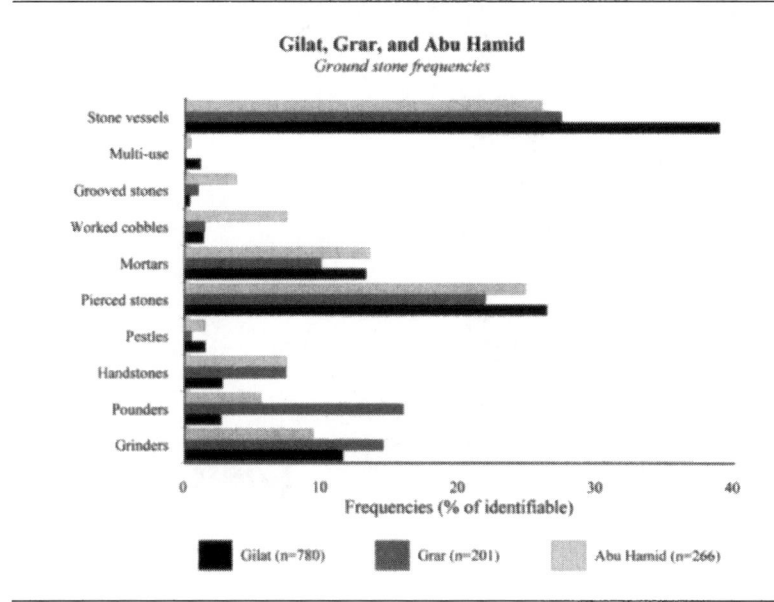

Figure 12.16. Spindle whorls from Area Y, Gilat: L. 584 (left) and L. 535 (right).

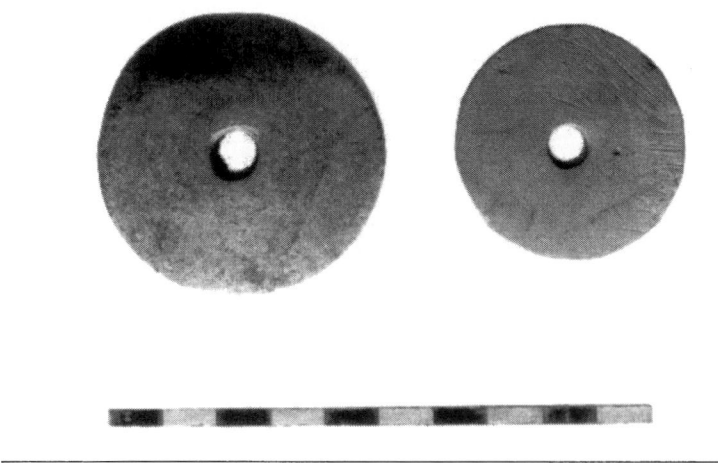

Figure 12.17. Gilat ground stone artefacts (stone rings, etc.).

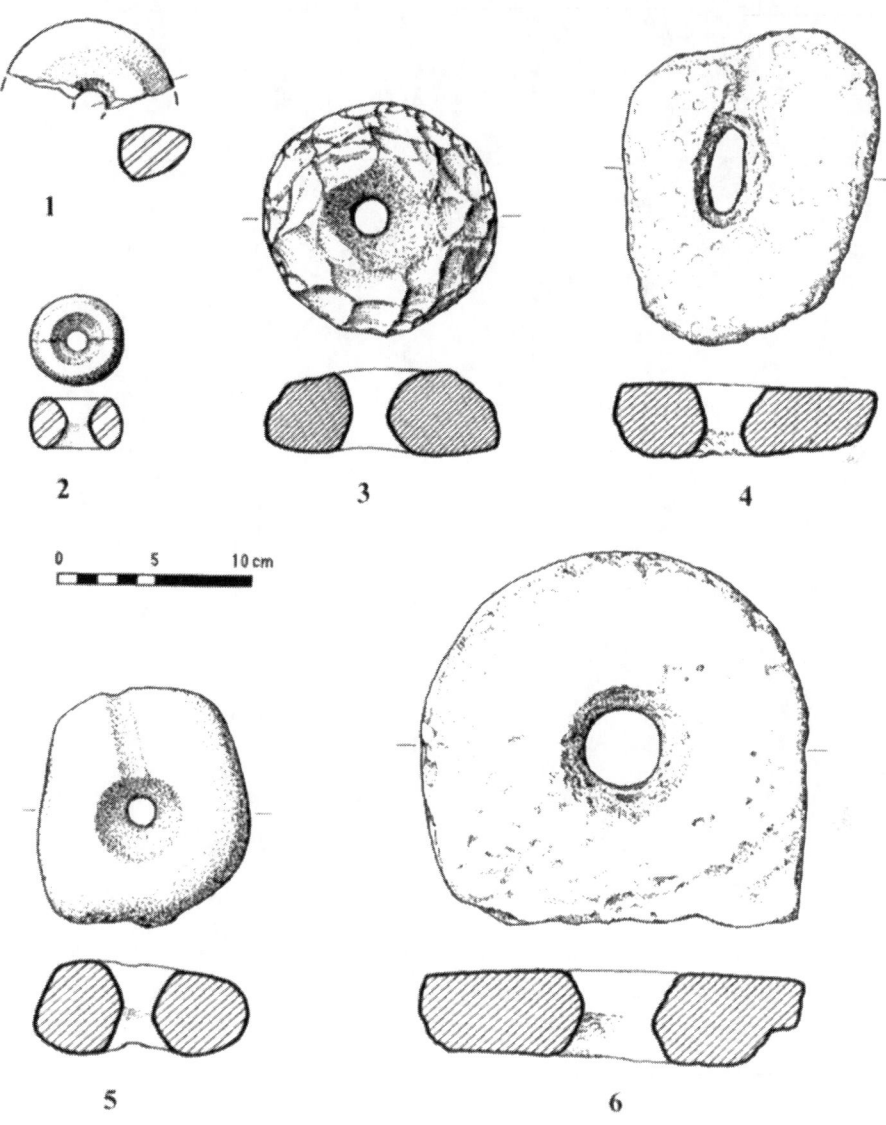

No.	Artifact	Reg. No.	Locus	Basket	Stratum	Description
1	macehead fragment	49/90	007	3027	2	basalt, disc-shaped
2	small stone ring	49/90	508/ 1029	1039/3256	1	basalt, 2 conjoined fragments, pump drill?
3	large stone ring	49/90	827	2313	2c	limestone, chipped and ground
4	large stone ring	19/91	1027	3245	1	beachrock
5	large stone ring	49/90	508	1083	1	limestone, grooved
6	large stone ring	19/91	1031	3254	2a	beachrock

Figure 12.18. Gilat ground stone artifacts (mortars, etc.).

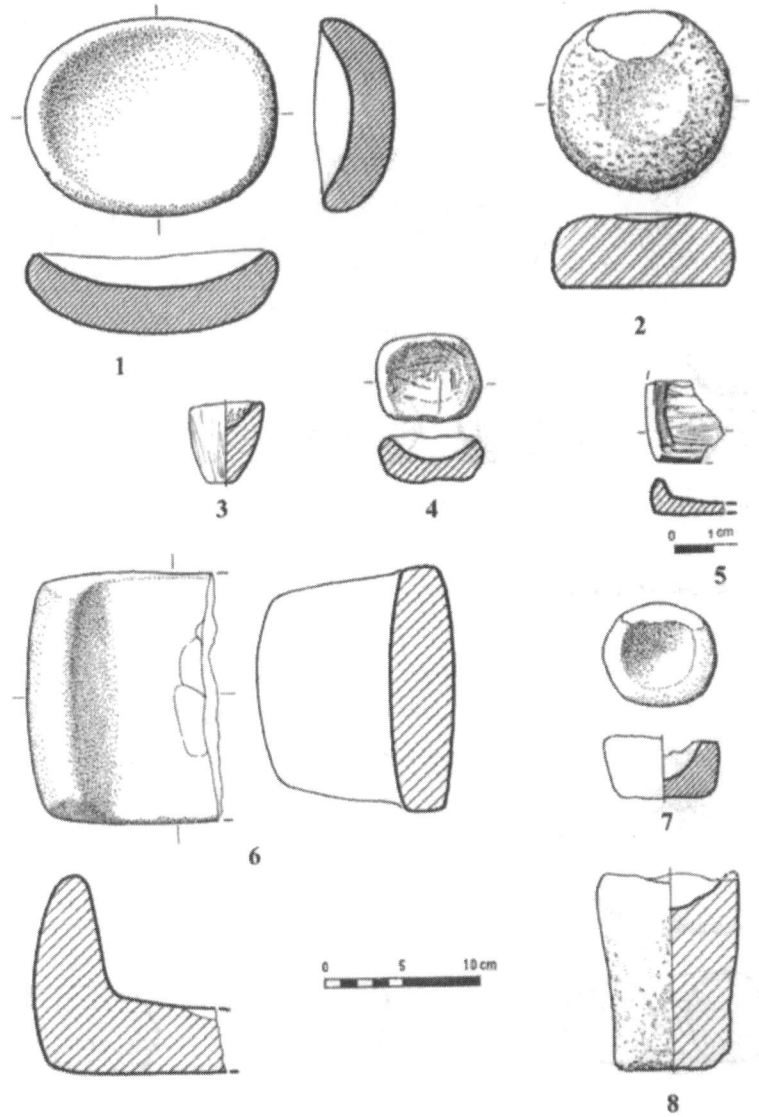

No.	Artifact	Reg. No.	Locus	Basket	Stratum	Description
1	bowl/basin	19/91	700	5311	2a	granite, polished
2	miscellaneous	19/91	1150	3747	3a	basalt, ground, possibly modified vessel base fragment
3	mortar?	49/90	838	2495	2b	chalk, striated exterior and interior
4	mortar	49/90	509	1054	1	chalk, small, shallow, interior striae
5	miscellaneous fragment	49-90	813	2296	2a	corner, low rim, interior striae
6	miscellaneous fragment	57/92	777	-	2c	limestone, well-ground
7	mortar					
8	pedestaled vessel	?	?	?	none	chalk

Figure 12.19. Gilat ground stone artefacts (tokens, etc.).

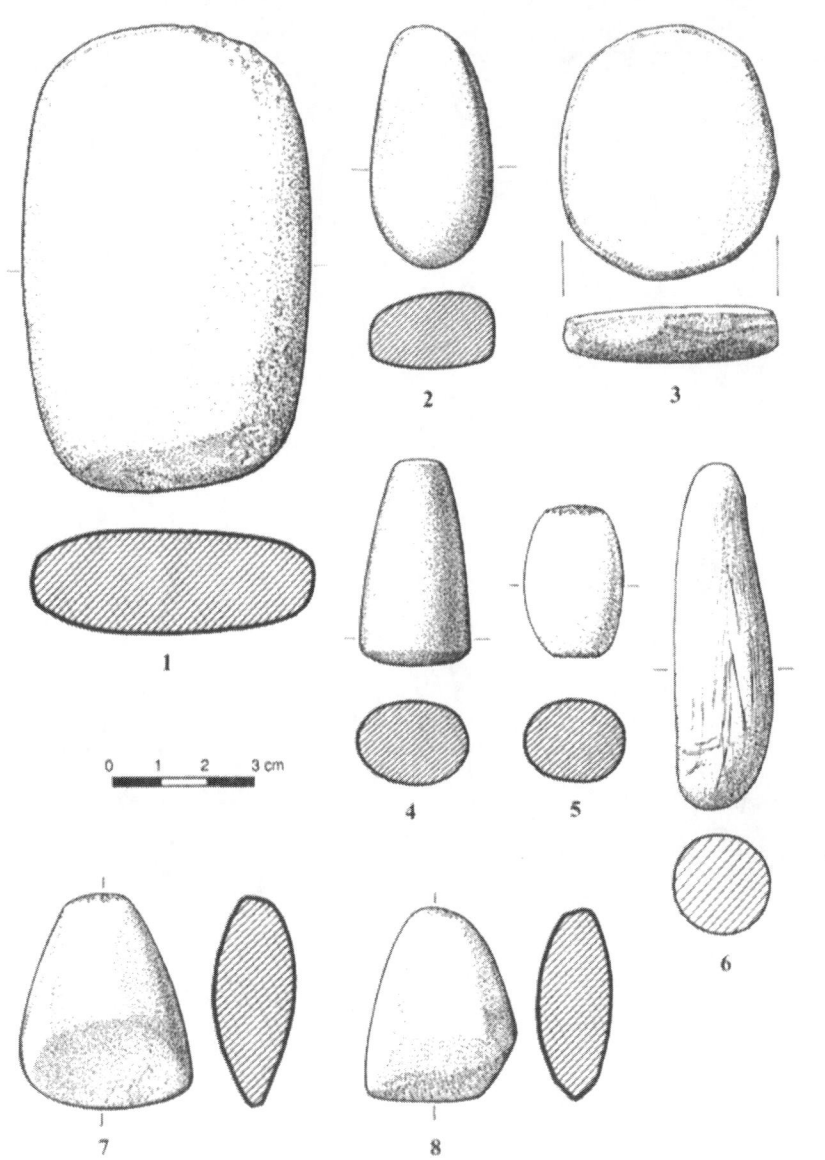

No.	Artifact	Reg. No.	Locus	Basket	Stratum	Description
1	palette	57/92	1223	3900	2a	granite, smooth, no concavity
2	token	57/92	1236	3926	2b	chalk, well-ground
3	token	19/91	649	5172	2c	ferruginous sandstone, chamfered edge
4	token	57/92	761	5427	2a	chlorite schist, conical, polished
5	multi-use tool	727	86	292	2b	bi-polar pecked, lateral grinding wear
6	miscellaneous	49/90	800	2197	1	chalk, striated and ground nodule
7	votive axe	19/91	1147	3689	3a	amphibolite, polished
8	votive axe	19/91	620	5082	2a	amphibolite, polished

Figure 12.20. Gilat ground stone artefacts (pendants, etc.).

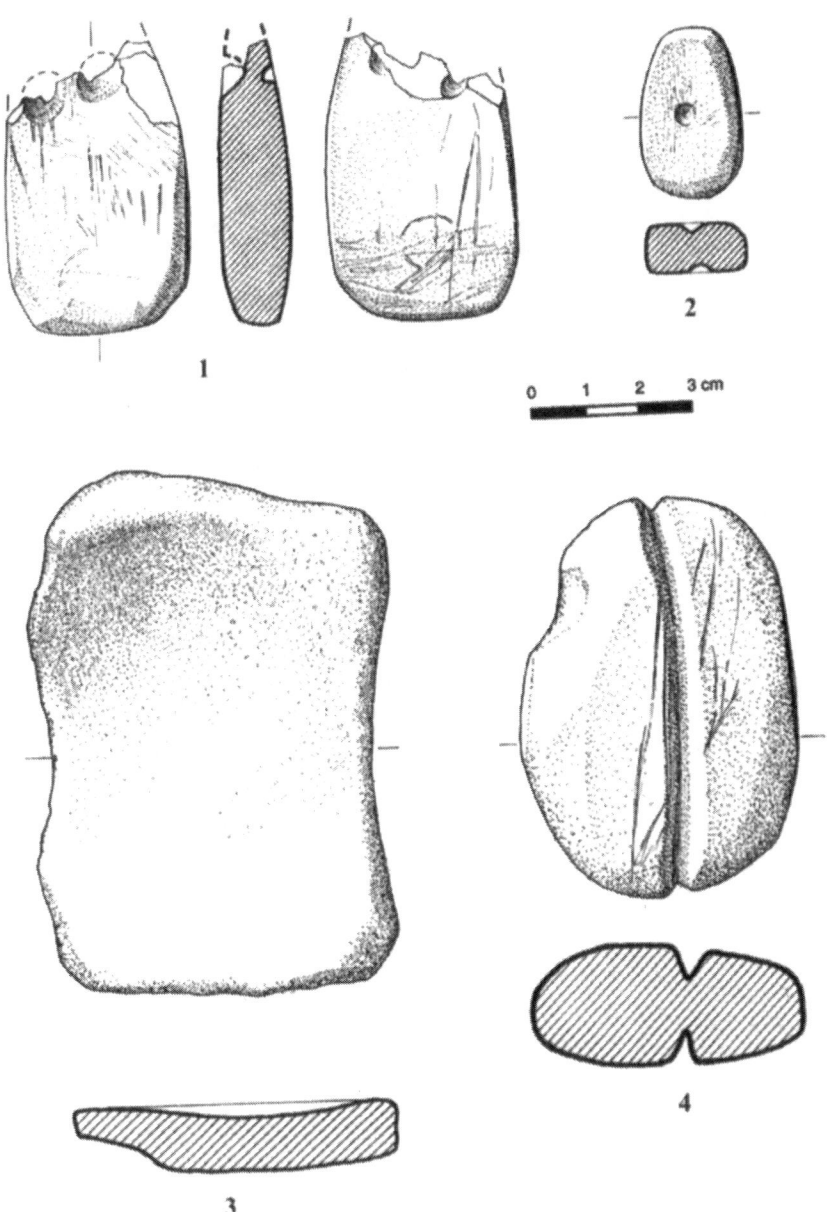

No.	Artifact	Reg. No.	Locus	Basket	Stratum	Description
1	pendant	57/92	798	5566	2a	double perforations, bifacially ground with striae
2	pendant?	57/92	1321	4169	2b	bifacial drill marks, not perforated, well ground
3	grinding slab	49/90	586	1381	3b	unifacial use
4	grooved stone	19/91	1135	3587	2c	chalk, circumferential groove

Figure 12.21. Gilat ground stone artefacts (tokens, etc.).

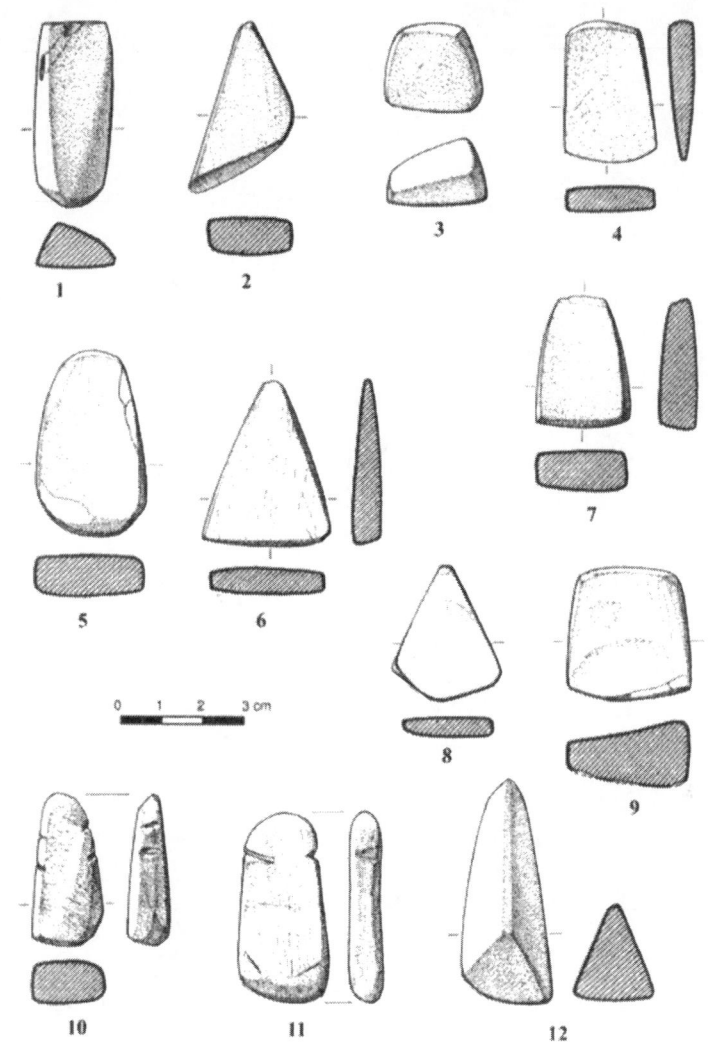

No.	Artifact	Reg. No.	Locus	Basket	Stratum	Description
1	pendant	49/90	895	2597	2b	ferruginous sandstone, chamfered trapezoid
2	ochre	57/92	786	5759	2c	modified, triangular
3	ochre	57/92	1214	3912	1	modified, trapezoidal
4	token	57/92	1207	3829	2b	chlorite schist, trapezoidal
5	token	49/90	005	3016	1	chalk, well-ground
6	token	19/91	633	5128	2b	chalk, well-ground, bifacial striae
7	token	49/90	006	3052	1	sandstone, green, well-ground
8	ochre	49/90	cleaning	1050	0	well-ground all over
9	ochre	57/92	786	5676	2c	modified, ground all over
10	pendant (?)	57/92	1547 (1056?)	7009 (5767?)	2c	limestone, 2 notches on each lateral edge
11	pendant (?)	57/92	1221	3868	2c	limestone, notches on edges
12	ochre	57/92	1562	5825	3b	well-ground all over

Figure 12.22. Gilat ground stone and related artifacts.

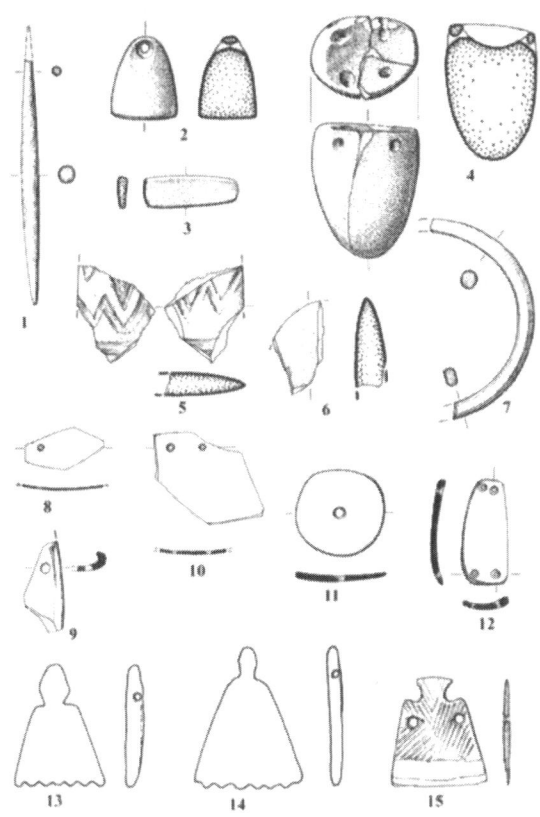

No.	Artifact	Reg. No.	Locus	Basket	Stratum	Description
1	hair pin/spacer?	19/91	1044	3358		finely ground bone, hair pin?
2	pendant	49/90	851	2427		bi-lateral perforation, finely ground
3	token?	49/90	838	2496		bone, finely ground
4	pendant	49/90	800	2093		ivory (hippo tusk), 4 holes drilled along edges
5		57/92	1369	4319		bifacially incised chevron designs
6	unknown		none	none	0	very finely ground, fine striae
7	shell bracelet fragment		1075	3451		
8	decorative object fragment	57/92	1393	4373		single perforation on mother of pearl fragment
9	decorative object fragment—pendant?	57/92	1558	5805		shell; single drilled perforation
10	pendant		none	none	0	mother-of-pearl; two perforations, possibly pendant fragment
11	pendant		0	3827	0	mother-of-pearl; ground edges, single drilled perforation
12	pendant/bracelet		908	2659		shell; ground edges, four drilled perforations
13	pendant		none	none	0	mother of pearl
14	pendant		none	none	0	mother of pearl
15	pendant		none	none	0	shell; bifacially ground, with fine incised lines

Figure 12.23. Gilat ground stone and related artifacts.

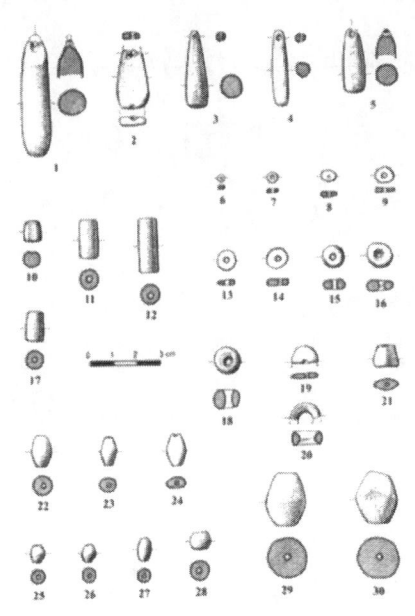

No.	Artifact	Reg. No.	Locus	Basket	Stratum	Description
1	pendant	19/91	1131	3756	3a	limestone,
2	pendant	19/91	1059	3399	2c	chlorite schist, trapezoidal
3	pendant	19/91	700	5286	2a	chlorite schist, elongate cone
4	pendant	57/92	1062	7026	2c	amazonite, conical
5	pendant		none	none	0	unknown
6	bead	19/91	1069	3459	2a	bone, cylindrical
7	bead	57/92	1214	3885	1	chlorite schist, disc
8	bead	19/91	608	5062	2a	turquoise, oval shaped, flat
9	bead	57/92	755	5470	2b/c	ostrich eggshell
10	bead, blank	57/92	1514	5654	2c	Tridacoua shell, undrilled
11	bead	49/90	957	2726	2a	limestone, cylindrical
12	bead	19/91	603	5022	1	limestone, cylindrical
13	bead	49/90	024	3112	3a	shell, disc
14	bead	57/92	1062	7025	2c	chlorite-schist, disc
15	bead	49/90	916	2742	3a	amazonite, disc
16	bead	49/90	555	1246	2c	carnelian, disc
17	bead	49/90	034	3140	3b	calcite, cylindrical
18	bead	19/91	1127	3579	2c	agate, flat sphere
19	bead	19/91	1059	3387	2a	amazonite, disc
20	bead?	57/92	1508	5611	2c	calcite, wide perforation
21	bead	57/92	1203	3816	3a	carnelian, trapezoidal, bi-convex cross-section
22	bead	49/90	883	2563	2b	limestone, biconvex
23	bead	57/92	787	5529	2b	amazonite, biconical
24	bead	19/91	1159	3691	2c	amazonite, biconical, plano-convex cross-section
25	bead	57/92	1322	4230	2c	chlorite schist, biconical
26	bead	57/92	1562	5824	3b	chlorite schist, biconical
27	bead	49/90	962	2834	2c	amazonite, bi-convex
28	bead	49/90	985	2845	2b	limestone, flattened sphere
29	bead	19/91	1037	3357	2a	limestone, biconical
30	bead	49/90	850	2550	2a	limestone, biconical

Figure 12.24. Gilat ground stone artefacts (pendant fragments, etc.).

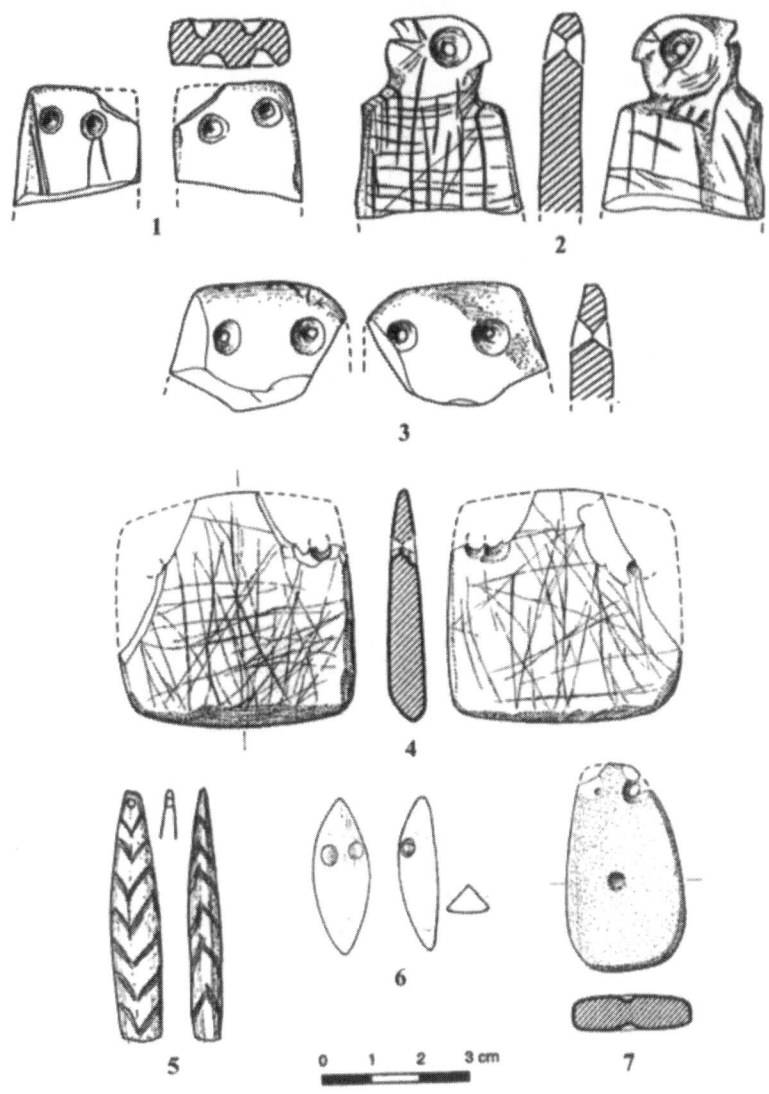

No.	Artifact	Reg. No.	Locus	Basket	Stratum	Description
1	pendant fragment	727		393		chalk; two incomplete perforations, bifacially
2	pendant fragment	727		393		chalk; single complete perforation, possible bird head motif? bifacial incisions
3	pendant fragment	727		436		chalk; two incomplete perforations, bifacially drilled
4	pendant-palette		800	2161		two drill marks, bifacially; multiple bifacial incisions
5	pendant	727		337		limestone; incised chevron design, both sides
6	pendant/bead	727				unidentified rock
7	pendant		961	2782		bifacially drilled; one complete

Figure 12.25. Gilat ground stone artefacts (maceheads, etc.).

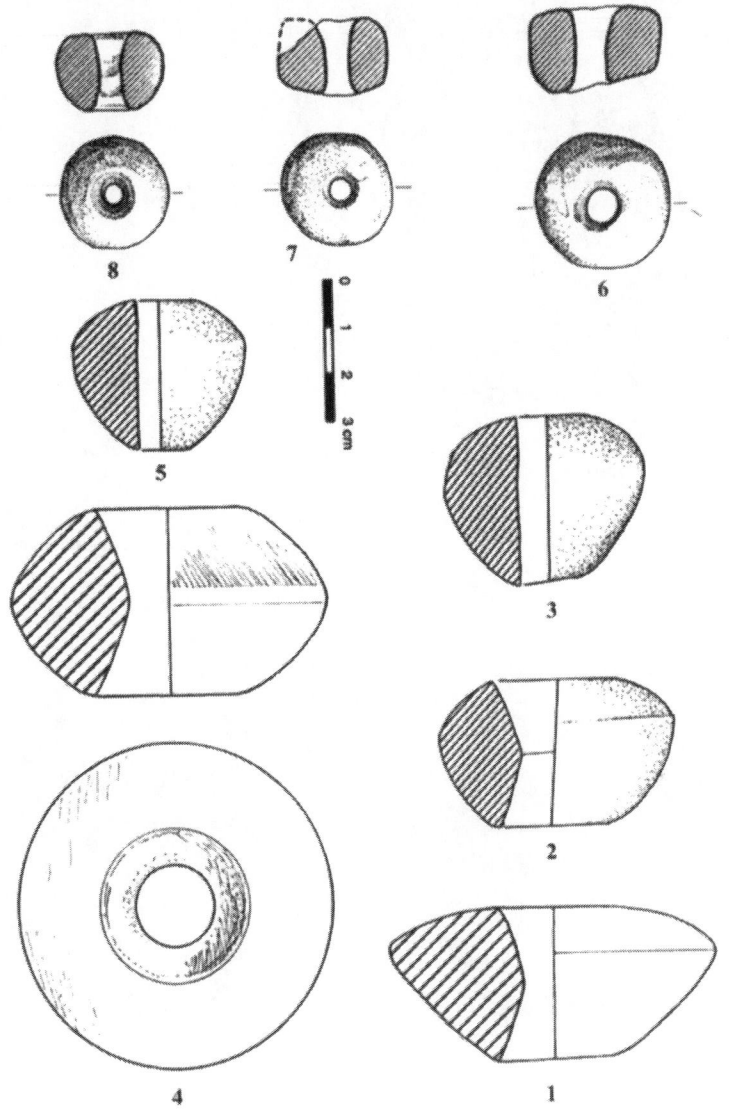

No.	Artifact	Reg. No.	Locus	Basket	Stratum	Description
1	macehead	568-13	75-1058	?	?	granite, convex-topped conical
2	macehead	none	none	none	0	chrysocolla, convex topped conical with carination
3	macehead	116	none	none	0	hematite, piriform
4	macehead	568-2				granite, biconical
5	macehead	727		371		
6	small perforated	57/92	1050	7004	0	limestone, roughly disc-shaped
7	small perforated	49/90	938	2763	2b	chalk, flattened sphere
8	small perforated	19/91	1147	3681	3a	limestone, flattened sphere

Figure 12.26. Gilat ground stone artefacts (palettes).

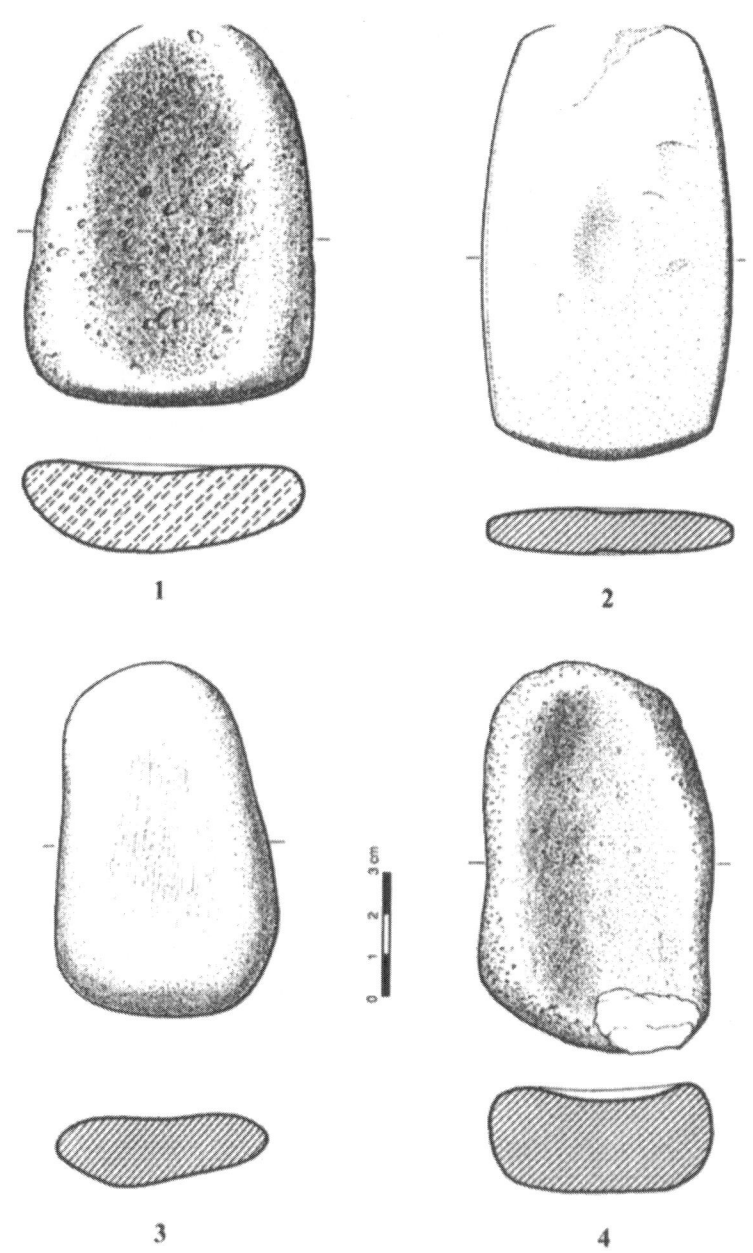

No.	Artifact	Reg. No.	Locus	Basket	Stratum	Description
1	palette	36/87	261	637	3a	scoria, unifacial use
2	palette	71-5203	none	none	surface	chlorite schist, bifacial use
3	palette	49/90	528	1162	2c	limestone
4	palette	57/92	1511	5712	2c	kurkar, unifacial use

Figure 12.27. Gilat ground stone artefacts (palettes, etc.).

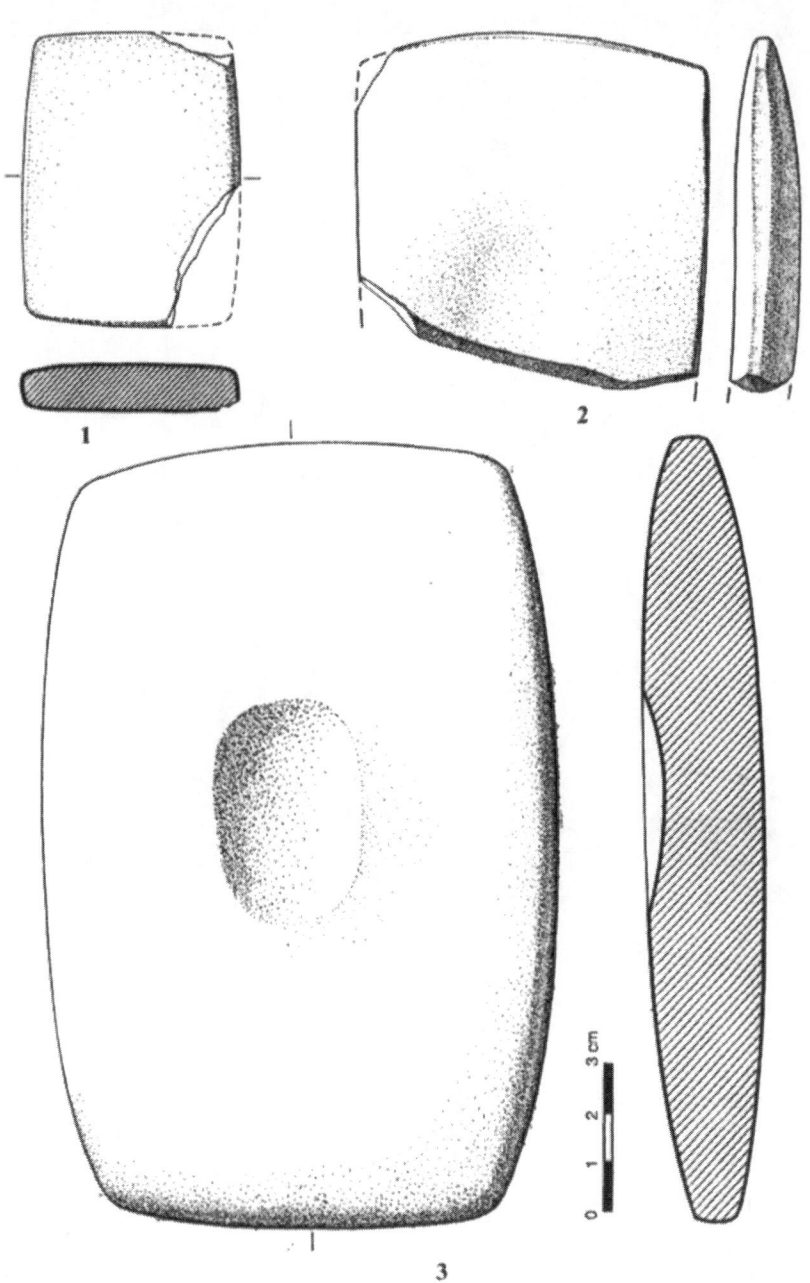

No.	Artifact	Reg. No.	Locus	Basket	Stratum	Description
1	palette	36/87-264	264?	?	3a?	Ferruginous limestone, unifacially worked
2	token/palette	49/90	0	1259	0	Red limestone
3	palette	36/87-519	261?	519?	2c	granite, unifacial concavity

Figure 12.28. Gilat ground stone artefacts (palettes, etc.).

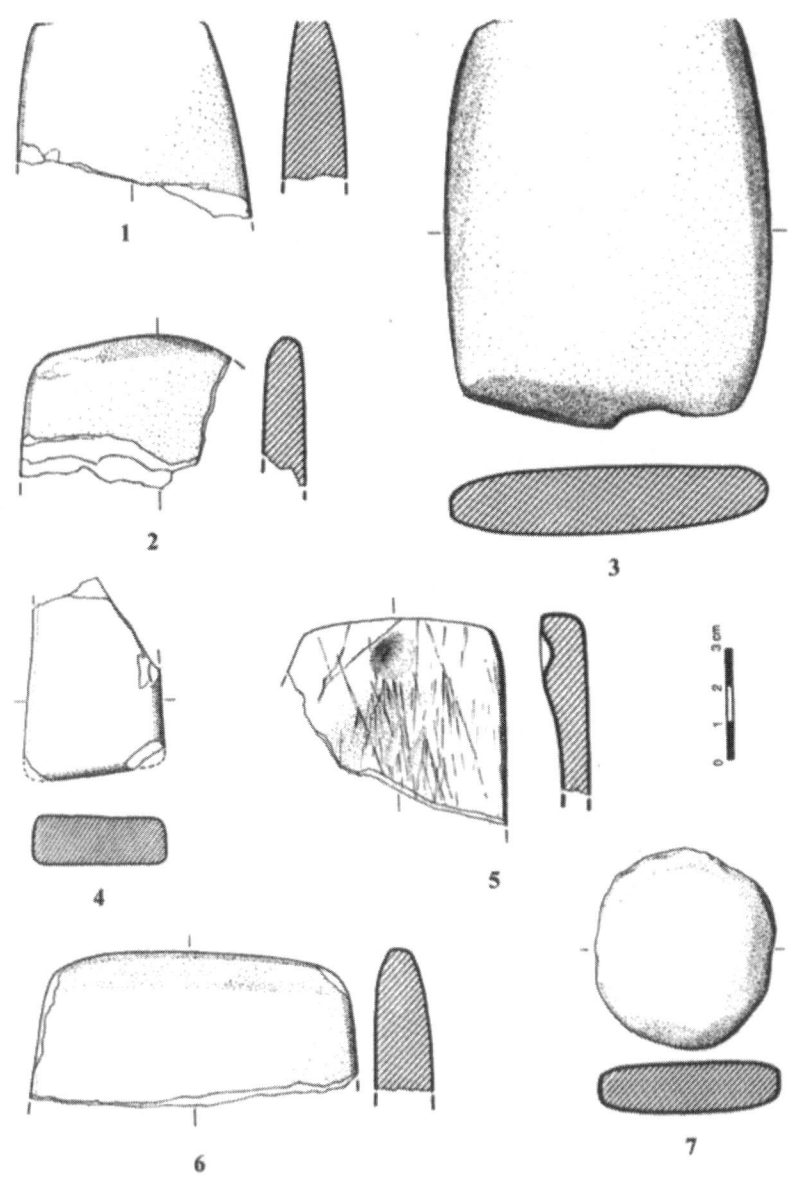

No.	Artifact	Reg. No.	Locus	Basket	Stratum	Description
1	palette, fragment	57/92	1223	3933	2a	limestone
2	palette, fragment					limestone
3	palette	36/87	92	597	2b	chlorite schist, smoothed, no traces of use-wear
4	miscellaneous, fragment	49/90	556	1390	3	limestone, slightly ground?
5	pendant?, fragment	19/91	1023	3226	1	chalk, unifacial concavity, unifacial drill mark, striae
6	palette, fragment	727-328	?	?	?	limestone, bifacially polished
7	token?	57/92	1153	3680	?	diorite, ground and polished bifacially

Figure 12.29. Gilat ground stone artefacts (palettes).

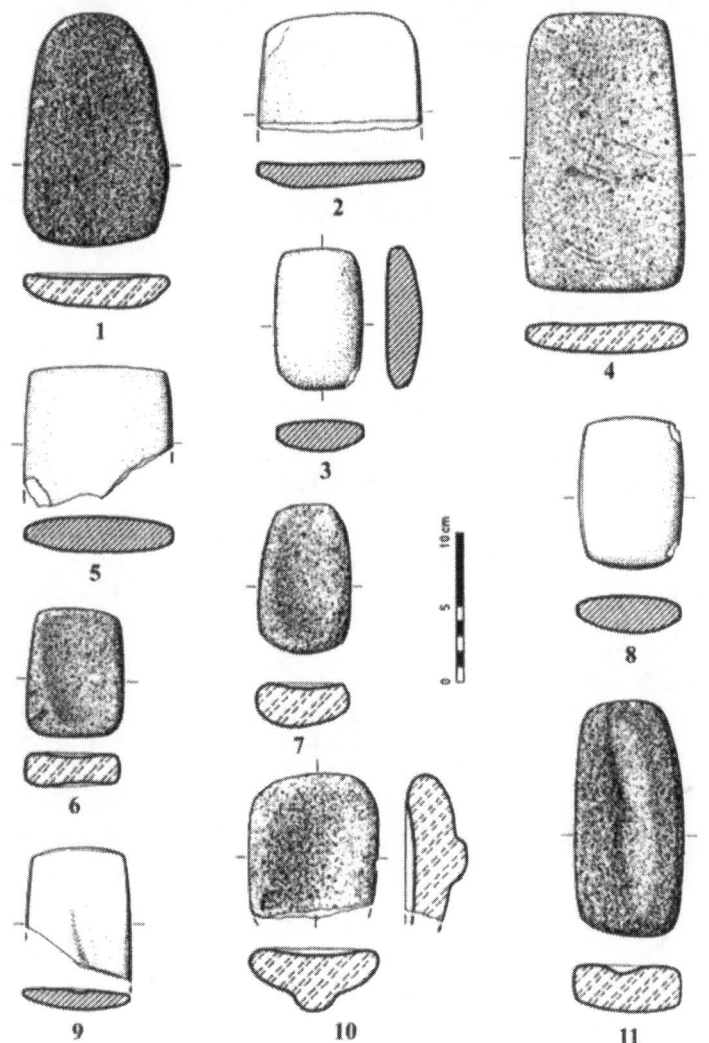

No.	Artifact	Reg. No.	Locus	Basket	Stratum	Description
1	palette	49/90	019?	3064?	3	scoria, unifacial use
2	palette, fragment	57/92	1034	3269	2a	mica schist
3	palette	49/90	817	2382	2a	granite, unifacially polished
4	palette	49/90	019	3066	3	scoria
5	palette, fragment	19/91	633	5153	2b	granite
6	palette	57/92	1337	4243	3a	scoria, bifacial use
7	palette	57/92	1062	7029	2c	scoria, unifacial use
8	palette	49/90	512	1068	1	granite
9	palette	57/92	1224	3901	2a	limestone, unifacial use
10	palette ?, fragment	19/91	800	2091	1	scoria, knob-like protrusion
11	palette	49/90	019	3065	3	scoria; unifacial, longitudinal groove

Figure 12.30. Gilat ground stone artefacts (spindle whorls).

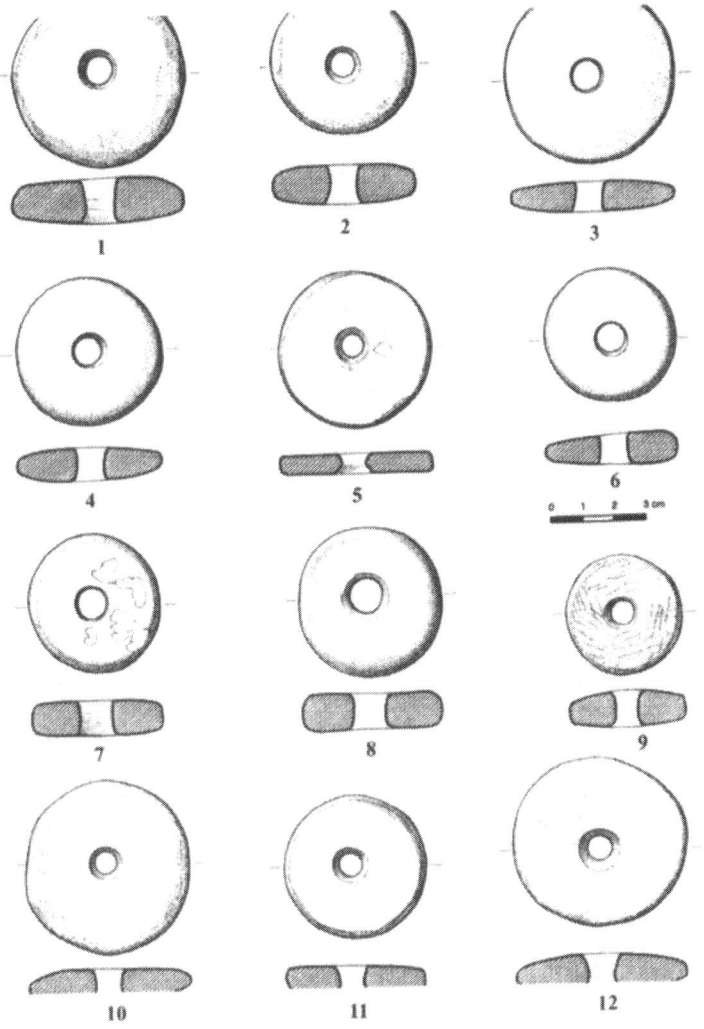

No.	Artifact	Reg. No.	Locus	Basket	Stratum	Description
1	spindle whorl	57/92	1505	5617	2c	limestone
2	spindle whorl	49/90	946	2701	2c	limestone
3	spindle whorl	19/91	1121	3673	2b	limestone
4	spindle whorl	19/91	1111	3553	2c	limestone (burned)
5	spindle whorl	49/90	803	2219	2a	ferruginous limestone
6	spindle whorl	57/92	751	5412	1	limestone
7	spindle whorl	49/90	503	1015	1	limestone
8	spindle whorl	19/91	1061	3617	2c	limestone
9	spindle whorl	49/90	880	2544	2b	chalk
10	spindle whorl	19/91	1064	3473	2a	chlorite-schist
11	spindle whorl	57/92	1505	5618	2c	chlorite-schist
12	spindle whorl	19/91	626	5106	2b	chlorite-schist

Figure 12.31. Gilat ground stone artifacts.

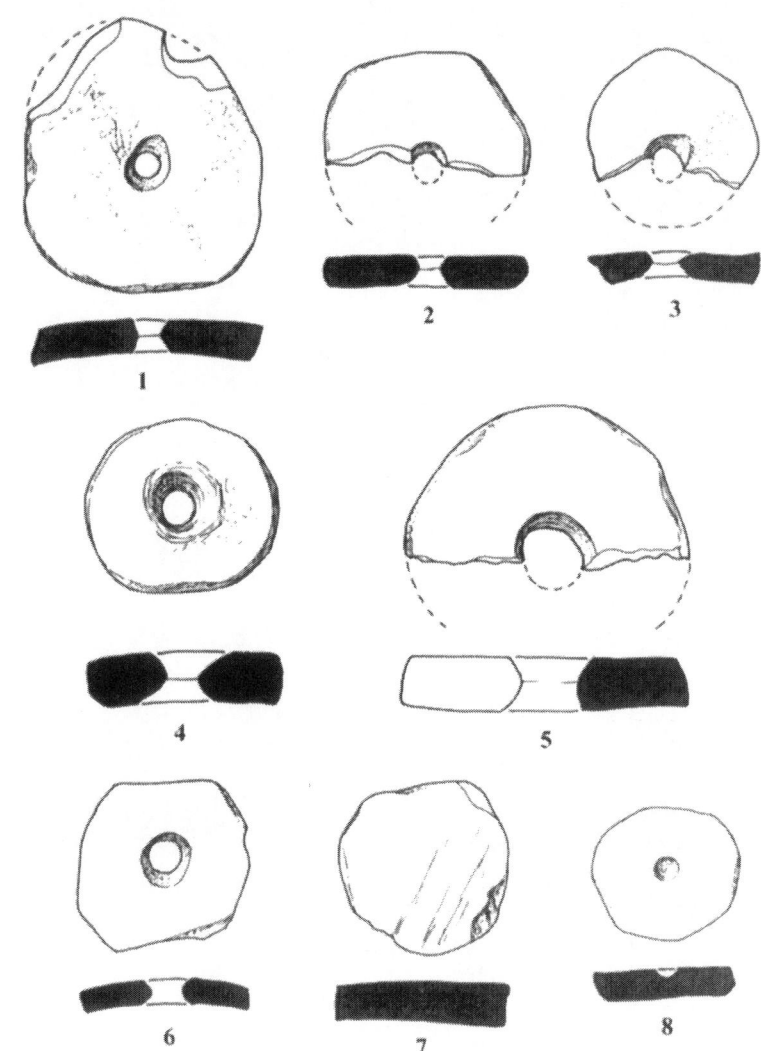

No.	Artifact	Reg. No.	Locus	Basket	Stratum	Description
1	spindle whorl	568				ceramic, vessel sherd with ground edges
2	spindle whorl fragment					ceramic, vessel sherd with ground edges
3	spindle whorl fragment					ceramic, vessel sherd with ground edges
4	spindle whorl					ceramic, vessel sherd with ground edges
5	spindle whorl fragment					ceramic, vessel sherd with ground edges
6	spindle whorl?					ceramic, vessel sherd with ground edges
7	spindle whorl blank?					ceramic, vessel sherd with ground edges, no drill marks
8	spindle whorl					ceramic, vessel sherd with ground edges, unifacial drill mark

Figure 12.32. Gilat ground stone artefacts (basalt vessels).

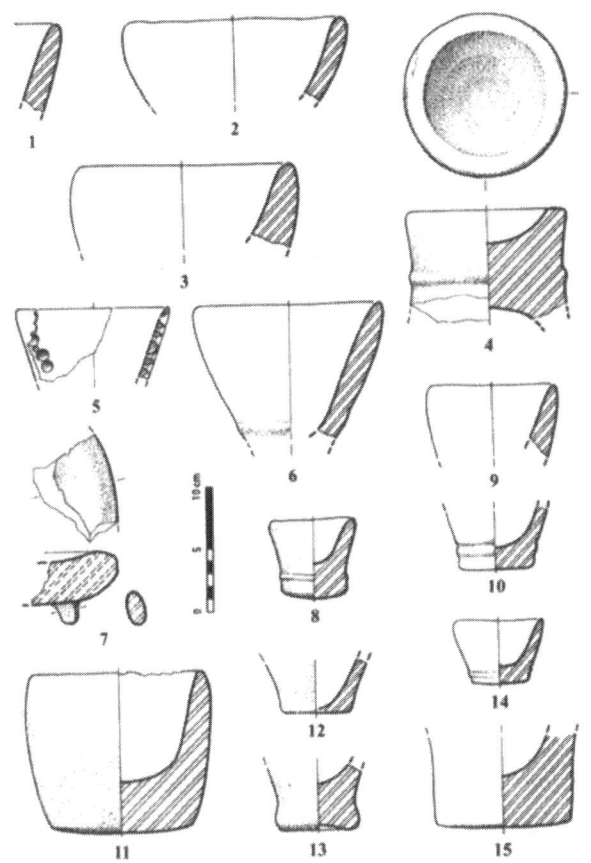

No.	Artifact	Reg. No.	Locus	Basket	Stratum	Description
1	rim fragment	19/91	704	5313	2b	basalt, open form, round rim
2	rim fragment	57/92	755	5423	2b/c	basalt, convex walls
3	rim fragment	57/92	786	5667	2c	basalt, bowl/mortar
4	fenestrated stand?	57/92	763	5532	2b	basalt, probably medial section of fenestrated stand; 'rim' re-ground, single band in relief
5	wall fragment	57/92	797	5803	2c	basalt, multiple drilled holes, for repair?
6	rim fragment	49/90	025	3131	3	basalt, faint medial band
7	footed platter?	57/92	755	5441	2b/c	scoria, knob or foot?
8	complete cup					basalt, single band in relief; re-ground fenestrated stand?
9	rim fragment	57/92	753	5407	2b	basalt
10	fenestrated stand?	49/90	018	3063	2b	basalt, re-ground medial section of fenestrated stand?
11	mortar/bowl	727/338	124?	338?	2c?	basalt?
12	base fragment	727/297	91?	297?	2	basalt, bowl base, hole worn through base
13	base fragment	727/413	155?	413?	4?	basalt, low pedestaled base fragment
14	complete cup	49/90	850	2533	2bii	basalt, single band in relief; re-ground fenestrated stand?
15	base fragment	49/90	840	2580	2a	basalt, thick bowl base

Figure 12.33. Gilat ground stone artifacts, basalt vessels.

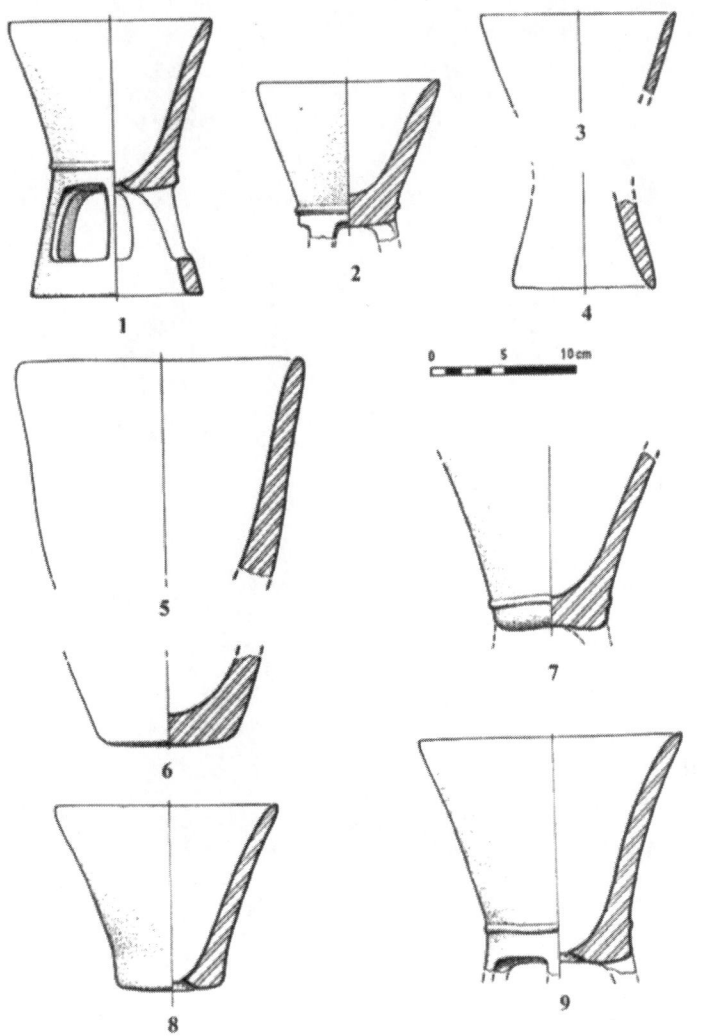

No.	Artifact	Reg. No.	Locus	Basket	Stratum	Description
1	fenestrated stand	57/92	1344	4301	2b	complete, hole through well, single medial band in relief
2	fenestrated stand	57/92	1572	5857	3a	upper section, single medial band in relief
3	rim fragment		42?	95?	3	thin, well-ground
4	rim fragment?	568/44	22?	44?	3	thin, well-ground, rim slightly ground flat
5	rim, deep bowl	19/91	640	5147	3b	undecorated
6	bowl base	57/92	1554	5817	2c/3a	well-ground
7	fenestrated stand	49/90	044	3150	2b	broken legs completely re-ground, single medial band in relief
8	bowl	36/87	270	567	2c	complete, hole worn through base
9	fenestrated stand	49/90	986	2838	2bi	upper section, single medial band in relief, hole worn through base

Figure 12.34. Gilat ground stone artefacts (standing stone?).

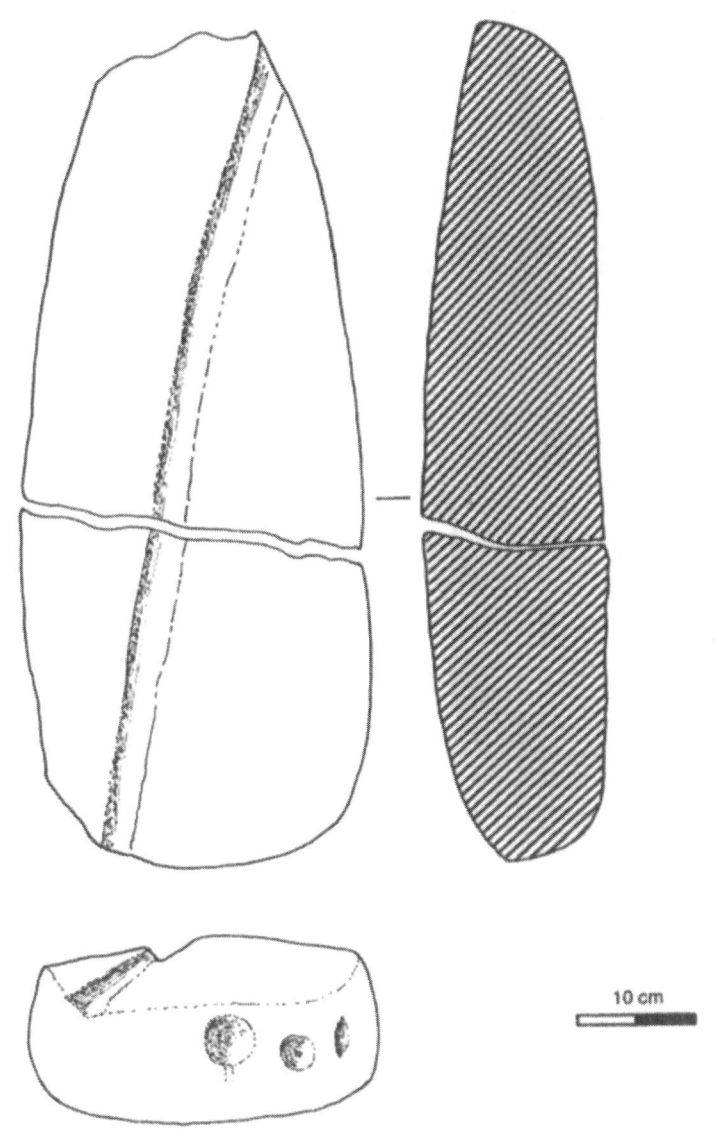

10 cm

No.	Artifact	Reg. No.	Locus	Basket	Stratum	Description
1	standing stone??	568-14	none	none	0	chalk, grooved, holes drilled in base

References

Adams J. (1989) Methods for improving ground stone artifacts analysis: experiments in mano wear patterns. In *Experiments in Lithic Technology*, edited by D.S. Amick and R.P. Mauldin. BAR International Series 528. Oxford: British Archaeological Reports, pp. 259–76.

Alon, D. (1990) Cult artifacts from Gilat and relations with Northern Edom in the Chalcolithic Period. *'Atiqot* 10:1–2*; 1–12 (Heb.)

Alon, D. and Levy, T.E. (1989) The archaeology of cult and the Chalcolithic sanctuary at Gilat. *Journal of Mediterranean Archaeology* 2/2:163–221.

Alon, D. and Yekutieli, Y. (1995) The Tel Halif Terrace 'Silo Site' and its implications for Early Bronze Age I. *'Atiqot* 27: 149–90.

Amiran, R., Paran, U., Shiloh, Y., Brown, R., Tsafrir, Y., and Ben-Tor, A. (1978) *Early Arad*. Jerusalem: Israel Exploration Society.

Amiran, R., and Porat, N. (1984) The basalt vessels of the Chalcolithic period and Early Bronze Age I. *Tel Aviv* 11:11–19.

Ayrton, E.R. and Loat, W.L.S. (1911) *Pre-dynastic Cemetery at El Mahasna*. Egypt Exploration Fund Memoirs 31. London: Egypt Exploration Fund.

Bar-Adon, P. (1980) *The Cave of the Treasure*. Jerusalem: Israel Exploration Society.

Bar-Yosef, O. (1998) Earliest Food Producers–Pre Pottery Neolithic (8000–5500). In *The Archaeology of Society in the Holy Land*, edited by T.E. Levy. London: Leicester University Press, pp. 190–204.

Barber, E.J.W. (1991) *Prehistoric Textiles*. Princeton: Princeton University Press.

Baumgartel, E.J. (1955) *The Cultures of Prehistoric Egypt I*. London: Oxford University Press.

Baumgartel, E.J. (1960) *The Cultures of Prehistoric Egypt II*. London: Oxford University Press.

Beck, H.C. (1928) Classification and nomenclature of beads and pendants. *Archaeologia* LXXVII:1–76.

Ben-Dor, I. (1936) Jericho: City and Necropolis (Report for Sixth and Concluding Season, 1936). Pottery of the Middle and Late Neolithic Periods. *Annals of Archaeology and Anthropology* XXIII: 77–90.

Bernbeck, J.E. (1999) Structure strikes back: Intuitive Meanings of Ceramics from Qale Rostam, Iran. In *Material Symbols: Culture and Economy in Prehistory*, edited by J.E. Robb. Carbondale: Southern Illinois University, pp. 90–111.

Betts, A., van der Borg, K., de Jong, A., McClintock, C., and van Strydonck, M. (1994) Early cotton in north Arabia. *Journal of Archaeological Science* 21:489–99.

Braun, E. (1985) *En Shadud: Salvage Excavations at a Farming Community in the Jezreel Valley, Israel*. BAR International Series 249. Oxford: British Archaeological Reports.

— (1990) Basalt bowls of the EB I horizon in the southern Levant. *Paleorient* 16(1):87–96.

— (1997) *Yiftah'el. Salvage and Rescue Excavations at a Prehistoric Village in Lower Galilee, Israel*. Jerusalem: Israel Antiquities Authority.

Brunton, G. (1937) *Mostegedda and the Tasian Culture*. London: Bernard Quaritch.

Brunton, G. and Caton-Thompson, G. (1928) *The Badarian Civilisation and Prehistoric Remains near Badari*. London: Quaritch.

Caton-Thompson, G. (1934) *The Desert Fayum*. London: Royal Anthropological Institute.

Cialowicz, K.M. (1989) Predynastic mace-heads in the Nile Valley. In *Late Prehistory of the Nile Basin and the Sahara*, edited by L. Kryzyzaniak and M. Kobusiewicz. Poznan: Poznan Archaeological Museum, pp. 261–6.

Commenge, C. (in press) *Le Mobilier des Sites de Beersheva. Neguev Septentrional, Israel*. Cahiers du Centre de Recherche Francais de Jerusalem 9. Paris: Association Paleorient.

Dayan, Y. (1969) Tell Turmus in the Huleh Valley. *Israel Exploration Journal* 19:65–78.

Dollfus, G., Z. Kafafi, J. Rewerski, N. Vaillant, E. Coqueugniot, J. Desse and R. Neef (1988) Abu Hamid, an early fourth millennium site in the Jordan Valley. In *The Prehistory of Jordan*, edited by A. Garrard and H.G. Gebel). BAR International Series 396. Oxford: British Archaeological Reports, pp. 567–601.

Dorrell, P. (1983) Appendix A: Stone vessels, tools and objects. In *Jericho V*, edited by K. Kenyon and T.A. Holland London: British School of Archaeology in Jerusalem, pp. 485–575.

Dothan, M. (1957) Excavations at Meser, 1956. Preliminary report on the first season. *Israel Exploration Journal* 7: 217–28.

— (1959a) Excavations at Horvat Beter (Beersheba). *'Atiqot* 2:1–42. (English series).

— (1959b) Excavations at Meser, 1957. Preliminary report on the second season. *Israel Exploration Journal* 9: 13–29.

Fitzgerald G.M. (1935) The Earliest Pottery of Beth Shan. *The Museum Journal* XXIV(1):5–32.

Foreman, R. (1978) Disc beads: Production by primitive techniques. *The Bead Journal* 3:17–22.

Fox, N.S. (1995) The striped Goddess from Gilat: Implications for the Chalcolithic Cult. *Israel Exploration Journal* 45(4):212–25.

Galili, E. and M. Weinstein-Evron (1985) Prehistory and paleoenvironments of submerged sites along the Carmel Coast of Israel. *Paleorient* 11/1:37–52.

Gilead, I. (1995) *Grar: A Chalcolithic Site in the Northern Negev.* Beersheva: Ben-Gurion University of the Negev Press.

Goodwin, A.J.H. (1947) The bored stones of South Africa. *Annals of the South African Museum* 37:1–210.

Gopher, A. and Greenberg, R. (1996) The Pottery Neolithic levels. In *Dan I: A Chronicle of the Excavations, the Pottery Neolithic, the Early Bronze Age, and the Middle Bronze Age Tombs*, edited by A. Biran. Jerusalem: Nelson Glueck School of Biblical Archaeology, pp. 67–81.

Gopher, A. and Tsuk, T. (1996) The Chalcolithic assemblage. In *The Nahal Qanah Cave: Earliest Gold in the Southern Levant*, edited by A. Gopher). Tel Aviv: Tel Aviv University, pp. 91–138.

Gophna, R. and Lifshitz, S. (1980) A Chalcolithic burial cave at Palmahim. *'Atiqot* XIV:1–8.

Goren, Y. (1991) Phosphorite vessels of the 4th millennium B.C. in the southern Levant: New data, new interpretations. *Journal of the Israel Prehistoric Society* 24: 102–11.

Grigson, C. (1987) Shiqmim: Pastoralism and other aspects of animal management in the Chalcolithic of the Northern Negev. In *Shiqmim I: Studies Concerning Chalcolithic Societies in the Northern Negev Desert, Israel*, edited by T.E. Levy. BAR International Series 356. Oxford: British Archaeological Reports, pp. 219–79.

Guy, P.L.O. and Engberg, R. (1938) *Megiddo Tombs.* Chicago: University of Chicago Press.

Hartenberg, R.S and Schmidt, J., Jr. (1969) The Egyptian drill and the origin of the crank. *Technology and Culture* 10:155–65.

Hassan, F.A. (1985) Radiocarbon chronology of Neolithic and Predynastic sites in Upper Egypt and the Delta. *The African Archaeological Review* 3:95–116.

Helms, S.W. (1991) Other Finds. In *Excavations at Jawa 1972–1986 Stratigraphy, Pottery and Other Finds*, edited by A.V.G. Betts. Edinburgh: Edinburgh University Press, pp. 155–67.

Hennessy, J. (1969) Preliminary report on the first season of excavations at Teleilat Ghassul. *Levant* 1:1–24.

Hoffman, M.A. (1991) *Egypt Before the Pharaohs.* Austin: University of Texas Press.

Hovers, E. (1996) The ground stone industry. In *Excavations at the City of David 1978–1985, Vol. IV*, edited by D.T. Ariel and A. De Groot. Jerusalem: Hebrew University, pp. 171–203.

Kantor, H. (1949) Book review of 'The Cultures of Prehistoric Egypt' by E.J. Baumgartel. *American Journal of Archaeology* 53:76–79.

Kaplan, J. (1963) Excavations at Benei Beraq, 1951. *Israel Exploration Journal* 13:300–12.

— (1969) Ein el Jarba: Chalcolithic remains in the Plain of Esdraelon. *Bulletin of the American School for Oriental Research* 194:2–39.

el-Khouli, A.A.-R.H (1978) *Egyptian Stone Vessels Predynastic Period to Dynasty III: Typology and Analysis.* Mainz am Rhein: von Zabern.

Koeppel, R. (1940) *Teleilat Ghassul II.* Rome: Pontifical Biblical Institute.

Lee, J.R. (1973) Chalcolithic Ghassul: New Aspects and Master Typology. Unpublished PhD dissertation, Hebrew University.

Leonard, A., Jr. (1992) The Jordan Valley Survey, 1953: some unpublished soundings conducted by James Mellaart. *Annual of the American Schools of Oriental Research* 50. Winona Lake: Eisenbrauns.

Levy, T.E. (1998) Cult, metallurgy, and rank societies–Chalcolithic Period (ca. 4500–3500 BCE). In *The Archaeology of Society in the Holy Land*, edited by T.E. Levy. London: Leicester University Press, pp. 226–44.

Levy, T.E., and D. Alon (1987) Excavations in Shiqmim Cemetery 3: Final Report on the 1982 Excavations. In *Shiqmim I: Studies Concerning Chalcolithic Societies in the Northern Negev Desert, Israel*, edited by T.E. Levy. BAR International Series 356. Oxford: British Archaeological Reports, pp. 333–5

Levy, T.E., and A. Holl (1987) Theory and practice in household archaeology: A case study from the Chalcolithic village at Shiqmim. In *Shiqmim I: Studies Concerning Chalcolithic Societies in the Northern Negev Desert, Israel*, edited by T.E. Levy. BAR International Series 356. Oxford: British Archaeological Reports, pp. 373–410.

Liu, R.K. (1978) Spindle whorls Part I: Some comments and speculations. *The Bead Journal* 3: 87–103.

MacDonald, E. (1932) Prehistoric Fara. *Beth Pelet II*. London: British School of Archaeology in Egypt.

Mallon, A., Koeppel, R.and Neuville, R. (1934) *Teleilat Ghassul I*. Rome: Pontifical Biblical Institute.

Needler, W. (1984) *Predynastic and Archaic Egypt in the Brooklyn Museum*. New York: Brooklyn Museum.

North, R.N. (1961) *Ghassul 1960: Excavation Report*. Analecta Biblica 14. Rome: Pontifical Biblical Institute.

Peet, T.E. (1914) *The Cemeteries of Abydos Part II. 1911–1912*. London: The Egypt Exploration Fund.

Perrot, J. (1955) Excavations at Tell Abu Matar near Beersheba. *Israel Exploration Journal* 5:17–40, 73–84, 167–89.

— (1957) Les fouilles d'Abou Matar pres de Beersheba. *Syria* 34:1–38.

— (1979) *Syria-Palestine I. From the Origins to the Bronze Age*. (Trans. by J. Hogarth). Geneva: Nagel.

Perrot, J. and Ladiray, D. (1980) *Tombes a ossuaires de la région côtière Palestinniene au IVe millénaire avant l'ère chrètienne*. Paris: Association Paléorient.

Perrot, J., Zori, N., and Reich, Y. (1967) Neve Ur, un nouvel aspect du Ghassoulien. *Israel Exploration Journal* 17:201–32.

Petrie, W.M.F. 1896) *Naqada and Ballas*. Warminster: Aris and Philips Ltd.

— (1901) *Diospolis Parva: The Cemeteries of Abadiyeh and Hu*. The Egypt Exploration Fund, Memoir 20. London: Egypt Exploration Fund.

— (1921) *Prehistoric Egypt: Corpus of Prehistoric Pottery and Palettes*. Reprint of 1920–21 original. Warminster: Aris and Philips Ltd.

Prausnitz, M.W. (1969) The excavations at Kabri. *Eretz Israel* IX:122–29 (Hebrew, English Summary p. 137). Jerusalem: Israel Exploration Society.

— (1970) *From Hunter to Farmer and Trader*. Jerusalem: Sivan Press.

Rizkana, I. and Seeher, J. (1988) *Maadi II: The Lithic Industries of the Predynastic Settlement*. Mainz: von Zabern.

Roodenberg, J.J. (1986) *Le Mobilier en Pierre de Bouqras*. Leiden: Nederlands Instituut voor het Nabije Oosten.

Rosen, S.A. (1997) *Lithics After the Stone Age. A Handbook of Stone Tools from the Levant*. Walnut Creek, CA.

Roshwalb, A. (1981) Protohistory in Wadi Ghazzeh: a Typological and Technological Study Based on the Macdonald Excavations. Unpublished PhD dissertation. University of London.

Roux, V. (1985) *Le Materiel de broyage: etude ethnoarcheologique a Tichitt (R.I. Mauritanie)*. Paris: Editions Recherche sur les Civilisations, Memoire no. 58.

Rowan, Y.M. (forthcoming a) The ground stone assemblage of Qiryat 'Ata. Excavations at Qiryat 'Ata. Israel Antiquity Authority Reports. Jerusalem.

— (forthcoming b) The ground stone assemblage. *Excavations at Tel En-Assawir*. Israel Antiquity Authority Reports. Jerusalem.

— (in press a) Use-wear analysis of the palettes from Abu Matar and Bir es-Safadi. In *Le Mobilier des Sites de Beersheva. Neguev Septentrional, Israel*, edited by C. Commenge. Cahiers du Centre de Recherche Francais de Jerusalem no. 9. Paris: Association Paléorient.

— (in press b) Basalt bowls and ground stone assemblage. In *Shoham (North), Lod Valley, Israel: Excavations of Three Chalcolithic Burial Caves*, edited by E.C.M. van den Brink and R. Gophna. Israel Antiquity Authority Reports.

— (1998) Ancient Distribution and Deposition of Prestige Objects: Basalt Vessels During Late Prehistory in the Southern Levant. Unpublished PhD dissertation, University of Texas at Austin, Austin.

Schaub, R.T., and Rast, W.E. (1989) *Bab edh-Dhra. Excavations in the Cemetery Directed by Paul W. Lapp (1965–1967)*. Winona Lake: Eisenbrauns.

Schick, T. (1998) Red ochre: The material and its cultural background. In *The Cave of the Warrior*, edited by T. Schick. Jerusalem: Israel Antiquities Authority, pp. 63–4.

Schmandt-Besserat, D. (1980) Ochre in prehistory. In *The Coming of the Age of Iron*, edited by T.A Wertime and J.D. Muhly, pp. 127–50.

— (1992) *Before Writing*. Volumes I and II. Austin: University of Texas Press.

Sebbane, M. n.d. Ground stone assemblage from Arad.

Seger, J.D. (1988) The objects. In *Gezer V*, edited by J.D. Seger and H.D. Lance. Jerusalem: Hebrew Union College/Nelon Glueck School of Biblical Archaeology, pp. 34–6.

Ussishkin, D. (1980) The Ghassulian Shrine at En-Gedi. *Tel Aviv* 7:1–44.

Valla, F. (1998) The first settled societies–Natufian (12,500–10,200 BP). In *The Archaeology of Society in the Holy Land*, edited by T.E. Levy. London: Leicester University Press, pp. 169–87.

van den Brink, E.C.M. (in prep) Peqi'in Cave. The Chalcolithic Ground Stone Assemblage: Basalt Vessels.

van den Brink, E.C.M., Rowan, Y.M., and Braun, E. (1999) Pedestalled basalt bowls of the Chalcolithic: New variations. *Israel Exploration Journal* 49/3-...4:161–83.

van den Brink, E.C.M., and T.E. Levy (eds) (2002) *Egypt and the Levant: Interrelations from the 4th through the Early 3rd Millennium B.C.E. New Approaches to Anthropological Archaeology*. London and New York: Continuum.

Van der Merwe, N.J. (1987) Comment on Hromnik's bored stones. *The South African Archaeological Bulletin* 42:68–69.

Waldron, S.R. (1987) Weighted digging sticks in Ethiopia. *The South African Archaeological Bulletin* 42: 69–71.

Ward, W.A. (1964) Relations between Egypt and Mesopotamia from prehistoric times to the end of the Middle Kingdom. *Journal of the Economic and Social History of the Orient*. 7(1):1–45.

Wright, K. (1992a) Ground Stone Assemblage Variations and Subsistence Strategies in the Levant, 22,000–5,500 B.P. Unpublished PhD dissertation, Yale University.

— (1992b) A classification system for ground stone tools from the prehistoric Levant. *Paleorient* 18(2):53–81.

— (1993) Early Holocene ground stone assemblages in the Levant. *Levant* XXV:93–111.

— (1994) Ground-stone tools and hunter-gatherer subsistence in Southwest Asia: Implications for the transition to farming. *American Antiquity* 59(2):238–63.

13 The Worked Bone from the Chalcolithic Site of Gilat:

Interim Report

Caroline Grigson

Introduction

The intention of the present study is to establish which types of bone tools were present at Gilat, to quantify them, to look for diachronic change, and to discuss the function of the tools in the lives of the occupants in terms of craft and ritual activity. Comparison with bone tools from other Chalcolithic sites in the Negev and with some earlier assemblages in the Levant has necessitated drawing up a new scheme of classification of bone tools, based on those already existing, but with additions and modifications. The report is interim to the extent that traces of wear caused by the initial manufacture of the tools and by subsequent use have not been studied, although useful additional information might be gained from a microscopical examination such as that carried out by Campana (1989) on Natufian tools in the Levant. But it is more than a preliminary study as a new bone tool typology has been constructed based on a careful metric and stylistic study of the assemblage carried out in England.

Layout and Stratigraphy

Four main strata were identified at Gilat—IV, III, II and I, with III being sub-divided into IIIA and IIIB, and II into IIA, IIB and IIC. Stratum IV is the earliest and may be Late Neolithic (Wadi Rabah); each of the sub-strata IIIB, IIIA, IIC, IIB and IIA represents a successive period of time within the Chalcolithic. The eight radio carbon dates obtained (see Table 5.3) are confined to Sub-strata IIIA, IIC, IIB and IIA; two probably anomalous dates fall in the third millennium BC (uncalibrated), but the remainder lie within the first half of the fourth millennium (uncalibrated), or early fifth millennium BC (calibrated). Stratum I is largely Chalcolithic, but was very disturbed by modern ploughing. More details of the depositional history of the site are given in Chapter 5. It is hoped that more 14C dates will be forthcoming from Gilat. However, given that the nearby site of Grar (Gilead 1995) produced no radiocarbon dates, the small sample from Gilat does provide some radiometric means of linking our site to other Chalcolithic sites in the southern Levant (Burton and Levy 2001).

The unit for recording the finds was the locus, identified as some kind of feature within a particular area. Every locus was assigned to one of the 31 types of context recognized in the course of excavation, some relating to actual structures and others to fills of various kinds.

Worked Bone Retrieval

Many of the worked bones at Gilat are broken; some of the breakage seems to have occurred before deposition or *in situ*, but some seems to have occurred during excavation and retrieval. The problem with the retrieval of bone tools is that they are not always distinguished from unworked animal bones in the course of excavation; this is particularly true of epiphyses when they have been broken off the remainder of the tool. Such pieces were usually packed in with the animal bone and only those that show signs of working are likely to have been recognized during the faunal analysis.

Dry sieving, through a 5 mm mesh, was carried out on sediment from all pits, surfaces and any matrix associated with human burials—but even then retrieval was not 100 % efficient. The faunal study (Chapter 6, this volume) showed that many of the smallest bones were missed and this may be true of the bone tools, especially needles and tiny polished pieces, as well as small broken fragments. Nevertheless the worked bone assemblage from Gilat is important, not least because with 278 pieces it is one of the largest from the Chalcolithic to have been studied so far.

During the course of study, the worked bones were washed in a minimum quantity of water and dried very slowly for fear that removal of the calcium carbonate coating and gypsum crystals present on some of the worked bones would cause damage. To facilitate the study and curation of the collection, each bone tool was marked with a code indicating the site and the year of excavation, together with locus, basket and identification number.

Methods

Descriptions of all the bones with traces of working were entered initially into a *Lotus 123* spreadsheet, in which each bone had a unique identification number. The headings included site, year of excavation, area of site, locus, basket, excavation square, stratum, ID number, tool type, tool class, part present, tapered or parallel-sided, length, maximum breadth, shaft breadth, species, which bone, part of bone, left or right side of body, fusion of epiphysis, initial preparation, type of working, site of working and additional remarks. The analysis of the data involved sorting the spreadsheet data using *Microsoft Excel 5.0*. Additional manuscript notes were made on finds of particular interest.

Classification

A new classification of bone tools is set out in Box 13.1. It is based on the excellent scheme worked out by Garfinkel and Horwitz (1988) for the bone tools from the PPNB levels at Yiftahel, in which the main categories recognized were: points (A), spatulae (B), ornaments or beads (C) and varia (D). It was necessary to add two extra categories in the classification of the Gilat Chalcolithic material: smoothing tools as (D)—varia now being listed as (E)—and miscellaneous worked bone as (F). Other categories not represented at Gilat, such as sickle hafts, chisels, harpoons, gorgets and fish hooks were excluded. One important terminological distinction is that Garfinkel and Horwitz (1988) follow Bar-Yosef and Tchernov (1970) in using the term 'awl' only for points on what they describe as 'unworked shaft fragments' (A2), whereas the term is so widely used in almost all other reports on bone tools for the A3 category (that is 'halved metapodial shafts' in the Yiftahel classification, although they are not necessarily halved and may also be made from distal tibiae) that it has been retained for all the (A3) items in the present study.

A different wide-ranging scheme was used by Marshall (1982) in her classic work on the very large bone tool assemblage at Jericho, which dates from the PPNA to the Bronze Age; however she had very few tools of Chalcolithic date and the modified Yiftahel scheme is simpler and easier to follow. Stordeur (1979, 1982, 1988, 1995a, 1995b) has studied much of the bone tool material from Natufian and Pre-Pottery Neolithic sites in the northern Levant and has produced a classification which is rather different from the others, but in which most of the main categories set out below can be recognized. Yet another scheme is that of Campana (1989) who in his study of bone tools from the Natufian of the southern Levant and the Proto-Neolithic of the Zagros recognised some, though by no means all, of the main categories in the present scheme (Box 13.1).

Box 13.1. A new classification of bone tools in the Levant based on the scheme devised for the PPNB levels at Yiftahel by Garfinkel and Horwitz (1988)

A = POINTS

A1 = Solid points

large mammal long bone or antler, worked all over, pointed at one or both ends (Fig. 13.2: A & B).

A2 = Irregular points

A2/1 - partially worked irregular points, unworked at handle end, vertically split, only tip worked, shaft thin, broad, tapering to the pointed tip, but irregularly.

A2/2 - totally worked irregular points, vertically split, worked all over, shaft thin, broad, tapering to the pointed tip, but irregularly (Fig. 13.2: C)

A3 = Awls

A3/1 - parallel-sided awls, usually sheep or goat metapodial, vertically split, includes half epiphysis (usually distal) as handle end, polish on outer surface, edges and point, medium or thin (except handle), broad, edges parallel, tip shouldered and wide angled (Fig. 13.2: D & E).

A3/2 - tapered awls with entire epiphysis, usually sheep or goat distal tibia, split diagonally, includes entire epiphysis as the handle end, thick, broad, tapering, tip continuous with taper, i.e. no shoulder (Fig. 13.2: F)

A3/3 - tapered awls with part epiphysis, usually sheep or goat distal tibia; as A3/2 but split vertically, includes half epiphysis as the handle end, medium thickness, broad, tapering, tip continuous with taper i.e. no shoulder (Fig. 13.2: G).

A4 = Points on shaft

A4/1 - single point on shaft, usually sheep or goat long bone shaft, without epiphysis, split vertically, worked all over; medullary cavity almost entirely obliterated, thin, narrow, edges parallel, tip shouldered and wide angled (less than in A3/1), handle end rounded (Fig. 13.2: H).

A4/2 - bipoints, usually sheep or goat long bone shaft without epiphysis, split vertically, worked all over; medullary cavity almost or entirely obliterated, thin, narrow, edges tapering, tip continuous with taper (i.e. no shoulder), handle end also pointed (but often only one end preserved) (Fig. 13.2: I). Small bipoints are usually termed gorgets (Campana 1989), but none were recognized at Gilat.

A4/3 - needles, usually sheep or goat long-bone shaft, without epiphysis, split vertically, worked all over, medullary cavity entirely obliterated, very thin and narrow, edges parallel or slightly tapering, tip continuous with taper (i.e. no shoulder), handle end rounded and perforated (Fig. 13.2: J).

A4/4 - bodkins, as A4/3 but wider.

A5 = Broken tips of points or awls of uncertain type

usually sheep or goat long-bone shaft, no epiphysis.

B = SPATULAE

Flat, spatulate tools with a rounded working end.

B1 = Perforated spatulae (none found at Gilat).

sometimes referred to as needle shuttles.

B2 = Narrow spatulae

on ribs of small mammals (e.g. fox), <10mm broad.

B3 = Medium spatulae

on ribs of medium mammals (e.g. sheep, goat or gazelle), 10–15mm broad.

B4 = Broad spatulae

on ribs or long-bone strips of large mammals (e.g. cattle), >15mm broad. Broken examples may not be distinguishable from perforated spatulae (B1).

B4/1 - spatulae made from unsplit ribs, polished both sides

B4/2 - spatulae made from split ribs, trabecular bone extant on one side, polished one or both sides (Fig. 13.3: A)

B4/3 - spatulae made from long-bone strips.

C = *ORNAMENTS and BEADS*

None found at Gilat.

D = SMOOTHING TOOLS

D1 = large bevelled tools

usually referred to as polishers, usually made from cattle long bones - distal or proximal metapodial, proximal radius or distal tibia. Epiphysis forms handle, with shaft tapering towards a rounded bevelled tip. Tip and inner part of shaft often highly polished. Outer surface and handle sometimes polished. Often only the tip survives (Fig. 13.2: C).

D/2 = small bevelled tools

usually referred to as burnishers, usually made from sheep or goat long-bones. Epiphysis forms handle, with shaft tapering towards a rounded bevelled tip. Often only the tip survives.

E = VARIA

(Fig. 13.3: D-G).

F = MISCELLANEOUS WORKED BONES

Usually fragmentary bones with traces of working or polishing, which cannot be assigned to type.

Bone Tools at Gilat and Other Chalcolithic Sites

The total number of bone tools excavated at Gilat was 278; the numbers of each type found in each of the strata and substrata are set out in Table 13.1 and summarized as percentages in Figure 13.1. Each type will now be discussed individually.

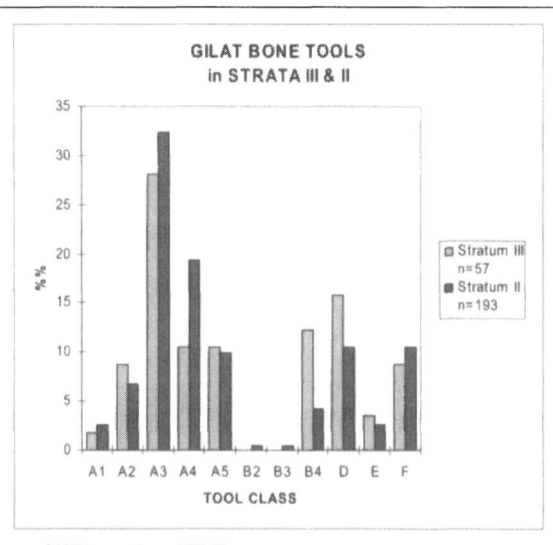

Figure 13.1. Bone Tool Distribution for Strata III and II from Gilat.

A1. Solid Points

Six solid points made from long-bone shafts, all probably of cattle, were found at Gilat; most could not be identified to bone element, but one included the proximal end of a metatarsal of an ox (Fig. 13.3: B). The seventh point (BT 206, L. 154, a pit, Sub-stratum IIIA, Area T, Fig. 13.2: A) was of much the same form, but very unusual in that it appears to have been made from an ostrich bone. It has not been possible to identify the actual bone element as no sectioned ostrich bones were available for comparison—this tentative identification is based on the very dense, smooth texture of the bone. It was 9.9 cm long, with a maximum width of 2.6 cm, and with patchy areas of polish.

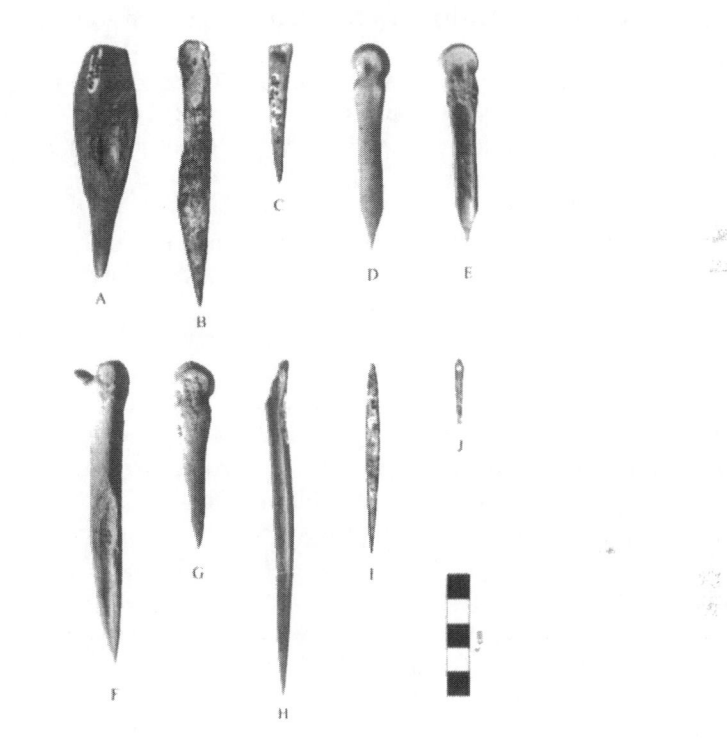

Figure 13.2. Bone Tools from Gilat.

A2. Irregular Points

Most of the 20 irregular points at Gilat could be assigned to subtype A2/1 or A2/2 (Fig. 13.2: C) with roughly equal numbers of each evenly scattered through the strata. All seem to have been made from sheep or goat long-bones. Irregular points are referred to by Campana (1989) as 'coarse perforators'.

A3. Awls

At least 86 (31%) of the bone tools from Gilat have been classed as awls, making them the most numerous tool type. The division of awls into several sub-types has already been suggested by Stordeur (1988, 1995a). She distinguishes between points which are vertically split ('Poinçon à poignée intégrée naturelle partielle sur os fendu longitudinalement') equivalent to my categories A3/1 and A3/3, and those in which the epiphysis is entire and the shaft is split diagonally ('Poinçon à poignée intégrée naturelle entière'), the equivalent of A3/2. Campana (1989) also recognises the difference between points which he calls most robust, that is points in which the epiphysis is entire, and smaller, lighter tools in which the epiphysis has been split lengthwise.

The main characteristic of A3/1 is that the shaft of the tool is parallel-sided and shouldered at the tip so that the angle between the sides of the tip is large, even though the extreme point may be sharp (Fig. 13.2: D and E). This means that, unlike the other sorts of awl and points, they could have only pierced holes of small diameter. They may have been used to aid the weaving of weft fibres between the warp fibres, in the weaving of reeds or coarse vegetable fibres in mats or similar items, or in weaving wool or linen fabrics. Thirty-two awls of type A3/1 were found at Gilat and were the most numerous type of tool; the original number was almost certainly much higher as many of the awls and points (types A3 and A5) that were too damaged to be assigned to sub-type must on grounds of probability have been of this type.

In sub-types A3/2 (Fig. 13.2: F) and A3/3 (Fig. 13.2: G) the tip and shaft form a continuous taper, but A3/2 have an entire epiphysis (usually distal) as the handle end, whereas in A3/3 the epiphysis has been split; consequently these tools are rather flat. It is probable that these were true awls used for piercing materials, particularly leather, by means of a rotary movement, as suggested by Campana (1989). The broad handle end of sub-type A3/2 would have facilitated the piercing action by improving the transmission of power from the hand. With 7 and 10 occurrences respectively these two types were not particularly common at Gilat, but these figures would be increased if more of the awls and points of types A3 and A5 could be assigned to sub-type.

Bone awls of all three types described simply as points were found at Grar (Gilead 1995: Fig. 8.5, nos. 4, 11, 12 and 13) and were also present in virtually all Chalcolithic and Neolithic sites in which bone tools have been analyzed. They were particularly common in the Chalcolithic of Site O in the Nahal Besor (Wadi Gaza - MacDonald 1932) and two were present in the Chalcolithic level at Arad (Amiran 1978). Awls of sub-types A3/2 and A3/3 are illustrated by Mallon *et al.* (1934: Fig. 30, nos. 3–6) from Teleilat Ghassul, by Bar Adon (1980: Ill. 51) at the Cave of the Treasure, and by Hennessy (1969: Fig. 11, nos 1, 2, 8) at the renewed excavations at Teleilat Ghassul.

A4. Points on Shafts

These tools have been worked over the entire surface with the removal of the epiphyses and near obliteration of the medullary cavity. Sub-type A4/1 (Fig. 13.2: H) is pointed at one end and rounded at the other, A4/2 are bi-points—pointed at either end (Fig. 13.2: I). The function of both types is unknown although a wide variety of uses is possible—perhaps they were used as netting needles or in weaving. With 17 and about 12 examples respectively, they were quite common at Gilat.

The most spectacular find amongst the bone tools were the remains of four points of sub-type A4/1 (BT 121, 123-125) retrieved from the ash fill in the multi-use, 'ritual' pit (L. 1344, Sub-stratum IIBi, Area J) which also contained nine burnt horncores of male gazelles. Some of these seem not to have been recognized in excavation as their remains were packed in with the animal bones, and some parts were missing. They were made from long-bone shafts—probably of sheep or goat—and though they were too broken to be reconstructed *in toto*, one was 12.7 cm long and another was longer. The maximum width of each was just over 1 cm. Each of the points was highly polished on the outer face and edges and all were burnt to the colour of ebony. Their original function can only be guessed at; perhaps they were projectile points used to hunt the gazelles, although there is no sign of hafting. Clearly they had more than a utilitarian function in this very special deposit (see below).

At least one point of sub-type A4/1 or 4/2 was present at Grar (Gilead 1995: Fig.8.5, no.4), but it was too broken to be categorized further.

Needles (A4/3) are by their very nature likely to be broken before, during or after discard, so it is not surprising that only four were identified at Gilat (Fig. 13.2J). With a small hole piercing the blunt end they were obviously used in some form of sewing with a thin thread. A needle was part of the small bone tool assemblage found at the Nahal Qanah burial cave (Gopher and Tsuk 1996).

There was one definite, though broken, bodkin (A4/4) at Gilat that had a hole at one end. It was made from a long-bone shaft and its length exceeded 7 cm. There was also another broken piece which was probably part of a bodkin. Not surprisingly there were many broken tips of point or awls (type A5) at Gilat which could not be assigned to sub-type.

B. Flat Spatulate Tools

Spatulae of sub-type B1 are often called needle shuttles because they have a small perforation at one end and so were almost certainly used in weaving with thread, but not with coarser materials. This was true in the Chalcolithic at the Cave of the Treasure (Bar Adon 1980: Ill.50, no.2 and enlarged detail) where the hole of such an implement still contained a small length of thread and the implement itself was associated with the remains of a wooden ground loom (*ibid*. Ill. 56). Although no spatulae of this sub-type were recognised at Gilat, some of the damaged broad shuttles (B4) mentioned below may have been of this sub-type.

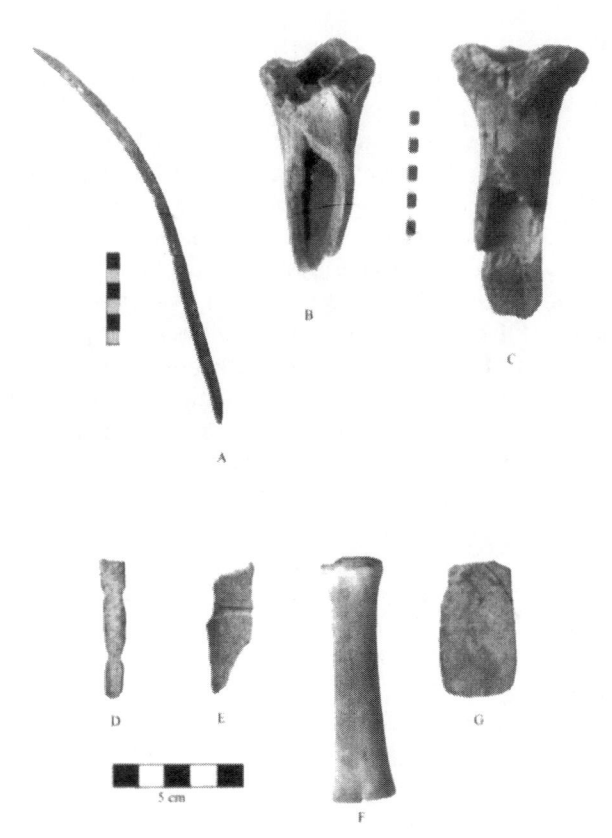

Figure 13.3. Worked Bone from Gilat.

A needle shuttle made on a rib was described and illustrated by MacDonald (1932, Pl. xxvi) from the Early Bronze IA Site H in the Nahal Besor, though described in the report as a netting mesh. Several from Teleilat Ghassul were illustrated by Mallon *et al.* (1934: Fig. 31, nos. 6, 7, 12–15) and by

Hennessy (1969: Fig. 11, no. 13), two from Horvat Beter by Dothan (1959: Fig. 18, nos. 40 and 44) and one from Shiqmim (Levy and Alon 1987: Fig. 6.11, no. 6). One of the needle shuttles at Teleilat Ghassul, had two holes, one at each end (Mallon, Koeppel and Neuville 1934: Fig. 30, no. 9). Needle shuttles were clearly usually a significant, if infrequent, part of the Chalcolithic bone tool kit.

Only one narrow (B2) and one medium (B3) spatula were found at Gilat, both made from long-bone shafts and probably of sheep or goat, but there were 16 large spatulae (B4) made from cattle ribs or long-bone shafts, of which six were un-split (B4/1) and seven were split (B4/2, Fig. 13.3: A). They were all neatly finished and were probably used in fine weaving for separating warp threads to facilitate the passage between them of weft threads. As some were broken it is possible that the missing parts were pierced, that is they were actually needle shuttles (see type B1 above). Three spatulae were found at Nahal Qanah (Gopher and Tsuk 1996).

C. Ornaments and Beads

No ornaments or bone beads were found at Gilat, although the plaque noted under varia should perhaps be considered under this heading.

D. Smoothing Tools

The remains of 36 polishers were found at Gilat, almost all consisting of small fragments of the working end. Five were of the smaller type (D2) made from sheep or goat long-bones. All the remaining 31 were of the large type (D1) made of cattle long-bones (Fig. 13.3: B and C); only five of these were at all complete. In each, the epiphysis formed the handle end and with the shaft tapering towards a highly polished bevelled tip. The lengths of these substantial tools varied from about 11 to 20 cm. Three were made from proximal radii, one from a proximal metatarsal and one from a distal tibia. This last polisher (BT 235) was retrieved from the ash fill in the 'multi-use pit' (L. 1344, Sub-stratum IIBi, Area J) which also contained nine burnt horncores of male gazelle and the four burnt points referred to above. It was burnt to a dark ebony colour and was highly polished.

Although polishers are almost always made from cattle bones, one on a distal metapodial of an equid is illustrated in the monograph on the classic Chalcolithic site of Teleilat Ghassul (Mallon *et al*. 1934: Fig. 31, no. 11). Identical tools of Type D formed a large proportion of the bone tool assemblage at Grar where they were referred to as polishers (Gilead 1995: Figs 8.5, nos. 1, 2 and 3, and Fig. 8.6, nos. 4, 5, 6 and 7) and another from one of the Beersheva sites is illustrated by Perrot (1968: Fig. 849).

E. Varia

The varia found at Gilat included:

BT 5 (L.1061, Stratum IIC) a highly polished long-bone of a sheep or goat, possibly a spatula (B2), but made from long-bone rather than rib (Fig. 13.3: D).

BT 10 (L. 16, Stratum IIB) a bone ring made from a section of a long-bone shaft, probably from a sheep or goat. It was polished all over the outer surface and was 5.3 mm in diameter.

BT 227 (L. 1320, Stratum IIC) a piece of long-bone shaft, probably of an ox, which had been ground flat all over forming a flat, oblong, rectangular plaque (Fig. 13.3: G). There were signs that a narrower extension or 'head' had been present, but was broken off. Although lacking decoration, it is similar in form to the complete plaque or amulet from Horvat Beter, described by Dothan (1959: Fig. 18, no. 59).

BT 87 (L. 524, Stratum II) a nearly complete proximal phalanx of an ox, with an oval hole right through it from the proximal end to the distal end.

BT 98 (L. 528, Stratum IIC) a nearly complete sheep metatarsal with two vertical grooves, one in the anterior face and one in the posterior face; perhaps a stage in bone working.

BT 165 (L. 1147, Stratum IIIA) a piece of long bone shaft, probably of sheep or goat with a circumferential groove, perhaps an intermediate stage in bone working (Fig. 13.3: E).

BT 218 (L. 1369, Stratum IIIA) is a polished metacarpal of a sheep or goat, lacking the distal end which appears to have been sawn off (Fig. 13.3: F).

F. Bones with some Degree of Working

Twenty-six bones showed some degree of working, but were too broken or damaged to be assigned to any bone tool type or sub-type.

Animal Species Utilized

It is hardly surprising that the raw material chosen for the manufacture of bone tools at Gilat (and elsewhere) is that which has the greatest tensile strength and density, that is the compact bone which forms the shafts of weight-bearing bones in those ungulates in which the limbs are elongated for speed, especially small bovids (sheep and goats, and gazelles in earlier sites) and large bovids (cattle). The relative rarity of tools made from perissodactyl, that is, equid, bones reflects the fact that their remains are usually present in very small numbers, so this potential raw material was only available in small amounts. The possible identification of a tool made from an ostrich (*Struthio camelus*) bone at Gilat is also a further example of the use of dense, weight-bearing bone, derived from the tibia of a heavy, bipedal and flightless bird which depends on speed to escape from predators.

Diachronic, Spatial and Contextual Analyses

Unlike the animal bones, in which the numbers of burnt and unburnt elements were unrelated to the burning or otherwise of the loci in which they were found, there does seem to have been a correlation between burning and context in the bone tools (Figure 13.2). These differences are significant in a 2 x 2 Chi square test, which suggests that many of the bone tools are in primary deposition. If that is the case, there may be some significance in the fact that while Stratum IV does not contain enough bone tools for comparison, the composition of the bone tool kits in Stratum III and Stratum II differs from each other (Table 13.1 and Figure 13.3). Points of various types predominate in both strata, but Stratum III contains more spatulae and burnishers than Stratum II, whereas Stratum II has more awls and points on shafts. This may be a functional difference, possibly related to a decline in leather working.

Deposition and Disposal

On first inspection the bone tools at Gilat appear to have been distributed haphazardly throughout the site. The high proportion found in pit contexts reflects their deposition in discard or refuse contexts; and, because of the relatively small number of bone tools, many loci lacked them altogether (see Chapter 14, this volume, for a full discussion of the spatial implications of the bone tools). The highest numbers were found in L. 528 (a pit) and L. 1044 (a pit), which had seven each, 1054 (a fill) 11, and L. 1344 (the pit with the gazelle horncores) five. There seems to be no particular significance in the relatively high number of bone tools in L. 528 (Sub-stratum IIC, Area Y), as this was a large ashy fill containing a pit with a poorly preserved, and possibly intrusive, human burial, and the same is true for the tools in L. 1044 (a pit in Sub-stratum IIBii, Area J) and L. 1054 (a fill in Sub-stratum IIIA, Area J). However the concentration of burnt tools in L. 1344 (a pit in Sub-stratum IIBi, Area J) is related to the deposit of burnt gazelle horncores and is of great interest. It is discussed further below.

The only deliberate deposit of bone tools seems to have been four points of sub-type A4/1 (BT 121, 123-125) and a burnt polisher (BT 235) retrieved from the ash fill in the 'multi-use pit' (L. 1344, Sub-stratum IIBi, Area J). This pit also contained nine burnt horncores of male gazelles, an animal figurine (cf. Chapter 15, this volume) and a fenestrated stand, all sealed beneath a clay cap (Chapter 5, this volume). All four points and the polisher were highly polished and burnt to the colour of ebony. The gazelle horncores are thought to be the remains of entire heads incinerated in a single episode and the points and polisher were probably burnt with them. Stordeur (1988) has established a sequence of colour change in bone when subject to different temperatures, she found that bone burns black between 525–625°C—so these items must have been exposed to very great heat. One wonders how such burning was produced. The points might have been projectile points used to hunt the gazelles, although there is no sign of hafting, and the polisher might have been used in the preparation of their skins. Clearly these tools in this very special deposit had more than a utilitarian function. As suggested in Chapter 5, the close location of this multi-use pit with the multiple human burial feature points to the ritual burning of the awls, the gazelle heads and the figurine.

Discussion

In order to discuss the use of bone tools in the Chalcolithic it is necessary to compare them with tools from earlier assemblages, when it might be supposed that different requirements resulted in different bone tool kits. So an attempt has been made in the following paragraphs to relate the tools excavated at Gilat with those found in earlier sites in the southern Levant from the Natufian to the Pottery Neolithic. Tracing the types of bone implements back in time in the Levant is sometimes limited by poor retrieval, small sample sizes, inconsistent terminology, scanty description and innumerate listings, but the main problem in relating the Chalcolithic to earlier assemblages is the dearth of material from the immediately preceding period, the Pottery Neolithic. Even at Jericho, with its large Pre-Pottery Neolithic samples, the Pottery Neolithic assemblage is so small as to be almost completely uninformative.

Some irregular points (A2) were excavated from Hayonim in the Natufian level and from Yiftahel in the PPNB, though described by the authors (Bar-Yosef and Tchernov 1970; Garfinkel and Horwitz 1988) as awls. They were also present at Jericho in the PPNA (Marshall 1982: Fig. 233). Stordeur (1988: Fig. 4) illustrates some partially worked irregular points from the Natufian of Mallaha in which only the tips were worked (A2/1) and makes the interesting observation that they were 'débité par percussion'. Little can be said about their function, except that they were probably used for making holes, especially in leather.

As already mentioned the distinction between awls which were vertically split through the epiphysis (A3/3) and those in which the epiphysis was entire and the shaft was split diagonally (A3/2) has been made by Stordeur (1988) in the Natufian at Mallaha and examples of each are illustrated in her Figures 2 and 3. A similar distinction was noted by Bar-Yosef and Tchernov (1970) at Hayonim Cave also in the Natufian and Valla (1995: Fig. 2) illustrates an awl of sub-type A3/3 from the Natufian. Marshall (1982: Figs 232, 249, 251) illustrates tools of the same sub-type from the PPNA, PPNB and Pottery Neolithic. Stordeur (1995a) also recognized both types in the PPNB levels at Aswad in Syria.

Clearly awls would have had a variety of uses, but those with sharp points and broad handles (A3/2) would have been most used in piercing materials such as leather, as Australian aborigines did into modern times, though the !Kung used bone awls for sewing (Sollas 1911). Awls are often described as weaving implements and they were probably also used to pierce or manipulate rushes and other fibrous materials in weaving, netting, mat-making or basketry (Campana 1989). It seems likely that these tools were used for a variety of tasks. Without detailed microscopic use-ware studies in the future, no definitive functions can be ascribed for these bone tools.

Awls of type A3/1, in which the main body of the tool is flat and parallel-sided and terminates in a shouldered point seem to have been first recognised in the present study, but they may have been present, even if unrecognized as a sub-type, in earlier assemblages. Such points might have been used in weaving, possible even weaving linen or wool.

Some points on shafts (A4/1) were noted by Stordeur (1988: Fig. 5) from Mallaha in the Natufian and many were excavated at Jericho in the PPNA (Marshall 1982: Fig. 234). There was only one at Yiftahel in the PPNB (Garfinkel and Horwitz 1988: Fig. 3, no. 1), but from the illustration it seems to be cruder in form and shorter than the burnt points at Gilat.

Bi-points (A4/2), apparently made from gazelle horncores, were noted from the Natufian at Hayonim cave by Bar-Yosef and Tchernov (1970), and many fine Natufian examples made from long-bones are illustrated by Stordeur (1988: Fig. 6) as well as by Valla (1995: Fig. 2). Bi-points of much the same form as those from Gilat were found in the PPNA at Jericho (Marshall 1982: Fig. 234).

Points on shafts and bi-points may have had a variety of function, but probably many were used as arrow or spear points in hunting.

Needles (A4/3) go back to at least the PPNA as shown by Marshall 1982 (Fig. 231, no. 12) at Jericho, where a great many pins (that is needles without holes) were also found. Two fine needles (A4/3 and a broad bodkin (A4/4) were found at Aswad in the PPNB (Stordeur 1995a).

Ofer Bar-Yosef (pers. comm.) has suggested that any of these sharply pointed tools might have been used to pierce human skin in the process of tattooing. This observation compliments the idea that some of the markings on the 'Gilat Woman' statuette represent tattoos (cf. Chapter 15, this volume). There are numerous other possible uses.

Many pierced spatulae (B1) were found in the Natufian at Mallaha, Stordeur (1988: Figs 12 and 13); they are short and rather coarse with large perforations, quite different from those of later periods and presumably with a completely different function, indeed Stordeur refers to them as 'retouchoirs'. Pierced spatulae (B1) of the more usual type were found in the PPNA at Jericho (Marshall 1982, Fig. 237). They were also utilised in the PPNB at Yiftahel (Garfinkel and Horwitz 1988) and Aswad, where rather oddly Stordeur (1995a) refers to them as flat knives (couteaux plats). Narrow, medium and broad spatulae were all identified from the PPNB at Yiftahel (Garfinkel and Horwitz 1988). Spatulae are usually thought of as weaving tools, and this seems eminently logical; however, that implies that weaving was already being practised in the Natufian. Perhaps the technology was extended from basketry and mat weaving to the weaving of linen and woollen fabrics at a subsequent period. It should be noted that actual items of cordage, matting and basketry were retrieved from the PPNB of Nahal Hemar Cave, the materials used were split reeds or grass, split rushes and linen yarn, sewn from a single thread probably with a needle (=crochet?). The most frequent of the bone tools were 281 spatulae, but there were also 12 beautifully preserved perforated shuttles and four points (Bar-Yosef 1985, 1995; Bar-Yosef and Alon 1988; Bar Yosef and Schick 1989). How the linen thread at Nahal Hemar was spun is not clear, but what seems to be the first appearance of clay spindle whorls, in the Wadi Rabah phase of the Pottery Neolithic at Nahal Zehora (Gopher 1995), may be significant (see also Chapter 14, this volume).

Broad spatulae (B4) made on cattle ribs were present in the Natufian at Hayonim Cave (Bar-Yosef and Tchernov 1970) and some of long-bone at Mallaha (Stordeur 1988: Figs 18 and 20); Mellaart (1975: 31) has made the rather odd suggestion in the Natufian they were used to scrape flour off querns.

Some tools which may have been used as burnishers are smoothed antler fragments found in the Natufian at Hayonim (Bar-Yosef and Tchernov 1970) and others made of long bones are illustrated by Stordeur (1988: Fig. 10) at Mallaha, but they bear little resemblance to those from Gilat and other Chalcolithic sites. No polishers or burnishers (D1 or D2) were found in the PPNB at Yiftahel or Nahal Hemar (Bar-Yosef 1985, 1995; Bar-Yosef and Alon 1988; Bar Yosef and Schick 1989; Garfinkel and

Horwitz 1988), but both were present at Aswad in the same period (Stordeur 1995a). Their absence at Yiftahel may be a consequence of smaller sample size, but at Nahal Hemar there is perhaps a functional explanation, as the bone tool assemblage there seems largely related to weaving. None of those at Aswad had the handle end, that is the epiphysis, intact, so it is not at all certain that the tools were of the same shape as those found at Gilat and other Chalcolithic sites. The 'smoothing tools' in the PPNA at Jericho (Marshall 1982: Figs 240–44) are fragments of large, presumably cattle, bones with rounded ends, they may have been polishers, but they are quite unlike those of the Chalcolithic. The polishers at Gilat and other Chalcolithic sites are characterised by broad handle ends involving an epiphysis—the distal or proximal metapodial, the proximal radius, or the distal tibia—with the shaft tapering towards a rounded bevelled tip. The inner part of shaft and the tip are highly polished. Similar tools have been found as far away as England (in the near contemporary Early Neolithic site of Windmill Hill for example) where they have been interpreted as burnishers for smoothing leather or polishing other materials (Smith 1965: Fig. 53, no. B1). These may be a particular development of the fourth millennium. It is worth noting that Inuit (Eskimos) used similar tools for scraping away excess hair and fat from skins (Sollas 1911).

It is clear that almost all the types of bone tools present in the Chalcolithic of the southern Levant were also in use in the Pre-Pottery Neolithic and often in the Natufian as well. Some of these tools probably had a multiplicity of uses, so it is necessary to exercise great caution in relating particular tools to particular functions, particularly when looking for signs of innovation. For example the presence of awls does not necessarily imply the weaving of fabrics, as they can be used in weaving, basketry and matting, and for piercing holes in materials such as leather; indeed Campana (1989) has shown that recent native North American people might use the same individual tool for more than one purpose. The existence of tools with more specialized uses over several thousand years implies a long-lasting continuity in function. What may be significant in attempting to compare tool kits of various sites and periods is the composition of the assemblages in terms of relative numbers of different types of tool excavated, but there are few sites in which preservation, retrieval and recording have been of a high enough standard to allow this to be done with any degree of reliability.

Conclusions

It is clear that the bone tools at Gilat represent much activity related to craft, weaving in the widest sense and the processing of leather. These are domestic activities and, as with the animal bones (see Chapter 6 where I suggest the animal remains were spread about the site in a haphazard manner). However, as shown in Chapter 14, when the bone tools are studied in relation to other realms of material culture, such as spindle whorls, tabular scrapers and other remains, they provide an important additional data source linking craft activities with ritual at Gilat. The 'sacred' and the 'profane' cannot be easily separated at Gilat. In addition to the bone tools within the habitation debris, there was one deliberate deposit involving four burnt bone points and a polisher in a pit with charred gazelle horncores and frontlets. This apparent offering represents an individual episode of human activity, an 'evenement' in Braudel's terminology (Levy and Holl 1995), an extraordinary event, probably of ritual significance, embedded within the vestiges of ordinary domestic activity. This dichotomy is also apparent in other classes of find at Gilat, for example the pottery assemblage with both domestic wares and ritual objects (Chapter 10). It is this combination of the ordinary and the extraordinary which characterises the site of Gilat.

Table 13.1. Gilat: bone tools by type, sub-type and sub-stratum.

Class	Type/sub-type	Stratum IV	Stratum III				Stratum IIIA/IIC	Stratum II					Stratum I	Stratum ?	Totals
		IV	IIIB	IIIA	III	all III	IIIA/IIC	IIC	IIB	IIA	II	all II	I	?	
A1	Solid point			1		1		2	1	1	1	5		1	7
A2	Irregular point														
A2/1	partially worked		1	2		3	1	1	3			5		1	10
A2/2	totally worked			2		2		3	2	2		7			9
A3	Awl	1		7	3	10	1	6	9	7	2	24	2		37
A3/1	parallel-sided			3	1	4		8	11	7		26	1		32
A3/2	tapered, epiphysis entire			1		1		1	1	2		4			7
A3/3	tapered, epiphysis split			1		1		2	2	4		8		1	10
A4	Point on shaft				1	1		2	7	4		13		2	16
A4/1	single point			2		2		1	13		1	14	1		17
A4/2	bipoint			1	1	2		1	6			8		2	12
A4/3	needle			1		1			1	1		2	1		4
A4/4	bodkin								1	1		2			2
A5	Point fragment			4	2	6		2	14	2	1	19		1	26
B2	Narrow spatula							1				1			1
B3	Medium spatula							1				1			1
B4	Broad spatula			1		1									1
B4/1	on unsplit rib		1	1	1	3		1	1	1		3			6
B4/2	on split rib		1	2		3		1	1			2		1	6
B4/3	on long bone strip						1	3				3			4
D1	Polisher	1	1	1	2	4		3	4	1	1	9	1	1	15
D1?	Polisher?	1	2	1	2	5		1	4	2		7	1	2	16
D2	Burnisher								4			4			5
E	Varia			2		2		2	2	1		5			7
F	Misc worked bone			4	1	5		9	7	2	2	20		1	26
totals		3	6	37	14	57	3	50	96	39	8	193	9	13	278

Table 13.2. Gilat: measurements of bone tools.

Class	Type	Sub-type	ID no	Length	Max b	Shaft b	Species	Bone	Part
A1	solid point		49	c84	17.2		cattle??	long-bone	shaft
A1	solid point		93	>99	c23		cattle	metatarsal	proximal
A1	solid point		206	99.1	26.0		ostrich?	tibia?	shaft
A1	solid point		207	111.8	15.5		cattle?	long-bone	shaft
A1	solid point		217	e116	17.1		cattle?	long-bone	shaft
A2/1	irregular point	partially worked	2	90.0	21.0		sheep/goat?	tibia?	distal shaft
A2/1	irregular point	partially worked	9	79			sheep/goat	metacarpal	proximal half
A2/1	irregular point	partially worked	40		15.3		sheep/goat?	tibia?	distal+shaft
A2/1	irregular point	partially worked	88	>160			cattle?	ulna	shaft+proximal
A2/2	irregular point	totally worked	19	58.2	13.2		sheep/goat?	metatarsal	proximal
A2/2	irregular point	totally worked	23	c74	17.5		sheep/goat?	tibia	proximal shaft
A2/2	irregular point	totally worked	28	85.6	c16		sheep/goat?	metapodial?	distal shaft
A2/2	irregular point	totally worked	33	e106			sheep/goat?	tibia	proximal shaft
A2/2	irregular point	totally worked	38	51.4	14.3		sheep/goat?	metapodial	proximal
A2/2	irregular point	totally worked	92		15.6		sheep/goat?	metatarsal	proximal
A2/2	irregular point	totally worked	109		16.0		sheep/goat?	metatarsal?	proximal shaft
A3/1		parallel-sided	4	>60	>13	10.7	sheep/goat?	long-bone	shaft
A3/1		parallel-sided	11	63.5		10.4	sheep/goat?	long-bone	shaft
A3/1		parallel-sided	56	81.5	14.5	10.4	sheep/goat?	metapodial	distal shaft
A3/1		parallel-sided	69	58.7	15.5	9.5	sheep/goat	metapodial	distal
A3/1		parallel-sided	70	e83.8	17.0	10.7	sheep	metapodial	distal
A3/1		parallel-sided	90	68.0	16.7	9.0	sheep/goat	metatarsal	proximal+shaft
A3/1		parallel-sided	151	63.7	16.1		sheep/goat?	long-bone	shaft
A3/1		parallel-sided	171	95.6	18.3	11.2	sheep	metacarpal	distal
A3/1		parallel-sided	191	98.8	16.6	11.4	sheep/goat?	metacarpal	distal
A3/1		parallel-sided	192	78.5	17.0	10.1	sheep/goat?	metacarpal	distal
A3/1		parallel-sided	194	104.0		11.5	sheep/goat?	metapodial?	distal shaft
A3/1		parallel-sided	222	79.9	16.6	10.2	goat	metacarpal	distal
A3/1		parallel-sided	271	66.7		10.1	sheep/goat?	metapodial	distal shaft
A3	awl?		64	>101		10.9	sheep/goat?	metacarpal?	shaft+proximal?
A3	awl?		91		18.1		sheep	metacarpal	shaft+distal
A3	awl?		133	94	14.1		sheep/goat?	tibia	proximal shaft
A3	awl?		257	56.4			sheep/goat?	long-bone	shaft
A3	awl?		272		15.5		sheep	metacarpal	distal

Context	Category	Form	No.	Length	Width		Species	Element	Part
A3/2	awl	taper, epiphysis entire	31	118	25.6		sheep/goat	tibia	distal+shaft
A3/2	awl	taper, epiphysis entire	60	73.7	29.3		sheep/goat	tibia	distal
A3/2	awl	taper, epiphysis entire	168	e88	24.2		sheep/goat	tibia	distal
A3/2	awl	taper, epiphysis entire	214		e31.3		goat	metacarpal	distal cyl
A3/2	awl	taper, epiphysis entire	234	69.7	16.2	10.8	sheep/goat?	metapodial	distal shaft
A3/3	awl	taper, epiphysis split	3	74.5	18.2		sheep/goat?	radius	distal
A3/3	awl	taper, epiphysis split	12	e69.5	18.2		sheep	metacarpal	distal
A3/3	awl	taper, epiphysis split	32	72.7	18.0		sheep	metacarpal	distal+shaft
A3/3	awl	taper, epiphysis split	84		20.2		sheep/goat?	radius	distal
A3/3	awl	taper, epiphysis split	174		16.0		sheep/goat?	tibia?	distal
A3/3	awl	taper, epiphysis split	185	81.0	19.8		sheep/goat?	tibia	distal
A3/3	awl	taper, epiphysis split	199	86.6	21.4		sheep/goat?	tibia	distal
A3/3	awl	taper, epiphysis split	277		16.8		sheep/goat?	tibia	distal
A4/1	point on shaft	single point	6	>115	7.9		?	long-bone	shaft
A4/1	point on shaft	single point	26		>7.7		sheep/goat?	long-bone	shaft
A4/1	point on shaft	single point	121	>84	11.1		sheep/goat?	long-bone	shaft
A4/1	point on shaft	single point	123	127	11.5		sheep/goat?	long-bone	shaft
A4/1	point on shaft	single point	124		12.3		sheep/goat?	long-bone	shaft
A4/1	point on shaft	single point	125	>127	12.0		sheep/goat?	long-bone	shaft
A4/1	point on shaft	single point	132	72	11.5	11.5	sheep/goat?	long-bone	shaft
A4/1	point on shaft	single point	137	71.8	10.8		sheep/goat?	long-bone	shaft
A4/1	point on shaft	single point	138	140	11.2		sheep/goat?	tibia?	shaft
A4/1?	point on shaft	single point	140		8.7		sheep/goat?	long-bone	shaft
A4/2	point on shaft	bipoint	42	51.3	6.6		sheep/goat?	long-bone	shaft
A4/2	point on shaft	bipoint	68	92.3	12.1		sheep/goat?	long-bone	shaft
A4/2	point on shaft	bipoint	118	80.7	6.8		sheep/goat?	long-bone	shaft
A4/2	point on shaft	bipoint	193		8.5		sheep/goat?	long-bone	shaft
A4/2	point on shaft	bipoint	196	102.2	10.6		sheep/goat?	long-bone	shaft
A4/2	point on shaft	bipoint	225	e65	7.0		sheep/goat?	long-bone	shaft
A4/3	point on shaft	needle	189		4.2		sheep/goat?	long-bone	shaft
A4/4	point on shaft	bodkin	71	>70	7.2			long-bone	shaft
B4/1	broad spatula	on rib	85	>160	c19		cattle?	rib	
B4/1	broad spatula	on unsplit rib	53	>138	27.8		cattle?	rib	distal
B4/1	broad spatula	on unsplit rib	153		17.5		cattle?	rib	
B4/1	broad spatula	on unsplit rib	175		20.5		cattle?	rib	
B4/1	broad spatula	on unsplit rib	213	118.5		23.1	cattle?	rib	shaft

B4/2	broad spatula	on split rib	27	e300	15.6		cattle?	rib	
B4/2	broad spatula	on split rib	29		21		cattle?	rib	
B4/3	broad spatula	on long bone strip	14	113	15		cattle?	long-bone	shaft
D1?	smoothing tool	polisher?	16	c126			cattle	metatarsal	proximal
D1?	smoothing tool	polisher?	51	c160	81		cattle	radius	proximal
D1?	smoothing tool	polisher?	54	200	75.4		cattle	radius	proximal
D1?	smoothing tool	polisher?	96	c145		c59	cattle	radius	proximal+shaft
D1?	smoothing tool	polisher?	235	c114			cattle	tibia	distal
D1?	smoothing tool	polisher?	263	62.9			cattle??	long-bone	shaft
D2?	smoothing tool	burnisher?	216	68.5	28.9		sheep/goat?	tibia	distal
D2?	smoothing tool	burnisher	262	63.6			sheep/goat?	long-bone	shaft

all measurements in millimetres; b. =breadth

Acknowledgments

I thank Tom Levy for accepting my offer to study the bone tools from Gilat. Which would not have been possible to place them in a wider context without access to the excellent library of the Institute of Archaeology at University College London. I owe a particular debt to Liora Kolska-Horwitz for supplying me with the paper of which she was a joint author on the bone tools from Yiftahel (Garfinkel and Horwitz 1988), with its straightforward classification of bone tools which was the inspiration for the present article. The bone tool assemblage is stored at the Nelson Glueck School of Biblical Archaeology at the Hebrew Union College-Jewish Institute of Religion in Jerusalem.

References

Amiran, R. (1978) *Early Arad, the Chalcolithic Settlement and and Early Bronze Age City*. Jerusalem: Israel Exploration Society.

Bar-Adon, P. (1980) The *Cave of the Treasure*. Jerusalem: Israel Exploration Society.

Bar-Yosef, O. (1985) *A cave in the desert: Nahal Hemar 9,000-year-old-finds*. Jerusalem: The Israel Museum.

— (1995) Earliest food producers—pre-pottery Neolithic (8000–5500). In *The Archaeology of Society in the Holy Land*, edited by T.E. Levy. London: Leicester University Press, pp. 190–204.

Bar-Yosef, O., and Alon, D. (1988) Excavations in the Nahal Hemar Cave. *Atiqot* 18: 1–30.

Bar-Yosef, O., and Schick, T. (1989) Early Neolithic organic remains from Nahal Hemar Cave. *National Geographic Research* 5(2):176–90.

Bar-Yosef, O. and Tchernov, E. (1970) The Natufian bone industry of ha-Yonim Cave. *Israel Exploration Journal* 20:141–50 & Figs 2–4.

Burton, M., and T.E. Levy (2001) The Chalcolithic radiocarbon record and its use in southern Levantine archaeology. *Radiocarbon* 43:1223–46

Campana, D.V. (1989) *Natufian and Protoneolithic Bone Tools*. BAR International Series 494. Oxford: British Archaeological Reports.

Dothan, M. (1959) Excavations at Horvat Beter (Beersheba). *Atiqot* 2:1–71.

Garfinkel, Y. and Horwitz, L.K. (1988) The pre-pottery Neolithic B bone industry from Yiftahel, Israel. *Paleorient* 14/1:73–85.

Gilead, I. (ed.) (1995) *Grar: A Chalcolithic Site in the Northern Negev*. Beer-Sheva: Ben-Gurion University of the Negev Press

Gilead, I. (1995). The weights and small finds from Grar. In *Grar: A Chalcolithic Site in the Northern Negev*, edited by I. Gilead. Beer-Sheva: Ben-Gurion University of the Negev Press, pp. 335–55.

Gopher, A. (1995) Early pottery-bearing groups in Israel—the Pottery Neolithic period. In *The Archaeology of Society in the Holy Land*, edited by T.E. Levy. London: Leicester University Press, pp. 205–25.

Gopher, A., and Tsuk, T. (1996) *The Nahal Qanah Cave: Earliest gold in the southern Levant*. Monograph Series of the Institute of Archaeology, Tel Aviv University 12. Tel Aviv: University of Tel Aviv.

Hennessy, J.B. (1969) Preliminary report on on the first season of excavations at Teleilat Ghassul. *Levant* 1:1–24.

Levy, T.E., and Alon, D. (1987) Excavations in the Shiqmim village. In *Shiqmim*, edited by T.E. Levy. BAR International Series 356. Oxford: British Archaeological Reports, vol. 1, pp. 153–218 and vol. 2, 6.1–12 and plates 6.1–18.

Levy, T.E., and Holl, A.F.C. (1995) Social change and the archaeology of the Holy Land. In *The Archaeology of Society in the Holy Land*, edited by T.E. Levy. London: Leicester University Press, pp. 2–8.

Macdonald, E. *et al.* (1932) *Beth Pelet II. Prehistoric Fara*. London: The British School of Archaeology in Egypt.

Mallon, A., Koeppel, S., and Neuville, R. (1934) *Teleilat Ghassul, 1*. Rome: Pontifical Institute.

Marshall, D.N. (1982) Jericho bone tools and objects. In *Excavations in Jericho 4*, edited by K.M. Kenyon and T.A. Holland. London: British School of Archaeology in Jerusalem, pp. 570–622.

Mellaart, J. (1975) *The Neolithic of the Near East*. London: Thames and Hudson.

Perrot, J. (1968) Prehistoire Palestinienne. In *Supplement au Dictionnaire de la Bible*. Paris, Letouzey & Ané, pp. 186–446.

Smith, I.F. (1965) *Windmill Hill and Avebury: Excavations by Alexander Keiller 1925–1939*. Oxford: Clarendon Press.

Sollas, W.J. (1911) *Ancient Hunters and their Modern Representatives*. London: MacMillan.

Stordeur, D. (1979) Quelques remarques prÇliminaires sur l'industrie de l'os du Proche-Orient du Xäme au VIäme millÇnaire. In *L'Industrie en Os et Bois de Cervide durant le Neolithique et l'Age des Metaux*, edited by H. Camps-Fabrer, 1:37–45.

— (1982). L'industrie osseuse de la Damascene du VIIIe au Vie millÇnnaire. In *L'Industrie en Os et Bois de Cervide durant le Neolithique et l'Age des Metaux*, edited by H. Camps-Fabrer, 2:9–23.

— (1988) *Outils et armes en os du gisement natoufien de Mallaha (Eynan) Israel*. Memoires et Travaux du Centre de Recherche francais de Jerusalem 6. Paris: Association Paleorient.

— (1995a) L'industrie osseuse de Tell Aswad. In *Aswad et Ghoraife, Sites neolithiques en Damascene (Syrie) aux IXäme et VIIIäme millenaires avant l'äre chretienne*, edited by H. de Cotenson. Beyrouth: Institut Francais d'Archaeologie du Proche Orient, pp. 163–77.

— (1995b) L'industrie osseuse de Goraife. In *Aswad et Ghoraife, Sites neolithiques en Damascene (Syrie) aux IXäme et VIIIäme millenaires avant l'äre chretienne*, edited by H. de Cotenson. Beyrouth: Institut Francais d'Archaeologie du Proche Orient, pp. 311–17.

Valla, F. (1995) The first settled societies–Natufian (12,500–10,200 BP). In *The Archaeology of Society in the Holy Land*, edited by T.E. Levy. London: Leicester University Press, pp. 169–85.

V.
PROCESSES OF INTEGRATION:
THE EMERGENCE OF A
PAN-REGIONAL RITUAL CENTER

14 The Intensification of Production at Gilat:

Textile Production

Thomas E. Levy, Wendy Conner, Yorke Rowan, and David Alon[†]

He also tore down the quarters of the male shrine prostitutes, which were in the temple of the Lord and where women did weaving for Asherah. (II Kings 23:7)

Introduction

Spinning and weaving were important industries and crafts carried out in the palaces and temples of the ancient Near East. The excavations at Gilat provide a window on the importance of weaving for late fifth–fourth millennia economies and social organization in the southern Levant.[1] However, to understand the significance of textiles in the prehistoric Levant, some general reference to textile production in the ancient Near East is needed to help contextualize the data discussed here. In one of the most comprehensive studies of prehistoric textiles, E.J.W. Barber (Barber 1991) points out that in Mesopotamia, spinning and weaving for the palaces, temples and wealthy households was done mainly by 'workshops of women' having the status either of servants or of slaves. For example, the link between temples/palaces, women and textiles is evidenced at Lagash during the time of Lugalanda and Urukagina around the early twenty-fourth century BC (Lambert 1961), at Ur during the end of the third Dynasty (c. 2000 BC; (Jacobsen 1970), and at Karana during the nineteenth Century BC (Dalley 1977). In Greece, roughly contemporaneous with the Egyptian evidence mentioned below, Linear B tablets show that textile production was linked to the palace economy (Killen 1966).

Palestine has a long tradition of producing prestigious textiles that were used by elites, both locally and abroad. During the Late Bronze Age, one of Pharaoh Thutmose III's greatest achievements was the destruction of Megiddo (biblical Armageddon) where he took vast quantities of clothing as booty back to Egypt (Breasted 1906). At this same time, Thutmose III took Syrian captives to Egypt to serve as artisans at the Temple of Amon, possibly to work as weavers (Lutz 1923). In Iron Age Judea, before Josiah's reforms, women wove vestments in the Temple in Jerusalem for the Asherah cult figure. In the quotation at the beginning of this chapter, II Kings provides ethnohistorical data making reference to the close link between weaving and temple organizations in the ancient Levant. In this chapter, we will argue that the production of textiles carried out in the

Chalcolithic sanctuary at Gilat went beyond what Marshall Sahlins (Sahlins 1974) refers to as the 'Domestic Mode of Production'. By examining the data both spatially and statistically, it is possible to understand the links between textile production and the emergence and maintenance of the early regional cult of Gilat during the late fifth and early fourth millennia. It will be suggested that the 'profane' practice of textile manufacture in the sanctuary complex at Gilat arose against the background of new socioeconomic developments associate with the 'secondary products revolution' that crystallized during the Chalcolithic period in the Levant (Levy 1983; Sherratt 1981).

The textile discoveries in the 'Cave of the Warrior' in the Judean Desert near Jericho (Schick 1998a) highlight the symbolic and social value of cloth in Levantine Chalcolithic societies and provide an important source of data for understanding the nature of textile production at Gilat. This rich of assemblage of Chalcolithic textiles from this Judean Desert site provides a unique glimpse of the importance of these perishable goods to the communities who made and used them. As Joy McCorriston (McCorriston 1997) points out in her stimulating paper *'The Fiber Revolution—Textile Extensification, Alienation, and Social Stratification in Ancient Mesopotamia'*, when considering third millennium BC Mesopotamia, changes in both the use of textile fibers and in textile production, it is possible to understand changes in land tenure, social relations, labor roles, and labor specialization which culminated in the great Mesopotamian households, temples, palaces, and classes of people that worked in them. The 'Fiber Revolution' may be too strong a metaphor for Chalcolithic Palestine; however, the fundamental socioeconomic changes that emerged in third millennium Mesopotamia had their roots in the proceeding late fifth–fourth millennia. It is in this context that the processual underpinnings of the 'Fiber Revolution' can be considered for Palestine. When all of these data are coupled together with ethnographic and ethnohistorical information concerning the role of fibers in pre-industrial societies, it is possible to infer how spinning and weaving may have contributed to some of the major social transformations that occurred during the late fifth–fourth millennia in the southern Levant.

The word textile derives from the Latin 'texture' and literally means anything woven or capable of being woven (Barber 1991:5). In Palestine, evidence that weaving became a common activity appears only in the Pre-Pottery Neolithic B (c. 7500–6000 BC). Marshall (1982) reports weaving tools in both PPNA and PPNB levels at Jericho but the PPNA samples appear to be more similar to skin burnishers than weaving tools. The assemblage of textiles and weaving tools found at Nahal Hemar in the Judean desert by Ofer Bar-Yosef and David Alon corroborates this. These excavators compared the PPNB assemblage for the Nahal Hemar cave with the PPNA collections from Netiv Hagdud (Bar-Yosef and Alon 1988:14) and suggest that evidence for weaving (over hide work) increases through time during the Neolithic. A similar increase in PPNB weaving tools has been found at Yiftahel (Garfinkel 1987a), Beidha (Kirkbride 1966; Marshall 1982), and Cayönü (Marshall 1982) in Turkey. However, intensification of spinning activities begins to take off during the Chalcolithic period and maybe associated with the new intensification and the exploitation of secondary animal products. This process has been referred to as the 'Secondary Products Revolution' by Andrew Sherratt (Sherratt 1981) and has been linked to the Chalcolithic period in Palestine in a number of studies by Levy (Levy 1983, 1992, 1998). As discussed throughout this study of Gilat, the 'secondary products revolution' refers to a time when the secondary product of animals—milk, wool, hair and traction—was systematically and intensively exploited for the first time. This shift in animal husbandry strategies had a fundamental impact on the economies, and ultimately—social organization, of those societies engaged in this process.

Recovering actual textile remains from open-air village sites is difficult owing to the organic nature of the material. Exceptions of course are the well-preserved textiles from cave sites such as the PPNB remains found at Nahal Hemar (Bar Yosef and Alon 1988). More recently, archaeologists working in the Judean Desert discovered a 'trove' of Chalcolithic textiles in what is now called 'The

Cave of the Warrior' mentioned above and located along the Wadi el-Makkukh near Jericho (Schick 1998a). The incredible trove of textiles was found in a 'burial bundle' included: a) a wrapping sheet (c. 7 × 2 m) made of woven linen yarn. Each edge is well preserved and the details of technique, weave and decoration have been determined by Schick (*ibid.*); b) a smaller rectangular linen cloth (c. 1.40 × 0.88 mm), found inside the wrapping sheet. This may have been part of a shroud that wrapped the deceased or a dress item placed on or next to him (*ibid.*); c) a linen sash (c. 2.0 × 0.20 m) that has retained its natural light beige color; d) a linen 'bandage' (c. 1.43 m long and 6.8–8.2 cm wide) that resembles modern bandages; e) three textile fragments; and f) a small yellowish-beige textile. Whether the Chalcolithic burial was actually a prehistoric 'warrior' is debatable. However, there seems little doubt concerning Schick's interpretation that, given the energy and expertise that went into the manufacture of the textiles, a high ranking male was buried in this Judean desert cave site. Besides the exceptional textiles remains, there were a considerable number of artifacts relating to weaving and possibly hide-working that have survived the millennia since their primary deposition. Some of these include loom weights, remains of the loom itself, natural impressions of textiles on pottery vessels, spindle whorls, and bone tools such as shuttles and awls. The fortuitous discovery of the Judean desert Cave of the Treasure provides an important benchmark for measuring some textiles as special prestige objects during the Chalcolithic period. As bone tools, fan scrapers and spindle whorls (Table 14.1) form our primary database for reconstructing textile production and hide-working at Gilat (see Chapters 12, 13, this volume), we present an overview of these objects, followed by a discussion of their role in the production of textile goods for exchange at the Gilat regional center.

Bone Tools in the Archaeological Record

It is problematic to conduct a comparative analysis of bone tools between Gilat and other sites because there is no uniform typology and method of classification among researchers in the Near East (see Grigson's discussion of these problems, Chapter 13, this volume). Some scholars (Garfinkel and Horwitz 1988) have attempted to create a standardized typology for earlier periods (PPNB) with the idea that it could be used in comparative studies within the same time period; however, for later periods there still lacks a cohesive method of classification as well as a developmental sequence in bone tools for the Near East. In the following discussion, we summarize the existing data for the Protohistoric periods in Palestine. A more comprehensive discussion of the Gilat bone tool assemblage is presented by Grigson (Appendix 13.1; Chapter 13, this volume).

At Nahal Mishmars Cave of the Treasure 11 bone awls were recorded and six bone needles/ shuttles, which researchers assume were used to create the textiles and fabrics found in that cave site. A piece of thread found in one of the holes of a needle/shuttle corroborates this assumption (Bar Adon 1980). It is assumed that bone tools were also related to hide working and essential for piercing leather and for the threading of thongs (Marshall 1982:576). As explained below, awls may have been also have been used in the actual manufacture of textiles. The ethnographic evidence suggests that bone tools may also have been utilized in fastening the flaps of Bedouin tents (Doughty 1888). The discovery of a pair of leather sandals from the Cave of the Warrior (Schick 1998b) and other cave sites (Bar Adon 1980), suggest that footwear must have been important apparel for the Chalcolithic inhabitants of the southern Levant in spite of the rarity of these perishable finds and that bone tools may have been used in their manufacture.

Thirty-four different bone tools were recorded at Jericho from the Late Pottery Neolithic to the early stages of the Early Bronze age. The total count, however, does not include the broken bone fragments retrieved so that the actual number may be much higher (Garfinkel and Horwitz 1988:83). The tool assemblage contains awls, points and various tools with flat sections.

At Mersin in Anatolia, researchers observed there was a decrease in the quantity and variety of bone tools from Neolithic levels to the Chalcolithic (Garstang 1953). Jericho also exhibits a similar pattern of decrease in the number and variety of tool types; however, there is a paucity of Chalcolithic deposits at the site. While there are no comparable Neolithic bone tool assemblages that can be used to facilitate such a comparison with Gilat, it appears that as a Chalcolithic site, Gilat has less of a variety of bone tools both in style and material than some of the earlier Neolithic sites in the region, thus providing some support for Garstang's perceived trend of decreasing variety through time. This may indicate a greater degree of specialization at Gilat with its smaller range of bone tool types.

The Gilat Bone Tool Assemblage

At Gilat a total provisional count of 240 bone tools were recorded and classified into five basic groups from all the strata (see Fig. 14.1).[2] An additional category of 'tool fragment' is included for those unidentifiable bone tool pieces, which could not be ascribed to one of the five major types. Bone awls composed the largest group with a total of 166 (68%). A total of 57 (24%) tool fragments were recorded as well as 9 (4%) shuttles, 4 (2%) spatulas and 4 (2%) needles. The majority of the bone tools were fashioned from the metapodial bones of sheep or goat. While a number of horn cores were found (see Chapter 6, this volume), they displayed no evidence of being worked. In studies of bone tool replications, it was shown that tools such as the Gilat bone tool assemblage are most likely carved from the malleable bones of freshly killed animals (Marshall 1982:570).

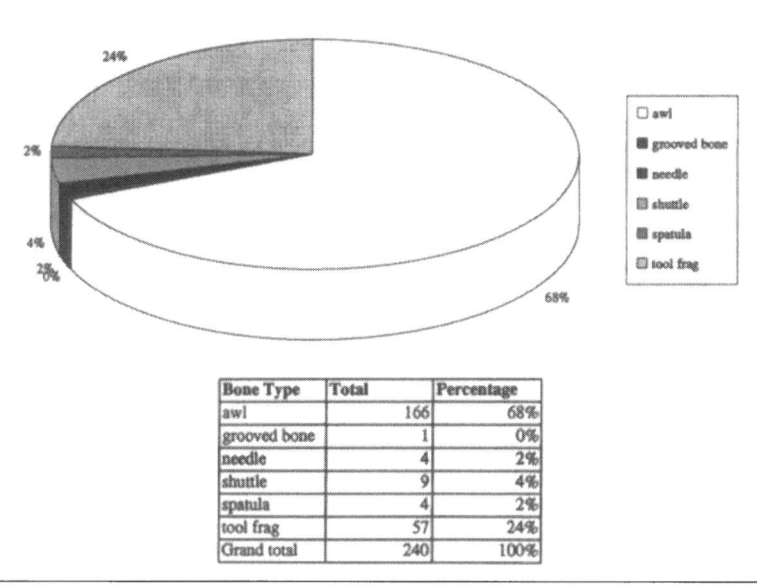

Bone Type	Total	Percentage
awl	166	68%
grooved bone	1	0%
needle	4	2%
shuttle	9	4%
spatula	4	2%
tool frag	57	24%
Grand total	240	100%

Figure 14.1. Bone Tool Type Distribution.

The length of complete bone tools recorded measured from 1.5–6.9 cm with average of 6.37 cm, a mode of 3.2 cm, and a standard deviation of 5.81. The width ranged from 3–44 mm with an average of 11.2 mm, a mode of 11 mm, and a standard deviation of 5.7. The thickness ranged from 2–23 mm with an average of 5.5 mm, a mode of 5 and a standard deviation of 2.7 (Table 14.2).

Table 14.1. Gilat spindle whorl data and projected weight data.

	Year	Locus	Basket	Square	Area	Context	Stratum	Material	Description	Length	Width	Thick	H. Dia	WT.	Proj. Wt
1	?	11	31	Rm A S5	D	floor	2C	limestone	-	-	-	-	-	-	-
2	1975	19	33	N5	D	floor	2C	sandstone	-	-	0.9	-	5	-	-
3	1975	-	-	-	D	surface	unknown	red sandstone	-	-	0.7	-	5.5	-	-
4	1975	19	40	N5	D	floor	2C	sandstone	-	-	-	-	4.9	-	-
5	1975	23	45	Rm A S5-S6	D	floor	2C	sandstone	-	-	1.4	-	1.4	-	-
6	1975	19	40	N5	D	floor	2C	sandstone	-	-	1.1	-	6	-	-
7	1975	29	56	Rm B S4	D	fill	2B	sandstone	-	-	-	-	4.4	-	-
8	1975	35	72	N5	D	floor	2C	sandstone	-	-	1.1	-	4.5	-	-
9	1975	SURF	-	-	D	surface	unknown	sandstone	-	-	-	-	4.9	-	-
10	1975	14	29	Ai6	D	floor	3A	unknown	-	-	-	-	-	-	-
11	1975	13	24	Ai5	D	floor	3A	limestone	-	-	-	-	-	-	-
12	1975	13	25	Ai5	D	floor	3A	limestone	-	-	-	-	-	-	-
13	1975	36	67	Rm B S4	D	floor	2C	limestone	-	-	-	-	-	-	-
14	1975	5	12	Ai6	D	floor	2B-2C	limestone	-	-	-	-	-	-	-
15	1976	35	66	N5	D	floor	2C	limestone	-	-	-	-	4.1	-	-
16	1976	69	213	Rm A/B N7	D	surface	2C	chalk w/oxides	-	-	-	-	-	-	-
17	1976	83	179	S3	D	floor	2C	limestone	-	-	-	-	-	-	-
18	1976	64	206	Rm C N4	D	pit	2C	limestone	-	-	-	-	-	-	-
19	1977	150	394	Rm A/B S4-S5	D	pit	2B	unknown	-	-	-	-	-	-	-
20	1977	159	424	M3	D	pit	2A	limestone w/oxides	-	-	-	-	-	-	-
21	1977	144	388	N3	D	fill	3A	limestone	-	-	-	-	-	-	-
22	1977	112	351	M6-N6	D	surface	3B	limestone	-	-	-	-	-	-	-
23	1977	137	371	M4	D	floor	2C	limestone	-	-	-	-	-	-	-
24	1977	29	56	Rm B 2C	D	fill	2B	sandstone	-	-	1.1	-	5.3	-	-
25	1987	301	622	N5	D	cleaning	3A	chalk	complete	32	14	11	6.5	13	13
26	1987	128	518	N6	D	pit	2C	ceramic	complete	35	16	6	7	10	10
27	1987	257	515	N5	D	floor	2C	ceramic	half	39	19	7	6	11	22
28	1990	558	1403	k7-J7	Y	mb struc.	2C	ceramic	complete	63	7	16	7	71	71
29	1990	800	2031	J3	J	topsoil	I	ceramic	half	27	7	6.5	7	1.5	3
30	1990	548	1198	J6	Y	pit	3	limestone	half	43	21	9	21	17	34
31	1990	509	1054	?	Y	fill	I	limestone	half	50	26	19	20	20.5	41
32	1987	258	522	L6	D	fill	I	ceramic	complete	40	30	8	5.5	15	15
33	1987	283	577	L5	D	fill	2C	gabbro	complete	58	9.5	11.5	9.5	63	63
34	1987	266	535	?	D	fill	2B	limestone	complete	42	6	7.5	6	15	15

No.	Year			Grid		Context	Group	Material	Completeness						
35	1987	278	278	L5	D	fill	2B	limestone	complete	49-50	5.5	9	9	36	36
36	1987	286	584	L6	D	fill	1	limestone	complete	50-52	7	16.5	7	50	50
37	1990	503	1013	J6	Y	topsoil	1	ceramic	complete	46	4	10	4	26	26
38	1990	024	3090	C4	M	pit	3A	ceramic	half	48.5	7	8	7	12	20
39	1990	021	3076	C4	M	fill	3A	ceramic	half	48	6.6	9	6.6	6	24
40	1990	556	1396	J7	Y	pit	3	ceramic	half	40	5	7.5	5	3	12
41	1990	025	3089	B6	M	pit	3A	ceramic	half	38	21	6	-	4	6
42	1990	853	2479	L3	J	pit	2C	ceramic	half	40	6	6	6	10	8
43	1990	882	2688	K4	J	silo	2B	ceramic	complete	39	6	6.5	6	7	10
44	1990	958	2746	J2-H2-H3	J	pit	2A	ceramic	half	40	6	8	6	4	14
45	1990	815	2352	J3	J	fill	2A	ceramic	half	37	5	6	6	11	8
46	1990	506	1035	K7	Y	topsoil	1	ceramic	half	37	4.5	9	5	6	22
47	1990	527	1148	K5	Y	fill	2	ceramic	half	34	5	8	4.5	2	12
48	1990	806	2821	J2-3,H2-3	J	pit	2A	ceramic	half	30	6	6.5	5	8	4
49	1990	800	2232	K3	J	topsoil	1	ceramic	half	37	6	10	6	4	16
50	1990	007	3039	C6	M	fill	2	ceramic	half	35	6	5.5	6	3	8
51	1990	030	3104	B5	M	ash	2	ceramic	half	30	20	7	6	4	6
52	1990	016	3059	B5	M	pit	2B	limestone	three quarter	25	4.5	6	-	4	5.3
53	1990	527	1110	K5	Y	fill	2	chalk	complete	37.5	5	27	5	31	31
54	1990	519	1094	K7	Y	pit	2	chalk	complete	39	9	15	9	18	18
55	1990	812	2362	K3	J	pit	2A	limestone	complete	37	17	20	17	27	27
56	1990	021	3076	C4	M	fill	2	chalk	three quarter	35	8.5	17	8.5	14	18.6
57	1990	509	1054	K6	Y	fill	1	limestone	one third	50	-	20	-	21	63
58	1990	024	3090	C4	M	pit	2	limestone	three quarter	40	32	22	-	13	17.3
59	1990	021	3076	C4	M	fill	2	limestone	three quarter	61	5	17	5	60	80
60	1990	009	3030	C5	M	pit	2B	limestone	half	49	8.5	19	8.5	32	64
61	1990	507	1042	K5	Y	fill	1	limestone	half	53	6	14	6	29	58
62	1990	503	1015	J6	Y	topsoil	1	limestone	complete	43	9	11	9	33	33
63	1990	528	1182	K6	Y	pit	2C	limestone	complete	46.5	7	11	7	36	36
64	1990	800	2108	J4	J	topsoil	1	limestone	half	46.5	6	11.5	6	18	36
65	1990	800	2170	L3	J	topsoil	1	limestone	half	45	10	11	10	18	36
66	1990	802	2165	L4	J	burial	1	limestone	half	53	7	11.5	7	25	50
67	1990	900	2742	J3-J4	J	burial	2B	chalk	one quarter	44	35	20	-	33	132
68	1990	802	2172	J4	J	burial	1	chalk	half	40	9	18	9	11	22
69	1990	946	2701	J4	J	surface (wall)	2C	limestone	complete	46	7.5	12	7.5	38	38
70	1990	858	2469	J3	J	pit	2A	limestone	complete	61	48	18	8.5	61	61

71	1990	040	3145	B4	M	rubbish dump	2C	limestone	complete	52.5	9	10.5	9	49	49
72	1990	872	2766	L4	J	wall	2A	chalk	complete	46.5	12.5	18.5	12.5	48	48
73	1990	880	2544	J3	J	structure	2B	chalk	complete	38	7.5	11	7.5	12	12
74	1990	803	2219	J4	J	ash	2A	ferr	complete	48	7	6	7	23	23
75	1990	501	1005	J5	Y	topsoil	1	limestone	complete	50	9	13	9	38	38
76	1990	800	2017	J4	J	topsoil	1	limestone	one third	14	7	13	7	7	21
77	1990	024	3082	C6	M	pit	2	chalk	one third	36	8.5	15	8.5	8	24
78	1991	696	5301	MO	T	feature/collapse	2A	ceramic	half	28	4	5	4	1	2
79	1991	701	5292	SO	T	dead locus	2A	ceramic	complete	29	4	7	4	7	7
80	1991	618	5083	S1	T	pit	2A	ceramic	half	41	27	10	5	11	22
81	1991	681	5226	S1	T	hearth	2B	ceramic	half	38	18	6	-	3	6
82	1991	693	5337	MO	T	fill	2B	ceramic	complete	38	6.5	6.5	6.5	10	10
83	1991	639	5146	S1	T	pit	2A	ceramic	half	35	6.5	7	6.5	2	4
84	1991	675	5214	Ai2	T	pit	2B	ceramic	one quarter	22.5	13	4	-	0.5	2
85	1991	617	5075	M1	T	fill	2	ceramic	quarter	48	5.5	5.5	5.5	12	12
86	1991	1041	3305	L2	J	pit	2A	ceramic	complete	31.5	17	5	17	9	9
87	1991	1041	3305	L2	J	pit	2B	ceramic	complete	44	5	8	5	11	22
88	1991	1052	3386	K1	J	surface	2A	ceramic	half	55	5.5	7	5.5	12	24
89	1991	1039	3282	H1	J	ash	2A	ceramic	half	35	5	6.5	5	4	8
90	1991	1041	3305	L2	J	pit	2A	ceramic	one third	24	6.5	8.5	6.5	3	9
91	1991	1050	3339	L1	J	pit	2A	ceramic	one	37	5	8	5	3	12
92	1991	1050	3339	L1	J	pit	2A	ceramic	quarter	20	5.5	7	5.5	5	20
93	1991	1124	3564	H1	J	pit	2B	ceramic	half	42	9	8	9	8	16
94	1991	1147	3736	K2	J	fill	3A	ceramic	half	51	-	9	-	12	24
95	1991	1051	3365	L2	J	pit	2A	ceramic	complete	53.5	7	6.5	7	20	20
96	1991	1074	3438	J1	J	hearth	2A	ceramic	complete	34	6	7	6	10	10
97	1991	1102	3520	H1	J	surface	2B	ceramic	half	40	6	8	6	5	10
98	1991	1049	3342	J2	J	fill	2C	ceramic	complete	40.5	3.5	10	3.5	20	20
99	1991	1029	3309	L2	J	pit	2A	ceramic	one	34	26	5	5	3	12
100	1991	1029	3272	L2	J	pit	2A	ceramic	quarter	40	3	8	3	15	15
101	1991	1029	3309	L2	J	pit	2A	ceramic	complete	20	21	21	-	3	9
102	1991	1147	3679	K2	J	fill	3A	ceramic	one third	37	5	5	5	5	5
103	1991	1144	3654	H2	J	fill	2C	ceramic	half	44	21	6	-	6	10
104	1991	1025	3236	L1	J	topsoil	1	ceramic	one third	14	5	7	5	1	12
105	1991	1105	3528	S2	J	pit	2C	limestone	three quarter	58	29.5	9	-	-	-

106	1991	639	5143	S1	T	pit	2A	limestone	half	35	6	6.5	6	4	8
107	1991	1029	3263	L2	J	pit	2A	chalk	half	30.5	18	11	11	5	10
108	1991	1116	3549	L1	J	structure	2A	chalk	complete	55	45	23	10	50	50
109	1991	1050	3344	L1	J	pit	2A	chalk	half	54	8.5	24	8.5	45	90
110	1991	1054	3570	H3	J	fill	3A	limestone	complete	45	10	8	10	30	30
111	1991	1111	3553	K1	J	fill	2C	limestone burned	complete	45	8	10	8	31	31
112	1991	649	5175	2C	T	pit	2C	limestone	complete	60	16.5	18	16.5	86	86
113	1991	616	5171	2A	T	fill	2A	masonite (feldspar)	complete	37	6.5	6	6.5	16	16
114	1991	626	5106	Ai1	T	pit	2B	chlorite schist	complete	53.5	9	11.5	9	52	52
115	1991	1064	3473	L4 or J2	J	surface	2A	chlorite schist	complete	53	7	11	7	41	41
116	1991	1028	3304	J1	J	ash	2B	chalk	one third	15	-	7.5	-	1.5	4.5
117	1991	1052	3343	K1	J	surface	2B	chalk	three quarter	26	5	12	5	1	1.33
118	1991	1059	3408	L1-L2	J	pit	2A	sandstone	one fourth	22	-	9	-	6	24
119	1991	639	5143	S1	T	pit	2A	limestone	one third	39	18	16	-	10	30
120	1991	1037	3484	H1	J	ash	2A	limestone	one half	51.5	5	11	5	20	40
121	1991	684	5249	M0	T	topsoil	I	limestone	one	21	33	7	8	5	20

AREA 87

122	1991	0	0	M6			I	limestone	quarter complete	54	45	19	5	50	50
123	1991	700	5322	M0	T	pit	2A	limestone	complete	45	8	24	8	56	56
124	1991	649	5324	Ai1	T	pit	2C	limestone	complete	50	6.5	7	6.5	21	21
125	1991	700	5288	M0	T	pit	2A	limestone	complete	53	#5-14	19	#5-14	71	71
126	1991	1064	3473	L4	J	surface	2A	limestone	complete	46	10	12	-	40	40
127	1991	1128	3592	J1	J	pit	2C	chalk	three quarter	60	9	18	-	37	49.3
128	1991	601	5059	Ai1	T	topsoil	I	limestone	half	45	8.5	6.5	8.5	10	20
129	1991	1023	3244	J1	J	topsoil	I	limestone	complete	38.5	38.5	10	5.5	20	20
130	1991	1044	3316	J1	J	pit	2B	limestone	complete	41	8	9.5	8	25	25
131	1991	649	5181	Ai1	T	pit	2C	limestone	complete	33.5	5.5	7	5.5	10	10
132	1991	1121	3673	L1	J	surface	2B	limestone	complete	55	9	10	9	40	40
133	1991	697	5294	S0	T	pit	2A	limestone	half	53	9	23	9	60	120
134	1991	1057	3379	J1	J	pit	2B	chalk	complete	45x45	9	12.5	9	21	21
135	1991	1022	3233	H1	J	topsoil	I	limestone	three quarter	38	26	17	-	22	29.3
136	1991	607	5031	N1	T	topsoil	I	limestone	half	51	19	18	14	26	52

137	1991	1037	3345	H1	J	fill	2A	chalk	half	21	20	12	17	3	6
138	1991	1160	3706	L1	J	pit	2A	chalk	quarter	40	15	14	15	9	36
139	1991	1034	3275	L2	J	pit	2A	limestone	half	38	18	19	16	12	24
140	1991	0	5004	J6	J	surface	unknown	chalk	half	36	25	14	20	17	34
141	1992	1294	4075	H2	J	fill	4	limestone	three quarter	60	29	31	23	43	57.3
142	1992	1346	4298	H4	J	pit	2B	ceramic	complete	27.5	5	6.5	5	6	6
143	1992	1259	4066	K0	J	fill	2C	ceramic	complete	37	31.5	7	4	8	8
144	1992	1309	4118	L0	J	pit	2C	chalk	one third	30	19	16	-	-	-
145	1992	1052	7006	N5	D	removal	2B	ceramic	complete	37.5	5	7	5	12	12
146	1992	1050	1050	M5	D	cleaning	2A	chalk	complete	29	8	16	8	11	11
147	1992	1250	3978	H4	J	pit	2B	chalk	complete	44	35	23	10	30	30
148	1992	1052	7006	N5	D	removal	2C	limestone	one third	36	14	8	10	5	15
149	1992	786	5583	S0-S1	T	fill	2C	chalk	complete	44	9.5	19	9.5	30	30
150	1992	1221	3857	L4	J	removal	2C	chalk	one third	50	9	21	17	11	33
151	1992	1505	5617	N1-M1	T	pit	2C	limestone	complete	56	11	14	11	47	47
152	1992	1236	3938	K0	J	fill	2B	flint	complete	53	6	9	6	52	52
153	1992	1056	7021	N5	D	pit	2C	ceramic	complete	50	6	11	6	36	36
154	1992	1223	3894	L4	J	fill	2A	limestone	complete	51.5	10	18	10	52	52
155	1992	1223	3930	L4	J	fill	2A	limestone	complete	45	8	14	8	36	36
156	1992	751	5412	M0	T	topsoil	1	limestone	complete	43	8.5	10	8.5	30	30
157	1992	1266	4025	L0	J	surface	2A	limestone	half	37	18	10	-	6	12
158	1992	1374	4366	H5	J	pit	2A	chalk	complete	46	15	19	-	58	58
159	1992	1505	5618	N1-M1	T	pit	2C	chlorite schist	complete	45	7	10	7	35	35
160	1992	1259	4069	K0	J	fill	2C	chalk	one quarter	20	-	6.2	-	-	-
161	1992	1052	7002	M5	D	surface	2B	limestone	half	20	10	14	6	4	8
162	1992	1310	4128	L0	T	pit	2C	chalk	half	39	18	25	18	18	36
163	1992	0	4394	H0	J	surface	unknown	chalk	three quarters	52	49	33	24	80	106.6

While bone tools appear to have been used for many different purposes, given the contextual evidence for their clustering around plaza areas, we suggest one of the main functions of bone tools was for use in textile production. As Grigson notes (Chapter 13, this volume), awls are often described as weaving implements and they were probably also used to pierce or manipulate rushes and other fibrous materials in weaving, netting, mat-making or basketry (Campana 1989). According to Grigson (*ibid.*) awls of her type A3/1, 'might have been used in weaving, possible even weaving linen or wool'. These are the most numerous sub-type of awl found in both Stratum II and III at Gilat. Bone awls and needles serve to 'undo knots or tangles, and to tighten or loosen the weave' (Bar Adon 1980:178). In order to test the correlation over time of these two artifact types, we ran a simple chi-square test between bone tool and spindle whorl totals and stratum layers (See Table 14.2). A chi-squares goodness of fit test measures the disagreement between the observed and expected frequencies of the data (Madrigal 1998). Conducting the tests on our two artifact types and the stratum totals a very small p value was produced, 2E - 05 .00005. This suggests that bone tools and spindle whorls could be distributed as such in the stratum by a .00005 chance alone. Thus, we conclude that these two artifact classes were used in the same activity areas at Gilat (mostly open plazas). Based on this test, we suggest that one of the primary uses for the majority of bone tools was in fact textile manufacture and production. The possibility that the bone tools were also used for leather work cannot be excluded; however, given their close association with spindle whorls, the spatial analyses suggests that they were more likely used in conjunction with textile production activities.

Table 14.2. Chi-Squared Test of Bone Tools-Spindle Whorls.

	1	2	2A	2B	2C	3	3A	3B	4	unknown	Total
Spindle Whorl	24	10	44	28	38	2	11	1	1	4	163
Bone Tool	12	8	43	84	43	7	36	5	0	2	240
	36	18	87	112	81	9	47	6	1	6	403
Expected Values	14.5	7.23	34.9	45	32.5	3.61	18.9	2.41	0.4	2.408867	
	21.4	10.7	51.8	66.7	48.2	5.36	28	3.57	0.6	3.57320099	
CHITEST=	0										

Spindle Whorls

Spindle whorls, or flywheels as they are sometimes called, are disc-shaped objects with a hole in the center through which a shaft or spindle is attached during spinning. They are made of a range of materials including clay, stone, wood and metal. Because the shaft is usually a narrow piece of wood, it rarely survives, leaving behind only the whorl. The spindle whorls' function in spinning is twofold: first, it absorbs some of the twisting of the thread, leaving one hand free for the constant drafting required for spinning. It also helps to expedite the spinning process and lengthen the continuous twist of the thread (Barber 1991:42–3). Today, traditional peasant and nomadic communities around the Middle East continue to use spindle whorls to produce different kinds of thread.

As spindle whorls (and loom weights) can be used for different purposes other than spinning and weaving, researchers are faced with the problem of how to determine if an object is indeed a spindle whorl. In order to address this problem Robert Liu (Liu 1978) has developed a criterion for identifying spindle whorls based on their functionality in spinning. The diameter of the shaft for example, must be large enough so that a shaft will fit through it. In research conducted by Liu, it was found that the diameter of the holes in spindle whorls ranged from 3 to 10 mm (Liu 1978:97). Weight is also another important factor in determining if an object is indeed a spindle whorl.

According to Liu's (*ibid.*) research, the maximum weight recorded for a spindle whorl is approximately 150 gm (*ibid.* 90); however, they can weigh as little as 5 gm. At Gilat all of the objects classified as 'complete' spindle whorls weighed between 5–68 gm with an average of 31.6 and a standard deviation of 18.6. In order to illuminate more patterns of weight data we also calculated a projected weight database (See Table 14.1) that combined the complete spindle whorl data with estimated total spindle whorl weights from the fragments. The newly completed data from the average projected weight for spindle whorls was 27.7 gm with a standard deviation of 23.9. The hole diameter of most spindle whorls was found to be within Liu's range for classifying spindle whorls although in many cases the hole diameter was not reported. There was an average of 8 mm for the hole diameter of the spindle whorls although in many cases this data was missing.

Spindle Whorls in the Middle Eastern Archaeological Record

According to Barber, spindle whorls begin to appear in the Aceramic and early ceramic Neolithic levels at sites such as Catal Huyuk (Mellaart 1962b) in Anatolia and Jarmo in Iraq (Singh 1974). In the fourth millennium there is a number of representations and reliefs depicting spinning and weaving including a Protoliterate cylinder seals from Choga Mish in Khuzistan (Barber 1991:56) and a design on a bowl from Badari in Egypt depicting a ground loom.

In Palestine, spindle whorls appear in small numbers during the Pre-Pottery Neolithic, begin to increase during the Pottery Neolithic at sites such as Sha'ar Ha'golan and Tell Abu Zureig (Anati 1963), and then occur in large numbers in the following Chalcolithic period. Evidence for Chalcolithic spindle whorls in Palestine have been found at most sites including the Cave of Treasure at Nahal Mishmar in the Judean Desert (Bar Adon 1980). Like the recently discovered Cave of the Warrior (Schick 1998), the cave in Nahal Mishmar provides important insights into Chalcolithic textile manufacture. A total of eight spindle whorls were reported by Bar Adon (1980) including four stone spindle whorls, two composed of basalt and two composed of limestone, and four made of pottery. Several other objects discovered in the cave were connected with weaving activities. These included shuttles and other parts of what researchers concluded were a horizontal ground loom (Bar-Adon 1980:177–78), possibly the earliest form of loom used in the southern Levant. Besides the pieces of the loom, archaeologists also recovered a number of needles and bone awls which may have been used for 'separating and tightening the threads and for undoing knots' (*ibid.*) as well as a rare group of well-preserved linen and wool fabrics.

Excavations at Jericho produced only two stone spindle whorls from the PPN layers; this does not necessarily imply that there was no spinning completed during these levels as thread may have been produced using the 'thigh spinning' method (Wheeler 1982). In contrast to the PPN levels, the Pottery Neolithic at Jericho provided a number of spindle whorls including nine made of pottery, 18 made from recycled potsherds, and two made of stone. Sophisticated stone shaping techniques for spindle whorl manufacture were later developed in the Early Bronze levels as evidenced by the 49 stone whorls recovered; however, reused pottery sherds were still utilized (Wheeler 1982:627). Jericho's data thus suggests that with the aid of the spindle whorl, spinning became standard in the Pottery Neolithic period and gained momentum in the subsequent Early Bronze Age (*ibid.*). The virtual absence of Chalcolithic deposits at Jericho does not preclude our suggesting that by the Chalcolithic period (as shown by the Gilat study here and evidence from other sites), spinning was an integral part of both the domestic and non-domestic economies of the late fifth–early fourth millennia BC in the southern Levant. Other Palestinian Chalcolithic sites with spindle whorls include Tell Abu Matar (Perrot 1955), Nahal Qanah (Gopher and Tsuk 1996), Abu Hamid (Dollfus and Kafafi 1988), and Horvat Beter (Dothan 1959).

At Arad in the northern Negev researchers recorded virtually no spindle whorls from the Chalcolithic stratum judging from the 1978 publication (Amiran 1978). While they recovered some objects defined as 'stone rings' (Amiran 1978:9; Pl. 67), few of the artifacts resemble what we define as spindle whorls. When the small finds are published from the Arad excavations, this observation may change. However, in the early excavations at Teleilat Ghassul, a total of 310 spindle whorls were found. The sample includes 114 finished and 66 unfinished perforated stone spindle whorls and 130 composed of fired clay (Mallon *et al.* 1934). Three of the fired clay/terra cotta spindle whorls from Ghassul strongly resemble the spindle whorls found in a domestic dwelling at Shiqmim in the northern Negev (Levy and Holl 1987). While totals are still unavailable for spindle whorls found at most late prehistoric sites, researchers at Shiqmim studying the house-hold as an archaeological unit of analysis found two whorls within a well-preserved room used for domestic purposes. Taking into consideration cultural formation processes affecting the archaeo-logical record, they assume that two spindle whorls were probably the norm for a Chalcolithic household unit (Levy 1987b).

As we suggest, parallels in Anatolia are relatively abundant for the Chalcolithic. A few were found at the site of Beycesultan in the Civril Valley in the late Chalcolithic periods (Lloyd and Mellaart 1962). Throughout the earlier Chalcolithic levels in Mersin, the archaeological record is saturated with a crude bulbous type of spindle whorl (Garstang 1953:76) that contrasts with a flatter whorl in later Chalcolithic stratum. No sequence of types has been established and it is possible that the flat spindle whorls were used for wool while the bulbous ones were used for flax (Garstang 1953:75–6). The fact that no bulbous whorls were found at Gilat could mean that no flax was spun there or perhaps that Gilat's inhabitants warranted a higher quality whorl as well as textile than that associated with the cruder spindle whorl production.

At Mersin researchers also identified Room 112 as a 'weaver's workshop' and dated it to the uppermost Chalcolithic level XII. Among the objects found in the 'workshop' were three heavy bone pointed tools, warp weights *in situ*, a shell receptacle and four clay spindle whorls (Garstang 1953:172–3). Clay spindle whorls were recovered from all layers representing the Middle and Upper Chalcolithic cultures between levels XIX and XIIb (Garstang 1953:177). The Mersin example is important because it highlights the link between bone tools, and textile production that has yet to be fully explored by researchers in the past. Mersin also provides an example of the emergence of textile manufacture during the Chalcolithic period that went beyond the domestic mode of production.

Spindle Whorls at Gilat

A total of 163 spindle whorls were found at Gilat from all of the excavation seasons at Gilat (See Table 14.1 and Chapter 12 this volume for illustrations). The number of spindle whorls is impressive considering the relatively small size of the areas excavated at Gilat, the relatively small number from other sites noted above, and in light of the household data from Shiqmim. With c. 1755 sqm excavated, the average number of spindle whorls per square meter of spindle whorls recovered at Gilat totals eight whereas at Shiqmim that number is significantly lower. As outlined above, the study of a Chalcolithic household unit at Shiqmim suggests that an average of two to four spindle whorls per household was characteristic of a domestic archaeological unit. The fact that four spindle whorls were found within the confines of the 'weaver's workshop' at Mersin also suggests that for domestic purposes, 2–4 spindle whorls was all that was needed to work. However, in the later strata at Gilat, spindle whorls and bone tools are found in greater numbers in relatively defined activity areas. The question which arises focuses on the implications of such a large number of spindle whorls at one site. After noting a large number of whorls in Early Bronze and later periods in the circum-Mediterranean and Near East, Barber concluded that the primary reason for having such a large number was to save the step of rewinding the thread by using the spindle as a shuttle in a loom (Barber 1991:305). However, to pass through the loom easily the spindle whorl would most likely possess a cone shape which is not the case with the large spindle whorl assemblage at Gilat. How, then, are we to explain the large number of whorls? It appears that the whorls were used for producing yarns and threads at a scale beyond the domestic mode of production.

Tabular Scrapers: Implications for Textile Production

In addition to bone tools and spindle whorls that were used to produce Chalcolithic textiles, tabular flint scrapers may also have been used for processing wool. This is not to suggest that these scrapers were not used for other purposes (Rowan and Levy 1991). However, given the contextual relationship between tabular scrapers and these other artifacts, it seems reasonable to put forward a hypothesis linking these tools to textile production. First appearing in the Late Neolithic throughout the Levant, perhaps concentrating in the south, tabular scrapers continue through the Chalcolithic and into the Early Bronze Age (Rosen 1983). Although termed 'scrapers', the term is something of a misnomer because of the lack of resemblance between the tabular 'fan' scrapers and other flake scrapers. As discussed in Chapter 11 (this volume), tabular scrapers from Gilat are rarely fan-shaped, and are typically much thinner than other scrapers. Although there is ethnographic evidence for endscrapers in use to scrape the inside of hides (Hayden 1979; Murdoch 1892; Nelson 1983(1899)), these are typically thick, heavy scrapers, typically hafted. The tabular scrapers from late prehistoric contexts in the southern Levant show no evidence for hafting and probably would have been very difficult to haft. In addition, the intentionally thinned cross-section of the tabular scrapers also argues against scraping of hides. In other words, tabular scrapers bear little resemblance to other scrapers (Henry 1995).

Very few use-wear analyses specific to examining tabular scraper function have been conducted. McConaughy (McConaughy 1979) suggested that tabular scrapers were not used as scrapers, but rather for cutting, or butchering. Similar to McConaughy's study, Rowan and Levy (1994: 132) also suggested that many tabular scrapers were used in a cutting fashion, but that others showed some wear commiserate with use on soft materials, similar to scrapers. Both studies lacked the rigorous replication of tools, experimental use on a variety of materials, and subsequent blind tests considered a necessity to current use wear analyses.[3] Nevertheless, the concurrence that few tabular scrapers exhibit typical scraper wear supports Henry's (1995:372) contention that these were not used as scrapers but rather as tools to shear wool and hair from sheep and goats. Whether or not ancient breeds would be shorn with flints is an open question (Ryder 1983), and the microscopic usewear on a tabular scraper used for cutting spun fibers might look very similar to that of shearing. In fact, wear traces used to shear a Shetland sheep were found to be similar to that of cutting sinew (Unger-Hamilton 1988).

Based on morphology and a test using two replicated tabular scrapers for sheep shearing, Henry (*ibid.*) argues that tabular scrapers could have served as sheep shears, and found them highly effective. Moreover, he contends that the thin cross-section would be effective for cutting, while the cortex allowed the user to maintain a grip against the lanolin soon coating the implements. As he further points out, the emergence of tabular scrapers and the secondary products revolution is consistent with their use for sheep shearing.

The relatively high frequency of tabular scrapers found in the limited excavated area of Gilat may be an additional element supporting the hypothesis that the production of textiles when beyond the domestic mode of production at the site. Polish observed on some tabular scrapers (see Chapter 11, this volume; also Lee 1973) may derive from this use, and does not resemble the brightness of sickle sheen. The numerous fragments and varied shapes and sizes of the tabular scrapers could result from the constant resharpening necessary in the task of sheep shearing, as Henry notes (*ibid.*).

The association of tabular scrapers with ritualized contexts at other Levantine sites has been noted for the Chalcolithic period (Levy 1987a), but is more common from Early Bronze Age contexts (McConaughy 1979; Rosen 1989 and references therein). The large number of tabular scrapers (n = 108, see Chapter 11, this volume) is a far greater number (double) than that of much larger excavation areas, such as Shiqmim. It seems unlikely that this could be the result of proximity to source material, because both sites are roughly the same distance to the potential western Negev and southern Jordan sources (Rosen 1983, 1989; Levy, personal observation). It seems more likely that this high number, in relative and absolute terms, reflects a functional capacity of the tool, rather than a ritual one.

Textile Production as a Medium of Exchange

From the beginning of the excavations at Gilat we identified the importance of the site for ritual activities and as a center for ceremonial exchange during the Chalcolithic. We placed it along with Tuleilat Ghassul and Ein Gedi as one of the few known regional Chalcolithic cult centers (cf. Alon 1976, 1977; Levy 1997). With future excavations in Israel, Palestine and Jordan, new centers of ritual may be found. Gal's (Gal *et al.* 1997a, 1997b) recent excavations at the Peqi'in cave in the Galilee may provide evidence of a burial cave whose function went beyond its use as a burial site. After careful analyses of the rich assemblage of non-local preciosities and imported items at Peqi'in, the site may join Gilat, Ein Gedi and Teleilat Ghassul as one of the few regional shrines or sanctuaries during this formative period. At Gilat, using petrographic analysis and spatial distribution techniques, it was concluded that Gilat housed a range of cult activities with materials indicative of participation from beyond the local level (Goren 1995). In addition, in our earlier work it was suggested that, 'cult objects seem to be brought to the site in a complete state, which suggests that they were traded for some material commodity, socio-religious services, or both' (Alon and Levy 1989). Some of the ritual items brought to the site and used in exchange included violin-shaped figurines, stone fenestrated stands, and torpedo-shaped vessels. Commenge's careful analysis of the violin shaped figurines (Chapter 15, this volume) adds further weight to the interpretation that these objects were brought to the site from different source areas. If these and other preciosities were brought to Gilat by visitors or 'pilgrims', what could have been taken away from Gilat besides the experience of having participated in ritual activities offered at the site (cf. Chapters 1, 5 and 16, this volume)? What is the nature of exchange in middle range societies and how might this have worked at Gilat?

Textile Exchange in Cultural and Geographic Context

By placing textile production in a socio-economic context, it may be possible to better understand the significance that the large assemblage of textile related objects had in exchange systems at the Gilat ritual center. Until recently, little attention was given to spindle whorls and their role in exchange networks that may have focused on Gilat (Alon and Levy 1989; Fox 1995; Joffe *et al.* 2001; Weippert 1998). In considering the archaeological record, spinning and textile production is often classified as 'domestic' activities and the contribution of this craft activity to ceremonial exchange networks has generally been ignored. This view is changing, however, with research from anthropologists such as Annette Weiner and Jane Schneider (Weiner and Schneider 1989) who write in their edited book *Cloth and the Human Experience*:

In addition to its seemingly endless variability and related semiotic potential, cloth is a repository for prized fibers and dyes, dedicated human labor, and the virtuoso artistry of competitive aesthetic development. As such, it attracts the attention of power holders, including those who would build chiefdoms and states. Throughout history, the architects of centralizing polities have awed spectators with sartorial splendor, strategically distributed beautiful fabrics among clients, and exported the textile output of royal and peasant workshops to earn foreign exchange. Cloth has often become a standard of value, circulating as money, so it should come as no surprise that cloth wealth has enriched the treasuries of many kingdoms and chiefdoms, conferring credibility on political elites along with gold, silver, jewels, and exotic shells.

Even when the first cities arose in the Middle East, it is doubtful that monetary economies based on the kind of currency systems alluded to above existed. This is especially true of the preceding Chalcolithic period. In considering the notion of 'currency' and pre-industrial societies, it is more useful to use the term 'traditional currencies' as employed by anthropologists Joel Robbins and David Akin (Robbins and Akin 1999), in regions such as Papua New Guinea where 'traditional currencies' existed until quite recently and included materials such as stone, shell and fiber. The traditional currencies were essential to local social economies and human relations (Liep 1999). What is clear from the growing body of ethnographic, ethnohistoric and historic data assembled by researchers such as Weiner and Schneider (*ibid.*) is the intrinsic value of textiles across time and space due in part to the energy put into cloth production, the expertise and the inherent beauty of these crafts. The profound impact of exchange in structuring human relations was first highlighted in the early work of Marcel Mauss (Mauss 1954) and his book *Essai sur la Don*. In pre-industrial societies (and often in industrial societies) the exchange of gifts went beyond monetary considerations—it is the ritual of exchange which is imbedded in these gifts that has value. Thus, gift exchange and the role of reciprocity and especially redistribution are essential models for understanding the role of textile manufacture at the Gilat ritual center. When people begin to produce beyond their domestic mode of production, reciprocity—where exchange takes place between individual s who are equals—begins to dwindle and redistribution—an exchange system where some central authority is involved—becomes more central to local economies. As Marvin Harris points out (Harris 1978; 1977:94), from a social evolutionary perspective,

> Redistribution began to appear as people worked harder in order to maintain a reciprocal balance with prestige-hungry, overzealous producers. As the reciprocal exchanges became unbalanced, they became gifts; and as the gifts piled up, the gift-givers were rewarded with prestige and counter-gifts. Soon redistribution predominated over reciprocity and highest prestige went to the most boastful, calculating gift-givers, who cajoled, shamed, and ultimately forced everybody to work harder than the Bushman ever dreamed was possible.

While Harris is referring specifically to the materialist underpinnings of the role of feasting and especially potlatch amongst the Kwakiutl of Vancouver Island, some of the root causes of prestige gift-giving redistributive economies can be gleaned here. More recent economic anthropological studies have emphasized the importance of the social relationships that characterize the exchange of goods in traditional societies. As Robbins and Akins (1999:2) point out, the key social relationships tied to exchange and can be tracked through the study of gift items, value (Appadurai 1986a; Miller 1995; Philibert 1989), consumption (Douglas and Isherwood 1981), and for some societies, money (Bloch and Parry 1989). Each of these variables is culturally constructed and can vary across time and space; however, in order to parse out meaning from the archaeological record, as emphasized throughout this book, interpretive models must first be contextually linked to the local ancient Near Eastern setting.

The proposition here is that objects such as violin-shaped figurines, stone palettes, torpedo jars and fenestrated stands were brought to Gilat as prestige gifts or offerings from various source areas in the southern Levant and that cloth was manufactured locally to be used in ritual activities in the Gilat sanctuary, as adornments for the ritual leaders at the site and as one medium of trade in a gift-based exchange system (see Chapters 9, 10, 12, 15, Appendix 1, this volume). Like copper in the Beersheva valley Chalcolithic chiefdom to the south, high quality textiles at Gilat could have been exchanged with visitors (pilgrims?) to the sanctuary to create social debt between the inhabitants of Gilat and visitors from the 'outside' (Levy 1992, 1998). This would have created a situation of social debt and the consolidation of what Chris Gosden (Gosden 1989) calls 'Debt-based Societies'. This builds on the anthropological understanding of gift giving first suggested by Mauss, as noted above, which is characteristic of some of the processes linked to the rise of chiefdom organizations (see Chapter 1, this volume). While remains of actual cloth are non-existent at Gilat, spindle whorls and other textile related artifacts are numerous at the site and lend support for viewing textiles as a medium of exchange. When this is coupled with the spectacular textile discoveries found recently in the Cave of the Warrior described above (Schick 1998), the special socioeconomic role of Chalcolithic textile production in helping to promote Gilat's role as a regional ritual center is even more apparent.

In our earlier study (Alon and Levy 1989), we proposed a distance model that helped explain patterns of prehistoric Levantine exchange through the petrographic and geological source analysis of various stone and ceramic objects found at Gilat. The model is still useful and it is applied in our discussion of figurative stone artifacts (Chapter 15, this volume). With our earlier distance model, we could approximate the distance an object traveled by identifying its material composition and its geologic source area. A three tiered model for identifying the source areas for objects was developed and included: 1) a local range of materials found near Gilat, 2) a medium range tier for materials found between 10–50 km and 3) a long-distance range for materials that came over 50 km. (Alon and Levy: 1989). A large percentage of spindle whorls are composed of materials whose source is located between c. 10–50 km, classifying them in the medium range of material compositions. 39 % of the whorls are composed of limestone and limestone with oxides (see Fig. 14.2; Chapter 12, this volume) that originate in the Judean hills between c. 10–50 km from Gilat. Another 17 % of the whorls comes from chalk and chalk with oxides which also is found between 10–50 km. Thus, the majority of the material used to make spindle whorls are not found in the immediate vicinity of Gilat suggesting that 'high quality' spindle whorls were made from many non-local sources like other more valuable stone objects such as violin-shape figurines and stone palettes. Like the violin-shape figurines (Chapter 15, this volume), there is no evidence for the on-site manufacture of the stone spindle whorls, suggesting that the whorls were not manufactured locally but were brought to the site completed.

As discussed above, there are a relatively large number of spindle whorls for the size of the Gilat excavation in comparison with other contemporary sites. When compared to the household analysis at Shiqmim where it was concluded that two spindle whorls per Chalcolithic household was probably the norm (Levy and Holl 1987), the large number of spindle whorls initially seems enigmatic. However, deeper analysis suggests that textile production went beyond household manufacture (Sahlins' DMP – Domestic Mode of Production) and entered a more complex system of production and exchange. Further archaeological support for this model comes from Mesoamerica and studies completed by Elizabeth Brumfiel (Brumfiel 1991). In her article 'Weaving and Cooking: Women's Production in Aztec Mexico', Brumfiel addresses the high frequency of spindle whorls found in certain sites in Mesoamerica. In pre-Aztec Mexico, large agricultural sites in rural areas such as Xico and Huexotla produced textiles just for domestic consumption. After these sites came under Aztec dominance there was a sharp decline in spindle whorl frequency (Brumfiel 1991:234). Those sites lying outside of the Valley of Mexico however, show a drastic increase in spindle whorl frequency after the Aztec conquest. Brumfiel postulates that the less intensive manufacture of textiles in the rural areas adjacent to the power center was made possible by increasing participation in local market exchange (*ibid.*). However, those sites lying at distances outside the Valley of Mexico and too far from Tenotchtitlan to deliver perishable agricultural goods, engaged in a heavy increase in cloth manufacture, as evidenced by the sharp increase in spindle whorls. What occurred then was what Brumfiel (1980) characterizes as a rational realloca-tion of labor.

In dealing with the Aztec empire, Brumfiel's elaborate and impressive model is based on a total of only 282 spindle whorls. This seems like an exceedingly small sample size for such a vast area with many sites; however, the patterns suggested by the Aztec model and their social implications are of great interest to the Gilat sanctuary analysis which has a spindle whorl sample size roughly four times as large than the Valley of Mexico study. In order to test some aspects of Brumfiel's model at Gilat and the nature of textile production, we examined the spatial distributions of spindle whorls and other artifacts throughout most of the strata identified at Gilat.

Spatial Distributions through Time of Spindle Whorls and Bone Tools at Gilat

As noted above, a total of 163 spindle whorls (cf. Table 14.1) and 240 bone tools were found at Gilat.[4] The distribution patterns of both artifact types over time suggest a sharp increase in industrial activity and a stronger organization of such activities through time

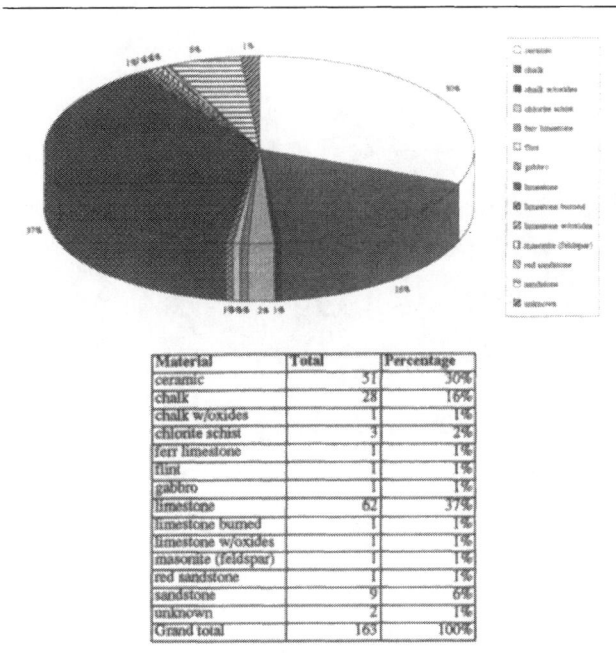

Material	Total	Percentage
ceramic	31	30%
chalk	28	16%
chalk w/oxides	1	1%
chlorite schist	3	2%
ferr limestone	1	1%
flint	1	1%
gabbro	1	1%
limestone	62	37%
limestone burned	1	1%
limestone w/oxides	1	1%
masonite (feldspar)	1	1%
red sandstone	1	1%
sandstone	9	6%
unknown	2	1%
Grand total	163	100%

Figure 14.2. Material Distribution of Spindle Whorls.

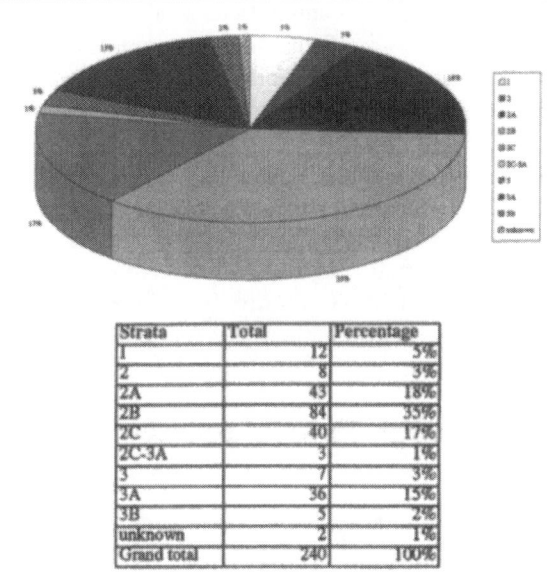

Strata	Total	Percentage
1	12	5%
2	8	3%
2A	43	18%
2B	84	35%
2C	40	17%
2C-3A	3	1%
3	7	3%
3A	36	15%
3B	5	2%
unknown	2	1%
Grand total	240	100%

Figure 14.3. Bone Tool Distribution by Stratum.

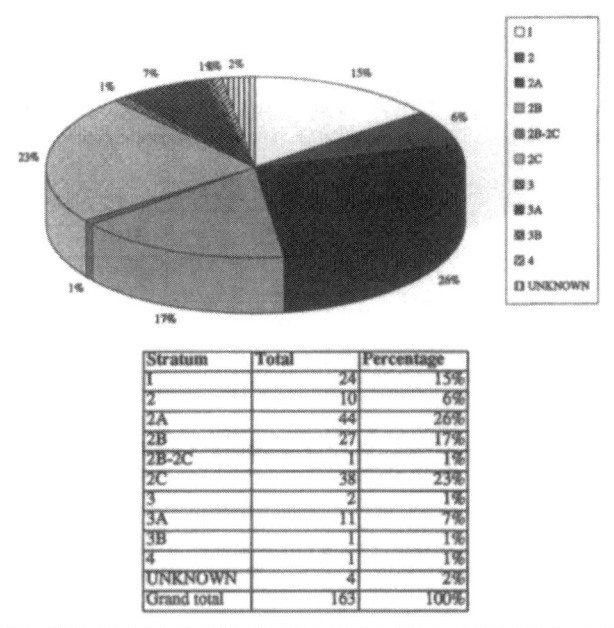

Stratum	Total	Percentage
1	24	15%
2	10	6%
2A	44	26%
2B	27	17%
2B-2C	1	1%
2C	38	23%
3	2	1%
3A	11	7%
3B	1	1%
4	1	1%
UNKNOWN	4	2%
Grand total	163	100%

Figure 14.4. Spindle Whorl Distribution by Stratum.

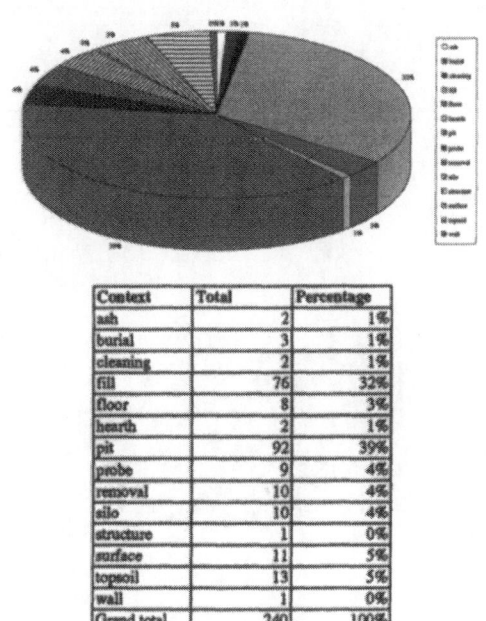

Context	Total	Percentage
ash	2	1%
burial	3	1%
cleaning	2	1%
fill	76	32%
floor	8	3%
hearth	2	1%
pit	92	39%
probe	9	4%
removal	10	4%
silo	10	4%
structure	1	0%
surface	11	5%
topsoil	13	5%
wall	1	0%
Grand total	240	100%

Figure 14.5. Bone Tool Distribution by Context.

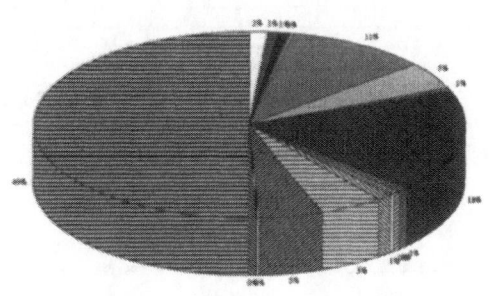

Context	Total	Percentage
ash	5	3%
burial	3	2%
cleaning	2	1%
dead locus	1	1%
fill	35	21%
floor	15	9%
hearth	2	1%
pit	58	35%
removal	3	2%
rubbish dump	1	1%
silo	1	1%
structure	4	2%
surface	15	9%
topsoil	16	10%
wall	1	1%
unknown	1	1%
Grand total	163	100%

Figure 14.6. Spindle Whorl Distribution by Context.

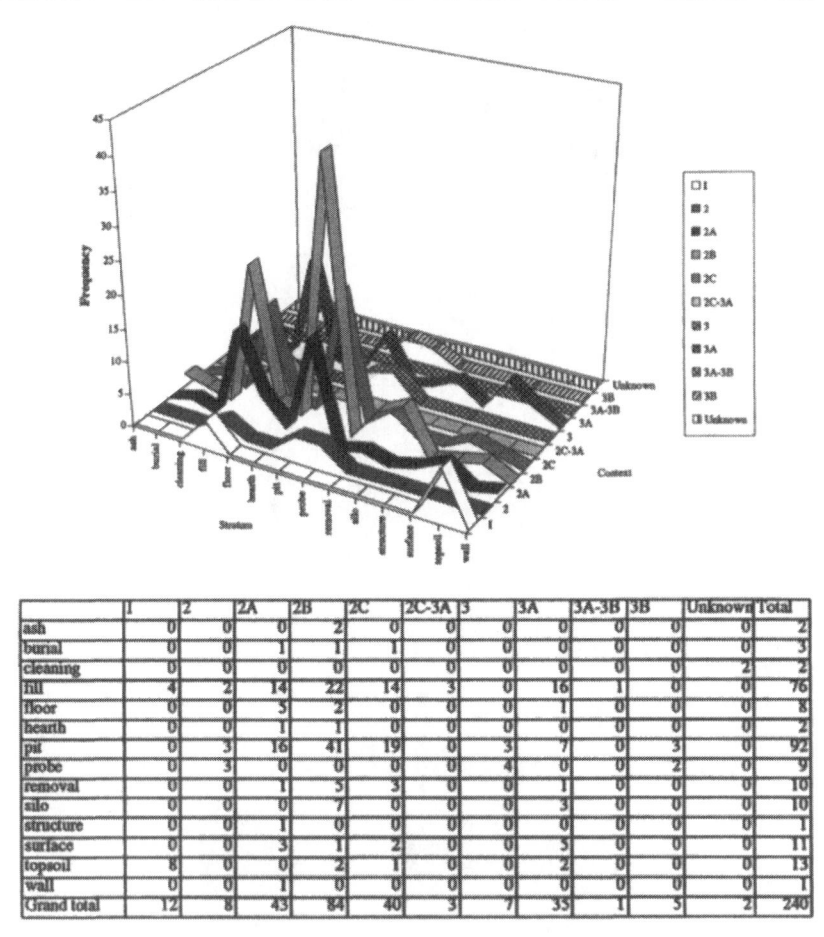

	1	2	2A	2B	2C	2C-3A	3	3A	3A-3B	3B	Unknown	Total
ash	0	0	0	2	0	0	0	0	0	0	0	2
burial	0	0	1	1	1	0	0	0	0	0	0	3
cleaning	0	0	0	0	0	0	0	0	0	0	2	2
hill	4	2	14	22	14	3	0	16	1	0	0	76
floor	0	0	5	2	0	0	0	1	0	0	0	8
hearth	0	0	1	1	0	0	0	0	0	0	0	2
pit	0	3	16	41	19	0	3	7	0	3	0	92
probe	0	3	0	0	0	0	4	0	0	2	0	9
removal	0	0	1	5	3	0	0	1	0	0	0	10
silo	0	0	0	7	0	0	0	3	0	0	0	10
structure	0	0	1	0	0	0	0	0	0	0	0	1
surface	0	0	3	1	2	0	0	5	0	0	0	11
topsoil	8	0	0	2	1	0	0	2	0	0	0	13
wall	0	0	1	0	0	0	0	0	0	0	0	1
Grand total	12	8	43	84	40	3	7	35	1	5	2	240

Figure 14.7. Bone Tool Distribution by Context and Stratum.

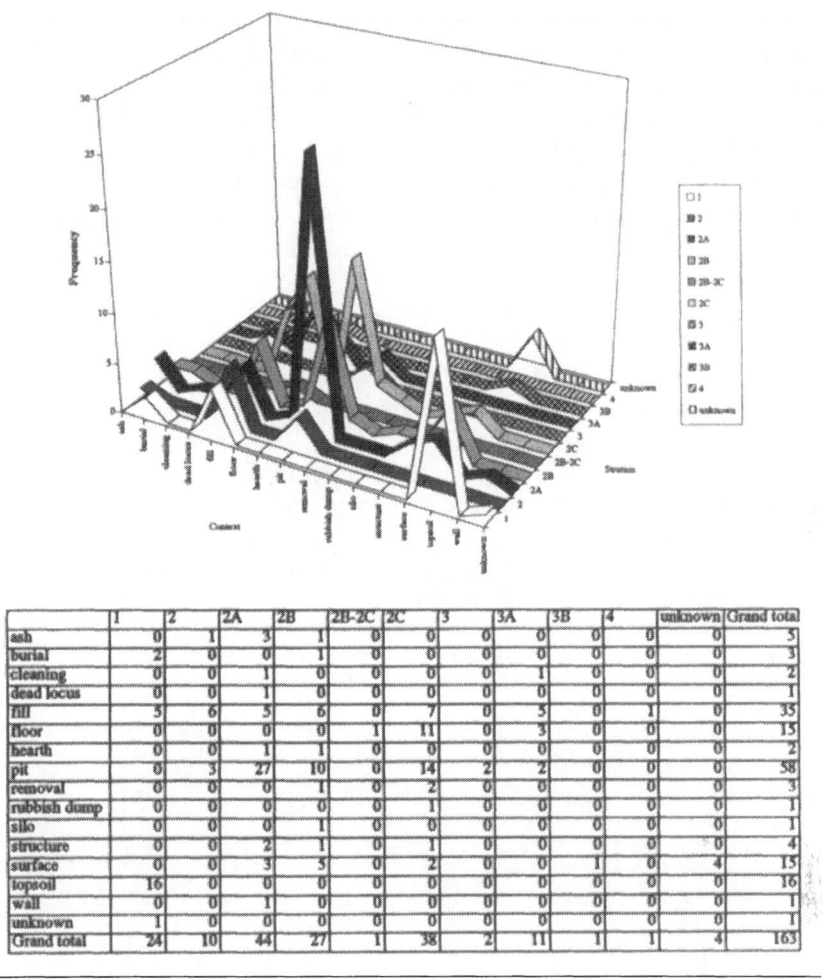

	1	2	2A	2B	2B-2C	2C	3	3A	3B	4	unknown	Grand total
ash	0	1	3	1	0	0	0	0	0	0	0	5
burial	2	0	0	1	0	0	0	0	0	0	0	3
cleaning	0	0	1	0	0	0	0	1	0	0	0	2
dead locus	0	0	1	0	0	0	0	0	0	0	0	1
fill	5	6	5	6	0	7	0	5	0	1	0	35
floor	0	0	0	0	1	11	0	3	0	0	0	15
hearth	0	0	1	1	0	0	0	0	0	0	0	2
pit	0	3	27	10	0	14	2	2	0	0	0	58
removal	0	0	0	1	0	2	0	0	0	0	0	3
rubbish dump	0	0	0	0	0	1	0	0	0	0	0	1
silo	0	0	0	1	0	0	0	0	0	0	0	1
structure	0	0	2	1	0	1	0	0	0	0	0	4
surface	0	0	3	5	0	2	0	0	1	0	4	15
topsoil	16	0	0	0	0	0	0	0	0	0	0	16
wall	0	0	1	0	0	0	0	0	0	0	0	1
unknown	1	0	0	0	0	0	0	0	0	0	0	1
Grand total	24	10	44	27	1	38	2	11	1	1	4	163

Figure 14.8. Spindle Whorl Distribution by Context and Stratum.

Early Strata

In the earliest strata represented by IV, IIIC and IIIB, very few spindle whorls and bone tools were recovered. Only five scattered bone tools and one spindle whorl were recorded from Stratum IIIB (see Figs. 14.3, 14.4). Stratum IIIA however, shows an increase in the frequency of both artifacts although there exists only slight clustering between the two themselves over the site area (see Figs 14.9, 14.10). 7 % (n = 10) of the total spindle whorls were recovered in this stratum (see Fig 14.4), five of which were found in fills as opposed to pits and other miscellaneous contexts. Bone tools however, appear frequently in this stratum and compose 15 % (n = 36) of all the bone tools collected. Like the spindle whorls, the majority were found in fill and cleaning contexts (see Fig. 14.7).

The only significant cluster of bone tools in Stratum IIIA was found in Sq. H3 with 14 bone tools and one spindle whorl (see Fig 14.5). This cluster is surrounded by wall 97, wall 98 and a silo identified as Locus 1369. As indicated in Chapter 5 (this volume), wall 98 is probably part of a large, incomplete, circle of mudbrick that was part of a circular platform like the ones that characterize Stratum IIB. While the purpose of this structure is still unknown, it is interesting that so many bone tools were found in its immediate vicinity. Of importance here is the fact that Stratum IIIA represents the first attempt by the inhabitants of Gilat to build large open plaza areas, unrelated to domestic activities. It is here in these public areas that for the first time we begin to detect evidence of non-domestic activities. In Stratum IIIA, there is a spatial division between the public plaza and the adjacent areas in the west and south where craft and other activities took place. As seen in Figure 14.9 and Figure 14.10 spindle whorls are found mostly in the west side of the site and bone tools are found in the south, both distributed away from the plaza. This spatial segregation suggests that two separate activities related to textile manufacture (and possibly hide working) were carried out by different areas of the site during this early occupation phase at the site.

Stratum IIC

While the frequency of spindle whorls (n = 38; 23 %) and bone tools (n = 40; 17 %) in Stratum IIC increases, there exists only slight cluster patterns and virtually no spatial parallels between bone tools and spindle whorls in the data (see Figs 14.11, 14.12). The artifacts are distributed much more evenly over the site's area and rarely are they found in groups of more than two. Stratum IIC is marked by hard surface areas which the excavators hypothesize were the floors of structures (see Chapter 5, this volume). Three spindle whorls and one bone tool were found on surfaces from Loci 1049, 1105 and 1144 of Sq. J2. In a pit identified as Locus 1118 a spindle whorl, bone awl, and palette were found with ash and animal bones.

Stratum IIB

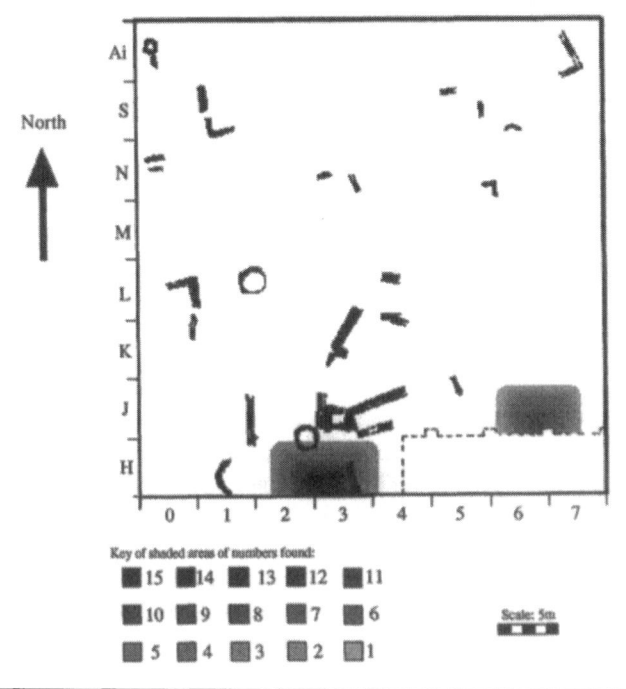

Figure 14.9. Bone Tool Distribution of Stratum IIIA.

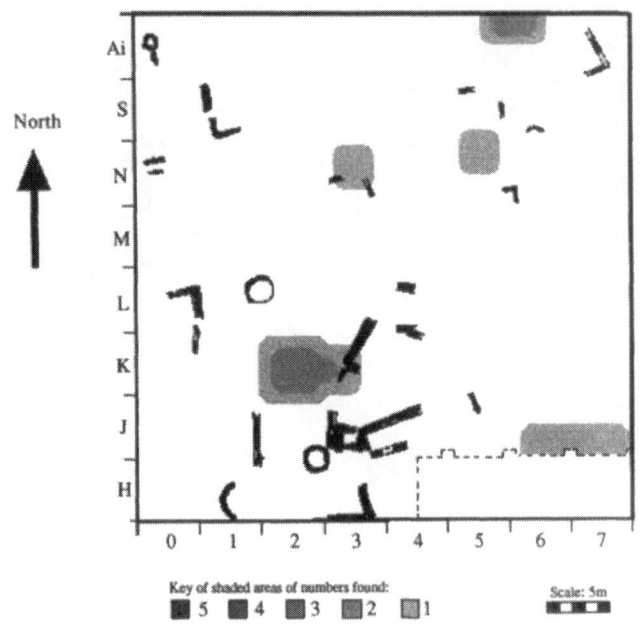

Figure 14.10. Spindle Whorl Distribution of Stratum IIIA.

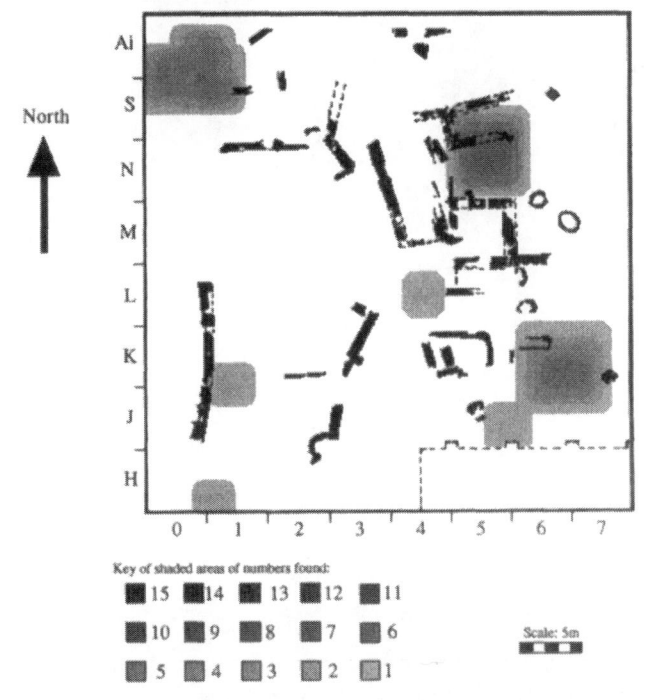

Figure 14.11. Bone Tool Distribution of Stratum IIC.

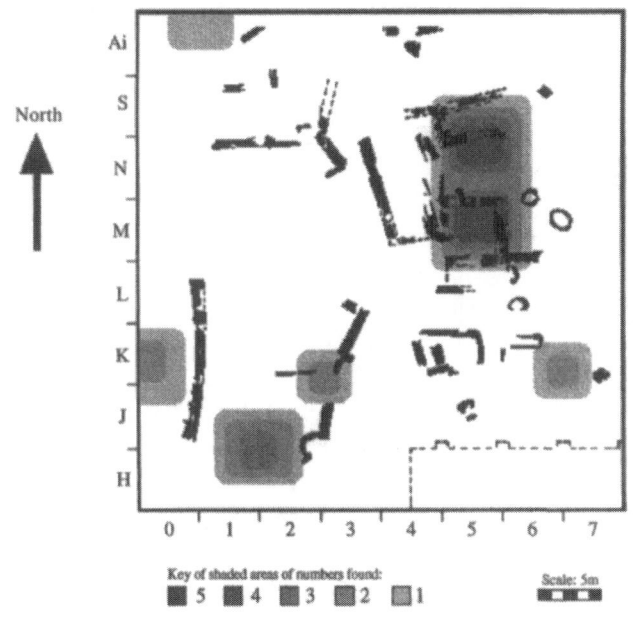

Figure 14.12. Spindle Whorl Distribution of Stratum IIC.

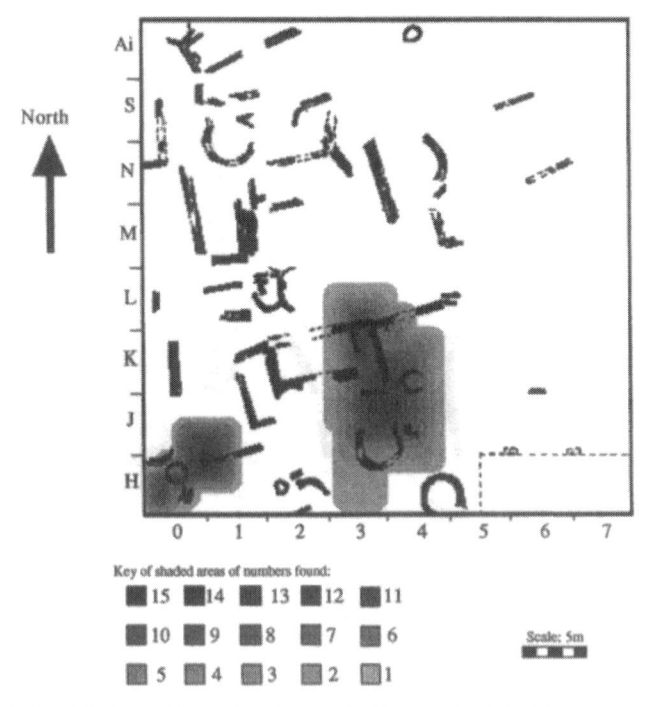

Figure 14.13. Bone Tool Distribution of Stratum IIB.

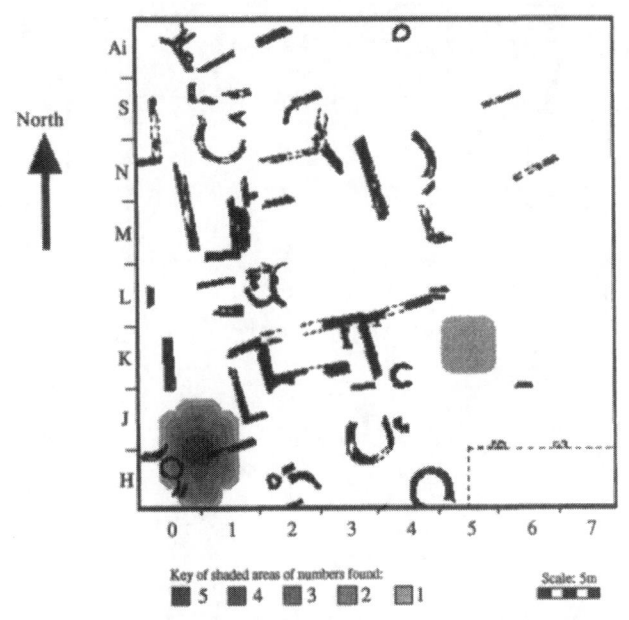

Figure 14.14. Spindle Whorl Distribution of Stratum IIB.

The distribution of spindle whorls and bone tools in IIIA and IIC is more stochastic and relatively few clusters appear in the data. This is apparent when each of these artifact types is examined together or individually. However there appears to be a drastic shift in distribution patterns within Stratum IIB. Stratum IIB contains the majority 35 % (n = 84) of the bone tools and 17 % (n = 27) of the spindle whorls from Gilat (see Figs. 14.3, 14.4). Stratum IIB represents the rebuilding of the cult complex at Gilat and the shift of the main architecture toward the west of the site. As described in Chapter 5 at least four large circular platforms, courtyards, cult buildings, a mortuary structure and other features are found here. As noted in the architectural analysis of Stratum IIB, this is the period of sanctuary construction seems to represent the most centralized period of planning and organization of the site. Similarly, the more centralized organization of textile production seems to have occurred at this time at Gilat.

The spatial analysis of Stratum IIB reveal the first instance in the stratigraphic sequence where there is a striking similarity between clusters of bone tools and spindle whorls (see Figs. 14.13, 14.14; see footnote 1 below). The corresponding clusters stretch from squares K3–K4. A large cluster of tools was found in a silo located at Square K4, Locus 882 whose rim was strengthened with stones and mudbrick and which excavators believe was designed for perennial use (see Chapter 5, this volume). Six bone tools were recovered here and suggest an industrial activity area. Another notable cluster was located at adjacent pits 1052 and 1044 of square J1. Locus 1052 which composed the floor of Room 10 produced three spindle whorls and three bone tools while Locus 1044 produced five bone tools and two spindle whorls. Excavations in Room 2 also revealed five bone tools and no spindle whorls although fragments of violin-shaped figures were found.

In IIB both artifact types were found predominantly in pits with the number of bone tools found in pits totaling 41 (17 %; Fig 14.7) and spindle whorls numbering 10 (6 %; Fig. 14.12). The large presence of spindle whorls and especially bone tools in this stratum strongly suggest the presence of industrial activities.

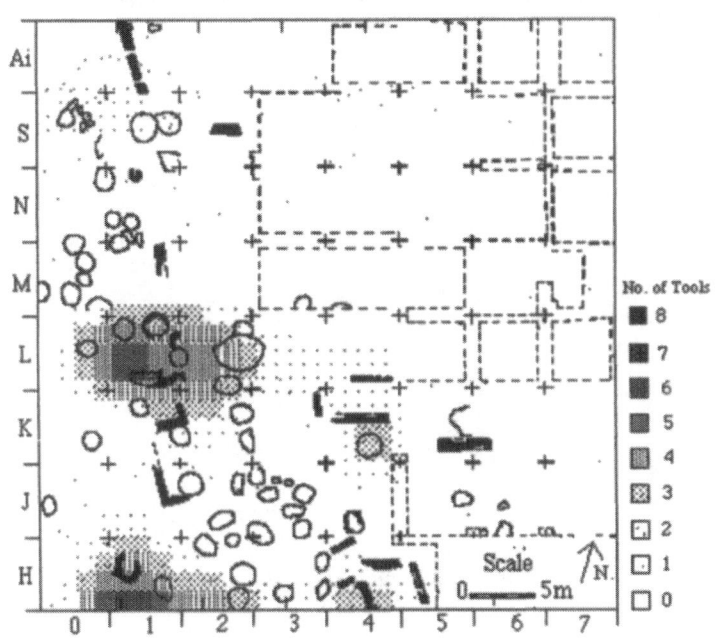

Figure 14.15. Bone Tool Distribution of Stratum IIA.

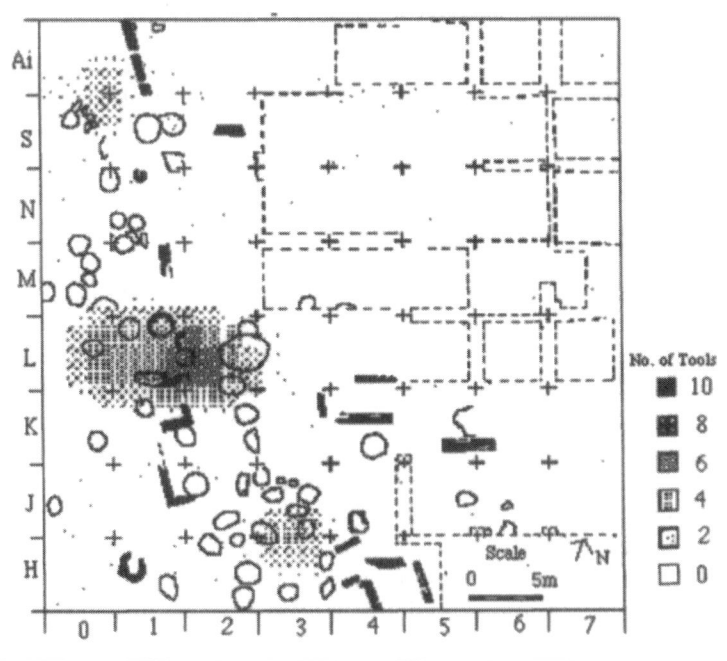

Figure 14.16. Spindle Whorl Distribution of Stratum IIA.

One of the most interesting pits in Stratum IIB was Locus 1344 in area H0. The 'multi-use' pit was linked to two different brief phases of use during the IIB occupation. The amount of time that elapsed between these two 'micro' depositional events is difficult to say. However, time between these two events can probably be measured in hours. The earlier phase was characterized by ashy deposits and the cluster of horn cores from gazelle (see Chapter 6, this volume), seven bone tools and an animal figurine. The latter phase produced seven bone awls that had been charred by fire and a fenestrated stand. The clustering of these artifacts in the pit, the careful mudbrick coating representing the first depositional event and the addition of more bone tools to the pit are indicative of a ritual event. Just why such large numbers of bone tools were included in the pit may be impossible to understand. However, the juxtaposition of the 'wild' gazelle and the 'domestic' bone tools that probably played a role in textile activities during the Stratum IIB occupation may be a kind of metaphor for some of the cognitive issues that concerned the people of Gilat—most probably linked to the growing distance between the sanctuary economy and earlier ones linked to hunting.

Stratum IIA

Although Stratum IIA is characterized by a more ephemeral architectural layout and is interpreted as less intensely occupied, there is still evidence for the continuation of textile production activities at this time. Stratum IIA represents the first occupation phase which has archaeological deposits that are relatively undisturbed in the Gilat sequence (see Chapter 5, this volume). IIA contains 18 % (n = 43) of the total bone tools and 26 % (n = 44; see Figs. 14.3, 14.4), of the total spindle whorls. Within this stratum a definite activity area manifests between squares L1 and L3 as evidenced by the superimposed clusters of bone tools and spindle whorls (see Figs 14.15, 14.16). A cluster of bone tools was also detected in square H1 from Loci 1037 and 1038 in ashy deposits. Most of the spindle whorls and bone tools in these squares are found in pits as in Stratum IIB (see Figs 14.7, 14.8). In pit Locus 1029, excavations revealed four spindle whorls and five bone tools alone. With few exceptions, the majority of these pits are 'secondary use' pits (Chapter 5). They are shallow, unlined pits which most likely were created for temporary storage and then later used as rubbish dumps. Most of the spindle whorls and bone tools are found in these types of pits. Some spindle whorls were found associated with unusual features in Stratum IIA such as the 'snake' structure composed of stone and mudbrick lying in a twisting pattern from Locus 1116 in square L1.

Stratum I

While Stratum I was largely disturbed by ploughing activities, a large amount of cultural material was recovered including 24 spindle whorls and 12 bone tools (see Figs 14.3, 14.4). It is interesting to note that while this layer was exposed to recent farming activities, it was still possible to identify superimposed clusters of bone tools and spindle whorls (see Figs. 14.17, 14.18). This is seen in a cluster of these two artifact types within the squares of J/K-5/6 indicating some sort of activity area within these deposits. Within these squares the majority of spindle whorls were recovered in groups of twos and threes. As all architecture had been destroyed within Stratum I, the only context in which artifacts were recovered was in topsoil and fills.

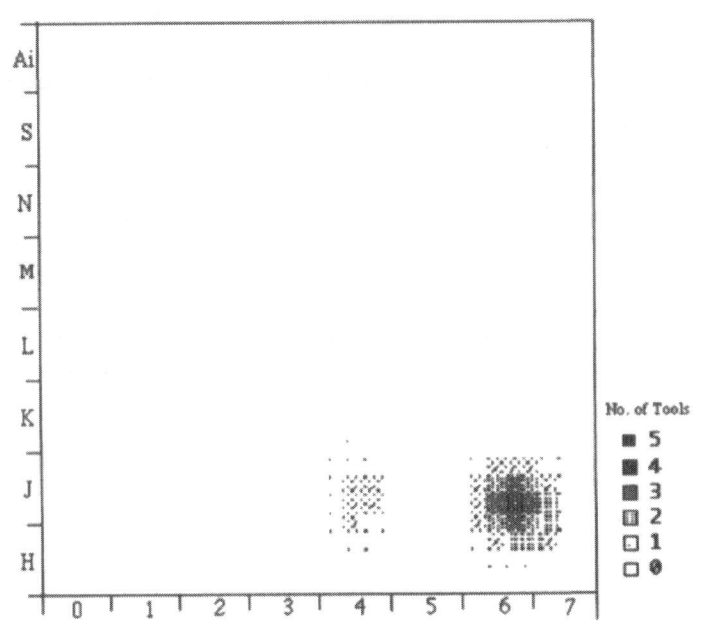

Figure 14.17. Bone Tool Distribution of Stratum I (note: no architectural remains were found here due to post-depositional disturbance).

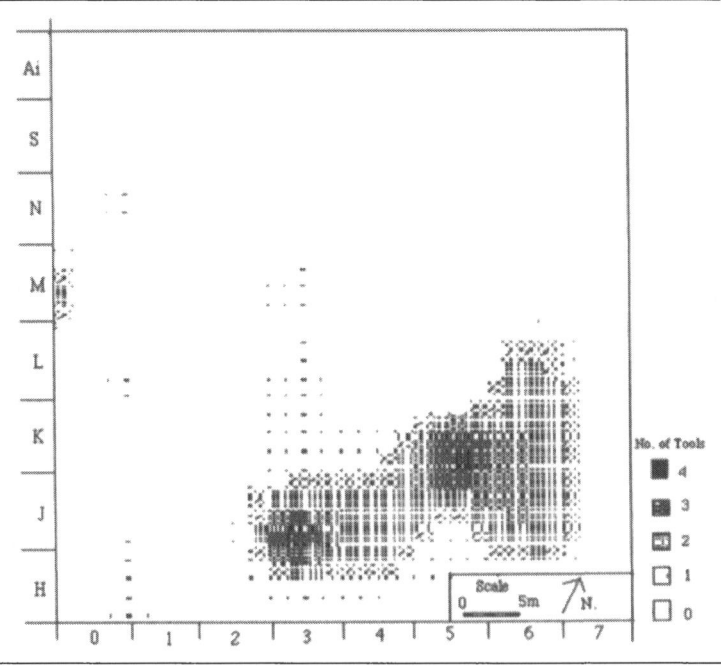

Figure 14.18. Spindle Whorl Distribution of Stratum I.

Gilat Textile Production through Time: An Overview

Over the course of time from the earliest strata to the most recent there appears to be a heightened intensity in textile production as evidenced by the increase in numbers of artifacts. Coinciding with an increase in numbers is a centralization of and 'clustering' of tools and whorls, thus suggesting that production may have been more centrally organized in the plaza areas as opposed to domestic organization of labor and resources. In the earlier strata (IV, IIIB), there are few spindle whorls or bone tools; however, in Stratum IIIA and IIC those numbers begin to climb and small clusters of bone tools and spindle whorls are manifest throughout the site. While the number of spindle whorls drops slightly from 36 in Stratum IIC to 27 in Stratum IIB, one can see a trend of clustering beginning in Stratum IIB between bone tools and spindle whorls. The number of bone tools increases dramatically from 32 in IIC to 74 in IIB and 40 in IIA, thus suggesting an increase in the production output as well an organizational capacity from the inhabitants at Gilat.

The main activity areas for textile production that we identified at Gilat include squares L1 and L2 of Stratum IIA and J1 of Stratum IIB. In light of Brumfiel's model, we can hypothesize that over time, the inhabitants of Gilat moved from a domestic form of textile production during the initial settlement phases (Strata IV and IIIB) to a more organized and intensified form. We can speculate that this intensification of production emerged from Gilat's peripheral location to the major area of Chalcolithic settlement in the Beersheva Valley to the south and the Chalcolithic 'heartland' in the lower Jordan valley to the east. As Gilat was situated in an ecotone setting (see Chapter 1, this volume) between the rich grazing lands of the Negev coastal plain and agriculturally viable valley bottom lands in the Beersheva valley and other Negev trough-shape valleys, Gilat's inhabitants may have found it economically rewarding to specialize in textile production to import some of its agricultural products. Much like the peripheral towns of Mexico, Gilat could have chosen to participate in a fairly developed Chalcolithic exchange system and use its own textile products (embedded with ritual and symbolic value and prestige) to trade for food stuffs, staples, and other prestige goods to support the specialized religious community at this site. Once Gilat's reputation as a regional center was established in Stratum IIC, the layout of the buildings, courtyards and other architectural features at the site suggest that textile production became more systematic and centralized during this period when the site experienced its organizational zenith.

One of the most interesting patterns to emerge concerns Strata 2A, the last well preserved strata, where industrial level textile production is found in association with sporadic evidence of architectural features. Although the main cultic functions of the site that were characteristic of Strata IIB and IIC diminished, textile production may have been maintained in order to continue to attract outsiders to the site. This enabled Gilat's inhabitants to preserve Gilat's place as a center in the onslaught of culture change near the end of its occupation history in the northern Negev.

Linking Cult, Status and Spinning

While the textiles produced beyond the DMP probably served as a medium of exchange they may have also helped to enhance Gilat's reputation as a center of cultic activities. In this volume, we have argued that Gilat was an important cultic site that drew pilgrims from across the northern Negev and southern Judean hills with offerings (see also, Alon and Levy 1989). Non-local ritual artifacts such as violin-shaped figurines, basalt fenestrated stands, and the anthropomorphic and zoomorphic statuettes made in the Judean hills support this assertion. However, the spindle whorls themselves may also possess an element of cultic significance. As Weiner and Schneider (1989:3) explain:

> The ritual and discourse that surround its manufacture establish cloth as a convincing analog for the regenerative and degenerative processes of life, and as a great connector, binding humans not only to each other but to the ancestors of their past and the progeny who constitute their future.

The researcher then cannot limit themselves to simply associating textile production with the quotidian and 'domestic'. While textile production is a practical outgrowth of the human experience, it also harbors symbolic meaning for cultures worldwide. Cloth and its productive components such as spindle whorls can symbolize life, fertility, and a pantheon of human attributes. This may explain the use of exotic imported stone, the same stone used to make violin-shape figurines, to manufacture some of the finest spindle whorls found at Gilat.

Does the boon in textile manufacture reflect Joy McCorriston's (McCorriston 1997) model of the late fourth–third millennium 'Fiber Revolution' that occurred in Mesopotamia? Not exactly; the fiber revolution according to McCorriston (*ibid.* 517ff) was tied to the shift from a dependence on flax for fiber to its replacement by wool at the principal textile fiber. This shift also coincided with the development of large textile-producing workshops alongside the earlier ubiquitous small-scale, household-based producers. The shift to wool was also linked to changes in land tenure, social relations, and labor roles that culminated in the establishment of the great Mesopotamian temple, palaces and class based societies of the third millennium. In the southern Levant we know that, like Mesopotamia, during the Pre-Pottery Neolithic flax was alrready the primary fiber used for textile manufacture (Schick 1988:38, 1995:202). Linen fibers were obtained from flax (*Linum usitatissimum L.*) by cutting the fruiting flax plants and steeping them in water for a few weeks. Thus the fibers were separated from the soft tissues, and were then dried and bleached in the sun (Zohary 1982:73). By the Chalcolithic period, as seen by the evidence from numerous caves in the Judean desert (Bar Adon 1980:153; Schick 1998) linen textiles were manufactured in abundance and it is assumed that flax was cultivated in humid areas such as the Beth Shean and Jericho valleys, and the Ein Gedi region where water was abundant (Schick 1998:128). It is certainly possible that flax could have been grown in the water retentive soils around springs on the Negev coastal plain or in the moist valley bottoms of the inland foothill zone. Unfortunately, the Gilat archaeobotanical samples submitted for analysis were not processed in time for this publication. However, it is worth noting that in the Beersheva valley (Kislev 1987:266–71), some 16 km south of Gilat at the site of Shiqmim, during detailed studies of more than 50 identified plant species obtained through flotation sampling of archaeological deposits, no evidence of flax came to light.

While the majority of Chalcolithic textiles are made from linen, this does not rule out the importance that wool may have played in textile manufacture during the late fifth–fourth millennium. Chalcolithic linens have been found specifically associated with human burials—an ancient Middle Eastern (Jewish) burial tradition reflected in both the Hebrew Bible and the New Testament ('They took the body of Jesus, and bound it in linen cloths with the spices, as is the burial custom of the Jews', John 19:40). According to Grigson (Chapter 6, this volume)

> Exactly where Gilat fits on the continuum of meat, to meat + milk, to meat + milk + wool is difficult to ascertain, but what is clear is that the ageing and sexing analysis of sheep and goats does not indicate a highly specialized herding strategy. The most likely scenario, taking all the results together, is an unspecialized economy based primarily on meat production and herd security, but with secondary products such as milk and wool also being utilized.

Thus, the animal remains do not indicate a highly specialized pastoral production system that supplied large amounts of wool to the Gilat sanctuary. These results lend support to the idea that both linen and wool were used to produce textiles at Gilat—something that may also be reflected in the size distribution of the spindle whorls outlined above. During the Stratum IIB sanctuary sequence when the organizational aspects of the site were at their most complex level, two enigmatic 'concave mudbrick basins'—CMBs—were constructed which may actually have functioned as fiber processing installations for linen (see Chapter 5, this volume). Clearly, the Gilat subsistence and textile production system took the 'shot gun' approach to adaptation. Sheep and goats were certainly exploited for both milk and fibers at Gilat. However, given the ubiquitous nature of linen in Chalcolithic burial contexts in Palestine, the possibility that flax was also used in textile manufacture at Gilat cannot be discounted. Like the 'secondary products revolution' which crystallized during the late fourth–third millennium, in the southern Levant, the 'fiber revolution' began to take shape during the Chalcolithic period when so many new technological (craft specialization, metallurgy, horticulture) and social institutions (chiefdoms, regional ritual centers) emerged.

Finally, what can be said in conclusion about the social role of textiles in Chalcolithic society? The textiles found in association with the Cave of the Warrior provide the best interpretive models for understanding the meaning of textiles for identifying the social personae of the deceased. According to Schick (1998:21ff) who studied the textiles in detail and is relied on here, the burial bundle probably represents the owner's 'Sunday best' and were never used as ordinary daily garb. This is seen from the complete parts of the textiles that indicate they were not in use for a long period of time. There are no darns, patches or signs of extensive wear. The quality of production indicates that the same workshop was responsible for manufacturing the various cloth pieces in the 'burial bundle'. Accordingly (*ibid.* 21) the regularity of the spinning and the accomplished weaving, with attention to color details and decorative designs indicate 'a skilled spinning and weaving establishment was engaged in the production of cloth, with an outstanding craftsperson in charge of special assignments—with the band decoration indicating a workshop signature or a mark of ownership or clanship. The ethnohistorical record of the Levant indicates that rank, authority and holiness were often expressed by fringes on garments (Milgrom 1981, 1983). Ornate hems with tassels were considered a symbolic extension of the owner and especially of rank and authority (*ibid.* 61). With specific reference to the male burial in the Cave of the Warrior, Schick (1998:22) suggests that the 'particularities of decoration are suggestive of a cloth designated for a person of high social standing—a "chief"', a ruler or a religious personality. If the Cave of the Warrior represents the final prestige laden textile product without a production address, Gilat certainly contained a textile workshop but lacks evidence of its final products. However, these two Chalcolithic textile-related sites provide complementary evidence that help us appreciate the role of textile manufactory in the social world of emergent middle range societies in this part of the Middle East.

Acknowledgments

Thanks to Robert McC. Adams for reading and commenting on an earlier version of this chapter. We are grateful to Eric Kansa, Preston Addison, Jeff Moorhead, David Phillips, and Guillermo Algaze for their insights as well. However, the views expressed here, and any factual errors, are the authors.

Notes

1.   There are slight discrepancies in the absolute number of bone tools and spindle whorls used in the spatial analyses in this chapter and the numbers given in Chapters 12 and 13 (this volume). This is because the data sets used here were collected shortly after the 1992 excavation season and before the final inventories were made. In addition, the fact that the Israel Antiquities Authority storage facility moved during this period resulted in the temporary misplacement of some Gilat data. Given this provision, the general artifact patterns observed here will not change. Researchers interested in testing results presented here should use the data sets published in Chapters 12 and 13 (this volume).

2. In Grigson's more detailed study (see Chapter 13, this volume), a total of 278 bone tools were analyzed. At the time of the study presented in this chapter, the remaining 38 tools were unavailable for analysis. However, the general trends observed in both Grigson's and our study are quite similar.

3. For replication experiments, McConaughy used pine dowels and white-tailed deer antler. This limits the potential identification of wear produced when used on softer materials.

4. See footnote 1 concerning the sample size of bone tools and other artifacts described in this chapter. This research was carried out before more robust spatial analysis methods based on GIS were available to the researchers. For the preferred methodology based on GIS, see Levy *et al*. 2001.

References

Alon, D. (1976) Two cult figurines from Gilat. *Atiqot* 11:116–18.

— (1977) A Chalcolithic temple at Gilat. *Biblical Archaeologist* 40:63–65.

Alon, D., and Levy, T.E. (1989) The Archaeology of Cult and Chalcolithic Sanctuary at Gilat. *Journal of Mediterranean Archeology* 2:163–221.

Amiran, R. (1978) *Early Arad: The Chalcolithic Settlement and Early Bronze City*. Jerusalem: The Israel Exploration Society.

Anati, E. (1963) *Palestine before the Hebrews*. London: Jonathan Cape.

Appadurai, A. (1986a) Introduction: commodities and the politics of value. In *The Social Life of Things: Commodities in Cultural Perspective*, edited by A. Appadurai. Cambridge: Cambridge University Press, pp. 3–63.

Bar Adon, P. (1980) *The Cave of the Treasure*. Jerusalem: Israel Exploration Society.

Bar Yosef, O., and Alon, D. (1988) Nahal Hemar Cave. *Atiqot* 18.

Barber, E.J.W. (1991) *Prehistoric Textiles: The Development of Cloth in the Neolithic and Bronze Ages*. Princeton: Princeton University Press.

Bloch, M., and Parry, J. (1989) Introduction: money and the morality of exchange. In *Money and the Morality of Exchange*, edited by M. Bloch. Cambridge: Cambridge University Press, pp. 1–32.

Breasted, (1906) *Ancient Records of Egypt II*. Chicago.

Brumfiel, E.M. (1980) Specialization, market exchange, and the Aztec State: a view from Huexotla. *Current Anthropology* 21:459–78.

— (1991) Weaving and cooking: women's production in Aztec Mexico. In *Engendering Archaeology: Women and Prehistory*, edited by M.W. Conkey. Oxford and New York: Blackwell, pp. 224–51.

Campana, D.V. (1989) *Natufian and Protoneolithic Bone Tools*. BAR International Series 494. Oxford: British Archaeological Reports.

Dalley, S. (1977) Old Babylonian trade in textiles at Tell al Rimah. *Iraq* 39:155–9.

Dollfus, G., and Kafafi, Z. (1988) *Abu Hamid: Village du 4e Millenaire de la Vallee du Jourdain*. Amman: Centre Culturel Francais et Department des Antiquities de Jourdanie.

Dothan, M. (1959) Excavations at Horvat Beter (Beersheba). *Atiqot* II:1–42.

Doughty, C.M. (1888) *Travels in Arabia Deserta*. Cambridge: Cambridge University Press.

Douglas, M., and Isherwood, B. (1981) *The World of Goods*. New York: Basic Books.

Fox, N.S. (1995) The striped goddess from Gilat: implications for the Chalcolithic cult. *Israel Exploration Journal* V45:212–25.

Gal, Z., Smithline, H., and Shalem D. (1997a) A Chalcolithic burial cave in Peqi'in, Upper Galilee. *Israel Exploration Journal* 47:145–54.

— (1997b) A chalcolithic burial cave in Peqi'in, Upper-Galilee (Early artistic development of figurative anthropomorphic and iconographic sculpture from a fifth-millennium BCE Galilean culture). *Israel Exploration Journal* V47:145–54.

Garfinkel, Y. (1987a) Yiftahel: a Neolithic village from the seventh millennium B.C. in the Lower Galilee, Israel. *Journal of Field Archaeology* 14:199–212.

Garfinkel, Y., and Horwitz, L.K. (1988) The Pre-Pottery Neolithic B bone industry from Yitahel, Israel. *Paleorient* 14:73–85.

Garstang, J. (1953) *Prehistoric Mersin: Yumuk Tepe in Southern Turkey*. Oxford: Clarendon Press.

Gopher, A., and Tsuk, T. (eds.) (1996) *The Nahal Qanah Cave: Earliest Gold in the Southern Levant.* Monograph Series of the Institute of Archaeology. Tel Aviv: Tel Aviv University.

Goren, Y. (1995) Shrines and ceramics in Chalcolithic Israel: the view through the petrographic microscope. *Archaeometry* 37:287–305.

Gosden, C. (1989) Debt, production and prehistory. *Journal of Anthropological Archaeology* 8:355–87.

Harris, M. (1978) *Cows, Pigs, Wars, and Witches.* Glasgow: Collins.

Hayden, B. (1979) Snap, shatter and superfractures: use-wear of stone skin scrapers. In *Lithic Use-Wear Analysis,* edited by B. Hayden. New York: Academic Press, pp. 207–29.

Henry, D.O. (1995) *Prehistoric Cultural Ecology and Evolution: Insights from Southern Jordan.* New York: Plenum Press.

Jacobsen, T. (1970) *Toward the Image of Tammuz and Other Essays.* Cambridge, MA.

Joffe, A.H., Dessel, J.P., and Hallote, R.S. (2001) The 'Gilat Woman': female iconography, chalcolithic cult, and the end of southern Levantine prehistory. *Near Eastern Archaeology* V64:8–23.

Killen, J.T. (1966) The Knossos Lc (Cloth) Tablets. *University of London Institute of Classical Studies* 13:105–9.

Kirkbride, D. (1966) Five seasons at the pre-pottery Neolithic village of Beidha in Jordan. *Palestine Exploration Quarterly* 8:8–72.

Kislev, M. (1987) Chalcolithic plant husbandry and ancient vegetation at Shiqmim. In *Shiqmim I,* edited by T.E. Levy. BAR International Series 356.Oxford: British Archaeological Reports, pp. 251–79

Lambert, M. (1961) Recherches sur la vie ouvriere: les Ateliers de tissage de Lagash. *Archiv Orientalni* 29:422–43.

Lee, R. (1973) Chalcolithic Ghassul: New Aspects and Master Typology. Ph.D, Hebrew University, Jerusalem.

Levy, T.E. (1983) The emergence of specialized pastoralism in the southern Levant. *World Archaeology* 15:15–36.

— (ed.) (1987a) *Shiqmim I: Studies Concerning Chalcolithic Societies in the Northern Negev Desert, Israel (1982–1984).* BAR International Series 356.Oxford: British Archaeological Reports.

— (1992) Transhumance, subsistence, and social evolution in the northern Negev Desert. In *Pastoralsim in the Levant: Archaeological Material in Anthropological Perspective,* edited by A. Khaznov and O.B. Yosef. Madison, Wisconsin: Prehistory Press.

— (1997) 'Gilat', in *The Oxford Encyclopedia of Archaeology in the Near East,* edited by E. Meyers, pp. 404–05. Oxford: Oxford University Press.

— (1998) Cult, metallurgy and rank societies: Chalcolithic Period (ca. 4500–3500 BCE). In *The Archaeology of Society in the Holy Land,* edited by T.E. Levy. London: Leicester University Press, pp. 226–44.

Levy, T.E., Anderson, J. D., Waggoner, M.. Smith, N., Muniz, A., and Adams, R.B. (2001) Interface: archaeology and technology: digital archaeology 2001: GIS-based excavation recording in Jordan. *The SAA Archaeological Record* 1:23–9.

Levy, T. E., and Holl, A. (1987) Theory and practice in household archaeology: a case study from the Chalcolithic village at Shiqmim. In *Shiqmim I: Studies Concerning Chalcolithic Societies in the Northern Negev Desert, Israel (1982–1984),* edited by T.E. Levy. BAR International Series 356.Oxford: British Archaeological Reports, pp. 373–410.

Liep, J. (1999) Pecuniary Schismogenesis in the Massim', in *Money and Modernity.* Edited by J. Robbins, pp. 131 - 150. Pittsburgh: Pittsburgh University Press.

Liu, R.K. (1978) Spindle Whorls part I: some comments and speculations. *The Bead Journal* 3:87–103.

Lloyd, S., and Mellaart, J. (1962) Beycesultan, vol. I. *Occasional Oublications of the British Institute of Archaeology at Ankara.*

Lutz, J. (1923) *Textiles and Costumes among the Peopoles of the Ancient Near East.* Leipzig.

Madrigal, L. (1998) *Statistics for Anthropology.* Cambridge: Cambridge University Press.

Mallon, A., Koeppel, R. and Neuville, R. (1934) *Teleilat Ghassul I, 1929–32.* Rome: Pontifical Biblical Institute.

Marshall, D.N. (1982) Jericho bone tools and objects. In *Excavations at Jericho IV,* edited by K.M. Kenyon and T.A. Holland. Jerusalem, London: Brittish School of Archaeology, pp. 570–622.

Mauss, M. (1954) *The Gift: Forms and Functions of Exchange in Archaic Society.* London: Routledge.

McConaughy, M. (1979) Formal and Functional Analysis of Chipped Stone Tools from Bab edh-Dhra, University of Pittsburgh.

McCorriston, J. (1997) The fiber revolution: textile extensification, alienation, and social stratification in Ancient Mesopotamia. *Current Anthropology* 38:517–48.

Mellaart, J. (1962b) Excavations at Catal Huyuk. *Anatolian Studies* 12:41–65.

Milgrom, J. (1981) *The Tassel and the Tallith*. Cincinnati: Judaic Studies program University of Cincinnati.

— (1983) Of hems and tassels. *Biblical Archaeological Review* 19:61–5.

Miller, D. (1995) Consumption and commodities. *Annual Review of Anthropology* 24:141–61.

Murdoch, J. (1892) *Ethnological Results of the Point Barrow Expedition. Ninth Annual Report of the Bureau of Ethnology*. Washington, D.C.: Government Printing Office.

Nelson, E.W. (1983) (1899). *The Eskimo about Bering Strait*. Washington, D.C.: Smithsonian Institution Press.

Perrot, J. (1955) The excavations at Tell Abu Matar, near Beersheba. *Israel Exploration Journal* 5:17–41, 73–84, 167–89.

Philibert, J.-M. (1989) 'Consuming culture: a study of simple commodity consumption. In *The Social Economy of Consumption*, edited by B.J. Orlove. Lanham, Md.: University Press of America, pp. 59–84.

Robbins, J., and Akin, D. (1999) An introduction to Melanesian currencies: agency, identity, and social reproduction. In *Money and Modernity: State and Local Currencies in Melansia*, edited by J. Robbins. Pittsburgh: University of Pittsburgh Press, pp. 1–40.

Rosen, S.A. (1983) Tabular scraper trade: a model of material cultural dispersion. *Bulletin of the American Schools of Oriental Research* 249:79–86.

Rowan, Y.M., and Levy, T.E. (1991) Use wear analysis of a Chalcolithic scraper assemblage from Shiqmim. *Journal of the Israel Prehistoric Society (Mitekufat Haeven)* 24:112–34.

Ryder, M.L. (1983) Sheep and Man. London: Gerald Duckworth.

Sahlins, M. (1974) *Stone Age Economics*. London: Tavistock Publications.

Schick, T. (1988) Nahal Hemar cave: cordage, basketry and fabrics. *Atiqot* 18:31–43.

— (1995) A 10,000-year-old comb from Wadi Marabba'at in the Judean Desert. *Atiqot* 27:199–202.

— (ed.) (1998a) *The Cave of the Warrior: A Fourth Millennium Burial in the Judean Desert*. Jerusalem: Israel Antiquities Authority.

— (1998b) The sandals. In *The Cave of the Warrior: A Fourth Millennium Burial in the Judean Desert*, vol. 6, edited by T. Schick. Jerusalem: Israel Antiquities Authority, pp. 34–8.

Sherratt, A.G. (1981) Plough and pastoralism: aspects of the secondary products revolution. In *Patterns of the Past: Studies in Honour of David Clarke*, edited by I. Hodder, G. Isaac, and N. Hammond. Cambridge: Cambridge University Press, pp. 261–305.

Singh, P. (1974) *Neolithic Cultures of Western Asia*. London and New York: Seminar Press.

Unger-Hamilton, R. (1988) *Method in Microwear Analysis. Prehistoric Sickles and Other Stone Tools from Arjoune, Syria*. BAR International Series 435. Oxford: British Archaeological Reports.

Weiner, A.B., and Schneider, J. (1989) *Cloth and Human Experience*. Smithsonian series in ethnographic inquiry. Washington: Smithsonian Institution Press.

Weippert, H. (1998) Sanctuary as meeting place: an example of a chalcolithic sacred shrine at Gilat. *Zeitschrift des Deutschen Palastina-Vereins* V114:106–36.

Wheeler, M. (1982) Loomweights and Spindle Whorls. In *Excavations at Jericho IV*, edited by K.M. Kenyon and T.A. Holland. Jerusalem, London: Brittish School of Archaeology, pp. 623–37.

Zohary, M. (1982) *Plants of the Bible: A Complete Handbook*. Cambridge: Cambridge University Press.

15 Gilat's Figurines:

Exploring the Social and Symbolic Dimensions of Representation

Catherine Commenge, Thomas E. Levy, David Alon†, and Eric Kansa

We are dealing with something more than a set of themes, more than institutional elements, more than institutions, more even than systems of institutions divisible into legal, economic, religious and other parts. We are concerned with 'wholes', with systems in their entirety.

Marcel MAUSS (1923–24)

Introduction

The source of imagery is both varied and abundant at Gilat. A fortuitous and auspicious discovery of figurines in the early 1950s announced the later harvest of 69 figural representations yielded by seven seasons of excavations (Alon 1961, 1976, 1977; Alon and Levy 1989). This composite collection is commensurate with the wealth of evidence for ritual activities gathered at the site. Fifty-three violin-shaped figurines[1] (VSF) are soberly chiseled in fine plates of limestone and of more exotic sandstone, schist and granodiorite, or delicately silhouetted in bone. Spirited human and animal effigies are embodied in pottery vessels (see Fig. 15.1a for the distribution of VSF for the entire Levant). Thirteen zoomorphic figurines are modeled in clay and one is carved in exogenous peridotite. This concentration of small-scale representations, varied in media and style, contrasts with the discrete presence of figurines at other sites, as it sheds light on the singularity of Gilat in the background of the Chalcolithic southern Levant.

This chapter explores the processes that initiated the reification of the tangible and intangible world by means of human and animal representation during the Chalcolithic period. The present study of Gilat's figurines attempts to identify the explicit processes used by this prehistoric community in the construction of meaning in the figurative art at the site. It aims to clarify the social background that inspired and fostered them. Hermeneutics of latent or manifest meaning assume that, through the intervention of representation, form is an introductory step to understanding the symbolic content of an object. This assumption is not as inclusive as it may seem. The *medium* of representation is of prominent import with regard to the specific knowledge or meanings it conveys. Action on matter *and* mind in action are infused into the pregnant moment of artifacts' materialization (Lemonnier 1986:174; Leroi-Gourhan 1965:29, 66, 260; Pfaffenberger

1992:500; Schlanger 1994). The cognitive and behavioral processes and choices that operate in the conception and the construction of artifacts—the very channels of representation of knowledge— seem all the more significant when elaborated for figural representation.

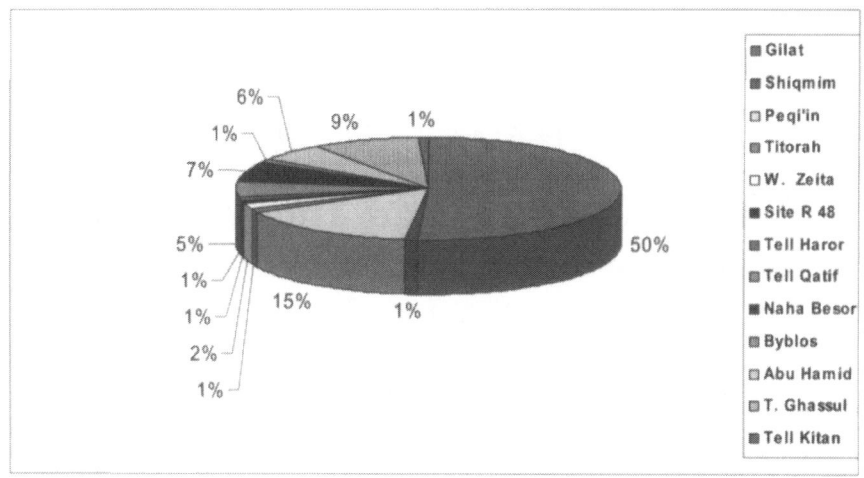

Figure 15.1a. Regional distribution of VSF for the Levant (N = 106).

Figurines do not offer obvious features indicative of direct action on the material world. The polysemous character of figurines has sometimes acted as a methodological aporia in interpreting them. However, the probable social and ideological role of figurines has invited discussion on their use, encouraging an exploration of their ritual and/or secular function (cf. Bailey 1996; Broman-Morales 1990, 1983; Cauvin 1994; Haaland and Haaland 1996; Hamilton 1996; Houmourziadis 1973; Marcus 1996; Mellaart 1970; Talalay 1993; Ucko 1968, 1996). In a recent study of Neolithic figurines from Greece, Talalay stressed the analytical need to distinguish between meaning and use of any figurine as she acknowledged that these notions were 'connected in the mind of the users' (Talalay 1993:38). Thus, there are some elementary steps to take in order, perhaps, to avoid the familiar 'minefields' of intellectual codes contrived by literary interpretive schemes. Structural evaluation that ponders the nature of figurines may entail systems of inference to circumscribe their status as signs, and the level at which symbols operated. The interaction between figurines and their users, between agents and actors in ritual performance, can only be founded on a large contextual spectrum of direct and indirect archaeological evidence. While the analytical framework presented here considers figural representation in action, a number of other variables are investigated in depth here. These include the place of figurine producers, the incidence of standardization (and its eventual digression), the organization of figurative object production and the nature of the demand and consumption of these objects. Reference to other realms of the material culture of the Chalcolithic Southern Levant—and to different means of symbolic elaboration—set the stage for Gilat's figurines. Quest for affiliate components will follow the complex web of earlier Neolithic societies, as the building blocks of the northern Negev intermediary societies. Ethnographic analogies eventually intervene, 'en contrepoint'.

The same analytical approach is applicable for many kinds of representations, both human and animal. The chasm that opposes culture *versus* nature cannot be *a priori* extended to the human *versus* animal condition, insofar as representation itself integrates them in the same realm of humanity.

As prologue to Gilat's figurines, this study should be understood as experimental and exploratory.

Anthropomorphic and Zoomorphic Vessels: The 'Lady' and the 'Ram' Effigies (Catherine Commenge)

The discovery of the statuettes or figurative vessels from Gilat generated widespread discussion within the Levantine archaeological community. Although there is a general consensus on the legibility of the vessels' cultic function, the commentators privileged an interpretive approach that considered selected iconographic details (Amiran 1976, 1989; Amiran and Tadmor 1980; Epstein 1982; Merhav 1993; Fox 1995; Tadmor 1988) and made erudite references to the mythology of early Near Eastern historical periods (Amiran 1976:120l; Alon 1977:64). A rather different approach is proposed here that, while referring to Neolithic symbolism for historical background, tries to determine, from the structure of both statuettes, how symbols could have been elaborated and used.

Embodying characters opposed in nature, the Ram and the Lady encapsulate a narrative depiction that locks them both in a similar 'angiophorous', pot-bearer role. By definition, effigy vessels are altogether subject and object, and as such, provide some evidence for literal and symbolical intricacy of form and content. They are characters and agents, foci of elaboration. As these objects are also receptacles, it can be assumed that they were instrumental in ritual performance (see Chapter 1, this volume). Definition and identification from physical and conceptual mechanisms involved in representation are critical in interpreting figurines (Bailey 1996:291). Here, the specificity of each represented character needs to be defined. Moreover, as both of these statuettes were found together in the same cult room of Stratum IIC (Room A), their possible reciprocal interplay needs to be ascertained.

The binary nature of ritual activity results in duplication of immutable actions, rooted in tradition, and in negotiation of the present social situation. The elaborate shape of these vessels, both seemingly designed for symbolical expression and practical use could reflect this dual strategy in ritual performance. Redundancy of elements by the way of analogy and homology is inherent to symbolic systems. The instilled components of imagery could thus be traced in other artifacts of the contemporary material culture, just as they already could be ground into previous ones. However, unique in the repertory of prehistoric Levantine 'art', these figurative vessels cannot be separated from the sociocultural context of the site, or from intra-regional and, perhaps, extra-regional late fifth–fourth millennium contexts.

Structural Conception and Vessel Embodiment

Figures 15.1 through 15.6 complete the fine-grained description and comments given by Alon (Alon 1976) shortly after the discovery of these statuettes. Petrographic studies indicate that the vessels were not made locally, but rather more than 50 km away in the Shephela region (Goren, Chapter 9).[2] Alon accurately remarked that both figurative vessels are made in sections built with different and connected miniature pots. The manufacture of miniature pottery vessels was common in the Chalcolithic period (Chapter 10, this volume). The height of the Woman is 31 cm (preserved), the total height of the Ram is 23 cm and its preserved length reaches 27.5 cm. Each figurine is skillfully shaped and has walls of regular thickness which are reinforced at the weakest places such as the connection between the pedestal seat and the pointed-base body of the Gilat Woman (Fig. 15. 1). Here, as with the zoomorphic figurines described below, skillful potter(s) made both statuettes. They are partly made from recognizable Chalcolithic pottery shapes, including the 'churn', beaker, cornet,[3] and pedestal bowl, already defined as ceremonial vessels (cf. Chapter 10, this volume). Miniaturization is also exclusive to these categories of vessels in the Gilat ceramic assemblage.

The opposite nature of their respective referent, one animal and the other human, is reflected in the *inverse* structure used to build the statuettes: three vessels carrying one to construct the Woman and one vessel carrying three to fabricate the Ram. The conception of these pot-bearer characters finds resonance in the Gilat pottery assemblage and this consideration can, perhaps, be stretched further than an obvious and predictable similitude of shapes. These figurative vessels are embodied shapes, decorated with organized painted designs, and completed with artifact attributes (pedestal seat, beakers, etc.). The allusive features of zoomorphic and of anthropomorphic nature, applied to some exclusive vessels, were presented and discussed in the ceramic analysis (Chapter 10).

The Gilat woman (incomplete height: 31 cm; Figs 15.1–15.3). The Gilat Woman is perhaps the most significant human representation in the site's material culture. The means of anthropomorphic representation are antithetical to those used for shaping the violin-shaped figurines. This figurative vessel is not conceived like the transfer in three-dimensions of the silhouetted surfaces of the stone violin figurines. Thus far, there is no precedent for this kind of gynecomorphous vessel or for any representation of women with explicit sexual depiction, together with artifact attributes, in the late prehistory of Palestine.[4] By the beginning of the sixth millennium, gynecomorphous vessels can be traced as far as northern Iraq, at Yarim Tepe II (Merpert *et al.* 1981). Closer to our Levantine specimen, jars representing a seated woman holding a vessel were uncovered at the Anatolian site of Hacilar (level I; Mellaart 1970:525: 1).[5] With this last representation, the jar entirely shapes the woman and homologous volumes reinforce the metaphorical relation between the receptacle and the referent. The neck, the body of the jar and of the woman is one and the same. The embodiment suggested in the case of the Lady of Gilat pertains from another nature. It remains a structure of pots with head and body shaped like individual pots. The metaphor of the embodiment is here based on analogous and not on homologous terms. The explicit character of the Lady is enhanced by the construction of separate elements—seat, body, head, churn-shaped vessel. Conversely, the seated figurative vessels from Hacilar are conceived as a 'wholes'.

The gynecomorphous vessel from Gilat presents a dramatized sexuality—tumescent pudenda, set off with red painted dots and incisions—that contradict an otherwise subdued feminity where breasts are reduced to the dimension of the button-shaped navel (Fig. 15.1). Realistic sexual characters can express sexual arousal, menstruation, defloration or parturition.[6] In terms of female characterization, they seem here the parts that stand for the whole. In order to be seen, pudenda are centered and exhibited on the lower abdomen. Hair, similar to the wavy hair of the Hacilar figurative vessels, is flowing down the back of the statuette and thus could be intended as a sexual metaphor. The limbs, although modeled in clay, are curiously emaciated and fingers and toes are misshaped and suggested by simple incisions.

The pedestal vessel used as a seat and the churn placed on the Woman's head are set off with plain red painting. A small pedestalled vessel is placed under the left arm. The inside of the bowl, shown from a frontal position, is decorated with red painted crossed lines, organized like a sunburst. The rather informal position of this small pedestal vessel was perhaps meant to show off this design and (or) to complete the narrative depiction with another distinctive although ostensibly passive accessory.

The linear designs applied to the body and limbs of the lady of Gilat have been interpreted as tattoos (Alon 1976; Fox 1995 and see Fig. 15. 1 and 15. 2). It can be assumed that for a vessel embodying a woman, decoration reflects and enhances the implied metaphor and is thus reciprocally meaningful. The observation in the Mafa society of Cameroon that the metaphor of the body and its adornment is the original source for decorating pots (David *et al.* 1988) may be reasonably stressed to anthropomorphic vessels in general. Moreover, Talalay (1993:35) clearly established that the decoration of pottery and clay figurines from Neolithic Franchti are 'markedly similar' and that this similarity creates 'explicit symbolic links between them'. Yet, with the exception of ossuaries, designs rarely occur on Chalcolithic vessels from the southern Levant and Gilat's assemblage is no exception.

Figure 15.1. The lady of Gilat with red-painted designs.

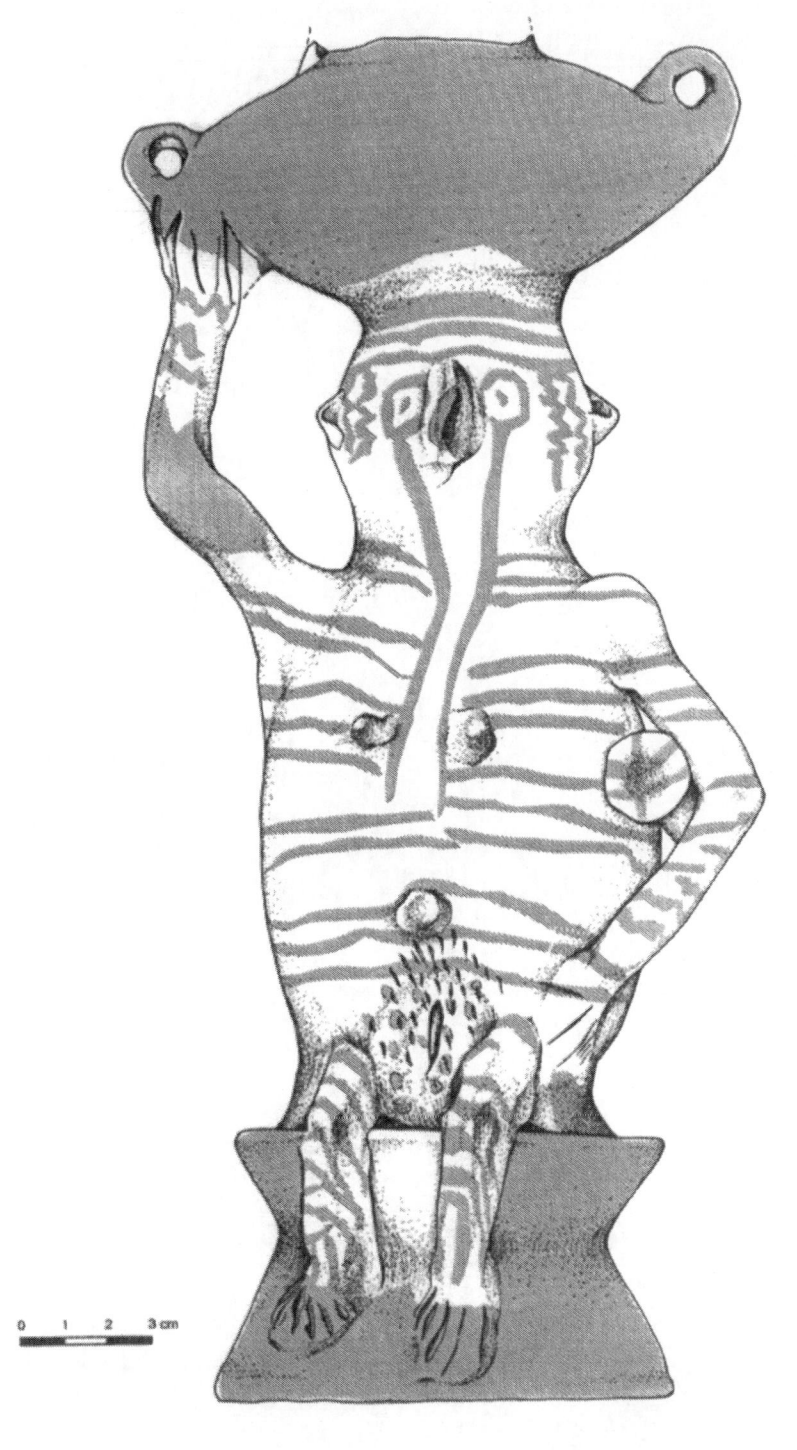

Figure 15.2. Side view of the Lady of Gilat.

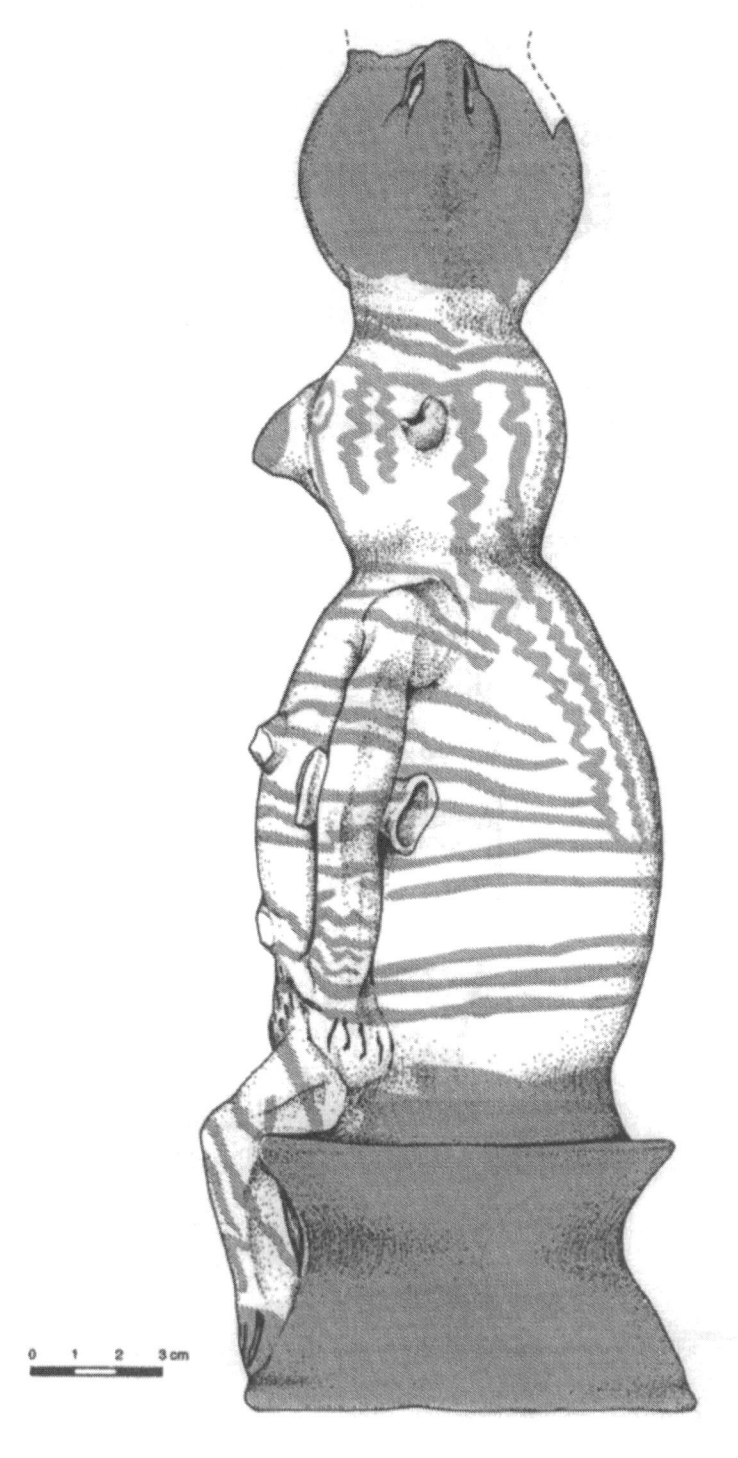

Figure 15.3. Profile of Gilat Lady.

Human features observed on Gilat ceremonial vessels refer to facial features (see Chapter 10, this volume).[7] References documenting elaborated designs or anatomical allusions on vessels are thus rather limited (or perhaps were not deciphered). However, horizontal bands of impressed designs placed on the maximal diameter of necked-jars is a common feature (Chapter 10, Fig. 10:19), and red painted bands are still characteristic of necked-jars at the Beersheva sites (Commenge-Pellerin 1987, 1990 Figs 42–49). The analogy between necked-jars and women (or any curvy profile) is obvious and a 'well-worn' interpretation.[8] Whether they give evidence for female tattooing or not, painted designs on the Gilat Lady are clearly organized from head to toe and will be scrutinized as potent symbolic expression.

Diachronic recurrence of designs and composition on Near-Eastern figurative vessels, beyond designating them as symbols, could confirm that the 'realistic' style of the Lady of Gilat is not structured from casual elements, but from conventional ones. Horizontal and vertical lines are conceived separately in different registers. Horizontal stripes of red paint cover the top of the head, the neck, body and limbs. Vertical and wavy lines cover the cheeks, back head and half of the back of the figurine. Eyes are circled and two vertical lines, which stop below the figurine's breasts, spring from them. Flowing liquid elements representing hair and tears (?) were painted first. Similar organization of painted designs is observed on one seated gynecomorphous jar from Hacilar I (Mellaart 1970:525: 1). The face and the back of the figurative jar are painted with vertical chevrons, neatly reserved from the body's painting. Similar vertical chevrons fill the pot held by the woman on her bosom, again suggesting a flowing, liquid element. The upper and lower parts of the body are painted with horizontal lines that emphasize the hips and the lower belly. Similar elements structure the organization of painted designs on both Anatolian and Levantine figurative vessels, suggesting that, despite contrasts in conception and the anteriority of the Anatolian specimen, they might allude to a common referent.

The specific representation of females by way of pots could result from one exclusive and metaphorical identification (Hodder 1982:67; Levi-Strauss 1985:238; Petrequin 1995:43). The example of the Gilat Ram implies that this identification is not exclusive here, or that gender identification could have applied to (specific?) shapes. We will then emphasize the fact that the topological conception of spindle-shaped vessels (the 'churn' shape embodied by the Ram) is horizontal and thus inverse to the topological conception of jars.[9]

The Gilat ram (length: 27.5 cm; see Figs 15.4–15.6). Zoomorphic vessels are rare in the Chalcolithic of Palestine. One fragmented head of a bovid (?) comes from Locus 727 (see Fig. 15.25.2) at Gilat. Its perforated snout is a characteristic also found on a figurative bull vessel from Abu Hamid, in Jordan, that has a fenestrated pedestal bowl. This short inventory is completed by one bull carrying churns that comes from the sanctuary of Ein Gedi, in the Judean Desert.[10]

The Ram vessel from Gilat is conceived like the body of a miniature spindle-shaped vessel ('churn'). The head, reduced in scale in comparison to the body, stands for the ogive handle of a churn while the tail stands for the opposite 'heel' handle. Ogive handles from churns of regular size are often 'horned handles', while heel handles can be triangular in profile (see this volume Fig. 10.31.3; and cf. Commenge-Pellerin 1987: Fig. 38.18; 1990: Fig. 55.9 and 12, Fig. 56.2–3). There is also a redundant equation between miniature spindle-shaped vessels ('churns') and some physical attributes of the Ram. In the pottery assemblage, miniature churns present twin lug-handles shaped and placed like a pair of horns either on the ogive or heel side of the vessel (Figs 10.31.4,7, 9 and 11). This homomorphism between ram representation and spindle-shaped vessels may indicate a hierophantic function for the figurative vessel insofar as it unveils the implicit meaning of a category of vessels already interpreted as ceremonial. The function of the so-called 'churns' is discussed in the ceramic analysis (cf Chapter 10, this volume; and Commenge-Pellerin 1990).

Figure 15.4. Front view of the Gilat Ram with red-painted designs.

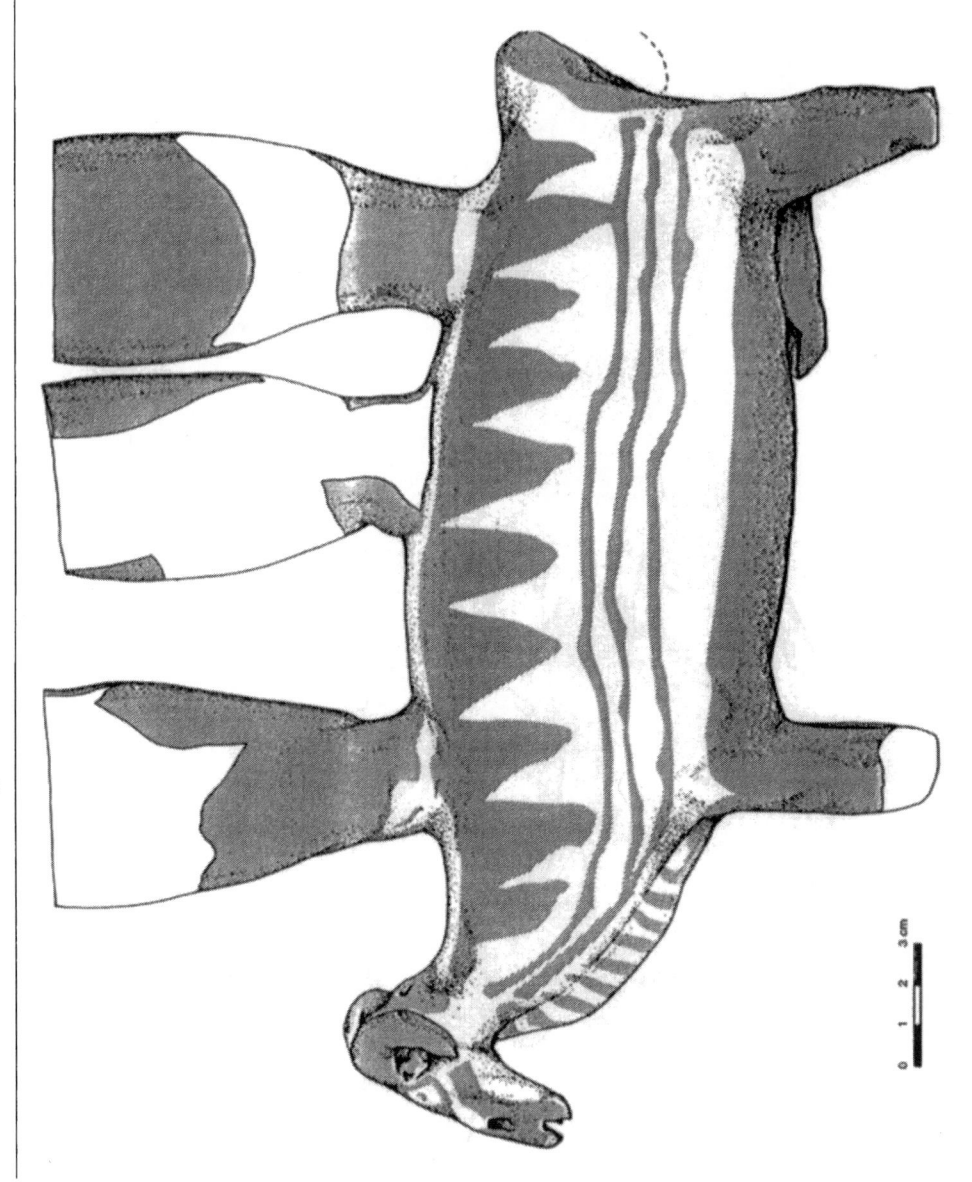

Figure 15.5. Side view of the Gilat Ram.

0   1   2   3 cm

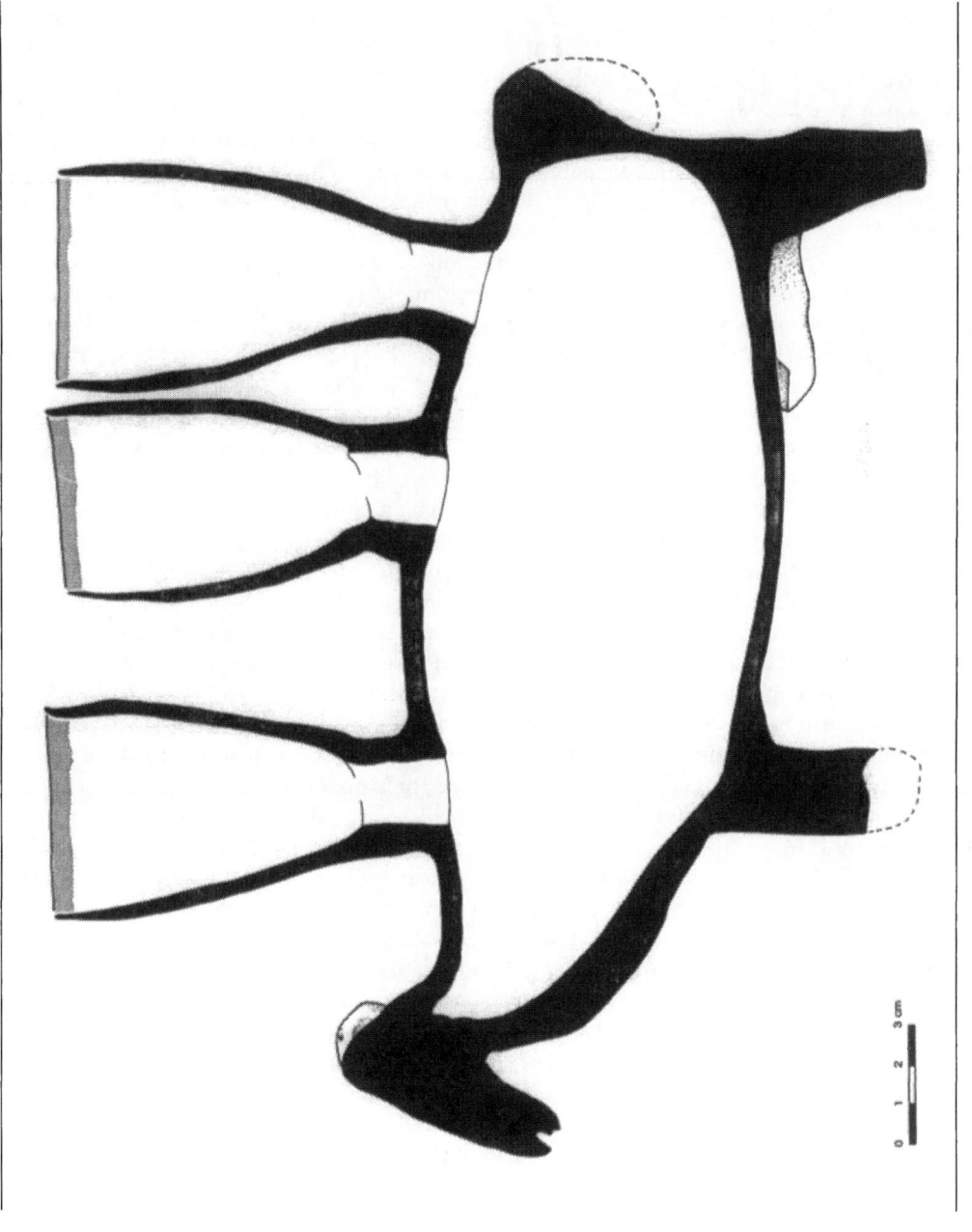

Figure 15.6. Profile of the Gilat Ram.

0 1 2 3 cm

'Churns' are usually interpreted as clues for a 'cult of milk' sets in the context of the development of pastoralism and the advent of the 'secondary products revolution' (Epstein 1982; Grigson 1987). However, the embodiment of spindle-shaped vessels refers to the male and not the female of the ovicaprine species. The Ram figurine is explicitly sexed, in contrast with other zoomorphic representations from Gilat (see below). The red painted decoration applied to the ram figurine is remarkably organized, while irregular and uncertain dots adorned the bull from Ein Gedi and chaotic painting the bull from Abu Hamid. Enhanced by a thorough design, the painted spikes that decorate the Ram's body can be seen like redundant symbols of virility. This rather Freudian interpretation finds—among many—parallels in the analysis of Mafa symbolism that makes primary analogies between horn,[11] penis and spike designs which both decorate persons or pots (David *et al*. 1988: 377).

At this stage of analysis, there is a metonymic link between the Ram and spindle-shaped vessels which is reinforced by symbols that could be metaphors for male sex. Therefore, there is a risk in arbitrarily focusing on a cult centered on milk production, based on the assumed function of spindle-shaped vessels ('churns') and thus at a secondary level of interpretation, that the very elaboration of symbols might actually be curtailed or distorted.

Agents in ritual performance. Does the oft stated assumption concerning the universality of the Mother Goddess image, who begets and promotes fertility, and under whose aegis, in the case of the Gilat Lady, the flocks are placed, resist a thorough examination of the symbols materialized in these two figurative vessels? The very hierophantism of these figurines induces other realms of symbolism that involve perhaps the fundamental dynamics for social cohesion and its reproduction or transformation, and could here be expressed through a possible 'mythical discourse' (cf. Ricoeur 1971; Douglas 1975). Some iconographic processes and elements of the Gilat Lady's representation give evidence for its congruence with initiation at a double level, in referring to the circumstances of initiation and in imparting symbolical knowledge about it.

Symbols are meant to elicit interpretation by the viewer. The pertinence of argumentation in interpreting symbols set in these effigies has to be tested for validity, however perilous the task. The Gilat Lady is generally linked to tangible evidence for a goddess representation. This figurative vessel has been viewed in different convergent roles, heralding an archaic Ashtarot, goddess of flocks and milk (Alon 1977: 65) or related to a Dumuzi-like myth illustrating 'a pastoral and incipient agricultural cult connected with milk' (Amiran 1976:119). Some authors insisted that the birth-giving goddess reveals 'a connection with feminity and the promotion of fertility among milk-giving flocks' (Epstein 1998:231).[12] There is a general agreement that these figurative vessels were used for libations within a cultic context. Identification and interpretation refer altogether to archetypical symbols rooted in what has been ascribed elsewhere to 'common humanity', like the notion of fertility (Haaland and Haaland 1996:299) which involves here metaphorical connections related to milk production. This gynecomorphous vessel is thus considered like a device dedicated to the proliferation and the prosperity that it supposedly illustrates, yet votive in nature to perpetuate abundance. The distance between identification and interpretation encompassed in these views finds some shortcomings that need to be scrutinized and challenged.

Vision and 'blindness', what is displayed and what is concealed by means of mystification, are central in ritual performance. Ritual performance acts for ordering and transforming while creating ambiguity and evoking a powerful consensus (Rappaport 1979:217, Fernandez 1965:922, Bell 1992:112; see also Chapter 1, this volume). The Gilat statuettes whose possible symbolic and ritualistic function is discussed below, possess the prime characteristics of focusing devices (Alon and Levy 1989). The Ram and the Lady are standing representations of fair dimensions for statuettes. Attributes are set off with red paint and can be seen at a distance. These effigy vessels achieve the primary design of ritual which is communication (Douglas 1973:97; Leach 1976:45). Convergent evidence for this purpose could be stressed from the hierophantic nature displayed by each figurative vessel. The woman's pudenda, placed to be viewed, are 'hyper-realistic' and certainly do not claim abstraction or a need for decipherment inherent to symbols. Unequivocal morphological details characterized the ram representation that fits the naturalistic category defined for zoomorphic figurines (see below). Painted spikes imply a first level of symbolism in representing virility. From a stylistic point of view, these iconographic means cannot denote 'archaism' in representation as both naturalistic animal figurines and highly stylized violin-shaped figurines are part of the material at Gilat.

In social terms, hierophantic focusing devices implies a double hierarchy that considers initiated and profane persons and, in terms of spirituality, different degrees of knowledge. Duality is also implicit insofar as representation induces a symmetrical or asymmetrical reflection of its related referent.

The emphasized pudenda could represent either sexuality, menstruation, defloration or parturition, situations that respectively insist and signal formative or transformative ontogenic stages in women's physiological development but also thresholds in their social life (cf. Marshack 1991:282). The female body could thus be viewed as mediating a relevant social structure. Preeminence of female forms in Neolithic representation has been construed as sufficient enough to evoke association to male contribution (Haaland and Haaland 1996). The Lady and the Ram, coming from the same context (Alon 1976, Chapter 5 this volume) are generally interpreted like separate entities (cf. Amiran 1976; Epstein 1985; Fox 1995; Merhav 1993). That approach neglects the contextual meaning of the pair of effigies, their inverse structure and different nature (human *versus* animal), their common provenance and their harmonized dimensions, their common character in being pot-bearers and the complementary nature of their sexual identity. These two last characters could represent, through binary contrasts, a combination and correlation of interacting forces and values.

Two preeminent symbolic figures emerge from the symbolical shift marking the initiation of Neolithic subsistence strategies in the Near East. One is 'the Goddess' who rules creation. The other is the Bull, generated by the Goddess herself (Mellaart 1975; Cauvin 1972, 1994). The Lady of Gilat and her ram acolyte could be reminiscent of this 'primary myth', illustrated at Çatal Hüyük, where the Goddess gives birth to bulls or, exceptionally, to rams (Mellaart 1967, 1975).[13] The Lady carries on her head a spindle-shaped vessel (the so-called 'churn') that, according to the analysis proposed *supra*, symbolically stands for the Ram itself. The presentation on the head refers to a privileged attribute. If the proposed homology to the Anatolian myth is correct, the Lady representation could be self-sufficient in recounting it. Her radiant sexuality insists on the source of her power that results in producing an animal and genesis-like force. There could thus be a fundamental substitution between bearing a child and bearing a ram. If the Woman representation from Gilat was, as suggested *supra,* a possible medium for social structure, it could signify that women were central in producing wealth for these Chalcolithic societies where specialized pastoralism was becoming an important part of the subsistence base.

This last assumption can perhaps find some plausible illustration in studies concerning the relation between symbolic thought and social reality (Levi-Strauss 1962:284). Evidence for this relation was proposed by Levi-Strauss (1979) in a unique essay on the structure of myths that is based on elements of material culture, namely masks. Levi-Strauss analyses some myths and rites pertaining to prosperous village-based Kwakiutl tribes that were settled along the Alaska gulf to the south of Vancouver, at the end of the nineteenth century. One of these myths elaborates upon the tight relation between a female, a supernatural being, Dzonokwa, and accumulated and distributed goods. The myth recounts that Dzonokwa acts like an ogress, who abducts children yet gives back, *mutatis mutandis*, copper artifacts. Nubile young women are symbolically assimilated to Dzonokwa. The bride-to-be subtracts from her family a dowry of copper artifacts, yet her future children belong *de facto* to her own kin (and thus are taken away from her husband's kin that receives the dowry). 'The young woman thus fulfils a social role and an economic function that makes her appear like a *tamed* Dzonokwa' (Levi-Strauss 1979:76—my translation, his italics). Thus, Dzonokwa gives and takes the very means of potlatch and so portrays her nubile reflection. The processual underpinnings of this myth can perhaps be used as a key for deciphering the meaning of the Gilat Lady. Two major foci of elaboration, the radiant pudenda and the presentation of the spindle/ram vessel serve as a vehicle reflecting the substance and symbolism of a fundamental exchange—children provided by women and kept for lineage by their own kin, flocks provided through women and abstract from their own kin[14]—with the result of justifying and securing the social contract and its *reproduction*. A fundamental image of Early Chalcolithic society could thus be inscribed in these two representations: whether this image reflects social reality or is the formalized imagination of an idealistic one is an open question. It might add credit to an assumption for matrilineality, opposed to matriarchy, proposed from the Neolithic onward (Cauvin 1985:15). Still, any premature conclusion suggesting a matrilinear structure of Chalcolithic societies should be here withheld until there is more unequivocal evidence.[15] In terms of social domination, discrepancy between ideological domains and social reality are frequent in matrilineal systems and that 'women may have been valued as producers of wealth and children (labor) in a hierarchical system in which women were not necessarily in control' (Hayden 1992:38) must be considered.

During their initiation, Kwakiutl young women wear a ritual dress that imitates Dzonokwa's. They are tightly bound with strips made of bark or of goat wool, a costume that finds parallels in many other nubility rites by the means of incisions or tattoos and are perhaps signified here in the stripes of red paint adorning the Gilat Lady.

A subsidiary remark addresses the fact that the Lady and the Ram are also vessels used as cultic utensils. The body of each character was conceived for total impletion. Insistence on their use for libation has perhaps neglected the preliminary and essential action of impletion. Impletion can *fulfill* the vessels function, whose contained and reciprocal forces can later have been poured out for consumption or dedication. Metonymic channels can link the container to the contained (Barley 1994), dilating further the scope of *substantial* metaphors. This last remark leads us back to the spindle-ram vessel carried by the Gilat Woman because it will certainly give more ground for further elaboration upon its functional identification as a churn. A supposed function cannot provide a generic definition for a vessel (Commenge-Pellerin 1987 and Chapter 10, this volume). Here we stress that the interpretation of the Gilat Woman statuette established channels of reciprocity between shape and gender and their symmetrical, redundant and symbolic representation. Whether milk—a female by-product—is metonymically related to the ram representation (and to semen?), and to the spindle-shaped vessel possibly used as a churn, remains, to our viewpoint, still an open question. Whether this figurative vessel, whose structure and features appeared bound by many threads to the Near Eastern Neolithic culture, and more specifically to the Anatolian Neolithic, heralds the advent of the Secondary Products Revolution is consequently a statement that still needs to be demonstrated and corroborated by further evidence. There are though, tenuous yet redundant elements that, perhaps, outline at Gilat a 'prior claim' for specialized sheep-goat husbandry, expressed by spindle-shaped miniature vessels bearing ram horns (Chapter 10, Fig. 10.31.4, 7, 9, 11 and Chapter 6, this volume), complemented by the unique ram head pendant from peridotite (see below and Fig. 15.26). Yet, any statement on economic choices through cultural expression might be corroborated by unequivocal evidence. Like numerous pottery vessels from Gilat, the provenance of the Ram and the Woman is situated in the Shephela. With the exception of one fragmented vessel,[16] these figurative vessels are unique at Gilat. Thus far, systems of exchange for figurative vessels such as inter-regional alliances, pilgrimage offerings or trade are immaterial. However, their hierophantic nature bolsters their instrumental dedication to the sanctuary cultic activities.

One of the main functions of symbolism lies in providing humankind with an intelligible key to understand the universe and to define its own place in it. The symbols encapsulated in the Lady and the Ram certainly illustrate this. Yet, a winding sequence of mediated, symbolic elements probably remains undeciphered, and possibly here reduces the proposed hermeneutical analysis to 'how the said is rescued from its saying' (Geertz 1983:32; Ricoeur 1971:558). The ideology of fertility (Cauvin 1982), of maternity, of hegemony, of harnessing and supremacy over animals, illustrated at Hacilar and Çatal Hüyük during the seventh millennium by the Goddess's potent representations (Cauvin 1994:49) could here find a counterpoised and countervailed assimilation in social development. In the same way as in mythical thought, matter is here a tool and not an object of signification.

Violin Figurines (Catherine Commenge)

Violin-shape figurines are numerous at Gilat yet relatively rare in Palestine as a whole. These objects were crucial components in relaying the complex system of cultic activities experienced at the site. More shadow than flesh, violin figurines initiated a new visual order for anthropomorphic representation that challenges our notion of Levantine imagery in late prehistory. Knowledge involved in mental and substantial construction of representation, tangible forms of belief and ritual action will here be observed in functional, spatial, temporal and diachronic perspectives.

Substantially, anthropomorphic representation is fostered by a reflective and reflexive conception that selects and shapes, and cryptically alters morphological elements that might be highly meaningful. For any aspect of material culture, and thus for any artifact production, action on matter and the production of meaning are fundamentally and tightly interwoven (Lemonnier 1991:17, Pfaffenberger 1992:505). By the means of technical choices and operations, cognitive constituents are encoded in matter, as mental perception first contrives reality, and then bridges it anew to the realm of the sensible. This process, which results in significant 'stylistic' investment, seems critical in the making of figurines. From technical imperative to conceptual schemes, the following analysis aims to explore conformance to and digression from 'standards', and their significance in social terms with consideration to the organization of production and consumption. Tentative extraction of the figurines' significance will here be operated not like a separate empirical entity, but examined within intricate segments of contextual information of this emergent ranking society, and observed from a diachronic perspective, in order to bridge symbolic domains in the time-continuum of thought.

In order to narrow and to secure the scope of analysis and discussion, a preliminary definition of the violin figurine is here proposed for the archaeological context of the Early Chalcolithic period in Palestine. In the Aegean world, the earliest examples of violin figurines are found at the Neolithic settlement at Saliagos (5000 BC). They precede by some 1,500 years those of Grotta-Pelos culture in the Early Cycladic period (Evans and Renfrew 1968; Renfrew 1969, 1972, 1991; Sherratt 2000). *Lato sensu*, this term tends to apply to any figurine whose curvaceous outline suggests a standing, most probably feminine, representation. It was chosen to describe, for instance, the round clay figurines from Hacilar I (Mellaart 1970).[17] However, violin-shaped figurines from the southern Levant are made from a thin and tabular support, cut out to produce a basically 'two-dimensional' representation. It presents two plane, to slightly plano-convex, faces. Longitudinal and transversal cross-sections are thus rectangular to elliptical and are characterized by their narrowness. The thickness of a figurine is equivalent to less than one-fifth of its maximal width. In accordance to its musical pseudo-referent, the length of the schematic head is emphasized, and the body silhouette is nipped at the waist. Protruding shoulders stand for arms. A compact, sub-rectangular base figures the lower part of the body below the horizontal waist-hips line.[18] In the corpus of Gilat, relative proportions to the total height of the figurine average one third for head, one-fifth for torso and one-half for base.

The excavations at Gilat recovered a grand total of 76 specimens that includes complete and incomplete figurines and fragments (Table 15.3). They represent a minimum number of 53 figurines made from local or exogenous stone (MNI: 48 figurines) but also made from bone (mni:3) or pottery sherds (MNI:2). Precocious and rare specimens of violin figurines appear in the archaeological record of Palestine in limited Wadi Rabah contexts (Dollfus and Kafafi 1995). They are discretely present at Chalcolithic sites, inland from the Jordan Valley to Judea and along the Mediterranean coast from Lebanon to northern Egypt (Table 15.1). In most cases, their chrono-stratigraphic context lacks precise definition. At two sites though, Titorah at Modi'in near Jerusalem (E. Lass pers. com.), and Wadi Zeita (C. Commenge, pers. evaluation), violin figurines are associated with pottery assemblages that present multiple similarities to Gilat's pottery assemblage and can thus be together assigned to an early phase of the Chalcolithic period (see Chapter 10). Although two figurines from Shiqmim, one from clay (Building Phase (BP) III) and one from bone (BP IIa), present some morphological elements derived from violin figurines (Levy 1987: Fig. 6.12: 4; Levy and Golden 1996), they are not typical of the material culture of the Beersheva sites. The regional distribution (Table 15. 1) shows figurines from different provenance. Some sites are still under investigation (Abu Hamid, Teleilat Ghassul) while others were only tested (Tell Kitan and one cave at Titorah). Investigations are still in progress with materials from other sites (Tel Sheva, Peqi'in). Keeping in mind the limiting factors, the number of violin-shaped figurines recovered at Gilat still exceeds the total of violin-shaped figurines collected, so far, in Palestine.

Table 15.1. Regional Levantine distribution of violin figurines.

Location	Description	References
site R48	1, limestone	Oren and Gilead 1981:15
Tel Qatif	5, small to medium, limestone?	Oren and Gilead pers.com.
Byblos	1, small, ivory	Dunand 1973
Abu Hamid	6 small, limestone	Dollfus *et al.* 1988 Dollfus and Kafafi 1995
Tel Kitan	1 fgt	Eisenberg 1993
Peqi'in	16 (mni?) among them miniatures	Gal *et al.* 1997 and Gal pers. com.
Tel Haror	1 small	Oren pers. com.
Tel Sheva	2?	-
Teleilat Ghassul	9 small to medium, limestone	Lee 1973, Koeppel *et al.* 1940 Mallon *et al.* 1934, Blackham 1999
Shiqmim*	1 small, clay 1 medium, bone	Levy 1987 Levy and Golden 1996
Wadi Zeita (Gat Govrin)	1 small 1 medium	Perrot pers.com.
Nahal Besor	7 small to medium 1 from bone, site H	Mac Donald 1932 Kibbutz Urim coll. Perrot pers. com.
Titorah	1 medium, limestone	Lass, pers. com.

*both with parts in slight relief, hybrid types

Table 15.2: Simplified evaluation of artifact types for production at Gilat*

artifacts	grinding implements			vessels	tabular artifacts		spherical perforated artifacts	
Raw material	Eocene limestone	beachstone	limestone	basalt	Cen. Turon. limestone	granodiorite talc-schist sandstone…	Cen. Turon. limestone	granite, schist
Spatial distribution of sources	regionally clustered	regionally clustered	regionally clustered	highly localized	regionally clustered	highly localized	regionally clustered	highly localized
Extraction difficulties	minimal	minimal	minimal	minimal	minimal	minimal	minimal	minimal
Location of production	local?	?	?	at source	?	?	?	?
Know-how (knowledge)	expedient/ moderate	moderate	elaborate	highly elaborate	very elaborate / highly elaborate		moderate/highly elaborate	
Technical investment	timesaving procedures	timesaving procedures	time-cons. procedures	highly time-cons. procedures	time-consuming procedures	time-consuming procedures	time-consuming procedures	
Stylistic investment	absent	absent	minimal	very high	moderate to very high		moderate to high	
Quantities produced	domestic consumption	domestic consumption	domestic consumption	low	low	low	low	low
Origin of consumed by-products	local	source at 30 km	local	source at 200 km	regional sources at 20+ kms	sources at 150 km*	regional sources at 20+ kms	sources at 150 km*
Use context	utilitarian	utilitarian	utilitarian	social/ritual	social/ritual		utilitarian/social	social
Inter-intra site distribution	present at all sites			present at all sites	unequal on-site distribution			

* The closest source is here considered. Sandstone were possibly collected in the Negev craters, at a shorter distance from Gilat (80 kilometers).

Context and Means of Production

Outstanding in quality, the violin figurines production should be analyzed within the general context of groundstone production. Within the groundstone assemblage of Gilat, several parameters (Table 15.2) distinguish different types of production that met diverse socioeconomic functions. The Gilat groundstone assemblage was structured around distinct units of production that reflect incipient elements of general south Levantine Chalcolithic groundstone assemblages. Each type of production used assorted rock sources (local and non-local), which necessitated different degrees of proficiency and stylistic investment. The bulk of the assemblage is represented by the local production of grinding implements and vessels that efficiently exploited mostly local limestone resources by operating with time-saving procedures and moderately elaborate techniques (Plate 12.3:4, 12.11:3). By contrast, the exogenous artifacts from basalt were most probably manufactured at workshops located near the Trans-Jordanian sources (Philip and Williams-Thorpe 1993, 2000). There, time-consuming labor, highly elaborate technical skill and stylistic investment were required for manufacturing fenestrated pedestal vessels. Eclectic raw materials, from ubiquitous limestone to exogenous and rare granite, schist or chlorite characterized a third unit of production. This unit can be divided into two distinct technical sub-groups. One sub-group includes spherical and perforated artifacts such as mace heads, weights, spindle-whorls and beads. There is a large range in the technical input, in particular for limestone artifacts that could be anything from 'prestige', labor-intensive mace-heads to simple weights. However, exogenous materials were exclusively used for manufacturing elaborate artifacts. The second sub-group achieves innovative, time-consuming and exclusive technical patterns on both local and exogenous materials. This sub-group includes the violin-shaped figurines, where the prevailing techniques reduce, plane off faces and chamfer edges (Plate 15.11.1–2 and 12, 15.13.6) of portable artifacts. This technical and stylistic trend produces tabular and geometric shapes such as rectangular or circular palettes (see Chapter 12, Plate 12.6; 12.7; 12.8), trapeze or triangular tokens (Fig. 12 9.2–9), circular spindle-whorls (see Chapter 14) and pendants.

The location of violin-shaped figurine production is still a question that needs clarification (i.e. was it on-site, off-site, at the sources? Was there a 'down-the-line production' concerning either raw blocks, pre-formed support or manufactured by-products?). Some evidence and subsequent assumptions concerning the organization of production of the violin-shape figurines are investigated below.

For sculpture, like for any artifact manufacture, choices of medium impose technical constraints. In the case of violin figurines, these constraints are both emphasized and limited by the desired thin, tabular volume selected to 'give body' to representation. 93.3% of the violin figurine specimens are made from stone (90.5 of the figurines minimum number of individuals). Rocks that naturally present tabular qualities, for instance an aptitude to schistosity, were first selected. Yet, the thinness of the requisite support required aleatory precautious reduction and abrading operations. Then, the 'two-dimensional' by-product obliged an outcut operation that considered the vertical symmetry and the proportions of the silhouetted features. To rescue here a term more adapted and genuine to chipped stone production, two major stages in the 'conceptual operative strategy' (Karlin 1992) involved first the conception of the tabular support and then the frame and composition of the formal and cadenced delineation of the figurine's silhouette.

Violin figurines from stone (Table 15.3)

Sources. The range of rocks employed in manufacturing violin-shaped figurines includes limestone, chalk, marl, granodiorite, sandstone and talc-schist (that includes phyllite).

The inventory of raw material shows that 48 figurines or 93.3 % of the minimal number of artifacts (70 stone specimens represent 90.5 % of all figurine specimens; see Table 15.3) are made from stone, either from regional or distant sources. These materials present different texture and structure and thus different capability in resisting percussion and abrasion.20

The identification of sources for raw material examines either the spatial distribution of a particular kind of raw material and/or ascribes a location to raw materials identified in an artifact assemblage. This two-pronged approach has been achieved for instance, in attempting to identify the original sources of south Levantine basalt artifacts (Amiran and Porat 1984; Philip and Williams-Thorpe 1993, 2000; Weinstein-Evron *et al*. 1995). For Gilat, an examination of the figurine specimens identified a variety of rock-types—sedimentary, metamorphic or plutonic rocks—used in the assemblage. Those identifications are completed here with consideration as to the rocks capacity for providing (or being worked to) tabular supports.

Limestone is a sedimentary, calcareous rock. Ridges of Cenomanian to Turonian platforms straggle over the northern Negev, at some 20 km east of Gilat. Tabular rocks of convenient dimensions can easily be collected from their outcrops. This indurated rock has a very compact texture and homogenous structure (Mohs 3–3.5). One can already note the absence of local Eocene limestone, whose deposits are located less than 10 km east of Gilat and whose rocks are carried along the wadi system.

Chalk is here represented by not very indurated, yet compact and fine-grained, specimens. *Marl* is a lithified variety of clay. Although friable, its laminous structure makes it suitable for the manufacturing of tabular artifacts. Chalk and marl are both sedimentary rocks of mainly Maastrichtian origin, and exposed near Lahav, 20 km away from Gilat.

Sandstone formations are usually layered. The joint system runs perpendicularly to the horizontal bedding planes, and weathering results in rectangular blocks. It is characterized by a very fine grained structure and rather compact texture (Mohs 2–3). Sources are numerous and well circumscribed. Paleozoic Nubian sandstones are spread in Jordan (from the Wadi Mujib area southwards) and in the southern Sinai. Lower Cretaceous sandstones are found in southern Lebanon, in Jordan from Wadi Zarqa southwards, in the area of Wadi Fa'ra and Wadi el Malikh in eastern Samaria, in the Sinai or closer to Gilat, in the Negev makhteshim. Their location into a specific geological formation cannot be further established. However, one greenish sandstone, coated with copper carbonates, comes either from Timna, from Wadi Faynan or from southeastern Sinai (cf. Fig. 15.16.3).

Talc-schist is a metamorphic rock that offers good cleavage (by inherent schistosity) and a very fine grained compactness (Mohs 2–3). *Phyllite* (from the Greek 'leaf') is a silky talc-schist with a laminated structure and a fine-grained texture that can be split into very thin sheets. These igneous rocks are exposed south of Faynan, in the Eastern Desert, near Eilat and in southern Sinai.

Plutonic *granodiorite* is a heterogeneous rock of high mafic content. It has a coarse grained texture and a very compact structure (Mohs 6.5). As for granite, the high proportion of feldspars allows the winning of parallepipedic blocks and the splitting of planes.[21] Granodiorite is exposed in the same locations as igneous-metamorphic talc-schists.

Eclectic yet purposive choices structure this inventory of raw materials. Regional sources, located at a minimal radius of twenty kilometers from Gilat, are exploited to manufacture almost 75% of the figurines specimens and 68.6% of the minimal number of figurines from stone (limestone: 65.7%/58.3%,[22] chalk: 7%/8.3% and marl: 1.4%/2%). Exogenous rocks from circumscribed sources were exploited at radius that may vary between middle-range distance if sandstones were collected in the Negev craters—the Makhtesh Ramon is at a minimal distance of 90 km from Gilat—to long-range distance, up to 150 km for other igneous-metamorphic rock sources of the Arabic shield. Sandstone specimens represents 11.4%/12.5%, talc-schist specimens represents

11.4%/14.5%, and granodiorite specimens represents 2.8%/4.1% of Gilat's assemblage of figurines from stone (see Table 15.9a for all percentages, lines set in bold characters). Extraction or mining of rocks for the making of violin-shaped figurines seem improbable. Choice of raw material concerned rocks that could be collected in blocks of suitable dimensions, along the wadi banks or at the denritic bases of sedimentary or metamorphic outcrops. There is an obvious demand for schistose, laminous or layered rocks whose structure facilitates the debitage of tabular supports.

Besides physical qualities, aesthetic appearance of rocks was certainly considered, such as the greenish surface of schists and copper-sandstone, the soft pink, bright purple or yellow shades of sandstone, or the peppered, mottled aspect of granodiorite. The blocks of limestone were also often chosen for their dappled or veined nature. Two figurines were made from pink limestone, commonly known as 'Jerusalem stone' (Figs 15.17.2 and 15.19.5).

While there is no evidence for the utilization of exogenous materials such as basalt, scoria or pumice for figurine production, these materials are well represented at Gilat by small sized, thinned and squared artifacts such as palettes (Pl. 12.6.1, 3, 7–8, 11).

Reconstitution of the operational sequence. There is a lack of direct evidence for documenting activities of production in Chalcolithic groundstone industries. Extensively excavated sites such as Safadi, Shiqmim or Abu Matar, where wadi pebbles were intensely exploited, give no evidence for groundstone workshops. It is possible that the absence of on-site production evidence was due to the excavation sampling strategy. Alternatively, local production may have been located along the wadi banks that offer raw material together with easy access to water for abrasion and/or polishing operations. Pre-formed slabs or rough-shapes are also rare, perhaps for the same reasons. Similarly —and the question of on-site or off-site violin figurines production would have to be addressed later—there is no evidence for groundstone (and *a fortiori* for figurine) workshops at Gilat. Given these parameters, the following is a provisional reconstruction of the operative sequence for tabular artifact manufacturing in general, and violin-shaped figurines in particular.

Labor-intensive techniques were used to shape the initial slab. This suggestion is based on analysis of a pre-formed, trapeze palette from siliceous limestone, recovered at Abu Matar (Commenge, forthcoming). A thorough, perpendicular pecking has reduced both faces and sides. This technique of preliminary reduction before abrasion is highly probable for rocks of compact texture such as limestone and granite, or granodiorite. The definitive thickness of the figurine seems more correlated to the hardness of the stone than to compactness and texture. An evaluation of the thickest section of each figurine and of each fragment gives a neat peak of thickness at 0.6 cm for artifacts made from limestone and for the group of schists. The hardness rather than the heterogeneous structure of granodiorite may have limited the operations of reduction. The thickness peak is at 1.6 cm for figurines made from this metamorphic rock. In some cases (limestone and schist), one face of the figurine is slightly better worked than the other. This can be due to the original state of the former slab, presenting an even natural face and an opposite, rougher face obtained by the perpendicular split of the block, exposing a local and weaker compaction of minerals. The fact that intensive reduction, followed by skillful abrasion does not conceal this original imperfection can suggest that a 'frontal' exhibition of the figurines has been intended (cf. Alon and Levy 1989).

It is probable that the cutout operation for shaping the general outline of the figurines was achieved, in order to limit risks of breakage, during the reduction process. The outcut operation observed on a sandstone rough-shape was achieved—with more or less success—on a 1.2 cm thick tabulated form whose two preserved faces were already evenly abraded (this specimen has no archaeological context, Fig. 15.22.5). In this case, the cutout was done by strokes operated from one face at a slightly perpendicular angle. Chipping along the edges of the opposite face evened the cutout. In vertical or transversal section, the faces of figurines are slightly convex along the edges, a reducing process masking former chopping marks. Yet, if a thorough abrasion of the lateral edges obliterated manufacturing traces on finished specimens, perpendicular chamfers are deliberately preserved, enhancing the thinness of the plate. Wear analysis concerning the palettes from Abu Matar and Safadi demonstrated that 'many edges were first ground parallel to the faces, then re-ground in a perpendicular to oblique motion. Chamfering sometimes produced striae running onto the planar faces that are generally differentiated on the basis of their intensity and shallowness' (Rowan in Commenge forthcoming). The carved breasts of a unique specimen have been facetted to present plane top surfaces (Fig. 15.20.1). Some specimens show a discrete attempt at creating some 'relief'. Overlapping, concentric traces of reduction can superficially 'nip' the waist (Fig. 15.15.1, Fig. 15.16.1). In spite of a lack of direct evidence, the punctual use of sawing or of multiple drilling, in particular for the hardest stone specimens, are here not excluded as processes involved in the cutting out of the figurine's silhouette. The rounded yet sharp angles at the waist (Fig. 15.15.1, 15.16.1–2), the delicate concavity of flaring heads (Fig. 15.12.6) suggest sophisticated processes of manufacturing for such fragile (yet hard) supports.

Faces and chamfers are evenly polished. As suggested by Roodenberg (1986:160), spherical and faceted 'pounders' from cortical flint or expedient chunks from basalt—rocks harder than materials used for the figurines' manufacture—could have been used like polishers. Some finishing abrasion might have been carried out with the use of mineral powder such as ground hematite (cf. Hahn 1986).

Some fragments have been carefully re-ground but none of them gives evidence for skilled craftsmanship, capable or ready to chamfer anew a broken piece. The base of broken heads have been simply ground (Fig. 15.17.1 and 9), like the breakage surfaces of a torso, symmetrically evened before the operation (Fig. 15.19.6). However, the transformation of a (broken) figurine into an outcut animal shape required a perfect visualization of volume and mastering of technique (Fig. 15.19.5).

Violin figurines are also made from other media offering tabular supports: bone and pottery sherds whose secondary-use operates by shape analogy.

Violin figurines from bone. Although rare, bone, and especially scapulae (Levy and Golden 1996), offer the possibility to cut out a plane support, suitable for manufacturing violin figurines. In spite of some slight difference in proportions (see *infra*), figurines from bone show morphological elements such as a characteristic elliptical transversal section, and chamfered lateral edges that characterized the whole assemblage (Fig. 15.19.7 and 10). On one complete figurine, the chamfering of the head and shoulders is not perpendicular but oblique, from the face to the back, creating an optical effect that underlines and lightens the contours of the head (Fig. 15.19.10). On both faces, striae, mostly oblique, result from a thorough polishing. Stordeur identifies two techniques for polishing bone artifacts (1988:77–78) that could have been selectively used on different parts of this figurine. Abrasion on a grinding and inactive stone implement was probably used on the plane and large surfaces of the front and the back. It is characterized here by long and oblique striae. Chamfers and face edges are covered by short and multidirectional striae that suggest polishing with a (active) hand-stone, more convenient for narrow or convex surfaces. In contrast to other raw materials, bone is not otherwise represented in the inventory of tabular artifacts.

Violin figurines from pottery. These figurines are made from sherds of buff, smooth-surfaced vessels. The three recovered fragments belong to locally produced, well made large vessels, possibly basins or jars. Two semi-circular notches mark the waist. Perpendicular strokes shaped the outline, and created angular, faceted edges reminiscent of the chamfered edges of stone specimens. All chamfers are thoroughly polished.

Table 15.3. Rocks used in the making of violin figurines at Gilat

Complete and fragmented violin-shaped figurines from **limestone**; m.n.i= 28, specimens= 46						
locus	*basket*	*square*	*area*	*stratum*	*context*	*description*
969	2776	J4	J	IIIA	pit	torso, reworked, red limestone
556	1390	J7	Y	III	pit	head, fgt
946	2900	J4	J	IIC	surface	torso
25	3096	B6	M	II	pit	shoulder
827	2303	L4	J	IIC	pit	shoulder and neck
896	2596.2+2613	J4	J	II B 2	pit	head missing
896	2596.1	J4	J	IIB2	pit	torso
25	3089.1	Ai5	D	IIIA	pit	base, phosphatic limestone
-	3200.2	H2	J	topsoil	-	head, fgt, Jerusalem limestone
820	2295	L3	J	IIA	floor	torso
017	3069.2	B6	M	II	ashy fill	base, fgt
-	3200.1	H2	J	I	topsoil	head
1022	3220	H1	J	I	topsoil	head
686	5256	NO	T	I	topsoil	base
1511	5738	S2	T	IIC	pit	head
1539	5724	Ai0	Y	IIIA	ash layer	torso
1212	3838	HO	J	I	topsoil	base
51	16.1	N4/5	D	IIB	fill	complete
51	186	N4/5	D	IIB	fill	head missing
50	28	Ai4	D	IIB	fill	torso
52	516	S4/5	D	-	topsoil	torso, fgt
50	14	Ai4	D	IIB	fill	torso, fgt
-	520	-	D	-	-	torso-base, fgt
50	384	Ai4	D	IIB	fill	head missing
151	389	M4/5	D	IIB	pit	body, fgt
515	1127	J6	Y	I-II	fill	torso
810	2284	K4	J	IIA	pit	base, grey, dense limestone
532	1133	J7	Y	II	pit	head, grey, dense limestone
806	2379	J3	J	IIA	pit	?
1236	3968.1	K0	J	IIB	fill	base, fgt
1236	3968.2+3	K0	J	IIB	fill	torso
860	2818	K4	J	IIB	surface	base
8	27	S5	D	IIC	fill	torso, fgt
11	37	D5	D	IIC	floor	torso, fgt
23	49	N6	D	IIC	fill	torso, fgt
30	52.1	S5	D	IIC	fill	torso, fgt
30	52.2	S5	D	IIC	fill	torso, fgt
14	56	Ai6	D	IIIA	floor	base,fgt
-	-	N5	-	-	topsoil	base
040	3141	B4	M	IIC	fill	perforated head
?	31?					head
?	516/568					base, fgt
-	232					base,fgt
1534	5713	S0	Y	IIIA	pit	head
1341	4262	L1/2	J	IIIA	silo	body, black limestone
-	5174					reshaped fgt

Fragmented violin-shaped figurines from **chalk**; m.n.i.= 4, specimens= 5						
locus	*basket*	*square*	*area*	*stratum*	*context*	*description*
826	2375	K3	J	IIB1	pit	body fgt
604	5024	M2	T	I	topsoil	base
1321	4208	H0	J	IIB1	fill	perforated shoulder, bituminous
800	2029	F4	J	I	topsoil	torso
1201	3807	K4	J	IIC	surface	fgt of base?

						Fragmented figurine from **marl**; m.n.i.= 1
locus	*basket*	*square*	*area*	*stratum*	*context*	*description*
697	5294	S0	Y	IIA	pit	torso, laminated marl

					Complete and fragmented violin-shaped figurines from **granodiorite**; m.n.i.= 2	
locus	*basket*	*square*	*area*	*stratum*	*context*	*description*
52	71	S4/5	D	-	topsoil	complete
50	186	Ai4	D	IIB	fill	body, fgt

				Complete and fragmented violin-shaped figurines from **sandstone**; m.n.i.= 6, specimens= 8		
locus	*basket*	*square*	*area*	*stratum*	*context*	*description*
-	5017	N7	Y	IIC-III	baulk	complete, copper carbonates
1036	3270	H1	J	IIA	fill	probably head, yellow sandstone
841	2357	K3	J	IIB1	floor	base, red-banded sandstone
52	16.2	S4/5	D		topsoil	head, fgt
-	3277	K3	J	I	topsoil	rough shape?
1084	1534	L3	J	IIB	floor	torso
1522	5658	N5	Y	IIC2	pit	base, fine purplish sandstone
99	237	N3	D	IIC	ashy floor	head

				Complete and fragmented violin-shaped figurines from **talc-schist (phyllite)**; m.n.i.= 7, specimens= 8		
locus	*basket*	*square*	*area*	*stratum*	*context*	*description*
307	633	L7	D	IIC	fill	complete
1212	3835	HO	J	I	topsoil	base, slatey, phyllite
1222	3879	L4	J	IIC2	floor	head missing
1322	4222	LO	J	IIC	pit	head missing
1213	3854. 1+2	JO	J	I	topsoil	base
2	25	-	D	-	-	base, fgt
7	20	S4	D	-	fill	torso
025	3089. 2	B6	M	III	pit	head?

Table 15.4. Violin figurines from bone

				Complete and fragmented violin-shaped figurines from **bone**; m.n.i=3		
locus	*basket*	*square*	*area*	*stratum*	*context*	*description*
961	2795.1+2	H2/J3	J	IIA	two pits	almost complete
806	2384	J3	J	IIA	pit	base, fgt
1215	3830	L3	J	IIB1	wall	base, fgt

Table 15.5. Violin figurines from pottery sherds

				Complete and fragmented violin-shaped figurines from **pottery**; m.n.i.=2		
locus	*basket*	*square*	*area*	*stratum*	*context*	*description*
50	437	Ai4	D	IIB	fill	head, fgt
1064	3474	L3	J	IIA	surface	body
19	40	N5	D	IIC	fill	head, fgt

Within the Early Chalcolithic technical system, the choice that led to the selection or the manufacturing of tabular supports can be considered as an innovative and relatively expansive trend.[23] This technical trend finds a parallel in the lithic assemblage, with the making of tabular scrapers (Fig. 11.28.1). One should note that those scrapers are made from exogenous flint (Roshwalb 1981; Rosen 1983; Rowan and Levy 1991) whose source can also be located in Negev Highlands (Rosen 1983), the Sinai peninsula (Kosloff 1972/73) or possibly Transjordan (Faynan district, Levy, pers. observation; Jafr basin, Wilke and L. Quintero, pers. com.). Among the exogenous rocks selected for the making of figurines, the choice of copper-sandstone pinpoints the exploitation of rock sources located near Eilat (Rothenberg 1972), in the Faynan district (Hauptmann and Weisgerber 1987; Levy *et al.* 1999) or in southeastern Sinai (Rothenberg *et al.* 1979; Ilani and Rosenfeld 1994). In the context of pre-metal Chalcolithic phase (or culture?) at Gilat, the interest in copper mineralization areas suggests a nascent interest in and utilization of copper ores.

Conceptual Schemes: Standards and Digression

To achieve these shapes, there was some technical anticipation in the selection of raw material. The subtle ability to evaluate the resistance of the block while reduced and abraded, to plane off opposite surfaces of determinate extension and leveled, horizontal and constant spatial direction implies both pre-visualization and high-skill know-how. Once the tabular support was made, other conceptual schemes intervene to shape the figurines' outline. Being 'two dimensional', the shape of the figurine is essentially determined by its framework or in other terms by its frontal contour line. Figure 15.8 demonstrates that the figurines' over-all shape and proportions tend to standardization. There are thus also anticipated, stereotyped and contrived patterns that supervise and regulate this technical course of procedure.

As Leroi-Gourhan (1970) points out, the framework of a figurine is structured around its vertical axis of symmetry and its maximal transverse diameter. In the case of the violin figurines, the maximal transverse diameter is equivalent to the hip line and is placed at a median position on the vertical axis of symmetry. The hip-line, central in the spatial definition of the figurine, divides asymmetrical volumes. The maximal width is kept constant below the hip-line, defining a plain and rectangular volume that forms the base of the figurine. It seems probable that the initial block was first cut into a parallelepipedic volume, and that its rectangular shape was conceived in two halves, one for the base and one for the figurine's upper part. Such a geometrical spatial definition would help in keeping proportions and equidistant points along the vertical axis of symmetry. Together with implicit knowledge and know-how, with capability and capacity, the regularity of practice represents a third dimension required in the manufacturing of figurines that should be considered. Henceforth, any classification of the figurines cannot be restrained to a typology enhancing differences in morphological details, but should examine all parameters involved in their manufacturing, and address the inferences of perceptible differences within or off the cadre of standardization to flesh out possible social implications.

Fields of uniformity: toward standardization (T.E. Levy and E. Kansa). For this analysis, it is important to determine, as objectively as possible, the meaningful size-categories of the violin figurines (if these categories even exist). Unfortunately, the data is very fragmentary and the analysis presented here was made in 1993 before the complete VSF dataset was assembled as presented above. However, the difference in total VSF numbers is minimal. Most examples of figurines are only broken fragments of the complete statuettes. In order to be able to meaningfully class these figurines by size, we must have a method to estimate complete figurine size based on their fragmentary remains.

Based on an examination of complete and large fragments of these statuettes, we can generally divide the form of figurines into three main parts: 'head', 'shoulders', and 'body' segments (Fig.

15.7). The 'head' segment varies from a slight trapezoidal shape (with a slightly wider crown than neck) to a rectangle. Generally, the 'shoulders' segment is trapezoidal, being widest at the shoulders and tapering at the waist. And finally, the 'body' segment is roughly rectangular in shape. Of course, the characterization of the 'head', 'shoulders' and 'body' of these figurines as rectangles and trapezoids is an act of approximation, necessary at this stage of our task. By computing the areas of these three simple shapes that make up the VSF's, we can gain a workable approximation of the size of violin figurines and compare them. The area of a figurine is simply approximated as the area of the head (A_h), plus the area of the shoulders region (A_s), plus the area of the body region (A_b). Size was not computed in three dimensions. As already stated, the most important form of the violin figurine is located on the plane in which the 'head', 'shoulders' and 'body' are fully visible. This plane carries by far the most visual information and is the plane most likely intended for display. Thickness, therefore, is not an important variable. Thus the total area of the violin figurine is: $A_{total} = A_h + A_s + A_b$. The area of the head is described as: $A_h = l_h * w_h$. l_h is the length of the head, from its crown to the shoulders; w_h is the width of the head. The area of the shoulders is described as: $A_s = l_s * (w_s + w_w) * .5$; l_h is the length from the shoulders to the waist; w_s is the width of the head; w_w is the width of the waist. The area of the head is described as: $A_b = l_b * w_b$. l_b is the length of the body, from the waist to the lowest edge; w_b is the width of the body, the maximum width of the figurine.

Having established a method for determining the approximate size of the figurine (in cm^2), we still face the problem of how to cope with the fact that the majority of the violin figurines assemblage consists only of fragments. To deal with this issue, we must again turn to the complete and nearly complete examples of these statuettes. In this small sample, it seems as if the proportions of these three segments ('head', 'shoulders' and 'body') are fairly standard. In the four complete examples the head length (l_h) ranges between about 27% to 35% of the total length of the figurine. The shoulders to waist length (l_s) ranges between about 19% to 25% of the total length of the figurine, and the body length (l_b) ranges between about 45% and 50% of the total length. The widths are similarly standardized, with the maximum width being the width of the body (w_b). The head width ranges between about 25% and 30% of this maximum width, the shoulder's width (w_s) range between 75% and 90% of the body width, and the waist width (w_w) between 52% and 58% of the maximum width. Using this data, an estimate of the standard proportions of the violin figurines were computed by averaging the proportions of the complete examples. Figure 15.8 illustrates both the approximate shapes of the segments that make up the violin figurines and the estimated standard proportions of these segments.

One measurement that has considerably more variability is the ratio of width to length. The maximum width varies from about 50% to 80% of the total length. This variability was considered when estimated sizes of complete figurines were computed from the proportions of the fragments. The total length and the maximum width of the figurines were treated independently. The method for estimating the complete size of a figurine from the measurements of a fragment was as follows:

1. Examine the fragment and determine which segment(s) of the figurine it came from.
2. If the fragment includes a complete segment ('head', 'shoulders', or 'body') or segments, then an estimate of the total length and the maximum width is computed based on the estimated standard proportions. For example, if the fragment represents all of the 'head' of a figurine, then its length is 31% of the total length and its width is 28% of the maximum width of the violin figurine.
3. If the piece is only a fragment of a 'head', 'shoulders' or 'body', an estimate of the complete size of the segment is made. Once we have estimated the complete size of the segment, then we can compute the complete size of the whole figurine. Those fragments which are two small to clearly identify or to approximate proportions are not considered.

Figure 15.7. Violin shape figure model:
approximate proportions of the segments that make up an idealized figurine.

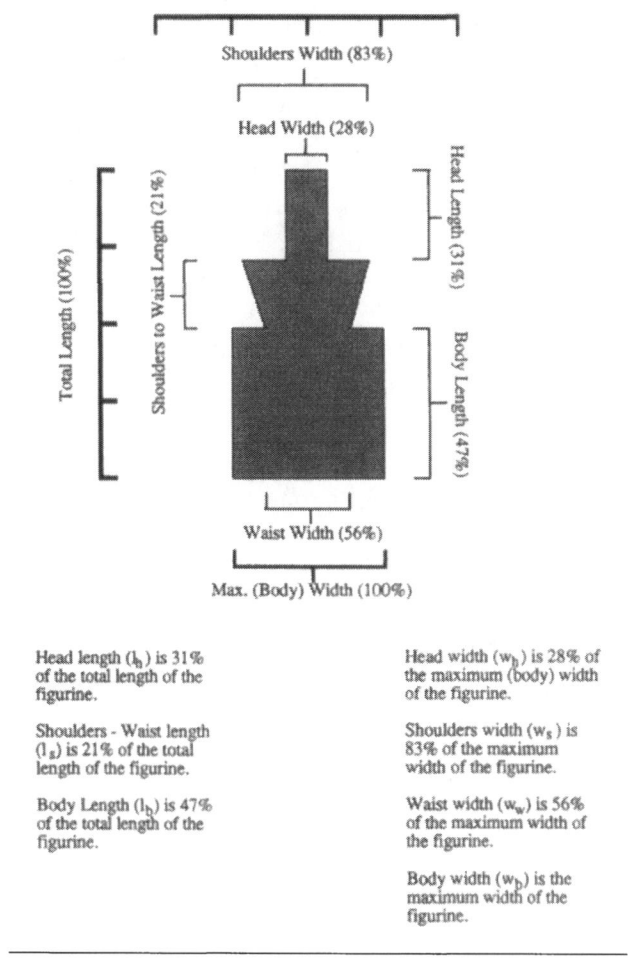

Head length (l_h) is 31% of the total length of the figurine.

Shoulders - Waist length (l_s) is 21% of the total length of the figurine.

Body Length (l_b) is 47% of the total length of the figurine.

Head width (w_h) is 28% of the maximum (body) width of the figurine.

Shoulders width (w_s) is 83% of the maximum width of the figurine.

Waist width (w_w) is 56% of the maximum width of the figurine.

Body width (w_b) is the maximum width of the figurine.

Figure 15.8. Distribution of approximate complete size categories
of the Violin shape figurines.

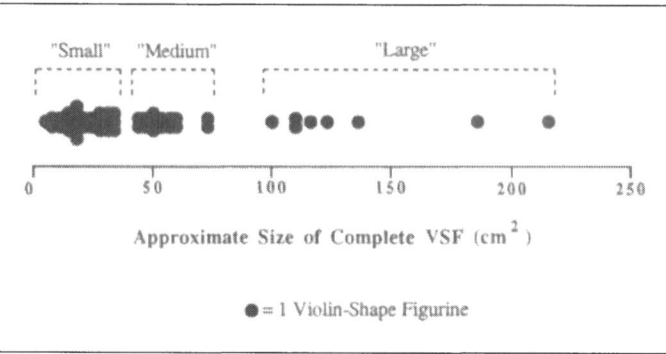

Approximate Size of Complete VSF (cm^2)

● = 1 Violin-Shape Figurine

Figure 15.9. Tree-diagram illustrating cluster analysis
of the approximated Gilat Violin figurine sizes

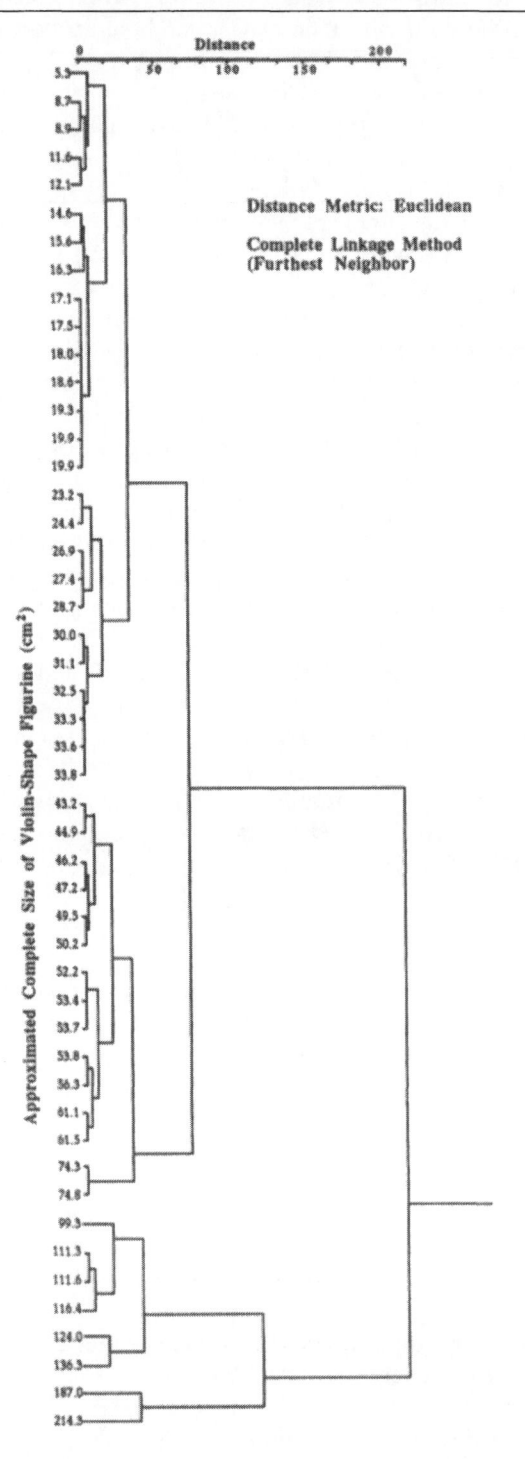

Once all of the figurines fragments were analyzed, they were classified according to size. Figure 15.8 illustrates the distribution of the approximated complete size categories of the violin figurines. The distribution is presented in the form of a 'dot-plot' in order to see size clusters more easily. From visual inspection of the plot, two main classes can be quickly recognized: the smaller one ranging from 5 cm^2 to 75 cm^2 and the larger one ranging from 99 cm^2 and 137 cm^2. It seems appropriate to further subdivide the smaller size class into two categories. When this is done the smallest ranges from 5 cm^2 to 34 cm^2, the 'medium' class ranges from 45 cm^2 to 75 cm^2, and the largest is between 99 cm^2 and 137 cm^2. Two figurines with the huge sizes of 187 cm^2 and 214 cm^2 are probably outliers, and should certainly fall into the 'large' range.

Another method to examine the sample of projected complete violin figurines' sizes for different size groupings is cluster analysis (Figure 15.9). The cluster analysis method used here (Euclidean distances, furthest neighbor linkage) groups the sample into larger and larger groupings based on their distance from each other in one dimension (size). Groups are progressively combined into larger and larger groups, whose elements are further and further apart. This type of cluster analysis lends itself to a 'tree diagram', which shows the relationships between such groups. The tree diagram (Fig. 15.9) illustrates the cluster analysis of the approximated Gilat violin figurines' sizes. This diagram shows groupings similar to those seen in the dot-plot (Fig. 15.8). We can split the sample into three groups, a 'small' with sizes ranging from 5 cm^2 to 34 cm^2, a 'medium' group with sizes ranging from 45 cm^2 to 75 cm^2, and a 'large' group with sizes greater than 99 cm^2.

While the over-all shape and proportions were fairly standardized, the variable of over-all size probably was not, as indicated by the polymodal size distribution. Alternatively, the polymodal size distribution may reflect the aims of the violin figurines' crafts-people. Unfortunately, because of our small sample size, there is no readily available, reliable way to statistically test for the probability that these groups were 'real' categories in the minds of the skilled artisans who created them. However, these proposed classifications are one of the most objective ways to deal with a small but important element of the cult activities carried out at the Gilat sanctuary.

Fields of variability (C. Commenge). Examination of complete figurines and fragments introduces variability among the corpus of figurines and brings forth some contrast to a (statistically) standardized assemblage. Different degrees of consistency and competence are involved in the project and its realization.

Morphological elements

Heads. A morphological classification recognizes two major types of heads.[24] With *type 1* (1a and 1b), the top of the head is horizontal to slightly concave, the sides of the head are parallel, the base is thus as large as its top. The cross-section is elliptical, each edge being marked by the short plan of chamfering. *Type 1a* presents straight and parallel sides (Figs 15.17.1). *Type 1b* presents concave and parallel sides (Figs 15.15; 15.16.3; 15.17.1–2).

With *type 2* (2a and 2b), the top of the head is horizontal to slightly convex, the sides of the head are flaring (divergent from base to top), the base is smaller than the top. The cross-section is elliptical with flattened edges for the top, sub-rectangular to oval for the base. *Type 2a* includes heads with straight and divergent sides (Figs 15.17. 3, 15.19.10). *Type 2b* presents concave and divergent sides (Fig. 15.17.5–6). It is unfortunate that no complete type 2 specimen was found. However, type 2 heads (especially type 2b heads) introduce, through evidence for complexity of technical achievement, another kind of hierarchy in the figurines corpus that goes beyond simple size or raw material variables. One complete head (Fig. 15.17.6) as well as one fragment both made from limestone and collected in Stratum IIC, document high technical achievement. They show a mastered and complete modification of shape on a very small volume. The slender and rounded neck gives way to a spatulate crown. Such heads can belong to medium to large size figurines (whose restituted length average 14 cm). One yellow sandstone fragment has been interpreted as a square, large and unique head of a figurine (Fig. 15.22.2). Sharp angles at the base of this specimen suggest a shoulder line and not a waist line, but the notches at the base of the neck make it difficult to decide upon the orientation of this fragment.

Bases. Most of the bases of figurines are conceived like palettes. They present the same subrectangular shape, plane faces and chamfered edges. Yet the shape and volume of the base, that represents one half of the figurine's length and almost two-third of its mass, is an essential element that balances the composition of the silhouette. Bases of complete figurines and fragments can be divided into three main groups. Each group is defined by the ratio of width (the horizontal median of the base) and height (the vertical median of the base: see Table 15. 8).

Type 1 includes bases whose width is shorter than height (ratio <1, see Figs 15.15, 15.16. 3). *Type 1a* can be described like 'non-angular' and presents straight vertical sides and a continuous and convex base (Fig. 15.17.12, Fig. 15.19.10). With *type 1 b* the junction of straight sides to convex base is angular, sides are slightly convergent (Fig. 15.15, 15.17.7) or divergent (Fig. 15.16.3), the surface of the base is slightly trapezoidal. With the exception of one specimen from bone, symmetrical angles of 90° form the hips and the hip line is horizontal. Yet one fragment can belong to a (so far) unique variant of this type of base (Fig. 15.22.4). It presents two straight and convergent sides that narrow the waist.

Type 2 includes bases whose width is longer than the height (ratio >1, see Figs 15.16.2, 15.18, 15.19.8). Sides are straight, vertical or slightly convergent (Fig. 15.19.8) or divergent (Fig. 15.16.2). The base is convex and slightly rounded. Angles at hip-line are slightly higher than 90° and the hip line is oblique, sloping downward (Fig 15.16.2). One type 2 base was grooved around the waist (Fig. 15.22.9).

Type 3 includes bases whose width and height are equal (ratio=1, Figs 15.16.1, 15.19.6). Sides are straight to slightly convex, the base is convex, and angles are marked. Angles at hip line are slightly higher than 90° and the hip line is oblique, sloping downward.

Torsos. This part seems less subject to morphological modification and varies more in terms of symmetry or of proportion. The torso is trapezoidal; the shoulder line is straight and horizontal. Sides are straight and oblique (to the exception of Fig. 15.16.3). The external angle to the base varies between 75° and 80°.

Several fragmented specimens, either torsos or bases, may suggest apprenticeship. One is the upper part of a figurine, whose chamfers are uneven and do not mask the former chipping of the shoulder line. The contour of the torso is asymmetrical, the broken head was chamfered on top (Fig. 15.17.8). On another specimen, the top of the head, perhaps broken during extreme reduction, is re-shaped with a double chamfer. The torso is also asymmetrical (Fig. 15.19.3). One asymmetrical base, insufficiently dressed (Fig. 15.22.8) can perhaps complete this heteroclite inventory.

With consideration to the conventional shaping of the violin figurines and the relative high rate of fragmentation, tracing evidence from morphological variables might be more significant in a system of covariance of characters. The stratigraphic distribution of bases and heads according to morphological types is proposed in Table 15.6. Only fragments securely identified are recorded. Based on modest evidence, information comes from types illustrated at several levels of occupation. Absence of types is, with regard to the small sample, not seemingly reliable. While fragmented specimens suggest that limestone and exogenous material might indifferently present the same variety either of head or base types, one can prudently notice an apparent and exclusive correlation between type 1a heads and exogenous material (sandstone and granodiorite) (see Table 15.6). Among the five complete specimens, two figurines, one from limestone and one from sandstone, present the same type of base (1b) and head (1a) but this covariance cannot be extended to the figurines proportions (Fig. 15.15 and 15.16.3). Each of the three other complete figurines, all from different materials (bone, granodiorite and talc-schist) gives evidence for different combinations of morphological characters. However narrow, the sample of complete figurines tends to underscore the correlation of morphological characters and to enhance the critical incidence of variables such as the figurines' relative proportions and the material figurines are made from. While it precludes any attempt to establish an authentic typology, it introduces fields of variability that, beyond a perceptible trend to standardization, may be crucial in determining the organization of violin-shape figurines production.

Table 15.6. Stratigraphic distribution of morphological characters.

Stratum	material	types of bases				types of heads			
complete specimens		1a	1b	2	3	1a	1b	2a	2b
IIC-3	sandstone	-	1	-	-	-	1	-	-
IIC	talc-shist	-	-	-	1	1	-	-	-
IIB	limestone	-	1	-	-	-	1	-	-
IIA	bone	1	-	-	-	-	-	1	-
no context	granodiorite	-	-	1	-	1	-	-	-
fragmented specimens									
IIIA	limestone	-	-	1	-	-	-	1	-
IIC	talc schist	-	-	1	1				
	limestone					-	2	-	2
IIB	sandstone	-	1	-	-				
	limestone	1	-	2	1				
	bone	-	1	-	-				
IIA	limestone	-	1	-	-				
	bone	-	1	-	-				
II*	limestone	1	-	-	-				
	limestone					-	1	-	-
topsoil/no context	phylite	-	-	1	-				
	limestone	-	3	1	-	-	2	-	-
	chalk	1	-	-	-				
total=	36	4	9	7	3	2	7	2	2

* without sub stratum specification

Table 15.7. Stratigraphic distribution of violin figurine specimens*.

level	III**	IIIA	II**	IIC	IIB	IIA	topsoil/ no context
medium							
limestone	1	6	3	9	11	3	13
chalk	-	-	-	1	2	-	2
marl	-	-	-	-	-	1	-
granodiorite		-	-	-	-	-	2
sandstone	-	-	-	3	2	1	3
talc schist	1	-	-	4	-	-	2
bone	-	-	-	-	1	2	-
pottery	-	-	-	1	1	1	-
N per stratigraphic unit=	2	6	3	18	17	8	22

*number of specimens includes complete, incomplete figurines and fragments (the minimal number of individuals being statistical). **Some specimens are not ascribed to a specific sub-stratum.

Symmetry. Complete figurines and several of the largest fragments show that symmetry of profiles on both sides of the vertical axis was achieved, in most cases, with a tenuous level of discrepancy. By contrast, asymmetry can be a differential element in discriminating one singular figurine from talc schist, with breasts carved in relief (Fig. 15.20). Upper angles of the base are asymmetrical; one side of the base is convex, while the opposite side is straight. This is also the case for two fragmented figurines, one from limestone and one from Phyllite, whose lopsided bases are nevertheless chamfered (Fig. 15.22.8–9).

Challenging proportions (Table 15.8). Polymodal estimates indicate a perceptible trend to size and shape standardization (Figs 15.8–9). However, the degree of *variability* in the violin-shape figurines' assemblage has to be explored insofar as it may yield complementary information on the organization of production. The following analysis aims to establish whether dimensions and their ratio discriminate categories of figurines, and whether this discrimination is correlated to the kind of material used and/or to the regional provenance of the figurines. It can be stated that proportions define rhythms of sculpture that are the respected guidelines in the conception of violin figurines. Those rhythms can follow slightly different tempos. In the assemblage of Gilat the proportion of the head (28 to 33% of the total height of the figurine) is the least variable height proportion. Therefore complete specimens or specimens having at least the torso and the base preserved were selected in order to get significant proportions for height and width (Table 15.8). The raw material of each specimen was registered as well as the archaeological provenance of the figurine. Some figurines from other sites, available from publications or collections, are similarly listed.

An algorithmic program capable of emphasizing heterogeneity within a narrow sample of artifacts was kindly provided by Gilles and Nicole Fernandez (Fernandez and Fernandez 2000). By computing three categories of variables or *characters*—proportions of heights and widths of body part against the total height of the figurine, raw material and provenance—this program allowed us to cluster and order similar variations among the defined characters (method of rectangular distances). By quantifying similitude, expressed in terms of distance between each character and object, the program yields ranked matrices of artifacts. It also defines 'splits' in the progression of the ordering whose meaning (or insignificance) has to be evaluated. Charts ranking splits among classes of artifacts as well as the most discriminative characters are also available. Before beginning the computer program, some specific characters were weighted with no consideration to the state of specimens, complete or incomplete: 1 weighted heights (Fig. 15.10a and c) and heights and widths (Fig. 15.10b and d) of body parts while total height was kept down to 0. With consideration to the main goals of this enterprise, we gave a weight of 1 to raw materials (each of the five materials listed was weighted with 0.2). Alternatively, Fig. 15.10e and 15.10f present ranked matrices where heights and widths are weighted while materials were kept down to 0.

The foremost result of this analysis is the introduction of distinct groups of figurines within the assemblage of Gilat. Ranking of discriminative characters indicates that, to the contrary of what was expected, the heigth of the head is a critical character. It is placed at the second rank for splitting classes of complete figurines (Fig. 15.10a, b and e). Therefore, and although they present some convergent evidence, comments on the results for complete and incomplete figurines are formally separated.

Complete figurines. Ranked matrices of complete figurines emphasize the recurrence of the following classes: (71, granodiorite, Gilat), (100 limestone, Peqi'in, 16.1 limestone, Gilat and 633 talc schist, Gilat), (5017 sandstone, Gilat, 200 bone, W. Ghazzeh, 500 limestone, Abu Hamid, Chalcolithic), (2795 bone, Gilat). This last class is placed either at the beginning or the end of the list. Two figurines, one from talc schist (633) and from sandstone (5017) either introduce or follow splits. Both belong to the assemblage of Gilat. It is remarkable that ranked splits between classes of artifacts are systematically introduced after or followed by figurines made from exogenous rock (granodiorite, talc schist, sandstone) or rare medium (bone).

Table 15.8. Proportions of violin figurines (with reference to figurines from other sites).

Height (length) proportions
TH: total height; TH*: total preserved height, from shoulders to base
Hh: head height; Ht: torso height; Hb: base height
/:ratio

Ni		head			torso				base	
	TH	*Hh*	*Hh/TH*	*Ht*	*Ht/Hh*	*Ht/TH*	*Hb*	*Hb/Hh*	*Hb/Ht*	*Hb/TH*
	*Gilat: limestone, complete figurines*									
16.1	*20,5*	*6,5*	*0,31*	*3,5*	*0,5*	*0,17*	*10,5*	*1,6*	*3*	*0,51*
	*Peqi'in, limestone, complete figurine*									
100	12,9	5,3	0,25	3	0,9	0,23	6,3	1,9	2,1	0,48
	*Abu Hamid, limestone, complete figurine*									
500* Chalco	3,6	1,2	0,33	1	0,8	0,27	1,4	1,1	1,4	0,38

*Dollfus and Kafafi 1995: Fig. 4:4

Ni	TH	Hh	Hh/TH	Ht	Ht/Hh	Ht/TH	Hb	Hb/Hh	Hb/Ht	Hb/TH
	*Gilat: talc-schist, complete figurine*									
633	15,1	4,9	0,32	3	0,6	0,19	7,2	1,4	2,4	0,47
	*Gilat: sandstone, complete figurine*									
5017	19,9	6,7	0,33	4,7	0,7	0,23	8,5	1,2	1,8	0,42
	*Gilat: granodiorite, complete figurine*									
1532	21,9	6,2	0,28	4,8	0,7	0,21	10,9	1,7	2,3	0,49
	*Gilat: bone, (in)complete figurine*									
2795	(7,1)	(2)	0,28	(1,9)	0,9	0,26	3,2	1,6	1,6	0,45
	*Wadi Ghazzeh: complete bone figurine*									
200*	6,3	2,1	0,33	1,6	0,7	0,25	2,4	1,1	1,5	0,38

Ni	TH*			Ht		Ht/HT*	Hb		Hb/Ht	Hb/HT*
	*Gilat: limestone, head missing*									
	*TH*: height from shoulders to base*									
186	(5,6)	-	-	1,9	-	0,33	3,7	-	1,9	0,66
2596	(6,6)	-	-	2	-	0,3	4,6	2,-	2,3	0,69
384	(6,7)	-	-	2	-	0,29	4,7	-	2,3	0,70
	*R 48: limestone, head missing*									
300	(7,6)	-	-	3	-	0,39	4,6	-	1,5	0,58

Oren 1993:1387, no scale (here considered 1/1 for proportions)

Ni	TH*			Ht		Ht/HT*	Hb		Hb/Ht	Hb/HT*
	*Titorah: limestone, head missing*									
400 Lass, pers. com	(3,3)	-	-	1,3	-	0,39	2	-	1,4	0,60
	*Abu Hamid, limestone, head missing*									
501* W.Raba	(5,7)	-	-	2,3	-	0,40	3,4	-	1,4	0,59
502** W.Raba	(6,2)	-	-	3,3	-	0,53	2,8	-	0,8	0,46
503*** Chalco	(6,5)	-	-	4,3	-	0,69	1,7	-	0,3	0,19

*Dollfus and Kafafi 1995: Fig. 4:*1, **2; Dollfus 1988: Plate 3: ***3

Ni	TH*			Ht		Ht/HT*	Hb		Hb/Ht	Hb/HT*
	*Gilat: talc schist, head missing*									
4222	5,9	-	-	2,2	-	0,37	3,7	-	1,6	0,62
3879	8,1	-	-	3,1	-	0,38	5	-	1,6	0,61

GILAT'S FIGURINES **771**

Width proportions
Wh: head width (top); Wsh: shoulders width; Wb: base width (median); Ww: waist width; Hb: base height

Gilat: limestone, complete figurines

Ni	TH	head				torso				base			
		Wh	Wh/Wsh	Wh/Wb	Wh/TH	Wsh	Wsh//Ww	Wsh/Wb	Wsh/TH	Wb	Wb/Hb	Wb/Ww	Wb/TH
16,1	20,7	2,4	0,3	0,2	0,11	7,3	1,6	0,7	0,35	9,3	0,8	2,1	0,45

Peqi'in, limestone, complete figurine

| 100 | 12,9 | 2 | 0,3 | 0,3 | 0,15 | 6 | 1,2 | 0,9 | 0,46 | 6,3 | 0,8 | 1,3 | 0,48 |

Abu Hamid: complete limestone figurine

| 500* Chalco | 3,6 | 0,6 | 0,5 | 0,3 | 0,16 | 1,2 | 1,5 | 0,7 | 0,33 | 1,6 | 1,1 | 2 | 0,44 |

* Dollfus and Kafafi 1995: Fig. 4:4

Gilat: talc schist, complete figurine

| 633 | 15,1 | 2,2 | 0,3 | 0,3 | 0,14 | 6,6 | 1,7 | 0,9 | 0,43 | 7,3 | 1 | 2 | 0,48 |

Gilat: sandstone, complete figurine

| 5017 | 19,9 | 2,2 | 0,3 | 0,3 | 0,11 | 6,1 | 1,7 | 0,8 | 0,30 | 7,2 | 0,8 | 2,1 | 0,36 |

Gilat: granodiorite, complete figurine

| 1532 | 21,9 | 3,8 | 0,3 | 0,3 | 0,17 | 10,5 | 1,5 | 0,8 | 0,47 | 12 | 1,1 | 1,7 | 0,54 |

Gilat: bone, (in)complete figurine

| 2795 | (7) | (1,1) | 0,6 | 0,4 | 0,15 | 1,6 | 1,4 | 0,6 | 0,22 | 2,4 | 0,7 | 2,1 | 0,34 |

Wadi Ghazzeh: bone, complete figurine

| 200* | 6,3 | 0,8 | 0,4 | 0,4 | 0,12 | 1,8 | 1,8 | 0,9 | 0,28 | 2 | 0,8 | 2 | 0,38 |

Jean Perrot, pers. com.

limestone, head missing
TH*: height from shoulders to base

Ni	TH*					Wsh	Wsh:Ww	Wsh/Wb	Wsh/TH*	Wb	Wb/Hb	Wb/Ww	Wb/TH*
186	(5,6)	-	-	-	-	3,9	1,9	0,7	0,69	4,5	1,2	2,2	0,80
2596	(6,6)	-	-	-	-	4	1,5	0,8	0,60	4,6	1	1,7	0,69
384	(6,7)	-	-	-	-	4,2	1,8	0,9	0,62	4,6	0,9	2	0,68

Titorah: limestone, head missing

| 400* | (3,3) | - | - | - | - | 2,1 | 1,7 | 0,8 | 0,63 | 2,4 | 1,2 | 2 | 0,72 |

R 48: limestone, head missing

| 300* | (7,6) | - | - | - | - | 5 | 1,2 | 0,7 | 0,65 | 6,4 | 1,5 | 1,6 | 0,84 |

Oren 1993:1387, no scale (here considered 1/1 for proportions)

Abu Hamid, limestone, head missing

501* W.Raba	(5,7)	-	-	-	-	3,1	1,4	0,7	+	4	1,2	1,9	0,70
502* W.Raba	(6,2)	-	-	-	-	3,2	1,7	0,7	0,51	4	1,4	2,2	0,64
503* Chalco	(6,2)	-	-	-	-	6,9	1,1	0,8	1,1	7,9	5,2	1,2	1,2

*Dollfus and Kafafi 1995: Fig. 4:*1, **2; Dollfus 1988: Plate 3: ***3

talc schist, head missing

| 4222 | 5,9 | - | - | - | - | - | - | - | - | 4,2 | 1,1 | 1,8 | 0,71 |
| 3879 | 8,1 | - | - | - | - | 5,2 | 1,3 | 0,8 | 0,64 | 6 | 1,2 | 1,5 | 0,74 |

*arbitrary and convenient numbers have been given to material from other sites.

One can observe that the figurines from Gilat are highly susceptible to splitting. The variety of material employed in this assemblage seems significant yet it produces unexpected patterns. On the one hand, one bone figurine from Gilat (2795) is always cut off in the ordering, either by provoking a split or by being singularized by one, while one bone figurine from Wadi Ghazzeh aggregates with figurines from different medium (200). Moreover, two classes cluster figurines from varied materials and provenances (5017, 200, 500)–(100, 16.1, 633). On the other hand, the examination of the proposed splits between classes of characters emphasizes the preponderance of proportions over materials. Ranking of characters that splits classes of artifacts first examines base then head height ratio to the total height of the figurines. When listed, provenance is placed at a low discriminative rank (rank 7, see Fig. 15.10a), while width proportions seem here negligible. A matrix considering both heights and widths but with no weight for materials (Fig. 15.10e) produced (exception: Peqi'in figurine 100) the same classes of artifacts than with a weight of 1 for materials. The assemblage of 16 figurines from Peqi'in seems already promising to complete, confirm or infirm evidence provided by Gilat's assemblage of violin figurines (see Fig. 15.10a, b and e).

The examination of the complete figurine sample suggests a tight covariance between the proportions of the figurine and the medium it is made from. Bone can be considered like a technically restrictive medium in patterning the figurine's morphology, in terms of dimensions and thickness, and incidentally, of proportions. Such constraints may have been critical in determining the choice of this specific medium. The constant and close ranking of one Wadi Ghazzeh figurine from bone (200) to one Gilat figurine from sandstone (5017) suggests that either fortuitous or intended concerns have lead to convergent proportions. However, the unique bone figurine from Gilat appears quite incongruous. The hardness of granodiorite, that can explain the relative thickness of the specimen, cannot explain noticeable differences in rythmic proportions. Similarly, the intrinsic qualities of limestone, sandstone or talc schist rather offer unrestrictive possibilities as far as proportions are concerned. Material constraints (and here the compacity of granodiorite is to be opposed to talc schist and sandstone foliation) cannot be adduced in support for dissonances in proportions. These first observations suggest that source of production may be a critical factor that splits the assemblage of complete violin figurines from Gilat.

Incomplete figurines. The sample of incomplete figurines confirms those first observations and introduces some complementary contrasts with regard to the provenance of the figurines (Figs 15.10c, d and e). The classification of incomplete figurines introduced by ranked matrices with materials weighted can be summed up as follows: (503 limestone, Abu Hamid, Chalcolithic), (502, limestone, Abu Hamid, Wadi Rabah), (501, limestone, Abu Hamid, Wadi Rabah, 300 limestone, site R48, 400 limestone, Titorah, 186 limestone, Gilat, 2596 limestone, Gilat, 384 limestone, Gilat), (4222, 3879 both from talc schist, Gilat). The computation of data with no weight on materials produced identical results, but with a significative aggregation of figurines (300 limestone, site R48) to the cluster formed by the two talc schist figurines from Gilat (3879, 300, 4222, see Fig. 15.10e).

Here also proportions are preponderant in ranking figurines with a preference for the base width/total height ratio (total height: from shoulder line to base). The base height is still placed in second rank. The range of represented materials is narrowed to limestone, largely represented, and talc schist. Ranked splits between classes of figurines recurrently isolate one group of Gilat figurines from exogenous material (3879, 4222 see Figs 15.10c and d) but also systematically singularized three limestone figurines from Abu Hamid (501, 502, 503, see Figs 15.10c, d and f)). Limestone figurines from Gilat keep together in the three ranked matrices. This observation emphasizes the tight correlation of their proportions. The first-ranked split introduced by one of those limestone figurines (384) in Fig. 15.10c sharply dissociates them from two talc schist figurines, also from Gilat (4222, 3879). The second-ranked split that occurs with one talc schist figurine (3879, Fig. 15.10d), marks a specimen already segregated in Gilat's assemblage: it is the unique specimen with carved breasts. Keeping in mind that the head of the figurine is seemingly a discriminative component, the covariance—already underscored with the assemblage of complete figurines—between the figurines' proportions and their medium is here compounded. Intrasite differentiation is corroborated. Another intrasite differentiation is suggested by the recurrent splitting of figurines recovered at Abu Hamid, all made from the same material. In this case, the interference of the chronological context is perhaps critical. However, one can observe the close and recurrent association of one limestone figurine (400) from Titorah in Judea with the group of limestone figurines from Gilat (384, 2596, 186). One limestone figurine from site R48, in north coastal Sinai, finds its way between two talc schist figurines from Gilat (Fig. 15.10f, no weight for materials). With consideration to otherwise recurrent evidence from ranked matrices, this ordering, that is not marked by a split, is interpreted as irrelevant.

This examination enhances the variability of violin figurines as they are segregated rather than aggregated by ranking. This especially applies in the assemblage of figurines from Gilat. Standards and morphological variables are tightly linked in shaping the violin figurines. In terms of production, the standardization of figurines perhaps finds its best definition with what Costin described 'as socially rather than economically mandated' (Costin 1991:34). Variables, insofar as they represent digression or interpretation of standards, tend to singularize sources of production. This, and the fact that raw material resources are all located off-site, apparently contests any centralization of figurine production at Gilat.

Figure 15.10a–f. Algorithmic matrices for complete and incomplete figurines.

Figure 15.10a. ranked matrix for complete figurines, heights and materials weighted.

16. 1: limestone, Gilat; 633: talc-schist, Gilat;	2	7	1	1	6	5	2	5
71: granodiorite, Gilat;	7	1	0	6	3	0	0	0
5017: sandstone, Gilat;	9		0	1	3	1	0	0
2795: bone, Gilat; 100: limestone,Peqi'in;	5					7		
200: bone, W. Ghazzeh;								
500: limestone, Chalcolithic, A. Hamid								
bone								
torso height/total height								
head width/total height								
base width/total height								
torso width/total height								
Total height								
base height/total height								
talc-schist								
granodiorite								
sandstone								
site								
limestone								
head height/total height								
ranked splits	3	1			2			
proposed splits between classes of artifacts	split to be introduced after: 1= 71; 2= 633; 3= 2795							
proposed splits between classes of characters	1= base height/total height 2= head height/total height 3= limestone 4= torso height/total height 5= bone 6= talc-schist 7= site							

Figure 15.10b. ranked matrix for complete figurines, heights, widths and materials weighted.

16. 1: limestone, Gilat; 633: talc-schist, Gilat; 71: granodiorite, Gilat; 5017: sandstone, Gilat; 2795: bone, Gilat; 100: limestone, Peqi'in; 200: bone, W. Ghazzeh; 500: limestone, Chalcolithic, A. Hamid	71	633	100	16.1	5017	200	500	2795
bone								
torso height/total height								
head width/total height								
base width/total height								
torso width/total height								
Total height								
base height/total height								
talc-schist								
granodiorite								
sandstone								
site								
limestone								
head height/total height								
ranked splits	3			2			1	

proposed splits between classes of artifacts	split to be introduced after: 1: 500; 2: 16. 1; 3: 71
proposed splits between classes of characters	1 = base height/total height 2 = head height/total height 3 = limestone 4 = torso height/total height 5 = bone 6 = sandstone

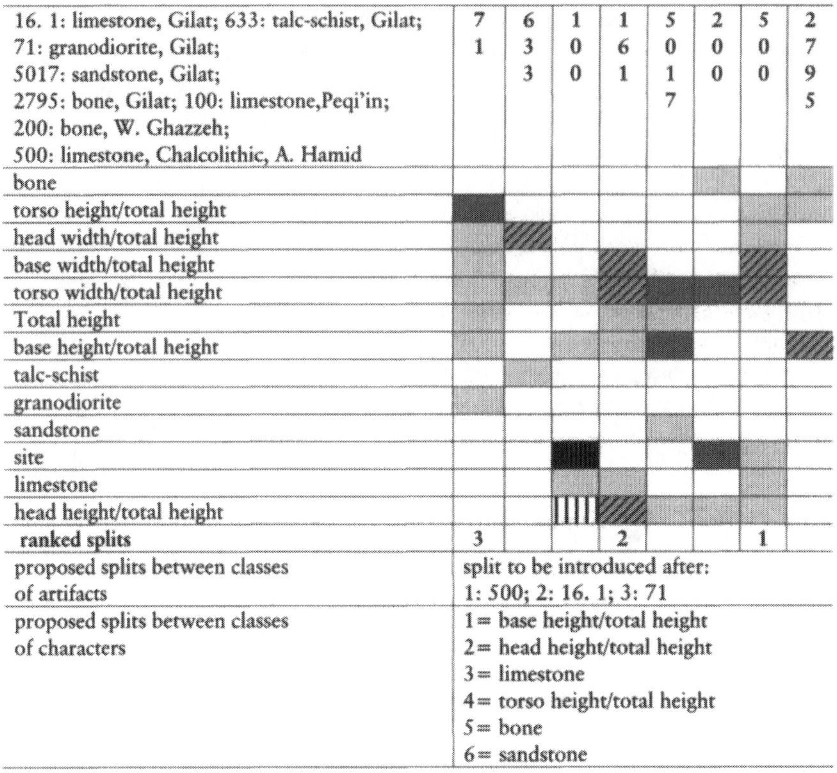

Figure 15.10c. ranked matrix for incomplete figurines, heights and materials weighted.

186, 2596 & 384: limestone, Gilat; 3879 & 4222: talc-schist, Gilat; 300: limestone, R48; 400: limestone, Titorah; 501 & 502: limestone, W. Rabah, A. Hamid; 503: limestone, Chalco, A. Hamid	503	502	501	300	400	2596	186	384	4222	3879
base height/(total height)										
talc-schist										
limestone										
site										
torso height/(total height)										
torso width/(total height)										
base width/(total height)										
(Total height)										
ranked splits	2	3						1		

proposed splits between classes of artifacts	splits to be introduced after: 1 = 384; 2 = 503; 3 = 502
proposed splits between classes of characters	1 = base width/(total height) 2 = base height/(total height) 3 = limestone 4 = torso width/(total height) 5 = talc schist

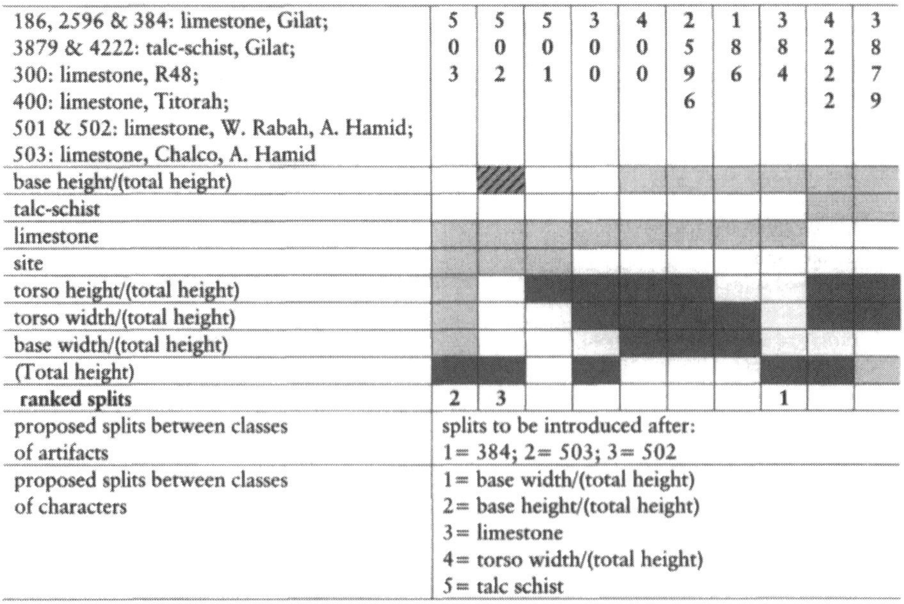

Figure 15.10d. ranked matrix for incomplete figurines, heights, widths and materials weighted.

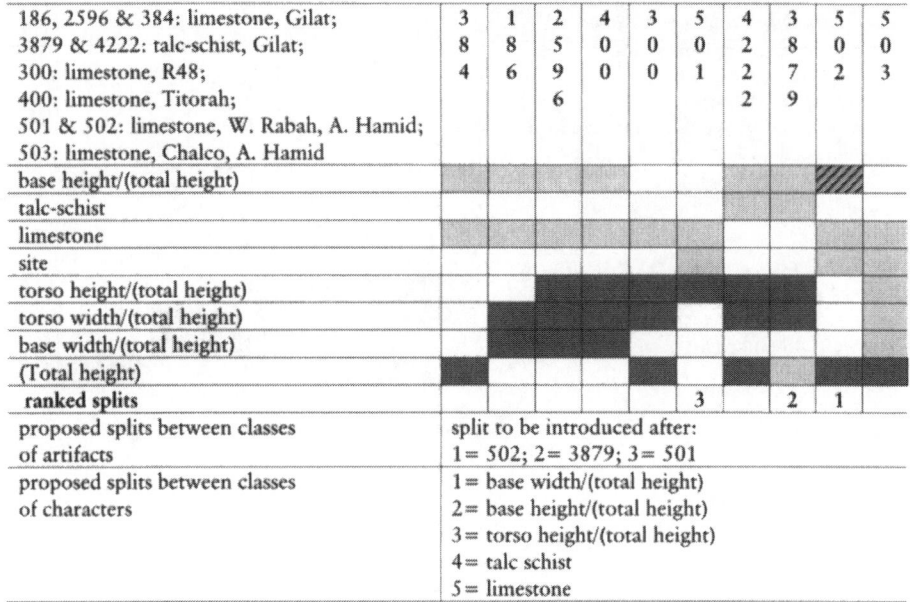

186, 2596 & 384: limestone, Gilat;	3	1	2	4	3	5	4	3	5	5
3879 & 4222: talc-schist, Gilat;	8	8	5	0	0	0	2	8	0	0
300: limestone, R48;	4	6	9	0	0	1	2	7	2	3
400: limestone, Titorah;			6				2	9		
501 & 502: limestone, W. Rabah, A. Hamid;
503: limestone, Chalco, A. Hamid

- base height/(total height)
- talc-schist
- limestone
- site
- torso height/(total height)
- torso width/(total height)
- base width/(total height)
- (Total height)
- **ranked splits**   3   2   1

proposed splits between classes
of artifacts
split to be introduced after:
1= 502; 2= 3879; 3= 501

proposed splits between classes
of characters
1= base width/(total height)
2= base height/(total height)
3= torso height/(total height)
4= talc schist
5= limestone

Figure 15.10e. ranked matrix for complete figurines, heights, widths weighted, no weight for materials.

16. 1: limestone, Gilat; 633: talc-schist, Gilat;	7	1	6	1	5	2	5	2
71: granodiorite, Gilat;	1	0	3	6	0	0	0	7
5017: sandstone, Gilat; 2795: bone, Gilat;		0	3	3	1	1	0	9
100: limestone, Peqi'in;					7			5
200: bone, W. Ghazzeh;
500: limestone, Chalcolithic, A. Hamid

- bone
- torso height/total height
- head width/total height
- base width/total height
- torso width/total height
- Total height
- base height/total height
- talc-schist
- granodiorite
- sandstone
- site
- limestone
- head height/total height
- **ranked splits**   2   3   1

proposed splits between classes
of artifacts
split to be introduced after:
1= 500; 2= 100; 3= 16.1

proposed splits between classes
of characters
1= base height/total height
2= head height/total height
3= limestone
4= bone

Figure 15.10f. ranked matrix for incomplete figurines, heights, widths weighted, no weight for materials.

186, 2596 & 384: limestone, Gilat;	3	3	4	5	4	2	1	3	5	5
3879 & 4222: talc-schist, Gilat;	8	0	2	0	0	5	8	8	0	0
300: limestone, R48;	7	0	2	1	0	9	6	4	2	3
400: limestone, Titorah;	9		2			6				
501 & 502: limestone, W. Rabah, A. Hamid;										
503: limestone, Chalco, A. Hamid										
base height/(total height)										
talc-schist										
limestone										
site										
torso height/(total height)										
torso width/(total height)										
base width/(total height)										
(Total height)										
ranked splits			2					3	1	
proposed splits between classes of artifacts	split to be introduced after: 1= 502; 2= 4222; 3= 384									
proposed splits between classes of characters	1= base width/total height 2= base height/(total height) 3= talc schist									

System and Organization of Production

Ever since the preliminary presentation of data from Gilat over a decade ago, the cultic function of the site has been a central theme (Alon 1976; Alon and Levy 1989). Violin figurines, abundant at the site while extremely rare elsewhere, have been a privileged element of elaboration with regard to the intensity in time and in space of cultic activities at the site. The very status of figurines, together with their unusual abundance, *de facto* raises the question as to the *nature* and the *level* of the demand as scrupulously defined by Costin (1991: 3) for such elaborate artifacts. The density of elaborate artifacts, the neglect of local sources, the relatively large percentages of artifacts made from exogenous materials, and the context of production (Tables 15.2 and 15.9b) first suggest a number of questions about craft specialization. Central to this problem is the organization of production and distribution, whose interdependent structures are fostered by socio-economic and political systems (Arnold and Munns 1994; D'Altroy and Earle 1985; Johnson 1973; Trigger 1974). Specialization, defined by Arnold (1987), Brumfiel and Earle (1987), and Costin (1991), is conceived and achieved to satisfy demands well beyond those of the production group itself (Perles 1992). Production is organized and standardized (Arnold and Munns 1994), and products designed to be exchanged and acquired by consumers that do not produce themselves. *Independent specialization* is defined as meeting utilitarian needs of goods or services and requires a sufficiently large, open-ended demand to support the specialists (see Costin 1991; Smith 1975). *Attached specialization* implies the production of high-status goods, and develops within political processes, as 'production on command for elites and the social and political institutions they control' (Costin 1991:7, and cf. Brumfiel and Earle 1987; Earle 1981; Russell 1988). Noticeable differences that promote a dichotomy between figurines from regional yet non-local materials and figurines from 'exogenous' materials, available at distant sources, are explored in terms of organization of production and distribution and might document the role of specialization within the socioeconomic context of emergent ranking at Gilat.

Table 15.9a. Comparative estimation of the output in the production* of tabular artefacts.

N=116 tabular artifacts*	limestone	marl	chalk	granodiorite	sandstone	talc-schist	totals
FIGURINES	28	1	4	2	6	7	= 48
mni: 48, % on N= 41. 3%							
specimens: 70							
per category of material:							
% on n	50.9%	50%	30.7%	15.3%	46.1%	35%	
% on N	24.1%	0.8%	3.4%	1.7%	5.1%	6%	
% on mni	58.3%	2%	8.3%	4.1%	12.5%	14.5%	= 99.7%
% on specimens	65.7%	1.4%	7%	2.8%	11.4%	11.4%	= 99.7%
TOKENS	17	-	9	1	5	4	= 36
mni: 36, % on N= 31%							
per category of material:		-					
% on n	30.9%		69.2%	7.6%	38.4%	20%	
% on N	14.6%		7. 7%	0.8%	4.3%	3.4%	
% on mni	47.2%		25%	2.7%	13.8%	11%	= 99.7%
PALETTES	10	1	-	10**	2	9	= 32
mni: 32, % on N= 27. 5%							
per category of material:							
% on n	18.1%	50%	-	76.9%	15.3%	45%	
% on N	8.6%	0.8%	-	8.6%	1. 7%	7.7%	
% on mni	31.2%	3.1%	-	31.2%	6.2%	28.1%	= 99.8%
N=	n= 55	n= 2	n= 13	n= 13	n= 13	n= 20	= 116
% on N=	47.4%	1.7%	11.2%	11.2%	11.2%	17.2%	= 99.9%

9 scoria palettes complete this inventory. This specific rock was not used for manufacturing figurines. ** One is from amphibolite, whose probable sources overlap that of granodiorite.

Table 15.9 b. Some variables in the organization of production* with consideration to the source location.

Variables in the Organization of Production of Tabular Artifacts				
distribution of types of tabular artifacts (N= 116)				
regional sources	total/N			
distribution of artifacts:	= 60. 2%	figurines= 28. 4%	tokens= 22. 4%	palettes= 9. 4%
distant sources	total/N			
distribution of artifacts	= 39. 6%	figurines= 12. 9%	tokens= 8. 6%	palettes= 18. 1%
distribution of artifacts,				
total, all materials merged	= 99. 8%	figurines= 41. 3%	tokens= 31%	palettes= 27. 5%
intra-distribution of tabular artifacts per type of source				
regional sources, n=70				
intra-distribution of artifacts from		figurines= 47. 1%	tokens= 37. 1%	palettes= 15. 7%
limestone, chalk and marl				
distant sources, n= 46				
intra-distribution of artifacts from		figurines= 32. 6%	tokens= 21. 7%	palettes= 45. 6%
granodiorite, sandstone and talc-schist				

* based on consumption of tabular artifacts at Gilat

The production of violin figurines exploited either regional sources of limestone (58.3%), chalk (8.3%) and marl (2%) or various sandstones (12.5%), talc schist or phyllite (14. 5%) and granodiorite (4.1%), available at distant sources of apparently geographically circumscribed deposits (see Table 15.9a where statistics are also given for numbers of specimens). In general, those same types of resources apply to one bipartite unit of production (see Table 15.2). From evidence based on similitude of sources and techniques, the production of violin figurines belongs to a larger group of production, characterized by tabular by-products (Table 15.2). Some statistics in Tables 15.9a-b show variables that consider all tabular artifacts recovered at Gilat, with the exception of scoria or pumice. Scoria and pumice were not used in manufacturing figurines (also their plausible sources do not overlap with proposed sources for exogenous materials used in the making of figurines). These statistics establish basic evidence for the distribution of tabular artifacts at the site, in terms of consumption. *De facto*, the archaeological context here defines *consumption*, evidenced by material in use at the site, rather than production that would be demonstrated by artifacts in the process of manufacture at the site, in workshop contexts. Although direct evidence for patterns of production is of paramount significance and thus sorely missing for this kind of analysis, consumption patterns, by definition, clarify the nature of the demand and as such establish the social and economic role of by-products.

Estimation within the whole assemblage of tabular artifacts indicates that demand favors figurines (41.3%, see Table 15.9a and b). Provision of figurines made from regional materials overrides provision of figurines made from exogenous ones, in a ratio that averages 2.33 to 1. *Per contra*, the demand for palettes gives a ratio of 1 limestone palette for 2 exogenous ones (this ratio almost raises to 1 to 3 if one takes scoria palettes into consideration). Representation of tokens made from regional materials is 3 to 1 made from exogenous ones. The demand for exogenous palettes (18.1%) overrides the demand for exogenous figurines (12.9%) while the demand for exogenous tokens is low (8.6%). This general and contrasted situation is mirrored in the intra-distribution of tabular artifacts made from regional materials ranging from *figurines* and *tokens* to *palettes* (see Table 15.9b). For comparison, in considering the intra-distribution of exogenous tabular artifacts as a whole, the range of by-products gives: *palettes, figurines, tokens*. The competing presence of similar artifacts from regional and distant sources at Gilat suggests some specific and certainly complementary patterns of production and of distribution for the whole assemblage of tabular by-products, and more specifically for violin figurines. The localization of the workshops must be ascertained together with the nature of their role in the social context of the organization of production. Regional distribution of sources and the quantity of resources they offer (limited or widespread) do not necessarily induce the localization of production centers, nor the degree of centralization of production (cf. Costin 1991; Perles 1990; Torrence 1986). Finally, the *context* of production considers the nature of control—if any—over production and distribution (Costin 1991). At Gilat, emergent ranking society and the specific context of intensive cultic activities may have determined particular patterns for organizing production. What, then, was the affiliation of producers to consumers with regard to the violin figurines?

In Table 15.9a, n defined the total of artifacts per raw material category; N defined the grand total of tabular artifacts. The statistical mni (minimal number of individuals) is considered for violin figurines while it accounts for the actual number of palettes and tokens (their index of fragmentation being lower); mni defines the minimal number of individuals per category of artifacts (see Table 15.3). As previously indicated, the mni of limestone figurines tends to be low, while the mni for other (rarer) materials tends to be high. Hereby statistics first concern raw materials used for figurines. The mni of palettes and tokens were kindly provided by Yorke Rowan. Small differences in sums are due to keeping to one number after decimal point.

Limestone, chalk and marl figurines: variables in managing regional production. The long-range exploitation of limestone—from expedient grinding implements to elaborate mace heads—seemingly indicates different units and scales of production together with different degrees of specialization (see Table 15.2). High-skilled, time-consuming techniques, high risks for breakage during the manufacture process, together with exclusivity of distribution, certainly rank the violin figurines production at the higher grade for technical specialization. The selective exploitation of sources along the Hebron hills ridge, while local and available Eocene deposits are disregarded, suggests an off-site production.

The following remarks are proposed with reservations as statistics are mostly based on incomplete limestone specimens (Figs 15.10c, d and f). Morphological and complementary information is provided by fragmented ones. The relative stereotype of conceptual patterns, apparent in the proportions of limestone figurines suggests that their making is guided by a common and referential knowledge. Although parameters of reference are still tenuous, certain latitude seems possible in morphological details like the shape of a base or head, insofar as overall proportions were not digressed. Those might be considered like a trademark of transmitted tradition through apprenticeship, all the more effective as the social requirement, and the nature of the demand was assertive. It seems also reasonable to assume that the making of violin figurines, given the complexity of the conceptual schemes, was concentrated amongst competent and knowledgeable craftspeople (or at least gifted apprentices). However, despite the relatively limited number of limestone figurines recovered at the site, different degrees of know-how (from high-skilled craftsmanship to obvious lack in dexterity) are observed. Elected artisans were perhaps invested with specific and ritualistic power in the circumstance. The prominent role of potters in the making of other representational and cultic artifacts may give some credit to this last assumption (see elsewhere in this chapter). It can also be assumed that a trend to standardization (that apparently concerns also figurine size, see Levy and Kansa, above) results altogether from canons of representation and from technical seriation. This last term refers here more to the fact that a few skilled producers were involved than to a logical result of basic economic forces.

Scale of production is also a parameter to consider (Table 15.9a-b). Violin figurines are portable and fragile artifacts and thus submitted to a potentially high rate of breakage. Evidence for intentional breakage is ambiguous as most breaks occurred at the weakest places (neck, protruding shoulders and waist). An absolute estimate of production output is impossible. However, violin figurines represent 50.9% of the limestone tabular artifacts. It is noticeable that limestone palettes represent a small part of this assemblage, with a ratio of one palette for almost three figurines (2.8). Tokens, technically small by-products that result from the manufacture of either figurines or palettes, are well represented (30.9%). Assuming that this distribution of tabular artifacts may reflect the organization of production, it will be interesting to test it against results obtained for exogenous materials (Table 15.9b).

The sample of marl and chalk figurines is narrow and eclectic. While one chalk base (from the topsoil) presents uncharacteristic slopping hips (Fig. 15.22.4 but see one figurine from bone Fig. 15.19.10), there is no decisive evidence to determine whether production sources were distinct from limestone ones. The few figurines from chalk recovered at Gilat tend to indicate that they were either less accessible or less favored by-products.

Exogenous violin figurines: variables in managing production. Exogenous materials present, in their diversity, higher constraints on production than limestone. Moreover, the proposed definition for technical seriation is inadequate for this assemblage. In the limits of the sample registered for computer analysis, it appears that figurines from different exogenous materials never cluster together to form a distinctive class, linked by a certain degree of similitude. Only two talc-schist figurines (incomplete specimens) stay together in the analysis (Fig. 15.10b and c). Bearing in mind the limited sample studied, one might assume that conceptual patterns were less stringent than in the limestone production. It can also be stressed that figurines might have been manufactured at different production-sources. This last assumption finds some corroboration. One limestone figurine and one talc-schist figurine from Gilat recurrently merge in the same class of complete figurines (Fig. 15.10a, b and e), together with one limestone figurine from Peqi'in, a funerary cave in Galilee (Fig. 15.10a and b). There is a single occurrence of one limestone figurine (100, from site R48) rallying talc-schist figurines from Gilat (Fig. 15.10f) that may indicate a common southern origin.

Again, the following propositions are conditional, insofar as they are induced from patterns of consumption at Gilat and are interpreted as indicative of the organization of production. Violin figurines represent 32.6% of the exogenous tabular artifacts (evaluation made on the mni, i.e. 15 figurines). This rate is lower than the percentage of figurines in the assemblage of limestone tabular artifacts (50.9%), but is seemingly counter-balanced by an intense production of palettes (45.6%, all exogenous materials except scoria and pumice considered). The situation appears more contrasted when considering each assemblage of exogenous material (Table 15.9b). The physical qualities of exogenous raw material noticeably interfere with patterns of production. Granodiorite figurines represent 15.3% of the assemblage. Granodiorite (or amphibolite) hardness is adequate for repercussion implements, a physical quality that privileges the manufacture of palettes. The distribution of tabular artifacts from less indurated sandstone illustrates another situation. Figurines are well represented (46.1%), while small artifacts like tokens represent an important part of the production (38.4%) and palettes only 15.3%. Talc-schist tabular artifacts show another pattern of rock exploitation as laminated and finely compact schist is highly adequate for shaping tabular artifacts. The neat discrepancy observed between records of palettes and figurines from all types of rocks—limestone included—is deadened for talc-schist artifacts (35% of figurines and 45% of palettes). But is the nature of the rock the only critical factor that determines patterns of production or consumption?

In considering 132 cubic cm as the maximal volume of a figurine, a maximal initial volume of 0.025 cubic m may have been necessary to manufacture the 19 figurines from exogenous material recovered at the site. The specific gravity of those exogenous materials varies from 2.6 to 2.8 gr/cubic cm. Thus a maximal weight of 60 to 65 kilograms of rocks may have been necessary for the making of those figurines. An estimation of 0.12 cubic m of exogenous raw material for the whole assemblage of tabular artifacts seems maximal. A maximal weight of 312 to 336 kg may have been necessary to manufacture the whole assemblage. A maximal estimation of 20 to 25 kg of exogenous material, used for making the figurines from level 2 at Gilat, can be proposed.[25]

On the general background of all tabular artifacts, sandstone and granodiorite artifacts are represented in equal proportions (11.2%, see Table 15.9a; note again that non-local chalk is similarly represented), while talc-schist artifacts show a higher, although modest, representation (17.2%). This suggests a certain regulation that concerns either demand or availability. In this context, random expeditions and/or aleatory patterns of acquisition for exogenous materials, appear dubious. This view seems to be corroborated by apparently 'organized' internal patterns of tabular artifacts' consumption at Gilat (see above and Table 15.9a). Exogenous materials used for tabular artifacts average 40% at Gilat (39.9% to 44% with pumice and scoria included). They efficiently compete with limestone as far as 'prestige' artifacts are considered, while they are prominent in the production of palettes (see Table 15.9a and b). Expeditions, either from Gilat or from plausible workshops in the vicinity of Cenomanian limestone deposits, for direct procurement at distant sources would have involved accurate knowledge of remote deposits. Only regular expeditions would have warranted the transmission of this knowledge from generation to generation. Moreover, the requested tabular support for the finished by-product implies a fair knowledge of the capacity of the blocks in resisting the reduction process. Besides, the relative long distances to varied sources together with the relatively modest and regular quantity of artifacts representing each of them in the technical subgroup of tabular artifacts, suggest trade rather than direct procurement (cf. Feblot-Augustins and Perles 1992; Perles 1992). Direct and occasional procurement by non-specialists is thus improbable.

Thus far there is no available evidence for documenting source exploitation or fall-off patterns of diffusion for either raw materials or manufactured violin figurines. One rough-shaped (?) from sandstone (with no archaeological context, Fig. 15.22.5) is tenuous evidence for documenting on-site manufacturing. Sites from the Nahal Besor (Macdonald *et al*. 1932 and with the exception of site M, a flint blade production center) to northeastern Sinai (site R 48, see Oren and Gilead 1981), or along the Nahal Sekher (Gilead and Goren 1986) or northern Arava (Beit Arieh and Gophna 1977) are recorded as seasonal sites with limited-range activities. They were apparently settled by herders or pig-raisers and have given little evidence for craft specialization. However, source-exploitation settlements are not absent in the Sinai. The southern site of Serabit el-Khadim (Beit Arieh 1981) presents evidence for contemporaneity to Gilat (see Chapter 10) together with evidence for mining and polishing turquoise nodules.[26] On the one hand, source-production sites of manufactured figurines in the vicinity of rock deposits seem likely. The isolation of sandstone or granodiorite violin figurines and the grouping of some talc-schist figurines tend to corroborate this view. Insofar as one considers manufactured artifacts, this type of production at remote sources parallels what can be assumed for other prestige goods made from igneous rocks, and in particular for basalt. On the other hand, the aggregation of one talc-schist figurine (633) with limestone ones, tends to evidence one common source-production for materials of either close or distant provenance. Convergent conceptual schemes and their imprints within spatial representation seem, through the cross-crossing of proportions, relevant to what is perhaps the trademark of affiliated know-how. They also seem to act as a buffer for stylistic morphological characters (Fig. 15.15.1 has a type 1b head and a type 1 base while figurine 633 (Fig, 15.16.1) has a type 1a head and a type 3 base).

Organization, distribution and context of production. A monolithic view of systems of production and distribution seems here inadequate. Historical and archaeological examples confirm the co-occurrence of different production systems for a specific category of artifacts (see Perles 1990). Although the location of production centers and the systems of production cannot be circumscribed with certitude, some propositions can be drawn to untangle and clarify the nature of the organization of production of violin figurines recovered at Gilat.

The following propositions can help outline a hypothetical reconstruction of the organization of production.

On-site production. There is no sufficient and decisive evidence that supports on-site production of violin figurines. Locally, available Eocene limestone sources are not exploited. Some limestone figurines or fragments of figurines have been re-shaped after breakage (see above and Fig. 15.17.8, 15.19.3, 5–7). Although it cannot be ruled out that some of these post-breakage operations can be the result of the source-production, this caring for damaged specimens or for precious fragments finds a parallel, for example, in the frequent re-shaping and re-utilization of imported basalt vessel fragments at Bir es-Safadi (Commenge forthcoming). Direct evidence for actual work on raw material at the site is very limited and, significantly, concerns exogenous materials. One plausible rough-shaped figurine from sandstone (Fig. 15.22.5) and one plausible rough-shaped mace head, a sub-spherical and picked lump of granite (see Chapter 12), might document the on-site process of raw or pre-shaped blocks. The fact that both are loose finds with no archaeological context should be noted. If one considers a hypothetical—and apparently exclusive—on-site production based on the indirect procurement of raw or pre-shaped blocks (see above), how then can one explain the apparent discrepancy, both in proportions and style, of these violin figurines (Fig. 15.15 and Figs 15.16.3, 15.18, 15.20 and 15.22.9)?

The highly proficient bone industry at the site supports the assumption of local production of bone violin figurines at Gilat (see Chapter 13, this volume). One unique bone figurine, whose body part height proportions are deliberate and not related to technical constraints, might be a referential 'local style' (Figs 15.10a, b and e and see Fig. 15.19.10). Figurines re-shaped from sherds are made from locally produced vessels. Although rare, small sized figurines expediently made from pottery sherds can acknowledge a paltry, local (and occasional?) production in this medium.

Off-site regional production. Evidence for regional production sources, located along the Hebron Hills range (at a minimal distance of a few dozens of kilometers to the east of Gilat) is supported by 60.2% of tabular artifacts made either from limestone, marl or chalk (Table 15.9b) and 68.6% of the minimal number of individual figurines recovered at the site (Table 15.9a). Limestone specimens tightly cluster together, seemingly indicating a common production-source, or at least a convergent trend in conceptual know-how. With consideration to the many pottery vessels brought to the site from Judea, one can observe that one figurine from Titorah (a small site in Judea) recurrently rally the limestone specimens recovered at Gilat (Figs 15.10c, d, f). Regional source-production could here be the most adequate term insofar as it may encapsulate several workshops located over Cenomanian limestone deposits of Western and Northern Judea. The high technical level of tabular artifacts and the trend to standardization perceptible in size and morphological proportions of violin figurines altogether suggest the specialization and nucleation of production (Costin 1991:7, 13). One talc-schist figurine (633) clusters with limestone figurines. It might evidence the (undifferentiated and integrated?) production from exogenous material(s), probably obtained by indirect procurement. Marl and chalk figurines are too fragmented to be included in any algorithmic matrix. Their modest representation, similar to the representation of granodiorite or sandstone (11.2%), points either to independent production-sources trading directly with Gilat, or to their production at workshops specializing in limestone artifacts (and indirect procurement of chalk and marl by these centers). Either mode of exploitation can also have concerned non-tabular artifacts from chalk. This last assumption finds some corroboration with one curious bent 'limb', either arm or leg, subquadrangular in section, that might have belonged to one small statue (Fig. 15.19.4). One can also observe that the relativly high rate of chalk tokens still does not compete with the limestone one (see Table 15.9a). Last, the exact location of production centers in western Judea is still *terra incognita*.

Off-site long-distance production. Bringing together all information concerning exogenous violin figurines at Gilat suggests varied—and plausibly competing—systems of production. The Saharo-Arabian area offers some mosaic concentrations of heterogeneous rock deposits where workshops could have been located. However, differences observed among exogenous figurines made from various materials impart different production-sources. Available data may fit more closely concentration rather than centralization of production. An investigation on the degree of standardization of exogenous palettes—a major by-product—would either confirm or temper this view. There is also evidence that the operational sequence was, at least for part of the exogenous production, spatially discontinuous. The specificity of the high-skilled although ubiquitous technical trend for producing tabular artifacts (that also concerns the flint industry) seemingly prompted the raising of the competitive value of by-products made from exotic material. While these assumed parameters call for more evidence on time, space and scale of production, bijective inducements between exogenous materials and one single form of trade or the assimilation of source deposits and production-sources are, with Gilat's figurines, certainly challenged.[27]

The specificity of evidence recovered at Gilat, as a sanctuary site, leads us to ponder the nature of demand, the patterns of consumption, and the *context*[28] of figurines production. Insights into the organization of production have already suggested that on-site production of figurines must have been marginal and occasional, and concerns bone and only possibly exogenous materials. One remarkable fact has to be, once again, noted: the quasi absence of on-site production at Gilat and the disinterest for competition and lower cost in exploiting local Eocene limestone deposits.

Therefore, demand for tabular artifacts in general and for violin-shaped figurines in particular, implies exchange. Moreover, inter-site distribution indicates a high concentration of figurines at Gilat and thus intense local consumption. In other terms, Gilat can be considered as a 'center' for consumption of tabular artifacts not produced on-site. With consideration to the frameworks sketched for the organization of production, what, then, was the nature of exchange and the context of production?

Considerable skill, high quality and regularity of by-products, the relatively high output of either palettes or figurines, and the regional concentration of production-sources and the spatial, interregional extent of distribution combine to evidence craft specialization. A hierarchy of media is perceptible, from regional to extra-regional sources but also in the extreme rarity and excellence of work applied to bone. The social component for violin figurines is highly selective. It can be stated that the perceptible trend for figurine standardization pertains to efficiency of production, but most certainly also to the prerogatives of demand that involved social and symbolic stereotypes (cf. Hodder 1983). These parameters are more congruent with what is observed for the assemblage of regionally produced figurines as a whole (limestone yet also schist figurines) than with the exogenous production. Provision from distant locations of exotic artifacts increases cost parameters and thus the artifacts' value. In the case of palettes, the local production is modest, while demand for exogenous ones is very high (Table 15.9b). In the case of figurines, the local level of output for limestone figurines seems high (Table 15.9a)[29] while the demand for exogenous figurines is important and consistent with the demand for palettes. Competition could thus have initiated and stimulated dynamics in concurrent systems of production. High demand for violin figurines at Gilat most probably promoted proficient and efficient off-site production. Stringent rules of representation, while satisfying the strict nature of the demand at the site, could have offset high-valued and exotic artifacts while restraining and surpassing on-going competition, with the best challenger in line, schist production, at either regional production centers or far-distance production-sources.

Considering the nature of Gilat, the assumption that figurines might have been brought to the sanctuary for different occasions and through channels of social exchange, rather than traded, cannot be definitely ruled out. The outstanding accumulation of either fine or common foreign wares at the site should here again be mentioned (see Chapter 10, this volume). Moreover, the two effigy vessels analyzed at the beginning of the chapter were made in the Shephela, while one peridotite ram head (see below, this chapter) might have been imported from Syria. Complex patterns of organization and distribution of exogenous artifacts should be individualized for each category of materials, of local or foreign provenance, in order to identify marked differences in the degrees to which resources were mobilized and exchanged.

One can assume that, at Gilat, a rising elite component promoted intensity of off-site production. The theoretical dichotomy between independent and attached specialization is perhaps inadequate to most pre-urban contexts. That workshops of attached specialists are located in close proximity to elite' compounds is generally acknowledged (Brumfiel and Earle 1987:5). However, distance to production-source settlements challenges the hypothesis of control over off-site production. That control can be exercised over distribution rather than production, while specialists at source exploitation sites are unmonitored, was demonstrated for sedentary complex hunter-gatherer societies (Arnold and Munns 1994). Rather than monitoring production, elite management might have encompassed distribution and consumption of high-valued artifacts 'through control over mechanisms related to distribution networks' (Arnold and Munns 1994:478). As already stated, the regular quantities of exogenous tabular artifacts represented in the Gilat assemblage suggest a certain regulation of availability. 'Control over mechanisms of distribution networks' is difficult to identify in the Gilat archaeological evidence as no specialized means of transportation seems to have been involved.

The nature of middle range societies makes physical control over off-site production unlikely. The relatively small quantities of material used for tabular artifacts production suggest that 'herders' from camp-sites in the Negev may have played a role in the circulation of manufactured artifacts. Whether they operated as middle-men in *freelance* trade (Renfrew 1984:127) or were sponsored by patrons is an open question.[30] Control over off-site resources, means of transportation—donkeys being the main beast of burden (cf. Levy pers. observation)—and extensive on-site production is evidenced by metal working at Chalcolithic settlements of the Beersheva valley (Levy and Shalev 1989). The very nature of metallurgy, involving transportation of large volumes of exogenous material for an exclusive on-site exploitation, finds no parallel at Gilat, at the threshold of the Chalcolithic period.

The operative mechanisms of local to long-distance exchange, through tribute or trade, have to be related to competitive involution and to the emulating yet demanding cycle of competition and prestige that characterizes chiefdom-level societies (cf. Commenge 2002). The 'commodity' status of highly elaborated basalt bowls imported to the Beersheva sites has recently been challenged in favor of a gift practice system that leads to the 'right to reciprocate…to participate further within the exchange system' (Philip and Williams-Thorpe 2000:1386–7). In this social context, one can also consider that the exclusive needs of a sanctuary could have been the most effective way to channel distribution. Last, the proficient production of limestone figurines in western Judea might have prevented aleatory shortages of exogenous figurines whose sources elites could not control.

Patronage and (or) religious prerogatives could thus have been effective means for controlling the distribution of violin figurines. So far, inter-site distribution in the southern Levant corroborates the high concentration of violin figurines at Gilat. This supplements the eloquent intra-site distribution which points to the same process. Patterns of spatial distribution indicate, in most cases, post-functional context (pits). However, a spatial hierarchy based on the size of figurines from local and exogenous materials, is apparent in and around room A in Stratum IIC (see below Levy and Kansa, and Fig. 15.13). Production is defined by consumption and one can argue that the nature of demand was hierarchical, especially for portable and prestige artifacts that may be evaluated for individual artifacts. However, in a cultic context, as defined by the concentration of artifacts in Stratum IIC, one cannot eliminate the assumption of a spatial hierarchy that indicates the eventual integrative—from holy center to periphery—sanctity of the place. That such a disposition would have worked as a cosmology reflecting social hierarchy and induced selective access is illustrated elsewhere (see Chapters 1, 5 and 10). This may eventually imply that control over acquisition of violin figurines, and therefore the power of priests or ritual specialists at Gilat, would have mediated resultant prestige.

Statistical Insights for the Spatial Distribution of Violin Figurines (E. Kansa and T.E. Levy)

Simple statistical analysis establishes the contextual distribution of figurines per stratum, with regard to their different size classes, in order to define valuable insights into plausible uses of space. A few strata provide insufficiently reliable data for detailed analysis. Although a large portion of the violin figurines were recovered in Stratum I, this occupation phase was heavily disturbed by deep-plowing, resulting in the mixture of the topsoil and ploughed architectural remains. A different problem concerns Strata IIIB and IV. In these strata, the excavation sample area is extremely small. In Stratum IIIB, only one figurine was recovered and in Stratum IV, none. Given these constraints, spatial analysis was only possible for Strata IIA, IIB, IIC, and IIIA.

Stratum IIA (Fig. 15.11)

In Stratum IIA, only six specimens were recovered. They are quite fragmentary (as measured by the ratio of fragment size to projected complete size) and this adds to the difficulty in determining any clear spatial patterns of distribution. Figure 15.11 shows an apparently random distribution of the violin figurines in relation to architecture. They appear to be incidentally embedded in fill context or most likely, in disposal contexts (such as pits). The fragments found in pit contexts tend to be the most incomplete. However, two fragments of a bone figurine were recovered in different pits (Fig. 15.19.10). Whether this accounts for random or intentional disposal after breakage is an open question. Contextual information for Stratum IIa, that shows an apparently random distribution of fragmented figurines together with comparatively scant architectural remains, is rather ambiguous on cult activity.

Figure 15.11. Spatial distribution of Violin shape figurines by size and material, Stratum IIA.

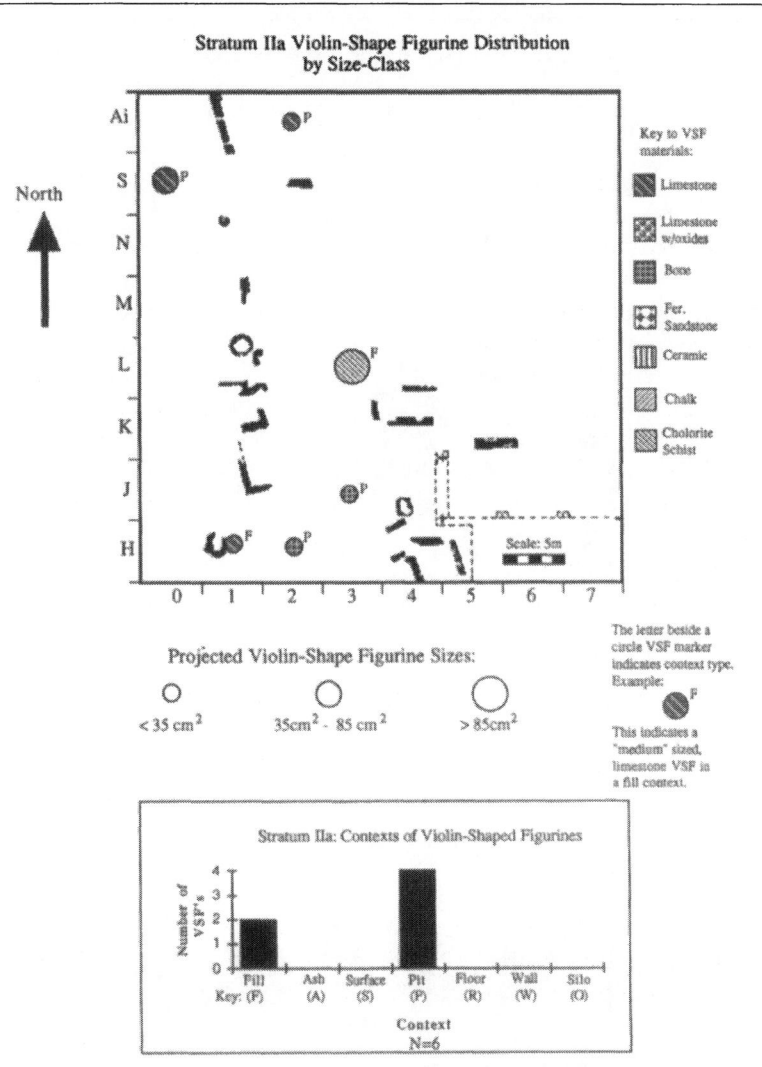

Stratum IIB (Fig. 15.12)

A different picture emerges from Stratum IIB. This stratum shows a wealth of preserved architectural data. Figure 15.12 reveals a cluster of six of the seven specimens found in this occupation phase in and around Room 3. However these are mostly fragments in disposal context (a large limestone base was found on the floor of Room 3). This spatial picture can be completed with the distribution map of ceremonial vessels. Ceremonial vessels are clustered around Room 3 (Chapter 10, this volume). Room 3 and its immediate surroundings appear as a focus of cult activity. However, while clusters of pottery are neatly defined—two clusters of cornets north and south of Room 3, two clusters of pedestal bowls and tubular vessels east and southeast of Room 3—they do not overlap with the figurines' distribution, with the exception of an area east of Room 3, where one cluster of pedestal bowls and tubular vessels includes the base of small limestone violin figurine.

Figure 15.12. Spatial distribution of Violin shape figurines by size and material, Stratum IIB.

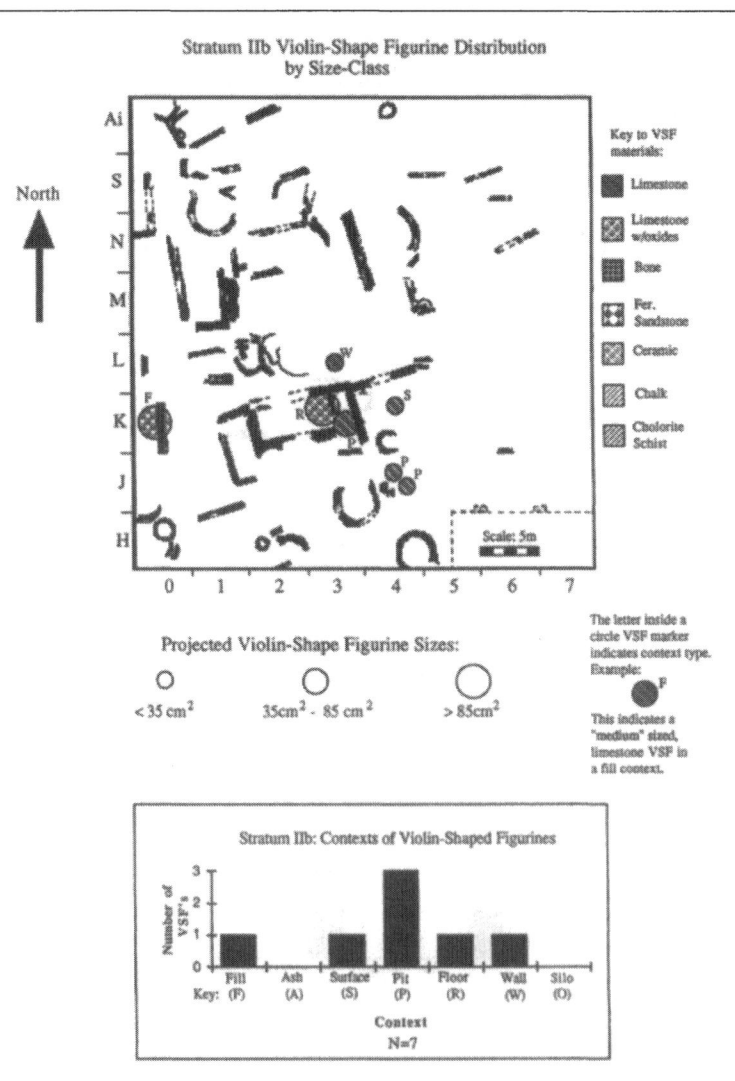

Figure 15.13. Spatial distribution of Violin shape figurines
by size and material, Stratum IIC.

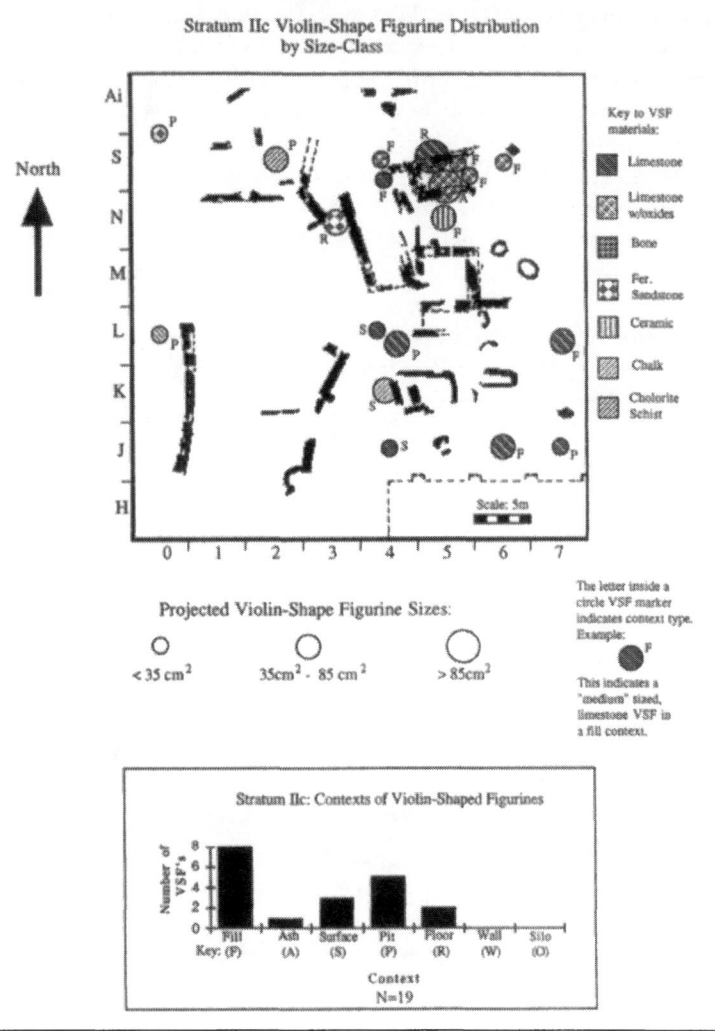

Stratum IIC (Fig. 15.13)

The distribution pattern in Stratum IIC is quite different, and provides some of the strongest evidence for the concentration of cult activity in the Gilat sanctuary. 42% of the violin figurine specimens, among them the most complete specimens, were recovered in this stratum. The violin figurines clearly cluster in and immediately around Room A, to a far greater degree of intensity than in Room 3 in Stratum IIb. Moreover, the largest of the figurines are also located in this cluster, while figurine size drops off radiating out from Room A. This concentration of figurines in and around Room A is quite isolated from the ceremonial vessel clusters. In Squares K5/6, where tubular and pedestal vessels and cornets are densely aggregated, no figurine specimens were recovered. However, far off the periphery of Room A, in squares A10/S0 and S2, pits producing fragmented figurines are associated with areas of intense concentration of pedestal bowls and torpedoes. In Square LO, a pit produced an incomplete chlorite figurine (Fig. 15.19.6) surrounded by tubular vessels.

In Stratum IIC, some of the fragmentary figurines were found on floors outside and inside the building, yet most of them belong to fill context, to the decayed mudbrick layer that buried the floors. Whether those figurines were somehow affixed to the walls, or were processed by other site formation conditions cannot be established. However, figurines from fills 'doubled' the clustering of figurines recovered on floors with no interference from other associated materials. How can one explain this recurrent clustering? The fall-off size patterns observed in and around Room A points to a spatial hierarchy, from center to periphery, that might have concerned the degree of 'sanctity' of the area and of its use. Figurines may have acted as symbols for display *to* or *by* individuals with access rights inside these structures. They may also have been stored in Room A and occasionally displayed in the nearby courtyards. The large size of some figurines may have facilitated the later function. The absence of post-functional contexts such as pits in the vicinity of Room A may emphasize primary, selective and intensive use of figurines in this privileged area.

Figure 15.14. Spatial distribution of Violin shape figurines by size and material, Stratum IIIA.

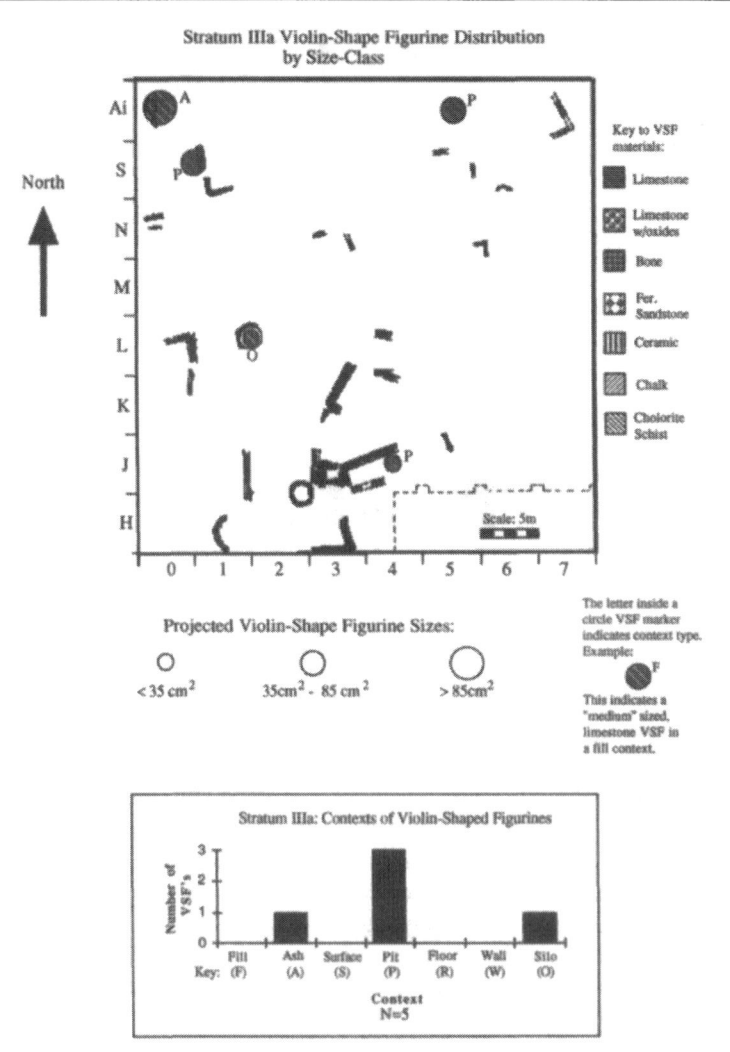

Stratum IIIA (Fig. 15.14).

The spatial picture of this stratum is similar to that seen with Stratum IIA. The small number of specimens, four in all, appears randomly scattered, as seen in Figure 15.14). The fragmentary nature of the figurine sample also parallels the situation in Stratum IIA. Additionally, these fragments were also mostly recovered from disposal contexts.

Spatial and contextual information documents either segregate clustering in and around architectural structures or post-functional disposal of figurines. Spatial distribution differences observed between Stratum IIB and Stratum IIC might concern shifts in the scale or organization of cult activity. Those insights on spatial distribution of violin figurines are primarily statistical and express trends that relate to 'observed effects' at distant focal length. Inferred causes may translate into a dynamic appreciation of the '*in situ*' function of violin figurines.

In the Quest for Meaning

It is here assumed that violin figurines act as a *medium* which shapes a mental image of a referent that must be substantiated and conveys social concerns that must also be defined for the participants. Opposition and contrast between the naturalistic embodiment of the 'Gilat Lady', fraught with orchestrated and suggestive attributes, and the austere, chiseled profile and recondite nature of the violin figurines give evidence for high versatility with regard to human representation in the cultic context of Gilat. 'Abstraction' disclosed by parsimony in substance and gain in illusion can here modify the terms and thus the gist of intended symbolic construction, giving access to other fields of cognition.

Few topics concerning prehistoric material culture have generated more debate than gynecomorphous figurines. Fields of interpretation have captured feminity through the lens of ideology and/or cognition. Among the questions addressed concerning the significance of figurines, agnostic ימְסִילפּ emphasizes the need for a theoretical approach that avoids 'monolithic classificatory categories' (Ucko 1968, 1996) while prevailing or prevalent epistemes still insist in addressing the very nature of figurines, either as subjects or objects, either as 'image of' or 'image for' (cf. Conkey 1987; Haaland and Haaland 1996; Marshack 1991; Mc Dermott 1996). The ingrained 'Mother Goddess' interpretation, that offers convenient adequacy between meaning and consequential function, yet also improper claim for universality (e.g. Gimbutas 1982), tends to be considered as an obsolescent option (Bailey 1996:292; Haaland and Haaland 1996:297 and cf. Meskell 1995; Ucko 1968). This opposition to divine hegemony perhaps implies more reluctance to support unquestioned universality than a fashionable dismissal. The philosophical vision of the Mother Goddess promoted by Jacques Cauvin takes its measure of monumental representations from Neolithic Anatolian sanctuaries (Cauvin 1994:100–101, and cf. Forest 1993; Mellaart 1967) yet presumed that this divine notion was kept intact for millennia while disseminated through multifarious Neolithic figurines from varied contexts. Restrictive weakness and biased excess in the 'andocentric paradigm' (Dobres 1992) that permeated interpretation of gynecomorphous figurines, have been underscored by feminist archaeologists (Conkey and Spector 1984; Hamilton 1994). However, biological condition (sex) and cultural condition (gender) merge in cognitive approaches to gynecomorphous figurines that mainly develop functionalist interpretations. Female representation is seen like a conceptual formation of ontological processes, instrumental in obstetrical pedagogy (Gorring 1991) or for increasing birth-rate (Gopher and Orelle 1996) or like metaphoric surrogates to economical and social mutation stress (Bolger 1993; Haaland and Haaland 1996). Some alternative interpretations reconcile figurines with being altogether subject and object of social elaboration in insisting on the figurines' function of communication, as instruments of social manipulation and negotiation (Bailey 1996; Conkey 1985) or vehicles of material information maintaining regional alliances (Gamble 1982) and/or social networks (Talalay 1987).

Addressing the Referent

Stylistic memories. However different from a stylistic point-of-view, the conceptual schemes of violin figurines bear diagnostic characters that relate to a long symbolic tradition embedded in the spatial definition of their body parts. Violin figurines display a certain disinclination toward realism in shaping human form, and this reiterates, in another conceptual context, a remark uttered in analyzing means of representation for the Gilat gynecomorphous cult vessel. Differential emphasis on anatomical features, pruned and distorted by geometrization, re-composes anatomical proportions resulting in hypertrophy of the head, atrophy of the arms and torso, and merging of hips and lower limbs. For modern individuals, it has been established that patterns of mental body-image generally underestimate the distance from the waist to the feet while they overestimate the importance of the upper-body (cf. McDermott 1996:237). This 'natural' inaccuracy tends to emphasize, by contrast, the utmost *conventionality* of patterns of proportions applied to violin figurines. Those standards appear similar to ones applied to clay figurines of the Pottery Neolithic period. Height proportions for body parts of one complete figurine from the Sha'ar Ha'Golan culture (Munhata 2B, see Garfinkel 1995: Fig. 24; Garfinkel and Miller 2002), are 30% for head, 23% for torso and 47% from hips to feet, proportions similar to the violin figurines standard (Fig. 15.7).[31] Evidence from incomplete specimens (heads and torsos, cf. Garfinkel 1995; Stekelis 1972) tends to corroborate this fact. The structure of the anatomic scheme seems identical for anthropomorphic representations radically opposed in conception (composite volumes *versus* two-dimensional outcut) that are made from media offering fundamental physical differences (clay *versus* stone). Proportions observed on complete (male) ivory figurines from the Beersheva sites are different (see Perrot 1959: Pl.II, 1968: Pl.V: 8).[32] The lower body part (from hips to feet) still represents 50%, or slightly over, of the total figurine height while torso dimensions profit from the reduction of the head (torso averages 30% while the head averages 15 to 20% of the figurine total height).

Hypertrophy of the head is a character shared by Neolithic and Early Chalcolithic figurines. The head of violin figurines, whose majestic elongation is sometimes delicately fanned at the top, is always perfectly delineated by a clear-cut shoulder-line. Hypertrophy of the head of figurines is idiosyncratic to some prehistoric Levantine figurines. Figurines with strobilaceous heads are found, for example, at Byblos ('Neolithique Ancien', Dunand 1973, Plate 113: 29567), at Ramad III (Contenson 1983: Fig. 14) and are characteristic of the Sha'ar Ha'Golan clay figurines (Garfinkel 1995: Fig. 24–29; Stekelis 1972: Plates 49, 65, 67).[33] For Neolithic specimens, current interpretations either consider the representation of a high hairdress or of a 'tall hat' (see Garfinkel 1995:31). However, keeping to the spirit rather than to the letter of the means, realism can perhaps give way to tentative significance of hypertrophy whatever its materialization.[34] Together with figurines, two other examples retain our attention. One elongated net used as a headdress was recovered in the Pre-Pottery Neolithic B Nahal Hemar Cave in the Judean Desert together with (and among a long list of well-preserved artifacts) asphalt coated skulls, human figurines and one human clay statue (Bar Yosef and Alon 1988; Fig. 12; Schick 1988). The second example of human depiction with elongated neck and/or head is found on the wall paintings from Teleilat Ghassul and these are contemporary with the violin figurines discussed here (see chapter 10, this volume; Mallon *et al.* 1934, frontispice: la Grande Peinture ^ l'Etoile; Cameron 1981: Fig. 14).[35] Both Neolithic and Chalcolithic examples of head hypertrophy, simulated or depicted, have been related to obvious cultic contexts. Magnification of the violin figurines' head supports the convention that might have enthroned a dignified agent or patient. Such a convention might have been insignificant for slightly later human representation illustrated at the Beersheva sites, especially for a bone violin-like figurine from Shiqmim (Golden and Levy 1997), or for the ivory statuettes from Safadi (Perrot 1959, 1964). In both case, there is overestimation of the head's dimension although no apparent elongation.[36]

Exploring gender. Addressing gender identification of violin figurines is a preliminary and necessary task. The chosen substantive that describes these figurines as *violin* figurines calls for redundant analogies (such as Man Ray's famous work), that are intuitively evocative—at least to the mind of western-educated archaeologists—of a feminine silhouette with distinctive narrow waist and curvy hips. Statements of universal and unequivocal encoded feminity were challenged for Natufian representation (Weinstein-Evron and Belfer-Cohen 1993:104) and more recently for the Sha'ar Ha'Golan corpus of clay statuettes and incised pebbles (Gopher and Orelle 1996:273). That latter assemblage draws our attention insofar as the Sha'ar Ha'Golan figurines are the immediate predecessors of violin figurines.

The Gilat figurine with carved breasts (Fig. 15.20) is unique in the assemblage of Gilat. One violin figurine with breasts is recorded at Peqi'in (out of ten specimens, see Gal *et al.* 1997:152). The unique violin figurine from clay at Shiqmim presents breasts (level III, Levy 1987:515, Fig. 6.12:4).[37] In the violin figurine assemblage of Gilat, 31 preserved torsos have no breasts. The absence of breasts is an intended omission, and thus may contest an unequivocal gender—namely female—for the violin figurines. The conception of violin figurines strictly avoids any indication of volume. Technical imperative of the selected tabular support permits, by means of outcut surfaces defining body contour, the extension in space of a standing figurine that seems meant to be only displayed from a frontal view. The intended frontal silhouette sketches in suggestive, yet spare lines, human anatomy—head, shoulder, waist, lower body parts. The basic process of geometrization acts by means of surfaces that are not conceived absolutely apart from concrete reality, or at least from rules that are generally thought to be applied to female representation, insofar as emphasis of the hips is concerned. The unique figurine with breasts in Gilat's assemblage thus appears like the exception to the rule, yet the rule was persuasive enough to demand tabulation of the breasts (Fig. 15.20). Asymmetry and discrepancy in proportions also isolate this chlorite figurine from the rest of the corpus. Its ostensible feminity, heretic by means, can then be suggestive for a digressive behavior from the prevaling code of representation. Rather than a challenge to the violin figurines' gender, it can here operate *a contrario* like a device apt to unveil and to confirm female gender for the whole assemblage.

Absence of explicit sexual indication on violin figurines thus offers resistance to the ideological sphere of influence that considers 'the fluidity of sex and gender' for figurines (Hamilton 1996:285, and cf. Ucko 1968). Androgyny has been suggested for Pottery Neolithic figurines of the Sha'ar Ha'Golan culture (Gopher and Orelle 1996). Heads of clay figurines are seen as composed of different representations of male and female genitals while incisions on the legs are interpreted as 'indicative of foreskin folds and not of obesity'[38] (Gopher and Orelle 1996:273). Androgyny is certainly a misleading term here for what is usually referred to as dual sex characteristics (cf. Hamilton 1996). Those dual characters could have been meant as a 'pictorial pun',[39] intended in this case to underscore gender complementary. These observations are drawn from fragments of figurines. It is notable that on the most complete figurines with explicit gender characters, one female from Munhata 2B (cf. Garfinkel 1995: Fig. 24, see also Fig. 25:1) and one male from Byblos (Dunand 1973: Pl.113, 21160), such 'sexually hybrid facial features' are absent. Moreover, heavy hips and 'obese' legs belong, as far as the preserved Neolithic figurines specimens demonstrate, to female figurines (Garfinkel 1995: Fig. 24 and Fig. 27:7). Idiosyncratic narrow hips and slim legs depict male figurines (Garfinkel 1995: Fig. 30). With consideration to the sober outcut technique involved in the conception of the violin figurines, emphasis of the hip line might have been the only comprehensible and visual 'vocal' to encode female gender identity on the viewer.

The interactive nature of evidence is as crucial as its sequential temporality. In other words, diachronic webs of information might indicate filiation in convention rather than in conception—this postulate has already been demonstrated for gynecomorphous vessels (see above, this chapter).

However, stratification of meaning is eminently contextual. Edging forward to make out the violin figurines' referent nature, one more step can be made, *ex nihilo*, toward absence of evidence for human male figuration in the inventory of artifacts recorded at Gilat. It can be stressed that emphasis of female sexual character was unnecessary insofar as it was not ascribed in gender duality. Yarmukian male figurines were recovered in post-depositional context that are similar to female figurines' context, and even in one case, in the same pit (Munhata 2B, loc. 643, Commenge pers. observation).[40] Male and female ivory figurines from the Beersheva culture present similar sculpted volumes yet explicit gender attributes. At the interface of the Neolithic and Chalcolithic symbolic systems, violin figurines elicit another mental image that seems 'self-sufficient' in its pared down nature. Mute sexuality in the violin figurines dissuades from prefatory interpretive scaffolding between biological and cultural representation of the commonly asserted notion of fertility.[41] Meaning, that is always susceptible to generating further elaboration, is here elliptically encoded and disclosed.

Who is Who?

Representation can operate for various referents, whose identity boundaries may be porous. The symbolic reflection of the self taken as an individual or as a social elementary unit, or the symbolic embodiment of an abstract notion like a prosopopoeia, or of a distinctive supranatural, divinized anthropomorphic entity.

Self and social-self. Total individualization of the referent would induce portrait and even, as lately debated, autogenous self-portrait (cf. McDermott 1996). The silhouetted, standardized nature of violin figurines obviously does not match this definition. The assumption made by Bailey that with figurines *'reality marked by dissimilarity can be replaced by a delusion defined by similarity'* (Bailey 1996:293) offers a seductive raison d'etre to 'social-self' representation. The representation of a 'social-self' notion engulfs a generic and/or gendered definition that may be respectively illustrated, in the case of the violin figurines, by hypertrophy of the head and large hips. With violin figurines, 'social-self' refers to female dignified images, to a female 'gens' or to an exalted, transcended female principle. The fundamental social role in wealth distribution that might be illustrated by the Lady of Gilat (see above) may thus find another mode of expression, here manifested like an allegory. Anthropological exploration of the code systems of body symbolism emphasizes its assimilation to the cultural principles that structure society (*fons* and *origo* for Turner 1967:90, and cf. Douglas 1973:174), while the realm of illusion is claimed as a major mechanism of social manipulation and negotiation (Turner 1967:28–9). At Gilat, violin figurines might thus allude to women's magnified status, apparently unchallenged by male representation or any evidence for men's symbolically preponderant role (this social message being accurate or consensually fabricated).[42] In this case, the unitary social principle metaphorically merges with the social elementary unit (women?).

Supranatural being. In this particular context of representation, the representation's referent belongs to an exactly opposite realm of thought, where symbols of metaphysical essence are impersonated. Whether this impersonation represents and exerts an universal and hegemonic power or is a supranatural entity in a mythical discourse, it is eminently religious.[43] For Cauvin, by the tenth millennium BC, at the threshold of the Near Eastern Neolithic Revolution, a new imaginary order was forged where human and divine universes were hierarchically divided. With this new order that defined 'a vertical topology' (Cauvin 1994:100), worship and invocation could have been the means of (collective and metaphysical?) subjection. More than a fertility symbol, the Goddess, *Mater Genetrix*, subordinates humanity to her magnanimous and intimidating power, arouses fear and adoration, in a religious system perceived like a kind of 'female monotheism' (Cauvin 1994:51).

Some violin figurine characters may purposely adapt in this interpretive framework. Head hypertrophy can represent a credible elaboration of marked divine transcendence. Mute sexuality and allusive feminity might have gained persuasive and pervading power while muffled and elliptically absorbed and concealed in forms subtly understood by initiated individuals. Identification of the violin figurines' reference to 'the Goddess' would thus be supported by an assumed and veiled hieratic code and plausible hierarchy of their spatial display and sanctity (see above).

Violin figurines in context: toward a functional interpretation. Representation can be considered like the spatial definition of knowledge (Foucault 1966). The introduction of a crucial distinction between figurines as 'images of' and figurines as 'images for', and the pronounced choice for the last definition in elaborating interpretation (Haaland and Haaland 1996:297) may altogether obliterate evidence for meaning and function interaction, and considerably narrow the field of knowledge elaboration. Moreover, with this functionalist perspective, the very notion of archaeological context —from the mode of deposition to the whole symbolic realm of material culture—is often biased by the assumption that the theoretical model of interpretation represents the context of the figurines' action. The nature of the violin figurines' referent and their plausible sphere of action are interactive elements within the symbolic system. These elements might mingle meaning and function, altogether performing in society and setting society on stage, and as such, prompting consideration of any contextual evidence, from field observation to other components of Early Chalcolithic cultural system.

At Gilat, fragmented violin figurines are most frequently recovered in disposal contexts and thus most probably post-functional context. Zoomorphic figurines, which apparently have no pretentions as prestige artifacts, are discarded in a similar way (see below, this chapter). Therefore figurines whose referents are opposed in nature, whose quality of medium and technical investment form striking contrast, have shared the same fate yet more notably, the same *temporality*. Some fragmented figurines have been re-shaped (see above and Figs 15.17.1, 8–9, 15.18.3, 5–7), and one head fragment has been redesigned as a pendant (Fig. 15.17.9). A large majority have been discarded with no further attention. The case of one valuable bone violin figurine whose fragments were recovered in two different pits gives a good illustration of the violin figurines' posterity (Fig. 15.19.10). Casual (?) discard of anthropomorphic figurines in supposedly innocuous contexts (such as pits, ashy areas, fill) is commonly reported at Neolithic Middle Eastern sites (Broman-Morales 1983:385; Eygun 1992:114; Garfinkel 1995; Le Brun 1989:177–8). However costly in technical and aesthetical investment, violin figurines were not confined to eternity. Ritualization is fundamentally a construction of power relationships (Bell 1992). Efficacy that empowers violin figurines might thus have acted like a transitory alchemy, cast between actors in ritual and the potent representations. While repetitive sequences are instrumental in ritual activities (Rappaport 1999:218–19), the performance timing of figurines is clearly beyond reach. However, the spell broken, disabled and thus depreciated, violin figurines might have been finally discarded.

With consideration to the spatial distribution of violin figurines, contextual data are ambivalent. It has already been observed that the statistical fall-off in size pattern of figurines in and around Room A (see above, Levy and Kansa, Stratum IIC) may indicate their display *to* or *by* a selected congregation. Again, figurines are portable and thus appear essentially like individual prestige artifacts. It may thus be assumed that, at least part of their function reflects some (ideal or real?) social order. Yet, this structure operates at a miniature scale, like a modelled world, apparently inherent to Gilat's ceremonial and cultic paraphernalia (see chapter 10, this volume), with no evidence for large statuary. As intense as cultic activities might have been at Gilat, monumentalism by means of iconographic depiction seems nonexistent. In the same Early Chalcolithic context, linked to Gilat by many cultural and symbolic threads (see below, this chapter), the large wall-paintings of

Teleilat Ghassul's sanctuaries display perplexing and perhaps masked characters (Cameron 1981). The most striking painting is a large star with composite and intricate inside patterns. This very elaborate design contrasts with the paucity of decorative patterns already acknowledged for all the material culture of this period. Another symbol is introduced here, 'monumental' and abstract. With consideration to its recurrence and preeminent location in the 'Peinture aux Personnages' (Mallon *et al.* 1934: Pl. 66), this mural design may introduce a cosmological dimension into a symbolic system so far comprehended from the sole point-of-view of naturalistic representation and centered on gendered concepts that have elicited mostly literal interpretation.

From this broader archaeological context, it is perhaps possible to draw some lines that sketch out alternative perspectives for meaning and function concerning the violin figurines. The 'discourse imposed by the force of imagery' (Cauvin 1994:100, my translation), with Neolithic monumental iconographic features displayed for the Anatolian Goddess (Mellaart 1967, 1970), could have given the measure of a two-tier metaphysical division of the world. It has been assumed above that the Lady of Gilat's narrative may represent assimilation at a social level, an 'ingested' version of the Anatolian mythical figure. However, as a whole, Early Chalcolithic anthropomorphic representation—insofar as it offers tangibility—seems to deliver an image of a society that reflects upon itself and represents itself. Hence figural and hierophantic vessels, whose didactic processes might have concerned dialectics in social foundations. Hence the 'Peinture aux Personnages', which introduces the representation of a ranked audience, a well individualized, dark-painted character facing it and most probably acting as an intermediary to the abstract and stellar figure set at his back. Hiero-phantism inherent in the structure of cult vessels as *agents*, is fully developed and enacted, yet from the points-of-view of *actors* within this painted scene. Variations are orchestrated around themes, and somehow, a monothetic theophany transcended in an emblematic mythogram, however spiritually elevating, seems inadequate to the leveled, manifold character of symbolic system and cultic activities at Gilat,[44] at Ghassul or at the Ein Gedi sanctuary (Usshiskin 1980).

What can we then suggest about the significance of Chalcolithic violin figurines? Relations between symbols and social categories tend to be erected through homologies or disparities among different levels and areas of experience (cf. Turner 1984). Violin figurines still possess morphological characters of Yarmukian figurines, and they are, similarly, temporal artifacts.[45] Yet, while Neolithic figurines are set up in a dual gendered system,[46] violin figurines appear to symbolize a unique and perhaps 'hegemonic' (female) entity. Whether this hegemony results from ritual logic that 'facilitate(s) subtle shifts in the ability of some symbols to dominate others' (Bell 1992:105), or whether it tends to underscore the primacy yet versatile transfiguration of the mythical Goddess is an open question. However, an *assumption* of the Goddess, prefigured in a vertical and metaphysical topology, appears inadequate with the violin figurines' temporal function. As seen at Ghassul, empyreal manifestation might concern the realm of cosmological abstraction. Part of an Early Chalcolithic symbolic system in which society may generate a mental image of itself, violin figurines may represent its unitary principle and/or its elementary unit, that, with consideration to the many threads still woven in Neolithic tradition, crystallizes and transforms an essential notion, ancestral and probably mythical, portrayed as a woman.

Sailing through the shoals and reefs of channels linking the conceptual realm of symbols to the functional realm of ritual, one can consider the use of violin figurines at Gilat. Contextual evidence indicates that the function of violin figurines is ascribed in time by temporal action, and in space by hierarchical distribution. Consecration of violin figurines for collective veneration, or dedication of violin figurines out of individual devotion is congruent with spatial hierarchy although not seemingly with transitory action and consequential periodic de-consecration. Violin figurines may imply collective tenet yet individual action. They might have been ritually set into action by individuals for individual purposes. Votive offerings, infused by occult efficacy, fulfill a pre-emptive function, topically and temporarily effective. Human effigies might be 'the channel through which magical influences are conveyed to the human individual '(Postgate 1994:179), as magical devices that fuse action and thought for granting vows, for curing diseases, or for apotropaic purposes. With regard to Talalay's comprehensive exploration of the ethnographic record, figurines that achieve those goals are not prestige artifacts, but rather wooden or clay figurines hastily shaped for the occasion by 'Philistine' hands. Although little attention is paid in literature to post-functional disposal of figurines, their eventual sweeping into rubbish heaps is recorded, after having performed in initiation ceremonies or in fertility rites[47] (Talalay 1993:42–3). Those ritual performances imply an individual, self-referential participation, yet they both refer to social legitimacy. We have already established that Gilat's violin figurines are mainly prestige artifacts, and thus that the nature of the demand is highly selective. Modest specimens like misshaped stone specimens or re-shaped pottery sherds are rare (see above). Violin figurines may thus elicit an essential dilemma with concern to their prerequisite durable and precious nature and their 'post-requisite' perishability. The virtual absence of expediently made violin figurines seems, from a functional point-of-view, subsidiary to this dilemma. One can argue that access to violin figurines was socially restricted to an elite and that the spatial hierarchy of figurines' size—if it does reflect social hierarchy—does not encompass society as a whole. This statement seems premature and insufficiently documented by the archaeological record (and with regard to the scarcity of violin figurines recorded at many other sites). However, all this contextual information converges to indicate that the use of violin figurines as prophylatic or curative *ex-votos* is improbable. Those *ex-votos*, whose occult efficacy seems more dependant on the intensity of action than on the quality of medium (see also below), generally present a compliant morphology that is either adapted to the nature of the disease or specifically portrays the patient (cf. Postgate 1994:179; Talalay 1993:42). The size of the offering can plausibly match either the importance of the wish or the supplicant's means, yet those necessities cannot seemingly be reflected in the hierarchical distribution of violin figurines.

Formalization and periodization, time and space, are essential to the deployment and efficiency of ritual activities. From a systemic point-of-view, there is, in the spatial pattern of the violin figurines at Gilat, a kind of reverberation of the spatial composition set for the congregation depicted in the Ghassulian 'Peinture aux Personnages'. Specific context might, in each case, indicate that both patterns respectively refer to the organization of a ritual system which, by definition, aims at controlling 'the contention and negotiation involved in the appropriation of symbols' (Bell 1992:130). It is impossible to definitely state a collective accomplishment, like a congregation gathering, for setting the circumstances of the violin figurines' use at Gilat. Yet, with consideration to information obtained through statistical analysis, it appears that the modality of their use was recurrent enough to etch in space a hierarchical patterning. A situational, expedient and thus strategic 'practice' enacting the figurines may explain their transitory efficiency. Rappaport observed that artifacts (or any substances or gestures) used in performative or meta-performative acts 'seem to bring into being institutional facts' (Rappaport 1999:167; see Chapter 1, this volume). If we assume that violin figurines transcend society's unitary principle and/or its elementary unit, whether mythical, ancestral and/or divine in essence, they could have been used in a contractual fashion, to predicate, through physical and spiritual conviction, acceptance and/or allegiance to this principle.[48] The condition and the circumstances of this experience (which might have been periodically reproduced or renewed?) as a self-referential message projected in articulate spatial ordering, might have forged a homeostatic vision of the community order that was, at an individual level, gratifying and perhaps empowering.

The use of violin figurines might have caused thought and action while it contrived to negotiate, integrate and differentiate self and society. Rather than being instrumental for ideology, potent violin figurines might have themselves represented and embodied a system in which knowledge was appropriated and negotiated.

The author is most grateful to Nicole and Gilles Fernandez for providing kind help and striking competence in data processing. Their web-site introducing the program they provided can be found in the bibliography below.

Catalogue of violin figurines (figs. 15.15 to 15.23)
*object drawn by Daniel Ladiray, CNRS

Figure 15.15. Complete violin shape figurine.

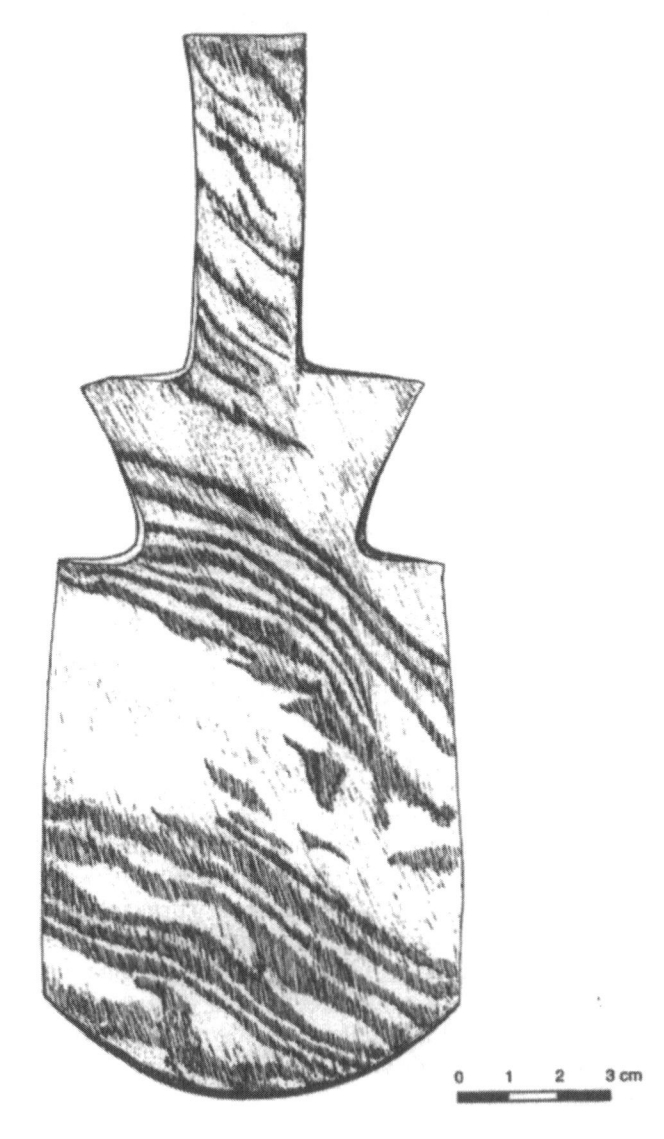

0   1   2   3 cm

basket	locus	stratum	material		description
16.1	51	IIB	limestone with oxydes		complete figurine

Figure 15.16. Three violin shape figurines.

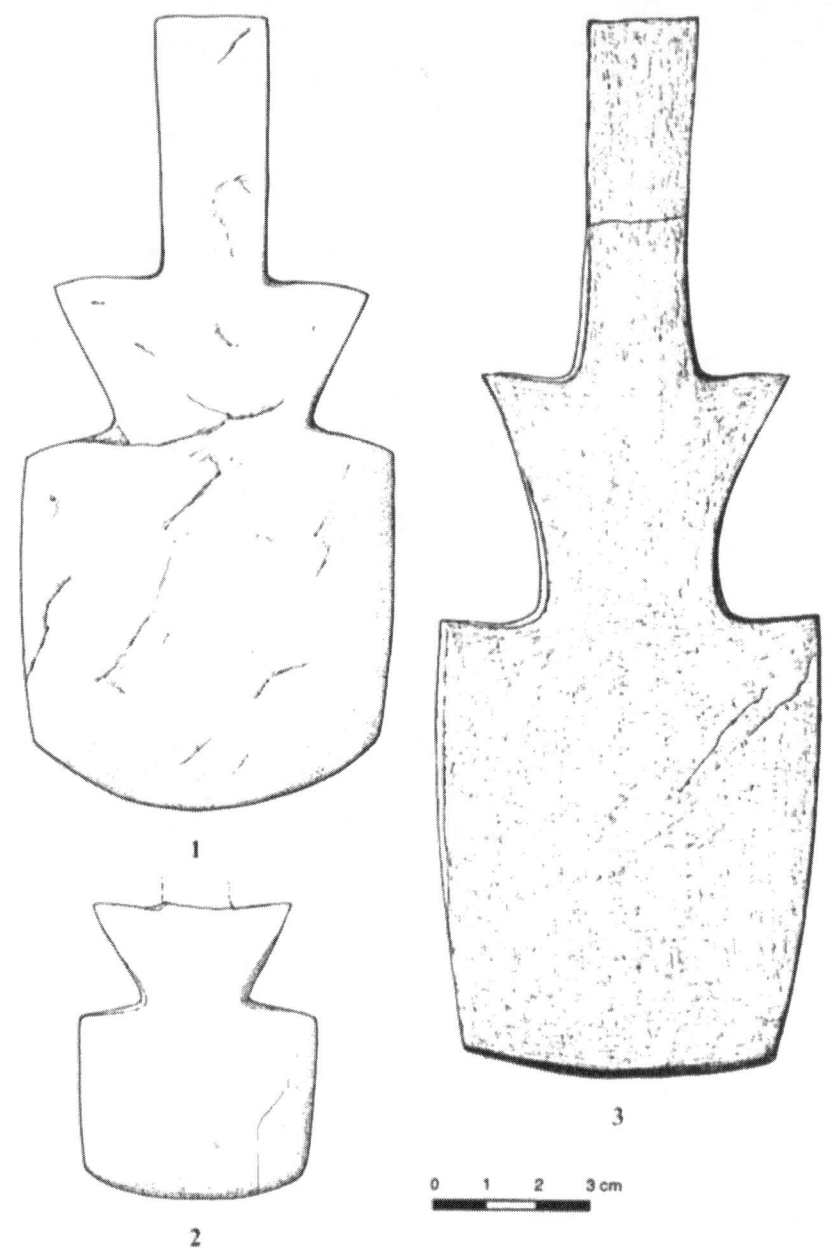

	basket	locus	stratum	material	description
1	633	307	IIC	talc-schist	complete, medium- sized figurine
2	186	51	IIB	limestone	head missing, small-sized figurine
3	5017	baulk	IIC-3	sandstone	complete figurine, greenish

Figure 15.17. Group of 12 violin shape figurine fragments.

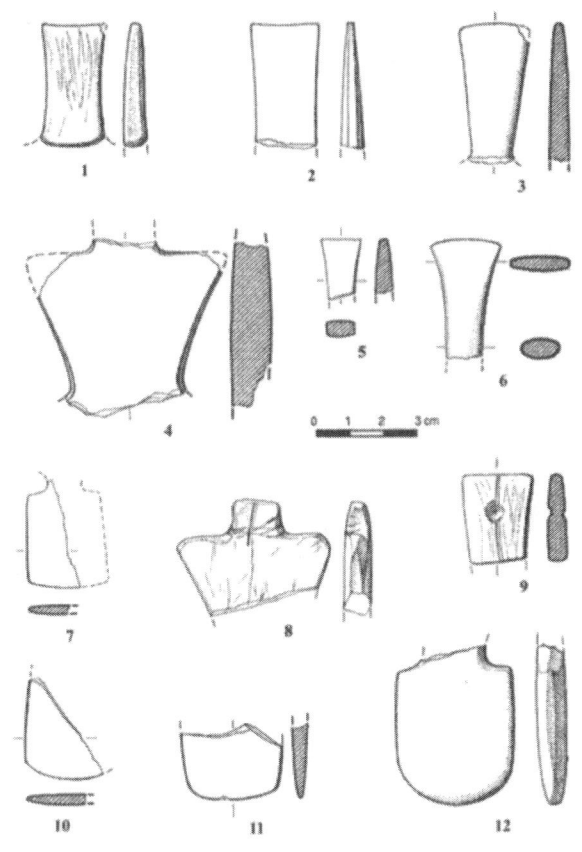

	basket	locus	stratum	material	description
1*	3220	1022	topsoil	limestone	head, type 1b, longitudinal and superficial striae, base ground after breakage
2*	3200.2	-	topsoil	'Jerusalem' limestone	head, type 1b, thorough polishing, angular chamfers
3*	5713	1534	IIIA	coarse limestone	head, type 2a, thorough polishing and no chamfer
4*	2295	820	IIA	limestone	torso
5*	1133	532	II	limestone	small fragmented head, type 2b, rectangular section due to sharp chamfering
6*	5738	1511	IIC	limestone	head, type 2b, spatulate on top, oval section at the neck, subrectangular at the top
7*	2384	806	IIA	bone	fragmented base (type 1b) of a small figurine
8*	1127	515	I-II	limestone	torso and neck, all edges reduced by grinding, asymmetrical. Shallow perpendicular groove and incisions around the neck
9*	3141	040	IIC	limestone	fragmented head, median perpendicular groove and attempt at perforating, base of fragment ground after breakage
10*	3830	1215	IIB1	bone	fragmented base of a small figurine
11*	2284	810	IIA	limestone	fragmented base of a small figurine
12*	3019	017	II	coarse limestone	base, type 1a, delicately chamfered

Figure 15.18. Complete violin shape figurine found by Alon in the 1950s.

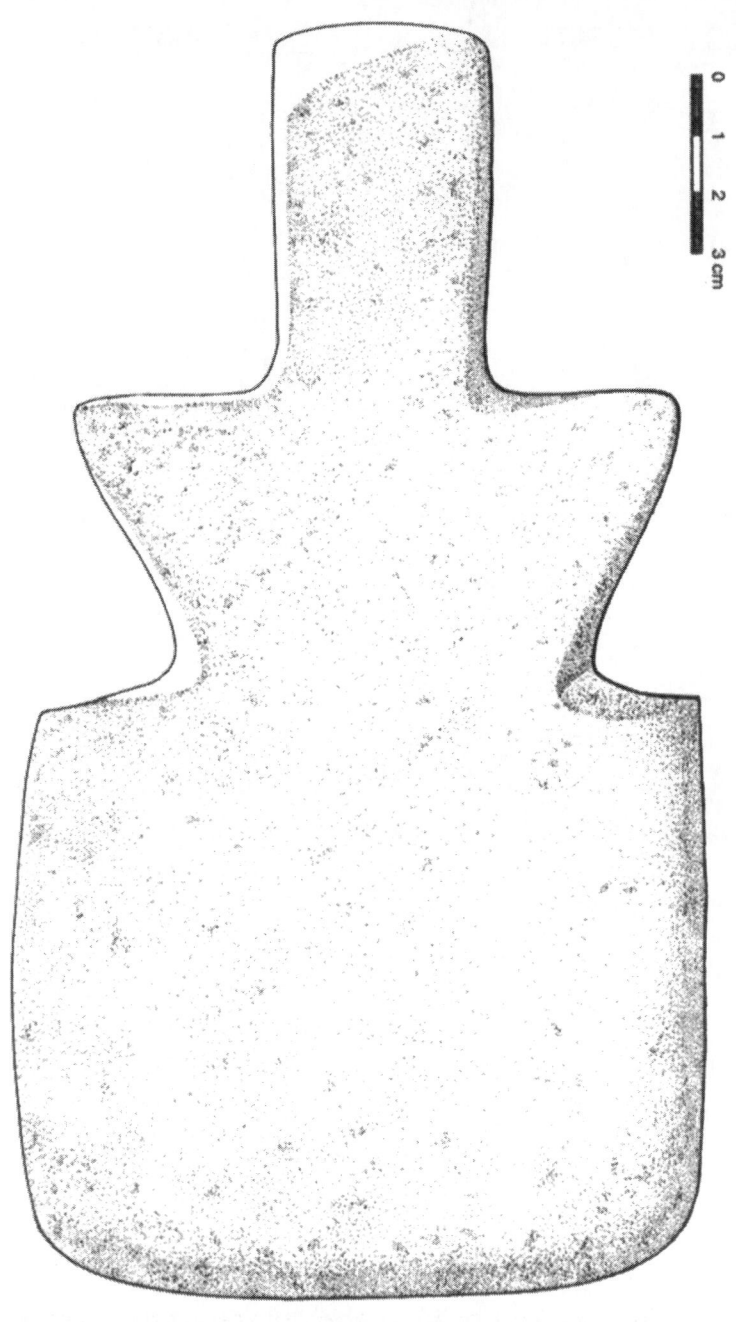

basket	locus	stratum	material	description
71	52	topsoil	granodiorite	complete figurine

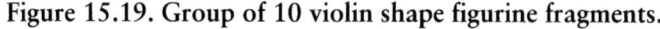

Figure 15.19. Group of 10 violin shape figurine fragments.

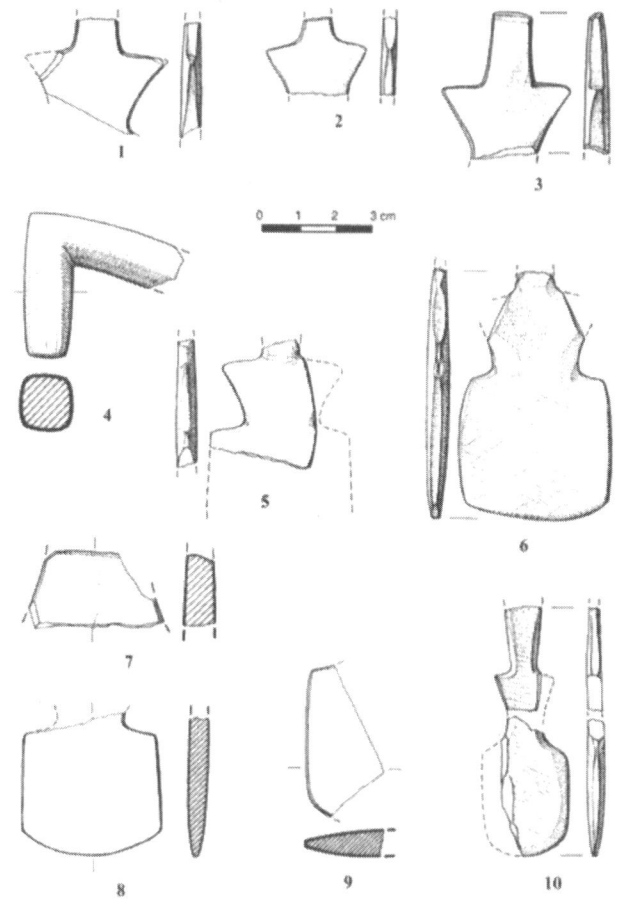

	basket	locus	stratum	material	description
1*	2596	896	IIB2	limestone	fragmented torso and neck
2*	2029	800	topsoil	chalk	torso, asymmetrical
3*	2900	946	IIC	limestone	head and torso, top of head reduced and ground after breakage
4*	5038	608	IIA	chalk	arm or leg ? sharply elbowed, light facettes produced by longitudinal reduction
5*	2776	969	IIIA	'Jerusalem' limestone	fragmented figurine from neck to waist, reworked to shape an animal
6*	1322	4222	IIC	talc-schist	head missing, shoulders symmetrically broken and ground, double chamfer nipping the waist, and oblique, crossed striae from polishing
7*	5174			limestone	fragment (torso?), one edge ground after breakage
8*	sq. N5	-	topsoil	limestone	base, type 2
9*	3968	1236	IIB	limestone	fragmented base
10*	2795. 1+2	961	IIA	bone	base type 1a, elongated torso and oblique chamfers from shoulders to head, perpendicular striae

Figure 15.20. Asymmetrical figurine with breasts, pebble figurine with breasts.

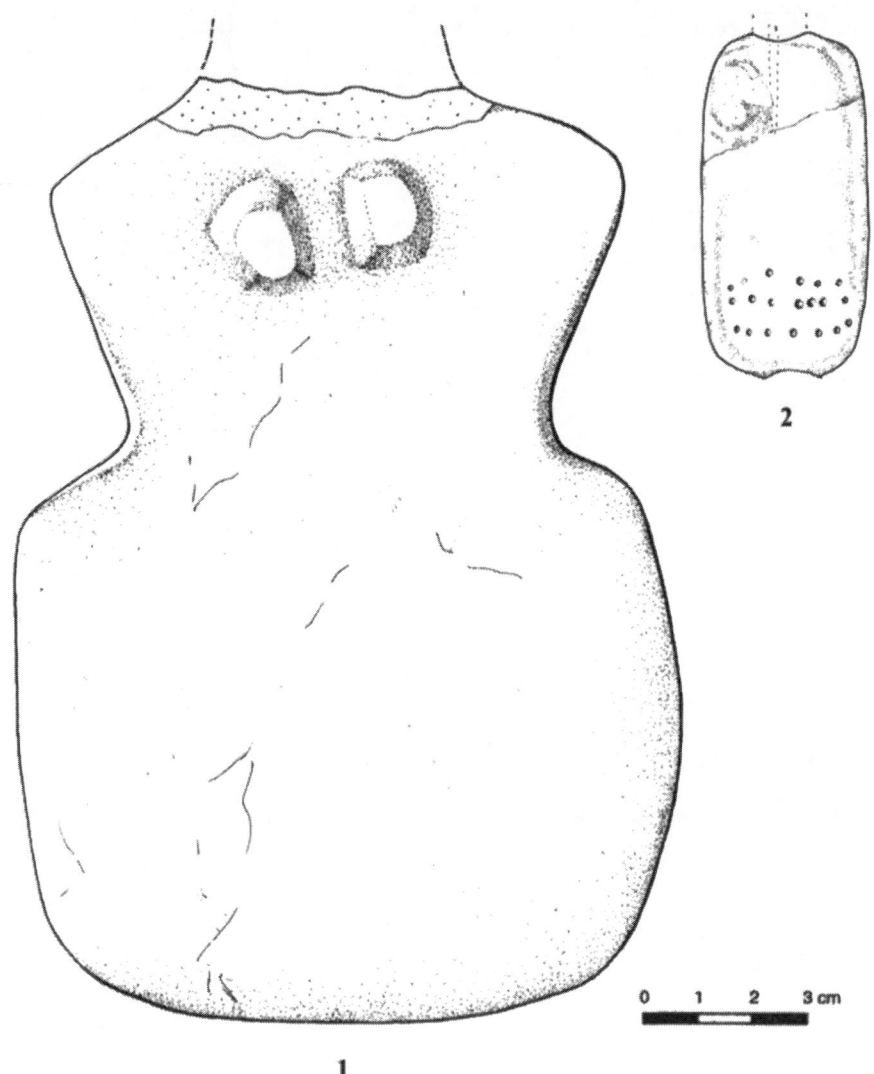

2

1

	basket	locus	stratum	material	description
1	3879	1222	2C	talc-schist	asymmetrical figurine, small facetted breasts
2	568	3601	III	limestone	pebble-like figurine, incised dots

Figure 15.21. Two violin shape figurines.

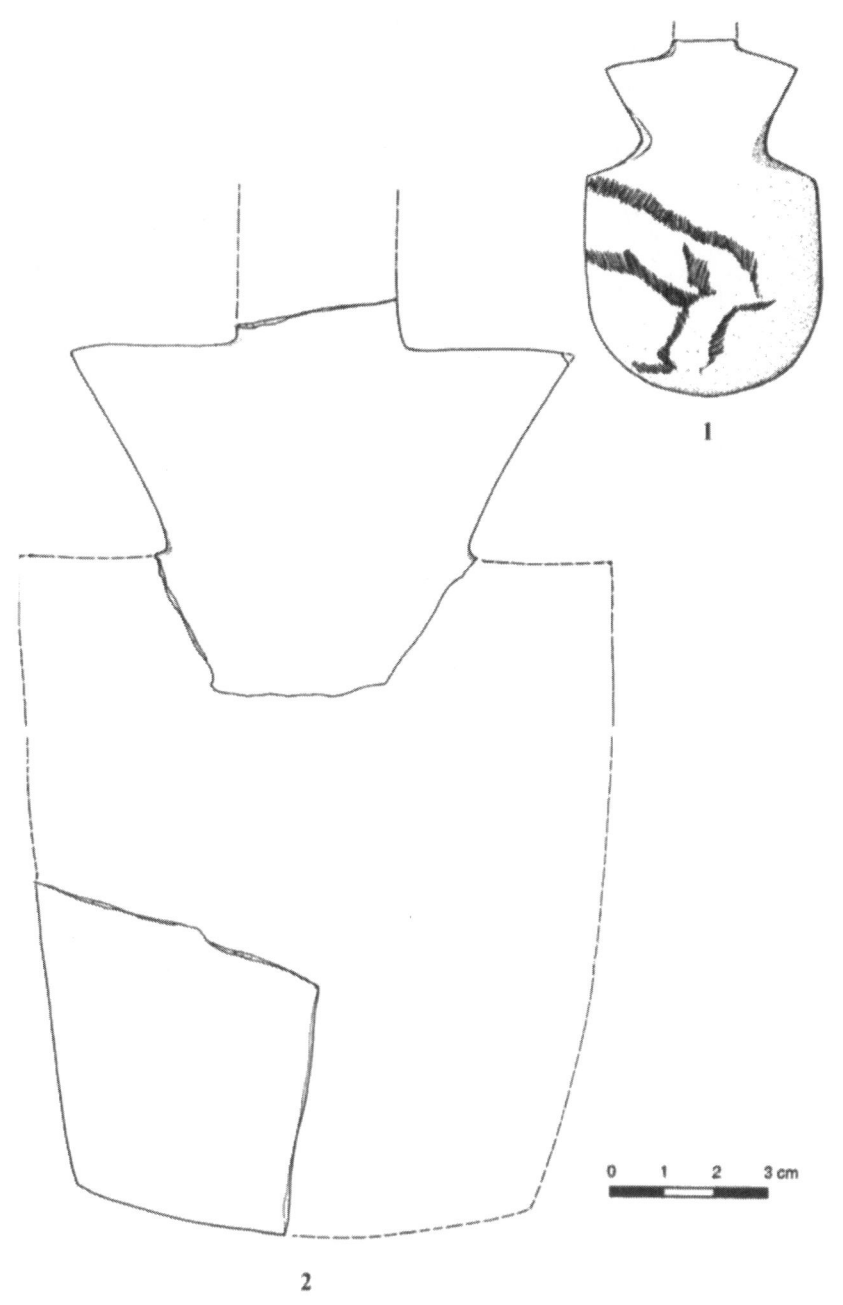

	basket	locus	stratum	material	description
1	384	50	IIB	limestone with oxydes	head missing, small-sized figurine
2	3854	1213	topsoil	talc-schist	torso and fragment of base (the reconstituted size is dubious)

Figure 15.22. Group of nine violin shape figurine fragments.

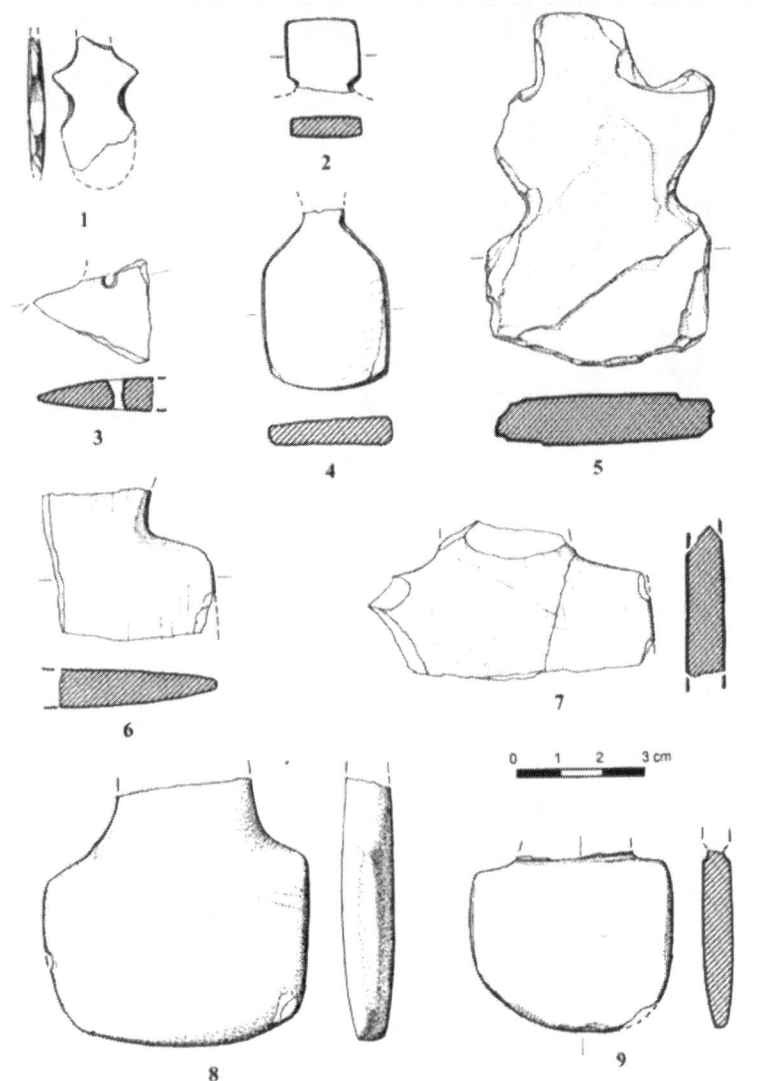

	basket	locus	stratum	material	description
1*	4262	1341	IIIA	black limestone	very small specimen, chamfered 'coches' at the waist
2*	3270	1036	IIA	sandstone	head?
3*	4208	1321	topsoil	chalk	fragmented shoulder, perforated
4*	5024	604	topsoil	chalk	base, long-waisted
5*	3277	-	topsoil	sandstone	rough-shape of a figurine (?), chipped edges—deteriorated at the base
6*	2375	826	IIB1	chalk	fragment, waist part, longitudinal striae
7*	3968	1236	IIB	limestone	fragment, roughly chipped
8*	3089	025	IIIA	limestone	fragmented figurine, lopsided base, one side chamfered
9*	3835	1212	topsoil	phyllite	base, type 2, groove around the waist

Figure 15.23. Group of three figurative objects (Violin shape figurine bases?).

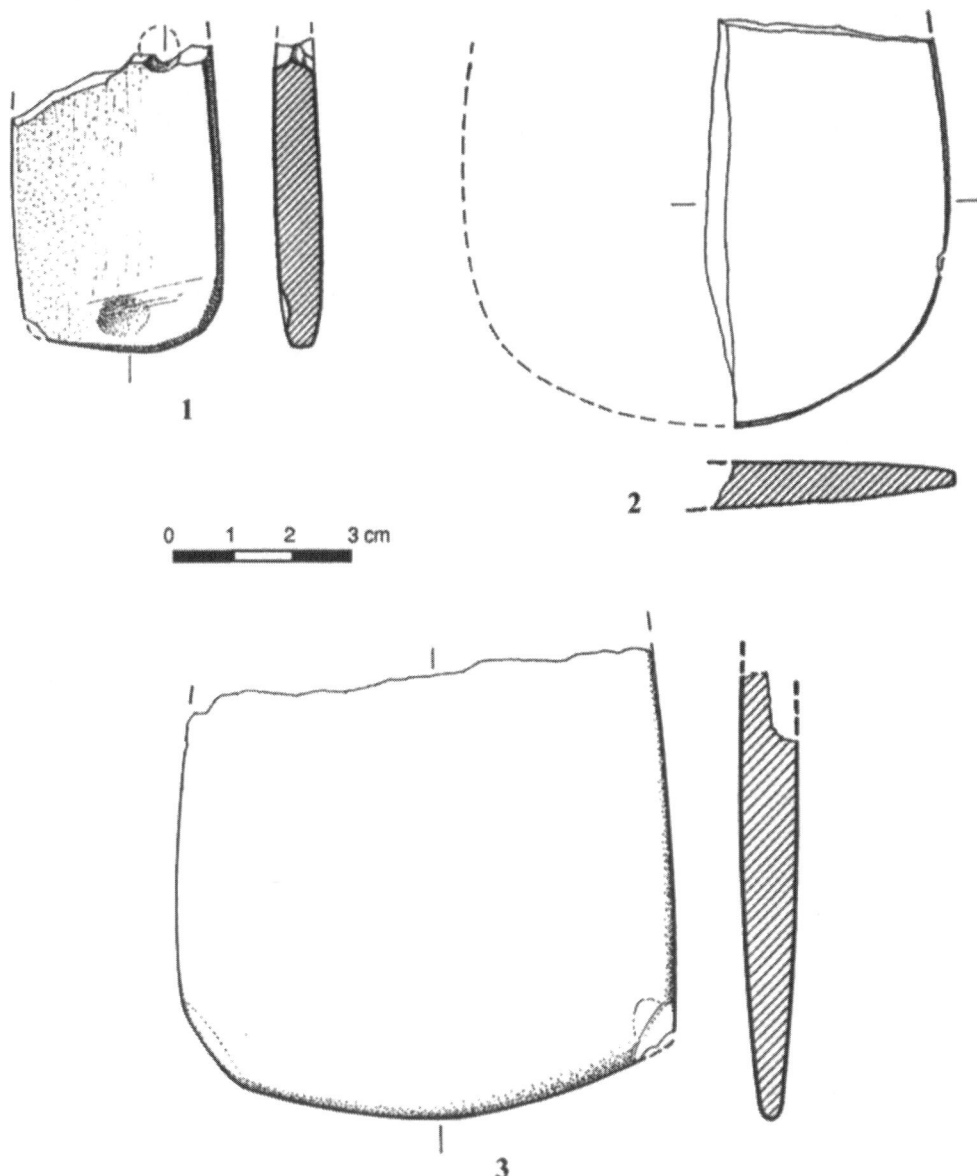

	basket	locus	stratum	material	description
1*	3123	014	II	chalk	perforated pendant or token, natural cupule at the base
2	3807	1201	IIC	chalk	fragmented, rounded base
3*	2357	841	IIB1	sandstone	fragmented base?

III a. Zoomorphic Clay Figurines (Catherine Commenge)

The representation of animals could be a most promising way toward an understanding of how prehistoric societies, ideologically or symbolically, comprehended their environment and related to it. During the Natufian period, this relation was expressed by ritual activities, involving elaborate patterns for burying humans together with animals—dog, gazelle and tortoise—and probably referring to the same myth (Tchernov and Valla 1997: 103). On a more theoretical basis, the powerful imagery of the Bull was interpreted as an essential vehicle for ideology and religion which, by the means of potent yet latent cognition, would have lead up to the advent of the Neolithic achievements in animal domestication (Cauvin 1994, 1972). Although the Early Chalcolithic period is, obviously, a less crucial context for the man/animal relation than the formative Natufian or PPN periods, the husbanding economy of Gilat reached a major economic threshold. The emergence of specialized pastoralism in the northern Negev Desert (Levy 1983) and the evidence for the use of ovicaprid secondary products at Safadi (Ducos 1973; Grigson 1987, 1988) and Grar (Grigson 1995) place Gilat's economic context at the threshold of what has been coined the 'secondary products revolution' (Alon and Levy 1989; Davis 1984; Sherratt 1981). Further, the impressive ritual practices inferred by the animal burials at Gilat (Cf. Chapter 6, this volume) are the most eloquent testimony to the renewed and pregnant significance of the investment in animals achieved by these Early Chalcolithic communities.

Significantly, the Natufians carved the first three-dimensional representations of animals in the Near East (Neuville 1951; Stekelis and Yzraeli 1963). A neat expansion in the spectrum of species illustrated by zoomorphic figurines, modeled from sun-baked or baked clay long before the generalized used of pottery,[49] is associated with the emergence of animal husbandry. Although erratically documented in the literature, over the two last decades Neolithic animal figurines have been found in large quantities and in diverse and most likely ambiguous contexts (Broman-Morales 1983; Eygun 1992; Garfinkel 1995). The example from PPNB Ain Ghazzal, providing caches of animal figurines (Rollefson 1986:49–50), some of which were interpreted as ritually killed cattle (Rollefson and Simmons 1986:50), or one Early Pottery Neolithic ritual deposit from Basta (Hermansen 1997), offer an exceptional contribution to the non-secular significance of zoomorphic figurines (Kohler-Rollefson 1992; McAdam 1997; Rollefson 1986; Rollefson and Simmons 1985). The lack of zoomorphic figurines for the end of the Late Neolithic period certainly reflects the general state of data for this period in the southern Levant (Garfinkel 1995; Gopher 1994). However, Gilat's zoomorphic figurines confirm the perduration of their production at the interface of the Neolithic and Chalcolithic periods.

Although objective analytical tools offer no guarantee for absolute neutrality, in considering Gilat's socio-economic, chronological and regional context, additional analytical methods need to be investigated with reference to the function of these figurines. The way in which animals are represented reflects a completely different concept from the human representation considered above. The conception of animal figurines differs in terms of medium, dimension and iconic processes that render matter explicit.

Zoomorphic figurines acknowledge a relation to 'otherness', which seems in many ways, from production to depiction, a more accessible referent that one's own kind. The very notion of 'otherness' implies the cognitive ways by which societies relate to animals. This process has been emphasized in the ethnographic record (Levi-Strauss 1962; Willis 1974; Fernandez 1974) yet also challenged as a dichotomist perspective between nature and culture (Descola 1987).

The notion of realism is relative in this specific corpus. The intention is to represent animals and not to reproduce them with natural exactitude. One can consider that reproduction requires skill and that representation calls for knowledge. Each stage in the making of zoomorphic figurines needs to be scrutinized as a conceptual step, as a 'channel' for information (Davis 1986) in tracking symbolic knowledge. As for the Ram effigy vessel, a multi-contextual and historical approach in observing the most material manifestations, in which thought and action are inseparable, from the 'momentous nature' (Renfrew 1994:9) of the manufacturing of figurines to the concepts involved in their iconic variety (Broman-Morales 1983), narrows the field of polyvalent interpretation and provides compelling evidence against the mundane utilization of the zoomorphic figurines.

The Zoomorphic Figurines Corpus (Figs 15.24–25)

Gilat produced a modest corpus of zoomorphic figurines, all but one made from evenly baked clay. All are small-sized (3 to 7 cm). Of the 13 pieces recovered, five are sufficiently complete or significant to be identified to taxon. Seven fragments, recognized as fore or hind part of animals, complete this assemblage. The figurines are thoroughly but lightly baked and thus fragile. They are all slightly damaged or broken. Fractures occur to the most salient tips, such as horns, neck, tail and legs, and thus unfortunately obliterate our ability to obtain relevant information.

Two zoomorphic artifacts have been used as pendants. The clay pendant that represents a complete bull is presented within the corpus of figurines. A topical emphasis is given, at the end of this chapter, to one ram head pendant made from non-local peridotite.

All the figurines are modeled from well levigated, homogeneous and untempered[50] clay. The quality of the clay matrix is slightly calcic. The absence of temper is due to the need to obtain 'fat' and slimy clay in which plasticity aids the modeling. In most of the cases, broken sections reveal a uniform buffed color (Munsell 5YR 7/3). The same process of manufacture may have been practiced at Abu Hamid, in the Jordan Valley, where about 50 lumps of clay, flattened and roughly circular or rectangular in shape, were excavated from a pit. These lumps were rolled and patted to pre-form animal figurines (Dollfus and Kafafi 1995:450). Gilat's figurines show that finger modeling followed by scraping of some part of the clay with a piece of wood, of bone or a blunt piece of flint, has refined the rough shapes. Clay plasticity and clever finger pinching and squeezing helped to outline the curve of the backbone, or the tilt of a muzzle or tail. Horns and, in one case, the fat tail of a sheep were separately made and then fixed to the body. All the figurines have a very smooth-textured surface.

Six figurines or fragments of figurines come from Stratum IIB2. Stratum IIC produced three of them. Four other specimens were recovered in Strata I, IIA, III and IV.

Sheep. Two figurines can be identified as sheep. One is a rather stocky animal with broken forelegs and horns (Fig 15.24.6). The hind-quarters are damaged. The sloping and parallel lines of the back and belly could indicate that the hind legs were not represented at all. This, and the straight position of the animal's head suggest that the figurine was shaped for a frontal presentation, standing by itself or being fixed like a *protome* (attached to the rim of a vessel, for example cf. Mallon *et al.* 1934:87 and Fig. 36.7–8).

The second sheep figurine seems a vivacious juvenile, stopped short when capering about, the head tilted, the hind quarters slightly lopsided (Fig. 15.24.1). Its tail, and the pocketed fat tail at its base, is finely shaped. The most remarkable character of this sheep figurine is its unique foreleg which is conical and longer than the two hind legs. It shows no sign of partition which might indicate that the forelegs were jointed. Three other figurines have this idiosyncratic 'anatomical' character (Figs 15.24.1 and 7 and one fragmented figurine which is not illustrated). The horns of both these sheep figurines are broken, but they appear to have been directed sideways at the base. Their large size suggests that both were rams, as ewes had much smaller horns or may even have sometimes been hornless (Ducos 1968; Grigson 1987, 1988). It is not possible to say whether the horns were coiled or spiral.

Figure 15.24. Selection of seven zoomorphic figurines and fragments.

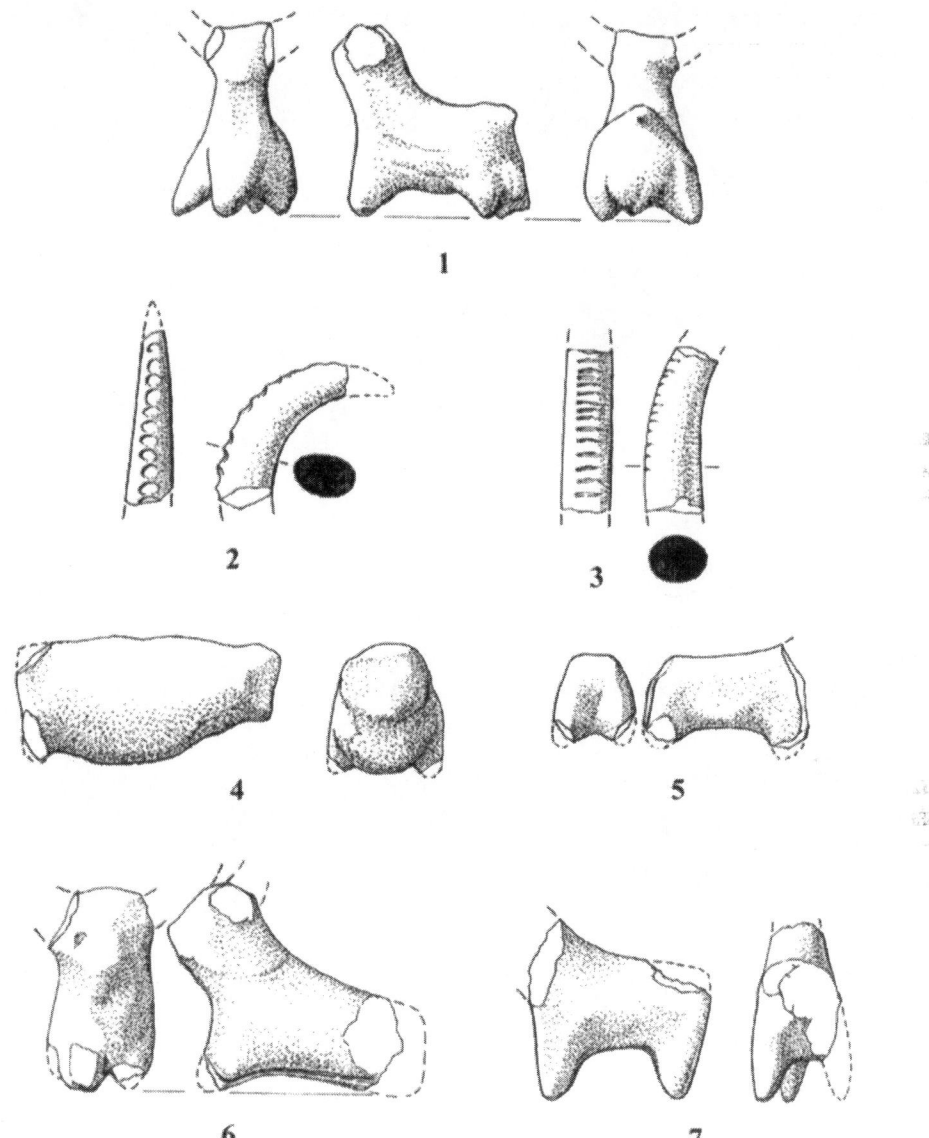

	basket	locus	level	description
1	3584	1126 pit	2C	male sheep, one fore-leg, blackened baked clay
2	5485	775 pit	2B2	Incised horn of an ibex buck, fragment, baked clay
3	5511	787 pit	2B2	Incised horn of a male gazelle, fragment, baked clay
4	5026	605	Topsoil	Rounded face figurine, no fore legs, hind legs and tail broken, baked clay
5	5859	1578 pit	2B2	one fore-leg (bovid?), fragmented, baked clay
6	4342	1344 pit	2B1	male sheep, broken hind, no evidence for hind legs, baked clay
7	5490	772 fill	2B	One fore-leg, probably bovid, fragmented, baked clay

Figure 15.25. Three zoomorphic clay figurines.

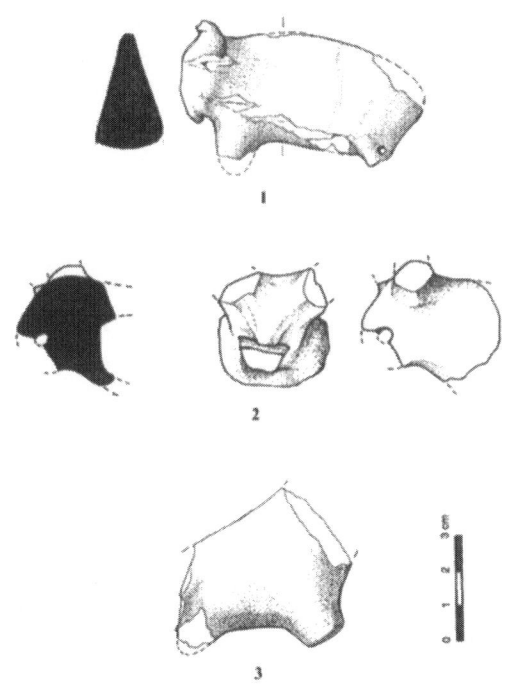

	basket	locus	level	description
1	5336	708 fill	3B	Bull, left hind leg perforated, lightly baked
2	277	727	?	Fragment of a zoomorphic vessel, bovid?? head, perforated snout (cf. Dollfus & Kafafi 1995, Fig.4: 6)
3	4199	1306 surface	3A2	fragmented and stubby figurine, baked clay

Clay figurines of sheep and goats were found in PPNB levels at Beidha (Kirkbride 1966, 1968), and Munhata (Garfinkel 1995: Fig. 17:4 and 7), then later in the sequence of this site (Garfinkel 1995: Fig. 32:5, 38:1). Fat-tailed sheep were already present in the Late Neolithic as shown by figurines from Munhata 2A (Wadi Rabah phase) (Garfinkel 1995: Fig. 38:1). The inventory of clay figurines found in Chalcolithic contexts is rather limited. One sheep figurine is recorded in the Cave of the Treasure (Bar Adon 1980) and one comes from Abu Matar (Perrot 1955).[51] At Gilat, sheep are well represented by one ram head in basalt and by one cultic vessel (see this chapter).

Cattle. One figurine of a bull was found at Gilat. It is made of very pure clay and was only lightly baked (Fig. 15.25.1). It presumably represents one of the small cattle described by Ducos (1968) and Grigson (1989, 1995) for the Chalcolithic period in the northern Negev. The rendering of the twisted horns and the frontal position of the head suggest stubbornness and power. The body's outline is massive and curiously triangular in section. The flanks are flattened and the backbone is prominent. The hind legs are broken. The left one is perforated. This bull figurine was probably used as a pendant or sewn on a garment; a fact which could explain the flatness of the flanks.

Bull figurines were already present at Aswad I (Syria) in a PPNA context, together with ibex and gazelle (Contenson 1989) and were ubiquitous in the corpus of Levantine sites during the PPNB period. They have been identified at Abu Gosh (Lechevallier 1978: Fig. 35:1–2) and are recorded as 'numerous' in the PPNB levels of Jericho (Holland 1982: Fig. 224:6–9 and pp. 553–4) as well as at Ain Ghazzal (Rollefson *et al*. 1992) or Wadi Fidan 001 (Levy pers. observation). Pottery Neolithic figurines of cattle were also identified at Byblos (Dunand 1973), Sha'ar Ha'Golan (Garfinkel 1995) and Jebel Abu Thawwab (Kafafi 1988). They represent the largest part of animal representation in the assemblage of Munhata, from the PPNB levels until the Wadi Rabah occupation (Garfinkel 1995:56). Two Chalcolithic cult vessels, one from Ein Gedi and one from Abu Hamid, represent bulls (Ussishkin 1980; Dollfus and Kafafi 1995).

Pig?. One comparatively large, incomplete figurine perhaps represents a pig (as suggested by C. Grigson, with consideration to the extreme slope of the back)[52] (Fig. 15.24.4). Body and legs are stubby, the neck is thick. More complete figurines recorded at other sites show that comparable features depicted pig (cf. Garfinkel 1995: Fig 17:5), but also sheep (cf. Garfinkel 1995: Fig. 17:4) or cattle (cf. Garfinkel 1995: Fig. 39:2).

Wild species.[53] Two fragmented horns belong to wild bovids. One, upright and sub-circular in cross-section, is slightly curved and its fore-edge is adorned with short, shallow and parallel incisions suggesting the lower part of the horn of a male gazelle (Fig. 15.24.3). Gazelles were a common component of animal bone assemblages in the southern Levant from the Upper Paleolithic, decreasing in importance in the PPNB with the introduction of domestic sheep and goat, and represented only in very small numbers in Late Neolithic and Chalcolithic sites. However, the find of nine burnt horncores of male gazelles at Gilat in what was clearly a ritual context (Locus 1344) suggests that they had a much greater significance than their small number suggests. At Teleilat Ghassul, a gazelle's head is well depicted in the 'Star fresco' and was described mysteriously by Mallon as 'un dragon' (Mallon *et al*. 1934:132).

The second horn belongs to an ibex buck (Fig 15.24.2). It is strongly curved, oval in cross-section, and has parallel, oval incisions indicating ridges on the fore-edge. It is not possible to distinguish between the bones of ibex (*Capra ibex*) and wild goats (*Capra hircus*), except from the horncores of males. A few bones have been found on some sites in the Negev and are identified as ibex rather than goat, since it is that taxon which is found today in the area. Ibex and (or) gazelle are found in the earliest assemblages at Aswad I and, later, at Beidha. Ibex received special attention in the Levantine Chalcolithic bestiary. Ibex is represented on many prestige copper artifacts from the Nahal Mishmar Cave (Bar Adon 1980). Ibex horns are depicted on the crown of the ossuaries from Chalcolithic funerary sites of the Israel coastal plain (Perrot and Ladiray 1980: 113 and Tableau X).

Unidentified and fragmentary figurines. One small animal, with a single fore leg, has rather high conical legs as compared to the two sheep figurines (Fig 15.24.7). Another also with only one fore leg, has angular hind quarters and perhaps a long, thin tail. Both characters suggest an ox (Fig. 15.24.5). One last specimen is odd-looking and in contrast with the general expressiveness of the corpus, is remarkably expressionless (Fig.15.24.4). The head is rounded and flattened. It has no fore legs and the hind legs, which are broken, appear to have been rather short. The tail is broken.

Three fragments of hind quarter parts (5712, 4246, 4309) and one fragment of a fore part bearing a unique leg (5367) have to be added to this short inventory.

Except the stocky animal with stubby fore legs (Fig. 15.25.3) and the bull pendant, the more complete figurines have an average length of c. 3.5 cm and a width of c. 1.8 cm. Compared to this diminutive scale and considering the natural range in stature of the depicted animals, the dimensions of the bull pendant figurine are slightly reduced.

Most of the hind quarter parts of the animals are preserved and it is thus noticeable that none of the figurines present any natural orifices or indication of genitalia. According to Caroline Grigson, most of the animals depicted seem to be male.

The *Momentous nature* of Production

By the end of the Levantine Neolithic period, the mode of production of zoomorphic figurines appears specialized as well as nucleated in contrast to what has been recorded at Middle Eastern Pre-Pottery Neolithic sites. At Jarmo, figurines were considered to have been made by different individuals in and around their home. Quantities of lumps of clay (350) were scattered all over the excavated area (Broman-Morales 1983:391). The 'standardization' of the 812 animal figurines found at Ganj Dareh only applies to some of their stylistic elements and not, apparently, to the making of regular and 'calibrated' modules (Eygun 1992:113–14).

Direct evidence for the production of zoomorphic figurines was recovered at Teleilat Ghassul and at Abu Hamid, in Jordan. Mallon mentioned that most of the zoomorphic figurines from Tell 3 (level IV) were found altogether with lumps of clay, thus indicating *un atelier de ceramiste* (Mallon *et al.* 1934:83). The recent discovery of 50 pre-shaped figurines in a pit at Abu Hamid, in a level contemporary to the Wadi Rabah phase (Dollfus and Kafafi 1995), also points to an organized sequence of production. Whether these places of production were part of pottery workshops has unfortunately not been established. Although tenuous, there is a degree of centralization in this mode of production that rules out expediency and that implies more than casual demand. The conception of this type of production involves the making of modular lumps, all prepared before being shaped. This sequential and rationalized conception fits in the technical milieu defined for pottery making at Gilat insofar as the mental and physical processes are the same (Commenge-Pellerin 1990, and see Chapter 10, this volume). However cursory the means and modest the size of the production of zoomorphic figurines at Gilat, it should not be described as expedient. Most of Gilat's zoomorphic figurines are made out of modules of c. 3.5 cm in length. One can reasonably assume that the figurines of Gilat were made by a potter, yet 13 figurines are present out of ten tons of pottery recovered at Gilat.

It is difficult to establish when, in this productive context, the representation would be 'invested with (partial) meaning' (Conkey 1987; Preziosi 1982:325). The circumstances of a nucleated, serial production could be related to particular needs of a particular time and place, thus defining a specific context—the actual commencement of ritual performance—for this production. Modeling a lump of clay reduces to the minimum the technical interval between the material and the shape of an artifact. It is probable that the ideas encapsulated in the representation were strong enough to be supported by a medium requiring light means of manufacturing and that, as a corollary, these ideas were reinforced by the easiness in multiplying representations. The conceptual endeavor embedded in clay representations might be understood as a metaphorical scheme. One could assume that the act of conception, even by means of simple suggestive modeling, of the representation of an animal from a shapeless mass of clay was, by itself, a techno-symbolic protocol. The shaping and storage of lumps of clay in a pit could also implicitly refer to mythical and cosmological meanings involved in pottery making and explain its origins (Levi-Strauss 1985:23–38). For physical reasons, tempered and already shaped lumps of clay (length c. 5–6 cm, diameter c. 1–2 cm, cf. Dollfus and Kafafi 1995:450)[54] dehydrate quickly and a pit only offers temporary protection against this process (Rice 1987:63 and 115). The storage of pre-shaped modules rather than of large and practical wedges of clay could thus indicate selective and punctual circumstances for a serial production. Giving shape to figurines could be the first step involving symbolic and intended thought and action, set in a ritual performance.

The assumption that the makers of zoomorphic figurines were potters[55] is strengthened by evidence for specialized and standardized production at Teleilat Ghassul and Abu Hamid. Further, we have established for certain that figurative vessels from Gilat, the Ram and the Lady, were each actually made by an experienced potter (see above). The study of Gilat's pottery assemblage has demonstrated the co-existence of technical variants and of a double-ranked production in which ceremonial vessels composed a large part. Whether this complex system of production mirrored ranking for potters and (or) social sub-systems was discussed *supra* (Chapter 10). The production of zoomorphic figurines at Gilat could have been devolved to specialists among the potters—most probably those using modular techniques—or even, among this specific group, to figurine specialists.[56] However, the modest amount of zoomorphic figurines recovered at the site does not help in corroborating this latter view.

Toward a Typology of Representation

The outlines of body, legs, tail, ears and muzzle are morphological characteristics whose presence, covariance or absence seems to be independent of the represented species. With reference to Davis' statement (1986) that by definition a representation refers to its object iconically, Gilat's specimens pertain to different 'iconic' conceptions. Different degrees of naturalism in representation divides the corpus of figurines into three categories, defined as *naturalistic* (morphological elements are all naturalistic), *para-naturalistic* (most of the elements are amorphous, some morphological elements are naturalistic) and *pseudo-naturalistic* (all elements but one are naturalistic).

The bull figurine fits into the naturalistic category. It has four legs, horns, and an outline immediately identifiable as a bull representation (Fig. 15.25.1). Considering the small size of the Gilat corpus, it is notable that the naturalistic category is represented by a relatively large figurine, which is the only one with a well-defined primary function, being used as a pendant. The opposite para-naturalistic group is represented by a complete although deliberately allusive representation (Fig. 15.24.4). The depiction in this specimen is elliptical and only conveys the presence of an animal. The amorphism found in some zoomorphic figurines is in contrast to the degree of abstraction reached with the violin-shaped figurines, which sublimates human representation into the canonical outlines of allusion. Yet, one noticeable digression to this opposition is the re-shaping of a violin-shaped figurine, made from ochre-red limestone, into a two-dimensional animal representation (Fig. 15.19.5). Whether undertaken on an already broken and (or) discarded violin-shaped figurine (which cannot be asserted), this skillful re-shaping can certainly be seen as more than expedient on such a valuable medium. This could give evidence for a new embodiment of the support that enhances the importance of animal representation.

The third category, the pseudo-naturalistic group, includes most of the identifiable figurines. This category includes the idiosyncratic animals with one leg, which can be referred to as teratological figurines. They represent about one-third of the corpus. Their anatomical particularity cannot be dismissed as 'neutral'. The single leg has no obvious practical purpose; on the contrary it contributes to the certain instability of the figurine. One cannot discount an eventual stylistic convention, yet the diversity in representation argues against such artistic restrictions. These representations proceed *de facto* from teratologism even if the representational and former intention was not restricted to the representation of a natural abnormality, *sensu stricto*. References to human and physical abnormality generally show a multiplication of genetic characters and are sometimes interpreted as signs of transcendence.[57] The meaning of this anatomical character, which defines the pseudo-naturalistic category, is considered metaphoric, as a referent to symbolic knowledge. This meaning could refer to some analogical substitution, as a metaphor would operate in a mythical system. As the hind legs of the small sheep represented in Fig. 15.24.6 appear to be absent, it falls in the pseudo-naturalistic category. If the interpretation of this plain hind part as a feature allowing a presentational posture of the figurine is correct, this element parallels the interpretation given to ring-based or 'faced' vessels, as features ritualizing their function (see Chapter 10, this volume).

The relative polymorphism of these representations should be noted. Although a degree of standardization in production could have been reached, it is not reflected in narrow stylistic standards. However, it is not obvious whether different degrees in naturalism could signify different functions. Broman-Morales remarked that, at Jarmo, abstract and figurative specimens were found together (Broman-Morales 1983:384). This kind of evidence certainly renders dubious any functionally oriented interpretation based on figurative categorization. The efficiency of thought and action could have prevailed over the quality of the iconic representation.

Zoomorphic Figurines in Context

Three fragmented zoomorphic figurines were found in ritual burial pits. The hind part of a sheep was found together with nine burnt gazelle horn cores, a fenestrated basalt stand and four bone tools in the bottom part of a pit, partially sealed by a cap of clay (Loc. 1344, Fig. 15.24.6) and linked to a human burial installation (see Chapter 5, this volume). That pottery sherds, which are ubiquitous at the site, were not found in this pit argues in favor for the intentional deposition of this fragmented zoomorphic figurine. The association in this ritual burial of animals in *nature* (horn cores), animals in *culture* (the manufacture of bone tools) and animals in representation (figurine) is remarkable. Less impressive but nevertheless significant is the find of the horns of ibex and gazelle in ritual burial pits. Although they are tiny fragments, they could have been placed there intentionally. The ibex horn fragment was in pit 787, in which discarded ceremonial vessels were placed above a dog's cranium. The gazelle horn was in pit 775, which also yielded discarded ceremonial vessels within each of its four layers, associated to three beads, one fragmented shell pendant and an ivory (?) half-ring. As with all the fragments of animal figurines recovered at Gilat, the fractured surfaces of the clay horns are worn and it is not possible to state whether breakage was intentional or not. Figurines (human or animal) found in refuse contexts (ashy areas, pits) are generally described as 'casually discarded' (Broman-Morales 1983:384–5; Eygun 1992:114). Referring to the discard of (human) representations in contexts 'which don't provide evidence for their utilization' at Khirokitia, Le Brun (1989:177–8) insists that the very banality of these contexts indicates the lack of attention paid to the figurines after their utilization. Thus, after fulfilling their specific purpose, figurines lost their *anima*. It can be argued that, at Gilat, selective fills of discarded artifacts used in ritual performance could represent more than 'post-functional' refuse. Parts of zoomorphic figurines could have been valued enough—and perhaps were still efficient if intended as votive items—to find their way to such 'final resting locations'. The proposed interpretation of a probable hoard deposit in an Early Pottery Neolithic (and perhaps PPNC) context, suggests that Basta inhabitants were 'engaged in ritual and reciprocal gift exchange with "the other world"' (Hermansen 1997:339). A plausible continuum within an ultimate redistributive scheme might be intended in Gilat's ritual practice.

Within an enlarged regional context, other threads could be followed in making consistent, though not explicit correlations, all pointing to a ritual utilization of some species that are modeled in clay. The animal figurines from Teleilat Ghassul are mostly identified as dogs (Mallon *et al.* 1934; Koeppel *et al.* 1940). This fact provides an unexpected clue to a mutual symbolic bestiary at Teleilat Ghassul and at Gilat. Several dogs skeletons and skulls were buried at Gilat, one of the skeleton, which had an unhealed fracture on a foreleg, was associated with a large double-handed tubular vessel (Loc. 692 and 698), probably imported from Ghassul (see this volume, Chapters 5, 9 and 10).

There is no other direct evidence for documenting how these figurines were used or rather, how they fulfill their role in ritual performance. Zoomorphic figurines are interpreted, with reference to ethnographical records, as items of sympathetic magic by Talalay (Talalay 1993 and cf. Parsons 1919). Some fragmented figurines could have been used as focusing devices and perhaps also as *protomes* affixed to pottery artifacts. That animal representation was active in ritual performance at Gilat and was primarily meant to be seen is illustrated to a remarkable degree by the Ram figurative vessel (see above). It is impossible to assert whether (hypothetical) *protomes* were meant for apotropaic purposes, symbolically referring to the artifact's use and content, or, perhaps, to the owner's identity within the group. Once again, the rarity of these (hypothetical) protruding devices at Gilat and the general paucity of pottery design—even on ceremonial vessels—seem to rule out a merely decorative purpose.

The system of animal husbandry at Gilat also provides a contextual background for these zoomorphic specimens (Grigson, Chapter 6). Analyses on animal representation in earlier prehistoric Middle Eastern contexts usually show that there are inconsistencies between the spectrum of species exploited and the animals elected into prehistoric bestiaries (Cauvin 1994). The same has been observed for hunter-gatherers in the ethnographic record (Guenther 1988). In contrast to what was proposed for the preceding Pottery Neolithic period (Garfinkel 1995:56), the ram and the bull are central figures (in association with wild species represented by gazelle and bear) in ritual practice at the very beginning of the Early Pottery period (Hermansen 1997:334). The cattle, the ovicaprids (and perhaps pigs) exploited at Gilat are the main taxa illustrated by the zoomorphic figurines. The small number of figurines recovered at the site precludes any further interpretation of the relative numbers of each taxon and any consideration of the relevance of the apparent absence of species (for example, dogs, equids and possibly goats).

Dimorphic morphological characters like the traces of large horns on some of the figurines indicate that most, if not all, of both the domestic and the wild animals depicted were male (this information could find a parallel with the ram figurine vessel that has explicit and implicit male sexual features). A realistic (?) expectation for female character depiction—such as udders—in the context of the 'secondary products revolution'[58] fails to materialize. However, with only 13 fragmentary figurines, this sample is far too limited for further discussion. The presence of ibex indicates another interpretive dimension. Unlike gazelles, which are almost ubiquitous in the southern Levant, ibex are found only in a few localities further south, at Ein Gedi in the Judean Desert and at Avdat in the Negev. The integration of ibex into Gilat's bestiary from an outer, though not very distant, world, and from a mineral, barren universe contrasting to the rich pasture lands of the Nahal Patish, is noteworthy. The Chalcolithic Ein Gedi sanctuary, in the immediate vicinity of the Dead Sea, yielded one large (male) horn of an ibex and two smaller (female) horns in an upturned bowl (Ussishkin 1980:28).

Zoomorphic figurines were numerous at Late Neolithic–Chalcolithic sites of the southern Levant such as Teleilat Ghassul and Abu Hamid. Although evaluating and comparing inventories from different sites is a peṣrilous enterprise, one can stress that animal figurines occurred in noticeable quantity at sites where intensive cultural activities are recorded, for example the Ein Gedi sanctuary and Teleilat Ghassul. At Ein Gedi, where the sanctuary compound was excavated in its entirety, the zoomorphic figurines (including one figurative vessel mentioned above, a figurine of a bull carrying a 'churn') represent more than 1% of the ware artifacts recovered at the site.[59]

One has to try and go beyond ecological and economic explanatory schemes when interpreting figurative artifacts. Tenuous, disparate data document the corpus of animal figurines; nevertheless they provide unexpected evidence for their place in the sociocultural background of Gilat. Unimpressive in size and style and made from an ordinary medium, these figurines may be the byproducts of occasional sympathetic magic. Yet an organized and specialized production is highly probable that, with regard to the modesty of the assemblage, can be described as nucleated rather than attesting mass-production. This kind of production could have been organized on a cyclical basis and related to the rythms of cultic events.

In considering Neolithic and Chalcolithic zoomorphic figurines, one can notice that some attitudes, ascribed to the conceptual endeavor involved in making the animal representation, could have changed through time. The most significant momentum could have been reached during the manufacturing process for Neolithic figurines: perforations with flakes (Ain Ghazal) or pocked-marks (Ganj Dareh, Munhata 2B) are made into wet clay (Rollefson 1983; Eygun 1992; Garfinkel 1995). Clay plasticity gives way to immediate action, shortening the distance between the meaning of the figurine and its use. If significance is defined as a way for establishing a relation between terms, Gilat's pseudo-naturalistic figurines could illustrate an enlargement of the field of meanings, the single foreleg referring to a conceptual order, beyond naturalism and beyond direct action, materializing more 'tacit knowledge'(cf. Polanyi and Prosch 1975).

Seen through the looking-glass of the apparent shift intervening in the system of husbandry at the time, these figurines resist the candid expectation of finding a symbolic resonance for any such change. Domesticated and wild species are represented in the corpus of zoomorphic figurines and, when found in explicit context, they are associated with selected and egregious remains of dog and gazelle. This tends to corroborate the full integration of zoomorphic figurines into the symbolic system and cultic activities at the site.

I would like to express here my gratitude to Francois VALLA *and Caroline* GRIGSON *for their competent advice and indulgent comments.*

III b. Ram Head Pendant from Peridotite (C. Commenge)

A spectacular small carved ram's head adds important data for studying the role of animals in Chalcolithic ritual at Gilat (Fig. 15.26). Sculpted in the round, this ram head is a unique masterwork in the inventory of stone artifacts of the southern Levantine Chalcolithic. It is 4.2 cm wide from horn to horn; its height is 2.8 cm. As a value-laden and personal adornment, it might anchor the construction of meaning in another version of symbolism, one that encapsulates social identity.

Figure 15.26. Ram's head.

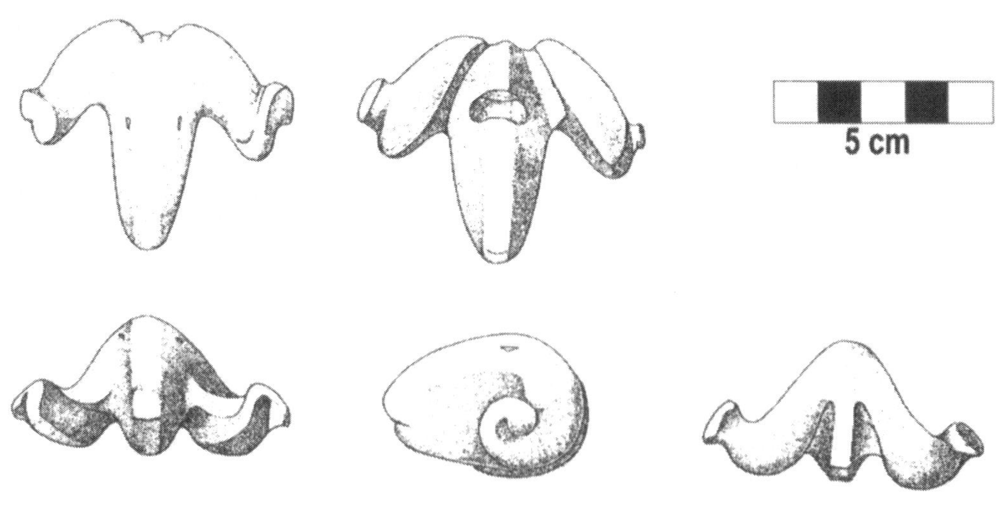

The ram's head is carved in a fine-grained peridotite. This igneous rock is part of ophiolites rock assemblage whose closest source deposit seems to be the Eastern. However, archaeological evidence challenges this possibility.

The highly-skilled craftsmanship involved in the making of this artifact reflects mastery of heavy technical constraints. A very firm grip has been necessary for carrying out a three-dimensional carving at such a small scale. The flat, angular surfaces that are still apparent at the top and at the base of the head (Fig 15.26) might give evidence for the grip of the jaws of a vise-like device. Pecking with a flint (?) tool (Mohs scale: 7) has reduced and shaped the head volumes. Two narrow grooves have set apart the two horns from the head at the back (Fig. 15.26). The ribbon-like and shallow grooves that suggest the twist of the horns are still apparent at the top of the head. The slight asymmetry of the tips of the horns is perhaps intentional yet symmetry was certainly a challenge considering constraints inherent to carving a hard material at such a very small scale. Diffuse pecking has shaped the head while the reduction of two lateral zones enhances the curve of the muzzle and the jaw-line. The mouth is clearly delineated. In contrast to the intended realism of the representation, two pecked and small eyes are placed on the front and not on the sides of the head. On the back of the head, a longitudinal ridge was reserved in order to allow and secure the drilling of a perforation whose bridge has been broken (Fig. 15.26). The piece was thoroughly sanded by the mechanical action of either an abrasive lapidary from hard rock, or abrasive powder of similar nature. In both case, running water was probably necessary to avoid warming and the risk of cracks. However, the sanding operation was more intensive on the front of the head than over its back, top and base.

The judicious use of reduced plane surfaces appears here related to techniques involved in the manufacture of other stone artifacts, such as violin figurines, but also to techniques that were later developed to relieve angles and planes on fenestrated pedestals of some basalt vessels (see, for example, one fenestrated pedestal from Abu Matar).[60] This and the mastering of in-the-round carving on this tiny pendant indicate the work of a long-trained craftsperson, and thus might suggest an off-site by-product, most probably at an ultrabasic rock-source workshop. This peridotite pendant finds a contemporary parallel at Ras Shamra. A ram head pendant from steatite was recovered at Late Obeid level III B1 (Contenson 1992:118–19, 196 and see Fig. 146: 7).[61] Its dimensions (3.7 × 2.3 cm) are slightly smaller than those of the Gilat pendant. Although its horns are broken, exquisite carving has shaped the head. Steatite, whose source can be the Ba'r et Bassit located 20 km away from Ras Shamra, was used from the earliest occupation at the site (PPNB, level VC) onward. It was reserved for valued artifacts such as seals and 'buttons' (Contenson 1992: Plate LXXXVIII: 4–5, XCIV: 1–2 and 5, XCV: 1–3), or shallow bowls ('coupelles 'or palettes, Pl. XCVII: 3, CIII: 1–2). However, ophiolites rocks are also found in the Ba'r et Bassit area (Courtois 1992:212). It can thus be argued that, although the Eastern Desert might be considered as one of the main source for exogenous artifacts at Gilat, especially for violin figurines, a northern Syrian source cannot here be excluded for the ram head pendant. This view finds some further support in reference to one seal from phyllite recovered at the Chalcolithic site of Grar (see Gilead 1995:361–3).[62] The presence of obsidian artifacts at Gilat (Yellin *et al.* 1996) also helps to document Chalcolithic trade between Gilat and Syro-Anatolia.

From a broader diachronic perspective, ram head pendants or amulets have been recorded at Early Bronze Age En Besor (Gophna 1976: Fig. 15 and Plate XLV) and in Predynastic Egypt (Petrie 1914: Plate XXXVIII. 212: a–m; 1920: Plate IX: 1–6, that have also been identified as ox representations, see Petrie 1920:11). However, means of representation cannot be paralleled with the in-the-round, three dimensional head from Gilat.

As documented by social anthropology, personal adornment is an effective medium 'in which humans construct and represent beliefs' (White 1992:539 and see Turner 1975). Here, the pendant's function seems to have been as an amulet worn by a person and to be seen by his or her peers. This small pendant has been conceived for visual display. The horns are widely spaced and the eyes are slightly misplaced in order to stare at the viewer (Fig. 15.26). One can note that, among animal representation at Gilat, pendants show the most detailed and naturalistic depiction. The exclusive depiction of the head, sufficient for evocating a generic representation, again emphasizes the importance of the Ram in Gilat's symbolic realm. The discovery at Basta, in an Early Pottery Neolithic hoard deposit, of one ram head pendant from limestone (Hermansen 1997) might give some clues for the signification of Gilat's specimen. The ram pendant from Basta is so shaped that it is also a phallic representation. Another green 'marble' pendant from Basta, assigned to a contemporary context, represents altogether a finely shaped man head and a phallus. These two pendants were prepared to be worn for two orientations and thus expressed alternative—and obviously bound—meanings. While such 'double entendre' or, picking up Alain Le Brun's word, such a 'pun' is not uncommon from the PPNB onward for human head representation (see Le Brun 1989; Gopher and Orelle 1996, its reverberation or extension to a ram head has been underscored (Hermansen 1997:339). The very elaboration of symbolism could have determined an implicit sexual reference with the ram head pendant from Gilat. However, evidence from other figurative artifacts tends here to indicate that representation refers more to gender than to a virile and primary force. With reference to the corpus of zoomorphic figurines, there is a certain propensity to represent male rather than female animals. There is no sexual indication on one complete bull pendant (Fig. 15.25.1). While the Ram figurative vessel is clearly sexed, sexual emphasis that can be related to a genesis-like force is with no contest the prerogative of the Woman representation (Fig. 15.1–15.3).

The ram head pendant suggests a personal bond established between the representation and its bearer, presumably expressed in terms of identification. Worn as a sign, the ram pendant might stand *aliquid pro aliquo*, as a substitute, and be a process to empower its owner with the animal's metaphorical values. Worn as an emblem, this personal retention of the Ram image might be designed, with consideration to the pendant's intrinsic value, for a display of social identity, that appears to assert authority and prestige together with solemn exaltation of belief. With reference to the interpretive scheme proposed above for the Ram persona and anima, a legitimating of lineage identification might also be intended. The bull pendant from clay adds some credit to these assumptions, and might have represented a multi-leveled challenger for Ram supremacy.[63]

This ram head could also be seen like a forbear for cognitive shifts that became more assertive with animal representation in the later Chalcolithic. Other precious and exogenous media such as copper or ivory were then used in representation of animals. Other conceptual formations were chosen by way of a pervasive animal imagery which seems to have filled an emblematic—and thus still metaphorical—function on many personal prestige artifacts (crowns, scepters, clay ossuaries, etc.). In this later emblematic and ostentatious bestiary, though, the Ram seems absent, having perhaps, at least temporarily, exhausted his symbolic hegemony.

Conclusion

This investigation of Gilat's figurines implicitly assumes that patterns of social behavior can be shaped by external circumstances yet also by the ideological milieu that encapsulates the yeast of sub-conscious forces. There are still, as painstakingly demonstrated above, rocky paths to cross in translating patterns of material evidence, and especially symbolic expression, into evidence for social action.

Heralded by figural representation, two major symbolic themes emerge at Gilat. One female figure and one ram figure appear at the heart of symbolic expression and perhaps at the heart of the web of social relations. As apparent hierophantism unveils plausible meaning, multi-leveled frameworks of inference point to the entwinement of those two characters' fate, perhaps as a commemorative image of a fundamental genesis. Seemingly, these two images appear coiled in, yet transfixed from, the ancient, certainly ancestral and probably mythical, Anatolian symbolic vision. However, magnified by emphatic transfiguration and omnipresence, the precious silhouettes of violin-shaped figurines usher in the pivotal signification and role of the female character, here interpreted as mirroring the society's unitary principle and/or elementary unit, and perhaps the converted and metamorphosed avatar of some mythical figure. Gender, expressed by the subdued female nature of the violin figurines is not conceptualized within a thrusting notion that entails symmetrical sexual opposition and complementarities. Plausibly transmogrified into the Ram, male representation is metaphoric and if one refers to the head pendant, probably emblematic. Multifarious and modest representation put on stage domestic and wild animals. Among those, as a supplementary indication, teratomorphism singles out sheep, thus unfolding more symbolic interest for this species.

The orchestration of ritual establishes a symbolically defined, temporal and spatial environment within which social interaction operates. At Gilat, symbolic representation in action, as (partially) reconstituted from the archaeological record, yields to different systemic and ritual strategies and experiences, that fold or unfold symbols while they might define (and secure?) the place of social agents. Through ritual practice, subtle distillation of knowledge etches different patterns that could have range from initiation to the ultimate coherence of the order of existence (the gynecomorphous vessel), appropriation, organized and hierarchical display of symbols (violin-shaped figurines), and their probable situational and temporal enactment (violin-shaped figurines and zoomorphic figurines). The noticeable reluctance to naturalization in human representation, the avoidance to signal personal resemblance and individual attributes (like social and/or personal markers) emphasizes the reference to a transcended 'constituted body' either by hierophantism or symbolism. In this context, social projection and eventual public comment, yet also significant individual implication or resistance, are beyond our reach. One can only suggest that mythopoeia could have been instrumental in reifying, enacting and perhaps negotiating cycles of *corporate* reproduction.

It is always tempting to elaborate on dependence of intensification or concentration of cultic activities with events modifying social organization. The current archaeological evidence or lack of evidence makes aleatory a diachronic epidemiology (cf. Sperber 1992) of figural representation in southern Palestine from the Neolithic period onward. Moreover, the reduction of symbolism to its social function, as a mirror of social existence, may drastically prune the extent of cognitive construction. Issues on the eventual waxing and waning of human representation through the Neolithic period should consider all contextual socioeconomic parameters, yet also the nature and the status of representation. On the one hand, one can prudently remark that the 'explosion' of female figurines at Early Chalcolithic Gilat may follow and precede periods whose material evidence seems to signal waning in female representation (namely the Wadi Rabah Late Neolithic phase and the latter Chalcolithic as regionally illustrated by the Beersheva sites). On the other hand, synchronic and regional epidemiology gives Early Chalcolithic Gilat as an active source. At the threshold of specialized pastoralism, emergent intermediate societies may have explored and challenged any isomorphism between social agents and contextual economical spheres erected as a cosmology, to claim and legitimate a new pact with natural forces that ensured the perpetuation of the social nexus.

Notes

1. Minimum number of individuals (73 specimens of violin-shaped figurines, some of which are fragments, have been recovered)
2. Chemical analysis is still not available
3. The cylindrical and funnel-like bases indicate beakers or cornets. Miriam Tadmor challenged this view and suggested that simple jars were represented (Tadmor 1986). The three funnel bases of the vessels are unnecessarily fragile if jars were intended. The pottery analysis demonstrates that beakers and pointed-base vessels are numerous at the site, and represent an important alternative to the 'ubiquitous' V-shaped bowls. All were most probably individual and ceremonial vessels (cf. Chapter 10).

4. One miniature churn, with no direct archaeological context, could have been part of a figurative vessel, see Tadmor 1990: Fig. 1.

5. One miniature churn, with no direct archaeological context, could have been part of a figurative vessel, see Tadmor 1990: Fig. 1.

6. Parturition has generally been selected to interpret this figurine sitting on a 'birth-stool' (Epstein, Amiran, Tadmor, Alon, Levy). Lack of evidence for the depiction of parturition on a figurine whose pudenda are very realistic, together with the parallel position of the legs, indicate that parturition cannot be directly depicted here. Contemporary birth figurines from Cyprus, some sitting on stools, are all squatting (a birth posture) and, besides, showing different stages of labour (see Gorring 1991 and below note 14).

7. This is also the case at Hacilar I: 'That Hacilar I people did see faces in their pots is abundantly clear from the extremely rich series of anthropomorphic vases': Mellaart 1970:141.

8. e.g. Among many, gynecomorphous jars made by Picasso.

9. The topological conception of the jar here refers to the orientation of the vessel's axis of revolution. Ovoid jars ('like churns', once again this is rather confusing) described by Mellaart (1975) might stand for women: their painting designs are evocative of breasts, or even figure women. Indeed, their topological conception is vertical.

10. Dollfus and Kafafi 1995: Fig. 4.6; Ussishkin 1980: Fig. 11.

11. Etymologically cornet means horn-shaped (latin *cornu* and from Medieval French, *see* the Webster dictionary). With the exception of Grar's pottery assemblage, spikes often decorate cornets rims (Fig. 4.4, 5 and 9, and see Commenge-Pellerin 1990: Fig. 36.6).

12. In addition to this more common interpretation that associates Gilat's figurative vessels with a cult of milk, Amiran (1989:56) substituted a cult promoting water and thus rain.

13. At Hacilar, the Goddess seated on a panther, cuddles a child or a baby panther.

14. Incidentally, E. Peltenberg, referring to a model proposed by Friedman and Rowlands, suggests that the Kissornerga birth figurines can stand for 'bride-price' and be part of a hierarchical system of exchange in a feasting context (Peltenberg 1993:14).

15. Discussing Boas, and in reference to the myth described above, Levi-Strauss shows that matrilinear and patrilinear active elements structure the Kwakiutl society fostering the goddess Dzonokwa (Levi-Strauss 1979:77, 142–6). See also, for insight on Kwakiult as an intermediate society: Arnold 1996:64.

16. That, unfortunately, was not available for petrographic investigation.

17. Hacilar I figurines are mostly incomplete and with no possible contest, are three-dimensional representations. With the exception of the name 'violin figurines' (see Weippert 1998), they bear little in common with Gilat's figurines.

18. To that typological extent, the proposed definition fits both Aegean and south Levantine specimens. However, the temporal disparity between the two assemblages precludes establishing any cultural link between the two regions at this time.

19.

20. The hardness scale established by Mohs and based on relative scratch hardness of rocks certainly does not offer a sufficient scientific basis. We consider here that it is convenient for establishing, empirically, a relative scale of hardness between the listed rocks.

21. A rough, tabular fragment of porphyric granite recovered at Abu Matar (thickness: 4.1 cm) can illustrate this process (Commenge forthcoming).

22. For all the percentages registered in this paragraph and cf. Table 15.9a percentage on total of stone specimens (stone vsf specimens=71)/ percentage total of minimal number of individuals (stone vsf m.n.i. = 48).

23. This technique is perhaps rooted in the Neolithic tradition- and by then already dedicated to elaborate and symbolic artifacts. From a techno-cultural and diachronical point of view, the choice of angular and tabular artifacts as a valuable medium for symbolic representation, can perhaps be traced to the Sha'ar Ha'Golan phase of the Pottery Neolithic (Munhata 2B). Very rare in this Neolithic groundstone assemblage,

technical and stylistic investment is reflected in complex and organized patterns of incisions that cover the plane faces (Gopher and Orelle 1995: Fig x:2–3).

24.   The figurines are not perfectly plane, leading to a slightly lateral view for some of them when drawn. Typological consideration is given from a 90° angle view of each part of the figurine.

25.   These estimates are based on the assumption that the initial rock represented six times the final by-product. Thus, one VSF of $12 \times 5 \times 0.5$ cm$= 30$cm^3 is estimated coming out of a block whose length and width was only one third larger than the VSF, and the thickness three times larger $= 18 \times 7.5 \times 1.5$cm $= 202.5$cm^3, and $202.5/30 = 6.75$. From my own experience at chipping stone, reduction to one-third of the original thickness seems reasonable as one should anticipate and carefully negotiate risks of breakage.

26.   Diffusion of turquoise from this southern Sinai site could have primarily concerned Egypt.

27.   The production and the distribution of artifacts made from igneous rocks (basalt, scoriae and pumice) indicate at least two systems of production. Basalt vessels, that require high-skilled and time-consuming techniques, are the by-products of workshops located at the source-deposits, most probably in Transjordan or in northern Palestine (cf. Philip *et al.* 2000). Scoria or pumice palettes are light pieces of rocks, which may have been collected from tumbles and/or from secondary deposits such as wadi beds. They are *ad hoc* artifacts whose original smooth and flattened shape has necessitated little reduction work.

28.   As defined by Costin 1991:11.

29.   The fact that the minimal number of limestone specimens is probably under-estimated should be reiterated here. It is easy to isolate colored exogenous fragments, less easy to decide, besides counting bases and heads, whether limestone fragmented shoulders belong to the same specimen or not.

30.   Being not involved in manufacturing processes, evidence of trade would thus be absent at their camps.

31.   Heights obtained along the vertical and median axis of each body part, whatever its orientation.

32.   Ivory statuettes present proportions that strikingly contrast with the ones of violin-shaped figurines. More specifically they have a rather regular and relatively static frontal outline due to the original and cylindrical shape of the tusk that determines the framing, while the profile displays a more audacious and rhythmic shift of volumes (Perrot 1959: Fig. Pl. II). By the end of the Chalcolithic period in the Beersheva area, the range of tabular artifacts made from both local or exogenous rocks excluded violin figurines and tokens and narrowed to palettes, spindle-whorls and pendants.

33.   But also, on the same chronological horizon, in the cultures of Hassuna or Samarra.

34.   Means of representation are elliptical. It seems perhaps immaterial to dwell on an elongated neck for violin figurines, and on the absence of neck for Sha'ar Ha'Golan figurines (Garfinkel 1995:33) insofar as the importance given to the head is a common character.

35.There are no grounds for asserting the reconstitution of horns at the top of heads.

36.   Hair or some kind of hair-dress was set by means of 'eyelets' around the head of ivory figurines.

37.   Some other Chalcolithic figurines that do not belong to the violin figurine category, as defined in our introduction, are represented with breasts (Mallon *et al.* 1934:84 Fig. 34:2 and one, from Gilat see Fig. 15. 20:2).

38.   We are referring here to the authors' Group V figurines, of the type of the famous Venus of Munhata.

39.   Borrowing here a term used by Le Brun in another context, Le Brun 1989:178).

40.   Exploitation of 'gendered' context seems not yet exploited for new excavations data such as Nahal Zehora (Gopher and Orelle 1996:273).

41.   Fertility rites in the ethnographic record use *infant* figurines rather than women representation (Talalay 1993:43).

42.   Violin figurines in their two-dimensional, impalpable appearance would indeed transcend and deny reality–in the way Lewis Carroll's deck of cards characters do.

43.   Here following Durkheim (Durkheim 1912).

44.   Whose polymorphism seems related to mythic references cf. Sperber 1979.

45. Munhata figurines were recovered from pits in a large area plastered with *pise*, a small 'plazza' surrounded by buildings (Munhata 2A). Commenge, pers. obs.

46. Based on Neolithic representation and not on a pre-supposed universal binary nature of symbolism.

47. Those, once again being here excluded.

48. The recent discovery of violin figurines in a funerary context (Gal pers.com.) may indicate that allegiance was directed at ancestral entities. Peqi'in will certainly provide many clues to our understanding of Chalcolithic societies.

49. One animal figurine from Mureybet IIIA (PPNA) is made from clay.

50. That is with not obvious and intentional addition of temper.

51. Two additional and unidentified fragments come respectively from Abu Matar and Safadi, and one Wadi Ghazzeh, site H (collections of the Centre de Recherche Français de Jérusalem, J. Perrot excavations n.d.).

52. Pigs were common at Gilat and Grar although entirely absent from the Beersheva sites, in the Beersheva basin (see Chapter 6, this volume).

53. Our thanks to Caroline Grigson for providing all information concerning gazelle and ibex.

54. Flattened balls of clay presenting a centered cupule and which were set on the back of large (length c. 16 cm) animal figurines, were also prepared in this pit: Dollfus and Kafafi 1995: Fig 3:3.

55. A similar conclusion has been proposed for Middle and Late Neolithic figurines (human and animal) from Franchti (Talalay 1993:33).

56. Evidence for differentiation of products and differentiation between social groups involved in pottery making was observed in Uttar-Pradesh and Bihar (India) in a technical milieu not so different from Gilat's. Mahias notes that '(no) group could hope to attain the status of those who model figurines of deities and claim superiority over the pot-makers' (Mahias 1993:174, cf. Saraswati 1978:32).

57. Prehistoric examples relate to human physical abnormality, such as the six-toed statues from Ain Ghazzal (Rollefson 1986).

58. In Late Neolithic contexts, one sexed ewe and one ewe with udders are recorded at Munahata (Garfinkel 1995: Fig. 33:2 and Fig. 38:1).

59. 367 vessels (complete vessels and bases) are recorded at Ein Gedi, see Chapter 10, and Ussishkin 1980.

60. Unpublished and exhibited at the Louvre Museum; Commenge forthcoming.

61. Stratum IIIB is characterized by an industry of blades (with a characteristic canaanean technique, see for Gilat: Rowan and Levy 1991) and a nascent metallurgy. Ras Shamra level IIIB represents either an occupation site roughly contemporary to Gilat or slightly latter.

62. This seal should be replaced in the Neolithic northern tradition.

63. A bucranium pendant from baked clay was associated (together with one gazelle and one bear figurine) the ram head/phallus pendant from Basta (Hermansen 1997: 333–4).

References

Aldenderfer, M. (1993) Ritual, hierarchy, and change in foraging societies. *Journal of Anthropological Archaeology* 12: 1–40.

Alon, D. (1961) Early settlement along the Nahal Garar and Nahal Patish. *M'befnim* 1: 87–96

— (1976) Two cult vessels from Gilat. *Atiqot* 11: 116–18.

— (1977) A Chalcolithic temple at Gilat. *The Biblical Archaeologist* 40/2: 63–5.

Alon, D., and Levy, T.E. (1989) The archaeology of cult and the Chalcolithic sanctuary at Gilat. *Journal of Mediterranean Archaeology* 2: 163–221.

Amiran, R. (1976) Note on the Gilat vessels. *Atiqot* 11: 119–20.

— (1989) The Gilat goddess, and the temples of Gilat, En-Gedi and Ai. In *L'Urbanisation de la Palestine de l'Age du Bronze Ancien. Bilan et Perspectives des Recherches Actuelles*, edited by P. de Miroschedji. BAR International Series 527/1. Oxford: British Archaeological Reports, pp. 53–60.

Amiran, R., and Porat, N. (1984) The basalt bowls of the Chalcolithic period and the Early Bronze Age I. *Tel Aviv* 11: 11–19.

Amiran, R., and Tadmor, M. (1980) A female cult statuette from Chalcolithic Beer-sheba. *Israel Exploration Journal* 30: 140–7.

Arnold, J.E. (1987) *Craft specialization in the Prehistoric Channel Islands, California*. Berkeley: University of California Press.

— (1996) Organizational transformations: power and labor among complex hunter-gatherers and other intermediate societies. In *Emergent Complexity: The Evolution of Complex Societies*, edited by J.E. Arnold. International Monographs in Prehistory, Archaeological Series 9. Ann Arbor: pp. 59–73.

Arnold, J. E., and Munns, A. (1994) Independent or attached specialization: the organization of shell bead production in California. *Journal of Field Archaeology* 21: 473–87.

Bahn, P. (1986) No sex please, we are Aurignacians. *Rock Art Research* 3: 99–120.

Bailey, D.W. (1994) Reading prehistoric figurines as individuals. *World Archaeology* 25/3: 321–31.

— (1996) The interpretation of figurines: the emergence of illusion and new ways of seeing, In Viewpoint: Can we interpret figurines? *Cambridge Archaeological Journal* 6/2: 291–5.

Bar Adon, P. (1980) *The Cave of the Treasure*. The Israel Exploration Society: Jerusalem

Barley, N. (1994) *Smashing Pots: Feats of Clay from Africa*. London: British Museum Press.

Bar Yosef, O., and Alon, D. (1988) *Nahal Hemar Cave. Atiqot* 18. Jerusalem: Israel Department of Antiquities and Museums.

Beaudry, M., Cook, L., and Mrozowski, S. (1991) Artefacts and active voices: material culture as social discourse. In *The Archaeology of Inequality*, edited by R. McGuire and R. Paynter. Oxford: Blackwell, pp. 150–91.

Bednarik, R.G. (1990–91) Epistemology in paleoart studies. *Origini* 15: 57–78.

Bell, C. (1992) *Ritual Theory, Ritual Practice*. Oxford and New York: Oxford University Press.

Beit Arieh, I. (1975) A Chalcolithic work station near Serabit el Khadem. *Qadmoniot* 8: 62–4 (Hebrew).

— (1980) A Chalcolithic site near Serabit el-Khadim. *Tel Aviv* 7: 45–65.

Beit Arieh, I. and Gophna, R. (1977) A note on a Chalcolithic site in Wadi Araba. *Tel Aviv* 4: 105–9.

Bernstein, R.J. (1983) *Beyond objectivism and relativism: science, hermeneutics and praxis*. Philadelphia: University of Pennsylvania Press.

Bessac, J.-C. (1986) *L'Outillage Traditionnel du Tailleur de Pierre, de l'Antiquité de nos Jours*. Paris: Editions du CNRS.

Blackham, M. (1999) Tulaylat Ghassul: an appraisal of Robert North's excavations (1959–60). *Levant* 31: 19–64.

Bolger, D. (1993) The feminine mystique: gender and society in prehistoric Cyprus studies. *Report of the Department of Antiquities, Cyprus*: 29–41.

— (1996) Figurines, fertility, and the emergence of complex society in Prehistoric Cyprus. *Current Anthropology* 37/2: 365–73.

Bonnano, A. (1985) Archaeology and Fertility Cult in ancient Mediterranea. *Papers presented at the First International Conference on Archaeology of the Ancient Mediterranea*. Amsterdam: B.R. Gruner.

Broman Morales, V. (1983) Jarmo figurines and other clay objects. In *Prehistoric Archaeology along the Zagros Flanks*, edited by L.S. Braidwood, R.J. Braidwood, B. Howe, C.A. Reed and P.J. Watson. University of Chicago, Oriental Institute Publications 105. Chicago: Chicago University Press, pp. 369–423.

— (1990) *Figurines and other Clay Objects from Sarab and Cay_nŸ*. Chicago: University of Chicago Press.

Brumfiel, E.M., and Earle, T.K. (eds) (1987) *Specialization, Exchange and Complex Societies*. New Directions in Archaeology. Cambridge: Cambridge University Press.

Cameron. D.O. (1981) *The Ghassulian Walls Paintings*. London: Kenyon-Deane.

Cauvin, J. (1972) *Religions Neolithiques de Syrie-Palestine*. Paris: Librairie d'Amérique et d'Orient, Jean Maisonneuve.

— (1978) *Les Premiers Villages de Syrie-Palestine du IXi au VIIi millenaire avant J. -C.* Collection de la Maison de l'Orient Mediterraneen Ancien 4, s_rie Archeologique 3. Lyon: Maison de l'Orient; Paris: de Boccard.

— (1979) Les fouilles de Mureybet (1971–1974) et leur signification pour la sedentaristation au Proche-Orient. *Annual of the American School for Oriental Research* 44: 19–48.

— (1980) Mureybet et Cheikh Hassan. In *Le Moyen Euphrate, zone de contacts et d'echanges*, edited by J. Margueron. Strasbourg: Universite des Sciences Humaines, pp. 21–34.

— (1985) La question du 'matriarcat prehistorique' et le r™le de la femme dans la Prehistoire. In *La Femme dans le Monde Mediterraneen. I. Antiquite*, edited by A.-M. V_rilhac. Lyon: Maison de l'Orient Mediterraneen, pp. 7–18.

— (1994) *Naissance des Divinites, Naissance de l'Agriculture: La Revolution des Symboles au Neolithique.* Paris: CNRS Editions.

Cauvin, M.-C. (ed.) (1990) *Rites et Rythmes Agraires.* Collection Travaux de la Maison de l'Orient 20. Lyon: Maison de l'Orient.

Clark, J.E. and Parry, W. J. (1990) Craft specialization and cultural complexity. *Research in Economic Anthropology* 12: 289–346.

Commenge-Pellerin, C. (1987) *La Poterie d'Abou Matar et de l'Ouadi Zoumeili (Beersheva) au IVi millénaire avant l'ére chrétienne.* Cahiers du Centre de Recherche Français de Jérusalem 3. Paris: Association Paléorient.

— (1990) *La Poterie de Safadi (Beersheva) au IVi millénaire avant l'ére chrétienne.* Cahiers du Centre de Recherche Français de Jérusalem 5. Paris: Association Paléorient.

— (2002) Competitive involution and expanded horizons: exploring the nature of interaction between northern Negev and Lower Egypt (ca. 4500–3600 b.c.e) In *Egypt and the Levant Interrelations from the 4th through the Early 3rd Millennium BCE*, edited by E.C.M. van den Brink and T.E. Levy. New Approaches to Anthropological Archaeology. London and New York: Continuum, pp. 139–53.

— (forthcoming) *The Chalcolithic Groundstone Assemblage of the Beersheva Sites, Israel.*

Conkey, M.W. (1978) Style and information in cultural evolution: towards a predictive model for the Paleolithic. In *Social Archaeology, Beyond Subsistence and Dating*, edited by C. Redman *et al.* New York: Academic Press, pp. 61–85.

— (1985) Ritual communication, social elaboration and the variable trajectories of Paleolithic material culture. In *Prehistoric Hunters-Gatherers: The Emergence of Social and Cultural Complexity*, edited by T.D. Price and J.A. Brown. New York: Academic Press, pp. 299–323.

— (1987) New approaches in the search of meaning, a review of research in 'Paleolithic Art'. *Journal of Field Archaeology* 14/4: 413–30.

Conkey, M. and Spector, J. (1984) Archaeology and the study of gender. In *Advances in Archaeological Method and Theory*, 7, edited by M. Schiffer. Orlando: Academic Press, pp. 1–38.

Contenson de, H. (1983) Early agriculture in Western Asia. In *The Hilly Flanks and Beyond, Essays on the Prehistory of Southwestern Asia, Presented to R.J. Braidwood*, edited by T.C. Young, P.E.L. Smith and P. Mortensen. Studies in Ancient Oriental Civilization 36. Chicago: Chicago University Press, pp. 57–74.

— (1989) L'Aswadien, un nouveau faciés du Néolithique syrien. *Paléorient* 15/1, pp. 259–61.

— (ed) (1992) *Préhistoire de Ras Shamra. Les sondages stratigraphiques de 1955 à 1976.* Ras Shamra-Ougarit VIII (2 volumes). Paris: Editions Recherche sur les Civilisations.

Costin, C. L. (1991) Craft specialization: issues in defining, documenting, and explaining the organization of production. In *Archaeological Methods and Theory* 3, edited by M.B. Schiffer. Tucson: The University of Arizona Press, pp. 1–56.

Courtois, L. (1992) Examen au microscope pétrographique de poteries néolithiques de Ras Shamra V et IV. In *Préhistoire de Ras Shamra. Les sondages stratigraphiques de 1955 à 1976*, edited by H. de Contenson. Ras Shamra-Ougarit VIII (2 volumes). Paris: Editions Recherche sur les Civilisations, pp. 209–22.

D'Altroy, T. and Earle, T.K. (1985) Staple finance, wealth finance, and storage in the Inca political economy. *Current Anthropology* 26/2: 187–206.

David, N., Sterner, J., and Gavua, K. (1988) Why pots are decorated. *Current Anthropology* 29: 365–89

Davis, S. (1984) The advent of milk and wool production in western Iran: some speculations. In *Animals and Archaeology 3. Early Herders and their Flocks*, edited by J. Clutton-Brock and C. Grigson. BAR International Series 202. Oxford: British Archaeological Reports, pp. 265–78.

Davis, W. (1986) The origins of image making. *Current Anthropology* 27/3: 193–216.

Descola, P. (1987) *La Nature Domestique: Symbolism et Praxis dans l'Ecologie des Achuars*. Paris: Editions de la Maison des Sciences de l'Homme.

Détienne, M. (1981) *L'Invention de la Mythologie*. Paris: Gallimard.

Digard, J.-P. (1990) *L'Homme et les Animaux Domestiques. Anthropologie d'une Passion*. Paris: Fayard.

Dobres, M.-A. (1992) Re-considering Venus figurines: a feminist-inspired re-analysis. In *Ancient Images, Ancient Thoughts: The Archaeology of Ideology*, edited by A.S. Goldsmith, S. Garvie, D. Selin and J. Smith. Calgary: University of Calgary Archaeological Association, pp. 245–62.

Dollfus, G., Kafafi, Z., Rewerski, J., Vaillant, N., Coqueugniot, E., Desse, J. and Neef, R. (1988) Abu Hamid, an early fourth millenium site in the Jordan Valley. Preliminary results. In *The Prehistory of Jordan. The State of Research in 1986*, edited by A.N. Garrard and H.G. Gebel, pp. 567–601. BAR International Series 396 (2 volumes). Oxford: British Archaeological Reports.

Dollfus, G. and Kafafi, Z. (1995) Représentations humaines et animales sur le site d'Abu Hamid (mi-7i-début 6i millénaire BP). In *Studies in the History and Archaeology of Jordan 5*, edited by K. Amr, F. Zayadine and M. Zaghloul, pp. 449–56.

Douglas, M. (1973) *Natural Symbols*. New York: Random House.

— (1975) *Implicit Meanings: Essays in Anthropology*. Routledge: London & New York.

Ducos, P. (1968) *L'Origine des Animaux Domestiques en Palestine*. Bordeaux: Delmas.

— (1973) Sur quelques problèmes posés par l'étude des premiers élevages en Asie du sud-ouest. In *Domestikationsforschung und Geschichte der Haustiere*, edited by J. Matolcsi. Akademiai Kiado.

Dunand, M. (1973) L'Architecture, les tombes, le matériel domestique, des origines néolithiques à l'avénement urbaine. In *Fouilles de Byblos*, tome V (2 vols). Paris: Jean Maisonneuve.

Durkheim, E. (1912) *Les Formes Elémentaires de la Vie Religieuse*. Paris (1965 *The Elementary Forms of Religious Life*. New York: Free Press).

Earle, T. (1981) Comment on P. Rice: Evolution of specialized pottery production: a trial model. *Current Anthropology* 22/3: 230–31.

Eisenberg, E. (1993) Kitan, Tell. In *The New Encyclopedia of Archaeological Excavations in the Holy Land*, 3, edited by E. Stern. New York & Jerusalem: The Israel Exploration Society and Carta, pp. 878–81.

Epstein, C. (1978) A new aspect of Chalcolithic culture. *Bulletin of the American Schools of Oriental Research* 229: 27–45.

— (1982) Cult symbols in Chalcolithic Palestine. *Bolletino del Centro Camuno di Studi Preistorici* 19: 63–81.

— (1985) Laden animal figures from Chalcolithic Palestine. *Bulletin of the American Schools of Oriental Research* 258: 53–60.

— (1998) *The Chalcolithic Culture of the Golan*. Israel Antiquities Authority Reports 4. Jerusalem: IAA publications.

Evans, J. and Renfrew, C. (1968) *Excavations at Saliagos, near Antiparos*. London: Thames & Hudson.

Eygun, G. (1992) Les figurines humaines et animales du site néolithique de Ganj Dareh(Iran). *Paléorient* 18/1: 109–17

Feblot-Augustins J. and Perles, C. (1992) Perspectives ethno-archeologiques sur les changes à longue distance. In *Ethno-archeologie, Justification, Problemes et Limites*, edited by F. Audouze, A. Gallay and V. RouxJuan-les-Pins: APDCA, pp. 195–209.

Fernandez, J.W. (1965) Symbolic consensus in a Fang reformative cult. *American Anthropologist* 67: 902–29.

— (1974) The mission of the metaphor in expressive culture. *Current Anthropology* 15: 119–45.

— (1977) The performance of ritual metaphors. In *The Social Use of Metaphor: Essays on the Anthropology of Rhetoric*, edited by J. David Sapir and C. Crocker. Philadelphia: University of Pennsylvania Press, pp. 100–31.

Fernandez, G. and Fernandez, N. (2000) http://ourworld.compuserve.com/homepages/Nic_Frndz/typolofr. htm.

Forest, J.-D. (1993) Çatal Hüyük et son décor: pour le déchiffrement d'un code symbolique. *Anatolica Antiqua* 2: 1–42.

Foucault, M. (1966) *Les Mots et les Choses*. Paris: Gallimard (1994 *The Order of Things—an Archaeology of the Human Sciences*. Vintage Books Editions).

Gal, Z., Smithline, H., and Shalem, D. (1997) A Chalcolithic burial Cave in Peqi'in, Upper Galilee. *Israel Exploration Journal*, 47/3-4: 145–54.

Gamble, C. (1982) Interaction and alliance in Paleolithic society. *Man* 17: 92–107.

Garfinkel, Y. (1994) Ritual burial of cultic objects: the earliest evidence. *Cambridge Archaeological Journal* 4/2: 159–88.

— (1995) *Human and Animal Fi gurines of Munhata (Israel)*. Cahiers du Centre de Recherche Français de Jérusalem 8. Paris: Association Paléorient.

— (1999) *The Yarmukians: Neolithic Art from Sha'ar Hagolan*. Jerusalem: Bible Lands Museum.

Garfinkel, Y., and Miller, M. (2002) *Sha'ar Hagolan: Neolithic Art in Context*. Oxford: Oxbow.

Gell, A. (1993) *Wrapping in Images: tattooing in Polynesia*. Oxford: Clarendon Press.

Geertz, C. (1973) *The Interpretation of Cultures*. New York: Basic Books.

— (1983) *Local Knowledge: Further Essays in Interpretive Anthropology*. New York: Basic Books.

Gilead, I. (1995) *Grar, a Chalcolithic Site in the Northern Negev*. Studies by the Department of Bible and Ancient Near-East, 7. Beersheva: Ben Gurion University of the Negev Press.

Gilead, I., and Goren, Y. (1986) Stations of the Chalcolithic period in Nahal Sekher, Northern Negev. *Paléorient* 12/1: 83–90.

Gill, D.W. and Chippendale, C. (1993) Material and intellectual consequences of esteem for Cycladic figurines. *American Journal of Archaeology* 97: 601–59.

Gimbutas, M. (1982) *The Goddess and Gods from Old Europe, 6500–3500 BC: Myths, Cult and Images*. London: Thames & Hudson.

Gopher A. and Orelle, E. (1996) An alternative interpration for the material imagery of the Yarmukian, a Neolithic culture of the sixth millenium BC in the Southern Levant. *Cambridge Archaeological Journal*, 6/2: 255–79.

Gophna, R. (1976) Excavations at En Besor. *Atiqot* 14: 9–16.

Gorring, E. (1991) The anthropomorphic figurines. In *Lemba Archaeological Project, vol. II, 2. A ceremonial area at Kissonerga*, edited by E. Peltenburg *et al.* Studies in Mediterranean Archaeology 73/3. Göteborg: Paul Astroms, pp. 39–60.

Graves-Brown, P.M. (1995) Fearful symmetry. *World Archaeology* 27 (1): 88–9.

Grigson, C. (1987) Pastoralism and other aspects of animal management in the Chalcolithic of the Northern Negev. In *Shiqmim I, Studies concerning Chalcolithic Societies in the Northern Negev Desert, Israel (1982–1984)*, edited by T.E. Levy. BAR International Series 356 (2 volumes). Oxford: British Archaeological Reports, pp. 219–42.

— (1988) Different herding strategies for sheep and goats in the Chalcolithic of Beersheva. *Archaeozoologia* 1/2: 115–25.

— (1989) Size and sex-morphometric evidence for the domestication of cattle in the Near- East. In *The Beginnings of Agriculture*, edited by A. Milles, D. Williams and N. Gardner. BAR International Series 496. Oxford: British Archaeological Reports, pp. 77–91.

— (1993) The earliest domestic horses in the Levant? New finds from the Fourth millenium of the Negev. *Journal of Archaeological Science* 20: 645–55.

— (1995) Cattle keepers of the northern Negev: animal remains from the Chalcolithic site of Grar. In *Grar, a Chalcolithic site in the Northern Negev*, edited by I. Gilead. Beersheva: Ben Gurion University Press, pp. 377–452.

Guenther, M. (1988) Animals in Bushman thought, myth and art. In *Hunters and Gatherers, 2: Property, Power and Ideology*, edited by T. Ingold, D. Riches and J. Woodburn. Berg: New York and Oxford, pp. 192–202.

Haaland G. and Haaland, R. (1996) Levels of meaning in symbolic objects, In Viewpoint: Can we interpret figurines? *Cambridge Archaeological Journal* 6/2: 295–300.

Hahn, J. (1986) *Kraft und aggression: die Botschaft der Eiszeitkunst im Aurignacien suddeutschlands?* Tübingen: Archeologia Venatoria.

Hamilton, N. (1994) A fresh look at the 'seated-gentleman' in the Pierides Foundation Museum, Republic of Cyprus. *Cambridge Archaeological Journal* 4/2: 302–12.

— (1996) The personal is political, In Viewpoint: Can we interpret figurines? *Cambridge Archaeological Journal* 6/2: 282–5.

Hauptmann, H. (1993) Ein Kult GebaŸde in Nevali Cori. In *Between the Rivers and over the Mountains*, edited by M. Frangipane, H. Hauptmann, H. Liveratti, P. Matthiae and P. Mellink. Rome: Universita di Roma 'La Sapienza', pp. 37–69.

Hauptmann, A. and Weisgerber, G. (1987) Archaeometallurgical and mining archaeological investigations in the area of Feinan, Wadi Arabah (Jordan). *Annual of The Department of Antiquities of Jordan* 31: 419–35.

Hayden, B. (1992) Observing Prehistoric women. In *Exploring Gender through Archaeology, Selected Papers from the 1991 Boone Conference*, edited by C. Claassen. Monographs in Prehistory 11, Prehistory Press: Madison, Wisconsin, pp. 33–48.

Hermansen, B. Dahl (1997) Art and ritual behaviour in Neolithic Basta. In *The Prehistory of Jordan, II. Perspectives from 1997*, edited by H.G.K. Gebel, Z. Kafafi and G. Rollefson. Studies in the Early Production, Subsistence and Environment 4. Berlin: Ex Oriente, pp. 333–43.

Hodder, I. (1982) *Symbolic and Structural Archaeology*. Cambridge: Cambridge University Press.

— (1983) *Symbols in Action*. Cambridge: Cambridge University Press.

— (ed.) (1989) *The Meaning of Things*. London: Unwin Hyman.

Holland, T.A. (1982) Figurines and miscellaneous objects. In *Excavations at Jericho*, vol 4, edited by K.M. Kenyon and T.A. Holland. London & The British School of Archaeology, pp. 551–63.

Houmourziadis, G. (1973) *I Anthropomorphi Idoloplastiki tis Neolithikis Thessalias*. Volos.

Ilani, S. and Rosenfeld, A. (1994) Ore sources of arsenic copper tools from Israel during Chalcolithic and Early Bronze ages. *Terra Research*: 177–9.

Ingold, T. (1986) *The Appropriation of Nature: essays on human ecology and social relations*. Manchester: Manchester University Press.

Johnson, G.A. (1973) *Local Exchange and Early State Development in Southwest Iran*. Anthropological Papers 51. Ann Arbor: The University of Michigan Museum of Anthropology.

Johnson, M. (1987) *The Body in the Mind: the Bodily Basis of Meaning, Imagination and Reason*. Chicago and London: Chicago University Press.

Kafafi, Z. (1988) Jebel Abu Thawwab. A pottery Neolithic village in north Jordan. In *The Prehistory of Jordan: The State of Research in 1986*, edited by A. Garrard and H.G. Gebel. BAR International Series 396 (2 volumes). Oxford: British Archaeological Reports, pp. 451–71.

Karlin, C. (1992) Connaissance et savoir faire: comment analyser un processus technique en Préhistoire. In *Reunion Internacional, Tecnologia y cadenas operativas liticas*. Barcelona: Universita autonoma, pp. 99–124.

Kirkbride, D. (1966) Five seasons at the Pre-Pottery Neolithic village of Beidha in Jordan. A summary. *Palestine Exploration Quaterly* 98/1: 8–61.

— (1968) Beidha 1967: an interim report. *Palestine Exploration Quaterly* 99: 90–6.

Koeppel, R., Mallon, R., Neuville, R. (1940) *Teleilat Ghassul II*. Rome: Pontifical Biblical Institute.

Köhler-Rollefson, I. (1992) A model for the development of nomadic pastoralism on the Transjordanian plateau. In *Pastoralism in the Levant, Archaeological Materials in Anthropological Perspectives*, edited by O. Bar-Yosef and A. Khazanov. Monographs in World Archaeology 10. Madison: Prehistory Press, pp. 11–18.

Kosloff, B. (1972/73) A brief note on the lithic industries of Sinai. *Museum Ha'aretz Yearbook* 15/16: 35–49.

Lawson, E.T. and McCauley, R.N. (1990) *Rethinking Religion: Connecting Cognition and Culture*. Cambridge: Cambridge University Press.

Leach, E. (1976) *Culture and Communication*. Cambridge: Cambridge University Press.

Le Brun, A (1989) *Fouilles Récentes à Khirokitia (Chypre): 1983–1986*. Paris: Editions Recherche sur les Civilisations.

Lechevallier, M. (1978) *Abou Gosh et Beisamoun, Deux Gisements du VIIi millénaire avant l'ére chrétienne en Israél*. Mémoires et Travaux du Centre de Recherche Français de Jérusalem 2. Paris: Association Paléorient.

Lee, R. (1973) *Chalcolithic Ghassul: New Aspects and Master Typology*. PhD thesis. Jerusalem: Hebrew University.

Lemonnier, P. (1986) The study of material culture today: towards an anthropology of technical systems. *Journal of Anthropological Archaeology* 5: 147–86.

— (1991) De la culture matérielle ˆ la culture? Ethnologie des techniques et Préhistoire. In *25 ans d'Etudes Technologiques en Préhistoire*. XIi Rencontres d'Arch_ologie et d'Histoire d'Antibes. Juan-les-Pins: Editions APDCA, pp. 15–20.

— (1992) *Elements for an Anthropology of Technology*. Anthropological Papers 88. Ann Arbor: The University of Michigan Museum of Anthropology.

— (ed.) (1992) *Technological Choices. Transformation in Material Cultures since the Neolithic*. London and New York: Routledge.

Leroi-Gourhan, A. (1945) (reprinted in 1973) *Evolution et Techniques: Milieu et Techniques*. Paris: Albin Michel.

— (1964) (reprinted 1983) *Les Religions de la Préhistoire*. Paris. Presses Universitaires de France.

— (1965) *Le Geste et la Parole - I, Technique et Langage. -II, la Mémoire et les Rythmes*. Paris: Albin Michel.

— (1970) Observations technologiques sur le rythme statuaire. *Echanges et Communications, Mélanges offerts à Claude Lévi-Strauss*. La Haye: Mouton, pp. 658–76.

Levi-Strauss, C. (1962) Le Totémisme aujourd'hui. Paris: Payot (*Totemism*. London: Merlin Press).

— (1979) *La Voie des Masques*. Paris: Plon. (1982 *The Way of the Masks*. Seattle: University of Washington Press).

— (1985) *La Potiere Jalouse*. Paris: Plon. (1988 *The Jealous Potter*. Chicago: University of Chicago Press).

Levy, T.E. (1983) The emergence of specialized pastoralism in the Southern Levant. *World Archaeology* 15: 15–36.

— (ed.) (1987) Shiqmim I. *Studies Concerning Chalcolithic Societies in the Norhern Negev Desert, Israel (1982–1984)*. BAR International Series 356 (2 volumes). Oxford: British Archaeological Reports.

Levy, T.E., Adams, R.B., and Najjar, M.
(1999) *Early metallurgy and social evolution: Jabal Hamrat Fidan*. ACOR Newletter 11(1): 1–3.

Levy, T.E., and Golden, J. (1996) Syncretistic and mnemonic dimensions of Chalcolithic art: a New human figurine from Shiqmim. *The Biblical Archaeologist* 59/3: 150–9.

Levy, T.E., and Shalev, S. (1989) Prehistoric metalworking in the Southern Levant: archaeometallurgical and social perspectives. *World Archaeology* 20: 353–72.

Macdonald, E., Starkey, J. L., and Lankester-Harding, G.L. (1932) *Beth-Pelet II. Prehistoric Fara*. Series of the British School of Archaeology in Egypt, 52. London: Bernard Qaritch and British Shool of Archaeology in Egypt.

Mahias, M.-C. (1993) Pottery techniques in India. Technical variants and social choice. In *Technological Choices: Transformation in Material Cultures since the Neolithic*, edited by P. Lemonnier. Routledge: London and New York, pp. 157–80.

Mallon, S.J., Koeppel, R., and Neuville, R. (1934) *Teleilat Ghassul I, Compte-Rendu des Fouilles de l'Institut Biblique Pontifical 1929–1932*. Rome.

Marangou, Ch. (1992) *Eidolia, Figurines et Miniatures du Neolithique Recent et du Bronze Ancient en Grece*. BAR International Series 576. Oxford: British Archaeological Reports.

Marcus, J. (1996) The importance of context in interpreting figurines, in Viewpoint: Can we interpreter figurines? *Cambridge Archaeological Journal* 6/2: 285–91

Marshack, A. (1991) *The Roots of Civilization*. 2nd edn. Mt Kisco-New York: Moyer Bell.

— (1992) The analytical problems of subjectivity in the maker and user. In *The Limitations of Archaeological Knowledge*, edited by T. Shay and J. Clottes. Liége: Université de Liége, pp. 181–210.

— (1995) On the 'geological' explanation of the Berekhat Ram figurine. *Current Anthropology* 36/3: 495.

— (1996) A Middle Paleolithic symbolic composition from the Golan Heights: the earliest known depictive image. *Current Anthropology* 37/2: 357–65.

Mauss, M. (1923–24) Essai sur le don. Forme et raison d'être de l'échange dans les sociétés archaiques. *Année Sociologique*, seconde série, tome I. (1967 The Gift: Forms and Functions of Exchange in Archaic Societies. New York: Norton).

McAdam, E. (1997) The figurines from the 1982–1985 seasons of excavations at Ain Ghazal. *Levant* 29: 115–52.

McDermott, L. (1996) Self-representation in Upper Paleolithic female figurines. *Current Anthropology* 37/2: 227–75.

Mellaart, J. (1967) *Çatal Hüyük, A Neolithic Town in Anatolia*. London: Mortimer Wheeler.

— (1970) *Excavations at Hacilar*. The British School of Archaeology at Ankara Occasionnal Publication 9 (2 vols). Edinburgh: Edinburgh University Press.

— (1975) *The Neolithic of the Near-East*. London: Thames and Hudson.

Merhav, R. (1993) Scepters of the divine from the Cave of the Treasure at Nahal Mishmar. In *Studies in the Archaeology and History of Ancient Israel in Honour of Moshe Dothan*, edited by M. Heltzer, A. Segal and D. Kaufman. Haifa: Haifa University Press, pp. 21–42 (in Hebrew).

Merpert, N.Y., Munchaev, R.M., and Bader, N.O. (1981) Investigation of the Soviet expedition in northern Iraq, 1976. *Sumer* 37: 22–54.

Meskell, L. (1995) Goddesses, Gimbutas and 'New Age' archaeology. *Antiquity* 69: 74–86.

Neuville, R. (1951) Le Paléolithique et le Mésolithique du Désert de Judée. *Archives de l'Institut de Paléonlotologie Humaine* 24. Paris: Masson and Cie.

Noy, T. (1985) Seated clay figurines from the Neolithic period, Israel. In *Archaeology and Fertility Cult in the Ancient Mediterranean: Papers presented at the First International Conference on Archaeology in the Ancient Mediterranean*, edited by A. Bonanno. Amsterdam: B. C. Gruner, pp. 63–7.

Oren, E. and Gilead, I. (1981) Chalcolithic sites in Northeastern Sinai. *Tel Aviv* 8: 25–44.

Özdogan, M., and Özdogan A. (1990) Cay_nŸ, a conspectus of recent works. In *Préhistoire du Levant: Processus des Changements Culturels*, edited by O. Aurenche, M.-C. and P. Sanlavile. Paris: Editions du CNRS, pp. 68–77.

Parsons, E.C. (1919) Increase by magic: a Zuni pattern. *American Anthropologist* 21: 279–86.

Peatfield, A. (1994) Cognitive aspects of religious symbolism: an archaelogist's perspective (review article). *Cambridge Archaeological Journal* 4/1: 149–55.

Peltenburg, E. (1988) A Cypriot model for Prehistoric ritual. *Antiquity* 62: 289–93.

— (1993) Settlement discontinuity and resistance to complexity in Cyprus, ca. 4500–2500 B.C. *Bulletin of the American Schools of Research* 292: 9–24.

Perles, C. (1990) L'outillage de pierre taillée neolithique en Grece: approvisionnement et exploitation des matieres premieres. *Bulletin de Correspondance Hellenique* 114: 1–42.

— (1992) Systems of exchange and organization of production in Neolithic Greece. *Journal of Mediterranean Archaeology* 5/2: 115–64.

Perrot, J. (1955) The excavations at Abu Matar, near Beersheba. *Israel Exploration Journal* 5/3: 167–89.

— (1959) Statuettes en ivoire et autres objets en ivoire et en os provenant de gisements prehistoriques de la region de Beershéba. *Syria* 36:1–2: 7–19.

— (1964) Les ivoires de la 7icampagne de fouilles à Safadi, près de Beersheva. *Eretz-Israel* 7: 92–3.

— (1968) Prehistoire palestinienne. In *Supplement au Dictonnaire de la Bible*, fascicule 43. Paris: Letouze and Ane, pp. 286–479.

Perrot, J. and Ladiray, D. (1980) *Tombes ^ Ossuaires de la Region C™tiere Palestinienne au IVi millénaire avant l'ére chrétienne*. Mémoires et Travaux du Centre de Recherches Préhistoriques Français de Jérusalem 1. Paris: Association Paléorient.

Petrequin, P. (1995) North wind, south wind. In *Technological Choices, Transformation in Material Culture since the Neolithic*, edited by P. Lemonnier. London and New York: Routledge, pp. 36–76.

Petrie, W.M. Flinders (1914) *Amulets*. London: Constable.

— (1920) (1974) *Prehistoric Egypt with corpus of Prehistoric Pottery and Palettes*. London: Aris and Phillips.

Pfaffenberger, B. (1992) The social anthropology of technology. *Annual Review of Anthropology* 21: 491–516.

Philip, G., and Williams-Thorpe, O. (1993) A provenance study of Jordanian basalt vessels of the Chalcolithic and Early Bronze Age periods. *Paléorient* 19/2: 51–63.

— (2000) The production and distribution of ground stone artefacts in the Southern Levant during the 5th–4th milleniua BC: some implications of geochimical and petrographic analysis. In *Proceedings of the First International Congress on the Archaeology of the Ancient Near-East (Rome, May 18th–23rd 1998)*, edited by P. Matthiae, A. Enea, L. Peyronel, and F. Pinnock. Rome, pp. 1380–96.

Postgate, J.N. (1994) Text and figure in ancient Mesopotamia: match and mismatch, In *The Ancient Mind: Elements of Cognitive Archaeology*, edited by C. Renfrew and E.B.W. Zubrow. New Directions in Archaeology. Cambridge: Cambridge University Press, pp. 176–84.

Preziosi, D. (1982) Constructing the origins of Art. *Art Journal* (Winter): 320–5.

Rappaport, R.A. (1979) *Ecology, Meaning and Religion*. Richmond California: North Atlantic Books.

— (1999) *Ritual and Religion in the Making of Humanity*. Cambridge: Cambridge University Press.

Redman, C.L. (1978) *The Rise of Civilization. From Early Farmers to Urban Societies in the Ancient Near East*. San Francisco: W.H. Freeman.

Renfrew, C. (1969) The development and chronology of the Early Cycladic figurines. *American Journal of Archaeology* 73: 1–32.

— (1972) *The Emergence of Civilization: The Cyclads and the Aegean in the Third Millenium BC*. London: Methuen.

— (1984) Trade as action at distance. In *Approaches to Social Archaeology*, edited by C. Renfrew. Cambridge: Harvard University Press, pp. 86–134.

— (1985) *The Archaeology of Cult. -The Sanctuary at Phylakopi*. London: Thames and Hudson.

— (1991) *The Cycladic Spirit: Masterpieces from the P. Goulandris Collection*. New York: Harry N. Abrams.

— (1993) Cognitive archaeology: some thought on the archaeology of thought. *Cambridge Archaeological Journal* 3/2: 247–70.

— (1994) Towards a cognitive archaeology. In *The Archaeology of the Mind. Elements of Cognitive Archaeology*, edited by C. Renfrew and E.B.W. Zubrow. New Directions in Archaeology. Cambridge: Cambridge University Press, pp. 3–12.

Renfrew, C. and Scarre, C. (1998) *Cognition and Material Culture: The Archaeology of Symbolic Storage*. McDonald Institute.

Rice, M. (1997) *The Power of the Bull*. London: Routledge.

Rice, P. (1987) *Pottery Analysis, a Source Book*. Chicago: Chicago University Press.

Ricoeur, P. (1971) The model of the text: meaningful action considered as a text. *Social Research* 38: 529–62.

Rollefson, G.O. (1983) Ritual and ceremonial at Neolithic Ain Ghazal. *Paléorient* 9/2: 29–38.

— (1986) Neolithic at Ain Ghazal: Ritual and ceremonial, II. *Paléorient* 12/1: 45–52.

Rollefson, G. and Simmons, A. (1985) Excavations at 'Ain Ghazal 1984. Preliminary report. *Annual of the Department of Antiquities of Jordan* 29: 11–30.

— (1986) The Neolithic Village of 'Ain Ghazal, Jordan. Preliminary report of the 1984 season. *Bulletin of the American Schools of Oriental Research* suppl. 24: 145–64.

Rollefson, G.O., Simmons, A. and Kafafi, Z. (1992) Neolithic cultures at 'Ain Ghazal, Jordan. *Journal of Field Archaeology* 19: 443–70.

Roodenberg, J.J. (1986) *Le Mobilier en Pierre de Bouqras. Utilisation de la Pierre dans un Site Néolithique sur le Moyen-Euphrate (Syrie)*. Istanbul: Nederlands Historisch-Archaeologisch Instituut; Leiden: Nederlands Instituut voor het Nabije Oosten Witte Singel.

Rosen, S. (1983) The tabular scrapers trade: a model for material culture dispersion. *Bulletin of the American Schools of Research* 249: 79–86.

Roshwalb, A. (1981) *Protohistory in Wadi Ghazzeh: a typological and technological study based on the Macdonald excavations*. Unpublished PhD Dissertation. University of London.

Rothenberg, B. (1972) *Timna: Valley of the Biblical Copper Mines*. London: Thames and Hudson.

Rothenberg, B., Danin, A., Garfunkel, Z., Huber, P., Klopfenstein, M. A., Oren, E., Tchernov, E., and Walser, G. (1979) *Pharaohs, Miners, Pilgrims and Soldiers*. Berne: Kummerly and Frey.

Rowan, Y., and Levy, T.E. (1991) Use-wear analysis of a Chalcolithic scrapers assemblage from Shiqmim. *Mi'tekufat Haeven* 24: 112–34.

Russell, G. (1988) *The Impact of Inka Policy on the Domestic Economy of the Wanka, Peru: Stone Tool Production and Use*. Los Angeles: University of California Press.

Sacher Fox, N. (1995) The striped goddess from Gilat. Implications for the Chalcolithic cult. *Israel Exploration Journal* 45: 212–25.

Saraswati, B.N. (1978) *Pottery-making Cultures and Indian Civilization*. New Dehli: Abhinav Publications.

Schick, T. (1988) A Neolithic cult headdress from the Nahal Hemar Cave. *Israel Museum Journal* 7: 25–33.

Schlanger, N. (1994) Mindful technology: unleashing the *chaine opératoire* for an archaeology of mind. In *The Ancient Mind: Elements of Cognitive Archaeology*, edited by C. Renfrew and E.B.W. Zubrow. New Directions in Archeology. Cambridge: Cambridge University Press, pp. 143–51.

Schmandt-Besserat, D. (1998) 'Ain Ghazzal monumental figurines, *Bulletin of the American Schools of Oriental Research* 310: 1–18.

Sherrat, A. (1981) Plough and pastoralism: aspects of the secondary products revolution, In *Patterns of the Past: Studies in Honour of David Clarke*, edited by I. Hodder, G. Isaac and N. Hammond. Cambridge: Cambridge University Press, pp. 261–305.

Sherratt, S. (2000) *Catalogue of Cycladic antiquities in the Ashmolean Museum: the Captive Spirit*. Mortimer and Theresa Sackler Foundation. Oxford: Oxford University Press.

Smith, C. (1975) Production in western Guatemala: a test of Von Thunen and Boserup. In *Formal Methods in Economic Anthropology*, edited by S. Pallner. American Anthropological Association Special Publication 4. Washington DC: American Anthropological Association, pp. 5–38.

Sperber, D. (1979) La pensée symbolique est-elle pré-rationelle? In *La Fonction Symbolique. Essai d'Anthropologie*, edited by M. Izard and P. Smith. Paris, pp. 17–42.

— (1992) Culture and matter. In *Representations in Archaeology*, edited by J.-C. Gardin and C. Peebles. Bloomington: Indiana University Press, pp. 56–65.

Stekelis, M. (1972) *The Yarmukian Culture of the Neolithic Period*. Jerusalem: The Hebrew University and Magnes Press.

Stekelis, M. and Ysraeli, T. (1963) Excavations at Nahal Oren. Preliminary report. *Israel Exploration Journal* 13/1: 1–17.

Stordeur, D. (1988) *Outils et Armes en Os du Gisement Natoufien de Mallaha (Eynan), Israel*. Mémoires et Travaux du Centre de Recherche Français de Jérusalem 6. Paris: Association Paléorient.

Tadmor, M. (1988) Naturalistic depiction in the Gilat sculpture vessels. *Israel Museum Journal* 5: 7–12.

— (1990) A group of figurines and miniature vessels from the Chalcolithic period. *Eretz Israel* 21: 249–58 (Hebrew).

Talalay, L.E. (1987) Rethinking the function of clay figurines legs from Neolithic Greece: an argument by analogy. *American Journal of Archaeology* 91: 161–9.

— (1993) *Deities, Dolls, and Devices: Neolithic Figurines from Franchti Cave, Greece*. Excavations at Franchti Cave, Greece, Fascicule 9. Bloomington and Indianapolis: Indiana University Press.

Tchernov, E. and Valla, F. (1997) Two new dogs, and other Natufian dogs, from the Southern Levant. *Journal of Archaeological Science* 24: 65–95.

Tilley, C. (1999) *Metaphor and Material Culture*. Oxford: Blackwell.

Torrence, R. (1986) *Production and Exchange of Stone Tools: Prehistoric Obsidian in the Aegean*. Cambridge: Cambridge University Press.

Trigger, B. (1974) The archaeology of government. *World Archaeology* 6: 95–106.

Turner, T.S. (1984) Dual opposition, hierarchy and value. In *Différences, Valeurs et Hierarchie: Textes offerts à Louis Dumont*, edited by J.-C. Galey. Paris: Ecole des Hautes Etudes en Sciences Sociales, pp. 335–70.

Turner, V. (1967) *Forest of Symbols: Aspects of Ndembu Ritual*. New York: Cornell University Press.

— (1969) *The Ritual Process*. Chicago: Aldine.

— (1975) Ritual as communication and potency: a Ndembu case study. In *Symbols and Society: Essays on Belief systems in action*, edited by C.E. Hill. Athens: University of Georgia Press, pp. 58–81.

Ucko, P.J (1968) *Anthropomorphic Figurines of Predynastic Egypt and Neolithic Crete with Comparative Material from Prehistoric Near East and Mainland Greece*. Royal Institute Occasional Papers 24. London: Andrew Szmidla.

— (1996) Mother, are you there, In Viewpoint: Can we interpret figurines? *Cambridge Archaeological Journal* 6/2: 300–4.

Ussishkin, D. (1980) The Ghassulian shrine at Ein Gedi. *Tel Aviv* 7/1–2: 1–44.

Voigt, M. (1983) Hajji Firuz Tepe, Iran: the Neolithic Settlement. Philadelphia: University Museum, University of Pennsylvania.

Weinstein-Evron, M., and Belfer- Cohen, A. (1993) Natufian figurines from the new excavations of the El-Wad cave, Mt Carmel, Israel. *Rock Art Research* 10/2: 102–6.

Weinstein-Evron, M., Lang, B., Ilani, S., Steinitz, G., and Kaufman, D. (1995) K/ar dating as a mean of sourcing Levantine Epipaleolithic basalt implements. *Archaeometry* 114/2: 106–36.

Weippert, H. (1998) Die chalkolithische Kultst_tte von Gilat als Ort der Begegnung. *Zeitschrift des deutschen Pal_stina-Vereins*: 106–35.

Willis, R. (1974) *Man and beast*. London: Hart-Davis, MacGibbon.

White, R. (1992) Beyond Art: Toward an understanding of the origins of material representation in Europe. *Annual Review of Anthropology* 21: 537–64.

Yellin, J., Levy, T.E., and Rowan, Y.M. (1996) New evidence on Prehistoric trade routes: the obsidian evidence from Gilat, Israel. *Journal of Field Archaeology* 23: 361.

16 Conclusion:

The Evolution of a Levantine Prehistoric Regional Cult Center

Thomas E. Levy

Introduction

The rise of sanctuary institutions that served regions, rather than simply local communities, represents a new threshold in the evolution of religion and society. From a social evolutionary perspective, this phenomenon can be linked cross-culturally to increasing social complexity and the emergence of chiefdom or rank societies. In the southern Levant, the surfacing of the first pan-regional ritual centers during the Chalcolithic period was tied to a web of new social processes that began to take shape during the late fifth–early fourth millennia BC. Some of these formative processes that began to crystallize at this time include the 'secondary products revolution' (Levy 1983, 1992; Sherratt 1981, 1997), the 'fiber revolution' (McCorriston 1997), the beginnings of metallurgy in the Levant (Golden 2005; Levy 1998; Shalev 1994; Shugar 2003), the first 'popu-lation explosion' in this part of the Middle East and other changes. Of the three of these new religio-social institutions that have been identified and excavated to date (Tuleilat Ghassul, En Gedi and Gilat), only Gilat has produced extensive assemblages of cult paraphernalia that can be used to examine questions related to late prehistoric ritual practice, ideology and belief underlying cult and ritual practices, and, ultimately, the role of ritual and religion in Chalcolithic Society. The rituals that were carried out at pan-regional sanctuaries such as Gilat provided the 'social glue' which helped integrate regional polities. To understand this process at Gilat, we have adopted the Durk-heimian (Durkheim 1933, 1995 [orig. 1912]) view of religion as powerfully strengthening a society's social structure as well as serving as a mechanism for controlling change based on the sacred authority of the social group's values and rules. In this way, regional religions or regional ritual (cult) organizations emerged out of the need to promote social solidarity. But this does not answer the specific question as to why Gilat emerged as the only Chalcolithic ritual center in the northern Negev desert when there were hundreds of contemporary 'secular' settlements in the region. Or why there was only one regional ritual center in the northern Negev and not the others? What was the nature of the various ritual acts and cults that focused on Gilat? And how was Gilat drawn into being a major player in promoting regional integration? This chapter will summarize many of the research conclusions presented earlier in this book by relying on the functionalist approach to the study of religion and society discussed earlier (Chapter 1, this volume).

Many of the interpretative models suggested throughout this volume have been based on comparisons with data from archaeology in the New and Old World, ethnohistoric texts, late nineteenth–twentieth-century cultural evolutionary studies, and ethnographic accounts. The use of the comparative method is part and parcel of anthropological archaeology. This is where we depart, to a degree, from the post-processual archaeology (Hodder 1987, 1999) of the previous two decades, which takes a more relativistic view of human culture. Throughout this book we have tried to identify underlying processes of social change related to the study of religion and ritual. While a number of the authors (cf. Marx, Chapter 3; Levy, Chapter 1, this volume) have found use for some nineteenth-century evolutionary scholars such as Robertson Smith, we have by no means accepted the unilinear evolutionary assumptions that so many of these pioneers held. Long ago, Franz Boas (1940) defined what was wrong with the Victorian cultural evolutionists who wrongly assumed that the occurrence of similar traits in different cultures implied participation in a universal cultural evolutionary step-ladder. Boas' influential paper helped change the course of anthropology by stressing that 'uncontrolled, uniformed, preconceived, and prejudicial cultural comparisons' (Gregor and Tuzin 2001a) ignored the fact that 'the identical result may have been reached on... different lines of development and from an infinite number of starting points' (Boas 1940). In a recent major exploration of the comparative method anew by cultural anthropologists, T.A. Gregor and D. Tuzin (Gregor and Tuzin 2001a) point out that Boas was not opposed to the existence of some cultural laws. As they suggest, Boas (*ibid.* 276) wrote that there were cultural laws that 'govern the growth of human culture, and it is our endeavor to discover these laws'. Boas (1940 [1896]: 280) concluded his critique of the comparative method with the following prophetic remarks:

> The comparative method, notwithstanding all that has been said and written in its praise, has been remarkably barren of definite results, and I believe it will not become fruitful until we renounce the vain endeavor to construct a uniform systematic history of the evolution of culture, and until we begin to make our comparison on the broader and sounder basis [of documented cultural-historical processes]. Up to this time we have too much reveled in more or less ingenious vagaries. The solid work is still all before us.

By situating our study of anthropology, archaeology and ritual deep within the details of the Gilat archaeological record, we have drawn on the reconfigured comparative method that has been so important to anthropological archaeology (Earle 1991; Feinman and Marcus 1998; Flannery 1999; Renfrew and Bahn 2000) and of renewed interest to cultural anthropology (Gregor and Tuzin 2001b; Johnson and Earle 1987).

Before trying to answer some of the processual questions noted above, it is important to summarize Gilat's place in the chronological framework of the Levantine Chalcolithic. This has direct bearing on the construction of any social models to explain developmental trajectories, social relations and the role of religion during this formative period.

Temporal Setting: Radiocarbon Dating and Divergent Evolution

To model the socioeconomic relations between Gilat and other Chalcolithic sites, it is important to place Gilat within the general southern Levantine chronological sequence. Based on stratigraphic data and stylistic trends in the Gilat pottery sequence presented in Chapter 10 (this volume), we suggest that the general ceramic assemblage of Gilat grew out of the late Neolithic, normative Wadi Rabah tradition (Gopher 1998). Gilead and Goren's (Gilead and Goren 1989; Goren 1995) suggestion that the Chalcolithic cultures of the northern Negev grew out of a 'Qatifian' Late Neolithic complex that came from the Faynan district in Jordan is highly suspect and a diffusion model that is not testable. Any similarities in pottery styles between the Faynan district and the northern Negev could be a result of similar pottery technologies or trade between these two regions. The parsimonious explanation rests on the Wadi Rabah pottery sherds found in the basal layers at Gilat which points to a 'Palestinian' rather than 'Trans-Jordanian' source area for the earliest settlers. As shown in Chapter 5, the earliest occupation (Stratum IV) at Gilat is characterized by pit houses. The main chronological question is: once the Gilat settlement and sanctuary sequence were established in Strata IIIA–IIA, how did it relate temporally to vibrant Chalcolithic cultures in other parts of the southern Levant such as the Beersheva valley culture, the lower Jordan valley and Teleilat Ghassul and the rest of the region?

The most compelling dating evidence comes from radiocarbon studies both of Gilat and of the other regions of the southern Levant (Bourke *et al.* 2001; Burton and Levy 2001). Researchers such as Joffe and Dessel (1995) and Gilead (1988) have gone to great efforts to divide the Chalcolithic cultures of the Levant into a well-defined temporal sequence with 'Early–Middle–Late–Developed' sub-phases. In Burton and Levy's (*ibid.*) recent analysis of more than 200 radiocarbon dates from Chalcolithic sites in the southern Levant, the most striking feature of this suite of dates is the overlap in the sigma values (standard deviations) for virtually the entire date list. With this kind of overlap, it is impossible to separate dates into meaningful categories of 'Early–Middle–Late–Developed'. In an ideal world, the dates would neatly cluster into these developmental phases and it would be possible to monitor growth, stability and collapse of Chalcolithic cultures across the region. Unfortunately, this is impossible with the existing data. With regard to Gilat, Figure Appendix 1.1 (also Table 5.3) shows that the eight available calibrated dates range (1 sigma) from c. 4,774–3,093 BC. Of these, two seem to be late intrusions (RT-860B = 3,705–3,377 BC; RT-2058 = 3,367–3,093 BC). The earliest date from Stratum IIB (OxA-3556 = 4,774–4,499 BC) may come from an earlier stratum at Gilat that was mixed with Stratum IIB material as a result of site formation processes. The largest suite of ¹⁴C dates from the southern Levant comes from nearby Shiqmim in the Beersheva valley (Burton and Levy 2001) with 40 samples. As argued by Burton and Levy (*ibid.*), given the problem of overlapping sigma values for the Levantine Chalcolithic ¹⁴C assemblage as a whole, the best way of documenting social change is through the standard stratigraphic analyses at deeply stratified sites such as Shiqmim, Teleilat Ghassul (Bourke *et al. ibid.*), and now Gilat. However, when the Gilat ¹⁴C suite is compared with the Shiqmim dates (Figure Appendix 1.2), the same problem exists of not being able to subdivide the temporal sequence of these two neighboring Chalcolithic polities. Based on available dates from these two neighboring geographic zones, the most that can be said is that that both Gilat and Shiqmim (and most of the Chalcolithic cultures of the southern Levant) were all contemporary. Perhaps in the future, more dates will be processed with smaller standard deviations and it will be possible to establish a finer dating sequence.

Based on the ¹⁴C dating evidence, cultural modeling of the main occupation strata at Gilat (Strata IIIA, IIC, IIB and IIA) must assume that this sanctuary site was contemporary with neighboring Chalcolithic cultures in the northern Negev along the Nahal Beersheva (Levy 1987), Nahal Besor [Wadi Gaza] (Macdonald, Starkey, and Lankester-Harding 1932), Nahal Grar (Gilead 1995) and other regions such as the lower Jordan valley (Mallon, Koeppel and Neuville 1934; Seaton 2000). Currently, it is not possible to determine a more fine-grain diachronic sequence for the northern Negev and temporal details concerning the beginning and end of the Chalcolithic period cannot yet be distinguished. The small number of radiocarbon dates from Gilat is a problem and it is hoped that a major research project of radiocarbon dating and the Chalcolithic period in the Levant will take place in the future. However, given the radiometric evidence, how then would the northern Negev Chalcolithic cultural landscape look in terms of regional settlement patterns?

During the Chalcolithic period, the southern Levant was a tapestry of small regional cultures that were often located along seasonal drainages, valleys and discrete geophysical zones that might extend for around 40 km across the landscape. Small regional cultural areas with settlement centers that integrate multiple communities through social, economic and religious activities are characteristic of chiefdom level societies (Johnson and Earle 1987). This is one of the hallmarks of the

Chalcolithic period in Palestine (Levy 1986). In the northern Negev, there were at least four distinct regional Chalcolithic cultures (see above). Other contemporary material cultural traditions (assumed to represent different social groups) existed in the lower Jordan valley, Golan Heights (Epstein 1998), the Jezreel valley (Engberg and Shipton 1934), Galilee (Gal, Smithline and Shalem 1997a; Gopher and Tsuk 1996) and other regions of the southern Levant. One of the most perplexing cultural occurrences relates to how four distinct Chalcolithic material cultures evolved and coexisted in such a relatively small area. The main 'Besor' catchment basin for the northern Negev where the Beersheva, Nahal Besor, Nahal Grar and Nahal Patish cultural traditions are located is only 3,390 sqkm in area (Israel. Ma*hle*ket ha-medidot 1970). At the center of these contemporary Chalcolithic polities was Gilat (Fig. 16.1), which lacked many of the resources of the olive oil rich Judean mountains or copper production of the Beersheva valley to the south, but 'capitalized' on manipulating ritual to propel itself as a settlement center that rivaled these more resource rich areas.

Figure 16.1 Thiessen polygon map with major Chalcolithic settlements in the northern Negev.
Note: 1 = Ze'elim, 2 = Shiqmim, 3 = Bir es-Safadi, 4 = Nevatim,
5 = Grar, 6 = Gilat, and 7 = Abu Hof.

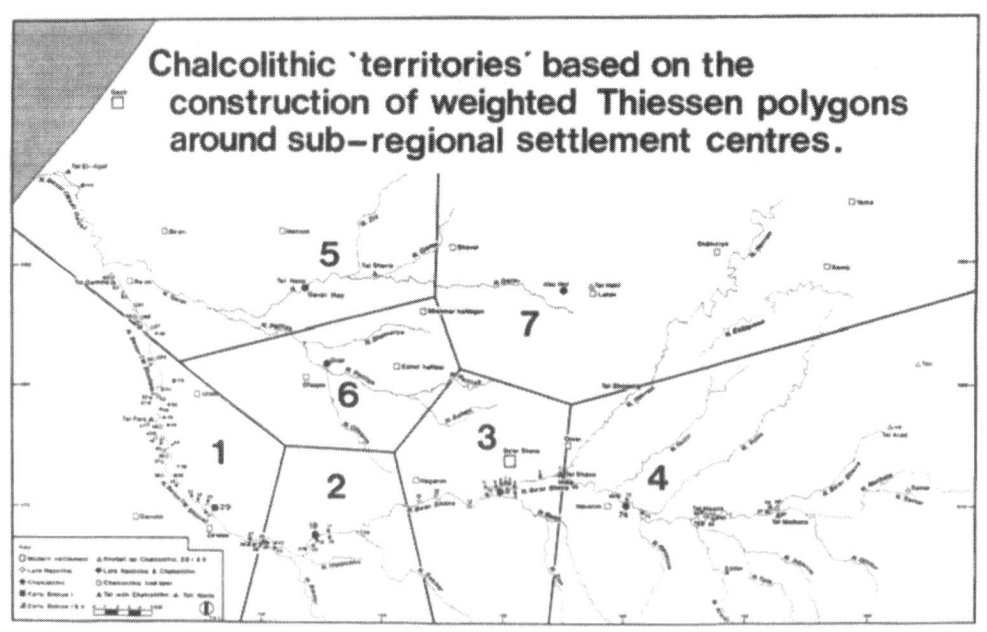

Perhaps the best solution to this problem is the notion of divergent cultural evolution used by Flannery and Marcus (1983) to explain the development of two distinct neighboring regional cultures in the Valley of Oaxaca, Mexico. Divergence in cultural evolution is based on the notion that every organism represents a complex combination of attributes that are 'legacies from different stages in its evolutionary past, and only a few of which can be explained on the basis of its current adaptation' (Flannery 1983). Flannery (*ibid.*) highlights how divergence from a common ancestor is one of the basic aspects of biological evolution, but 'undoubtedly played a major role in the evolution of the bewildering variety of human cultures with which the anthropologist is confronted'. Flannery uses ethnographic case studies to show how different cultures in the same geographic region can have similar kinship, social organization, ritual and certain religious concepts based on the sharing of the same ancestral roots. This is supported with ethnographic data from Chiapas

Mexico, (McQuown and Pitt-Rivers 1970), Panama (Linares 1977) and Madagascar (Kottak 1972). The ethnographic data from Madagascar is especially pertinent to cultural evolutionary models because they identify the processes of *parallel* and *convergent* evolution. Accordingly, when two neighboring populations are in continuous contact, innovations can be exchanged with such regularity that a sort of parallel evolution takes place over a given period of time. As shown in Chapter 10 of this volume, the general similarities in pottery vessel forms throughout the northern Negev and lower Jordan valley may be explained by this process. Alternatively, as Flannery (*ibid.*) points out, after a long separation, two societies 'may converge either as the result of a similar adaptation or of the acculturative effect of a third society'. In the case of the northern Negev, instances of cultural convergence can be identified through the establishment of pan-regional cults such as the one featuring violin-shape figurines (see Chapter 15, this volume). However, the differences in the sub-regional character between the various Chalcolithic cultures that occupied the different northern Negev wadi habitats argues for the central role of divergent evolutionary processes to explain the material differences between these cultures that grew out of the Late Neolithic ancestral tradition.

The vibrant Beersheva valley Chalcolithic culture, first made famous through Perrot's (1955, 1959, 1984) excavations at Abu Matar and Bir es-Safadi, has been shown by Levy (1992, 1998; Levy and Shalev 1989; but see also Golden 2005, Shugar 2003) and others to have had a virtual 'monopoly' on the procurement of copper ore, as well as the processing, casting and distribution of copper objects. This production and trade system was used to build, maintain and project the Beersheva valley chiefdom in a way that is not evidenced at any other regional Chalcolithic polity (Lovell 2001). How the Beersheva chiefdom maintained this copper monopoly is treated elsewhere (Levy 1998). What is important for understanding Gilat's emergence as one of the earliest pan-regional ritual centers in the Levant in general and the northern Negev specifically, is that through divergent evolutionary processes based on the manipulation of the Chalcolithic ritual world of symbols and ritual practice, it constructed itself into an important late fifth–early fourth millennia ritual center. What Gilat lacked in terms of the control of technology, it made up for by manipulating Chalcolithic ideology.

The Rise of Chalcolithic 'Priesthoods'—Evolutionary Perspectives

To paint a picture of some aspects of the ritual organization of the Gilat sanctuary and processes that led to its growth, it is important to clarify the changing roles and personae of magico-religious practitioners through social evolutionary time. Here again, we rely on the comparative method, but this time in a series of quantitative studies carried out by a psychological anthropologist interested in the anthropology of religion. By understanding the characteristics and differences between 'priests' who organized ritual activities at Gilat and magico-religious practitioners in less complex societies, it will be possible to appreciate some of the underlying socioeconomic variables that led to emergence of the Gilat ritual center. Michael Winkelman's (1986, 1992) cross-cultural research into the biological and social foundations of shamanism provide the most comprehensive statistically grounded data concerning the evolution of a full range of idealized 'types' of magico-religious practitioners that can be conveniently linked to the social evolutionary sequence of the southern Levant (cf. Table 16.1). Just as social evolutionary typologies are fraught with difficulties and should not be considered as specific pathways to culture change, the typology of magico-religious practitioners (shaman–shaman/healer–healers–mediums–priests) should not be taken as a strict evolutionary sequence. As shown by Bilu (Bilu and Ben-Ari 1992), some of these socioreligious personae can exist within the most modern and complex social systems. However, in terms of helping to identify various ideological processes linked to the rise of some of the earliest Levantine chiefdoms, Winkelman's cross-cultural results are extremely useful.

Table 16.1. General model of social evolution in the southern Levant and suggested changes in magico-religious practitioners based on M. Winkelman (2000). Note: ASC = Altered States of Consciousness.

Characteristics	Paleolithic	Natufian	Pre-Pottery Neolithic	Pottery Neolithic	Chalcolithic and Early Bronze Age
	Shaman	Shaman/Healer	Healer	Spirit Medium	Priest
Societal Conditions	Hunting and Gathering, nomadic; No local political integration; No social classes	Agricultural subsistence, Sedentary	Agricultural subsistence, sedentary; political integration	Agricultural Subsistence; sedentary; political integration	Agriculture, semi-sedentary or permanent residency; political integration
Magico-Religious Activity	Healing and divination; Protection from spirits and malevolent magic; Hunting magic; Malevolent acts	Healing and divination; Protection from spirits and malevolent magic; Hunting magic and agricultural rites; Minor malevolent acts	Healing and divination. Agricultural and socio-economic rites. Propitiation	Healing and divination; protection from spirits and malevolent magic; agricultural magic; propitiation	Protection and purification; Agricultural and socio-economic rites. Propitiation and worship
Socio-political Power	Charismatic leader, communal and war leader	Informal political power; Moderate judiciary decisions	Judicial, legislative, and economic power. Life-cycle rituals	Informal political power; moderate judiciary decisions	Political, legislative, judicial, economic, and military power
Social Characteristics	Mostly male, female secondary. High social status amongst 'equals'; Ambiguous moral status	Predominately male, moderate socioeconomic status, mostly moral status	Primarily male, female rare; high socio-economic status; mostly moral.	Predominantly female, male secondary/rare; Low socio-economic status; exclusively moral	Exclusively male. High social and economic status. Exclusively male
Professional Characteristics	Part-time; No group – individual practice	Part-time, collective/group practice; specialized role	Full-time. Collective – group practice. Highly specialized role.	Part-time, collective/group practice; temporal lobe syndrome	Full-time. Organized practitioner group. Hierarchically ranked roles
Selection and Training	Vision quests, dreams, illness, and spirit's request. ASC and spirit training or individual practitioner. Status recognized by clients	Vision quests, dreams, illness, and spirit's request. ASC and spirit training or individual practitioner. Ceremony recognizes status	Voluntary selection, 'payment' to trainer. Learns rituals and techniques. Ceremony recognizes status	Spontaneous possession by spirit; training in practitioner group; ceremony recognizes status	Social inheritance or succession. Political action
Motive and Context	Acts as client request for client, local community	Acts at client request in client group	Acts at client request in client group. Performs at public collective rituals	Acts primarily for clients; performs public ceremonies	Acts to fulfill public functions. Calendrical rites

Supernatural Power	Animal spirits, spirit allies. Spirit power, usually controlled	Spirits' allies and impersonal power (man). Power controlled	Superior gods and impersonal power (man). Ritual techniques and formulas. Power under control	Possessing spirits dominate; power out of control, unconscious	Power from superior spirits or gods. Has no control over spirit power
Special abilities	Weather control, flying, fire immunity, death and rebirth, transformation into animal	Occasional flight, animal transformation	Prevent future illness	None	Affect weather
Techniques	Spirit control; Physical and empirical medicine; Massaging and plants	Physical and empirical medicine. Massaging, herbal, cleanse wounds. Charms, spells, exorcisms, and rituals. Spirit control and propitiation	Charms, spells, exorcisms, rituals, and sacrifice. Propitiation and command of spirits	Propitiation and spirit control; exorcisms and sacrifices	Propitiation and collective rites. Sacrifice and consumption
Altered States of Consciousness (ASC) Conditions and spirit relations	ASC training and practice. Shamanic soul flight/journey. Isolation, austerities, fasting, hallucinogens, chanting and singing, extensive drumming and percussion, and, frequently, collapse and unconsciousness	ASC training and practice. Isolation, austerities, fasting, hallucinogens, chanting and singing, extensive percussion, and frequently, collapse/unconsciousness	ASC limited or absent. Social isolation; fasting; minor austerities; limited singing, chanting, or percussion	ASC – possession; spontaneous onset, tremors, convulsions, seizures, compulsive motor behavior, amnesia, temporal lobe discharge.	Generally no ASC or very limited. Occasionally alcohol consumption, sexual abstinence, social isolation, sleep deprivation

Briefly, the most significant socioeconomic variables that underlay the evolution of priests are: 1) the absence of hunting and gathering as the major source of subsistence and a reliance on agriculture; 2) permanence of settlement (an absence of a nomadic lifestyle); 3) settlement systems where sociopolitical integration goes beyond the level of the local community; and 4) social ranking and stratification. Based on the use of autocorrelation multiple-regression analysis, Winkelman and others (Dow *et al.* 1984; Winkelman 1992) were able to show that these relationships of socioeconomic conditions to the forms of magico-religious practitioners (shaman–shaman/healer–healers–mediums–priests) were independent of processes of cultural diffusion. Chalcolithic societies in the northern Negev possessed all of these socioeconomic conditions (Levy 1998) that would have facilitated the evolution of priests as a magico-religious type during the late fifth–early fourth millennia BC.

The following is a concise description of the evolution of magico-religious personae (based on Winkelman, above) in relation to the Levantine archaeological record from the Paleolithic period, to the beginnings of sedentism during the Natufian period and through the emergence of chiefdoms (Chalcolithic) and urban communities (Early Bronze Age). It is important to set the evolutionary stage for the rise of priests rather than various other magico-religious practitioner types, in Gilat during the Chalcolithic period.

Paleolithic: *Shamans*

Although not discussed in this book, Shamans should be mentioned as they are probably the earliest type of magico-religious practitioner to evolve. Shamans are found throughout the ethnographic world with the exception of the circum-Mediterranean zone and the Insular Pacific regions, where there is an absence of contemporary hunter-gatherer societies. Most shamanic traditions correlate with hunting, gathering or fishing subsistence economies; however, some were identified with pastoral societies of Eurasia and in some Amerindian groups who practiced agriculture. Shamans are characteristic of egalitarian societies that have political organization at the local community level and would have been typical of the numerous Paleolithic cultures of the Levant (Table 16.1). The adoption of agriculture and more complex forms of sociopolitical integration led to the disappearance of shamans.

Natufian: *Shaman/Healers*

With the emergence of sedentism during the Natufian period, c. 10,000 bp (Valla 1998), the classic shaman magico-religious practitioner would have evolved into a shaman/healer (see, Table 16.1 for attributes). Shaman/healers occur mostly in sedentary societies that rely on agriculture. According to Winkelman (*ibid.*), the adoption of agriculture is the primary cause of this transformation. The increase in human population size at this time is linked to larger scale ritual ceremonies that can also be linked to the shaman/healer.

Pre-Pottery Neolithic: *Healers*

By the Pre-Pottery Neolithic periods and the solidification of agricultural-based subsistence and village-based herding (Bar Yosef 1998; Byrd 1994), the emergence of healers can be linked to the presence of political integration that went beyond the local community. Whether or not chiefdoms existed at this time is debated (Kuijt 2000). However, the presence of large village settlements such as Jericho, Ain Ghazal, Basta, and other sites with possible satellite hamlets during PPNB phase may argue for the rise of polities of regional scale. According to Winkelman (*ibid.*) almost all healers are associated with societies such as the PPNB, with agriculture as a primary food source. The social and other characteristics listed in Table 16.1 all point to the existence of healers during the PPN rather than full time priests.

Pottery Neolithic: *Spirit Mediums*

The presence of spirit mediums (involved in healing, divination, the protection from spirits and malevolent magic, as well as agricultural magic and propitiation) is significantly correlated with the presence of political integration beyond the local community and by social stratification, but only political integration is an independently significant predictor (Winkelman 2000:74). Agriculture does not predict the occurrence of medium and many agricultural societies lack mediums. The primary reasons for linking spirit mediums with the Pottery Neolithic are the social characteristics of spirit mediums that Winkelman's cross-cultural study linked predominantly with females rather than males (Table 16.1). Unlike any other archaeological period, the overwhelming dominance of unambiguous female motifs in Pottery Neolithic figurative art (Garfinkel 1999) argues for the central role of women as magico-religious practitioners at this time. This is in contrast with the following Chalcolithic period when a wider range of ritual art appears and the depiction of females (see Chapter 15, discussion of violin figurines) is abstract and ambiguous.

Chalcolithic/Early Bronze Age: *Priests*

Priests are generally associated with sedentary agricultural societies or pastoral societies with political integration beyond the local community level. Amongst other factors, the emergence of priests can be linked to the Chalcolithic period in the southern Levant because it is the first time that two-tier settlement hierarchies and regional settlement systems can be defined (Joffe 1991; Levy and Alon 1987) and specialized sanctuary complexes appear in the archaeological record (Alon and Levy 1989; Alon 1990; Seaton 2000; Ussishkin 1980). According to Winkelman (2000:74), independently significant predictions of priest were found with agriculture and political integration. Cross-cultural evidence, as well as the archaeological evidence at Gilat (Chapters 5, 15 this volume; Table 16.1), indicates that the magico-religious activities of priests focus on agricultural and socioeconomic rites (Chapter 14, this volume), propitiation and worship. The social characteristics of priesthoods tend to reflect exclusively male, high social and economic personae. These are full-time ritual positions that are hierarchically organized where ritual acts to fulfill public functions and is often related to calendrical rites (see Chapter 1, this volume, for discussion of agricultural implications of Chalcolithic pilgrimage and below). Priests in traditional societies are also characterized as having special abilities to affect weather—a key power for agro-pastoral societies. Alcohol consumption also becomes important for enhancing altered states of consciousness (ASC; Winkelman 2000). However, as the production of alcoholic beverages seems to be as old as the 'Neolithic revolution' (Joffe 1998), alcohol may have played a role in ritual activities as early as the beginnings of plant domestication. By the following Early Bronze Age, the establishment of fortified towns marks the widespread establishment of formal sanctuaries in the Levant and, no doubt, the consolidation of priests as an institutional form of magico-religious practitioner in these societies. The creation of full-time priests in agriculturally based societies that were based on multi-community regional polities led to the rise of permanent facilities to house the priesthood and deities where a wide range of ritual acts could take place. The identification of 'regional cults' in the ethnographic record (Werbner 1977) provide an important source of data for exploring the dynamics of religion in middle range societies where living priests and dead saints inhabited centers of ritual activity.

Regional Cults: Networks and Change through Time

From the perspective of social evolution, the phenomenon of regional cults intersects with the emergence of middle range, rank or chiefdom level societies. With the rise of regional polities (Johnson and Earle 1987) new religious institutions were needed to link formerly disparate local groups into multi-community societies. The Gilat study shows that the rise of regional cults helped provide the bonds that linked widespread settlements into a *cultural* web that provided solutions to persistent problems related to agro-pastoral risk management, warfare, the control of technology and trade. As Werbner (1977) points out, in regional cults flows of goods, services information and people move across major political and ethnic boundaries. The investigation of regional cults at Gilat has clarified a number of issues. For example, it was possible to identify ritual activities that may not coincide with the spatial boundaries and hierarchies of local regional and sub-regional Levantine cultures. The petrographic (Chapter 9, this volume) and geological provenance identifications (Chapters 12, 15) of various imported vessels, figurines, and other objects illustrate the direction of exchange from diverse south Levantine geographic areas stretching over distances of more than 150 km that included the lower Jordan valley, Edom in Transjordan, the southern Judean mountains and other areas in the northern Negev. Each of these regions is characterized by its own distinct Chalcolithic material culture, reflecting the different ethnic character of groups that participated in a web of regional cults focused on Gilat. Chief amongst the regional cults was one that focused on the worship of the enigmatic violin-shape figurines (Chapter 15, this volume).

Another dimension of regional cults that can be traced to a limited degree at Gilat is the definition of how the regional cult web changed through time during the late fifth–fourth millennia BCE. In some respects, this relates to the evolution of magico-religious practitioners through time at the site. Seen against the Late Neolithic ancestor model for the earliest occupation at Gilat (Stratum IV, Chapter 5, this volume), the sporadic pit house occupation at the site suggests that habitation may not have been as permanent as the occupation during Strata IIIA, IIC and IIB. If this observation is correct, it can be assumed that Stratum IV magico-religious practitioners were most likely part-time 'mediums' and not full-time priests (Table 16.1). The smaller quantities of imported 'cult' paraphernalia is certainly related to the smaller excavation sample size from the earliest levels, but based on the excavation of three complete 5 x 5m units in Area T, the small number of ritual objects found in the early levels can also be linked fewer pan-regional exchange relations. The absence of full-time priests at the sanctuary at this time may indicate less 'demand' for exotica and less visibility of Gilat as a ritual center during its initial settlement phases. By Stratum IIC (Figs 5.99E and 99F) and the construction of the first well-defined sanctuary complex, there is an exponential increase in the number of imported ritual related artifacts (Chapters 5, 10, 12, 15). The construction of the *domus ecclesiae* (Turner 1979) for the first time at Gilat probably marks the formal emergence of full-time priests and the establishment of regional political integration based on ritual precepts. By Stratum IIB (Figs 5.20a–b), when the architectural plan is at its most complex, the Gilat priests seem to have institutionalized ritual practice to an even greater degree and no doubt established their reputation throughout an extensive regional ritual catchment zone that covered most of what is today southern Israel, Palestine and parts of southern Jordan. Whereas Stratum IIB represented a major reorganization of the site on the ruins of Stratum IIC, by Stratum IIA (Figs 5.19a–b) Gilat suffered a major organizational decline as evidenced by the paucity of architectural remains. While craft activities continued at the site, such as the production of textiles (Chapter 14, this volume), it is doubtful that full-time priests were still in residence. The regional significance of Gilat as a cult center had declined.

The Gilat study also attempted to examine how regional and local cults interact through time. The ethnographic study by Bilu (Chapter 4, this volume) of the Baba Sali regional cult, on the periphery of the more traditional Ashkenazi and Sephardic religious establishment in Jerusalem, provides important comparative material concerning some of cultural processes underlying the production of regional cults in the Middle East today. Based on the material remains found in the excavations at Gilat (Chapter 5, this volume), it is possible to identify a number of ritual facilities that may relate to 'cults' that operated at the site in the different strata. By strata, these activities include the following:

- *Stratum IV* small open-air mud brick altars for local ritual practice;
- *Stratum IIIB* small open-air mudbrick altars, intentional dog burials with offerings, human burials around settlement. Ritual activities still seem to focus on the local community, but cult activities begin to become regularized;
- *Stratum IIIA* open-air plaza for public ritual, open-air mudbrick altar, dog burials, human burials beneath plaza and other contexts, increase in ceramic vessels related to ritual activities (Chapter 10). With the construction of the first large plaza, ritual may have begun to take on a regional dimension;
- *Stratum IIC* construction of sanctuary architecture for hidden rites related to the worship of anthropomorphic and zoomorphic statuettes (Chapter 15, this volume), public court-yard with standing stone installation, dog skull burials (Chapter 6, this volume), ritual burial of cache of ostrich eggs, wide-spread introduction of violin-shape figurine worship with links to other south Levantine regions (see above; Chapter 15, this volume), beginning of textile production beyond the DMP in the sanctuary precinct, increase in human burials within the sanctuary compound, import of 'torpedo' vessels with olive oil offerings (Chapter 10, this volume). At this time, the local cult practices at the Gilat ritual center interfaced with the increasing importance of pan-regional cult practices that brought ritual contacts between Gilat, the southern Judean hills, lower Jordan valley, and other areas. These relations were possibly linked to the exchange of textiles manufactured in the sanctuary.
- *Stratum IIB* construction of intricate sanctuary architectural plan and facilities to accommodate and organize larger numbers of participants in ritual activities took place, construction of large circular platforms with infant burials for ritual acts in the open-air, continuation of widespread use of violin shape figurines, construction of mortuary facility within the sanctuary complex for multiple human burial with associated 'multi-use ritual pit', evidence of ritual feasting linked to mass human burial (Dietler and Hayden 2001), numerous human burials throughout sanctuary complex (Chapter 8, this volume), further increase in textile production and related organization for exchange, import of 'torpedo' vessels with olive oil offerings (Chapter 10, this volume). The multiple burial, where all the individuals died and were buried at the same time (Chapter 8, this volume) in a special burial monument within the sanctuary complex may have worked to promote regional pilgrimage to Gilat like the saintly burial pilgrimage site discussed by Bilu (Chapter 4) for today's town of Netivot located c. 7 km from Gilat (see below for discussion of pilgrimage and Gilat). Regional cult activities seem to have been at their apex at this time, with limited evidence of local cult
- *Stratum IIA* marked decrease in evidence for inter-regional exchange of cult-related objects, less evidence of public ritual activities, construction of small open-air altars with stone foundations. The paucity of architectural and artifact evidence indicates reversion to more local oriented cult activities.

The influx of large quantities of ritual exotica into Gilat suggests that pilgrimage played an important role in promoting this site into a pan-regional ritual center. In the concluding section, the role of pilgrimage is explored as having been a key factor in promoting ideological adaptation (Conrad and Demarest 1984) to the northern Negev environment and the important socioeconomic transformations that were taking place during the late fifth–early fourth millennia.

Pilgrimage and the Construction of Ideological Networks and *communitas*

In this study of ritual, religion and social change in formative societies, pilgrimage is viewed as perhaps the single most important ritual act for promoting *communitas* (see Chapter 1, this volume). While much of V. Turner's (1969, 1982) influential analysis of pilgrimage focuses on the individual and how the experience of pilgrimage is translated into a rite of passage (Gennep 1960 [orig. 1908]), here we are more interested in how pilgrimage affects larger social groups. Turner's work on pilgrimage suggests that there are common cross-cultural elements such as liminality and *communitas*. As Kunin (1998) points out, as would be expected, some scholars have questioned the role of *communitas* as a universal characteristic of pilgrimage. However, of interest here is Bowman's (Jha 1985) observation that emphasis on *communitas* in pilgrimage rites may actually be created by the religious hierarchy that organizes these rituals rather than something that the pilgrims themselves aspire to or actually achieve. By promoting *communitas* through pilgrimage, the priests build their own power base and enhance their prestige. Elements of this were shown in Bilu's study (Chapter 4, this volume) of the Baba Sali pilgrimage organization in Netivot. Based on these processual parallels, we assume that the priests at Gilat took an active role in promoting *communitas* through pilgrimage to their site.

The most conclusive evidence for pilgrimage to Gilat from distances of up 100 km are the petrographic studies of the Gilat 'torpedo' vessels (Chapter 9 and Appendix 2, this volume). Most of these unusual 'amphorae-like' jars that were tested petrographically and shown by Yuval Goren (Chapter 9, this volume) to come from the southern Judean mountains which is home to wild olives (Zohary 1975) and presumably was a prime region for olive growing and the production of olive oil during the Chalcolithic period. Margie Burton's organic residue analysis (Appendix 2, this volume) provides evidence that the sampled torpedo jars contained olive oil. The exotic shape of these large storage jars, the fact that they are found only at Gilat, made in non-local regions, and that they contained olive oil, a rare preciosity, have led us to assume that these vessels and their contents were offerings brought to the sanctuary as part of the pilgrimage process. Presumably other exotica such as violin-shape figurines, stone fenestrated stands, palettes and other 'valuable' objects were part of similar exchange networks to the Gilat sanctuary.

How then did the pilgrimage work? Using local Iron Age ethnohistoric data from the Hebrew Bible, the three main Jewish pilgrimage festivals (Passover [Fig. 16.2, B2 - spring], Shavuot [Fig. 16.2, C2, summer] and Sukkot [Fig. 16.2, A1, fall]), can been seen as originally tied to the agricultural cycle (Kunin 1998). When the Hebrew Bible was codified, these holidays took on historical associations with Passover linked to the Exodus from Egypt, Shavuot linked with the giving of the commandments on Mount Sinai, and Sukkot with the 40 years of wandering in the wilderness. The historic ramifications of these pilgrimage celebrations are overlain with covenantal aspects that promoted *communitas*. Thus, these pilgrimage holidays represent a syncretism between ancient agricultural festivals in the southern Levant with newer covenantal structures that contributed to the strengthening of the Iron Age temple elite in Jerusalem which was the main ritual center at that time. The dictates of the calendrical growing and harvesting seasons in the marginal lands of the southern Levant (see Figure 16.2) were monitored by the priests whose specialized knowledge of the rituals needed to insure crop and pasture success helped to solidify their power and prestige. Similarly, in earlier periods like the Chalcolithic, we can assume that a similar agro-pastoral calendar was in place and that the priests at sanctuaries like Gilat fulfilled public social functions by organizing calendrical rites. Thus, at certain times of the year, especially the spring growing season and fall harvesting season, Gilat must have been an active center of pilgrimage.

Figure 16.2 Cropping model for Levant. Pastoral and agricultural practices are determined by seasonal variation in the semi-arid lands of the northern Negev.

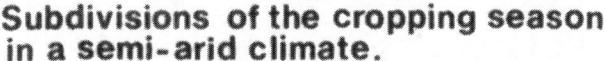

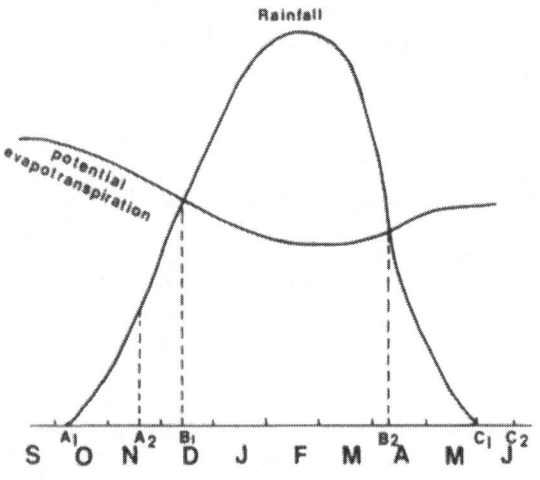

Subdivisions of the cropping season in a semi-arid climate.

A_1: Beginning of rainy season;

A_2: Beginning of transition period (precipitation = half of P.E.T.);

B_1: End of transition period, beginning of humid period;

B_2: End of humid period;

C_1: End of rainy season;

C_2: Exhaustion of moisture reserves in the soil.

(after Cochemé & Franquin 1967; Atlas of Israel 1970)

Ethnographic data from the Negev shows how Bedouin pastoralists had to move their herd westward from the eastern and southern Negev to the rich annual grazing lands on the Negev coastal plain (Marx 1967). Based on the paleoenvironmental data discussed earlier (see Chapter 1, this volume), it was shown that even during the Chalcolithic, the northern Negev was characterized by a semi-arid environment. Thus, it can be assumed that similar annual nomadic treks, from the arid east to the more humid west, in search of pasture existed during the late fifth–fourth millennia. Gilat, then, was a 'gateway' to the rich grazing lands of the Negev coastal plain. Gilat's own harvesting activities around the site (Chapter 11, this volume, on sickle blades) would have produced excellent stubble for sheep and goat grazing. During the Stratum IIB occupation, one scenario suggests that the people buried in the mortuary monument (and their curious deaths) within the sanctuary compound at the same time, must have drawn pilgrims from near and far to participate in propitiation and collective rites organized by the Gilat priests. Like the ethnographic case studies presented in this volume concerning Bedouin pilgrimage to saints' tombs in southern Sinai and Jewish pilgrimage to the new Baba Sali sacred site in Netivot in the northern Negev, Gilat as sacred center should be conceptualized as having been constructed not only out of 'bricks and mortar', but also through the manipulation of symbols and ritual to draw pilgrims and believers to the site.

In conclusion, the manipulation of late fifth–fourth millennia religious concepts and rituals played crucial roles in the emergence, maintenance and ultimate collapse of the Gilat sanctuary. By taking a comparative, anthropological and archaeological approach to the study of religion and social evolution, we have seen how divergent evolutionary processes propelled Gilat into a ritual center unlike any other place in the Negev desert.

Acknowledgments

I am very grateful to my colleague, Donald Tuzin, for reading and commenting on an earlier draft of this chapter. I have benefited greatly over the years by his deep synthetic views of anthropology.

References

Alon, D., and T.E. Levy (1989) The archaeology of cult and Chalcolithic sanctuary at Gilat. *Journal of Mediterranean Archeology* 2:163–221.

Alon, D. and Levy, T.E. (1990) The Gilat Sanctuary: its centrality and influence in the southern Levant during the late 5th–early 4th Millennium B.C.E. (Hebrew). *Eretz Israel* 21:23–36.

Bar Yosef, O. (1998) Earliest food producers: Pre-Pottery Neolithic (8000–5500 BCE). In *The Archaeology of Society in the Holy Land*, edited by T.E. Levy. London: Leicester University Press, pp. 190–204.

Bilu, Y., and Ben-Ari, E. (1992) Making of modern saints: manufactured charisma and the Abu-Hatseiras of Israel. *American Ethnologist* 19:672–87.

Boas, F. (1940) The limitations of the comparative method of anthropology. In *Race, Language and Culture*, edited by F. Boas. New York: Macmillan, pp. 270–80.

Bourke, S., Lawson, E., Lovell, J., Hua, Q., Zoppi, U., and Barbetti, M. (2001) The chronology of the Ghassulian Chalcolithic period in the southern Levant: New C-14 determinations from Teleilat Ghassul, Jordan. *Radiocarbon* V43:1217–22.

Burton, M., and Levy, T.E. (2001) The Chalcolithic radiocarbon record and its use in southern Levantine archaeology. *Radiocarbon* V43:1223–46.

Byrd, B.F. (1994) From early humans to farmers and herders: recent progress on key transitions in southwest Asia. *Journal of Archaeological Research* 2:221–53.

Conrad, G.W., and Demarest, A.A. (1984) *Religion and Empire: The Dynamics of Aztec and Inca Expansionism*. Cambridge: Cambridge University Press.

Dietler, M., and Hayden, B. (eds) (2001) *Feasts: Archaeological and Ethnographic Perspectives on Food, Politics, and Power*. Washington and London: Smithsonian Institution Press.

Dow, M., Burton, M., White, D., and Reitz, K. (1984) Galton's problem as network autocorrelation. *American Ethnologist* 11:754–70.

Durkheim, E. (1933) *The Division of Labor in Society*. Glencoe: Free Press.

— (1995) [orig. 1912] *The Elementary Forms of Religious Life (Translated and with an Introduction by Karen E. Fields)*. New York and others: The Free Press.

Earle, T. (1991) The evolution of chiefdoms. In *Chiefdoms: Power, Economy, and Ideology*, edited by T. Earle. Cambridge: Cambridge University Press, pp. 1–15.

Engberg, A.M., and Shipton, G.M. (1934) *Notes on the Chalcolithic and Early Bronze Age Pottery of Megiddo*. Chicago: The Oriental Institute of the University.

Epstein, C. (1998) *The Chalcolithic Culture of the Golan*. Jerusalem: Israel Antiquities Authority.

Feinman, G.M., and Marcus, J. (eds) (1998) *Archaic States*. Santa Fe: School of American Research Press.

Flannery, K.V. (1983) Theoretical framework: topic 1—divergent evolution. In *The Cloud People: Divergent Evolution of the Zapotec and Mixtec Civilizations*, edited by K.V. Flannery and J. Marcus. London and others: Academic Press, pp. 1–4.

— (1999) Process and Agency in Early State Formation. *Cambridge Archaeological Journal* 9:3–21.

Flannery, K.V., and Marcus, J. (eds) (1983) *The Cloud People: Divergent Evolution of the Zapotec and Mixtec Civilizations*. New York: Academic Press.

Gal, Z., Smithline, H., and Shalem, D. (1997a) A Chalcolithic burial cave in Peqi'in, Upper Galilee. *Israel Exploration Journal* 47:145–54.

Garfinkel, Y. (1999) *The Yarmukians: Neolithic art from Sha'ar Hagolan.* Jerusalem: Bible Lands Museum Jerusalem.

Gennep, A. van (1960) [orig 1908] *The Rites of Passage.* London: Routledge and Kegan Paul.

Gilead, I. (1988) The Chalcolithic period in the levant. *Journal of World Prehistory* 2:397–443.

— (ed.) (1995) *Grar: A Chalcolithic Site in the Northern Negev.* Beer-Sheva: Ben-Gurion University of the Negev Press.

Gilead, I., and Goren, Y. (1989) Petrographic analyses of 4th Millenium B.C. Pottery and stone vessels from the northern Negev, Israel. *Bulletin of the American Schools of Oriental Research* 275:5–14.

Golden, J. (2005) *Dawn of the Metal Age.* London: Equinox.

Gopher, A. (1998) Early pottery-bearing groups in Israel: the Pottery Neolithic Period. In *The Archaeology of Society in the Holy Land*, edited by T.E. Levy. London: Leicester University Press, pp. 205–25.

Gopher, A., and Tsuk, T. (eds) (1996) *The Nahal Qanah Cave: Earliest Gold in the Southern Levant.* Tel Aviv: Monograph Series of the Institute of Archaeology Tel Aviv University.

Goren, Y. (1995) Shrines and ceramics in Chalcolithic Israel: the view through the petrographic microscope. *Archaeometry* 37:287–305.

Gregor, T. A., and Tuzin, D.F. (2001a) Comparing gender in Amazonia and Melanesia. In *Gender in Amazonia and Melanesia: An Exploration of the Comparative Method*, edited by T.A. Gregor and D.F. Tuzin. Berkeley: University of California Press, pp. 1–16.

— (eds) (2001b) *Gender in Amazonia and Melanesia: An Exploration of the Comparative Method.* Berkeley: University of California Press.

Hodder, I. (1987) The contextual analysis of symbolic meanings. In *The Archaeology of Contextual Meanings*, edited by I. Hodder. Cambridge: Cambridge University Press, pp. 1–10.

— (1999) *The Archaeological Process: An Introduction.* Oxford: Blackwell.

Israel. Ma'hle'ket ha-medidot (1970) *Atlas of Israel; cartography, physical geography, human and economic geography, history.* 2nd edn. Jerusalem: Survey of Israel Ministry of Labour.

Jha, M. (ed.) (1985) *Dimensions of Pilgrimage.* New Dehli: Inter-India Publications.

Joffe, A.H. (1991) *Settlement and Society in Early Bronze I and II in the Southern Levant: Complementarity and Contradiction in a Small-Scale Complex Society. Monographs in Mediterranean Archaeology.* Sheffield: Sheffield Academic Press.

— (1998) Alcohol and social complexity in ancient western Asia. *Current Anthropology* V39:297–322.

Joffe, A.H., and Dessel, J.P. (1995) Redefining chronology and terminology for the Chalcolithic of the southern Levant. *Current Anthropology* V36:507–18.

Johnson, A.W., and Earle, T. (1987) *The Evolution of Human Societies: From Foraging Group to Agrarian State.* Stanford: Stanford University Press.

Kottak, C.P. (1972) A cultural adaptive approach to Malagasy political organization. In *Social Exchange and Interaction*, vol. 46, edited by E.N. Wilmsen. Ann Arbor: Anthropological Papers of the University of Michigan Museum of Anthropology, pp. 107–28.

Kuijt, I. (2000) *Life in Neolithic Farming Communities: Social Organization, Identity, and Differentiation. Fundamental issues in archaeology.* New York: Kluwer Academic/Plenum Publishers.

Kunin, S.D. (1998) *God's Place in the World: Sacred Space and Sacred Place in Judaism.* London: Cassell.

Levy, T.E. (1983) The emergence of specialized pastoralism in the southern Levant. *World Archaeology* 15:15–36.

— (1986) Archaeological sources for the history of Palestine: the Chalcolithic Period. *Biblical Archaeologist* 49:83–108.

— (ed.) (1987) *Shiqmim I: Studies Concerning Chalcolithic Societies in the Northern Negev Desert, Israel (1982–1984).* BAR International Series 356. Oxford: British Archaeological Reports.

— (1992) Transhumance, subsistence, and social evolution in the northern Negev desert. In *Pastoralsim in the Levant: Archaeological Material in Anthropological Perspective*, edited by A. Khaznov and O.B. Yosef. Madison, Wisconsin: Prehistory Press.

— (1998) Cult, Metallurgy and Rank Societies: Chalcolithic Period (c. 4500–3500 BCE). In *The Archaeology of Society in the Holy Land*, edited by T.E. Levy. London: Leicester University Press, pp. 226–44.

Levy, T.E., and Alon, D. (1987) Settlement patterns along the Nahal Beersheva–Lower Nahal Besor: models of subsistence in the northern Negev. In *Shiqmim I*, edited by T.E. Levy. BAR International Series 356. Oxford: British Archaeological Reports, pp. 45–138.

Levy, T.E., and Shalev, S. (1989) Prehistoric metalworking in the southern Levant: archaeometallurgy and social perspectives. *World Archaeology* 20:353–72.

Linares, O.F. (1977) Adaptive strategies in Western Panama. *World Archaeology* 8:304–19.

Lovell, J.L. (2001) *The Late Neolithic and Chalcolithic Periods in the Southern Levant - New Data from the Site of Teleilat Ghassul, Jordan. Monographs of the Sydney University Teleilat Ghassul Project 1.* BAR International Series 974. Oxford: British Archaeological Reports.

Macdonald, E., Starkey, J.L., and Lankester-Harding, G. (1932) *Beth Pelet* II:Prehistoric Fava. London: British School of Archaeology.

Mallon, A., Koeppel, R., and Neuville, R. (1934) *Teleilat Ghassul I, 1929–32.* Rome: Pontifical Biblical Institute.

Marx, E. (1967) *Bedouin of the Negev.* Manchester: Manchester University Press.

McCorriston, J. (1997) The fiber revolution: textile extensification, alienation, and social stratification in Ancient Mesopotamia. *Current Anthropology* 38:517–48.

McQuown, N.A., and Pitt-Rivers, J. (eds) (1970) *Ensayos de Antropologia en la Zona Central de Chiapas.* Mexico, D.F.: Instituto Nacional Indigenista.

Perrot, J. (1955) The excavations at Tell Abu Matar, near Beersheba. *Israel Exploration Journal* 5:17–41, 73–84, 167–89.

— (1959) Statuettes en ivoire et autre objets en ivoire et en os provenant des gisements prehistoriques de la region de Beersheba. *Syria* 36:8–19.

Perrot, P. (1984) Structures d'habitat mode de vie et environnement. les villages souterrains des pasteurs de Beersheva, dans le sud D'Israel, au IVe millenaire avant l'ere chretienne. *Paleorient* 10:75–96.

Renfrew, C., and Bahn, P. (2000) *Archaeology: Theories, Methods, and Practice.* 3rd edn. New York: Thames and Hudson.

Seaton, P. (2000) Aspects of new research at the Chalcolithic sanctuary precinct at Teleilat Ghassul, In *Proceedings of the First International Congress on the Archaeology of the Ancient Near East, Rome, May 18th–23rd, 1998,* edited by P. Matthiae, A. Enea, L. Peyronel, and F. Pinnock. Rome, pp. 1503–14.

Shalev, S. (1994) Change in metal production from the Chalcolithic period to the Early Bronze Age in Israel and Jordan. *Antiquity* 68:630–7.

Sherratt, A.G. (1981) Plough and pastoralism: aspects of the secondary products revolution. In *Patterns of the Past: Studies in Honour of David Clarke,* edited by I. Hodder, G. Isaac, and N. Hammond. Cambridge: Cambridge University Press, pp. 261–305.

— (1997) *Economy and Society in Prehistoric Europe: Changing Perspectives.* Princeton, New Jersey: Princeton University Press.

Shugar, A.N. (2003) Reconstructing the Chalcolithic metallurgical process at Abu Matar, Israel. *Archaeometallurgy in Europe* 1: 449–58.

Turner, H.W. (1979) *From Temple to Meeting House: The Phenomenology and Theology of Places of Worship.* The Hague; New York: Mouton.

Turner, V.W. (1969) *The Ritual Process: Structure and Anti-structure. The Lewis Henry Morgan Lectures 1966.* Chicago: Aldine.

— (1982) *Celebration, Studies in Festivity and Ritual.* Washington DC: Smithsonian Institution Press.

Ussishkin, D. (1980) The Ghassulian shrine at En-Gedi. *Tel Aviv*:1–44.

Valla, F.R. (1998) The first settled societies–Natufian (12,5000–10,200 BP). In *The Archaeology of Society in the Holy Land,* edited by T.E. Levy. London: Leicester University Press, pp. 169–87.

Werbner, R.P. (1977) Introduction. In *Regional Cults, Association of Social Anthropologists Monograph 16,* edited by R.P. Werbner. London, New York, San Francisco: Academic Press, pp. ix–xxxvii.

Winkelman, M. (1986) Magico-religious practitioner types and socioeconomic analysis. *Behavior Science Research* 20:17–46.

— (1992) Shamans, priests, and witches: a cross-cultural study of magico-religious practioners. *Anthropological Research Papers* 44.

Zohary, D. (1975) Beginnings of Fruit Growing in the Old World. *Science* 187:319–27.

VI.
APPENDICES

Appendix I
Organic Residue Analysis of Selected Vessels from Gilat— Gilat Torpedo Jars

Margie Burton and Thomas E. Levy

Introduction

The significance of the 'torpedo jar' as an integral part of the Gilat ritual assemblage came to light during the second phase of excavations at the site that were jointly directed by T. E. Levy and D. Alon in 1987 and from 1990 to 1992. The name 'torpedo jar' was coined during the Gulf War when missiles of a variety of shapes and forms were in the consciousness of most people living in Israel at the time. The discovery of numerous torpedo jar fragments around the Gilat sanctuary led to the identification of this vessel as a new Chalcolithic ceramic type (Alon and Levy 1989: 200). The exceptional nature of the Gilat torpedo jar within the Chalcolithic ceramic assemblage was emphasized by Y. Goren's (1987, 1995, see Chapter 9 for a full discussion of the petrography of these vessels) petrographic studies that demonstrated their origin in a large number of petrographic zones in the southern Levant—especially in the northern Negev and southern Judean hills). Given local ethnohistorical data from the southern Levant, the unusual shape and size of the vessels resembling later Greek and Roman olive oil and wine amphorae (Will 1977: 265), and the context in which they were found at the site, the excavators suggested that the torpedo jars were associated with ritual activities and may have been used to contain special liquids such as olive oil, wine, or other psychotropic substances (Alon and Levy 1989: 202). Direct testing of such hypotheses concerning the function of ancient ceramic vessels is now possible through techniques of organic residue analysis. In this section, the results of organic residue studies conducted by M. Burton at the laboratories of the University of California, San Diego—Scripps Institution of Oceanography (UCSD-SIO) are presented for the torpedo jars from Gilat.

Methodology

With improvements in experimental protocols and instrumentation over the last three decades, organic residue analysis has become a powerful tool for identifying archaeological vessel contents (e.g. Charters et al. 1993, 1995; Condamin et al. 1976; Copley et al. 2001, 2003; Dudd et al.

1998; Evershed et al. 1991, 1999; Fankhauser 1994, 1997; Malainey et al. 1999; McGovern et al. 1999; Patrick et al. 1985; Reber and Evershed 2004, Skibo 1992). In particular, lipids absorbed during the storage and processing of foodstuffs in ceramic vessels have been shown to be relatively well-preserved, in some cases for thousands of years. A pilot study of torpedo jar lipid extracts was recently completed at the University of California, San Diego. The experimental approach was to characterize torpedo jar lipid profiles by Gas Chromatography/Mass Spectrometry (GC/MS) and to compare these profiles to those of laboratory-degraded olive oil and wine, the two most likely candidates for torpedo jar contents.

Samples

Archaeological samples. Pieces (ca. 20 g) were cut from eight different torpedo jar vessels excavated during the Phase I (1975–77, 1987) operations at Gilat, Area D (Table 1, Plate 1). The vessels had been stored at Hebrew Union College, Jerusalem, Israel since the time of their excavation. Seven of the samples were taken from the mid-wall portion near the vessel handles, with the eighth cut from the vessel base. Samples were prepared for extraction by first removing the outer surface with the sanding bit of a Dremel tool (to avoid any contamination from adhering sediment or handling during excavation and storage), and then crushed to a fine powder in a glazed ceramic mortar and pestle. Testing of surrounding sediments is desirable to confirm that archaeological vessel residues derive from vessel use rather than from lipids in the depositional environment. In this study, sediment samples corresponding to these particular vessels were not available, however, one sample of sediment from inside a Gilat torpedo jar excavated in 1990 (Area Y, L. 534, B. 1409) was analyzed for lipid content as an environmental control.

Experimental samples. In order to simulate the absorbed lipid content of archaeological ceramic vessels used to store olive oil and wine, pottery blanks (unglazed, fired ceramic rods weighing ca. 6 g each) were soaked in commercial olive oil and red wine for three days. The excess liquid was then poured off, and the pottery rods were placed in glass jars and surrounded with moist garden soil. The capped jars were incubated at 37 degrees C. Surrounding soil was periodically re-moistened. Pottery rods were removed for analysis after 95 days and 358 days. They were then prepared for extraction in the same manner as were the archaeological samples: the outer surface was removed and the remaining ceramic crushed in a mortar and pestle.

All equipment used was rinsed (x3) with organic solvent (2:1 chloroform/methanol) between samples.

Extraction of Lipids

Lipids were extracted by adding 5–10 ml of solvent (2:1 chloroform/methanol) to the powdered ceramic material or sediment (ca. 7 g for archaeological samples and ca. 2–7 g for experimental samples) in test tubes, followed by ultrasonication with a probe (2 x 1 min). The samples were then centrifuged (5 min or longer, as needed) and the supernatant was removed to clean test tubes. Samples were dried under nitrogen to obtain the Total Lipid Extract (TLE) and frozen until derivatization and analysis.

Only disposable glass test tubes were used and these were rinsed (x3) with solvent prior to use. The ultrasonic probe was also rinsed (x3) with solvent between samples. Solvent blanks were extracted in parallel with the experimental samples to control for the introduction of contaminant lipids during laboratory procedures.

Instrumentation and Analysis

All sample TLEs were analyzed by Gas Chromatography/Mass Spectrometry (GC/MS) at the University of California, San Diego—Scripps Institution of Oceanography Analytical Facilities.

Analysis was performed on a Hewlett-Packard 5890A gas chromatograph/mass spectrometer system. Instrument control, data acquisition, and data analysis was conducted via a PC with HP Chemstation software linked to the GC/MS system.

An AT-1 column (Alltech part #13753, 15m, 0.25mm ID, 0.25μm film thickness) was used to separate the biomolecular components of the archaeological and experimental sample TLEs immediately following derivatization to their trimethylsilyl (TMS) esters (by treatment with Sil-Prep reagent or BSTFA + 1% TMCS [Alltech]). The temperature program began with a 2 minute hold at 50 °C, followed by steps of 10 °C/min up to a maximum temperature of 330°C with a 10 minute isothermal hold. The injector temperature was set at 280°C. The carrier gas was helium at a column head pressure of 15 psi and a flow rate of 15 ml/min.

The archaeological sample TLEs were analyzed a second time using a slower temperature program on an EC-Wax column (Alltech part #19654, 30m, 0.32mm ID, 0.25 μm film thickness) to confirm the AT-1 results and to improve resolution of short chain fatty acids. In this case, methyl ester derivatives were prepared by treatment of the TLEs with Meth-Prep II reagent (Alltech). The temperature program was 50 to 260°C at 5°C/min with an initial 2 minute hold and a final hold at 260°C for 20 min. The injector port temperature was 250°C. The helium carrier gas flow rate was 10 ml/min with a column head pressure of 15 psi.

Injection volume was 2μl. Solvent blanks were run between samples in order to completely clear the column. Peak identifications were based on matching of mass spectra with an on-line library of known compounds and on retention times of purchased standards (lauric, palmitic, and behenic acids; cholesterol [Alltech]). The fatty acid molar ratios were calculated using peak areas of the major characteristic ion (74 or 75 for methyl ester or TMS derivatives, respectively) as integrated by the online software.

Results and Discussion

Results for Archaeological Samples

Fatty acids were detected in all eight of the torpedo jar TLEs. Figure 1 shows a typical EC-Wax column chromatogram. The relative abundances of the Fatty Acid Methyl Esters (FAME) in each sample based on the EC-Wax column chromatograms are given in Table 2 (by convention, the value for C16:0, the most common naturally occurring saturated fatty acid, is set equal to one). Six of the eight jars sampled contained a range of fatty acids from C16:0 to C7:0. Fatty acid profiles for all the torpedo jar samples are dominated by saturated carbon chains of lengths 7, 8, and 9. Only a trace amount of C16:0 (ca. 5% of that found in the torpedo jars) was detected in the sediment sample that was tested, suggesting that the depositional environment is not the source of the fatty acids extracted from the pottery walls, consistent with the conclusions of other researchers (e.g. Heron et al. 1991: 649). The AT-1 column results for the archaeological samples were similar to the EC-Wax column analyses, with the exception that fatty acids of chain lengths shorter than 8 are not reliably identified due to the steeper temperature gradient.

In addition to fatty acids, GC/MS analysis of the torpedo jar TLEs revealed the presence of plastic contaminants (phthalates and benzenedicarboxylic acids). This is a common finding in residue analyses of archaeological materials, where plastic-related compounds (especially phthalates) frequently appear in the lipid profiles (Fankhauser and Hocart 1995: 7). These volatile synthesized compounds are most likely absorbed from the depositional environment and/or during post-excavation storage.

Results for Experimental Samples

Comparison of GC/MS results for the experimentally-aged olive oil and wine samples shows that absorbed lipid content derived from these two sources differs dramatically. Table 3 presents the lipid composition of the olive oil- and wine-soaked pottery blank TLEs as revealed by the AT-1 column chromatograms. Chromatograms for the specimens aged for 358 days are shown in Figure 2. As expected based on published fatty acid content for olive oil and red wine (USDA Nutrient Data Base <www.nal.usda.gov>), the total weight of the TLEs from the olive oil-soaked pottery is much greater than from the wine-soaked pottery (ca. 67:1 after 358 days). Wine itself has no fat content; however, yeast used in the fermentation process may be the source of the trace amounts of C8:0 and C9:0 detected in the wine-soaked pottery.

Results from the olive-oil soaked pottery obtained after 95 and 358 days of incubation in moist garden soil clearly indicate the microbially-mediated process of lipid degradation and consumption that can be expected to occur in archaeological ceramic vessels (cf. Dudd et al. 1998). The level of oleic acid (C18:1 n=9), the principle component of olive oil (ca. 80% by weight), rapidly declines (by 95% over a 263 day period) while its breakdown products, saturated short-chain fatty acids— especially C9:0 and C8:0, accumulate (note that C7:0 is not identifiable using the AT-1 protocol due to the steep temperature gradient). A possible scenario for the diagenesis of oleic acid is shown in Figure 3. Such a process of hydroxylation at the double bond followed by chain-scission would give rise to intermediate products C14:0, C12:0, and C10:0, as well as the predominant C9:0 and C8:0, seen in the aged samples. A similar process could be expected to result in the breakdown of olive oil's linoleic (C18:2) and linolenic (C18:3) acids. Polyunsaturated fatty acids are thought to be the most susceptible to alteration and almost never survive in archaeological specimens (Heron and Evershed 1993: 268). In this experiment, no appreciable polyunsaturated fatty acids were present after 358 days of simulated burial. Dicarboxylic acids, dominated by the C7, C8, and C9 moieties (heptanedioic, octanedioic, and azelaic acids), were also detected in the experimentally-aged olive oil specimens. These are likewise expected oxidation products of unsaturated fatty acids (Regert et al. 1998). The amount of total lipid in the aged olive oil-soaked samples decreased by 47% over the course of 263 days. Loss of lipid from the pottery probably occurs through groundwater elution of the short-chain fatty acid degradation products which are readily water soluble and also as a result of consumption by micro-organisms (Dudd et al. 1998: 1345). The latter is confirmed by the appearance of microbial lipids (pentadecanoic C15:0 and heptadecanoic C17:0 acids) at very low levels in the olive oil-soaked specimen aged for 358 days.

Discussion

The fatty acid composition of the Gilat torpedo jar TLEs, with more components and at levels significantly greater than found in background sediment, suggest that the residues derive from the original contents of the vessel. This finding is consistent with previous studies carried out by other researchers (e.g. Charters et al. 1993; Evershed et al. 1992; Heron et al. 1991). It is clear from the fatty acid profiles of the archaeological samples, however, that extensive degradation of the source lipid has taken place during more than 6000 years of burial. This degradation is evidenced by the complete absence of any unsaturated fatty acids and the high levels of short-chain fatty acids such as are not found in any known organism (see for example Gunstone et al. 1986). The presence of C13:0 in one of the torpedo jar samples (#37), suggests that bacteria may have played a role in lipid breakdown since odd-chain fatty acids are common only in microorganisms (Harwood and Russell 1984: 9). Diagenetic processes of oxidation, hydrogenation, hydroxylation, and microbial degradation are commonly observed in archaeological specimens (Heron and Evershed 1993: 268), and lead to altered fatty acid profiles that cannot be matched directly to the original vessel contents.

As noted above, in the case of the torpedo jars, Alon and Levy (1989: 202) initially proposed that these vessels may have contained special liquids, such as olive oil or wine, brought to Gilat as ritual offerings. Examination of the lipid profiles of the experimentally-aged samples of olive oil- and red wine-infused pottery indicate that olive oil, and not wine, is the likely source of the torpedo jar absorbed residues. Although torpedo jar fatty acid profiles do not resemble the composition of fresh olive oil, the very high levels of C8:0, and especially C7:0 and C9:0, observed in the archaeological specimens are logical end products of its degradation as shown by the aged olive oil specimens. In contrast, wine contains virtually no fatty acids and therefore could not be the source of the torpedo jar residues. The trace amounts of C8:0 and C9:0 found in the wine-soaked experimental sample were less than 1% of those detected in the archaeological pottery.

The presence of significant levels of C7, C8, and C9 lipid moieties in archaeological residues has been associated with high concentrations of oleic acid (C18:1 n=9) in the postulated source material by other researchers. B. Fankhauser and C. Hocart (1995) found fatty acid ratios similar to those seen in the torpedo jar TLEs in lipid extracts of soil samples taken from an olive press at Pylos, Greece (ca. 1200 BC). They attributed the unusually high levels of C7:0, C8:0, and C9:0 to the breakdown of oleic acid that would have been present in sediments surrounding the olive press. A lipid extract from a 6th century AD ceramic oil lamp from Qasr Ibrim, Egyptian Nubia, contained short-chain dicarboxylic acids dominated by C9 azelaic acid and C8 octanedioic acid (Regert et al. (1998: 2031). According to the researchers, relative abundance profiles of the short-chain diagenetic end-products in archaeological materials should reflect the positions of unsaturation in the precursors; i.e. an abundance of C9 should indicate unsaturation at position 9 in the source biomolecule (Op. cit.: 2030). The experimental results of the current study generally confirm this expected relationship between the source lipid profile (in this case, olive oil) and its simulated archaeological manifestation. Both aged olive oil specimens showed high levels of C9:0. However, the observed relationship between levels of C8:0 and C9:0 appears to be somewhat variable-- C8:0 was the major component in the 95-day sample, while C9:0 dominated the 358-day sample. This suggests that molar abundance ratios between particular short-chain diagenetic products at any given point in time may shift, perhaps due to differential rates of progressive breakdown, microbial consumption, and/or elution.

Summary

Since their initial discovery and publication in the late 1980s, the size, unique form, and restricted spatial distribution of the Gilat torpedo jar have stimulated interest in its possible function within southern Levantine Chalcolithic society. Based on morphological analogy, archaeological context, petrographic analyses, and ethnohistoric evidence, the torpedo jar is thought to have played an important role in cult-related activities and inter-community exchange during the 5th–4th millennium BCE. The organic residue study reported in this section was designed to investigate the possible contents of these vessels, which may have been intended as ritual offerings. The results of extraction and GC/MS analysis of absorbed lipids from eight Gilat torpedo jars revealed appreciable levels of fatty acids that were distinguishable from a background sediment sample. In spite of the degraded nature of the fatty acid profiles, it was possible, through comparison with experimentally-aged samples of olive oil- and wine-soaked pottery, to identify olive oil as the likely source of the torpedo jar lipid residues. This is the first direct evidence for the function of the Gilat torpedo jars.

The significance of this finding must be viewed within the context of agrotechnological development related to olive cultivation and processing during the 5th –4th millennium BCE, an innovative period that witnessed the 'secondary products revolution' in the Levant (Levy 1983, Sherratt 1981). In fact, the precise time frame for the domestication of the olive in the Near East remains controversial. It is generally agreed that this was achieved only after Neolithic grain agriculture was in place—approximately 1000 years after the collapse of Pre-Pottery Neolithic cultures in the Levant. The presence of olive pits in collections from the early excavations at Tuleilat Ghassul led D. Zohary (Zohary 1975) to suggest that olive domestication occurred during the Chalcolithic period. Some time after Zohary's writing, large quantities of olive pits were discovered in underwater Late Neolithic sites along Israel's Carmel coast by E. Galili and his colleagues (Galili et al. 1989). They proposed that olives were already domesticated during the Late Neolithic. However, M. Kislev (Kislev 1994–95) carried out a metric analysis of the olive pits from these submerged sites and argued that the recovered specimens were in fact from wild trees. Although there may not be a consensus as to exactly when olives were domesticated, it is clear that sometime during the Late Neolithic/Chalcolithic interface the processing and consumption of these fruits and their oils became increasingly important to Levantine societies. The best evidence for olive oil extraction during the Late Neolithic period comes from the submerged site of Kfar Samir off the coast of Haifa (Galili et al. 1997). In the following Chalcolithic period, there is limited evidence of olive-oil extraction at some sites in the Jordan valley (Neef 1990), the Golan Heights (Epstein 1993), and Samaria (Eitam 1993). Present evidence thus implies that olives, and we may assume olive oil, were still rare and probably highly valued commodities during the Chalcolithic period. In this context, the identification of olive oil residues in the Gilat torpedo vessels takes on a greater poignancy in terms of the social, economic, and religious significance of olive oil at the Gilat Chalcolithic sanctuary. The symbolic meaning of olive oil and its role in the Gilat sanctuary is discussed in the concluding chapter of this volume.

Acknowledgements

M. Burton would like to thank Professor Avram Biran and the staff of the Nelson Glueck School of Biblical Archaeology–Hebrew Union College, Jerusalem, Israel for facilitating access to the Gilat pottery collections. Thanks to Dr Ron Burton, Director of the Marine Biology Research Division at UCSD-SIO, for providing laboratory space and assistance. Dr Kevin Walda and Charles Limm of the UCSD-SIO Analytical Facilities provided essential technical support, and their attention and advice was very much appreciated. Special thanks to Dr Barry Fankhauser, Australian Department of Health and Aging, for making valuable suggestions regarding experimental procedures for the torpedo jar lipid analysis. Thanks also to Dr Jeffrey Bada of UCSD-SIO for reviewing the results and their interpretation. The project could not have gone forward without the generous funds provided by the Department of Anthropology at UCSD and the Wenner-Gren Foundation for Anthropological Research (Pre-doctoral Grant #6496 to M. Burton).

Tables

Table Appendix 1.1. Gilat torpedo jars tested for lipid residues.

GC/MS Sample #	Year/Lic#/ Locus	Plate #	Munsell Code	Inclusions	Description
5	1975/568/L.16	1	2.5YR 6/6	Fine dolomitic sand	Thick-walled (20mm). Layered construction
6	1975/568/L.31	2	5 YR 7/4	Coarse, angular black, gray, white grits; some refractive	Thin-walled (8mm). Gray core.
7	1975/568/L.39	3	2.5YR 6/4	Coarse white and light gray grits	Medium-thick wall (12.5 mm).
8	1970/25-6/L.13	4	2.5YR 7/3	Medium-coarse (0.5–3mm diam.) black, gray angular grits with some white grits	Thick-walled (20mm). Black core.
35	1975/568/L.19	5	2.5YR 7/4	Coarse angular white grits and dolomitic sand	Thick-walled (28mm).
36	1975/568/L.54	6	2.5YR 7/3	Medium coarse (ca. 1mm diam.) rounded gray grits	Thick-walled (25mm).
37	1975/568/L.41	7	2.5YR 7/3	Medium coarse (ca. 1mm diam.) angular white and light gray grits; some refractive	Thick walled (18mm).
38	1987/36-87/ L. 585-53	Not illustrated	5 YR 7/4	Medium coarse (ca. 1mm diam.) angular dark to light gray grits; some refractive	Thick-walled (23mm). Dark gray core.

Table Appendix 1.2. FAME molar ratios for Gilat torpedo jars.

	Sample 5	Sample 6	Sample 7	Sample 8	Sample 35	Sample 36	Sample 37	Sample 38
C4:0	0	0	0	0	0	0	0	0
C6:0	0	0	0	0	0	0	0	0
C7:0	1.49	2.18	1.51	1.52	present	3.25	3.84	present
C8:0	2.99	4.09	2.80	3.02	present	5.52	9.45	present
C9:0	1.92	5.25	5.24	1.14	0	8.30	11.12	0
C10:0	0	0.39	0.16	0.20	0	0.89	1.60	0
C12:0	0	0.93	0.26	0.60	0	0.96	1.79	0
C13:0	0	0	0	0	0	0	0.35	0
C14:0	0	0	0.54	0.58	0	0	0	0
C16:0	1.00	1.00	1.00	1.00	0	1.00	1.00	0
C18:0	0.86	0.30	0.42	0.45	0	0	0.29	0

Table Appendix 1.3. Components of Experimental Sample TLEs (AT-1 Column).

	Olive Oil (A)	Olive Oil-Soaked Pottery	Olive Oil-Soaked Pottery	Red Wine (B)	Red Wine-Soaked Pottery
Number of Days Aged (C)		95	358		358
TLE ug/Powdered ceramic g		40869	25776		386
C6:0	0.00	N/A	N/A	0.00	N/A
C7:0	0.00	N/A	N/A	0.00	N/A
C8:0	0.00	2.97	1.34	0.00	trace
C9:0	0.00	2.36	1.88	0.00	trace
C10:0	0.00	0.19	0.04	0.00	0.00
C12:0	0.00	0.03	0.01	0.00	0.00
C14:0	0.00	0.01	0.01	0.00	0.00
C16:0	1.00	1.00	1.00	0.00	0.00
C16:1	0.07	0.00	0.00	0.00	0.00
C18:0	0.20	0.16	0.08	0.00	0.00
C18:1	6.87	0.19	0.01	0.00	0.00
C18:2	0.65	0.02	0.00	0.00	0.00
C18:3	0.05	0.00	0.00	0.00	0.00
C20:0	0.03	0.00	0.02	0.00	0.00
C20:1	0.02	0.00	0.00	0.00	0.00
Sterols		no	no		no
Phthalates		yes	no		no
Other Compounds		Glycerol			Benzoic acid, TMS ester
		Propanedioic acid, methyl-, bis (TMS) ester			
		Hexanedioic acid, 3-methyl, bis (TMS) ester	Hexanedioic acid, bis (TMS) ester		
		Heptanedioic acid, bis (TMS) ester	Heptanedioic acid, bis (TMS) ester		
		Octanedioic acid, bis (TMS) ester	Octanedioic acid, bis (TMS) ester		

Figures

Figure Appendix 1.1. EC-Wax chromatogram for torpedo jar sample 37
Compound key: C7:0-C18:0 fatty acids
P Phthalate and benzenedicarboxylic acid contaminants.

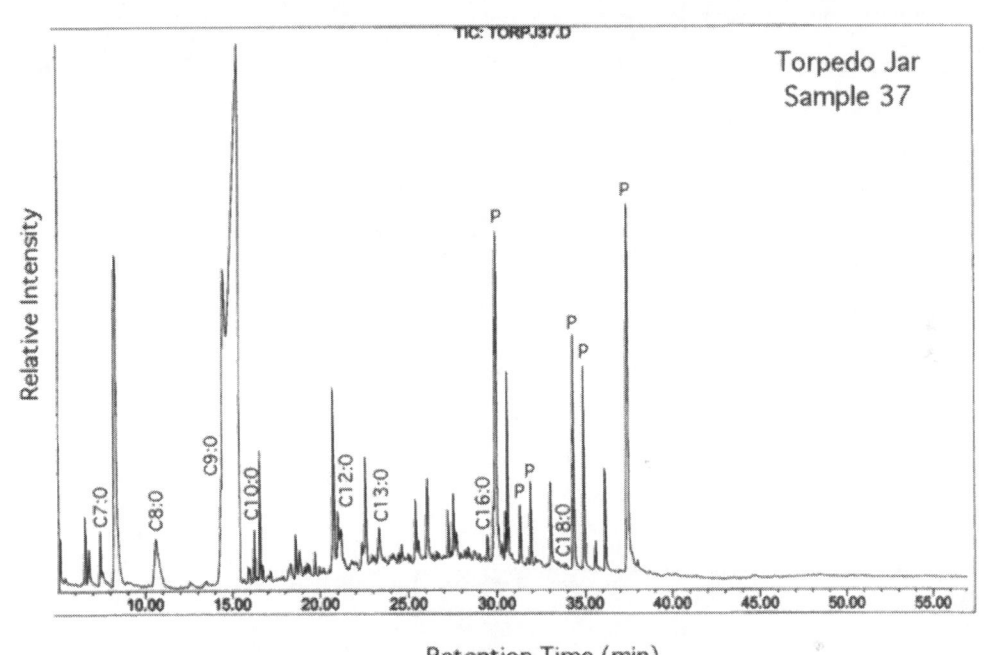

Figure Appendix 1.2. AT-1 Chromatograms for 358-day aged samples: A, olive oil; B, wine
Compound key: C8:0-C20:0 Fatty acids
D6-D10 Dicarboxylic acids
MP Monopalmitin
IS Internal standard (n-Tetratriacontane)

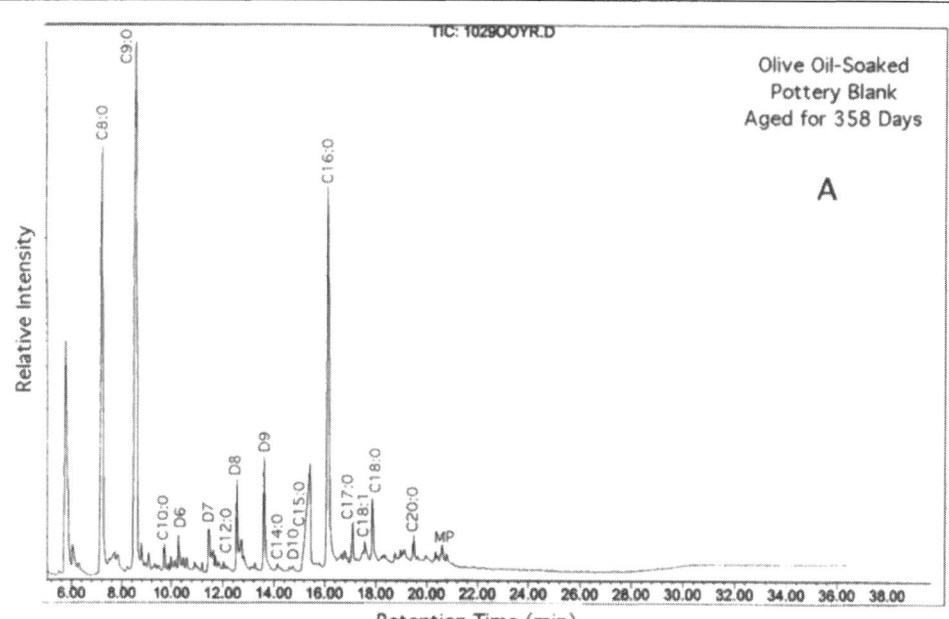

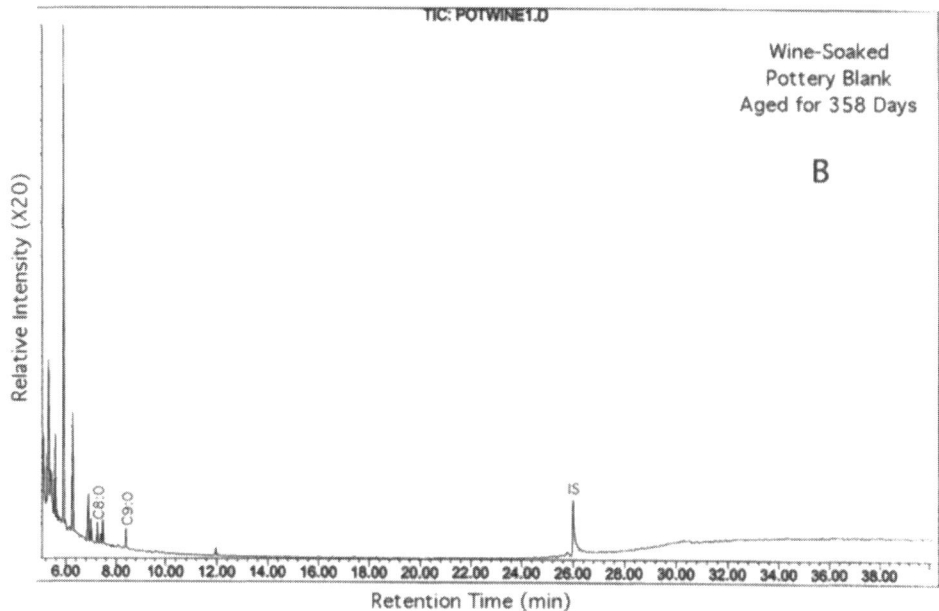

Figure Appendix 1.3. One proposed degradation pathway for the formation of short-chain fatty acids from oleic acid.

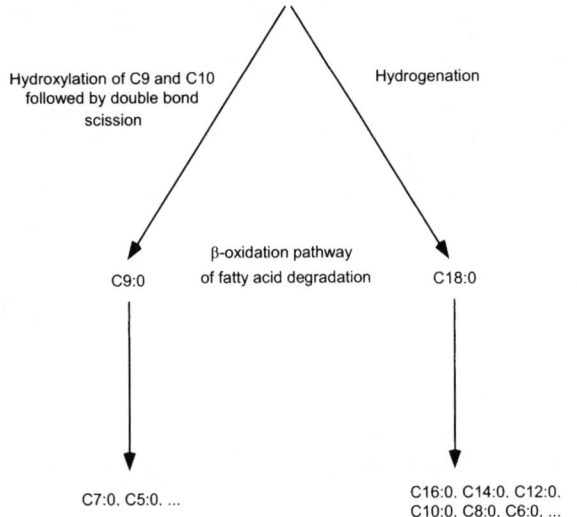

Degradation of Oleic Acid
C18:1 (n=9)

CH_3-CH_2-CH_2-CH_2-CH_2-CH_2-CH_2-CH_2-CH=CH-CH_2-CH_2-CH_2-CH_2-CH_2-CH_2-CH_2-COOH

Hydroxylation of C9 and C10
followed by double bond
scission

Hydrogenation

β-oxidation pathway
of fatty acid degradation

C9:0

C18:0

C7:0. C5:0. ...

C16:0. C14:0. C12:0.
C10:0. C8:0. C6:0. ...

Plates

Plate Appendix 1.1. Torpedo jar vessels sampled for residual analysis
(illustrations from Alon 1990).

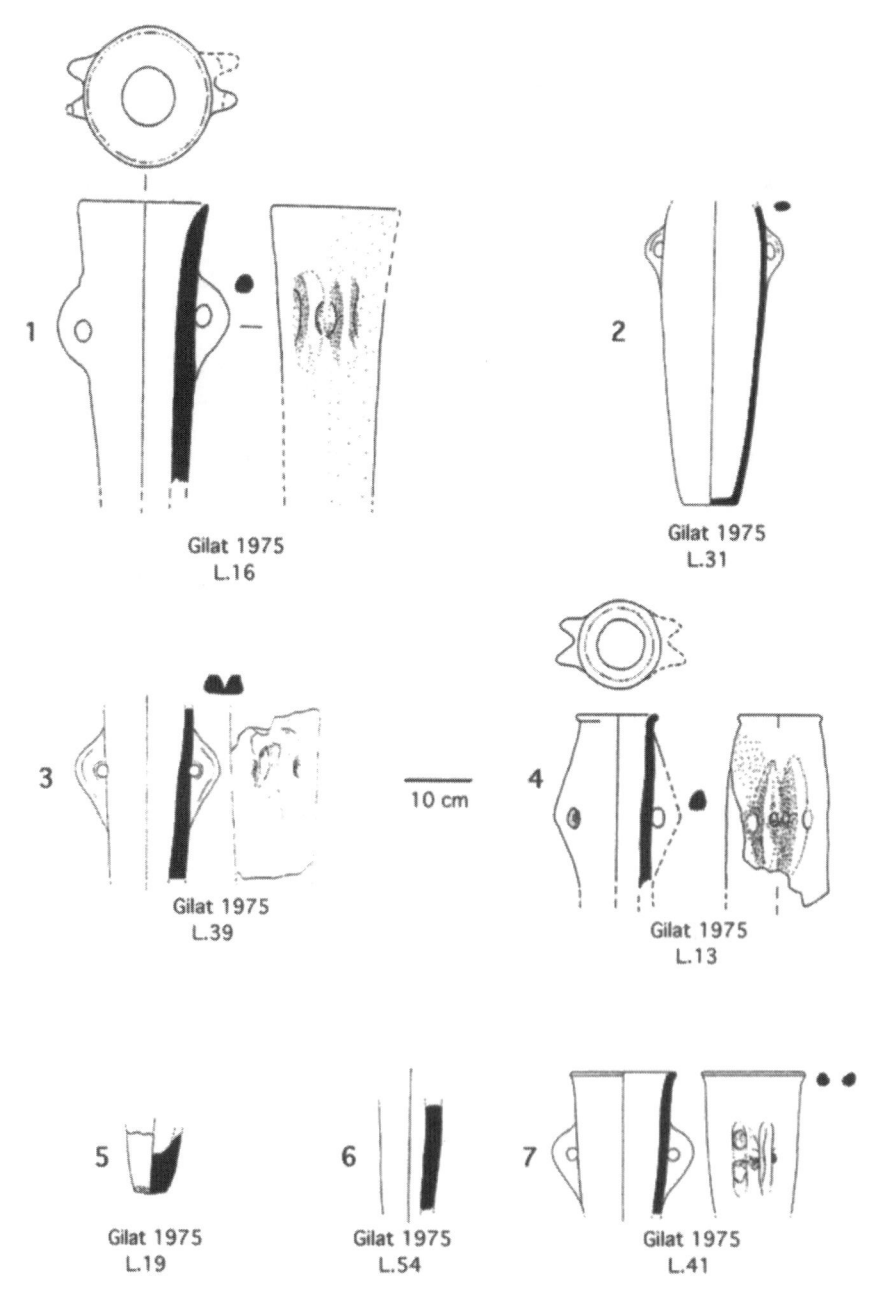

References

Alon, D. (1990) Cult Artifacts from Gilat and relations with Northern Edom in the Chalcolithic Period. *'Atiqot* (Hebrew Series) 10:1–12.

Alon, D., and T.E. Levy (1989) The Archaeology of Cult and the Chalcolithic Sanctuary at Gilat. *Journal of Mediterranean Archaeology* 2(2):163–221.

Condamin, J.F., M. Formenti, O. Metais, M. Michel and P. Blond (1976) The application of gas chromatography to the tracing of oil in ancient amphorae. *Archaeometry* 18:195–201.

Charters, S., R.P. Evershed, L.J. Goad, P.W. Blinkhorn and V. Denham (1993) Quantification and distribution of lipid in archaeological ceramics: implications for studying potsherds for organic residue analysis and the classification of vessel use. *Archaeometry* 35:211–23.

Charters, S., R.P. Evershed, P.W. Blinkhorn, and V. Denham (1995) Evidence for the mixing of fats and waxes in archaeological ceramics. *Archaeometry* 37:113–27.

Copley, M.S., R. Berstan, S.N. Dudd, G. Docherty, A.J. Mukherjee, V. Straker and S. Payne (2003) Direct chemical evidence for widespread dairying in prehistoric Britain. *Proceedings of the National Academy of Sciences* 100(4):1524–529.

Copley, M.S., P.J. Rose, A. Clapham, D.N. Edwards, M.C. Horton, and R.P. Evershed (2001) Processing palm fruits in the Nile Valley--biomolecular evidence from Qasr Ibrim. *Antiquity* 75:538–42.

Dudd, S.N., M. Regert and R.P. Evershed (1998) Assessing microbial lipid contributions during laboratory degradations of fats and oils and pure triacylglycerols absorbed in ceramic potsherds. *Organic Geochemistry* 29(5–7):1345–354.

Eitam, D. (1993) 'Between the [olive] rows, oil will be produced, presses will be trod...' (Job 24, 11). *Oil and Wine Production in the Mediterranean Area.* XXVI:65.

Epstein, C. (1993) Oil production in the Golan Heights during the Chalcolithic period. *Tel Aviv* 20:133.

Evershed, R.P., S.N. Dudd, S. Charters, H. Mottram, A.W. Stott, A. Raven, P.F. van Bergen and H.A. Bland (1999) Lipids as carriers of anthropogenic signals from prehistory. *Philosophical Transactions of the Royal Society of London* 354:19–31.

Evershed, R.P., C. Heron, S. Charters and L.J. Goad (1992) The Survival of Food Residues: New Methods of Interpretation and Application. *Proceedings of the British Academy* 77:187–208.

Evershed, R.P., C. Heron, and L.J. Goad (1991) Epicuticular wax components preserved in potsherds as chemical indicators of leafy vegetables in ancient diets. *Antiquity* 65:540–44.

Fankhauser, B. (1994) Protein and lipid analysis of food residues. In *Tropical Archaeobotany: Applications and New Developments*, edited by J.G. Hather. New York: Routledge, pp. 227–50.

— (1997) Amino acid analysis of food residues in pottery: a field and laboratory study. *Archaeology in Oceania* 32(1):131–40.

Fankhauser, B., and C. Hocart (1995) *Gas Chromatography/Mass Spectrometry Analyses of Pylos Soil Samples: A Report to the Pylos Project.* George Rapp, Coordinator. 15pp.

Galili, E., D.J. Stanley, J. Sharvit and M. Weinstein-Evron (1997) Evidence for Earliest Olive-Oil Production in Submerged Settlements off the Carmel Coast, Israel. *Journal of Archaeological Science* 24:1141–50.

Galili, E., D. Zohary and M. Weinstein-Evron (1989) Appearance of olives in submerged Neolithic sites along the Carmel coast. *Mitekufat Haeven* 22:95–97.

Goren, Y. (1987) *The Petrography of Ceramic Assemblages from the Chalcolithic Period of Southern Eretz Isarael.* Unpublished M.A. thesis. The Hebrew University of Jerusalem.

— (1995) Shrines and ceramics in Chalcolithic Israel: the view through the petrographic microscope. *Archaeometry* 37(2):287–305.

Gunstone, F.D., J.L. Harwood and F.B. Padley (eds.) (1986) *The Lipid Handbook.* New York: Chapman and Hall.

Harwood, J.L. and N.J. Russell (1984) *Lipids in Plants and Microbes.* London: George Allen & Unwin.

Heron, C., and R.P. Evershed (1993) The analysis of organicresidues and the study ofpottery use. In *Archaeological Method and Theory.* Vol. 5, edited by M.B. Schiffer. Tucson: University of Arizona Press, pp. 247–84.

Heron, C., R.P. Evershed and L.J. Goad (1991) Effects of migrationof soil lipids onorganic residues associated with buried potsherds. *Journal of Archaeological Science* 18:641–59.

Kislev, M.E. (1994–95) Wild Olive Stones at Submerged Chalcolithic Kfar Samir, Haifa, Israel. *Journal of the Israel Prehistoric Society* 26:134–45.

Levy, T.E. (1983) The Emergence of Specialized Pastoralism in the Southern Levant. *World Archaeology* 15:15–36.

McGovern, P., D.L. Glusker, R.A. Moreau, A. Nunez, C.W. Beck, E. Simpson, E.D. Butrym, L.J. Exner and E.C. Stout (1999) A funerary feast fit for King Midas. *Nature* 402 (23/30 December): 863–64.

Malainey, M.E., R. Przybylski and B.L. Sherriff (1999) The Effectsof Thermal and Oxidative Degradation on the Fatty Acid Composition of Food Plants and Animals of Western Canada: Implications for the Identification of Archaeological Vessel Residues. *Journal of Archaeological Science* 26:95–103.

Neef, R. (1990) Introduction, development, and environmental implications of olive culture: the evidence from Jordan. In *Man's Role in the Shaping of the Eastern Mediterranean Landscape*, edited by S.G. Bottema, G. Entjes-Nieborg and W. van Zeist. Rotterdam: Brookfield, pp. 295–306.

Patrick, M., A.J. deKoning and A.B. Smith (1985) Gas liquid chromatographic analysis of fatty acids in food residues from ceramics found in the southwestern cape, South Africa. *Archaeometry* 27(3):231–36.

Reber, E.A., and R.P. Evershed (2004) How did Mississipians prepare maize? The application of compound-specific carbon isotope analysis to absorbed pottery residues from several Mississippi Valley sites. *Archaeometry* 46(1):19–33.

Regert, M., H.A. Bland, S.N. Dudd, P.F. van Bergen and R.P. Evershed (1998) Free and bound fatty acid oxidation products in archaeological ceramic vessels. *Proceedings of the Royal Society of London*. B 265:2027–32.

Sherratt, A.G. (1981) Plough and Pastoralism: Aspects of the secondary products revolution. In *Patterns of the Past: Studies in Honour of David Clarke*, edited by I. Hodder, G. Isaac and N. Hammond. Cambridge: Cambridge University Press, pp. 261–305.

Skibo, J.M. (1992) *Pottery Function: a use-alteration perspective*. Interdisciplinary Contributions to Archaeology. New York: Plenum Press.

USDA Nutrient Data Base <www.nal.usda.gov>.

Will, E.L. (1977) The Ancient Commercial Amphora. *Archaeology* 30(4):264–70.

Zohary, D. (1975) Beginnings of Fruit Growing in the Old World. *Science* 187:319–27.

Appendix 2
Radiocarbon Dating of Gilat

Thomas E. Levy and Margie Burton

The settlement history of the northern Negev desert in Israel during the Chalcolithic period has been a controversial issue for some time (Burton and Levy 2001: 1232; Gilead 1994; Joffe and Dessel 1995). The distinctive material assemblages discussed in this volume suggest that Gilat had a special role in the evolution of Chalcolithic social systems in this region and further that it may represent an early phase in the developmental trajectory. The purpose of the radiocarbon dating of Gilat is to verify the age of the material remains and to place the site in chronological context with other 14C-dated sites of the northern Negev Chalcolithic. The sample of radiocarbon dates (n = 8) is small and problematic as will be discussed below. The relative paucity of carbonized material found during the excavations made it impossible to find an abundance of short-life samples. However, the dates described here are important in that they help place the Gilat Chalcolithic occupation within the northern Negev chronological sequence with an objective radiometric method. Some major Chalcolithic research projects have failed to produce any radiocarbon dates (cf. Gilead 1995) making it extremely difficult to objectively order those assemblages within the social evolutionary trajectory of the late 5th–early 4th millennium BCE southern Levant. Finally, given the small sample size and rather random process of selecting material for radiocarbon dating, it is not useful to model these dates using wiggle-matching or other statistical methods (Bronk Ramsey 2001).

Eight samples (seven of charcoal, one of burnt seeds) from Gilat have been radiocarbon-dated. Details of the sample provenience are shown in Table Appendix 2.1. The radiocarbon determinations are shown in Table Appendix 2.2. The one- and two-sigma limits for the calibrated dates from Gilat are graphically represented in Figure Appendix 1.1 in comparison with the set of 40 dates from Shiqmim (Levy et al., in prep.), which currently has the best radiometric record of any northern Negev Chalcolithic site.

Table Appendix 2.1. Gilat 14C Sample Descriptions

Sample	Material	Year	Locus	Basket	Stratum	Context
OxA-4011	Charred seeds (wheat/barley)	1992	1369	4359	IIIA	Silo
RT-860A	Charcoal	1987	128	518	IIC	Silo
RT-2058					IIC	
OxA-3556	Charcoal	1991	1044	3348	IIB	Pit
OxA-3555	Charcoal	1991	709	5350	IIB	Pit
Beta-131730	Charcoal	1992	1265	3991	IIB	Hearth
RT-860B	Charcoal	1987	92	595	IIB	Pit
Beta-131729	Charcoal	1991	696	5275	IIA	Pit

Table Appendix 2.2. ^{14}C Determinations of the Gilat Samples

Sample	Radiocarbon Age BP	$\delta^{13}C‰$	Calibrated BC* 68.3% area (1-sigma)	Relative Area under Probability Distribution	Calibrated BC* 95.4% area (2-sigma)	Relative Area under Probability Distribution	Reference
OxA-4011	5540 ± 70	-20.9	4455-4335	1.00	4524-4508	0.013	Burton and Levy 2001: 1244
					4503-4247	0.987	
RT-860A	5440 ± 180	-24.3	4453-4416	0.085	4689-3938	0.985	Alon and Levy 1989: 169
			4408-4215	0.528	3860-3810	0.015	Carmi and Segal 1992: 125
			4204-4044	0.387			
RT-2058	4530 ± 85		3363-3255	0.399	3503-3429	0.075	Burton and Levy 2001: 1244
			3252-3098	0.601	3381-3006	0.874	
					2994-2923	0.050	
OxA-3556	5790 ± 105	-23.2	4772-4750	0.081	4902-4888	0.008	Burton and Levy 2001: 1244
			4726-4522	0.896	4879-4874	0.003	
			4509-4503	0.023	4852-4446	0.964	
					4421-4397	0.017	
					4383-4365	0.009	
OxA-3555	5710 ± 100	-15.2	4687-4630	0.226	4774-4748	0.030	Burton and Levy 2001: 1244
			4623-4457	0.774	4732-4352	0.970	
Beta-131730	5730 ± 40	-23.3	4668-4662	0.042	4688-4489	0.963	Burton and Levy 2001: 1244
			4647-4643	0.027	4477-4461	0.037	
			4616-4518	0.843			
			4512-4501	0.089			
RT-860B	4800 ± 135	-24.3	3706-3497	0.743	3943-3330	0.974	Alon and Levy 1989: 169
			3463-3376	0.257	3218-3180	0.013	Carmi and Segal 1992: 125
					3157-3121	0.013	
Beta-131729	5560 ± 50	-22.7	4451-4418	0.389	4496-4468	0.049	Burton and Levy 2001: 1244
			4403-4351	0.611	4464-4330	0.943	
					4269-4263	0.007	

* Calibrated using CALIB v4.4 (Stuiver and Reimer 1993) and INTCAL 98.14c calibration data set (Stuiver et al.1998)

Figure Appendix 2.2. Calibrated 14C Dates from Gilat and Shiqmim Village
(See Table Appendix 2.2)

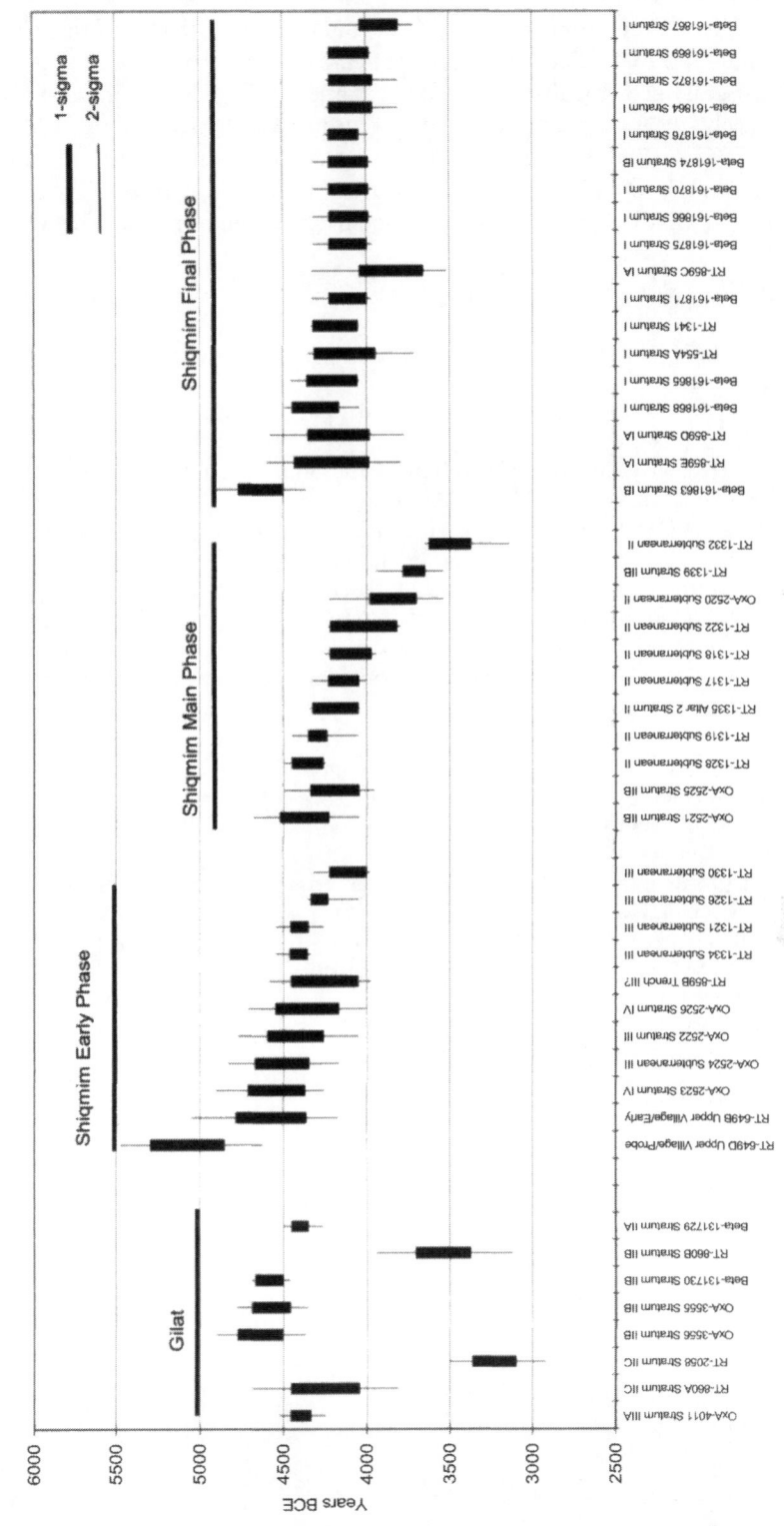

Six of the eight ^{14}C determinations for Gilat indicate activity within three or four centuries centered around 4500 BCE. This time frame appears to correspond with the initial settlement of Shiqmim. Substantial growth of the planned rectilinear village at Shiqmim onto the floodplain terrace (Levy et al. 1991) may have occurred some time later, between about 4200 and 4000 BCE. Two of the Gilat dates (RT-2058 and RT-860B) appear to be outliers and may represent disturbed depositional contexts. Overall, Gilat's radiocarbon dates are consistent with a chronological placement early in the Chalcolithic settlement sequence of the northern Negev.

References

Alon, D., and T.E. Levy (1989) The Archaeology of Cult and the Chalcolithic Sanctuary at Gilat. *Journal of Mediterranean Archaeology* 2(2):163–221.

Bronk Ramsey, C. (2001) Development of the radiocarbon calibration program OxCal. *Radiocarbon* 43 355–63.

Burton, M., and T.E. Levy (2001) The Chalcolithic Radiocarbon Record and Its Use in Southern Levantine Archaeology. *Radiocarbon* 43(3):1223–46.

Carmi, I., and D. Segal (1992) Rehovot radiocarbon measurements IV. *Radiocarbon* 34(1):115–32.

Gilead, I. (1994) The History of the Chalcolithic Settlement in the Nahal Beer Sheva Area: The Radiocarbon Aspect. *Bulletin of the American Schools of Oriental Research* 296:1–13.

Gilead, I. (ed.) (1995) *Grar, A Chalcolithic Site in the Northern Negev*. Studies by the Department of Bible and the Ancient Near East. Vol. VII. Beer-Sheva, Israel. Ben Gurion University of the Negev Press.

Joffe, A.H., and J.P. Dessel (1995) Redefining Chronology and Terminology for the Chalcolithic of the Southern Levant. *Current Anthropology* 36:507–18.

Levy, T.E., D. Alon, C. Grigson, A. Holl, P. Goldberg, Y. Rowan, and P. Smith (1991) Subterranean Negev Settlement. *National Geographic Research & Exploration* 7(4):394–413.

Levy, T.E., Y.M. Rowan, and M.M. Burton (in prep.) Desert Chiefdom: Dimensions of Subterranean Settlement and Society in Israel's Desert (ca. 4500–3600 BC) Based on New Data from Shiqmim. London: Equinox.

Stuiver, M., and P.J. Reimer (1993) Extended 14C database and revised CALIB radiocarbon calibration program. *Radiocarbon* 35:215–30.

Stuiver, M., P.J. Reimer, E. Bard, J.W. Beck, G.S. Burr, K.A. Hughen, B. Kromer, F.G. McCormac, J. van der Plicht, and M. Spurk (1998) INTCAL98 Radiocarbon age calibration 24,000 - 0 cal BP. *Radiocarbon* 40:1041–83.

Index

A

Abu Hamid, 136, 211, 402, 407, 442, 443, 496, 502, 578, 596, 597, 599, 659, 678, 712, 733, 743, 747, 751, 766, 767, 768, 769, 770, 803, 806, 807, 810, 820
Abu Matar, 133, 136, 212, 242, 245, 323, 324, 337, 364, 369, 376, 388, 393, 394, 403, 426, 427, 434, 443, 456, 500, 521, 577, 580, 584, 585, 593, 594, 595, 598, 680, 712, 735, 755, 756, 805, 812, 815, 817, 824, 832, 843
Abu-Hatseira, 26, 76, 79, 81, 82, 86, 87, 90, 91, 841
agents, 348, 737, 738, 791, 814
agro-technology, 5, 15
Alon, D., 25, 211, 316, 324, 363, 388, 390, 495, 499, 569, 570, 678, 698, 733, 817, 818, 841, 842, 857, 861
Amiran, R., 25, 211, 495, 678, 698, 733, 817, 818
Amuq, 221, 222
anthropomorphic, 10, 97, 136, 593, 730, 733, 739, 750, 787, 789, 790, 791, 815, 821, 838
Appadurai, A., 495, 733
Arad, 22, 98, 211, 313, 374, 511, 571, 575, 576, 577, 578, 579, 584, 592, 598, 678, 680, 687, 698, 713, 733
Asherah, 702
axe, 106, 114, 118, 119, 148, 443, 505, 565, 580, 583, 619, 620, 662
Azor, 323, 324, 440, 588

B

Baba Baruch, 82, 83, 84, 85, 86, 88, 89, 90
Baba Sali, 75, 76, 78, 81, 82, 83, 84, 85, 86, 87, 88, 89, 90, 837, 839, 840
Bar-Adon, P., 313, 324, 388, 678, 698
Barber, E., 678, 733
Bar-Yosef, O., 324, 363, 678, 698
beads, 101, 122, 132, 320, 518, 522, 572, 573, 577, 582, 584, 585, 586, 592, 599, 600, 628, 655, 678, 679, 683, 689, 753, 809

Bedouin, 14, 16, 18, 25, 29, 30, 54, 55, 56, 57, 58, 59, 60, 61, 62, 63, 64, 65, 66, 67, 68, 69, 70, 71, 72, 73, 74, 88, 90, 100, 245, 338, 441, 500, 519, 571, 704, 840, 843
beer, 437
Beersheva, 5, 6, 22, 23, 24, 25, 30, 31, 130, 137, 211, 212, 215, 221, 242, 313, 315, 316, 323, 327, 390, 392, 393, 402, 403, 405, 408, 409, 411, 417, 421, 424, 434, 436, 439, 440, 441, 443, 451, 496, 497, 498, 506, 513, 518, 519, 520, 521, 587, 595, 598, 599, 601, 678, 679, 680, 689, 717, 730, 731, 743, 751, 781, 787, 789, 814, 816, 817, 819, 821, 824, 830, 831, 832, 842, 843
belief, 3, 5, 6, 7, 10, 16, 23, 24, 26, 29, 33, 35, 56, 65, 69, 70, 74, 89, 750, 813, 828
Bell, C., 25, 495, 818
Ben Shemen, 323, 339, 340, 341, 343, 344, 345, 346, 364, 585
Besorian, 378, 379, 381, 521, 522
Bilu, Y., 26, 91, 841
Bir es-Safadi, 133, 137, 216, 227, 241, 245, 316, 337, 338, 339, 394, 402, 403, 434, 443, 444, 453, 506, 507, 513, 521, 585, 588, 589, 593, 594, 595, 598, 680, 778, 831, 832
Boas, F., 841
bone element analysis, 216, 234, 235, 258, 259, 260, 261, 265, 286
Bordes, F., 569
Bourke, S., 26, 211, 363, 495, 569, 841
Braun, E., 678, 681
Brumfiel, E., 495, 733, 818
burial, 28, 80, 82, 83, 84, 100, 101, 102, 103, 104, 105, 108, 109, 114, 118, 119, 124, 126, 127, 128, 130, 131, 134, 137, 138, 144, 145, 146, 147, 149, 150, 152, 177, 180, 218, 219, 234, 235, 243, 244, 249, 259, 268, 270, 282, 283, 285, 290, 323, 327, 329, 330, 331, 333, 334, 335, 336, 337, 338, 339, 340, 347, 349, 350, 351, 363, 373, 386, 438, 439, 440, 443, 456, 457, 488, 496, 497, 510, 550, 581, 582, 584, 599, 601, 622, 624, 631, 632, 642,

643, 679, 688, 690, 704, 708, 715, 731, 732, 733, 809, 821, 838, 842, 848
Byblos, 341, 364, 496, 751, 787, 788, 806, 820

C

Canaan, T., 26, 73
Capra, 219, 240, 244, 313, 806
Carneiro, R., 26
Catal Huyuk, 712, 735
cattle, 72, 79, 218, 219, 220, 221, 222, 223, 225, 227, 228, 229, 230, 231, 232, 233, 234, 235, 236, 237, 240, 243, 244, 247, 250, 255, 256, 261, 262, 268, 274, 280, 284, 285, 304, 305, 306, 313, 314, 315, 442, 684, 685, 686, 689, 690, 692, 693, 695, 696, 697, 802, 805, 806, 810, 821
Cauvin, J., 818
Cave of the Treasure, 245, 313, 324, 388, 389, 390, 495, 678, 687, 688, 698, 704, 733, 805, 818, 824
cemetery, 81, 82, 87, 315, 327, 336, 339, 349, 364, 435, 439, 510, 512, 581
Central Hill Country, 373
ceremonial centers, 21
ceremonial ware, 393
chiefdom, 5, 6, 16, 20, 23, 24, 717, 781, 828, 830, 832, 836
chipped stone, 504, 505, 506, 517, 519, 520, 521, 522, 570, 574, 578, 753
churn, 110, 112, 129, 148, 187, 192, 216, 231, 232, 386, 399, 409, 421, 422, 426, 442, 450, 451, 455, 489, 490, 491, 492, 738, 739, 743, 748, 749, 810, 815
City of David, 373, 679
cognitive, 15, 24, 31, 368, 370, 501, 728, 737, 750, 786, 802, 813, 814, 825
collective burial, 330, 336, 337, 347, 352
Commenge, C., 678
Communitas, 31
community-based pilgrimage, 80
Confucius, 3
Conkey, M., 819
consumption, 14, 89, 227, 229, 233, 245, 393, 398, 406, 407, 408, 409, 423, 434, 435, 436, 439, 449, 450, 452, 453, 456, 497, 716, 717, 735, 737, 749, 750, 774, 775, 777, 779, 780, 781, 836, 848, 849, 850
cooking, 54, 67, 108, 113, 136, 216, 391, 437, 438, 443, 444, 449, 457, 503, 733
cornet, 136, 208, 232, 414, 430, 449, 461, 738, 815

courtyard, 97, 98, 108, 112, 114, 115, 117, 120, 121, 135, 136, 137, 176, 177, 178, 331, 445, 448, 450, 453, 455, 520, 838
Crapanzano, V., 91
cult, 8, 9, 10, 11, 12, 13, 14, 15, 16, 18, 19, 23, 24, 25, 31, 35, 37, 38, 39, 43, 45, 47, 48, 49, 50, 51, 52, 55, 56, 71, 75, 76, 81, 87, 88, 89, 90, 91, 96, 97, 98, 99, 100, 102, 110, 119, 133, 134, 136, 137, 138, 211, 323, 327, 338, 363, 367, 368, 388, 495, 569, 589, 594, 678, 702, 715, 726, 733, 734, 738, 747, 763, 782, 783, 784, 786, 787, 791, 806, 815, 817, 818, 820, 825, 828, 837, 838, 841, 849
culture, 4, 5, 6, 9, 10, 11, 12, 15, 18, 19, 21, 24, 32, 37, 48, 53, 80, 96, 99, 102, 103, 106, 110, 112, 115, 116, 117, 133, 139, 368, 377, 381, 390, 392, 408, 434, 438, 443, 495, 497, 499, 500, 501, 502, 503, 504, 518, 570, 572, 693, 730, 733, 735, 737, 738, 739, 748, 749, 750, 751, 759, 786, 787, 788, 789, 790, 791, 802, 809, 818, 820, 821, 823, 825, 829, 830, 832, 837, 858

D

Danin, A., 27, 825
David, N., 496, 819
debitage, 101, 110, 112, 504, 505, 506, 507, 512, 513, 515, 516, 517, 518, 519, 522, 523, 755
Dessel, J., 569, 734, 842
diachronic, 215, 217, 218, 219, 234, 268, 269, 271, 313, 392, 682, 750, 788, 812, 814, 830
divergent cultural evolution, 5, 831
dog burial, 126, 127, 134, 135, 199, 237, 238, 239, 318, 398, 399, 416, 431, 438, 484, 838
Domestic Mode of Production (DMP), 703, 717
domestic ware, 246, 393, 693
Donald, M., 27
donkey, 57, 220, 224, 247, 275, 313
Dothan, M., 211, 324, 679, 698, 733
Dumuzi, 747
Durkheim, E., 27, 820, 841

E

Earle, T., 27, 495, 496, 497, 818, 819, 820, 841, 842
Early Bronze Age, 8, 25, 26, 29, 30, 31, 97, 98, 211, 215, 221, 233, 313, 339, 347, 365, 367, 372, 373, 374, 375, 381, 389, 440,

456, 501, 510, 511, 570, 571, 588, 678, 679, 698, 712, 714, 715, 812, 818, 824, 835, 836, 841, 843

Egypt, 16, 18, 26, 32, 61, 62, 63, 65, 233, 324, 325, 339, 363, 365, 371, 374, 376, 390, 400, 496, 500, 570, 580, 581, 588, 589, 591, 593, 595, 600, 678, 679, 680, 681, 698, 702, 712, 733, 751, 812, 816, 819, 823, 824, 826, 839

Ein Gedi, 98, 232, 240, 245, 318, 326, 435, 439, 440, 503, 715, 731, 743, 747, 791, 806, 810, 817, 826

Eliade, M., 27, 91

Epstein, C., 27, 314, 388, 497, 820, 841, 857

equid, 128, 220, 223, 224, 231, 233, 247, 250, 262, 275, 287, 309, 318, 689, 690

ethnography, 24, 52, 72, 91

Evershed, R., 857

exchange, 11, 16, 19, 24, 34, 42, 43, 48, 49, 64, 232, 319, 323, 393, 398, 399, 400, 406, 407, 452, 500, 522, 573, 582, 585, 587, 591, 593, 704, 715, 716, 717, 718, 730, 733, 749, 780, 781, 809, 815, 824, 837, 838, 839, 849

F

Fabian, P., 389, 498

farming, 69, 71, 215, 245, 315, 364, 502, 572, 681, 728

feasting, 13, 17, 43, 236, 406, 407, 449, 453, 454, 455, 716, 815, 838

fenestrated stand, 14, 105, 107, 110, 118, 122, 132, 136, 137, 138, 181, 183, 195, 243, 244, 291, 323, 369, 594, 595, 596, 597, 598, 599, 601, 658, 675, 676, 691, 715, 716, 728, 730, 839

fertility, 10, 14, 36, 37, 731, 747, 750, 789, 792, 818

Fiber Revolution, 703, 731

figurine, 105, 106, 110, 119, 124, 128, 138, 171, 186, 216, 233, 243, 244, 291, 329, 336, 419, 434, 452, 494, 499, 580, 587, 620, 691, 728, 737, 738, 743, 747, 750, 751, 753, 754, 755, 756, 758, 759, 760, 761, 762, 764, 765, 766, 767, 768, 769, 770, 776, 777, 778, 779, 780, 781, 782, 783, 784, 786, 787, 788, 790, 793, 794, 795, 796, 797, 798, 799, 800, 803, 804, 805, 806, 808, 809, 810, 811, 815, 816, 817, 823, 838

Flannery, K., 28, 314, 841

foothill, 21, 22, 39, 95, 215, 242, 731

Fox, R., 28

Frazer, J., 28

Friedman, R.E., 28

functionalist, 4, 8, 11, 17, 786, 790, 828

G

Gal, Z., 28, 363, 497, 733, 821, 842

Ganj Dareh, 316, 807, 811, 820

Garfinkel, Y., 314, 497, 698, 733, 821, 842

Garstang, J., 733

gazelle, 105, 138, 210, 220, 237, 239, 241, 243, 244, 245, 246, 247, 262, 286, 289, 291, 301, 336, 684, 689, 690, 691, 692, 693, 728, 802, 804, 805, 806, 809, 810, 811, 817

Geertz, C., 28, 73, 91, 821

Gellner, E., 28, 73, 91

gender, 10, 51, 336, 340, 436, 438, 453, 457, 743, 749, 786, 788, 789, 813, 818, 819, 842

geography, 19, 21, 24, 29, 38, 42, 81, 88, 133, 842

geomorphology, 22

Gilat Lady, 174, 206, 742, 743, 747, 749, 786

Gilat Ram, 136, 174, 743, 744

Gilead, I., 211, 314, 363, 389, 390, 497, 500, 569, 679, 698, 821, 824, 842, 861

goat, 67, 101, 105, 218, 219, 220, 221, 225, 226, 227, 228, 232, 234, 235, 240, 244, 245, 246, 247, 249, 250, 253, 254, 258, 259, 262, 276, 277, 283, 285, 294, 295, 296, 297, 298, 299, 301, 302, 303, 317, 334, 336, 350, 441, 684, 685, 686, 687, 689, 690, 695, 696, 697, 705, 749, 806, 840

Goldberg, P., 28, 314, 316

Goodfriend, G., 28

Gopher, A., 28, 211, 363, 389, 679, 698, 733, 842

Goren, Y., 211, 314, 389, 390, 497, 498, 679, 733, 821, 842, 857

Grar, 121, 139, 211, 216, 220, 221, 222, 224, 225, 226, 229, 230, 245, 314, 315, 324, 337, 339, 363, 376, 378, 394, 408, 414, 421, 424, 434, 435, 439, 440, 441, 443, 460, 497, 498, 504, 505, 506, 507, 508, 511, 512, 513, 515, 517, 518, 519, 520, 521, 523, 539, 569, 575, 576, 577, 579, 585, 591, 592, 594, 595, 598, 599, 600, 601, 659, 679, 682, 687, 689, 698, 802, 812, 815, 817, 821, 830, 831, 842, 861

Grigson, C., 314, 315, 316, 317, 318, 498, 679, 821

grinding stone, 129, 130, 198, 201, 575, 576

ground stone, 19, 24, 123, 501, 513, 518, 572, 573, 574, 575, 577, 579, 580, 582, 583, 592, 594, 599, 600, 609, 619, 620, 628, 645, 659, 660, 661, 662, 663, 664, 665, 666, 667, 668, 669, 670, 671, 672, 673, 674, 675, 676, 677, 678, 679, 680, 681, 824

H

Habad, 78
Harris, M., 29, 734
Hauptmann, A., 389, 822
healer, 832, 835
herding, 14, 58, 61, 62, 64, 66, 225, 228, 239, 245, 279, 315, 498, 731, 821, 835
heterogeneity, 500, 766
hillula, 78, 79, 80, 81, 84, 85
Hodder, I., 29, 363, 498, 822, 842
horn core, 105, 138, 210, 229, 451, 705, 728, 809
Horvat Beter, 121, 136, 137, 211, 216, 221, 245, 313, 315, 323, 324, 518, 521, 571, 575, 577, 578, 579, 580, 583, 584, 585, 591, 593, 598, 679, 689, 698, 712, 733
Horvat Hor, 341, 365
human remains, 24, 104, 327
hunting, 7, 8, 14, 35, 37, 239, 241, 243, 692, 728, 835

I

ideology, 4, 5, 9, 10, 14, 16, 31, 38, 45, 51, 71, 78, 80, 91, 96, 582, 750, 786, 792, 802, 828, 832
Ilan, O., 389
immigration, 79, 80
incense burner, 13, 129, 136, 440
inter-regional, 369, 393, 398, 400, 406, 407, 749, 838
intra-mural inhumation, 338
Islam, 54, 55, 56, 57, 71, 73, 74, 78, 90, 91

J

Jericho, 221, 238, 263, 313, 318, 369, 377, 379, 381, 511, 575, 577, 578, 579, 583, 598, 601, 678, 683, 691, 692, 693, 698, 703, 704, 705, 712, 731, 734, 735, 806, 822, 835
Jerusalem, 25, 26, 27, 29, 30, 73, 74, 78, 85, 87, 90, 91, 92, 96, 211, 212, 239, 246, 313, 314, 317, 324, 363, 364, 371, 373, 388, 389, 390, 391, 399, 443, 495, 497, 498, 499, 502, 522, 523, 569, 570, 571, 591, 678, 679, 680, 681, 698, 699, 702, 733, 734, 735, 751, 755, 757, 795, 797, 818, 820, 821, 823, 826, 837, 839, 841, 842, 846, 850, 857
Jewish, 19, 21, 76, 78, 79, 80, 81, 82, 83, 84, 85, 86, 88, 89, 90, 91, 92, 96, 338, 698, 731, 839, 840
Jezreel valley, 831
Joffe, A., 569, 734, 842, 861
Jordan, 6, 11, 30, 31, 96, 134, 211, 212, 241, 242, 316, 363, 364, 371, 376, 377, 379, 381, 388, 389, 399, 401, 402, 407, 434, 442, 443, 495, 496, 498, 500, 510, 511, 523, 569, 570, 600, 678, 679, 715, 730, 734, 743, 751, 754, 803, 807, 820, 822, 825, 829, 830, 831, 832, 837, 838, 841, 843, 850, 858
Jordan Valley, 134, 371, 376, 399, 401, 402, 407, 434, 442, 443, 496, 511, 678, 679, 751, 803, 820
Judean Mountains, 369, 374, 376, 381, 382, 442

K

Kabbalah, 78, 92
Kabri, 377, 497, 596, 597, 680
Kafafi, Z., 496, 498, 733, 820, 822, 825
Kangas, S., 498
Kerner, S., 29, 211
Koeppel, R., 498, 500, 570, 679, 680, 734, 822, 823, 843
Kopytoff, I., 498
Kramer, C., 496, 498
Kuijt, I., 364, 842
Kunin, S., 29, 842

L

Lambis, 320, 323, 587
Leach, E., 499, 822
Lemonnier, P., 499, 823
Levi-Strauss, C., 499, 823
Levy, T.E., 29, 30, 316, 318, 324, 364, 388, 389, 390, 495, 499, 502, 503, 569, 570, 571, 678, 679, 680, 698, 733, 734, 735, 817, 823, 825, 827, 841, 842, 843, 858, 861
linen, 232, 687, 692, 704, 711, 712, 731, 732
Liverani, M., 30
Lod, 377, 680
loess, 131, 133, 369, 370, 371, 372, 398, 399
Lovell, J., 212, 500, 841, 843

M

Macdonald, E., 500, 698, 823, 843
mace head, 31, 95, 124, 137, 209, 390, 522, 572, 573, 574, 580, 581, 582, 587, 588, 589, 592, 599, 600, 601, 753, 775, 778
magico-religious, 33, 832, 835, 836, 837, 843
Mallaha, 317, 691, 692, 699, 826
Mallon, A., 212, 316, 324, 364, 570, 680, 698, 734, 843
mammals, 241, 248, 684
Marcus, J., 30, 823, 841
marine shell, 323
Maring, 11, 47
Marshall, D., 698, 734
Marx, E., 30, 74, 843
Marx, K., 30
massebot, 95
Mauss, M., 734, 823
McCorriston, J., 735, 843
Mediterranean, 8, 12, 22, 25, 33, 73, 90, 211, 242, 319, 322, 323, 324, 325, 363, 388, 392, 393, 407, 410, 495, 500, 504, 518, 569, 678, 714, 733, 751, 817, 821, 824, 835, 841, 842, 857, 858, 861
Megiddo, 27, 98, 212, 592, 679, 702, 841
Mellaart, J., 699, 734, 735, 824
Melos, 8
Meser, 577, 591, 598, 679
Mezad Aluf, 340, 349, 364, 435, 439
milking, 228
miniature churns, 395, 399, 422, 423, 426, 427, 429, 442, 455, 743
mortuary practices, 326, 338
Mountain Ok, 36, 37, 38, 39, 48
Moza marl, 369, 370, 373, 374, 382, 383, 384, 385, 386, 387
multiple human burial, 336, 691, 838
Munhata, 222, 314, 377, 389, 401, 433, 457, 480, 787, 788, 789, 805, 806, 811, 815, 816, 817, 821
Muniz, A., 734
Musil, A., 30, 74

N

Nahal Beersheva, 30, 130, 316, 390, 519, 830, 842
Nahal Grar, 139, 216, 519, 830, 831
Nahal Mishmar, 31, 245, 323, 341, 363, 367, 368, 378, 389, 390, 391, 585, 587, 588, 704, 712, 806, 824

Nahal Patish, 5, 25, 95, 99, 133, 134, 139, 211, 242, 381, 399, 408, 433, 434, 495, 506, 519, 810, 817, 831
Nahal Qanah, 6, 28, 211, 363, 584, 599, 679, 688, 689, 698, 712, 733, 842
Nahal Refaim, 372, 373
Nahshoni, P., 390
Najjar, M., 363, 499, 823
Natufian, 6, 134, 238, 263, 317, 338, 339, 341, 343, 363, 365, 438, 570, 572, 579, 600, 681, 682, 683, 684, 691, 692, 693, 698, 699, 733, 788, 802, 826, 835, 843
Netivot, 19, 75, 76, 78, 81, 82, 83, 84, 85, 86, 87, 88, 89, 90, 838, 839, 840
Neve Ur, 576, 589, 591, 680
Nile mud, 371, 376, 387
Northwest Semitic, 4
nutritional needs, 231

O

obsidian, 33, 503, 512, 518, 521, 571, 812, 827
ochre, 121, 429, 578, 580, 581, 593, 620, 621, 622, 664, 680, 808
Ofakim, 81, 86, 95
off-site production, 393, 400, 402, 403, 406, 407, 408, 435, 441, 442, 456, 776, 780, 781
olive oil, 14, 138, 392, 407, 408, 439, 442, 450, 452, 497, 499, 831, 838, 839, 845, 846, 848, 849, 850, 854
Oren, E., 390, 500, 824, 825
organic residue, 24, 839, 845, 846, 849, 857
ostrich egg, 110, 136, 152, 188, 241, 243, 244, 246, 322, 586, 587, 628, 629, 666, 838
Ovis, 219, 222, 313

P

palette, 125, 128, 329, 336, 451, 494, 580, 587, 593, 620, 662, 667, 669, 670, 671, 672, 723, 755, 775, 776
Papua New Guinea, 11, 12, 16, 18, 35, 36, 39, 53, 716
pastoral, 8, 22, 58, 63, 71, 225, 227, 228, 232, 731, 747, 835, 836, 837, 839
pathology, 217, 231, 347
pendant, 118, 122, 411, 518, 584, 585, 592, 663, 664, 665, 666, 667, 671, 749, 790, 801, 803, 805, 806, 808, 809, 812, 813, 814, 817
performance, 9, 11, 12, 20, 68, 86, 96, 98, 438, 440, 500, 737, 738, 747, 790, 807, 809, 810, 820

Perles, C., 820, 824
Perrot, J., 212, 324, 364, 390, 500, 501, 570, 680, 699, 735, 824, 843
petrography, 370, 399, 845
Phase I excavations, 95, 96
Phase II excavations, 95, 97, 99, 571
pigs, 37, 40, 47, 218, 219, 221, 223, 230, 231, 234, 235, 236, 242, 244, 245, 246, 249, 256, 257, 261, 269, 275, 281, 284, 285, 313, 315, 316, 810
pilgrimage, 5, 16, 18, 19, 20, 21, 23, 24, 26, 30, 31, 32, 38, 40, 49, 50, 51, 56, 57, 59, 60, 64, 65, 67, 68, 69, 70, 71, 74, 76, 78, 79, 80, 81, 86, 87, 89, 90, 91, 338, 749, 836, 838, 839, 840
pithos, 192, 204, 205, 420, 443, 468, 469, 470, 471, 472, 473, 474, 477, 481, 482
platform, 98, 100, 103, 104, 106, 107, 109, 110, 111, 113, 116, 118, 120, 121, 123, 128, 129, 130, 137, 138, 140, 143, 144, 145, 146, 147, 149, 151, 152, 179, 201, 333, 335, 455, 467, 480, 488, 507, 540, 541, 542, 634, 722
plaza, 99, 105, 109, 110, 112, 123, 135, 136, 137, 184, 185, 186, 197, 241, 243, 331, 336, 444, 448, 711, 723, 730, 838
Pleistocene, 22, 28, 101, 111, 115, 116, 117, 123, 124, 125, 127, 130, 131, 133, 134, 200, 202, 223, 313, 365
Porat, N., 390, 678, 818
Pottery Neolithic, 221, 222, 245, 263, 316, 338, 363, 377, 378, 381, 405, 423, 497, 583, 678, 679, 683, 691, 692, 693, 698, 703, 704, 712, 731, 733, 787, 788, 802, 806, 807, 809, 810, 813, 815, 822, 835, 836, 841, 842, 849
prestige, 16, 21, 40, 49, 233, 236, 326, 339, 406, 408, 452, 498, 591, 600, 704, 716, 730, 732, 753, 777, 778, 781, 790, 792, 806, 813, 839
priest, 50, 66, 836
priesthood, 49, 836
production, 5, 26, 31, 83, 84, 89, 91, 102, 105, 110, 224, 226, 227, 228, 232, 245, 279, 316, 329, 367, 368, 373, 374, 375, 376, 392, 393, 397, 398, 399, 400, 402, 403, 405, 406, 407, 408, 409, 411, 421, 426, 429, 431, 434, 439, 441, 442, 443, 452, 457, 495, 496, 497, 500, 501, 502, 505, 506, 507, 508, 510, 511, 513, 516, 518, 519, 520, 522, 569, 573, 577, 580, 581, 589, 591, 599, 600, 702, 703, 704, 711, 713, 714, 715, 716, 717, 730, 731, 732,
733, 734, 737, 747, 750, 753, 755, 765, 766, 769, 770, 773, 774, 775, 776, 777, 778, 779, 780, 781, 802, 807, 808, 809, 810, 816, 818, 819, 820, 824, 831, 832, 836, 837, 839, 843, 857
systems, 393, 405, 406, 421, 434, 452, 778
production systems, 393, 405, 406, 421, 434, 452, 778
Proto-Canaanean blades, 571
provenance, 13, 19, 367, 368, 369, 370, 371, 381, 382, 438, 441, 442, 456, 501, 748, 749, 751, 766, 769, 778, 780, 824, 837

Q

Qatif, 216, 240, 242, 245, 315, 368, 370, 377, 378, 381, 434, 506, 507, 518, 751

R

radiocarbon dating, 117, 363, 589, 830, 858
rainfall, 16, 22, 28, 29, 57, 242
ram, 244, 386, 437, 743, 747, 748, 749, 780, 803, 805, 810, 811, 812, 813, 817
Ramot Nof, 378, 386, 387, 388, 390
ranking, 338, 348, 393, 425, 433, 436, 438, 449, 456, 704, 750, 766, 769, 770, 773, 775, 808, 835
Rappaport, R., 31, 501, 825
regional, 3, 4, 5, 6, 8, 10, 12, 16, 18, 19, 21, 22, 23, 24, 34, 38, 39, 40, 43, 45, 46, 47, 48, 49, 79, 80, 86, 88, 89, 96, 135, 136, 138, 139, 326, 339, 368, 369, 392, 393, 398, 400, 403, 406, 407, 435, 505, 520, 521, 599, 703, 704, 715, 717, 730, 732, 738, 749, 751, 754, 766, 773, 774, 775, 779, 780, 786, 802, 809, 814, 828, 830, 831, 832, 835, 836, 837, 838
Regional
    integration, 43, 828
    production, 400, 406, 407, 775, 779, 780
regional cult, 8, 10, 18, 19, 23, 24, 46, 89, 96, 135, 136, 703, 830, 831, 832, 836, 837, 838
regional integration, 43, 828
regional production, 400, 406, 775, 779, 780
regression analysis, 8, 835
Renfrew, C., 31, 212, 325, 364, 501, 820, 825, 843
risk management, 23, 231, 232, 837
ritual, 3, 5, 6, 7, 8, 9, 10, 11, 12, 13, 14, 15, 16, 17, 18, 19, 20, 21, 22, 23, 24, 26, 34, 35, 36, 37, 38, 40, 43, 45, 46, 47, 48, 49, 50, 52, 53, 60, 76, 80, 82, 89, 90, 96, 102, 105,

109, 110, 126, 129, 134, 135, 136, 137, 138, 139, 232, 236, 237, 243, 244, 245, 246, 323, 326, 327, 329, 334, 338, 339, 368, 381, 392, 407, 408, 436, 444, 445, 453, 454, 455, 504, 510, 511, 582, 682, 687, 691, 693, 715, 716, 717, 728, 730, 731, 732, 736, 737, 738, 747, 749, 750, 781, 790, 791, 792, 802, 806, 807, 809, 810, 811, 814, 820, 822, 824, 828, 829, 831, 832, 835, 836, 837, 838, 839, 840, 841, 845, 848, 849
   centers, 3, 12, 16, 20, 48, 326, 732, 828, 832
   practice, 8, 9, 10, 14, 24, 80, 126, 326, 802, 809, 810, 814, 828, 832, 837, 838
ritual centers, 3, 12, 16, 20, 48, 326, 732, 828, 832
ritual practice, 8, 9, 10, 14, 24, 80, 126, 326, 802, 809, 810, 814, 828, 832, 837, 838
Robbins, J., 31, 735
Robertson Smith, 3, 17, 18, 24, 31, 55, 71, 72, 829
Rosen, A., 31, 500
Rosen, S., 389, 390, 501, 570, 680, 735, 825
Roshwalb, A., 317, 502, 570, 680, 825
Roux, V., 496, 502, 680
Rowan, Y., 316, 502, 503, 571, 680, 681, 735, 825, 827

S

sacrifice, 10, 13, 17, 23, 64, 67, 496
Sahlins, M., 31, 735
Samaria, 6, 339, 369, 371, 374, 375, 754, 850
Schick, T., 212, 364, 571, 680, 698, 735, 825
Schiffer, M., 31, 212, 502
Seaton, P., 31, 212, 364, 390, 843
secondary burial, 327, 336, 338, 339, 340, 349, 443, 599
Secondary Products Revolution, 245, 441, 703, 749
Section, 117, 160, 161, 162, 524, 527, 582
Shalev, S., 31, 212, 364, 390, 391, 499, 570, 823, 843
shaman, 7, 832, 835
sheep, 58, 61, 62, 67, 101, 105, 216, 218, 219, 220, 221, 222, 225, 226, 227, 228, 230, 231, 232, 234, 235, 236, 237, 239, 240, 243, 244, 245, 246, 247, 249, 250, 252, 253, 254, 261, 262, 268, 270, 271, 273, 276, 277, 278, 279, 282, 283, 284, 285, 294, 295, 296, 297, 298, 299, 302, 303, 313, 315, 317, 334, 336, 350, 498, 684,

685, 686, 687, 689, 690, 695, 696, 697, 705, 714, 715, 731, 749, 803, 804, 805, 806, 808, 809, 814, 821, 840
sheikh, 460
Sherratt, A., 317, 502, 735, 843, 858
Shiqmim, 21, 25, 28, 29, 30, 121, 122, 128, 133, 136, 137, 209, 211, 212, 215, 216, 224, 242, 245, 314, 315, 316, 318, 323, 324, 337, 339, 343, 344, 345, 346, 347, 349, 364, 376, 378, 389, 390, 434, 435, 439, 440, 441, 498, 499, 502, 504, 505, 506, 507, 510, 511, 512, 513, 514, 515, 517, 518, 519, 520, 521, 522, 539, 569, 570, 571, 577, 584, 585, 589, 591, 596, 598, 679, 680, 689, 698, 713, 715, 717, 731, 734, 735, 751, 755, 787, 788, 821, 823, 825, 830, 831, 842, 859, 861, 863
shrine center, 34, 35, 36, 38, 39, 40, 45, 46, 48, 49, 50, 51
Shugar, A., 843
sickle blade, 116, 377, 508, 509, 511, 513, 514, 520, 522, 548, 840
silo, 98, 100, 105, 106, 107, 110, 114, 115, 133, 135, 138, 142, 143, 147, 175, 183, 189, 193, 243, 244, 331, 332, 335, 336, 445, 451, 452, 458, 459, 460, 462, 481, 482, 483, 490, 575, 621, 622, 624, 632, 634, 642, 707, 722, 726, 757
Sinai, 16, 18, 26, 27, 30, 32, 54, 55, 56, 57, 58, 59, 60, 61, 62, 63, 64, 65, 66, 67, 68, 69, 70, 71, 72, 73, 74, 89, 98, 129, 211, 314, 315, 323, 324, 325, 338, 363, 368, 370, 373, 374, 375, 377, 378, 379, 387, 388, 389, 390, 408, 434, 500, 510, 518, 569, 600, 754, 759, 770, 778, 816, 822, 824, 839, 840
social
   exchange, 406, 780
   organization, 3, 6, 11, 18, 50, 60, 71, 215, 326, 702, 703, 814, 831
   production, 392, 397
Sopher, D., 32, 212
spatial analysis, 99, 437, 454, 726, 733, 781
spatial distribution, 21, 57, 399, 406, 407, 408, 431, 436, 437, 443, 445, 448, 449, 450, 452, 456, 715, 718, 754, 781, 786, 790, 849
spindle whorl, 101, 118, 121, 123, 132, 136, 138, 139, 197, 207, 232, 246, 518, 522, 573, 574, 582, 589, 590, 591, 592, 596, 599, 600, 601, 631, 634, 673, 674, 692, 693, 704, 706, 711, 712, 713, 714, 715, 717, 718, 722, 723, 726, 728, 730, 731, 732

spinning, 216, 232, 246, 590, 591, 702, 703, 711, 712, 715, 732
spirit medium, 836
Spiro, M., 32
spring, 13, 50, 63, 64, 95, 743, 839
Stager, L., 32, 212
standing stone, 14, 89, 95, 99, 110, 129, 136, 144, 146, 150, 176, 185, 202, 677, 838
statuette, 222, 232, 692, 739, 749, 818
status, 14, 21, 39, 78, 92, 221, 224, 233, 326, 338, 339, 348, 408, 431, 438, 450, 454, 456, 702, 737, 773, 781, 789, 814, 817
stone circle, 101, 104, 108, 135, 137, 149
stone vessel, 233, 314, 389, 573, 579, 594, 595, 596, 597, 598, 636, 641, 842
storage, 5, 14, 15, 16, 31, 98, 100, 102, 112, 114, 124, 131, 132, 134, 175, 193, 219, 231, 232, 375, 393, 394, 406, 407, 423, 425, 435, 436, 437, 438, 439, 442, 443, 449, 450, 452, 453, 454, 455, 496, 504, 506, 519, 728, 732, 807, 819, 839, 846, 847
Stordeur, D., 317, 699, 826
stratigraphy, 12, 95, 99, 104, 216, 378, 394
Sus scrofa, 220, 240
symbolism, 10, 38, 53, 68, 326, 388, 738, 747, 748, 749, 750, 789, 811, 813, 814, 817, 824
syncretism, 11, 839

T

Talalay, L., 826
Taqiya marl, 369, 371, 374, 375
Telefolip, 36, 37, 38, 39, 40, 45, 51
Tell en-Nasbeh, 373
Tell Turmus, 591, 678
Teluliot Batashi, 377
temples, 14, 27, 38, 702, 703, 818
territory, 40, 54, 56, 58, 59, 61, 62, 64, 65, 66, 69, 71, 72, 85, 588
textile production, 702, 703, 704, 711, 713, 714, 715, 717, 718, 726, 728, 730, 731, 732, 838
Titorah, 399, 419, 420, 433, 443, 457, 751, 767, 768, 769, 770, 771, 772, 773, 779
token, 51, 73, 122, 123, 126, 455, 583, 662, 664, 665, 670, 671, 801
tomb, 54, 60, 64, 65, 66, 67, 68, 69, 70, 78, 79, 80, 81, 83, 88, 89, 338, 339, 387
torpedo jar, 19, 98, 111, 136, 137, 177, 381, 395, 398, 399, 400, 401, 402, 405, 419, 420, 421, 425, 429, 442, 443, 445, 448, 453, 455, 486, 716, 839, 845, 846, 847, 848, 849, 850, 851, 853

Totemism, 7, 28, 823
traction, 215, 231, 232, 703
Transjordan, 233, 363, 375, 389, 393, 402, 438, 569, 582, 585, 759, 816, 837
Tuleilat Ghassul, 6, 136, 323, 324, 337, 510, 518, 521, 575, 576, 577, 578, 579, 581, 583, 584, 585, 588, 589, 591, 593, 594, 596, 597, 598, 715, 828, 849
Turner, H., 32, 365, 843
Tuzin, D., 32, 842
typological
    classification; lithic, 5, 133, 368, 370, 376, 378, 379, 381, 393, 397, 399, 402, 409, 423, 424, 425, 428, 429, 450, 499, 502, 504, 505, 512, 569, 574, 590, 594, 601, 815, 825

U

Ucko, P., 365, 826
ungulate, 218, 235, 236, 238, 244, 268, 269, 270, 271, 285
urban, 15, 17, 20, 25, 78, 86, 91, 780, 835
Uruk, 233, 317, 454
Ussishkin, D., 32, 212, 318, 365, 391, 503, 681, 826, 843

V

Valla, F., 317, 571, 681, 699, 826, 843
van den Brink, E., 365, 681
Van der Leeuw, S., 503

veneration, 74, 78, 79, 81, 86, 90, 233, 244, 791
violin shape figurine, 136, 793, 794, 795, 797, 799, 800, 838

W

Wadi Beersheva, 327
Wadi Gaza, 504, 507, 508, 510, 519, 520, 521, 583, 585, 586, 591, 593, 599, 687, 830
Wadi Makkuk, 341, 349
Wadi Rabah, 133, 134, 206, 222, 405, 411, 412, 419, 423, 424, 433, 434, 498, 511, 520, 521, 573, 583, 589, 600, 601, 682, 692, 751, 769, 805, 806, 807, 814, 829
Wadi Zeita, 370, 379, 387, 408, 420, 433, 434, 443, 456, 598, 751
Wadi Zumeili, 399
Weingrod, A., 32
Werbner, R., 32, 74, 92, 843

wild animals, 225, 244, 810, 814
Wilkinson, T., 33
women, 50, 52, 67, 69, 438, 457, 702, 733,
    739, 743, 748, 749, 789, 815, 816, 822, 836
wool, 138, 215, 225, 226, 227, 228, 232, 236,
    246, 277, 279, 496, 504, 590, 687, 692,
    703, 711, 712, 713, 714, 731, 749, 819
worked bone, 101, 683, 694

Y

Yellin, J., 33, 390, 503, 571, 827
yoghurt, 231, 232

Z

Zapotec, 5, 28, 30, 841
Zevit, Z., 33
ziara, 78
Zohary, D., 318, 497, 503, 843, 858
zoomorphic, 10, 97, 136, 244, 587, 730, 736,
    738, 739, 747, 748, 802, 803, 804, 805,
    807, 808, 809, 810, 811, 813, 814, 838
Zubrow, E.B., 503